D1189884

Human *Sexuality*

MAKING INFORMED DECISIONS

Sixth Edition

David **KNOX**   Susan **MILSTEIN**

BVT Publishing

Better textbooks, better prices

www.BVTPublishing.com

Publisher and Managing Director: Richard Schofield
Production and Fulfillment Manager: Janai Escobedo
Permissions Coordinator: Jade Elk
Designers: Stephanie Elliott and Tim Gerlach
Managing Editor: Anne Serbulea
Copyeditor: Regina Roths
Proofreader: Teresa Daly
Ancillary Coordinator: Tiffany Ballard

Cover Images Credit: Shutterstock
Technology and Sexuality Icon Credit: Andrea Sosa

All rights reserved. Printed in the United States of America. No part of this book may be used or reproduced in any manner whatsoever without written permission, except in the case of brief quotations embodied in critical articles and reviews. For information address BVT Publishing, P.O. Box 492831, Redding, CA 96049-2831.

Some ancillaries, including electronic and printed components, may not be available to customers outside of the United States.

LAB BOOK[Plus] ISBN: 978-1-5178-0968-3
TEXTBOOK[Plus] (Loose-Leaf Bundle) ISBN: 978-1-5178-0967-6
eBook[Plus] ISBN: 978-1-5178-0966-9
Loose-Leaf ISBN: 978-1-5178-0964-5
Soft Cover ISBN: 978-1-5178-0965-2

Copyright © 2021 by BVT Publishing

About the Authors

David Knox, PhD, is professor of sociology at East Carolina University, in Greenville, North Carolina, where he teaches human sexuality and marriage and family courses. He is the author or coauthor of five textbooks and more than 130 research articles. He presents regularly at professional conferences and mentors graduate students in relationship/sexual therapy. In addition, Dr. Knox is a member of the Society for the Scientific Study of Sexuality.

Susan Milstein, PhD, is a clinical assistant professor in the Department of Health Enhancement and Kinesiology at Texas A&M University. She is the founder and lead consultant at Milstein Health Consulting, a member of the advisory council for the Woodhull Freedom Foundation, and a member of the Advisory Board for the Men's Health Network.

Dr. Milstein earned her PhD in human sexuality from Widener University in Pennsylvania, the only accredited PhD program in human sexuality in the US. She is a Master Certified Health Education Specialist and a Certified Sexuality Educator. Her memberships include the American Association of Sexuality Educators, Counselors and Therapists; the Society for the Scientific Study of Sexuality; and the Society for Public Health Education.

Brief Contents

Table of contents vii

Preface xxi

1 *Human Sexuality: An Introduction* **2**

2 *Sex Research and Theory* **28**

3 *Female Sexual Anatomy, Physiology, and Response* **60**

4 *Male Sexual Anatomy, Physiology, and Response* **90**

5 *Gender and Sexuality* **106**

6 *Love and Sexuality* **134**

7 *Communication and Sexuality* **162**

8 *Individual and Interpersonal Sexuality* **188**

9 *Lifespan View of Sexuality* **214**

10 *Diversity—LGBTQIA* **248**

11 *Health and Sexuality* **280**

12 *Contraception and Abortion* **306**

13 *Pregnancy and Childbirth* **336**

14 *Sexual Dysfunctions and Sex Therapy* **358**

15 *Variant Sexual Behavior* **394**

16 *Sexually Transmitted Infections* **424**

17 *Sexual Coercion* **456**

18 *Commercialization of Sex* **498**

Glossary 535

References 555

Author Index 595

Subject Index 603

Table of Contents

Chapter 1

Human Sexuality: An Introduction 2

Self-Assessment 1-1: Sexual Importance Scale 5

1.1 **Defining Human Sexuality** 6
   1.1a Thoughts 6
   1.1b Sexual Self-Concept 6
   1.1c Values 7
   1.1d Emotions 11
   1.1e Behaviors 11
   1.1f Anatomy and Physiology 12
   1.1g Reproduction 12
   1.1h Interpersonal Relationships 13
   Technology and Sexuality 1-1: There's an App for That! 13
   1.1i Sexual Health 14
   1.1j Still Other Views 14

1.2 **Nature of Sexual Decisions** 14
   1.2a Not to Decide Is to Decide 14
   1.2b Decisions Involve Trade-Offs 15
   1.2c Decisions Include Selecting a Positive or Negative View 15
   1.2d Decisions Can Produce Ambivalence and Uncertainty 15
   1.2e Some Decisions Are Revocable; Some Are Not 15

1.3 **Making Sexual Decisions** 16
   1.3a Four Themes of Sexual Decision-Making by Women 16
   1.3b Deciding to Improve One's Sexual Growth 16
   Self-Assessment 1-2: Sexual Growth Beliefs Measure 17
   1.3c Spatial Context of Sex 18

1.4 **Influences on Sexual Decisions** 18
   1.4a Culture 18
   1.4b Media 18
   1.4c Peers and Parents 19
   1.4d Technology 20
   1.4e Education 21
   1.4f Religion 21
   Social Policy 1-1: Sex Education in Public Schools 23
   1.4g Alcohol/Substance Use 24
   1.4h Psychological Factors 24
   Personal Decisions 1-1: Do You or Other Factors Control Your Sexual Decisions? 25

Chapter 2

Sex Research and Theory 28

2.1 **The Nature of Sex Research** 31

2.2 **The Interdisciplinary Nature of Sexology** 32

2.3 **Theories of Sexuality** 32
   2.3a Biological Theories 33
   2.3b Psychological Theories 33
   Self-Assessment 2-1: Need for Sexual Intimacy Scale 36
   2.3c Sociological Theories 37

2.4   Eclectic View of Human Sexuality 40

2.4a   Early Sex Researchers **40**

2.5   Conducting Sex Research: A Step-by-Step Process 42

2.5a   Identifying a Research Question **42**
2.5b   Reviewing the Literature **42**
2.5c   Formulating a Hypothesis and Operationalizing Variables **42**
2.5d   Caveats in Sex Research **44**
Technology and Sexuality 2-1: Online Surveys **46**
2.5e   Research Ethics: Protection of Human Subjects **46**

2.6   Methods of Data Collection 48

2.6a   Experimental Research **48**
2.6b   Survey Research **48**
2.6c   Field Research **50**
2.6d   Direct Laboratory Observation **51**
Social Policy 2-1: Public Funding for Sex Research? **51**
2.6e   Case Studies **52**

2.7   Levels of Data Analysis 52

2.7a   Descriptive **52**
2.7b   Correlation **52**
2.7c   Causation **54**
2.7d   Expanding Statistical Frontiers **54**

2.8   Interpretation and Discussion 55

Chapter 3

Female Sexual Anatomy, Physiology, and Response **60**

3.1   Female External Anatomy and Physiology 62

3.1a   Mons Veneris **62**
3.1b   Labia **63**
3.1c   Clitoris **63**
Technology and Sexuality 3-1: Cosmetic Surgery **64**
Personal Decisions 3-1: Shaving Pubic Hair **64**
3.1d   Vaginal Opening **65**
3.1e   Urethral Opening **66**
3.1f   Female Genital Alteration **66**
3.1g   The Female Breasts **69**
Social Policy 3-1: Breastfeeding in Public? **69**
Personal Decisions 3-2: Breast Self-Examination and Mammogram? **71**

3.2   Female Internal Anatomy and Physiology 72

3.2a   Vagina **72**
3.2b   The "G-Spot" **73**
Personal Decisions 3-3: Pap Test and Pelvic Exam **74**
3.2c   Uterus **74**
3.2d   Fallopian Tubes **74**
3.2e   Ovaries **75**

3.3   Menstruation 75

3.3a   Phases of the Menstrual Cycle **76**
3.3b   Attitudes Toward Menstruation **77**
Self-Assessment 3-1: Menstrual Attitude Questionnaire **77**
3.3c   Problems of the Menstrual Cycle **79**

3.4 Models of Sexual Response 81

3.4a   Masters and Johnson's Four-Stage Model of Sexual Response **81**
3.4b   Kaplan's Three-Stage Model of Sexual Response **84**
3.4c   Basson's Model of Sexual Response **84**
Personal Decisions 3-4: Having Sex with a Partner When Desire Is Low **84**

3.5 Hormones and Sexual Response 85

3.6 Pheromones, Aphrodisiacs, and Sexual Response 86

Chapter 4
Male Sexual Anatomy, Physiology, and Response **90**

4.1 Male External Anatomy and Physiology 91

4.1a   Penis **92**
Technology and Sexuality 4-1: Promises to Increase Penis Length **94**
Social Policy 4-1: Male Circumcision **95**
4.1b   Scrotum **96**

4.2 Male Internal Anatomy and Physiology 96

4.2a   Testes **96**
4.2b   Duct System **98**
4.2c   Seminal Vesicles, Prostate Gland, and Bulbourethral Gland **99**
Personal Decisions 4.1: Assessing Prostate Cancer **100**

4.3 Sexual Response Cycle of Men 100

4.3a   Masters and Johnson's Four-Stage Model of Sexual Response **100**
4.3b   Differences in the Sexual Response Cycle of Men and Women **103**

Chapter 5
Gender and Sexuality **106**

5.1 Terminology 108

5.1a   Sex **108**
5.1b   Gender **108**
5.1c   Gender Identity **110**
5.1d   Transgender **111**
5.1e   Gender Roles **112**
Self-Assessment 5-1: Transgender Inclusive Behavior Scale **113**
Technology and Sexuality 5-1: Transgender Options **114**
5.1f   Gender Role Ideology **115**
Self-Assessment 5-2: Sexual Assertiveness Questionnaire **115**

5.2 Biological Beginnings 116

5.2a   Chromosomes **116**
5.2b   Disorders of Sex Development **116**
Social Policy 5-1: Selecting the Sex of an Unborn Child **117**
5.2c   Atypical Chromosomal Development **118**
5.2d   Fetal Hormones **118**
5.2e   Atypical Anatomical Development **120**
5.2f   Pubertal Hormones **120**
5.2g   The Mosaic Brain **121**

5.3　Theories of Gender Role Development 122
　5.3a　Sociobiology **122**
　5.3b　Social Learning Theory **123**
　5.3c　Cognitive-Developmental Theory **123**

5.4　Agents of Gender Role Socialization 124
　5.4a　Parents **124**
　5.4b　Peers and Partners **125**
　5.4c　Teachers **125**
　5.4d　Religion **125**
　5.4e　Media **126**

5.5　Effects of Gender Role Socialization on Sexuality 126
　5.5a　Female Sexuality **126**
　5.5b　Male Sexuality **128**

5.6　Gender Role Changes 129
　5.6a　Androgyny **129**
　5.6b　Gender Role Transcendence **129**
　5.6c　Gender Postmodernism **130**

Chapter 6

Love and Sexuality **134**

6.1　Ways of Viewing Love 136
　6.1a　Love on a Continuum from Romanticism to Realism **136**
　Self-Assessment 6-1: The Love Attitudes Scale **137**
　6.1b　Three Elements of Love **138**
　6.1c　Love Languages **139**

6.2　Love Styles 140
　Technology and Sexuality 6-1:
　Technology and Romantic Relationships **140**
　6.2a　Love and Sex: Similarities and Differences **141**
　Personal Decisions 6-1: Sex With or Without Love **143**

6.3　Contexts for Sex and Love 143
　6.3a　Hooking Up **143**
　6.3b　Friends with Benefits **145**

6.4　Polyamory and Open Relationships 146
　Social Policy 6-1: Love in the Workplace **147**
　6.4a　Advantages and Disadvantages of Polyamory **149**
　6.4b　Rules of an Open Relationship **150**
　6.4c　Consensually Non-Monogamous Relationships **151**
　Self-Assessment 6-2: Consensual Non-Monogamy Scale **152**

6.5　Factors Involved in Selecting a Long-Term Partner 153
　6.5a　Cultural Factors in Selecting a Partner **153**
　6.5b　Sociological Forces in Selecting a Partner: Homogamy **153**
　6.5c　Psychological Factors in Selecting a Partner **154**

6.6　Challenges Related to Intimate Sexual Relationships 155
　6.6a　Jealousy **155**
　6.6b　Guilt **156**
　6.6c　Obsession **156**
　6.6d　Stalking **157**
　6.6e　Romantic Breakup—Change in Sexual Values **158**

Chapter 7
Communication and Sexuality 162

7.1 Principles of Relationship/Sexual Communication 164
7.1a Initiate Discussion of Important Issues 165
7.1b Choose Good Timing 165
7.1c Give Congruent Messages 166
Self-Assessment 7-1: The Sexual Signaling Behaviors Inventory 167
7.1d Minimize Criticism; Maximize Compliments 168
7.1e Communicate Feelings 169
7.1f Tell Your Partner What You Want (or Don't) 169
7.1g Make Statements Instead of Asking Questions 170
7.1h Ask Open-Ended Questions 170
7.1i Use Reflective Listening 171
7.1j Use "I" Statements 172
7.1k Keep the Process Going 172
7.1l Take Responsibility for Being Understood 172
Personal Decisions 7-1: What to Do When Your Partner Will
                               Not Communicate 173
7.1m Avoid Rehashing/Stay Focused 173

7.2 Technology, Communication, and Relationships 173
7.2a Texting and Interpersonal Communication 174
7.2b When Social Media Sites Become a Relationship Problem 174
7.2c Dick Pics 174
Technology and Sexuality 7-1: Sexting 175

7.3 Communication Theory 176
7.3a Identity Formation Theory 176
7.3b Social Learning Theory 176
7.3c Social Exchange Theory 176
Social Policy 7-1: The Law and Sexting 177

**7.4 Honesty and Dishonesty in
      Interpersonal Communication 177**
7.4a Privacy Versus Secrecy and Deception 178
7.4b Extent of Dishonesty Among College Students 179
7.4c Catfishing 179
Personal Decisions 7-2: Is Honesty Always the Best Policy? 180

7.5 Resolving Conflict in Relationships 181
7.5a Approach Communication from a Place of Respect and Negotiation 181
7.5b Address Recurring Issues 181
7.5c Focus on What You Want (Rather Than What You Don't Want) 182
7.5d Find Out Your Partner's Point of View 182
7.5e Generate Win-Win Solutions to the Conflict 182
7.5f Evaluate and Select a Solution 183

7.6 Gender Differences in Communication 184

Chapter 8
Individual and Interpersonal Sexuality 188

8.1 Erotophilia and Erotophobia 189

8.2   Virginity, Chastity, Celibacy, and Abstinence 190

Self-Assessment 8-1: Erotophilia versus Erotophobia Scale **191**

8.2a   Voluntary Abstinence **193**
8.2b   Involuntary Abstinence **193**

Social Policy 8-1: Institutional Restrictions on Sexual Expression **194**

8.2c   Asexuality **194**

8.3   Masturbation 194

8.3a   Origins of Negative Attitudes Toward Masturbation **195**
8.3b   Pros and Cons of Masturbation **198**
8.3c   Vibrators **200**

Technology and Sexuality 8-1: Sex Toy Update **201**

8.4   Sexual Fantasies 201

8.5   Interpersonal Sexuality 202

8.5a   Kissing **202**
8.5b   Sexual Touching **203**
8.5c   Fellatio **203**
8.5d   Cunnilingus **204**
8.5e   Penile-Clitoral Stimulation **204**
8.5f   Anal Stimulation **205**
8.5g   Anal Intercourse **205**
8.5h   Vaginal Intercourse **206**

Personal Decisions 8-1: Deciding to Have Sex in a New Relationship **209**

8.5i   Threesomes **211**

Chapter 9

Lifespan View of Sexuality **214**

9.1   Sexuality in Infancy and Childhood 216

9.1a   Infancy **216**
9.1b   Sexual Behaviors of Children **216**
9.1c   Parents as Sex Educators for Their Children **218**
9.1d   Public and Parochial Sex Education **218**

Personal Decisions 9-1: Exposing Children to Parental Nudity **220**

9.2   Sexuality in Adolescence 220

9.2a   Adolescence **220**
9.2b   Physiological and Physical Changes **221**
9.2c   Psychological Changes **222**
9.2d   Sexual Debut of Adolescents **222**
9.2e   Talking with Teens About Sex **223**
9.2f   Teen Pregnancy and Births **224**

9.3   Sexuality in Adulthood 224

Social Policy 9-1: Plan B for Adolescents? **225**
Technology and Sexuality 9-1: Effect of Reality TV on Viewers **226**

9.3a   Sexuality Among Singles **227**
9.3b   Sexuality Among Cohabitants **227**

Self-Assessment 9-1: Student Sexual Risks Scale (SSRS) **228**

9.3c   Sexuality Among Spouses **230**
9.3d   Sexuality Among the Divorced **231**
9.3e   Sexuality Among the Widowed **231**
9.3f   Sexual Compliance **232**

9.4 Extramarital and Extradyadic Affairs 232

    9.4a Types of Extramarital, Extradyadic Encounters **233**
    Self-Assessment 9-2: Attitudes Toward Infidelity Scale **234**
    9.4b Motivations for Extramarital/Extradyadic Affairs **235**
    9.4c Avoiding an Affair **237**
    9.4d Recovery from an Affair/Betrayal **237**
    Personal Decisions 9-2: We Both Had Affairs and Decided to
            Remain Married **238**

9.5 Sexuality in the Middle Years 238

    9.5a Women: Menopause and Hormone Replacement Therapy **239**
    9.5b Men and Testosterone Replacement Therapy **241**

9.6 Love and Sexuality in the Later Years 241

    Social Policy 9-2: Restricting Sexuality in Elder-Care Facilities **244**

Chapter 10

Diversity—LGBTQIA **248**

10.1 LGBTQIA Terminology 250

10.2 Conceptual Models of Sexual Orientation 251

    10.2a Dichotomous Model **251**
    10.2b Unidimensional Continuum Model **251**
    10.2c Multidimensional Model **253**

10.3 Prevalence by Sexual Orientation 253

10.4 Theories of Sexual Orientation 254

    10.4a Biological Explanations **254**
    10.4b Is There a Social/Cultural Influence? **255**

10.5 Dangers of Conversion Therapy 255

10.6 Coming Out or Concealment? 256

    10.6a Coming Out to Yourself and Others **258**
    Personal Decisions 10-1: Benefits and Risks of Coming Out **258**
    Technology and Sexuality 10-1: Online LGBTQIA Support Groups **259**
    10.6b Mixed-Orientation Relationships **260**

10.7 Relationships 260

    10.7a Gay Male Relationships **261**
    10.7b Lesbian Relationships **262**
    10.7c Bisexual Relationships **262**
    10.7d Pansexual Relationships **263**
    10.7e Trans Partner Relationships **263**

10.8 Health, Health Behavior, HIV, and Sexual Orientation 265

10.9 Heterosexism, Homonegativity, and Homophobia 266

    Self-Assessment 10-1: Sexual Prejudice Scale **267**
    10.9a Homonegativity and Homophobia **269**
    Social Policy 10-1: Same-Sex Marriage **272**
    10.9b Discrimination against Homosexuals **273**
    10.9c Biphobia **274**

10.10 How Heterosexuals Are Affected by Homophobia 274

**10.11 What to Do About Anti-LGBTQIA Prejudice
and Discrimination 276**

Chapter 11

Health and Sexuality **280**

11.1 **Effects of Illness and Disability on Sexuality** **282**

11.2 **Effects of Illness and Disability on Self-Concept and Body Image** **283**

Personal Decisions 11-1: Would You Date or Marry a Person in a Wheelchair? **283**

11.3 **Impaired Sensory-Motor Function and Sexuality** **283**

11.3a Spinal Cord Injury **283**
11.3b Multiple Sclerosis and Cerebral Palsy **285**

11.4 **Diabetes and Sexuality** **286**

Technology and Sexuality 11-1: Online Self-Diagnosis & Treatment **287**

11.5 **Impaired Cognitive Function and Sexuality** **288**

11.5a Alzheimer's Disease and Other Forms of Dementia **288**
11.5b Traumatic Brain Injury **289**
11.5c Intellectual and Developmental Disability **289**
Self-Assessment 11-1: Attitudes Toward Sexuality of People with an Intellectual Disability **291**

11.6 **Mental Illness and Sexuality** **292**

11.6a Mental Illness and Sexual Dysfunction **292**
11.6b Mental Illness and Barriers to Sexual Expression, Safer Sex, and Contraception **292**

11.7 **Effects of Pain and Fatigue on Sexuality** **293**

11.7a Pain and Sexuality **293**
11.7b Fatigue and Sexuality **294**

11.8 **Effects of Medical Treatment on Sexuality** **295**

11.8a Effects of Surgery on Sexuality **295**

11.9 **Effects of Medication and Radiation on Sexuality** **297**

11.10 **Alcohol, Other Drugs, and Sexuality** **298**

Social Policy 11-1: Alcohol Abuse on Campus **298**
11.10a Alcohol and Sexuality **299**
11.10b Other Recreational Drugs and Sexuality **299**
Self-Assessment 11-2: Motives for Drinking Alcohol Scale **300**
11.10c Alcohol, Drugs, and Unsafe Sex **301**

Chapter 12

Contraception and Abortion **306**

12.1 **Contraception** **308**

Self-Assessment 12-1: Contraceptive Behavior Scale (CBS) **309**
12.1a Hormonal Methods **309**
12.1b Barrier Methods **312**
12.1c Natural Family Planning Methods **317**
12.1d Withdrawal **319**
12.1e Emergency Contraception **319**
Technology and Sexuality 12-1: Contraception **321**

12.2 **Sterilization** **321**

12.2a Female Sterilization **322**
12.2b Male Sterilization **322**

12.3 Abortion 324

    12.3a Methods of Abortion **324**
    12.3b Abortion Rights in the United States: Activism, Court Rulings, and Legislation **328**
    12.3c Attitudes Toward Abortion **330**
    12.3d International Access **331**
    12.3e Physical and Psychological Effects **332**
    Personal Decisions 12-1: Deciding Whether to Have an Abortion **333**

Chapter 13

Pregnancy and Childbirth **336**

13.1 Pregnancy 338

    13.1a Pregnancy Intention **338**
    13.1b Beginning of Pregnancy **338**
    Personal Decisions 13-1: I Am an Egg Donor* **339**
    13.1c Pregnancy Testing **340**
    13.1d Physical Changes During Pregnancy **340**
    13.1e Maternal Mortality **340**
    13.1f Prenatal Care and Exercise **342**
    13.1g Alcohol, Cigarette, and Drug Use **342**
    Social Policy 13-1: Criminal Prosecution for Fetal Abuse? **344**
    13.1h Prenatal Testing **344**
    13.1i Miscarriage **346**
    13.1j Sex During Pregnancy **346**

13.2 Infertility 347

    13.2a Causes of Infertility **348**
    Technology and Sexuality 13-1: Infertility, Birth Defects, and Information Sharing **349**

13.3 Childbirth: Preparation and Reality 349

    13.3a Childbirth Preparation—Lamaze **349**
    13.3b Trends: Classes, Birth Centers, Home Birth, and VBAC **351**
    13.3c Pain Control in Labor and Delivery **351**
    13.3d First Stage of Labor **352**
    13.3e Second Stage of Labor **352**
    13.3f Third Stage of Labor **354**
    13.3g Cesarean Childbirth **354**
    13.3h Reactions to the Baby **355**
    13.3i Dangers of Childbirth for the Mother **355**

Chapter 14

Sexual Dysfunctions and Sex Therapy **358**

14.1 Definitions of Sexual Dysfunctions 360

14.2 Causes and Contributing Factors of Sexual Dysfunctions 362

    14.2a Organic Factors **362**
    14.2b Sociocultural Factors **363**
    14.2c Psychological Factors **364**
    14.2d Relationship Factors **365**
    14.2e Cognitive Factors **365**
    14.2f Sexual Destiny? **366**
    Self-Assessment 14-1: Sexual Destiny Beliefs Measure **366**

14.3   Interest/Arousal Dysfunctions   367

14.3a   Female Sexual Interest/Arousal Disorder   **367**
Social Policy 14-1: "Even the Score" Debate   **371**
14.3b   Male Hypoactive Sexual Desire Disorder   **372**
14.3c   Couple Discrepancy in Desire for Frequency of Sex   **373**

14.4   Other Male Sexual Dysfunctions   373

14.4a   Premature Ejaculation   **373**
14.4b   Erectile Disorder   **375**

14.5   Orgasm Dysfunctions   378

14.5a   Female Orgasmic Disorder   **378**
14.5b   Delayed Ejaculation   **381**

14.6   Genito-Pelvic Pain/Penetration Disorder   383

14.6a   Vaginismus   **384**
14.6b   Dyspareunia   **384**

14.7   Sex Therapy   386

14.7a   Sex Therapist Requirements/Status of the Profession   **386**
14.7b   Cognitive Behavioral Sex Therapy   **386**
Personal Decisions 14-1: Finding a Sex Therapist   **387**
14.7c   Masters and Johnson's Approach   **387**
14.7d   Kaplan's Approach   **388**
14.7e   PLISSIT Model Approach   **389**
14.7f   LoPiccolo's Approach   **389**
14.7g   Effectiveness of Sex Therapy   **389**
Technology and Sexuality 14-1: The Medicalization of
Sexual Dysfunctions   **390**

Chapter 15

Variant Sexual Behavior   **394**

15.1   What Is Normal Sexual Behavior?   396

15.1a   Criteria Used to Define Normal Sexual Behavior   **396**
15.1b   Historical Variations in Definitions of Normal Sexual Behavior   **397**
15.1c   Nudism   **398**

15.2   Variant Sexual Behavior: Definitions and Overview   398

15.2a   Legal Versus Illegal Paraphilias   **400**
Personal Decisions 15-1: Whose Business Is a Paraphilia?   **401**

15.3   Types of Paraphilic Disorders   401

15.3a   Voyeuristic Disorder   **402**
15.3b   Exhibitionistic Disorder   **403**
15.3c   Frotteuristic Disorder   **404**
15.3d   Sexual Masochism Disorder   **405**
15.3e   Sadism Disorder   **407**
15.3f   Pedophilic Disorder   **408**
15.3g   Fetishistic Disorder   **410**
Self-Assessment 15-1: Salience of Fetishism Scale   **410**
Technology and Sexuality 15-1: Finding Paraphilia Partners via
the Internet   **411**
15.3h   Transvestic Disorder   **412**
15.3i   Other Paraphilias   **412**
15.3j   Pathologizing Kink   **414**
15.3k   "Sexual Addiction"   **414**

15.4   The Origins of Paraphilias: Theoretical Perspectives   415

15.4a Psychoanalytic Theory   **415**
Self-Assessment 15-2: Sexual Compulsivity Scale   **416**
15.4b Feminist Theory   **417**
15.4c Learning Theory   **417**
15.4d Biological Theory   **418**

15.5   Treatment of Paraphilias   418

15.5a Decreasing Deviant Sexual Arousal   **419**
Social Policy 15-1: Treating Paraphilic Sex Offenders with Hormones   **419**
15.5b Aversive Conditioning   **420**
15.5c Covert Sensitization   **420**
15.5d Learning Social Skills   **420**
Personal Decisions 15-2: Can People Control Their Paraphilias?   **421**
15.5e Changing Faulty Cognitions   **421**
15.5f Resolving Sexual Dysfunctions   **421**

Chapter16
Sexually Transmitted Infections   **424**

16.1   Sexually Transmitted Infections: An Overview   426

16.1a Prevalence and Incidence of STIs in the United States   **426**
16.1b Ignorance Promotes Infection   **426**
16.1c Risk Factors for Sexually Transmitted Infections   **427**
16.1d STI Testing   **430**
Technology and Sexuality 16-1: Notification of Partners   **431**
16.1e Consequences of Sexually Transmitted Infections   **432**

16.2   Sexually Transmitted Infections: A Pandemic   434

16.3   Types of STIs   434

16.3a Ectoparasitic Infections   **434**
16.3b Bacterial Infections   **435**
16.3c Viral Infections   **439**

16.4   HIV and AIDS   442

16.4a Definitions of HIV and AIDS   **442**
16.4b Transmission   **442**
16.4c Prevention and Control   **445**

16.5   Protecting Yourself from STIs   445

16.5a Abstaining from Sex   **446**
16.5b Reducing the Number of Sexual Partners and Mutual Monogamy   **446**
16.5c Using Condoms Consistently and Effectively   **446**
Self-Assessment 16-1: The UCLA Multidimensional Condom
Attitudes Scale   **448**
16.5d Preexposure Vaccination   **449**
Social Policy 16-1: Condom Availability in High Schools   **450**
16.5e Seeking STI Screening and Prompt Treatment   **451**
Personal Decisions 16-1: Should You Be Screened for STIs?   **451**
Social Policy 16-2: Legal Aspects of Disclosing an STI   **452**

16.6   Accessing Sexual Health Services   453

Chapter 17
Sexual Coercion   **456**

17.1   Sexual Coercion: Rape and Sexual Assault   458

17.1a   Definitions of Rape   **459**

Self-Assessment 17-1: Revised Sexual Coercion Inventory*   **460**

Personal Experience 17-1: "And the Lights Went Out"   **462**

17.1b   Prevalence and Contexts of Rape   **462**

17.1c   Characteristics of Men Who Rape Women   **463**

17.1d   Men as Victims of Rape   **466**

17.2   Theories of Rape   467

17.2a   Evolutionary and Biological Theories of Rape   **467**

17.2b   Psychopathological Theory of Rape   **468**

Technology and Sexuality 17-1: Resources for Safety, Information, and Support   **468**

17.2c   Feminist Theory of Rape   **469**

17.2d   Social Learning Theory of Rape   **469**

Self-Assessment 17-2: Rape Supportive Attitude Scale   **470**

17.2e   Rape Culture   **471**

17.2f   Sexual Assault and Harassment in the Military   **472**

17.3   Consequences of Rape and Treatment for Rape Survivors   473

17.3a   Reporting a Rape and Title IX   **473**

17.3b   Consequences of Rape   **474**

17.3c   Treatment for Rape Survivors   **475**

17.4   Prevention of Rape   475

17.4a   Teaching Women to Avoid Rape   **476**

17.4b   Teaching Men Not to Rape   **476**

17.4c   Campaigns to Address Rape   **477**

Social Policy 17-1: The #MeToo Movement—Have We Gone Too Far?   **478**

17.5   Child Sexual Abuse   479

17.5a   Intrafamilial Child Sexual Abuse   **480**

Personal Experience 17-2: "Child Sex Abuse by My Father"   **481**

17.5b   Extrafamilial Child Sexual Abuse   **483**

17.5c   Stages of Grooming   **483**

17.5d   Recovered Memories of Abuse   **483**

17.6   Consequences and Treatment of Child Sexual Abuse   484

17.6a   Impact of Child Sexual Abuse   **484**

17.6b   Treatment of Sexually Abused Children and Adults Sexually Abused as Children   **485**

17.7   Prevention of Child Sexual Abuse   485

Social Policy 17-2: Megan's Law   **486**

17.8   Treatment of Rape and Child Sexual Abuse Perpetrators   486

17.9   Sexual Harassment   487

17.9a   Definition and Incidence of Sexual Harassment   **488**

17.9b   Theories of Sexual Harassment   **489**

17.9c   Profile of Sexually Harassed Victims and Perpetrators   **490**

Social Policy 17-3: Sexual Harassment Policy in the Workplace   **490**

17.9d   Consequences of Sexual Harassment   **491**

17.9e   Responses to Sexual Harassment   **491**

Personal Decisions 17-1: Confronting Someone Who Sexually Harasses You   **492**

Chapter 18
Commercialization of Sex **498**

18.1 Sex in Advertising **500**

18.2 Sexuality Online **500**

18.2a Benefits of Sexuality Online **500**
Social Policy 18-1: Government Control of Online Sexual Content **501**
18.2b Disadvantages of Sexuality Online **504**

18.3 Sex and the Law **506**

18.4 Sex-Related Businesses **507**

18.4a Phone Sex **507**
18.4b Camming **507**
18.4c Strip Clubs **507**
Personal Decisions 18-1: "Camming from My Apartment" **508**
Personal Decisions 18-2: What It's Like to Be a Stripper—Two Stories **509**
18.4d Erotic Massage Parlors **510**
18.4e Community Attitudes toward Adult Businesses **510**

18.5 Pornography **511**

18.5a Defining Pornography and Erotica **511**
Technology and Sexuality 18-1:
Online Porn, Commercial vs. Amateur, and "Pornification" **512**
Self-Assessment 18-1: The Problematic Pornography
Consumption Scale (PPCS) **513**
18.5b Pornography and the Law **514**
18.5c Effects of Pornography on Individuals and Relationships **515**
Personal Experience 18-1: Porn in My Marriage* **517**

18.6 Sex Work **517**

18.6a Definition of Prostitution as Sex Work **517**
18.6b Types of Sex Workers **518**
18.6c Becoming a Sex Worker **521**
18.6d Life as a Sex Worker **523**
18.6e Impact of Sex Work on Personal Intimate Relationships **523**
Personal Decisions 18-3: Sex Workers Speak Out **524**
18.6f Clients of Sex Workers **524**
18.6g Prostitution and the Law **526**
18.6h Sex Workers and STIs/HIV **526**
Social Policy 18-2: Should Sex Work Be Decriminalized? **527**
18.6i Sex Trafficking **528**

Glossary **535**

References **555**

Author Index **595**

Subject Index **603**

Preface

Why another edition of *Human Sexuality: Making Informed Decisions?* One sexuality teacher noted that giving the same tests every year was routine—while the questions were the same, the answers kept changing. The chapters in this sixth edition have been thoroughly revised, with more than 400 new research citations (many 2019 references). The revision also features original data from over 13,000 undergraduates who revealed their sexual attitudes and behaviors.

Finally, this sixth edition reflects an awareness of changes in gender terminology in our society. Where appropriate, the term cisgender (meaning one's genitalia matches their gender identity) has been used. The term has not been used when referring to some research because not all researchers indicated whether their respondents were asked their gender or their gender identity.

The theme of the text remains the same: to encourage you to make informed, deliberate sexual decisions. Young adults might recognize that by not making a decision (e.g. to use a condom/safe sex), they have already made a decision by default (e.g. not using a condom/unsafe sex). In this regard, making informed/deliberate decisions involves being aware of the options/consequences of the various choices, making a decision, and following through.

Examples of new content for this edition include:

New to this Edition

Chapter 1: Human Sexuality: An Introduction

- Concept of sex positivity explained
- Sexual health as part of the definition of human sexuality
- The experience of casual sex
- Deciding to improve one's sexual growth
- Self-Assessment: Sexual Growth Beliefs Measure
- Being in a dating/romantic relationship with an older partner
- Decreasing double standard
- Hedonism is contextual (e.g. sexual tourism)
- Spatial context for sex (e.g. in a parked car)
- Abstinence-only-until-marriage programs funded in spite of ineffectiveness
- Impact of religion on sexual attitudes and behaviors
- Effect of time spent on social media on one's relationship fidelity
- Exposure to media (women's magazines) associated with negative self-sexualization
- World Association for Sexual Health
- Definitions of virginity among LGBTQIA members
- Conditions of sexual agency
- Sexual values of 13,000-plus undergraduates
- Happier reported marital satisfaction with fewer previous sexual partners
- The sexual behavior of dating app users compared to non-app users
- Japan's Rorikon as "Lolita Complex"
- Mischievous research responders and outrageous responses
- Sexual well-being and freedom not to be sexual
- Romantic breakups associated with sexual values becoming more liberal
- Snapchat sexual messaging
- Double standard reflected by Asian American men
- Religious persons, lower mental health, and less ability to control sex thoughts
- Gang members' expectations of "sexing-in" and "running trains"
- Alcohol's role in getting a woman to have sexual intercourse without a condom

Chapter 2: Sex Research and Theory

- Profile of respondents who typically participate in sex research
- Sexuality throughout the world—China
- Problems associated with sex research on black males
- Sociobiology becoming more tenuous as an accepted theory
- Effect on individuals who become involved in "sensitive sex research topics"
- Federal funding as a reflection of values of administration in power
- Theories used to interpret analysis of the data
- New statistical opportunities through open-source software: taxometric analysis, tests of measurement variability, differential item functioning, and equivalence testing

Chapter 3: Female Sexual Anatomy, Physiology, and Response

- Female genital cutting experienced by millions of women worldwide
- Variability of female sexual response
- Gambian men compare the sexuality of cut and uncut partners
- Criminalization of menstrual huts in Nepal
- Female orgasm discrepancy—what husbands think versus reality
- Increased sexual self-esteem in men when their partner has an orgasm
- Alternative rights of passage (to genital cutting)
- View of female breasts by sexual minority women of Taiwan
- Menstrual equality legislation
- Clitoral stimulation's role during sexual intercourse for orgasm
- The use of sex toys by sex educators to close orgasm gap in heterosexual relationships

Chapter 4: Male Sexual Anatomy, Physiology, and Response

- Recommendations to ban male circumcision by Icelandic and Danish health officials
- Penis length of sexually experienced college males
- Preferences of 1,592 women in regard to circumcised/uncircumcised penis

Chapter 5: Gender and Sexuality

- New terminology for gender-fluid individuals/relationships
- Need for sensitivity for intersex individuals in regard to genital exams
- Inconsistencies in parental attitudes toward egalitarian gender role socialization and actual behavior (traditional)
- What constitutes being a woman—the case of the 2012 Miss Universe pageant
- Transgender Inclusive Behavior Scale (TIBS)
- Male sexuality described as negative (e.g. rape) with little focus on sex positivity
- Women and men preferences regarding egalitarian relationships/women in subordinate role
- Effect of telling contemporary intersex youth of their intersex status
- Percent reporting satisfaction with sex reassignment surgery
- Higher levels of sex guilt in women versus men
- Limited public acceptance of transgender individuals using public restrooms
- How bisexual parents socialize their children in regard to gender
- Number of lifetime sex partners reported by British women
- Higher sexual inactivity among transfeminine individuals without surgery
- How bisexual mothers rear their children in regard to gender
- Minimizing stigma and trauma on individuals identified as intersex
- Body perception by black women versus white women
- High sex agency (assertiveness) and higher positivity about sex in some women
- Male sexuality discussion as negative (e.g. men rape) more than positive
- Preferences about child gender by undergraduates

Chapter 6: Love and Sexuality

- Love languages
- Updated data from Annual Office Romance Survey of Vault.com
- Consensually non-monogamous relationships linked to positive sexual health outcomes
- Self-Assessment: Consensual Non-Monogamy Scale
- Comparison of relationship quality among monogamists and polyamorists
- Comparison of sexual satisfaction between consensual non-monogamous and monogamous couples
- Love relationship with a robot?
- Sex as primary motive for friends with benefits relationship
- Likelihood of marriage by persons who first hook up
- Persons in a friends with benefits relationship
- Love at first sight versus strong attraction labeled as love
- Rates of sexual satisfaction (and orgasm) in monogamous relationships versus consensually non-monogamous relationships
- Equal relationship satisfaction
- Sexual satisfaction rates in swingers versus persons in monogamous relationships
- How the motivation for hooking up impacts emotional outcome (pleasure versus coping)
- How sexual values change as a result of a romantic breakup

Chapter 7: Communication and Sexuality

- Impact on the relationship of rejecting the partner kindly versus having sex reluctantly
- Catfishing
- Feminist openness about what they want sexually/frequency of fake orgasm
- Sexting as both objectifying and liberating
- Receiving unwanted sexting/coerced sexting associated with depression, anxiety
- Discussing sexual exclusivity
- Self-disclosure and sexual satisfaction
- Sexual compatibility and sexual satisfaction
- Importance of discussing condom use—reasons for not using condom
- Sexual communication associated with desire, arousal, orgasm, and less pain
- Research on words lovers say and the noises they make during sex
- Sexting in long-distance relationships
- Goal of men who sent dick pics

Chapter 8: Individual and Interpersonal Sexuality

- Percent of US adults reporting interpersonal sex at least once a week
- Threesomes with two males and one female reflect expanding boundaries of male sexuality
- Sex toy use: frequency, types, demographics of users, frequency of cleaning
- View of manual, oral, and anal sex as not "having sex"
- Potential violence and danger in the "incel community" (involuntary celibate)
- Vibrator use among Chinese women
- Online availability of fully functional sex dolls

Chapter 9: Lifespan View of Sexuality

- Numbers of 18–29 year olds reporting no partner sex in the last 12 months
- Patterns of number of sexual partners ages 16–22
- Sexual bereavement of persons who lose a long-term partner
- Being realistic about monogamy and whether to end a relationship
- Reasons for extradyadic emotional, sexual, cybersexual involvement
- Romantic love in late life of 14 previously divorced/widowed women (ages 65–84)
- Primary reasons spouses give for remaining faithful
- Similarity of adolescent precocious sexual behavior in single-parent homes
- Focus of sexual debut education on making deliberate sexual decisions
- Sexual compliance
- Japan's rent-a-family industry
- Use of synthetic surrogates by couples for threesomes
- Partner's reaction to infidelity
- Content analysis of *Hot in Cleveland* by women over 50
- Divorce as a time of empowerment for women in both exploration and satisfaction
- Avoiding involvement in an affair
- Identification of 77 motivations for sexual intercourse
- Adolescent girls' preference of mothers and sisters (over friends) when talking about dating and sex
- Sexual guilt associated with engaging in sexual behavior in adolescence
- Parental discussion with adolescents about sex associated with delay in first intercourse
- Likelihood of office workers over age 50 to have romantic relationship with a coworker
- Variety for men and neglect for women as top reasons identified for having an affair
- No mention of sex in online dating profiles of those over 60
- The role of better health in sexual functioning and satisfaction
- Social construction of menopause as an illness rather than empowerment

Chapter 10: Diversity—LGBTQIA

- Trans partner relationships
- Korean acceptance of homosexuality across a 5-year period
- How asexuals are impacted by a compulsory sexuality-focused society
- Effect of religion on gays and lesbians
- Five facts about same-sex marriage
- Lower sexual satisfaction among same-sex individuals than heterosexuals
- Increasing bans of conversion therapy by states
- Higher depression/anxiety among bisexuals than heterosexuals or lesbians/gay males
- How age impacts openness (being out of the closet)
- Discrimination of LGBT individuals in elder-care settings
- Relationship quality of same-sex couples versus other-sex and bisexual couples
- Prison as a context that blurs genders and sexualities
- Health, health behavior, and sexual orientation
- Longitudinal study comparing children of lesbian mothers and normative scale
- "Bear" identity
- Negative outcomes for mental health in gay and religious persons
- Higher incidence of internet hate targeting experienced by LGBT in the South
- Asexuals and discovery of interest/desire on first experience
- Higher mental distress by pansexuals versus bisexuals
- Low percentage of men and women reporting minimal interest in sex
- Preferences in elementary school children for children with other-sex parents

Chapter 11: Health and Sexuality

- Disabled individuals not an automatic determinant of asexuality
- Sexual frequencies of those with lower cognitive ability
- Positive association of cannabis use with sexual functioning and sexual satisfaction
- Association of diabetes in women to sexual satisfaction/higher sexual dysfunction

Chapter 12: Contraception and Abortion

- Condom use resistance among men with history of sex aggression/alcohol abuse
- Stealthing as a form of abuse
- Georgia's "Fetal Heartbeat Bill" outlawing abortion once heartbeat in womb detected
- Increase in states passing legislation to ban most abortions at every stage and criminalize the procedure for physicians
- Availability of safe, reliable hormonal male contraception in 2030
- Number of states regarded as hostile toward abortion rights

Chapter 13: Pregnancy and Childbirth

- Factors in decision of lesbians and gays to have a biological child
- Drop in sexual frequency and satisfaction for parents after birth of their child
- Annual use of donor sperm (alone or mixed) by women
- Limited research support for including partners in postpartum depression interventions
- Dangers of childbirth for the mother
- Peripartum depression
- Association of vaginal delivery with lower frequency of orgasm/intensity when compared to Caesarean delivery

Chapter 14: Sexual Dysfunctions and Sex Therapy

- Vyleesi, designed to boost female desire, being touted as "female Viagra"
- Self-Assessment: Sexual Destiny Beliefs Measure
- Group mindfulness-based cognitive therapy for sexuality (MBCT-S) and low libido
- Number of sexuality courses required for marriage and family therapy graduate programs
- Use of the "good enough" model for sexual enjoyment/satisfaction
- Treatment of discrepancy in desired sex frequency
- Reasons women give for not having an orgasm during partnered sex
- Surrogate partners in therapy
- Use of synthetic surrogate in sex therapy
- Impact of genitopelvic pain on self-worth in women
- Personal and relationship distress impacted by presence of sexual dysfunctions
- Effects of age on sexual frequency and dysfunctions
- Effects of chronic disease on one's desire/sexual functioning
- Lower interest in sex by women who breastfeed
- Percentage of couples seeing a marriage/family therapist for a sexual problem

Chapter 15: Variant Sexual Behavior

- Nudism
- International data from Quebec on paraphiliac desires and behavior
- Making out: frequencies, motivations, and outcomes
- Concept of "virtuous pedophile"
- Use of the internet by pedophiles to find minors to have sex with
- Fluidity/switching in gendered bondage, discipline, sadism, masochism (BDSM) roles
- Age-play (e.g. littles) and how it has been pathologized

Chapter 16: Sexually Transmitted Infections

- PEP (post-exposure prophylaxis)
- Outcomes of HIV prevention messages about self/partner benefits of antiretroviral therapy
- Frequency of condom use among more involved/committed partners in a relationship
- Tourism as a context of increased sexual risk taking
- Condom assertiveness
- Stealthing
- Use of video games to improve use on condoms

Chapter 17: Sexual Coercion

- Revised Sexual Coercion Inventory
- How sexual consent is best understood along a continuum rather than a dichotomy
- Personal Experience: "And the Lights Went Out"
- Stages of grooming
- Personal Experience: Child Sex Abuse by My Father
- Gang rapes in the Second Congo War (1998–2003) and Bosnian War (1992–1995) and kidnapping by Boko Haram
- Broad definition of sexual harassment
- Cyberstalkers
- Increased reporting of sexual harassment due to Harvey Weinstein exposure
- Use of protective behavioral strategies to help prevent rape
- Personal Decisions: Spring Break at the Beach
- Comparison of testosterone levels of sex offenders and non-sex offenders
- Benefits of polygraph testing while perpetrator is in supervision
- Delay of new Pentagon data on sexual assault based on fears of slowed recruiting
- Pennsylvania Grand Jury Report of over 300 priests sexually assaulting over 1,000 children in massive cover up
- #MeToo Movement—Have we gone too far?
- Themes of treatment in child sexual abuse
- Sexual agency—importance of females being assertive

Chapter 18: Commercialization of Sex

- Sex worker motivation for getting into the business
- Nuances of sugar baby and sugar daddy—chemistry or prostitution?
- Global view of male escort websites
- Tunisian professional boyfriends
- Potential lockdown, restricted mobility of sex workers in Nevada's brothels
- Egyptian parents allowing children to "marry" tourists for legal sex
- Feminist porn
- Revenge porn—men violence against women?
- Cybersex addiction
- Advertisements of escorts on the internet
- Erotic Review as a source of information and socialization of the novice client
- Primary reason sex workers want to exit the business
- Positive effects of online pornography for women
- Effects of pornography use related to shared (watch together), concordant (watch separately), or discordant use (only one watches)
- The Problematic Pornography Consumption Scale (PPCS)
- State–level anti-trafficking legislation
- "Strichplatz" areas—"sex boxes"— in Zurich, Switzerland for "drive-in" sex
- Male escorts offering emotional intimacy, interaction, personality—the "boyfriend" experience
- Downloaded pornography content primarily women pleasuring men
- 2018 FOSTA (Fight Online Sex Trafficking Act) and SESTA (Stop Enabling Sex Traffickers Act) bills

Supplements and Resources

Instructor Supplements

A complete teaching package is available for instructors who adopt this book. This package includes an **online lab**, *Instructor's Manual,* **exam bank, PowerPoint® slides, LMS integration,** and **LMS exam bank files.**

Online Lab	BVT's online lab is available for this textbook on two different platforms—BVT*Lab* (at www.BVTLab.com), and LAB BOOK™ (at www.BVTLabBook.com). These are described in more detail in the corresponding sections below. Both platforms allow instructors to set up graded homework, quizzes, and exams.
Instructor's Manual	The *Instructor's Manual* helps first-time instructors develop the course, while also offering seasoned instructors a new perspective on the materials. Each section of the *Instructor's Manual* coincides with a chapter in the textbook. The user-friendly format begins by providing learning objectives and detailed outlines for each chapter. Then, the manual presents lecture discussions, class activities, and/or sample answers to the end-of-chapter review questions, along with citations that provide the rationale for the answers. Lastly, additional resources—books, articles, websites—are listed to help instructors review the materials covered in each chapter.
Exam Bank	An extensive exam bank is available to instructors in both hard-copy and electronic form. Each chapter has approximately 50 multiple-choice, 25 true/false, 10 short-answer, and 5 essay questions ranked by difficulty and style. Each question is referenced to the appropriate section of the text to make test creation quick and easy.
PowerPoint Slides	A set of PowerPoint slides with about 40 slides per chapter is available and includes a chapter overview, learning objectives, slides covering all key topics, key figures and charts, and summary and conclusion slides.
LMS Integration	BVT offers basic integration with Learning Management Systems (LMSs), providing single-sign-on links (often called LTI links) from Blackboard, Canvas, Moodle (or any other LMS) directly into BVT*Lab*, eBookPlus or the LAB BOOK platform. Gradebooks from BVT*Lab* and the LAB BOOK can be imported into most LMSs.
LMS Exam Bank Files	Exam banks are available as Blackboard files, QTI files (for Canvas) and Respondus files (for other LMSs) so they can easily be imported into a wide variety of course management systems.

Student Resources

Student resources are available for this textbook at both the BVT*Lab* platform and the LAB BOOK platform, as described below. These resources are geared toward students needing additional assistance, as well as those seeking complete mastery of the content. The following resources are available:

Practice Questions	Students can work through hundreds of practice questions online. Questions are multiple choice or true/false in format and are graded instantly for immediate feedback.
Flashcards	BVT*Lab* includes sets of flashcards that reinforce the key terms and concepts from each chapter.
PowerPoint Slides	For a study recap, students can view all of the instructor PowerPoint slides online.
Additional LAB BOOK Resources	On the LAB BOOK platform, comprehension questions are sprinkled throughout each chapter of the eBook, and detailed section summaries are included in the lab. Study tools such as text highlighting and margin notes are also available. These resources are not available in BVT*Lab*.

BVT*Lab*

BVT*Lab* is an affordable online lab for instructors and their students. It includes an online classroom with grade book and class forum, a homework grading system, extensive test banks for quizzes and exams, and a host of student study resources.

Course Setup	BVT*Lab* has an easy-to-use, intuitive interface that allows instructors to quickly set up their courses and grade books and to replicate them from section to section and semester to semester.
Grade Book	Using an assigned passcode, students register into their section's grade book, which automatically grades and records all homework, quizzes, and tests.
Class Forum	Instructors can post discussion threads to a class forum and then monitor and moderate student replies.
Student Resources	All student resources for this textbook are available in digital form within BVT*Lab*. Even if a class is not taught in the lab, students who have purchased lab access can still use the student resources in the lab.
eBook	BVT*Lab* includes both a webBook™ and a downloadable eBook (on the VitalSource® platform). For some product bundles, BVT's LAB BOOK can also be accessed from within BVT*Lab*, offering enhanced eBook features and study tools for students, as described below.

LAB BOOK

LAB BOOK is a web-based eBook platform with an integrated lab providing comprehension tools and interactive student resources. Instructors can build homework and quizzes right into the eBook. LAB BOOK is either included with eBOOK^Plus or offered as a stand-alone product.

Course Setup	LAB BOOK uses the BVT*Lab* interface to allow instructors to set up their courses and grade books and to replicate them from section to section and semester to semester.
Grade Book	Using an assigned passcode, students register into their section's grade book, which automatically grades and records all homework, quizzes, and tests.
Advanced eBook	LAB BOOK is a mobile-friendly, web-based eBook platform designed for PCs, Macs, tablets, and smartphones. LAB BOOK allows highlighting, margin notes, and a host of other study tools.
Student Resources	All student resources for this textbook are available in the LAB BOOK, as described in the Student Resources section above.

Customization

BVT's Custom Publishing Division can help you modify this book's content to satisfy your specific instructional needs. The following are examples of customization:

- Rearrangement of chapters to follow the order of your syllabus
- Deletion of chapters not covered in your course
- Addition of paragraphs, sections, or chapters you or your colleagues have written for this course
- Editing of the existing content, down to the word level
- Customization of the accompanying student resources and online lab
- Addition of handouts, lecture notes, syllabus, and so forth
- Incorporation of student worksheets into the textbook

All of these customizations will be professionally typeset to produce a seamless textbook of the highest quality, with an updated table of contents and index to reflect the customized content.

Acknowledgments

Human Sexuality: Making Informed Decisions 6th edition is the result of the work of many people. We are indebted to members of the BVT Publishing team for their focused professionalism. Specifically, that includes Publisher and Managing Director Richard Schofield; Production and Fulfillment Manager Janai Escobedo; Permissions Coordinator Jade Elk; Designers Stephanie Elliott and Tim Gerlach; Managing Editor Anne Serbulea; Copyeditor Regina Roths; Proofreader Teresa Daly; and Ancillary Coordinator Tiffany Koopal.

Appreciation is also expressed to Dr. Robert Sammons, who continues to provide awareness of cutting-edge sexuality content, and to Dr. Lindsay Briggs for her suggestions regarding Chapter 5.

We are always interested in ways to improve the text. As such, we invite your feedback and suggestions for material to include in subsequent editions. We welcome dialogue with professors and students about sexuality issues, and we encourage you to e-mail us.

David Knox: knoxd@ecu.edu

Susan Milstein: drsuemilstein@gmail.com

Chapter Outline

Defining Human Sexuality 6
  Thoughts 6
  Sexual Self-Concept 7
  Values 8
  Emotions 11
  Behaviors 12
Anatomy and Physiology 13
Reproduction 13
Interpersonal Relationships 13

Sexual Health 14
and Other Views 18
Sexual Decisions 18
To Decide Is to Decide 18
Involve Trade-Offs 18

CHAPTER

1

Human Sexuality: An Introduction

Sex is perfectly natural. It's something that's pleasurable. It's enjoyable and it enhances a relationship. So why don't we learn as much as we can about it and become comfortable with ourselves as sexual human beings because we are all sexual?

Sue Johanson, Canadian sex educator

Chapter Outline

Self-Assessment 1-1:
  Sexual Importance Scale **5**
1.1 Defining Human Sexuality 6
1.1a Thoughts **6**
1.1b Sexual Self-Concept **7**
1.1c Values **8**
1.1d Emotions **11**
1.1e Behaviors **12**
1.1f Anatomy and Physiology **13**
1.1g Reproduction **13**
1.1h Interpersonal Relationships **13**
Technology and Sexuality 1-1:
  There's an App for That! **13**
1.1i Sexual Health **14**
1.1j Still Other Views **14**
1.2 Nature of Sexual Decisions 15
1.2a Not to Decide Is to Decide **15**
1.2b Decisions Involve Trade-Offs **15**
1.2c Decisions Include Selecting a Positive or Negative View **15**
1.2d Decisions Can Produce Ambivalence and Uncertainty **16**
1.2e Some Decisions Are Revocable; Some Are Not **16**

1.3 Making Sexual Decisions 16
1.3a Four Themes of Sexual Decision-Making by Women **16**
1.3b Deciding to Improve One's Sexual Growth **17**
Self-Assessment 1-2:
  Sexual Growth Beliefs Measure **17**
1.3c Spatial Context of Sex **18**
1.4 Influences on Sexual Decisions 18
1.4a Culture **19**
1.4b Media **19**
1.4c Peers and Parents **20**
1.4d Technology **21**
1.4e Education **22**
1.4f Religion **22**
Social Policy 1-1
  Sex Education in Public Schools **24**
1.4g Alcohol/Substance Use **25**
1.4h Psychological Factors **25**
Personal Decisions 1-1
  Do You or Other Factors Control Your Sexual Decisions? **26**
Web Links 27
Key Terms 27

Objectives

1. Identify the various elements that make up the concept of human sexuality
2. Know the importance of body image for your sexuality
3. Review the nature of sexual decisions and the four themes of making sexual decisions
4. Discuss technology, sexuality, and apps
5. Review the various influences on making sexual decisions
6. Understand the evolution and status of sex education programs in the United States

Truth —— OR —— Fiction?

T / F   1. Women make and break virginity pledges more than men.

T / F   2. The "hookup culture" (casual sex) is now the predominant sexual value.

T / F   3. Comprehensive sex education is mandated in the UK from the primary grades through high school.

T / F   4. Believing that a good sexual relationship is something you need to work at is negatively associated with sexual quality.

T / F   5. In a high school, if there are more females than males, males are less likely to be romantic or to commit to one partner.

Answers: 1. T   2. F   3. T   4. F   5. T

Courses in human sexuality always fill quickly to capacity and are viewed as "more interesting than other courses" (King et al., 2019b). Sexuality is a core aspect of our being, from reproduction to a sense of self to exhilarating experiences. That sexuality is of prime importance in our lives is the reason for our focus on making informed decisions. Below are examples of situations requiring informed decisions about our sexuality:

- You have just met someone at a party or bar. You've had a couple of drinks and are flirting. Your partner flirts back. How soon and what types of sexual activities are appropriate with this person?

- Your partner watches a lot of porn. Do you join in? Confront your partner? Ignore the behavior?

- You have a sexually transmitted infection (STI), have had an abortion, or have previously engaged in sexual behavior your partner does not know about. Do you tell your partner?

These scenarios reflect the need to make decisions about dilemmas such as the timing of introducing sex into a new relationship, the role of pornography, and the timing of revealing sexual secrets. A primary goal of this text is to emphasize the relentlessness of the sexual challenges that confront us and the importance of making deliberate and informed sexual decisions throughout our lives.

Our society also makes decisions about social policies on sexuality, including the availability of abortions, emergency contraception as an over-the-counter medication, the legalization of same-sex marriages, and the nature of sex education in the public school system.

Sexual decisions remain at the core of who we are as individuals and as a nation. Making informed decisions involves knowledge of the psychological, physical, and social consequences of those decisions. Having a partner comfortable with their own sexuality was important to 92% of the 5,500 respondents in Match.com's *Singles in America survey* (2016).

In relation to making sexual decisions, a major theme of this text is positive sexuality (see insert).

Themes of Positive Sexuality

Another term for positive sexuality is sex positivity. The themes behind the term were identified by Ivanski and Kohut (2017). These were based on the thoughts of 52 professionals in sexuality and relationships:

Personal beliefs about sexuality—these include that sex is good as long as no one is being harmed, it encompasses beliefs about women's rights (e.g. to enjoy sex free of negative labeling), and it requires consent of the parties.

Education about sexuality—individuals are informed of basic aspects of sex, anatomy, pregnancy, pregnancy prevention, abortion, STIs. Information emphasizes diversity in ages and sexual orientations and is presented in an open, nonjudgmental way.

Health and safety—individuals use contraception and condoms.

Respect for the individual—includes respect for individual choice, abstinence as a valid option, self-acceptance about your own choices and the choices of others.

Positive relationships with others—includes being accepting of the diversity in genders, sexual identities, and preferences of others.

Negative aspects—sex positivity can lead to oversexualization, particularly in the media; it can promote the idea that everyone should have sex, be judgmental of those who do not have a positive relationship with sex, and cause people to feel pressured into doing things they are not comfortable with.

Self-Assessment 1-1: Sexual Importance Scale

Instructions

Respond to the following questions as truthfully as you can. There are no wrong or right answers. Use the following criteria as you place a check mark above the number indicating the extent to which you agree or disagree with that statement.

1 (Disagree strongly), 2 (Mostly disagree), 3 (Disagree a little), 4 (Neither agree nor diagree),
5 (Agree a little), 6 (Mostly agree), 7 (Agree strongly)

1. __ Having a regular sex partner is one of the most important benefits of marriage or other long-term relationships.

2. __ I expect my partner to make being a good lover a high priority in our relationship.

3.* __ Paying attention to each other sexually is one of the most important things couples should do to be happy together.

4. __ Couples would be happier if they spent more time making love.

5. __ When I am choosing a partner, average looks are okay as long as they are a good lover.

6. __ If I knew that I would not get caught, I could see myself doing something illegal to obtain sex.

7. __ When I am choosing a partner, it is okay if they are not that smart as long as they are a good lover.

8. __ If my partner wanted me to work less and spend more time making love, I would try to do as they wished.

9. __ I would feel justified in getting a divorce if I were not sexually satisfied.

10. __ If my partner refused to have sex with me after a reasonable amount of time in a dating relationship, I would feel justified in dumping them.

11. __ I would dump someone that I liked if I thought they were not good in bed.

12. __ When I am choosing a partner, it is okay if they don't have much money as long as they are a good lover.

13. __ I would do almost anything to obtain a peak sexual experience.

14.* __ Paying attention to each other sexually is the most important thing couples should do to be happy together.

15. __ I would *not* endanger my health for sex.

16. __ There is nothing more important in a long-term relationship than a good sex life.

17. __ Sex is *not* that big of a deal to me.

Scoring Instructions and Norms

Reverse-score items 15 and 17. If you selected a 1 for these items, write a 7; if you selected a 2 for these items, write a 6; and so on. After reverse-scoring, add the items. Your score will range from 17 to 119, with a midpoint of 68. Of 89 males, the average score was 60.28; of 150 females, the average score was 50.47. The higher the score, the more important sex is to the individual.

Source: Dossett, J. (2014, November). *How important is sex? The development and validation of the sexual importance scale.* Presented at the annual meeting of the Society for the Scientific Study of Sexuality, Omaha, NE. Used by permission of J. Dossett.

* Psychological surveys sometimes contain duplicate entries to help researchers control for individuals who answer the questions at random or without much thought.

Comfort with visible body parts varies by culture. In the United States, the naked breasts of an adult female are viewed as erotic and are not to be displayed in public, as demonstrated in recent debates about breastfeeding in public. However, among the Xavante Indian tribe in Brazil, women's breasts are openly displayed and have a neutral erotic stimulus value. In the United States, we feel the penis should not be exposed in public, whereas in European cultures, it is seen as neutral. Consider public statuary: Michelangelo's *David-Apollo* caused an uproar when it was exhibited on tour in the United States.

1.1 Defining Human Sexuality

Human sexuality is a multifaceted concept. No one definition can capture its complexity. Instead, human sexuality can best be understood in terms of various factors.

1.1a Thoughts

The thoughts we have about sexual phenomena are a major component of human sexuality. Indeed, the major "sex organ" of the human body is the brain. The thoughts a person has about sexual behavior—through previous experience, pornography, movies, and the media—will impact the behavior that person is motivated to engage in. Thoughts about sex are important since they may be inaccurate. For example, males tend to think that "Sex is meant to be quick, without foreplay, and that the man should always be on top." Similarly, females tend to think that they "should play a passive and receptive role in sexual activities" (Nobre et al., 2003). Having positive thoughts about your sexual well-being, particularly among women, is also associated with life satisfaction (Stephenson & Meston, 2015).

Each person looks in the mirror and "sees" the degree to which they are a sexual person.

(Amberlynn Bishop)

1.1b Sexual Self-Concept

Your **sexual self-concept** is the way you think or feel about your body, while your **sexual self-efficacy** is how you feel about your own competence to function sexually and be a good sexual partner (Rowland et al., 2015). For women, Frost et al. (2018) used "body scent, buttocks, chest or breasts, appearance of eyes, sex drive, sex activities, face, head hair, and skin condition" as a measure of "sexual attractiveness" in their revision of the Body Esteem Scale. Komarnicky et al. (2019) also found that viewing one's genitals positively influenced one's body image. Feeling positively about one's body is related to the quality of one's romantic relationship via their own sexual satisfaction (Van den Brink et al., 2018). A study of 53 women ages 29–47 in heterosexual relationships revealed that a poor body image was associated with low dyadic and solitary sexual desire. A low body image also promoted distracting thoughts (e.g. "Does he think I'm fat?") while engaged in sexual activity with one's partner (Dosch et al., 2016). Other researchers have confirmed low body image among women (Carvalheira et al., 2017). However, men also struggle with body-satisfaction concerns (particularly penis size), which sometimes translates into not seeking early intervention for sex-related illnesses

Sexual self-concept
The way you think and feel about your body, self-evaluation of your interest in sex, and evaluation of yourself as a sexual partner

Sexual self-efficacy
The way you think and feel about your own competence to function sexually or to be a good sexual partner

such as testicular cancer (Johnston et al., 2014). Research indicates that body image may also be an issue for trans men and women, and this may put trans men at higher risks of developing an eating disorder (Witcomb et al., 2015).

Self-love is about respecting and appreciating every single part of who you are, and being proud to be you.
Miya Yamanouchi, *Embrace Your Sexual Self: A Practical Guide for Women*

For women, Frost et al. (2018) used "waist, thighs, body build, hips, legs, figure or physique, appearance of stomach, weight" as a measure of "weight concern" in their revision of the Body Esteem Scale. Being "over" weight is a major issue in US dating culture. Women often think they are less valuable and attractive if their weight does not approximate the cultural ideal. Morotti and colleagues (2013) noted that lean women reported more frequent intercourse and more orgasms than obese women. Similarly, in a survey of 1,357 heterosexual women between the ages of 18 and 29, respondents reported that sexual satisfaction increased as body image improved (Breuer & Pericak, 2014).

A major source of your body image is your romantic partner. Meltzer and McNulty (2014) emphasized that:

> ... body valuation by a committed male partner is positively associated with women's relationship satisfaction when that partner also values them for their nonphysical qualities, but negatively associated with women's relationship satisfaction when that partner is not committed or does not value them for their nonphysical qualities. (p. 68)

Hence, one's relationship and the partner's level of commitment have a powerful effect on one's sexual self-concept.

In the United States, entire industries encourage people to feel bad about their physical attributes, such as weight, breast size, hair loss, wrinkles, and varicose veins, with advertising designed to create body shame and urge consumers to seek relief through buying the latest products for dieting or skin care. When actress Jane Fonda, now in her late 80s, was asked how she could look so young, she replied, "A lot of money."

We don't want to eat hot fudge sundaes as much as we want our lives to be hot fudge sundaes.
Geneen Roth, *Women, Food and God: An Unexpected Path to Almost Everything*

Sex is like money—only too much is enough.
John Updike, novelist

1.1c Values

Sexual values are moral guidelines for making sexual decisions in one's relationships. Among the various sexual values are absolutism, relativism, and hedonism.

Sexual values
Moral guidelines for making sexual decisions

Personal REFLECTION

Take a moment to express your thoughts about the following questions. Sexual values and sexual behavior may not always be consistent. How often (if ever) have you made a sexual decision that was not consistent with your sexual values? If so, what influenced you to do so (alcohol, peer influence)? How did you feel about your decision then, and how do you feel about it now (guilt, regret, indifference)? There is a gender difference in regard to sexual regret: Women are more likely to regret casual sex, and men are more likely to regret missed sexual opportunities (Galperin et al., 2013).

Absolutism refers to a belief system based on the unconditional power and authority of religion, law, or tradition. Table 1-1 lists a breakdown of the sexual values of 13,070 undergraduate students surveyed on sexual values. Absolutist sexual values were reported by 13% of 3,068 male students and 15% of 10,002 female students queried (Hall & Knox, 2019).

What are the primary reasons for delaying one's sexual debut (the first time one has sexual/anal intercourse)? Of Australians who reported never having had sexual or anal intercourse, the primary reasons for doing so were being proud of being a virgin, not being ready, fearing negative outcomes (e.g. STI), and religion. However, over half of the respondents reported that they had engaged in some form of sexual activity, including deep kissing, sexual touching, or oral sex (Heywood et al., 2018). While religion was not the major influence for virginity among these adolescents, it remains a powerful social influence in that some religions teach that sexual intercourse is permissible only in marriage. An example is True Love Waits, an international campaign designed to challenge teenagers and college students to remain sexually abstinent until marriage. Sponsored by LifeWay Christian Resources, the program requires young people to agree to the absolutist position and sign a commitment to the following:

> Believing that true love waits, I make a commitment to God, myself, my family, my friends, my future mate, and my future children to a lifetime of purity including sexual abstinence from this day until the day I enter a biblical marriage relationship. (Lifeway, 2014)

In a sample of 961 undergraduates, 39% of women and 21% of men (34% total) reported having made an abstinence pledge. Among those who made an abstinence pledge, 65% of women and 52% of men (62% total) reported breaking their pledge (Barnett et al., 2018).

I am not saying renounce sex, I am saying transform it. It need not remain just biological: bring some spirituality to it.

Osho, Indian mystic (1931–1990)

To have her here in bed with me, breathing on me, her hair in my mouth — I count that something of a miracle.

Henry Miller, novelist and playwright

Eighty college students at a Christian university were surveyed about the disparity between what they had been taught and what they personally believed. While 60% reported that they were taught to abstain from sexual intercourse until marriage, about one-third were comfortable with, were engaging in, or were contemplating premarital sex. Reflecting this transition, one respondent noted, "I know that premarital sex is wrong; however, I think it should depend on the couple and relationship." A conservative Christian student who was asked how she reconciled her sexual relationship with her religious teachings replied, "That's easy. I just ignore the teachings and do what works for us" (Williams et al., 2014). In regard to sexual values over time, researchers have found an increase in premarital permissiveness over a 30-year period, with a decrease in religious attendance and an increase in education as influential variables (Elias et al., 2015).

Relativism

Relativism is a value system emphasizing that sexual decisions should be made in the context of a particular situation. Table 1-1 reveals that 55% of the male respondents and 62% of the females reported having relativist sexual values. Whereas an absolutist might feel that it is wrong for unmarried people to have intercourse, a relativist might feel that the moral correctness of sex outside marriage depends on the particular situation. For example, a relativist might feel that sex between casual dating partners is wrong in some situations, such as when one partner pressures or lies to the partner in

Absolutism
A belief system based on the unconditional power and authority of religion, law, or tradition

Relativism
Sexual value that emphasizes that sexual decisions should be made in the context of a particular situation

order to persuade them to have sex. Yet in other cases, when there is no deception or coercion and the dating partners are practicing safer sex, intercourse between casual dating partners may be viewed as acceptable.

Netting and Reynolds (2018) reported on the changes in sexual values among Canadians over a 30-year period. Contrary to the claims of popular media, casual sex ("hookup culture") has not replaced romantic relationships as the most common context for student sexual behavior. While individuals may go through a period of hedonism, relationship sex is the preferred value.

TABLE 1-1	Sexual Values of 13,070 Undergraduates		
Respondents	Absolutism	Relativism	Hedonism
Male students (N = 3,068)	13%	55%	32%
Female students (N = 10,002)	15%	62%	23%

Data Source: Hall, S., & Knox, D. (2019). [Relationship and sexual behaviors of a sample of 13,070 university students.] Unpublished raw data, Ball State University, Muncie, IN, and East Carolina University, Greenville, NC.

Hedonism

Hedonism is the sexual value that reflects the philosophy that the pursuit of pleasure and the avoidance of pain provide the ultimate value and motivation for sexual behavior. Table 1-1 reveals that, of the 3,068 undergraduate males studied, 32% reported having hedonist sexual values, as did 23% of the 10,002 undergraduate females. Hedonism is sometimes contextual. Tourists sometimes regard being on vacation as being in a "hedonistic zone of exception" (Berdychevsky, 2017). The slogan, "What happens in Vegas, stays in Vegas" is a commercial for hedonism.

You have exactly one life in which to do everything you'll ever do. Act accordingly.

Colin Wright, international speaker

The hedonist's sexual values are reflected in the creed, "If it feels good, do it." Hedonists are sensation seekers. They tend to pursue novel, exciting, and optimal levels of stimulation and arousal, and their goal is pleasure.

Data analysis from 30 institutions across the United States on single heterosexual college students (N = 3,907), ages 18–25, revealed that in a month prior to the survey, more men (19%) than women (7%) reported having had casual sex. The researchers also found that casual sex was negatively associated with psychological well-being (defined in reference to self-esteem and life satisfaction) and positively associated with psychological distress such as anxiety and depression, with no gender differences (Bersamin et al., 2014). In a sample of 12,401 adolescents, suicide ideation was more frequent among individuals in casual sexual relationships compared to those in stable relationships (Sandberg-Thoma & Kamp Dush, 2014). See the insert on *The Experience of Casual Sex.*

What is the impact of one's sexual history on divorce and marital satisfaction? Wolfinger (2018) confirmed that virgins who marry have the lowest divorce rate, although that might be related to one's religious beliefs about divorce. Beyond that finding, having multiple or a few sexual partners does not seem to make a significant difference in the divorce rate. But what about the impact of one's sexual history on marital satisfaction? Analysis of national data revealed that for both women and men the fewer the sexual partners, the more likely the person is to report being very happily married. This finding was truer for men than women. For example, for women who had one sexual partner, 64% reported being very happily married; for men, 71% reported being very happily married. For women reporting having had 6–10 partners, 52% reported being very happily married; men, 62%.

Hedonism
Sexual value that reflects a philosophy that the pursuit of pleasure and the avoidance of pain are the ultimate values and motivation for sexual behavior

The Experience of Casual Sex*

Researchers Farvid and Braun (2017) interviewed 30 ethnically diverse, heterosexual women and men (ages 18 to 46) in New Zealand about their experiences with casual sex. Various themes emerged.

Thrilling Context to Be/Do Whatever

Aside from casual sex being a new, anxious, thrilling experience, one 25-year-old female reported that she enjoyed the fact that she could be completely uninhibited and do whatever she wanted. She noted that, with a boyfriend, she felt scripted but with someone she did not know and who did not know her, "We can do lots of things I don't normally do ... cause I don't care what his image is of me."

Newness in Contrast to the Usual and Dull

Casual sex was also described as a departure from the mundane. One 33-year-old male said, "... things with the same person would get kinda dull but you can do the same things you like with different people and it never gets boring."

The Value of Flirting

For some, the casual sex was fun due to the flirting beforehand. "... it's the talking about it without talking about it" thing, where you hint to each other that you're gonna go home and have sex. For many, the actual sex was disappointing in terms of physical pleasure; the fun was the new partner, the context, the flirting.

Forbidden, Naughty, Unusual

Others said that casual sex crossed boundaries, such as sex with a friend, sex in public, or sex in a van. It was the deviousness that made the encounter exciting.

Ego Boost

Some men thought of casual sex as an ego boost, that they were able to take a woman down. "... I scored this cheerleader from Alabama University or something." Some women had a similar ego experience in that they were able to get a "really good looking, really popular guy" to take them home for sex. The meaning was in the conquest.

Awkward and Tricky

Feeling anxious, awkward, and uncomfortable are terms used by some to describe their casual sex experience. "Not awkward, awkward ... but it becomes better if you know someone over a period of time." The difficulty of negotiating the sex and the morning after were sometimes uncomfortable.

Casual Sex as Deficient

Women respondents often talked of the downside of casual sex–quick, unemotional, drunken. "... there's just nothing there." Some men had a similar experience, comparing casual sex to meeting a need, like eating to reduce hunger ... not fulfilling. "... in some ways it's actually nice to even just spend close comfortable time with someone you really care about than to have sex with someone you don't ..."

Summary

The researchers summarized the reactions to casual sex by saying that the participants identified both positives and negatives but "ultimately claimed a preference for relationship sex as more pleasureable, more meaningful, and better than casual sex" (p.86).

*Adapted and abridged from Farvid P. and V. Braun 2017. Unpacking the "pleasures" and "pains" of heterosexual casual sex: Beyond singular understandings. *The Journal of Sex Research, 54* (1), pp. 73–90.

Sexual double standard

One standard for women and another for men regarding sexual behavior (In the United States, for example, it is normative for men to have more sexual partners than women do.)

The **sexual double standard**—the view that encourages and accepts the sexual expression of men more than women—is reflected in Table 1-1. The double standard was also evident in a sample of Asian Americans with men expressing more liberal values for men initiating sex, having more sexual partners, and selecting a more conservative spouse (than single playgirl) (Guo, 2019).

Cultural labels for male hedonists include "real men," "stud," and "player," whereas the cultural labels for female hedonists include "whore" and "slut." It appears that men in the United States gain status from having sex with a number of partners, while women are more vulnerable to gaining a bad reputation. However, the double standard is decreasing. Stewart-Williams et al. (2017) found that both women and men were reluctant to get involved in a long-term relationship with someone who had an extensive sexual history.

> *If a girl gets a random hookup, it's like "Oh, she's a whore," but if a guy gets a hookup, it's like "Bump my fist."*
>
> Respondents in hookup research by Yazedjian, Toews, and Daniel (2014)

Another example of the double standard revealed that women respondents reported discomfort in initiating sexual interaction for fear of disapproval (Fetterolf & Sanchez, 2015). After sex, some women may also feel guilty and ashamed and experience a drop in self-esteem if they believe that permissive sexual attitudes are unacceptable (Coffman & Jozkowski, 2015). These studies reflect the proverbial "walk of shame" ... the morning after the night that the woman slept over at the guy's dorm and is walking back to her place.

Finally, sexually hedonistic women use various strategies to mitigate their exposure to disapproval and stigma: detach from religion, withhold information about their sexual behavior from significant others, and reduce their expectations of a future relationship developing from a hookup encounter (Fulle et al., 2015). On the other hand, some women don't buy into the double standard and feel that seeking sexual pleasure gives them a sense of empowerment (Grose, 2014).

1.1d Emotions

Love and intimacy are contexts that influence the expression of sexual behavior (Jardin et al., 2017). Intimacy is a multidimensional concept that includes being

> *We want things not because we have reasons for them; we have reasons for them because we want them.*
>
> Arthur Schoepenhauer, German philosopher

sensitive to the needs of another, feeling emotional closeness with another, sharing thoughts and feelings with another, and listening reflectively/empathetically to what another is experiencing. Women have traditionally been socialized to experience sex in the context of an emotional relationship. The fact that men are more often hedonists and women are more often absolutists and relativists indicates that an emotional context has value for a higher proportion of women than for men.

Emotional heartbreak is also associated with changes in sexual values. Analysis of data on 286 never-married undergraduates who reported having experienced one or more romantic breakups revealed significant changes in regard to becoming more liberal. Specifically, respondents who were absolutist became more relativistic and those who were relativistic became more hedonistic (Hilliard et al., 2019c).

1.1e Behaviors

The term *human sexuality* implies a variety of behaviors. Definitions of what constitutes having had sex vary, with most heterosexuals agreeing that vaginal (5.9 on a 6 point scale) and anal (5.6 on a 6 point scale) intercourse constitute "having had sex," but less agreement (3.8) on oral sex being defined as "having sex." These data are from an analysis of 300 heterosexual respondents ages 18–30 (Horowitz & Bedford, 2017). The meanings and behavioral definitions of sex presented here refer to the heteronormative model. The "gold standard" for sex to gay men is anal sex, with no clear standard for lesbians (Sewell, 2017).

Virginity is a concept that is often muddled. Rather than dichotomous—you are or are not a virgin—a three-part view of virginity might be adopted: oral sex, vaginal sex, and anal sex. No longer is the term *virgin* synonymous with absence of sexual behaviors in any one of these three areas. Rather, whether an individual has engaged in each of the three behaviors must be identified. Hence, an individual would not just say, "I am a virgin." Rather, the individual would state, "I am an oral virgin," or "intercourse virgin," or "anal virgin," as the case may be. We have been referring to heterosexual virginity. Huang (2018) confirmed that homosexual males refer to experiencing receptive or penetrative anal sex as having lost their virginity. Lesbians are more diffuse with some reporting that genital fondling could count as loss of virginity (Ellis & Walters, 2018). Regardless, virginity loss is not a salient topic in the LGBTQIA community and is superseded by topics such as coming out.

Another way to express becoming sexually active is by saying that you have made your sexual debut. This has a less negative connotation than the common phrase "lost my virginity," as you have not lost something by becoming sexually active.

National DATA

Based on a survey of 5,865 adult respondents ages 20–24 in the United States, 83% of men and 64% of women reported having masturbated alone (rather than with a partner) in the past 12 months. In addition, 63% of the men and 70% of the women reported having received oral sex from their heterosexual partner, and 6% of the men and 9% of the women received oral sex in same-sex encounters. "Having experienced vaginal intercourse" was reported by 63% of men and 80% of women, and 23% of women reported engaging in penile-anal intercourse with their male partner (Reece et al., 2012).

1.1f Anatomy and Physiology

The idea of sex often brings to mind the thought of naked bodies or anatomy. Hence, the term *human sexuality* implies sexual anatomy, referring to external genitalia, secondary sex characteristics such as a deepened voice in males and breast development in females, and internal reproductive organs, including ovaries and testes. *Physiology* refers to how the parts work or the functioning of the genitals and reproductive system.

1.1g Reproduction

The term human sexuality includes reproduction of the species. Sociobiologists, who believe that social behavior has a biological basis, emphasize that much of the sexual interaction that occurs between men and women has its basis in the drive to procreate. Indeed, the perpetuation of the species depends on the sperm and egg uniting. Ferreira et al. (2019) analyzed 16 years of data of calls and emails to "Sex Sense," an information referral source in Canada. Women asked more about contraception, emergency contraceptive pills, and pregnancy, while men asked about sexually transmitted infections, general sexual health, and pleasure. Hence, the focus of women was on preventing reproduction while men focused on avoiding the negative outcomes (STIs).

1.1h Interpersonal Relationships

Although masturbation and sexual fantasies can occur outside the context of a relationship, much of sexuality occurs in the context of interpersonal relationships. Such relationships vary—heterosexual, bisexual, pansexual or homosexual; nonmarital, marital, or extramarital; casual or intimate; personal or business-related (as in webcam sex or sex work); and brief or long-term. The type of emotional and social relationship a couple has affects the definition and quality of their sexual relationship. Indeed, relationship satisfaction is associated with

They told me, "Be sensible with your new love
Don't be fooled thinking this is the last you'll find"
But they never stood in the dark with you, love
When you take me in your arms and drive me slowly out of my mind.

Mel Carter, "Hold Me, Thrill Me, Kiss Me,"
written and arranged by David Noble (1952).
Vocal Popular Sheet Music Collection, score 1067,
via the Digital Commons.

sexual satisfaction (Stephenson et al., 2013). The comment to a partner, "I can't fight with you all day and want to have sex with you at night" illustrates the impact of the social context on the sexual experience.

Partners in committed relationships report the highest sexual satisfaction (Farvid & Braun, 2017). Whitton and colleagues (2013) found that female college students who were involved in committed dating relationships reported fewer depressive symptoms. Sexuality in the context of a romantic relationship has also been associated with general health (Becasen et al., 2015).

Technology and Sexuality 1-1: There's an App for That!

How people interact with the world around them has changed dramatically over the last 20 years. Instead of relying on newspapers, magazines, and radio to get information, people now turn to their smartphones and tablets, where they can access everything the internet has to offer. Young adults 18–29 are the most connected group in the United States, with 99% of that population owning a cell phone (Pew Research Center, 2019c). Apps may be used for casual sex, but also for dating and networking for people of all sexual orientations (Wu & Ward, 2018). Sawyer (2018) surveyed 509 heterosexual undergraduates, 40% of whom reported having used a dating app. When compared to non-app users, dating app users were more likely to report having unprotected vaginal and anal sex in the last 3 months, more lifetime sexual partners, and using drugs before having sex.

While not every app is related to sexuality, many are. You can find spreadsheets to help you keep track of how often you're having sex, truth-or-dare games, guides to new sexual positions, and interactive apps sponsored by condom manufacturers that include everything from sex trivia to product information. There seems to be no limit to the type of app available, which might explain why the expression "There's an app for that" has become part of our culture. With sexuality apps, and social networking and dating apps like Tinder™, people are accessing sexuality content more often than ever before. What are the individual, relationship, and societal impacts of this avalanche of sexuality apps?

Research helps to evaluate the impact of apps on sexuality. Some argue that because apps make it easier for people to hook up, they may increase the risk of contracting an STI. Hahn et al. (2018) noted that the more time individuals spent interacting on their app before meeting the person, the less likely they were to engage in high-risk sexual behavior.

There might be some benefits to sex apps. They can be used as sources of sexual health education, since some provide answers to questions about everything from sexual positions to contraceptive options. Using apps as a means of providing sexual health education can be vital in a country where comprehensive sexuality education is not available to everyone. Some apps that list local health clinics providing free condoms might help to reduce the transmission of STIs.

Apps may be attractive in large part because users can explore their questions and interests from the privacy of their own smartphones. It's important to keep in mind that sexuality-related apps are not always inherently good or bad—often, it's how they are used that makes a difference in one's life. Hence the presence of app technology is independent of the values that determine how it is used. For example, using a hookup app to cheat in a monogamous relationship is using technology in a way that is likely to have negative consequences for the couple's relationship. But that same app may be used to find one's lifetime partner.

1.1i Sexual Health

One's sexual health is also tied to the concept of sexuality. Having a positive view of one's sexuality, being free of STIs, guilt, and force are all part of one's sexual health. Campa et al. (2018) emphasized the need for sexual health programs to be available for a wide spectrum of populations. Epstein and Mamo (2017) noted that an academic focus on sexual health also serves to legitimize the study of sexuality.

Related to sexual health is sexual pleasure. According to the World Association for Sexual Health, the first 3 of 6 aspects to sexual pleasure are:

- Fundamental to anyone's sexual health and well-being is that the experience should be pleasurable, safe, and "free of discrimination, coercion, and violence";
- The human experience includes access to sources of sexual pleasure;
- Human rights include sexual rights. (World Association for Sexual Health, 2019)

1.1j Still Other Views

Silver et al. (2018) identified nine themes of sex including male-centric view (penis in vagina), heteronormative, orgasm imperative, interaction (consensual), and humor ("slip the P in the V"). These themes reflect the complexity of human sexuality. Increasingly, to be free of being sexually active is also considered having sexual well-being (Lorimer et al., 2019).

1.2 Nature of Sexual Decisions

Whenever we are confronted with a sexual decision, at least five factors are involved:

1. Not to decide is to decide.
2. Decisions involve trade-offs.
3. Decisions include selecting a positive or negative view.
4. Decisions can produce ambivalence and uncertainty.
5. Some decisions are revocable; some are not.

1.2a Not to Decide Is to Decide

Not making a decision is a decision by default. For example, if you are having oral, vaginal, or anal intercourse and do not make a conscious decision to use a condom or dental dam, you have inadvertently made a decision to increase your risk for contracting a sexually transmitted infection—including HIV. If you are having vaginal intercourse and do not decide to use contraception, you have decided to risk pregnancy. If you do not monitor and restrict your alcohol or drug use at parties or in a new relationship, you have made a decision to drift toward unprotected sex (or increase the risk of sexual assault). Widman et al. (2018) noted that individuals can learn to make conscious decisions about their sexual behavior (e.g. being sexually assertive to alert a partner what you do not want/what you want, STI protection).

1.2b Decisions Involve Trade-Offs

All the decisions you make will involve trade-offs or disadvantages and advantages. The decision to cheat on your partner may provide excitement, but it may also produce feelings of guilt and lead to the breakup of your relationship. The decision to tell your partner of an indiscretion may deepen your feelings of intimacy, but by doing so, you may run the risk of your partner leaving you. The decision to have an abortion may enable you to avoid the hardship of continuing an unwanted pregnancy; however, it can sometimes involve feelings of guilt, anxiety, or regret—especially in a social context in which abortion is stigmatized or where access is limited. Likewise, the decision to continue an unwanted pregnancy may enable you to experience the joy of having a child, but it may also involve the hardships of inopportune parenting.

1.2c Decisions Include Selecting a Positive or Negative View

Regardless of your circumstances, you can choose to focus on the positive aspects of a difficult situation and to approach it as a problem to be solved. A positive problem-solving approach can be used in every situation. For example, the discovery of your partner having an affair can be viewed as an opportunity to open channels of communication and strengthen your relationship. Another example of choosing a positive view is a woman who contracted genital herpes due to repeated casual sex. She viewed her STI as a wake-up call to be more discriminating in the selection of her sexual partners. "It was a wake-up call to sexual responsibility," she said.

1.2d Decisions Can Produce Ambivalence and Uncertainty

Deciding among options often creates **ambivalence**—conflicting feelings that produce uncertainty or indecisiveness about your course of action.

Ambivalence can occur in the presence of many options. In the United States, for example, a young unmarried couple facing an unplanned pregnancy has several options. The woman can choose to have an abortion, place the baby up for adoption, or rear the baby in a single-parent home. The couple can decide to stay together, perhaps even marry, and keep the baby. While many people navigate these choices without regret, for some, choosing any one of these options can cause ambivalence. Long after the fact, some people may still wonder if they made the right choice.

1.2e Some Decisions Are Revocable; Some Are Not

Some sexual decisions are revocable—they can be changed. For example, a person who has chosen to have sex with multiple partners can subsequently decide to be faithful to one partner or to abstain from sexual relations. An individual who has accepted being sexually unsatisfied in an ongoing relationship ("I never told him how to get me off") can decide to address the issue or seek sex therapy with that partner.

Although many sexual decisions can be modified or changed, some cannot. You cannot eliminate the effects of some sexually transmissible infections or undo an abortion. However, it is possible to learn from past decisions. Reflecting on good and poor decisions can provide useful information for current and future decisions.

Ambivalence
Conflicting feelings that coexist, producing uncertainty or indecisiveness about a person, object, idea, or course of action

1.3 **Making Sexual Decisions**

1.3a Four Themes of Sexual Decision-Making by Women

Various themes are involved in making a sexual decision. In 2015, two researchers (Cooper & Gordon, 2015) surveyed the sexual decision-making process of a group of New Zealand women who had previously participated in casual sex without a condom. In interviews with 11 respondents, four major themes of sexual decision-making emerged. Although the sample was small, it revealed a pattern of unhealthy decisions specific to women.

The first theme was the importance of being in a relationship:

I have sex with someone to date them ... and hope they will call again. ... [T]he idea is that you're having casual sex with a guy ... and then it will turn into a relationship, if you have sex often enough—that's mental. But a lot of girls see it as a way into a relationship with someone.

A second theme was the influence of alcohol:

It loosens you up, and your inhibitions run wild. ... [Y]ou're freer, you would go and talk to strangers, and be more confident and flirt a bit more, and stuff like that, because you sort of think you can do anything when you're drunk; there's no consequences.

A third theme was the need to be seen as normal:

When all your friends are having sex, you feel like you are missing out 'cause you are not doing it; ... you're not cool because you are not doing [it]. ... [I]t kind of felt okay to do it because everyone else was doing it.

A final theme was a feeling of powerlessness in negotiating condom use:

If you say no to them, they might not like you; or think, "Oh, if I say no, that's going to be the end of our night ... and then they won't call me [the] next day, or whatever." And I suppose you don't want them going back to their friends ... and tell them what happened; ... they might be like, "That dumb bitch didn't give me any."

Showing a pattern of disempowered decisions about sexual involvement—as a means of securing affection, involving the abuse of alcohol to reduce inhibition, yielding to cultural and peer pressure, and submitting to unprotected sex for fear of rejection or public shaming—these findings reveal a disturbing inequity and lack of agency in women's experience of sexual relationships.

1.3b Deciding to Improve One's Sexual Growth

Sexual growth
The term for sexual satisfaction that results from work and effort with one's partner for a good sex life

How important is working on your sexual relationship to make it a good one? **Sexual growth** is the term for sexual satisfaction that results from work and effort with one's partner with the goal of a mutually satisfying sexual relationship. *Self-assessment 1–2* provides a way to determine the degree of your sexual growth beliefs.

Self-Assessment 1-2: Sexual Growth Beliefs Measure

Write the number to the left of each item that reflects your level of disagreement/agreement:

1 (Disagree strongly), 2 (Mostly disagree), 3 (Disagree a little), 4 (Neither agree nor diagree),
5 (Agree a little), 6 (Mostly agree), 7 (Agree strongly)

1. __ Sexual satisfaction often fluctuates over the course of a relationship.

2. __ A satisfying sexual relationship evolves through hard work and resolution of incompatibilities.

3 __ In order to maintain a good sexual relationship, a couple needs to exert time and energy.

4. __ Successful sexual relationships require regular maintenance.

5. __ Without acknowledging romantic partners' different sexual interests, a sexual relationship cannot improve.

6. __ A satisfying sexual relationship is partly a matter of learning to resolve sexual differences with a partner.

7. __ Making compromises for a partner is part of a good sexual relationship.

8. __ Working through sexual problems is a sign that a couple has a strong bond.

9. __ In a relationship, maintaining a satisfying sex life requires effort.

10. __ Sexual desire is likely to ebb and flow (i.e., change) over the course of a relationship.

11. __ Communicating about sexual issues can bring partners closer together.

12. __ Acknowledging each other's differing sexual interests is important for a couple to enhance their sex life.

13. __ Even satisfied couples will experience sexual challenges at times.

Total score _____

Scoring

Add the numbers you wrote before each item to obtain a total score. The higher your total score (91 is the highest possible score), the greater your beliefs in sexual growth—that sexual satisfaction is a function of hard work and effort with your partner to resolve sexual incompatibilities. The lower your score (13 is the lowest possible score), the less you believe that sexual growth results from effort. A score of 49 places you at the midpoint between not believing that hard work and effort is necessary for sexual growth and believing that effort is important. Maxwell et al. (2017) conducted several studies and found that sexual growth beliefs were moderately positively associated with both sexual and relationship quality.

Source: Maxwell, J. A., A. Muise, G. MacDonald, l. C. Day, N. O. Rosen, & E. A. Impett, 2017, How implicit theories of sexuality shape sexual and relationship well-being. *Journal of Personality & Social Psychology*, 112(2), pp. 238–279.

1.3c Spatial Context of Sex

Sexual decisions are made in a spatial context. While the most frequent context for sex is in a bed at night, Struckman-Johnson et al. (2017) reported on sex in parked cars. Analysis of data from 195 men and 511 women revealed about 60% reported engaging in sexual behavior while in a parked car. Most respondents were in serious but noncohabiting romantic relationships (not hookups), penile-vaginal intercourse/genital touching were the most common sexual behaviors, and the back seat of a standard car was the most frequent context. Most respondents regarded the experience as positive both sexually and romantically, however 2.5 percent of the men and 4.3 percent of the women reporting being coerced.

1.4 **Influences on Sexual Decisions**

Whether sexual decisions operate at the micro (individual) or macro (societal) level, various cultural, social, and psychological influences are involved.

1.4a Culture

The culture in which individuals grow up and live impacts their ideas about sex and interpersonal behavior. In Japan, Rorikon, is an abbreviation for "Lolita Complex." In a sex shop in Tokyo, life-size models of girls, their breasts at various stages of puberty, are for sale. Young Japanese females learn early that to be sexual is to be wanted.

Rickman (2018) noted the degree to which being interested in celebrity culture has an impact on romantic relationships. The ratio of females to males in one's high school is also influential. Harknett and Cranney (2017) analyzed the behavior of 12,617 high school students and noted that when female classmates were more numerous than male classmates and boys have the upper hand from a bargaining standpoint, the males are less likely to express desire for a romantic relationship (hence less commitment).

There are also cross-cultural variations in sexuality. For example, while premarital sex is increasing in India, it is still not widespread (Majumdar, 2018). And, although homosexual behavior has struggled for acceptance in the United States, in some other cultures, same-gender sexual behavior is regarded as a pathway to heterosexuality. Among the Sambia people of New Guinea's Eastern Highlands province, preadolescent boys are taught to perform fellatio (oral sex) on older unmarried males and to ingest their sperm. They are told that it enables them to produce their own sperm in adulthood, thereby ensuring their ability to impregnate their wives (Mead, 1928).

1.4b Media

Media projects images of all types of genders, relationships, and sexuality. And these may have negative associations. Ward et al. (2018) found that undergraduate women who reported heavy exposure to women's magazines, lifestyle reality TV, and situation comedies also reported greater self-sexualization, which in turn predicted more use of alcohol to feel sexual and more negative sexual affect. Similarly, social media has been criticized for contributing to women's negative body images and self-concepts. Social media, specifically Snapchat®, conveys messages about sexuality. In a content analysis of 394 screenshots ("snaps") involving sexuality, 87% were of females … and mostly (78%) selfies (consensual). Forty percent were nudes, mostly of the breasts and buttocks (Yockery et al., 2019). Use of Facebook® can also be a source of negative emotions about body image and consciousness. In a survey of 467 undergraduate women and 348 undergraduate men, Manago and colleagues (2015) found that Facebook involvement predicted objectified body consciousness, which in turn predicted greater body shame, particularly for women. For women, looking at images of peers and celebrity images on Instagram has been linked to dissatisfaction with their own bodies (Brown & Tiggemannn, 2016).

Modern media also creates and reflects sexual norms. Lulu & Alkaff (2018) conducted a content analysis of the content of 60 articles in women's magazines from three contexts—Malaysia, the US, and Egypt—and found that empowerment of the female was the main theme but always in the context of traditional male-female roles in heterosexist relationships. Jozkowski et al. (2016) reported on how consent and negotiation of sex was reflected in 50 PG-rated films. Nonverbal cues predominated and previous penetrative sex made future sexual intercourse more likely.

Talk shows such as *Jerry Springer* regularly broadcast programs on infidelity, acquaintance rape, and porn addiction. And on MTV®, college students are shown on spring break amid a frenzy of alcohol and sex. Music videos often convey questionable sexual messages. Bleakley (2017) found an association between adolescent media exposure and combining alcohol and sex. Wolfe (2016a) also emphasized how the media creates dread and fear among those who have genital herpes.

1.4c Peers and Parents

Peers and parents are major influences on sexual behavior. Regarding peers, Montes et al. (2017) found that the perceived hookup attitudes of one's friends is associated with one's own hookup attitudes. Researchers have also confirmed that the perception of peer approval of hooking-up behavior influenced engaging in the behavior for both sexes (Napper et al., 2015). While peer approval is operative on both sexes, it is more often a motive for hooking up for male rather than female college students (Snapp et al., 2014). Peers are also a major source of sexual knowledge and sexual values. Your first source of information about sex was likely to have been your peers, and the sexual values of your closest friends are probably very similar to your own.

Quinn et al. (2019) emphasized the power of peers operative in gang contexts. They conducted 58 interviews with adolescent members of six gangs and identified the unspoken norms and expectations, including "sexing-in" (female gang members expected to have sex with members of the gang) and "running trains," whereby members would line up and have sex with one female. Despite the prevalence of such practices, many gang members felt regret and remorse over their participation but noted it was just part of "the life"—confirming the power of context and group norms.

Various family factors—including parental behavior, family composition closeness/ relationships, values, and economic resources—influence sexual decisions. For example, Weiser & Weigel (2017) found that parental infidelity is associated with an individual's own infidelity. How parents treat adolescents also impacts sexual behavior—adolescents who report child maltreatment or neglect also note higher numbers of sexual partners, casual sexual behavior, and being younger at first intercourse (Thibodeau et al., 2017). Also, a family's economic resources may influence one's decisions about what type of birth control to use, whether to seek sexual health care (such as Pap smears and mammograms), and whether to continue an unplanned pregnancy.

Communication is also important. "Clear communication between parents and their youth about sex is associated with higher rates of sexual abstinence, condom use, and intent to delay initiation of sexual intercourse, which can prevent STIs and unintended pregnancy" (Coakley et al., 2017b). An example of what a father said to his son follows:

We had this talk about how sex is like jail. I said, "You can do something for 10 seconds and be in an orange suit before the night is over if the condom breaks— hole in the condom—something happens. And you hope that she's not pregnant." (Coakley et al., 2017a, pp. 355–368)

Klein et al. (2018) found that adolescent females displaying sexual agency (making decisions and being assertive) reported parents who discussed sexuality with them and provided emotional support and encouraged autonomy. Grossman et al. (2018) reported that delay of first sexual intercourse and avoiding pregnancy are the primary topics messaged by parents. The researchers also noted the importance of extended kin as sources of sex education and that they are sometimes perceived as easier to talk to.

New cultural experiences also impact family values. Bacchus (2017) confirmed that second-generation South Asian American women were in conflict between tradition and current social forces. Often they would engage in premarital sexual behavior, lie to their parents, and live a double life. Hilliard et al. (2018) also found that the acquisition of new cultural values can strain family relationships. About a quarter of the 111 international students in their study who became involved in a romantic relationship with someone who they met in the United States did not tell their parents (e.g. they feared disapproval).

(Stacy Huff)

Texting permeates the lives of couples, often to the point of ignoring each other.

1.4d Technology

Digisexuality, the use of radical new sexual technologies (e.g. teledildonics, virtual sex, sex robots), is increasing (McArthur & Twist, 2016). Knox et al. (2017) surveyed 345 undergraduates about their attitudes toward the use of a sex doll. About 1 in 5 (17%) reported that they understood how someone could use a doll for sex. Cindy Gallop is an advertising consultant who emphasizes that the major impact of technology today (through its distribution of pornography on the internet) undermines young people's capacity to connect emotionally and sexually with a partner. Her YouTube™ discussion (http://bvtlab.com/8v88M) exposes the atrocious myths that youth are buying as reality (such as the fallacy that all girls love to have their partner ejaculate on their faces) and the associated behaviors and lies some women feel are obligatory in order to maintain their relationships. Even "benign" pornography that is devoid of degradation or rape scenarios can set up unrealistic expectations that make real-life intimacy seem a diminished or "less than" experience for both sexes.

A man cannot really be called (sexually) confident if he has never bought his woman a vibrator.

Mokokoma Mokhonoana,
"On Masturbation: A Satirical Essay"

Has the internet changed anything about sexuality? Only this: Our obsession with the constant, intense, novel stimulation of the internet has rendered real sex with an actual person a bit less all-compelling than it used to be. We actually have to remember to pay attention during sex now.

Abbasi and Alghamdi (2018) noted how social media impacts relationship fidelity. Not only does spending a lot of time on social media decrease the amount of time available to one's partner, such time is spent looking at and even considering alternatives available to the current partner.

Digisexuality
The use of radical new sexual technologies (e.g. teledildonics, virtual sex, sex robots)

National DATA

Ninety-six percent of Americans 18–29 own a smartphone.

Source: Pew Research Center. (2019, June 12). Mobile Fact Sheet: Who owns cellphones and smartphones? Retrieved from http://www.pewinternet.org/fact-sheet/mobile.

Cultural Diversity

Döring et al. (2017) compared the online activity of college males and females in four countries—Canada, Germany, Sweden, and the United States (N = 2,690). Finding sexual information (90%) and sexual entertainment (77%) were the most common behaviors. Browsing for sexual products (49%) and cybersex (31%) were also popular. Men showed both higher prevalence and frequency of use of sexually stimulating material online than did women. Students in all four countries were similar in their online sexual activity experiences.

Wolfe (2016b) noted that while daters on OKCupid® may start out seeking one partner, they are soon overwhelmed with a variety of partners. "Swiping through the Tinder® app fills the respondents' brains with multiple possibilities."

1.4e Education

Education level is a demographic that can help predict sexual behavior. Over 65 years ago, Alfred Kinsey and colleagues (1948) observed that college-educated men reported higher masturbation rates than those with only a high school education. The following *Social Policy 1–1* feature emphasizes the controversy over sex education in the public school system and the outcome of sex education for students. (The efficacy of human sexuality instruction at the college level has already been demonstrated by Angel et al., 2016).

Before the child ever gets to school it will have received crucial, almost irrevocable sex education and this will have been taught by the parents, who are not aware of what they are doing.

Mary Calderone, sex educator

1.4f Religion

We tried ignorance for a very long time and it's time we try education.

Joycelyn Elders, former surgeon general of the United States

Religion has a profound influence on one's experience with sexuality. Longest and Uecker (2018) found that religious salience in individuals was related to delayed first sexual intercourse and fewer sexual partners. Similarly, Fox and Kuck (2018) found that undergraduates who reported higher levels of religiosity reported having fewer sexual partners in the last year. High religiosity is also associated with disapproval of the following: homosexuality, being involved in a "friends with benefits" relationship, cohabitation, hooking up, cheating, abortion, and using the internet to find a partner (e.g. internet partners would not be "heaven sent") (Fox et al., 2019). Sexual guilt is also associated with higher religious attendance (Pearson, 2018). In this regard, Grubbs and Perry (2019) noted that religious individuals reported the most distress in viewing pornography. Langlais & Schwanz (2018) examined the degree to which couples

All religions have something to say about sex, and it rarely coincides with scientific knowledge about sex and sexuality.

Darrel Ray, *Sex & God: How Religion Distorts Sexuality*

Religion typically emphasizes the restraint of sexual behavior.

were involved in religion. They used the term "centrality of religiosity of relationship (CRR)" and found that greater CRR was related to lower intimate touching, oral sex, and vaginal intercourse.

Religion may also be associated with unsuccessful repression of sexual thoughts and urges. Efrati (2019) found that religious adolescents reported higher episodes of compulsive sexual behavior (fantasies, urges), distress in coping with these intrusive thoughts, and lower mental health. In effect, their biological urges were at odds with their religious teachings that such urges and thoughts were sinful.

Williams et al. (2018) also observed three ways in which Muslim, Hindu, and Protestant Christian groups influence the sexuality of their youth, including: (a) prescribed avoidance, in which young men and women are segregated in many religious and educational settings and encouraged to moderate any cross-gender contact in public; (b) self-restraint supplemented with peer surveillance, in which young people are repeatedly encouraged not only to learn to control themselves through internal moral codes but also to enlist their peers to monitor each other's conduct and call them to account for violations of those codes; and (c) "classed" disengagement, in which highly educated, middle-class families do little to address sex directly, but treat it as but one aspect of developing individual ethical principles that will assist their educational and class mobility (e.g. avoid premarital pregnancy).

Finally, religion can dictate one's sexual behavior in reference to a spouse. Hernandez-Kane and Mahoney (2018) emphasized that religion sanctifies marital sex suggesting that it has a divine quality, is a deeply spiritual experience, holy, and reflects a sacred sexual bond. Spouses who have greater perceived sanctity of marital sexuality also report higher frequencies of sex, sexual satisfaction and marital satisfaction. In another study of interviews with 15 married Iranian women, they reported that it was their sacred duty to be a frequent and willing sexual partner for their husbands. Indeed, they believed that their status with God depended on their being a good wife (pleasing their husband sexually). The researchers summarized the interviews with the Iranian wives as follows:

> Most women mentioned that satisfying their husband's sexual needs was a divine rule. They also believed that rejecting such desires was a sin. They claimed they met their husband's sexual needs to save themselves from hell and sinfulness; ... pleasing God meant pleasing their husbands, especially their sexual needs. If their husbands desired to have sex, their wives could not refuse without any acceptable reason. They believed it was a sin not to follow God's rules. In some cases, the husbands misused such beliefs to force their wives to have sex. (Ravanipour et al., 2013, p. 185)

Sanjakdar (2018) noted that religion is often thought of as intolerant and incompatible with today's progressive and modern society but argued that inclusion of religion in a national conversation about sex education can be used to create a more inclusive learning experience.

Social Policy 1-1

Sex Education in Public Schools

While comprehensive sex education in the UK is mandated from primary school through high school, sex education in the US is required in only 24 states and the District of Columbia, and in many states is not required to be medically accurate (SIECUS, 2018b). Sex education was introduced in the US public school system in the late 19th century with the goal of combating STIs (sexually transmitted infections) and instilling sexual morality (typically understood as abstinence until marriage). Over time, the abstinence agenda became more evident. The Trump administration has been in favor of abstinence–only teaching in the nation's public schools and sought to defund any federal programs to the contrary. Valerie Huber, the Department of Health and Human Services official overseeing this effort, explained, "As public health and policymakers, we must normalize sexual delay" (Hellman, 2017). Hence, programs that discuss contraception and other means of pregnancy protection (in addition to abstinence), referred to as **comprehensive sex education programs**, such as the Teen Pregnancy Prevention Program set up by the Obama administration in 2010, have been targets for defunding.

> **Comprehensive sex education programs**
> Programs that discuss abstinence as well as the use of contraception

Santelli et al. (2017) emphasized that the abstinence-only-until-marriage (AOUM) theme continues to be promoted and funded (for the past 35 years) even though the weight of scientific evidence finds that these programs are not effective in delaying initiation of sexual intercourse or changing other sexual risk behaviors (use of condoms). AOUM programs threaten fundamental human rights to health, information, and life. Santelli et al. (2019) noted that a comparison of the sexual AOUM program to the Teen Pregnancy Prevention (TPP) revealed that the former resulted in an increase in state adolescent birthrates, whereas TPP resulted in a decrease in those rates. Indeed, young people need access to accurate and comprehensive sexual health information to protect their health and lives, which are not being provided by the federal government.

A majority of 560 undergraduates noted approval for all 18 topics (including sexual pleasure) typically included in sexual health education programs (Canan & Jozkowski, 2017). However, existing sex education programs generally exclude content relevant to lesbian, gay, bisexual, transgender, and queer/questioning youth. This deficit disenfranchises these populations by ignoring LGBTQ issues, such as emphasizing STI prevention and addressing healthy relationships (Gowen & Winges-Yanez, 2014). Research has revealed that exposure to transgender issues for only 3–4 hours in a sexuality class reduced anti-transgender prejudice (Green, 2014). Online education has also been an effective educational medium, particularly for LGBTQ individuals (Mustanski et al., 2015).

Levin (2016) emphasized that it is sometimes the impact of a particular teacher that is more influential than the content. Beyond the public school system, Butler et al. (2014) reported in a national survey of 1,101 colleges and universities that 86% made male latex condoms available to their students via the student health center. However, only 27% advertised condom availability.

International sex education is lacking, particularly in LGBT issues. In 2018, Scotland became the first county in the world to include LGBT issues in its curriculum.

1.4g Alcohol/Substance Use

Alcohol is the drug most frequently used by college students. Alcohol and other substance use are associated with reducing inhibitions, resulting in higher frequencies of casual sex encounters. Bleakley et al. (2017) found that 21% of their adolescent respondents reported drinking alcohol before their most recent sexual intercourse. In a study of 7,020 students, 35% of those who said that they agreed to unwanted sex during their most recent sexual experience also noted that they were drunk or high (Fishburn et al., 2016). Women who had been drinking were particularly vulnerable to unsafe, unplanned sexual behavior that they regretted (Haas et al., 2017). In addition, alcohol use is associated with lower condom use in that men use it to get the woman to have sexual intercourse without a condom (George, 2019). The lower the substance use, the higher the self-regulation (Moilanen & Manuel, 2018).

1.4h Psychological Factors

Many psychological constructs are believed to influence sexuality, including sexual self-concept, self-esteem, attachment style, and personality characteristics such as impulsiveness, sensation seeking, and dependency. They also affect the **locus of control**, an individual's beliefs about the source or cause of their successes and failures. A person with an **internal locus of control** believes that successes and failures in life are attributable to their own abilities and efforts. A person with an **external locus of control** believes that successes and failures are determined by fate, chance, or some powerful external source, such as other individuals. See *Personal Decisions 1-1* to determine what factors control sexual decisions.

Locus of control
An individual's beliefs about the source or cause (internal or external) of his or her successes and failures

Internal locus of control
The belief that successes and failures in life are attributable to one's own abilities and efforts

External locus of control
The perspective that successes and failures are determined by fate, chance, or some powerful external source

---

TABLE 1-2 | Who Controls Our Decisions? Advantages and Disadvantages of Different Views

Are you wondering if taking a human sexuality course will influence your sexual attitude and behaviors?

Views	Advantages	Disadvantages
View 1: We control our decisions.	Gives individuals a sense of control over their lives and encourages them to take responsibility for their decisions	Blames individuals for their unwise sexual decisions and fails to acknowledge the influence of social and cultural factors on sexual decisions
View 2: Other factors influence our decisions.	Recognizes how emotions, peers, and cultural factors influence individuals' lives and decisions; implies that making changes in the social and cultural environment may be necessary to help people make better decisions	Blames social and cultural factors for sexual decisions and discourages individuals from taking responsibility for their behaviors and decisions

PERSONAL DECISIONS 1-1

Do You or Other Factors Control Your Sexual Decisions?

What do the following questions have in common?

- Is sex with an attractive stranger worth the risk of contracting HIV or other sexually transmitted infections?
- How and when do I bring up the issue of using a condom with a new partner?
- Can I find partners who will honor my value of being abstinent until marriage?
- How much do I tell my new partner about my previous sexual experiences (including masturbation, number of sexual partners, gender of past partners)?
- Do I disclose to my partner that I have fantasies about sex with other people?
- Can I make a thoughtful decision about having sexual contact with a partner if I've been drinking alcohol?
- What type of birth control should my partner and I use?

Each of these questions involves making a sexual decision. One of the main goals of this text is to emphasize the importance of making deliberate and informed decisions about your sexuality. The alternative is to let circumstances and others decide for you. Informed decision-making involves knowledge of the psychological, physiological, and social components of sexual functioning and personal values and of the interaction between cultural values and sexual behaviors.

Decisions may be the result of **free will**. The belief in free will implies that although heredity and environment may influence our decisions, as individuals we are ultimately in charge of our own destinies. Even when our lives are affected by circumstances or events that we do not choose, we can still decide how to view and respond to them.

An alternative and competing assumption about making deliberate decisions is **determinism**—the idea that human nature is largely determined by heredity and environment. Being born with a particular sexual orientation reflects determinism in the sense that sexual orientation may have a biological or genetic base. Determinism may also have a social basis. Sociologists emphasize that social forces—such as the society in which one lives, one's family, and one's peers—all heavily influence decisions. This is the social-context view of decision-making. Hence, some homosexuals do not feel free to be open about their sexual identity for fear of social disapproval.

Rather than viewing sexual decisions as an either/or situation, each view contributes to a broader understanding.

Free will
Belief that individuals are ultimately in charge of their own destinies

Determinism
Belief that one's nature is largely determined by heredity and environment

Chapter Summary

Defining Human Sexuality

THIS CHAPTER DEFINED human sexuality in terms of its various components, delineated the nature of sexuality, identified the steps in sexual decision-making, and reviewed the influences on sexual decisions.

Human sexuality can best be defined in terms of its various components: thoughts, sexual self-concept, values, emotions, behaviors, anatomy and physiology, reproduction, and interpersonal relationships. The key to sexual satisfaction is a positive interpersonal relationship.

Interdisciplinary Nature of Sexual Decisions

WE ARE CONTINUALLY MAKING DECISIONS, many of which are difficult because they involve tradeoffs—disadvantages as well as advantages. Such decisions can produce ambivalence or uncertainty. Decisions that result in irrevocable outcomes, such as becoming a parent, are among the most difficult choices individuals may face. However, we cannot avoid making decisions, because not to choose is itself a decision. For example, if we have oral, vaginal, or anal sex without using a condom or dental dam, we have made a decision to risk contracting and transmitting HIV.

Another factor involved in sexual decision-making is that we can always choose a positive view ("Contracting an STI has taught me to use a condom in the future.") Some ambivalence and uncertainty are inherent in making most decisions.

Influences on Sexual Decisions

ALTHOUGH WE LIKE TO THINK we make our own sexual decisions and have free will to do so, we are actually strongly influenced by a number of factors. These influences include culture, media, peers and family, technology, education, religion, and mind-altering substances, such as alcohol.

Web Links

Go Ask Alice

> http://www.goaskalice.columbia.edu/

Make Love Not Porn

> http://makelovenotporn.com/

SIECUS

> http://www.siecus.org

Sexual Health Network

> http://www.sexualhealthnetwork.co.uk

World Association for Sexual Health

> https://worldsexualhealth.net/

Key Terms

Absolutism **8**

Ambivalence **15**

Comprehensive sex
    education programs **23**

Determinism **25**

Digisexuality **20**

External locus of control **24**

Free will **25**

Hedonism **9**

Internal locus of control **24**

Locus of control **24**

Relativism **8**

Sexual double standard **10**

Sexual growth **16**

Sexual self-concept **6**

Sexual self-efficacy **6**

Sexual values **7**

CHAPTER
2

Sex Research and Theory

Sex lies at the root of life, and we can never learn to reverence life until we know how to understand sex.

Havelock Ellis, pioneer sex researcher

Chapter Outline

2.1 **The Nature of Sex Research** **31**
2.2 **The Interdisciplinary Nature of Sexology** **32**
2.3 **Theories of Sexuality** **32**
   2.3a Biological Theories **33**
   2.3b Psychological Theories **33**
   Self-Assessment 2-1:
      Need for Sexual Intimacy Scale **36**
   2.3c Sociological Theories **37**
2.4 **Eclectic View of Human Sexuality** **40**
   2.4a Early Sex Researchers **40**
2.5 **Conducting Sex Research: A Step-by-Step Process** **42**
   2.5a Identifying a Research Question **42**
   2.5b Reviewing the Literature **42**
   2.5c Formulating a Hypothesis and Operationalizing Variables **42**
   2.5d Caveats in Sex Research **44**
   Technology and Sexuality 2-1:
      Online Surveys **46**
   2.5e Research Ethics: Protection of Human Subjects **46**

2.6 **Methods of Data Collection** **48**
   2.6a Experimental Research **48**
   2.6b Survey Research **48**
   2.6c Field Research **50**
   2.6d Direct Laboratory Observation **51**
   Social Policy 2-1
      Public Funding for Sex Research? **51**
   2.6e Case Studies **52**
2.7 **Levels of Data Analysis** **52**
   2.7a Descriptive **52**
   2.7b Correlation **52**
   2.7c Causation **54**
   2.7d Expanding Statistical Frontiers **54**
2.8 **Interpretation and Discussion** **55**

Web Links **57**
Key Terms **58**

Objectives

1. Know how scientific knowledge is different from other sources of knowledge
2. Identify and distinguish between deductive and inductive research
3. Review the various biological, psychological, and sociological theories used to study sexuality
4. Review the contributions of early sex researchers
5. Summarize the problems associated with Masters and Johnson's research
6. Explain the five methods of data collection and the pros and cons of each
7. Discuss the three levels of data analysis
8. Review the arguments for and against federal funding of sex research

Truth — OR — Fiction?

T / F   1. Research respondents are typically older, noncollege, and conservative.

T / F   2. Professors who conduct research and who teach sexuality are often assumed to have a certain sexual identity.

T / F   3. Respondents to a survey who provide their sexual history end up with lower sexual self-esteem on follow-up.

T / F   4. The Masters and Johnson Institute has over 5,000 affiliates in America today.

T / F   5. There are over 35 fully accredited programs offering a PhD in sexuality in America today.

Answers: 1. F   2. T   3. F   4. F   5. F

Students taking courses in human sexuality are often kidded about taking such classes. Peers may tease and ask questions like, "Does the class have a lab?" Biologists, psychologists, sociologists, health-care professionals, and others who study human sexuality in their occupational fields may also be subjected to ridicule or sarcasm. One sexuality teacher reported, "I have been at times reluctant to see myself as a 'sexualities scholar' because many of my colleagues leap to conclusions about my sexual identity, and they treat me differently" (Irvine, 2015, p. 120). Of 69 graduate programs in marriage and family therapy, 41% had no faculty members who identified sexuality as their primary area of expertise (Zamboni & Zaid, 2017).

Nevertheless, the study of human sexuality is based on research. Professional organizations such as the Society for the Scientific Study of Sexuality, academic programs such as a doctorate in Human Sexuality Studies at Widener University, the Kinsey Institute at Indiana University, and upward of 20 sexuality journals testify to the emphasis on training and research to understand human sexuality.

Critical sexuality studies reflect the commitment of academia to the scientific study of sexuality. Critical sexuality studies identify core sexuality areas of research. These include (1) HIV and AIDS, (2) gender, (3) sexology, (4) sexual and reproductive health (as distinct from HIV and AIDS), and (5) human rights. Although Widener University, in Pennsylvania, currently offers the only fully accredited doctoral program in human sexuality studies in the United States, various levels of training in sexology are available in other universities as part of other programs, such as psychology or gender studies. Due to the influence of conservative ideology and religious authority focusing on the dangers of sexuality and the need for social control and chastity in the United States, the majority of sex research has dealt with the negative aspects of sexuality (Arakawa et al., 2013). In a content analysis of articles appearing in four prestigious journals *(Journal of Sex Research, Archives of Sexual Behavior, The New England Journal of Medicine, and Obstetrics and Gynecology)* from 1960 to the present, the researchers revealed that "only a slim minority of articles investigated the delights of love, sex, and intimacy." Indeed, "the vast majority focused on the problems associated with sexual behavior." Much content has also focused on the disease aspects of sexuality—specifically, HIV and other STIs. An exception is the *Journal of Positive Sexuality,* which emphasizes sexual diversity; sexual identities, orientations, and practices; open and safe communication; empowerment of sexual minorities; and collaboration to help resolve sexual problems in society. According to the journal, "sex positivity is consistent with the World Health Organization definition of sexual health," which is: "a state of physical, emotional, mental and social well-being in relation to sexuality; it is not merely the absence of disease, dysfunction or infirmity" (Center for Positive Sexuality, 2019).

Finally, there is a need to move beyond print journals in academia to the dissemination of sex research content to lay audiences via the use of social media—blogs, podcasts, YouTube, Twitter®, etc.—as well as articles in popular magazines and sexuality workshops in local communities (Lehmiller et al., 2014).

> *Research is formalized curiosity. It is poking and prying with a purpose.*
>
> Nora Neal Hurston, Anthropologist

Critical sexuality studies
Generic term for current core content of sexuality theory and research that is multifaceted and multidisciplinary (crossing several social science and humanities disciplines)

Cultural Diversity

Research on sexuality is conducted throughout the world, including China. Ho et al. (2018) reviewed how sexuality researchers have had to navigate the tension between neoliberal and authoritarian styles of government, noting that some forms of sexual conduct are officially "deviant."

2.1 **The Nature of Sex Research**

Scientific research involves collecting and analyzing **empirical evidence**—data that can be observed, measured, and quantified. There are various sources of knowledge: common sense (living together before marriage means that people get to know each other better and results in happier marriages), intuition (it just feels like cohabitants would have happier marriages), tradition (Icelanders have always lived together before marriage), and authority (religious leaders disapprove of cohabitation). Scientific knowledge is different from all of these in that it is based on observable or empirical evidence. For example, in contrast to the assumption that hooking up is associated with no subsequent romantic relationship, Erichsen and Dignam (2016) found that almost a quarter (23%) of their hookup respondents reported that they had transitioned to a long-term romantic relationship.

> *I don't know. It is an empirical question. Let's see what the data show.*
>
> Jack Turner, psychologist

Researchers are expected to not only connect theory to their data (see Figure 2-1) but also publish their findings. Other researchers and academicians can then replicate, scrutinize, and critically examine these findings.

Thus, theory and research are both parts of the scientific process. Theory and empirical research are linked through two forms of reasoning: deductive and inductive.

FIGURE **2-1** ‖ Links Between Theory and Research: Deductive and Inductive Reasoning

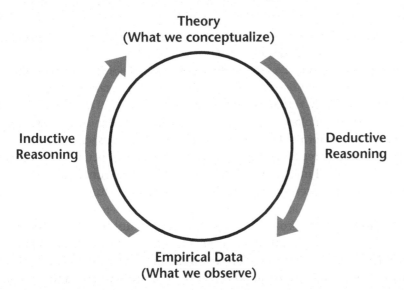

Deductive research involves starting with a specific theory, generating a specific expectation or hypothesis based on that theory, and then gathering data that will either support or refute the theory. For example, researchers may hypothesize that men might move a new acquaintance faster toward sex than women would do in the same situation; thus, the researchers may ask university students to complete a questionnaire on hooking-up scripts and pacing sexual behavior.

Alternatively, researchers might engage in **inductive research**, which begins with specific data that are then used to formulate (induce) an explanation (or theory). In this case, researchers might have a data set that shows that men are more aggressive sexually and might hypothesize that such aggressiveness is biologically and socially induced.

Empirical evidence
Data that can be observed, measured, and quantified

Deductive research
Sequence of research starting with a specific theory, generating a specific expectation or hypothesis based on that theory, and then gathering data that will either support or refute the theory

Inductive research
Sequence of research that begins with specific empirical data, which are then used to formulate a theory to explain the data

In this chapter, after summarizing basic theories of sexuality, we describe how researchers conduct scientific studies of sexuality. First, however, we review the interdisciplinary nature of the study of sexology.

2.2 The Interdisciplinary Nature of Sexology

Sex researchers represent a broad range of disciplines. The study of sexuality is an interdisciplinary field, including psychology, sociology, family studies, medicine, public health, social work, counseling and therapy, history, and education. While courses in human sexuality are most often taught in departments of psychology, health, sociology, and family studies, the three major sources of content are biosexology, psychosexology, and sociosexology. Researchers often share their work with each other at local and national conferences. Sex research is also international in that the World Association for Sexual Health as well as the International Academy of Sex Research feature annual conferences.

Biosexology is the study of the biological aspects of sexuality. Studies in this field focus on such topics as the physiological and endocrinological aspects of sexual development and sexual response, the biological processes involved in sexually transmitted infections, the role of evolution and genetics in sexual development, the physiology of reproduction, and the development of new contraceptives. Biosexology is also concerned with the effects of drugs, medications, disease, and exercise on sexuality.

Psychosexology involves the study of how psychological processes influence and are influenced by sexual development and behavior. For example, how do emotions and motivations affect sexual performance, the use of contraception, and safer sex practices? What psychological processes are involved in the development of sexual aggression and other forms of sexual deviance? How do various sexual and reproductive experiences (such as pregnancy, rape, infertility, sexual dysfunction, and acquisition of a sexually transmitted infection) affect an individual's emotional state?

Sociosexology is concerned with the way social and cultural forces influence and are influenced by sexual attitudes, beliefs, and behaviors—for example, how culture, age, race, ethnicity, socioeconomic status, and gender are related to attitudes, beliefs, and behaviors regarding masturbation, homosexuality, abortion, nonmarital sexual relationships, and HIV infection. Thus, **sexology** may be thought of as a unique discipline that identifies important questions related to sexuality issues and finds and integrates answers from biology, psychology, and sociology based on scientific methods of investigation.

2.3 Theories of Sexuality

A **theory** is a set of ideas designed to answer a question or explain a particular phenomenon (such as, "Why does one person rape another?" and "Why do some individuals of one gender like to dress up in clothes traditionally associated with the other gender?"). In the following sections we review various theoretical perspectives and their applications to human sexuality.

The evolution of sex is the hardest problem in evolutionary biology.

John Maynard Smith, biologist

The study of sexuality is an interdisciplinary and international endeavor.

Biosexology
Study of the biological aspects of sexuality

Psychosexology
Area of sexology focused on how psychological processes influence and are influenced by sexual development and behavior

Sociosexology
Aspect of sexology that is concerned with the way social and cultural forces influence and are influenced by sexual attitudes, beliefs, and behaviors

Sexology
Unique discipline that identifies important questions related to sexuality issues and finds and integrates answers from biology, psychology, and sociology based on scientific methods of investigation

Theory
Set of ideas designed to answer a question or explain a particular phenomenon

Personal **REFLECTION**

Take a moment to express your thoughts about the following question.
How much of your knowledge about human sexuality is based on each of the various sources of knowledge: common sense, intuition, tradition, authority, and scientific research?

2.3a Biological Theories

Biological theories of sexuality include both physiological and evolutionary theories. **Physiological theories** of sexuality describe and explain how physiological processes affect and are affected by sexual behavior. Cardiovascular, respiratory, neurological and endocrinological functioning, and genetic factors are all involved in sexual processes and behaviors.

Evolutionary or **sociobiological theories** of sexuality explain human sexual behavior on the basis of human evolution. According to evolutionary theories of sexuality, sexual behaviors and traits evolve through **natural selection**. Through this process, individuals who have genetic traits that are adaptive for survival and reproduction are more likely to survive and pass on those traits to their offspring. For cisgender women, it is in their sociobiological interest to discriminate among potential partners and mate with one who provides resources for supporting the development of their offspring. Dennis (2018) noted that sociobiology in recent years has become more tenuous as a theory to explain sexual behavior.

The **biosocial framework**, which emphasizes the interaction of biological/genetic inheritance with the social environment to explain and predict human behavior, is related to evolutionary sociobiological theories. Borrowing from evolutionary psychology, sociobiology, and psychobiology, biosocial theory uses the concept of natural selection to explain such phenomena as mate selection. Natural selection emphasizes that it is natural for the individual to want to survive. Cisgender men's tendency to seek young cisgender women with whom to procreate is related to the biological fact that young cisgender women are more fertile and produce more healthy offspring than older cisgender women. Cisgender women, on the other hand, tend to seek cisgender men who are older and more economically stable because they can provide economic resources for their offspring. Hence, both biological (youth/fertility) and social (economic stability) factors combine to explain the mate selection process.

2.3b Psychological Theories

Biological theories do not account for the influence of personality, learning, thoughts, and emotions on human sexuality. These aspects are explained by psychological theory, including psychoanalytic theory, learning theory, and cognitive/affective theory.

Psychoanalytic Theories

Psychoanalytic theory, originally developed by Sigmund Freud (1856–1939), emphasizes the role of unconscious processes in our lives. This theory dominated early views on the nature of human sexuality. A basic knowledge of Freud's ideas about personality structure is important to understand his theories of sexuality.

Physiological theory
Theory that describes and explains how physiological processes affect and are affected by sexual behavior

Evolutionary theory
Theory that explains human sexual behavior and sexual anatomy on the basis of human evolution (See also *sociobiological theory.*)

Sociobiological theory
Framework that explains human sexual behavior and sexual anatomy as functional for human evolution (See also *evolutionary theory.*)

Natural selection
Theory that individuals who have genetic traits that are adaptive for survival are more likely to survive and pass on their genetic traits to their offspring

Biosocial framework
Theoretical framework that emphasizes the interaction of one's biological/genetic inheritance with one's social environment to explain and predict human behavior

Psychoanalytic theory
Sigmund Freud's theory that emphasizes the role of unconscious processes in life

> *Don't become a mere recorder of facts, but try to penetrate the mystery of their origin.*
>
> Ivan Pavlov, pioneer in classical conditioning

Freud believed that each person's personality consists of the id, ego, and superego. The **id** comprises instinctive biological drives such as the need for sex, food, and water. Freud saw human sexuality as a biological force that drives individuals toward the satisfaction of sexual needs and desires. Indeed, one of Freud's most important contributions was his belief that infants and children are sexual beings who possess a positive sexual drive that is biologically wired into their systems.

Another part of the personality, the **ego** deals with objective reality as the individual figures out how to obtain the desires of the id. The ego also must be realistic about social expectations. Whereas the id is self-centered and uninhibited, the ego is that part of the personality that inhibits the id in order to conform to social expectations. While the id operates on what Freud called the *pleasure principle*, the ego operates on the *reality principle*. The ego ensures that individuals do not attempt to fulfill every need and desire whenever they occur. Freud saw rape as a failure of the ego to function properly.

The **superego** is the conscience, which functions by guiding the individual to do what is morally right and good. The superego creates feelings of guilt when the ego fails to inhibit the id and the individual engages in socially unacceptable behavior.

Freud emphasized that personality develops in stages. When we successfully complete one stage, we are able to develop to the next one. If we fail to successfully complete any given stage, we become fixated or stuck in it. The four basic psychosexual stages Freud identified are the oral, anal, phallic, and genital stages.

Although Freud developed his theories during an era of sexual repression, he proposed that **libido** was the most important of human instincts. While his libido theory was an important contribution, Freud has been criticized as overemphasizing sexual motivation for behavior. His clinical observations were based on people who came to him with their problems, but he often generalized broadly from them. His work would not meet the standards of scientific objectivity required today.

Karen Horney (1885–1952) recognized the importance of childhood personality development, but she believed that social—rather than sexual—factors are dominant in personality formation. She felt that the need to emerge from the helpless, controlled state of an infant to that of an independent, autonomous individual is the driving force of the development of the individual. To Horney, sex played a minor role in the drive for independence.

Erik Erikson (1902–1994) believed that individuals progress through a series of stages as they develop. However, unlike Freud, he felt that the states are psychosocial, not psychosexual. He believed that central developmental tasks do not involve seeking oral, anal, and genital pleasures; rather they focus on establishing basic trust with people. Also, Erikson felt that personality formation does not end in adolescence but is a lifelong process—and most contemporary psychologists agree.

In contrast to Freud's psychoanalytic view of sexuality, other psychological theories explain human sexual attitudes and behaviors as learned. Learning theories include classical conditioning theory, operant learning theory, and social learning theory.

Classical Conditioning Theories

Classical conditioning is a process whereby a stimulus and a response that are not originally linked become connected. Ivan Pavlov (1849–1936), a Russian physician, observed that the presence of food caused dogs to salivate. Because salivation is a natural reflex to the presence of food, we call food an *unconditioned stimulus*. However, if Pavlov rang a bell and then gave the dogs food, the dogs soon learned that the bell meant food was forthcoming and would salivate at the sound of the bell. Hence, the bell became a *conditioned stimulus* because it had become associated with the food and was now capable of producing the same response as the food (an unconditioned stimulus).

Id
Freud's term that refers to instinctive biological drives, such as the need for sex, food, and water

Ego
Freud's term for that part of the individual's psyche that deals with objective reality

Superego
Freud's term for the conscience, which functions by guiding the individual to do what is morally right and good

Libido
The sex drive

Classical conditioning
Behavior modification technique whereby an unconditioned stimulus and a neutral stimulus are linked to elicit a desired response

Sexual fetishes can be explained on the basis of classical conditioning. A fetish is a previously neutral stimulus that becomes a conditioned stimulus for erotic feelings. For example, some people have a feather, foot, or leather fetish and respond to these stimuli in erotic ways. However, there is nothing about a feather that would serve to elicit erotic feelings unless it was associated with erotic feelings in the past.

Operant Learning Theories

Operant learning theory, largely developed by B. F. Skinner (1904–1990), is also referred to as operant conditioning or radical behaviorism; it emphasizes that the consequences of a behavior influence whether that behavior will occur in the future. Consequences that follow a behavior may maintain, increase, or decrease (including terminate) the frequency of the behavior. A consequence that maintains or increases a behavior is known as **reinforcement**; a consequence that decreases or terminates a behavior is known as **punishment**. A partner who has been reinforced for initiating sexual behavior is likely to do so again. A partner who has been punished for initiating sexual behavior is less likely to do so in the future. Operant conditioning has not been applied in sexuality research as much as classical conditioning and has mainly been used in the treatment of sexual dysfunctions and in unsuccessful attempts to alter sexual preferences.

(Laura Zuber)

Social learning theory may be used to explain the interaction of these individuals. The smiling, hand–holding, and flirting with each other is mutually reinforcing and will increase their physical intimacy (contingent on an acceptable value system).

Social Learning Theories

Another learning-based approach to understanding human sexuality is **social learning theory**, also referred to as modeling, observational learning, or vicarious learning. It emphasizes that a behavior may be increased without direct reinforcement but in antic-ipation of reinforcement. For example, sexual pleasure and the anticipation of it can be potent reinforcers. Social psychologist Albert Bandura (1925–) put less emphasis on anticipated reward; instead, he emphasized *social learning*, also known *as observational learning*, which posits that we learn by observing and imitating another. For example, we imitate the sexual attitudes and behaviors that we observe in our parents, our peers, and the media. Advertisers are aware of the power of this modeling and hire known, accepted, and approved celebrities to sell products.

Cognitive/Affective Theories

Cognitive/affective theories of sexuality emphasize the role of thought processes and emotions in sexual behavior. The importance of cognitions, or thoughts, in human life was recognized nearly 2,000 years ago by the philosopher Epictetus (55–135), who said, "Man is disturbed not by things, but by the view that he takes of them." Cognitive therapists Aaron Beck and Albert Ellis emphasized that maladaptive or irra-tional thoughts may result in sexual problems. Thoughts such as "I must always have an orgasm" or "I should always be interested in sex" may result in unnecessary frus-tration. Through cognitive therapy, which is based on cognitive theory, these cogni-tions may be examined and changed.

Emotions are related to cognitions. As the preceding example illustrates, changing a person's cognitions will affect the way they feel about sexuality. Affective theories of sexuality emphasize the fact that emotions, such as love, jealousy, fear, anxiety, embar-rassment, and frustration, may precede sexual expression, may be a component of sexual expression, and/or may be a consequence of sexual activity. *Self-Assessment 2-1* may be used to assess your need for sexual intimacy.

Operant learning theory
Explanation of human behavior that emphasizes that the consequences of a behavior influence whether that behavior will occur in the future

Reinforcement
Consequence that maintains or increases a behavior

Punishment
Consequence that decreases or terminates a behavior

Social learning theory
Framework that emphasizes the process of learning through observation and imitation

Cognitive/affective theory
As related to sexuality, a theory that emphasizes the role of thought processes and emotions in sexual behavior

Self-Assessment 2-1:
Need for Sexual Intimacy Scale

Directions

The items that follow address things we may need in life. Some people say we need many things in order to survive (food, shelter, etc.). In the following series of items, rate each one by how much you agree or disagree with it as being something you may need. The term *partner* here refers to a sexual partner (short-term, dating, committed, long-term).

For each item, identify a number that reflects your level of agreement with the statement given and write that number in the space provided.

1 (Disagree definitely), 2 (Disagree mostly), 3 (Neither disagree nor agree), 4 (Agree mostly), 5 (Agree definitely)

Three Areas of Sexual Intimacy

1. Need for Sex

1. __ I need to have more sex.
2. __ I need sex every day.
3. __ I need to have an orgasm every day.
4. __ I need to let myself go sexually with someone.
5. __ I need to have sex every couple of days.
6. __ I need someone who is "great in bed."
7. __ I need sex with a lot of partners.
8. __ I need to take control of my partner when we are intimate.

Scoring

Add up the scores for all eight statements (each should have a value between 1 and 5) and divide by 8.
The lowest possible score is 1, suggesting a low need for sex; the highest possible score is 5, suggesting a high need for sex.

2. Need for Affiliation

1. __ I need a partner who loves me.
2. __ I need someone to love.
3. __ I need companionship.
4. __ I need a companion in life.
5. __ I need to have complete trust in the people I am intimate with.
6. __ I don't need anyone special in my life.
7. __ I need somebody to hold my hand.
8. __ I need a few really good friends.
9. __ I need someone to sleep next to me.

Scoring

Reverse score number 6. (If you selected a 5, replace the 5 with a 1. If you selected a 1, replace it with a 5, etc.) Add each of the nine items (from 1 to 5) and divide by 9. The lowest possible score is 1, suggesting a low need for affiliation; the highest possible score is 5, suggesting a high need for affiliation.

3. Need for Dominance

1. __ I need my partner to tell me where they are at all times.
2. __ I need control over my partner.
3. __ I need my partner to give me what I want (such as financial support, clothes, a car).
4. __ I need a partner I can manipulate.
5. __ I need the ability to order my partner to have sex with me if I want to.

Scoring

Add each of the five items (from 1 to 5) and divide by 5. The lowest possible score is 1, suggesting a low need for dominance; the highest possible score is 5, suggesting a high need for dominance.

Participants

Participants in the initial scale study conducted in 2008 were 347 students with a mean age of 21, mostly female (61%) and single (92%). Seventy-nine percent reported at least one sexual experience (Marelich & Lundquist, 2008). A second set (Marelich et al., 2013) of 422 psychology undergraduates also took the scale study. The respondents were at least 18 years of age and reported having had at least one experience of sexual intercourse.

Results

In Marelich and Lundquist's (2008) study, individuals showing a higher need for sex reported more lifetime sexual partners, more one-night stands, less condom use, less ability to discuss condoms with their partners, and greater use of intoxicants during sex. Those showing a higher need for affiliation had a preference for being in a relationship (women more than men), were more likely to be consumed with thinking about their partners, and were less likely to mislead their partners about a positive HIV test. Those showing a high need for dominance had a preference for dominating their partner sexually and were more likely to ask their partners about past sexual experiences and to report that sex is an important part of a relationship.

The second study (Marelich et al., 2013) revealed that individuals who had a higher need for sex also had higher levels of sexual desire, more unrestricted sexual attitudes, and higher sexual awareness. Those reporting a higher need for dominance engaged in more dominant behaviors, and those reporting a higher need for affiliation had more positive attitudes about emotional support and closeness in relationships. Males reported a higher need for sex and dominance than females.

Validity and Reliability

Details on the validity and reliability of the scale study's findings are available from the author, as noted in the source.

Source: "Motivations for Sexual Intimacy: Development of a Needs-Based Sexual Intimacy Scale," by William D. Marelich and Jessica Lundquist, *International Journal of Sexual Health, 20*(3), 2008. Scale is used with the permission of William D. Marelich, Department of Psychology, California State University—Fullerton.

2.3c Sociological Theories

Sociological theories of human sexuality explain how society and social groups affect and are affected by sexual attitudes and behaviors. The various sociological theoretical perspectives on human sexuality include symbolic interaction, structural-functional, conflict, feminist, and systems theories.

... both gender and sexuality are learned forms of social practice, and ... looking to "natural differences" between women and men for lessons of sexual conduct is an error.

John Gagnon, sociologist

Symbolic Interaction Theories

Symbolic interaction theory, which was developed by Max Weber, Georg Simmel, and Charles Horton Cooley, focuses on how meanings, labels, and definitions that are learned through interactions affect our attitudes, self-concept, and behavior.

Being alluring is an advantage in attracting others. This woman is applying makeup to match what she understands to be the female physical presentation for femininity in American culture.

In addition, our definitions of what constitutes appropriate and inappropriate sexual behavior are learned through our relationships with others. Sexual self-concepts, including body image and perception of one's self as an emotional and sexual partner, are also influenced by interactions with others.

An important component of symbolic interaction theory is the concept of **social scripts**, developed by John Gagnon (Gagnon, 1977; Gagnon & Simon, 1973). Social scripts are shared interpretations that have three functions: define situations, name actors, and plot behaviors. For example, the social script operative in someone buying sex from a sex worker is to define the situation (sex for money), name actors (sex worker and client), and plot behaviors (sex worker will perform requested sexual behaviors for money).

Sexual social scripts operate on three levels—cultural, interpersonal, and intrapsychic (Montemurro, 2014a). In a binary gender world, the traditional *cultural script* for sexual expression has been that women are passive and men are aggressive (the takeaway cultural message is that women who are aggressive are deviant). *Interpersonal scripts* dictate behavior, so that due to cultural constraints, women approach desirable men less often than men approach desirable women. *Intrapsychic scripts* are conversations that individuals have with themselves about their behavior—women who are sexually aggressive and/or find pleasure in casual sex must contend with being slut-shamed.

An example of a traditional heterosexual social script is that the female is expected to view sex as a relationship, and the male is expected to view sex as recreation.

She really had, uh, deep feelings for me, … but I didn't have the same deep feelings for her. I think it was more of a sexual thing for me, but for her it was more of a relationship thing. So I feel kind of bad in that part. Most of my relationships have been like that, where, um, I've broken their hearts. … I've had, I've made plenty, I've made, you know, a couple girls cry. (Masters et al., 2013, p. 416)

Research has revealed traditional gender-role social scripting in hookups. Men are expected to initiate sexual activity and women are expected to take a more passive role (Yazedjian et al., 2014).

While there are general sexual social scripts for women and men, scripts are not uniform; rather, they are complex and diverse. For example, some men expect and prefer sex in the context of a relationship (Morrison et al., 2015), and some women view sex as sport and pleasure (Fulle et al., 2015).

Structural-Functional Theories

Structural-functional theory, developed by Talcott Parsons (1902–1979) and Robert Merton (1910–2003), views society as a system of interrelated parts that influence each other and work together to achieve social stability. The various parts include family, religion, government, economics, and education. Structural-functional theory

Symbolic interaction theory
Sociological theory that focuses on how meanings, labels, and definitions learned through interaction affect one's attitudes, self-concept, and behavior

Social scripts
Shared interpretations that have three functions: define situations, name actors, and plot behaviors

Structural-functional theory
Framework that views society as a system of interrelated parts that influence each other and work together to achieve social stability

suggests that social behavior may be either functional or dysfunctional. Functional behavior contributes to social stability; dysfunctional behavior disrupts social stability. The institution of marriage, which is based on the emotional and sexual bonding of individuals, may be viewed as functional for society because it provides a structure in which children are born and socialized to be productive members of society. Hence, in the United States, there is greater social approval for sex within marriage—children born to a married couple are cared for by the parents and not by social services (as is more common of children born to single parents). Extramarital sex is viewed as dysfunctional because it is associated with divorce, which can affect the emotional well-being of children and disrupt their care and socialization.

Structural-functional theory also focuses on how parts of society influence each other and how changes in one area produce or necessitate changes in another. For example, the educational system in a society affects its birthrate in that women with low levels of education tend to have high birthrates. Hence, reducing population growth may involve increasing education for women. In another example of the structural-functional connection, the changing socioeconomics of the working world in the United States—which includes more women in the workforce today than in previous generations—has influenced the government to establish laws concerning sexual harassment and family leave.

Conflict Theories

Whereas structural-functional theory views society as composed of different parts working together, **conflict theory**, developed by Karl Marx and Ralf Dahrendorf, views society as composed of different parts competing for power and resources. For example, antiabortion groups are in conflict with pro-choice groups; gay rights advocates are in conflict with groups who oppose gay rights; and insurance companies are in conflict with consumers about whether abortion care, contraceptives, and sexual enhancement medications such as Viagra® should be covered in health insurance plans.

Feminist Theories

Feminist theory, which overlaps with conflict theory, focuses on the imbalance of power and resources between women and men, exploring its effect on sexuality, with a wider view of gender inequity in both domestic and public life.

In the feminist view, women's subordination is reflected in limitation of reproductive health care (denial of or reduced access to contraceptives and abortion); restrictions on and objectification of women's appearance, behavior, and sexual activity; stigma associated with the unmarried state; and imbalance in domestic responsibilities and child-rearing, in some cultures completely restricting women to the home (purdah in the Muslim community). Women are also underrepresented in the public sphere, with both law and custom restricting their political power, education, and workforce participation and remuneration.

Feminist analysis targets the **patriarchy**—the global system in which females are subordinate to or the property of a male, usually their husbands and/or fathers. This sociopolitical framework, based on familial descent traced through the male as the head of the family, defines women's and girls' worth in relation to male interests and has resulted in abuse (including sexual assault) of the human rights of women and children around the globe.

Mary Wollstonecraft's (1759–1797) historic 1792 treatise, "Vindication of the Rights of Women," set the stage for modern feminist theory, which developed in three stages. The late 19th century "first-wave" feminists Elizabeth Cady Stanton (1815–1902) and Susan B. Anthony (1820–1906), among others, risked imprisonment and

Conflict theory
Sociological theory that views society as consisting of different parts competing for power and resources

Feminist theory
Perspectives that analyze discrepancies in equality between men and women and how these imbalances affect sexuality, research studies in sexuality, and sexual health-care delivery

Patriarchy
The global system in which females are subordinate to or the property of a male, usually their husbands and/or fathers

The greatest feminists have also been the greatest lovers.

Erika Jong, feminist

physical assault in their struggle for suffrage. In the second wave of the 1960s and 1970s, reproductive rights and equal treatment under the law were dominant concerns. Feminism's third wave, from the 1990s to the present, champions intersectionality, including the voices of women of color and LGBTQ rights.

Systems Theories

Systems theory, developed by Murray Bowen (1913–1990), emphasizes the interpersonal and relationship aspects of sexuality. For example, whereas a biological view of low sexual desire emphasizes the role of hormones or medications and a psychological view might emphasize negative cognitions and emotions regarding sexual arousal, a systems perspective views low sexual desire as a product of the interaction between two partners. Negative interaction between partners can affect their interest in having sex with each other.

Table 2-1 presents different theoretical explanations for various observations of sexuality.

2.4 **Eclectic View of Human Sexuality**

Whereas some scholars who study human sexuality focus on one theoretical approach, others propose an **eclectic view** that recognizes the contributions of multiple perspectives. For example, sexuality of the aging can be understood in terms of a comprehensive view of the various biological, psychological, and social aspects of the aging process. For example, in the eclectic view, decreased libido in older people is not only a function of decreased testosterone/progesterone, but also of other factors such as altered self-concept ("I am no longer sexually attractive") and cultural expectations that deny a strong libido among the elderly.

2.4a **Early Sex Researchers**

Several early 20th-century scientists were instrumental in shifting society's ideas about sex from a religious perspective toward the consideration of scientific ideologies and discoveries. These pioneers include Richard von Krafft-Ebing, Havelock Ellis, Alfred Kinsey, and William Masters and Virginia Johnson.

Richard von Krafft-Ebing (1840–1902) was a Viennese psychiatrist and sexologist who focused on the study of abnormal, or *pathological*, sexuality. Originally published in 1886, *Psychopathia Sexualis* (1965) contains Krafft-Ebing's case histories of more than 200 individuals—some of them bizarre. For example, he revealed that some parents applied a white-hot iron to the clitoris of young girls for "treatment" of masturbation.

Havelock Ellis (1859–1939) emphasized that sexual behavior was learned social behavior, that deviant sexual behavior was merely that which society labeled as abnormal, and that an enjoyable sex life (a desirable goal) was not something that just happened, but rather had to be achieved.

Alfred Kinsey (1894–1956) is regarded as the pioneer of human sexuality research. His marriage course at Indiana University became too controversial because of its explicit nature, so he was given the choice to tone it down or collect sex research full-time. His choice of the latter resulted in the Institute for Sex Research, which housed the sexual histories of more than 18,000 people. Kinsey personally interviewed 8,000 individuals in extensive interviews that lasted 1.5–2 hours each. His major impact was in influencing society to consider sex as an acceptable topic of social conversation.

Systems theory
Theoretical framework that emphasizes the interpersonal and relationship aspects of sexuality

Eclectic view
View that recognizes the contribution of multiple perspectives to the understanding of sexuality

TABLE 2-1	Sexuality Observations and Theoretical Explanations
Observation	**Theory**
1. Men are more sexually aggressive than women.	**Operant Learning** Men have been reinforced for being sexually aggressive. Women have been punished for being sexually aggressive. **Social Script** Our society teaches men to be more aggressive and women to be more passive sexually. Each gender learns through interactions with parents, peers, and partners that this is normative behavior. **Physiological** Men have large amounts of androgen, and women have larger amounts of progesterone, which accounts for male aggressiveness and female passivity.
2. Pornography is consumed primarily by men.	**Operant Learning** Men derive erotic pleasure (reinforcement) from pornography. **Social Script** Men influence each other to regard pornography as desired entertainment. Men share information about internet porn sites; this reflects a norm regarding pornography among males. Women rarely discuss pornography with each other. **Evolutionary** Men are biologically wired to become erect in response to visual sexual stimuli.
3. In most societies, men are allowed to have a number of sexual partners.	**Structural-Functional** In many societies, women outnumber men. Polygyny potentially provides a mate for every woman. **Feminist** The social, political, and economic power of men provides the context for men to exploit women sexually by making rules in favor of polygyny. **Evolutionary** Men are biologically wired for variety; women, for monogamy. These respective wirings produce reproductive success for the respective sexes.
4. Women and men tend to report lower levels of sexual desire in their elderly years.	**Social Script** Aging women and men learn social scripts that teach them that elderly persons are not expected to be sexual. **Systems** Elderly persons are often not in a relationship that elicits sexual desire. **Biological** Hormonal changes in the elderly account for decreased or absent sexual desire (physiological). There is no reproductive advantage for elderly women to be sexually active; there is minimal reproductive advantage for elderly men to be sexually active (evolutionary).
5. Extradyadic relationships, including marital infidelity, are common.	**Operant Learning** Immediate interpersonal reinforcement for extradyadic sex is stronger than delayed punishment for infidelity. **Biological** Humans (especially men) are biologically wired to be sexually receptive to numerous partners. **Structural-Functional** Infidelity reflects the weakening of the family institution. **Systems** Emotional and sexual interactions between couples are failing to meet the needs of one or both partners.

But Kinsey's data have been criticized as not being representative of the general public. In the 1940s and 1950s, he drove to Chicago from Indiana University to interview anyone who would allow him to do so. This resulted in prostitutes, homosexuals, substance abusers, and individuals with lower socioeconomic backgrounds being overrepresented in his research. The National Sex Study at Indiana University updated his research in 2012.

While Kinsey and his predecessors researched the cultural attitudes on and frequency of sexual behavior, Masters and Johnson provided data on physiological responses during sex. *Up Close 2-1* details the credentials, research, and relationship of Masters and Johnson.

2.5 Conducting Sex Research: A Step-by-Step Process

Research is valuable because it helps provide evidence for or against a hypothesis. For example, while it is hypothesized that hookups are recreation and rarely transition to sustained romantic relationships, almost a quarter of the respondents in a 2015 study reported such an experience (Erichsen et al., 2015). The steps in conducting research are identifying a research question, reviewing the literature, formulating hypotheses, operationalizing the research variables, collecting data, and analyzing and interpreting the results.

> *We are recorders and reporters of the facts—not judges of the behavior we describe.*
>
> Alfred Kinsey, early sex researcher

2.5a Identifying a Research Question

A researcher's interest in a particular research question may be based on a personal life experience or may involve concern about certain human or social problems. Researchers are generally hired by the government, by industry, or by some other organization to conduct research and investigate questions of interest.

2.5b Reviewing the Literature

Numerous journals (some identified earlier in this chapter) publish research on human sexuality. Reviewing the articles in these and other journals enables researchers to discover what other researchers have already learned about a topic, provides them with ideas about new research questions, and suggests ways to conduct research.

Hypothesis
A tentative and testable proposal or an educated guess about the outcome of a research study

Variable
Any measurable event or characteristic that varies or is subject to change

Independent variable
Variable that is presumed to cause or influence the dependent variable

Dependent variable
Variable that is measured to assess what, if any, effect the independent variable has on it

2.5c Formulating a Hypothesis and Operationalizing Variables

To answer their research questions, researchers must transform their questions into testable **hypotheses**, a tentative or educated guess designed to test a theory. Hypotheses involve predictions about the relationship between two or more variables—for example, alcohol and condom use. A **variable** is any measurable event or characteristic that varies or is subject to change. There are two types of variables. The **independent variable** is presumed to cause or influence the dependent variable. The **dependent variable** is measured to assess what, if any, effect the independent variable has on it. The following is an example of a sex research hypothesis and its variables:

Masters and Johnson

William Masters and Virginia Johnson are best known for their book *Human Sexual Response* (1966), which detailed their 11-year research study in which they observed over 10,000 orgasms (via sexual intercourse and masturbation) experienced by almost 700 volunteers (382 females and 312 males) at Washington University in St. Louis, Missouri. They identified and provided data on the sexual response cycle (excitement, plateau, orgasm, resolution) and the physiological changes that occur during each stage (heart rate, breathing, muscle contractions).

Dr. Masters initiated the sex research and soon recognized the need for a female assistant. Virginia Johnson, a twice-divorced mother of two, was soon hired and became aware that having sex with Dr. Masters was expected, because he told her that they needed to know what their volunteers were experiencing physiologically when connected to the various machines. She accepted the position without protest, and they became Masters and Johnson. Today, his behavior would be regarded as blatant sexual harassment.

The couple married 5 years after the publication of their blockbuster best seller. Their biographer, Thomas Maier (2009), suggested that their marriage was more of a business than a love connection. Johnson said, "I probably never loved him" (p. 222), and Masters later said of the marriage, "It was convenient" (p. 238). The couple launched a lucrative private practice in sex therapy, charging $5,000 for 2 weeks in their offices in St. Louis. At one time, they had a 6-month waiting list with over 400 names. Their influence on sex therapy was dramatic. Across America in the 1970s, there were over 5,000 sex therapy clinics offering variations of Masters and Johnson therapy, but only 50 sex therapists were actually trained by Masters and Johnson.

Behind the Masters and Johnson enterprise there were questions and problems. Johnson had no formal training—she was a high school graduate who wanted to go to college but never did. Indeed, Masters, an obstetrician, had no sex therapy training. The extent of his education as a clinician was a few weeks with a psychiatrist during his residency. Hence, the world-famous sex therapists had no clinical training at all.

Another concern was the lack of training of the clinical staff of the Masters and Johnson Institute. While initial staff members Robert Kolodny and Sallie Schumacher were credentialed, some subsequent staff members had questionable qualifications. For example, in the later years, researcher Robert Meyners had a PhD in theology—and was the son-in-law of Virginia Johnson.

The allegation that Masters cooked the data for his and Johnson's controversial book *Homosexuality in Perspective* (1979) is even more disturbing than their lack of formal training. In the book, theoretically based on 67 cases (54 men and 13 women) of homosexuals who wanted to convert to heterosexuality, Masters boasted a 70% success rate. However, when clinic director/physician Robert Kolodny of the Masters and Johnson Institute asked to see the data and hear the tape recordings, Masters refused. "He made it up," Johnson said (Maier, 2009, p. 294).

There were other problems. In the 1970s, the use of sex surrogates (who worked with 41 men with problems of premature ejaculation and erectile dysfunction) became visible with a $2.5 million federal lawsuit filed by the husband of Barbara Calvert. He claimed that he and his wife had been patients of Masters and Johnson and that the use of his wife as a sex surrogate was a violation of the patient-therapist relationship. Details of the out-of-court settlement were never made public.

After 21 years of marriage, Masters and Johnson divorced (initiated by Masters, who wanted to marry a previous partner), and their collaboration began to unravel. By the end of the 1980s, the Masters and Johnson Institute was losing money. Numerous books, such as *The Pleasure Bond* (1976), *Masters and Johnson on Sex and Human Loving* (1986), and *Crisis: Heterosexual Behavior in the Age of HIV* (1988), never matched the sales of *Human Sexual Response*. *Crisis*, cowritten by Robert Kolodny, gained notoriety for its bizarre views on AIDS, including the false claim that it could be acquired by casual contact. The subsequent critical backlash was a factor in Masters's 1992 decision to resign as the Institute's director and its subsequent closure in 1994.

Howie Masters, the son of Bill Masters by his first wife, said, "In the end my father walked away as a pauper" (Maier, 2009, p. 362). Suffering from Parkinson's disease and dementia, William Masters died in 2001. Johnson did not remarry and died in 2013.

Despite these and other problems, Masters and Johnson's research on the physiology of sexual response made a unique contribution to the literature, and some of their procedures, such as sensate focus, are standard sex therapy techniques today. Masters and Johnson, like Alfred Kinsey, remain pioneers in the field of human sexuality. Their lives and work were featured in the 2013 Showtime® television series *Masters of Sex*, based on the 2009 book by Thomas Maier.

1. *Hypothesis*: High alcohol consumption is associated with lower condom use.
2. *Independent Variable:* Alcohol consumption
3. *Dependent Variable:* Condom use

Because human sexual behavior and attitudes are complex and influenced by many factors, researchers often assess the effects of several independent variables on one or more dependent variables. For example, condom use is also influenced by the status of the relationship and whether the couple reports being in love. Partners who are hooking up are more likely to use a condom than cohabiting couples who report being in love.

Researchers must also specify how they will **operationalize** variables and develop an **operational definition** (working definition) of their terms. They must also apply working definitions to such terms as *sexual satisfaction*, *sexual desire*, *pornography*, *sexual orientation*, *rape*, and *cohabitation*. An operational definition of cohabitation is "two unrelated adults of the opposite sex who live in the same residence overnight for four nights a week for at least three months." Such specifics will eliminate lovers who stay over at each other's apartment on the weekend, but it would also eliminate same gender couples.

2.5d Caveats in Sex Research

Research bias operates in various ways, including the selection of topics. Pham (2017) noted an overabundance of research on the hookup culture to the neglect of other areas of sexuality research. Researchers themselves are also not immune to bias. Alfred Kinsey, as a biologist and international expert on the gall wasp, was a taxonomist. As such, he classified and described variations within and across species. In trying to find all the variations in human sexual behaviors and validate sexual variety, he pursued unusual sexualities and may have spent more time revealing the extremes of sexuality (for example, pedophilia) than reflecting the population as a whole.

Researchers are also biased by their own socialization and cultural context. Bowleg et al. (2017) noted that most research on the sexuality of black males has assumed white male heterosexuality as normative, which has posited black males as hypersexual and deviant.

Another source of potential bias occurs when researchers present an interpretation of what other researchers have done. Two layers of bias may be operative here: (a) when the original data are collected and interpreted and (b) when the second researcher reads the study of the original researcher and makes their own interpretation. Much of this text is based on the authors' representations of someone else's research. As a consumer, you should be alert to the potential bias in reading such secondary sources. To help control for this bias, we have provided references to the original sources for your own reading.

Some researchers are deliberately dishonest, unethical, and deceptive. Earlier in this chapter we noted that William Masters falsified his data on reparative therapy. In Chapter 5, Gender and Sexuality, we note that Dr. John Money of Johns Hopkins University published research that related the opposite of what his subject reported. More recently, Theranos Corporation, valued at $10 billion at its zenith, was found to have presented faulty data to investors, consumers, and patients. Elizabeth Holmes, CEO, made up the claims of the company's research for the blood-testing machine of Theranos; today the stock is worth zero (O'Donnell, 2018). Table 2-2 summarizes other caveats to keep in mind when dealing with research reports.

Operationalize
Define how a variable will be measured

Operational definition
Working definition; how a variable is defined in a particular study

TABLE 2-2 | **Caveats in Sex Research**

Caveat	Consequences	Example
The sample wasn't random.	Cannot generalize the findings	The sexual attitudes and behaviors of college students are not the same as those of other adults.
There was no control group.	Inaccurate conclusions	For purposes of comparison, studies on the effect of exposure to pornography on sexual satisfaction need a control group of respondents not exposed to pornography.
There were differences (such as age) between groups of respondents.	Inaccurate conclusions	May be due to passage of time or to cohort differences.
The terms were not operationally defined.	Inability to measure what is not clearly defined	What are "hooking up," "sexual satisfaction," "open sexual communication," and "orgasm"?
A research bias was present.	Slanted conclusions	A researcher studying the preference for sex toy use should not be funded by a maker of sex toys.
There has been a time lag since the original research.	Outdated conclusions	The often-quoted Kinsey sex research is over 60 years old.
The data are distorted.	Invalid conclusions	Research subjects exaggerate, omit information, and/or recall facts or events inaccurately. Respondents may remember what they wish rather than what really happened.
Mischievous responders	Invalidate data	Some respondents provide outrageous answers (e.g. "I have had 1,000 partners") since they think it is "funny" to do so.

An additional research concern is participation bias suggesting that those who agree to become involved in sex research are younger, college educated, liberal and do not attend church (Zapien, 2017). In addition, there is the question of whether those who do not respond to internet surveys are different from those who do. In a study of 2,049 individuals about whom extensive information was known, Busby and Yoshida (2015) found virtually no differences (of 18 factors, such as personality, family of origin measures, etc.) between those who had valid email addresses and those who did not. Rinehart et al. (2017) also confirmed that collecting research from undergraduates on "sensitive topics" (e.g. rape) does not unduly increase participant distress. Indeed, subjects may benefit from their participation in research. Bay-Chen found increased sexual self-esteem from participants who revealed their sexual history. Fahs (2016) also emphasized that there are "margins of the interview" that are challenging insights to identify and that are easily missed. For example, discussions of "first sex" (which is sometimes assumed to be first intercourse) may evoke stories of sexual trauma or nonpenetrative sex.

Cimpian et al. (2018) discussed the concept of "mischievous responders"—respondents who mislead researchers by providing extreme and untruthful responses to multiple items, perhaps because they find it "funny" to do so.

Finally, surveys sometimes overlook important data. McClelland & Holland (2016) identified 136 instances in which respondents diagnosed with late-stage breast cancer had taken the Female Sexual Function Index and made clarifications and corrections or noted items as "not applicable" in the margins of the survey printout. These marginalia give the researcher important feedback about the respondent's life and the research design that are often ignored.

Technology and Sexuality 2-1: Online Surveys

Although the internet has existed for over 25 years, some researchers remain skeptical of using it as a resource for collecting data. Concerns include the time investment involved in online research, the limitations of a sample (demographic bias), and a low response rate. Are these valid concerns?

Twenty years ago, the online population was different than it is today. Previously, many individuals connected to the internet with a dial-up connection, so only those who could afford to pay the internet service provider for a faster connection would be included in the survey. Today, more than 90% of Americans use the internet (Pew Research Center, 2019c). A higher percentage have cell phone access. In regard to the previous concern by researchers that certain groups, such as lower-income individuals who lack online access, would be underrepresented in online research, the reality is that today's youth from lower socioeconomic backgrounds do have access to the internet, but it tends to be through mobile devices rather than traditional desktop computers (Madden et al., 2013). Online research has also proved valuable in reaching populations that have previously been difficult to access, such as people who identify as LGBTQ or those who engage in high-risk health behaviors, including substance abuse (Matthews & Cramer, 2008; Ramo & Prochaska, 2012).

Online research tools have also improved. No longer must researchers know how to write html code in order to develop surveys. Today, a variety of apps and online survey companies can create a survey from the researcher's questions. Universities also provide research assistance, including survey development, online hosting of surveys for respondent convenience, and data analysis format tools, such as SPSS statistics software.

While online surveys have numerous advantages, problems do remain, including a lower response rate than paper surveys (Kongsved et al., 2007). Anonymity is another concern. If a survey link is emailed to a potential respondent, the researcher can link the answers to the email, thus compromising anonymity (Sue & Ritter, 2012). This problem has been solved by posting the survey on a website and providing respondents with a password to input their responses.

Despite such concerns, technology is increasingly used to conduct research in sexuality. Social networking sites such as Facebook and Twitter are being used to recruit participants to complete surveys, blogs are being used as references for qualitative research, and therapy is being offered online via Skype™ sessions (Andersson & Titov, 2014; Ramo & Prochaska, 2012; Sato et al., 2015). Indeed, the internet has become the researcher's tool of choice.

2.5e Research Ethics: Protection of Human Subjects

It is important to protect the individuals who participate in research. The American Psychological Association charges psychologists to uphold high standards of ethics, conduct, education, and achievement. While these ethics often focus on issues relevant to clinical work (APA, 2010), they are equally important in reference to participants involved in research projects. A major principle of ethics in regard to conducting research is **informed consent**: The person participating in the research project must be fully informed as to the risks and dangers and must voluntarily agree to participate. While Nazi Germany provides egregious examples of forcing patients to submit to various research projects against their will, the United States has also been guilty of exposing subjects to physical harm without their knowledge.

In 1932, the U.S. Public Health Service launched a research study known as the Tuskegee syphilis experiment at Tuskegee Institute in Tuskegee, Alabama. Nearly 400 black men who had syphilis were enrolled in the project to determine how the disease spreads, progresses, and kills. The men were not told that they had syphilis, and they were not treated for it—even when penicillin became a standard cure in 1947, while the study was still active. The participants were told that they had "bad blood," a euphemism to describe several illnesses, including syphilis, anemia, and fatigue. For their willingness to be involved in the study, the men were given free meals and free burial insurance (Jones, 1993).

Informed consent
In the context of participants in a research project, voluntary agreement to participate based on the provision of full information as to the project's risks and dangers

The experiment lasted 4 decades, until public health workers leaked the story to the media. By then, dozens of the men had died, and many of their wives and children had been infected. In 1973, the National Association for the Advancement of Colored People (NAACP) filed a class-action lawsuit. The suit culminated in a $9 million settlement divided among the study's surviving participants, who received free health care, as did infected wives, widows, and children (NPR, 2002).

The National Research Act, the National Commission for the Protection of Human Subjects of Biomedical and Behavioral Research, and the Office for Human Research Protections set ethical standards and guidelines for supervising federally funded clinical trials. Central to these guidelines is individual informed consent (Mays, 2012). In 1997, President Bill Clinton apologized to the survivors of the Tuskegee experiment, pledging to ensure that such unethical research would never be repeated.

Another egregious example of deceptive research occurred in Guatemala from 1946 to 1948. U.S. Public Health Service physicians deliberately infected prisoners, soldiers, and patients in a mental hospital with syphilis and, in some cases, gonorrhea. A total of 696 men and women were exposed to syphilis without their knowledge. When the subjects contracted the disease, they were given antibiotics, although it is unclear if all infected parties were cured. This study was hidden from public exposure for even longer than Tuskegee, since there were only a few articles published in Spanish—in contrast to 13 published reports on the Tuskegee example of "malfeasance and ethical failings" (Reverby, 2012, p. 493). In October 2010, the United States formally apologized to the citizens of Guatemala for conducting these experiments.

While not a government-funded study, independent researcher Laud Humphreys's participant-observer study of the British "tearoom trade" also violated the principle of informed consent. Humphreys served as a "watch queen" (lookout) during the study, observing sexual encounters between same-sex strangers in public bathrooms without revealing his research role. He recorded participants' automobile license numbers and used them to trace the owners' identities and addresses. A year later, he included these men as participants in an unrelated social health survey that he conducted with a colleague. In this way, he not only participated in the study himself, but he also obtained background and personal information on tearoom clients without their knowledge or approval. In a retrospective discussion of his research, Humphreys (1975) responded to ethical critiques and agreed with the criticism of the tracing of license numbers to interview men in their homes, admitting that he put these men at risk of arrest by law enforcement officers.

Per the National Research Act, to ensure compliance with human research protocol, researchers are required to obtain approval from the Institutional Review Board (IRB) of their university or institutional affiliation. These panels review each research proposal requesting federal funding to ensure that the expected research ethics are being followed—including informed consent. Research involving human subjects is required to meet the requirements published in "Ethical Principles and Guidelines for the Protection of Human Subjects of Research," also known as the Belmont Report (http://bvtlab.com/NR99q), named after the Belmont Conference Center, where the commission met when drafting the report in 1976.

The three basic principles protecting human subjects are respect of persons, beneficence, and justice. *Respect of persons* includes protecting those with diminished capacity. *Beneficence* means doing no harm, maximizing possible benefits, and minimizing possible harms. *Justice* requires the researcher to treat all subjects equally.

Research is the process of going up alleys to see if they are blind.

Marston Bates, zoologist

2.6 Methods of Data Collection

After identifying a research question, reviewing the literature, formulating a hypothesis, and operationalizing variables, researchers collect data. Methods of data collection include experimental research, survey research, field research, direct laboratory observations, and case studies.

2.6a Experimental Research

Experimental research involves manipulating the independent variable to determine how it affects the dependent variable. In conducting an experiment, the researcher recruits participants and randomly assigns them to either an experimental group or a control group. After measuring the dependent variable in both groups, the researcher exposes participants in the experimental group to the independent variable—also known as the experimental treatment. Then the researcher measures the dependent variable in both groups again and compares the experimental group with the control group. Any differences between the groups may be due to the experimental treatment.

The importance of a control group was illustrated in the research of Willoughby and colleagues (2014b), who found a link between pornography consumption and diminished self-worth and increased depressive symptoms. However, no such associations were found when control variables were taken into consideration.

The major strength of the experimental method is that it provides information on causal relationships, showing how one variable affects another. Its primary weakness is that experiments are often conducted on small samples, usually in artificial laboratory settings. For this reason, the findings may not be generalizable to other people in natural settings.

2.6b Survey Research

Most research in sexuality is **survey research** (Fletcher et al., 2013), which involves eliciting information from respondents using questions. An important part of survey research is selecting a **sample**, or a portion of the population in which the researcher is interested. Ideally, samples are representative of the population being studied. A **representative sample** allows the researcher to assume that responses obtained from the sample are similar to those that would be obtained from the larger population.

Most sex research studies are self-reported and are not based on representative samples. Instead, they are conducted on convenient samples, such as college students to whom researchers have easy access. The problem with convenience samples is that they may not be representative of the larger population.

A problem with research is the nature of volunteers. Students who volunteer for sexuality research have been shown to be more likely to have had sexual intercourse, have performed oral sex, score higher on sexual esteem and sexual sensation-seeking, and report sexual attitudes that are less traditional than those of nonvolunteers (Wiederman, 1999). Wiederman cautioned that if such volunteers are not representative, the validity of sexuality research might be particularly suspect. Notwithstanding these issues with samples, there are several kinds of survey research.

Experimental research
Research methodology that involves manipulating the independent variable to determine how it affects the dependent variable

Survey research
Research that involves eliciting information from respondents using questions

Sample
Portion of the population that the researcher studies to attempt to make inferences about the whole population

Representative sample
Sample the researcher studies that is representative of the population from which it is taken

Interviews

After selecting their sample, survey researchers interview people or ask them to complete written or online questionnaires, as is seen, for example, in researcher Beth Montemurro's (2014a) interviews of 95 females in regard to their sexual socialization. Adeagbo (2018) also interviewed 20 interracial gay men about their intimate relationships. O'Callaghan et al. (2019) interviewed 45 survivors of sexual assault. In **interview survey research**, trained interviewers ask respondents a series of questions and take written notes or record the respondents' answers. Interviews may be conducted over the telephone, face-to-face, or online via an application such as Skype. Interview survey research enables the researcher to clarify questions for the respondent and follow up on answers to particular questions. Face-to-face interviews are an effective method of surveying individuals who do not have a telephone, internet connection, or mailing address.

A major disadvantage of interview research is the lack of privacy and anonymity involved. Respondents may feel embarrassed or threatened when asked to answer questions about sexual attitudes and behaviors. As a result, some may choose not to participate, and those who do may conceal or alter information to give socially desirable answers such as, "No, I have never had intercourse with someone other than my spouse during my marriage" or "Yes, I use condoms every time I have sex."

Other disadvantages of interview survey research include the time and expense required. Interviews can easily last over an hour, with some ongoing studies taking far longer, and the cost can be enormous when including interviewer training, transportation to the respondents' homes, and computer data entry. Telephone interviews are less time consuming and cost less but may yield less information since nonverbal behavior, which may prompt follow-up questions, cannot be observed.

Although face-to-face interviews are often conducted one-on-one, sometimes they are held in a small group called a **focus group**. Advantages of focus group research include the minimal expense of time and money and the fact that it allows participants to interact and raise new issues for the researcher to investigate. Respondents can clarify their responses and respond in more depth than they would in a survey. A disadvantage of the focus group is its limited sample size, which means that the data may not be representative of the larger research population.

Interview survey research
Type of research in which trained interviewers ask respondents a series of questions and either take written notes or record the respondents' answers, over the telephone, online, or face-to-face

Focus group
Interviews conducted in a small group and typically focused on one subject

Questionnaires

Instead of conducting face-to-face or phone interviews, researchers may develop questionnaires that they give to a sample of respondents taking a survey on the internet where respondents answer in private. The digital version of the Sexual Life History Calendar (d/SLHC) is a web-based questionnaire that asks the respondents about past sexual and relationship experiences, and their circumstances, meanings, and ramifications (Bay-Cheng, 2017). Surveys such as this provide large quantities of data that can be analyzed relatively inexpensively as compared to face-to-face interviews or telephone surveys (which take a great deal of the respondents'/researchers' time).

(Amberlynn Bishop)

Sex surveys are often completed online by undergraduates in their room.

Because researchers do not ask respondents to write their names on questionnaires, questionnaire research provides privacy and anonymity for the research participants, although online surveys linked to a person's email or IP address are not anonymous. However, respondents sometimes do provide inaccurate answers to questionnaires. Data collected on the results of the honesty of a question on a self-administered questionnaire have found that between 5% and 20% (varying by sex and race) admitted that they had lied during previous interviews. Many respondents were also incorrect in remembering their previous answers (Udry, 1998).

When sexual information is sensitive or potentially stigmatizing, obtaining accurate information may be especially challenging. For example, given the social pressure to avoid behaviors that increase risk to HIV exposure, respondents may find it difficult to admit they perform such behaviors.

Studies on sexuality and relationships are commonly found in popular magazines such as *Cosmopolitan* and online. Sometimes these magazines or websites conduct their own research by asking readers/visitors to complete questionnaires and mail them to the magazine editors or to take a survey online. The survey results are published in subsequent issues of the magazine or on the website.

The results of magazine and online surveys should be viewed with caution because the data are not based on representative samples. Other problems include the inadequacy of some questions, the methods of analysis, and the inherent bias of the publication or website, which wants to reflect a positive image of its readership. Results that show the respondents in a negative light are not likely to be published.

2.6c Field Research

Field research, or *fieldwork*, involves observing and studying social behaviors in the settings in which they occur naturally. Field research is conducted in two ways. In **participant observation** research, to obtain an insider's perspective of the people and/or behavior being observed, the researcher takes part in the phenomenon being studied. For example, a researcher might go nude at a nudist resort to observe client behavior patterns.

In **nonparticipant observation** research, the investigators observe the phenomenon being studied but do not actively participate in the group or the activity.

For example, researchers could study nude beaches and strip clubs as observers, without taking off their clothes.

The primary advantage of field research of both types is that it yields detailed, descriptive, and direct information about the behaviors, values, emotions, and norms of those being studied. However, the individuals being studied may alter their behaviors if they know they are being observed, and researchers who do not let the individuals know they are being studied may be violating ethical codes of research conduct. Another potential problem with field research is that the researchers' observations are subjective and may be biased. In addition, because field research is usually based on small samples, the findings may not be generalizable.

Field research
Method of data collection that involves observing and studying social behaviors in settings in which they occur naturally

Participant observation
Type of observation in which the researcher participates in the phenomenon being studied to obtain an insider's perspective of the people and/or behavior being observed

Nonparticipant observation
Type of research in which investigators observe the phenomenon being studied but do not actively participate in the group or the activity

(Amberlynn Bishop)

An example of participant observation of gambling would be to join a card game and observe the behavior of the players. In sexuality research, it would be to go to a nudist camp.

2.6d Direct Laboratory Observation

We previously discussed the work of William Masters and Virginia Johnson, who provided laboratory data on human sexual response. It was not until their work that laboratory analysis of sexual behavior/response became legitimate.

Problems with laboratory-based research include the use of volunteers. Are those who volunteer to participate in such research similar to those who do not? Research volunteers are more likely to be sexually experienced, more interested in sexual variety, and less guilty about sex than nonvolunteers. Thus, volunteer samples may not be representative of the group from which they are recruited, and caution should be used in making generalizations based on the findings.

Social Policy 2-1

Public Funding for Sex Research?

Conducting large-scale sex research is expensive. Staff members are needed to draw samples, conduct interviews, analyze data, interpret findings, and write up the results. Who pays for sex research? Funding may come from private organizations and corporations, universities, or government agencies. Using government funds is a controversial practice in the United States.

Congress is often not convinced of the validity of providing funding for sex research and fears the retribution of the voting public. Members of Congress also cite morality issues and suggest that funding should be used for more pressing concerns, such as finding the cure for cancer or for veterans' needs. Sex researchers, such as Heather Rupp of the Kinsey Institute, note that sexuality research has a greater chance of being funded when tied to health-related issues (Merta, 2010). Sex research also reflects the values of the administration in power. During the Obama Administration, federal funds were available for comprehensive sexual health. With social conservatives in power in the Trump Administration, federal dollars were more directed toward abstinence-only-until-marriage programs (Donovan, 2017).

Typical Arguments for Funding Sex Research

Taxpayers fund projects all the time. Most of our tax money goes to things that we do not understand and to things that do not benefit the population as a whole. Sex research is something that can benefit people on every level of society. Sexual dysfunctions, STIs, AIDS, and other sexual concerns do not discriminate—they are problems that affect the old and the young, the rich and the poor. Sex research has given us answers and solutions to many problems about sex and related issues. New drugs have been discovered to treat sexual problems such as AIDS and erectile dysfunction. Without sex research, we would not have these medications to treat life-threatening disease or to enhance sexual encounters. The more funding sex research gets, the more we learn about sexuality. The more we know about sex and sexuality, the better.

Typical Arguments Against Public Funding for Sex Research

People pay enough taxes already; sex research is the last thing people need to be throwing their money away on. Therefore, the public should not fund sex research. There are more important things to be putting tax money toward—like education and health care. Sex researchers seem to be doing fine being funded by private organizations, so there's no reason for the public to help with funding. Why do we need to research sex anyway? We all know what sex is and what purpose it serves. What more is there to research?

2.6e Case Studies

A **case study** is a research approach that involves conducting an in-depth, detailed analysis of an individual, group, relationship, or event. Data obtained in a case study may come from interviews, observations, or analysis of records (medical, educational, and legal). Like field research, case studies yield detailed qualitative or descriptive information about the experiences of individuals. An example of a case study is that of a 29-year-old man who was anxious about talking with, touching, or kissing a woman. Surrogates were used to help him feel more comfortable with women, which subsequently enabled him to participate in a happy cohabiting relationship (Zentner & Knox, 2013).

Case studies are valuable in providing detailed qualitative information about the experiences of individuals and groups. The main disadvantage of the case study method is that findings based on a small sample size (in some cases, a sample size of one) are not generalizable.

2.7 Levels of Data Analysis

After collecting data on a research question, researchers analyze the data to test their hypotheses. There are three levels of data analysis: descriptive, correlation, and causation.

2.7a Descriptive

The goal of many sexuality research studies is to describe sexual processes, behaviors, and attitudes, as well as the people who experience them. **Descriptive research** may be qualitative or quantitative. *Qualitative descriptions* of sexuality are verbal narratives that describe details and nuances of sexual phenomena. For example, Ashton et al. (2018) emphasized the value of qualitative research on women's pornography use including revealing differences between how the respondents saw themselves as different from the female pornography actors and the differences in how they perceived the effects of pornography on their intimate relationships. The respondents also experienced tensions between their own arousal to pornography and their values. *Quantitative descriptions* of sexuality are numerical representations of sexual phenomena. Quantitative descriptive data analysis may involve computing the following: mean (average), frequency, mode (the most frequently occurring observation in the data), and median (the middle data point).

2.7b Correlation

Researchers are often interested in the relationships among variables. **Correlation** refers to a relationship among two or more variables. Correlational research may answer such questions as "What factors (such as alcohol/drug use) are associated with contracting a sexually transmitted infection?" Figure 2-2 shows three types of correlations described here.

If a correlation or relationship exists between two variables, a change in one variable is associated with a change in the other. A **positive correlation** exists when both variables change in the same direction. For example, in general, the greater the number of sexual partners a person has, the greater the chance of contracting a sexually transmitted infection. As variable *A* (number of sexual partners) increases, variable *B* (chances of contracting an STI) also increases, revealing a positive correlation between

Case study
Research method that involves conducting an in-depth, detailed analysis of an individual, group, relationship, or event

Descriptive research
Qualitative or quantitative research that describes sexual processes, behaviors, and attitudes, as well as the people who experience them

Correlation
Statistical index that represents the degree of relationship between two variables

Positive correlation
Relationship between two variables that exists when both variables change in the same direction

the number of sexual partners and the chance of contracting an STI. Similarly, as the number of sexual partners decreases, the chance of contracting an STI decreases. Notice that in both cases, the variables change in the same direction.

A **negative correlation** exists when two variables change in opposite directions. For example, there is a negative correlation between condom use and the chance of contracting an STI. This means that as condom use increases, the chance of contracting an STI decreases.

Students often make the mistake of thinking that if two variables decrease, the correlation is negative. To avoid making this error, remember that in a positive correlation, it does not matter whether the variables increase or decrease, as long as they change in the same direction.

Sometimes the relationship between variables is curvilinear. A **curvilinear correlation** exists when two variables vary in both the same and opposite directions. For example, suppose that if you have one alcoholic beverage, your desire for sex increases. With two drinks, your sexual desire increases more, and three drinks raise your interest even higher. So far, there is a positive correlation between alcohol consumption (variable *A*) and sexual desire (variable *B*): As one variable increases, the other also increases. Now suppose that after four drinks, you start feeling sleepy, dizzy, or nauseated, and your interest in sex decreases. After five drinks, you are either vomiting or semiconscious, and sex is of no interest to you. There is now a negative correlation between alcohol consumption and sexual desire: As alcohol consumption increases, sexual interest decreases.

A fourth type of correlation, a **spurious correlation**, is present when two variables appear to be related, but only because they are both related to a third variable. When the third variable is controlled through a statistical method in which a variable is held constant, the apparent relationship between the dependent and independent variables disappear. For example, suppose a researcher finds that the more devout you are, the more likely you are to contract a sexually transmitted infection. How can that be? Is there something about religious fervor that, in and of itself, leads to STIs? The explanation is that devout unmarried individuals are less likely to plan sex; and therefore, when they do have intercourse, they often are not prepared with contraception, such as a condom, or would feel guilty about using one. Therefore, the correlation between devoutness and STIs is spurious. These variables appear to be related only because they are both related to a third variable (in this case, condom use).

Negative correlation
Relationship between two variables that change in opposite directions

Curvilinear correlation
Relationship that exists when two variables vary in both the same and opposite directions

Spurious correlation
Pattern that exists when two variables appear to be related but only because they are both related to a third variable

FIGURE **2-2** ‖ Graphs Depicting Positive, Negative, and Curvilinear Relationships

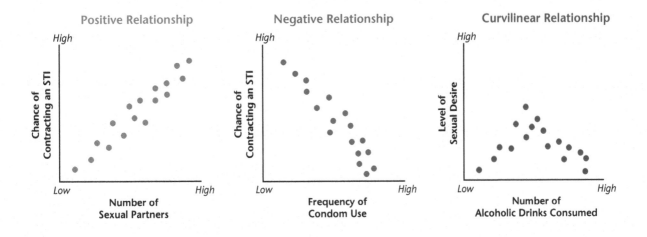

2.7c Causation

If data analysis reveals that two variables are correlated, we know only that a change in one variable is associated with a change in the other. We cannot assume, however, that a change in one variable *causes* a change in the other unless our data collection and analysis are specifically designed to assess causation. The research method that best allows us to assess causal relationships is the experimental method.

To demonstrate causality, three conditions must be met. First, the research must demonstrate that variable *A* is correlated with variable *B*. In other words, a change in variable *A* must be associated with a change in variable *B*. Second, the researcher must demonstrate that the presumed cause (variable *A*) occurs or changes prior to the presumed effect (variable *B*). The cause must precede the effect.

For example, suppose a researcher finds that a negative correlation exists between marital conflict and frequency of marital intercourse: As marital conflict increases, frequency of marital intercourse decreases. To demonstrate that marital conflict causes the frequency of marital intercourse to decrease, the researcher must show that the marital conflict preceded the decrease in marital intercourse. Otherwise, they cannot be sure whether marital conflict causes a decrease in marital intercourse or a decrease in marital intercourse causes marital conflict.

Third, the researcher must demonstrate that the observed correlation is not spurious. A *nonspurious correlation* is a relationship between two variables that cannot be explained by a third variable. This kind of correlation suggests that an inherent causal link exists between the two variables. As we discussed earlier, the correlation between devoutness and sexually transmitted infections is spurious because a third variable—condom use—explains the correlation. Another example of a spurious correlation is the relationship between sexual assault history and current marital status. Suppose a study finds that people with sexual assault history are less likely to be married. While it may seem reasonable to speculate that the previous assault history caused anxiety about being intimate in a marriage relationship, an alternative possibility cannot be ruled out that a third variable—low assertiveness skills, for example—may increase both sexual assault risk and less attractiveness as a potential marriage partner.

2.7d Expanding Statistical Frontiers

Sakaluk (2019) emphasized that recently developed open-source software provides new statistical opportunities, including taxometric analysis, tests of measurement variability, differential item functioning, and equivalence testing. Some researches, unfamiliar with these techniques, may be reluctant to use them.

2.8 Interpretation and Discussion

Following analysis of the data, the researcher evaluates and interprets the results using various theories. Muise et al. (2018) suggested that the theories used by researchers to explain relationships could also be used to explain sexuality. These include attachment theory (relationship satisfaction can be enhanced by close emotional attachments), implicit theory (beliefs about relationships, such as they are products of work rather than destiny and can be extended to fulfilling relationships), exchange theory (the ratio of positive and negatives in a couple's relationship impact their sexual relationship) and interdependence theory. The latter refers to partners being differentially invested in each other with each seeking ways to increase their mutuality. Such a sexual dilemma may be resolved by meeting the partner's sexual needs to increase the sexual satisfaction of the relationship, which may increase relationship satisfaction. The ebb and flow of these commitment patterns and how they result in sexual decisions and outcomes in a relationship is instructive.

Following theoretical interpretation of the data, the researcher will draw implications and possible applications. Limitations of the data are also identified. Most often these involve a small, nonrandom sample or a sample that is specific to one group (such as college students), where analysis of the data is not generalizable, revealing very little about other groups (e.g. other older adults). Finally, the researcher often suggests new ideas, topics, or variables to be explored and examined in future research. Figure 2-3 provides an overview of the research process.

FIGURE **2-3** ‖ Steps Involved in Conducting a Research Project

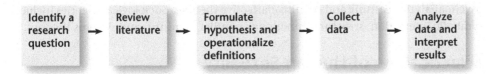

Chapter Summary

Research and Theory

RESEARCH AND THEORY provide ways of discovering and explaining new information about human sexuality. They are the bedrock of sexology as a discipline.

Nature of Sex Research

SCIENTIFIC RESEARCH involves methods of collecting and analyzing empirical evidence or data that can be observed. Scientific knowledge is different from common sense, intuition, tradition, and authority in that it is supported by observable evidence. Theory and empirical data are linked through two forms of reasoning: deductive and inductive.

Interdisciplinary Nature of Sex Research

SEXOLOGY, THE SCIENTIFIC STUDY OF SEXUALITY, is an interdisciplinary field that incorporates various other fields. Sexology can be divided into three broad approaches: biosexology, psychosexology, and sociosexology.

Theories of Sexuality

BIOLOGICAL, PSYCHOLOGICAL, AND SOCIOLOGICAL THEORIES each contribute unique insights to our understanding of various aspects of sexuality. Biological theories include physiological and evolutionary theories. Psychological theories include psychoanalytic, learning and cognitive/affective theories. Sociological theories include symbolic interaction, structural-functional, conflict, feminist, and systems theories.

Eclectic View of Human Sexuality

MANY ASPECTS OF HUMAN SEXUALITY ARE BEST EXPLAINED by using an eclectic theoretical approach that considers biological, psychological, and sociological explanations.

Conducting Sex Research: A Step-by-Step Process

UNLIKE CASUAL OBSERVATIONS of sexuality, scientific sex research is conducted according to a systematic process. After identifying a research question, the researcher reviews the literature on the subject, formulates hypotheses, operationalizes research variables, collects data, and analyzes and interprets the results. Researchers are obliged to follow ethical research protocol, which includes informed consent.

Methods of Data Collection

EXPERIMENTAL RESEARCH, SURVEY RESEARCH, FIELD RESEARCH, DIRECT LABORATORY OBSERVATION, AND CASE STUDIES each have advantages and disadvantages. For example, the major strength of the experimental method is that it provides information on causal relationships, showing how one variable affects another. This method's primary weakness is that experiments are often conducted on small samples in artificial laboratory settings, so the findings may not be generalized to other people in natural settings.

Levels of Data Analysis

LEVELS OF DATA ANALYSIS include descriptive (qualitative or quantitative), correlation (positive, negative, curvilinear, or spurious), and causation. Determining causation is difficult because human experiences are influenced by so many factors, making it difficult to isolate one factor to assess its effects.

Interpretation and Discussion

FINALLY, FOLLOWING DATA ANALYSIS, the researcher evaluates and interprets the results and their implications. This may entail qualifying the results, drawing inferences from them, assessing the theoretical implications, and discussing possible applications.

Web Links

American Association of Sexuality Educators, Counselors and Therapists

    http://www.aasect.org/

International Academy of Sex Research

    www.iasr.org

Journal of Positive Sexuality

    http://journalofpositivesexuality.org

Kinsey Institute

    http://www.indiana.edu/~kinsey/

Kinsey Reporter

    http://www.kinseyreporter.org/

Psychological Research on the Net

    http://psych.hanover.edu/research/exponnet.html

Sexuality Information and Education Council of the United States

    http://www.siecus.org/

Society for the Scientific Study of Sexuality

    http://www.sexscience.org

Widener University: Center for Human Sexuality Studies

    https://www.widener.edu/academics/graduate-studies
        /human-sexuality-studies-med

World Association for Sexual Health

    https://worldsexualhealth.net/

Key Terms

Biosexology **32**

Biosocial framework **33**

Case study **52**

Classical conditioning **34**

Cognitive/affective theory **35**

Conflict theory **39**

Correlation **52**

Critical sexuality studies **30**

Curvilinear correlation **53**

Deductive research **31**

Dependent variable **42**

Descriptive research **52**

Eclectic view **40**

Ego **34**

Empirical evidence **31**

Evolutionary theory **33**

Experimental research **48**

Feminist theory **39**

Field research **50**

Focus group **49**

Hypothesis **42**

Id **34**

Independent variable **42**

Inductive research **31**

Informed consent **46**

Interview survey research **49**

Libido **34**

Natural selection **33**

Negative correlation **53**

Nonparticipant observation **50**

Operant learning theory **35**

Operational definition **44**

Operationalize **44**

Participant observation **50**

Patriarchy **39**

Physiological theory **33**

Positive correlation **52**

Psychoanalytic theory **33**

Psychosexology **32**

Punishment **35**

Reinforcement **35**

Representative sample **48**

Sample **48**

Sexology **32**

Social learning theory **35**

Social scripts **38**

Sociobiological theory **33**

Sociosexology **32**

Spurious correlation **53**

Structural-functional theory **38**

Superego **34**

Survey research **48**

Symbolic interaction theory **38**

Systems theory **40**

Theory **32**

Variable **42**

CHAPTER

3

Female Sexual Anatomy, Physiology, and Response

It's work having a vagina. Guys don't think that it's work but it is. You think it shows up like that to the event? It doesn't. Every night it's like getting it ready for its first quinceanera, believe me.

Amy Schumer, comedian

Chapter Outline

3.1 **Female External Anatomy and Physiology 62**
  3.1a Mons Veneris **62**
  3.1b Labia **63**
  3.1c Clitoris **63**
  Technology and Sexuality 3-1:
    Cosmetic Surgery **64**
  Personal Decisions 3-1
    Shaving Pubic Hair **64**
  3.1d Vaginal Opening **65**
  3.1e Urethral Opening **66**
  3.1f Female Genital Alteration **66**
  3.1g The Female Breasts **69**
  Social Policy 3-1
    Breastfeeding in Public? **69**
  Personal Decisions 3-2
    Breast Self-Examination
    and Mammogram? **71**
3.2 **Female Internal Anatomy and Physiology 72**
  3.2a Vagina **72**
  3.2b The "G-Spot" **73**
  Personal Decisions 3-3
    Pap Test and Pelvic Exam **74**
  3.2c Uterus **74**

  3.2d Fallopian Tubes **74**
  3.2e Ovaries **75**
3.3 **Menstruation 75**
  3.3a Phases of the Menstrual Cycle **76**
  3.3b Attitudes Toward Menstruation **77**
  Self-Assessment 3-1:
    Menstrual Attitude
    Questionnaire **77**
  3.3c Problems of the Menstrual Cycle **79**
3.4 **Models of Sexual Response 81**
  3.4a Masters and Johnson's Four-Stage
    Model of Sexual Response **81**
  3.4b Kaplan's Three-Stage Model of
    Sexual Response **84**
  3.4c Basson's Model of
    Sexual Response **84**
  Personal Decisions 3-4
    Having Sex with a Partner When
    Desire Is Low **84**
3.5 **Hormones and Sexual Response 85**
3.6 **Pheromones, Aphrodisiacs, and Sexual Response 86**

Web Links 89
Key Terms 89

Objectives

1. Identify and label the internal and external female anatomy
2. Understand female physiology
3. Know the social issues surrounding breastfeeding in public, including the various legal changes
4. Be aware of the importance of breast examinations, self and otherwise

5. Review the guidelines about who should have mammograms and how often
6. Describe the phases of the menstrual cycle
7. List the potential problems of the menstrual cycle
8. Discuss three models of sexual response
9. Know how hormones influence sexual response

Truth — OR — Fiction?

T / F   1. Gambian men report a preference for "uncut" rather than "cut" women, whom they describe as less interested in sex.

T / F   2. Nepal criminalizes the practice of menstrual huts, isolating women to sheds outside the home during menstruation.

T / F   3. The primary reason for pretending orgasm for both women and men is that it feels good (caught up in the moment).

T / F   4. A woman's orgasm is associated with the man's enhanced feeling of sexual self-esteem.

T / F   5. Women who have sex with women report having an orgasm more often than women who report having sex with men.

Answers: 1. T   2. T   3. F   4. T   5. T

Female sexuality continues to be a cultural concern. Not only do females struggle with meeting the culturally defined definitions of body type, but navigating the cultural scripts of "appropriate" behavior/coping with the double standard remain a challenge. In this chapter we review the basics of anatomy and physiology. Technically, anatomy is the study of body structure, and physiology is the study of bodily functions. **Sexual anatomy** refers to internal and external genitals, which are also called *sex organs*. **Sexual physiology**

Sexual anatomy
Term referring to internal and external genitals, also called sex organs

Sexual physiology
Vascular, hormonal, and central nervous system processes involved in genital functioning

refers to the vascular, hormonal, and central nervous system processes involved in genital functioning. Sexual sensations involve the whole body—not just the sex organs. Furthermore, what happens above the neck—in the brain—largely influences sexual functioning.

3.1 Female External Anatomy and Physiology

Despite living in a culture that seems sexually obsessed, some women in the United States don't know the correct scientific names for their genitalia. Girls are often not taught names for their external genital parts; instead, they are instilled with shame about them, with vague references to "down there."

The external female genitalia are collectively known as the **vulva**, a Latin term meaning "covering." The female external sex organs include the mons veneris, labia, clitoris, urethral opening, and vaginal opening (see Figure 3-1). Female genitalia differ in size, shape, and color, resulting in considerable variability in appearance (see Figure 3-2)

FIGURE **3-1** ‖ **External Female Genitalia**

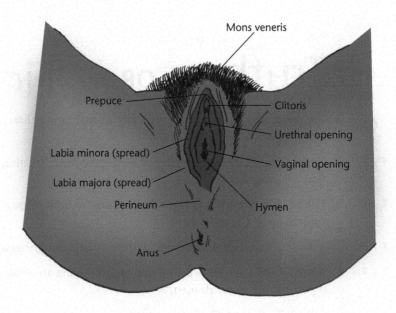

Mons veneris

Prepuce

Clitoris

Urethral opening

Labia minora (spread)

Vaginal opening

Labia majora (spread)

Perineum

Hymen

Anus

3.1a Mons Veneris

The soft cushion of fatty tissue that lies over the *pubic symphysis* (the joint between the left and right pubic bones) is called the **mons veneris** (mahns vuh-NAIR-ihs), which is Latin for mound of Venus, in honor of the Roman goddess of love, sex, fertility, and beauty.

The mons acts as a cushion to protect the pubic region during intercourse. Because this area is filled with many nerve endings, women often find gentle stimulation highly pleasurable. Also known as the *mons pubis*, this area becomes covered with hair during puberty. The evolutionary function of this hair may be to trap and concentrate pelvic odors for attracting a mate, although increasingly, shaving has become a trend for young women in the United States (see *Personal Decisions 3-1*).

Vulva
External female genitalia

Mons veneris
Soft cushion of fatty tissue that lies over the pubic symphysis (joint between the left and right pubic bones)

FIGURE **3-2** ‖ Variations in the Vulva

3.1b Labia

The **labia majora** (LAY-bee-uh mih-JOR-uh), or *major lips,* are two elongated folds of fatty tissue that extend from the mons veneris to the **perineum** (PEHR-ih-NEE-um)—the area of skin between the opening of the vagina and the anus. The outer sides of these labia may be covered with hair, whereas the inner sides are smooth and supplied with oil and sweat glands. Located between the labia majora lie two hairless, flat folds of skin called the **labia minora** (mih-NOR-uh), or *little lips,* that enfold the urethral and vaginal openings. The labia minora join at the top to form the prepuce, or hood, of the clitoris. It is not uncommon for the labia minora to protrude beyond the labia majora, as they vary considerably in size from woman to woman.

The labia minora have numerous nerve endings, making them very sensitive to tactile stimulation. They also have a rich supply of blood vessels. During sexual stimulation, they become engorged with blood, which causes them to swell and change color. With prolonged stimulation, the inner surfaces of the labia minora receive a small amount of mucous secretion from the small **Bartholin** (BAR-toe-lin) **glands**, which are located at the base of the minor lips. This does not significantly contribute to vaginal lubrication, however; the main function of these glands remains unknown.

The labia and the entire vulval area perspire and also secrete a blend of oils, fats, waxes, cholesterol, and discarded cells called *sebum,* which gives the area a slippery feel.

3.1c Clitoris

The most sensitive organ of the female genitalia is the **clitoris** (KLIH-ter-iss)—a sensory organ located at the top of the labia minora (see Figure 3-3) and equipped with 8,000 nerve fibers. The word *clitoris* is derived from the Greek *kleitoris.* The clitoris is extremely sensitive to touch, pressure, and temperature and is unique in that it is an organ whose only known function is to provide sexual sensations and erotic pleasure. In a sexually unaroused woman, the only visible part of the clitoris is the glans—a small external knob of tissue located just below the clitoral hood. The size of the clitoral glans, about 1/4 inch in diameter and 1/4 to 1 inch in length, is not related to the subjective experience of pleasure.

The clitoris is pure in purpose. It is the only organ in the body designed purely for pleasure.

Eve Ensler, *The Vagina Monologues*

Labia majora ("major lips")
Two elongated folds of fatty tissue that extend from the mons veneris to the perineum

Perineum
Area of skin between the opening of the vagina and the anus

Labia minora ("little lips")
Two smaller elongated folds of fatty tissue that enfold the urethral and vaginal openings

Bartholin glands
Glands located at the base of the minor lips of the female genitalia that secrete a small amount of mucus to the inner surfaces of the labia minora

Clitoris
Sensory organ located at the top of the labia minora of the female genitalia

Technology and Sexuality 3-1: Cosmetic Surgery

Dolly Parton is known for saying, "If I see something saggin', baggin', or draggin', I'll get it nipped, tucked, or sucked." From shaving to Brazilian waxes to "vajazzling" (decorating the pubic area with glitter or crystals), women's desire to change the look of their vulva is not new. What is becoming more popular, and is of concern, is the increase in women having plastic surgery on their vulvas and vaginas.

Such surgeries include vaginal "rejuvenation" surgery, or vaginoplasty, designed to reduce and make the labia minora symmetrical, augment the labia majora, and tighten the vagina. These operations, which produce what is sometimes called the "designer vagina," have been critiqued by the American Congress of Obstetricians and Gynecologists (ACOG) for their multiple health risks.

While surgery for reconstructive reasons is understandable, there is alarm when the reason is cosmetic. ACOG notes that the "absence of data supporting the safety and efficacy of these procedures makes the recommendation untenable; … negative health effects of vaginal rejuvenation procedures and products include hemorrhaging, scarring, infection, altered sensation, and dyspareunia" (American College of Obstetricians and Gynecologists, 2007). Nevertheless, many physicians are willing to perform these surgeries. In 2017, there were 10,253, labiaplasty procedures performed in the United States, a decrease from 12,666 the previous year (American Society of Plastic Surgeons, 2018).

Why do women seek labiaplasty? Some have identified pornography as the culprit for women's desire to have a "normal"-looking vulva. In a study of American, British, and Dutch women, 71% wanted a labiaplasty for emotional reasons, including fear of ridicule, fear of partner reaction, and self-loathing (Zwier, 2014). These reasons may be related to the consumption of porn by their partners, as well as by the women themselves, who absorb it as a new norm.

The women who completed the questionnaire were members of online communities on labial surgery. What this study did not examine was the impact that the other women in the community may have had—encouraging these surgeries by implied rejection from their partners if the women did not get them. Pro-anorexia sites (commonly referred to as pro-ana) are further evidence of unhealthy behavior provoked by misogynistic cultural norms.

In addition to the emotional reasons and the possible negative impact of online communities, there is also concern about the role of the physicians who are performing these surgeries and the associated marketing (American College of Obstetricians and Gynecologists, 2007). Women who are searching for answers and options online may be lured into agreeing to genital cosmetic surgery through aggressive marketing rather than careful consideration of the procedure (Liao et al., 2012). U.S. culture also promotes the idea that vaginas are "dirty" and smell bad (as seen in feminine spray or douche advertisements); yet there is no discussion of the adverse health consequences that can result from using these products (Martino et al., 2004). What is needed is information about such procedures and an emphasis on self-acceptance and the natural variation in human bodies—including labias!

PERSONAL DECISIONS 3-1

Shaving Pubic Hair

Increasingly, women are shaving their pubic hair. Based on a survey of 436 undergraduates in the United States, 97% of both women and men reported that they shaved their pubic region, and 51% of the women had removed all of their pubic hair (Caron, 2013). Pubic hair removal was significantly associated with younger age, a greater interest in sex, vaginal fingering, finger-clitoral stimulation, having a casual sex partner, using vaginal hygiene products, and applying cream to the genitals (Herbenick et al., 2013).

Reasons for shaving pubic hair include the rise in skimpy bathing suits, oral sex, porn actors and actresses shaving to increase/enhance the view of their genitals, perception that other women shave, personal preference for the way it looks/feels, preference of partner, and sharing the ritual of shaving with a partner. Burris and Munteanu (2015) found that the less the female pubic hair, the greater the reported arousal by the undergraduate heterosexual male.

Kelly and Hoerl (2015) suggested that both proponents of sexual liberation and abstinence-until-marriage advocates convey to women that the appearance of a prepubescent and pure vagina is essential to sexual appeal: "Waxing and other vaginal cosmetic procedures are marketed as enactments of personal choice, sexual autonomy, and proper self-care." Alternatively, the abstinence movement has rendered chastity "sexy" and "worth the wait." Both camps focus on male sexual pleasure devoid of concerns of the woman.

The clitoris is a far larger organ than most people are aware, and much of its erectile tissue extends inside the body and surrounds the vagina. The shaft of the clitoris, which is hidden from view by the clitoral hood, divides into two much larger structures called *crura* (Kroo-ra), erectile tissue; they are about 3 inches long. It is thought that this may be why some women reach orgasm with intercourse and why rubbing along the sides of the vulva feels pleasurable—it stimulates the crura. The clitoris develops embryologically from the same tissue as the penis but has twice the number of nerve endings. The body of the clitoris consists of spongy tissue that fills with blood during sexual arousal. This results in a doubling or tripling of its original size; it becomes swollen and springy, but not rigid. Stimulation of any part of the female body may result in engorgement or swelling of the clitoris.

Towne (2019) interviewed women in regard to orgasm during sexual intercourse and confirmed that they orgasmed as a function of clitoral stimulation during penetration by themselves or their partner: Variations in specific masturbation techniques included the area(s) of the clitoris stimulated, the involvement of the labia in stimulation, the area of the hand(s) or vibrator used, the type of movement they preferred, and whether or not vaginal penetration was included.

FIGURE 3-3 ‖ Anatomy of the Clitoris

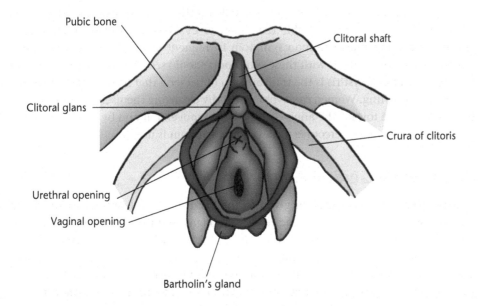

Pubic bone

Clitoral shaft

Clitoral glans

Crura of clitoris

Urethral opening

Vaginal opening

Bartholin's gland

3.1d Vaginal Opening

The area between the labia minora, called the **vestibule**, includes the urethral opening and the vaginal opening, or **introitus** (in-TRO-ih-tus). The vaginal opening, like the anus, is surrounded by a ring of sphincter muscles. The vaginal opening can expand to accommodate the passage of a baby at childbirth.

The vaginal opening is sometimes partially covered by a thin mucous membrane called the **hymen**. Throughout history, and in some countries today, the hymen has been regarded as proof of virginity (Sommers & Abboud, 2014). A newlywed woman in the country of Jordan—as well as many other countries in the Middle East, Africa, and elsewhere—who is found to be without a hymen may be returned to her parents, disgraced by exile, or killed (referred to as **honor killing**, since she has brought dishonor and disgrace to her parents, and they need to reclaim their honor by killing her). It has also been a common practice in many societies to display a bloody bed sheet

Vestibule
Smooth tissue surrounding a woman's urethral opening

Introitus
Vaginal opening

Hymen
Thin mucous membrane that may partially cover the vaginal opening

Honor killing
The killing of an unmarried female who has had sex (which is thought to bring dishonor to her parents) by the parents or another family member in order to restore the family's honor (The practice occurs in Middle Eastern countries such as Jordan.)

after the wedding night as proof of the bride's virginity. In Japan, sexually experienced women sometimes have plastic surgeons reconstruct their hymens before marriage. In Sweden, teenage women suffer under "oppressive demands to preserve their virginity" (Cinthio, 2015), with some resorting to surgery to appear chaste.

The hymen is, however, a poor indicator of virginity. Some women are born without hymens or with incomplete hymens. For other women, the hymen is accidentally ruptured by vigorous physical activity or by the insertion of a tampon. In some women, the hymen stretches during sexual intercourse without tearing. Most doctors cannot determine whether a woman is a virgin by simply examining her vaginal opening.

3.1e Urethral Opening

Above the vaginal opening but below the clitoris is the urethral opening, which allows urine to pass from the body. A short tube called the **urethra** connects the bladder (where urine collects) with the urethral opening. Small glands called *Skene* glands (also called the *paraurethral glands*), which are just inside the urethral opening, drain into the urethra and near the urethral opening. Usually, these glands are not seen or felt; however, when infected, they may become enlarged and tender. It has been speculated that the Skene glands are the source of female ejaculate.

Because of the shorter length of the female urethra and its close proximity to the anus, women are more susceptible than men to **cystitis**, or bladder inflammation and infection. The most common symptom is frequent urination accompanied by a burning sensation. Anyone with these symptoms should see a health-care practitioner. A common cause of cystitis is the transmission of bacteria that live in the intestines to the urethral opening. Women can avoid cystitis by cleansing themselves from "front to back"—the vulva toward the anus—after a bowel movement and by avoiding vaginal intercourse after anal intercourse (unless a new condom is used).

3.1f Female Genital Alteration

Considerable attention has been given to the occurrence and severity of the global human rights crisis and widespread health problems resulting from cutting off parts (or total removal) of a female's external genitalia. **Female genital cutting** (FGC) involves cutting off the clitoris and/or excising (partially or totally) the labia minora. The practice is not confined to a particular religion, but spans at least three faiths practiced in 30 countries across three continents. Worldwide, up to 140 million women have undergone FGC (Nakku, 2019). In the US, half a million females have had or are at risk for this procedure. Among them is Renee Bergstrom who reported that a fundamentalist Christian physician mutilated her genitals to prevent her from masturbating (Baldas, 2017). Federal law criminalizes the performance of FGC on females under 18 in the United States; however, the procedure is not unknown in this country. Dr. Jumana Nagarwala of Detroit was arrested for performing the operation, which was the first female genital mutilation case in the United States. (Baldas, 2017).

In its August 2016 report on FGC, the U.S. Government Accountability Office (GAO) noted that the Centers for Disease Control and Prevention (CDC) estimates that over half a million women and girls in the United States—mainly those from immigrant families—have had or are at risk for the procedure. This represents a threefold increase from its 1990 estimate.

Although federal law and many state laws criminalize FGC and offer federal protection for women and girls who have had the procedure or are at risk in their

Urethra
Short tube that connects the bladder with the urethral opening

Cystitis
Bladder inflammation

Female genital cutting
Cutting or amputating some or all of the female external genitalia: the prepuce (or hood) of the clitoris and shaft of the clitoris, the labia minora, and the labia majora (also called female genital alteration)

home countries, the GAO found that few domestic prosecutions or even investigations have been carried out. It recommends that the U.S. Department of State offer further information to visa recipients and that each federal agency document its work on FGC. The United Kingdom also criminalizes the procedure. However, FGC continues around the world (Onwu, 2019).

Most often, young women in the West are sent back to their country of origin for the procedure. Over 90% of women from Egypt, Eritrea, Ethiopia, Mali, Sierra Leone, and Northern Sudan have "been cut" (Nicoletti, 2007), as well as 98% of the women in Somalia (Simister, 2010) and Djibouti (Youssouf, 2013). The American Academy of Pediatrics condemns all types of female genital cutting (Policy Statement, 2012), citing its life-threatening risks of physical and psychological harm. The Academy counsels its physician members not to perform such procedures and to provide "compassionate education" about the harms of FGC.

The reasons for the practice include the following beliefs:

1. *Sociological/cultural:* Parents believe that FGC makes their daughters lose their desire for sex, which helps them maintain their virginity and enhances their acceptability as a marriage partner, as well as future fidelity to their husbands. FGC is considered a rite of passage that initiates a girl into womanhood and cements her status as subordinate to her husband and in social cohesion with other females.

2. *Hygiene/aesthetics:* Female genitalia are considered dirty and unsightly; thus, their removal promotes hygiene and enhances appearance. In actuality, it often has life-threatening sequelae to the women's health.

3. *Religion:* Some Muslim communities practice FGC in the belief that the Islamic faith demands it. Though it is not mentioned in the Quran, it is implicitly approved in a hadith, and many practitioners and families believe it is a religious requirement. FGC is also practiced in many Christian Coptic and animist communities (von der Osten-Sacken & Uwer, 2007).

4. *Myths:* FGC is thought to enhance fertility and promote child survival (Nicoletti, 2007), whereas it is actually a primary threat to both. Aside from the associated severe pain and infection, many girls die or sustain lifelong injuries and disease, including HIV, menstrual and urinary problems, due to urethral injury, and pain and difficulty in sex. Women with FGC can also have prolonged and difficult labors that increase the chance of obstetric complications and fetal death, as well as fistula (fecal matter leaking into the damaged vaginal canal).

Oyefara (2015) analyzed data from 350 married women. Results revealed that those who had experienced female genital cutting reported defective sexuality (absence of arousal/pleasure) and sexual dysfunctions (pain, no orgasm). Interviews with 30 Somali women living in the United States revealed that 93% had been genitally cut, with half of these reporting negative effects on their relationship and 40% reporting pain during intercourse. Lien (2017) interviewed Gambian men in regard to the sexuality of their women partners who were cut and uncut. Most preferred uncut partners, citing low sexual interest, rare orgasm, lack of responsiveness in cut women. Examples of comments:

There are big differences between cut and uncut women. The cut women don't have feelings so I was not happy with them. Both partner need to have feeling. You are not 100% satisfied with them. The thing that give them feeling is taken away. (Wolof, 34 years)

I have two wives. One is completely flat and levelled. We have sexual problems. She never becomes aroused. It is boring. I am not satisfied and she is not either. She is always dry and never wet. I must use a very long time with her, and I get confused. (Mandinka, 50 years) (Lien, 2017)

The usual treatment for vaginal pain, such as suggesting other options for sexual expression (e.g., oral sex), would not be culturally accepted (Robinson & Connor, 2014).

Changing deeply held cultural beliefs and values concerning this practice cannot be achieved by denigration. Such efforts in Senegal have been less than effective where there has been resistance; in some cases, the practice has been driven underground (Bettina et al., 2013). The practice has also been outlawed in Kenya but continues in the rural communities (Onyulo, 2018). More effective approaches to discouraging the practice acknowledge the following:

1. In many cultures that practice FGC, the female has lower status and less power than the male, and girls are commonly considered a resource that increases the family wealth, with marriage as their primary purpose. With this in mind, many nongovernmental organizations focused on ending FGC employ a multifaceted, culturally appropriate approach similar to the methods of organizations working to end child marriage. This approach comprises education of both women and men on the practice's health risks and the human rights of girl children. It also educates them to serve as anti-FGC mentors in their community. Positive reinforcement, such as payment, community development, and training for alternate income sources, can serve as a strong motivational background to the educational effort. Without accepting the practice morally, progress has been made with a sensitive communication style that avoids judgmental language and focuses on commonalities and positive outcomes.

2. Education is key. An analysis of national samples of FGC in Kenya revealed that the higher the education level of the mother, the lower the incidence of genital cutting in daughters (Simister, 2010). Hence, increasing the educational level of women in the community is a structural way to reduce FGC. McChesney (2015) also noted that community-led programs and the empowerment of women are the most effective techniques.

3. Although older women usually perform the procedure, men are the gatekeepers of the practice of FGC. The men believe that FGC serves their purpose for ensuring virginity, providing the man confidence in his paternity, and ensuring the wife's fidelity in marriage. They believe that with her sexuality thus impaired, she will not seek other partners. Eradication of female genital cutting can be achieved only with both women's and men's participation (Diop & Stewart, 2014).

4. Hughes (2018) emphasized Alternative Rites of Passage (ARP) which allows females entry into womanhood without female genital cutting. These are becoming increasingly popular in Kenya. These attempt to combine the girls' human rights (life, health, education, protection) and cultural rights (manifested in teachings and ritual elements that aim to mimic the cultural traditions of the community). Acceptance is slow but increasing.

I cried till I passed out. I bled profusely. I was thereafter treated with herbs, salt, and water.

Rachael Chepsal, age 14 (from Iten, Kenya, of her illegal circumcision)

3.1g The Female Breasts

The female breasts are designed to provide milk for infants and young children (see *Social Policy 3-1: Breastfeeding in Public?*). They are not considered part of the reproductive system, and their development is viewed as a secondary sex characteristic, like pubic hair. **Secondary sex characteristics** are those that differentiate males and females but are not linked to reproduction. Female breasts begin to develop during puberty in response to increasing levels of estrogen, which has a similar effect if injected into males. Breast augmentation surgery is the most frequently performed cosmetic plastic surgery performed annually—300,378 in 2017 (American Society of Plastic Surgeons, 2018).

> **Secondary sex characteristics**
> Characteristics that differentiate males and females that are not linked to reproduction (facial hair in men, breasts in women)

Social Policy 3-1

Breastfeeding in Public?

Approximately 75% of mothers in the United States begin breastfeeding their infants, but less than 15% are breastfeeding exclusively 6 months later. One reason for this is that, in the United States, "breastfeeding remains a problematic social act, despite its agreed importance for child health" (Leeming et al., 2013, p. 450). Hospitals also aggressively market baby formula (Laura, 2018).

Reaction to breastfeeding in public varies from acceptance to toleration. Although it is not against the law to breastfeed in public in any state, nursing mothers can experience harassment, intimidation, and discrimination for breastfeeding in public. This causes many to feel uncomfortable about the practice. Nursing mothers have been asked to either stop breastfeeding or to leave public places—including restaurants, malls, libraries, parks, bus stations, pools, movie theaters, hotel lobbies, department stores, and even doctors' offices.

Studies show that breast milk has significant benefits for both mother and infant. Children who are fed breast milk have lower rates of death, meningitis, childhood leukemia and other cancers, diabetes, respiratory illnesses, bacterial and viral infections, ear infections, allergies, obesity, and developmental delays. In addition, women who breastfeed have a lower risk for breast and ovarian cancers. They also have lower rates of depression and are more likely to emotionally bond with their infants (Meese, 2013).

Researchers calculated the effects of breastfeeding and low/very low birth-weight rates in Louisiana (Ma et al., 2013) and estimated that if 90% of newborns in Louisiana were exclusively breastfed for the first 6 months of life with only 80% compliance, there would be $186,371,125 in savings and 16 infant deaths prevented. As our society and legal system continue to recognize and encourage breastfeeding, a message is sent to the public at large that breastfeeding is an important issue—one that has an impact on our lives and the futures of our children. In spite of the benefits of breastfeeding, some women do not like to breastfeed—they regard it as a painful ordeal, they may be bored with it, or the baby may not be cooperative. These women resent the social pressure to engage in a behavior they do not enjoy (Símonardóttir, S. & Gíslason, 2018).

There is national and federal support in the United States for babies getting breast milk. The Healthy People 2020 initiative identified the national goal to increase the proportion of mothers who breastfeed their babies in the early postpartum period to 81.9% by the year 2020. Since one of the major reasons mothers stop breastfeeding is to return to work (Bonet et al., 2013), employers are required to provide reasonable break time for an employee, for 1 year after the child's birth, to express breast milk for her nursing child each time such employee has the need to express milk. Mothers are also legally allowed to breastfeed their babies on government property.

Breastfeeding is an international issue. Canada and Norway are among the countries that have relatively high rates of breastfeeding and have favorable structural conditions, as well as strong cultural expectations, surrounding breastfeeding (Andrews & Knaak, 2013).

(Jaylen Rodgers)

Despite the satisfaction to couples and benefits of breastfeeding for the baby, disapproval of breastfeeding in public still exists.

Each adult female breast consists of 15–20 mammary, or milk-producing, glands that are connected to the nipple by separate ducts (see Figure 3-4). The soft consistency and size of the breasts are due to fatty tissues loosely packed between the glands. The amount of fat in the breasts is partly determined by heredity. Breasts vary in size and shape; it is common for a woman to have one breast that is slightly larger than the other. Breast size also varies as overall body size varies.

There is no relation between breast size and shape and their sensitivity or sexual responsiveness. Many women notice changes during their menstrual cycle, with breasts larger and fuller right before menstruation. Some women experience subjective enjoyment in having their breasts stimulated, while others may not experience the sensation as pleasurable.

The nipples are made up of smooth muscle fibers with numerous nerve endings, making them sensitive to touch. The nipples are kept lubricated during breastfeeding by secretions of oil from the **areola** (EH-ree-OH-luh), the darkened area around the nipple. This area becomes permanently darker after pregnancy.

FIGURE 3-4 ‖ Internal and External Anatomy of the Female Breast

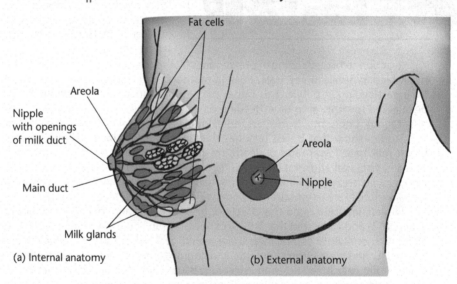

Fat cells

Areola

Nipple with openings of milk duct

Main duct

Milk glands

(a) Internal anatomy

Areola

Nipple

(b) External anatomy

Areola
Darkened ring around the nipple that keeps the nipples lubricated by secretions of oil during breastfeeding

PERSONAL DECISIONS 3-2

Breast Self-Examination and Mammogram?

Breast cancer is the most common cancer in women. The American Cancer Society (2019a) notes that around 268,600 new breast cancer cases and 41,760 deaths occur annually. A woman with breast cancer is much more likely to survive if the cancer is detected and treated early, before it develops to an advanced stage and spreads to other parts of the body.

The figure below shows the quadrants of the breast most likely to develop cancer: upper left, 50%; lower left, 11%; upper right, 15%; and lower right, 6%. Breast cancers in the center of the breast account for 18% of cancer cases.

Some breast tumors are too small to feel during a physical breast examination. A **mammogram** is a low-dose X-ray technique (similar to that for a dental exam) used by a radiologist to detect small tumors inside the breast. A breast biopsy, which involves removing breast tissue for examination under the microscope, is taken if a lump or nodule is found. In October 2015, the American Cancer Society changed its guidelines for mammograms, raising the baseline age from 40 to 45 (Oeffinger et al., 2015), while the Mayo Clinic continued to recommend that all women should have a mammogram yearly starting at age 45 (Pruthi, 2019). Although it has been documented that routine mammography screening can save lives, risks include radiation exposure; the stress, pain, and possible overtreatment of having diagnostic tests to follow up on false positives; or abnormal mammogram results that are not breast cancer or that detect cancers that would not be lethal.

> **Mammogram**
> Low-dose X-ray technique used by radiologists to detect small tumors inside the breast

---

FIGURE **3-5** ‖ **Breast Cancer Quadrants**

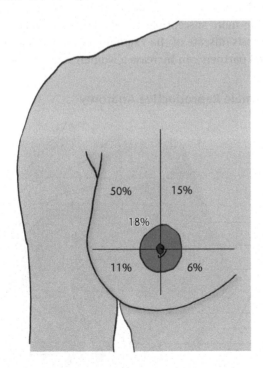

3.2 **Female Internal Anatomy and Physiology**

The internal sex organs of the female include the vagina, uterus, and paired fallopian tubes and ovaries (see Figure 3-6).

3.2a Vagina

The word *vagina* is derived from a Latin word meaning "sheath." The **vagina** is a 3- to 5-inch long muscular tube that extends from the vulva to the cervix of the uterus. The vagina is located behind the bladder and in front of the rectum and points at a 45-degree angle toward the small of the back. The walls of the vagina are normally collapsed; thus, the vagina is really a potential space rather than an actual one. The walls of the vagina have a soft, pliable, mucosal surface similar to that of the mouth. During sexual arousal, the vaginal walls become engorged with blood, and the consequent pressure causes the mucous lining to secrete drops of fluid.

The vagina functions as a pathway for menstrual flow and as the birth canal, as well as an organ for sexual activity. The vagina can expand by as much as 2 inches in length and diameter during intercourse.

Some people erroneously believe that the vagina is a dirty part of the body. In fact, the vagina is a self-cleansing organ. The bacteria that are found naturally in the vagina help destroy other potentially harmful bacteria. In addition, secretions from the vaginal walls help maintain the vagina's normally acidic environment. The use of feminine hygiene sprays, as well as douches, can cause irritation, allergic reactions, and vaginal infection by altering the vagina's natural chemical balance.

If a woman experiences a strong and unpleasant vaginal odor, she may have an infection and should seek medical evaluation. Some women (such as those taking birth control pills) may be more susceptible to imbalances in vaginal flora and are more susceptible to vaginosis (disease of the vagina) and yeast infection. In addition, intercourse with infected partners can increase a woman's susceptibility to various STIs.

FIGURE **3-6** ‖ **Female Reproductive Anatomy**

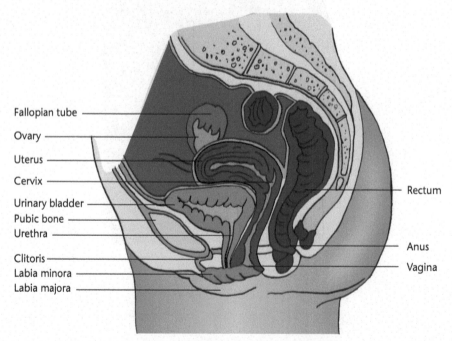

Fallopian tube
Ovary
Uterus
Cervix
Urinary bladder
Pubic bone
Urethra
Clitoris
Labia minora
Labia majora
Rectum
Anus
Vagina

Vagina
Muscular tube 3–5 inches long that extends from the vulva to the cervix of the uterus

The muscles of the pelvic floor, including the **pubococcygeus** (pyoo-boh-kahk-SIH-jee-us, or PC) and the levator ani, surround the lower third of the vagina. These muscles can influence sexual functioning. If they are too tense, vaginal entry may be difficult or impossible. However, some degree of muscle tone is probably desirable. Some sex therapists have advocated performing **Kegel exercises** (named after Dr. Arnold Kegel). They may also be used to improve bladder control and treat vulvar pain. Kegel exercises involve voluntarily contracting the PC muscle, as though stopping the flow of urine after beginning to urinate, several times at several sessions per day. Another way to find the pelvic floor muscles is to insert a finger halfway into the vagina and try to grip the finger with the vagina. Tense the PC muscle up and in, relaxing the muscles of the abdomen and buttocks. Squeeze up and in for 10 seconds and then relax for 10 seconds. Some women practice Kegel exercises while waiting at a red light or during class.

3.2b The "G-Spot"

In 1950, German gynecologist Ernst Gräfenberg reported that he found a highly sensitive area on the anterior wall of the vagina, 1–2 inches into the vaginal canal. This area, named in 1981 as the "Gräfenberg spot," or "**G-spot**," reportedly swells during stimulation, resulting in high arousal and orgasm (see Figure 3-7).

> *For women, the best aphrodisiacs are words. The G-spot is in the ears. He who looks for it below there is wasting his time.*
>
> Isabel Allende, Chilean-American writer

There is disagreement about the existence of the G-spot. Hines (2001) reviewed the literature on the G-spot and concluded the following: "The evidence is far too weak to support the reality of the G-spot. Specifically, anecdotal observations and case studies made on the basis of a tiny number of subjects are not supported by subsequent anatomic and biochemical studies" (p. 359). Hines characterized the G-spot as "a sort of gynecologic UFO: much sought for, much discussed, but unverified by objective means" (p. 361).

Some women report that they experience an orgasm not by clitoral or G-spot stimulation but via exercise. Referred to as exercise-induced orgasm (EIO) or exercise-induced sexual pleasure (EISP), various exercises, such as weight lifting (26.5%), yoga (20%), bicycling (15.8%), running (13.2%), and walking/hiking (9.6%), triggered an orgasm (Herbenick, 2012).

FIGURE **3-7** ‖ **Location of the Alleged Gräfenberg Spot**

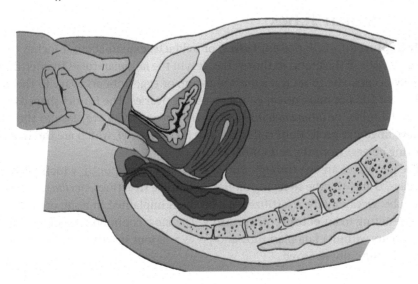

Pubococcygeus
Muscle surrounding the opening to the vagina that can influence sexual functioning; if it is too tense, vaginal entry may be difficult or impossible

Kegel exercise
Voluntary contraction of the PC muscle, as though stopping the flow of urine after beginning to urinate, that may be performed several times at several sessions per day

G-spot
Alleged highly sensitive area on the front wall of the vagina, 1–2 inches into the vaginal canal (also called the Gräfenberg spot)

PERSONAL DECISIONS 3-3

Pap Test and Pelvic Exam

A **Pap test** is valuable in the detection of cervical cancer. The test, named after Dr. Georgios Papanikolaou, who originated the technique, involves swabbing a small sample of cells from the cervix. Women who smoke, have first intercourse at an early age, have specific strains of human papillomavirus (HPV—the virus that causes genital warts), have multiple sex partners, or have partners who have had multiple sex partners are at increased risk for cervical cancer. Cervical cancer is almost 100% curable when detected and treated early.

In 2015, updated screening guidelines for cervical cancer were released by the American Cancer Society. These guidelines recommend that women have their first Pap test at age 21. Women ages 21–29 should be screened with a Pap test every 3 years. Women ages 30–65 can then be screened every 5 years with Pap and HPV co-testing or every 3 years with a Pap test alone.

> **Pap test**
> Procedure in which surface cells are scraped from the vaginal walls and cervix, transferred to a slide, and examined under a microscope to detect the presence of cancer cells

3.2c Uterus

The **uterus** (YOO-ter-us), or *womb*, resembles a small, inverted pear. In women who have not given birth, it measures about 3 inches long and 3 inches wide at the top. It is in the uterus that a fertilized ovum implants and develops into a fetus. No other organ is capable of expanding as much as the uterus does during pregnancy. Held in the pelvic cavity by ligaments, the uterus is generally perpendicular to the vagina. However, 1 in every 10 women has a uterus that tilts backward. Although this poses no serious problems, it may cause discomfort with some positions during intercourse.

The broad, rounded part of the uterus is the **fundus**, and the narrower portion, which projects into the vagina, is the **cervix**. The cervix feels like a small, slippery bump (like the tip of the nose) at the top of the vagina. The **os**, or opening of the cervix (through which semen and menstrual flow both pass), is normally the diameter of a pencil; however, in childbirth it dilates to about 4 inches and stretches further to allow the passage of the baby. Secretory glands located in the cervical canal produce mucus that differs in consistency at different stages of the menstrual cycle.

3.2d Fallopian Tubes

The **fallopian** (fuh-LOE-pee-en) **tubes**, or oviducts, extend about 4 inches laterally from either side of the uterus to the ovaries. It is in the fallopian tubes that fertilization normally occurs. The tubes transport the ovum, or egg, from an ovary to the uterus, but the tubes do not make direct contact with the ovaries. The funnel-shaped ovarian ends of the tubes, or *infundibulums* (IN-fun-DIH-byoo-lumz), are close to the ovaries and have fingerlike projections called *fimbriae* (FIM-bree-ay), which are thought to aid in picking up eggs from the abdominal cavity.

The passage of an egg through one of the tubes each month, which takes about three days, is aided by the sweeping motion of hairlike structures, or *cilia*, on the inside of the tube. Occasionally, a fertilized egg becomes implanted in a site other than the uterus, resulting in an **ectopic pregnancy**. The most common type of ectopic pregnancy occurs within a fallopian tube and poses a serious health threat to the woman unless it is surgically removed.

Uterus
Also called the womb, the hollow, muscular organ in which a fertilized egg may implant and develop

Fundus
Broad, rounded part of the uterus

Cervix
Narrower portion of the uterus that projects into the vagina

Os
Opening of the cervix (opening to the uterus)

Fallopian tubes
Oviducts, or tubes, that extend about 4 inches laterally from either side of the uterus to the ovaries; they transport the ovum from an ovary to the uterus

Ectopic pregnancy
Condition in which a fertilized egg becomes implanted in a site other than the uterus

Tying off the fallopian tubes so that egg and sperm cannot meet is a common type of female sterilization. The tubes can also be blocked by inflammation, and serious infections can result in permanent scarring and even sterility.

3.2e Ovaries

The **ovaries** (OH-ver-reez), which are attached by ligaments on both sides of the uterus, are the female gonads. These two almond-shaped structures have two functions: producing ova and producing the female hormones—estrogen and progesterone. At birth, the ovaries combined have about 2 million immature ova, each contained within a thin capsule to form a *follicle*. Some of the follicles begin to mature at puberty, but only about 400–500 mature ova will be released in a woman's lifetime.

An ovarian cyst is a fluid-filled sac in the ovary. Many cysts are normal and are referred to as *functional cysts*, in that they occur as a result of ovulation. Functional cysts usually shrink within 1–3 months, though checkups are essential to ensure that the cysts are shrinking. In some cases, birth control pills are recommended because cysts do not form unless the woman ovulates.

"I was beginning to think that Simon just had a bad case of OCD, ADD, and PMS. With a little BS and OMG mixed in."

Dannika Dark, Gravity

While ovarian cancer is rare (3% of cancer among women), it is the cause of more deaths than any other cancer in the female reproductive systems. Typically there are no symptoms, so any irregularity, such as pelvic or abdominal pain, that is beyond what the woman normally experiences should be investigated by her health-care provider.

3.3 Menstruation

When girls reach about age 12, a part of the brain called the *hypothalamus* signals the pituitary gland at the base of the brain to begin releasing **follicle-stimulating hormone** (FSH) into the bloodstream. This hormone stimulates a follicle to develop and release a mature egg from the ovary. If the egg is fertilized, it will implant itself in the endometrium of the uterus, which has become thick and engorged with blood vessels in preparation for implantation. If the egg is not fertilized, the thickened tissue of the uterus is sloughed off. This flow of blood, mucus, and dead tissue (about 2–3 ounces worth) is called **menstruation**, or **menses**, from the Latin *mensis* (or month). The time of first menstruation is called **menarche**. Except during pregnancy, this process will repeat at monthly intervals until menopause. The average menstrual cycle is 28 days, but this varies from cycle to cycle and woman to woman. Some cycles range anywhere from 22 to 35 days. "Menstrual equality" legislation has been debated in congress to allow payment from health flexible spending accounts for menstrual products regarded as important as soap to hygiene.

Nearly 50 years ago, researcher Martha McClintock (1971) found evidence for what she termed **menstrual synchrony** among the 135 undergraduates in her dorm at Wellesley College. Roommates and close friends had an increased likelihood of their menstrual cycles occurring at relatively the same time. However, subsequent research has failed to consistently confirm that close cohabitation draws menstrual cycles closer together.

Ovaries
Female gonads, attached by ligaments on both sides of the uterus, that have the following two functions: producing ova and producing the female hormones—estrogen and progesterone

Follicle-stimulating hormone
Hormone responsible for the release of an egg from the ovary

Menstruation or menses
Sloughing off of blood, mucus, and lining of the uterus

Menarche
First menstruation

Menstrual synchrony
Increased tendency for women living in close proximity to have their menstrual cycles occur at relatively the same time

(Vicki Oliver)

Adolescent females are beginning their periods and developing into young women earlier than in previous years.

3.3a Phases of the Menstrual Cycle

The menstrual cycle can be divided into four phases: preovulatory (follicular), ovulatory, postovulatory (luteal), and menstrual. In the preovulatory phase, a signal is sent from the hypothalamus for the release of FSH from the pituitary gland, stimulating the growth of about 20 follicles in one ovary. In about 10 days, one follicle continues to grow and secretes increasing amounts of estrogen. This causes growth of the endometrium in the uterus, along with an increase in the cervical mucus, providing a hospitable environment for sperm. Estrogen also signals the pituitary gland to stop any further release of FSH and to begin secreting *luteinizing hormone* (LH). When the levels of estrogen reach a critical point, there is a surge in blood levels of LH, followed by ovulation within 36 hours. During ovulation, the follicle moves to the periphery of the ovary and expels the ovum into the abdominal cavity. Ovulation occurs about 14 days before the start of menstruation, regardless of cycle length.

In the postovulatory phase, the empty follicular sac (now called the *corpus luteum*, from the Latin, meaning "yellow body") secretes hormones causing the endometrium to thicken further, building up nutrients. The breasts are also stimulated and may swell or become tender.

If the egg is fertilized and implants in the uterine wall, the lining of the uterus is maintained during pregnancy by continuous secretions of hormones from the ovary. If fertilization does not occur, the corpus luteum disintegrates 10 days after ovulation, the levels of the hormones maintaining the endometrium decrease, and menstruation begins. The day menstruation begins is counted as Day 1 of the menstrual cycle.

During menstruation, which lasts 2–8 days, the endometrial matter is shed. The "fertile window" is about 6 days long, principally spanning the day of ovulation and the previous 5 days (Harris & Vitzthum, 2013).

Menstrual suppression, or the use of hormones or drugs to suppress menstruation, is an option for women. Contraceptives such as Seasonale® reduce period frequency to once every 4 months. A woman may also choose to not take the placebo pills in a pack of oral contraceptives, in which case she would not get her period at all.

A nonpharmaceutical procedure, **menstrual extraction** is a manual suction technique using the Del-Em, a simple device invented in the early 1970s by Lorraine Rothman and Carol Downer of the Feminist Women's Health Centers of California (Women's Health Specialists of California, n.d.) to help women gain and maintain control over their menstrual cycles and reproductive choices. It can be used as a method of very early termination of pregnancy, expediting menstrual onset, and removing menstrual blood for convenience or to avoid period pain (Chalker & Downer, 1998).

Women who experience menstrual symptoms as painful or bothersome may be pleased not to menstruate, but women who consider their monthly cycle a sign of health may not want to have fewer periods or intervene to stop them altogether. Women should discuss their options for menstrual suppression with their health-care provider.

Menstrual suppression
Use of hormones or drugs to inhibit menstruation

Menstrual extraction
Self-help manual suction technique to control the menstrual cycle or provide very early termination of pregnancy

Cultural Diversity

An ancient tradition in Nepal of menstrual or period huts required the woman who was menstruating or who had just given birth to live in an animal shed outside their homes since they were considered impure. For a couple of days to a month, the woman was barred from entering their home and could not touch men, cattle, or some foods. In 2017, Nepal criminalized the practice and required anyone enforcing the tradition to face a three-month jail sentence and a fine.

3.3b Attitudes Toward Menstruation

People can explore their own attitudes about menstruation by completing the Menstrual Attitude Questionnaire in *Self-Assessment 3-1.*

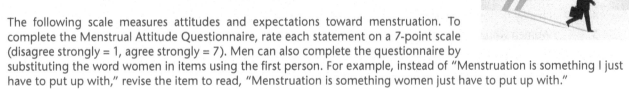

Self-Assessment 3-1:
Menstrual Attitude Questionnaire

The following scale measures attitudes and expectations toward menstruation. To complete the Menstrual Attitude Questionnaire, rate each statement on a 7-point scale (disagree strongly = 1, agree strongly = 7). Men can also complete the questionnaire by substituting the word women in items using the first person. For example, instead of "Menstruation is something I just have to put up with," revise the item to read, "Menstruation is something women just have to put up with."

Subscale 1

1. __ A woman's performance in sports is not affected negatively by menstruation.*
2. __ Women are more tired than usual when they are menstruating.
3. __ I expect extra consideration from my friends when I am menstruating.
4. __ The physiological effects of menstruation are normally no greater than other usual fluctuations in physical state.*
5. __ Menstruation can adversely affect my performance in sports.
6. __ I feel as fit during menstruation as I do any other time of the month.*
7. __ I don't allow the fact that I'm menstruating to interfere with my usual activities.*
8. __ Avoiding certain activities during menstruation is often very wise.
9. __ I am more easily upset during my premenstrual or menstrual periods than at other times of the month.
10. __ I don't believe my menstrual period affects how well I do on intellectual tasks.*
11. __ I realize that I cannot expect as much of myself during menstruation, compared to the rest of the month.
12. — Women just have to accept the fact that they may not perform as well when they are menstruating.

Subscale 2

1. __ Menstruation is something I just have to put up with.
2. __ In some ways, I enjoy my menstrual periods.*
3. __ Men have a real advantage in not having the monthly interruption of a menstrual period.
4. __ I hope it will be possible someday to get a menstrual period over within a few minutes.
5. __ The only thing menstruation is good for is to let me know I'm not pregnant.
6. — Menstruation provides a way for me to keep in touch with my body.*

Subscale 3

1. — Menstruation is a recurring affirmation of womanhood.
2. — Menstruation allows women to be more aware of their bodies.
3. — Menstruation provides a way for me to keep in touch with my body.
4. — Menstruation is an obvious example of the rhythmicity that pervades all of life.
5. — The recurrent monthly flow of menstruation is an external indication of a woman's general good health.

Subscale 4

1. — I can tell my period is approaching because of breast tenderness, backache, cramps, or other physical signs.
2. __ I have learned to anticipate my menstrual period by the mood changes that precede it.
3. __ My own moods are not influenced in any major way by the phase of my menstrual cycle.*
4. __ I am more easily upset during my premenstrual or menstrual periods than at other times of the month.
5. — Most women show a weight gain just before or during menstruation.

Subscale 5

1. — Others should not be critical of a woman who is easily upset before or during her menstrual period.*
2. — Cramps are bothersome only if one pays attention to them.
3. — A woman who attributes her irritability to her approaching menstrual period is neurotic.
4. — I barely notice the minor physiological effects of my menstrual periods.
5. — Women who complain of menstrual distress are just using that as an excuse.
6. — Premenstrual tension/irritability is all in a woman's head.
7. — Most women make too much of the minor physiological effects of menstruation.

Scoring

A mean is computed for each subscale by dividing the sum of items by the number of items in each factor (reversing the scoring of items where necessary). An * indicates items for reverse scoring (a rating of 1 is changed to 7, 2 is changed to 6, 3 is changed to 5).

Interpretation

A higher score indicates stronger endorsement of the concept measured by each subscale. The following is a summary of data obtained from four different samples. You may want to compare your scores with these groups.

Source: Brooks-Gunn, J., & Ruble, D. N. (1980). The menstrual attitude questionnaire. *Psychosomatic Medicine, 42*(5), 503–512. Reprinted with permission of the author.

TABLE 3-1	Summary Statistics for the Menstrual Attitude Questionnaire							
		College Women (Sample 1)		College Women (Sample 2)		College Men		Adolescent Girls
Factor Scores		**(N = 191)**		**(N = 154)**		**(N = 82)**		**(N = 72)**
		mean	SD	mean	SD	mean	SD	mean	SD
1. Menstruating as a debilitating event		3.39	1.09	3.61	0.98	4.45	0.73	3.75	1.28
2. Menstruation as a bothersome event		4.18	1.26	4.65	1.09	4.13	0.93	3.99	1.54
3. Menstruation as a natural event		4.64	1.09	4.51	1.04	4.55	0.93	4.62	0.84
4. Anticipation and prediction of the onset of menstruation		3.79	1.16	4.98	1.11	5.04	0.74	3.85	1.34
5. Denial of any effect of menstruation		2.73	0.96	3.17	1.05	2.83	0.79	3.12	1.08

Data source: Brooks-Gunn, J., & Ruble, D. N. (1980). The menstrual attitude questionnaire. *Psychosomatic Medicine*, 42(5), pp. 503–512.

3.3c Problems of the Menstrual Cycle

Various problems have been associated with the menstrual cycle. Although most adolescent girls have regular monthly periods, irregularity or **oligomenorrhea** is not unusual. The interval between periods may be highly variable. A missed period may or may not indicate pregnancy. Issues such as anxiety, overwork, relationship problems with a partner, or fear of being pregnant can cause a woman to miss her period, as can intense training for competitive athletics. Some women have periods only once a year. If the menstrual cycle has not stabilized by age 17, a gynecologist should be consulted. Spotting or bleeding between periods also indicates the need for a checkup.

Amenorrhea is the absence of menstruation for 3 or more months when a woman is not pregnant, menopausal, or breastfeeding. Pituitary or ovarian tumors or metabolic diseases are possible causes of amenorrhea; hence, a physician should be consulted. Excessive or prolonged menstruation, or **menorrhagia**, may suggest other problems, such as possible uterine infection and tumors.

Some women experience painful menstruation, or **dysmenorrhea**, symptoms of which can include spasmodic pelvic cramping and bloating, headaches, and backaches. In addition, they may feel tense, irritable, nauseated, and depressed. As the result of the hormone changes, some women retain excess body fluids and experience painful swelling of the breasts during menstruation.

Painful menstruation can also be caused by endometrial tissue growing outside the uterus (in the fallopian tubes or abdominal cavity, for example). This condition is known as **endometriosis**. These tissues deteriorate during menstruation, just as the lining of the uterus normally does, and a painful infection can result when the tissue cannot be expelled. Treatment includes herbal remedies, aspirin and other nonsteroidal anti-inflammatory drugs (NSAIDS), hormonal pharmaceuticals, and surgery.

Finally, some women experience **premenstrual syndrome** (PMS)—physical and psychological symptoms caused by hormonal changes from the time of ovulation to the beginning of, and sometimes during, menstruation. To assess the degree to which university females reported various symptoms before and during menstruation, Guler and colleagues (2013) asked a series of open-ended questions to 202 participants enrolled in the study (the mean age was 20.5 years). Among the respondents, the five most common complaints reported were irritability (76.7%), breast fullness (68.6%), back pain (67.4%), abdominal distension (60.5%), and sentimentalism (56.4%). Almost

Oligomenorrhea
Irregular monthly periods

Amenorrhea
Absence of menstruation for 3 or more months during which a woman is not pregnant, is menopausal, or is breastfeeding

Menorrhagia
Excessive or prolonged menstruation

Dysmenorrhea
Painful menstruation

Endometriosis
Growth of endometrial tissue outside the uterus (in the fallopian tubes or abdominal cavity) that may cause pain

Premenstrual syndrome
Physical and psychological symptoms caused by hormonal changes from the time of ovulation to the beginning of, and sometimes during, menstruation

1 in 5 (19.4%) reported having impaired sexuality (predicted by headache and sentimentalism). Over three-fourths (77.3%) reported that they have been using some medication (e.g., analgesics), but most (57.6%) had never sought help. The authors concluded, "A majority of women experience mild to severe physical and psychological discomfort during the premenstrual period, which may affect their life quality" (p. 93). Doyle and colleagues (2015) studied the medical records of 500 regularly cycling women and found both medical and psychological (e.g., depression and pain) associations with PMS.

Debate still remains about PMS. Harris and Vitzthum (2013) reviewed the studies on PMS and behavior and concluded the following:

> In sum, of those studies in which investigators measured hormone concentrations throughout the course of the ovarian cycle in samples of women with and/or without cycle-attributed symptoms, all failed to find unequivocal evidence of any relationship between baseline and/or fluctuations in hormone levels and changes in mood or physical indicators. (Harris & Vitzthum, 2013, p. 234)

It is also instructive to note that PMS primarily exists in heterosexual contexts where hetero-patriarchal constructions of both femininity and premenstrual issues may occur and women are pathologized premenstrually (Ussher & Perz, 2013).

In lesbian relationships, the context allows women to engage in coping strategies premenstrually, such as taking time out to be alone or to engage in self-care with understanding. Hence, premenstrual change can be "contextualized within broader cultural representations of hetero-normativity, which provide the context for gendered roles and coping" (Ussher & Perz, 2013, p. 132).

Premenstrual dysphoric disorder (PMDD) is a proposed diagnostic category indicating a more severe form of PMS that interferes with work, social activities, and relationships. The essential features of PMDD are symptoms such as markedly depressed mood and mood swings, marked irritability/anger, marked anxiety, and decreased interest in activities. Other symptoms include difficulty concentrating, lethargy, and a sense of being out of control. For diagnosis, the duration of the symptoms must have occurred most months for the previous 12 months (American Psychiatric Association, 2013, p. 172). The difference between premenstrual syndrome and premenstrual dysphoric disorder is that a minimum of five symptoms is not required for the former. Pilver and colleagues (2013) analyzed data of 3,965 American women ages 18–40 who were part of the Collaborative Psychiatric Epidemiology Survey to assess the relationship between PMDD and suicide ideation. The researchers did find such an association.

Premenstrual dysphoric disorder
A proposed diagnostic category indicating a more severe form of PMS that interferes with work, social activities, and the relationships of a woman

National DATA

Between 2% and 6% of menstruating women reported the prevalence of premenstrual dysphoric disorder in the past 12 months (American Psychiatric Association, 2013, p. 173).

3.4 **Models of Sexual Response**

Genital sexual response in women has been measured by assessing vascular changes (increased blood volume) in the blood vessels of the vagina and temperature changes in the labia. The device most frequently used to assess vascular changes is the photometer, made of clear plastic and shaped like a tampon. Temperature of the labia is monitored with surface temperature probes that also measure the temperature of comparison sites, such as skin on the chest. MRI (magnetic resonance imaging) has also been used to assess changes in clitoral volume and as a way to quantitatively assess the sexual arousal response in women.

3.4a Masters and Johnson's Four-Stage Model of Sexual Response

Masters and Johnson proposed a four-stage model describing sexual response, or the sequence of sexual events (Masters & Johnson, 1966). Their model focused on four stages of genital response: excitement, plateau, orgasm, and resolution. In this chapter we focus on the female sexual response and, in Chapter 4, on the male sexual response.

Excitement Phase

During the **excitement phase**, individuals become sexually aroused in response to hormonal, tactile, auditory, visual, olfactory, cognitive, and relationship stimuli. For both women and men, the excitement phase of sexual response is characterized by peripheral arousal (increases in heart rate, blood pressure, respiration, and overall muscle tension) and genital arousal (**vasocongestion**, or increased blood flow to the genital region). In women, vasocongestion results in vaginal lubrication and engorgement of external genitals (labia majora, labia minora, and clitoris). During sexual excitement, the labia turn a darker color, and the upper two-thirds of the vagina expands in width and depth.

Physiological signs of sexual excitement are not always linked to feeling sexually aroused. Women can become lubricated without feeling aroused—for example, they can become lubricated as a response to nervousness, excitement, or fear. The source of the vaginal lubrication in women is the moisture from the small blood vessels that lie in the vaginal walls. This moisture is forced through the walls as the vaginal tissues engorge and produce a "sweating" of the vaginal barrel. Individual droplets merge to form a glistening coating of the vagina.

Plateau Phase

After reaching a high level of sexual arousal, women enter the **plateau phase** of the sexual response cycle. The lower third of the vagina constricts and the upper two-thirds expands, presumably to form a pool to catch the semen. At the same time, the clitoris withdraws behind the clitoral hood, providing insulation for the extremely sensitive glans of the clitoris. Direct clitoral stimulation at this time may be painful or unpleasant because the glans has a tremendous number of nerve endings concentrated in a small area. Even though the clitoris is under the hood, it continues to respond to stimulation of the area surrounding it.

Other changes occur as well: **myotonia** (muscle contractions), **hyperventilation** (heavy breathing), **tachycardia** (heart rate increase), and blood pressure elevation. Some women also experience a "sex flush" that looks like a measles rash on parts of the chest, neck, face, and forehead. This flush sometimes suggests a high level of sexual excitement or tension.

Excitement phase
Phase of sexual response cycle whereby increasing arousal is manifested by increases in heart rate, blood pressure, respiration, overall muscle tension, and vasocongestion, or increased blood flow to the genital region

Vasocongestion
Increased blood flow to the genital region

Plateau phase
Second phase of Masters and Johnson's model of the sexual response cycle, which involves the continuation of sexual arousal, including myotonia (muscle contractions), hyperventilation (heavy breathing), tachycardia (heart rate increase), and blood pressure elevation

Myotonia
Muscle contractions

Hyperventilation
Abnormally heavy breathing, resulting in loss of carbon dioxide from the blood, sometimes resulting in lowered blood pressure and fainting

Tachycardia
Increased heart rate

Remember, sex is like a Chinese dinner. It ain't over "till you both get your cookie."

Alec Baldwin, actor

Cognitive factors are also important in the maintenance of the plateau phase. Individuals in this stage must continue to focus on the experience in an erotic sense to avoid a return to prearousal levels of physiological indicators.

Orgasm Phase

Orgasm is the climax of sexual excitement and is experienced as a release of tension involving intense pleasure. Perhaps the easiest aspects of an orgasm to identify are the physiological changes that, in both women and men, involve an increase in respiration, heart rate, and blood pressure. Although everyone is different, as is each person's experience of orgasm, researchers have provided some information on the various experiences.

Physiologically, the orgasmic experience for women involves simultaneous rhythmic contractions of the uterus, the outer third of the vagina, and the rectal sphincter. These contractions begin at 0.8-second intervals and then diminish in intensity, duration, and regularity. A mild orgasm may have only 3–5 contractions, whereas an intense one may have 10–15 contractions.

Although there has been considerable debate on "clitoral versus vaginal" orgasm, Masters and Johnson (1966) stated that clitoral stimulation (either direct or indirect) is necessary for orgasm. They identified only one type of orgasm, refuting the categories of clitoral and vaginal orgasm.

Subsequently, Singer (1973) contradicted Masters and Johnson and identified two variations in female orgasmic experiences: *vulval orgasms* and *uterine orgasms*. **Vulval orgasms** (also known as *clitoral orgasms*) result primarily from manual stimulation of the clitoris and are characterized by spastic contractions of the outer third of the vagina. In contrast, **uterine orgasms** are caused by deep intravaginal stimulation and involve contractions in the uterus as well as the vagina. **Blended orgasms** are those in which women experience both vulval contractions and deep uterine enjoyment.

Some females express liquid from their urethra at orgasm, sometimes referred to as female ejaculation. In some women the amount of the substance is small, usually milky white, and technically referred to as female ejaculate. The substance is prostatic-specific antigen (PSA) and is produced by the Skene glands. In other women, the woman squirts fluid (enough to make it appear as though she has wet the bed) that may contain PSA but is mostly urine (Thompson, 2015).

People may sometimes wonder if their sexual partner is faking orgasm. Seguin and colleagues (2015) studied feigning orgasm and found that 43% of 94 women and 17% of 53 men reported that they had pretended to have an orgasm with their current relationship partner. In regard to motivation, men were more likely than women to report pretending orgasm due to intoxication, discomfort, or displeasure attributable to their sexual partner and feelings of insecurity. Based on three studies (total of 1,472 respondents) the primary reasons for pretending orgasm reported by both men and women were: feels good (e.g. caught up in the moment), for the partner, not into sex, manipulation/power, insecurity, and emotional communication (e.g. closeness) (Goodman, 2017). Leonhardt et al. (2017) surveyed 1,683 heterosexual newlywed couples about the discrepancy/misperception of how often a husband reported that his wife had an orgasm with how often she actually had an orgasm. Forty-two percent of husbands misperceived how often their wives were orgasmic. A wife's orgasm was very much related to her sexual satisfaction but not so much to her marital satisfaction. Men who perceived their wife as having an orgasm reported higher sexual satisfaction themselves and their masculinity was enhanced via their wife's sexual pleasure. Chadwick and Van Anders (2017) confirmed that men reported higher sexual self-esteem after their partner's imagined orgasm during sexual intercourse. Hence, the woman's orgasm is not just about her pleasure but the man's masculinity.

Orgasm
Climax of sexual excitement, experienced as a release of tension involving intense pleasure

Vulval orgasm
An orgasm that results primarily from manual stimulation of the clitoris and is characterized by contractions of the outer third of the vagina (also called *clitoral orgasm*)

Uterine orgasm
In contrast to clitoral orgasm, an orgasm caused by deep intravaginal stimulation and involving contractions in the uterus as well as the vagina

Blended orgasm
Orgasm whereby the woman experiences both vulval contractions and deep uterine enjoyment

Resolution Phase

After orgasm, the **resolution phase** of the sexual response cycle begins, which involves the body's return to its pre-excitement condition. In women, the vagina begins to shorten in both width and length, and the clitoris returns to its normal anatomic position. Breathing, heart rate, and blood pressure return to normal. A thin layer of perspiration may appear over the entire body.

In the resolution phase, individuals may prefer to avoid additional genital stimulation: "My clitoris feels very sensitive—almost burns—and I don't want it touched after I orgasm" (case files of first author). This statement characterizes the feelings of some women. Others say their clitoris tickles when touched after orgasm. When sexual arousal does not result in orgasm, resolution still takes place but more gradually. Some women experience an unpleasant sensation of sexual tension or fullness in the genital area due to prolonged vasocongestion in the absence of orgasm.

Alternative Cycles in Women

Masters and Johnson (1966) stated that a woman might experience the sexual response cycle in one of three ways. When there is sufficient and continuous stimulation, the most usual pattern is a progression from excitement through plateau to orgasm to resolution, passing through all phases and returning to none of these stages for a second time. Experientially, the woman gets excited, enjoys a climax, and cuddles in her partner's arms after one orgasm. If she is masturbating, she relaxes and savors the experience.

In another pattern (again, assuming sufficient and continuous stimulation), the woman goes from excitement to plateau to orgasm to another or several orgasms and then to resolution. The interval between orgasms varies—in some cases, it is only a few seconds. In effect, the woman gets excited, climbs through the plateau phase, and bounces from orgasm to orgasm while briefly reaching the plateau phase between orgasms.

Still another pattern of female sexual response is to move through the sequence of phases of the sexual response cycle but skip the orgasm phase. The woman gets excited and climbs to the plateau phase but does not have an orgasm. Insufficient stimulation, distraction, and/or lack of interest in the partner (if one is involved) are some of the reasons for not reaching orgasm. The woman moves from the plateau phase directly to the resolution phase.

Although the Masters and Johnson model is the most widely presented model of human sexual response, it has been criticized on several counts. First, the idea of a four-stage process is arbitrary and imprecise. Whereas Masters and Johnson, as well as Helen Kaplan, reported only one reflex pathway in sexual responding, Perry and Whipple described a second reflex pathway that might account for the ability of some women to experience the vulval, uterine, or blended orgasms as described by Singer (Whipple & Komisaruk, 1999). Also, the Masters and Johnson model virtually ignores cognitive and emotional states, focusing almost exclusively on objective physiological measures (Basson, 2001a). The measurement of the physiological changes (primarily changes in the genitals) deals with bodily response, which is just one aspect of sexuality. Masters and Johnson's model of sexual response was not designed to assess the emotional and intimacy aspects of sexuality and sexual interaction.

Leavitt et al. (2019) reported evidence of variability in the female sexual response cycle such that women (769 in their sample) may experience desire and arousal similarly. However, although variability may exist, healthy relational and sexual outcomes were reported by most women. The message is to accept and embrace variability of sexual response. No differences in sexual orientation were found.

Resolution phase
Final phase of Masters and Johnson's model of the sexual response cycle that describes the body's return to its pre-excitement condition

3.4b Kaplan's Three-Stage Model of Sexual Response

In an effort to emphasize the motivational and psychological aspects of human sexual response, Helen Kaplan (1979) proposed a three-stage model consisting of desire, excitement, and orgasm. The first stage, sexual desire, involves feeling "horny," sexy, or interested in sex; this stage may be accompanied by genital sensations. Kaplan's excitement and orgasm phases are very similar to those of Masters and Johnson—both models focus on vasocongestion and genital contractions in these two phases. However, Kaplan focused more attention on the motivational and psychological aspects of sexual response. The primary criticism of Kaplan's model is her suggestion that desire is a necessary prerequisite for excitement. However, desire is not necessary for arousal or orgasm to occur.

3.4c Basson's Model of Sexual Response

Rosemary Basson (2001a, 2001b) emphasized that psychological factors, as well as biological factors, affect the processing of sexual stimuli. She suggested that, for many women, the beginning of sexual response in sex with a partner is emotional intimacy, which may begin with sexual neutrality and openness to sexual involvement and that leads to sexual stimulation and then sexual arousal. So, for many women, it is not sexual desire that is the beginning point of sexual response (in a sexual interaction that is wanted, not coerced), but rather a willingness to be receptive to sexual stimuli. Their desire to share physical pleasure may be more for the sake of sharing than for satisfying sexual hunger. Men sometimes also experience intimacy-based desire; but more often than women, they experience spontaneous desire (probably largely biologically based).

PERSONAL DECISIONS 3-4

Having Sex with a Partner When Desire Is Low

It is not unusual when one partner wants to engage in sex that the other does not (Kleinplatz et al., 2018). Should the partner who has low sex interest or desire agree to participate anyway?

Sex therapists confronted with a couple who have discrepant sexual desires may note that the less interested partner need not be interested in sex but rather receptive to sexual stimulation, which may then be labeled in positive sexual terms. Such labeling may result in enjoyment, which may lead to continuation of the stimulation and sexual involvement.

Indeed, aside from pleasing the partner, a potential positive outcome from choosing to engage in sexual behavior independent of desire is that the individual may experience desire following involvement in sexual behavior. Cognitive behavior therapists conceptualize this phenomenon as "acting yourself into a new way of feeling, rather than feeling yourself into a new way of acting."

Rather than wait for the feelings of sexual desire to occur before engaging in sexual behavior, the person acts as though there is feeling, only to discover that the feeling sometimes follows. An old French saying reflects this phenomenon: "L'appetit vient avec mangent," which translates into "The appetite comes with eating."

We are not suggesting that an individual who lacks sexual desire routinely be open to sexual stimulation with their partner or always comply with the partner's wishes. As we will emphasize in Chapter 14 on sexual dysfunctions and sex therapy, sometimes it is the behavior of the partner that fails to entice you to participate in sex through a lack of skill or context. Hence, the discrepancy in a couple's sexual relationship may not be due to the partner with the low sexual interest, but to the other partner. This is why the relationship of the couple becomes the focus of the sex therapist.

3.5 Hormones and Sexual Response

Hormones are chemical messengers that typically travel from cell to cell via the bloodstream. The hypothalamus and pituitary gland near the center of the brain regulate the endocrine system's secretion of hormones into the bloodstream (see Figure 3-8). The reproductive hormones (estrogens, progesterone, and androgens) are mainly produced in the gonads. They influence reproductive development through organizing and activating effects. Organizing effects include anatomical differentiation (the development of male or female genitals) and some differentiation of brain structure. At puberty, they lead to the development of secondary sex characteristics.

Activating effects include influences on behavior and affective states. For example, researchers have studied the role of reproductive hormones and their possible influence on adolescent aggression and behavior problems, adolescent sexuality, the menstrual cycle, and related mood changes.

Endocrine factors relevant to sexual response are androgens, estrogens, progesterone, prolactin, oxytocin, cortisol, and pheromones. Free testosterone (1%–2% of all testosterone in the body, may help account for the experience of feeling lusty) and bound testosterone (bound to sex hormone binding proteins called *globulins*) may also be related to sex drive. Yet researchers do not agree on a direct link between hormones in the bloodstream and sex drive. Harris and Vitzthum (2013) reviewed the effect of hormones on sexual behavior and emphasized the lack of credible research (due to the challenges of controlling for variables, definitions, and time). Hence, while hormones may have an effect on sexual behavior, so might social factors—for example, sexual activity increases on the weekend and on vacation. The conclusion on the relationship between hormones and sexual desire is that social (one's partner/peers), psychological (sexual self-concept/previous positive sexual experiences), and cultural (Is it okay to be sexual?) factors may be far more important than hormone levels.

FIGURE 3-8 ‖ **Endocrine System**

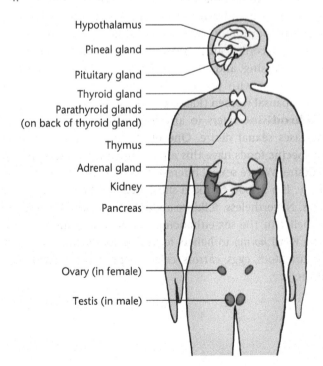

Hypothalamus
Pineal gland
Pituitary gland
Thyroid gland
Parathyroid glands
(on back of thyroid gland)
Thymus
Adrenal gland
Kidney
Pancreas
Ovary (in female)
Testis (in male)

Hormones
Chemical messengers that travel from cell to cell via the bloodstream

3.6 Pheromones, Aphrodisiacs, and Sexual Response

The term *pheromone* comes from the Greek words *pherein*, meaning "to carry," and *hormone*, meaning to "excite." **Pheromones** are chemicals that activate the behavior of same species organisms. Niehuis and colleagues (2013) confirmed the existence of sex pheromones in many sexually reproducing organisms—their focus was on wasps! Research on sex pheromones in humans has been less convincing.

Coffee is often an aphrodisiac.

The functions of human pheromones include attracting the opposite sex, repelling the same sex, and bonding mother and infant. Pheromones typically operate without the person's awareness; however, researchers disagree about whether they do, in fact, influence human sociosexual behaviors. Two older studies are instructive. One examined the effect of hormones on sexual behavior—it involved 38 male volunteers who applied a male hormone to their aftershave lotion. They reported significant increases in sexual intercourse and sleeping next to a partner when compared to men who had a placebo in their aftershave lotion (Cutler et al., 1998). Hence, presumably, women were attracted to the male with the pheromone.

Coffee (with caffeine) has been confirmed as having a positive effect on maintaining sexual involvement. Diokno and colleagues (1990) observed that at least one cup of coffee per day is significantly associated with a higher prevalence of sexual activity in women (age 60 and over) and with a higher potency rate in men (age 60 and over).

In research on 44 postmenopausal women (mean age 57) who volunteered for a double-blind placebo-controlled study designed "to test an odorless pheromone, added to their preferred fragrance, to learn if it might increase the romance in your life," a significantly greater proportion of participants using the pheromone formula (40.9%) than placebo (13.6%) recorded an increase over their own weekly average baseline frequency of petting, kissing, and affection. The researchers concluded that the pheromone formulation worn with perfume for a period of 6 weeks had sex-attractant effects for postmenopausal women (Rako & Friebely, 2004).

The term **aphrodisiac** refers to any food, drink, drug, scent, or device that arouses and increases sexual desire. One of the more prevalent myths of human sexuality is that specific foods have this effect. In reality, no food reliably increases a person's sexual desire. Where sexual interest does increase, it is often a result of a self-fulfilling prophecy. If a person thinks a substance will have a desire-inducing effect, it sometimes does. Nevertheless, folklore about aphrodisiacs has a long history, from the Vietnamese belief in the sex-enhancing power of a ground-up rhinoceros horn (the origin of the word *horny*) to beliefs regarding foods and other substances, such as oysters, crabs, tomatoes, eggs, carrots, celery, pepper, turtle soup, paprika, nutmeg, ginger, and saffron.

Pheromones
Chemicals that activate the behavior of same-species organisms

Aphrodisiac
Any food, drink, drug, scent, or device that arouses and increases sexual desire

Beyond the use of any alleged aphrodisiac, the use of a sex toy has been identified as having a high probability of inducing an orgasm. Schulz et al. (2019) noted that sex educators and sex therapists should recommend the use of sex toys to close the existing orgasm gap in heterosexual relationships.

(Amberlynn Bishop)

Body lotions and perfumes are often used as pheromones to provide an attractant scent.

Chapter Summary

Female External Anatomy and Physiology

FEMALE EXTERNAL SEXUAL ANATOMY includes the mons veneris, labia, clitoris, vaginal opening, and urethral opening. The clitoris is the most sensitive part of a woman's sexual anatomy. Even though the female breasts provide the important function of nourishing offspring, they are secondary sex characteristics and are not considered part of the female reproductive anatomy.

Female Internal Anatomy and Physiology

THE VAGINA, UTERUS, FALLOPIAN TUBES, OVARIES, AND THE SUPPOSED "G-SPOT" make up the internal sexual anatomy of the female. Fertilization of the female egg, or ovum, usually occurs in the fallopian tubes.

Models of Sexual Response

THE MASTERS AND JOHNSON MODEL OF SEXUAL RESPONSE involves four phases: excitement, plateau, orgasm, and resolution. This cycle has been criticized in that it is biologically and genitally focused. In contrast, Helen Kaplan proposed a three-stage model consisting of desire, excitement, and orgasm. Kaplan focused more attention on the motivational and psychological aspects of sexual response. The primary criticism of Kaplan's model is her suggestion that desire is a necessary prerequisite for excitement.

Rosemary Basson emphasized that the floor, or basin, of sexual response for many women is emotional intimacy, whereby they are open to sexual involvement that leads to sexual stimuli and then sexual arousal.

Hormones and Sexual Response

RESEARCHERS DISAGREE on the link between hormones in the bloodstream and sexual desire. The best evidence suggests that social, psychological, and cultural factors may be more important than hormone levels.

Pheromones, Aphrodisiacs, and Sexual Response

THE FUNCTIONS OF HUMAN PHEROMONES include attracting the opposite sex, repelling the same sex, and bonding the mother and infant. Although there is evidence of pheromone-induced sex attraction or behavior in other organisms, researchers disagree about whether pheromones do, in fact, influence human socio-sexual behaviors. The term *aphrodisiac* refers to any substance that increases sexual desire. Despite popular belief, no food reliably increases a person's sexual desire.

Web Links

American Cancer Society

http://www.cancer.org

Breastfeeding

http://www.thebump.com/topics/parenting-breastfeeding

Female Genital Cutting Education and Networking Project

http://www.hollyfeld.org/~fgm/index.php

Engerotics

www.engerotics.com

Society for Menstrual Cycle Research

http://www.menstruationresearch.org

Our Bodies, Ourselves

http://www.ourbodiesourselves.org

Key Terms

Amenorrhea **79**

Aphrodisiac **86**

Areola **70**

Bartholin glands **63**

Blended orgasm **82**

Cervix **74**

Clitoris **63**

Cystitis **66**

Dysmenorrhea **79**

Ectopic pregnancy **74**

Endometriosis **79**

Excitement phase **81**

Fallopian tubes **74**

Female genital cutting **66**

Follicle-stimulating hormone **75**

Fundus **74**

G-spot **73**

Honor killing **65**

Hormones **85**

Hymen **65**

Hyperventilation **81**

Introitus **65**

Kegel exercise **73**

Labia majora ("major lips") **63**

Labia minora ("little lips") **63**

Mammogram **71**

Menarche **75**

Menorrhagia **79**

Menstrual extraction **76**

Menstrual suppression **76**

Menstrual synchrony **75**

Menstruation or menses **75**

Mons veneris **62**

Myotonia **81**

Oligomenorrhea **79**

Orgasm **82**

Os **74**

Ovaries **75**

Pap test **74**

Perineum **63**

Pheromones **86**

Plateau phase **81**

Premenstrual dysphoric disorder **80**

Premenstrual syndrome **79**

Pubococcygeus **73**

Resolution phase **83**

Secondary sex characteristics **69**

Sexual anatomy **61**

Sexual physiology **61**

Tachycardia **81**

Urethra **66**

Uterine orgasm **82**

Uterus **74**

Vagina **72**

Vasocongestion **81**

Vestibule **65**

Vulva **62**

Vulval orgasm **82**

CHAPTER
4

Male Sexual Anatomy, Physiology, and Response

The noblest pleasure is the joy of understanding

Leonardo da Vinci

Chapter Outline

4.1 Male External Anatomy and Physiology 91
4.1a   Penis **92**
Technology and Sexuality 4-1:
        Promises to Increase
        Penis Length **94**
Social Policy 4-1
        Male Circumcision **95**
4.1b   Scrotum **96**
4.2 Male Internal Anatomy and Physiology 96
4.2a   Testes **96**
4.2b   Duct System **98**

4.2c   Seminal Vesicles, Prostate Gland, and
        Bulbourethral Gland **99**
Personal Decisions 4.1
        Assessing Prostate Cancer **100**
4.3 Sexual Response Cycle of Men 100
4.3a   Masters and Johnson's Four-Stage
        Model of Sexual Response **100**
4.3b   Differences in the Sexual Response
        Cycle of Men and Women **103**

Web Links 104
Key Terms 105

Objectives

1. Identify and label male external anatomy
2. Describe male external physiology
3. Identify and label male internal anatomy
4. Review male internal physiology
5. Know how males should perform a genital self-exam

6. Understand the likelihood of contracting testicular cancer and know how to do a testicular self-exam
7. Learn the sexual response cycle of men according to Masters and Johnson
8. Discuss the prevalence of prostate cancer and the ways in which it is detected
9. Explain the differences in the male and female sexual response cycles

(Shuang Li / Shutterstock)

Truth — OR — Fiction?

T / F   1. When asked to evaluate their bodies, men are least satisfied with the length of their penis.

T / F   2. The American Academy of Pediatrics recommends routine circumcision for all male newborns.

T / F   3. Men dissatisfied with the length of their penis are the least satisfied with their sex lives.

T / F   4. The majority of semen is composed of sperm.

T / F   5. Orgasm and ejaculation are the same thing.

Answers: 1. F   2. F   3. T   4. F   5. F

One of men's greatest fears is that they will not "measure up." This obsession with the size of their penis is one of the body issues common to most men. They must also feel pressure to be tall enough and muscular enough, and they may have performance expectations that can devastate their self-concept if they can't "keep it up." In this chapter, we review male anatomy and physiology, as well as the sexual response cycle.

4.1 Male External Anatomy and Physiology

Male external sexual and reproductive anatomy includes the penis and scrotum. Like the vulva, male genitalia differ in appearance, and no single example can be labeled "normal" (see Figure 4-1).

FIGURE **4-1** ‖ The Male Penis Varies in Appearance

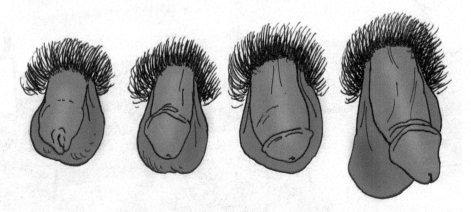

I hate those e-mails where they try to sell you penis enhancers. I got 10 just the other day. Eight of them from my girlfriend.

Jimmy Carr, comedian

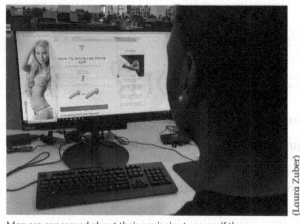

Men are concerned about their penis size to assess if they "measure up."

(Laura Zuber)

4.1a Penis

The **penis** (PEE-nis) is the primary male sex organ that, in its unaroused state, is soft and hangs between the legs. When sexually stimulated, the penis enlarges, hardens, and becomes erect, enabling penetration of the female's vagina. The penis not only functions reproductively (depositing sperm in the vagina) and sexually; it also contains the passageway from the bladder to eliminate urine.

Penis size refers to both length and circumference. Of 463 gay and bisexual men, 86% had measured their penile length, and 69% their penile circumference. More than half (51%) reported penile length as 6–8 inches, and 32% reported penile circumference as 4–6 inches around (Grov et al., 2013b). King et al. (2019a) found that 130 sexually experienced college men reported their penis length to be an average of 6.62 inches with only 26.9% of the sexually experienced men's self-reported penis lengths of less than 6 inches.

A continuing trend among young men is *manscaping*. While waxing has been common among young single women, single men are now shaving, waxing, and trimming their body hair. Some feel that their partners expect it and will be pleased at their presentation. Some feel that manscaping makes the penis appear longer, though there are also other motives. Hall (2015) noted that modern masculine scripts include caring (e.g., shaving so as not to scratch the sensitive skin of the female) and equality ("Why should women be expected to shave down there, but not guys? It's a matter of respect.")

Does penis size matter to female partners? Some research confirms that longer penises are associated with increased likelihood of vaginal orgasm (Costa et al., 2012). In an online survey, 323 women reported their past month's frequency of various sexual outcomes (vaginal and clitoral orgasms). Results revealed that the likelihood of vaginal orgasm was related to a longer penis. However, data provided by 43 women in a study on penis size preferences revealed that they did not prefer a larger-than-average penis—their ideal lengths were comparable with population norms (Johnston et al., 2014). The women in this study did not provide information on the effect of penis size on their overall sexual satisfaction.

Penis
Primary male external sex organ that, in the unaroused state, is soft and hangs between the legs

National **DATA**

The average size of the adult male penis (based on a sample of 15,521 men) is 5.1 inches (Veale et al., 2015).

Males are socialized to believe "the bigger, the better" and think that potential partners would prefer a longer, thicker penis. The plethora of advertisements targeting men to "increase your penis size" testifies to this male desire for a larger penis. In a survey of 67 men about penis size and satisfaction, dissatisfaction was still common among men, even though many perceived themselves to be of average size (Johnston et al., 2014). In a nationally representative survey of noninstitutionalized adult males aged 18–65 years residing in the U.S., 27% reported the least amount of satisfaction with the length of their penis. Such dissatisfaction was associated with being less sexually active and less sexually satisfied (Gaither et al., 2017).

Though the male concern with penis size is an ancient one, as depicted in frescoes in the ruins of Pompeii (Morgentaler, 2009), the modern source of this widespread obsession is attributed to the males seen in pornography, who often have unusually long penises. Famed porn star John Holmes was said to have "a third leg." Some men who feel that their penis is too short seek various methods of increasing its length. Penile-lengthening surgery is sometimes performed, but it is still considered experimental. See *Technology and Sexuality 4–1* for more information.

The visible, free-hanging portion of the penis consists of the body, or shaft, and the smooth, rounded **glans** at the tip. Like the glans of the female clitoris, the glans of the penis has numerous nerve endings. The penis is especially sensitive to touch on the raised rim, or **corona**, and on the **frenulum** (the thin strip of skin on the underside), which connects the glans with the body. The body of the penis is not nearly as sensitive as the glans. The urethral opening, or **meatus**, through which urine is expelled from the body, is normally located at the tip of the glans. Occasionally, the urethral opening is located at the side of the glans, a minor anatomical defect that may prevent depositing sperm at the cervical opening; this can be surgically corrected.

The penis is not a muscle, in that the man cannot contract the penis and cause an erection. In cross section, the penis can be seen to consist of three parallel cylinders of tissue containing many cavities: two *corpora cavernosa* (cavernous bodies) and a *corpus spongiosum* (spongy body) through which the urethra passes (see Figure 4-2). Each is bound in its own fibrous sheath. The spongy body can be felt on the underside when the penis is erect. The penis has numerous blood vessels. When the penis is flaccid, blood coming in through the arteries is drained by veins deep within the penis and bypasses the spongy tissues. However, during arousal, the arteries dilate, blood enters faster than it can leave, and venous outflow is reduced, so the blood is diverted into the spongy tissue. As the cavities of the cavernous and spongy bodies fill with blood, pressure against the fibrous membranes causes the corpora cavernosa to expand and the penis to become erect.

Like the clitoris, the penis is attached to the pubic bone by the inner tips of the cavernous bodies, called *crura*. Unlike the penises of some other mammalian species, the human penis has no bone—men can't really have a "boner." However, the fibrous sheath of the corpora of the erect penis can fracture as a result of being abruptly bent during sexual intercourse or masturbation.

Glans
Small, rounded body of tissue on the head of the penis that can swell and harden

Corona
Raised rim on the glans of the penis that is especially sensitive to touch

Frenulum
Thin strip of skin on the underside of the head of the penis that connects the glans with the shaft

Meatus
Opening to the urethra at the tip of the penis

Technology and Sexuality 4-1: Promises to Increase Penis Length

We've all seen the ads for products that promise to increase penis length. Many people may wonder: Do these products work? For those considering pills and creams to lengthen the penis, caveat emptor: There is no research to show that these work (Mayo Clinic Staff, 2014).

Alternatively, some people consider a vacuum pump. These devices may be effective for men with erectile dysfunction. A review of treatment options has shown that when males with erectile dysfunction use a vacuum erection device, they report successfully engaging in intercourse more often than with any other treatment option, including oral drugs like Viagra (Pahlajani et al., 2012). However, for those who don't have erectile dysfunction, all the vacuum pumps can do is temporarily change the size that an erect penis appears to be—the length is not affected (Mayo Clinic Staff, 2017).

Other options for men who want a longer penis include traction or surgery. There is limited research on the use of traction. One study showed that men who wore a traction extender for at least 4 hours a day, every day for 6 months, showed an increase in penis size of 1.7 cm—a little over half an inch (Gontero et al., 2009). However, more research needs to be conducted before it can be concluded that traction results in increased penis length (Ghanem et al., 2013). In regard to surgical options for cosmetic reasons, the "results are modest, the rate of complications significant, and the satisfaction low" (Chevallier et al., 2013, p. 685).

While there may not be a lot of promise for making the penis longer, there might be some newer options for making it wider. Doctors have tried doing penile injections using different substances, including hyaluronic acid, a carbohydrate produced by the body. The substance can be bought over the counter to help with arthritis and as a skin moisturizer. In a recent study, 41 men had hyaluronic acid injected into their penises and smoothed out with a roller (Kwak et al., 2011). The researchers measured penis girth at 1 month and 18 months after injection. The study found an increase in penis girth that was attained after injection and maintained for 18 months (Kwak et al., 2011).

CyberSkin® has also been used in increasing penis size and girth. This material feels like human skin and is designed to warm up to body temperature (Topco, n.d.). CyberSkin has been used for a variety of sex toys, including dildos and Fleshlights® (artificial vaginas). While technological devices offer some options to those wanting to increase their penis size, a more natural alternative for men is to learn to appreciate their body/penis size and to talk with their partner about what each can do to please the other. The goal is to take the focus off of anatomy and replace it with interpersonal communication, affection, and pleasure—something no pill, injection, pump, or extender can do.

FIGURE **4-2** ‖ Male Reproductive Anatomy, Side View

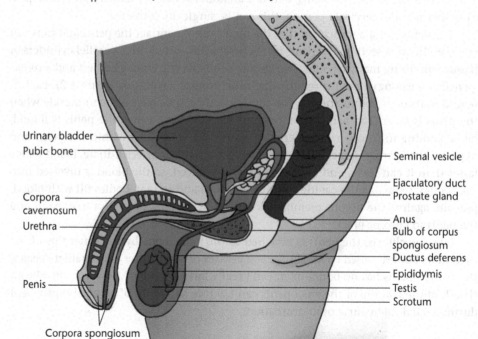

Peyronie's Disease (PD) produces a curved or deformed penis that is a result of accumulated scar tissue. In a review of the literature regarding the psychological impact of the male having Peyronie's Disease, 81% of men with PD report emotional difficulties, with about half reporting depression (48%) and relationship problems (54%). "The challenges imposed by PD include alterations in sexual relationships, restrictions on intimacy, social isolation, and stigmatization—all of which are linked and reinforce each other" (Nelson & Mulhall, 2013, p. 653).

The root of the penis consists of the crura and the inner end of the spongy body, which is expanded to form the bulb. Two muscles surround the root of the penis and aid in ejaculation and urination. Voluntary and involuntary contractions of these muscles result in a slight jerking of the erect penis.

The glans of the penis is actually the expanded front end of the spongy body. The skin of the penis, which is extremely loose to enable expansion during erection, folds over most of the glans. This foreskin, or *prepuce*, is fixed at the border between the glans and body of the penis. Small glands beneath the foreskin secrete small amounts of oils that have no known physiological function. These oily secretions can become mixed with sweat and bacteria to form *smegma*, a cheesy substance similar to that which can build up under the clitoral hood in women.

Circumcision is a surgical procedure in which the foreskin of the penis is pulled forward and cut off. About 81% of adult males in the United States have been circumcised. Male circumcision is a religious or cultural rite for members of the Jewish and Muslim faiths. In some societies, circumcision is often performed by a traditional (instead of a medical) circumciser, and without anesthesia, as a puberty rite to symbolize the passage into manhood. Of 1,592 women, 58% preferred a circumcised penis, 35% no preference, and 7% an uncircumcised penis (Michel & Mark, 2019).

Peyronie's disease
A curved or deformed penis that is a result of accumulated scar tissue

Circumcision
Surgical procedure in which the foreskin of the penis is pulled forward and cut off (also known as *male genital mutilation*)

Social Policy 4-1

Male Circumcision

In the United States, where male circumcision is performed on about 81% of male children within the first few days after birth (Introcaso et al., 2013), the primary reasons are to maintain tradition and to promote hygiene. The American Academy of Pediatrics (AAP) formed a multidisciplinary task force of AAP members in 2007 to evaluate the evidence on male circumcision. On the basis of this evaluation, the AAP reversed its earlier position and emphasized that the health benefits of newborn male circumcision may outweigh the risks and that the benefits of the procedure may justify access to this procedure for families who choose it. Specific benefits include prevention of urinary tract infections, penile cancer, and transmission of some sexually transmitted infections, including HIV and HPV, a virus that can cause cervical cancer. The AAP (2012) also stated, "The procedure is well tolerated when performed by trained professionals under sterile conditions with appropriate pain management."

However, Jenkins (2014) noted that the AAP's position is not without controversy both within the United States and internationally. Indeed, despite the evaluation's acknowledgment of the health benefits of circumcision, the AAP concludes that the benefits are "not great enough to recommend routine circumcision for all male newborns."

Cultural Diversity

In Europe, fewer than 20% of men have been circumcised (Ingraham, 2015). British and German courts have decreed that children may decide for themselves if they want to be circumcized. Danish and Icelandic health officials recommend banning the procedure. In contrast, religious leaders oppose the ban. Jewish and Muslim newborns are routinely circumcised for cultural and religious reasons.

4.1b Scrotum

The **scrotum** (SKROH-tum) is the sac that is located below the penis and contains the testicles. Beneath the skin is a thin layer of muscle fibers that contract in the cold, helping to draw the testicles closer to the body. In hot environments, the muscle fibers relax, and the testicles are suspended farther away from the body. The numerous glands in the skin of the scrotum produce sweat. These responses help regulate the temperature of the testicles. The temperature in the scrotum is 2–3 degrees Fahrenheit lower than in the interior of the body. Sperm can be produced only at a temperature several degrees lower than normal body temperature, and any variation can result in sterility. The impact of temperature has been known for some time, with reports dating back to Roman use of very hot baths as a form of birth control (though it was far from consistently effective).

4.2 Male Internal Anatomy and Physiology

The male internal organs include the testicles (where sperm is produced), a duct system to transport the sperm out of the body, the seminal vesicles, and the prostate gland (see Figure 4-3).

4.2a Testes

The paired **testes**, or *testicles*, are the male gonads, which develop from the same embryonic tissue as the female gonads (the ovaries). The two oval-shaped testicles are suspended in the scrotum by the spermatic cord and enclosed within a fibrous sheath. It is normal for the left testicle to hang lower than the right one in right-handed men, and the reverse in left-handed men. However, the two testicles should be about the same size; if one is noticeably larger, a physician should be consulted. The testes are very sensitive to pressure. Some men find gentle touching of the scrotum to be sexually arousing, whereas others find this type of stimulation unpleasant.

Following puberty, the function of the testes is to produce spermatozoa and androgens, mainly testosterone. The pituitary hormones LH (luteinizing hormone) and FSH (follicle-stimulating hormone) regulate sperm production. Stimulated by LH, the male hormone testosterone is produced in the **interstitial** (or Leydig **cells**), which are located between the seminiferous tubules (see Figure 4-4). The testes produce sperm—about 300 million are released with each ejaculation.

Testosterone and another androgen, dihydrotestosterone (DHT), are important for more than their sexual functions. Testosterone increases the size of muscle cells, thus increasing lean body mass and body weight. That is why some athletes use synthetic

Scrotum
The sac located below the penis that contains the testicles

Testes
Male glands that develop from the same embryonic tissue as the female gonads (the ovaries) and produce spermatozoa and male hormones (They are also called *testicles*)

Interstitial cells
Cells that are housed in the testes and produce testosterone (They are also known as Leydig cells)

androgens (anabolic steroids) to build muscle mass and enhance performance. Androgens also regulate blood-clotting factors and liver enzymes and regulate the ratio of high-density lipoprotein (HDL) to low-density lipoprotein (LDL) , which affects the risk of coronary heart disease.

FIGURE **4-3** ‖ Male Internal Reproductive System, Posterior

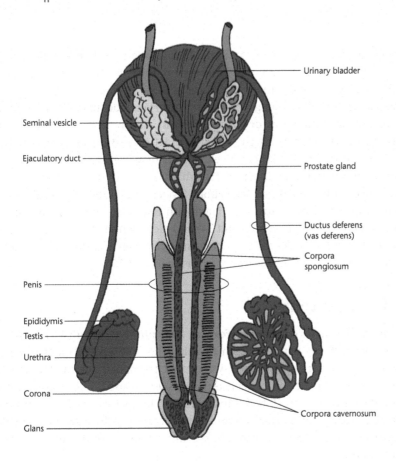

FIGURE **4-4** ‖ Cross-Section of Testicle

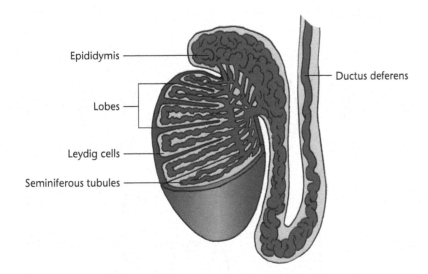

National **DATA**

Annually in the United States, there are about 9,560 new cases of testicular cancer. The median age of diagnosis is 33, and about 410 men will die annually from the disease (American Cancer Society, 2019c).

Testicular cancer is not very common. A man's lifetime chance of developing it is about 1 in 280. Because treatment is so successful, the risk of dying from this cancer is very low: about 1 in 5,000 (American Cancer Society, 2019c).

Risk factors for developing testicular cancer include having an undescended testicle or testicles (known as **cryptorchidism**), family history (father or brothers who have had testicular cancer), the presence of HIV infection, and carcinoma in situ. The latter means that testicular germ-cell cancers may begin as a noninvasive form of the disease called carcinoma in situ (CIS), which may or may not progress to become invasive cancer. If it does, it can take about 5 years. It is difficult to find CIS because it has no symptoms. Risk factors associated with testicular cancer are age (half of the cases are found in men between 20 and 34) and race—white males are five times more likely to get testicular cancer than African American men and three times more likely than Asian American men (American Cancer Society, 2016b).

4.2b Duct System

Sperm are produced in the **seminiferous** (SEH-mih-NIH-fer-uhs) **tubules**, which come together to form a tube in each testicle called the **epididymis** (EH-pih-DID-ih-muss)—the first part of the duct system that transports sperm. The epididymis, which can be felt on the top of each testicle, is a C-shaped, highly convoluted tube with a total length of up to 20 feet (Pinon, 2002). The sperm spend 2–6 days traveling through the epididymis as they mature, and the body will reabsorb them if ejaculation does not occur. Movement of the sperm through these tissues depends on the androgen supply.

FIGURE **4-5** ‖ Testicular Self-Exam

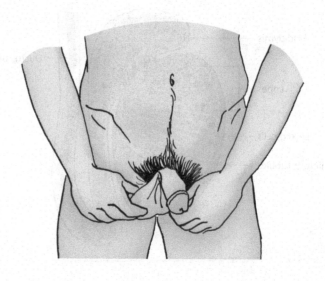

Cryptorchidism
Undescended testes

Seminiferous tubules
Part of the spermatic duct system, located within the testicles

Epididymis
Part of the spermatic duct system connecting the testicles with the vas deferens

The sperm (which actually account for a relatively small amount of semen) leave the scrotum through the second part of the duct system, the **vas deferens** (VASS-DEH-fer-enz), or *ductus deferens*. These 14- to 16-inch-long paired ducts transport the sperm from the epididymis up and over the bladder to the prostate gland, where the sperm mix with seminal fluid to form semen. One form of male sterilization, vasectomy, involves cutting and tying off each vas deferens.

4.2c Seminal Vesicles, Prostate Gland, and Bulbourethral Gland

The **seminal vesicles** resemble two small sacs about 2 inches in length located behind the bladder. They are mistakenly called vesicles because it was once believed that they were storage areas for semen. The seminal vesicles, however, secrete their own fluids, which mix with sperm and fluids from the prostate gland. Substances secreted from the seminal vesicles include a sugar-rich fluid (fructose) that provides sperm with a source of energy and helps with the sperms' motility. Most of semen consists of fluid from the seminal vesicles. The rest of semen consists of fluid from the **prostate gland**, which mixes with the fluid from the seminal vesicles. The prostate is a chestnut-sized structure located below the bladder and in front of the rectum. It contains smooth muscle fibers and glandular tissue. Prostaglandins, the hormones secreted by the prostate and other tissues, stimulate contractility of smooth muscles. Sperm, which reach the ejaculatory duct as a result of both the muscular contractions of the epididymis and vas deferens and the sweeping motion of hairlike cilia on their inner walls, are made active by fructose. Prostaglandins induce contractions of the uterus, possibly aiding movement of the sperm within the female.

The prostate gland has also been referred to as the *male pleasure gland* or the **male "G-spot."** A partner seeking to stimulate this gland would reach down between the man's legs, insert the index finger into the anus to the second knuckle, and press forward in a firm "come hither" motion. This stimulation can cause some men to have an explosive orgasm; others will feel very little.

In the prostate, the ejaculatory ducts join the initial portion of the urethra from the bladder to form a single common passageway for urine and semen. The prostate enlarges at puberty as the result of increasing hormone levels. As the man ages, in some cases the prostate becomes larger and constricts the urethra, interfering with urination. Treatments involve doing nothing, taking medication, receiving radiation, or surgically removing the prostate. The prostate is also a common site of infection, resulting in an inflamed condition called *prostatitis*. Major symptoms are painful ejaculation or defecation; this condition is easily treated with antibiotics.

Second to skin cancer, prostate cancer is the most common type of cancer in men, and the risk increases with age. Radical surgery for prostate cancer typically results in an inability to get an erection. Radiation therapy is an alternative to radical surgery for prostate cancer. In a survey of 252 men who had radiation therapy, 89% had lost their ability to ejaculate at a 5-year follow-up (Sullivan et al., 2013b). All men should have their prostate checked annually after age 50, or before if there is a family history of prostate cancer.

Benign prostatic hyperplasia (BPH) refers to the normal enlargement of the man's prostate as he ages. The most common symptoms of BPH are a hesitant, interrupted, weak stream of urine; urgency and leaking or dribbling; and/or more frequent urination, especially at night. Sometimes a man may not know there is a problem until he suddenly finds himself unable to urinate at all.

Vas deferens
Tube from the ejaculatory ducts to the testes that transports sperm

Seminal vesicles
Two small glands about 2 inches in length, located behind the bladder in the male, that secrete fluids that mix with sperm to become semen

Prostate gland
Chestnut-sized structure in the male, located below the bladder and in front of the rectum, that produces much of the seminal fluid

Male "G-spot"
The prostate gland, which can be stimulated by a partner who inserts an index finger, up to the second knuckle (facing the partner) into the anus, and bends the finger in a "come hither" motion

Benign prostatic hyperplasia
Normal enlargement of the man's prostate as he ages that may eventually require treatment

PERSONAL DECISIONS 4.1

Assessing Prostate Cancer

It is estimated that there will be 174,650 new cases of prostate cancer and that 31,620 men will die from prostate cancer in 2019. Nearly two-thirds of all prostate cancers are diagnosed in men over the age of 65. The average age of diagnosis is 66. (American Cancer Society, 2019b).

One way to detect prostate cancer is a digital rectal exam. The health-care professional inserts a gloved, lubricated finger into the rectal canal and then rotates the finger to see if the size of the prostate is normal and to check for any unusual lumps in the rectum. While a blood test (PSA) has been the traditional way to assess prostate cancer, a prostate biopsy is the only way to accurately assess the presence of prostate cancer.

Men who have BPH with symptoms usually need some kind of treatment at some time. However, treatment may not be indicated when the gland is mildly enlarged because the symptoms may clear up without treatment. Instead of immediate treatment, physicians suggest regular checkups to watch for early problems. If the condition begins to pose a danger to the patient's health or causes a major inconvenience, treatment is usually recommended.

The **Cowper glands** (also called *bulbourethral glands*) are two structures attached through their tiny ducts to the urethra in the penis. These pea-sized structures secrete a clear, sticky fluid during sexual arousal, called **pre-ejaculatory fluid**. While this fluid is not rich in sperm, they are nevertheless present. If a man is using a condom for contraception, he should put it on prior to beginning intercourse.

Cowper glands
Pea-sized structures attached to the urethra in the penis that secrete droplets of clear, sticky fluid prior to ejaculation (also known as *bulbourethral glands*)

Pre-ejaculatory fluid
Fluid released from the Cowper glands during sexual arousal

Penile strain gauge
Flexible band that fits around the base of the penis and expands as the penis enlarges, measuring circumference—a way of measuring male arousal via penis size

4.3 Sexual Response Cycle of Men

The physiology of sexual response in men may be measured by examining changes in the size of the penis (increases in length, circumference, or rigidity). The most common way of measuring an increase in penile size is the **penile strain gauge**, composed of a flexible band that fits around the base of the penis and expands as the penis enlarges, measuring circumference. Useful outside the laboratory or in a lab connected to a computer, a RigiScan® monitor continuously monitors penile circumference and rigidity. Although expensive, it is the most broadly used instrument for measuring male genital response.

4.3a Masters and Johnson's Four-Stage Model of Sexual Response

Recall from Chapter 3, section 3.4a, the four-stage model of female sexual response described by Masters and Johnson (1966): excitement, plateau, orgasm, and resolution. Here, we focus on male sexual response.

Excitement Phase

During the excitement phase, men become sexually aroused in response to hormonal, tactile, auditory, visual, olfactory, cognitive, and relationship stimuli. Peripheral arousal (increased heart rate, blood pressure, respiration, and overall muscle tension) occurs. Genital arousal (vasocongestion, or increased blood flow to the genital region) causes erection, or *tumescence.*

Physiological signs of sexual excitement are not always linked to feeling sexually aroused. Although erection is usually indicative of sexual arousal, it is possible for men to feel aroused without becoming erect and they can have erections without feeling sexually aroused. For example, a man can have an erection as a response to fear, anger, exercise, or REM sleep.

In Chapter 14 we discuss erectile dysfunction. For now we note that medications such as Viagra, Levitra®, and Cialis® are routinely used to increase blood flow to the penis (physical stimulation is necessary to produce an erection). These medications do not induce arousal; instead, they allow for arousal to occur when the context and stimulation are sexual.

Plateau Phase

After reaching a high level of sexual arousal, men enter the plateau phase, during which the penis increases slightly in diameter and the size of the testes increases considerably—from 50% to 100%. In some men, the head (glans) of the penis turns a darker color. Other changes also include myotonia (muscle contractions), hyperventilation (heavy breathing), tachycardia (heart rate increase), and blood pressure elevation. Also, some men experience a "sex flush" that looks like a measles rash on parts of the chest, neck, face, and forehead. This flush sometimes suggests a high level of sexual excitement or tension.

> *She finally understood that sex was never about orgasms. Sex was merely a vehicle to achieve connection. It wasn't the destination that mattered—only the journey.*
>
> Joshua Edward Smith, *Duality*

Orgasm Phase

Male orgasm and ejaculation are not one and the same process, although in most men the two occur simultaneously. *Orgasm* refers specifically to the pleasurable, rhythmic muscular contractions in the pelvic region and the release of sexual tension. *Ejaculation* refers to the release of semen that usually accompanies orgasm. Orgasm without ejaculation is not uncommon in boys before puberty. It also can occur if the prostate is diseased or as a side effect of some medications.

Ejaculation in men occurs in two stages. In the first stage, **emission**, there is a buildup of fluid from the prostate, seminal vesicles, and vas deferens in the *prostatic urethra* (the area behind the base of the penis and above the testes). When this pool of semen collects, the man enters a stage of **ejaculatory inevitability**—he knows he is going to ejaculate and cannot control or stop the process. Due to the distance the semen must travel through the urethra, the external appearance of semen does not occur until several seconds after the man experiences ejaculatory inevitability.

In the second stage, **expulsion**, the penile muscles contract two to three times at 0.8-second intervals, propelling the semen from the penis. The contractions may then continue at longer intervals. The more time that has passed since the last ejaculation, the greater the number of contractions, and the greater the volume of ejaculate and sperm count. The anal sphincter contracts, as well.

Emission
First phase of a male orgasm in which semen pools in the urethral bulb and ejaculatory pressure builds

Ejaculatory inevitability
The feeling a male has when he becomes aware that he is going to ejaculate and cannot stop the process

Expulsion
Second phase of a male orgasm in which semen is expelled by vigorous contractions of the muscles surrounding the root of the penis, pelvic region, and genital ducts

The subjective experience of orgasm in men begins with the sensation of deep warmth or pressure that accompanies ejaculatory inevitability, followed by intensely pleasurable contractions involving the genitals, perineum (the area between the anus and scrotum), rectum, and anal sphincter. The process of semen traveling through the urethra may be experienced as a warm rush of fluid or a shooting sensation.

Some men experience the orgasmic contractions but are able to inhibit the emission of semen and experience *nonejaculatory orgasm*. Such orgasms are not usually followed by a refractory period, so the man may have consecutive, or multiple, orgasms.

It is also possible for a man to experience the sensation of orgasm but not see any ejaculate come from the penis. In some illnesses, and as a side effect of some tranquilizers and blood pressure medications, the ejaculate empties into the urinary bladder instead of flowing out through the urethra. This is called **retrograde ejaculation**.

The probability of experiencing an orgasm for men (as well as for women) is related to the frequency of being touched sexually. In a survey of 1,352 men and women ages 57–85, the odds of being unable to climax were greater by 2.4 times among men and 2.8 times among women who sometimes, rarely, or never engaged in sexual touching compared to those who always engaged in it (Galinsky, 2012).

While orgasm is typically associated with pleasure, Lee and colleagues (2013) documented the existence of **orgasmic headache**, or OH, which occurs as a sudden and severe headache at the time of orgasm or shortly afterward. The researchers discussed the case history of a 34-year-old man who complained of a severe headache that developed abruptly with orgasm and decreased over a period of 4–8 hours with the use of a calcium channel blocker.

Ejaculating before a man's partner wants him to is commonly referred to as *premature ejaculation*. In Chapter 14, Sexual Dysfunctions and Sex Therapy, we discuss premature ejaculation in detail. Here, we note that 25% of 3,016 men in five cities in China reported experiencing premature ejaculation. Older men, men who smoked, and those with higher body mass indexes were more likely to report the malady (Gao et al., 2013).

Resolution Phase

Retrograde ejaculation
Ejaculation during which a man experiences an orgasm where the ejaculate does not come out of the penis, but is emptied, instead, into the bladder

Orgasmic headache
A sudden and severe headache that occurs at the time of orgasm or shortly afterward

After orgasm, the resolution phase—which involves the body's return to its pre-excitement condition of the sexual response cycle—begins. There is usually, although not always, a loss of erection, and the testes decrease in size and descend into the scrotum. Breathing, heart rate, and blood pressure return to normal. A thin layer of perspiration may appear over the entire body.

In the resolution phase, individuals may prefer to avoid additional genital stimulation. A man often wants to lie still and avoid stimulation of the head of the penis. Men experience a *refractory period*, which is a time when it is physiologically impossible to have additional orgasms. When sexual arousal does not result in orgasm, resolution still takes place, but more gradually. Some men experience an unpleasant sensation of sexual tension or fullness in the genital area due to prolonged vasocongestion in the absence of orgasm.

4.3b Differences in the Sexual Response Cycle of Men and Women

In the sexual response cycles of women and men, there are three differences:

1. Whereas men usually climax once (and some men report multiple orgasms whereby they have an orgasm but do not ejaculate), women's responses are more variable. They may have an orgasm once, more than once, or not at all.

2. When the woman does experience more than one climax, she may be capable of doing so throughout her lifespan, although this may vary, depending on the type of orgasm. In contrast, the man's refractory period gets longer, especially as he ages.

3. Orgasm in men is never accompanied by urination, whereas this may occur in women.

As noted in the discussion in Chapter 3, section 3.4a, the Masters and Johnson model focuses almost exclusively on objective, physiological measures and does not address the emotional, spiritual, and intimacy aspects of sexuality and sexual interaction.

Chapter Summary

Male External Anatomy and Physiology

THE PENIS AND SCROTUM make up the external anatomy of the male. Penile erection is caused by dilation of the numerous blood vessels within the penis, which results in blood entering the penis faster than it can leave. The trapped blood within the penis creates pressure and results in penile erection.

Male Internal Anatomy and Physiology

THE TESTES, DUCT SYSTEM, SEMINAL VESICLES, AND PROSTATE GLAND make up the internal sexual anatomy of the male. Sperm are produced in the testes. Semen is the mixture of sperm and seminal fluid. Most seminal fluid comes from the seminal vesicles and the prostate gland, but a small amount is also secreted by the two Cowper glands, or bulbourethral glands, that are located below the prostate gland.

Sexual Response Cycle of Men

MASTERS AND JOHNSON'S MODEL OF SEXUAL RESPONSE involves four phases: excitement, plateau, orgasm, and resolution. There are three major differences in the sexual response cycles of men and women.

Web Links

American Cancer Society

    http://www.cancer.org

Circumcision Resource Center

    http://www.circumcision.org

National Organization of Circumcision Information Resource Centers

    http://www.nocirc.org

Human Anatomy and Physiology Society

    http://www.hapsweb.org/

Key Terms

Benign prostatic hyperplasia **99**

Circumcision **95**

Corona **93**

Cowper glands **100**

Cryptorchidism **98**

Ejaculatory inevitability **101**

Emission **101**

Epididymis **98**

Expulsion **101**

Frenulum **93**

Glans **93**

Interstitial cells **96**

Male "G-spot" **99**

Meatus **93**

Orgasmic headache **102**

Penile strain gauge **100**

Penis **92**

Peyronie's disease **95**

Pre-ejaculatory fluid **100**

Prostate gland **99**

Retrograde ejaculation **102**

Scrotum **96**

Seminal vesicles **99**

Seminiferous tubules **98**

Testes **96**

Vas deferens **99**

CHAPTER
5
Gender and Sexuality

The woman most in need of liberation is the woman in every man and the man in every woman.

William Sloan Coffin, clergyman and political activist

Chapter Outline

5.1 **Terminology 108**
  5.1a Sex **108**
  5.1b Gender **108**
  5.1c Gender Identity **110**
  5.1d Transgender **111**
  5.1e Gender Roles **112**
  Self-Assessment 5-1:
    Transgender Inclusive
    Behavior Scale **113**
  Technology and Sexuality 5-1:
    Transgender Options **114**
  5.1f Gender Role Ideology **115**
  Self-Assessment 5-2:
    Sexual Assertiveness
    Questionnaire **115**
5.2 **Biological Beginnings 116**
  5.2a Chromosomes **116**
  5.2b Disorders of Sex Development **116**
  Social Policy 5-1
    Selecting the Sex of an
    Unborn Child **117**
  5.2c Atypical Chromosomal
    Development **118**
  5.2d Fetal Hormones **118**
  5.2e Atypical Anatomical
    Development **120**

5.2f Pubertal Hormones **120**
5.2g The Mosaic Brain **121**
5.3 **Theories of Gender
Role Development 122**
  5.3a Sociobiology **122**
  5.3b Social Learning Theory **123**
  5.3c Cognitive-Developmental
    Theory **123**
5.4 **Agents of Gender
Role Socialization 124**
  5.4a Parents **124**
  5.4b Peers and Partners **125**
  5.4c Teachers **125**
  5.4d Religion **125**
  5.4e Media **126**
5.5 **Effects of Gender Role Socialization
on Sexuality 126**
  5.5a Female Sexuality **126**
  5.5b Male Sexuality **128**
5.6 **Gender Role Changes 129**
  5.6a Androgyny **129**
  5.6b Gender Role Transcendence **129**
  5.6c Gender Postmodernism **130**

Web Links 132
Key Terms 133

Objectives

1. Explain the factors typically used to identify a person's sex
2. Define the terms *gender, gender identity, transgender, gender role,* and *gender role ideology*
3. Review how being male or female may be viewed on a continuum
4. Describe preconception sex selection and the reasons for and against the process
5. List the most common chromosomal abnormalities
6. Discuss the role of fetal hormones
7. Describe the theories of gender role development
8. Review the various effects of gender role socialization on relationships and sexuality
9. Define the terms *androgyny, gender role transcendence,* and *gender postmodernism*

(Shutterstock)

Truth — OR — Fiction?

T / F   1. Women report greater physical pleasure and positive emotional affect from casual sex than men.

T / F   2. The FDA has not approved any technique for gender selection.

T / F   3. Gender dysphoric individuals who have had hormone therapy only have higher life satisfaction than those who have had surgery.

T / F   4. The majority of dialogue in movies is written for women.

T / F   5. Increasingly, emerging adults prefer egalitarian relationships, which are seen as the context for highest couple satisfaction.

Answers: 1. F   2. T   3. F   4. F   5. T

From the moment we are born, we are subjected to the constraints of traditional gender roles. Cultural programming affects everything from the color of our nursery (blue for a boy and pink for a girl) to our name (names are typically considered masculine or feminine); how we're treated at home and at school; and, as an adult, our personal, social, and occupational opportunities and limitations. While our culture is undergoing reevaluation and change, remnants of the past remain.

Egalitarian gender roles are associated with frequency of sexual intimacy and relationship satisfaction. Carlson et al. (2016a) found that heterosexual couples who are egalitarian in their division of labor reported higher sexual frequencies/satisfaction than traditional couples. Carlson et al. (2016b) also found that men in heterosexual marriages who are equal partners with their spouses in child care report more satisfying sexual relationships, intimacy, and relationship quality. In this chapter, we examine gender roles and how these roles impact sexuality. We begin by looking at the terms used to discuss gender issues.

Using Gender Inclusive Pronouns

If you are unsure what gender pronouns you should use for your friends, just ask politely. For example, say something like "How would you like to be addressed?" or "Please remind me what pronouns you prefer again?" Some people include gender pronoun preferences in their e-mail signatures. For example, below your e-mail signature line, add your preferred pronouns such as "pronouns: she/her/hers." You can also include your gender pronouns when introducing yourself. For example, "Hi, my name is Terry and I am from Springfield. My pronouns are they/them/theirs."

5.1 Terminology

In common usage, the terms *sex* and *gender* are often used interchangeably. To health educators, psychologists, sociologists, sexologists, and sex therapists, however, these terms are not synonymous. After clarifying the distinction between sex and gender, we discuss other relevant terminology—including *gender identity, gender role,* and *gender role ideology.*

5.1a Sex

Sex
The biological distinction between female and male, usually categorized on the basis of the reproductive organs and genetic makeup

Primary sex characteristics
Characteristics that differentiate women and men, such as external genitalia (vulva and penis), gonads (ovaries and testes), sex chromosomes (XX and XY), and hormones (estrogen, progesterone, and testosterone)

Gender
Social and psychological characteristics associated with being female or male

Gender binary
An either/or concept of gender as feminine or masculine, used by previous generations

Sex refers to a person's biological distinction. The **primary sex characteristics** that differentiate people are sex chromosomes (XX, XY, XXX, XO, and XXY), hormones (estrogen, progesterone, and testosterone), external genitalia (vulva and penis), internal sex organs (fallopian tubes, uterus, and vagina for females; epididymis, vas deferens, and seminal vesicles for males), and gonads (ovaries and testes). Secondary sex characteristics include larger breasts in women and facial hair and deeper voice in men.

Even though we commonly think of biological sex as consisting of two dichotomous categories (female and male), current views suggest that biological sex exists on a continuum. This view is supported by the existence of individuals with mixed or ambiguous genitals. Indeed, some males produce fewer androgens than some females, just as some females produce fewer estrogens than some males.

5.1b Gender

Gender refers to the social and psychological characteristics associated with being a specific gender. Characteristics typically associated with the traditional female gender include being gentle, emotional, and cooperative. Characteristics typically associated with the traditional male gender include being aggressive, rational, and competitive. In previous generations, gender was dichotomized (**gender binary**) as an either/or concept (feminine or masculine). This conception is limiting in that not all individuals fit neatly into either/or categories, suggesting that gender might be viewed from a gender nonbinary perspective. The airline industry allows customers to identify themselves as M(ale), F(emale), U(undisclosed) or X(unspecified). Those who do not identify with a gender have the option of selecting "Mx." as a title, rather than Mr. or Ms.

Whereas some researchers emphasize the role of social influences, others emphasize a biological imperative as the basis of gender role behavior. While some studies point to social influence as the major factor in gender roles, the research of John Money inadvertently made clear the powerful impact of biological wiring. Dr. Money, a psychologist and former director of the now-defunct Gender Identity Clinic at Johns Hopkins Medical School, encouraged the parents of a boy (David) to rear him as a girl (Brenda) because of a botched circumcision that rendered the infant without a penis. Money argued that social mirrors dictate gender identity; thus, if the parents treated the child as a girl (name, dress, toys, etc.), the child would adopt the role of a girl and later that of a woman. The child was castrated, and sex reassignment began.

The experiment failed miserably. At the age of 14, the child was finally informed of his medical history and made the decision (after much distress and struggle) to reclaim his life as a male. Indeed, David reported that he had never felt like a girl (Colapinto, 2000). Although David did marry and was the adoptive father of two children, he later committed suicide.

FIGURE **5-1** ‖ **The Gender Unicorn**

The Gender Unicorn is a way to visualize the various aspects of one's gender identity, gender expression, sex assigned at birth, category of those to whom one is physically attracted, and the category of those to whom one is emotionally attracted. See The Gender Unicorn – Trans Student Educational Resources at www.transstudent.org/gender for more information.

Put a marker (e.g. dot) on the arrow line to indicate your reality.

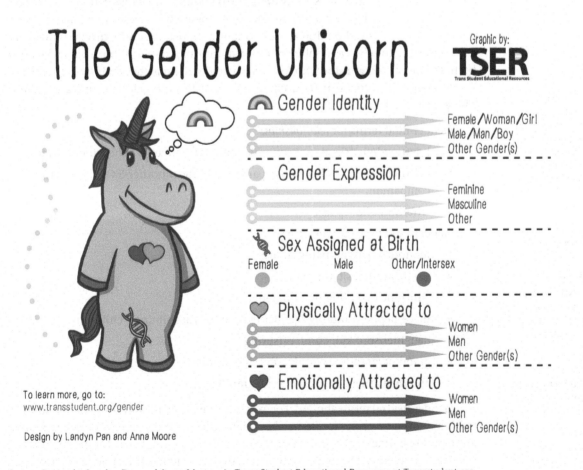

Source: Design by Landyn Pan and Anna Moore, via Trans Student Educational Resources at Transstudent.org. Reprinted with permission.

David's situation is at the heart of the scientific nature-versus-nurture debate as it relates to gender. In Dr. Money's early publications, written before David's suicide, David's situation was described as a textbook example of how nurture is the more important influence in gender identity, if a reassignment is done early enough.

Dr. Milton Diamond followed up on David's case and concluded that Money had falsified his data. After meeting David, Diamond wrote a paper in 1994 with Keith Sigmundson (who had been one of David's psychiatrists), revealing the discrepant outcome. Their paper (Diamond & Sigmundson, 1997), which was published 3 years later, challenged Money's articles and asserted that while nurture may influence a person's degree of masculinity or femininity, nature is the stronger force in forming gender identity and sexual orientation. Genetic influences on the brain and nervous system emphasize the neurobiological basis of sex and caution against early surgical intervention for infants with ambiguous genitals.

5.1c Gender Identity

Gender identity is the psychological state of viewing yourself as a specific gender. Such identity is largely learned and is a reflection of society's conceptions of gender and gender roles. Some individuals are **agender** in that they do not identify as having a gender identity. Still others are **gender fluid** in that they change conceptions of how they feel and how they view themselves (these variations may vary by the minute, week, month, or year). **Genderqueer** individuals can consider themselves as nonbinary (not feminine or masculine) but a varied blend of both. Persons are **cisgender** who feel that their identity matches their biological sex.

Gender-fluid terms can be used in reference to both relationships and family. These include (Dolan, 2019):

Gender-fluid terms for *relationships:*

- boyfriend/girlfriend (not serious): date, lover, sweetie, babe, cuddle buddy
- boyfriend/girlfriend (serious): partner, significant other/S.O., other half, companion,
- wife/husband: spouse

Gender-fluid terms for *family* are:

- mom/dad: parent, parental unit
- sister/brother: sibling, sib
- aunt/uncle: pibling (your parent's sibling)
- niece/nephew: nibling (gender neutral for your siblings' children)
- daughter/son: kid, child, offspring
- grandma/grandpa: grandparent, bibi or nini
- granddaughter/son: grandchild, grandkid

Gender-neutral terms abound. For example, the U.S. Food and Drug Administration (FDA) approved new rules for "female" condoms that not only change the device's name but ease some other strict regulations. Now called the "single-use internal condom," the device is approved for both vaginal and anal sex and has the same regulatory classification as the "male" condom.

Feminism isn't about hating men. It's about challenging the absurd gender distinctions that boys and girls learn from childhood and carry into their adult lives.

Robert Webb, English comedian

(Trevor Werb)

This gender fluid person notes that they never know which gender they are going to be upon awakening.

Gender identity
Psychological state of viewing yourself as a girl or a boy, and later as a woman or man, or in the case of genderqueer individuals, as a blend of the two

Agender
Individuals who do not identify as having a gender identity

Gender fluid
Individuals who change conceptions of how they feel and how they view themselves

Genderqueer
Individuals who consider themselves a blend of both feminine and masculine

Cisgender
Individuals who feel that their identity matches their biological sex

Individuals learn gender roles and gender expression from society. *Gender expression* is how you present yourself and may include external items, like your clothing and hairstyle.

While gender roles for children in the United States have become increasingly separate from a commercial standpoint, awareness of the issue has spurred some changes: Target® stores, for example, have removed offensive signage distinguishing "Building Toys" from "Girls' Building Toys." Early objectification of girls and gender-segregated aisles in toy stores remain the norm, offering a stereo-typed plethora of decorative pink products and an armory of automatic weapons. In addition, many girls' clothes are highly sexualized (Miller, 2015).

I am not male or female. I think I float somewhere in between.

Sam Smith, British singer

5.1d Transgender

The term **transgender** (also referred to as trans or gender variant or gender expansive) refers to individuals of one biological sex (female or male) who express behavior that is "different from cultural expectations based on the sex they were assigned at birth" (Human Rights Campaign, n.d.) and who identify with the other sex. Caitlyn Jenner brought nationwide visibility to the issue of transgender individuals in her *20/20* interview in 2015 with the announcement, "I have always thought of myself as more of a woman." Kattari et al. (2018) developed the Transgender Inclusive Behavior Scale (TIBS) to identify the degree to which individuals use language that does not reinforce the gender binary assumption and acknowledge cisgender (non-transgender) privilege. Hargie et al. (2017) noted that sports is a context when transgender individuals feel particularly excluded. **Transsexual** is an older term for the person who has had hormonal or surgical intervention to change their body to align with their gender identity. While still used as an identity label by some, the term transgender has become the term of choice by many organizations, while the term trans is often used by individuals.

(Shutterstock)

A transgender person identifies with being a particular sex and seeks to outwardly look like the person culturally identified as that sex.

Although The Williams Institute estimates that 0.58% of the US population is transgender, there are difficulties in determining an accurate percentage (Flores et al., 2016). The U.S. Census offers no option to self-identify as transgender. People who identify as transgender may currently be in a stage of transition, whether social or medical, or may choose not to publicly identify as transgender. See *Technology and Sexuality 5-1* for further discussion of transition. Some transgender people experience extreme *gender dysphoria*, or unhappiness with their biological sex. In one study, gender-dysphoric transgender men who had not had surgical interventions had the highest scores on body dislike/uneasiness (Bandini et al., 2013). Data on 1,093 male-to-female and female-to-male transgender people from another study revealed clinical depression (44.1%), anxiety (33.2%), and body complaints (27.5%) (Bockting et al., 2013). The source of these maladies was identified as social stigma, which was moderated by peer support. Klein & Golub (2016) noted that 42% of 3,458 self-identified transgender/gender nonconforming individuals reported having attempted suicide. Rejection by parents and misuse of drugs/alcohol increased the risk of an attempt. Sexual inactivity, particular for transfeminine individuals who have not had surgery, was found to be higher by Scheim and Bauer (2019).

Transgender
Term that refers to individuals of one biological sex (female or male) who identify with the other and express behavior that "is different from cultural expectations based on the sex they were assigned at birth"

Transsexual
An older term for a person who has had hormonal or surgical intervention to change their body to align with their gender identity

THINK ABOUT IT

Tamilin et al. (2017) reviewed the disqualification of Jenna Talackova from the Miss Universe Canada pageant in 2012 on the grounds that she was not a "naturally born" female. She had transitioned from male to female, contested her exclusion, and was allowed to compete. Her experience challenged the notion of womanhood along three themes—bodily markers (e.g. curves), legal markers (e.g. she was legally identified as female), and beauty markers (e.g. smooth skin). In 2018, Angela Ponce (transgender) competed as the Miss Universe Spain contestant. When do you think being a transgender contestant will no longer be unusual?

Simbar et al. (2018) studied 90 gender dysphoric individuals in various stages of transition, persons with no treatment, those with hormone therapy only, and those who had completed gender-affirming surgery. Those in the latter category reported the more positive body image and quality of life. In a study of 136 gender-sysphotic individuals who had had sex-reassignment surgery (also known as gender-affirming surgery), 94%–100%, depending on the surgery performed (e.g. genital, chest, facial, vocal cord and/or thyroid cartilage surgery), reported postoperative satisfaction; 6% reported dissatisfaction and/or regret (van de Grift et al. 2018).

Prevention models emphasize changing social structures, norms, and attitudes that produce minority stress for gender-variant people. *Self-Assessment 5-1* helps to identify the degree to which a person is transgender inclusive.

When a transgender person comes out, it impacts all interpersonal relationships, including those with sexual partners, families, and friends. Parents may struggle with the physical and psychological "loss" of their child. Wahlig (2015) noted this is ambiguous in that it is not clear-cut, as in the death of a child. The physical loss is to another gender, and the psychological loss is related to the ambiguity of their child's new identification with a different gender.

> *Your gender identity is about who you are, how you feel, the sex that you feel yourself to be. Sexual orientation is who you are attracted to.*
>
> Chaz Bono

As our society moves toward more tolerance, a variety of children's books on transgender concepts have emerged, such as *My Princess Boy, Jacob's New Dress,* and *When Kayla Was Kyle.* Search online for "transgender-friendly young children's books" for a list. These books provide a context of acceptance for whoever you are and enlighten parents in terms of the importance of accepting their transgender children. Per a survey of 3,458 self-identified transgender respondents, parental rejection triples the rate of transgender adolescent suicide (Klein & Golub, 2016), as in the tragic 2014 suicide of 17-year-old Leelah (birth name Joshua) Alcorn, who felt that she had always been a girl and could no longer tolerate her parents' rejection.

5.1e Gender Roles

Gender roles
Social norms that dictate culturally appropriate female and male behavior

Gender roles are behaviors people are expected to engage in. All societies have social norms that dictate how people should behave, based on their gender. In the United States, gender roles associated with being a "real man" include emotional control, self-reliance, being a "stud" or "player," a focus on winning, dominance over women, violence, risk taking, and disdain for homosexuals. In regard to sexuality, being a player, risk-taking, and a focus on winning are related to a higher number of sexual partners (Iwamoto et al., 2014).

Self-Assessment 5-1:
Transgender Inclusive Behavior Scale

Directions:

Using the following scale, how frequently do you participate in each of these behaviors?

Please circle: 1 (never), 2 (rarely), 3 (sometimes), and 4 (often), or 5 (always)

I ask for pronouns when I meet someone new.	1 2 3 4 5
I use gender-neutral language to refer to people whose pronouns I do not know.	1 2 3 4 5
I ensure spaces where I host/attend events offer gender-neutral bathrooms.	1 2 3 4 5
I use the terms "nontransgender" or "cisgender" to refer to people whose sex they were assigned at birth matches their current gender identity.	1 2 3 4 5
I have participated in discussions about the effects and/or benefits of cisgender or nontransgender privilege.	1 2 3 4 5
I share my pronouns when I introduce myself to someone new.	1 2 3 4 5
I have asked my friends, coworkers, and/or family members what their pronouns are.	1 2 3 4 5
I read books/blogs/articles by transgender women, transgender men, and gender nonconforming/nonbinary individuals.	1 2 3 4 5
I speak out against "womyn born womyn" or transgender-exclusive policies (such as those offered by certain "women's retreats" or "men's groups").	1 2 3 4 5
I initiate conversations about how my community can support transgender individuals.	1 2 3 4 5
I try to keep myself updated on ongoing conversations about acceptable language to use when referring to transgender individuals.	1 2 3 4 5
I work to educate myself on issues regarding transgender communities.	1 2 3 4 5
I am aware of local resources that offer support to transgender people.	1 2 3 4 5
I keep myself updated on whether employment policies in my state/city include transgender people.	1 2 3 4 5
I keep myself updated on whether housing policies in my state/city include transgender people.	1 2 3 4 5

Scoring:

Add the scores and divide by 15 to get your average. This is your TIBS score.

Interpretation:

Lower scores (15 is the lowest possible score) reflect less transgender-inclusive behavior and higher scores (75 is the highest possible score) reflect greater transgender-inclusive behavior. Forty-five is the midpoint between the lowest and highest scores.

Source: Shanna K. Kattari, et al, (2018). "Development and Validation of the Transgender Inclusive Behavior Scale (TIBS)," *Journal of Homosexuality*, 65(2). Copyright 2018 by Taylor & Francis Ltd., http://www.tandfonline.com. Reprinted by permission of the publisher and Dr. Kattari. Developed and validated by Shanna K. Kattari, PhD, MEd; Ashley A. O'Connor, MSW; Leonardo Kattari, MSW. Email Dr. Kattari at skattari@umich.edu for validation data.

Occupational sex segregation
Tendency for women and men to pursue different occupations

Sex roles
Roles filled by women or men that are defined by biological constraints and can be enacted by members of one biological sex only, such as wet nurse or sperm donor

In the United States and globally, gender roles for females generally include greater emotional response, prioritization of relationships, and greater allegiance to family and child care. Women have also been socialized to enter "female" occupations—such as elementary school teaching, day-care work, and nursing. Men are discouraged from entering "female" fields such as elementary education and may be stigmatized as gay if they do so (Moss-Racusin & Johnson, 2016). **Occupational sex segregation** reflects how people choose or drift into certain occupations and avoid others.

The term **sex roles** is often confused with and used interchangeably with the term *gender roles*. However, whereas gender roles are socially defined and can be enacted by either women or men, sex roles are defined by biological constraints and can be enacted by members of one biological sex only, as with wet nurse and sperm donor.

Technology and Sexuality 5-1: Transgender Options

Due to the increased media presence of transgender people, Americans are becoming more aware of transgender issues. However, many do not understand the issues that many transgender people face, including discrimination, violence, difficulty accessing health care, and making decisions about transitioning.

Transition is not a sex change operation, as many people believe it is, though it may include surgery. It is a process of changing so that the body, presentation, and how others view the person are more congruent with the person's gender identity. No two people have the same transition experience. While some may opt for surgery, others may not. Money, access to medical care, cultural environment, and perceived social support influence the transitioning experience. It is also important to emphasize that not everyone who identifies as transgender feels the need to transition.

The three types of transitioning are legal, social, and physical. Legal transition is obtaining documents like a driver's license or a birth certificate that accurately reflects a person's gender. In January 2019, New York City passed legislation allowing for a third option for gender on birth certificates. Other states—currently Oregon, Maine, Washington, New Jersey, and California—and Washington, DC, also allow for a nonbinary option on either birth certificates or driver's licenses. For many people living in these states and cities, the process of obtaining new documents may be made easier by being able to access information and forms online. Social transition for transgender people involves changing how they dress, using makeup (or not), selecting a new name, and using new gender-affirming pronouns to refer to themselves.

Physical transitioning may involve surgery and/or the use of hormones. Thanks to advances in technology and the surgical techniques that exist today, transgender people have more surgical options. They may opt to have breast removal or implants (known as "top" surgery), or genital surgery ("bottom" surgery). Possible feminizing surgeries may include vaginoplasty and labiaplasty, while possible masculinizing surgeries include phalloplasty or metoidioplasty. Metoidioplasty involves enlarging the clitoris with testosterone, with subsequent surgery on the clitoris and surrounding tissue to create a penis. While there have been some improvements in how these masculinizing surgeries are performed, they are still more likely to result in more complications than feminizing surgeries do (Selvaggi & Bellringer, 2011).

Other options include plastic surgery to change facial shape or a tracheal shave, which changes the size and appearance of the Adam's apple. Other surgeries can help adjust the vocal pitch, though speech therapy is recommended as a better option (Schneider & Courey, 2016).

Hormones can either be combined with surgery or utilized independently. While transgender people have been using hormones as adults for many years, the use of hormones to suppress pubertal changes is an option. In these situations, transgender children, in conjunction with their doctors and caregivers, consider whether to take "puberty blockers."

Sequelae from the use of these medications in children and adolescents, including permanent sterility, as well as long-term side effects, are a concern. Research on adults who went through hormonal pubertal suppression as adolescents has revealed positive emotional effects (de Vries et al., 2014), although the health risks are still under discussion (Humphries-Waa, 2014). Also, some studies show that a significant percentage of children's gender dysphoria does not persist into adulthood (Wallien & Cohen-Kettenis, 2008).

Whether it is peer support, hormonal treatments, surgical options, or information about trans-friendly health-care practitioners online, technology has helped the transgender community find resources and reinforcement.

5.1f Gender Role Ideology

Gender role ideology refers to the socially prescribed role relationships between people in society. These role relationship norms become important since they may have an impact on social scripts for a couple's behavior. Egalitarian social scripts are presumed to be more prevalent in contemporary society, but examples continue that suggest traditional roles are still prevalent. Shared power between partners is associated with relationship satisfaction in both heterosexual and gay relationships (Pollitt et al. 2018). Similarly, there is an emerging preference among both women and men for egalitarian relationships (Sells & Ganong, 2017). However, women in heterosexual relationships more often report that they feel subordinate in a relationship (Bay-Cheng et al., 2018). Heterosexual women, in general, are less aggressive in initiating sex than are lesbians (Gonzalez-Rivas et al., 2016) with their partners. However, heterosexual women still take the lead in moving the relationship toward commitment—having "the talk" (Nelms et al., 2012). *Self-Assessment 5-2: The Sexual Assertiveness Questionnaire,* provides a way to assess your comfort and style in relationships.

Gender role ideology
Socially prescribed role relationships between women and men in any given society

Self-Assessment 5-2:
Sexual Assertiveness Questionnaire

1. __ I feel uncomfortable telling my partner what feels good. (R)
2. __ I feel uncomfortable talking during sex. (R)
3. __ I am open with my partner about my sexual needs.
4. __ I let my partner know if I want to have sex.
5. __ I feel shy when it comes to sex.
6. — I approach my partner for sex when I desire.
7. __ I begin sex with my partner if I want to.
8. __ It is easy for me to discuss sex with my partner.
9. __ I refuse to have sex if I don't want to.
10. __ I find myself having sex when I do not really want it.
11. __ I give in and kiss if my partner pressures me, even if I already said no.
12. __ I have sex if my partner wants me to, even if I don't want to.
13. __ It is easy for me to say no if I don't want to have sex.
14. __ I would ask my partner about his or her risk of HIV.
15. __ I would ask my partner if he or she has had sex with someone who shoots drugs with needles.
16. __ I ask my partner if he or she has practiced safe sex with other partners.
17. __ I ask my partners about their sexual history.
18. __ I ask my partners whether they have ever had a sexually transmitted infection/disease.

Items 1 through 8 make up the communication about sexual initiation and satisfaction subscale; items 9 through 13 make up the refusal of unwanted sex subscale; items 14 through 18 make up the sexual history communication subscale. Participants indicated their level of endorsement for each item on a Likert-type scale that ranged from 1 (strongly disagree) to 7 (strongly agree). Higher scores reflected higher assertiveness. (Note: (R) = Item was reverse-coded.)

Source: Loshek, E., & Terrell, H. K. (2015). The development of the Sexual Assertiveness Questionnaire (SAQ): A comprehensive measure of sexual assertiveness for women. *Journal of Sex Research,* 52(9), 1017–1027, Taylor and Francis Ltd, http://www.tandfonline.com. Reprinted by permission of the publisher and Heather Terrell.

THINK ABOUT IT

Take a moment to answer the following question. Whereas traditional heterosexual relationships have reflected male dominance, homosexual relationships tend to be more equal, with greater gender role flexibility. When gender role ideology in homosexual relationships is assessed, lesbian relationships are more egalitarian and flexible than male relationships. How do you explain these differences?

I was more of a man as a woman than I've ever been as a man with a woman. I've just got to learn to do it without the dress.

Dustin Hoffman, in *Tootsie*

Nature, we are starting to realize, is every bit as important as nurture. Genetic influences, brain chemistry, and neurological development contribute strongly to who we are as children and what we become as adults.

Stanley Turecki, family psychiatrist

Increasingly, couples today are egalitarian.

Chromosomes
Threadlike structures of DNA within the cell nucleus that carry genes and transmit hereditary information

Disorders of sex development
An umbrella term that includes many different conditions that occur when "a less-common path of sex development is taken"

5.2 Biological Beginnings

The distinction between the sexes begins at the moment of fertilization, when the sperm and the egg unite to form a zygote. Both chromosomal and hormonal factors contribute to the development of the zygote.

5.2a Chromosomes

Chromosomes are threadlike structures located within the nucleus of every cell in the body. Each cell contains 23 pairs of chromosomes—a total of 46 chromosomes per cell. Chromosomes contain genes, the basic units of heredity, that determine not only such physical characteristics as eye color, hair color, and body type, but also predispositions for such characteristics as baldness, color blindness, and hemophilia. Within these 23 pairs of chromosomes are *sex chromosomes*, which play a role in determining an individual's physical characteristics. There are two types of sex chromosomes: X and Y. Normally, females have two X chromosomes, whereas males have one X and one Y chromosome. The human X chromosome contains about 3,000–4,000 genes and is 2–3 times longer than the Y chromosome.

When the egg and sperm meet in the fallopian tube, each contains only half the normal number of chromosomes (one from each of the 23 pairs). The union of sperm and egg results in a single cell called a *zygote*, which has the normal 46 chromosomes. The egg will always have an X chromosome, but the sperm will have either an X or Y chromosome. Because the sex chromosome in the egg is always X (the female chromosome), the sex chromosome in the sperm will determine the sex of a child. If the sperm contains an X chromosome, the match with the female chromosome will be XX, and the child will be genetically female. If the sperm contains a Y chromosome, the match with the female chromosome will be XY, and the child will be genetically male.

The fact that chromosomes control the biological sex of a child has enabled some parents to select the sex of their offspring. Whether or not this decision should be an option is discussed in *Social Policy 5-1*.

5.2b Disorders of Sex Development

Disorders of sex development (DSD) is an umbrella term that includes many different conditions that occur when "a less-common path of sex development is taken" (Consortium on the Management of Disorders of Sex Development, 2006). DSD includes nonstandard chromosomal development and ambiguous genitalia.

Social Policy 5-1

Selecting the Sex of an Unborn Child

In a survey of 598 undergraduates, if they could have only one child, 35% reported that they wanted a male, 23% wanted a female, and 42% "couldn't care less" about the child's sex. (Bragg et al. 2018). **Preconception sex selection**, also called **family balancing**, is a way to select the sex of a child. MicroSort® technology involves a sperm-sorting technique that identifies sperm cells that correspond to the desired sex. The pregnancy probability with the desired sex of child will vary according to the amount of motile cells and the sex selected. As of 2017, in terms of the number of babies of the desired sex born, MicroSort has been 93% effective for girls and 82% effective for boys. The Genetics and IVF Institute in Fairfax, Virginia, and Bethesda, Maryland, developed MicroSort®. Other providers such as The Fertility Institutes have offered sex selection but there is no FDA approval for any sex-selection technique.

Arguments for nonmedical sex selection via sperm sorting include an individual's right to choose the sex of their child because doing so harms neither the individual making the choice nor the child. Preconception sperm sorting avoids abortion of fetuses or destruction of embryos based on sex and results in positive outcomes for the child, since the child will be of the desired sex. In addition, people in child-rationed societies such as China may benefit, since female infanticide could be avoided.

Arguments against sperm sorting include the prediction that an imbalanced sex ratio will occur (fewer females), resulting in more men without female partners, which may lead to a loss of opportunity to have children, less church attendance, and more violence/wars. These arguments may not be valid, as researchers have found that in the larger society, "there is little evidence to suggest that there is a sex preference in industrialized countries. Instead, families that have a preference want to have children of both sexes" (Kalfoglou et al., 2013).

If preconception sex selection is not employed, a couple that wants a child of a particular sex can use amniocentesis to determine the sex of the fetus. Best performed in the 16th or 17th week of pregnancy, **amniocentesis** involves inserting a needle into the pregnant woman's uterus to withdraw fluid, which is then analyzed to determine if the cells carry XX or XY chromosomes.

Alternatively, chorionic villi sampling can be used to detect fetal sex as early as 8 weeks into gestation. Depending on the position of the fetus, an ultrasound may reveal the fetus's genital area; however, this is not considered a reliable test to determine a child's sex.

After use of one or more of these various tests, the parents may allow the fetus to develop if it is the biological sex that they desire. Otherwise, the fetus may be aborted. Such a decision is not widely practiced in the United States by either physicians or parents, but it does occur elsewhere. This process of selecting the child's sex through **prenatal sex selection** is highly controversial.

The strongest argument for prenatal sex selection is that it can prevent the birth of an infant with a serious or fatal sex-linked genetic disease. Another argument is that aborting a fetus of the "undesired sex" is less objectionable than killing the infant after it is born. The practice of female infanticide—the killing of female infants by drowning, strangling, or exposure—has been well-documented in Eastern countries, including China and India. It occurs because of the widespread cultural value placed on having male children.

In China, India, and many other Eastern countries, boys are seen as an asset because they provide labor in the fields and take care of elderly parents. Girls are considered economic liabilities because they require a dowry and then leave the family to care for their own husbands and children. Sex selection in the form of abortion of female fetuses continues to occur among South and East Asian immigrants.

Preconception sex selection
Selection of the sex of a child before it is conceived (See also *family balancing*)

Family balancing
Act of selecting the sex of a child before it is conceived, ostensibly for a "balanced" one boy/one girl family; involves separating sperm carrying the X and Y chromosomes

Amniocentesis
Prenatal test in which a needle is inserted (usually in the 16th or 17th week of pregnancy) into the pregnant woman's uterus to withdraw fluid that is analyzed to determine if the cells carry XX (female) or XY (male) chromosomes, and to identify chromosomal defects

Prenatal sex selection
Selection of whether to continue the pregnancy based on the sex of the fetus

5.2c Atypical Chromosomal Development

As we have seen, expected development in babies requires that the correct number of chromosomes be present in the developing fetus. In some instances, the fetus may exhibit atypical sexual development. For every sex chromosome from the mother (X), there must be a corresponding sex chromosome from the father (X or Y) for normal sexual development to occur. Atypical development is the result of too many or too few sex chromosomes. Either the father or the mother may contribute an abnormal or extra sex chromosome.

Two of the most common of these genetic conditions are Klinefelter syndrome and Turner syndrome. **Klinefelter syndrome** occurs in males and results from the presence of an extra X sex chromosome (XXY). The result is aberrant testicular development, infertility, and low interest in sex (low libido), and, in some cases, mental disability. Males with an extra X chromosome often experience language deficits, neuromaturational lag, academic difficulties, and psychological distress. Common characteristics also include abnormally long legs and lack of a deep voice and beard. The main therapy involves androgen replacement, which may help with muscle strength but does not restore fertility. This syndrome occurs in about 1 in 800 male births.

Turner syndrome occurs in females and results from the absence of an X chromosome (XO). It is characterized by abnormal ovarian development, failure to menstruate, infertility, and the lack of secondary sexual characteristics such as armpit and pubic hair. Turner syndrome is also associated with short stature, a short, webbed neck, and a predisposition to heart and kidney defects. It occurs with a frequency of about 1 in 25,000 girls. Treatment for Turner syndrome includes hormone replacement therapy to develop secondary sexual characteristics and the use of a biosynthetic human growth hormone to promote growth. Such treatment directs girls with Turner syndrome toward normal female development.

5.2d Fetal Hormones

Hormones are also important in the development of the fetus. Embryos are indistinguishable by genitalia during the first several weeks of intrauterine life (described as the *indifferent gonadal stage*). In expected fetal development, two primitive gonads and two paired duct systems form at about the fifth or sixth week of development. While the reproductive system of the male (epididymis, vas deferens, ejaculatory duct) develops from the Wolffian ducts and the female reproductive system (fallopian tubes, uterus, vagina) from the Mullerian ducts, both ducts are present in the developing embryo at this stage (see Figure 5-2).

If the embryo is genetically a male (XY), a chemical substance controlled by the Y chromosome (H-Y antigen) stimulates the primitive gonads to develop into testes. The development of a female requires that no additional testosterone be present (referred to as the *default pathway*). Without the controlling substance from the Y chromosome, the primitive gonads will develop into ovaries and the Mullerian duct system into fallopian tubes, uterus, and vagina; without testosterone, the Wolffian duct system will degenerate or become blind tubules. Differentiation of the female gonads begins at about the end of the eighth week and takes place over a longer period than in the male. In the female, the genital tubercle does not enlarge; it forms the clitoris. The urogenital sinus and urogenital folds differentiate into the vagina and the labia.

Klinefelter syndrome
Condition that occurs in males and results from the presence of an extra X sex chromosome (XXY), resulting in aberrant testicular development, infertility, low interest in sex (low libido), and, in some cases, mental disability

Turner syndrome
Condition that occurs in females resulting from the absence of an X chromosome (XO)

FIGURE **5-2** || **Sexual Differentiation of External Genitalia**

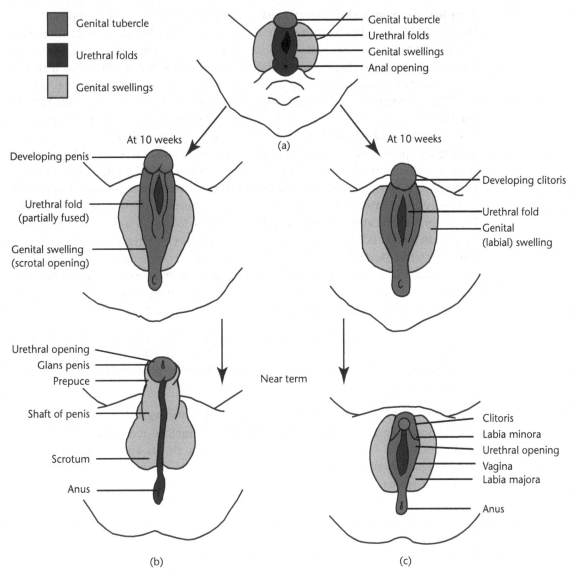

(a) Undifferentiated stage (7 weeks) (b) Male development (c) Female development

Although the infant's gonads (testes and ovaries) produce the sex hormones (testosterone and estrogen), these hormones are regulated by the pituitary gland, which is located at the base of the brain about 2 inches behind the eyes. The release of pituitary hormones, as it turns out, is controlled by additional hormones (also called *releasing factors*) from the hypothalamus, a part of the brain just above the pituitary. It is the hypothalamus that differs in males and females, in both the connections between cells and the size of various groups of cells. The presence of testosterone before birth stimulates not only the development of the male reproductive system but also, apparently, the development of the male hypothalamus. The female hypothalamus develops in the absence of testosterone.

5.2e Atypical Anatomical Development

Atypical anatomical development, also known as diverse sex development (dsd), (Roen, 2019), refers to congenital variations in the reproductive system, sometimes resulting in ambiguous genitals. The term intersex may be used to describe ambiguous genitalia. Even if the chromosomal makeup is XX or XY, too much or too little of a certain kind of hormone during gestation can cause variations in sex development.

When ambiguous genitals are detected at birth, parents and physicians face the decision of assigning either the male or female gender to the intersex infant. In the past, infants with ambiguous genitals were reared in the gender most closely approximating the appearance of a particular sex. Current guidelines recommend that, unless there is a genuine medical need, surgical alteration of a child's genitalia should not be performed. When the child is of age to realistically understand the risks and benefits of surgery and is capable of giving consent, then cosmetic surgeries may be performed. Finally, more education, therapeutic support, and follow-up are recommended for these individuals and their families. In the past, intersex children were not told of their intersex status. Davis & Wakefield (2017) surveyed 16 contemporary intersex youth who revealed they were not deeply troubled by their diagnosis and they were open with their peers and teachers. Dating as an intersex person is fraught with anxiety and rejection. One male shared his rejection experience (Frank, 2018):

> [...] girls most definitely aren't attracted to me. Well, not true ... initially they are, just not after they discover how I'm put together. Their reaction isn't just negative, it's, "I'm sorry, I have to go now!" And they do, hastily throwing on their clothes, never to be seen or heard from again.

Roen (2019) explicated the enormous complexity regarding the management of a person who is intersex. Such considerations include reducing the number of genital exams to help minimize their stigmatizing effects and lower anxiety, and engaging parents in programs to educate them prior to any surgical consent for their intersex offspring.

5.2f Pubertal Hormones

Marked changes in growth and maturation occur during puberty as a consequence of gonadal development and hormonal output (see Figure 5-3). In girls, increased estrogen and dihydrotestosterone (DHT) are responsible for changes in physique, while increased androgens are responsible for changes in boys. Although almost all tissues of the body are affected, the most notable changes are the maturation of the reproductive system and the development of secondary sexual characteristics. The timing of pubertal onset varies across individuals, but begins earlier for girls than for boys. *Menarche* (a girl's first menstruation) ranges in timing from 9.7 to 16.7 years, with a mean onset of 12.3 years. Puberty ends when reproductive capacity is established, with regular ovulatory and menstrual cycles for girls and high levels of sperm production and erectile function in boys.

Atypical anatomical development
Refers to congenital variations in the reproductive system, sometimes resulting in ambiguous genitalia

FIGURE **5-3** ‖ Effects of Hormones on Sexual Development During Puberty

The body's endocrine system produces hormones that trigger body changes in male and female youths.

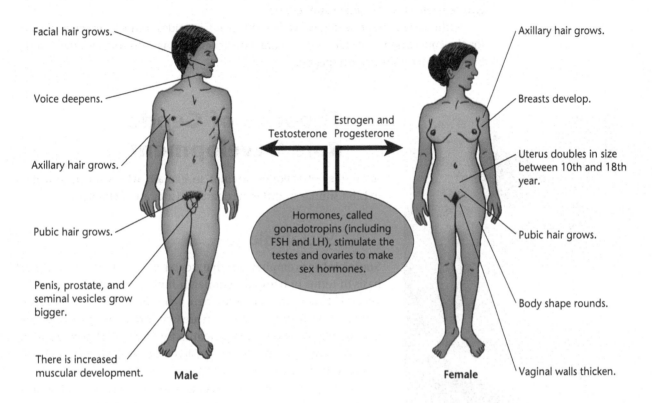

5.2g The Mosaic Brain

Over the past half century, most research on the connection between gender and the brain has focused on hormonal influence and anatomical differences between male and female brains to explain the disparities in male and female gender roles and treatment as largely the product of biology (Brizendine, 2006). But more recently, serious questions about the ethics and methodology of this orthodox "hardwired" male-versus-female brain research have been examined, resulting in a less sex-linked, more flexible view (Jordan-Young & Rumiati, 2012).

There's no such thing as a male or female brain. That's not to say there are no sex differences in the brain, but these differences are not uniformly different in any one individual.

Margaret McCarthy, neuroscientist

An international research team (Joel et al., 2015) conducted a comprehensive study based on MRIs (magnetic resonance images) of the brains of more than 1,400 male and female subjects. From their analysis of these data, supported by corresponding documentation of the interests, behavior, and personality traits of 5,500 male and female subjects, the researchers arrived at a more nuanced and complex assessment.

The previous sexual dimorphic model did not hold up against the new findings of extensive overlap in the characteristics of male and female gray matter, white matter, and neural connections. The study also found that brains with consistently "male" or "female" characteristics were rare; instead, most brains consist of what the researchers called a "mosaic," with variances observed within each gender and commonalities observed in both males and females.

These findings were corroborated by the study's personality analysis segment, which revealed that internal consistency per gender was "extremely rare." Based on these results, the research team concluded that the human brain cannot be regarded as two separate classes of male and female.

Although further research is needed, this study provides compelling scientific data for the conception of gender as a cultural construct, calling into further question the biological determinism perspective.

5.3 Theories of Gender Role Development

A number of theories attempt to explain why women and men exhibit similar or different characteristics and behaviors.

5.3a Sociobiology

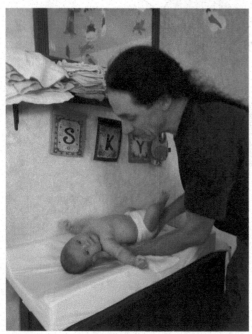

Men are increasingly challenging sociobiology and are involved in taking care of babies.

Sociobiology emphasizes that social behavior has a biological basis in terms of being functional in human evolution. The differences between women and men were functional for survival. Women stayed in the nest, nurtured children, and gathered food nearby, whereas men could go afar to find food. Such a conceptualization focuses on the division of labor between women and men as functional for the survival of the species.

Although there is little agreement (even among sociologists) on the merits of sociobiology, as well as the relevance of evolutionary roles to modern life, the theory emphasizes that biological differences (such as hormonal and chromosomal differences) between women and men account for the social and psychological differences in female and male characteristics, behaviors, and roles. For example, testosterone is a male hormone associated with aggression, and progesterone is a female hormone associated with nurturance. Such hormonal differences are used to partially explain that men have more sexual partners than women, are more likely to engage in casual sex, and are the perpetrators of most acts of sexual coercion as well as sexual harassment.

In the sociobiological model of mate selection, heterosexual men tend to seek and mate with women who are youthful and attractive. These characteristics are associated with fertility, health, and reproductive potential for women. Similarly, women tend to select and mate with men whom they deem will provide the maximum parental investment in their offspring. The term **parental investment** refers to any investment by a parent that increases the offspring's chance of surviving and thus increases reproductive success. Parental investments require time and energy. Women have a great deal of parental investment in their offspring (9 months' gestation, the physical energy and risks of childbirth, breastfeeding, and caretaking of dependent offspring) and tend to mate with men who have economic resources and are willing to share them. The pattern of men seeking physically attractive young women and women seeking economically ambitious men was found in 37 groups of women and men in 33 different societies (Buss, 1989).

Sociobiology
Framework in which social behavior is viewed as having a biological basis in terms of being functional in human evolution

Parental investment
Any investment by a parent that increases the offspring's chance of surviving and thus increases reproductive success

The sociobiological explanation for mate selection is controversial. Critics argue that women may show concern for the earning capacity of a potential mate because they have been systematically denied access to similar economic resources, and selecting a mate with these resources is one of their remaining options. In addition, it is argued that both women and men, when selecting a mate, think more about their partners as companions than as future parents of their offspring. Finally, the sociobiological perspective fails to acknowledge the degree to which social and psychological factors influence our behavior. It also fails to acknowledge anyone who does not identify as male or female.

> *I hope the 21st century sees an end to the nature-nurture argument. ... We need to move forward and investigate how nature and culture interact.*
>
> Helen Fisher, anthropologist

5.3b Social Learning Theory

Derived from the school of behavioral psychology, **social learning theory** emphasizes the role of reward and punishment in explaining how a child learns gender role behavior. For example, two young brothers who enjoyed playing "lady" put on dresses and high-heeled shoes, and carried pocketbooks. Their father came home early one day and angrily demanded they "take those clothes off and never put them on again! Those things are for women." The boys were punished for playing "lady," but rewarded with their father's approval for playing "cowboys," with plastic guns and "Bang! You're dead!" dialogue.

Reward and punishment alone are not sufficient to account for the way in which children learn gender roles. Direct instruction ("Girls wear dresses" and "Men walk on the outside when walking with a woman") is another way children learn through social interaction with others. The famous "Baby X" experiment of the 1970s, repeated in the 1980s, showed that adults who thought an infant was either male or female offered them only gender-specific toys (Seavey et al., 1975). From infancy, girl babies are held and spoken to in different ways than boys, and this gender typing continues throughout childhood, to powerful effect (Begley, 2009). In addition, many of society's gender rules are learned through modeling, in which the child observes another's behavior and imitates that behavior. Gender role models include parents, peers, siblings, and characters portrayed in the media.

> *Find out what a child will work for and will work to avoid, systematically manipulate these contingencies and you can change behavior.*
>
> Jack Turner, psychologist

The impact of modeling on the development of gender role behavior is controversial. For example, a modeling perspective implies that children will tend to imitate the parent of the same gender. However, though mainly women rear children in all cultures, this persistent female model does not seem to interfere with the male's development of the behavior that is considered appropriate for his gender. One explanation suggests that boys learn early that our society generally grants boys and men more status and privileges than girls and women; therefore, they devalue the feminine and emphasize the learning of masculine behavior.

5.3c Cognitive-Developmental Theory

The **cognitive-developmental theory** of gender role acquisition reflects a blend of biological and social learning views. According to this theory, biological readiness (in terms of the cognitive development of the child) influences how the child responds to gender cues in the environment (Kohlberg, 1966, 1976). For example, gender discrimination (the ability to identify social and psychological characteristics associated with being female and male) begins at about 30 months of age. At that age, toddlers are able

Social learning theory
Theory that emphasizes the role of reward and punishment in acquisition of gender role behavior

Cognitive-developmental theory
Theory that views gender role acquisition as based on both biology and social learning

to assign a "boy's toy" to a boy and a "girl's toy" to a girl. However, at this age, children do not view gender as a permanent characteristic. Thus, while young children may define people who wear long hair as girls and those who never wear dresses as boys, they also believe they can change their gender by altering their hair or changing clothes.

Not until age 6 or 7 does the child view gender as permanent (Kohlberg, 1966, 1969). In Kohlberg's view, this cognitive understanding is not a result of social learning. Rather, it involves the development of a specific mental ability to grasp the idea that certain basic characteristics of people do not change. When children learn the concept of gender permanence, they seek to become competent and proper members of their gender group. For example, a child standing on the edge of a school playground may observe one group of children jumping rope while another group is playing football. That child's gender identity as either a girl or a boy connects with the observed *gender-appropriate* behavior, and they join one of the two groups. Once in the group, the child seeks to develop the behaviors that are socially defined as appropriate for their gender.

5.4 **Agents of Gender Role Socialization**

Although biology may provide a basis for some roles (being 7 feet tall is helpful for becoming a basketball player), cultural influences in the form of various socialization agents (parents, peers, teachers, religion, and the media) shape the individual toward various gender roles. These powerful influences, in large part, dictate what people think, feel, and do in their gender roles.

5.4a **Parents**

The family may be the first gendered institution a child encounters, with female and male roles often highly structured by gender. The gendered world begins with the color of the nursery, names for children, the toys put in the crib, and the different ways people interact with boy and girl babies.

It continues as the children age. The sex talk parents give their daughters and sons is different, with daughters being encouraged to be more restrictive in providing sexual access and to be more abstinent than sons (Kuhle et al., 2015). But although adolescent males may be directed to cut the grass, and adolescent females to clean the kitchen, over the last few decades, mothers and fathers have been transitioning from modeling traditional gender roles toward co-parenting practices (Kwon et al., 2013). Hence, today's children are more likely to have exposure to egalitarian role models. However, in interviews with 60 parents who reported on the gender role socialization behavior of their adolescents, Blodgett et al. (2019) revealed that parental gender role attitudes may conflict with their socialization gender role behavior. For example, parents reported holding gender role attitudes but socialized their adolescents according to traditional gender norms (e.g. girls wash dishes, boys mow the lawn).

> *We've begun to raise daughters more like sons, ... but few have the courage to raise our sons more like our daughters.*
> Gloria Steinem

There is some question about how bisexual parents socialize their children in regard to gender. Flanders et al. (2019b) interviewed 25 nonmonosexual-minority women in different gender relationships about their parenting practices. Results revealed that the participants expressed an openness to deviating from gender norms in the socialization of their children by providing both same- and cross-gender opportunities, as well as in being open to the potential their children would identify as trans.

5.4b Peers and Partners

Although parents are usually the first socializing agents who influence a child's gender role development, peers become increasingly important during the school years. Researchers have confirmed that children influence one another's engagement in gender-typed activities (Martin et al., 2013).

Whereas boys are encouraged to restrict their emotional expression, female adolescents are under tremendous pressure to be trim, pretty, and popular rather than athletic, intelligent, or independent. In class, they speak less often than boys, receive less attention, and are called on less often by their teachers (Fass & Mason, 1995). Female adolescents are sometimes in great conflict, as high academic success may be viewed as being less than feminine.

Peer disapproval for failure to conform to traditional gender stereotypes can be a powerful force and is reflected in the terms *sissy* and *tomboy*. These terms are used pejoratively to refer to children who exhibit behaviors stereotypically associated with the other gender.

Partners are also influential as agents of female socialization. Based on survey data of 222 female undergraduates (plus a 90-minute focus group with 12 undergraduates), significant differences in body image emerged, with black women expressing greater insecurity about the shape of their buttocks and having breasts that were too large compared to white women. However, black women were significantly more likely to believe that they had sexier bodies than white women. Black males (according to black females) were also "more open to being like 'oh you have a fat ass' while white guys, like, will talk about it privately with their guy friends." Of "white guys," a black respondent said, "You can see them watching and talking about you and stuff, but they won't, like, say anything" (Hilliard et al. 2019a).

5.4c Teachers

Teachers are important influences on gender role development. They not only serve as models in the classroom, but the textbooks used in their courses provide images of gender roles. Modern textbooks present a continuum of gender identities, which include transformative gendered roles for women that are congruent with a wider scope of behavior for women and men, reflecting the reality of evolving gender roles throughout the Western world. In the United States and abroad, women work in prestigious and powerful positions as scientists, physicians, researchers, CEOs of major corporations, artists, entrepreneurs, and a host of other careers, and many have egalitarian husbands, some of whom keep to the domestic sphere, leaving the breadwinning role to their wives.

5.4d Religion

Religion developed to provide answers to questions about the meaning of birth, life, and death. Traditional Western religions are patriarchal—male dominance is indisputable in the hierarchy of both the dogma and the organizational structure, where power and status have been accorded mostly to men. Until recently, only men could be priests, ministers, and rabbis. The Catholic Church still prohibits females from serving as clergy, and men dominate the top positions in the U.S. dioceses.

Male bias is also reflected in the terminology used to refer to God in Jewish, Christian, and Islamic religions. For example, God is traditionally referred to as *He, Father, Lord*, and *King*.

Evangelical and fundamentalist religious groups endorse a set of rigid beliefs about gender roles, insisting that a woman's place is in the home (Lazo & Cole, 2014). Religiosity in general is also associated with "benevolent" sexism toward women—the belief that women are to be protected and cared for (Mikolajczak & Pietrzak, 2014).

5.4e Media

Media—such as movies, videos, television, magazines, newspapers, books, and music—both reflects and shapes gender roles. Media images of women and men typically conform to traditional, misogynistic gender stereotypes, and media portrayals depicting the exploitation, victimization, and sexual objectification of women are common. For example, Kirsch and Murnen (2015) examined media messages of seven popular American children's TV programs. The most common theme was boys objectifying and valuing girls solely for their appearance, and girls engaging in self-objectification and the ego-stroking of boys. In regard to movies, a content analysis of 2,000 screenplays revealed that 60% of the dialogue was written for men (Anderson & Daniels, 2016). As for music, a qualitative analysis of lyrics of 30 popular songs revealed a view of women as being childlike, a possession of men, and valuable only for their physical characteristics (Jasper, 2015).

Radio and blogs also provide information about gender. Radio personality/blogger August McLaughlin (2015) emphasized three myths about female sexuality that have been debunked by recent research. These myths are that women rarely orgasm (indeed, most do), that they have their sexual peak in their 30s (positive attitudes toward sexuality are associated with an active libido into the 40s, 50s, and beyond), and that they are not as visual as men in regard to sexual arousal (the porn industry survives on the male dollar, but women can also be aroused visually).

However, the media also allows the opportunity to expose people to different ideas about gender. Commercials are challenging what it means to "run like a girl." Some TV shows and movies depict women in positions of power, either in the corporate world or in government. And in a sign of increasing mainstream acceptance of transgender topics, the critically acclaimed Amazon TV series *Transparent* won four Emmy awards in 2016.

5.5 Effects of Gender Role Socialization on Sexuality

Gender role socialization influences virtually every sphere of life, including self-concept, educational achievement, occupation, income, and health. People learn their gender roles from the society and culture in which they are socialized. They also learn values, such as **sexism**, which is prejudice and discrimination based on sex. In the following sections, we look at gender roles in other societies as well as the effects of traditional gender role socialization on women and men in the United States.

5.5a Female Sexuality

Women differ from men in regard to relationships and sexuality in a number of ways.

1. *Importance of relationship involvement and commitment, and body image*: Females are socialized to be involved in a committed romantic relationship as the context for their personal happiness and sexual fulfillment. When they are not, they are more likely to feel stigmatized (Fulle et al., 2016) and

Sexism
Prejudice and discrimination, typically against women, on the basis of sex

depressed (Whitton et al., 2013). Regarding body image, beauty pageants for children emphasize the degree to which very young girls are socialized to focus on beauty and appearance for approval. A look at the cover of women's magazines (such as *Women's Health* and *Cosmopolitan*) begs the question, "Are these body images healthy or realistic?" These powerful stereotypes have a negative effect on body image in the many women who do not match the cultural ideal. In a study of 63 undergraduate females, researchers found that women held conflicting beliefs about the body they would like to have and the body they actually had. The result was depression and anxiety (Heron & Smyth, 2013). Body dissatisfaction among females occurs not only during the college years; it also persists from childhood throughout the adult lifespan (Runfola et al., 2013). It affects sexuality, as women with a positive body image are more likely to report positive sexual functioning in terms of sexual desire, arousal, lubrication, orgasm, and satisfaction (Erbil, 2013).

2. *Masturbation*: In a national sample of 5,865 adults between the ages of 20 and 29 living in the United States, 68% of the women, compared to 84% of the men, reported having masturbated in the past year (Reece et al., 2012). While traditional female socialization has taught women that it is "dirty" to touch themselves "down there," contemporary cultural messages indicate that women are responsible for their sexual pleasure and that masturbation is normative among their female peers. Many women have a vibrator in the bedside cabinet.

3. *Expressing love:* In heterosexual relationships, women are significantly more likely than men to tell their partners that they love them (Williams & Russell, 2013).

4. *Sexual thoughts*: Based on a national sample, women are much less preoccupied with sex than men. Nineteen percent of women, in contrast to 54% of men, reported thinking about sex every day or several times a day (Michael et al., 1994).

5. *Orgasm*: Women are less likely than men to experience orgasm. This is particularly true at first intercourse. Seven percent of women, in contrast to 79% of men, reported orgasm during their first intercourse experience (Sprecher et al., 1995). Lower orgasmic frequency is related not only to sexual technique (less contact with the clitoris), but also to traditional female role socialization in heterosexual relationships—women are expected to be more attentive to their partner's sexual enjoyment and pleasure than their own.

6. *Number of partners*: Women report having fewer sexual partners than men. In a British national probability survey, women reported 7 lifetime sexual partners (men, 14) (Mitchell, et al. (2019). Traditional female role socialization teaches women to limit the number of sexual partners so they will not be perceived as being "loose" or immoral. In addition, men may report higher numbers to reflect their masculinity.

7. *Sexual assertiveness*: Women who are sexually assertive initiate and communicate about the sex they desire ("I feel comfortable telling my partner what feels good"), refuse unwanted sex ("I refuse to have sex if I don't want to"), and communicate with their partners about sexual history and risk ("I ask my partner if he or she has practiced safe sex with other partners") (Loshek & Terrell, 2015). Kettrey (2018) noted that women who are high on sexual agency (assertive) report a more positive sexual experience. Traditional gender roles may be associated with lower assertiveness.

8. *Other sexual differences*: Table 5-1 reveals several additional differences between women and men, including that women are less likely to report that they are hedonistic about sex, less likely to have hooked up, more likely to have been cheated on, more likely to have been stalked, and more likely to have been pressured to have sex by a person they were dating.

> *I don't think boys, in general, watch the emotional world of relationships as closely as girls do. Girls track that world all day long, like watching the weather.*
>
> Carol Gilligan, gender researcher

TABLE 5-1 | Differences in Reported Sexual Behavior Between Undergraduate Females and Males (N = 13,070)

	Female (10,002)	Male (3,068)
"I am a hedonist."	23%	32%
"I have hooked up or had sex the first night I met someone."	25%	35%
"A romantic partner cheated on me."	55%	51%
"I have been stalked."	28%	19%
"I have been pressured to have sex by a person I was dating."	39%	21%

Data source: Hall, S., & Knox, D. (2019). [Relationship and sexual behaviors of a sample of 13,070 university students.] Unpublished raw data, Ball State University, Muncie, IN, and East Carolina University, Greenville, NC.

5.5b Male Sexuality

Male sexuality differs from female sexuality in a number of ways, including a reverse of the findings for women identified above. These differences indicate that men are less likely to value being in a committed relationship, more likely to masturbate, less likely to say "I love you," more likely to report thinking about sex, more likely to orgasm, and more likely to report a higher number of sexual partners than women. Fulle and colleagues (2016) also observed that men were less likely to feel remorse or regret following a hookup. In a review of 30 sex surveys around the world, significant differences were observed between men and women in both sexual desire and sexual behavior (Hakim, 2015).

In addition, undergraduate males are more likely to report being hedonistic, having hooked up, cheated, stalked a partner, and pressured a dating partner to have sex. Indeed Karioris & Allan (2019) noted that men and sexuality are usually discussed in the negative—it is men who rape, are violent, have ideas of entitlement, hire sex workers, consume pornography. There is little to no discussion of a "sex positive" vision of males.

Men and women are also held to different sexual standards. The *double standard* encompasses one set of rules for men and another for women. Men who have a high number of sexual partners are viewed with more approval than women who have a high number of sexual partners. Terms such as *whore* and *slut* are specific to women. Having a high number of penetrative sex partners is also associated with higher self-esteem in men, but not in women (Maas & Lefkowitz, 2015). Men also report more sexual pleasure and positive affect from casual sex than women (Woerner and Abbey, 2017).

5.6 **Gender Role Changes**

Imagine a society in which people develop characteristics, lifestyles, and values that are independent of gender role stereotypes. Characteristics such as strength, independence, logical thinking, and sexual aggressiveness are no longer associated solely with maleness, just as sexual passivity, dependence, emotions, intuitiveness, and nurturance are no longer associated solely with femaleness. All genders are considered equal: Anyone may pursue any occupational, political, and domestic role. Some gender scholars have suggested that people in such a society would be neither feminine nor masculine, but would be described as androgynous.

The next sections discuss androgyny, gender role transcendence, and gender postmodernism.

5.6a Androgyny

Androgyny is a blend of traits that are stereotypically associated with masculinity and femininity. Singer/songwriter Lady Gaga is androgynous: Sometimes she appears publicly as a woman and other times as a man.

Other androgynous celebrities include David Bowie, Boy George, Patti Smith, and Annie Lennox. The following explains the two forms of androgyny:

1. *Physiological androgyny* refers to intersexed individuals, discussed earlier in the chapter. The genitals are neither clearly male nor female, and there is a mixing of female and male chromosomes and hormones.

2. *Behavioral androgyny* refers to the blending or reversal of traditional male and female behavior, so that a biological male may be very passive, gentle, and nurturing, and a biological female may be very assertive, rough, and selfish.

Androgyny may also imply flexibility of traits; for example, an androgynous individual may be emotional in one situation, logical in another, assertive in another, and so forth. Gender role identity (androgyny, masculinity, femininity) was assessed in a sample of Korean and American college students, with androgyny emerging as the largest proportion in the American sample and the femininity group in the Korean sample (Shin et al., 2010). In one study, the gender roles (masculine, feminine, androgynous, undifferentiated) of 434 undergraduates were predominately two types: androgynous and undifferentiated. Of these, the androgynous group had the highest self-esteem and used positive coping strategies—for example, exercise rather than drinking (Xishan et al., 2012).

5.6b **Gender Role Transcendence**

Beyond the concept of androgyny is that of gender role transcendence. We associate many aspects of our world—including colors, foods, social and occupational roles, and personality traits—with either masculinity or femininity. The concept of **gender role transcendence** means abandoning gender frameworks (becoming *gender aschematic*), so that personality traits, social and occupational roles, and other aspects of life are independent from traditional gender categories. Transcendence is not equal for women and men. Although females are becoming more masculine—in part because our society values whatever is masculine—men are not becoming more feminine. Indeed, adolescent boys may be described as very gender-entrenched.

Androgyny
Having traits stereotypically associated with both masculinity and femininity

Gender role transcendence
Abandonment of gender schema, or becoming gender aschematic, so that personality traits, social and occupational roles, and other aspects of life are independent from gender categories

5.6c Gender Postmodernism

Beyond gender role transcendence is **gender postmodernism**, which abandons the notion of gender as natural and emphasizes that gender is socially constructed. More than 15 years ago, Monro (2000) noted that people in the postmodern society would no longer be categorized as male or female, but would be recognized as capable of many identities—"a third sex" (p. 37). A new conceptualization of trans people calls for new social structures "based on the principles of equality, diversity, and the right to self determination" (p. 42). No longer would our society telegraph transphobia or misogyny; instead, it would embrace pluralization "as an indication of social evolution, allowing greater choice and means of self-expression concerning gender" (p. 42).

There is some evidence that societies are changing globally. In Juchitán in Mexico, Thailand and Burma in Southeast Asia, and Samoa in Polynesia, there is tolerance for gender variance and cross-gender behavior (Coleman & Allen, 2014). The socialization of arbitrary gender attitudes and behaviors is subtle yet profound, exerting powerful influence from infancy—even in something as ephemeral as color. Researchers have provided evidence of the effect of manipulating color on toy preference. Infant and toddler males ages 20–48 months tended to avoid pink toys. The researchers predict that in the absence of gender color-coded toys, infants and children would become more equal in their toy selection (Wong & Hines, 2015). In the 19th and early 20th centuries, pink was considered a masculine color. The Pink and Blue project emphasizes the extent of culturally embedded color preference in our society (see website link at end of chapter).

Gender postmodernism
Abandonment of the notion of gender as natural and recognition that gender is socially constructed; dissolution of male and female categories as currently conceptualized in Western capitalist society

Chapter Summary

Terminology

SEX REFERS TO THE BIOLOGICAL DISTINCTION between females and males, whereas *gender* refers to the social and psychological characteristics often associated with being female or male. For example, characteristics typically associated with the female gender include gentleness, emotionality, and cooperation. Characteristics associated with the male gender include aggression, rationality, and competitiveness. Other terms related to sex and gender include *gender identity, gender expression, transgender, gender role,* and *gender role ideology.*

Biological Beginnings

THE BIOLOGICAL SEX OF AN INDIVIDUAL is determined by chromosomes, gonads, internal sex organs, and external genitals.

Chromosomal abnormalities and fetal hormones have significant physical and psychological outcomes for the individual. Individuals may also be intersex, which suggests that males and females exist on a continuum with the possibility of having characteristics of both.

Theories of Gender Role Development

SOCIOBIOLOGY EMPHASIZES biological sources of social behavior, such as sexual aggression on the part of males due to higher levels of testosterone. Social learning theory discusses how children are rewarded and punished for expressing various gender role behaviors. Cognitive-developmental theorists are concerned with the developmental ages at which children are capable of learning social roles.

Agents of Gender Role Socialization

PARENTS, PEERS, TEACHERS/EDUCATIONAL MATERIALS, RELIGION, AND THE MEDIA often project and encourage traditional gender roles for women and men. The cumulative effect is the perpetuation of gender stereotypes. Each agent of socialization reinforces gender roles that are learned from other agents of socialization, thereby creating a gender role system that is deeply embedded in our culture.

Effects of Gender Role Socialization on Relationships and Sexuality

FEMALE GENDER ROLE SOCIALIZATION usually results in the desire for relationship commitment, a negative body image, lower frequency of masturbation, greater comfort in expressing love, lower frequency of sexual thoughts, less frequent orgasms, fewer sexual partners than males, and sexual passiveness. In contrast, men are less likely to value being in a committed relationship, more likely to masturbate, less likely to say "I love you," more likely to report thinking about sex, more likely to orgasm, and more likely to report a higher number of sexual partners than women.

Gender Role Changes

ANDROGYNY **REFERS TO** a blend of traits that are stereotypically associated with masculinity and femininity. Androgyny may also imply flexibility of traits and is associated with high self-esteem. Gender role transcendence involves abandoning gender frameworks to live and look at phenomena independent of traditional gender categories. Gender postmodernism predicts a new era in which people are no longer characterized as male or female, but will be recognized as capable of many characteristics and identities.

Web Links

Differences in Men and Women

http://bvtlab.com/96898

GLAAD Media Reference Guide: Transgender

http://www.glaad.org/reference/transgender

Genetics and IVF Institute

http://www.givf.com/contactus/index.shtml

Intersex Initiative

http://www.intersexinitiative.org

MicroSort®

http://www.microsort.com/

Intersex Society of North America: "North American Task Force on Intersex Formed"

http://www.isna.org/node/153

Pink and Blue Project

http://www.jeongmeeyoon.com/aw_pinkblue.htm

The United Kingdom Intersex Association

http://www.ukia.co.uk/

Key Terms

Agender **110**

Amniocentesis **117**

Androgyny **129**

Atypical anatomical development **120**

Chromosomes **116**

Cisgender **110**

Cognitive-developmental theory **123**

Disorders of sex development **116**

Family balancing **117**

Gender **108**

Gender binary **108**

Gender fluid **110**

Gender identity **110**

Gender postmodernism **130**

Genderqueer **110**

Gender role ideology **115**

Gender roles **112**

Gender role transcendence **129**

Klinefelter syndrome **118**

Occupational sex segregation **114**

Parental investment **122**

Preconception sex selection **117**

Prenatal sex selection **117**

Primary sex characteristics **108**

Sex **108**

Sexism **126**

Sex roles **114**

Social learning theory **123**

Sociobiology **122**

Transgender **111**

Transsexual **111**

Turner syndrome **118**

CHAPTER

6

Love and Sexuality

Love and sex do indeed go together.

Edward O. Wilson, biologist

Chapter Outline

6.1 Ways of Viewing Love 136
6.1a Love on a Continuum from Romanticism to Realism 136
Self-Assessment 6-1: The Love Attitudes Scale 137
6.1b Three Elements of Love 138
6.1c Love Languages 139

6.2 Love Styles 140
Technology and Sexuality 6-1: Technology and Romantic Relationships 140
6.2a Love and Sex: Similarities and Differences 141
Personal Decisions 6-1 Sex With or Without Love 143

6.3 Contexts for Sex and Love 143
6.3a Hooking Up 143
6.3b Friends with Benefits 145

6.4 Polyamory and Open Relationships 146
Social Policy 6-1 Love in the Workplace 147
6.4a Advantages and Disadvantages of Polyamory 149
6.4b Rules of an Open Relationship 150

6.4c Consensually Non-Monogamous Relationships 151
Self-Assessment 6-2: Consensual Non-Monogamy Scale 152

6.5 Factors Involved in Selecting a Long-Term Partner 153
6.5a Cultural Factors in Selecting a Partner 153
6.5b Sociological Forces in Selecting a Partner: Homogamy 153
6.5c Psychological Factors in Selecting a Partner 154

6.6 Challenges Related to Intimate Sexual Relationships 155
6.6a Jealousy 155
6.6b Guilt 156
6.6c Obsession 156
6.6d Stalking 157
6.6e Romantic Breakup—Change in Sexual Values 158

Web Links 160
Key Terms 160

Objectives

1. Differentiate between the family of origin and the family of procreation
2. Explain the differences between romanticism and realism
3. List the three central elements of love
4. Review the various love styles
5. Know the similarities and differences of love and sex
6. Identify the latest research on hooking up and on friends with benefits
7. Discuss the impact of technology on love relationships
8. Identify the cultural, sociological, and psychological factors involved in finding a partner
9. Explain polyamory and the advantages and disadvantages associated with it
10. List the various challenges related to intimate relationships

Truth — OR — Fiction?

T / F 1. Couples who have first intercourse as friends are likely to transition to a romantic relationship.

T / F 2. Couples who have the same "love language" report higher relationship satisfaction than couples who do not.

T / F 3. Monogamous couples report significantly higher relationship quality than polyamorous couples/"open" couples.

T / F 4. Sex in casual relationships is associated with decreases in emotional health.

T / F 5. Developing an emotional relationship with a robot is possible.

Answers: 1. T 2. F 3. F 4. T 5. T

The above photo is of locks that lovers in Paris have secured on a bridge over the Seine river. They have thrown the keys into the river to symbolize they are locked in love forever. The drive to love and to be loved is fundamental to human existence. Sex is also a core element of life. It is the basis of our existence, where we came from in terms of our **family of origin** (the family in which we were born and reared), and where we are going in terms of our **family of procreation** (the family we begin, which provides the context for having our own children, if desired). One of the contexts in which sex occurs is love—the context most individuals report as being the most fulfilling. Indeed, love

Family of origin
Family into which an individual is born

Family of procreation
Family you begin by finding a mate and having and rearing children

"Lift your hips for me, love."

Tahereh Mafi, *Ignite Me*

(Trevor Werb)

While lovers do not always view love in the same way, most undergraduates view love in terms of romance and companionship.

is the top reason for engaging in partnered sex, as identified by a nationally representative study of Americans between the ages of 14 and 94 (Collazo & Barnhart, 2014). Additionally, the greater the emotional involvement of a couple, the more likely they are to have engaged in all forms of sex—kissing, touching, oral, and penetrative sex (Lefkowitz & Wesche, 2014). Finally, there is an urgency in falling in love. One-third of 5,509 Match.com (2017) respondents reported that they expected to feel romantic chemistry on the first date. We begin this chapter by reviewing the various ways love is conceptualized.

6.1 Ways of Viewing Love

Ask your friends or peers in your sexuality class to identify the characteristics of love. You will hear such words as *caring, commitment, trust, companionship, affection, happiness,* and *security.* The most notable characteristic of love is diversity—people have different conceptions of love, identify different elements associated with love, and categorize love as representing different styles. Lomas (2018) regarded love as a polysemous concept and examined its nature and presence across the world's cultures reflected in published and internet sources. He found 609 words associated with "love," which he grouped into 14 categories representing 14 "flavours" of love. Examples included familial love, passionate love (sensual/physical desire), compassionate love, possessive love, and star-crossed love. Emotional expression also differs by gender and sexual orientation, with gay men tending to the highest expression of "soft" emotions and heterosexual men the lowest level of such expression (Zeigler & Muscarella, 2019).

I don't want to live—I want to love first, and live incidentally.

Zelda Fitzgerald

6.1a Love on a Continuum from Romanticism to Realism

Romantic love today may be conceptualized as existing on a continuum from romanticism to realism. Romantics believe in love at first sight, in one true love, and in the idea that love conquers all. Realists disagree with all these beliefs. Realists believe that love takes time to develop, that there are numerous people with whom you may fall in love, and that love does not conquer all. *Self-Assessment 6-1: The Love Attitudes Scale* provides a way for you to assess where you fall on the continuum from romanticism to realism.

THINK ABOUT IT

Take a moment to answer the following questions. Do you and your partner tend to be romantics or realists? Is it important that you agree on your view of love? Can a romantic and a realist live happily ever after?

Self-Assessment 6-1: The Love Attitudes Scale

This scale is designed to assess the degree to which you are romantic or realistic in your attitudes toward love. There are no right or wrong answers.

Directions

After reading each sentence carefully, write the number that best represents the degree to which you agree or disagree with the sentence.

1 (Strongly agree), 2 (Mildly agree), 3 (Undecided), 4 (Mildly disagree), 5 (Strongly disagree)

1. ___ Love doesn't make sense. It just is.

2. ___ When you fall "head over heels" in love, it's sure to be the real thing.

3. ___ To be in love with someone you would like to marry but can't is a tragedy.

4. ___ When love hits, you know it.

5. ___ Common interests are really unimportant. As long as each of you is truly in love, you will adjust.

6. ___ It doesn't matter if you marry after you have known your partner for only a short time, as long as you know you are in love.

7. ___ If you are going to love a person, you will know after a short time.

8. ___ As long as two people love each other, the educational differences they have really do not matter.

9. ___ You can love someone even though you do not like any of that person's friends.

10. ___ When you are in love, you are usually in a daze.

11. ___ "Love at first sight" is often the deepest and most enduring type of love.

12. ___ When you are in love, it really does not matter what your partner does because you will love him or her anyway.

13. ___ As long as you really love a person, you will be able to solve the problems you have with the person.

14. ___ Usually you can really love and be happy with only one or two people in the world.

15. ___ Regardless of other factors, truly loving a person is a good enough reason to marry that person.

16. ___ It is necessary to be in love with the one you marry to be happy.

17. ___ Love is more of a feeling than a relationship.

18. ___ People should not get married unless they are in love.

19. __ Most people truly love only once during their lives.

20. __ Somewhere there is an ideal mate for most people.

21. __ In most cases, you will "know it" when you meet the right partner.

22. __ Jealousy usually varies directly with love; that is, the more you are in love, the greater your tendency to become jealous will be.

23. __ When you are in love, you are motivated by what you feel rather than by what you think.

24. __ Love is best described as an exciting rather than a calm thing.

25. __ Most divorces probably result from falling out of love rather than failing to adjust.

26. __ When you are in love, your judgment is usually not too clear.

27. __ Love comes only once in a lifetime.

28. __ Love is often a violent and uncontrollable emotion.

29. __ When selecting a marriage partner, differences in social class and religion are of small importance compared with love.

30. __ No matter what anyone says, love cannot be understood.

Scoring

Add the numbers you wrote down: 1 (strongly agree) is the most romantic response, and 5 (strongly disagree) is the most realistic response. The lower your total score (30 is the lowest possible score), the more romantic your attitudes toward love. The higher your total score (150 is the highest possible score), the more realistic your attitudes toward love. A score of 90 places you at the midpoint between being an extreme romantic and an extreme realist. Both men and women undergraduates typically score above 90, with men scoring closer to 90 than women.

Source: Knox, D. (1970). Conceptions of love at three developmental levels. *The Family Coordinator, 19*(2), 151–157. Permission to use the scale for research is granted from David Knox.

I fell in love the way you fall asleep: slowly, then all at once.

John Green, *The Fault in Our Stars*

6.1b Three Elements of Love

Robert Sternberg (1986) identified several states of love on the basis of the presence or absence of three elements: intimacy, passion, and commitment. Sternberg defined the following three elements in his triangular theory of love:

- Intimacy: emotional connectedness
- Passion: romantic feelings and physical sexual desire
- Commitment: desire to maintain the relationship

According to Sternberg (1986), various types of love can be described on the basis of the three elements he identified:

1. *Nonlove:* absence of all three components
2. *Liking:* intimacy without passion or commitment
3. *Infatuation:* passion without intimacy or commitment
4. *Romantic love:* intimacy and passion without commitment
5. *Companionate love:* intimacy and commitment without passion

6. *Fatuous love:* passion and commitment without intimacy

7. *Empty love:* commitment without passion or intimacy

8. *Consummate love:* combination of intimacy, passion, and commitment

Sternberg's love types might also be viewed as stages. As individuals change, their relationship changes. For example, what begins as *liking* may develop into *companionate love* over time. Some individuals report that they fall in love "at first sight." Zsok et al. (2017) found that love at first sight is not love, intimacy, or commitment but a strong attraction that some may label as love.

Love is the only disease that makes you feel better.

Sam Shepard, playwright

6.1c Love Languages

Gary Chapman's (2010) five love languages have become part of American love culture. These five languages are gifts, quality time, words of affirmation, acts of service, and physical touch. Chapman encourages individuals to use the language of love most desired by the partner rather than the one preferred by the individual providing the love. Bland and McQueen (2018) studied the love languages in 100 couples and found that congruent love languages between the partners was associated with their reporting less distress in their relationship. In a previous study, Bunt and Hazelwood (2017) compared love languages in 67 heterosexual couples and found that 61% had the same primary love language. However, there was no significant relationship between having the same love language and reported relationship satisfaction. Rather it was the self-regulation, the adaptability in adjusting to the different perceptions, particularly for women, that was associated with relationship satisfaction. Finally, having a mutual love language of quality time was positively related to relationship satisfaction

(Chelsea Curry Edwards)

This couple reflect three of the love languages: quality time, words of affirmation, and physical touch.

and commitment. Having a love language of receiving gifts was negatively associated with low relationship satisfaction and commitment. Hence, enjoying spending time with one's partner not the gifts one's partner provides is associated with positive relationship outcomes (Taff & Limke-McLean, 2019).

Cultural Diversity

Love in the West and love in the East differ. Those in individualistic America tend to be more romantic, expect love to be present before marriage, and believe that love continues as a prerequisite for staying together. Those in familistic Eastern countries (China, India, Indonesia) tend to be more realistic in their view of love, expect love to follow rather than precede marriage, and do not require love to continue for the couple to stay together. Love between partners in Western society is considered a criterion for marital success (Turetsky et al., 2014). The result is that Western societies (including the United States) have a very high divorce rate (40%–50%) compared to Eastern societies, which have very low divorce rates (under 10%).

Being romantic about love is also more likely among American undergraduates than Icelandic undergraduates. In a comparison of data from the respective countries, not only were Americans more likely to have experienced love at first sight, but they were also more willing to marry within a short time after meeting the person if they were in love (Freysteinsdóttir et al., 2014).

6.2 **Love Styles**

Hendrick and Hendrick (1992) described and studied another schema for looking at types of love relationships or orientations toward love, based on a theory of Canadian sociologist John Alan Lee. Although people may show characteristics of more than one love style, they are often characterized as exhibiting one of six different love styles:

- *Eros:* passionate love; not limited to physical passion
- *Ludus:* game-playing love—for mutual enjoyment without serious intent
- *Storge:* friendship; companionate love
- *Pragma:* pragmatic and practical love
- *Mania:* manic, jealous, obsessive love
- *Agape:* selfless, idealistic love

Women tend to reflect eros and pragma styles, and men the ludus style. The love styles associated with the lowest relationship satisfaction are ludus and mania styles; eros and agape love styles are associated with the highest relationship satisfaction (Montgomery & Sorell, 1997).

Technology and Sexuality 6-1: Technology and Romantic Relationships

Technology has changed the way individuals initiate, escalate, and end their relationships. Those who want a date tonight open their Tinder® app, scroll through several photos, swipe right for those that look good, ask if the person wants to hang out, and wait a few minutes for a response. Other apps to find a partner include OkCupid, PURE™, Hinge™, Love Flutter™, Glimpse™, Tastebuds™, Skout™, and Bumble™. The latter is unique in that the woman must make the first move or there is no relationship.

Technology impacts romantic relationships in both positive and negative ways. On the positive side, technology (as in texting) allows individuals to have an instant and continuous connection throughout the day so that they are, in effect, together all the time. Texting is particularly valuable for couples in long-distance relationships, providing a way for the partners to maintain their connection via constant communication.

On the negative side, texting discourages talking on the phone and face-to-face communication. The scene of two people sitting at a table, both texting and neither talking to the other, is all too familiar.

Some college students have reached their limit with technology in relationships and want more human inter-action. In a study of 1,003 undergraduates, the respondents believed that talking, hanging out, and sharing intimate details were more important than using communication technologies to establish a relationship (Rappleyea et al., 2014). Indeed, an extreme example of technology going too far is *nomophobia,* in which the individual is dependent on virtual environments to the point of having a social phobia. These individuals experience personal interaction as irrelevant and difficult.

Marriage and family therapist and professor Lori Schade and colleagues (2013) studied relationship satisfaction and technology in romantic relationships. Analyzing data from 276 adults (ages 18–25) in committed relationships, they found that male texting frequency was negatively associated with relationship satisfaction and stability scores for both partners, while female texting frequency was positively associated with their own relationship stability scores. Hence, females thrived on texting, which had a positive relationship effect. Males tolerated it, which had the opposite/negative effect. One man, said, "I'm afraid to see a woman more than three times since she will start this drama of 'Why didn't you text me when you first woke up this morning?'"

6.2a Love and Sex: Similarities and Differences

In this section, we review the similarities and differences between love and sex. In general, love and sex are more similar than they are different.

Similarities Between Love and Sex

1. *Both love and sex are characterized by intense, enjoyable feelings.* To be involved in a love relationship is one of the most intense, enjoyable human experiences. Sex is also an intense and enjoyable experience. Being told that you are loved and experiencing an orgasm are both intense and enjoyable.

2. *Both love and sex involve physiological changes.* When a person is in an intense love relationship, their brain produces phenylethylamine (PEA), a chemical correlate of amphetamine, which may result in a giddy feeling similar to an amphetamine high. PEA, as well as serotonin, the feel-good brain chemical (both are present in chocolate), is also released at the time of orgasm. The physiological changes the body experiences during sexual excitement have been well documented by Masters and Johnson (1966) in their observations of more than 10,000 orgasms. Such changes include increased heart rate, blood pressure, and breathing.

3. *Both love and sex have a cognitive component.* To experience the maximum pleasure from both, the person must label or interpret the experience in positive terms. For love to develop, each person in the relationship must define being together, looking at each other, sharing activities, and talking as enjoyable.

   Positive labeling is also important in sex. Each person's touch, kiss, caress, and body type are different; sexual pleasure depends on labeling sexual interaction with that person as enjoyable. "I can't stand the way he kisses me" and "I love the way he kisses me" are two interpretations of kissing the same person, but only one of these interpretations makes the event pleasurable.

4. *Both love and sex may be expressed in various ways.* Expressions of love may include words ("I love you"), gifts (flowers or candy), behaviors (being on time, a surprise text message, washing the partner's car), or touch (holding hands, tickling). Similarly, sex and love may both be expressed through a glance, embrace, kiss, massage, or intercourse.

5. *The need for love and sex increases with deprivation.* The more we get, the less we feel we need; the less we get, the more we feel we need. The all-consuming passion of Romeo and Juliet, perhaps the most celebrated love story of all time, undoubtedly was fed by their enforced separation.

   Deprivation has the same effect on the need for sex. Statements of people who have been separated from their lovers may be similar to "I'm horny as a mountain goat," "We're going to spend the weekend in bed," and "The second thing we're going to do when we get together is take a drive out in the country."

Differences Between Love and Sex

There are several differences between love and sex.

1. *Love is crucial for human happiness; sex is important, but not crucial.* Although sex is regarded as a life-enhancing experience, no one has suggested that its value supersedes love.

2. *Love is pervasive, whereas sex tends to be localized.* Love is felt all over, but sexual feeling is most often associated with various body parts (lips, breasts, or genitals). People do not speak of love as they do of sex: "It feels good here."

3. *Love tends to be more selective than sex.* The standards that people have for a love partner are generally higher than those they have for a sex partner. Expressions like "I'll take anything wearing pants," "Just show me a room full of skirts," and "I wouldn't kick him out of bed" reflect the desire to have sex with someone—anyone. Love wants the person rather than a person.

    The standards for a love partner may also be different from those for a sexual partner. For example, some people develop relationships to meet emotional/intimacy needs that are not met by their sexual partners. A sexual component need not be a part of the love relationship they have with those they love.

Sex without love is not unusual. In a sample of 3,066 undergraduate males, 53% reported that they had had sex without love, as did 49% of 10,008 undergraduate females (Hall & Knox, 2019). However, uninvolved sex seems to be lacking. In a study by Thomsen and Chang (2000), 292 undergraduate respondents identified the two most frequent regrets about their first intercourse experience as wishing they had waited and wishing they had been in a committed relationship. In a survey of 315 undergraduates, both men and women reported that they wanted to delay sex with partners that they were romantically interested in (Hunt & Jozkowski, 2014).

However, the ideal that sex with love is wholesome and sex without love is exploitative may be an untenable position. For example, two strangers can meet, share each other sexually, have a deep mutual admiration for each other's sensuous qualities, and then go their separate ways. Such an encounter is not necessarily sexual exploitation. Rather, it may be an example of two individuals who have a preference for independence and singlehood rather than deep emotional involvement, commitment, or marriage. They may also not have time for a relationship. "I have a full-time job and go to school full time," reported one of our students. "I don't have time for a relationship, but I'll take a hookup when I can get it."

Each person in a sexual encounter will undoubtedly experience different degrees of love feelings, and the experience of each may differ across time. One woman reported that the first time she had intercourse with her future husband occurred shortly after they had met in a bar. She described their first sexual encounter as "raw, naked sex" with no emotional feelings. But as they continued to see each other over a period of months, an emotional relationship developed, and "sex took on a love meaning for us." Sex with love can also drift into sex without love. One man said he had been deeply in love with his wife, but that they had gradually drifted apart. Sex between them was no longer sex with love. Both love and sex can be viewed on a continuum. Love feelings can range from nonexistent to intense, and relationships can range from limited to intense sexual interaction.

> *"I want you to spend the night," you said. And it was definitely your phrasing that ensured it. If you had said, "Let's have sex," or "Let's go to my place," or even "I really want you," I'm not sure we would have gone quite as far as we did. But I loved the notion that the night was mine to spend, and I immediately decided to spend it with you.*
>
> David Levithan, *The Lover's Dictionary*

PERSONAL DECISIONS 6-1

Sex With or Without Love

Most sexual encounters occur on a continuum from no love involvement to love involvement. Opinions vary with regard to whether an emotional relationship is a worthy prerequisite for sexual involvement:

Sex is good and beautiful when both parties want it; but when one person wants sex only, that's bad. I love sex, but I like to feel that the man cares about me. I can't handle the type of sexual relationship where one night I spend the night with him and the next night he spends the night with someone else. I feel like I am being used. There are still a few women around, like me, who need the commitment before sex.

Source: Authors' files

6.3 Contexts for Sex and Love

Hooking up and *friends with benefits* continue to be phenomena among university students. We now examine both of these contexts.

6.3a Hooking Up

Hooking up is a sexual encounter that occurs between individuals who have no relationship commitment. Between 70% and 85% of college students report having hooked up (Hudson et al., 2018). The definitions of hooking up vary from a one-night encounter to repetitive sexual experiences with a nonromantic partner periodically over time (Vrangalova, 2015). Most often the individuals will have met that evening, had drinks, and gone back to one of the partners' apartments for sex. There is generally no expectation of seeing each other again, and alcohol is often involved. Broader definitions of hooking up (such as making out or deep kissing) tend to be used by women, whereas men see hooking up as involving intercourse (Yazedjian et al., 2014).

Chang et al. (2012) identified the unspoken rules of hooking up: Doing so is not dating or a romantic relationship. Hooking up is physical and secret. Someone who hooks up is to expect no subsequent phone calls from their hookup partner, and condoms/protection should always be used (though only 57% of their sample reported condom use on hookups). Aubrey and Smith (2013) also noted that hooking up reflects a set of cultural beliefs. These beliefs include that hooking up is shameless fun, will enhance your status in your peer group, and reflects your sexual freedom/control over your sexuality.

Data on the frequency of college students having experienced a hookup varies. In their review of literature, Barriger and Velez-Blasini (2013) found that between 77% and 85% of undergraduates reported having hooked up within the previous year, suggesting that hooking up may be becoming a primary context for learning about intimate relationships.

Allison and Risman (2017) confirmed that the delay in ideal marriage is associated with hooking up and with more hookup partners. But such hooking up from this delay occurs less often for working-class women (particularly black women) and Asian men

Hooking up
Meeting someone and becoming sexually involved that same evening with no commitment or expectation beyond the encounter

who do not benefit from the white, male, more class-privileged hookup college culture. Hence, hookups are affected by gender, race, and class.

In one study, men reported having 10 hookups; women reported having 7 (Jayson, 2011). The higher ratio of women to men on campus is associated with a higher frequency of hooking up (Adkins et al., 2015). National data from 2004 to 2012 on the sexual behavior of young adults revealed no evidence of partners reporting more sexual partners or more frequent sex across the years (Monto & Carey, 2014). The notion of a new hookup cultural wave was not substantiated by the data.

Chang and colleagues (2012) surveyed 369 undergraduates (69% reported having hooked up) and found that those with pro-feminist attitudes were not more likely to hook up. However, women who hooked up were more likely than men to agree with the unspoken rules of hooking up: no commitment, no emotional intimacy, and no future obligation to each other. They were clear that hooking up was about sex with no future. These data reflect that hooking up may be common on college and university campuses. The exceptions are campuses, such as Liberty University, that provide a religious context for students.

In study of 477 first year college students, those reporting sexual intercourse in casual relationships reported decreases in emotional health compared to those engaging in no sexual behavior (Wesche et al. 2019). Fielder and colleagues (2013) studied hookups in first-year college women and found an association with experiencing depression, sexual victimization, and STIs. De Jong et al. (2018) found that female emotional reaction to hooking up was related to motivation—if the goal was fun/pleasure/enhancement, the outcome was positive. If the hookup was used as a coping mechanism, the outcome was negative. Women and men often experience hooking up differently. Women in hookup contexts were less likely to experience cunnilingus but were frequently expected to provide fellatio (Blackstrom et al., 2012). However, Vrangalova (2015) analyzed data on 872 undergraduates that revealed a positive outcome in regard to psychological well-being for females (they may have felt empowered) and a negative outcome for men (they may have felt threatened/pressure to perform).

While it is often assumed that hookups do not result in long-term love relationships, Erichsen and Dignam (2016) found that 1 in 5 (23%) undergraduates who had hooked up reported that they had transitioned to an exclusive romantic relationship. The primary strategies for transitioning included defining the relationship as more than a hookup ("We care about each other"), expressing personal interest in a relationship beyond sex ("I want more than a sexual relationship with you"), and spending time together doing things of mutual interest. There was no significant gender difference in reporting that a relationship had transitioned from a hookup to an exclusive emotional one. The older the undergraduate, the more likely the student wanted the hookup to become a romantic relationship (Stuhlsatz & Lohman, 2014). Additionally, having repeated sex with a person is related to forming an attachment with that person (Hazan et al., 2014). Hence, hookup couples who transition to a relationship are more likely to be those who keep hooking up/having sex with the same person. Timmermans and Courtois (2018) confirmed that hookups may transition to committed relationships. They reported on 1,038 Tinder users and found that one-third of the conversations on Tinder led to casual sex and more than a fourth led to a committed relationship. The authors concluded, "... sexual encounters will eventually lead to committed relationships in a society where initiation of relationship formation with dating has been replaced by hooking up" (p. 59).

As is apparent, the research is mixed on the impact of hooking up. To add to the research inconsistences, there has been a concern that the "hookup culture" has undermined and been associated with the devaluation of marriage. But James-Kangal et al.

(2018) surveyed 248 emerging adults and confirmed that "Contrary to concerns about the devaluation of marriage, results indicated that level of engagement in hooking up was not associated with expectations for involvement in future committed relationships, including marriage."

6.3b Friends with Benefits

"Friends with benefits" has become part of the relational sexual landscape. A **friends with benefits** relationship (FWBR) is one in which the friends do not have a romantic relationship but get together regularly for sex. This sexual activity could range from kissing to sexual intercourse and is a repeated part of a friendship, not just a one-night stand. Forty-nine percent of 3,007 undergraduate males reported that they had been in a FWBR (43% of 9,902 undergraduate females) (Hall & Knox, 2019). Stein et al. (2019) identified the primary motivation for involvement in an FWBR—sex. In addition, there are gender differences, with men more focused on the sex and women more focused on the relationship aspects. Cashman & Walters (2018) found that persons who reported having been in an FWBR (compared to those who had not experienced an FWBR) reported having had more lifetime sexual partners, more partners since beginning college, and higher rates of masturbation (particularly women).

Jovanovic and Williams (2018) conducted focus groups of women and men about involvement in an FWBR and found several themes: empowerment in which the woman (like the man) was free to have sex, control (e.g. the woman could depart from traditional roles and initiate sex with the guy), and safety (e.g. a comfortable friend not a random hookup). In addition to having a "safe" sexual partner (low STI exposure and partner not an unpredictable hookup), other advantages of involvement in an FWBR were having a predictably "good" sexual partner who knows likes/dislikes, and not increasing one's "body count" (number of sexual partners). Other advantages include having a regular sex partner, not being burdened with having to devote the time that an emotional relationship would require, and being free to date/find one's true love while still having one's sexual needs met.

Mongeau and colleagues (2013) surveyed 258 people who were in an FWBR. Based on this survey, they identified seven types and stated the percentages of each.

1. *True friends:* These are close friends who have sex on multiple occasions (similar to but not labeled as romantic partners); the largest percentage (26%) of the 258 respondents reported this type of FWBR.

2. *Just sex:* The focus is sex and a serial hookup with the same person, with no care about that person other than as a sexual partner (12%).

3. *Network opportunism:* As part of the same social network, network opportunists hang out together and sometimes go home to have sex together when there is no better option—a sort of sexual failsafe (15%).

4. *Successful transition:* This type uses an FWBR to transition into a romantic relationship (8%). Laverty et al. (2016) analyzed data on 803 individuals who had their first intercourse as friends. Over a third of the men and women (36% and 38%) expected that they would end up as potential partners. In 61% of the cases, their expectations were realized.

5. *Unintentional transition:* This sexual relationship morphs into a romantic relationship without the transition being the initial intent; the relationship results from regular sex, hanging out together, and so forth (8%).

Friends with benefits
Friends who get together regularly for sex but who do not have a romantic relationship

6. *Failed transition:* One partner becomes involved, while the other does not. As a result, the relationship stalls; the lowest percentage (7%) of the 258 respondents reported this type of FWBR.

7. *Transition out:* The couple was romantic, but the relationship ended; however, the sexual relationship continued (11%). Advantages to ex-sex include having a safe sexual partner, having a predictably good sexual partner who knows your likes/dislikes, not increasing the number of lifetime sexual partners, and "fanning sexual flames that might facilitate rekindling partners' emotional connections" (Mongeau et al., 2013).

Advantages of being in an FWBR involve having a regular sexual partner, not feeling vulnerable to having to hook up with a stranger just to have sex, minimizing your exposure to STIs, not increasing the number of sexual partners, and feeling free to have other relationships (including sexual ones). Disadvantages include developing a bad reputation as someone who does not really care about emotional involvement, coping with the discrepancy of becoming more or less involved than the partner, and losing the capacity to give yourself emotionally. Dube et al. (2017) surveyed 2,304 adolescents, 17% of whom reported being in an FWBR. Psychological distress and increased alcohol and drug use were associated with penetrative involvement in an FWBR for the girls (but not for the boys).

> *True Love in this differs from gold and clay,/That to divide is not to take away.*
>
> Percy Bysshe Shelley, English romantic poet

These individuals are in a polyamorous relationship whereby they have a relationship with each other while also having emotional and sexual relationships with others.

Polyamory
Involvement of more than two individuals in a pair-bonded relationship (some of the individuals may be married to each other) who have an emotional, sexual, and sometimes parenting relationship

Swingers
Spouses who agree that they will have sexual encounters with other couples

6.4 Polyamory and Open Relationships

Interest in polyamory continues to increase (Moors, 2017). **Polyamory** means multiple loves (in Latin, *poly* means "many" and *amor* means "love"). By agreement, each partner may have numerous emotional and sexual relationships. Between 4% and 5% of individuals report involvement in a polyamorous relationship, also referred to as *consensual non-monogamy* (Moors et al., 2014; Blumer et al., 2015). Balzarini et al. (2016) reported on a sample of 3,530 adults who identified as polyamorous and found that 77% of the females and 40% of the males identified as something other than heterosexual—the most prominent was bisexual and pansexual. The respondents were also well-educated and nonreligious.

Polyamorists and monogamists differ from **swingers** (spouses who agree that they will have sexual encounters with other couples) in that the latter are more focused on recreational sex. Swingers also tend to be older, more educated, and have higher incomes. A qualitative study on swinging was conducted by Vaillancourt and Few-Demo (2014), whereby each spouse of 10 couples responded to a series of questions online. In most cases, the husband became aware of swinging first and introduced the idea to the spouse. Over several discussions, a joint decision was made to pursue other swinging couples. Most couples were private about their swinging behavior and felt that it had a positive outcome for their relationship. Kimberly and Hans (2015) interviewed 16 couples and identified the steps or stages through which couples pass to get to swinging. A beginning point occurs when one or both spouses reveal an interest in sex with others, trying new non-monogamous experiences (such as hiring a sex worker to join the couple) or going to a swinging convention and finding a *mentor* who explains the swinging lifestyle. Couples maintain/enhance their marital satisfaction by being open about their thoughts/feelings/jealousies and through sharing the swinging experience rather than cheating. Estimates of the number of swingers in the United States range from 4 to 15 million. Some swinging occurs in the context of sex parties, defined as a gathering of 6 or more people where full nudity is allowed and people openly engage in sexual and/or kinky activities. Wells et al. (2016) identified 1,389 individuals who reported having attended at least one **sex party** in the past year. Eight was the median number of sex parties the respondents reported having attended.

Sex party
The gathering of 6 or more people where full nudity is allowed and people openly engage in sexual and/or kinky activities

Social Policy 6-1

Love in the Workplace

Although media attention on the workplace has been more about sexual harassment than finding a love partner, it remains a context where romantic relationships develop. Faith Hill and Tim McGraw, Blake Shelton and Gwen Stefani, and Bill and Melinda Gates met on the job. In a national survey of workers, over half (57%) revealed that they had become involved in a romance with a coworker; 10% said that they met the person they married there (Vault Careers, 2017).

Advantages of a Workplace Romance

The energy that both fuels and results from intense love feelings can also fuel productivity on the job. If the coworkers eventually marry or enter a nonmarital but committed, long-term relationship, they may be more satisfied with and committed to their jobs than spouses whose partners work elsewhere. Working at the same location enables married couples to commute together, go to company-sponsored events together, share projects, and talk shop together. Workplaces, such as academia, often try to hire both partners since they are more likely to become permanent workers since they can both work at the same place.

In recognizing the potential benefits of increased job satisfaction, morale, productivity, creativity, and commitment, some companies encourage love relationships among employees. Aware that its single employees are interested in relationships, Hitachi Insurance Service provides a dating service, called Tie the Knot, for its 400,000 employees (many of whom are unmarried) in Tokyo, Japan. Those interested in finding a partner complete an application, and a meeting or lunch is arranged with a suitable candidate through the Wedding Commander. In America, some companies hire married employees, reflecting a focus on the value of each employee to the firm rather than on their love relationship outside work.

Disadvantages of a Workplace Romance

Workplace romances can also be problematic for the individuals involved, as well as for their employers. When a workplace romance involves a supervisor/subordinate relationship, other employees might make claims of favoritism or differential treatment. In a typical differential-treatment allegation, an employee (usually a woman) claims that the company denied her a job benefit because her supervisor favored another female coworker who happened to be the supervisor's girlfriend.

If a workplace relationship breaks up, it may be difficult to continue to work in the same environment (and others at work may experience the fallout). A breakup that is less than amicable may result in efforts by partners to sabotage each other's work relationships and performance, and incidents of workplace violence, harassment, and/or allegations of sexual harassment are not uncommon. But breakups with bad outcomes may not be the norm; of employees in the 2017 Vault.com Romance Survey, two-thirds (more men than women) who had become involved in an office romance said that they would do so again.

Company Policies on Workplace Romances

Some companies, such as Disney, Universal, and Columbia, have anti-fraternization clauses that impose a cap on workers talking about private issues or sending personal emails. Some British firms even have "love contracts" that require workers to tell their managers if they are involved with anyone from the workplace.

Most companies do not prohibit romantic relationships among employees. However, the company may have a policy prohibiting open displays of affection between employees in the workplace, romantic relationships between supervisor and subordinate, and relationships in which one of the participants is married. These policies may be enforced by transferring or dismissing employees who don't play by the rules. But most companies have no policy regarding love relationships at work and generally regard romances between coworkers as none of the company's business.

Antipolygamy legislation has framed polyamory as a sexual orientation, arguing that some people are immutably predisposed toward forming multiple relationships. Robinson (2013) interviewed 40 bisexual women and suggested that polyamory and monogamy are better viewed as strategies of sexual expression rather than as immutable orientations. Hence, you are not born to seek polyamory, but you may seek a context of multiple partners independent of sexual orientation. Aguilar (2013) was a participant observer at two communes where polyamory was practiced. She noted how the social context in which people live influences them to follow the group norms. In regard to the psychological well-being of the partners involved in consensual nonmonogamy, as well as to relationship quality and stability, a review of literature has revealed no significant differences compared with people in monogamous relationships (Rubel & Bogaert, 2015).

About 80% of the 100 members of Twin Oaks Community (www.twinoaks.org) in Louisa, Virginia, are polyamorous—each partner may have several emotional or physical relationships with others at the same time. Although most are not legally married, these adults view themselves as emotionally bonded to each other and may even rear children together. Concerned about enduring, intimate relationships that include sex, people in polyamorous relationships seek to rid themselves of jealous feelings and to increase their level of **compersion**—feeling happy for a partner who enjoys an emotional and sexual relationship with another.

Sheff (2014) identified the benefits and difficulties of poly families—multipartner relationships that raise children and function as families. Benefits included shared resources, honesty/emotional intimacy among family members, and multiple role models for children: "Many parents say that their children's lives, experiences, and self-concepts are richer for the multiple loving adults in their families" (p. 201). The difficulties of poly families include social stigma and teenage leverage against poly parents in which a disgruntled teen might blackmail parents, threatening to reveal their unconventional lifestyle to authorities, employers, or teachers.

Sheff's (2014) research reveals that the nonsexual emotional ties that bind people in poly families are far more important than the sexual connections between the adults:

> While the sexual relationships polys establish with each other get the most attention from the media, ... they are not the ... most important aspect of poly relationships. ... Much like heterosexual families, poly families spend far more time hanging out together, doing homework, making dinner, carpooling, folding laundry, and having family meetings or relationship talks than they do having sex. (pp. 206–207)

Compersion
The opposite of jealousy, whereby a person feels positive about a lover's emotional and sexual enjoyment with another

Up Close 6-1

Compersion Is My Challenge

My name is Kate, and one of the guys I'm in love with is Paxus. We live at Twin Oaks, and we are polyamorous, which means we're open to having intimate relationships with more than one person. We're not swingers, and we aren't polygamists. Our relationships are not quick-sex-overnight encounters, but instead deeply committed relationships that we nurture over time.

Compersion is when one feels good about one's lover getting romantically involved with someone else. It is one of the key aspects that can help poly relationships function well. It's important for me to celebrate and honor the happiness of my partners when they're getting involved with other people. It's taken me awhile to develop my capacity for compersion—it certainly isn't something we learn from popular culture!

When Paxus (or another of my partners) is developing a relationship with someone else, I sometimes worry that she is more interesting than me or better in bed, or that he is more attracted to her. When those feelings come up for me, I communicate openly and directly with my partner about my fears, and we work together to address the fears and to strengthen our relationship. It's not easy, and it takes commitment to do the deep emotional processing. For me, the benefits of polyamory (having rich relationships with several wonderful people, and moving away from the idea of love as possession) are well worth the effort (Adamson, 2014).

6.4a Advantages and Disadvantages of Polyamory

Embracing polyamory has both advantages and disadvantages. It can offer greater variety in your emotional and sexual life; the avoidance of hidden affairs and the attendant feelings of deception, mistrust, or betrayal; and the opportunity to have different needs met by different people. The disadvantages of polyamory involve having to manage your feelings of jealousy and limited time with each partner. Of the latter, one polyamorous partner said, "With three relationships and a full-time job, I just don't have much time to spend with each partner, so I'm frustrated about who I'll be with next. And managing the feelings of the other partners who want to spend time with me is a challenge."[*]

Sexual Exclusivity

Polyfidelity differs from polyamory in that polyfideles (the term for someone who practices polyfidelity) expect their partners to remain sexually exclusive within a group that is larger than two people, though some polyfidelitous groups have members who do not have sex with each other. Almost all polyfideles see each other as family members, regardless of the degree of sexual contact within their relationships. Not all polys in a relationship have sex with each other, and I call those who are emotionally intimate but not sexually connected *polyaffective*.

Polygeometry

The number of people involved in poly relationships varies and can include open couples, vees, triads, quads, and moresomes. The most common form is the *open couple*, which is usually composed of two people who often are in a long-term relationship, cohabitate (some married, others unmarried), and have extradyadic sexual

Polyfidelity
Partners in the group remain faithful (sexually exclusive) to everyone else in the group

---

[*] The remainder of this section was written by and used with the permission of Dr. Elizabeth Sheff, Department of Sociology, Georgia State University, Atlanta. Dr. Sheff conducted more than 40 interviews with persons involved in polyamory.

relationships. **Vees** are three-person relationships in which one member is sexually connected to each of the two others. The relationship between the two nonlovers can range from strangers (who are aware of and cordial with each other), to casual friends, to enemies. A *triad*, commonly understood as *ménage à trois*, generally includes three sexually involved adults. Sometimes triads begin as threesomes—15% of 196 undergraduates reported having participated in a threesome (Morris et al. 2016). But, more often, threesomes form when a single joins an open couple or a larger group loses one or more members. *Quads,* as the name implies, are groups of four adults most commonly formed when two couples join, although sometimes they develop when a triad adds a fourth or a moresome loses member(s). Quads are notoriously unstable, frequently losing someone to poly-style divorce. *Moresomes*, groups with five or more adult members, are larger, more fragile, and more complicated than quads.

Emotional Intimacy

Polys frequently use the terms *primary, secondary*, and *tertiary* to describe their varied levels of intimacy. *Primary* partners—sometimes corresponding to the larger cultural conception of a spouse—usually have long-term relationships, joint finances, cohabitate, make major life decisions together, and sometimes they have children. *Secondary* partners tend to keep their lives more separate than primary partners, frequently maintain separate finances and residences, may have less intense emotional connections than primaries, and usually discuss major life decisions, though they generally do not make those decisions jointly. *Tertiary* relationships are often less emotionally intimate, sometimes with long-distance or more casual partners. Some tertiary relationships closely resemble swinging. Some poly families have *spice*, the poly word for more than one spouse. Emotional relationships may even be possible with robots. Hiroshi Ishiguro of Japan builds androids—"beautiful, realistic, uncannily convincing human replicas." He has suggested that developing love feelings for an android is now a possibility (Mar, 2017).

6.4b Rules of an Open Relationship

While polyamorous relationships involve emotional as well as sexual involvement with others, **open relationships,** traditionally called *swinging*, are more sexually and recreationally focused. These relationships involve individuals agreeing that they may have sexual encounters with others. Over two-thirds (72%) of 12,081 undergraduates reported that they could not feel good about their partner being involved in an emotional/sexual relationship with someone else (Hall & Knox, 2019). These may be more generic feelings of allowing the partner to have had positive emotional/sexual experiences with others rather than current feelings about a love/sex partner. Where a couple is involved in an open relationship, they often agree to certain rules:

1. *Honesty:* "We tell each other everything we do with someone outside the relationship. If we flirt, we even tell that. Openness about our feelings is a must; if we get uncomfortable or jealous, we must talk about it."

2. *Recreational sex:* "Sex with the other person will be purely recreational—it is not love, and the relationship with the other person is going nowhere. The people we choose to have sex with must know that we have a loving, committed relationship with someone else."

3. *Condom use:* "This is a requirement every time."

Vees
Three-person relationships in which one member is sexually connected to each of the two others

Open relationship
Each partner agrees that the other can have sexual (and sometimes emotional) relationships with someone outside the couple relationship

4. *Approval:* "Every person we have sex with must be approved by the partner in advance. Each partner has the right to veto a selection. The person in question must not be into partner snatching, looking for romance, or jealous. Persons off the list are coworkers, family, old lovers, and old friends."

5. *Online hunting:* "This is prohibited. Each agrees not to go looking on the internet for sex partners."

6. *Social media:* "No photos on social media of partner with others."

7. *Priority:* "We are each other's priority. We also spend vacations and holidays together."

8. *Feelings end contact with other:* "If either of us catch feelings for someone we are having sex with, we stop seeing that person ASAP."

9. *Friends and sex:* "No sex with friends or people who are included in our network of friendships."

10. *Number:* "Maximum of three other people having sex with at one time."

11. *Pregnancy/STI scare*: "Partner must be made aware of pregnancy or STI scare immediately."

Other rules of swingers identified by Kimberly and Hans (2015) who interviewed 32 swingers (16 husband-wife dyads), included excluding overly aggressive men and agreeing on privacy issues concerning family/non-swinger friends.

6.4c Consensually Non-Monogamous Relationships

Individuals differ on the degree to which they prefer a monogamous versus a non-monogamous relationship. The Self-Assessment to follow allows you to identify your attitudes toward these relationships.

Wood et al. (2018) revealed that about 4% of adults in North America participate in consensually non-monogamous (CNM) relationships. Furthermore, there are no differences in mean levels of relationship and sexual satisfaction between CNM and monogamous individuals. Cohen (2016a) studied 122 CNM partners in which the partners agreed that each could become involved with others outside the dyad. Almost two-thirds (73%) of the CNM relationships were by mutual agreement. The greatest advantages were "to experience something new," to be "free," and to not be "tied down." Males were attracted by the opportunity to have sex with others; females were attracted by the notion of not being stuck in a relationship. The greatest disadvantage was the stigma associated with the lifestyle followed by problems in communication, jealousy, and trust. Following the rules, such as not seeing the same person twice, was an important agreement for the partners involved in CNM.

Seguin et al. (2017) examined the relationship quality of 3,463 individuals in monogamous, open, and polyamorous relationships and found no significant differences in reported relationship quality and equity. The researchers concluded that "these results strongly suggest that these types of relationship agreements are equally healthy viable options." Conley et al. (2018) compared the sexual satisfaction of individuals in monogamous and CNM relationships and found slightly lower sexual satisfaction and orgasm rates among monogamous individuals. Swingers reported higher sexual satisfaction than monogamous individuals; those in open relationships had equal sexual satisfaction rates with those in monogamous relationships. Also, relationship satisfaction did not differ between monogamous and CNM groups.

Self-Assessment 6-2: Consensual Non-Monogamy Scale

The purpose of this scale is to assess the degree to which you have a positive, neutral, or negative view of consensual non-monogamy (CNM) when compared to monogamy (M).

Directions

After reading each sentence carefully, circle the number that best represents the degree to which you strongly disagree to strongly agree with the sentence. There are no right or wrong answers.

1 (Strongly agree), 2 (Mildly agree), 3 (Undecided), 4 (Mildly disagree), 5 (Strongly disagree)

1. Monogamy is out of date.	1 2 3 4 5
2. Engaging in CNM is more honest than monogamy.	1 2 3 4 5
3. CNM individuals are happier than monogamists.	1 2 3 4 5
4. CNM relationships are happier than M relationships.	1 2 3 4 5
5. CNM is more associated with mental health than M.	1 2 3 4 5
6. Increasingly, more individuals are choosing CNM.	1 2 3 4 5
7. Most people secretly prefer CNM over M.	1 2 3 4 5
8. You can be in love and in a CNM relationship.	1 2 3 4 5
9. CNM is becoming more acceptable.	1 2 3 4 5
10. I can imagine being in a CNM relationship.	1 2 3 4 5

Scoring

Add the numbers you circled. The lower your total score (10 is the lowest possible score), the less approving you are of CNM. The higher your total score (50 is the highest possible score) the more approving you are of CNM. A score of 30 places you at the midpoint between being the extremes.

Source: This scale was developed for this text. It is to be used for general assessment and is not designed to be a clinical diagnostic tool or as a research instrument.

Rodrigues et al. (2017) found that if persons who are attracted to having a number of sexual partners are able to negotiate with a love partner to allow such encounters, relationship quality with that person does not seem to be negatively affected and can improve relationship stability. Such a finding is counter to research that suggests non-monogamous relationships are doomed. Finally, Haupert et al. (2017) investigated engagement in CNM relationships and found that it was linked to positive aspects of sexual health, including open conversations about sexual needs and risk (with greater condom use).

National **DATA**

Married couples in which one spouse is black and the other white make up less than 1% of the 63.3 million marriages in the United States (ProQuest *Statistical Abstract of the United States*, 2019, Table 60).

6.5 Factors Involved in Selecting a Long-Term Partner

In this section, we review the cultural, sociological, and psychological factors that influence the attraction of two people to each other.

6.5a Cultural Factors in Selecting a Partner

Individuals are not free to marry whomever they please—their culture and society influence their decisions. Two forms of cultural pressure operative in mate selection are endogamy and exogamy. **Endogamy** is the cultural expectation to select a marriage partner within your own social group—such as race, religion, and social class. Endogamous pressures involve social approval and disapproval to encourage you to select a partner within your own group. The pressure toward an endogamous mate choice is especially strong when race is concerned.

These spouses have much in common—age, race, religion, and three children.

(Chelsea Curry Edwards)

Residential, religious, and educational segregation, coupled with parental disapproval for cross-racial pairings, helps to explain the low frequency of interracial marriages. The result is that most people marry within their own racial group. However, in the first decade of the 21st century, the number of interethnic marriages soared nearly 30% to make up nearly 1 in 10 opposite-sex unions, suggesting that the future may be color blind (Wang, 2014). This trend of increased multiracial unity may help ameliorate the disturbing concurrent rise in white racism and hate groups in the United States , which has been aided by online platforms, as reported in the Southern Poverty Law Center's recent research (Hankes, 2016).

In contrast to endogamy, **exogamy** is the cultural expectation to marry outside your own family group. Incest taboos are universal. In no society are children permitted to marry the parent of the other sex. In the United States, siblings and, in some states, first cousins are also prohibited from marrying each other. The reason for such restrictions is fear of genetic defects in children whose parents are too closely related.

6.5b Sociological Forces in Selecting a Partner: Homogamy

The **homogamy theory** of mate selection states that we tend to be attracted to and become involved with those who are similar to ourselves in such characteristics as age, race, religion, social class, grade point average, alcohol and tobacco consumption, IQ, and sexual experience.

Endogamy
The cultural expectation to select a marriage partner within one's own social group

Exogamy
The cultural expectation to marry outside your own family group

Homogamy theory
Individuals tend to be attracted to and involved with persons similar to themselves in age, race, religion, and so on

Birds of a feather, flock together.

William Turner,
Rescuing of Romish Fox

6.5c Psychological Factors in Selecting a Partner

Psychologists have focused on complementary needs, exchanges, parental characteristics, and personality types with regard to pair bonding.

Complementary Needs Theory

Complementary needs theory (opposites attract) states that we tend to select mates whose needs are opposite and complementary to our own needs. Partners can also be drawn to each other on the basis of nurturance versus receptivity. These complementary needs suggest that one person likes to give and take care of another, whereas the other likes to be the beneficiary of such care.

Exchange Theory

Exchange theory emphasizes that mate selection is based on assessing who offers the greatest rewards at the lowest cost. Five concepts help explain the exchange process in mate selection:

1. *Rewards* are the behaviors (your partner looking at you with the eyes of love), words (saying "I love you"), and resources (being beautiful or handsome; having a car, condo, and money; helping around the house or running errands for you) that you value and that influence you to continue the relationship.

2. *Costs* are the unpleasant aspects of a relationship. A woman identified the costs associated with being involved with her partner: "He abuses drugs, doesn't have a job, and lives 9 hours away." The costs her partner associated with being involved with this woman included "she nags me," "she doesn't like sex," and "she wants her mother to live with us if we marry."

3. *Profit* occurs when the rewards exceed the costs. Unless the couple referred to in concept number 2 derives a profit from staying together, they are likely to end their relationship.

4. *Loss* occurs when the costs exceed the rewards.

5. It is also necessary that no other person who offers a higher profit is currently available.

Most people have definite ideas about what they are looking for in a partner. The currency used in the marriage market consists of the socially valued characteristics of the persons involved, such as age, physical characteristics, and economic status. In our free-choice system of partner selection, we typically get as much in return for our social attributes as we can.

When you identify a person who offers you a good exchange for what you have to offer, other bargains are made about the conditions of your continued relationship. Waller and Hill (1951) observed that the person who has the least interest in continuing the relationship can control it. This **principle of least interest** is illustrated by the woman who says, "He wants to date me more than I want to date him, so we end up going where I want to go and doing what I want to do." In this case, the woman trades her company for the man's acquiescence to her decisions.

The exchange theory of mate selection may be criticized on the basis that people do not consciously think of what they have and what they can trade. Rather, they have some vague notion of who they are attracted to and rely on past experience to know if the person would be interested in them. People also rarely think in terms of profit and loss—that is, they don't think, "I will stay in this relationship as long as there is profit and leave it when there is loss." Rather, they may think more in terms of love, commitment, and working out whatever issues may confront them.

Complementary needs theory
Individuals tend to select a mate whose needs are opposite or complementary to their own needs

Exchange theory
In mate selection, refers to selecting a partner who offers the greatest rewards at the lowest cost

Principle of least interest
The person with the least interest controls the relationship

6.6 Challenges Related to Intimate Sexual Relationships

Shakespeare said that the course of true love never did run smooth. But when an intimate relationship is superseded by negative emotions, it can veer into distressing and even physically threatening territory, encompassing jealousy, guilt, obsession, and stalking.

6.6a Jealousy

Jealousy can be defined as an emotional response to a perceived or real threat to an important or valued relationship. People experiencing jealousy fear being abandoned or replaced and feel anger at the partner or the perceived competition. Jealousy is not uncommon among undergraduates. Of 3,005 university males, 51% agreed with the statement "I am a jealous person"; of 9,888 undergraduate females, 54% agreed with that statement (Hall & Knox, 2019). Jealousy is also more likely to occur early in a couple's relationship, such as when new couples are working out their trust/levels of commitment. When noncohabiting, cohabiting, and married couples are compared in regard to jealously, married couples are the least likely to report jealousy in their relationship (Gatzeva & Paik, 2011).

Jealousy, that dragon which slays love under the pretense of keeping it alive.

Havelock Ellis, sexuality pioneer

(Trevor Werb)

One source of jealousy is the perception that one's previous partner is interested in someone else.

Causes of Jealousy

Jealousy can be triggered by external or internal factors. External factors can include behaviors a partner engages in that are interpreted as an emotional and/or sexual interest in someone (or something) else or a lack of emotional and/or sexual interest in the primary partner. Per traditional gender roles, women can become jealous of a rival's physical attractiveness ("She's a beautiful woman. No wonder my partner is interested"), and male jealousy can be provoked by the rival's physical dominance ("I'm a runt compared to that guy") (Buunk et al., 2010).

Internal causes of jealousy refer to characteristics that predispose individuals to jealous feelings independent of their partner's behavior. Internal causes of jealousy include mistrust, lack of perceived alternatives, feeling insecure in the relationship, and low self-esteem. The latter (low self-esteem) is also associated with fears concerning sexuality, such as "Is my partner attracted to me sexually?" (Favez et al., 2016).

Positive Consequences of Jealousy

Jealousy may also signal to the partner that they are valued and telegraph parameters for interaction with others, such as a ban on communicating with previous lovers. A woman said of her jealous partner:

> When I started spending extra time with this guy at the office, my partner got jealous and told me he thought I was getting in over my head and asked me to cut back on the relationship because it was "tearing him up." I felt he really loved me when he told me this, so I stopped having lunch with the guy at work and distanced myself from him. (Source: Authors' files)

Jealousy
Emotional reaction to a perceived or real threat to a valued love relationship

Negative Consequences of Jealousy

Jealousy, with its obsessive ruminations about the partner's alleged infidelity, can make people miserable. They may obsessively worry about the partner being with the new person, which they interpret as confirmation of their own inadequacy. Jealousy also conveys "I don't trust you" to the partner, and it is this insidious mistrust that may destroy the relationship. If jealousy results in repeated, unwarranted accusations, a partner can tire of such attacks and seek to end the relationship with the accuser.

In its extreme form, jealousy can have devastating consequences. Possessive jealousy involves an attack on a partner or the person to whom the partner is allegedly showing attention. In some instances, people have stalked or killed their partners and then killed themselves due to jealousy or feelings of rejection.

There is no greater glory than love, nor any greater punishment than jealousy.

Lope de Vega, Spanish playwright

6.6b Guilt

Guilt is another emotion that may affect the quality of relationships and influence sexual behavior. **Sexual guilt** is the feeling that results from the violation of your own sexual values or those that you have grown up with. Guilt may result when you go against what you think you should not do ("I should not have gotten drunk and had intercourse")—students often refer to returning home the morning after a hookup as the "walk of shame." Emmers-Sommer (2018) found higher levels of sex guilt in women than men as well as guilt being associated with negative attitudes toward sex and lower sex frequencies. Beale et al. (2016) emphasized guilt as a consequence of religion and that some are very conflicted by their religion and sexual behavior. Research by Fulle et al. (2015) revealed that women reported more guilt over their sexual behavior than men. This finding is related to the double standard, which labels women who have multiple sexual partners as a slut, whereas men experience approval for having sex with numerous women.

In some cases, sexual guilt may interfere with a person's sexual well-being. For example, some women feel guilty about experiencing sexual pleasure because they have been taught that sex is bad and that "good" women do not enjoy sex. In this situation, sexual guilt may interfere with a woman's ability to become sexually aroused and experience orgasm, even within a loving and committed relationship. One woman in the authors' classes said, "I never felt sex was okay, not even after I was married. I think my Catholic background and prudish parents did me in."

Sexual guilt
Feeling that results from violating your sexual values

Obsessive relational intrusion
Stranger or acquaintance repeatedly invades the physical or symbolic space of another with the goal of having an intimate relationship

6.6c Obsession

In the name of love, people have stalked the beloved, shot the beloved, and killed themselves in reaction to rejected love. Although most instances of unrequited love are resolved adequately, **obsessive relational intrusion** (ORI) has come to be recognized in various forms. A stranger or an acquaintance may employ ORI by repeatedly invading one's physical or symbolic privacy in their attempts to have an intimate relationship. Activities may include sending text messages, calls, gifts, and repeated requests for dates, or they may escalate into stalking and violence.

6.6d Stalking

Stalking is an extreme form of ORI, defined as the repeated, willful, and malicious following or harassment of one person by another. It may involve watching a victim, property damage, home invasion, or threats of physical harm. It usually causes great emotional distress and impairs the recipient's social and work activities. Of 3,028 male respondents in a survey of undergraduates, 19% reported that someone had stalked them, whereas 28% of 9,942 undergraduate females reported being stalked (Hall & Knox, 2019).

Maybe there's more we all could have done, but we just have to let the guilt remind us to do better next time.

Veronica Roth, *Divergent*

Love can turn into an obsession requiring constant contact with the beloved ("blowing up the partner's cell phone").

(Amberlynn Bishop)

Various theories—patriarchal, social learning, and social conflict—provide explanations for men stalking women. As an expression of male authority, men learn to be dominant, feel a sense of entitlement to women's bodies, and use physical power to control women. People who stalk are obsessional and very controlling. They are typically mentally ill and have one or more personality disorders involving paranoid, antisocial, or obsessive-compulsive behaviors.

Here are some coping strategies for dealing with a stalker, abuser, or obsessional partner:

1. Make a direct statement to the person: "I am not interested in dating you." "Stay away from me."

2. Seek protection through formal channels, such as assistance from law enforcement and legal means (legal aid advice, restraining order) and shelter options to avoid the situation accelerating into crisis, and inform the stalker: "I am calling the cops if you bother me again."

3. Avoid the perpetrator. Do not respond to text messages or telephone calls, and avoid in-person encounters.

4. Change phone numbers, address, and so forth, and seek shelter situations as necessary.

5. Keep trusted friends or family members apprised of your whereabouts and any concerns you may have about a potential stalker.

6. Train in the use of and carry personal security in the form of pepper spray, stun guns, or other forms of protection, per state law.

> **Stalking**
> An extreme form of obsessive relational intrusion that may involve behaviors like home invasion or threats of physical harm

Women never stalk men; they just research them intensely.

Matshona Dhliwayo, Canadian author

6.6e Romantic Breakup—Change in Sexual Values

Hilliard et al. (2019c) investigated the degree to which the sexual values of absolutism (no intercourse before marriage), relativism (sexual involvement in the context of a relationship), and hedonism (sex for pleasure) change when a romantic relationship ends. A 32-item internet questionnaire (completed by 286 never-married undergraduates who had experienced one or more romantic breakups) and a focus group were the data sources. Analysis revealed, in general, significant changes from absolutism to relativism and from relativism to hedonism after a romantic breakup. Examples of comments from undergraduates who were asked to talk about how the breakup changed their sexual values:

- *I've always kinda been a relativist since when I was in a relationship the sex was good and I enjoyed that. After the relationship ended, it didn't make me an absolutist, but it definitely made me more hesitant … made me want to wait longer.*

- *My previous relationship lasted 7 years (all of high school and most of college) so when it was over, I wanted to get out there, so I guess I was more hedonistic than anything. My sexual values didn't really change, I still thought that sex is sex, you don't have to wait until marriage.*

- *In my last relationship I didn't want to have sex unless I was with him. But once we broke up, within a few days I was sleeping with someone else and then someone else the next day.*

- *I've only ever been in two serious relationships and had sex in both of them. After my last relationship ended, I decided that I wasn't going to date for a long time. But I did hook up with someone after my last relationship to see what it was like, but I don't think I am going to continue to do that—I just wanted to see how it was but it's not really for me.*

- *I was in a two-and-a-half-year relationship and I ended up getting cheated on. Before the relationship, I would've considered myself a relativist but after I got cheated on, I realized that maybe people don't really care about getting to know you before they have sex with you so I decided I was going to try it and it took off from there and I slept with a few people.*

Chapter Summary

Love

LOVE IS a profound emotion that bonds individuals to each other. It is also a context for sexual intimacy.

Love may be conceptualized on a continuum from romanticism to realism. Sternberg's (1986) triangular theory of love identifies types of love based on the presence or absence of three elements: intimacy, passion, and commitment. John Alan Lee described various love styles: eros, ludus, storge, pragma, mania, and agape.

Sex and love have similarities (both involve intense feelings and physiological changes; need increases with deprivation) and differences (love is crucial to human happiness, but sex is not).

Contexts for Sex and Love: Hooking Up, Friends with Benefits, the Workplace

SEXUALITY OCCURS in relationship contexts, such as hooking up and friends with benefits. The former involves an understanding that the focus is on sexual fun with no future commitment. The status of friends with benefits is more vague and may involve both romance and a future.

Polyamory and Open Relationships

POLYAMORY INVOLVES multiple loves on the part of both partners in a relationship. Swinging is different from polyamory relationships in that the focus is more on recreational sex. It involves rules, such as alerting the partner of a new sexual encounter, not falling in love, and the partner getting the right to nix a specific selection.

Finding a Long-Term Partner

INDIVIDUALS ARE ATTRACTED to each other in reference to cultural (endogamy, exogamy), sociological (homogamy), and psychological (complementary needs, exchange theory, parental characteristics, and personality types) factors.

Challenges Related to Intimate Sexual Relationships

JEALOUSY RESULTS from feeling that one's love relationship is being threatened. Feelings of jealousy may ignite from both external and internal sources. Sexual guilt is the feeling that results from the violation of your own sexual values. Obsessive relational intrusion and stalking involve unwanted pursuit and invasion of the target person's privacy, sometimes extending to their bodily safety and survival.

Web Links

Polyamory

> http://www.polyamorysociety.org/

Stalking Resource Center: The National Center for Victims of Crime

> http://www.ncvc.org/src/

Twin Oaks Community

> http://www.twinoaks.org

Key Terms

Compersion **148**

Complementary needs theory **154**

Endogamy **153**

Exchange theory **154**

Exogamy **153**

Family of origin **135**

Family of procreation **135**

Friends with benefits **145**

Homogamy theory **153**

Hooking up **143**

Jealousy **155**

Obsessive relational intrusion **156**

Open relationship **150**

Polyamory **146**

Polyfidelity **149**

Principle of least interest **154**

Sex party **147**

Sexual guilt **156**

Stalking **157**

Swingers **146**

Vees **150**

CHAPTER

7

Communication and Sexuality

Sex should be a deepening of communication, not a substitute for it.

Marianne Williamson, author/lecturer

Chapter Outline

7.1 **Principles of Relationship/ Sexual Communication 164**
   7.1a Initiate Discussion of Important Issues **165**
   7.1b Choose Good Timing **165**
   7.1c Give Congruent Messages **166**
   Self-Assessment 7-1:
      The Sexual Signaling Behaviors Inventory **167**
   7.1d Minimize Criticism; Maximize Compliments **168**
   7.1e Communicate Feelings **169**
   7.1f Tell Your Partner What You Want (or Don't) **169**
   7.1g Make Statements Instead of Asking Questions **170**
   7.1h Ask Open-Ended Questions **170**
   7.1i Use Reflective Listening **171**
   7.1j Use "I" Statements **172**
   7.1k Keep the Process Going **172**
   7.1l Take Responsibility for Being Understood **172**
   Personal Decisions 7-1
      What to Do When Your Partner Will Not Communicate **173**
   7.1m Avoid Rehashing/Stay Focused **173**
7.2 **Technology, Communication, and Relationships 173**
   7.2a Texting and Interpersonal Communication **174**
   7.2b When Social Media Sites Become a Relationship Problem **174**
   7.2c Dick Pics **174**
   Technology and Sexuality 7-1:
      Sexting **175**

7.3 **Communication Theory 176**
   7.3a Identity Formation Theory **176**
   7.3b Social Learning Theory **176**
   7.3c Social Exchange Theory **176**
   Social Policy 7-1
      The Law and Sexting **177**
7.4 **Honesty and Dishonesty in Interpersonal Communication 177**
   7.4a Privacy Versus Secrecy and Deception **178**
   7.4b Extent of Dishonesty Among College Students **179**
   7.4c Catfishing **179**
   Personal Decisions 7-2
      Is Honesty Always the Best Policy? **180**
7.5 **Resolving Conflict in Relationships 181**
   7.5a Approach Communication from a Place of Respect and Negotiation **181**
   7.5b Address Recurring Issues **181**
   7.5c Focus on What You Want (Rather Than What You Don't Want) **182**
   7.5d Find Out Your Partner's Point of View **182**
   7.5e Generate Win-Win Solutions to the Conflict **182**
   7.5f Evaluate and Select a Solution **183**
7.6 **Gender Differences in Communication 184**

Web Links 186
Key Terms 186

(Amberlynn Bishop)

Objectives

1. Review the various relationship/sexual principles of effective communication
2. Give examples of congruent messages
3. Know how technology/texting is used to initiate, cultivate, maintain, and end relationships
4. Discuss sexting in relationships and the legal implications
5. Explain the difference between open-ended and closed-ended questions (give examples)
6. Discuss and explain the various communication theories
7. Explain the difference between privacy, secrecy, and deception. Is honesty always the best policy?
8. Understand the extent of dishonesty among college students
9. Describe how to resolve conflict in relationships
10. Review various gender differences in communication

Truth OR Fiction?

T / F 1. Most romantic partners tell each other their expectations regarding sexual exclusivity.

T / F 2. The more couples depend on texting to communicate, the lower their relationship satisfaction.

T / F 3. Disclosing an affair is always the right thing to do.

T / F 4. Dick pics are most often regarded as funny and sexy.

T / F 5. Feminists are more likely to be open with their partners about what they want sexually and to fake orgasm less often.

Answers: 1. F 2. T 3. F 4. F 5. T

Communication, not sex, is the one factor that distinguishes a mediocre relationship from a great one. Notice that when people are proud of their relationship and want others to know how good it is, they will say, "We talked all night." When their relationship has turned sour, however, they say, "We have nothing to say to each other." Just as communication, in general, facilitates a very satisfying relationship, sexual intimacy is enhanced by good sexual communication. Based on a meta-analysis across 48 studies, a positive relationship was found between a couples' sexual communication and all dimensions of sexual function—desire, arousal, erection, lubrication, orgasm, and less pain (Mallory et al., 2019). In addition, Murray et al. (2019) surveyed lovers who reported lower relationship satisfaction if they did not discuss with their partners the decision to have sex/use contraception.

The following provides other examples of the need for communicating about sexuality:

- Mary is involved in an emotional and sexual relationship with Tom. Cunnilingus or a vibrator are the only ways she can experience an orgasm, but she is reluctant to tell Tom what she needs. She has a dilemma: If she tells Tom, she risks his disapproval and his refusal to do what she asks. If she does not tell Tom about her need, she risks growing resentful and feeling dissatisfied in their sexual relationship.

- José has drifted into a flirtatious relationship with a man in his office. He is emotionally and sexually attracted to him. He knows he feels the same. José is also in love with his partner of 3 years, Mateo, and is committed to him emotionally and sexually. Should he tell Mateo about his attraction to the man at work? Should he disclose that he has dreamed about him? That he has sexual fantasies about him? How open should he be?

- Sherry and her husband, Gary, get into frequent arguments. Their pattern is that after arguing, they cool off by not talking to each other for a few hours. But Gary sometimes approaches Sherry for sex as a way to make up. Sherry prefers to talk about their conflict and resolve it before having sex, but she is afraid that if she rejects Gary's sexual advances, he will become angry again. What should she do?

If you can find the time to discuss groceries and domestic tasks with your partner, you can find the time to talk about sexual role-play.

Miya Yamanouchi, *Embrace Your Sexual Self: A Practical Guide for Women*

Resolution of the above dilemmas involves talking about sexual expectations, attraction to others, and the timing of sex after an argument. In this chapter we focus on the details of communicating about sexuality in a relationship. We begin by focusing on basic principles.

7.1 Principles of Relationship/ Sexual Communication

Communication involves both information and the process of exchanging information between individuals. The information, or the messages exchanged between individuals, is referred to as the *content*. The fact that the individuals are communicating, and the way in which they do so, is the *process*. Communication is the exchange of accurate and timely information with another person. If the information does not convey the speaker's intentions, the exchange is inadequate/inaccurate. If the information comes too late ("You never told me you loved me"), it can be as worthless as no information at all.

Communication
Exchange of messages between two or more people

As important as communication is for developing and sustaining fulfilling and enduring relationships, there are few contexts in which we learn the skills of communicating, and talking about sex and sexual issues may be even more difficult—especially for women. In interviews with 95 women ages 20–68, Montemurro and colleagues (2015) found that most were not comfortable talking about sex (doing so is "what men do"), and women who did talk about sex feared being judged negatively.

In this chapter, we review some of the principles of communication as they apply to relationships in general and to the sexual relationship specifically.

7.1a Initiate Discussion of Important Issues

In addition to being clear about when one wants to have sex with one's partner, which tends to be viewed accurately (Dobson et al., 2018), effective communication means addressing important issues. The three scenarios described earlier require talking about sexual expectations, attraction to others, and the timing of sex after an argument. Failure to deal with these issues leads to being frustrated sexually, leaving a relationship vulnerable to an affair, and creating a destructive pattern. Muise et al. (2017b) noted the importance of addressing differences in how much each partner wants sex and not being in the mood. The researchers emphasized that it is equally important to legitimize not being in the mood as well as the partner who wants sex. Indeed, greater sexual satisfaction and relationship quality were associated, particularly for young mothers transitioning to parenthood, when their partners recognized their need not to have sex. Alternatively, Braksmajer (2017) discussed situations in which one person has a dysfunction (e.g. pain during intercourse) and performs oral or manual sex for the partner as "sexual care work" and that this was done willingly for the partner and the relationship.

Sex with others is also an important issue. Londo and Thompson (2016) surveyed 563 respondents in a romantic relationship. Forty percent reported that they had discussed sexual exclusivity; 51% said that this expectation was implied. Sharma et al. (2019) studied the agreements between males in a relationship and found weak agreement about whether the partners had an agreement about sex/relationships outside the dyad and weak agreement on the specifics of those agreements. Discussion of condom use is also important. Couples who report that they become increasingly involved reduce their condom use on the premise that they trust each other to be exclusive (Fortenberry, 2019).

7.1b Choose Good Timing

The phrase "timing is everything" can be applied to interpersonal communication. In general, it is best to discuss important or difficult issues when partners are alone together in private with no distractions, have ample time to talk, and are rested and sober. Avoid discussing important issues when you or your partner are tired or under unusual stress. If one partner (or both) is upset, it may be best to wait until things have cooled off. If you aren't sure whether the timing is right, you can ask your partner, "Is this a good time for you to talk?" Likewise, if your partner brings up an issue you're not ready for, suggest a specific alternative time to have the discussion.

Good timing in communication also means that information should be communicated when the receiver can make an informed response. For example, discussions about sexual issues—such as pregnancy prevention, STI protection, and monogamy—should occur *before* partners engage in sexual activity.

7.1c Give Congruent Messages

The process of communication involves both verbal and nonverbal messages. **Verbal messages** are the words individuals say to each other. **Nonverbal messages** include facial expressions, gestures, bodily contact, and tone of voice. Kozin (2016) noted that flirting is most suggestive when it is nonverbal: "an inadvertent touch, a surreptitious smile, the floating, touch-and-go eye contact, the other-directed demeanor, and the closely set proxemics." When verbal and nonverbal messages match each other, they are considered *congruent messages*. Blunt-Vinti et al. (2019) found that the more the communication, both verbal and nonverbal, about sex the higher the reported sexual satisfaction. The researchers suggested it is more the presence and amount than the style of communication that matters.

The right thing at the wrong time is the wrong thing.

Joshua Harris, *I Kissed Dating Goodbye: A New Attitude Toward Relationships and Romance*

(Trevor Werb)

This couple is exchanging both verbal and nonverbal messages.

What happens when verbal and nonverbal messages don't match? For example, suppose Lashanda and Brian are giving feedback about the last time they had sex. Lashanda says to Brian, "It was good." However, with her sullen facial expression, lack of eye contact, and hesitant tone of voice, Lashanda's verbal and nonverbal messages are not congruent. When this happens, the other partner typically gives more weight to the nonverbal message. In this scenario, Brian would probably believe the nonverbal message, thinking that Lashanda didn't enjoy their encounter. He might also feel that she was not being honest with him.

Communication, both verbal and nonverbal, comes through loud and clear, even on a first date. Cohen (2016b) asked 390 undergraduates to rate their dates' verbal and nonverbal behaviors that signaled that their date was attracted to them. Results revealed differences between females and males. Behaviors that women viewed as signaling attraction included their dates making comments on their physical appearance ("You look nice"), centering the conversation on them ("Tell me about you"), referring to things in common ("We have the same major"), maintaining a lively conversation, discussing the future ("Maybe we could go to that concert"), paying for the meal, extending the date ("Want to take a walk?"), hugging/kissing them goodbye at the end of the date, and texting/calling shortly afterward.

Behaviors that men viewed as signaling that their date was attracted to them included the woman talking about herself—her own life, interests, and hobbies. Men perceived this as the woman letting her guard down and revealing herself. Other first-date behaviors men liked were steering the conversation to the topic of sex ("How do you feel about sex?") and hugging/kissing goodbye at the end of the date. The men did not want the women to initiate contact after the date, but to respond to their texts/calls.

Verbal messages
Words individuals say to each other

Nonverbal messages
Type of communication in which facial expressions, gestures, bodily contact, and tone of voice predominate

You say it best when you say nothing at all.

Alison Krauss, singer

Behaviors both genders noted that signaled that their dates were not attracted to them included waving hello and goodbye, talking about past relationships, focusing on differences, and having no subsequent contact after the date.

Self-Assessment 7-1:
The Sexual Signaling Behaviors Inventory

When you think your partner can be persuaded to have sex, even though they have not yet become aware of your desire, what do you usually do? Check all items that apply.

A. __ Ask directly

B. __ Use some code words with which the person is familiar

C. __ Use more eye contact

D. __ Use touching (snuggling, kissing, etc.)

E. __ Change appearance or clothing

F. __ Remove clothing

G. __ Change tone of voice

H. __ Make indirect talk of sex

I. __ Do more favors for the other

J. __ Set mood atmosphere (music, lighting, etc.)

K. __ Share a drink

L. __ Tease

M. __ Look at sexual material

N. __ Play games such as chase or light "roughhousing"

O. __ Give compliments ("I love you." "You're nice.")

P. __ Use some force

Q. __ Use "suggestive" body movements or postures

R. __ Allow hands to wander

S. __ Lie down

T. __ Other (describe _____)

Dr. Clinton Jesser (1978), a sociology professor who was interested in determining how college students communicate to their heterosexual partners when they want coitus (sexual intercourse), developed this scale. He examined the responses of 50 men and 75 women; 90% and 75%, respectively, were coitally experienced. The most frequently reported signals were "used touching (snuggling, kissing, etc.)" and "allowed hands to wander," which were both endorsed by more than 70% of the men and women as indicating a desire for intercourse. The next most frequent item was "asked directly," which was reported by 58% of the women and 56% of the men. Although there was essentially no difference in the reports of men and women who said they asked directly, women were more likely to report using eye contact, changing their appearance or clothing, and changing their tone of voice. The women who used the direct approach (42 of the 75) were no more likely to be rebuffed than those using an indirect approach.

Source: Jesser, C. J. (1978). Male responses to direct verbal sexual initiatives of females. *The Journal of Sex Research, 14*(2), pp. 118–128, Taylor & Francis Ltd, http://www.tandfonline.com Reprinted by permission of the publisher.

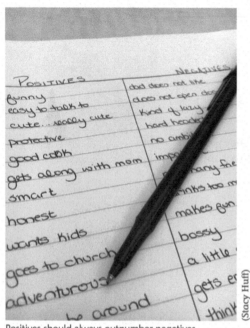

(Stacy Huff)

Positives should always outnumber negatives.

7.1d Minimize Criticism; Maximize Compliments

Research on marital interaction has consistently shown that one brutal zinger can erase 20 acts of kindness (Notarius & Markman, 1994). Because intimate partners are capable of hurting each other so deeply, it is important not to criticize your partner. McNeil et al. (2018) confirmed that partners who report being emotionally attached engage in less negative (hostility, negative affect, and critical of partner) communication.

Conversely, complimenting your partner and making positive remarks can enhance the relationship. Sincere compliments and positive remarks are not only good to hear, they can also create a **self-fulfilling prophecy** effect. A partner who is often told that they are an attentive and affectionate lover is more likely to behave accordingly to make these expectations come true than a partner who receives no feedback or negative feedback.

Gottman and colleagues (1998) studied 130 newlywed couples to examine marital communication patterns that are predictive of marital satisfaction. They found that a high positive-to-negative statement ratio predicted satisfaction among stable couples. In longitudinal studies with more than 2,000 married couples, happy couples, on the average, have five times as many positive interactions and expressions as negative expressions. This five-to-one ratio of positives to negatives is "the magic ratio," according to Gottman (1994, p. 56). He compares it to the pH of soil, the balance between acidity and alkalinity that is essential for fertility; likewise, a relationship must be balanced by a great deal more positivity than negativity for love/sexual interest to be nourished.

Gottman (1994) also identified four negative qualities that sabotage attempts at partner communication and are the strongest predictors of divorce: criticism, contempt, defensiveness, and stonewalling. These qualities are so potentially destructive to a relationship that he calls them "The Four Horsemen of the Apocalypse." Criticism involves an attack on the partner's personality or character rather than a specific behavior. Contempt is behind the intention to insult a partner and may involve psychological abuse. Examples include hostile humor, name-calling, and insults. Defensiveness—denying responsibility or making excuses—escalates conflict. The most symptomatic behavior of relationship disaster is stonewalling, or shutting the partner out. The stonewaller just stops interaction, turning into a "stone wall" (p. 94).

Making positive statements is particularly important at the beginning and end of a discussion. In psychology, the term **primacy/recency effect** refers to the human tendency to remember best what occurs first and last in a sequence. After discussing a difficult issue, partners may be more likely to come away with a positive feeling about the interaction if it begins and ends with positive comments. For example, suppose your partner tries a new sexual position with you that you find unpleasant. You might say, "I didn't enjoy that; please don't do it again." But instead, you could say, "I'm glad you want us to try new things, but that position was a bit uncomfortable/painful for me. I'd rather be on top. Being able to tell you what I like and don't like is one of the things I like most about our relationship." This might result in continued exploration/enjoyment of the sexual relationship, in contrast to the former statement, which could shut the sex down.

If you're so upset with your partner that you begin a discussion by blurting out a negative comment, you can still end the conversation on a positive note, such as, "Thank you for listening to my anger and allowing me to vent." Or, if your partner

Self-fulfilling prophecy
Behaving in such a way to make expectations come true; for example, caustically accusing a partner of infidelity may lead that partner to be unfaithful

Primacy/ recency effect
Tendency of individuals to remember best what occurs first and last in a sequence

begins a discussion with a negative remark such as, "Our sex life is so boring, you never want to try anything new," you can respond positively: "Thanks for telling me about your frustration with our sex life. I need to know when things aren't working. Let's talk about what we can do to spice things up."

7.1e Communicate Feelings

In intimate relationships, it is important to communicate emotions—feelings as well as thoughts. This advice sounds simple, but many people aren't in touch with their feelings or they confuse them with thoughts. If you listen to yourself and to others, you'll hear people communicating thoughts that are often labeled as feelings. For example, the statement "I feel that we should be tested for STIs" communicates a thought, not a feeling. Feelings include sadness, fear, anger, joy, excitement, guilt, boredom, anxiety, frustration, and depression. "We should be tested for STIs" is not a feeling. The statement "I am afraid to have sex with you because we haven't been tested for STIs" is expressing a feeling—fear.

To communicate emotions, you must first recognize and label, or describe, them. Unfortunately, many people learn to hide and repress unpleasant feelings. Before you can communicate your emotions to a partner, you must access your feelings and give yourself permission to feel them and talk about them. Attempts to cover up or minimize unpleasant feelings may be made with the best intentions, but repressing your emotions or stifling your partner's often serves to prolong the emotional state rather than to resolve it. What are your feelings about your sexual relationship with your partner—joy, excitement, adventurousness, sadness, fear, hopelessness, guilt, or apprehension?

Bennett (2019) emphasized the positive value of noises/words during sex and categorized 477 statements made by lovers during sexual activity. Examples included reflexive calls ("oh God!"), emotional bonding ("I love you"), instructive statements ("where should I cum?"), and sexual submission ("do me good baby"). Some statements revealed pain ("something hurts" "I'm cramping up").

7.1f Tell Your Partner What You Want (or Don't)

In a relationship, it is important for partners to decide what behaviors they want from each other, to tell each other in clear behavioral terms what they want, and to do so in a positive way. Table 7-1 provides examples of how complaints can be reframed into requests.

TABLE 7-1	**Rephrasing Complaints into Positive Requests**
Complaints	**Requests**
I don't like to make love when you haven't showered.	Please take a shower before we make love. I'll guarantee better sex if you shower first.
Don't rub so hard.	Please rub more softly … like this.
I don't want you to stay up so late at night.	How about coming to bed at 10:00 and letting me know how I can make it worth your while?
Leave me alone; I'm trying to get ready for work!	We can have some long, slow sex after a glass of wine later tonight.
Whenever I ask you to massage me, you end up wanting to have sex with me.	Just give me a massage, please. Tomorrow night I'll give you one as a prelude to fun sex.

One common error people make when communicating is not being specific enough about what they want. When you tell your partner what you want, use specific, behavioral terms; notice that the requests in Table 7-1 are specific.

Women may be less assertive about what they want sexually than men, particularly when they want oral sex. In a study of 237 sexually active women, the researchers observed that if they perceived that their partners would not be open to giving them oral sex, they were less likely to ask them to do so (Satinsky & Jozkowski, 2015). However, more recent research revealed that feminists and women endorsing feminist beliefs are more likely to be open about their sexual needs and to be less likely to fake orgasm since their sexual needs are being met (Hilliard et al. 2019c). Nevertheless, still other research reveals that women may also have sex reluctantly rather than kindly reject their partner. The outcome is negative for the relationship. It is better not to have sex (Kim et al. 2018).

7.1g Make Statements Instead of Asking Questions

When partners are uncomfortable or unwilling to express their feelings and behavioral desires, they may put their statements in the form of questions. For example, partners who have difficulty expressing what they want may ask the question, "Do you think we should see a sex therapist?" instead of making the statement "I think we might benefit from seeing a sex therapist."

Transforming statements into questions allows partners to mask or hide their true feelings, thoughts, and desires—and thus interferes with the development and maintenance of relationship intimacy. Try to discern which of your partner's and your own questions are really statements that are masking feelings, wants, or both, and rephrase the questions into statements.

7.1h Ask Open-Ended Questions

Open-ended question
Broad question designed to elicit a great deal of information

Closed-ended question
Type of question that yields little information and can be answered in one word

Touch-and-ask rule
Sexual technique whereby each touch and caress is accompanied by the question, "How does that feel?" and is followed by feedback from the partner

When you want information from your partner, open-ended questions will often yield more information than closed-ended ones. An **open-ended question** is a broad question designed to elicit a lot of information. In contrast, a **closed-ended question** can be answered in one word. Open-ended questions are useful in finding out your partner's feelings, thoughts, and desires. One way to use open-ended questions in a sexual relationship is to follow the **touch-and-ask rule**, whereby each touch and caress is accompanied by the question, "How does that feel?" The partner then gives feedback. By using this rule, a couple can learn a lot about how to please each other. Guiding and moving the partner's hand or body are also ways of giving feedback. Babin (2013) confirmed that verbal and nonverbal communication during sex were positively related to sexual satisfaction.

Table 7-2 provides examples of open- and closed-ended questions. Both may be valuable.

My wife said I don't listen to her—at least I think that's what she said.

Laurence J. Peter, author and educator

TABLE 7-2	Open-Ended and Closed-Ended Questions
Open-Ended Questions	**Closed-Ended Questions**
What are your thoughts about condom use?	Do you have a condom?
What can I do to please you sexually?	Would you like oral sex?
What do you think about having children?	Do you want to have children? How many? What interval?
How do you feel about trying something new?	Do you want to try anal sex? Do you want me to tie you up, blindfold you, and enjoy you orally?
What are your views on abortion?	Would you agree to have an abortion if we got pregnant?

7.1i Use Reflective Listening

One of the most important communication skills is the art of **reflective listening**: restating the meaning of what your partner has said to you in a conversation. With this technique, your partner is more likely to feel that you are listening and that you understand their feelings, thoughts, and desires. In practicing reflective listening, it is important to repeat the ideas or thoughts expressed by your partner, as well as the emotions that your partner has conveyed. For example, suppose that after you have made love, your partner says, "Next time, can we spend a little more time on foreplay?" You might respond by reflecting back your partner's message: "You're saying that you feel frustrated that we didn't take more time to be loving and affectionate before having intercourse and that more foreplay is something you definitely want us to include in our lovemaking."

Using the technique of reflective listening is challenging when one partner blames or criticizes the other. When people are blamed or criticized, they typically respond by withdrawing from the interaction, attacking back through blaming or criticizing the other person, or defending or explaining themselves. Each of these responses may produce further conflict and frustration. Alternatively, instead of withdrawing, attacking back, or defending and explaining, the listener can simply reflect back what the partner has said. At some point in the discussion, the criticized partner should express their own thoughts, feelings, and views. However, it is best to first acknowledge the other person's feelings and thoughts through reflective listening. Table 7-3 presents an example of a critical or accusatory remark, followed by four types of possible responses. Compare the reflective listening response with the other three.

Reflective listening
Communication technique in which one person restates the meaning of what their partner has said in a conversation

TABLE 7-3	Four Responses to a Critical or Accusatory Remark
Critical or Accusatory Remark	
"You told me you had only a couple of sexual partners before me. You lied."	
Four Possible Responses	
1. Withdraw from the interaction: "I can't handle this. I'm out of here."	
2. Attack back: "Well, you didn't tell me you had herpes. That's lying too."	
3. Defend or explain: "I was afraid you would break up with me if I told you the real number. ... I didn't want to hurt you or us."	
4. Reflective listening: "You are angry at me for telling you I had fewer previous sexual partners than I really did. You wish that I had been honest with you. I'm sorry."	

Making "I" statements of one's position/feelings and avoiding "you" accusatory statements are helpful in a difficult conversation.

7.1j Use "I" Statements

"I" statements focus on the feelings and thoughts of the communicator without making a judgment on others. Because "I" statements are a clear and nonthreatening way of expressing what you want and how you feel, they are likely to result in a positive change in the listener's behavior.

In contrast, **"you" statements** blame or criticize the listener and often result in increasing negative feelings and behavior in the relationship. For example, suppose you are angry with your partner for watching porn. Rather than saying, "You are very deceitful watching porn. ... I checked your history on the computer, and you've been indulging yourself since we have been together" (a "you" statement), you might say, "It upsets me that you watch porn when I am not here. I much prefer that we watch porn together." The latter focuses on your feelings and what you would like to happen.

7.1k Keep the Process Going

In the introduction to this chapter, we noted that communication involves both content (the words that are said) and process (the continued interaction/discussion). It is important to keep the process going and not allow the content to shut it down. For example, Angela says to Andy, "I don't trust you." Instead of Andy blurting, "I don't care what you think" while he leaves the room, a more helpful response might be, "I appreciate your telling me your feelings; tell me why you feel that way." In this way, the conversation continues, and the couple can move toward a resolution. Otherwise, the discussion stops, and nothing is resolved.

"I" statements
Statements that focus on the feelings and thoughts of the communicator without making a judgment on what the other person says or does

"You" statements
In communication theory, those statements that blame or criticize the listener and often result in increasing negative feelings and behavior in the relationship

7.1l Take Responsibility for Being Understood

Partners often blame each other for not understanding what is said. "Are you deaf? Didn't you hear what I said? Can't you understand anything?" are phrases that blame the partner. The result is that the partner feels bad, will become emotionally distant, and will be less interested in subsequent communication. To avoid these negative feelings, which are likely to increase the distance between partners, each partner should take full responsibility for making themselves heard: "I'm sorry; I'm not making myself clear. What I am trying to say is that I think we should stop talking about this issue and let it go." The partner may not like what is being said but doesn't feel belittled for not understanding.

Cultural Diversity

The culture in which a person is reared will influence the meaning of various words. An American woman was dating a man from Iceland. When she asked him, "Would you like to go out to dinner?" he responded, "Yes, maybe." She felt confused by this response and was uncertain whether he wanted to eat out. It was not until she visited his home in Iceland and asked his mother, "Would you like me to set the table?"—and his mother replied, "Yes, maybe"—that she discovered that "Yes, maybe" means "Yes, definitely."

PERSONAL DECISIONS 7-1

What to Do When Your Partner Will Not Communicate

One of the most frustrating experiences in relationships occurs when one partner wants and tries to communicate, but the other partner will not. Of course, partners always communicate—even not communicating is a way of communicating. What if your partner will not respond to something you say? You might try the following (Duncan & Rock, 1993):

1. *Change your strategy.* Rather than trying to coax your partner into talking, become less available for conversation and stop trying to initiate or maintain discussion. Keep it short if a discussion does start. This strategy removes the pressure on the partner to talk and shifts the power in the relationship.

2. *Interpret silence in a positive way.* For example, "We are so close that we don't always have to be talking" or "I feel good when you're quiet because I know that it means everything is all right between us." This negates any power your partner might be expressing through silence.

3. *Focus less on the relationship and more on satisfying yourself.* When you do things for yourself, you need less from others in the way of attention and assurance.

7.1m Avoid Rehashing/Stay Focused

Partners sometimes get off the subject and turn a discussion into a session of criticizing their partner. For example, if the topic is "Where is our relationship going?" the conversation can easily degenerate into accusations of "You never loved me," and "Let's break up." Alternatively, the partners can stay focused on what they do and don't want from their relationship.

Applying the communication principles presented in this chapter to everyday interactions can enhance both individual and relationship well-being and increase your sexual satisfaction with your partner. The principles and techniques are fairly simple but not necessarily easy to apply. For effective application, you must first abandon old patterns of communication and deliberately replace them with the new. Most couples report that the effort is worthwhile.

7.2 Technology, Communication, and Relationships

Text messages have become a primary means for flirting and for the initiation, escalation, and maintenance of romantic relationships in young adults (Gibbs, 2012; Bergdall et al., 2012).

(Trevor Werb)

Technology helps couples in long-distance relationships to see and talk with each other frequently via Skype or Zoom dates.

National **DATA**

Use of smartphones is pervasive. Ninety-six percent of Americans ages 18–29, and 81% of all adults in the US use a smartphone (Pew Research Center, 2019c).

7.2a Texting and Interpersonal Communication

While personal, portable, wirelessly networked technology in the form of iPhones, Androids, iPads, and so on have become commonplace, the use of technology in relationships has both positive and negative effects. On the positive side, it allows for instant and unabated connection—individuals can text each other throughout the day so that they are "in effect, together all the time." On the negative side is the lack of interpersonal skill development when technology-based communication is used more than face-to-face talking (Nesi et al., 2017). In addition, is the development of **nomophobia**, in which the individual is dependent on virtual environments to the point of having a social phobia (King et al., 2013) and finds personal interaction difficult. In addition, texting in the presence of your partner interrupts your face-to-face communication and encourages the intrusion of your work/job or other texting respondent into the emotional intimacy of your love relationship. "Even when we are alone, my partner is texting," said one undergraduate. When texting becomes *sexting*, with sexual photos, the behavior can have legal consequences (see *Technology and Sexuality 7–1*).

> *People have entire relationships via text messages now.*
>
> Danielle Steel, novelist

7.2b When Social Media Sites Become a Relationship Problem

Norton and Baptist (2012) identified how social networking sites (such as Facebook, with over 2 billion users) are problematic for couples—the sites are intrusive (one partner surfs while the other is talking), encourage compulsive use (partner checks social media during mealtimes and on vacation), and can facilitate infidelity (flirting/cheating online). The researchers identified how 205 married individuals mitigated the impact of technology on their relationship. Three strategies included openness (each spouse knew the other's passwords and online friends and they had access to each other's online social networking accounts, email, etc.), fidelity (flirting and online relationships were off limits), and appropriate people (knowing the friends of the partner, and no former partners allowed).

7.2c Dick Pics

Waling & Pym (2017) conceptualize dick pics as existing within two competing frameworks: (1) sexting and (2) sexual harassment. These two competing frameworks diverge on the axis of consent. The sexting framework positions dick pics as an extension of conventional and consensual sexting behaviors, while the second identifies dick pics as a form of nonconsensual sexual interaction, which can be categorized as sexual harassment, offensive, or abusive.

Nomophobia
Dependence on virtual reality environments to the point that one has a social phobia

Sexting is the sending of erotic text and photo images via cell phone, internet, or social media. Sexting begins in high school and continues into college. The behavior has become common in undergraduate relationships, particularly in long-distance dating relationships (Bridle & Humphreys, 2019). Weisskirch et al. (2017) surveyed 459 heterosexual, unmarried undergraduates: 80% reported sending a sexually suggestive text, 62% proposed a sexual activity, and 55% sent a sexually suggestive photo/video. The researchers noted that "sexting may emerge in romantic relationships when one individual feels comfortable in the romantic relationship, perceives the partner as desiring or receptive to sexting, and feels a degree of commitment" (p. 691). Drouin et al. (2018) noted that sexting with a romantic partner was accompanied by the expectation to engage in the sexual activities with the partner the next time they were together.

Sexting may be both objectifying and liberating (Liong & Cheng (2019): objectifying in that it reduces the individual to a sexual object, liberating in that it allows the individual to experience themselves as a free sexual being. Some research has shown that women who send sex photos to their male partners are pressured to do so. This finding has been questioned by Lee and Crofts (2015), who provided data that as few as 10% of females reported pressure from a male as the primary reason for sending sex photos, finding that fun and flirtatiousness were the more common reasons. However, Lippman and Campbell (2014), among other researchers, noted that females are both pressured to send sex photos and labeled as sluts for doing so. A study by Usigan (2011) also found that teen girls are pressured and shamed by peers for sexting, and Van Ouytsel et al. (2017) noted that adolescent females feel pressure to send sex text messages out of fear of losing their boyfriends. The downsides of sending sexting photos include: (1) they could be used to coerce/blackmail the partner, (2) they could be distributed out of revenge after a breakup, or (3) they could be forwarded to others to boast about having received the photographs. Klettke et al. (2019) found in a sample of 444 young adults that receiving unwanted sexts, or sexting under coercion, was associated with higher levels of depression and anxiety, symptoms of stress, and lower self-esteem.

Oswald et al. (2019) surveyed 1,087 men between the ages of 16 and 92 years, and found that almost half (48%) of these men reported having sent an unsolicited dick pic, or one that was not specifically requested. These men were motivated primarily by a desire to receive sexy pictures in return; men hoped to elicit positive feelings of sexual excitement in their recipients. Men who had sent unsolicited dick pics endorsed higher levels of narcissism as well as both hostile and benevolent sexism than men who had not sent such images. Many men reported that they viewed the sending of unsolicited dick pics as "a normal way of flirting." In tandem, these results suggest that senders of unsolicited dick pics conceptualize these as an extension of sexting culture more generally, rather than a form of harassment.

Vogels & Stewart (2018) surveyed 108 individuals, ages 9–54 (88% ciswomen, 12% trans) about having received a "dick pic." Almost three quarters (72%) reported having received a dick pic, with their predominant reaction being that the photos were "intrusive," "gross," and "harassing." Hence, dick pics were not viewed as fun and sexy, but rather as harassment. Further evidence (e.g., Ringrose & Lawrence, 2018; Vitis & Gilmour, 2017; Waling & Pym, 2017) suggests that many women do conceptualize dick pics as an intrusive form of sexual harassment.

The contrast between male senders' and women recipients' views on dick pics may be due in part to evolutionary forces, which have driven men to overperceive sexual intent (e.g., Farris et al., 2008; Haselton, 2003). Modern men may overestimate women's interest in receiving nude imagery based on their own receptivity in reversed roles (March & Wagstaff, 2017; Waling & Pym, 2017) and may thus send dick pics as a projection of their own sexual desires onto women.

7.3 Communication Theory

Because communication involves interaction in social contexts, we examine various theoretical frameworks for relationship communication. Models of communication come from the fields of mathematics, psychology, and sociology. Three that seem especially relevant to communication between partners are identity formation theory, social learning theory, and social exchange theory.

7.3a Identity Formation Theory

One reason that interpersonal communication is so important, according to such theorists as George Herbert Mead and Erik Erikson, is that our self-identity develops largely as a result of social interaction. We learn about ourselves from the responses of others—their communications give us cues about how important, capable, or inadequate we are. Cooley (1964) coined the term **looking-glass self** to describe the idea that the image people have of themselves is a reflection of what other people tell them about themselves. However, reflections from others that are inconsistent or contradictory with your self-image may cause tension or anxiety. Individuals may see themselves differently from the way others perceive them. For example, when a male hooks up nightly with a new partner, he may see himself as a stud that women love, but others may see him as a lonely guy who is incapable of intimacy.

7.3b Social Learning Theory

Verbal behavior, positive or negative, is decreased or increased depending on whether it is reinforced or punished. For example, if a person expresses an opinion ("I think that same-sex marriage should be legalized throughout the United States") and their partner reinforces this view with "I agree," the person is likely to continue talking about gay rights. On the other hand, the partner might say, "How can you say that? Marriage is for women and men who can reproduce/have children." That response is likely to punish expressing an opinion on same-sex marriage, so that the person may be more likely to change the subject.

Verbal statements may be discriminative or serve as cues for other types of responses. For example, a partner may say, "I am going upstairs to take a shower and will be ready for a glass of wine" (translation: "I am getting cleaned up for sexual intimacy"). A discriminative stimulus may also be used to cue that a behavior will not lead to reinforcement, as when the partner replies, "I am going to bed. See you tomorrow."

7.3c Social Exchange Theory

Social exchange theorists combine behavioral psychology and economic theory. Exchange theorists suggest that the interaction between partners can be described as a ratio of rewards to costs. For example, two strangers who meet with the possibility of hooking up will continue to interact only if each has a high ratio of rewards to cost.

Rewards are positive outcomes of the interaction—each smiles at the other, says nice things, touches the other gently and nondemandingly, and so on. *Costs* refer to negative outcomes, such as receiving criticism or feeling regret, which make the interaction painful. As long as the rewards outweigh the costs and there is a profit for the interaction, the relationship will continue. When the costs are higher than the rewards and there is a loss for the interaction, the relationship will stop. In long-term relationships, a person may forgo immediate rewards in anticipation of long-term gain, especially if there is reciprocity in the exchanges between the partners. Although this idea

Looking-glass self
Idea that the image people have of themselves is a reflection of what other people tell them they are

doesn't sound romantic, sociological theorists observe that even love relationships are established and continued on the basis of reciprocity—that is, exchanged benefits and costs. Social exchange theories have been applied to the study of relationships and sexuality, so that people who hook up can be understood as exchanging reinforcers throughout the evening as they move toward one apartment or the other—the partners smile at each other, they drink, they flirt, they touch each other, and so on. If either partner stops reinforcing, the interaction will stop, and no hooking up will occur.

Social Policy 7-1

The Law and Sexting

The transmission of sexual content—either words, photos, or video—from one person to another is common across all types of romantic relationships (committed, casually sexual, and cheating), with text messaging being the primary medium used to send sex pictures and videos (Drouin et al., 2013). Sexting may be positive, as a relationship enhancer, or negative—perhaps as a ticket to becoming a felon if the photos are of underage individuals.

In a survey of 1,652 undergraduates, 65% reported having sent sexually suggestive texts or photos to a current or potential partner, and 69% had received them. Approximately 31% shared these private communications with a third party. Contrary to Lee and Crofts's data (2015), females in this study were significantly more likely to feel pressured to send sex texts and photos than males (Burke Winkleman et al., 2014).

While most undergraduates are not at risk as long as the parties are age 18 or older, sending erotic photos of individuals younger than age 18 can be criminal. Former congressman Anthony Wiener was sentenced to 21 months in jail for sexting a 15-year-old. Many countries consider sexting to be child pornography, and laws related to child pornography have been applied in some cases. In the United States, six high school students in Greensburg, Pennsylvania, were charged with child pornography after three teenage girls allegedly took nude or seminude photos of themselves and shared them with male classmates via their cell phones.

While there is disagreement whether sexting by teenagers in romantic relationships constitutes child pornography, caution is warranted (Zhang, 2010; Jaishankar, 2009). Sexuality educators might do well to alert students to the catastrophic legal consequences of sexting (Burke et al., 2014). Ricketts et al. (2015) investigated the sexting behaviors of adolescents under the age of 18 and found that deviant peer associations and internet-related problems such as online addiction were associated with sexting by juveniles. Some students may view sending sexual images on Snapchat® as safer because the image disappears quickly, before it can be saved or sent to someone, but many third-party apps enable saving and sharing, so it's far from foolproof (Struckman-Johnson et al., 2014).

Sexting also has consequences for adult to adult messaging. In 2018, Army Major General Joseph Harrington lost a rank as punishment for sending over 1,000 messages to the wife of an enlisted man.

7.4 Honesty and Dishonesty in Interpersonal Communication

Deception, dishonesty, cheating, lying, and infidelity—whatever the label—have become major sources of emotional distress and sexual dissatisfaction in relationships. Being cheated on is not uncommon among undergraduates. Of 9,943 undergraduate females, 55% reported that they had been involved with a partner who cheated on them. Of 3,034 undergraduate males, 49% reported that they had been cheated on. Of those who reported having cheated on a partner, 27% were female and 26% were male (Hall & Knox, 2019). Definitions of cheating vary, with sexual behavior, such as oral sex, more likely to be identified as cheating than emotional behavior, such as being in love with someone else. Women are more likely than men to define emotional behaviors as cheating (Eiseman & Peterson, 2014).

> *We see the utter loss of shame among political leaders where they're caught in a lie and they just double down and they lie some more.*
>
> Former president Barack Obama

Dishonesty and deception take various forms. In addition to telling an outright lie, people may pretend, exaggerate, or conceal the truth. They may put up a good front, be two-faced, or tell a partial truth. People also engage in self-deception when they deny or fail to acknowledge their own thoughts, feelings, values, beliefs, priorities, goals, and desires.

7.4a Privacy Versus Secrecy and Deception

In virtually every relationship, partners avoid sharing some details about themselves or their past. Sometimes partners don't share their feelings and concerns with each other. However, it is worthwhile to distinguish when withholding information about ourselves is an act of privacy and when it is an act of secrecy or deception. When we withhold private information, we are creating or responding to boundaries between ourselves and other people. There may be no harm done in maintaining some aspects of ourselves as private, not to be disclosed to others. Indeed, it is healthy to have and maintain boundaries between the self and others. However, the more intimate the relationship, the greater your desire is to share your most personal and private self with your partner—and the greater the emotional consequences of not sharing.

College students also keep secrets from their partners. In a study of 431 under-graduates, Easterling et al. (2012) found the following:

1. *Most kept secrets.* Over 60% of respondents reported having kept a secret from a romantic partner, and over one-quarter of respondents reported that they are currently doing so. Some secrets were about sexual preferences: 20% of a sample of adults reported that they enjoyed the fetish of sexual role playing as an adult baby/diaper lover, or ABDL (Zamboni, 2018).

2. *Females kept more secrets.* Sensitivity to the partner's reaction, desire to avoid hurting the partner, and desire to avoid damaging the relationship may be the primary reasons females were more likely than males to keep a secret from a romantic partner.

3. *Spouses kept more secrets.* Spouses have a great deal to lose if there is an indiscretion or if one partner does something the other will disapprove of, such as spending too much money. Partners who are dating or "seeing each other" have less to lose and are less likely to keep secrets.

4. *Black people kept more secrets.* In the United States, black people are a minority who are still victimized by the white majority. One way to avoid such victimization is to keep your thoughts to yourself, keeping them secret for the purpose of self-preservation. This practice may generalize to romantic relationships.

5. *Homosexuals kept more secrets.* In response to a similar history of victimization, many homosexuals sought security in silence. Indeed, the phrase "in the closet" means keeping a secret.

Respondents were asked why they kept a personal secret from a romantic partner. "To avoid hurting the partner" was the top reason reported by 38.9% of the respondents. "It would alter our relationship," and "I feel so ashamed for what I did," were reported by 17.7% and 10.7% of the respondents, respectively.

7.4b Extent of Dishonesty Among College Students

Lying in relationships among college students is not uncommon. In one study, 77 college students kept diaries of their daily social interactions and reported telling two lies a day (DePaulo et al., 1996). Participants said they did not regard their lies as serious and did not plan them or worry about being caught. In another study, 137 students reported 21 lies they had told to a current or past partner. The most frequently told lie, reported by 31% of the respondents, was "the number of previous sex partners" (Knox et al., 1993). College students and community members reported the most serious lies they ever told were to their closest relationship partners (DePaulo et al., 2004). Their motivations were to get something they wanted, do something to which they felt entitled, avoid punishment or confrontation, keep up appearances, protect others, or avoid hurting others.

Walters and Burger (2013) studied individuals who defined themselves as having cheated on a romantic partner and who informed the partner about it. While some felt guilty, others wanted to come clean. Still others saw the infidelity as a sign that the relationship was not what it should be or considered it as a way to let the partner know that they wanted a polyamorous relationship. A significant portion of the respondents also felt that, out of respect for the partner and their relationship, they needed to disclose. Most disclosures were done in person (38%) or over the phone (38%). Other means of disclosure included being informed by a third party (12%), via email (6%), and through text messaging (6%). The following is an example of an interview with an undergraduate talking about disclosing to her partner:

I told him, you know, "You weren't there for me. You haven't been a boyfriend to me the last few months. I don't know what you expect from me and everything." He was mad, and I expected him to be. But I mean [pause] he kinda understood. He didn't really say much, so there really wasn't much said after [the disclosure]. But the next day he was talking to me again and everything, and he was like, "It's going to be okay. We're going to get past it." But, we didn't. (Walters & Burger, 2013, p. 36)

> *Often the difference between a successful marriage and a mediocre one consists of leaving about three or four things a day unsaid.*
>
> Harlan Miller, author

7.4c Catfishing

Catfishing is the process of luring someone into believing that a person they meet online (e.g. Tinder, Twitter, Facebook, etc.) is real when the "person" is fake and made up by someone who enjoys tricking them. With stolen pictures and false identities, those who catfish create fake social media accounts to lure victims into a romantic relationship. Impersonating a member of the military is one of the most common scams (Allan, 2018). In the military scenario, the person is presented as one who is deployed and not permitted to reveal where they are or to Skype. Then suddenly one day the person needs money to fly home and asks the now romantically involved person to pay. People who are lured into having a relationship with the catfisher and those who have their photos used by the catfish scammer are both victims (Flynn, 2019). In an interview of 27 self-identified catfish scammers, 41% mentioned being lonely and unable to connect socially with others (Vanman, 2018).

Catfishing
The process of luring someone into believing that a fake person they meet online is actually real

PERSONAL DECISIONS 7-2

Is Honesty Always the Best Policy?

Good communication often implies open communication, and there is a social script claiming that total honesty with your partner is always best. As evidence, there is an adage about marriage, "The secret of a good marriage is: no secrets." In reality, how much honesty is good for a marriage/relationship? Is honesty always the best policy?

Some individuals believe that relationships can be functional only when a certain amount of illusion is maintained. Not to be told that you are overweight or that you aren't the best of lovers allows you to maintain the illusion that your partner never thinks of your weight (particularly when you eat a second bag of potato chips) or your sexual inadequacy. You are happier, and your relationship is not hampered by your partner's honesty.

Complete, or "radical" honesty may carry negative consequences. Suppose you tell your partner about all of your previous partners or sexual relationships because you want an open and honest relationship. Later, during times of anger, your partner brings up this information in the future. Was your honesty worth the consequences?

Disclosing an extramarital affair requires special consideration—spouses might carefully consider the consequences before disclosing. While there are exceptions, in general, disclosure might result in a divorce, and the lives of any affected children might be changed forever. Some couples, however, may find that the disclosure of an affair by one partner forces them to examine problems in their relationship, seek marriage therapy, or both. In such cases, disclosure may ultimately result in bringing the couple closer together in an emotional sense. Caughlin and Bassinger (2015) question whether "completely open and honest communication is really what we want," suggesting that the value of openness should be "balanced against other values, such as politeness, respectfulness, and discretion" (p. f2).

Most individuals are careful about what they say to each other and deliberately withhold information, in some cases for fear of negative outcomes. Some information, however, should not be withheld from the partner, including previous marriages and children, a sexual orientation different from what the partner expects, alcohol or other drug addiction, a sexually transmitted infection (such as HIV or genital herpes) or possible exposure, and any known physical limitations (such as sterility). Disclosures of this nature include anything that would have a significant impact on the partner or the relationship.

Some individuals wait until after the marriage to disclose a secret. One example is a cross-dresser who, fearing his wife's disapproval, did not disclose his proclivity until years after the marriage. Indeed, he never disclosed; instead, his wife found his bra and panties and confronted him. Although she was ultimately able to accept his desire to cross-dress (and they would shop together), his lack of disclosure was a definite risk. In another case of a cross-dresser who also had not disclosed the practice, he later found that his wife could not overlook his secret. She found out because he had forgotten to remove his earrings one day after he had been cross-dressing. Although they had been married 16 years, had four children, and she viewed him as a good provider, good father, and faithful husband, she regarded his deception across the years as unforgivable.

One of our students reported on how she was "catfished":

I was on the app Tinder after a bad break up with my ex. It was a horrible heartbreak so I started chatting with this guy named Adam. We hung out a few times and then things became sexual (against my better judgement). After we had sex he completely dropped out of my life. His phone was disconnected. I tried searching him on social media. And I could not find anybody by his name from the location he said he was from. I even paid for a one-time phone background check and the name registered with the phone wasn't the name he gave me. He deactivated his Tinder account or deleted me off of his chat list so I couldn't contact him there. I finally was able to contact him over Snapchat but most of the time he would read my messages then not reply. I finally irritated him enough to where he finally talked to me. I asked him why he never came back after we had sex and his excuse was because he was gay. So that was the first and the last time I ever had sex with a guy that I didn't really know.

Which later caused me to be very scared that when I had sex with the man I'm dating now I was terrified that I would make the mistake of sleeping with someone who didn't care about me.

7.5 Resolving Conflict in Relationships

Being able to resolve conflict is an essential skill for relationship survival, maintenance, and satisfaction. More than half (56%) of the 343 university students surveyed reported having a very troublesome relationship within the past 5 years. Of those who had a troubled relationship, most (69%) reported talking to the partner in an attempt to resolve the problem, 19% avoided discussing the problem, and 18% avoided the partner (Levitt et al., 1996).

Be quick to resolve conflicts before they mature to become wars. The energetic crocodile was once a delicate egg!

Israelmore Ayivor, *The Great Hand Book of Quotes*

Howard Markman is head of the Center for Marital and Family Studies at the University of Denver. He and his colleagues have been studying 150 couples at yearly intervals (beginning before marriage) to determine the factors most responsible for marital success. They have found that communication skills that reflect the ability to handle conflict and disagreement are the single biggest predictor of marital success over time (Markman et al., 1994):

> Remember: It's not how much you love one another, how good your sex life is, or what problems you have with money that best predicts the future quality of your marriage. ... The key is for you to develop constructive tactics and ground rules for handling the conflicts and disagreements that are inevitable in any significant relationship. (p. 6)

There is also merit in developing and using conflict negotiation skills before problems develop. Not only are individuals more willing to work on issues when things are going well, but they also have not developed negative patterns of response that are difficult to change. In the following sections, we review principles and techniques that are helpful in resolving interpersonal conflict.

7.5a Approach Communication from a Place of Respect and Negotiation

Partners who care about each other and their relationship can best achieve their relationship goals by approaching communication on a particular issue or topic from a place of respect and negotiation. Each partner must regard the other as an equal and acknowledge that their perspectives and views deserve respect. Neither partner is to denigrate the other or dictate an outcome. Rather, the goal of a discussion is for each to have a positive feeling about the outcome rather than to have their position accepted. As one spouse said, "It is better for us to be right with each other than to be right in getting our own way." This context of respect and negotiation implies that denigrating the partner or being emotionally abusive are both counterproductive to discussion and conflict resolution.

7.5b Address Recurring Issues

Some couples are uncomfortable confronting each other to talk about issues that plague them. They fear that such confrontation will further weaken their relationship. Pam is jealous that Mark spends more time with other people at parties than with her.

"When we go someplace together," she blurts out, "he drops me and starts talking with someone else." Her jealousy is spreading to other areas of their relationship: "When we're walking down the street and he turns his head to look at another woman, I get furious." If Pam and Mark don't discuss her feelings about Mark's behavior, their relationship may deteriorate as a result of a negative response cycle: He looks at another woman, and she gets angry. Then he gets angry at her anger and finds that he is even more attracted to other women. She gets angrier because he escalates his attention to other women, and so on.

To bring the matter up, Pam might say, "I feel jealous when you spend more time with other women at parties than with me. I need some help in dealing with these feelings." By expressing her concern in this way, she has identified the problem from her perspective and asked for her partner's cooperation in handling it. (She did not attack; instead, she invited her partner's help in dealing with an issue.)

7.5c Focus on What You Want (Rather Than What You Don't Want)

Dealing with conflict is more likely to result in resolution if both partners focus on what they want rather than what they don't want. For example, rather than tell Mark she doesn't want him to spend so much time with other women at parties, Pam might tell him that she wants him to spend more time with her at parties. "I'd feel better if we go together and stay together," she said, "We don't need to be joined at the hip, and we will certainly want to talk with others; the bulk of our time there, however, should be spent with each other."

7.5d Find Out Your Partner's Point of View

We often assume that we know what our partner thinks and why they do things. Sometimes we are wrong. Rather than assume how they think and feel about a particular issue, we might ask them open-ended questions in an effort to get them to tell us thoughts and feelings about a particular situation. Pam's words to Mark might be, "What is it like for you when we go to parties? How do you feel about my jealousy?"

After your partner has shared their thoughts about an issue with you, it is important for you to summarize their perspective in a nonjudgmental way. After Mark has told Pam how he feels about their being at parties together, she can summarize his perspective by saying, "You feel that I cling to you more than I should, and you would like me to let you wander around without feeling like you're making me angry." (She may not agree with his view, but she knows exactly what it is—and Mark knows that she knows.)

7.5e Generate Win-Win Solutions to the Conflict

A **win-win solution** is one in which both people involved in a conflict feel satisfied with the agreement or resolution to the conflict. It is imperative to look for win-win solutions to conflicts. Solutions in which one person wins and the other person loses involve one person not getting their needs met. As a result, the person who loses may develop feelings of resentment, anger, hurt, and hostility toward the winner and may even look for ways to get even. In this way, the winner is also a loser. In intimate relationships, one winner really means two losers.

Win-win solution
Outcome of an interpersonal conflict whereby both people feel satisfied with the agreement or resolution

Generating win-win solutions to interpersonal conflicts often requires the technique of **brainstorming**, which involves suggesting as many alternatives as possible without evaluating them. Brainstorming is crucial to conflict resolution because it shifts the partners' focus from criticizing each other's perspective to working together to develop alternative solutions. Any solution may be acceptable as long as it is one of mutual agreement.

7.5f Evaluate and Select a Solution

After a number of solutions are generated, each solution should be evaluated, and the best one should be selected. In evaluating solutions to conflicts, it may be helpful to ask the following questions:

- Does the solution satisfy both individuals? Is it a win-win solution?
- Is the solution specific? Does the solution specify exactly who is to do what, how, and when?
- Is the solution realistic? Can both parties realistically follow through with what they have agreed upon?
- Does the solution prevent the problem from recurring?
- Does the solution specify what is to happen if the problem recurs?

FIGURE 7-1 || **Steps in Resolving Conflict**

Greeff and de Bruyne (2000) studied several styles of conflict and noted that the *collaborating style* was associated with the highest level of marital and spousal satisfaction. Each partner saying how they felt about a situation and cooperating to find a win-win solution characterized the collaborating style. Styles that were not helpful were the *competing style* (each partner tried to force their answer on the other—a win-lose approach) and the *avoiding style* (the partners would simply avoid addressing the issue and hope that it would go away). Depressed spouses who did not have the energy to engage their partners used this pattern of avoidance most frequently.

Brainstorming
Problem-solving strategy of suggesting as many alternatives as possible without evaluating them

7.6 Gender Differences in Communication

Females begin to excel in communication skills early. Haapsamo and colleagues (2013) found that females at age 8–36 months developed communication skills faster than males. Sociolinguistic scholar and popular author Deborah Tannen's (1990) research shows that men and women are socialized in different same-sex cultures, and when they talk to the other sex, they are talking to a member of another culture. Tannen also found that men and women differ in public and private speaking. She explained the differences using the terms *report talk* and *rapport talk*. Men generally approach communication, even in private situations, like public speaking or giving a report. They see talk as a way to convey information. In contrast, women generally engage in rapport talk, creating interaction and establishing connections. When there are problems in communicating with a partner, women are the first to notice. Pfeifer and colleagues (2013) studied 213 married couples in Taiwan and found that women were significantly more likely than men to report that communication was a problem. Such a communication problem means a drop in marital quality (Frye-Cox & Hesse, 2013).

In general, to men, communication emphasizes what is informative and competitive; to women, communication is more about emotion and interaction. To men, conversations are negotiations in which they try to "achieve and maintain the upper hand if they can, and to protect themselves from others' attempts to put them down and push them around" (Frye-Cox & Hesse, 2013, p. 25). However, to women, conversations are negotiations for closeness in which they try "to seek and give confirmations and support, and to reach consensus" (p. 25). A woman's goal is to preserve intimacy and avoid isolation. Greater use of social network sites by women emphasizes their goal to connect in regard to relationships. Based on a survey of 2,021 individuals ages 12 and over conducted by Arbitron and Edison Research, 27% of the respondents reported using social networking sites/services "several times a day" (Carey & Trap, 2013). Kimbrough and colleagues (2013) confirmed that women use social networking sites more frequently than men.

A team of researchers reviewed the literature on intimacy in communication and observed that men approach a problem in the relationship cognitively, whereas women approach it emotionally (Derlega et al., 1993). A husband might react to a seriously ill child by putting pressure on the wife to be mature (stop crying) about the situation and by encouraging stoicism (asking her not to worry). Women, on the other hand, tend to want their husbands to be more emotional (wanting him to cry to show that he really cares that their child is ill).

Men are also more likely to suppress their emotional expression to their wives. Velotti et al. (2016) studied emotional suppression by both husbands and wives in 229 newlywed couples at 5 months and 2 years after marriage. They found that husbands' habitual use of suppression was the most consistent predictor of lower marital quality over time.

As noted above, rather than avoidance, suppression, or competitiveness, the "female" style of communication—acknowledging other views, seeking consensus, and interaction—is associated with the best outcome for optimal communication between partners.

Chapter Summary

Principles of Relationship/Sexual Communication

PRINCIPLES include initiating discussions about important issues, giving congruent messages, minimizing negative and maximizing positive remarks, expressing feelings, practicing reflective listening, using "I" messages, and staying focused.

Technology, Communication, and Relationships

TEXT MESSAGES have become a primary means for flirting and for the initiation, escalation, and maintenance of romantic relationships in young adults. Indeed, technology can facilitate communication in relationships, but it can also lead to conflict.

Communication Theory

THEORIES, including identity formation (communication skills are learned through interaction with others), social learning (verbal statements are a consequence of reinforcers), and social exchange (people continue to interact or don't in reference to a rewards-to-costs ratio), may be used to help understand communication between partners.

Honesty and Dishonesty in Interpersonal Communication

HONEST COMMUNICATION is associated with trust and intimacy. Despite the importance of honesty in relationships, deception occurs frequently in interpersonal relationships.

Resolving Conflict in Relationships

HAVING A PLAN to communicate about conflicts is essential. Such a plan includes approaching a discussion from the point of view of respect for the partner and a willingness to negotiate an outcome rather than dictate a solution, addressing recurring issues rather than suppressing them, focusing on what you want rather than what you don't want, finding out your partner's point of view, generating win-win solutions to conflict, and evaluating and selecting the solution.

Gender Differences in Communication

SOCIOLINGUIST AND AUTHOR DEBORAH TANNEN observed that men and women are socialized in different same-sex cultures, and when they talk to the other sex, they are talking to a member of another culture. Men tend to approach communication, even in private situations, like public speaking or giving a report. They see talk as a way to convey information. In contrast, women tend to engage in rapport talk, using talk to interact and establish connections.

Web Links

American Association for Marriage and Family Therapy

http://aamft.org

The Gottman Institute

http://www.gottman.com/

Key Terms

Brainstorming **183**

Catfishing **179**

Closed-ended question **170**

Communication **164**

"I" statements **172**

Looking-glass self **176**

Nomophobia **174**

Nonverbal messages **166**

Open-ended question **170**

Primacy/recency effect **168**

Reflective listening **171**

Self-fulfilling prophecy **168**

Touch-and-ask rule **170**

Verbal messages **166**

Win-win solution **182**

"You" statements **172**

CHAPTER

8

Individual and Interpersonal Sexuality

Sex is a two-way treat.

Franklin P. Jones

Chapter Outline

8.1 **Erotophilia and Erotophobia 189**
8.2 **Virginity, Chastity, Celibacy, and Abstinence 190**
Self-Assessment 8-1:
Erotophilia versus
Erotophobia Scale **191**
8.2a Voluntary Abstinence **193**
8.2b Involuntary Abstinence **193**
Social Policy 8-1
Institutional Restrictions on
Sexual Expression **194**
8.2c Asexuality **194**
8.3 **Masturbation 194**
8.3a Origins of Negative Attitudes
Toward Masturbation **195**
8.3b Pros and Cons of Masturbation **198**
8.3c Vibrators **200**
Technology and Sexuality 8-1:
Sex Toy Update **201**

8.4 **Sexual Fantasies 201**
8.5 **Interpersonal Sexuality 202**
8.5a Kissing **202**
8.5b Sexual Touching **203**
8.5c Fellatio **203**
8.5d Cunnilingus **204**
8.5e Penile-Clitoral Stimulation **204**
8.5f Anal Stimulation **205**
8.5g Anal Intercourse **205**
8.5h Vaginal Intercourse **206**
Personal Decisions 8-1
Deciding to Have Sex in a
New Relationship **209**
8.5i Threesomes **211**

WebLinks 213
KeyTerms 213

Objectives

1. Differentiate between erotophilia and erotophobia
2. Review the concepts of voluntary and involuntary abstinence
3. Know how negative attitudes toward masturbation developed
4. Learn the demographics of who masturbates and the advantages and disadvantages

5. Explain sexual fantasies and dreams
6. List and discuss the various sexual behaviors
7. Discuss the use of vibrators, both individually and interpersonally
8. Identify what issues should be considered in deciding to have sex in a new relationship
9. Review new data on threesomes

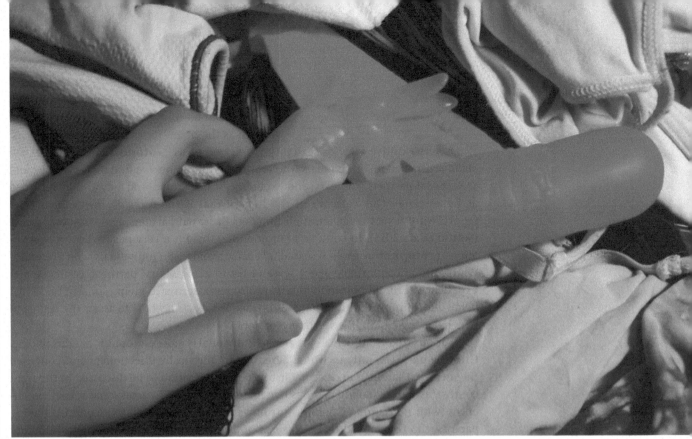

(Chelsea Curry Edwards)

Truth — OR — Fiction?

T / F   1. Research suggests that men regard virgins as desirable partners to become involved with.

T / F   2. Men tend to masturbate more out of compensation if partner sex is not occurring whereas women masturbate to complement the sex they are experiencing with a partner.

T / F   3. Ninety percent of women report that they are able to orgasm with a vibrator.

T / F   4. Incels may be referred to as diabolically misogynistic.

T / F   5. Most women who use sex toys report that they regularly clean them.

Answers: 1. F   2. T   3. T   4. T   5. T

Sexuality is not only individual but relational. In this chapter we focus on individual and interpersonal behaviors that are commonly recognized as sexual—including masturbation, touching, kissing, breast stimulation, manual- and oral-genital stimulation, anal stimulation and anal intercourse, and vaginal intercourse. We begin by looking at the continuum of sexual interest from erotophilia to erotophobia.

8.1 Erotophilia and Erotophobia

For most individuals, sexual behavior—both individual and interpersonal—generally involves pleasure and enjoyment. Yet, for a few individuals, how anyone could actually *enjoy* masturbation, oral sex, intercourse, and so forth is a mystery because they certainly don't find these behaviors to

> *Don't put off till tomorrow anyone you could be doing today.*
>
> Emma Chase, author

be pleasurable. The range of feelings toward sexual behavior can be conceptualized on a continuum known as the *erotophilic-erotophobic continuum*.

A very positive view of sexuality is referred to as **erotophilia** *(eroto* = sexual; *philia* = attracted to). Individuals who are erotophilic enjoy sex; find it pleasurable; and seek sexual partners, contexts, and experiences. The erotophilic may also be regarded as hypersexual. One category of the hypersexual is the *paraphilic hypersexual*, who reports early sexual behavior, high numbers of sexual partners, and substance abuse (Sutton et al., 2015). In contrast to erotophilia, there is a very negative view of sexuality—**erotophobia** *(eroto* = sexual; *phobia* = avoidance). Individuals who are erotophobic are uncomfortable about sex and try to avoid sexual partners, contexts, and experiences. Erotophobic individuals are also less assertive in giving consent for sexual behavior (Kilimnik & Humphreys, 2014). See *Self-Assessment 8-1* to assess the degree to which you are erotophilic versus erotophobic.

Various factors influence whether an individual is more erotophilic or erotophobic. Growing up in a family in which parents were physically affectionate and conveyed the message that sex is an acceptable topic of conversation to be discussed in the right context, as well as having had positive masturbatory and interpersonal sexual experiences (with no traumatic ones), contributes to being erotophilic. In contrast, having parents who telegraphed that sex is *bad* or *dirty*, having engaged in no masturbatory behavior, and having been forced to engage in sexual behavior (rape or molestation) are associated with erotophobia.

Individuals may move from one end of the continuum to the other. For example, an erotophilic person who delights in masturbation and who enjoys an intense reciprocal loving/sexual relationship can become erotophobic as a result of an intense negative sexual experience such as gang rape. On the other hand, an erotophobic person can learn to enjoy sex by means of repeated exposure to sexual behavior with a loving partner who provides a context of intense, positive, or frequent sex. Stewart-Williams et al. (2017) found that when selecting a partner for a long-term relationship, individuals "want a mate with a bit of a past, but not too much."

Before discussing specific sexual behaviors, we explore concepts related to the absence of or limitations on sexual behavior: virginity, chastity, celibacy, and abstinence.

8.2 Virginity, Chastity, Celibacy, and Abstinence

Erotophilia
Propensity to have very positive views of and emotional responses to sexuality

Erotophobia
Propensity to have very negative views of and emotional responses to sexuality

Virginity
State of not having experienced sexual intercourse

Virginity refers to an absence of experience of sexual intercourse. Virgins may or may not have experienced other forms of sexual interaction, such as oral sex. Indeed, some individuals still define themselves as virgins even though they have engaged in oral sex. Of 2,953 university males, 74% agreed that "If you have oral sex, you are still a virgin" (of 9,751 university females, 71% agreed). Hence, according to these undergraduates, having oral sex with someone is not really having sex (Hall & Knox, 2019). In addition to maintaining the self-concept that you are a virgin, engaging in oral sex rather than sexual intercourse may also be motivated by the desire to avoid getting pregnant or contracting an STI, to keep a partner interested, to avoid a bad reputation, or to avoid feeling guilty about having sexual intercourse (Vazsonyi & Jenkins, 2010). These are the typical motivations for virginity identified by females. Men tend to report "my partner was not willing" as the most frequent reason for being a virgin (Sprecher & Treger, 2015). Regardless of the motivation, a study of 5,000 single American adults revealed that the sexually inexperienced view themselves as stigmatized and that virgins are not desired as relationship partners. Gesselman et al.(2017) confirmed that others stigmatize virgins and view them as undesirable partners. The researchers concluded that the value of virginity "may result in negative interpersonal consequences such as limited opportunities for romantic relationships" (p. 202).

I used to be Snow White, but I drifted.

Mae West, actress of the 1930s

Self-Assessment 8-1:
Erotophilia versus Erotophobia Scale

The purpose of this scale is to assess the degree to which you tend to be erotophilic versus erotophobic.

Directions

After reading each sentence carefully, circle the number that best represents the degree to which you strongly disagree to strongly agree with the sentence. There are no right or wrong answers.

1 (Strongly disagree), 2 (Mildly disagree), 3 (Undecided), 4 (Mildly agree), 5 (Strongly agree)

1.	I think about sex a great deal.	1 2 3 4 5
2.	I look for opportunities to have sex with my partner.	1 2 3 4 5
3.	I enjoy watching pornography.	1 2 3 4 5
4.	I enjoy having sex.	1 2 3 4 5
5.	Masturbation improves one's physical/mental health.	1 2 3 4 5
6.	I would only marry someone who enjoyed sex.	1 2 3 4 5
7.	I would be unhappy with a nonsexual partner.	1 2 3 4 5
8.	Movies with some eroticism are more enjoyable.	1 2 3 4 5
9.	I think sex is good for your physical/mental health.	1 2 3 4 5
10.	Few things are more enjoyable than sex.	1 2 3 4 5

Scoring

Add the numbers you circled. The lower your total score (10 is the lowest possible score), the more erotophobic you are. The higher your total score (50 is the highest possible score) the more erotophilic you are. A score of 30 places you at the midpoint between being the extremes.

Source: This scale was developed for this text. It is to be used for general assessment and is not designed to be a clinical diagnostic tool or as a research instrument.

Individuals conceptualize their virginity in one of three ways—as a process, gift, or stigma. The *process view* regards first intercourse as a mechanism of learning about yourself, partner, and sexuality—it is a learning experience. The *gift view* regards being a virgin as a valuable, positive status wherein it is important to find the

(Breonna Gilbert-Love)

Religion is the primary source of the decision to remain a virgin until marriage for this woman (she has experienced no vaginal, oral, or anal sex and cites her faith as the reason for her waiting until marriage).

right person, since sharing the gift is special. The *stigma view* considers virginity as something to be ashamed of, to hide, and to rid yourself of. When 215 undergraduates were asked their view, 54% classified themselves as process oriented, 38% as gift oriented, and 8.4% as stigma oriented at the time of first coitus (Humphreys, 2013).

Most narratives about virginity refer to a heterosexual young woman and an older, experienced male. An exception is research on undergraduate males losing their virginity to an older female. In an article titled, "I Took His V-card," researchers identified 237 individuals (women and men) who provided 195 stories about the male losing his virginity. In most cases (58%), the woman knew ahead of time that the partner was a virgin, with a similar percentage (59%) of men reporting that it was a good first experience (12% said it was "really bad"). Gender roles were operative, with 71% reporting pressure to conform to traditional roles, but 49% said they enjoyed role reversal (Caron & Hinman, 2013).

People who are no longer virgins may wish to return to being a virgin. The concept of *secondary virginity* has emerged and refers to a sexually experienced person's deliberate decision to refrain from intimate encounters for a set period of time and to refer to that decision as a kind of virginity rather than mere abstinence. Secondary virginity may be a result of physically painful, emotionally distressing, or romantically disappointing sexual encounters. Of 61 young adults interviewed (most of whom were white, conservative, religious women), more than half believed that a person could, under some circumstances, be a virgin more than once. Fifteen people contended that people could resume their virginity in an emotional, psychological, or spiritual sense (Carpenter, 2011). Terence Duluca, a 27-year-old heterosexual, white Roman Catholic, explained:

> There is a different feeling when you love somebody and when you just care about somebody. So I would have to say if you feel that way, then I guess you could be a virgin again. Christians get born all the time again, so … When there's true love involved, yes, I believe that.

Asceticism
Belief that rising above carnal lust and the pursuit of sensual pleasure into a life of self-discipline and self-denial is desirable

Chastity
State of not having had sexual intercourse; also implies moral purity or virtuousness in both thought and conduct

Celibacy
Condition of refraining from sexual intercourse, especially by reason of religious vows; also used to refer to being unmarried

Those who follow **asceticism** believe that giving in to carnal lust is unnecessary and attempt to rise above the pursuit of sensual pleasure into a life of self-discipline and self-denial. Accordingly, spiritual life is viewed as the highest good, and self-denial helps one to achieve it. Catholic priests, monks, nuns, and some other celibate people have adopted the sexual value of asceticism.

The term **chastity** also refers to not having had sexual intercourse, but chastity also implies moral purity or virtuousness in both thought and conduct.

Celibacy often refers to the condition of being unmarried, especially by reason of religious vows, and also implies refraining from having sexual intercourse. The official position of the contemporary Catholic Church maintains that priests, nuns, and monks are expected to be celibate so that they might have the maximum time, freedom, and energy for the work of the church. However, due to the exposure of young males to the atrocities of sexual molestation by some priests, many parents and professionals are now on high alert. No longer is the priesthood a convenient place for the sex predator to hide. This fact, coupled with the prohibition of marriage and the requirement of celibacy, has led to a shortage of priests. As such, church leaders may be increasingly open to dialogue regarding married priesthood—a practice already adopted in the Episcopal Church.

The more commonly used term today that refers to refraining from sexual intercourse is **abstinence**. For some individuals, abstinence means refraining from sexual intercourse but not from other forms of sexual behavior such as masturbation or oral sex. Abstinence can be voluntary or involuntary and can last for short or extended periods of time.

> *I have nothing to give anyone, really. It's the one gift I can give that has any kind of value. It makes me feel worthy.*
>
> Fisher Amelie, *Callum & Harper*

8.2a Voluntary Abstinence

Voluntary abstinence can be motivated by a number of reasons, including the desire to avoid sexually transmitted infections and pregnancy. Other individuals practice abstinence to better focus their energy on personal, academic, or professional development without the distractions of sexual involvement. Still other individuals are voluntarily abstinent because they lack interest or sexual desire or may find sex aversive—for example, in cases in which sexual activity triggers negative emotions associated with prior sexual abuse. For some gay and lesbian individuals who do not accept their sexual orientation, abstinence may be a way to avoid dealing with the stigma of living as openly homosexual. Some couples choose to abstain from sexual intercourse as a way to enhance their enjoyment of the nonsexual aspects of their relationship. The practice of abstinence can also be related to cultural or religious beliefs and customs. For example, during the Muslim observation of Ramadan, in addition to fasting, believers abstain from sexual intercourse during daylight hours.

There are also a variety of reproductive and medical reasons for practicing short periods of abstinence. For example, some women use the *natural family planning method* (also known as the *ovulation* or *calendar method*) to abstain from sexual intercourse during the time of month they are most likely to conceive. Some cisgender men are temporarily abstinent to increase the chance of impregnating their partners, because the longer the time interval between ejaculations, the more volume and concentration of sperm are present in the semen. Medical conditions that can warrant short periods of abstinence include genital infections and pregnancy complications. In addition, a period of abstinence from sexual intercourse is recommended for cisgender women after abortion and childbirth.

8.2b Involuntary Abstinence

One of the most common reasons for **involuntary abstinence** is the lack of a sexual partner. This situation is common to many of us at different times in our lives. We may be between relationships, separated, divorced, or widowed; or we may be in a marriage or relationship in which our partner is unwilling to have sexual relations. Involuntary abstinence may also be induced by separation of partners due to military deployment, work-related travel, being in a long-distance relationship, or prison. *Hospital, nursing, and retirement homes* are also contexts that may increase the incidence of abstinence.

Experiencing involuntary abstinence over a long period of time can be a very difficult emotional experience. Ling et al. (2018) noted that some members of the male "incel" community (involuntary celibate) may blame women for rejecting them and become violent. In effect, incels:

> have constructed a violent political ideology around the injustice of young, beautiful women refusing to have sex with them. These men often subscribe to notions of white supremacy. They are, by their own judgment, mostly unattractive and socially inept. (They frequently call themselves "subhuman.") They're also diabolically misogynistic. (Tolentino, 2018)

Abstinence
State of refraining from having sexual intercourse

Voluntary abstinence
State of forgoing sexual intercourse for a period of time by choice

Involuntary abstinence
Condition of not having sexual relations due to environmental factors, such as not having a partner or being confined to an institution that does not encourage sexual expression

Social Policy 8-1

Institutional Restrictions on Sexual Expression

Hospitals are notorious for encouraging or enforcing abstinence. It is assumed that if you are in the hospital, you should have no sexual experience of any kind. There is no discussion of sexual activity, no privacy for masturbation (the nurse or physician can walk in at any time), and no accommodations for engaging in sexual relations with a partner.

Research also indicates that patients who are in palliative care want to discuss with their medical providers how their illness is impacting their physical opportunities (Kelemen et al., 2016). It is also important for patients in hospice to maintain physical intimacy with a partner, yet they may not be able to given the negative attitudes of the staff and the lack of privacy (Pinto et al., 2019). While many might not associate dying and palliative care with sexual activity and intimacy, it is important that patients be provided this opportunity.

Nursing homes also institutionalize abstinence. This will be discussed in more detail in Chapter 9.

This woman reports that while she is a romantic and loves emotional involvement, she has no sexual interest in or sexual attraction to a partner.

Elliot Rodger is the gunman who opened fire on students at the University of California, Santa Barbara in 2014, killing six. In a video posted before his attack, Rodger called his planned attack "retribution" for the women who rejected him and for "all you men for living a better life than me."

8.2c Asexuality

Related to celibacy and the issues of abstinence is **asexuality**, whereby the person reports a lack of sexual attraction to anyone. According to the Asexuality Visibility and Education Network, "Unlike celibacy, which is a choice, asexuality is a sexual orientation." Asexual people have "the same emotional needs as everybody else and are just as capable of forming intimate relationships." Between 8% and 10% of individuals (women more than men) self-identify as asexual (AVEN, 2016) We discuss asexuality in more detail in Chapter 10.

Asexuality
Absence of sexual attraction to anyone

Masturbation
Natural, common, and nonharmful means of sexual self-pleasuring that is engaged in by individuals of all ages, sexual orientations, and levels of functioning (also called autoerotic behavior)

8.3 Masturbation

Masturbation may begin in infancy. In a study of 19 healthy females from 3 months to an average of 8 years, the mean age for onset of masturbation was 10.4 months (Rodoo & Hellberg, 2013). In adults, Traeen et al. (2016) found that of 2,090 Norwegians ages 18–29, heterosexual women reported later first orgasm through masturbation than lesbian and bisexual women (median 15.2 versus 13.1 years), while heterosexual men reported earlier debut (median 13.5 years) than heterosexual women.

In a position statement, the Sexuality and Information Council of the United States (SIECUS, 2018a) described **masturbation** (also called *autoerotic behavior*) as:

A natural, common, and nonharmful means of experiencing sexual pleasure. Masturbation can be a way of becoming comfortable with one's body and enjoying one's sexuality, whether or not in a sexual relationship. Masturbation is a safe alternative to shared sexual behavior. SIECUS believes that no one should be made to feel guilty for choosing or not choosing to masturbate.

We have reason to believe that man first walked upright to free his hands for masturbation.

Lily Tomlin, comedian

If masturbation is a crime, I'd be on death row.

Gilbert Gottfried

National DATA

Based on a survey of American adults ages 18–64 of 7,648 men and 8,090 women, 61% of the men and 35% of the women reported having masturbated in the past two weeks. Not having a partner or not being content with one's sexual frequency with a partner, being white, and being college educated were associated with higher rates of masturbation. Men tended to masturbate more out of compensation if partner sex was not occurring; women were more likely to masturbate to complement their sex with a partner (Regnerus et al., 2017).

Terms other than *autoerotic behavior* for masturbation include *self-pleasuring, solo sex,* and *sex without a partner.* Several older, more pejorative terms for masturbation are *self-pollution, self-abuse, solitary vice, sin against nature, voluntary pollution,* and *onanism.* The negative connotations associated with these terms are a result of various accounts and myths that originated in religion, archaic medicine, and traditional psychotherapy. Traditionally, parents have also transmitted a negative view of masturbation to their children. Shame, guilt, and anxiety continue to be common feelings associated with masturbation in our society due to traditional negative attitudes toward the practice.

8.3a Origins of Negative Attitudes Toward Masturbation

While masturbation today is more often thought of in terms of its benefits, a historical analysis reveals that religion, medicine, and traditional psychotherapy have encouraged a negative view.

Religion and Masturbation

A number of religious traditions have associated masturbation with something evil or sinful. St. Augustine and other early Christians believed that sexual fantasies (which often accompany masturbation) were caused by demons who led their victims down a sinful path to hell. Medieval Jewish and Christian leaders believed that ejaculated semen would breed devils (Allen, 2000). Those guilty of masturbating could still be saved through prayer, abstinence, holy water, and absolution.

Negative religious views toward masturbation stemmed from the belief that any nonprocreative sexual act is morally wrong. Traditional religious doctrines also disapproved of other forms of nonprocreative sex—such as oral sex,

Religion has traditionally held a negative view of masturbation.

anal intercourse, and coitus interruptus (sex without orgasm). In the 21st century, tolerance for masturbation by some Jewish and Protestant groups suggests that there are conditions under which it is acceptable—to help prevent infidelity or premarital sex, or as a way of balancing the libidos of spouses.

Taking a cross-cultural view on masturbation, in ancient Chinese religious thought, life was viewed as a balance between the forces of yin and yang. Sex represented this harmonious balance: The essence of sexual **yang** was the male's semen, and the essence of sexual **yin** was the woman's vaginal fluid. Female masturbation was virtually ignored because vaginal fluid (yin) was thought to be inexhaustible. However, semen (yang) was viewed as precious, and masturbation was regarded as a waste of vital yang essence (Tannahill, 1982).

Medicine, Psychotherapy, and Masturbation

The **semen-conservation doctrine** (from early Ayurvedic teachings in India) held that general good health in both sexes depends on conserving the life-giving power of vital fluids. These fluids, which include both semen and vaginal fluid, were believed to be important for intelligence and memory and were derived from good nutrition. Wastage or depletion of semen (regarded as more important than female emissions) was discouraged because it was thought to result in a loss of resistance to illness and a decrease in well-being. The second-century physician Aretaeus of Cappadocia, for example, warned against men losing too much semen: "For it is the semen ... which makes us to be men—hot, well braced in limbs, hairy, well voiced, spirited, strong to think and to act" (quoted in Allen, 2000, p. 83).

Early medicine's negative view of masturbation can also be traced to the fact that for centuries, physicians did not clearly distinguish between masturbation and the sexually transmitted infection gonorrhea (which in Greek means *flow of seed*). One of the symptoms of gonorrhea in men is the discharge of thick pus from the penis. The failure to differentiate between semen ejaculated during masturbation or released during spontaneous nocturnal emissions and the penile discharge associated with gonorrhea led physicians to lump gonorrhea and masturbation into a single pathology until the 20th century: "Additionally, for a medical profession that was increasingly able to recognize problems it could not yet cure, self-abuse [masturbation] was an easy culprit to link with all kinds of diseases nobody could otherwise explain" (Allen, 2000, p. 86).

When Samuel Tissot, a highly respected 18th-century Swiss doctor, published a book on the diseases produced by masturbation (Tissot, 1758/1766), he added medical credibility to the view that masturbation was harmful. Tissot presented graphic and gruesome case studies depicting the horrific effects of masturbation and provided drawings of those affected, one of which portrays a man who had been reduced by the practice to, as described in the following:

> A being that less resembled a living creature than a corpse. ... A watery, palish blood issued from his nose; slaver constantly flowed from his mouth. Having diarrhea, he voided his excrement in bed without knowing it. He had a continual flux of semen ... The disorder of his mind was equal to that of his body. (Allen, 2000, p. 88)

By the mid-19th century, Tissot's admonitions against masturbation had made their way into medical textbooks, journals, and books for parents.

Adding to the medical bias against masturbation was Reverend Sylvester Graham, who also claimed that masturbation resulted in the loss of fluids that were vital to the body. In 1834, Graham wrote that losing an ounce of semen was equal to the loss of

Yang
In Chinese thought, the male force that is viewed as active

Yin
In Chinese thought, the female force that is seen as passive

Semen-conservation doctrine
From early Ayurvedic teachings in India, the belief that general good health in both sexes depends on conserving the life-giving power of vital fluids (semen and vaginal fluids)

several ounces of blood. He believed that every time a man ejaculated, he ran the risk of contracting a disease of the nervous system. Among his solutions were graham crackers, which he claimed would help prevent the development of carnal lust that resulted from eating animal flesh (Graham, 1848). John Harvey Kellogg, MD, had similar beliefs and suggested his own cure—corn flakes. Kellogg's Corn Flakes® were originally developed as a food to extinguish sexual desire and curb masturbation desires.

In the early 20th century, psychotherapy joined medicine and religion to convince people of the negative effects of masturbation. In 1893, Sigmund Freud claimed that masturbation caused *neurasthenia*—a widely diagnosed psychosomatic illness characterized by weakness and nervousness. Freud and other psychotherapists who followed his teachings viewed masturbation as an infantile form of sexual gratification, believing that people who masturbated to excess could fixate on themselves as a sexual object and would not be able to relate to others in a sexually mature way. The message was clear: If you want to be a good sexual partner in marriage, don't masturbate. If you do masturbate, don't do it too often.

The result of religious, medical, and therapeutic professions denigrating masturbation was devastating for individuals who succumbed to temptation, causing unnecessary shame, anxiety, fear, and guilt. The burden of these feelings was particularly heavy because there was no one with whom to share the guilt. In the case of a premarital pregnancy, responsibility could be shared. With masturbation, however, the "crime" had been committed alone.

The perceived dangers of masturbation warranted extreme measures to deter children and adults from engaging in this behavior. Physicians recommended mechanical restraints (such as straitjackets and chastity belts), tying children's hands and feet at night, and circumcision as preventive practices (Allen, 2000).

Because women who masturbated "could become obsessed with sex and thus unfit for their proper role in society," horseback riding, bicycling, and even using pedal-operated sewing machines, "which could stimulate working women until they became sexually sick," were to be avoided (Allen, 2000, p. 96). If preventive measures did not work, masturbators were often locked up in asylums, treated with drugs (such as sedatives and poisons), or subjected to a range of interventions designed to prevent masturbation by stimulating the genitals in painful ways, preventing genital sensation, or deadening it.

These physician-prescribed interventions included putting ice on the genitals; blistering and scalding the penis, vulva, inner thighs, or perineum; inserting electrodes into the rectum and urethra; cauterizing the clitoris by anointing it with pure carbolic acid; circumcising the penis; and surgically removing the clitoris, ovaries, and testicles. As late as the mid-20th century, even more extreme measures were employed. Famed gay Southern playwright Tennessee Williams's disturbed sister, Rose, who taunted their sexually repressed mother with talk of masturbating with altar candles, was subjected to lobotomy to "restore her innocence." This tragedy served as the dark inspiration of his play *Suddenly Last Summer*, and Williams himself was so terrified of masturbation that he claimed he never attempted it until he was 26 (Bailey, 2015).

One of the most important developments in reducing inaccurate assumptions about the outcomes of masturbation was the advancement of the germ theory of disease and the recognition of the gonococcus and spirochete as causes of gonorrhea and syphilis in the late 19th century (Bullough, 2003). However, sexuality historian Vern Bullough noted that what further promoted changes in attitudes toward masturbation was information provided by modern sex researchers in the 20th century.

Kinsey and his colleagues revealed that 92% of the men in their sample reported having masturbated (Kinsey et al., 1948), yet the researchers found no evidence of the dire consequences that had been earlier predicted for those who masturbate. These findings presented a major challenge to the prevailing medical views of masturbation as harmful.

In spite of Kinsey's evidence suggesting that masturbation was not physically, emotionally, or socially debilitating, many physicians continued to convey to their patients negative attitudes toward its practice. More recently, physicians' attitudes toward masturbation have become more positive—in part due to the inclusion of human sexuality courses in medical school curricula. Indeed, sex therapists commonly prescribe masturbation as a treatment.

Today, medical concerns about adverse health effects of masturbation are limited to special cases in which it can result in physical harm. One of these special cases is the practice of restricting the flow of blood to the brain by constricting one's neck with a rope or belt during masturbation, called **autoerotic asphyxiation**. This dangerous practice, designed to intensify orgasm, can result in accidental death by strangulation.

8.3b Pros and Cons of Masturbation

Some individuals feel very uncomfortable about masturbating, especially when their religious beliefs prohibit it. Deciding whether or not to masturbate is a very personal decision, and opting not to is just as legitimate a choice as the decision to masturbate. Nevertheless, in making one's own decisions regarding this form of sexual behavior, it may be helpful to consider the pros and cons.

Pros of Masturbation

1. *Self-knowledge*: Masturbation can provide immediate feedback about what you enjoy. Self-knowledge about what feels good enables a person to know what they need for sexual pleasure and what to teach a partner about how to provide pleasure.

2. *Increased body comfort*: Masturbation can increase an individual's comfort with their own body. People who are comfortable with their bodies are more confident and less anxious during sexual interactions, resulting in more overall sexual satisfaction with their partner. Not all individuals (particularly women) are comfortable when they begin masturbating, but comfort often develops with repeated experiences. Masturbation may also increase an individual's physical, as well as psychological, body comfort. Students in the authors' classes reported that they masturbate to relieve tension, to get to sleep, and to help abate menstrual cramps.

3. *Orgasm more likely*: Masturbation continues to be the way most women report experiencing an orgasm (Suschinsky & Chivers, 2018). The vast majority of women orgasm via masturbation compared to only 3%–10% of women who reliably orgasm via penetration (Mintz, 2017).

4. *Pressure taken off partner*: Inevitably, partners in a relationship will vary in their desire for having interpersonal sex. During such times, the partner wanting more sex may feel frustrated, and the partner wanting less sex may feel guilty for not wanting to accommodate the partner. Masturbation might provide an alternative means of sexual satisfaction for the partner wanting more sex, while taking the pressure off the other partner. The result may be less interpersonal stress for both people.

5. *No partner necessary*: Masturbation provides a way to enjoy a sexual experience or an orgasm when no partner is available. This can be an option when the person is ill or disabled.

Autoerotic asphyxiation
Cutting off one's air supply to enhance one's orgasm but misjudging the extent of doing so such that accidental death occurs

6. *Avoids risk of STI or pregnancy*: When masturbation is enjoyed as a solo activity, there is no risk of transmitting or acquiring a sexually transmitted infection, nor is there any risk of pregnancy.

7. *Unique, pleasurable experience*: Masturbation is a unique sexual experience, different from intercourse and oral stimulation of the genitals. Some people who have interpersonal sex on a regular basis with their partners may also enjoy masturbation because they regard it as a unique experience that partner sex cannot duplicate.

8. *Helpful in maintaining sexual fidelity*: For individuals in coupled relationships, masturbation can help the partners remain faithful when they are separated.

9. *Useful in treatment of sexual dysfunctions*: Sex therapists routinely recommend masturbation to women who report never having experienced orgasm as a means of learning the place(s), pressure, and rhythm of clitoral/genital stimulation that lead(s) to orgasm. Women who know how to pleasure themselves to orgasm are better able to teach their partners how to do so. As noted in the third point, women who masturbate to orgasm are more likely to report orgasm during intercourse. Masturbation is also used in the treatment of hypoactive sexual desire.

10. *Delayed ejaculation*: Frequent masturbation to orgasm on the part of the male is associated with his delay in ejaculation with each subsequent sexual stimulation session.

People who have not masturbated but wish to do so can find explicit directions on the internet. In any search engine, you can type in "how to masturbate" to identify several websites providing masturbatory information, including how to masturbate.

Cons of Masturbation

1. *Feeling of being abnormal*: Some people feel they are abnormal because they masturbate too frequently. If you worry that you masturbate too much, ask yourself this question: "Does masturbation interfere with my daily functioning?" If it interrupts or gets in the way of your job, your responsibilities, or your social life, you may want to talk with a therapist. There are no health risks with masturbation. Skin irritation is possible, but using plenty of lubrication will prevent that.

2. *Strengthened attraction to inappropriate stimuli*: Masturbation or fantasies related to an inappropriate stimulus may strengthen erotic feelings toward that stimulus. For example, adults who masturbate while fantasizing about sexual interactions with children are strengthening their erotic responses to children. Repeated rehearsal of such sexual fantasies and masturbatory behavior contributes to viewing children as sexual objects.

3. *Guilt:* Because social influences such as religion still communicate disapproval for masturbation, the person who does so is vulnerable to feeling guilty. These feelings may cause the person to have low self-esteem or to feel distressed.

4. *Problems with relationship*: If a couple has not discussed their views on solo masturbation, there can be issues if they find out their partner is masturbating. These can be addressed by talking about their feelings about mutual and solo masturbation.

8.3c Vibrators

Wood et al. (2017) assessed sex toy use of 1,435 Canadian women (ages 18–81), 52.3% of whom reported having used a sex toy (24% used once a week). Sex toy users were more likely to report a bisexual, lesbian, queer, or questioning identity. Participants used a variety of sex toys including vibrators; butt plugs; and bondage, discipline, sadism, masochism (BDSM) toys. Most reported cleaning their toys regularly using soap and water. In a study of 235 Chinese females ages 16–58, 69% reported having used a vibrator, with a third reporting having done so at least once in the past few weeks. Over a third (37%) were in a relationship with one partner; more than one-fourth (26.4%) were married. In contrast to the Canadian findings, over two-thirds (67%) of the Chinese sample reported that they were heterosexual (Jing et al. 2018).

Although commonly used by women (and couples) today, vibrators have a unique history. In the 1800s, physicians rubbed the clitoral area as a treatment for women presenting symptoms of hysteria, which was the catchall term for being anxious, nervous, irritable, and unable to sleep. These hand jobs were amazingly effective in curing the woman by producing what was labeled as a *paroxysm*—a word that meant sudden emotion but did not imply pleasure, since women were thought to have no libido.

I just want mind-boggling sex tonight, but I don't think you can beat my vibrator.

Anna Bayes, erotica author, *Snug Fit*

Open discussion of vibrators is routine in university courses on human sexuality.

However, physicians tired of manually providing this "healing" of hysteria. In 1880, an English physician, Joseph Granville, patented the electromechanical vibrator to save physicians the work. In the early 1900s, "personal massagers" were sold by Sears® and women could help themselves. However, it was not until the 1970s that their explicit use for producing orgasm became socially acceptable (Maines, 2001).

Vibrator use among women is common (Driemeyer et al. 2017). To meet the ever-increasing demand, sex toy parties such as Pure Romance™ are commonly held in sororities and private homes, and products are also available at sex shops such as Good Vibrations®, which offers storefront and mail-order sales of toys and related products, as well as product descriptions and reviews on its website.

Masturbation/vibrator use is big business. Betty Dodson is a pioneer in encouraging women to feel comfortable with their bodies, to masturbate, and to use a vibrator. One private sex coaching session with Dodson is $1,500, payable in cash. She also sells a number of books and videos and notes that private sessions may not be necessary. (See http://bvtlab.com/SmrQ7.)

Whereas most men recognize the value of a vibrator in helping the woman orgasm/experience sexual pleasure, some may be threatened by its use. One man, who said that his fiancée had made it clear that she enjoyed her vibrator, stated, "I think she prefers it to me." In response, the woman told him, "There is no replacing you … since you are my love/my partner. A vibrator is simply what I need to help me orgasm, enjoy sex, and be an involved sexual partner with you." Some couples shop together for their sex toys and have a drawer full. Others give each other sex toys for special events, such as birthdays and Christmas. There are hundreds of sex toys on the market, including sex toys for men, sold in intimate adult shops or online (search "sex toys" or "vibrators" online). Experimenting with the various options can be an enjoyable adventure. It may be helpful for both partners to openly discuss their feelings regarding the use of a vibrator in their relationship.

Technology and Sexuality 8-1: Sex Toy Update*

The first vibrators were used by physicians in the 19th century to treat "hysteria" in female patients. Since then, vibrators have become sex toys and have changed in terms of their power source, the materials they are made from, and how they are used. Modern technologies provide new options to enhance one's sexual experience. Sexual enhancement products, also known as sexual wellness products, refer to items used to aid sexual pleasure or experience during solo or partnered sex and range from supplements to massage oil to sex toys. With the availability of online shopping, increases in the sales of sexual enhancement products (e.g., sex toys) is expected to continue (Business Wire, 2018). This means one will be able to shop online for a fully functional sex doll with the hair, eyes, body type, and voice of one's choosing (Geher & Wedberg, 2019).

In the past, sex toys were made of hard vinyl or rubber. The newer generation of sex toys is made with more body-friendly materials such as silicone. Some items are even equipped with Bluetooth, so they can be programmed by your smartphone. Researchers have reported that vibrators and sex toys have potential therapeutic benefits (Döring & Pöschl, 2018; Rullo, et al., 2018). These sexual aids can be particularly valuable in helping individuals with disabilities meet their sexual needs/improve their sexual wellness (Morales, et al., 2018). While the good news of sexual enhancement products is their availability, insufficient attention has been placed on usage, safety, and regulations. For example, the type of lubrication needed with a particular sex toy will depend on what the sex toy is made of (e.g. water-based lubrication is needed rather than silicone-based for silicone sex toys). In addition, toxic materials (e.g. thermoplastic elastomer) are still used in production of some sex toys.

With the development of medical grade silicone, cyberskin (soft, stretchy material resembling human skin) and artificial intelligence, lifelike, responsive sex dolls/sexbots are now available (and some are used in brothels). Indeed, it is possible to create one's own sexbot by looking through a catalog and choosing different body parts such as head, lips, and breasts. Sexbots are frequently oversexualized and are programmed to be submissive sex slaves. Whether the development of sexbots further objectifies women and children remains unresolved. Attitudes toward the use of sex dolls have been primarily negative. In a study of 345 undergraduates, over two-thirds (68%) reported that they "could not understand how anyone could think of having sex with a doll" (Knox et al., 2017).

Augmented reality and haptic technology (kinestatic or telefeel technology) has also emerged to provide a realistic cybersex experience. Teledildonics, also known as cyberdildonics, involves the virtual control of sexual toys or vibrators. For example, individuals in long distance relationships may continue their sex life together by stimulating each other over the internet using these sex toys (Faustino, 2018; Farivar, 2018). Cybersex is no longer a purely virtual experience, it can also simulate touch and various sensations.

Technologies are embedded in modern life. The link between sexuality and technology is here, and the variations will continue as new technologies emerge. This strong union can enrich and expand human sexuality. At the same time, the merger between sex and technology poses ethical challenges for consideration and debate.

* Appreciation is expressed to Dr. I Joyce Chang for the update of this section.

8.4 Sexual Fantasies

Both **sexual fantasies** and dreams are part of individual sexuality. Sexual fantasies can be thought of as cognitive, erotic visual scripts often used in masturbation, though some people can achieve orgasm without physical stimulation. Mizrahi et al. (2018) found that individuals are more likely to have sexual fantasies of their partner if they feel secure in the relationship and if they view their partner as responsive.

Persons may also use sexual fantasies when having sex with a partner. Patterson et al. (2018) reported that 55% of their respondents who used fantasies while masturbating alone also used sexual fantasies when with a partner. *Thinking off* (also referred to as *energy orgasm*) is a term used to describe an orgasm that results from controlling one's breath and energy. Barbara Carrellas demonstrates

Sexual fantasies
Cognitions, thoughts, and/or images that are sexual in nature

A fantasy is something produced in the imagination, allowing you to indulge in a thought life that is very different from what you experience on a day-to-day basis. Within this realm there is no fear of discovery, no worry about being shamed; here there is only the deepest of pleasures.

K. Kiker, *White*

Synthetic Surrogates (http://syntheticsurrogates.com) features an array of sex dolls for companionship and sex. The dolls in this photo are on display at the annual conference of the American Association of Sexuality Educators, Counselors and Therapists.

The secret of a good sexual relationship is making love with *your partner, not* to *your partner.*

Dianna Lowe and Kenneth Lowe, married couple

this orgasm in her video available at http://bvtlab.com/8Ga8U. Researchers at Rutgers University conducted brain imaging of Carrellas's nongenital and genitally based orgasms; the imaging indicated that her brain activity was the same in both.

8.5 Interpersonal Sexuality

Most adult sexual behavior occurs in the context of a relationship. More people (70%) regard a good sexual relationship as very important for a successful romantic relationship than adequate income (53%) and shared interests (46%) (Muise, 2018). In the following sections, a variety of interpersonal sexual behaviors, from touching to anal intercourse, are discussed.

Cultural Diversity

A survey of 1,397 Chinese university students revealed higher rates of intrapersonal behaviors such as sexual fantasizing (65%), solitary masturbation (46%), and viewing pornography (57%) than interpersonal behaviors, such as petting (28%), oral sex (10%), and intercourse (13%). Males reported higher rates of these behaviors than females (Chi et al., 2015).

8.5a Kissing

Kissing is a common sexual behavior that may be performed with the mouth closed or open. Kinsey (1948, 53) referred to the latter as deep kissing, also known as *soul kissing, tongue kissing,* or *French kissing.*

In an analysis of data on kissing from 308 males and 594 females, ages 18–63, the researchers found that kissing served a useful mate-assessment function: Women placed a higher importance on kissing and noted that a kiss was more likely to affect their attraction to a potential mate than did men. Kissing also seemed to be important in increasing pair-bond attachments and was found to be related to relationship satisfaction (Wlodarski & Dunbar, 2013).

8.5b Sexual Touching

Sexual touching is a:

> broad category of activities which are usually undertaken with the goal of increasing one's own and/or one's partner's sexual arousal and pleasure. These activities can include, but are not limited to, kissing, stroking, massaging, and holding anywhere from one part to the entirety of a partner's body. (Galinsky, 2012, p. 876)

Many people regard touching as the most significant aspect of sex. Jenny McCarthy, former Playmate of the Year®, said in an interview that she did not care if she ever had an orgasm again. What she needed was to be held.

Both men and women report orgasmic benefits from sexual touching. Analysis of data on 1,352 adults revealed that the odds of being "unable to climax were greater by 2.4 times among men and 2.8 times among women who sometimes, rarely, or never engaged in sexual touching, compared to those who always engaged in sexual touching" (Galinsky, 2012).

The benefits of sexual touching have been identified by Galinsky (2012). For one, touching is not focused on genital performance, so the lovers can relax and enjoy. Second, there are physiological benefits from touching, which not only decreases stress but also increases a sense of calm and contentment. Third, sexual touching may promote a context of trust and connection, which has been linked to reduced sexual inhibition in women and reduced risk for erectile dysfunction in men. Sexual touching is, in effect, a signal for affection and the desire for greater intimacy.

In the past, sexual touching was sometimes referred to as foreplay, but this term implies that this takes place before intercourse, which is not the case for all people. Sexual touching may take place before, during, or after other sexual activities or it may happen by itself.

Orgasmic meditation (OM) is a holistic variation of partnered sexual touching that involves stroking the clitoris in what is described as a nonsexual way for 15 minutes, only to feel, connect, and be present. The goal is not orgasm, but to enhance the connection between partners. Nicole Daedone, the founder of OneTaste™, describes OM as the "cure for hunger in the Western woman" (Ted Talk, http://bvtlab.com/w87n4) and the OneTaste website (http://onetaste.us/what-is-om/) identifies OM as a consciousness practice designed for singles and couples to experience more connection, vitality, pleasure, and meaning.

8.5c Fellatio

Fellatio, which comes from the Latin *fellare*, meaning "to suck," is oral stimulation of the man's genitals. Fellatio may be a precursor to intercourse (vaginal or anal) or may be engaged in independently.

Although fellatio most often involves sucking the penis, it may also include licking the shaft, glans, frenulum, and scrotum. The partner's hands also may caress the scrotum and perineum during fellatio. If fellatio results in orgasm, the semen may be swallowed if the partner desires to do so. Fellatio is common among college students: 78% of 2,996 undergraduate males reported that they had received fellatio (Hall & Knox, 2019).

Some couples engage in oral sex simultaneously, whereby each partner is a giver and receiver at the same time. The term *69* has been used to describe the positions of two partners engaging in mutual oral-genital stimulation.

Sexual touching
The broad category of activities that are usually undertaken with the goal of increasing your own and/or your partner's sexual arousal and pleasure

Orgasmic meditation
Holistic practice whereby one individual strokes the clitoris of the partner in a way that is designed to increase the emotional connection between the partners, not to create an orgasm

Fellatio
Oral stimulation of a man's genitals

National DATA

Based on a survey of 5,865 respondents in the United States, of adults ages 20–29, 70% of the men reported that they had "received oral sex from a woman" in the past 12 months (Reece et al., 2012).

Fellatio can be used as a means of avoiding intercourse for moral reasons (to preserve virginity) or to avoid pregnancy. Some who engage in unprotected oral sex mistakenly believe it cannot transmit STIs. To reduce the risk of HIV and other STI transmission, the penis should be covered with a condom during fellatio. A primary motivation for fellatio is pleasure. Many people experience physical pleasure and satisfaction from receiving and/or giving fellatio.

If you're not into oral sex, keep your mouth shut.

Unknown

National DATA

Based on a survey of 5,865 respondents in the United States, of adults ages 20–29, 71% of the women reported that they had "received oral sex from a man" in the past 12 months (Reece et al., 2012).

8.5d Cunnilingus

Cunnilingus, translated from the Latin, means "he who licks the vulva." Cunnilingus involves the stimulation of the clitoris, labia, and vaginal opening of the woman by her partner's tongue and lips. The technique many women enjoy is gentle teasing by the tongue, with stronger, more rhythmic sucking or tongue stroking movements when orgasm approaches. While the partner's mouth is caressing and licking the clitoral shaft and glans, some women prefer additional stimulation by a dildo, finger, or vibrator in the vagina or anus. Cunnilingus is a common practice among college students. Of 9,856 undergraduate females, 78% reported that they had received cunnilingus (Hall & Knox, 2019). Vogels (2016) found that both men and women reported higher oral sex-giving behavior when they viewed individuals of their same sex engaging in the behavior.

Cunnilingus is a girl's best friend. Cunnilingus is life. Everything else is just waiting. An orgasm during cunnilingus turns you into an angel. You grow wings and glimpse paradise.

Chloe Thurlow, *Katie in Love*

Human papillomavirus (HPV) can be transmitted through oral sex, which can result in throat cancer. To reduce risk of STI transmission during cunnilingus, partners should use a **dental dam**, a thin piece of latex that covers the vulva. A latex condom that is cut into a flat piece may act as a substitute for a dental dam. Dental dams can also be purchased online. Another option is nonmicrowavable plastic wrap.

8.5e Penile-Clitoral Stimulation

In addition to stimulating the clitoral area by mouth, some heterosexual women rub their partner's penis across and around their clitoris. Such stimulation may or may not be followed by penetration. If the man is not wearing a condom, penile-clitoral stimulation carries a risk of pregnancy. If the man ejaculates near the woman's vaginal

Cunnilingus
Stimulation of the clitoris, labia, and vaginal opening of the woman by her partner's tongue and lips

Dental dam
Thin piece of latex that covers the vulva during cunnilingus or the anus during analingus

opening during penile-clitoral stimulation, or even if he emits just a small amount of pre-ejaculatory fluid (which may contain sperm), pregnancy is possible.

8.5f Anal Stimulation

Some individuals enjoy stimulation of the anus via the partner's finger, dildo, or vibrator. Another form of anal stimulation, called **fisting**, involves the insertion of several fingers or an entire closed fist and forearm (typically lubricated with a nonpetroleum-based lubricant) into a partner's rectum and sometimes the lower colon. Care during insertion is particularly important; it should not be abrupt or forceful so as to avoid damage to the rectum, colon, and anal sphincter. Although anyone can perform or receive fisting, this activity is usually associated with male homosexual activity.

Some partners enjoy oral-anal stimulation, or **analingus** (also referred to as *rimming*), which involves licking and/or insertion of the tongue into the partner's anus. Some avoid this behavior due to health concerns. For protection, a latex barrier (or nonmicrowavable plastic wrap) should be used during analingus. Branfman et al. (2018) surveyed 170 heterosexual undergraduate men in a US university and found that 24 percent reported having received anal pleasure.

National DATA

Based on a survey of 5,865 respondents in the United States, of adults ages 20–29, 5% of the men and 22% of the women reported having received a penis in the anus in the past 12 months (Reece et al., 2012).

8.5g Anal Intercourse

Molinares et al. (2016) analyzed data from a survey on anal sex completed by 205 undergraduates (primarily heterosexual females). Analysis revealed that 37% of the respondents had experienced anal sex, with over three-fourths (78%) reporting that their partner had brought up the idea. The primary reason for having anal sex was "to please the partner" (32%) with other motives identified as curiosity (26%) and "to spice things up" (11%).

Receptive anal intercourse is also experienced by males. Partners differ in their preference for and comfort in being the active or passive partner. Both partners may have orgasm during anal penetration—the active partner due to stimulation of the penis and the passive partner due to the fact that the partner's penis in his rectum exerts pressure on his prostate gland, which may trigger orgasm. However, females generally experience less pleasure due to the absence of a prostate.

The person receiving anal intercourse is at higher risk than the man who inserts his penis into his partner's rectum because anal intercourse often tears the rectum, allowing HIV-infected semen to come in contact with the bloodstream. In addition, the first few inches of the anus provide darkness, warmth, and moisture in the mucous membranes, so are a prime host for transmitting HIV. Couples who engage in anal intercourse should always use a condom to protect against transmission of HIV and other STIs. The use of water-based lubrication products, such as K-Y® Jelly, may also enable the penis to enter the partner's rectum more easily and thus minimize tearing of the rectal tissue. If vaginal intercourse or oral contact with the penis follows anal intercourse, the penis should first be thoroughly washed.

Fisting
Insertion of several fingers or an entire closed fist and forearm (typically lubricated with a nonpetroleum-based lubricant) into a partner's rectum and sometimes the lower colon; term also used to describe insertion of hand into vagina

Analingus
Licking and/or insertion of the tongue into the partner's anus (also known as *rimming*)

Another risk associated with anal intercourse (as well as with manual or oral stimulation of the anus) is **cystitis** (bladder infection). Cystitis may result from bacteria from the anal region being spread to the urethral opening. Symptoms of cystitis may include a persistent urge to urinate, pain during urination, and fever.

8.5h Vaginal Intercourse

Sexual intercourse, or **coitus**, refers to the sexual union of a penis and a vagina—the vagina encircles or surrounds the penis, and the penis penetrates the vagina (see Figure 8-1).

FIGURE **8-1** ‖ Sexual Intercourse

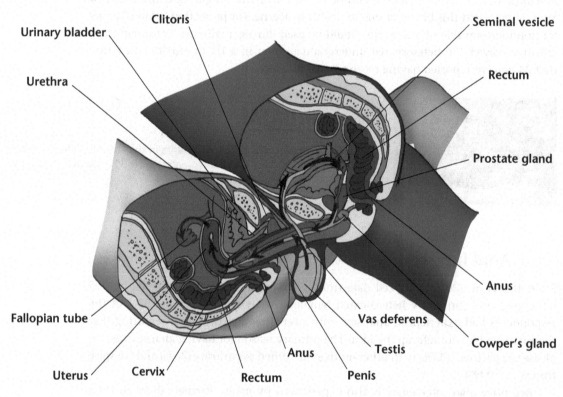

Milhausen et al. (2016) surveyed 1,466 adults ages 40–59 and found that 30 minutes was the reported length of time of the last sexual encounter (included was 10 or fewer minutes of pre- or post sex-affection behavior [SAB]). Frequency of penis vagina intercourse predicted sexual and emotional satisfaction for men and women. Post-SAB predicted emotional satisfaction in women only. In addition to how long intercourse lasts, another important variable to consider is frequency of intercourse. The coital frequency of 254 women, average age 34, was assessed by da Silva Lara and colleagues (2016). The women had been in a relationship an average of just under 9 years and had an average of 1.7 children. Ninety-eight percent were employed. Coital frequency was more than 3 times a week: 8.66%; 2–3 times per week: 38.58%; 1 time per week: 15.75%; 1 time per month: 5.51%; and never: 1.97%. Women who reported having coitus 3 times per week had significantly higher body mass index than those who had coitus 2–3 times per week. Obese women had higher frequencies than women of

Cystitis
Bladder infection

Sexual intercourse
Sexual union of a man's penis and a woman's vagina (also known as coitus)

Coitus
See sexual intercourse

normal weight and overweight women. Muise and colleagues (2016) analyzed data from 30,000 respondents and found that the once-weekly frequency of sexual intercourse for established couples is related to relationship satisfaction. This finding challenges the myth that more is better. There is also a myth that individuals have large numbers of sexual partners. However, data from the National Survey of Family Growth (2015) revealed that the median number of lifetime opposite-sex partners among sexually experienced individuals ages 25–44 in 2011–2015 was 6.1 for men and 4.2 for women.

Motives for engaging in sexual behavior include feeling valued by your partner, expressing value for your partner, relieving stress, providing nurturance, exerting power, and experiencing the power of your partner (Gunderson et al., 2014). Hernandez et al. (2018) studied factors associated with females (aged 15–19) making the decision to have their first sexual experience and noted the importance of being involved in a dating relationship with an older partner. Boislard et al. (2016) also noted that being in a romantic relationship was associated with first sexual intercourse.

Positions for Intercourse

There are numerous positions for penile vaginal intercourse. Some of the more common positions follow:

1. **Man-on-Top Position**

    The man-on-top position is the most frequently reported position used during intercourse. This is also referred to as the "missionary position." The woman reclines on her back, bends her knees, and spreads her legs. The man positions himself between her legs, supporting himself on his elbows and knees. The man or woman may guide his penis into her vagina. This position permits maximum male thrusting and facilitates eye contact, kissing, and caressing. Some partners may prefer to be on top or on bottom as an expression of their feelings about gender, dominance, and submission.

    Some women experience pain from the deep penetration. Giving feedback to the partner to thrust less deeply, the male using "donut rings" to decrease the depth of penetration, or the female closing her legs after penetration can serve as antidotes. For some women, the man-above position makes clitoral contact and orgasm difficult, although many women find ways of moving their hips or positioning their body to achieve clitoral stimulation and/or orgasm. Either the man's or the woman's hand or finger may also stimulate the woman's clitoris during man-on-top intercourse. For some men, the muscle tension produced by supporting their weight and active thrusting hastens ejaculation, which may be problematic for both the woman and man.

    A variation of the man-on-top position involves the woman lying on her back, with the man squatting or kneeling between the woman's spread legs. Body contact can be full and intimate or minimal.

2. **Woman-on-Top Position**

    In the woman-on-top position, the woman may either lie lengthwise so that her legs are between her partner's or kneel on top with her knees on either side of him. The primary advantage of this position is that it provides the woman with more control so that she can move in ways that provide her with maximum pleasure. Many women report that this position is more likely to lead to orgasm than the man-on-top position. In this position, partners can also touch each other (or themselves), kiss, and maintain eye contact.

Some women report drawbacks to the woman-above position. Some feel too shy in this position and do not enjoy "being on display." Others complain that the penis keeps falling out because the woman may lift too high before the downward stroke.

For both women and men, being on the bottom position during intercourse is easier and requires less energy and exertion, whereas being on the top position during intercourse is more work. Some partners' preferences for being on the bottom or the top may depend on how tired or energetic they feel.

3. Side-by-Side Position

A relaxing position for both partners is the side-by-side position. The partners lie on their sides, facing each other. The top legs are lifted and positioned to accommodate easy entry of the penis. Neither partner bears the strain of "doing all the work," and the partners have relative freedom to move their body as they wish to achieve the desired place of contact and rhythm of movement. This position may be preferred in the latter months of pregnancy.

4. Rear-Entry Position

There are several ways to achieve a rear-entry intercourse position. The woman may lie on her side with her back to her partner. She may also support herself on her knees and hands or forearms and elbows, or she may lie on her stomach and tilt her buttocks upward while the man enters her vagina from behind. In another rear-entry variation, the man may lie on his back and the woman may kneel or squat above him with her back toward her partner.

Many of the rear-entry intercourse positions permit the man or the woman to manually stimulate her breasts or clitoris or caress her legs and buttocks. Many women are unable to achieve orgasm using the rear-entry position. Although some women enjoy the deep penetration that results from rear-entry intercourse, others find it painful. Other disadvantages of rear-entry intercourse include a tendency for the penis to slip out and the loss of face-to-face contact. Sometimes the stigma of bestiality accompanies this position because it is often described with animal names, as in the Chinese "leaping tiger" and the American term "doggie position" or "doggie style."

5. Sitting Position

In the sitting position, the man sits on a chair or the edge of the bed with his partner sitting across his thighs. The woman can lower herself onto his erect penis or insert it after she is sitting. She may be facing him, or her back may be turned to him. The face-to-face sitting position involves maximum freedom to stimulate the breasts (manually or orally), to kiss, and to hug. It may allow the man to delay ejaculating because it doesn't involve pelvic thrusting. Chinese erotic art often depicts coitus in a sitting position, but this is not prominent in other cultures.

6. Standing Position

In the standing position, the woman raises one leg, or the man picks her leg/ legs up and places her onto his erect penis. She puts her legs around his waist and her arms around his neck while he is holding her. Both must be well coordinated and in good physical condition for this position.

An easier variation of the standing position is for the man to stand while the woman sits or reclines on a raised surface (a high bed, a table, or a chair). The woman's legs are spread, and the man inserts his penis into her vagina while standing between her legs. In most cultures of the world, standing positions are associated with brief (often illicit) encounters.

7. Variations

There are innumerable variations to the basic positions described here. For example, in the man-above position, the woman's legs may be closed or open, bent or straight, over his shoulders or around his neck. The woman may be on her back or raised on her elbows. The partners may face each other or be head-to-toe. Couples can choose different positions to add variety to their lovemaking and provide different types of stimulation and pleasure. Sexual intercourse positions may also vary according to pregnancy and health issues.

National DATA

Based on a survey of 5,865 respondents in the United States, of adults ages 20–29, 73% of the men and 84% of the women reported that they had experienced sexual intercourse in the past 12 months (Reece et al., 2012).

Racial/Ethnic Diversity

Analysis of data on 4,413 young women, ages 15–24, in the United States revealed a higher incidence of vaginal sex among women of black race/ethnicity. In regard to oral and anal sex, white women had higher incidences than nonwhites. Hispanic women had a lower incidence of oral sex, and Asian women had a lower incidence of anal sex (Hall et al., 2012).

The stereotype "Once you go black, you never go back" was the focus of research by Halligan and colleagues (2015). At a large southeastern university, 404 undergraduates provided data about racial stereotypes regarding black-white sexual experiences. Almost 1 in 5 (19%) white females had dated a black male, and 18% of black females had dated a white male. The average level (on a scale from 0 to 10) of sexual satisfaction reported by white females who had had sex with a black male was 7.62; with white males, it was 5.68. Black female sexual satisfaction with white males was 7.44; with black males, 5.00. The response rate for the question on sexual satisfaction was low, and there were no statistically significant differences in these broad group comparisons. However, the higher reports on sexual satisfaction in cross-racial relationships might possibly be related to the forbidden status of multicultural sexual experience.

PERSONAL DECISIONS 8-1

Deciding to Have Sex in a New Relationship

There are several issues you might consider in making the decision to have sexual intercourse with a new partner.

1. *Personal consequences:* How do you predict you will feel about yourself after you have had intercourse with a new partner? An increasing percentage of college students are relativists and feel that the outcome will be positive if they are in love. The following quote is from a student in our classes:

   I believe intercourse before marriage is okay under certain circumstances. I believe that when a person falls in love with another and the relationship is stable, it is then appropriate. This should be thought about very carefully for a long time, so as not to regret engaging in intercourse.

Those who are not in love and have sex in a casual context often report sexual regret about their decision.

> *When I have the chance to experience sex with someone new, my first thought is to jump right in, ask questions later. However, my very second thought is, "If we do this, will he think I'm slutty?" followed by "Is it too early to be doing this? What if I regret it?" Looking back at my dating experiences over the past several years, it seems that earlier on, I let a guy talk me into doing something sexual even though those questions were running circles in my head. However, in the most recent instances, I remained firm that sex wasn't going to happen so soon into dating someone, and I do not regret my decision.*

Lefkowitz et al. (2016) identified the consequences of the most recent vaginal sex experience reported by 253 first-year college students to be overwhelmingly positive: 89% reported feeling increased intimacy with the partner, and 81% reported feeling physically satisfied. Negative consequences were minimal—while 17% worried about pregnancy, only 11% felt that they had violated their morals, and only 5% regretted having had sexual intercourse.

2. *Timing:* In a sample of over 5,000 unmarried singles, about a third (28%) reported that they had sex by the third date, and almost half (46%) had done so by the sixth date (Jayson, 2013). Delaying intercourse with a new partner is important for achieving a positive outcome and avoiding regret. Table 8-1 reveals that a third of 429 undergraduates regretted having sexual intercourse too soon in a relationship (Merrill & Knox, 2010, p. 2).

TABLE 8-1	Regret for Engaging in Behavior Too Soon or Too Late (N = 429)			
Behavior	**Too Soon**	**Too Late**	**Perfect Timing**	**Did Not Do**
Sexual intercourse	33.3%	3.3%	48.4%	15.0%
Spent the night	26.6%	3.7%	58.8%	11.4%
Saying "I love you"	26.1%	3.9%	50.8%	19.2%
Kissing	11.1%	3.1%	82.8%	3.1%

Data source: *When I Fall In Love Again: A New Study on Finding and Keeping the Love of Your Life,* by Jane Merrill and David Knox, Praeger Publishing, (2010), p. 2.

3. *Partner consequences:* Because a basic moral principle is to do no harm to others, it is important to consider the effect of intercourse on your partner. Whereas intercourse may be a pleasurable experience with positive consequences for you, your partner may react differently. What is your partner's religious background and sexual values? A highly religious person with absolutist sexual values will typically have a very different reaction to sexual intercourse than a person with low religiosity and relativistic or hedonistic sexual values.

4. *Relationship consequences:* What is the effect of intercourse on a couple's relationship? In general, a good relationship enhances good sex (Breuer & Pericak, 2014).

5. *Contraception:* Another potential consequence of intercourse is pregnancy. Once a couple decides to have intercourse, a separate decision must be made as to whether intercourse should result in pregnancy. Most sexually active undergraduates do not want children. People who want to avoid pregnancy must choose and plan to use a contraceptive method.

6. *HIV and other sexually transmissible infections:* Avoiding HIV infection and other STIs is an important consideration in deciding whether to have intercourse in a new relationship. Couples should discuss their sexual histories and HIV and STI status before engaging in sexual activity.

   For most people, having an increased number of sex partners results in the rapid spread of the bacteria and viruses responsible for numerous varieties of STIs. However, in a sample of 2,933 undergraduate males, 29% reported consistent condom use, and of 9,635 undergraduate females, 26% reported consistent condom use (Hall & Knox, 2019).

7. *Influence of alcohol and other drugs:* A final consideration with regard to the decision to have intercourse in a new relationship is to be aware of the influence of alcohol and other drugs. A team of researchers found that the amount of alcohol consumed by undergraduates was associated with having sex with a stranger. The contexts of alcohol consumption included parties at fraternity and sorority houses, residence halls, off-campus, and bars/restaurants—in short, all places where students drink (Bersamin et al., 2013).

8. It's okay to change your mind about including intercourse in a relationship. Although most couples that include intercourse in their relationship continue the pattern, some decide to omit it from their sexual agenda. One female student said, "Since I did not want to go on the pill and would be frantic if I got pregnant, we decided the stress was not worth having intercourse. While we do have oral sex, we don't even think about having intercourse anymore."

8.5i Threesomes

Morris and colleagues (2016) reported analysis of data from 196 undergraduates who completed a 59-item online questionnaire designed to assess their attitudes/experience in regard to threesomes. Fifteen percent of the sample reported having experienced a threesome, and 49% reported knowing someone who had experienced a threesome. Their motivation was primarily curiosity, the third person was usually a friend/acquaintance, the outcome for the relationship was primarily either no effect or a positive effect, and the event happened only once. There were no gender differences in reported jealousy.

Scoats et al. (2018) also studied the threesome experience of 30 gay-friendly, heterosexual undergraduate men both with two women and one man (FFM) and with two men and one woman (MMF). Twelve of the respondents reported having had a threesome (seven with FFM combinations and five with MMF combinations). The researchers argued that threesomes today reflect a less sexual procreative and more playful/experimental focus of sexuality. In addition, the fact that two men and one woman were among the threesomes reflected that the cultural boundaries of heterosexuality are expanding for males.

Some couples use a synthetic surrogate, also referred to as a "companion doll," to have a threesome. Data posted on the synthetic surrogate note that 20% of users of synthetic surrogates are couples (www.syntheticsurrogates.com).

> *I like threesomes with two women, not because I'm a cynical sexual predator. Oh no! But because I'm a romantic. I'm looking for "The One." And I'll find her more quickly if I audition two at a time.*
>
> Russell Brand

Chapter Summary

Erotophilia and Erotophobia

THE RANGE OF FEELINGS toward sexual behavior can be conceptualized according to a continuum known as the *erotophilic-erotophobic continuum*. The propensity to have positive emotional responses to sexuality is referred to as *erotophilia*. The tendency to have negative emotional responses to sexuality is known as *erotophobia*. Individuals who are erotophobic tend to feel uncomfortable about sex and try to avoid sexual partners, contexts, and experiences.

Virginity, Chastity, Celibacy, and Abstinence

VIRGINITY refers to not having experienced sexual intercourse. Virgins may or may not have experienced other forms of sexual interaction, such as manual- and oral-genital stimulation or anal sex. The term *chastity* also refers to not having had sexual intercourse, but it also implies moral purity or virtuousness in both thought and conduct. *Celibacy* may refer to the condition of being unmarried, especially by reason of religious vows, and also implies refraining from having sexual intercourse. The more commonly used term today that refers to refraining from having sexual intercourse is *abstinence*. *Asexuality* is when a person reports a lack of sexual attraction to anyone.

Masturbation

AUTOEROTIC BEHAVIOR, commonly known as masturbation, involves sexual self-pleasuring. Due to traditional negative attitudes toward masturbation that originated in religion, medicine, and traditional psychotherapy, shame, guilt, and anxiety continue to be common feelings associated with masturbation in our society. Masturbation varies by sex, religion, race/ethnicity, and education. Partnered individuals, as well as singles, engage in masturbation as a solo activity or with a partner.

Sexual Fantasies

SEXUAL FANTASIES can be thought of as cognitive erotic visual scripts. They are often used in masturbation, and may be used during sex with a partner.

Interpersonal Sexuality

MOST ADULT SEXUAL BEHAVIOR occurs in the context of a relationship. These behaviors include kissing, sexual touching, oral-penile stimulation, oral-clitoral stimulation, penile-clitoral stimulation, anal stimulation, anal intercourse, and vaginal intercourse. These sexual behaviors and their many variations can be enjoyed by couples of all genders and orientations.

Web Links

The Asexual Visibility & Education Network

http://www.asexuality.org/home/

Animals That Masturbate (Other Than Humans)

http://bvtlab.com/79s8m

OMGYes: Learning About Women's Masturbation

https://www.omgyes.com/how-it-works

Synthetic Surrogates

https://syntheticsurrogates.com

Key Terms

Abstinence **193**

Analingus **205**

Asceticism **192**

Asexuality **194**

Autoerotic asphyxiation **198**

Celibacy **192**

Chastity **192**

Coitus **206**

Cunnilingus **204**

Cystitis **206**

Dental dam **204**

Erotophilia **190**

Erotophobia **190**

Fellatio **203**

Fisting **205**

Involuntary abstinence **193**

Masturbation **194**

Orgasmic meditation **203**

Semen-conservation doctrine **196**

Sexual fantasies **201**

Sexual intercourse **206**

Sexual touching **203**

Virginity **190**

Voluntary
    abstinence **193**

Yang **196**

Yin **196**

CHAPTER
9

Lifespan View of Sexuality

Your 40s are good. Your 50s are great. Your 60s are fab. And 70 is f@king awesome!*

Helen Mirren, actress

Chapter Outline

9.1 Sexuality in Infancy and Childhood 216
9.1a Infancy **216**
9.1b Sexual Behaviors of Children **216**
9.1c Parents as Sex Educators for Their Children **218**
9.1d Public and Parochial Sex Education **218**
Personal Decisions 9-1
Exposing Children to Parental Nudity **220**

9.2 Sexuality in Adolescence 220
9.2a Adolescence **220**
9.2b Physiological and Physical Changes **221**
9.2c Psychological Changes **222**
9.2d Sexual Debut of Adolescents **222**
9.2e Talking with Teens About Sex **223**
9.2f Teen Pregnancy and Births **224**

9.3 Sexuality in Adulthood 224
Social Policy 9-1
Plan B for Adolescents? **225**
Technology and Sexuality 9-1:
Effect of Reality TV on Viewers **226**
9.3a Sexuality Among Singles **227**
9.3b Sexuality Among Cohabitants **227**
Self-Assessment 9-1:
Student Sexual Risks Scale (SSRS) **228**
9.3c Sexuality Among Spouses **230**

9.3d Sexuality Among the Divorced **231**
9.3e Sexuality Among the Widowed **231**
9.3f Sexual Compliance **232**

9.4 Extramarital and Extradyadic Affairs 232
9.4a Types of Extramarital, Extradyadic Encounters **233**
Self-Assessment 9-2:
Attitudes Toward Infidelity Scale **234**
9.4b Motivations for Extramarital/Extradyadic Affairs **235**
9.4c Avoiding an Affair **237**
9.4d Recovery from an Affair/Betrayal **237**
Personal Decisions 9-2
We Both Had Affairs and Decided to Remain Married **238**

9.5 Sexuality in the Middle Years 238
9.5a Women: Menopause and Hormone Replacement Therapy **239**
9.5b Men and Testosterone Replacement Therapy **241**

9.6 Love and Sexuality in the Later Years 241
Social Policy 9-2
Restricting Sexuality in Elder-Care Facilities **244**

Web Links 246
Key Terms 247

Objectives

1. Describe the lifespan perspective of human sexuality
2. Understand how sexual development begins during infancy and is influenced by parental behaviors
3. Know how sexuality impacts adolescent development
4. Review Plan B® (levonorgestrel) for adolescents and the consequences of teen pregnancy
5. Discuss the various trends in sexuality among singles, cohabitants, married couples, and divorced individuals
6. Understand the types of affairs and motives for involvement in an affair
7. Learn how sexuality changes in the middle and later years

Truth OR Fiction?

T / F 1. Delay in sexual debut is associated with parents talking with their children about sex.

T / F 2. Morality and fear of being alone are primary reasons for making a conscious decision to remain faithful.

T / F 3. The frequency of sex reported by American adults reached an all-time high in 2018.

T / F 4. The primary message of mothers to their daughters about sex is to wait.

T / F 5. There is a lack of a safe sex culture among the elderly.

Answers: 1. T   2. T   3. F   4. T   5. T

exuality changes throughout a person's life. In a study assessing the motivations for sex of individuals 18–75 years of age, researchers found that younger age groups identified "fun," while older groups reported "mutual desire" (Collazo et al., 2014). In this chapter we take the long view of sexuality across time. We begin with sexuality in utero and expand our view to the various issues individuals face.

As noted in the Preface to the text, we are aware of the changes in the use of gender terminology and suggested a way to address this issue. Here, we reiterate that we ask that you interpret the terms to fit the context being discussed. For example, where we refer to "boy" or "girl," or "male" or "female," in most instances we are referring to cisgender male (cismale) or cisgender female (cisfemale).

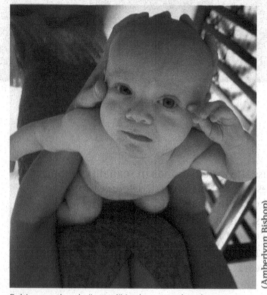

Youth has no age.

Plato

(Amberlynn Bishop)

Babies are already "sexual" in the sense that they are biologically wired as to which "sex" (male or female or where they will be on the continuum) and sexual orientation they will reflect. Socialization is yet to impact their sexual values and behaviors.

Infancy
First year of life
following birth

Childhood
Developmental time frame that extends from ages 2–12 and involves physical, cognitive, social, and sexual development

9.1 Sexuality in Infancy and Childhood

A life-cycle view of sexuality emphasizes that early experiences are important influences in subsequent sexual development.

9.1a Infancy

Infancy is the first year of life. Just as infants are born with digestive and respiratory systems, they also have a sexual response system that has already begun to function. Ultrasounds on those who are pregnant have been used to document penile and clitoral erections in the uterus. Hence, with the exception of the reproductive system (which does not mature until puberty), all the human body systems begin functioning prenatally.

Because sexual pleasure is an unconditioned, positive stimulus, infants are capable of learning associations via classical conditioning processes. Masturbation in infancy and childhood is normal, natural, and often frequent, so it is important for parents not to overreact when their children masturbate.

Parents who slap their infants for touching their own body parts and label such behaviors as "dirty" may teach their children to associate sexuality with anxiety and guilt. It is crucial to keep in mind that it is normal for babies and young children to find pleasure touching their own bodies. Later will come lessons about the body's private zones, relegating self-exploration to the appropriate "personal time," and not allowing others to touch them without consent.

9.1b Sexual Behaviors of Children

Childhood extends from ages 2–12 and involves physical, cognitive, social, and sexual development. Collecting data on the sexuality of children involves the observations of caretakers. Table 9-1 presents data from a seven-page questionnaire completed by caregivers of 917 children ages 2–12 of Belgian or Dutch origin and reveals selected sexual behaviors of various age groups (Schoentjes et al., 1999).

The selected behaviors in Table 9-1 can be sorted into various categories: exhibitionism, self-stimulation, other-focused gender role behavior, sexual anxiety, sexual interest, and voyeuristic behavior. Notice that the uninhibited behavior of 2–5-year-olds quickly abates as socialization takes place. For example, 30% of children in that age group were observed touching their sex parts in public, but only 9% of 10–12-year-olds exhibited this behavior. Similarly, 21% of 2–5-year-olds touched the sex parts of others, but only 2% of those ages 10–12 years did so.

TABLE 9-1	Sexual Behaviors of 917 Belgian and Dutch Children			
No.	Item	(n = 470)	(n = 311)	(n = 136)
1.	Touches sex parts in public	30.0%	16.1%	8.8%
2.	Masturbates with hands	9.2	6.1	5.2
3.	Masturbates with object	3.2	0.3	1.5
4.	Touches other people's sex parts	21.9	7.7	1.5
5.	Touches sex parts at home	78.3	56.0	31.6
6.	Uses words that describe sex acts	3.6	24.4	27.9
7.	Pretends to be opposite sex when playing	13.8	2.9	1.5
8.	Puts objects in vagina or rectum	3.0	0.3	0.0
9.	Tries to look at people when they are nude	37.2	28.9	19.1
10.	Undresses self in front of others	62.6	48.6	27.2
11.	Kisses other children not in the family	63.4	38.6	23.5
12.	Shows sex parts to children	13.2	7.1	2.2
13.	If boy, plays with girl's toys; if girl, plays with boy's toys	59.4	38.3	20.6
14.	Shy about undressing	15.3	30.2	32.4
15.	Plays doctor	53.0	39.2	15.4

Data source: Schoentjes, E., Deboutte, D., & Friedrich, W. (1999). Child sexual behavior inventory: A Dutch-speaking normative sample. *Pediatrics*, *104*(4–1), pp. 885–893.

Unlike adult sexuality, which is about eroticism and action, childhood sexuality is about curiosity and playfulness (Orozco-Lapray et al. 2016). "Doctor" is a favorite game among preschool children. This game involves one child assuming the role of patient and the other the role of doctor. The patient undresses, and the doctor examines the patient by making a visual inspection and by touching their body, often including the genitals. Some parents, believing such exploration is wrong, punish their children for playing doctor. Alternatively, parents might respond by saying something nonpunitive, such as, "It is interesting to find out how other people's bodies look, isn't it?" However, developmental psychologists suggest that parents should be concerned and should intervene if one child is unwilling or is coerced into playing doctor, if the children are not the same age (or within a couple of years), or if the activity is potentially harmful—such as inserting objects into themselves or each other. In such situations, parents might say something like, "Your body is wonderful, and it is natural that you are interested in your own body. But it is your body, and only you should touch yourself in private places."

9.1c Parents as Sex Educators for Their Children

Sexual socialization/sexuality education of children is a process by which knowledge, attitudes, and values about sexuality are learned. Parents are typically regarded as the first and most important source of sexual socialization for their children. Children are continually learning from parents about sex (even if parents don't talk about it), and parents may be concerned about what and when to talk with their children about sex. Many parents are afraid that doing so will spark experimentation and destroy their child's innocence/nonsexual state. Due to their own inadequate socialization, some parents also may be tense when engaging in a conversation about sex; when they do bring up the subject, it is more often about reproduction than relationships.

Pariera & Brody (2018) noted the importance of parents talking about sex early, often, and over a range of topics. Parents in the Christensen et al. (2017) research reported that they felt awkward in talking to their children about sex and noted that their parents never talked to them about it. Scroggs et al. (2019) noted the negative impact of sexual guilt on the self-esteem of adolescents across their years of youth and emphasized the need for parents to engage in sex-positive conversations about sexuality. Indeed, when parents talk with their children about sex there is strong evidence of positive outcomes for children, including delay of sexual debut and use of contraception/protection (Flores & Barroso, 2017). Delay of sex is also associated with a positive self-image in adolescence (Scroggs et al., 2019).

Timing is also important. Parent-child sexual communication is most effective when it is initiated prior to first intercourse, or **sexual debut**. When parents of adolescents encounter sexually charged scenes in media or notice their children listening to music with sexually explicit lyrics, they can use the experience as an opportunity to spur an open, age-appropriate discussion with their children to share information and foster a critical, nonsexist point of view. Specific books that parents might find helpful are Robie Harris's *It's So Amazing!* (ages 7 and up) and *It's Perfectly Normal* (ages 10 and up).

> *Parents are the sex educators of their children, whether they do it well or badly.*
>
> Sol Gordon, sex educator

> *Sex education in America is too little, too late, too biological.*
>
> Sandy Caron, sex educator

9.1d Public and Parochial Sex Education

The school system should also be involved in the education/socialization of children about sex. The National Sexuality Education Standards: core content and skills for K–12 can be found on the SIECUS.org website.

See Figure 9–1 for what children should be learning in kindergarten from Unhushed, a nonprofit that writes comprehensive, age-appropriate, innovative, up-to-date sexuality education curricula, programs, and supplementary materials.

Because the standards for sex education are not legally binding, many school districts offer insufficient or no sex education at all. Courses on sexual harassment and sexual respect are taught in some states' high school curricula. Aside from the basic "birds and the bees" content, age-appropriate information on the importance of nonsexist behavior should be available from the primary grades onward.

Some churches and other religious groups are also involved in sex education for children and youth. However, religious schools are not subject to state regulations, and the material can sometimes be doctrinaire or out of sync with current scientific knowledge. In the United States, states like North Dakota have proposed legislation overturning mandatory approval of curricula by a certified sex educator to enable religious groups to set their own standards. In these states, groups like Focus on the Family work with state governments to promulgate public-school sex-ed curricula that can be inaccurate and even dangerous (Weill, 2017).

Sexual debut
First sexual intercourse

FIGURE **9-1** ‖ Scope & Sequence—Kindergarten

Topic	Knowledge (As a result of the Unhushed program, participants will know the following content)	Skills (As a result of the Unhushed program, participants will be able to execute the following skills)	Attitudes (As a result of the Unhushed program, participants will move closer to the following positions)
Anatomy & Physiology	Proper names for external genitalia, including the vulva, clitoris, penis, testicles, and anus The body can feel both good and bad Human bodies develop and change over time Keeping your body clean is an important part of body care and health Each body is different and capable of many things	Name body parts Practice body care (e.g., washing body parts, brushing teeth) Identify actions their bodies are capable of Identify aspects of their body they view positively Express bodily needs and wishes	Positive body image Self-compassion A respect for differences
Puberty & Adolescent Development			
Identity	Every person is unique and special Some people feel like girls, some people feel like boys, and some people may feel like both or neither	Identify differences between self and others	Positive attitudes toward people of all genders A respect for differences
Pregnancy & Reproduction			
STIs & HIV			
Healthy Relationships	There are different family structures, and they can all be really great families People can become parents in many different ways, including birth and adoption Chosen families are another way to become family	Explain how people can become members of a family Name relationship bonds (e.g. friend, stepparent, etc.)	A respect for various family structures Value love and safety within familial relationships
Personal Safety	All people, including children, have the right to tell others not to touch their body when they do not want to be touched	Identify and express needs and wishes Say "yes" and no" Identify adults who can provide help and support Communicate need for help Listening to the no of others	Confidence in self to identify and express needs and wishes Awareness that it is okay to ask for help Positive feelings about ability to respect boundaries of others

Source: Smarr, J., & Francis, S. (2019). *Unhushed: The Elementary Curriculum*. (K. Rayne, Ed). Austin, Texas: Unhushed. Copyright Un|Hushed; reprinted with permission.

PERSONAL DECISIONS 9-1

Exposing Children to Parental Nudity

Some parents are concerned about the effects parental nudity may have on their children. Others are concerned that they may have damaged their children because the children have walked in on them and observed them having intercourse. (This is known as the *primal scene.*) To what degree should parents be concerned about these issues?

In general, children with parents who don't rush to cover up when they happen upon them changing clothes or parents who embrace nudism learn positive associations with their bodies. Harm in the form of negative feelings or guilt about the body results when parents shame children for being nude or for touching their own bodies. This is not the case with parents who embrace nudism or who are casual about occasional moments of nudity.

In contrast to these approaches, the Unitarian Universalist Association has developed a comprehensive, secular sex-education curriculum that champions diversity and presents scientifically up-to-date, nonjudgmental information. This lifespan sexuality education program, called Our Whole Lives (OWL), is available for use by public and private schools, as well as homeschool groups, faith communities, youth groups, and colleges (http://bvtlab.com/E9fM8). The program also offers an optional religious supplement, *Sexuality and Our Faith*, created by the Unitarian Universalist Association and the United Church of Christ.

Sex is a momentary itch, love never lets you go.
Kingsley Amis, English novelist

9.2 Sexuality in Adolescence

Adolescence is defined as the developmental period between puberty and adulthood. It is the time when the individual is transformed from a child to a young adult with a future adult life. In the United States and most other modern Western cultures, adolescence typically begins between the ages of 10 and 13 and ends between the ages of 18 and 22.

9.2a Adolescence

Early adolescence (middle school or junior high school age) includes the time of greatest pubertal change. Late adolescence (the mid to late teen years) involves identity exploration, interaction with romantic partners, and school performance with a possible career objective in mind. Adolescence is characterized by many social, psychological, and physical changes, although the most noticeable changes are physical. Adolescent children of single parents (in contrast to two-parent homes) are at greater risk for precocious sexual behavior, STIs, and premarital pregnancy, and these outcomes are true in both single-female and male-headed households (Dufur et al., 2018).

Adolescents use the internet as a major source of sex information. One area of adolescent online sex exploration is "fan communities." These use Harry Potter, Japanese manga and animation, or other popular-culture characters to imagine and explore sexual issues. "'Child abuse publications legislation' in Australia and elsewhere now criminalizes the representation of even imaginary characters who are or may only 'appear to be' under the age of 18 in sexual scenarios" (McLelland, 2017, p. 234). But

Adolescence
Developmental period in which a youth moves from childhood to adulthood

these "online sexual scenarios take no account of the nature of the interaction that takes place in these online communities and fail to address the educative value these communities could play in a young person's developing sexual identity" (p. 253).

In regard to whom adolescents talk with, Killoren et al. (2019) found that adolescent girls disclosed information about their dating and sexuality to their mothers and sisters before doing so to friends. Such disclosure was associated with a positive relationship with both family members.

9.2b Physiological and Physical Changes

The adolescent's body undergoes rapid physiological and anatomical change. The term **puberty** comes from the Latin *pubescere*, which means to be covered with hair. Pubic hair and axillary (underarm) hair in young cisgender girls and pubic, axillary, and facial hair in young cisgender boys are evidence that the hypothalamus is triggering the pituitary gland to release gonadotropins into the bloodstream. These hormones cause the testes in the cisgender male to increase testosterone production and the ovaries in the cisgender female to increase estrogen production. In a study of adolescent males in Finland, the primary sexual concern was the size and function of their penises; they were not as interested in sex education programs that focused on sexual risks and the effects of watching pornography (Kontula, 2014).

Further physical changes in adolescence include the development of secondary sex characteristics, such as breasts in cisgender females and facial hair and a deepened voice in cisgender males. A growth spurt also ensues, with cisgender girls preceding cisgender boys by about 2 years. Genitals of the respective sexes also enlarge (the penis and testes in the cisgender male and the labia in the cisgender female). Internally, the prostate gland and seminal vesicles begin to function, making it possible for the young adolescent cisgender male to ejaculate. First ejaculation, or **semenarche**, usually occurs around age 13 or 14, but the timing is variable. Sperm is present in the ejaculate at about age 14.

Cisgender girls experience their own internal changes. The uterus, cervix, and vaginal walls respond to hormone changes to produce the first menstruation, or *menarche*. This usually occurs between the ages of 12 and 13, but the timing is highly variable.

Adolescents are particularly concerned about the degree to which their bodies match the dominant cultural image, which can cause great stress. Girls are more likely to be dissatisfied with their body image than boys. Since many adolescent females are intent on matching the culture's rigid cultural appearance, weight, and body type ideals, the consequence of weight on sexual decisions and behavior is significant. National data on adolescents reveals that overweight or obese adolescent girls are less likely than their recommended-weight counterparts to be sexually active (Averett et al., 2013). However, even girls of age-appropriate weight are subjected to extreme commercial programming by the larger culture to obsess about their size, with more than 42% of first- to third-grade girls wanting to be thinner (Collins, 1991) and a third of age-appropriate-weight girls reporting dieting (Wertheim et al., 2009). Eating disorders affect 20 million women and girls in the United States, twice as many as men and boys, and the mortality rate of anorexic young women between ages 15 and 24 is 12 times higher than that of all other causes of death (National Eating Disorders Association, n.d.). Boys going through

(Amberlynn Bishop)

Adolescence is a delicate time of growing up.

Puberty
Developmental stage in which a youth achieves reproductive capacity

Semenarche
A boy's first seminal ejaculation

adolescence are also impacted by the images they see, particularly of muscular men. This is one of the factors that contributes to body dissatisfaction and binge eating among boys (Mitchison et al., 2017).

9.2c Psychological Changes

In addition to physical changes, adolescent psychological changes include moving from a state of childish dependence to a state of relative independence, ambivalence about the onset of adulthood, exploring and resolving sexual identity issues, and developing the security of feeling normal. An example of adolescent ambivalence about growing up is the adolescent female who experiments with makeup but still cuddles her stuffed teddy bear. Adolescents often want the freedom to play as children while at the same time exploring adult independence.

Risky sexual behaviors (early sexual debut, numerous sexual partners, absence of condoms/contraception) are normative during adolescence. In spite of their quest for independence and risk-taking, adolescents tend to be psychologically healthy. National data have revealed that, on average, all study participants had low levels of depression, perceptions of social rejection tended to decrease over time, and happiness tended to increase.

9.2d Sexual Debut of Adolescents

Based on a national survey of adolescents, 3.4% reported having had sexual intercourse by age 13 (Kann et al., 2018). In a study on ninth-grade urban Latino and African Americans (average age 15.2) in 10 Los Angeles area high schools, 19% reported having experienced vaginal sex; 16%, oral sex (Donatello et al., 2017). Adolescent sexual debut is an important step toward adulthood (Kuortti & Lindfors, 2014), but at very young ages, first intercourse is more likely to be nonconsensual (Finer & Philbin, 2013).

Early sexual debut is typically associated with high-risk sexual behavior, including alcohol/drug use, not using condoms, getting pregnant (or causing pregnancy), and violence in the form of (primarily girls) being hit/slapped or otherwise hurt by a partner. Peterson et al. (2016) revealed that women who planned their first intercourse reported more satisfaction and less regret. Goldfarb et al. (2016) reported that first sex among gay/bisexual/queer men was a way of "figuring out" their sexual orientation. They also reported that their first experience was not pleasurable and was painful/uncomfortable (they did not use lubrication).

Rossi et al. (2017) identified the number of sexual partners ages 16–22 of 332 participants and found four patterns—the abstainers group (9.1%), low-increasing group (30.6 %), medium-increasing group (53.0%), and multiple-partners group (7.3%). Only in the latter group did the number of partners exceed five. Lower numbers were associated with later pubertal development, being from a two-parent family, parental monitoring, and being female. Once sexual intercourse begins in adolescence, it generally continues. Abma and Martinez (2017) revealed that 42% of female teens and 44% of male teens report having had sexual intercourse with 81% of females reporting the use of a hormonal contraception and 80% of males reporting the use of a condom.

Vissing (2018) emphasizes a new approach to sexual debut education (SDE). Rather than emphasizing to wait until marriage or abstain from sex, SDE focuses on empowering the individual to think about and make choices regarding the who, relationship context, what, when, why, and where a person would like to have their first sexual experience. SDE also focuses on making decisions ahead of time about contraception and STI protection.

Sexual competence refers to four criteria—use of contraception, autonomy of decision, equally willing, and the "right time" (Palmer et al. 2017) that identify when a person is ready for first intercourse. It is these contextual factors, not age, that are the primary focus. Individuals not displaying sexual competence at first heterosexual intercourse were more likely to report having HPV, low sexual function in the last year, unplanned pregnancy, and nonvolitional sex.

9.2e Talking with Teens About Sex

Goldfarb et al. (2018) conducted focus groups of 74 first and second year undergraduates to find out what the sexual communication contexts and content they had with their parents were, prior to their first sexual intercourse. The contexts were mainly with mothers, awkward, and they feared their parents' reactions if they told them anything. The content was commonly about protection, and the message to women was to wait. There was a general lack of support for nonheterosexual orientations. Of course, parents are important sources of sexual learning for their children. Although children are constantly learning about relationships and sexuality through observing their parents, talking about sex when children are most vulnerable to risky sexual behavior (late childhood, early adolescence) is critical (Coakley et al. 2017b).

Karen Rayne (2015) is the author of *Breaking the Hush Factor: Ten Rules for Talking with Teenagers About Sex*. She is also the mother of two teenagers. Here are her rules for parents who want to communicate with their adolescents:

1. *Know yourself.* What are your expectations, your hopes, and your fears about your teenager's sexual and romantic development? You will have far more control over yourself and your interactions if you have a full understanding of these things.

2. *Remember that it's not about you.* Your teenager is, in fact, discovering sex for the first time. They want to talk about their current exciting, overwhelming path. So let them! That's how you'll find out what you can do to help your teenager walk this path—and remember, that's what matters most.

3. *Stop talking!* As the parent of a teenager, you are in the business of getting to know your teenager, not to give information. If you're talking, you can't hear anything your teenager is trying to tell you.

4. *Start listening!* Stop talking. Start listening. Remember what's most important about your role as a parent. And that can't happen if you don't really, really listen.

5. *You get only one question.* Since there's only one, you had better make it a good one that can't be answered with a yes or a no. Spend some time mulling over it. You can ask it when you're sure it's a good one. Open-ended questions are best: "What was it like when …"

6. *Do something else.* Anything else. Many teenagers, especially boys, will have an easier time talking about sexuality and romance if you're doing something side by side, like driving, walking, or playing a game, rather than sitting and looking at each other.

7. *About pleasure and pain.* You have to talk about both. If you don't acknowledge the physical and emotional pleasure associated with sexuality, your teenager will think you're completely out of touch, and so you will be completely out of touch.

Sexual competence
Refers to four criteria—use of contraception, autonomy of decision, equally willing, and the "right time" as to when a person is ready for first intercourse

8. *Be cool like a cucumber.* It is only when you manage to have a calm, loving demeanor that your teenager will feel comfortable talking with you. And remember—you're in the business of getting to know your teenager—and the only way to do that is if your teenager keeps talking.

9. *Bring it on!* Your teenagers have tough questions, some of them quite specific and technical. If you're able to answer these questions with honesty, humor, and without judgment, your teenager will feel much more at home coming to you with the increasingly difficult emotional questions that touch their heart.

10. *Never surrender.* There may be times you feel like quitting. Like the millionth time when you've tried to have an actual conversation with your teenager—about anything, much less sex!—and your teenager has once again completely avoided eye contact and has not even acknowledged your existence. But you can't. You're still doing some good, so keep going. Trust me.

9.2f Teen Pregnancy and Births

Just the mention of a teenage mom may sometimes carry the implication that she did not want to get pregnant and is struggling to cope with early motherhood; however, some sexually active adolescent females want to get pregnant. Sixteen percent of a sample of teenage girls ages 15–18 reported that they would be "a little pleased" or "very pleased" if they were to become pregnant. Factors associated with wanting to become pregnant included having had a prior pregnancy, being older in contrast to being younger, and having parents with a high school education or less (Cavazos-Rehg et al., 2013).

Sexuality in adulthood is more about coming into an awareness of one's own sexuality, comfort, and excitement for the future.

(Amberlynn Bishop)

In the United States, the teen birth rate is 18.8 births per 1,000 teen girls (ages 15–19) or about 195,000 births per year to teen girls (Power to Decide, 2019). The rates have been dropping for two decades, and increased use of contraceptives by teens is the primary explanation for their decline (Boonstra, 2014). Despite the continued drop, the rates remain far higher than in other developed countries.

9.3 Sexuality in Adulthood

The frequency of sex reported by American adults reached an all-time low in 2018. The percentage of Americans having sex at least once a week declined from 51% (1996) to 39% (2018). Almost a quarter (23%) of those ages 18–29 reported having no sex in the past year. Explanations include stress over labor force participation and the rise of technology, which constantly occupies the focus of many young adults (Ingraham, 2019). Soh (2019) also noted "toxic masculinity" (men perceived as not respecting women), individuals moving out of their parents' house later (no place to have sex), and #metoomovment fallout (men fearful of being accused of rape when sex was believed to be consensual).

In general, parents in the United States are fearful of sex education for their children and avoid any references to it, believing if they don't talk about sex, their children won't have sex. Such a view is nonsense to parents in the Netherlands, where the sexuality of children is acknowledged and accepted. Discussions about the normality of sex and the importance of responsibility permeate the dialogue. Indeed, some parents allow their adolescent to have a steady partner visit for the evening, including an overnight stay. Condoms are available in the bedside table, and there is coffee in the morning, along with typical dialogue concerning school, politics, and soccer.

Cultural Diversity

Social Policy 9-1

Plan B for Adolescents?

Some emergency contraception is available, without a prescription, to people of any age. Levonorgestrel (brand name Plan B One-Step); also sold as Next Choice One Dose® and My Way®) is a high-dose progestin pill that acts to prevent ovulation or fertilization of an egg. While it can be taken for up to 120 hours after unprotected intercourse, it becomes less effective the longer you wait. Taking it within 72 hours after unprotected sex, condom failure, or a missed period can reduce the chance of pregnancy by up to 89%. Plan B is most effective (approximately 95%) if taken within 24 hours after unprotected intercourse. It is not the abortion pill (RU-486).

Plan B—which costs $40 to $60 for one pill—can be used to reduce the occurrence of pregnancy in the 1 in 5 adolescent girls in the United States who report unprotected sexual intercourse. The Centers for Disease Control and Prevention reports that nearly a third (1 in 3) female victims were first raped between ages 11 and 17 (National Center for Injury Prevention and Control, 2019); for these young women, Plan B provides the valuable option of not becoming pregnant with their rapist's child. Some people claim that Plan B's over-the-counter availability will encourage teens to have sex since they can "just take a pill in the morning." In addition, some are against the Plan B option because they feel it encourages promiscuity. There is no evidence to support these beliefs.

Davis and Olmsted (2017) studied 601 emerging adults (18–29) who revealed that one of their motivations for becoming sexually intimate was to facilitate or explore their identity as a person. Sociologist Beth Montemurro (2014a) interviewed 95 women in their 20s, 30s, 40s, 50s, and 60s, identifying various developmental phases of their sexual subjectivity (awareness of sexual desire and acting on it) throughout their lifespan:

1. *Developing a stance:* Attitude toward sexuality is either positive or negative, something to hide/feel guilty about or something to embrace. Women born before 1960 tended to have negative, guilt-ridden, oppressive beginnings.

2. *Learning through doing:* Through encounters with others, a new view of sexuality evolves that confirms or changes your original stance.

3. *First sexual relationship of consequence:* The first serious sexual relationship or marriage provides a context of security in which the woman may learn it is safe to be sexual and to experience pleasure with approval.

4. *Self-discovery through role and relationship changes:* Motherhood (desexualizes the woman) and divorce (frees the woman to explore) are new roles, with concomitant changes.

5. *Self-discovery through embodied changes:* Hormonal changes (from motherhood, menopause and aging) allow women to reflect on earlier sexual learning, which may bring more freedom to be sexual or to embrace sexual desire.

6. *Self-acceptance:* Pleasing others may morph into pleasing yourself sexually.

Of course, neither marriage nor children are relevant to some women, who may prefer neither.

Television has a powerful effect on what a person learns about sex in our society. *Technology and Sexuality 9-1* looks at the effect of reality television on sexuality.

Technology and Sexuality 9-1:
Effect of Reality TV on Viewers

Reality television has been criticized as having a negative impact on viewers. Some of the criticism seemed unfounded when, in 2014, newspapers and websites highlighted a single study that claimed that MTV® shows like *16 and Pregnant* caused a decline in the teen birthrate in the United States. Is this one study consistent with other research about the impact of reality TV on individuals?

Osborn (2012) conducted a study of how watching television, including reality television, impacted married people. He found that spouses who viewed romantic programs believed that what they saw on television reflected reality in relationships. In addition, watching romantic programs was associated with lower marital commitment and favorable attitudes toward alternatives to their marriages, which might include being in a relationship with someone else or choosing not to be in a relationship at all.

Other studies have indicated that reality television shows impact our views on how individuals behave and how couples interact. Research by Riddle and De Simone (2013) revealed that individuals who watched reality television believed that women were more likely than men to engage in bad behaviors, such as gossiping and being verbally aggressive/argumentative. Respondents who watched a lot of romantic programming also overestimated the number of affairs spouses have and believed that spouses getting married would be more likely to divorce.

While research may indicate that watching reality television influences attitudes, what is its effect on behavior? A study of college students by Fogel and Kovalenko (2013) found that those students who watched reality television that specifically focused on sexual relationships were more likely to engage in one-night stands.

This research seems to contradict those headlines about the positive effects of MTV's programming—until we look beyond the headlines and examine the research itself. The study, conducted by Kearney and Levine (2014), examined the changes in what young people were searching for online and what they were tweeting about after *16 and Pregnant* aired, which showed an increase in the number of searches and posts about abortion and birth control.

From these data, the researchers surmised that *16 and Pregnant* contributed to the decline in the teen birthrate over an 18-month period. However, this claim is based on a faulty process, because correlation does not imply causality. Although the research did reveal increased interest in the topics of abortion and birth control, it cannot be concluded that the TV show itself resulted in a reduction in teen birthrates—the cause may have been related to new sex education programs in high school or any number of factors.

In another study on the impact of *16 and Pregnant*, Aubrey and colleagues (2014) found, based on objective self-reporting, that female viewers who watched a single episode of the show felt less likely that they would get pregnant and believed that for teen mothers being pregnant carried more benefits than risks.

What do we conclude? Do reality shows help or hurt the individuals who watch them? Objective studies suggest that these shows have an overall negative impact on beliefs about other people, about relationships, and about the risks of teen pregnancy. These outcomes do not necessarily mean you should stop watching reality television. However, it is important to recognize the potential impact of viewing these programs, in addition to all the other media messages you're exposed to.

National DATA

There are 45 million never-married men and 40 million never-married women over the age of 15 in the United States (ProQuest Statistical Abstract of the United States, 2019, Table 57).

Cultural Diversity

Based on analysis of data for 31 sub-Saharan African countries and 25,483 cases, most respondents reported being satisfied with their sex life, with males, those in a relationship, those late 20s to early 30s, and those more educated/higher incomes reporting higher satisfaction (Cranney, 2017).

9.3a Sexuality Among Singles

Never-married individuals have intercourse less frequently than those who are married or living together. In addition to having less sex and achieving less sexual satisfaction (Michael et al., 1994), singles may also be more vulnerable to engaging in high-risk sexual behavior. *Self-Assessment 9-1* allows you to determine the degree to which you engage in behavior that involves a high risk for STI infection.

9.3b Sexuality Among Cohabitants

Cohabitation, also known as living together, involves two adults—unrelated by blood or by law and involved in an emotional and sexual relationship—who sleep in the same residence at least 4 nights a week for 3 months. The endorsement of cohabitation by undergraduates is strongly associated with having more sexual partners, being permissive in sexual attitudes, and being less religious. Cohabitants also tend to have a higher frequency of sex, since the partners are often relatively new to each other (Willoughby & Carroll, 2012). The higher frequency of sex decreases after the birth of a child, which typically leads to marriage (more often for women) (Cho et al., 2018).

My boyfriend and I live together, which means we don't have sex—ever. Now that the milk is free, we've both become lactose intolerant.

Margaret Cho, comedian

Not all cohabitants are college students. Indeed, only 18% of all cohabitants are under the age of 25. The largest percentage (36%) are between the ages of 25 and 34 (Jayson, 2012). Recent data indicates a 75% increase, since 2007, in the number of people over 50 who report cohabiting (Stepler, 2017). Reasons for the increase in cohabitation include career or educational commitments; increased tolerance of society, parents, and peers; improved birth control technology; desire for a stable emotional and sexual relationship without legal ties; avoiding loneliness; and greater disregard for convention.

Cohabitation
Also known as living together, cohabitation is when two unrelated adults involved in a relationship sleep in the same residence at least 4 nights a week for 3 months.

Self-Assessment 9-1: Student Sexual Risks Scale (SSRS)

The following self-assessment allows you to evaluate the degree to which you may be at risk for engaging in behavior that exposes you to HIV. Safer sex means sexual activity that reduces the risk of transmitting the virus that causes AIDS. Using condoms is an example of safer sex. Unsafe, risky, or unprotected sex means sex without a condom or other sexual activity that might increase the risk of HIV transmission. For each of the following items, write the letter that best characterizes your belief:

A = Agree, U = Undecided, D = Disagree

1. __ If my partner wanted me to have unprotected sex, I would probably give in.
2. __ The proper use of a condom could enhance sexual pleasure.
3. __ I may have had sex with someone who was at risk for HIV/AIDS.
4. __ If I were going to have sex, I would take precautions to reduce my risk of HIV/AIDS.
5. __ Condoms ruin the natural sex act.
6. __ When I think that one of my friends might have sex on a date, I ask him/her if he/she has a condom.
7. __ I am at risk for HIV/AIDS.
8. __ I would try to use a condom when I had sex.
9. __ Condoms interfere with romance.
10. __ My friends talk a lot about safer sex.
11. __ If my partner wanted me to participate in risky sex, and I said that we needed to be safer, we would still probably end up having unsafe sex.
12. __ Generally, I am in favor of using condoms.
13. __ I would avoid using condoms if at all possible.
14. __ If a friend knew that I might have sex on a date, he/she would ask me whether I was carrying a condom.
15. __ There is a possibility that I have HIV/AIDS.
16. __ If I had a date, I would probably not drink alcohol or use drugs.
17. __ Safer sex reduces the mental pleasure of sex.
18. __ If I thought that one of my friends had sex on a date, I would ask him/her if he/she used a condom.
19. __ The idea of using a condom doesn't appeal to me.
20. __ Safer sex is a habit for me.
21. __ If a friend knew that I had sex on a date, he/she wouldn't care whether I had used a condom or not.
22. __ If my partner wanted me to participate in risky sex, and I suggested a lower-risk alternative, we would have the safer sex instead.
23. __ The sensory aspects (smell, touch, etc.) of condoms make them unpleasant.
24. __ I intend to follow safer sex guidelines within the next year.
25. __ With condoms, you can't really give yourself over to your partner.
26. __ I am determined to practice safer sex.
27. __ If my partner wanted me to have unprotected sex, and I made some excuse to use a condom, we would still end up having unprotected sex.
28. __ If I had sex and I told my friends that I did not use condoms, they would be angry or disappointed.
29. __ I think safer sex would get boring fast.
30. __ My sexual experiences do not put me at risk for HIV/AIDS.
31. __ Condoms are irritating.
32. __ My friends and I encourage each other before dates to practice safer sex.
33. __ When I socialize, I usually drink alcohol or use drugs.

34. ___ If I were going to have sex in the next year, I would use condoms.

35. ___ If a sexual partner didn't want to use condoms, we would have sex without using condoms.

36. ___ People can get the same pleasure from safer sex as from unprotected sex.

37. ___ Using condoms interrupts sex play.

38. ___ It is a hassle to use condoms.

Scoring

Begin by giving yourself 80 points. Subtract one point for every undecided response. Subtract two points every time that you disagreed with odd-numbered items or with item number 38. Subtract two points every time you agreed with even-numbered items 2 through 36.

Interpreting Your Score

Research shows that students who make higher scores on the SSRS are more likely to engage in risky sexual activities, such as having multiple sex partners or failing to consistently use condoms during sex. In contrast, students who practice safer sex tend to endorse more positive attitudes toward safer sex and tend to have peer networks that encourage safer sexual practices. These students usually plan on making sexual activity safer and feel confident in their ability to negotiate safer sex, even when a dating partner may press for riskier sex. Students who practice safer sex often refrain from using alcohol or drugs, which may impede negotiation of safer sex. They also often report having engaged in lower-risk activities in the past. How do you measure up?

Below 15: Lower Risk

Of 200 students surveyed by DeHart and Birkimer (1997), 16% were in this category. Congratulations! Your score on the SSRS indicates that, relative to other students, your thoughts and behaviors are more supportive of safer sex. Is there any room for improvement in your score? If so, you may want to examine items for which you lost points and try to build safer sexual strengths in those areas. You can help protect others from HIV by educating your peers about making sexual activity safer.

15–37: Average Risk

Of 200 students surveyed by DeHart and Birkimer (1997), 68% were in this category. Your score on the SSRS is about average in comparison with those of other college students. Although you don't fall into the higher-risk category, be aware that "average" people can get HIV too. Thus, you may want to enhance your sexual safety by figuring out where you lost points and working toward safer sexual strengths in those areas.

38 and Above: Higher Risk

Of 200 students surveyed by DeHart and Birkimer (1997), 16% were in this category. Relative to other students, your score on the SSRS indicates that your thoughts and behaviors are less supportive of safer sex. Such high scores tend to be associated with greater HIV-risk behavior. Rather than simply giving in to riskier attitudes and behaviors, you may want to empower yourself and reduce your risk by critically examining areas for improvement. On which items did you lose points? Think about how you can strengthen your sexual safety in these areas. Reading more about safer sex can help; sometimes colleges and health clinics offer courses or workshops on safer sex. You can get more information about resources in your area by contacting the Centers for Disease Control and Prevention AIDS Information Line at 1-800-HIV-0440 (448-0440) | 1-888-480-3739 TTY.

Reference: DeHart, D. D., & Birkimer, J. C. (1997). Trying to practice safer sex: Development of the sexual risks scale. *Journal of Sex Research, 34*(1), 11–25. Developed for this text by Dana D. DeHart, College of Social Work at the University of South Carolina, and John C. Birkimer, University of Louisville, Kentucky. Used by permission of Dana DeHart and John C. Birkimer.

9.3c Sexuality Among Spouses

In spite of the perceived benefits of singlehood and cohabitation, marriage remains the lifestyle most Americans eventually choose (among those over 65 years of age in the United States today, 96% have married at least once). We await data to ascertain if the same percent of today's youth eventually marry. Nine percent of 13,070 undergraduates reported that they want to maintain their freedom/never marry (Hall & Knox, 2019).

Marital sex is characterized by its social legitimacy, declining frequency, and superiority in terms of sexual and emotional satisfaction.

1. *Social legitimacy*: In our society, marital intercourse is the most legitimate form of sexual behavior. Premarital and extramarital intercourse do not rate as high a level of social approval as does marital sex. It is not only okay to have intercourse when married, it is expected. People assume that married couples make love and that something is wrong if they do not.

2. *Declining frequency*: Sexual intercourse between spouses occurs about six times a month and declines in frequency as they age. Pregnancy also decreases the frequency of sexual intercourse. In addition to biological changes due to aging and pregnancy, satiation contributes to the declining frequency of intercourse between spouses and partners in long-term relationships. Psychologists use the term **satiation** to refer to the repeated exposure of a particular stimulus (in this case, the partner), which results in the reduction of its ability to reinforce. The 500th time that a person has intercourse with the same partner is not as new and exciting as the first few times.

    A change in hormone levels may also be related to the decline in frequency of sexual intercourse between spouses. Testosterone levels (associated with higher levels of sexual approach behavior) are lower in men who are in committed or married relationships, as well as in women who are mothers (Barrett, et al., 2013).

    Some spouses do not have intercourse at all. In a nationwide study of sexuality, 1% of husbands and 3% of wives reported that they had not had intercourse in the past 12 months (Michael et al., 1994). Ill health, age, sexual orientation, stress, depression, and conflict were identified as some of the reasons for not having intercourse in marriage. Such an arrangement may be accompanied by a range of affection, from limited to extensive.

3. *Sexual and emotional satisfaction*: Despite declining frequency over time, marital sex remains a richly satisfying experience. Contrary to the popular belief that unattached singles have the best sex, married and pair-bonded adults enjoy the most satisfying sexual relationships. In the national sample referred to earlier, 88% of married people said they received great physical pleasure from their sexual lives, and almost 85% said they received great emotional satisfaction (Michael et al., 1994). Individuals least likely to report being physically and emotionally pleased in their sexual relationships are those who are not married, not living with anyone, or not in a stable relationship. Hence, the categories from most to least sexually satisfied are married people, cohabitants, and the uninvolved.

In interviews with 71 women who were married, separated, divorced, or widowed, marriage (for older women) was defined as the great turning point where these women learned about sex in detail. Those who had limited sex before marriage felt more secure to enjoy and explore their sexuality. Those who were sexually experienced may have

Satiation
A stimulus loses its value with repeated exposure

felt disappointed that their husband was not as interested in sex. Others felt it was time for them to settle down and be more "pure" in their sexual interest and expression (focus on the cultural script of marital sex). Some who had had negative sexual experiences as single women looked to marriage hoping to find a partner who was not too interested/too sexual (Montemurro, 2014b).

What marriage offers – and what fidelity is meant to protect – is the possibility of moments when what we have chosen and what we desire are the same.

Wendell Berry, *The Body and the Earth*

Cultural Diversity

What constitutes a marriage and a family varies by society and culture. Japan's rent-a-family industry involves one's ability to rent a wife, husband, child, sibling, you name it. Indeed, a Japanese woman who wants a traditional wedding but who has no man in her life can rent a stand-in groom, bridesmaids, ushers, etc. She need only show up with her parents to have the event of her lifetime (the cost is $47,000). Grieving widows/widowers can also rent a spouse, parents who are estranged from their children can rent engaged children, and the elderly can rent grandchildren. One such company is called Family Romance (founded by Yuichi Ishii, who has 1,200 freelance actors from which to choose). Ishii has played the husband to 100 women. These are social, not sexual relationships (Batuman, 2018).

9.3d Sexuality Among the Divorced

Of the over 800,000 people getting divorced annually, most have intercourse within 1 year of being separated from their spouses.

Morrissey Stahl et al. (2018) interviewed women following their divorce and found divorce empowering for them in both exploration and satisfaction. Of course, the meanings of intercourse for separated or divorced individuals vary. For many, intercourse is a way to reestablish—indeed, repair—a damaged sense of self-esteem. Barber and Cooper (2014) found that those who had been dumped used sex to cope with feelings of distress, anger, and diminished self-esteem. Additionally, those who had sex for these reasons were more likely (not initially, but over time) to continue having sex with different new partners. Caution about becoming involved with someone on the rebound may be warranted. One answer to the question "How fast should you run from a person on the rebound?" may be "As fast as you can." Waiting until the partner has 12–18 months of distance from the previous relationship provides for a more stable context for a new connection.

9.3e Sexuality Among the Widowed

Radosh and Simkin (2017) used the term "sexual bereavement" to refer to the unacknowledged loss of sexual and affectional activities when a long-time partner dies. They surveyed 104 women age 55 and older, 72% of whom reported they would miss sex if their partner predeceased them. Yet these respondents acknowledged the reluctance of friends and professionals to talk about this loss. Kimmons and Moore (2014) found that widows had more interest in cohabitation than remarriage but the researchers did not address the loss of sex. Kirkman and colleagues (2016) noted that the failure to acknowledge or emphasize the existence of sexual behavior in the later years results in insufficient attention to this area of research. The researchers suggested that social policy about sexuality should include older adult sexuality.

A good widow does not crave sex. She certainly doesn't talk about it. ... Apparently I stink at being a good widow.

Hunter, widowsvoice.blogsplot.com

9.3f Sexual Compliance

Given that partners may differ in sexual interest and desire, Vannier and O'Sullivan (2010) identified the concept of **sexual compliance** whereby an individual willingly agrees to participate in sexual behavior without having the desire to do so. Quinn-Nilas and Kennett (2018) noted that "upwards of 60% of young women report compliant sexual behaviors when unwanted sexual advances are conceptualized broadly to include unwanted dancing, kissing, petting, oral sex, and vaginal intercourse not involving coercion." In the Vannier and O'Sullivan (2010) research, sexual compliance was a strategy these individuals used in their committed relationships to cope with different levels of sexual desire.

There were no gender differences in sexual desire and no gender differences in providing sexual compliant behavior. The majority of participants reported enjoying the sexual activity despite not wanting to engage in it at first. Braksmajer (2017) studied partners who were unable to have sex (pain, disability) who engaged in sex for their partners as a way of maintaining intimacy, keeping the sexual relationship going, etc.

However, Muise et al. (2017b) emphasized that it is equally important to legitimize one partner not being in the mood as well as the partner who wants sex. Indeed, greater sexual satisfaction and relationship quality were associated, particularly for young mothers, when their partners recognized their need not to have sex.

9.4 Extramarital and Extradyadic Affairs

About one-fourth of husbands and 20% of wives report having had sex with someone other than their spouse during the marriage (Russell et al., 2013). Definitions of infidelity vary. Moller and Vossler (2015) surveyed clients and counselors and identified three main categories: infidelity as sexual intercourse, infidelity as extradyadic sexual activities (including cybersex/sexting), and infidelity as emotional betrayal (being in love with someone the partner is not aware of).

In modern times, couples are more concerned about loyalty than love.

Amit Kalantri, *Wealth of Words*

In regard to the latter, one of Zapien's respondents in a study on extramarital affairs noted: "I didn't have a physical affair, but I became very emotionally involved with someone for a couple of months whom I actively sought out in the early days of craigslist (can you believe it?!)" (Zapien, 2017). Jackman (2014) analyzed the answers of 512 internet respondents ages 18–59 in regard to identifying characteristics associated with being unfaithful: favorable attitudes toward infidelity, confidence in your ability to attract others, a social network that would support infidelity, lower levels of religiosity, being unfaithful in the past, and being male. Power is also associated with infidelity. Lammers and Maner (2016) found that power "releases people from the inhibiting effects of social norms and thus increases their appetite for counternormative forms of sexuality." Finally, Balderrama-Durbin et al. (2017) studied soldiers in the Air Force and found that being deployed was associated with infidelity. Hence, being separated from one's partner is associated with vulnerability to an affair.

Sexual compliance
The concept whereby an individual willingly agrees to participate in sexual behavior without having the desire to do so

9.4a Types of Extramarital, Extradyadic Encounters

The term **extramarital affair** refers to a spouse's sexual involvement with someone outside the marriage. **Extradyadic affair** refers to betrayal (sexual, emotional, cybersexual) by an individual in an "exclusive" relationship. Whether the partners are married or not, different types of affairs include the following:

1. *Brief encounter*: A partner meets and hooks up with a stranger. In this case, the encounter usually happens out of town, and alcohol is usually involved.

2. *Paid sex*: A partner seeks sexual variety with a sex worker who will do whatever that spouse wants. These encounters usually go undetected unless there is an STI, the person confesses, or the sex worker exposes the client.

3. *Instrumental or utilitarian affair*: This is sex in exchange for a job or promotion, an affair to get back at the partner, or an affair used to transition out of the relationship.

4. *Coping mechanism*: Sex can be used to enhance your self-concept or feeling of sexual inadequacy, compensate for failure in business, cope with the death of a family member, or test your sexual orientation.

5. *Paraphiliac affairs*: In these encounters, the on-the-side sex partner acts out sexual fantasies or participates in sexual practices that the person's spouse considers bizarre or abnormal, such as sexual masochism, sexual sadism, or transvestic fetishism.

6. *Office romance*: Two individuals who work together may fall in love or just drift into an affair. In a Vault Careers (2019) survey of more than 700 respondents, 30% of those 18–21 and 72% of those over 50 reported that they had been involved in an office romance.

7. *Internet or use of apps*: Although an extramarital affair does not exist legally unless two people (one of them married) have intercourse, connecting with someone via an app or online can be disruptive to a marriage or a couple's relationship.

    Virtual friendships may evolve to feelings of intimacy; involve secrecy (the partner doesn't know the level of involvement); include sexual tension (even though there is no physical sex); and take time, attention, energy, and affection away from the partner. *Self-Assessment 9-2* allows you to measure your attitude toward infidelity.

A man is basically as faithful as his options.

Chris Rock, comedian

Extramarital affair
Sexual involvement between a spouse and someone other than the person they are married to

Extradyadic affair
Betrayal (sexual, emotional, cybersexual) by an individual in an "exclusive" relationship

Diversity in Other Countries

Forty-three percent of 126 married men (mean age, 46) in Vietnam reported having had sex with someone other than their wife. Their doing so was unrelated to frequency of sex with their wives, their satisfaction in the marital relationship, or their frequency of orgasms with the wife. The divorce rate in Vietnam is less than 5 percent (Nguyen et al. 2016).

Self-Assessment 9-2:
Attitudes Toward Infidelity Scale

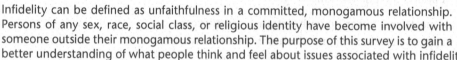

Infidelity can be defined as unfaithfulness in a committed, monogamous relationship. Persons of any sex, race, social class, or religious identity have become involved with someone outside their monogamous relationship. The purpose of this survey is to gain a better understanding of what people think and feel about issues associated with infidelity. There are no right or wrong answers. Provide your honest reaction to each statement.

Please read each statement carefully, and respond by using the following scale:

1 (Disagree strongly), 2 (Disagree mostly), 3 (Disagree a little), 4 (Neither disagree nor agree),

5 (Agree a little), 6 (Agree mostly), 7 (Agree strongly)

1. __ Being unfaithful never hurt anyone.
2.* __ Infidelity in a marital relationship is grounds for divorce.
3. __ Infidelity is acceptable for retaliation of infidelity.
4. __ It is natural for people to be unfaithful.
5.* __ Online/internet behavior (for example, visiting sex chat rooms, porn sites) is an act of infidelity.
6.* __ Infidelity is morally wrong in all circumstances, regardless of the situation.
7.* __ Being unfaithful in a relationship is one of the most dishonorable things a person can do.
8.* __ Infidelity is unacceptable, under any circumstances, if the couple is married.
9. __ I would not mind if my significant other had an affair as long as I did not know about it.
10. __ It would be acceptable for me to have an affair, but not my significant other.
11. __ I would have an affair if I knew my significant other would never find out.
12.* __ If I knew my significant other was guilty of infidelity, I would confront him/her.

Scoring

Selecting a 1 reflects the least acceptance of infidelity; selecting a 7 reflects the greatest acceptance of infidelity. Before adding the numbers you selected, reverse the scores for items with an asterisk (*). For example, if you responded to item 2 with a "6," change this number to a "2"; if you responded with a "3," change this number to a "5"; and so on. After making these changes, add the numbers. The lower your total score (12 is the lowest possible), the less accepting you are of infidelity; the higher your total score (84 is the highest possible), the greater your acceptance of infidelity. A score of 48 places you at the midpoint between being very disapproving and very accepting of infidelity.

Scores of Other Students Who Completed the Scale

The scale was completed by 150 male and 136 female student volunteers at Valdosta State University in Valdosta, Georgia. The average score on the scale was 27.85 with an SD (standard deviation) of 12.02. Their ages ranged from 18 to 49, with a mean age of 23.36 (SD = 5.13). Male participants reported more positive attitudes toward infidelity (mean = 31.53; SD = 11.86) than did female participants (mean = 23.78; SD = 10.86; $p < 0.05$). White participants had more negative attitudes toward infidelity (mean = 25.36; SD = 11.17) than did nonwhite participants (mean = 31.71; SD = 12.32; $p < 0.05$).

Source: Whatley, M. (2006). Attitudes toward infidelity scale [Survey]. Published data from Valdosta State University, Valdosta, GA. Retrieved from https://www.scribd.com/doc/152231639/Attitudes-Toward-Infidelity-Scale. Used by permission. Other uses of this scale by written permission of Dr. Whatley only (mwhatley@valdosta.edu). Information on the reliability and validity of this scale is available from Dr. Whatley.

9.4b Motivations for Extramarital/Extradyadic Affairs

Individuals in pair-bonded relationships report a number of reasons for emotional, sexual, or cybersex betrayal of a partner. A primary reason is the perception that one's needs are not being met in the primary relationship and looking elsewhere to meet those needs (Norona et al. 2018). Selterman et al. (2019) identified 77 motivations. Some of these follow:

1. *Variety, novelty, and excitement*: Most spouses enter marriage having had numerous sexual partners (12 for men, 7 for women), and many struggle with the transition of moving from a multiple-partner context to only one. Traditional marriage depends on fidelity. Indeed, traditional wedding vows state, "Hold myself only unto you as long as we both shall live." Selterman et al (2019) reported that "variety" was reported by 87% of the men in their sample (495) in contrast to 62% of the women. Table 9-2 identifies the lifestyle alternatives for resolving the transition from multiple sexual partners to only one at marriage. Consensual nonmonogamy, which includes swinging, polyamory, and threesomes, may be seen as attempts to maintain monogamy since the extradyadic sex is with the knowledge of the partner. And, in the case of swinging and threesomes, external partners may be physically brought into the relationship bed. Sizemore and Olmstead (2017) analyzed data on 890 emerging adults (ages 18–29) and found that a willingness to engage in consensual nonmonogamy was associated with an openness to sexual experimentation, exploring one's sexual identity, and having positive attitudes toward casual sex.

TABLE **9-2**	Sexual Lifestyle Alternatives		
Monogamy	Cheating	Swinging	Polyamory
Spouse is only sex partner.	One or both partners cheat.	Spouses agree to multiple sex partners.	Spouses agree to multiple love and sex partners.

Extradyadic betrayal may be motivated by the desire for variety, novelty, and excitement. One of the characteristics of long-term, committed relationships is the tendency for sex to become routine. Early in a relationship, partners generally cannot seem to have sex often enough. However, with constant availability, they may achieve a level of satiation; and the attractiveness and excitement of sex with the primary partner may wane. Some may be attracted to another person and may act on that attraction under the influence of alcohol (Norona et al., 2018).

The **Coolidge effect** is a term used to describe this waning of sexual excitement and the effect of novelty and variety on sexual arousal:

> One day President and Mrs. Coolidge were visiting a government farm. Soon after their arrival, they were taken off on separate tours. When Mrs. Coolidge passed the chicken pens, she paused to ask the man in charge if the rooster copulated more than once each day. "Dozens of times," was the reply. "Please tell that to the President," Mrs. Coolidge requested. When the President passed the pens and was told about the rooster, he asked, "Same hen every time?" "Oh no, Mr. President, a different one each time." The President nodded slowly and then said, "Tell that to Mrs. Coolidge." (Bermant, 1976, pp. 76–77)

Coolidge effect
The effect of novelty and variety on sexual arousal—for example, when a novel partner is available, a sexually satiated male regains capacity for arousal

Whether or not individuals are biologically wired for monogamy continues to be debated. Monogamy among mammals is rare (3%–10%), tending to be the exception more often than the rule (Morell, 1998). Unlike love, which is a feeling, monogamy is a social rule that most pair bond committed individuals choose to follow most of the time.

2. *Workplace friendships:* The workplace is a common place for extramarital involvements to develop. With daily interaction, a sense of compatibility, partnership, and accomplishment from working together on projects can lead to deeper feelings.

3. *Relationship dissatisfaction*: It is commonly believed that people who have affairs are not happy in their marriage. Spouses who feel misunderstood, unloved, and ignored sometimes turn to another who offers understanding, love, and attention. Selterman et al. (2019) reported that "neglect" was an important motivation for infidelity for 77% of the women; 62% of the men.

4. *Sexual dissatisfaction*: Some spouses engage in extramarital sex because their partner is not interested in sex. Others may go outside the relationship because their partners will not engage in the sexual behaviors they want and enjoy.

5. *Revenge*: Some extramarital sexual involvements are acts of revenge against a spouse for having an affair. When partners find out that their mate has had or is having an affair, they are often hurt and angry. One response to this hurt and anger is to have an affair to "get even" with the unfaithful partner.

6. *Homosexuality*: Some individuals marry as a front for their homosexuality. The songwriter Cole Porter, known for such romantic classics as "I've Got You Under My Skin," "Night and Day," and "Every Time We Say Goodbye," was a homosexual who feared no one would buy his music if his sexual orientation were known. He married Linda Lee Thomas (alleged to be a lesbian), and their marriage lasted until Porter's death 30 years later.

   Other gay and lesbian people marry as a way of denying their homosexuality. These individuals are likely to feel unfulfilled in their marriage and may seek involvement in an extramarital homosexual relationship. Other individuals may marry and then discover later in life that they desire a homosexual relationship. Such individuals are motivated by a range of reasons: Some feel that they have been homosexual or bisexual all along. Others feel that their sexual orientation has changed from heterosexual to homosexual or bisexual. Still others may be unsure of their sexual orientation and want to explore a homosexual relationship, or feel that they are predominantly heterosexual but wish to experience a homosexual relationship for variety. The term **down low** typically refers to the behavior of a married man who has sex with men in secret, not disclosing it to his spouse.

7. *Absence from partner:* One factor that may predispose a spouse to an affair is prolonged separation from their partner. Some wives whose husbands are away for military service report that the loneliness can become unbearable, and some husbands who are away say that remaining faithful is difficult. Partners in dual-career relationships that involve extensive travel or living in separate cities may be vulnerable to an affair.

8. *High androgen levels*: Men who have high levels of androgen have an increased likelihood of extradyadic involvement (Fisher et al., 2012).

Down low
Behavior of keeping sexual activity private; term used to describe men who have sex with men but do not label themselves as gay or bisexual

The above list focuses on the motivations for having an extramarital affair. In contrast, Ziv et al (2018) identified morality and fear of being alone as the primary reasons 423 spouses reported that they made a conscious choice to remain faithful. Spouses more likely to choose fidelity were female, religious, and had been married for a shorter period of time.

9.4c Avoiding an Affair

Jeanfreau and Mong (2019) interviewed 11 spouses about avoiding involvement in being unfaithful. All reported having had the opportunity for an affair (e.g. at a conference), had been flirted with or had a direct solicitation, and had an established relationship with the person. Five of the respondents reported having had an affair. Those who remained faithful reported intense love for their partner, religious values/commitment, and communication as factors operative in their fidelity. Regarding communication, one respondent said, "I tell my husband everything, we're honest with each other." Similarly, another commented, "I don't keep anything from him."

9.4d Recovery from an Affair/Betrayal

Shrout & Weigel (2018) studied the reaction to a partner's infidelity and found that the greater the partner blame, self-blame, and causal attribution of the infidelity, the greater the depression, anxiety, and distress symptoms, which in turn were associated with more health-compromising behaviors (e.g. greater alcohol use). How do therapists help couples move beyond an affair? Relationship therapist Robert Scuka (2015) provided guidelines for the involved partner, for the hurt partner, and for the couple. A rewording and summary of these guidelines follow:

- *Tasks for the partner who had the affair:* Acknowledge the hurt to their partner, express sorrow/contriteness, give up all interaction/contact with the person with whom they had the affair, provide complete information about whereabouts/text messages, get tested for STI and report results to partner, and be tolerant of the partner's moods/suspicions/struggle to get over the infidelity.

- *Tasks for the partner who was hurt:* Acknowledge the sorrow of their partner, have compassion for the partner's imperfection/be mindful of their own imperfections, make a commitment to forgive and get over their anger/resentment.

- *Tasks for the couple:* Accept that the healing will take time, maintain hope, be kind to each other (don't attack), listen/make reflective statements to each other, spend time together in activities of mutual enjoyment, reestablish sexual intimacy, be sensitive to different timetables of recovery.

Ester Perel (2017) also helps couples cope with an affair. She emphasizes the importance of being realistic about love, life, and relationships, that to expect one's partner to never cross the line with another in a lifetime relationship may be an idea attached to an unnecessary outcome, ending one's relationship. Rather, couples can become closer as a result of an affair by communicating about their relationship and how they can meet each other's needs.

Trust is a risk masquerading as a promise.

Adam Phillips, psychoanalyst

THINK ABOUT IT

Take a moment to answer the following question. The spouse who chooses to have an affair is often judged as being deceitful and unfaithful to the vows of the marriage and inflicting enormous pain on the partner (and children). What is often not considered is that when an affair is defined in terms of giving excessive emotional energy, time, and economic resources to something or someone outside the primary relationship, other types of "affairs," however nonsexual, may be equally devastating to a partner and relationship. Spouses who choose to devote their lives to their careers, children, parents, friends, or recreational interests to the exclusion of their partner may deprive them of emotional energy, time, and money, and the partner may choose to become involved with a person who provides more attention and interest. What relationships are you aware of in which a spouse felt neglected by a partner who was excessively focused on someone or something external to the marriage?

PERSONAL DECISIONS 9-2

We Both Had Affairs and Decided to Remain Married

We were like all couples who begin their lives together—in love, happy, and looking forward to a wonderful life together. We had a rocky beginning with an unplanned pregnancy, unsupportive parents for our wedding, unemployment, debt, etc. After 12 years of marriage, I (Jan, the wife) became involved with someone at work. What began as a harmless friendship at work escalated into emotions and sex. It blew up 2 months later when my lover's wife found out.

When I told Eric (my husband), he was in shock. Feeling devastated and betrayed, his reaction was, "Let's get through this," which was more difficult than we imagined. I changed jobs, we went to counseling, things were better, but we were both very busy with our two young children, working long hours, and spending little time together.

Two years later, Eric drifted into a relationship that was both emotional and sexual. His lover's husband found out and exposed the affair of 6 months. After months of coping with the fallout, I had a mental breakdown and was admitted to the hospital. Our younger daughter also became depressed, grades began to drop, etc.

It is now 4 years later. We are out of danger. We are both dreadfully sorry for the pain we inflicted on ourselves, our partner, and our children. We have become involved in counseling, learned to prioritize each other, spend time together, and talk openly about our relationship and our family.

Not a day goes by that we don't think about and regret the mess we caused. But we celebrate that we made it through this most difficult time and feel improved (personally and maritally) by our struggle. We think affairs are devastating but are glad that we were able to keep our marriage and our family together. While I wrote the above, my husband, Eric, acknowledges his agreement with every word.

Source: Jan Molinares (published with her permission)

9.5 Sexuality in the Middle Years

Middle age
Commonly thought to occur between the ages of 40 and 60

Middle age is commonly thought to occur between the ages of 40 and 60. Family life specialists define middle age as beginning when the last child leaves home and continuing until retirement or the death of either spouse. Middle age is a time of transition for people and their sexuality. A content analysis of the sexual scripts depicted of older women via the television program *Hot in Cleveland* over four seasons revealed that these over-50 women viewed sex as desirable. Thus, the cultural scripts for the elderly, particularly older women, sometimes reinforce the idea of lifelong sexual desire (Montemurro & Chewning, 2018).

Montemurro and Siefken (2014) interviewed 84 women (ages 20–60) about the meaning of the term **cougar**—an older woman who assertively pursues younger sexual partners. The researchers found that the majority of women viewed the label negatively, regarding it as predatory and aggressive. However, some women embraced the term as reflective of the reality of older women's sexuality and continued sexual desire. One respondent reflecting this feeling noted:

> *You know what, just physically, biologically—because men are at peak when they are younger, women are at peak when they are older, it's the perfect sexual relationship. You get the best of both worlds. You enjoy each other and maybe men can learn from you.*

Estill et al. (2018) reported data on 1,170 middle-age adults and found that feeling older and having less positive views of aging were associated with rating sexual activity as less enjoyable over time. Granville and Pregler (2018) reviewed sexuality of older women. While most note a decline in sexual desire with age, the majority rate sex as important in their lives (with emotional intimacy a paramount reason for sexual engagement). Primary sexual problems of older women are the absence of a partner and those partners who are available have difficulty maintaining erections. Other sexual problems of older women are problems of vulvovaginal atrophy and infrequent orgasm (most often tied to partner's sexual dysfunction). For men, sexual changes are associated with a decrease in testosterone. Other women and men, continue their interest/engagement in sexuality and sexual behavior. There has also been an increase in STIs and HIV for those 50 and over. Fileborn et al. (2018) emphasized that there is a lack of safer sex culture among older people, so it's important for people of all ages to practice safer sex. A website focused on this issue is http://www.safersex4seniors.org.

> *I don't have the same libido. It used to be that I didn't think I could go to sleep if I wasn't involved in some kind of amorous contact or another. Well, I spend a lot of time sleeping alone these days. That's different and it's very liberating. … My fear is that I'm beginning to prefer it.*
>
> Jack Nicholson, actor

National DATA

Reported sexual intercourse with a partner in the last 12 months: In their 50s: 50% of women and 60% of men; in their 60s: 40% of women and 50% of men; in their 70s+: 20% of women and 40% of men (Herbenick et al., 2010).

9.5a Women: Menopause and Hormone Replacement Therapy

Menopause is a primary physical event for middle-aged women. Defined as the permanent cessation of menstruation, menopause is caused by the gradual decline of estrogen produced by the ovaries. It occurs around age 50 for most women, but may begin much earlier or later. Signs that the woman may be nearing menopause include decreased menstrual flow and a less predictable cycle. After 12 months with no period, the woman is said to be through menopause. However, a woman who is

Cougar
Older woman who pursues younger sexual partners

Menopause
Permanent cessation of menstruation that occurs in middle age

sexually involved with a man and does not want to risk a pregnancy should use some form of contraception until her periods have stopped for 2 years, because she may not know until the second year whether periods have really ceased.

Although the term **climacteric** is often used synonymously with menopause, it refers to changes that both men and women experience. The term *menopause* refers only to the period when the menstrual flow permanently stops, whereas *climacteric* refers to the whole process of hormonal change induced by the ovaries or testes, pituitary gland, and hypothalamus. Reactions to such hormonal changes in women may include hot flashes, in which the woman feels a sudden rush of heat from the waist up. Hot flashes are often accompanied by an increased reddening of the skin surface and a drenching perspiration. Other symptoms may include heart palpitations, insomnia, dizziness, irritability, headaches, backache, and weight gain.

Menopause begins with perimenopause, usually occurring in the 40s. In this 3- to 5-year period, estrogen levels begin to drop, and women may experience irregular periods and the symptoms described above. Menopause itself occurs naturally after 12 months of missed periods (though it can also occur due to other causes, such as illness or medication). In the postmenopausal period, menopausal symptoms can persist for several years; for most women, however, they end within 1 year of the last period. Vaginal dryness and a tendency to accumulate fat in the abdominal area, as well as an increased risk of heart disease, osteoporosis, and osteopenia (low bone density), are ongoing factors in postmenopausal life due to the diminished estrogen in the body (Women's Health Research Institute, n.d.).

Some women find estrogen replacement therapy or hormone replacement therapy (HRT)—estrogen plus progestin—helpful to control hot flashes, night sweats, and vaginal dryness. However, research conducted by the Women's Health Initiative revealed an increased risk of heart disease and other illnesses, including cancer, among healthy postmenopausal women taking combination hormone replacement therapy (WHI, 2010). This and other WHI studies concluded that these and other HRT-related risks, including stroke and blood clots, outweigh HRT's benefits (WHI, 2008). But amid questions about the hormones used and the postmenopausal status of the women studied in the WHI surveys, recent research on women with hysterectomies who did not use HRT indicated that their mortality rate from coronary heart disease was higher than that of HRT users, suggesting a possible protective effect (Sarrel et al., 2013).

HRT can be administered by varied delivery systems, including pills, topical creams, gels or patches, intravaginal rings, and suppositories. Some women gain benefit from one modality over another.

The use of hormone replacement therapy continues to be debated and researched. Davies and colleagues (2013) reported the collective thinking of the Society for Women's Health at a research roundtable of 18 experts within the field, who discussed the evidence related to the risks and benefits of hormone therapy. Regarding quality of life, the panel noted that HRT initiated in midlife (around age 50) for healthy women (those without cancer or cardiac problems) could significantly increase their quality of life. However, HRT started in later years would not significantly increase quality of life or life expectancy. Any woman considering using either estrogen or HRT for treatment of menopausal symptoms is encouraged to review her individual health history and medical goals with her health-care provider.

Some women who choose not to use HRT explore other treatments, such as alternative and plant-based therapies. A recent systematic review and meta-analysis of plant-based phytoestrogens revealed improvement in hot flashes and vaginal dryness, but not night sweats. The researchers recommended further rigorous studies due to suboptimal current evidence (Franco et al., 2016).

Climacteric

Term often used synonymously with menopause; refers to changes that both men and women experience at midlife

THINK ABOUT IT

Take a moment to answer the following questions. How is the sexuality of aging women and men affected by cultural stereotypes and expectations? How might a generation of today's young women, who have grown up in a sexually open and permissive era, differ when they become elderly (in terms of their sexuality) from elderly women of today, who were reared in a more conservative, restrictive era?

9.5b Men and Testosterone Replacement Therapy

Some researchers suggest that men go through their own menopause because they also experience a drop in sex hormones similar to that in women. However, the drop in testosterone is highly variable. In some men, the level can sink so low that men may experience depression, anxiety, hot flashes, decreased libido, difficulty achieving or maintaining an erection, and diminished memory. Yet other men experience no profound drop, and those who do may or may not respond to hormonal intervention.

Indeed, the changes most men and women experience as they age occur over a long period of time, and any associated depression and anxiety seem to be as much related to their life situation (for example, lack of career success, waning status) as to hormonal alterations. Middle-aged women or men who are not successful in their careers or feel bereft as the children grow up and move away from home may fear that they may never achieve what they had hoped and will carry their unfulfilled dreams to the grave. This knowledge may be coupled with an awareness of diminishing sexual vigor and attractiveness. For women and men who have been taught that masculinity and femininity are measured by career success, childrearing, and sexual allure or prowess, middle age may be particularly difficult.

Nevertheless, "low testosterone level" and "testosterone replacement therapy" are common phrases in television commercials, reflecting the $5 billion market promising renewed sexual energy, renewed mental clarity, an upbeat mood, and reliable erections. Testosterone is available in gels, patches, or injections. The most reliable change is an improved libido for 80% of men.

An inordinate passion for pleasure is the secret of remaining young.

Oscar Wilde

However, as with hormone replacement for women, there is disagreement among physicians in regard to the health risks of hormones for men, including heart disease and prostate cancer. Most physicians agree that testosterone does not instigate prostate cancer, but they do not give testosterone to men who have prostate cancer. Testosterone levels in men range from 250–890. The FDA defines low testosterone as below 300, but some physicians will treat men with higher levels. The best advice to men considering testosterone replacement is to "consult with a physician who works with testosterone issues on a regular basis and ask a lot of questions" (Harvard Health Letter, 2013).

9.6 Love and Sexuality in the Later Years

Moore and Sailor (2018) interviewed 14 previously divorced/widowed women between the ages of 65 and 84 who talked of their new romantic love in late life. Various themes of their experience included being open to experience, feeling attracted to a partner, being committed, adjournment (dealing with romantic endings of previous or the current relationship), and generativity (nurturing new relationships, leaving a legacy). While some were shocked that their new

Use it or lose it, right?

Jane Fonda, using sex toys at age 80

Love and sex in the later years is often more about love and less about sex.

partner died after a short time, they all reported positive physical and emotional effects of loving in the later years.

There are numerous changes in the sexuality of women and men as they age. Frequency of intercourse drops from about once a week for those 40–59 to once every 6 weeks for those 70 and older. Changes in men include a decrease in the size of the penis from an average of 5 to about 4 inches. Elderly men also become more easily aroused by touch rather than visual stimulation, which was more arousing when they were younger (Vickers, 2010). Erections take longer to achieve and are less rigid, and it takes longer for the man to recover before he can have another erection. "It now takes me all night to do what I used to do all night" is the motto of the aging male. Kemerer et al. (2019) confirmed the impact of health on sexual functioning and satisfaction at midlife. As predicted, the greater one's health, the greater the reported sexual functioning and satisfaction.

Iveniuk and Waite (2018) surveyed both members of 953 older couples who reported that physical health and perceived marital quality were associated with greater interest in sex. Rutagumirwa and Bailey (2018) interviewed 15 older men (ages 60–82) who reported that they were emotionally distressed about the decline in their sexual performance. The majority experienced an inability to conform to male sexual scripts, which undermined their sense of masculinity. Fileborn et al. (2017) interviewed 27 Australian men aged 60 and over to discover their views and feelings about sex. Some examples follow:

Why is it important, what sort of question is that? It defines what a man is, doesn't it? (age 65)

If it didn't sort of happen [getting an erection] and you just had a nice intimate sort of encounter, then it was okay. But ... sexual satisfaction really to me is intercourse and of course ... for reaching your climax. (age 69)

If I have intercourse with somebody and it's extraordinarily unexciting, even though my penis might've had an orgasm, my brain has not had an orgasm and therefore I can go away feeling disappointed. (age 69)

Older men often seek Levitra, Cialis, and Viagra (prescription drugs that help a man obtain and maintain an erection), which are helpful for about 50% of men in their late 60s. Others with erectile dysfunction may benefit from a pump that inflates two small banana-shaped tubes that have been surgically implanted into the penis. Still others benefit from devices placed over the penis to trap blood so as to create an erection. Women also experience changes including menopause, which is associated with a surge of sexual libido, an interest in initiating sex, and greater orgasmic capacity. Not only are women free from worry about getting pregnant, but estrogen levels drop and testosterone levels increase. Vaginal walls become thinner and less lubricating. Lubricants like K-Y Jelly can resolve the latter issue. Krajewski (2019) emphasized how menopause is socially constructed as an illness (medicalized) and recommends a focus on empowerment.

The view that a person is old is socially induced, perpetuated by advertisements and corporations that profit by offering a return to youth. The pharmaceutical drug Osphena® is touted in its promotional literature as an innovative, hormone-free therapeutic option to cure two dysfunctions often experienced by menopausal women: vaginal atrophy and dyspareunia. However, the data to back up these claims are lacking. Per Emma Bedor's (2016) analysis, the Osphena campaign is a "clear contemporary illustration that the age-old rhetoric of women's bodies as requiring medical intervention to resist aging is far from passé."

Heywood et al. (2018) examined the sexual behavior of 1,583 men and women aged 60-plus and found that less than half (46%) reported that they were very or extremely satisfied with their sexual lives. Those who had sex more often and were more interested in sex were more likely to be satisfied, while those who wanted sex more often in the future were less likely to be satisfied, as were men who had experienced sexual difficulties. Sexual satisfaction was also associated with life satisfaction in men and positive mental health in women. How the elderly present themselves on dating sites may be instructive. Wada et al. (2019) examined 320 online profiles of heterosexual individuals over 60 who were seeking a partner on dating sites. The individuals characterized themselves as active, adventurous, healthy, and intellectually engaged. They were also involved in volunteer work, had a positive approach to live and presented themselves as happy, fun-loving, and humorous. References to sex were nonexistent.

As noted above, most sexually active individuals are in good health. Diabetes and hypertension are major causes of sexual dysfunction. Incontinence (leaking of urine) is an issue for some older women and can be a source of embarrassment. The most frequent sexual problem for men is erectile dysfunction; for women, the most frequent sexual problem is the lack of a partner.

Reasons for lack of sexual satisfaction in a relationship were identified by Syme and colleagues (2013). They surveyed older adults ages 63–67 and found that having a spouse in poor health, a history of diabetes, and feeling fatigued were the primary culprits. In contrast, those who were satisfied with their sexual relationship were male, reported positive marital support, and had a spouse in good health.

> *Sex at age 90 is like trying to shoot pool with a rope.*
>
> George Burns, lived to be 100

Under what conditions does sexual desire continue in a relationship? Two researchers interviewed heterosexual men and women, as well as lesbian women, about maintaining desire in long-term relationships (Milhausen & Murray, 2014). The respondents, who were ages 18–84, identified four factors that influenced their sexual desire: self factors (maintaining a positive body image), partner factors (initiating sex with a partner), relationship factors (emotional intimacy), and external factors (romantic setting). Forbes et al. (2017b) analyzed data on 6,278 individuals (ages 20–93) and found that, in general, the sexual quality of one's life declined over time (more true for women than men). However, when aging couples gave thought and effort to their sex life with a continued frequency, there were higher associations with sexual quality. Hence it is not age itself, but the behaviors of older persons and their partners who may continue to enjoy a high sexual quality of life.

Some older spouses are sexually inactive. Analysis of data on 1,502 men and women ages 57–85 revealed that 29% reported no sexual activity for the past 12 months or more (Karraker & DeLamater, 2013). The longer the couple had been married, the older the spouse, and the more compromised the spouse's health, the more likely the individual was to report no sexual activity.

Social Policy 9-2

Restricting Sexuality in Elder-Care Facilities

Yelland and Hosier (2017) assessed attitudes toward sexual expression by the elderly in a long-term care (LTC) facility. Almost 1 in 5 (19%) of the respondents said that LTC residents should not be allowed to have sexual relations with their spouse in the facility. Simpson et al. (2018) also noted sexuality was virtually nonexistent in the elder-care facility they studied. But the need for intimacy remained. One of the residents noted, "We had our sex life way back. But we need to cuddle."

Elder-care facilities have traditionally institutionalized abstinence. These facilities (under the operating assumption that the elderly are sexless) sometimes do not allow spouses to occupy the same room. Barriers to sexual activity among hospital and elder-care facilities may be removed by educating staff about the desire/need for sexual expression regardless of age, providing privacy ("do not disturb" signs, closed doors, private rooms designated for intimacy), allowing conjugal visits or home visits, changing medications that may impair sexual function, and providing information and counseling about sexuality to interested residents.

One resource for keeping visible the importance of sexuality in the later years is Joan Price's book *Naked at Our Age* (http://www.joanprice.com/nakedatourage.html).

Chapter Summary

Sexuality in Infancy and Childhood

SEXUALITY BEGINS EARLY. In the uterus, boys often have penile erections, and girls have clitoral erections and vaginal lubrication. Masturbation has been observed in both boys and girls as infants. Parents might be mindful of not reacting negatively to their infant's self-pleasuring. The sexual behaviors of children can be categorized into various areas, including exhibitionism, self-stimulation, and voyeuristic behavior.

Sexual socialization/sexuality education of children is the process by which knowledge, attitudes, and values about sex are learned. Parents are typically regarded as the first and most important source of sexual socialization for their children, but are often reluctant to talk with their children about sex. Not only may they feel inadequate in terms of their own knowledge, they may also fear that sexual discussions will spark experimentation and destroy their child's innocence/nonsexual state.

Sexuality in Adolescence

ADOLESCENCE IS DEFINED as the developmental period between puberty and adulthood. It is a time when a child's body and image transform into a young adult with a future adult life. Adolescence involves identity exploration, interaction with romantic partners, and school performance. Profound physiological, physical, and anatomical changes also occur. Psychological changes for adolescents include moving from a state of childish dependence to relative independence, resolving sexual identity issues, and feeling secure that they are normal.

Sexuality in Adulthood

THE FREQUENCY OF SEX reported by American adults reached an all-time low recently. Adults have a variety of options, including being single, living together, and getting married.

Marital sex is characterized by its social legitimacy, declining frequency, and superiority in terms of sexual and emotional satisfaction. Sexual intercourse between spouses occurs about six times a month and declines in frequency as the marriage progresses.

Of the almost 2 million people getting divorced annually, most will have intercourse within 1 year of being separated from their spouses. For many, intercourse is a way to reestablish—indeed, repair—their crippled self-esteem.

Extramarital and Extradyadic Affairs

SOME PEOPLE CHOOSE to have sexual intercourse outside their marriage or committed relationship. Reasons include the desire for variety, sexual unhappiness in the marriage, and falling in love or drifting into a sexual relationship with a coworker.

Sexuality in the Middle Years

THE PERIOD OF MIDDLE AGE is generally between 40 and 60. A majority of people in this age group rate sex as important in their lives. Women experience the end of their periods; men experience the loss of testosterone. Hormone replacement therapy and testosterone therapy can be indicated. However, the decision to use hormone/testosterone therapy is complex and should be undertaken under the guidance of a health-care professional.

Love and Sexuality in the Later Years

THERE ARE NUMEROUS CHANGES in the sexuality of women and men as they age. How people view these changes is often influenced by society. The most frequent sexual problem for men after 60 is erectile dysfunction; for women, the most frequent sexual problem is the lack of a partner.

Web Links

National Sex Ed Conference: Center for Sex Education

http://bvtlab.com/8747K

Talk About Sex: Gender Identity

http://www.seriouslysexuality.com

Power to Decide: The Campaign to Prevent Unplanned Pregnancy

https://thenationalcampaign.org/

Unhushed (Talking with Adolescents About Sex)

http://www.unhushed.org/

Sex and the Elderly: Information and Resources

http://www.caring-for-aging-parents.com/sex-and-the-elderly.html

Key Terms

Adolescence **220**

Childhood **216**

Climacteric **240**

Cohabitation **227**

Coolidge effect **235**

Cougar **239**

Down low **236**

Extradyadic affair **233**

Extramarital affair **233**

Infancy **216**

Menopause **239**

Middle age **238**

Puberty **221**

Satiation **230**

Semenarche **221**

Sexual competence **223**

Sexual compliance **232**

Sexual debut **218**

Diversity—LGBTQIA

It still strikes me as strange that anyone could have any moral objection to someone else's sexuality. It's like telling someone else how to clean their house.

River Phoenix

Chapter Outline

10.1 **LGBTQIA Terminology 250**

10.2 **Conceptual Models of Sexual Orientation 251**
  10.2a Dichotomous Model **251**
  10.2b Unidimensional Continuum Model **251**
  10.2c Multidimensional Model **253**

10.3 **Prevalence by Sexual Orientation 253**

10.4 **Theories of Sexual Orientation 254**
  10.4a Biological Explanations **254**
  10.4b Is There a Social/ Cultural Influence? **255**

10.5 **Dangers of Conversion Therapy 255**

10.6 **Coming Out or Concealment? 256**
  10.6a Coming Out to Yourself and Others **258**
  Personal Decisions 10-1
    Benefits and Risks of Coming Out **258**
  Technology and Sexuality 10-1:
    Online LGBTQIA Support Groups **259**
  10.6b Mixed-Orientation Relationships **260**

10.7 **Relationships 260**
  10.7a Gay Male Relationships **261**
  10.7b Lesbian Relationships **262**
  10.7c Bisexual Relationships **262**
  10.7d Pansexual Relationships **263**
  10.7e Trans Partner Relationships **263**

10.8 **Health, Health Behavior, HIV, and Sexual Orientation 265**

10.9 **Heterosexism, Homonegativity, and Homophobia 266**
  Self-Assessment 10-1:
    Sexual Prejudice Scale **267**
  10.9a Homonegativity and Homophobia **269**
  Social Policy 10-1
    Same-Sex Marriage **272**
  10.9b Discrimination against Homosexuals **273**
  10.9c Biphobia **274**

10.10 **How Heterosexuals Are Affected by Homophobia 274**

10.11 **What to Do About Anti-LGBTQIA Prejudice and Discrimination 276**

Web Links **279**
Key Terms **279**

Objectives

1. Differentiate the terms *sexual orientation* and *sexual preference*

2. Identify the meaning of LGBTQIA and review three conceptual models of sexual orientation

3. Know the prevalence of heterosexuality, being gay, and bisexuality

4. Review the theories of sexual orientation

5. Know the data on the lack of effectiveness of conversion therapy

6. Understand the process of coming out, including risks and benefits

7. Review gay/lesbian, bisexual, and pansexual relationships

8. Differentiate between heterosexism, homonegativity, and homophobia

9. Review how heterosexuals are affected by homophobia

(Maria Trull McDonald / Mia Bella Expressions)

Truth — OR — Fiction?

T / F 1. The college/university context is a positive/affirmative context in which to "come out."

T / F 2. Same-sex undergraduates report higher sexual satisfaction than heterosexual undergraduates.

T / F 3. The older the individual the more open (out of the closet) the individual.

T / F 4. Relationship quality in bisexual relationships is higher than same-sex and other-sex relationships.

T / F 5. Physical appearance is less important for gay men looking for a partner online than whether the partner is "out of the closet."

Answers: 1. T   2. F   3. T   4. F   5. F

Same-sex relationships and issues have become very much a part of US society and culture—Pete Buttigieg as a contender in the 2020 Democratic primary, the legalization of same-sex marriage, and the "coming out" of celebrities. Of 12,841 undergraduates, 89% reported that they were "comfortable around a person" they knew to be gay (Hall & Knox, 2019). While prejudice and discrimination still exist, they are waning.

I'm not a lesbian, but my girlfriend is.

Gina Gershon, actress

10.1 LGBTQIA Terminology

Sexual orientation refers to the classification of individuals as heterosexual, gay, lesbian, bisexual, pansexual, or asexual, based on their emotional and sexual attractions, relationships, self-identity, and lifestyle. With the exception of pansexuality, all of these classifications are based on a gender binary system of male and female. **Heterosexuality** refers to the predominance of emotional and sexual attraction to people of the other sex. The term **homosexuality** (an offensive term for some) refers to the predominance of emotional and sexual attractions to people of the same sex. Gay men and lesbians are the preferred terms. Within the gay community, there are further variations, such as "butch" and "femme" for lesbians. There is also a gay male subculture known as "bear," which is someone who is big, thick, and oftentimes hairy (Quidley-Rodriguez & De Santis, 2019). **Bisexuality** is the emotional and sexual attraction to members of both sexes (for a historical review of bisexuality, see Taylor, 2018). The *T* in LGBTQIA stands for transgender. **Queer** is a blanket term that many gender nonconforming individuals prefer. Hammack et al. (2019) emphasized a queer paradigm, which states that "intimacy may occur among individuals of any gender identity, may change across the life course, need not be restricted to a dyadic form, etc." (p. 583). Intersexed are those who have physical characteristics of both sexes. **LGBTQIA** is a term that has emerged to refer collectively to lesbians, gays, bisexuals, transgender people, those questioning their sexual orientation/sexual identity, intersexed, and those who are asexual and agender. It also refers to allies and friends of the cause.

The term **asexual** describes an absence of sexual attraction/arousal to a partner. However, people who identify as asexual may form emotional attachments, masturbate, and experience sexual pleasure (Hille, 2014) and orgasm (Van Houdenhove et al., 2015). Mitchell and Hunnicutt (2019) noted that those who are asexual often discover their lack of sexual interest/attraction after they have had sex. They also feel that telling others about their asexuality is a form of "coming out" for which they feel pathologized and disapproved of.

Gupta (2017) interviewed 30 asexuals and identified ways they saw themselves as affected by compulsory sexuality: pathologization (i.e. they were told something was wrong with them but that they would get over it), unwanted sex (i.e., having sex just to keep the partner), relationship conflict (i.e., the expectation of sex kept coming up), and the denial of epistemic authority (not being believed—saying that the asexual was a "late bloomer" and would get over having no interest in sex).

Some of the interviewees made clear that they never felt anything was wrong with them.

So I never felt like I needed to talk to someone about it, you know? I never felt like I needed to seek out mental health professionals or anything like that. You know, it wasn't bothering me. I wasn't feeling depressed or suicidal or anything like that, so I didn't feel like I needed a counselor. It's not something that I wanted to cure or anything like that. Furthermore, the asexual *challenged contemporary Western society's tendency to privilege sexual relationships over nonsexual relationships.*

Asexuality may be regarded as a sexual orientation. The Asexual Visibility and Education Network (AVEN) facilitates awareness of asexuality as an explicit identity category.

The term *LGBTQIA* does not take into account other sexual identities, including pansexual. **Pansexuality** is not based on a gender binary system. It is defined as sexual attraction to other people regardless of their biological sex, gender, or gender identity (Parks & Moore, 2016). Identifying as being pansexual or bisexual are sometimes

---

Sexual orientation
Classification of individuals as heterosexual, bisexual, or homosexual based on their emotional, cognitive, and sexual attractions, as well as their self-identity and lifestyle

Heterosexuality
Sexual orientation in which the predominance of emotional and sexual attraction is to people of the other sex

Homosexuality
Sexual orientation in which the predominance of emotional and sexual attraction is to people of the same sex

Bisexuality
Emotional and sexual attraction to members of both sexes

Queer
A blanket term that many gender nonconforming individuals prefer

Intersexed
Individuals who have characteristics of both sexes

LGBTQIA
Lesbian, gay, bisexual, transgender, questioning/ queer, intersex, asexual, or ally

Asexual
Refers to people who do not experience sexual attraction/arousal to a partner; however, they may form emotional attachments, masturbate, and experience sexual pleasure

Pansexuality
The state in which someone is attracted to people, regardless of their gender identity

viewed as the same. But Greaves et al. (2019) noted that pansexuals are more likely to be younger, gender diverse (transgender or nonbinary), and report higher psychological distress than bisexual individuals.

Longitudinal data on Korean perspectives on gay/lesbians of five cohorts, including 3,299 Korean men and women between 18 and 59 years of age, from 1994 through 2014, revealed greater acceptance of being gay and civil rights for gays. However, changes have been slow and Korean gays/lesbians remain subjects of social stigma and discrimination primarily due to increased Christian activism (Youn, 2018).

Cultural Diversity

THINK ABOUT IT

Take a moment to answer the following question. Although the terms *sexual preference and sexual orientation* are often used interchangeably, many sexuality researchers and academicians (including the authors of this text) prefer to use the latter term. Sexual preference implies that the individual is consciously choosing to whom they are attracted, whereas sexual orientation suggests that it is innate (as is handedness) or may be influenced by multiple factors. The term *sexual identity* may also be used rather than *sexual preference*. What is your feeling about using the respective terms, and what meaning does each have for you?

10.2 Conceptual Models of Sexual Orientation

Researchers have noted the difficulty of measuring sexual orientation (Wolff et al., 2017). There are three models of sexual orientation: the *dichotomous* model, in which people are either heterosexual or gay; the *unidimensional continuum* model, in which sexual orientation is viewed on a continuum; and the *multidimensional* model, in which sexuality is seen as a function of degrees of various components, such as emotions, behaviors, and cognitions.

10.2a Dichotomous Model

The **dichotomous model** (also referred to as the *either-or model of sexuality*) takes the position that a person is either gay or not. The major criticisms of the dichotomous model of sexual orientation are that it ignores the existence of bisexuality, asexuality, and pansexuality and that it does not allow for any gradations of sexual orientation as a continuum.

10.2b Unidimensional Continuum Model

In early research on sexual behavior, Kinsey and his colleagues (Kinsey et al., 1948, 1953) found that a substantial proportion of respondents reported having had same-sex sexual experiences, yet very few reported exclusive gay behavior. These data led Kinsey to conclude that, contrary to the commonly held dichotomous model of sexual orientation, most people are not exclusively heterosexual or gay. Thus, Kinsey suggested the **unidimensional continuum model** of sexual orientation and developed the Heterosexual-Homosexual Rating Scale to assess where on the continuum of sexual

Dichotomous model
(Also referred to as the *either-or model of sexuality*) Way of conceptualizing sexual orientation that prevails not only in views on sexual orientation but also in cultural understandings of biological sex (male versus female) and gender (masculine versus feminine)

Unidimensional continuum model
Identification of sexual orientation on a scale from 0 (exclusively heterosexual) to 6 (exclusively gay), suggesting that most people are not on the extremes but somewhere in between

orientation an individual is located (see Figure 10-1). Given that one's sexual orientation exists on a continuum, Savin-Williams (2018) sought greater clarity/differentiation of exclusively heterosexual, primarily heterosexual, and mostly heterosexual using sexual indicators of attraction, fantasy, genital contact, and romantic indicators of infatuation and romantic relationship. Findings revealed greater endorsement of same-sex sexuality as one identified with mostly heterosexual compared to exclusively or primarily heterosexual. Silva and Bridges Whaley (2018) estimated that about 7% of straight men have occasional sex with men.

The unidimensional continuum model recognizes that heterosexual and homosexual orientations are not mutually exclusive and that an individual's sexual orientation may have both heterosexual and homosexual elements. The criticism of the Kinsey scale is that it does not account for some important aspects of sexuality, such as self-identity, lifestyle, and social group preference. You could place yourself on the continuum, but the criteria for doing so are not clear.

FIGURE **10-1** ‖ The Heterosexual-Homosexual Rating Scale

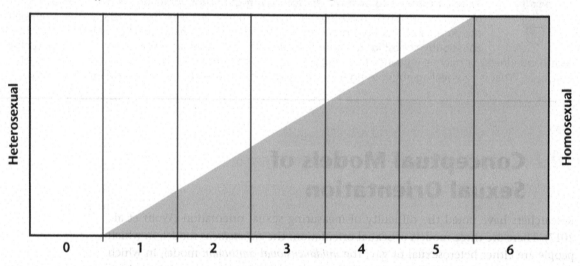

Based on both psychological reactions and overt experience, individuals rate as follows:

0   Exclusively heterosexual with no homosexual factors
1   Predominantly heterosexual, only incidentally homosexual
2   Predominantly heterosexual, but more than incidentally homosexual
3   Equally heterosexual and homosexual
4   Predominantly homosexual, but more than incidentally heterosexual
5   Predominantly homosexual, but incidentally heterosexual
6   Exclusively homosexual factors

Source: Kinsey, A. C., Pomeroy, W. B., Martin, C. E., & Gebhard, P. H. (1953). *Sexual behavior in the human female* (p. 470, Figure 93). Philadelphia, PA: W. B. Saunders. Copyright © 2017, The Trustees of Indiana University on behalf of the Kinsey Institute. All rights reserved. Reprinted with permission.

10.2c Multidimensional Model

The **multidimensional model** of sexual orientation suggests that orientation consists of various independent components—including emotional and social preferences, behavior, self-identification, sexual attraction, fantasy, and lifestyle—and that these components may change over time. The most important contribution of the multidimensional model is its incorporation of self-identity as a central element of sexual orientation. Thus, individuals can engage in same-sex sexual behavior but can self-identify as heterosexual and vice versa.

Sexual fluidity, the capacity for variation in erotic response depending on the situation, is another way to characterize sexual orientation. In this view, orientation is not fixed, but is subject to context, experiences, age, and so on. Gill (2014) noted the use of apps such as Manhunt® and Grindr® by individuals exploring the fluidity of their sexuality.

We're both the girl in the relationship. That's kinda the point.

Anonymous

Emotional expression also differs by gender and sexual orientation, with gay men reporting the highest expression of "soft" emotions (more subordinate and conciliatory) and heterosexual men (more dominant and controlling) reporting the lowest level of such expression (Zeigler & Muscarella, 2019).

10.3 **Prevalence by Sexual Orientation**

It is difficult to determine how many people identify as a specific orientation. Due to embarrassment, a desire for privacy, or fear of social disapproval, many individuals do not identify themselves as anything other than heterosexual. Self-identified sexual orientation is often incongruent with preference and behavior.

Estimates of the prevalence of various sexual orientations also vary due to differences in the way researchers define and measure orientation. For example gay, straight, and bisexual alternatives on questionnaires do not give a respondent the ability to choose something else, such as pansexual or asexual. Dimisexual is another term. Dimisexuality is the phenomenon of a person who cannot experience sexual attraction without first having a significant emotional attachment. Dimisexuality is recognized as a sexual orientation and on a continuum from allosexuals (sexually active individuals) to asexuals (no interest). Dimisexuals are midway (Fiorini, 2019).

Multidimensional model

Way of conceptualizing sexual orientation that suggests that a person's orientation consists of various independent components—including emotions, lifestyle, self-identification, sexual attraction, fantasy, and behavior—and that these components may change over time

Sexual fluidity

Capacity for variation in erotic responses depending on the situation

National **DATA**

Longitudinal data on 6,864 individuals from age 16 to the late 20s revealed for males: 87.4% straight males, 6.5% minimal sexual expression males, 3.8% mostly straight and bimales, and 2.4% emerging gay males. For females: 73.8% straight females, 7% minimal sexual expression females, 10.2% mostly straight discontinuous females, 7.5% emerging bifemales, and 1.5% emerging lesbian females (Kaestle, 2019). Bisexual women represent the largest demographic of sexual minority people in the United States with 5.5% of women between the ages of 18–44 reporting a bisexual identity (Flanders et al. 2019a).

10.4 Theories of Sexual Orientation

One of the prevailing questions raised regarding one's orientation centers on its origin or cause. Gay people are often irritated by the fact that heterosexual people seem overly concerned about finding the cause of homosexuality. The same question is rarely asked about heterosexuality because it is assumed that this sexual orientation is normal and needs no explanation. Questions about causation can imply that something is wrong with homosexuality.

Nevertheless, considerable research has been conducted on the origin of homosexuality and whether its basis is derived from nature (genetic, hormonal, innate) or nurture (learned through social experiences and cultural influences). Most researchers agree that an interaction of biological (nature) and social/cultural (environmental) forces is involved in the development of sexual orientation. It should be noted that little research has been conducted on the origins of bisexuality, pansexuality, and asexuality.

10.4a Biological Explanations

Biological explanations of the development of sexual orientation usually focus on genetic, neuroanatomical, or hormonal differences between heterosexuals and homosexuals. Fausto-Sterling (2019) notes that "the body tells the brain about how it is feeling" (p. 549). Several lines of evidence suggest that biological factors play a role (Breedlove, 2017; DuPree et al., 2004). A discussion of three biological explorations of sexual orientation follows.

> *Homosexuality is immutable, irreversible and nonpathological.*
> Abhijit Naskar, *Either Civilized or Phobic: A Treatise on Homosexuality*

Genetic Theories

Is sexual orientation an inborn trait that is transmitted genetically, like eye color? There does seem to be a genetic influence, although, unlike with the case of eye color, a single gene has not been confirmed. In the United States, a study of a national probability sample of twin and nontwin siblings concluded that "familial factors, which are at least partly genetic, influence sexual orientation" (Kendler et al., 2000). In this sample, 3.1% of the men and 1.5% of the women reported nonheterosexual sexual orientation. The concordance rate in monozygotic twins was 31.6% for nonheterosexual sexual orientation; so, if one identical twin was gay or lesbian, the co-twin was also gay or lesbian in 31.6% of the pairs.

Further support for a genetic influence on homosexuality has been provided by Cantor and colleagues (2002), who noted that men with older homosexual brothers are more likely to be homosexual themselves: "[R]oughly one gay man in seven owes his sexual orientation to the fraternal birth order effect" (p. 63).

How much of the link in sexual orientation between twins is accounted for by genetic inheritance? One large population-based twin study used the Australian National Health and Medical Research Council Twin Registry (Kirk et al., 2000) and measured behavioral and psychological aspects of sexual orientation. Of the 4,901 respondents, 2.6% of the women rated themselves as bisexual and 0.7% as homosexual; 3.2% of the men rated themselves as bisexual and 3.1% as homosexual. The researchers concluded that genetic influences were linked to homosexuality in both women and men, with estimates of 50%–60% heritability for women, about twice the men's rate of 30%.

Prenatal Hormonal Theories

In his discussion of prenatal influences on sexual orientation, Diamond (1995) discussed the effects of the maturation of the testes or ovaries and their release (or lack) of hormones. These hormones affect the structural development of the genitalia and other structures. At the gross and microscopic levels, they also organize the developing nervous system and influence sex-linked behaviors (biasing the individual toward male- or female-typical behaviors).

Hormonal and neurological factors operating prior to birth, between the second and fifth month of gestation, are the "main determinants of sexual orientation" (Ellis & Ames, 1987, p. 235). Fetal exposure to hormones such as testosterone is believed to impact the developing neural pathways of the brain. Sexual orientation is programmed into the brain during critical prenatal periods and early childhood (Money, 1987). Breedlove (2017) emphasized that lesbians, on average, show evidence of greater prenatal androgen exposure than groups of straight women. Hence there is some evidence to suggest the early biochemical lean toward one sexual orientation over another.

Postpubertal Hormonal Theories

Endocrinology (the study of hormones) research to determine whether the levels of sex hormones of gay men and lesbians resemble those of the other sex has yielded mixed results (Ellis, 1996). Ellis concluded that the connection between postpubertal sex hormone levels and homosexuality is complex and is probably applicable only to some subgroups of gay men and lesbians.

The belief in biological determinism of sexual orientation among homosexuals themselves is strong. In a national study of homosexual men, 90% believe that they were born with their homosexual orientation, while only 4% believe that environmental factors were the sole cause (Lever, 1994). Viewing sexual orientation as biologically based or essential is associated with less prejudice by heterosexuals and less internalized homonegativity by gays (Blaszcznski & Morandini, 2014). Although there are those who still believe that homosexuality is more of a choice, acceptance of a biological explanation is increasing.

> *I think being gay is a blessing, and it's something I am thankful for every single day.*
>
> Anderson Cooper, television news celebrity

10.4b Is There a Social/Cultural Influence?

Adrenal androgens provide the fuel for the sex drive (around age 10), but they do not provide the direction or sexual orientation. According to social/cultural theories of sexual orientation, sexual orientation is determined by forces such as peer group, parents, and the mass media. Because many of these forces encourage heterosexuality, proponents of these explanations posit that unique environmental influences account for homosexuality.

> *My sexual preference is often.*
>
> Bumper sticker

10.5 Dangers of Conversion Therapy

Individuals who believe that homosexual people choose their sexual orientation tend to think that they can and should change it. **Conversion therapy** (also called *reparative therapy*) is focused on this process. Articles published in *American Psychologist* and other journals in 2011–2012 reviewed 50 years of research and confirmed there

Conversion therapy
Therapy designed to change a person's sexual orientation, usually gay to heterosexual

is no evidence that sexual arousal in response to same-sex individuals can be changed to those of the other sex. In fact, per the Human Rights Campaign (2016), conversion therapy has been associated with depression, anxiety, drug use, homelessness, and suicide. The American Psychological Association (APA), American Academy of Pediatrics, and The American Counseling Association have recommended legislation to ban conversion therapy. Fifteen states have such a ban and 20 other states have similar legislation in progress (Miller, 2018). In 2015, the Obama administration called for a ban on conversion therapies for minors (Shear, 2015).

10.6 Coming Out or Concealment?

Nonheterosexual identity development may occur through the process of **coming out**. The term, a shortened form of "coming out of the closet," refers to the process of defining one's sexual orientation and disclosing one's self-identification to others. Villar et al. (2019) noted the unique issues of coming out in a retirement community. While most were supportive of such disclosures, one was never sure what the reaction would be. Brumbaugh-Johnson and Hull (2019) interviewed trans individuals and found another layer of coming out. One of the respondents noted that after he got his mother used to his being a bisexual, another disclosure was that he was a she. Schmitz and Tyler (2018) interviewed LGBTQ+ individuals, including undergraduates, and found that their educational contexts were conducive to helping them develop their identities, or "undo" rigid norms of gender and sexuality. Coming out may be also be a matter of degree. In interviews with gay men about how they dressed, the overriding theme was that they were not "hiding or shouting" but were just presenting their authentic selves (Clarke & Smith, 2015).

I consider being gay among the greatest gifts God has given me.

Tim Cook, Apple CEO

Coming out is also not a linear, one-time event, but a complicated, over-time experience to different people in different contexts (Klein et al., 2015). Coming out to yourself also necessitates identifying who you are. Individuals must merge their own experiences with the labels available in society, such as gay, cross-dresser, butch lesbian, and so on (Levitt & Ippolito, 2014). Coming out may occur in person or online. In one study, 63% of 61 LGB individuals reported that they were out online (referred to as *e-visibility*), most frequently on Facebook. About half (49%) did not care if their partners were also out online (Blumer & Bergdall, 2014). Wilson et al. (2018) found that being open about one's sexual orientation became particularly important for older LGBT adults. One reason is that they may be less concerned about what other people think.

In 2014, a team of researchers noted the difference between concealment and nondisclosure: With concealment, people deliberately attempt to keep their sexual orientation a secret; with nondisclosure, they are open to disclose their sexual orientation in various contexts. Interviews with 203 bisexual men who did not disclose their bisexuality to family, friends, and female partners stated that their reasons for nondisclosure, including their same-sex behaviors, were their own business and nobody else's; that others had no reason to know; that the topic of sexual behavior was too personal; that they were private people in general; and that it was inappropriate to discuss same-sex behavior in many contexts (Schrimshaw et al., 2014).

Coming out
(Shortened form of "coming out of the closet") Process of defining yourself as gay in sexual orientation and disclosing your self-identification to others

Previous research has documented the negative effects of being gay in a heterosexist society and discussed the differences in measuring concealment versus nondisclosure in various contexts. The researchers studied the concealment and nondisclosure patterns of lesbians and found that concealment was a stronger predictor of stress than nondisclosure (Hope & Meidlinger, 2014). Compared to heterosexual youth, sexual minority youth report drinking more alcohol during the week to eliminate personal worries (coping) and to avoid being excluded by peers (conformity) (DiPlacidio, 1998). Hence, being out seems to be associated with positive outcomes for the individual (particularly older individuals).

Closets are for clothes.

Bumper sticker

There are about half a million gay dads in the United States. One provided several suggestions for coming out to one's children, including becoming comfortable with one's own gayness, discussing it with them when they're young before they find out from someone outside the family, assuring one's child that they won't be gay just because their dad is gay, and helping them decide what they tell their friends.

Coming out as a bisexual is different from coming out as gay or lesbian. In a qualitative study of the coming-out experiences of 45 bisexuals, Scherrer and colleagues (2015) noted that bisexuals may come out to resolve their parents' confusion—for example, explaining why they spend a lot of time with and are moving in with a same-sex person. Others feel that use of the term *gay* is easier for parents/family than *bisexual*. One respondent said that her parents knew what *gay* meant but thought bisexuals were "weird," so the term *gay* was used. Regardless of the strategy or use of term, the predominant reaction of parents to coming out as a bisexual was to label the new identity as a phase ("You're just trying this out, but you will come to your senses"). Zivony and Saguy (2018) noted that bisexuals are stereotyped as being more confused and promiscuous than nonbisexual women. Bisexual women report bisexual stigma (from heterosexuals, gay men, and lesbians) which is associated with being victims of higher rates of sexual violence (Flanders et al. 2019).

There is little research to understand the coming-out process for those who are pansexual or asexual. A study by Belous and Bauman (2017) indicates that coming out as pansexual may be a distinctive process from coming out as either bisexual or gay.

Cultural Diversity

In a study of the coming-out experiences of 130 women ages 18–72 from countries throughout the world, the various categories of coming out included the following: (1) preplanned conversation (over half of the respondents deliberately selected a time to come out, as in "I have something to tell you."); (2) emergent conversation (in talking with someone who brings up hate crimes or someone who is gay, the individual said, "I'm gay too."); (3) coaxed conversations (the receiver asked the LGB person if they were gay or bisexual); (4) confrontational conversations (a parent stumbled across a child's nonheterosexual orientation and confronted the child in a negative/accusatory way); (5) romantic/sexual conversation ("I kind of like guys" or "I kind of like girls" or "Would you like to kiss?"); (6) educational/activist conversation (being on a panel of LGB individuals and coming out to the group); and (7) mediated conversation (coming out on Facebook) (Manning, 2015a). Positive reactions to coming out included openness to the disclosure, direct affirming statements, laughing, and joking. Negative reactions included denial, religious talk, criticism, and shaming statements (Manning, 2015b).

10.6a Coming Out to Yourself and Others

Defining yourself and coming out to yourself can be a frightening and confusing experience. Personal Decisions 10-1 examines the benefits and risks of coming out.

PERSONAL DECISIONS 10-1

Benefits and Risks of Coming Out

In a society in which heterosexuality is expected and considered the norm, heterosexuals rarely have to choose whether to tell others that they are heterosexual. However, decisions about coming out and being open and honest about your sexual orientation and identity (particularly to your parents) may create anxiety for individuals who are gay, bisexual, asexual, or pansexual. In a study of coming-out experiences of 53 young adults, the people to whom the individuals came out, in order, were friends, mothers, and fathers (Rossi, 2010).

Benefits of Coming Out

Coming out to parents is associated with decided benefits. In a comparison of 111 gay, lesbian, and bisexual youth who disclosed their sexual orientation to their parents with 53 individuals who had not come out, results showed that the former reported higher levels of acceptance from their parents, lower levels of alcohol and drug consumption, and fewer identity and adjustment problems (D'Amico & Julien, 2012). In another study, lesbians and bisexual females who did not come out to parents reported higher levels of illicit drug use, poorer self-reported health status, and being more depressed (Rothman et al., 2012). Individuals who join LGB groups also report less depression. In effect, these individuals have come out both to themselves and to others (McLaren et al., 2013).

Risks of Coming Out

The greatest risk of coming out is an increased suicide risk. Puckett et al. (2017) reported that LGB youth who lost friends when they came out were 29 times more likely to report suicide attempts. Whether or not LGB individuals come out is influenced by the degree to which they are tired of hiding their sexual orientation, the degree to which they feel more honest about being open, their assessment of the risks of coming out, and their prediction of how others will respond. Some of the overall risks involved in coming out include:

1. *Parental and family members:* Responses by family to an emerging adult who comes out to them include a range: supportive, denial, confused, or unsupportive (Gkyamerah et al., 2019). Researchers Mena and Vaccaro (2013) interviewed 24 gay and lesbian youth about their coming-out experience to their parents and reported a less than 100% affirmative ("We love you," "Being gay is irrelevant") reaction that resulted in varying degrees of sadness and depression (three became suicidal). Because parents are heavily invested in their children, most find a way to not make an issue of their son or daughter being gay. "We just don't talk about it," said one parent. Parents and other family members can learn more about orientation from the local chapter of Parents, Families, and Friends of Lesbians and Gays (PFLAG) and from books and online resources, such as those found at the Human Rights Campaign's National Coming Out Project. Education is important, as parental rejection of LGB individuals is related to suicide ideation and attempts (van Bergen et al., 2013). Because black individuals are more likely than white ones to view gay relations as always wrong, black lesbians and gay men are more likely to face disapproval from their families and straight friends than are white lesbians and gay men (Loiacano, 1993). The Resource Guide to Coming Out for African Americans (Human Rights Campaign, 2014) is a useful guide.

2. *Harassment and discrimination at school*: LGB students are more vulnerable to being bullied, harassed, and discriminated against both in school and online (Joshi et al., 2016). The negative effects are predictable and include a wide range of health and mental health concerns, including sexual health risk, substance abuse, and suicide, compared with their heterosexual peers (Russell et al., 2011).

3. *Discrimination and harassment in the workplace:* The workplace continues to be an environment in which the 8 million LGB individuals in the United States experience discrimination and harassment. While bills banning discrimination against gays in the workplace, such as the Employment Non-Discrimination Act (ENDA), have been submitted in Congress for 20 years, they have been voted down.

4. *Hate crime victimization:* Another risk of coming out is that of being a victim of antigay hate crimes against individuals or their property that are based on bias against the victims because of their perceived sexual orientation. Such crimes include verbal threats and intimidation, vandalism, sexual assault and rape, physical assault, and murder. Ramirez and Kim (2018) also found that lesbian and bisexual women were over two times more likely to experience lifetime sexual victimization as heterosexuals. Aside from transgender individuals, they may be the most victimized sexual minority.

Alonzo and Buttitta (2019) noted that the coming out process is more complex than simply having a conversation with one's peers or parents. They observe that the discussion must change from an individual, developmental perspective focused on stages to perspectives that are flexible, health focused, context driven, and inclusive (i.e., including perspectives for bisexuality and nonbinary sexualities). Because LGB individuals and their families must continue to resist the internalization of stigma, because the intersection of multiple identities has the potential to add stress to the family system, and because LGB individuals and their families must finesse their way through the reality of minority stress, LGB individuals must come into their identities in ways that fit best for them.

Technology and Sexuality 10-1: Online LGBTQIA Support Groups

There are several reasons someone might turn to the internet for support and information. One reason is the constant availability—an online connection provides continuous access to the online world. Anonymity is another reason—the internet enables people to seek resources and support from others with similar experiences without having to reveal their own identity. Being anonymous provides a safe way to explore fantasies that a person would never discuss with a partner. In addition, anonymity allows people to take on another persona, which provides an escape from everyday life. Finally, sexual and gender minorities fear lack of acceptance from health-care professionals so they turn to the internet for answers (Hoskins et al., 2016). For LGBTQIA individuals, being online may provide a source of support and help alleviate feelings of isolation and depression (Levine & Kantor, 2016; Varjas et al., 2013). Online interaction can also help people improve their offline lives. In a study of LGBT youth, researchers found that individuals were using the internet as a way of finding offline resources, including where to go for STI testing and finding physicians who were LGBTQ friendly (DeHaan et al., 2013). LGBTQ youth also went online to find parties and activities (DeHaan et al., 2013). Finally, the internet—and more specifically, social media—can be used as a forum to come out to others (Varjas et al., 2013).

For those who identify as LGBTQIA, there are a number of websites for resources and support. One of the more well-known sites is the It Gets Better Project®, started by columnist Dan Savage in response to LGBTQIA youth who died by suicide as a result of being bullied. The website http://www.itgetsbetter.org provides a place for people to share their stories and videos about their experiences, with the theme that no matter how difficult things may seem, circumstances get better. The website includes a "get help" page that lists both national and local resources.

One of the links is the Trevor Project® (https://www.thetrevorproject.org/). This project is specifically designed to help LGBTQIA youth who are in crises, including being suicidal.

Princeton University's Lesbian, Gay, Bisexual, and Transgender Center (http://lgbt.princeton.edu/resources/) is a general page that provides a multitude of links to online resources for the LGBTQIA community and their allies.

While the online world can feel like a safe place, there are still concerns about safety, and youth may be victims of cyberbullying (Varjas et al., 2013). For those who are using the internet and social media as a way of meeting romantic partners, it is important to keep in mind that people sometimes misrepresent themselves online.

For people of all orientations and genders, the real world can be a confusing, lonely, and challenging place. Seeking information and support online can help you connect with others, feel less isolated, and find resources that can help you lead a happier, healthier life.

10.6b Mixed-Orientation Relationships

Gay and bisexual people marry heterosexuals for some of the same reasons heterosexuals marry each other—deep love for their partner, desire for children in a socially approved heterosexual context, family pressure to marry, the desire to live a socially approved lifestyle, and belief that marriage is the only way to achieve a happy adult life. It is estimated that 20% of gay men are married to a woman (Strommen, 1989). A gay father (his daughter was in the first author's class) who married a heterosexual woman revealed his experience:

> *I had always known I was gay, but I knew coming out to my family was not an option. I had three older brothers, one who was in the ministry, my father was a minister, and so were his two brothers. My family had always been church fixtures, and a gay son would have ruined their reputation. I dated women in an attempt to turn myself and ended up getting my girlfriend at the time pregnant. I decided to marry her, even though I knew it wasn't going to work in the long run, because I wanted to give my child as normal of a childhood as possible.*

> *After 5 years of marriage, we separated, and it felt like I could maybe stop hiding who I was. My family was pressuring me to get back out there, and after holding them off, I met a woman who I believed would be my saving grace. I learned that she had been with other women during college and felt like she could be my cover-up. However, after we married, it was apparent that would not be the case. I began drinking because I was ashamed of who I was and what my life had become because of it. I made the decision to end my second marriage and come out to my family. My parents and grandparents had passed away at this point, so I didn't feel like I had to worry about rejection from them. Coming out to the older members of our family led to a few interesting conversations, but they all assured me that they still loved me, and their opinion of me as a person and as a father to my children had not changed. Once I was honest with everyone, I felt like a huge weight had been lifted off my shoulders.*

The immediate and long-term consequences for an LGBTQIA person coming out to a partner varies from couple to couple. Some who disclose are able to work though the revelation with their partner. In a study of 56 self-identified bisexual husbands and 51 heterosexual wives of bisexual men who maintained their marriage after disclosure, honest communication, peer support, therapy, and "taking time" were identified as factors associated with positive coping (Buxton, 2001). Eight heterosexual women in a relationship with a gay or bisexual partner emphasized that they were able to reframe the disclosure by their partner so as to maximize the positives of the relationship (Adler & Ben-Ari, 2018).

10.7 Relationships

Interviews with 36 LGB couples, in regard to their relationship histories, revealed that they noted more stress in coming out as individuals and as a couple (if and when), greater hesitancy to commit, and less family/institutional support for their relationship (hence, more vulnerability to breaking up) (Macapagal et al., 2015). Otherwise, gay and heterosexual couples are strikingly similar in regard to having equal power and control, being emotionally expressive, perceiving many attractions and few alternatives to the relationship, placing a high value on attachment, and sharing decision-making (Kurdek, 1994). In a comparison of relationship quality of cohabitants over a 10-year period involving both partners from 95 lesbian, 92 gay male, and

226 heterosexual couples living without children and both partners from 312 heterosexual couples living with children, the researcher found that lesbian couples showed the highest level of relationship quality (Kurdek, 2008). Gay and lesbian couples in general are particularly resilient to stress/difficulties in their relationship since they have been confronted with the need to cope with prejudice or discrimination throughout their relationship (Lyne, 2014).

Perales and Baxter (2018) analyzed data on 25,348 individuals in the United Kingdom, comparing same-sex couples with heterosexuals and found similar levels of relationship quality. Data analysis of 9,206 individuals in Australia revealed higher relationship quality among same-sex couples. The lowest relationship quality was reported by bisexual couples.

(Photo provided by Justin & Brandon)

This married couple enjoy the delights of Montana.

10.7a Gay Male Relationships

Research by Leickly et al. (2017) on what gay men look for in a partner online revealed "unreasonably high physical appearance expectations." And, a common stereotype about gay men is that they prefer casual sexual relationships with multiple partners (indeed, the term "dogging" refers to anonymous sex between males) versus monogamous, long-term relationships (Haywood, 2018). However, De Santis et al. (2017) surveyed a sample of 103 Hispanic men (50 heterosexual, 43 gay, and 10 bisexual) and found that one-third reported sex outside the primary relationship, and there were no differences between gay/bisexual and heterosexual men. In interviews with 36 gay men committed to monogamy in their relationships, respondents spoke of the benefits of emotional/sexual satisfaction, trust, security, and so forth (Duncan et al., 2015). National data confirm that gay males are increasingly preferring monogamous relationships (Ram & Devillers, 2016). Adeagbo (2018) interviewed 20 interracial gay men between the ages of 23 and 58 involved in an intimate relationship and found that their stable relationships reflected the same variables of stable heterosexual couples—effective communication, trust, and equality. The data from these interviews contradicted "the general stereotype that gay men are anti-family and averse to monogamy" (p. 17).

The degree to which gay men engage in casual sexual relationships is better explained by the fact that they are male than by the fact that they are gay. In this regard, gay and straight men have a lot in common, including that they both tend to have fewer barriers to engaging in casual sex than do women (heterosexual or lesbian). One way that gay men meet partners is through the internet (sites such as Grindr). A study of men who seek men online for sex revealed that these sites promote higher-risk sexual activities (Blackwell & Dziegielewski, 2012). *Party and play* (PNP), one such activity, involves using crystal methamphetamine and having unprotected anal sex. While the extent of this phenomenon is not known, Grindr is known for being a site where individuals seek drugs with T (for Tina = meth's street name) as in "ParTy and Play" and emojis such as snowflakes for cocaine.

Some men who don't identify as gay, but want to engage in same-sex gender sexual activities, may have "bud sex," which is between masculine, heterosexual males who choose other masculine, white, and straight or secretly bisexual men as partners for secretive sex without romantic involvement (Silva, 2017).

If male homosexuals are called "gay," then female homosexuals should be called "ecstatic."

Shelly Roberts

The wedding day—a joyous occasion.

This woman reports she is equally attracted emotionally and sexually to both women and men.

(Amberlynn Bishop)

10.7b Lesbian Relationships

Like many heterosexual women, most lesbian women value stable, monogamous relationships that are emotionally and sexually satisfying (Potarca et al., 2015). Lesbian and heterosexual women in US society are taught that sexual expression should occur in the context of emotional or romantic involvement. In a comparison of lesbian/bisexual women and heterosexual women, the former had higher sexual skill/efficacy scores (James, 2014). Lesbians and their partners also do more *emotion work* (caring about how the other is feeling and keeping the emotional relationship stable) than do heterosexual or gay males (Umberson et al., 2015).

Stereotypes and assumptions about what sexual behaviors various categories of lesbians engage in are unfounded. A sample of 214 women who self-identified as lesbian were surveyed regarding the relationship between lesbian labels (butch, soft butch, butch/femme, femme, and high femme) and attraction to sexual behavior (being on top, etc.). Researchers found no relationship between the label and the sexual behavior and emphasized that sexual behaviors in the lesbian community are fluid across labels (Walker et al., 2012).

Of 94 lesbian women in one study, 93% said their first lesbian experience was emotional—physical expression came later (Corbett & Morgan, 1983). Hence, for gay women, the formula is love first; for gay men, sex first—just as for their straight counterparts. Indeed, a joke in the lesbian community is that a lesbian couple's second date involves renting a U-Haul so they can move in and nest together. In a comparison of 52 lesbian couples with 50 gay male couples and 218 heterosexual married couples, Green and colleagues (1996) found that the lesbian couples were the closest, the most flexible in terms of their roles, and the most satisfied in their relationships.

Previous researchers have referred to *lesbian bed death*, the idea that since males typically drive the sexual frequency of a relationship, a relationship of two females would be devoid of regular sexual behavior. Research suggests that this is not an accurate portrayal of what occurs in lesbian relationships. Data on the sexual behavior of 586 women in a same-sex relationship (1–36 years) revealed that the majority of the women reported both genital and nongenital sexual behavior once a week or more. Moreover, the women reported satisfaction in their sexual behavior and sexual desire (Cohen & Byers, 2014).

10.7c Bisexual Relationships

Perales and Baxter (2018) found that relationship quality of bisexuals was lower than same-sex or other-sex couples. Heterosexuals and lesbian/gay men are less willing than bisexuals to engage in romantic/sexual activities with bisexual partners. Bisexuals reveal worse mental health profiles than their heterosexual and gay/lesbian counterparts. Minority stress and lifetime adversity contribute to this outcome (Persson & Pfaus,

2015). However, Jones et al. (2018) found that bisexuals may create/nurture close supportive networks, which contribute to their well-being.

Bisexuality immediately doubles your chances for a date on Saturday night.

Woody Allen

10.7d Pansexual Relationships

Pansexuals are individuals who are attracted to all people, regardless of their gender or orientation. In a study of the sexual satisfaction and sexual functioning of 403 pansexuals, both men and women reported very high sexual satisfaction; however, 26% of the female participants met the criteria for sexual dysfunctions (Watson & Pericak, 2014). But this study is about individuals who identify as pansexuals. An area in need of systematic research is on pansexuals.

10.7e Trans Partner Relationships

This section is based on the research of Platt and Bolland (2017). Trans* as used here, is a comprehensive term that encompasses all those within the diverse gender nonconforming population. Existing research reveals that trans* individuals are among the most discriminated, marginalized, and stigmatized, with high levels of mental and financial difficulties.

While this study is about trans relationships, not all of the respondents were in a relationship at the time of the interview. Data for this study came from interviews with 38 trans* individuals who self-identified as either (a) having transitioned or (b) having gender expression fluidity. As for sexual orientation, participants identified as lesbian, bisexual, demisexual, pansexual, straight, queer, and no label. Most were white, Euro-American and the remainder African American, Hispanic, or biracial. The respondents were recruited through widely placed advertisements on trans-oriented public pages on Facebook.

The participants completed a one-hour interview via Skype during which they responded to 13 prompt questions about their lives and relationships (e.g., Overall, what would you say are the pros and cons of being trans in regard to romantic relationships?). Five themes were identified in the answers from the respondents.

This woman reports that she is attracted to virtually everyone—men, women, gay/lesbian/bi, transgender.

(Amberlynn Bishop)

1. **The oppressive gender binary system**

    Thirty-three of the 38 participants (87%) noted the relentless stress of living within the oppressive and narrowly defined male or female gender role system. Examples of issues trans* individuals had to confront included the complexity of determining their own gender identity and how to present themselves (i.e., did they want to present as a male, female, or gender queer person?) and what type partner did the other person want? Jennifer, a 49-year-old trans* woman said:

    > *"My parents are going to be there" or "There will be people who I work with at this party." And I'm like, "So really? So yeah, I have to like hide?. ... We've had screaming matches on the way to a New Year's Eve party because I'm wearing stockings, heels, and a dress. And she doesn't want me to do that.*

2. **Coming out and disclosure decisions**

   Dealing with the complexity of disclosure of one's trans* identity to one's current and/or future partners was another major issue. Along with struggling with the disclosure was the problem of finding a partner who would truly accept them as trans*. Getting rejected is common.

   > *The heterosexual men protect their sexuality. So when I date a man I tell them initially, right away that I'm transgender. It's almost a guarantee that a relationship is going to stop at this point.* (Amy, age 40–55)

   Another concern is that some individuals seek a trans* person to have sex with them … as a fetish.

   > *The biggest obstacle that I've found is … a lot of guys see me as transgender, see me as … I don't know, a toy. They don't consider me to be a person.* (Taylor, age 27)

3. **Emotional and physical sexuality concerns**

   Participants talked about the challenges of sexual relations. Some comments included:

   > *It's hard for a partner to react to a body that they're not familiar with.* (Cris, age 25)

   Another issue is how one feels about one's body

   > *There's times when I feel like "Oh, I look okay, I look pretty good." And then a lot of other times where it's like "Oooh, look at that" and "Ooh, my God" and "Oh, he's going to look at this and I'm going to feel horrible."* (Quinn, age 60)

   Nikkelen & Kreukels (2018) emphasized that gender dysphoric individuals who completed GCT (gender confirming treatment including hormonal and genital surgery) reported significant body satisfaction compared to those who had not completed GCT.

4. **Healthy relationships are work**

   Trans* individuals must navigate all the issues that other couples do—where to live (is the city transgender friendly?), work priority/schedule issues and in-laws/extended family.

   > *We see them [extended family] in the summers and at Christmas time. So when we showed up—in the summer—nobody had told those three anything. So a year ago they met me as one person and now here I am and I'm not the same person. I mean, I'm the same person, but I don't look the same, I don't have the same name, I don't even sound the same, so … they were quite confused.* (Jake, age 37)

Another participant shared:

> [My dad] was kind of an uphill battle and I actually had to pull weekends
> away with my kids from [my dad and his wife]. So I was really worried
> because they started to make my daughter feel ashamed of us. And I was
> like no, we're not playing that game. (Cameron, age 27)

5. **Living an authentic life**

    In spite of the difficulty trans* people face there is joy in moving out of the
    shadows and being true to one's self. Some examples are:

> So the pros are that you're being completely authentic and I think that in a
> loving relationship … that is absolutely critical. (Aubrey, age 59)

Another participant shared:

> I feel more alive than I ever have felt. I feel, like … more complete and less
> anxious and less … just … completely lost. My anxiety has done a complete
> 180. (Michael, age 34)

*Researchers Platt and Bolland (2017) summarized their research by noting
the important issues trans* individuals face in their relationships (their fears
and rejections) but also their joy of authenticity.

10.8 Health, Health Behavior, HIV, and Sexual Orientation

Regarding the health (fair/poor/chronic conditions) and health behavior (exercise,
moderate drinker), when same-sex spouses are compared with different-sex spouses,
there is greater similarity between gay and lesbian couples than between heterosexual
couples. Hence, if one gay spouse exercises, the other is more likely to do so than would
be true in a heterosexual marriage. These findings were revealed when both spouses
in 121 gay, 168 lesbian, and 122 heterosexual married couples were compared (Holway
et al., 2018).

Most worldwide HIV infection occurs through heterosexual transmission.
However, in the United States, HIV infection remains the most threatening STI for
gay males and bisexuals. Men who have sex with men account for more new cases of
AIDS in the United States than do persons in any other transmission category. While
the exchange of semen in men who have unprotected anal intercourse ("bareback")
may meet emotional needs for the men, it remains a dangerous health practice. The
frequency of unprotected anal intercourse among men who have sex with men is under
5% (Kerr et al., 2015). These men typically meet in a variety of contexts—online/apps,
cruising, and bathhouses.

Women who have sex exclusively with other women have a much lower rate of
HIV infection than men (both gay and straight) and women who have sex with men.
However, since female-to-female transmission of HIV is theoretically possible through
exposure to the cervical and vaginal secretions of an HIV-infected woman, following
safer sex guidelines is recommended. Lesbians and bisexual women are most at risk for
HIV if they have sex with men who have been exposed to HIV or if they share needles
to inject drugs.

10.9 Heterosexism, Homonegativity, and Homophobia

Attitudes toward same-sex sexual behavior and relationships vary across cultures and historical time periods. Today, most countries throughout the world, including the United States, are predominantly heterosexist. **Heterosexism** is the belief, stated or implied, that heterosexuality is superior (morally, socially, emotionally, and behaviorally) to being gay. It involves the systematic degradation and stigmatization of any nonheterosexual form of behavior, identity, or relationship. Heterosexism results in prejudice and discrimination against nonheterosexuals. Buck et al. (2019) reviewed three studies on public displays of affection (PDA) and found that all studies of participants' reactions to videotaped heterosexual, homosexual, and transgender PDA revealed that participants were generally comfortable with viewing all PDA scenarios, but participants were most comfortable viewing heterosexual PDA and least comfortable viewing transgender PDA.

> *I am just becoming aware of how guilty I feel by being queer.*
>
> Susan Sontag, writer/feminist

Costello et al. (2019) analyzed data on a sample of 968 internet users aged 15–36 and found that individuals living in the southern region of the United States were nearly three times as likely to be targeted by hate related to sexual orientation. Heterosexism assumes that all people are or should be heterosexual. Heterosexism is pervasive. For example, even the dating games or newlywed games on cruise ships are limited to heterosexual couples. Gay individuals going on vacation often look for specific gay-friendly tourist spots, bed-and-breakfast establishments, and cities such as Key West and San Francisco. Such marginalization may have unforeseen effects. Ritter et al. (2018) compared self-reported sexual satisfaction of 87 sexual minority undergraduates with 193 heterosexual undergraduates and found that the former reported lower sexual satisfaction. The researchers suggested that the culprit may be that sexual minority relationships exist in a context of heterosexism, suppression, stigmatization, prejudice, discrimination, and violence, which may lower both relationship quality and sexual satisfaction.

Prejudice begins early and by one's peers. Farr et al. (2019) reported on 131 elementary school students (M_{age} = 7.79 years; 61 girls) who viewed images of same-sex (female and male) and other-sex couples with a child and then were asked about their perceptions of these families, particularly the children. Results indicated participants' preferences toward children with other-sex versus same-sex parents.

With the legalization of same-sex marriage, the heterosexist norms will eventually change, albeit slowly. Before reading further, you may wish to complete *Self-Assessment 10-1: Sexual Prejudice Scale*.

There are various dimensions to attitudes about homosexuality (Adolfsen et al., 2010):

1. *General attitude:* Is being gay considered to be normal or abnormal? Do people think that gay/lesbians should be allowed to live their lives just as freely as heterosexuals? According to a nationwide poll, 30% of Americans agreed that they would be "very" or "somewhat" uncomfortable if they learned that a family member was LGBTQ (Harris Poll/GLAAD, 2018).

2. *Equal rights:* Should gay individuals be granted the same rights as heterosexuals in regard to marriage and adoption?

3. *Close quarters:* What are the feelings in regard to having a gay neighbor or a lesbian colleague? According to a nationwide poll, 31% of Americans agreed that they would be "very" or "somewhat" uncomfortable to learn that their doctor was LGBTQ (Harris Poll, 2018).

Heterosexism
Belief, stated or implied, that heterosexuality is superior (morally, socially, emotionally, and behaviorally) to homosexuality

4. *Public display*: What are the reactions to a gay couple holding hands in public? According to a nationwide poll, 31% of Americans agreed that they were "very" or "somewhat" uncomfortable seeing a gay couple hold hands (Harris Poll, 2018).

5. *Modern homonegativity*: Feeling that being gay is accepted in society and that various special attentions are unnecessary.

In regard to reducing homonegativity, interacting with LGBT members either in person on online (the contact hypothesis) are alternatives (White et al. 2019).

Self-Assessment 10-1: Sexual Prejudice Scale

Directions

The items below provide a way to assess your level of prejudice against gay men and lesbians. For each item, identify a number from 1 to 6 that reflects your level of agreement, and write the number in the space provided.

1 (Strongly disagree), 2 (Disagree), 3 (Mildly disagree), 4 (Mildly agree), 5 (Agree), 6 (Strongly agree)

Gay Men Scale

1. __ You can tell a man is gay by the way he walks.
2. __ I think it's gross when I see two men who are clearly "together."
3.* __ Retirement benefits should include the partners of gay men.
4. __ Most gay men are flamboyant.
5. __ It's wrong for men to have sex with men.
6.* __ Family medical leave rules should include the domestic partners of gay men.
7. __ Most gay men are promiscuous.
8. __ Marriage between two men should be kept illegal.
9.* __ Health-care benefits should include partners of gay male employees.
10. __ Most gay men have HIV/AIDS.
11. __ Gay men are immoral.
12.* __ Hospitals should allow gay men to be involved in their partners' medical care.
13. __ A sexual relationship between two men is unnatural.
14. __ Most gay men like to have anonymous sex with men in public places.
15.* __ There's nothing wrong with being a gay man.

Scoring

*Reverse score items 3, 6, 9, 12, and 15. For example, if you selected a 6, replace the 6 with a 1. If you selected a 1, replace it with a 6. Add each score of the 15 items. The lowest possible score is 15, suggesting a very low level of prejudice against gay men; the highest possible score is 90, suggesting a very high level of prejudice against gay men. The midpoint between 15 and 90 is 52. Scores lower than 52 reflect less prejudice against gay men, while scores higher than this reflect more prejudice against gay men.

Participants

Both undergraduate and graduate students enrolled in social work courses made up a convenience sample (N = 851). The sample was predominantly women (83.1%), white (65.9%), heterosexual (89.8%), single (81.3%), nonparenting (81.1%), 25 years of age or under (69.3%), and majoring in social work (80.8%).

Results

The range of scores for the gay men scale was 15 to 84. (M = 31.53, SD = 15.30). The sample had relatively low levels of prejudice against gay men.

Lesbian Scale

1. __ Most lesbians don't wear makeup.
2. __ Lesbians are harming the traditional family.
3.* __ Lesbians should have the same civil rights as straight women.
4. __ Most lesbians prefer to dress like men.
5.* __ Being a lesbian is a normal expression of sexuality.
6. __ Lesbians want too many rights.
7. __ Most lesbians are more masculine than straight women.
8. __ It's morally wrong to be a lesbian.
9.* __ Employers should provide retirement benefits for lesbian partners.
10. __ Most lesbians look like men.
11. __ I disapprove of lesbians.
12.* __ Marriage between two women should be legal.
13. __ Lesbians are confused about their sexuality.
14. __ Most lesbians don't like men.
15.* __ Employers should provide health-care benefits to the partners of their lesbian employees.

Scoring

*Reverse score items 3, 5, 9, 12 and 15. For example, if you selected a 6, replace the 6 with a 1. If you selected a 1, replace it with a 6. Add each score of the 15 items. The lowest possible score is 15, suggesting a very low level of prejudice against lesbians; the highest possible score is 90, suggesting a very high level of prejudice against lesbians. The midpoint between 15 and 90 is 52. Scores lower than 52 would reflect less prejudice against lesbians, while scores higher than this would reflect more prejudice against lesbians.

Participants

Both undergraduate and graduate students enrolled in social work courses made up a convenience sample (N = 851). The sample was predominantly women (83.1%), white (65.9%), heterosexual (89.8%), single (81.3%), nonparenting (81.1%), 25 years of age or under (69.3%), and majoring in social work (80.8%).

Results

The range of scores for the lesbian scale was 15 to 86 (M = 30.41, SD = 15.60). The sample had relatively low levels of prejudice against lesbians.

Source: Chonody, J. M. (2013). Measuring sexual prejudice against gay men and lesbian women: Development of the Sexual Prejudice Scale (SPS). *Journal of Homosexuality, 60*(6), 895–926. Copyright 2013 Taylor and Francis, Ltd., http://www.tandfonline.com. Reprinted by permission of the publisher and Jill Chonody.

10.9a Homonegativity and Homophobia

The term **homophobia** is commonly used to refer to negative attitudes and emotions toward being gay and those who engage in same-sex behavior. Even photographs of two males kissing elicit a negative emotional reaction in some heterosexual males (Bishop, 2015). Persons who have had little contact with gays, who are male, and who believe that being gay is a choice are most likely to have negative attitudes toward gay individuals (Chonody, 2013). Other factors of college students associated with intolerance toward lesbians and gays include Christian religious values, being a first-year college student, and selecting a major other than the arts and sciences (Holland et al., 2012). Gay and lesbian college students looking to find support might assess the existence of an LGB student organization on campus (Kane, 2013).

Homophobia is not necessarily a clinical phobia (that is, one involving a compelling desire to avoid the feared object despite recognizing that the fear is unreasonable). Other terms that refer to negative attitudes and emotions toward gay individuals include **homonegativity** (attaching negative connotations to being gay) and *antigay bias*. Transgender people are targets of similar negativity. Puckett et al. (2018) revealed the difficulties transgender individuals experience when they engage the medical community to transition. Barriers can be significant, from lack of information provided by the health-care professionals to outright rejection.

The radical right is so homophobic that they're blaming global warming on the AIDS quilt.

Dennis Miller, comedian

There are several sources for homonegativity and homophobia in the United States:

1. *Religion:* Although the Presbyterian Church formally sanctions same-sex marriage and some others are tolerant (Episcopal), still other forms of organized religion prohibit such unions (United Methodists, Mormons, and American and Southern Baptists). Reform Judaism has a history of supporting the LGBT cause, while the far more conservative Orthodox Judaism takes a stand against it. Worldwide, there is considerable homonegativity from most religions of the world. A survey of attitudes toward homosexuality held by religions in 79 countries revealed negative attitudes toward homosexuality, with Islam being the most negative (Jäckle & Wenzelburger, 2015).

    Religious attitudes toward homosexuality vary and include: (1) "God hates fags" (loveless judgmentalism); (2) "God loves the sinner, hates the sin" (condemns homosexual behavior, not the individual); (3) "We don't talk about that" (homosexuals allowed to be invisible without judgment); (4) "They can't help it" (tolerant acceptance); (5) "God's good gift" (created by God and good); and (6) "Godly calling" (views homosexuality as a righteous choice) (Moon, 2014). Lomash and Galupo (2016) observed microinsults to gay individuals by religious individuals. One of the respondents noted: "She told me that even if I was gay, that 'God forgives you and you can change.' It made the process of finding a spiritual home in college very difficult." Finally, Rodriguez et al. (2019) found an association with one's gay identity struggle and negative mental health. And, when religion and spirituality influences (typically negative) were considered, the identity struggle was ongoing and active rather than a passive cognitive conflict.

Homophobia
Negative emotional responses toward, and aversion to, gay individuals

Homonegativity
Term that refers to antigay responses, including negative feelings (fear, disgust, anger), thoughts, and behavior

Cultural
Diversity

Twenty-six countries have legalized same-sex marriage, including Argentina, Belgium, Brazil, Canada, Denmark, France, Iceland, the Netherlands, New Zealand, Norway, Portugal, South Africa, Spain, Sweden, and Uruguay (Pew Research Center, 2019c). Seventy-nine countries have laws against being gay. In Gambia, homosexuality is regarded like rape or incest—a lifetime prison sentence may result. Under Sharia law, as practiced in Yemen, Iran, Mauritania, Nigeria, Qatar, Somalia, Sudan, Afghanistan, Saudi Arabia, and the United Arab Emirates, being gay is punishable by death (International Lesbian, Gay, Bisexual, Trans and Intersex Association, 2016). In 2017, the US voted against a resolution condemning the death penalty for LGBT individuals. The vote occurred October 4 at the Human Rights Council in Geneva, Switzerland, and was 27 in favor of condemning abuse of the death penalty, 13 against, and seven abstentions. The US vote was a complete reversal of President Donald Trump's earlier stated support for the LGBT community.

Aware that religion often has a more negative than positive view of homosexuality, SIECUS (2015) recommends, "Religious groups and spiritual leaders can helpfully involve themselves in sexuality education and in promoting the sexual health of their constituents, including those who are gay, lesbian, bisexual."

Scheitle and Wolf (2017) analyzed General Social Survey data to confirm that heterosexual and sexual minority individuals do not differ in terms of the religious traditions in which they were reared but do differ in whether they remain in conservative religions. Sexual minorities are "more likely than heterosexuals to move away from Christian traditions and towards disaffiliation or reaffiliation with 'other' traditions that include Judaism, Buddhism, and liberal nontraditional religions such as Unitarian Universalism."

2. *Marital and procreative bias:* Many societies have traditionally condoned sex only when it occurs in a marital context that provides for the possibility of reproducing and rearing children. Not until 2015 was same-sex marriage legal in every state in the United States (see *Social Policy 10-1* for a review of the pros and cons of same-sex marriage).

3. *Concern about HIV and AIDS:* Although most cases of HIV and AIDS worldwide are attributed to heterosexual transmission, the rates of HIV and AIDS in the United States are much higher among gay and bisexual men than among other groups. Because of this, many people in the United States associate HIV and AIDS with homosexuality and bisexuality. Lesbians, incidentally, have a very low risk for sexually transmitted HIV—a lower risk than heterosexual women.

4. *Rigid gender roles:* Antigay sentiments also stem from rigid gender roles. Lesbians are perceived as stepping out of line by relinquishing traditional female sexual and economic dependence on men. In the traditional patriarchal view, both gay men and lesbians are often viewed as betrayers of their gender who must be punished.

5. *Psychiatric labeling:* Prior to 1973, the American Psychiatric Association defined homosexuality as a mental disorder. When the third edition of the *Diagnostic and Statistical Manual of Mental Disorders (DSM-III)* was published in 1980, homosexuality was no longer included as a disorder. Homosexuality itself is not regarded as a psychiatric disorder, but persistent and marked distress over being homosexual is a concern.

6. *Myths and negative stereotypes:* Homonegativity may also stem from some of the unsupported beliefs and negative stereotypes regarding homosexuality. For example, many people believe that gays are child molesters, even though the ratio of heterosexual to homosexual child molesters is approximately 11:1 (Moser, 1992). Further, lesbians are stereotyped as women who want to be (or at least look and act like) men, whereas gay men are stereotyped as men who want to be (or at least look and act like) women. In reality, the gay and lesbian population is as diverse as the heterosexual population, not only in appearance, but also in social class, educational achievement, occupational status, race, ethnicity, and personality.

 **10-1**

APA Removal of Homosexuality as a Mental Disorder

Prior to 1973, the American Psychiatric Association listed homosexuality as a mental disorder with treatments including chemical castration, electric shock therapy, mental institutionalization, and lobotomies. The catalyst for the change was a presentation in 1972 by psychiatrist and member of the organization, John E. Fryer. He appeared as Dr. H. Anonymous at the Annual Convention in Dallas in 1972 wearing a mask and a big curly wig, and he used a voice-altering microphone.

"I am a homosexual. I am a psychiatrist," he said, and noted that he had to remain anonymous for fear of losing his job as an untenured professor at a major university. Earlier, he had been terminated from his psychiatry residency program at the University of Pennsylvania's School of Medicine when it was discovered he was gay.

A year after Dr. Fryer's presentation, the American Psychiatric Association removed homosexuality from the *Diagnostic and Statistical Manual of Mental Disorders*. Dr. Saul Levin (also gay) was the CEO/medical director in 2017 and gave a keynote presentation giving a tribute to Dr. Fryer (De Groot, 2017).

I know what it feels like to try to blend in so that everybody else will think that you're okay and they won't hurt you.

Ellen DeGeneres, American comedian

Social Policy 10-1

Same-Sex Marriage

Masci et al. (2017) identified several key facts about same-sex marriage:

1. Greater societal support. Every year since 2007 there has been an increase in public support for same-sex marriage. In 2017, 62% supported same-sex marriage, 32% opposed. Hoy (2018) confirmed that same-sex marriage increased the belongingness and inclusion of gays into mainstream society. Kennedy et al. (2018) confirmed emotional support same-sex spouses experienced from family, friends, and coworkers for their marriage.

2. Demographic differences in support. There is a demographic divide in support of same-sex marriage with religiously unaffiliated more supportive than the religiously affiliated. Younger individuals are also more supportive: 74% of millennials (now ages 18–36), 65% of Generation Xers (ages 37–52), 56% of baby boomers (ages 53–71), 41% of those in the Silent Generation (ages 72–89).

3. More same-sex marriages. Before legalization 38% of cohabiting same-sex couples were married. After the Supreme Court ruling, 61% of cohabiting same-sex couples are married.

4. Reasons for marriage. While both LGBT individuals and the general public cite love as the primary reason for marriage (84% and 88%), the LGBT individuals are more likely to cite rights and benefits as a reason for marriage (46% and 23%).

Defense of Marriage Act
Legislative act that denied federal recognition of same-sex marriage and allowed states to ignore same-sex marriages licensed elsewhere

In 2013, in a five-to-four ruling, the U.S. Supreme Court struck down the **Defense of Marriage Act** (DOMA), which had been passed in 1996 and which defined marriage as a "legal union between one man and one woman." DOMA was ruled unconstitutional on equal protection grounds, thus confirming that the almost 1 million legally married same-sex couples throughout the country would no longer be denied access to federal recognition and marriage benefits (Weise & Strauss, 2013).

This decision paved the way to another five-to-four decision, this time in June 2015, in which the Court ruled that state bans on same-sex marriage were unconstitutional, thereby legalizing same-sex marriage in all 50 states.

But even though same-sex marriage is the law of the land, debate for and against it continues.

Arguments in Favor of Same-Sex Marriage

Aside from the basic issue of equal protection under the law, the primary argument for same-sex marriage is that it will promote relationship stability among gay and lesbian couples. In a study of the long-term dating intentions and monogamy beliefs of gay and lesbian online daters across 53 regions in eight European countries (N = 24,598), the presence of pro-same-sex relationship legislation was found to also be associated with higher long-term dating intentions and stronger belief in monogamy (Potarca et al., 2015).

Positive outcomes for gay marriage have been documented (Setzer, 2015). In a sample of 225 lesbian married couples, the respondents reported physical, psychological, and financial well-being in their relationships. The researchers noted that these data support the finding in the heterosexual marriage literature that healthy marriage is associated with distinct well-being benefits (Ducharme & Kollar, 2012). Other researchers have found that same-sex married lesbian, gay, and bisexual people were significantly less distressed than lesbian, gay, and bisexual people who are not in a legally recognized relationship (Wright et al., 2013).

Children of same-sex parents also benefit from the legal recognition of same-sex marriage. These benefits include the right to health insurance coverage and Social Security survivor benefits from a nonbiological parent. It also provides the right to assist and represent the spouse in major health and end-of-life care and decisions.

While critics suggest that children reared by same-sex parents are disadvantaged (Kirby & Michaelson, 2015), there are no data to support this fear. Indeed, over a quarter of a million children being reared by same-sex couples (20%–25% of same-sex couples raise children) benefit from the legal recognition of the marriage of their parents (Van Willigen, 2015). Fedewa and colleagues (2015) reviewed 33 research articles representing 5,272 children from same-gender and different-gender parents. Few significant differences from children of heterosexuals were found, none of them deleterious to the child.

Children flourish in attentive, loving, nurturing contexts—and parents of same-sex and different-sex orientations can both provide this context. In a longitudinal study comparing children of lesbian mothers with a normative sample, there were no significant between-group differences with respect to adaptive functioning (family, friends, spouse or partner relationships, and educational or job performance), behavioral or emotional problems, scores on mental health diagnostic scales, or the percentage of participants with a score in the borderline or clinical range (Gartrell et al., 2018).

Arguments Against Same-Sex Marriage

The primary reason for disapproval of same-sex marriage is conservative morality. Gay marriage is viewed by some as "immoral, a sin, against the Bible." Opponents of same-sex marriage who view homosexuality as unnatural, sick, or immoral do not want their children to view homosexuality as socially acceptable. There is also a belief on the part of about half of Americans that same-sex parents cannot parent as well as male-female parents (Whithead, 2018).

10.9b Discrimination against Homosexuals

Behavioral homonegativity involves **discrimination**, behavior that involves treating categories of individuals unequally. Discrimination against lesbians and gays can occur at the individual level. The most severe form of behavioral homonegativity is antigay violence, in which gay men, lesbians, and anyone perceived to be gay are physically attacked, injured, tortured, and even killed.

The consequences of homophobia may not be death, but poor mental health instead. Platt et al. (2018) examined national health data, which confirmed that sexual minority individuals utilize mental health-care professionals at higher rates than heterosexual individuals. In a study of the mental health characteristics of lesbians and bisexual undergraduate college women compared with heterosexual college women, results revealed that the bisexual women reported the worst mental health in terms of anxiety, anger, depressive symptoms, self-injury, and suicidal ideation/suicide attempts. Both bisexual women and lesbians had a far greater likelihood of having these mental health issues when compared with heterosexual women (Kerr et al., 2013). A higher risk of depression, suicide ideation, and suicide attempts also occurs in adolescents who report same-sex attraction (Taylor et al., 2015).

Further evidence was found by Hequembourg and Dearing (2013), who analyzed data on 389 gays, lesbians, and bisexuals and found a tendency toward feelings of shame and guilt, as well as abuse of drugs, as a function of internalizing heterosexism. Hence, because a relentless sea of disapproval surrounds gays and lesbians for who they are and what they do, it is not unexpected that there would be negative psychological outcomes. Lyyerzapf et al. (2018) emphasized that discrimination and exclusion continue into elder-care settings where LGBT respondents reported the need to keep their sexual minority status a secret out of fear of social exclusion.

To counter the report of negative experiences of LGBT individuals, Flanders et al. (2017) revealed 278 positive experiences of 91 individuals about their sexual identity via daily diaries. An example recorded by one respondent follows:

Discrimination
Behavior that involves treating categories of individuals unequally

I talked more with my coworker who came out to me and he ended up saying he was poly[amorous] and pan[sexual], and I admitted I was bi rather than totally gay and he was like "rock on man, I hear you." We talked a bit about the semantics of bi vs pansexual because he's dating a transman, but all together it was a great and affirming experience. I did not expect to make a friend at work who got this stuff.

10.9c Biphobia

Just as the term *homophobia* is used to refer to negative attitudes and emotional responses and discriminatory behavior toward gay men and lesbians, **biphobia** refers to similar reactions and discrimination toward bisexuals. Bisexual men are viewed more negatively than bisexual women, gay men, or lesbians (Eliason, 2000). Bisexuals are thought to be homosexuals afraid to acknowledge their real identity or homosexuals maintaining heterosexual relationships to avoid rejection by the heterosexual mainstream. In addition, bisexual individuals are sometimes viewed as heterosexuals who are looking for exotic sexual experiences. Bisexuals may experience double discrimination in that neither the heterosexual nor the homosexual community fully accepts them. Ross et al. (2018) reviewed 52 studies comparing depression/anxiety rates by sexual orientation and found the lowest rates of depression and anxiety among heterosexuals and highest rates among bisexuals with in-between rates for lesbian or gay individuals. Lack of positive affirmative support for one's bisexual status was the context for high rates among bisexuals.

Gay women seem to exhibit greater levels of biphobia than do gay men. The reason may be that many lesbian women associate their identity with a political stance against sexism and patriarchy.

10.10 How Heterosexuals Are Affected by Homophobia

The antigay and heterosexist social climate of our society is often viewed in terms of how it victimizes the gay population. However, heterosexuals are also victimized by heterosexism and antigay prejudice and discrimination. Some of these effects follow:

1. *Heterosexual victims of hate crimes:* Extreme homophobia contributes to instances of violence against homosexuals—acts known as **hate crimes**. Such crimes include verbal harassment (the most frequent form of hate crime experienced by victims), vandalism, sexual assault and rape, physical assault, and murder.

   Because hate crimes are crimes of perception, victims may not be homosexual; they may just be perceived as being homosexual. The National Coalition of Anti-Violence Programs (2014) reported that in 2013, heterosexual individuals in the United States were victims of antigay hate crimes, representing 14% of all antigay hate crime victims.

Biphobia
Fearful, negative, discriminatory reactions toward bisexuals

Hate crimes
Bringing harm to an individual because they are viewed as belonging to a group you don't approve of

2. *Concern, fear, and grief over the well-being of gay, lesbian, or trans family members and friends:* Many heterosexual family members and friends of homosexual people experience concern, fear, and grief over the mistreatment of their gay or lesbian friends or family members; transsexual people are also at risk of abuse. In 2016, there were 77 murders of lesbian, gay, bisexual, transgender, queer or HIV-infected individuals in the United States (National Coalition of Anti-Violence Programs, 2016). Heterosexual parents who have a gay or lesbian teenager often worry about how the harassment, ridicule, rejection, and violence experienced at school might affect their child. Will their child be traumatized, make bad grades, or drop out of school to escape the harassment, violence, and alienation they endure there? Will the gay or lesbian child respond to antigay victimization by turning to drugs or alcohol or by dying by suicide, as there is an increased risk in this population (van Bergen et al., 2013)? Higher rates of anxiety, depression, and panic attacks are also associated with being gay (Oswalt & Wyatt, 2011). In 2010, four gay teens (Billy Lucas, Tyler Clementi, Asher Brown, and Seth Walsh) died by suicide in response to being bullied about their sexuality. Their suicides generated media attention and inspired the aforementioned "It Gets Better Project" (http://www.itgetsbetter.org/).

3. *Restriction of intimacy and self-expression:* Because of the antigay social climate, heterosexual individuals—especially males—are hindered in their own self-expression and intimacy in same-sex relationships. Males must be careful about how they hug each other so as not to appear gay. Homophobic scripts also frighten youth who do not conform to gender role expectations, leading some youth to avoid activities, such as arts for boys or athletics for girls, and professions, such as elementary education for males.

4. *Rape/sexual assault:* Men who participate in gang rape may entice each other into the act "by implying that those who do not participate are unmanly or homosexual" (Sanday, 1995, p. 399). Homonegativity also encourages early sexual activity among adolescent men. Adolescent male virgins are often teased by their male peers: "You mean you don't do it with girls yet? What are you, a fag or something?" Not wanting to be labeled and stigmatized as a "fag," some adolescent boys "prove" their heterosexuality by having sex with girls or even committing rape.

5. *School shootings:* Antigay harassment has also been a factor in many of the school shootings of recent years. For example, in 2001, 15-year-old Charles Andrew Williams fired more than 30 rounds in a San Diego, California, suburban high school, killing 2 and injuring 13 others. A woman who knew Williams reported that the students had teased him and called him gay.

10.11 What to Do About Anti-LGBTQIA Prejudice and Discrimination

Discrimination against LGBTQIA individuals continues. Pomeranz (2018) noted that several states and the federal government have proposed or enacted laws that permit residents to discriminate against LGBTQ individuals. In 2018, the Supreme Court ruled that baker Jake Phillips could refuse to bake a wedding cake for Charlie Craig and David Mullins on the grounds that it was "against his faith."

An **ally development model** has been suggested as a means of providing a new learning context for homophobic heterosexist students in grades K–12 (Zammitt et al., 2015). Such a model is multilayered and involves school counselors, school social workers, and school psychologists providing programs to expose K–12 children to the nature of prejudice and discrimination toward LGBTQIA individuals. In addition, LGBTQIA individuals should be provided with a framework for how to react to or perceive prejudice and discrimination. In some schools, the whole culture is LGBTQIA aware and supportive.

College is another context where acceptance of LGBTQIA individuals can increase. Research has demonstrated that interaction with gays and lesbians and taking courses related to these issues are associated with more accepting attitudes regarding same-sex relationships, voting for a gay presidential candidate, and comfort with a gay/lesbian roommate (Sevecke et al., 2015).

Medical school also serves as a context in which to socialize a new generation. However, Murphy (2016) emphasized how medical students at the top 20 medical schools are routinely exposed to a hidden curriculum of heteronormativity that repeatedly suggests some orientations are normal, natural, and obvious, while others are quietly excluded.

In 2017, the United States Army began compulsory transgender sensitivity training for soldiers to reflect Pentagon policies that accept transgender individuals. Previously, transgender individuals had been barred from military service. In April 2019, the policy was changed again; with this change, the armed services were instructed to begin discharging transgender service members.

Ally development model

Combating homophobia by exposing children in K–12 grades to the nature of prejudice and discrimination toward LGBTQIA individuals

Chapter Summary

GAY, LESBIAN, BISEXUAL, AND TRANSGENDER individuals are receiving increased visibility in our society, though challenges remain.

LGBTQIA Terminology

SEXUAL ORIENTATION refers to the classification of individuals as heterosexual, bisexual, homosexual, pansexual, or asexual based on their emotional and sexual attractions, relationships, self-identity, and lifestyle. *Heterosexuality* refers to the predominance of emotional and sexual attraction to persons of the other sex; homosexuality, to persons of the same sex; bisexuality, to both sexes. *LGBTQIA* is a term that has emerged to refer collectively to lesbians, gays, bisexuals, and transgender individuals; those questioning their sexual orientations/sexual identity those who are intersexed; those who are asexual; or those who are an ally/friend of the cause.

Conceptual Models of Sexual Orientation

THE THREE MODELS OF SEXUAL ORIENTATION are the dichotomous model (people are either heterosexual or homosexual), the unidimensional continuum model (sexual orientation is viewed on a continuum from heterosexuality to homosexuality), and the multidimensional model (orientation consists of various independent components).

Prevalence by Sexual Orientation

THE PREVALENCE OF VARIOUS orientations is difficult to determine due to fear of social disapproval and changing sexual attractions, behaviors, and identities over time. About 10 million individuals (4% of the population) in the United States are self-identified as LGBTQ, though the actual number may be higher.

Theories of Sexual Orientation

BASIC THEORIES OF SEXUAL ORIENTATION are biological (genetic, prenatal, and postpubertal hormonal) and social/cultural (parent-child interactions, peer groups, mass media). Most researchers agree that an interaction of biological and social/cultural forces is involved in the development of sexual orientation. *Conversion therapy is a forced attempt* to change the sexual orientation of homosexuals. There is no evidence that such therapy works; in fact, not only does it fail to change its subjects, but it has been associated with attempted suicide, depression, and anxiety.

Coming Out or Concealment?

COMING OUT is not a linear, one-time event, but a complicated, over-time experience to different people in different contexts. The reactions are unpredictable. Coming out is different for those who are bisexual, asexual or pansexual. Benefits of coming out to parents include higher levels of acceptance from their parents, lower levels of alcohol and drug consumption, and fewer identity and adjustment problems.

Relationships

HOMOSEXUAL, BISEXUAL, AND HETEROSEXUAL RELATIONSHIPS may be more similar than different, although those in nonheterosexual relationships are often more resilient to stress and difficulties in their relationships.

Gay male relationships are stereotyped as short-term and lacking closeness and intimacy. In reality, most gay men prefer long-term, close relationships. Many lesbians value monogamous, emotionally and sexually satisfying relationships. People who are pansexual report high sexual satisfaction. Those who are trans* face many challenges in society, and some of these may impact relationships.

Health, Health Behavior, HIV, and Sexual Orientation

WORLDWIDE, MOST HIV INFECTION occurs through heterosexual transmission. HIV infection remains the most threatening STI for male homosexuals and bisexuals. Women who have sex exclusively with other women have a much lower rate of HIV infection than men (both gay and straight) and women who have sex with men. However, lesbians and bisexual women may also be at risk for HIV if they have sex with men who have been exposed to HIV and/or inject drugs.

Heterosexism, Homonegativity, and Homophobia

HETEROSEXISM is the belief that heterosexuality is superior (morally, socially, emotionally, and behaviorally) to homosexuality and involves the systematic degradation and stigmatization of any nonheterosexual form of behavior, identity, or relationship. Homophobia refers to negative attitudes and emotions toward homosexuality and those who engage in homosexual behavior. Homonegativity includes negative feelings (fear, disgust, anger), thoughts, and behaviors.

How Heterosexuals Are Affected by Homophobia

HETEROSEXUALS are affected by how homosexuals are treated. For example, hate crimes directed toward gays may hurt heterosexuals because homophobes who beat up gays may also target heterosexuals whom they perceive as gay. The National Coalition of Anti-Violence Programs reported that heterosexual individuals in the United States were victims of antigay hate crimes, representing 14% of all antigay hate crime victims. Also, heterosexuals who have gay and lesbian friends and family members are subject to emotional stress and anxiety about their well-being in a hostile culture.

What to Do About Anti-LGBTQIA Prejudice and Discrimination

One of the ways to address the discrimination against LGBTQIA people is to create learning environments that are more supportive. These programs can be implemented in grades K–12. Research has shown that for college students, interacting with people who are LGBTQIA, and taking courses that address LGBTQIA issues can lead to more accepting attitudes.

Web Links

Advocate (Online Newspaper for LGBTQIA News)

http://www.advocate.com/

Bisexual Resource Center

http://www.biresource.net/

COLAGE: People with a Lesbian, Gay, Transgender, or Queer Parent

http://www.colage.org

Gay Parent Magazine

http://www.gayparentmag.com/

Out

http://www.out.com/

Parents, Families, Friends of Lesbians and Gays (PFLAG)

http://www.pflag.org

Key Terms

Ally development model **276**

Asexual **250**

Biphobia **274**

Bisexuality **250**

Coming out **256**

Conversion therapy **255**

Defense of Marriage Act **272**

Dichotomous model **251**

Discrimination **273**

Hate crimes **274**

Heterosexism **266**

Heterosexuality **250**

Homonegativity **269**

Homophobia **269**

Homosexuality **250**

Intersexed **250**

LGBTQIA **250**

Multidimensional model **253**

Pansexuality **250**

Queer **250**

Sexual fluidity **253**

Sexual orientation **250**

Unidimensional continuum
model **251**

CHAPTER
11

Health and Sexuality

Sexual health is more than freedom from sexual disease or disorders. ... Sexual health is nonexploitive and respectful of self and others. ... Sexual health is dependent upon an individual's well-being and sense of self-esteem. Sexual health requires trust, honesty, and communication.

Eli Coleman, director, program in Human Sexuality, University of Minnesota

Chapter Outline

11.1 **Effects of Illness and Disability on Sexuality** 282

11.2 **Effects of Illness and Disability on Self-Concept and Body Image** 283
Personal Decisions 11-1
Would You Date or Marry a Person in a Wheelchair? 283

11.3 **Impaired Sensory-Motor Function and Sexuality** 283
11.3a Spinal Cord Injury 283
11.3b Multiple Sclerosis and Cerebral Palsy 285

11.4 **Diabetes and Sexuality** 286
Technology and Sexuality 11-1:
Online Self-Diagnosis & Treatment 287

11.5 **Impaired Cognitive Function and Sexuality** 288
11.5a Alzheimer's Disease and Other Forms of Dementia 288
11.5b Traumatic Brain Injury 289
11.5c Intellectual and Developmental Disability 289
Self-Assessment 11-1:
Attitudes Toward Sexuality of People with an Intellectual Disability 291

11.6 **Mental Illness and Sexuality** 292
11.6a Mental Illness and Sexual Dysfunction 292
11.6b Mental Illness and Barriers to Sexual Expression, Safer Sex, and Contraception 292

11.7 **Effects of Pain and Fatigue on Sexuality** 293
11.7a Pain and Sexuality 293
11.7b Fatigue and Sexuality 294

11.8 **Effects of Medical Treatment on Sexuality** 295
11.8a Effects of Surgery on Sexuality 295

11.9 **Effects of Medication and Radiation on Sexuality** 297

11.10 **Alcohol, Other Drugs, and Sexuality** 298
Social Policy 11-1
Alcohol Abuse on Campus 298
11.10a Alcohol and Sexuality 299
11.10b Other Recreational Drugs and Sexuality 299
Self-Assessment 11-2:
Motives for Drinking Alcohol Scale 300
11.10c Alcohol, Drugs, and Unsafe Sex 301

Web Links 303
Key Terms 304

Objectives

1. Identify the effects of illness and disability on self-concept and body image
2. Understand the effects of impaired sensory-motor function on sexuality
3. Discuss the impact of diabetes on sexuality
4. Review the effects of impaired cognitive function on sexuality
5. Explain the effects of mental illness on sexuality
6. Learn how pain and fatigue impact sexuality
7. Know the effects of various medical treatments on sexuality
8. Identify how alcohol and other drugs impact sexuality

Truth — OR — Fiction?

T / F 1. Individuals who are hearing impaired have more sexual partners than the visually impaired/physically disabled.

T / F 2. Caretakers of spinal cord injured individuals may interfere with the psychological/sexual relationship with partners.

T / F 3. The disabled are often thought to be asexual.

T / F 4. Less than 10% of 810 undergraduates said they would be open to dating/marrying a person in a wheelchair.

T / F 5. The internet is often the most reliable way to diagnose and treat a disability, particularly in regard to sex.

Answers: 1. T 2. T 3. T 4. F 5. F

While exercise, diet, and maintaining an appropriate weight are critical to being physically healthy for sexual functioning, being out of shape, ill, or disabled are not unusual. Indeed, having a physical illness is likely for most of us, and the effect on our sexuality can be challenging. Having a **disability** is also not unusual and will necessitate communicating about the implications for sex with one's partner.

In this chapter we examine how illness, disease, and disability interfere with the quality of life in relationships and sexuality. We include information on the effects of alcohol and drugs on sexuality.

Disability
Health condition that involves functional deficits in performing activities of daily living

National DATA

Forty million individuals in the US have a disability (ProQuest Statistical Abstract of the United States, 2019, Table 202).

11.1 Effects of Illness and Disability on Sexuality

Some illnesses have a dramatic impact on the patient's sexuality. Since sexuality is vital to one's self-image and the quality of one's interpersonal relationships, the onset of an illness begins a major challenge for the individual and couple. Benoit et al. (2017b) focused on how cancer impacts a couple's sexual relationship and discussed stages and strategies of adjustment/coping. Women with gynecologic cancer noted severe decreases in sexual desire, arousal, frequency of intercourse, and orgasm (Bal et al., 2013).

The disabled struggle with how their disability will impact their sexual behavior. Some are able to shift the focus. One woman said: "I don't feel like it really affected my sexuality as much just because ... I never really defined my sexuality based on my physical body and stuff as much as my skills, my intelligence, my creativity" (Kattari, 2014). Others are matter-of-fact: "I tend to go with this is who I am, this is what I am, this is the package. If you don't like it and you want to leave, okay, I get it" (Kattari, 2014).

Retznik et al. (2017) interviewed 84 individuals (18–25) with a disability (hearing, visual, physical) who had been in a relationship at least once. Eighty percent of the women and two-thirds of the men reported having had sexual intercourse (average age = 16). The hearing impaired reported more sexual partners than the visually impaired or physically disabled. Those with a physical disability reported fewer relationships and delayed first sexual intercourse. Differences impacted sexuality in one of two ways— early sexuality activity to compensate for negative self-image or abstinence.

The disabled are sometimes assumed to be asexual—to have no interest in sexual expression with a partner (Lund & Johnson, 2015). This misconception contributes to the fact that physicians and health-care professionals generally ignore the sexuality of the ill or disabled. In a study of 137 females with multiple sclerosis, only 2% reported that they had ever discussed sexual concerns with a physician (Lew-Starowicz & Rola, 2013). Those who are disabled often report being abused and sexually victimized.

Health is the greatest gift.

Buddha

While some are traumatized by their victimization, others are resigned to it as just the way they are treated (Linton & Rueda, 2015). Minority adolescents with disabilities also report incidences of psychological and physical abuse, as well as sexual abuse (2015).

THINK ABOUT IT

Take a moment to answer the following question. Illness and disability can also enhance self-concept. For example, some childhood cancer survivors feel stronger and more confident as a result of surviving cancer. What are some other ways in which illness or disability might enhance self-concept?

11.2 **Effects of Illness and Disability on Self-Concept and Body Image**

In general, persons with chronic illness or disability are vulnerable to developing a negative self-concept and body image; they view themselves as undesirable or inadequate romantic and sexual partners. The paraplegic in the 2012 movie *The Sessions* was fearful that no female would be willing to touch him, let alone have sex with him. All too often, individuals with disabilities internalize negative social attitudes, which leads them to retreat from intimate relations and adopt a nonsexual lifestyle. Persons with disabilities or disease may also view themselves as physically flawed and sexually unattractive.

The only disability is a bad attitude.

Scott Hamilton, figure skater

PERSONAL DECISIONS 11-1

Would You Date or Marry a Person in a Wheelchair?

Access to public places has become law for those in wheelchairs, with the result of increasing their numbers and visibility. It is common for individuals in wheelchairs to be seen on campus or in class. Because of stigma and stereotypes, the able-bodied may be reluctant to engage the person in a wheelchair. *Do I speak to the person? Would I date the person? Would marriage be an option?*

A team of researchers (Marini et al., 2013) surveyed 810 undergraduates regarding their interest in being friends with, dating, or marrying a wheelchair user. Almost two-thirds (66%) reported that they would have no problem dating or marrying a wheelchair user. People with the personal traits of intelligence, humor, kindness, and pleasing physical appearance were rated most highly as potential dates/marriage partners. Students who were unwilling to date or marry an individual in a wheelchair noted that they feared the partner would require too much caregiving, would not be able to perform sexually, or would be sick too often.

11.3 **Impaired Sensory-Motor Function and Sexuality**

A number of neurological diseases and injuries, including spinal cord injury, can result in impaired sensory-motor functioning. The effects of sensory-motor impairment on sexuality are varied and depend, in part, on the type and severity of the illness or injury.

11.3a Spinal Cord Injury

The effect of spinal cord injury on sexual functioning depends on the level of injury and whether it is *complete* or *incomplete*. In a complete injury, there is no function below the level of the injury—no sensation and no voluntary movement. In an incomplete injury, there is some functioning below the primary level of the injury. There are major changes from spinal cord injury (depending on severity) to manage—loss of bladder, bowel, and sexual function are compounded by psychological outcomes such as feelings of bewilderment, disbelief, anger, fear, hope, and despair. McKinney (2018) noted the unusual context of the physically disabled who has both a partner and caretakers. She noted that while the caretakers are helpful (indeed indispensable) they may also be in the way of both psychological and physical intimacy. The triad is an unusual context to manage.

Cervical (neck) injuries usually result in **quadriplegia**—paralysis from the neck down. Very high cervical injuries can result in a loss of many involuntary functions, including the ability to breathe, necessitating breathing aids such as mechanical ventilators. Injuries at the thoracic level and below result in **paraplegia**—paralysis of the lower half of the body.

Interviews with four women who use a wheelchair revealed the challenges of sustaining themselves as sexual individuals, despite societal stereotypes of the disabled (Parker & Yau, 2012). Their struggle was to be perceived as a sexual being, not just as a woman with a disability in a wheelchair. Two of the women noted:

> You think that because you are in a wheelchair that nobody will want you. ... You have still got feelings, and you still want to experience your sexuality. But they [society and potential romantic partners] don't see you like that, because you are in a wheelchair. Which makes it very hard because you still feel like a woman. (Ms. C.)

> When you are trying to meet new people, the reality is they see you in the chair. ... After a few years I resorted to the fact that I was going to be alone for the rest of my life. (Ms. D.)

Nevertheless, the respondents reported that they had regained their sexual life and positive feelings regarding their sexuality. Peer support, masturbation, use of the internet to meet new partners, and communication were important factors. In people with spinal cord injury, orgasm may occur by direct stimulation of the genitals, by mentally reassigning sensations that can be felt in other areas of the body to the genitals, and/or by erotic imagery such as fantasizing. Peta et al. (2017) interviewed 16 disabled women who rejected the notion that they are asexual, and found that the ways in which they asserted their sexuality challenged dominant, restrictive, and ableist constructs.

The presence of and involvement with a partner are the major positive predictors of adjustment for a spinal cord-injured person. Freeman et al. (2017) interviewed five heterosexual couples in which the male had a sustained spinal cord injury. In all cases, the couple gave each other complete support during the rehabilitation process. A major complaint was the inpatient environment and presence of uninformed health professionals, which limited the couple's ability to engage in intimate behavior.

For men with spinal cord injury who are able to achieve erection, intercourse may take place with the partner sitting down on the erect penis. If erection is not achieved, some couples use the *stuffing technique*, in which partners push the soft penis into the woman's vagina, which she then contracts to hold the penis inside her. For some men with spinal cord injury, Viagra or an inflatable penile prosthesis implant can be helpful in achieving erection. *Up Close 11-1* reveals the experience of a man with a spinal cord injury and the effect on his marriage.

Parents with spinal cord injury (SCI) noted that while they could still have children, they were not immune to the stress and sexual dysfunctions that sometimes accompany SCI. Hence, SCI involves enormous challenges, which are often overcome with support, patience, and perseverance (Kaiser et al., 2012).

Quadriplegia
Paralysis from the neck down

Paraplegia
Paralysis of the lower half of the body

Effect of Spinal Cord Injury on Marriage and Sexuality

I was a happily married 25-year-old man with two children. I was in a car accident that left me paralyzed from the waist down and partially paralyzed from the waist up. I had a terrible time adjusting to the fact that I was in a wheel-chair. Plus, the accident messed up my marriage completely. My wife stayed with me for 5 years, but only because she felt sorry for me. As soon as I went to a rehabilitation center and began to manage for myself, she left me.

It has been very hard for me to find a woman who doesn't have hang-ups about men in wheelchairs, unless they are in one too. Because I'm not in an environment where there are a lot of disabled people, it has been difficult finding female companionship. The exception has been a nurse I met at the rehabilitation center. We had a great time together. After I left, we stayed in touch for a while, and then I just stopped hearing from her.

While women don't want me as a permanent companion/partner/husband, they are curious. I find that women try to pick me up in bars. They want to know what sex is like with a guy in a wheelchair. What they like me to do is drive them wild orally, but eventually they want intercourse, and that's something I can't do. It is a major problem.

11.3b Multiple Sclerosis and Cerebral Palsy

Multiple sclerosis (MS) is a progressive disease that attacks the central nervous system. Onset of MS usually occurs between the ages of 20 and 40, and the incidence of MS is two to three times higher in women than in men (Sahay et al., 2012). Symptoms of MS, which vary from person to person, may include lack of muscle coordination; weakness and fatigue; tremors; spasms; stiffness; slurred speech; impaired genital sensation; pain (stabbing pain in the face or down the spine; burning, aching, cramping, or pins-and-needles sensation); numbness in the face, body, or extremities; and cognitive impairment. Bladder (38%) and bowel (48%) problems have also been reported in a sample of 144 females with MS (Sahay et al., 2012).

Respondents (particularly women) with MS reported that fear of sexual rejection was a major concern (Quinn et al., 2015). Sexual dysfunction is common among women and men with MS and may involve reduced genital sensation, genital pain, vaginal dryness, loss of libido, erection problems, difficulty or inability to ejaculate, and difficulty reaching orgasm. Because of the progressive nature of the disease, symptoms of sexual dysfunction in women and men with MS tend to increase in severity and number over time. However, individuals with MS and their partners can improve marital and sexual satisfaction through counseling, communication about sexual issues with health-care providers, and interventions to improve sexual functioning, such as Viagra for men and personal lubricating products for women.

(Laura Zuber)

Relationships/sexuality remain a part of this woman's persona in spite of her having multiple sclerosis (MS).

Multiple sclerosis
Progressive disease that attacks the central nervous system

International **DATA**

More than 1 million individuals live with multiple sclerosis (National Multiple Sclerosis Society, 2019).

Cerebral palsy (CP)—a condition caused by brain damage that occurs before or during birth or in infancy—also involves symptoms that can interfere with sexual expression. Infancy symptoms can vary according to the area and degree of brain damage, but generally include uncontrollable movement, lack of coordination, spasms, and speech impairment. Problems with sight and hearing may also occur. Cerebral palsy may also result in cognitive impairment (learning and intellectual or developmental disabilities).

Adults with CP often require counseling and assistance in achieving sexual satisfaction. For example, one woman with severe spasticity due to cerebral palsy used her mouth to operate a specially designed vibrator that enabled her to reach orgasm (Donnelly, 1997).

National **DATA**

Cerebral palsy affects two to three children out of every 1,000 live births (Cerebralpalsy.org, 2018).

11.4 Diabetes and Sexuality

Cerebral palsy
Condition, often caused by brain damage that occurs before or during birth or in infancy, resulting in muscular impairment and sometimes speech and learning disabilities

Diabetes mellitus
Chronic disease in which the pancreas fails to produce sufficient insulin, which is necessary for metabolizing carbohydrates and fats

Diabetes mellitus is a chronic disease in which the pancreas fails to produce sufficient insulin, which is necessary for metabolizing carbohydrates and fats. The symptoms—which may be controlled through injections of insulin—include excess sugar in the blood and urine; excessive thirst, hunger, and urination; and weakness. Most people with diabetes have type 2 diabetes (associated with obesity in later life), which is increasing dramatically in the United States and worldwide as populations become more sedentary and obese.

In a study of the sexuality of 80 men and 80 women who had type 2 diabetes, 65% of the men reported male sexual dysfunction (erectile dysfunction), and 68% of the women reported female sexual dysfunction, such as lack of sexual desire and orgasmic dysfunction. Psychogenic factors were more operative in women than men (Hintistan & Cilingir, 2013). Type 1 diabetes may also be a problem. Flotynska et al. (2019) found among women with type 1 diabetes, lower sexual satisfaction and higher reported sexual dysfunction. Similarly, Yacan and Erol (2019) compared 30 women with type 1 diabetes, 30 women with type 2 diabetes, and 30 women without diabetes on their "Female Sexual Function Index (FSFI)" and found significantly lower scores of desire, arousal, lubrication, orgasm, and satisfaction for those with diabetes.

National **DATA**

Twenty-three million adults (18 years and over) have been diagnosed with diabetes (ProQuest Statistical Abstract of the United States, 2019, Table 2019).

Technology and Sexuality 11-1: Online Self-Diagnosis & Treatment

Since its inception, people have used the internet as a means to acquire information on a variety of topics, including their own health. Individuals use websites such as WebMD®, symptom checkers, and apps to diagnose a possible illness or ailment. While online searches may be a common way for people to try to discover what's wrong with them, it is not the most reliable method for diagnosing or identifying a treatment plan. The film critic Roger Ebert acknowledged that he made a fatal error in relying on the internet to guide him in finding a cure for his cancer.

In a study of symptom-checker apps, researchers found that the apps were not accurate and listed the correct diagnosis as the first diagnosis in only 34% of the cases (Semigran et al., 2015). These symptom checkers often include not just a first diagnosis but also a list of 20 other possible diagnoses—the correct diagnosis appeared in the top-20 list only 58% of the time (Semigran et al., 2015).

Additional research on websites that offer diagnosis and treatment advice found that these sites often lacked easily accessible information about when medical care should be sought (North et al., 2012). When this type of information was available, in a majority of cases it was either not available on the top half of the page or could only be obtained by clicking a link (North et al., 2012). The fact that this information was not more prominent might impact people accessing it, affecting their choice to seek medical care in a timely fashion.

Given the limitations of technology for providing correct medical diagnoses, why do individuals use the internet for self-diagnosis of sexual problems? One answer may be related to the fact that in contemporary US culture, people are not comfortable talking about sexuality. Discussing issues and concerns about sexual functioning face-to-face might be too embarrassing (van Lankveld & Mevissen, 2015). Feelings of shame, discomfort, or anxiety about using sexual terms may cause people to avoid talking to their health-care provider and instead use their smartphone or web browser. Not wanting to talk to a physician may also be related to not wanting to disclose sexual behaviors for fear of being judged.

Inaccurately self-diagnosing a sexual problem via the internet can have a negative impact on your sexual functioning and your relationships. For example, a woman may discover that she is unable to have an orgasm and goes online to find out the name of her concern. One diagnosis is "female orgasmic disorder." However, there are other factors that may cause her to have problems reaching orgasm—discomfort with her body, a lack of information about anatomy and physiological functioning, lack of communication, involvement in a relationship where she doesn't feel loved, or fear of becoming pregnant. Instead of examining other possible issues, people who consult only the internet may decide that they have a disorder and stop sexual activity, believing that there's something wrong with them. Of course, such a decision may result in problems with their partner.

While the internet is a valuable resource, it must be used as only one source of information. Consultation with a credentialed professional who can ask the person for details about their specific concern is more likely to lead to an accurate diagnosis and treatment. In the end, individuals must decide for themselves if the potential negatives of self-diagnosing a sexual problem outweigh the potential discomfort and embarrassment that may result in talking with a professional.

(Laura Zuber)

Increasingly, individuals use their cell phone to find information on health/sexuality.

11.5 Impaired Cognitive Function and Sexuality

Many illnesses and injuries result in impaired cognitive functioning—such as memory loss, language comprehension problems, learning disabilities, and confusion. Some illnesses and injuries, such as multiple sclerosis and cerebral palsy, may involve both sensory-motor impairment and cognitive impairment. Next, we examine impaired cognitive function and its effect on sexuality by more closely focusing on Alzheimer's disease and other forms of dementia, traumatic brain injury, and intellectual or developmental disabilities.

I think I'm getting a little bit of Alzheimer's. Just a little.

Christopher Walken, American actor

11.5a Alzheimer's Disease and Other Forms of Dementia

Dementia is a brain disorder involving memory impairment and at least one of the following: **aphasia** (impaired communicative ability); **agnosia** (loss of auditory, sensory, or visual comprehension); **apraxia** (inability to perform coordinated movements); or loss of ability to think abstractly and to plan, initiate, sequence, monitor, and stop complex behavior. Other symptoms of dementia include depression, personality changes, sleep disturbances, psychosis and agitation, and incontinence.

Causes of dementia include stroke, Parkinson's disease, head trauma, brain tumor, infectious disease (HIV and syphilis), and long-term alcohol abuse. Mild dementia is associated with reduced sexual activity, which is more likely to be noticed by men than women (Tsatali & Tsolaki, 2014). The most common cause of dementia, accounting for two thirds of all dementia cases, is **Alzheimer's disease**—a progressive and degenerative brain disease that typically progresses through stages from mild memory loss through significant cognitive impairment to very serious confusion and the loss of ability to manage activities of daily living, such as dressing, eating, and bathing. A person with end-stage Alzheimer's disease may be incontinent, unable to speak, and unable to walk.

It is not uncommon for persons with dementia to exhibit inappropriate sexual and social behavior, such as uninvited and intrusive touching and inappropriate sexual comments. For example, a hospitalized man diagnosed with Alzheimer's disease asked a female nurse who was giving him a bath if she would "jack me off." The nurse simply told him that she was giving him a bath, not performing a sexual service.

A study of the sexual behavior of 36 Alzheimer's patients and their spouses revealed that patients and spouses reported sexual dissatisfaction. Common causes of sexual dissatisfaction included erectile dysfunction and lack of female sexual desire. Men associated sexual dissatisfaction with sadness, and women reported feelings of lack of intimacy and increased anxiety (Dourado et al., 2010).

Dementia
Brain disorder involving multiple cognitive deficits, including memory impairment and at least one of the following: aphasia; agnosia; apraxia; or loss of ability to think abstractly and to plan, initiate, sequence, monitor, and stop complex behavior

Aphasia
Impaired communicative ability

Agnosia
Loss of auditory, sensory, or visual comprehension

Apraxia
Inability to perform coordinated movements

Alzheimer's disease
Progressive and degenerative brain disease progressing from mild memory loss, through significant cognitive impairment, to very serious confusion and the loss of ability to manage activities of daily living, such as dressing, eating, and bathing

---

National DATA

Nearly 6 million (5.8) Americans are living with Alzheimer's disease (Alzheimer's Association, 2019).

THINK ABOUT IT

Take a moment to answer the following question. Spouses or partners of individuals with Alzheimer's disease face a number of sexual concerns, such as the ethics of having sex with a partner who "has become a stranger," who is no longer aware of what is happening so cannot give consent, or who may think the spouse is someone else. In 2007, Supreme Court Justice Sandra Day O'Connor openly talked about her husband's affair with another woman. Both her husband and the other woman had Alzheimer's disease and were living in the same care facility. To the surprise of many, Justice O'Connor was happy for her husband that he had found happiness. What would you do in the same situation? What decisions would you make about your own sexuality if your partner no longer recognized you?

11.5b Traumatic Brain Injury

Traumatic brain injury (TBI) is a closed head injury that results from an exterior force and creates a temporary or enduring impairment in brain functioning. The nature of impairment varies according to the severity of the injury and the specific area of the brain that is affected. Sneha (2018) detailed the extensive/intensive cognitive process of recovering from brain injury after being thrown from a bike. Brain injury due to football concussion is a culturally visible topic.

Brain injury can directly and indirectly affect important aspects related to sexuality and sexual function. Following a traumatic brain injury, individuals may experience some type of problem in sexual functioning, such as reduced sexual drive and self-control, decreased erectile ability, inability to become aroused, or the development of new sexual interests such as masochism (Moreno et al., 2013). They may also experience changes that affect their social interactions: mood swings, depression, social withdrawal, and problems with anger control. Since TBI is most commonly experienced by those ages 15–25, those affected are often in a life stage of beginning to form and maintain intimate relationships.

11.5c Intellectual and Developmental Disability

In the United States, 4.6 million people have an intellectual or developmental disability (ARC, 2015). **Intellectual disability (ID)** involves subaverage intellectual functioning (with onset prior to age 18) and three functional deficits in adaptive behavior, such as needing assistance with bathing. Intellectual disability has replaced the term *mental retardation* (Rosa's Law, 2010). Severity of disability can be described as mild, moderate, severe, or profound. Increasingly, the emphasis in defining intellectual disability is focused on adaptive behavior—individuals are categorized in terms of their need for supportive services (intermittent, limited, extensive, and pervasive). Opinion is divided on attitudes toward sexuality of the ID (see *Self-Assessment 11-1*). Kahn and Halpern (2018) analyzed data on 13,845 respondents from adolescence (ages 12–18) to early adulthood (ages 28–34) and found that those with the lowest cognitive ability had lower frequencies of vaginal, oral, and anal sex than those with average cognitive ability.

A team of researchers emphasized the importance of sexuality (including sense of self, sexual role, sexual preference, eroticism, pleasure, intimacy, etc.) in human life, including for the intellectually disabled (Kijak et al., 2013). They surveyed 133 individuals with mild intellectual disability and found that sexual development was delayed by an average of 3 years. Autoerotic behavior was the most common sexual activity, which sometimes occurred in inappropriate places—schools, parks, squares, public toilets, shops, trams, buses, and forests, as well as health-care facilities.

Traumatic brain injury
Closed head injury that results from an exterior force and creates a temporary or enduring impairment in brain functioning

Intellectual disability
Condition that involves subaverage intellectual functioning and deficits in adaptive behavior (also referred to as *mental retardation*)

Petting and sexual intercourse also occurred, but less frequently and later than in a control group of adolescents. The petting/intercourse was typically initiated by the male with another intellectually disabled partner. One of the male respondents commented on his experience:

> *When Ann and I touched each other on the bottom—that was a cool feeling. I was 17 when I had sex with a girl for the first time. She was the same age as me. I did it out of curiosity. She was very scared and even cried. I thought that something bad had happened to her. It was not too good. But now, we have sex and it is really cool.*

The sexual knowledge of the respondents was limited, with only 10% understanding the notion of contraception. Balancing the rights of the intellectually disabled against the social norms of propriety and preventing pregnancy or STIs remain challenges. A review of 20 studies on the methods for teaching sex education to individuals with intellectual disabilities found that the generalization of skills to real-life situations was often not achieved (Schaafsma et al., 2015). In one study, researchers concluded that transitioning to adulthood for intellectually disabled persons is difficult. They "struggled for an 'as normal as possible' adult identity, and to develop sexual identity as a 'normal' identity, in the context of the overshadowing ID identity" (Wilkinson et al., 2015). Many still felt stigmatized, and their caretakers described ongoing challenges (Wilkinson et al., 2015).

There are two basic models for viewing the disabled: the medical model and the social model (Parchomiuk, 2013). The **medical model** (also called the *biological model*) views the individual as coping with a personal tragedy, which implies adjusting to limited functioning. The sexual needs of the individual are viewed as nonexistent. In contrast, the **social model** views intellectual disability as the product of specific social definitions that involve oppression of and discrimination against disabled people. The focus of the social model is to encourage the disabled to get control over their own lives by rejecting the social definitions that limit them.

Educators of individuals with intellectual or developmental disabilities view the sexuality of such individuals as a basic human right (Wilkenfeld & Ballan, 2011). However, these educators do have concerns about the capacity of this population to consent to and facilitate sexual behavior without negative consequences (pregnancy and STIs). People with intellectual disabilities often require extensive assistance in performing activities of daily living. People with autism also reported the need for specialized sex education and the lack of professionals trained to address their relationships and sexual issues/dysfunctions (Teter, 2014).

Becoming pregnant and having a child as an adolescent or adult with an intellectual disability becomes a very complicated endeavor—one that sexuality educators think requires serious consideration. While parents are the logical choice as sex educators for their children with intellectual disabilities, they often lack the specialized skills or choose not to fulfill this role.

A great deal is known about what professionals think about the sexuality of the intellectually disabled, but what do the intellectually disabled themselves think about sex and sexuality? Interviews with 10 women with intellectual disabilities revealed that many could not conceptualize themselves as sexual beings, and they tended to regard sex as a dirty and inappropriate activity for them. They generally believed that other people prohibited them from engaging in sexual activity. The women often considered themselves to be of little value, and the majority had no clear sense of identity (Fitzgerald & Withers, 2013).

Medical model (view of intellectual disability)
Views the intellectually disabled individual as coping with a personal tragedy—which implies adjusting to limited functioning; views their sexual needs as nonexistent (also called the biological model)

Social model (view of intellectual disability)
Views the intellectually disabled individual as the product of specific social definitions that involve oppression and discrimination

Self-Assessment 11-1:
Attitudes Toward Sexuality of
People with an Intellectual Disability

Directions

The items below provide a way to assess your attitudes and beliefs toward the sexuality of persons with an intellectual disability. For each item, identify a number from 0 to 5 that reflects your level of agreement, and write the number in the space provided.

X (Not able to tell), 0 (Completely disagree), 1 (Mostly disagree), 2 (Mildly disagree),

3 (Mildly agree), 4 (Mostly agree), 5 (Completely agree)

1. __ Intellectual disability eliminates sexual needs.
2. __ Individuals with intellectual disability are, in most cases, "forever children" and require constant care.
3. __ Individuals with intellectual disability are, in most cases, incapable of forming marital relationships.
4. __ Individuals with intellectual disability usually express their sexual needs in pathological forms.
5. __ Due to deficits in the cognitive and emotional spheres, individuals with intellectual disability are usually incapable of fidelity in a partnership.
6. __ Intellectual disability is always inherited; hence, individuals with disability should not be allowed to have children.
7. __ Love in a partnership of individuals with intellectual disability is, in most cases, only an attempt to copy observed models and not a genuine feeling.
8. __ Sterilization would protect individuals with intellectual disability from sexual harassment.
9. __ Individuals with intellectual disability tend to commit sex-related crimes.
10. __ Bringing up issues related to sexuality during school education may arouse dormant sexual needs.
11. __ Individuals with intellectual disabilities are very unlikely to form happy relationships with each other.

Scoring

Add each of the 11 items. Total scores ranged from 0–55, with lower scores reflecting more positive views. The lowest possible score is 0, suggesting a very high level of acceptance of sexuality among the intellectually disabled. The highest possible score is 55, suggesting a very low level of acceptance of sexuality among the disabled. The midpoint between 0 and 55 is 27.5. Scores lower than 27.5 would reflect greater approval for sexuality of the intellectually disabled; scores higher than this would reflect greater disapproval for sexuality of the intellectually disabled.

Source: Parchomiuk, M. (2013). Model of Intellectual Disability and the Relationship of Attitudes Towards the Sexuality of Persons with an Intellectual Disability. *Sexuality and Disability, 31*(2), 125–139. Reprinted courtesy of a CC 2.0 International license via Springer.com.

Another challenge for those with ID/DD is their vulnerability to abuse in their interpersonal relationships (Ward et al., 2013). The Friendships and Dating Program was designed to teach the social skills needed to develop healthy, meaningful relationships and to prevent violence in dating and partnered relationships. Thirty-one participant adults revealed that the program was successful in increasing social networks and reducing interpersonal violence.

There is also a prevalence of sexual abuse and assault of people with intellectual disabilities. The percentages range from 63% to 86%, with a high likelihood of repeat victimization. Statistics have also shown that most perpetrators of sexual violence are caregivers, family, and other staff (Muccigrosso, 1991; Tyiska, 1998; Cambridge et al., 2011).

11.6 Mental Illness and Sexuality

Mental disorders are characterized by mild to severe disturbances in thinking, mood, or behavior associated with distress or impaired functioning. *Mental illness* refers collectively to all mental disorders; there are more than 300 classified forms of mental illness.

11.6a Mental Illness and Sexual Dysfunction

Some mental illnesses and their treatments (such as medication) are associated with problems in sexual functioning. For example, major depression is associated with a higher risk of erectile dysfunction in men and lower sexual desire in both women and men. Antidepressant medications are widely recognized as affecting sexual desire and arousal. Patients sometimes stop taking their much-needed medications due to the side effects (Quinn et al., 2012).

Schizophrenia is a mental disorder characterized by social withdrawal and disturbances in thought, motor behavior, and interpersonal functioning. In a comparison of the sexual functioning of institutionalized patients with schizophrenia and noninstitutionalized adults, researchers found that 71.2% of males and 57.1% of females in the institutionalized group experienced sexual dysfunction, compared with 10% of males and 50% of females in the noninstitutionalized group. These dysfunctions included erectile dysfunction, ejaculatory difficulties, and difficulty achieving orgasm (Acuña et al., 2010). Persons with untreated schizophrenia may also report decreased sexual desire and thoughts and are likely to experience interference in their sexual communication and relationships with others. Schizophrenic women are often women of childbearing age and potential mothers who need to be informed by healthcare professionals about intimate relationships and contraception (Seeman, 2013).

11.6b Mental Illness and Barriers to Sexual Expression, Safer Sex, and Contraception

In residential settings for mentally ill persons, such as group homes, lack of privacy and "no sex between residents" policies limit opportunities for sexual expression. Among the noninstitutionalized mentally ill population, the formation of intimate relationships is hindered by the stigma associated with mental illness and by the impaired social skills associated with some disorders. For example, individuals with schizophrenia tend to have fewer sexual relationships than the normal population because of deficits in their social and relational abilities.

Mental disorders
Mental states characterized by mild to severe disturbances in thinking, mood, or behavior associated with distress or impaired functioning (sometimes called mental illness)

Schizophrenia
Mental disorder characterized by social withdrawal and disturbances in thought, motor behavior, and interpersonal functioning

A major barrier to the practice of safer sex and the use of contraception among individuals with mental illness is lack of knowledge and possible inability to provide consent. The families of mentally ill patients may disapprove of their relative's sexual activity, resulting in a lack of support from family members in communicating with the mentally ill about contraception and safer sex. People with mental illness may also have limited incomes and cannot afford the most effective methods of contraception, such as Long Acting Reversible Contraceptives (LARCs), despite insurance through the Affordable Care Act covering the cost in some states.

Some individuals with mental illness may lack the knowledge and the social skills needed to negotiate safer sex, such as persuasion or limit setting. Not only may they not know what contraception is, but they may also lack the skills to discuss contraceptive use with a potential partner. The result may be an unintended pregnancy or STI. Persson and colleagues (2016) reported on the development and implementation of a sex education group for patients admitted to a psychiatric day hospital in Montreal, Quebec, Canada. Patients attending the group noted that it normalized their sexual concerns by providing a safe place in which to learn and to talk about sexuality. Finally, women with serious mental illness often have histories of physical and sexual assault and are at risk for repeated victimization.

Some research suggests that nurses working in mental health are reluctant to discuss sexual issues with their patients (Quinn et al., 2013). Mental health and healthcare professionals are encouraged to be mindful of the need for education in this area.

11.7 Effects of Pain and Fatigue on Sexuality

Persons with illness or disability often experience pain and fatigue. Both of these impact sexuality negatively.

11.7a Pain and Sexuality

Pain can result from a disease or injury or from treatments for the disease or injury. Pain is associated with a number of health problems, including arthritis, migraine headaches, back injuries, multiple sclerosis, cancer, and **endometriosis**—the growth of endometrial tissue outside the uterus (in the fallopian tubes or abdominal cavity). Indeed, pain is a hallmark of endometriosis, a gynecological disorder. A comparison of 46 women with confirmed endometriosis and 80 healthy controls revealed significant differences such as lower arousal, lower orgasm, and higher pain (Ghajarzadeh et al., 2014).

Pain from burn injuries affects not only the physical interest in having sex but also the psychological well-being. Female burn patients in one study reported that they no longer felt sexy, did not want their partners to look at them/their body, and had an overall decrease in sexual behavior (Connell et al., 2015).

Most people with chronic pain have pain-related difficulty with sexual activity. Painful conditions can impair range of motion or make vigorous movement in sexual activity difficult. Pain decreases sexual desire and contributes to emotional distress, anxiety, fatigue, and depression, which interfere with sexual functioning. In one study, 81% of a sample of chronic low-back pain patients complained about sexual difficulties. Libido decrease and painful intercourse were reported, respectively, in 14.8% and 97.5% of the cases. The sexual quality of life reported by the patients was also affected (Bahouq et al., 2013).

Endometriosis
Growth of endometrial tissue outside the uterus, in the fallopian tubes or abdominal cavity, which may cause pain

Various medications can relieve pain, which can have a positive effect on sexuality. However, pain is often undertreated with inadequate doses of pain medication. Pain medication may also have a negative effect on sexual desire.

In addition to minimizing the effects of pain on sexual functioning, couples can explore alternative positions for comfort and substitute noncoital sexual activity. Some sexual positions involve less physical exertion, place little or no weight on painful areas, and permit more control of depth of penetration during intercourse. When pain makes intercourse uncomfortable, couples can explore the pleasures of kissing, massage, cuddling, and oral or manual genital stimulation. Indeed, one option for people suffering from various physical ailments is to redefine how they view sexuality. For some, there can be an increase in sexual satisfaction if focus is taken off of the genitals and placed on the whole-body experience.

Personal REFLECTION

Take a moment to express your thoughts about the following questions. Has pain ever prevented you from having sex? If so, did you discuss this issue with your partner? To what degree did your partner respond with understanding?

11.7b Fatigue and Sexuality

In addition to pain, chronic illness and disability are often accompanied by fatigue. Persons with fatigue feel exhausted, weak, and depleted of energy. Fatigue may result from the effects of an illness or disease on the various body organs. One of the factors that impacts sexuality during aging is fatigue. A team of researchers analyzed longitudinal data and found that low sexual satisfaction was associated with reported fatigue (Syme et al., 2013), which may have a substantial impact on heterosexual couples as they age. As men are traditionally the initiators of sexual activity, when they feel fatigued, there may be a sharp decrease in sexual activity if their female partners follow a traditional gender role and feel uncomfortable taking on the role of initiator.

Fatigue may also be related to a specific illness. For example, individuals with **chronic obstructive pulmonary disease (COPD)**—a collective term for diseases that affect the flow of air into the body, such as asthma, bronchitis, and emphysema— often experience fatigue due to decreased oxygen intake and the effort involved in breathing. Because breathing is difficult for COPD patients (some require an oxygen tank), any activity that increases respiration rate, including sexual activity, may be beyond the person's physical capability.

Fatigue may also result from medication or other medical treatments. The emotional and psychological stress that accompanies chronic illness and disability also produces fatigue, not only for patients but also for their intimate partners. Patients and their partners may spend a great deal of emotional energy trying to cope with the illness or disability.

When chronic fatigue interferes with sexual interest or functioning, several interventions may be helpful. First, the fatigued person might engage in sexual behavior at a time when they feel most rested and have the most energy. Second, the person may explore different positions for sexual activity and noncoital sexual behaviors that are less demanding. Third, counseling may help a person work through the conflicts of accepting the illness or disability in an effort to reduce psychological fatigue.

Chronic obstructive pulmonary disease
Collective term for diseases that affect the flow of air into the body, such as asthma, bronchitis, and emphysema (Individuals with COPD often experience fatigue due to decreased oxygen intake and the effort involved in breathing.)

11.8 Effects of Medical Treatment on Sexuality

Although medical treatments, such as medication, radiation, and surgery, can improve sexual functioning, they can also reduce sexual desire, produce erectile dysfunction or vaginal dryness, cause difficulty in reaching orgasm, and/or lead to ejaculation problems.

11.8a Effects of Surgery on Sexuality

Surgery can have positive effects on sexuality when it alleviates a condition that interferes with sexual functioning. For example, a man who lacks interest in sex due to chronic back pain may find renewed libido following successful back surgery. Or a woman who avoids sexual activity because she has endometriosis may be free of pain and able to enjoy intercourse again following surgery to remove the endometrial tissue.

However, surgical treatment of medical problems can also have a negative impact on sexuality. For example, surgery for gynecologic cancer can affect sexuality, reproductive function, and overall quality of life. Indeed, surgery can affect sexuality by removing a part of the body involved in sexual activity and causing negative changes in body image and self-concept (Carter et al., 2013).

Hysterectomy

Surgical removal of the uterus, known as a **hysterectomy**, is the second most common surgery performed on women in the United States (after the caesarean section). Surgical removal of the ovaries, called **oophorectomy**, alters estrogen levels in women, resulting in what is known as **surgical menopause**. The sudden decrease in estrogen can lead to decreased desire, vaginal dryness, and dyspareunia. Hormone replacement therapy can alleviate these sexual dysfunction symptoms.

Surgery does not inevitably result in changes such as loss of libido. In a survey of 258 women who had undergone one of five types of hysterectomy, no differences were observed in change in sexual desire among the various types (Lermann et al., 2013).

Mastectomy and Lumpectomy

Women and men with breast cancer may have **breast-conserving therapy** (BCT, commonly known as *lumpectomy*), a **mastectomy** (surgical removal of the breast), or a **double mastectomy** (removal of both breasts). Women who have a mastectomy commonly struggle to accept their body image and may choose to wear prosthetic breasts that are inserted into a bra or glued onto the body. Alternatively, they may choose to undergo reconstructive surgery to form a new breast (or two new breasts, if they have had a double mastectomy). In a reconstructed breast, feelings of pleasure from touching the breast and nipple are largely lost because the nerve that supplies feeling to the nipple is cut during surgery.

About 20% of women who have had mastectomies choose to "go flat"—avoid further surgery or wear prosthetics. This enables faster recovery from the mastectomy and prevents problems with reduced muscle strength and other risks of reconstructive surgery (BreastCancer.org, 2019).

Shaw and colleagues (2016) conducted interviews with 22 female breast cancer survivors who attempted to form new relationships post-breast cancer. Seven themes were revealed: the women's decision to consider dating, their ability/desire to commence a new relationship, cancer-related disclosure, changes to intimacy and sexuality, body image difficulties, changing values, and trusting a new partner.

Hysterectomy
Surgical removal of the uterus

Oophorectomy
Surgical removal of the ovaries

Surgical menopause
Sudden decrease in estrogen resulting from removal of the ovaries that can lead to decreased desire, vaginal dryness, and dyspareunia

Breast-conserving therapy
Removal of the cancerous lump rather than the whole breast (also called lumpectomy)

Mastectomy
Surgical removal of one breast

Double mastectomy
Removal of both breasts

In a study of the prevalence of sexual dysfunction in young women with breast cancer, Kedde and colleagues (2013) found that among women who were still undergoing treatment, 64% had a sexual dysfunction, and among those who had completed treatment, 45% had a sexual dysfunction. Radical mastectomy was associated with female orgasmic disorder and early menopause dyspareunia (Kedde et al., 2013).

Radical Prostatectomy, Orchiectomy, and Penectomy

Treatment for prostate cancer may involve surgical removal of the prostate—a procedure known as a **radical prostatectomy**—and/or surgical removal of the testicles, known as an **orchiectomy**. Removal of both testicles stops the production of the hormone testosterone that nourishes the cancer. These surgical procedures result in infertility. Other sexual effects of these surgeries include erection problems; low sexual desire; and lack of orgasm, dry orgasm, and weaker orgasm. A study of 28 heterosexual couples in which the husband had a prostatectomy revealed the challenges of coping with changes. Men reported mild erectile dysfunction, incontinence, and low sexual satisfaction. A major coping mechanism was placing a lower priority on sexual activity (Wittmann et al., 2015). Cryotherapy is an alternative to radical prostatectomy that typically does not result in loss of erection or loss of bladder function.

Orchiectomy is also performed for testicular cancer, although in this case, the surgeon usually removes only the affected testicle, leaving the man with one testicle. Fertility, sexual desire, and sexual functioning are rarely affected when only one testicle is removed. After undergoing surgical removal of a testicle, a man can have a silicone gel–filled prosthesis surgically implanted in his scrotum to regain a more natural look.

When a man has cancer of the penis or of the bottom part of the urethra, treatment may involve **penectomy**—surgical removal of part of or the entire penis. Following a partial penectomy, in which only the end of the penis is removed, the remaining shaft still becomes erect with excitement, and sexual penetration can usually be achieved. Even though the most sensitive area of the penis (the glans, or "head") is gone, a man can still experience orgasm and ejaculation. A total penectomy involves removing the entire penis. The surgeon creates a new opening for the urethra, and the man expels urine from a tube between his scrotum and his anus. The man can experience pleasure by stimulating the area between the anus and the scrotum. He can pleasure his partner through manual or oral stimulation or by stimulation with a vibrator.

Ostomy Surgery

During ostomy surgery, a portion of the large or small intestine or urinary system is rerouted and brought to the skin surface of the abdomen. The resulting protruding portion of bowel is called a **stoma** (also referred to as an *ostomy*) and has a moist, reddish appearance similar to the lining inside the mouth. Depending on the type of surgery, urine or stool leaves the body through the stoma and is collected in a pouch adhered to the abdomen and worn under clothing. The most common reason for **ostomy surgery** is cancer, usually of the colon, rectum, bladder, cervix, or ovaries.

Ostomy surgery affects sexuality primarily through its negative effects on sexual self-concept and body image. A person with a stoma cannot control the elimination of urine, gas, or stool from the body. Functions previously conducted in private (urination, defecation, and passage of gas) are now out of control in public situations. This loss of control can be unnerving. However, these inconveniences are viewed in context. In a study assessing the quality of life and changes in sexuality of patients with rectal cancer who had an ostomy, in-depth interviews with 26 patients (both male and female) revealed difficulty related to exercise, sleep, social activities, and sexuality. However, patients' perception of the quality of life with a stoma "appears to

Radical prostatectomy
Surgical removal of the prostate

Orchiectomy
Surgical removal of the testicles

Penectomy
Surgical removal of part or all of the penis

Stoma
Protruding portion of the large or small intestine (bowel) or urinary system that is rerouted and brought to the skin surface of the abdomen during ostomy surgery (also called ostomy)

Ostomy surgery
Surgery whereby a portion of the large or small intestine or urinary system is rerouted and brought to the skin surface of the abdomen, where the contents are collected in a bag (Cancers of the colon, rectum, bladder, cervix, or ovaries are typical causes of ostomy surgery.)

have undergone a response shift through recalibration of their standards for measuring quality of life" in the sense that these difficulties were viewed as less important in comparison with cancer-related mortality (Neuman et al., 2012).

Cardiovascular Disease

The American Heart Association issued new guidelines on sexual activity for individuals with cardiovascular disease and their partners (Steinke et al., 2013). The document emphasizes the social, psychological, and physical factors that cardiovascular patients are to consider in regard to sexual functioning. Basically, patients are advised to consult their physician about their level of health and the medications they are taking before resuming strenuous sexual activity. Hugging, holding, and physical intimacy focused on enjoying arousal is safe, but use of medications (such as Viagra) should occur only if recommended by a physician.

11.9 Effects of Medication and Radiation on Sexuality

Medication can improve sexual functioning either by (a) directly affecting sexual response (for example, Viagra, Levitra, and Cialis improve erectile functioning) or (b) alleviating the health problem that underlies the sexual dysfunction (aspirin relieves pain that interferes with sexual desire). However, many commonly prescribed medications, including antidepressants, antihypertensives (for high blood pressure), and drugs for heartburn, interfere with sexual desire and functioning. Some prescription pain medications produce sedation, constipation, and nausea—symptoms that diminish interest in sexual activity.

Chemotherapy medication and radiation treatment for cancer patients produce nausea and fatigue, which reduce sexual desire. Hair loss, weight loss, and paleness—other common effects of cancer treatment—can reduce sexual desire by creating feelings of unattractiveness.

Medications and radiation can also interfere with fertility and reproduction. For example, women who must take medication regularly to control a health condition—such as antiseizure medicine for epilepsy—are advised to avoid getting pregnant because the medication they must take could result in birth defects. In addition, this medicine can also disrupt certain types of hormonal contraceptives.

Chemotherapy drugs and radiation used to treat cancer of the pelvic area can either temporarily or permanently damage ovaries, affecting fertility in women, and can slow semen production, affecting fertility in men. Yaman and Ayaz (2016) interviewed 17 married women about their experience with gynecological cancer. The women reported psychological problems that included frustration/despair, depression, anger, negative body image, and problems with their sex lives. Coping mechanisms included prayer and support from family and others. The majority said that they were able to cope through denial.

When a medication has a negative sexual side effect, a doctor may suggest that the patient wait to see if the problem subsides, change the drug's schedule or dosage, switch to a different drug, or suggest taking another drug to counteract or neutralize the first drug's side effect. Alternative therapies that can relieve pain without the sexual side effects associated with medication include biofeedback, hypnosis, yoga, meditation, Pilates, and acupuncture.

11.10 **Alcohol, Other Drugs, and Sexuality**

Use of alcohol or other drugs is considered a mental illness when it meets the criteria for substance dependence or **substance abuse**—that is, the person no longer fulfills vital roles in work, relationships, and health (see Table 11-1). Alcohol is the most frequently used recreational drug in our society and on college and university campuses (see *Social Policy 11-1*). Eaton et al. (2015) estimated that 4.3 million American adults regularly drink alcohol prior to having sex and that doing so is associated with generalized anxiety disorder and alcohol dependence. Use of drugs and sex has been referred to as *chemsex* and thought to be a public health problem in that it may lead to HIV and STIs.

Substance abuse
The overuse or overdependence on drugs or chemicals that results in a failure to fulfill obligations at work, school, or home, the effects of which include danger (such as driving while impaired), recurrent substance-related legal problems, and continued substance use despite its negative effect on social or interpersonal relationships (also called substance dependence)

TABLE **11-1** | **Criteria for Substance Dependence and Abuse**

Substance Dependence	Substance Abuse
Drug tolerance (more and more of the drug is needed to experience the effects)	Failure to fulfill role obligations at work, school, or home due to substance use
Giving up important social, occupational, or recreational activities because of substance use	Recurrent substance-related legal problems
Continued substance use despite knowledge that such use contributes to a physical or psychological problem	Continued substance use despite its negative effect on social or interpersonal relationships

Social Policy 11-1

Alcohol Abuse on Campus

While some college students do not drink, most do. And, some have a problem with alcohol. Of 2,935 undergraduate males, 13% agreed that "I have a problem with alcohol" (of 9,749 undergraduate females, 9% agreed) (Hall & Knox, 2019).

At a northeastern university, increases in both frequency and volume were noted over a 6-year period—particularly in females, those over 21, those living off campus, and those performing well academically. Individuals with personalities characterized by urgency and sensation-seeking also drink more and have more binges and more alcohol problems (Shin et al., 2012). Alcohol and other drug use (Pedrelli et al., 2013), including energy drinks (Snipes & Benotsch, 2013), are correlated—as is the greater likelihood of cohabitation, early marriage, and divorce (Williams et al., 2012).

Campus policies throughout the United States include alcohol-free dorms; alcohol bans, enforcement, and sanctions; peer support; alerting parents; education; and alcohol-free events. An example of the latter is Western State Colorado University, which offers late-night movies, $1 breakfasts, dances, and a safe spring break alternative. The University of Albany also has a year-round campaign that addresses making healthy choices, not just a brochure distributed during freshmen orientation.

Most colleges and universities do not ban alcohol or its possession on campus. Indeed, some sell alcohol at football games to boost revenue. Some attorneys think colleges and universities can be held liable for not stopping dangerous drinking patterns, but others argue that college is a place for students to learn how to behave responsibly.

11.10a **Alcohol and Sexuality**

Alcohol is a central nervous system depressant that physiologically suppresses sexual response for anyone who drinks. It can interfere with sexual arousal, penile erection, vaginal lubrication, and ability to achieve orgasm. *Self-Assessment 11-2* allows you to identify your motives for drinking alcohol.

Whereas some partners consume alcohol to enhance sexual intimacy, others drink to suppress their negative feelings toward sex or toward their partner and to tolerate sexual relations. Long-term alcohol use in high doses can lead to cirrhosis and other diseases of the liver and a number of other health problems that affect sexual functioning and relationships. In men, alcoholism can lead to decreases in testosterone, loss of facial hair, breast enlargement, decreased libido, and erectile dysfunction. In women, alcoholism can interfere with menstruation and ovulation, leading to early menopause.

Alcohol—it provokes the desire, but takes away the performance.

Shakespeare

(Andrea Sosa)

Alcohol is the most commonly used drug by college students. Not only does it reduce inhibitions resulting in more sex with more partners it impacts sexual functioning of both partners.

11.10b **Other Recreational Drugs and Sexuality**

Recreational drugs are often used with the intention of enhancing sexual pleasure. Regarding marijuana (cannabis), Moser (2019) analyzed data from a survey completed by 811 social media respondents who revealed that cannabis use was associated with reporting both enhanced sexual functioning and satisfaction. Age and gender were not found to have significant effects on cannabis use and sexual functioning and satisfaction. Participants reported increased desire, orgasm intensity, and masturbation pleasure. Results indicated that taste and touch were enhanced when using cannabis.

Another drug sometimes used to enhance sexual pleasure is **ecstasy**, also known as *MDMA*, *X*, *Molly*, or *E*. Ecstasy has both stimulant and psychedelic effects that can result in increased energy; enhanced sense of pleasure and self-confidence; and feelings of peacefulness, acceptance, and closeness with others. Although these effects of ecstasy can enhance sexual pleasure, the drug is also associated with a number of dangerous risks, including dehydration, hyperthermia, seizures, and heart or kidney failure.

Cocaine (snorted or injected) or crack (smoked) use has a significant negative effect on sexual function and overall health. Although new users of cocaine may perceive a positive effect, this is not specifically a sexual effect; rather, it is likely a function of the overall feeling of confidence and energy associated with the use of the drug. However, regular or long-term use results in diminished sexual desire, erectile ability, and ability to have an orgasm. In addition, using cocaine increases the risk of heart attack, sudden death, and other cardiovascular conditions.

Crystal methamphetamine is a stimulant that decreases inhibitions, enhances libido, and heightens perceptions of sexual intensity. Although it constricts the blood vessels, interfering with prolonged erection, some users counter that effect by using Viagra or another similar drug. The hazards of crystal meth are great, and the drug is highly addictive. Its use promotes risky sexual behaviors and, especially among gay men, is substantially linked with HIV and other STIs. It causes long-term damage to the brain (to all users, not only addicts) and can result in heart failure, stroke, memory loss, paranoia, anorexia, malnutrition, and dehydration.

Ecstasy
Drug with both stimulant and psychedelic effects that can result in increased energy; enhanced sense of pleasure and self-confidence; and feelings of peacefulness, acceptance, and closeness with others; also known as MDMA, X, Molly, or E (use is also associated with dangerous risks, such as heart failure)

Self-Assessment 11-2: Motives for Drinking Alcohol Scale

Read the list of reasons people sometimes give for drinking alcohol.
Thinking of all the times you drink, how often would you say you drink for each of the following reasons?

Directions

Write the appropriate number after reading each item.

1 (never/almost never), 2 (some of the time), 3 (half of the time), 4 (most of the time), 5 (almost always)

1. __ To help me to enjoy a party
2. __ To be sociable
3. __ To make social gatherings more fun
4. __ To improve parties and celebrations
5. __ To celebrate a special occasion with friends
6. __ To forget my worries
7. __ To help my depression or nervousness
8. __ To cheer me up
9. __ To make me feel more self-confident
10. __ To help me forget about problems
11. __ Because the effects of alcohol feel good
12. __ Because it is exciting
13. __ To get high
14. __ Because it gives me a pleasant feeling
15. __ Because it is fun
16. __ Because of pressure from friends
17. __ To avoid disapproval for not drinking
18. __ To fit in with the group
19. __ To be liked
20. __ To avoid feeling left out

Scoring

The four basic drinking motives are social, coping, enhancement, and conformity. The items for these and the average scores from 1,243 respondents follow. The lowest score reflecting each motive is 1 = never; the highest score reflecting each motive is 5 = always. The most frequent motive for women and men is to be sociable. The least frequent motive for women and men is to conform. To compare your score with other respondents, add the numbers you circled for each of the following: social, coping, enhancement, and conformity reasons identified. For example, to ascertain the degree to which your motivation for drinking alcohol is to be sociable, add the numbers you circled for items 1 through 5.

Again, the basic reasons for drinking are social, coping, enhancement, and conformity. Items 1, 2, 3, 4, and 5 pertain to social drinking; items 6, 7, 8, 9, and 10 pertain to coping drinking; items 11, 12, 13, 14, and 15 pertain to enhancement drinking; and items 16, 17, 18, 19, and 20 pertain to conformity drinking. In this study, female respondents scored 2.29 for social drinking, 1.61 for coping drinking, 1.99 for enhancement drinking, and 1.34 for conformity drinking. Male respondents scored 2.63 for social drinking, 1.59 for coping drinking, 2.33 for enhancement drinking, and 1.43 for conformity drinking.

Source: Copyright ©1994, American Psychological Association; adapted with permission. Cooper, M. L. (1994). Motivations for alcohol use among adolescents: Development and validation of a four factor model. *Psychological Assessment, 6*(2), 117–128.

Drugs and Erectile Dysfunction

Here are some of the illicit, abused, prescription, and over-the-counter medications that have been associated with erectile dysfunction in some patients:

- Diuretics and high blood pressure drugs
- Antidepressants, anti-anxiety drugs, and antiepileptic drugs
- Antihistamines
- Muscle relaxants
- Non-steroidal anti-inflammatory drugs
- Parkinson's disease medications
- Antiarrythmics
- Prostate cancer medications
- Chemotherapy drugs
- Tobacco
- Alcohol
- Barbiturates

Source: WebMD. (2019, October). *Drugs Linked to Erectile Dysfunction*. Rev. by N. Q. Bandukwala. Retrieved from https://www.webmd.com/erectile-dysfunction/guide/drugs-linked-erectile-dysfunction

11.10c Alcohol, Drugs, and Unsafe Sex

Use of alcohol and other drugs is associated with having unprotected sex. High-risk sexual behavior associated with substance use may result from the disinhibiting effects of the substance, the effect of the substance on judgment, or the exchange of sex for drugs (or for money to buy drugs).

Chapter Summary

IN THIS CHAPTER, we examined the effects of physical and mental illness, disability, and substance use on sexuality.

Effects of Illness and Disability on Sexuality

THE DISABLED are assumed to be *asexual,* and health-care professionals often ignore their sexuality.

Effects of Illness and Disability on Self-Concept and Body Image

PERSONS WITH CHRONIC ILLNESS OR DISABILITY are vulnerable to developing a negative self-concept and body image. They are also susceptible to viewing themselves as undesirable or inadequate romantic and sexual partners.

Impaired Sensory-Motor Function and Sexuality

A NUMBER OF NEUROLOGICAL DISEASES AND INJURIES, including spinal cord injury, multiple sclerosis (MS), and cerebral palsy (CP)—can result in impaired sensory-motor functioning. The effects of sensory-motor impairment on sexuality are varied and depend, in part, on the type and severity of the illness or injury.

Diabetes and Sexuality

DIABETES MELLITUS is a chronic disease in which the pancreas fails to produce sufficient insulin. In women, diabetes can result in lack of sexual desire and orgasmic dysfunction. Diabetic men may have erectile dysfunction.

Impaired Cognitive Function and Sexuality

MANY ILLNESSES AND INJURIES, such as Alzheimer's disease and other forms of dementia, traumatic brain injury, and intellectual disability—result in impaired cognitive functioning, such as memory loss, language comprehension problems, learning disabilities, and confusion. Inappropriate sexual behavior is common among persons with cognitive impairment. Issues of pregnancy and STIs for the intellectually disabled are challenges for health-care professionals.

Mental Illness and Sexuality

MENTAL DISORDERS are characterized by mild to severe disturbances in thinking, mood, or behavior associated with distress or impaired functioning. Some mental illnesses and their treatments (medication) are associated with problems in sexual functioning. Major depression is associated with a higher risk of erectile dysfunction in men and lower sexual desire in both women and men. Some antidepressant medications used to treat depression interfere with sexual desire and arousal.

Effects of Pain and Fatigue on Sexuality

PAIN can impair range of motion or make vigorous movement difficult during sexual activity. Pain decreases sexual desire and contributes to emotional distress, anxiety, fatigue, and depression.

Effects of Medical Treatment on Sexuality

ALTHOUGH MEDICAL TREATMENTS such as medication, radiation, and surgery can improve sexual functioning, they can also reduce sexual desire, produce erectile dysfunction or vaginal dryness, cause difficulty in reaching orgasm, or lead to ejaculation problems. Surgery can also affect sexuality by removing a part of the body involved in sexual activity, causing negative changes in body image and self-concept, affecting hormonal levels, and causing infertility.

Effects of Medication and Radiation on Sexuality

Medication can improve sexual functioning either by directly affecting sexual response or by alleviating the health problem that underlies the sexual dysfunction. However, many commonly prescribed medications interfere with sexual desire and functioning.

Alcohol, Other Drugs, and Sexuality

ALCOHOL is a central nervous system depressant that physiologically suppresses sexual response. It can interfere with sexual arousal, penile erection, and ability to achieve orgasm. Long-term alcohol use in high doses can lead to cirrhosis and other diseases of the liver, as well as a number of other health problems that affect sexual functioning and relationships.

Recreational drugs, such as marijuana and ecstasy, are often used with the intention of enhancing sexual pleasure. Ecstasy is associated with a number of dangerous risks, including dehydration, hyperthermia, seizures, and heart or kidney failure. Use of alcohol and other drugs is associated with having unprotected sex.

Web Links

MedlinePlus®

> https://www.medlineplus.gov

HealthFinder

> https://www.healthfinder.gov

Key Terms

Agnosia **288**

Alzheimer's disease **288**

Aphasia **288**

Apraxia **288**

Breast-conserving therapy **295**

Cerebral palsy **286**

Chronic obstructive
    pulmonary disease **294**

Dementia **288**

Diabetes mellitus **286**

Disability **281**

Double mastectomy **295**

Ecstasy **299**

Endometriosis **293**

Hysterectomy **295**

Intellectual disability **289**

Mastectomy **295**

Medical model (view of
    intellectual disability) **290**

Mental disorders **292**

Multiple sclerosis **285**

Oophorectomy **295**

Orchiectomy **296**

Ostomy surgery **296**

Paraplegia **284**

Penectomy **296**

Quadriplegia **284**

Radical prostatectomy **296**

Schizophrenia **292**

Social model (view of
    intellectual disability) **290**

Stoma **296**

Substance abuse **298**

Surgical menopause **295**

Traumatic brain injury **289**

CHAPTER
12

Contraception and Abortion

If you have no control over your reproduction, you have no control over your life.

Joycelyn Elders, former surgeon general

Chapter Outline

12.1 Contraception 308
    Self-Assessment 12-1:
      Contraceptive Behavior
      Scale (CBS) **309**
    12.1a Hormonal Methods **309**
    12.1b Barrier Methods **312**
    12.1c Natural Family Planning
      Methods **317**
    12.1d Withdrawal **319**
    12.1e Emergency Contraception **319**
    Technology and Sexuality 12-1:
      Contraception **321**
12.2 Sterilization 321
    12.2a Female Sterilization **322**
    12.2b Male Sterilization **322**

12.3 Abortion 324
    12.3a Methods of Abortion **324**
    12.3b Abortion Rights in the United
      States: Activism, Court Rulings,
      and Legislation **328**
    12.3c Attitudes Toward Abortion **330**
    12.3d International Access **331**
    12.3e Physical and
      Psychological Effects **332**
    Personal Decisions 12-1
      Deciding Whether to Have
      an Abortion **333**

Web Links 335
Key Terms 335

Objectives

1. Define contraception and list the various methods
2. Identify the five most frequently used forms of contraception for college students
3. Identify the different types of abortion
4. Know the divergent attitudes and political positions in regard to abortion
5. Recognize and understand the physical and psychological effects of abortion

(Amberlynn Bishop)

Truth — OR — Fiction?

T / F 1. Web-based sexual health programs are effective for improving intentions to communicate about sexual health in relationships.

T / F 2. In contrast to hooking up, individuals in a relationship are less likely to use a condom.

T / F 3. The younger the person, the more likely the person to have had a repeat abortion.

T / F 4. Child maltreatment is associated with subsequent unintended pregnancy.

T / F 5. UPA (ulipristal acetate) is now recommended as the first choice for hormonal emergency contraception (EC).

Answers: 1. T   2. T   3. F   4. T   5. T

P ublic debate continues over the appropriateness of teaching about contraception in the public school system as well as access to abortion in the United States. In spite of the outcome of the Supreme Court's landmark *Roe v. Wade* decision legalizing abortion some states continue to restrict abortion.

The debates might be viewed in historical context—that women have forever sought to control the timing of their getting pregnant and having children. Ancient Roman and Greek records discuss women relying on dances and amulets to prevent pregnancy. Other examples of early contraception include lemons, cotton, rue, black cohosh, and papaya seeds. In this chapter we review the various methods of contraception, sometimes referred to as *family planning, fertility regulation,* or *birth control*.

The truth is that contraception saves lives, prevents unplanned pregnancies, improves outcomes for children and reduces the number of abortions.

Ann McLane Kuster, politician

While the terms male and female are socially constructed gender terms, they are used in this chapter to indicate body parts. The authors recognize that anyone with a uterus can get pregnant, no matter how they identify their gender. For the ease of language, the term "female" indicates a person with a uterus and "male" a person with a penis.

12.1 Contraception

About half of all pregnancies in the United States are unintended (Cassell, 2015). All contraceptive methods have one of three goals: to prevent the sperm from fertilizing the egg—(to prevent conception), to suppress ovulation, or to keep the fertilized egg from implanting in the uterus. The method used is not only an individual decision, but also ideally, one that is negotiated with a partner. Researchers have noted that power imbalances emanating from gender and age may impact a person's ability to negotiate safer sex practices (Taylor, 1995). Depression and psychological stress may also have a negative impact on contraceptive use (Wiley & Wilson, 2014). Social class is related to contraceptive use, as well as the education level—the more educated the individual, the more deliberate the use of contraception (Sassler & Miller, 2014). Gender also interacts with social class and the sex ratio on college campuses—women with lower socioeconomic status are less likely to report using condoms when more women than men are on campus (Bearak, 2014). Before reviewing the various types of contraception, consider taking *Self-Assessment 12-1: Contraceptive Behavior Scale* to assess your use of contraception.

Table 12-1 reflects the top five most commonly used contraceptives by college students in the United States. Over 50% also reported using the male condom with other methods. Such condom use emphasized that college students are mindful of preventing not only unintended pregnancy but also STIs. However, over time, most couples in a relationship stop using condoms and give "dislike using a condom" and "feels better without" as the primary reason (Mullinax et al., 2017).

TABLE 12-1	Reported Contraceptive Used by College Students During Last Vaginal Intercourse
Type of Contraceptive	**Percentage**
Male condom	58.8
Oral contraceptives	53.5
Withdrawal	31.1
Intrauterine device	14.1
Birth control implants	9.1

Data source: American College Health Association. (2018). American College Health Association-National College Health Assessment II: Reference Group Executive Summary Spring 2018. Silver Spring, MD: American College Health Association; 2018. Retrieved from https://www.acha.org/documents/ncha/NCHA-II_Spring_2018 _Reference_Group_Executive_Summary.pdf

Self-Assessment 12-1:
Contraceptive Behavior Scale (CBS)

In taking the CBS, participants respond according to the degree of consistency between their actual practice and the statement of the item, which is rated from 0 (totally no correspondence) to 4 (total correspondence). Higher scores (4 is the top score) indicate better contraceptive behaviors.

1. __ I practice contraception each time I have sex.
2. __ I have a preferred contraceptive method used to prevent pregnancy (safe period combined with condom or coitus interruptus combined with condom).
3. __ I pay attention to any contraceptive information that enables me to have good contraceptive practice.
4. __ When I am doubtful about the safety of a contraceptive method after having sex with my partners, I will take other compensatory methods (take emergency contraceptive pills or consult friends to take action).
5. __ I use a contraceptive method accurately.

Scoring

Add the numbers you gave for each item and divide by 5: 4 is the top score, indicating a high level of contraceptive behavior, and 0 is the lowest possible score.

Norms

The Contraceptive Behavior Scale was completed by 525 sexually active adolescents. The mean score was 2.72, with a standard deviation of 2.11.

Validity and Reliability

See article referenced below.

Republished with permission of John Wiley & Sons, from Wang, R. H., Jian, S. Y., & Yang, Y. M. (July, 2011). Psychometric testing of the Chinese version of the Contraceptive Behavior Scale: A preliminary study. *Journal of Clinical Nursing, 22*(7–8), 1066–1072; permission conveyed through Copyright Clearance Center, Inc.

12.1a Hormonal Methods

Hormonal methods of contraception currently available to women include "the pill," NEXPLANON® (its precursor, IMPLANON®, has been discontinued in the United States), Depo-Provera® or Depo-subQ Provera 104®, NuvaRing®, and Ortho Evra®. Women may choose to use different hormonal methods throughout their lives. Stern (2018) noted the importance of health practitioners being supportive of individuals making changes in their choice of contraceptive.

Oral Contraceptives

The birth control pill is the most commonly used method of all the nonsurgical forms of contraception. Although a small percentage of people who take the pill still become pregnant, it remains an effective birth control option for many.

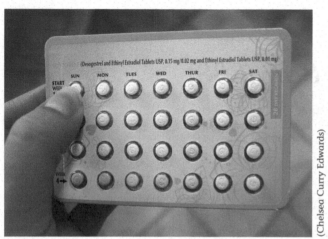

(Chelsea Curry Edwards)

The Pill remains the most commonly used contraceptive.

Oral contraceptives are available in two types: the combination pill and the minipill. There are many types of combination pills; however, they all contain estrogen and progestin and usually have both active and inactive pills. Most monthly combination pill packets have at least four inactive pills, or placebos, which have no hormones. These inactive pills are designed to keep the user in the routine of taking a pill while allowing them to have a few hormone-free days. They are not necessary to prevent pregnancy and can be skipped, although this should be discussed with a health-care provider.

The multiphasic combination pill varies in the amount of each hormone in each active pill. Monophasic combination pills have the same levels of hormones in every active pill. Both multiphasic and monophasic combination pills work by raising the natural level of hormones in a person's body, inhibiting ovulation, and creating an environment where sperm cannot easily reach the egg. The second type of birth control pill, the minipill, contains the same progesterone-like hormone found in the combination pill but does not contain estrogen. Progestin-only pills are taken every day, with no hormone-free interval. The progestin in the minipill creates a hostile environment for sperm and does not allow implantation of a fertilized egg in the uterus. Unlike the combination pill, however, the minipill does not always inhibit ovulation. The minipill has also been associated with a higher incidence of irregular bleeding.

In most states (excluding Oregon and California), neither the combination pill nor the minipill is available unless prescribed by a health-care provider. Contraindications—reasons for not using birth control pills—include hypertension, impaired liver function, known or suspected tumors that are estrogen-dependent, undiagnosed abnormal genital bleeding, pregnancy at the time of the examination, and a history of poor blood circulation or blood clotting.

The major complications associated with taking oral contraceptives are blood clots and high blood pressure. Also, the risk of heart attack is increased for those who smoke or have other risk factors for heart disease. Although the long-term negative consequences of taking birth control pills are still the subject of research, some people who use them experience short-term negative effects. These side effects include increased susceptibility to vaginal infections, nausea, slight weight gain, vaginal bleeding between periods, breast tenderness, headaches, and mood changes (some people become depressed and experience a loss of sexual desire). Users should also be aware of situations in which the pill is not effective, such as when combined with certain prescription medications and when pills are missed. The pill is also not as effective if it is not taken at the same time every day. On the positive side, pill use reduces the incidence of ectopic pregnancy and offers many noncontraceptive benefits including: regular menses, less dysmenorrhea, and reduced incidence of ovarian and endometrial cancers.

Finally, people should be aware that pill use is associated with an increased incidence of chlamydia and gonorrhea. One reason for the association of pill use and a higher incidence of STIs is that sexually active people who use the pill sometimes erroneously feel that because they are protected from becoming pregnant, they are also protected from contracting STIs. The pill provides no protection against STIs; the only methods that provide some protection against STIs are condoms.

For most people using the contraceptive pill for birth control, the chances of experiencing adverse effects are greatly outweighed by the very high protection against pregnancy, as well as other short- and possibly long-term health benefits (Hannaford, 2013).

An option for people using oral contraception is to skip the placebo pills and use the pill continuously. Some who like to experience vaginal bleeding a few times a year, may take a one-week hormone break every 12 weeks. This type of use is called extended use. Others may choose not to have vaginal bleeding, and will continuously take the pill. This is called continuous use (WHO/RHR & CCP, 2018). For those who choose to do either continuous or extended use, there may be problems with irregular bleeding for the first few months.

NEXPLANON

There have been various subdermal implants (such as Jadelle®), but only IMPLANON's replacement, **NEXPLANON**, is currently on the market in the United States. The difference between the products is an improved applicator and a small amount of barium sulfate added to NEXPLANON that makes the implant visible on x-ray, computed tomography (CT) scan, ultrasound scan, and magnetic resonance imaging (MRI). This helps health-care providers confirm the implant is correctly in place and aids them in locating it for removal. The NEXPLANON implant is a single, flexible plastic rod the size of a matchstick that releases a progestin hormone called etonogestrel that prevents ovaries from releasing eggs and that thickens the cervical mucus to help block sperm from reaching the egg.

A health-care provider inserts the implant just under the skin of the inner side of a woman's upper arm, and the implant provides pregnancy protection for up to 3 years—although it may be removed at any time. The implant contains no estrogen, which makes it a viable contraceptive solution for some women who have contraindications to estrogen use. Irregular bleeding is the most common side effect, especially in the first 6–12 months of use (Sharp & Dohme, 2016).

Depo-Provera or Depo-subQ Provera 104

Depo-Provera, also known as *Depo* or the *shot*, is a long-acting, reversible, hormonal contraceptive that is injected every 3 months. Side effects of Depo-Provera include menstrual spotting, irregular bleeding, and some heavy bleeding the first few months of use, although 8 out of 10 people using Depo-Provera will eventually experience amenorrhea, or the absence of a menstrual period. Mood changes, headaches, dizziness, and fatigue have also been observed. Some women report a weight gain of 5–10 pounds. Also, after the injections are stopped, it takes an average of 18 months before the person will become pregnant at the same rate as people who have not used Depo-Provera.

The thought of getting pregnant again is terrific birth control.

Bethany Lopez, *Indelible*

Depo-Provera has been associated with significant loss of bone density that may not be completely reversible after discontinuing use. The FDA recommends that Depo-Provera only be used for no longer than 2 years, hence the medication's black-box warning that prolonged use could result in a loss of bone density.

Similarly, Depo-subQ Provera 104 is an injection method that offers a 30% lower hormone dosage than Depo-Provera. While Depo-Provera is injected deep into the muscle, Depo-subQ Provera 104 is injected just beneath the skin. Depo-subQ Provera 104 has similar benefits, risks, and side effects, as well as the same black-box warning for risk of significant loss of bone density as described for Depo-Provera. However, the lower amount of hormone may mean slightly fewer progestin-related side effects. Less long-term information is available about its effectiveness, although short-term studies show

NEXPLANON
A single, flexible, plastic-rod subdermal implant the size of a matchstick that releases a progestin hormone called etonogestrel and provides up to 3 years of protection against pregnancy

Depo-Provera
A synthetic compound, similar to progesterone, injected into the woman's arm or buttock that protects her against pregnancy for 3 months by preventing ovulation

similar results to Depo-Provera. Depo-subQ Provera 104 injection is also FDA-approved for the treatment of endometriosis-related pain (Mayo Clinic Staff, 2019).

Vaginal Rings

NuvaRing, a soft, flexible, and transparent ring approximately 2 inches in diameter that is worn inside the vagina, provides 3-week-long pregnancy protection. NuvaRing has two major advantages. First, because the hormones are delivered locally rather than systemically, very low levels are administered (the lowest dose of any of the hormonal contraceptives). Second, unlike oral contraceptives, in which the hormone levels rise and fall depending on when the pill is taken, the hormone level from the NuvaRing remains constant. Out of 100 people using NuvaRing for a year under typical conditions, 9 will become pregnant. This method is self-administered. NuvaRing is inserted into the vagina and is designed to release hormones that are absorbed by the person's body for 3 weeks. The ring is then removed for a week, at which time the menstrual cycle will occur; afterward a new ring is inserted. Like extended and continuous use of the pill, users can opt to begin one ring right after the previous one; however, this option should be discussed with your health-care provider.

Transdermal Applications

Ortho Evra is a contraceptive transdermal patch (now available in the United States only as Xulane) that delivers hormones to a woman's body through skin absorption. A new contraceptive patch is applied and left on for a week. After a week, the old patch is removed and a new one is put on. This is repeated for 3 weeks. The patch can be placed anywhere on the butt, upper arm, lower abdomen, and upper body, though it should not be worn on the breasts. The fourth week is patch-free and the time when the menstrual cycle will occur.

An alternative to Xulane, the progestin-only **NEA-TDS (norethindrone acetate transdermal system)** is being developed. This contraceptive patch is worn continuously for 7 days and then replaced with a new patch (rotating sites on the abdomen, buttocks, or hips). Through daily paper diaries kept by 689 users ages 18–47, Simon and colleagues (2013) evaluated its use. While application site reactions (5%) and menstrual disturbances (6%) were the most common adverse reactions, the researchers found no "major safety concerns" that were evident following treatment for up to 1 year of use. NEA-TDS carries a lower risk of blood clots than Xulane and other contraceptive patches, though it has similar cardiovascular risk factors to those of oral contraceptives.

Male Hormonal Methods

There is still no male pill available, anywhere. Research to date suggests that the success rate of a male hormonal contraception using injectable testosterone alone in clinical trials is actually high and comparable to methods for women. Vasalgel™, a reversible, nonhormonal polymer that blocks the vas deferens, has proven effective in baboons and is being viewed as a possible contraceptive in human males.

12.1b Barrier Methods

Some people reject the use of hormonal contraceptives on the basis of not wanting to introduce chemicals into their bodies. Barrier methods provide several alternatives: internal and external condoms, spermicides, diaphragm, and cervical cap.

No glove, no love.

Lauren Oliver, *Before I Fall*

NuvaRing
Soft, flexible, and transparent ring, approximately 2 inches in diameter, that is worn inside the vagina and provides month-long pregnancy protection

NEA-TDS (norethindrone acetate transdermal system)
A contraceptive patch worn continuously for 7 days and then replaced with a new patch (rotating sites on the abdomen, buttocks, or hips)

External Condom

As noted in Table 12-1, the external condom, sometimes referred to as the male condom, is the most frequently reported contraception used by today's college student. The external condom is a thin sheath made of latex, polyurethane (they may also be flavored), polyisoprene, or natural membranes. Latex condoms, which can be used only with water-based lubricants, have been more popular historically. Polyisoprene condoms can be used with oil-based lubricants, are an option for some people who have latex-sensitive allergies, provide some protection against the HIV virus and other sexually transmitted infections, and allow for greater sensitivity during intercourse. Condoms made of natural membranes (sheep intestinal lining) are not recommended because they are not effective in preventing transmission of HIV or other STIs.

The condom works by being rolled over and down the shaft of the erect penis before intercourse (see Figure 12-1). After ejaculation, sperm are caught inside the condom. When used in combination with a spermicidal lubricant that is placed inside the reservoir tip of the condaom, as well as a spermicidal or sperm-killing agent that is inserted inside the vagina, the condom is a highly effective contraceptive. Nonoxynol-9 products, such as condoms that have N-9 as a lubricant, should not be used rectally during anal sex because doing so could *increase* the risk of getting HIV or other STIs.

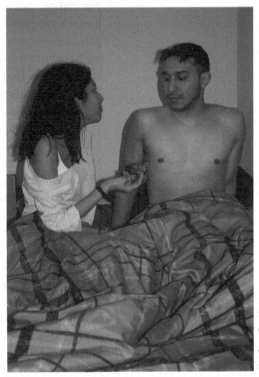

(Andrea Sosa)

Condom before sex is the pattern of most college students today.

FIGURE **12-1** ‖ How to Put on a Condom

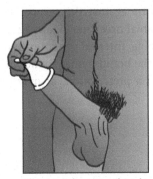

Place condom over head of the erect penis.
If condom does not have reservoir tip, pinch the top of the condom to leave room for semen.

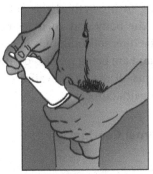

While holding the top, unroll the condom.

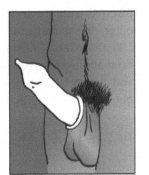

Continue unrolling the condom to the base of the penis.

Like any contraceptive, the condom is effective only when used properly. It should be placed on the penis early enough to avoid any seminal leakage into the vagina. Polyurethane, polyisoprene, or latex condoms with a reservoir tip are preferable because they are less likely to break. Even if the condom has a reservoir tip, air should be squeezed out of the tip as it is being placed on the penis to reduce the chance of breaking during ejaculation. Such breakage may occur, however. (Tip: If the condom breaks, immediately insert a spermicide into the vagina to reduce the risk of pregnancy.) Finally, the penis should be withdrawn from the vagina immediately after ejaculation, before the penis returns to its flaccid state. If the penis is not withdrawn and the erection subsides, semen may leak from the base of the condom into the labia. Alternatively, when the erection subsides, the condom will come off when the penis is withdrawn if the condom is not held onto. Either way, the sperm will begin to travel up the vagina to the reproductive tract, and fertilization may occur. Whenever a condom is used, a spermicide may also be used. In addition to furnishing extra protection, spermicides also provide lubrication, which permits easy entrance of the condom-covered penis into the vagina. If no spermicide is used and the condom is not of the prelubricated variety, a sterile lubricant (such as K-Y Jelly) may be needed. Vaseline or other kinds of petroleum jelly should not be used with condoms because vaginal infections or condom breakage may result. Prior to use, it's also important to check condoms for visible damage and for the date of expiration.

There is sometimes resistance by males to using a condom. **Condom use resistance**, defined as successful attempts to engage in unprotected sexual intercourse with a partner who wants to use a condom, was reported by 81% of men in a sample of 562. Tactics included lying ("I don't have an STI), emotional manipulation ("I love you, this will be good for us"), and stealthing (removing condom without the person's awareness). Males who had a history of sexual aggression and high alcohol consumption were more likely perpetrators of condom use resistance (Stappenbeck et al., 2019). Brodsky (2017) noted **stealthing** which exposes the victim to pregnancy and disease, is a form of abuse that attacks the partner's dignity and autonomy.

Internal Condom

The **internal condom**, sometimes referred to as an insertive or female condom, resembles the external condom except that it fits in the vagina to prevent pregnancy, HIV infection, and other STIs. The newest version of the internal condom, FC2®, is made of nitrile. It is about 6.5 inches long and has flexible rings at both ends. It is inserted with the inner ring fitting behind the pubic bone against the cervix; the outer ring remains outside the body and encircles the labial area (see Figure 12-2). Like the external version, the internal condom is not reusable. Internal condoms have been approved by the FDA and are being marketed under the brand names Femidom® and Reality®. The one-size-fits-all device is available with a prescription, or may be obtained at a reproductive health clinic.

FIGURE **12-2** ‖ The Internal Condom

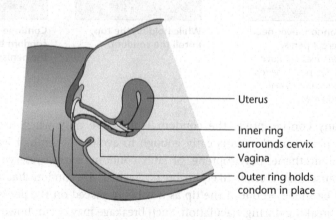

Uterus

Inner ring surrounds cervix

Vagina

Outer ring holds condom in place

Condom use resistance
Successful attempt to engage in unprotected sexual intercourse with a partner who wants to use a condom

Stealthing
Nonconsensual removal during sexual intercourse of a condom which exposes the victim to pregnancy and disease

Internal condom
Lubricated, polyurethane condom that is about 6.5 inches long and has flexible rings at both ends—one inserted vaginally, which covers the cervix, and one external, which partially covers the labia

Internal condoms are durable and may not tear as easily as latex external condoms. Some people may encounter some difficulty with first attempts at insertion. A major advantage of the internal condom is it helps protect against transmission of HIV and other STIs, giving people an option for protection if their partner refuses to wear a condom. Placement may occur up to 8 hours before use, allowing greater spontaneity. The internal condom may also be used during anal sex to help protect against STI and HIV transmission. To use it anally, the inner ring is removed and the condom put over the rectal opening.

There are problems with the internal condom. It can slip out of the vagina, and it is more expensive and harder to obtain since it was moved to prescription-only in 2017. A benefit of this type of condom is that it might be a better option for people with erectile dysfunction since it does not require a full erection.

Vaginal Spermicides

A **spermicide** is a chemical that kills sperm. Vaginal spermicides come in several forms, including foam, cream, jelly, film, and suppository. Current data suggest that spermicidal creams or gels should be used with a diaphragm. Spermicidal foams, creams, gels, suppositories, and films may be used alone or with a condom.

Spermicides must be applied before the penis enters the vagina, no more than 20 minutes before intercourse. Appropriate applicators are included when the product is purchased (see Figure 12-3). Foam is effective immediately. However, suppositories, creams, or jellies require a few minutes to allow the product to melt and spread inside the vagina (package instructions describe the exact time required). Each time intercourse is repeated more spermicide must be applied. Spermicide must be left in place for at least 6–8 hours after intercourse, and the vagina should not be douched or rinsed during this period.

FIGURE **12-3** ‖ Vaginal Spermicides

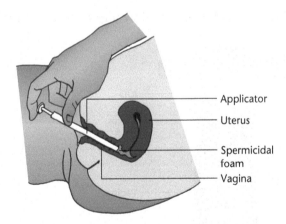

- Applicator
- Uterus
- Spermicidal foam
- Vagina

One advantage of using spermicides is that they are available without a prescription or medical examination. They also do not manipulate a person's hormonal system, and they have few side effects. It was believed that a major noncontraceptive benefit of some spermicides is that they offer some protection against sexually transmitted infections. However, guidelines for prevention and treatment of STIs from the Centers for Disease Control and Prevention (CDC) suggest that spermicides are not recommended for STI/HIV protection. Furthermore, the CDC emphasizes that condoms lubricated with spermicides offer no more protection from STIs than other lubricated condoms. Finally, spermicidal lubricated condoms have a shorter shelf life, cost more, and may be associated with increased urinary tract infections.

Spermicide
Chemical that kills sperm. It can be placed in a condom and/or deep in the vagina to prevent sperm from entering the cervix

THINK ABOUT IT

Take a moment to answer the following question. Individuals rarely use only one method of contraception throughout their fertile years. Which methods seem most suitable for you, and why, for each stage of your life?

A contraceptive used correctly and happily for a short time is better than one used incorrectly or unhappily for a long time.

Lisa Stern, health educator

Spermicides can also be found in the **Today Sponge®**, a disk-shaped polyurethane device. This small device is dampened with water to activate the spermicide and then inserted into the vagina before intercourse begins, providing protection for multiple acts of intercourse for a 24-hour period.

Intrauterine Device

Although not technically a barrier method, the **intrauterine device** (IUD) is a structural device that prevents implantation and may interfere with sperm and egg transport. The IUD is an object inserted into the uterus by a health-care professional to prevent the fertilized egg from implanting on the uterine wall or to dislodge the fertilized egg if it has already implanted (see Figure 12-4). The three most common IUDs are Skyla® (left in for up to 3 years), Mirena® (left in for up to 6 years), and Paragard®, also known as the copper T (left in for up to 12 years). Skyla and Mirena both contain hormones, while Paragard does not. All three are T-shaped devices that sit in the uterus and prevent more than 99 out of 100 pregnancies in a year. Liletta and Kyleena are the newest versions available in the US. Kyleena and Skyla are slightly smaller IUDs. IUDs are not for people who have a history of ectopic pregnancy or pelvic inflammatory disease. Once inserted, the IUD should be checked in about 6 weeks to confirm proper placement.

FIGURE **12-4** || The IUD, as It Is Inserted by a Health-care Practitioner

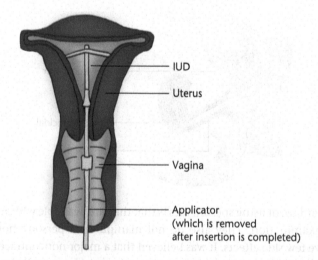

Today Sponge
Disk-shaped polyurethane device containing the spermicide nonoxynol-9 that protects for repeated acts of intercourse over 24 hours without the need for supplying additional spermicide

Intrauterine device
Object inserted into the uterus by a physician to prevent the fertilized egg from implanting on the uterine wall

Young adults are increasingly (now 12%) using Long-Acting, Reversible Contraceptives (LARCs), with IUDs and implants being used most often. Reasons for the shift are effectiveness, stability (no need to do anything such as buy and put on a condom, although they should still be used to prevent STIs), and nothing to remember (for at least 3 years). The result of the increase in LARCs by adults will be fewer unintended pregnancies (Guttmacher Institute, 2014a).

Cervical Barrier Devices

There are other cervical barrier devices available, including the diaphragm and cervical cap. The **diaphragm** is a shallow rubber dome attached to a flexible, circular steel spring. It covers the cervix and prevents sperm from moving beyond the vagina into the uterus. The older diaphragm must be fitted by a health-care provider and should be used with a spermicidal jelly or cream. The newest diaphragm on the market, the Caya® is latex free and has a nylon rim and a contoured shape. Since one size fits most, many women don't need to have a fitting done. The **cervical cap** is a thimble-shaped contraceptive device made of rubber or polyethylene that fits tightly over the cervix and is held in place by suction. It should also be used with spermicidal jelly or cream. A prescription is needed for both of these options.

12.1c Natural Family Planning Methods

Also referred to as **periodic abstinence**, *rhythm method*, and *fertility awareness*, natural family planning involves refraining from sexual intercourse during the 1–2 weeks each month when the woman is thought to be fertile. Women who use periodic abstinence must know their time of ovulation and avoid intercourse just before, during, and immediately after that time. Calculating the fertile period involves three assumptions: (1) ovulation occurs on day 14 (plus or minus 2 days) before the onset of the next menstrual period; (2) sperm typically remain viable for 2–3 days; and (3) the ovum survives for 24 hours.

The period during which the woman is fertile can be predicted in four ways: the calendar method, the basal body temperature method, the cervical mucus method, and the hormone-in-urine method. These methods may be used not only to avoid pregnancy but also to facilitate conception if the woman wants to become pregnant. We provide only basic instructions here for using periodic abstinence as a method of contraception. Individuals considering this method should consult with their health-care provider for more information.

Calendar Method

The calendar method is the oldest and most widely practiced method of avoiding pregnancy through periodic abstinence. This method allows people to calculate the onset and duration of their fertile period. When using the calendar method to predict when the egg is ready to be fertilized, people keep a record of the length of their menstrual cycles for 8 months. The menstrual cycle is counted from day one of the menstrual period through the last day before the onset of the next period. The fertile period is then calculated by subtracting 18 days from the length of the shortest cycle and 11 days from the length of the longest cycle. The resulting figures indicate the range of their fertility period. It is during this time that the person must abstain from intercourse if pregnancy is not desired.

For example, suppose that during an 8-month period, a person had cycle lengths of 26, 32, 27, 30, 28, 27, 28, and 29 days. Subtracting 18 from the shortest cycle (26) and 11 from the longest cycle (32) computes the days that the egg is likely to be in the fallopian tubes. To avoid getting pregnant, the person must avoid intercourse on days 8 through 21 of their cycle.

The calendar method of predicting the *safe period* may be unreliable for two reasons. First, the next month the person may ovulate at a different time than any of the previous 8 months. Second, sperm life varies—they may live up to 5 days, which is long enough to meet the next egg in the fallopian tubes.

Diaphragm
Shallow rubber dome attached to a flexible, circular steel spring, 2–4 inches in diameter, that can be inserted vaginally to cover the cervix and prevent sperm from entering the uterus

Cervical cap
Thimble-shaped contraceptive device made of rubber or polyethylene that fits tightly over the cervix and is held in place by suction

Periodic abstinence
Refraining from sexual intercourse during the 1 to 2 weeks each month when the woman is thought to be fertile; (also known as *rhythm method, fertility awareness,* and *natural family planning*)

Basal Body Temperature Method

The basal body temperature (BBT) method is based on determining the time of ovulation by measuring temperature changes that occur in a person's body shortly after ovulation. The basal body temperature is the temperature of the body, at rest, on waking in the morning. To establish BBT, the person's temperature must be taken before getting out of bed in the morning for 3 months. Shortly before, during, or right after ovulation, the person's BBT usually rises about 0.4°F–0.8°F. Some people notice a temperature drop about 12 to 24 hours before it begins to rise after ovulation. Intercourse must be avoided from the time the person's temperature drops until the temperature has remained elevated for 3 consecutive days. Intercourse may be resumed on the night of the third day after the BBT has risen and remained elevated for 3 consecutive days. Advantages of using this method include being natural and avoiding chemicals. Disadvantages include the higher pregnancy rate for persons using this method.

Cervical Mucus Method

The cervical mucus method, also known as the *Billings method* of natural family planning, is based on observations of changes in the cervical mucus during an individual's monthly cycle. The person may observe the cervical mucus by wiping themselves with toilet paper.

The person should abstain from intercourse during their menstrual period because the mucus is obscured by menstrual blood and cannot be observed and ovulation can occur during menstruation. After menstruation ceases, intercourse is permitted on days when no mucus is present or thick mucus is present in small amounts. Intercourse should be avoided just prior to, during, and immediately after ovulation if pregnancy is not desired. Before ovulation, mucus is cloudy, yellow or white, and sticky. During ovulation, cervical mucus is thin, clear, slippery, and stretchy and resembles raw egg white, which may be referred to as **Spinnbarkeit**. This phase is known as the *peak symptom*. During ovulation, some people experience ovulatory pain referred to as **Mittelschmerz**. Such pain may include feelings of heaviness, abdominal swelling, rectal pain or discomfort, and lower abdominal pain or discomfort on either side. Mittelschmerz is useful for identifying ovulation but not for predicting it. Intercourse may resume 4 days after the disappearance of the peak symptom and continue until the next menses. During this time, cervical mucus may be either clear and watery or cloudy and sticky, or there may be no mucus noticed at all.

Advantages of the cervical mucus method include that it requires people to become familiar with their reproductive system, and it can give early warning about some STIs (which can affect cervical mucus). However, the cervical mucus method requires people to distinguish between mucus and semen, spermicidal agents, lubrication, and infectious discharges. Also, people must not douche, because they will wash away what they are trying to observe.

Hormone-in-Urine Method

Luteinizing hormone (LH) is released in increasing amounts in the ovulating individual 12–24 hours prior to ovulation. People can purchase over-the-counter ovulation tests, such as First Response™ and Ovutime, which are designed to ascertain the surge of LH into the urine (signaling ovulation). This alerts the individual to avoid intercourse to maximize the chance of preventing pregnancy. Some test kits involve the

Spinnbarkeit
The slippery, elastic, raw egg white consistency of the cervical mucus that becomes evident at the time of ovulation and signals that it is likely a woman has ovulated

Mittelschmerz
Ovulatory pain

person exposing a test stick during urination, whereas others involve collecting the urine in a small cup and placing the test stick in the cup. In practice, a person conducts a number of urine tests over a period of days because each test kit comes supplied with five or six tests. Some people experience the LH hormone surge within a 10-hour span, so they may need to test themselves more than once a day. Of course, this method can also be used to predict the best time to have intercourse to maximize the chance of becoming pregnant.

12.1d Withdrawal

Coitus interruptus, also known as *withdrawal*, is the practice whereby the penis is withdrawn from the vagina before ejaculation. The advantages of coitus interruptus are that it requires no devices or chemicals, and it is always available. The disadvantages of withdrawal are that it does not provide protection from STIs, it may interrupt the sexual response cycle and diminish the pleasure for the couple, and it can be ineffective in preventing pregnancy if not used correctly.

Withdrawal is not a reliable form of contraception for two reasons. First, a small amount of pre-ejaculatory fluid can be unknowingly emitted which may contain sperm. One drop can contain millions of sperm. In addition, an individual may lack the self-control to withdraw the penis before ejaculation, or withdrawal may be delayed too long and some semen may be inadvertently ejaculated near the vaginal opening of their partner. Sperm deposited there can live in the moist labia and make their way up the vagina.

12.1e Emergency Contraception

Also called **postcoital contraception**, **emergency contraception** refers to various types of hormonal options or postcoital IUD insertion used primarily in three circumstances: when a person has unprotected intercourse, when a contraceptive method fails (such as condom breakage or slippage), and when a person is raped. Emergency contraception medication should be taken for those times when unprotected intercourse has occurred, preferably within 72 hours, though it can work [for up to] to 120 hours. Emergency contraception is not the same thing as the abortion pill (Hitchcock, personal communication, 2015).

Plan B One-Step® is a brand of hormonal emergency contraception that many people are familiar with, although generic versions of Plan B are also available over the counter. Plan B has reduced effectiveness for people with a BMI over 25. ella® is also a hormonal method of emergency contraception and is effective in people with a BMI up to 35; ella is available by prescription only. These options, known as the Yuzpe method after the physician who proposed them, involve ingesting a certain number of tablets of combined estrogen-progesterone. In higher doses, they serve to prevent ovulation, fertilization of the egg, or transportation of the egg to the uterus. They may also make the uterine lining inhospitable to implantation. Common side effects of combined estrogen-progesterone emergency contraception pills include nausea, vomiting, headaches, and breast tenderness; some people also experience abdominal pain, headache, and dizziness.

A nonhormonal option for emergency contraception is the insertion of the copper Paragard IUD, although this requires a doctor's visit.

Coitus interruptus
Practice whereby the man withdraws the penis from the vagina before he ejaculates (also known as *withdrawal*)

Postcoital contraception
See *emergency contraception*

Emergency contraception
Contraceptive administered within 72 hours following unprotected intercourse; referred to as the morning-after pill

TABLE 12-2 | Contraceptive Effectiveness, STI Protection, Benefits/Disadvantages, Cost

Method	Rates[1]	STI	Benefits	Disadvantages	Cost[2]
Oral contraceptive (the pill)	91%	No	High effectiveness rate, 24-hour protection, and menstrual regulation	Daily administration, side effects possible, medication interactions	For the oral contraceptive (the pill) row: $0–50 per month
NEXPLANON NXT (3-year implant)	99.95%	No	High effectiveness rate, long-term protection	Side effects possible, menstrual changes	For the Nexplanon NXT row: $40 every 3 years
Depo-Provera (3-month injection) or Depo-subQ Provera 104	94%	No	High effectiveness rate, long-term protection	Decreases body calcium, not recommended for use longer than 2 years for most users, side effects likely	For the Depo-Provera row: $0–50 for each shot
Transdermal patch	91%	No	Same as oral contraceptives except use is weekly, not daily	Patch changed weekly, side effects possible	$15–32 per month
NuvaRing (vaginal ring)	91%	No	Same as oral contraceptives except use is for 3 weeks not daily	Must be comfortable with body for insertion	$15–48 per month
External condom	82%	Yes	Few or no side effects, easy to purchase and use	Can interrupt spontaneity	$2–10 a box
Internal condom	79%	Yes	Few or no side effects	Decreased sensation and insertion takes practice	$4–10 a box
Spermicide	72%	No	Many forms to choose, easy to purchase and use	Can cause irritation, can be messy	$8–18 per box/tube/can
Today Sponge3	76–88%	No	Few side effects, effective for 24 hours after nsertion	Spermicide irritation possible	$3–5 per sponge
Diaphragm and Cervical cap	88% (diaphragm)	No	Few side effects, can be inserted within 2 hours before intercourse	Can be messy, increased risk of vaginal/UTI infections	$50–200 plus spermicide
Intrauterine device (IUD): Paragard or Mirena	99.2%	No	No/little maintenance, longer term protection	Risk of pelvic inflammatory disease (PID) increased, chance of expulsion	$150–300
Withdrawal	78%	No	Requires little planning, always available	Pre-ejaculatory fluid can contain sperm	$0
Periodic abstinence	76%	No	No side effects, accepted in all religions/cultures	Requires a lot of planning, need ability to interpret fertility signs	$0
Emergency contraception		No	Provides an option after intercourse has occurred	Must be taken within 120 hours, side effects likely	$10–32

1 Effectiveness rates are listed as percentages of women not experiencing an unintended pregnancy during the first year of typical use. Typical use refers to use under real-life conditions. Perfect use effectiveness rates are higher.

2 Costs may vary.

3 Lower percentages apply to parous women (women who have given birth). Higher rates apply to nulliparous women (women who have never given birth).

References: Hall, S. and D. Knox. (2019). College Student Attitudes and Behaviors Survey of 12,568 undergraduates. Unpublished data collected for this text. Department of Family, Consumer, and Technology Education Teachers College, Ball State University and Department of Sociology, East Carolina University, Greenville, NC.

Technology and Sexuality 12-1: Contraception

Since the oral contraceptive pill was introduced in 1960, the number of contraceptive options available for women has greatly increased. Scientific changes in hormone production and the technological delivery systems that are used to introduce those hormones into the human body have led to the increase in options.

The contraceptive pill has changed dramatically over the last 50 years. The dosage of hormones is significantly lower in today's pill, and people have a number of options to choose from. While the traditional pill pack consisted of 21 active hormone pills and 7 sugar pills (placebos), Seasonale® has 84 days of hormone pills before the traditional hormone-free week. Other pill options contain four sugar pills or no sugar pills. One type of pill, which used to be sold under the name brand name Lybrel® but is now available generically, contains 365 active pills.

Technology and research have changed not only the dosage of the hormones but also the delivery system used to introduce them into the body. The last 25 years have seen the advent of the transdermal patch, the vaginal ring, the implant, the injection, and the hormonal IUD.

So what do tomorrow's contraceptive options look like? Currently, new combinations of hormones are being used in implants. There has also been development of smaller IUDs and potentially ones that are frameless and not in the traditional "T" shape.

There has been some development of new barrier methods as well. The major change has been in the materials being used. The internal condom (FC2) is made of nitrile, and a new single-use diaphragm, made of silicone, was approved by the FDA in 2014. This new diaphragm is one size fits all, so there is no need to be fitted by a doctor.

Other contraceptive options include external condoms made of polyisoprene, which allow for condom use by those who are allergic to latex. Polyisoprene condoms also feel softer than latex, so individuals may enjoy using them more. An additional benefit of polyisoprene condoms is that they can be used with oil-based lubricants. Condom size options have also increased, which is important to be aware of since using the wrong size is one reason condoms slip or break. While many condom manufacturers provide a larger condom, a typical condom size, and a smaller condom, (often labeled as *snugger* or *close fit*), MyONE® condom has more specific sizing and comes in 60 sizes.

What about new hormonal contraceptive options for men? For years there has been talk about a male pill. The problem with the concept of a male pill is that while researchers have been able to use hormones to stop sperm production, this also reduces testosterone production. New research is being conducted to stop the release of sperm. Research on this and other male methods is still in the early stages of development. Researcher Christina Wang of LABio Med noted that "Safe, reliable hormonal male contraception should be available in about 10 years" (Hafner, 2019). The Male Contraceptive Initiative (http://www.malecontraceptive.org/) is a good resource for information on new male methods in development around the world.

12.2 Sterilization

Unlike the temporary and reversible methods of contraception discussed earlier in this chapter, **sterilization** is a permanent surgical procedure that prevents reproduction (Bartz & Greenberg, 2008). Sterilization may be a contraceptive method of choice when an individual should not have more children for health reasons or when individuals are certain about their desire to have no more children or to remain child-free. Most couples complete their intended childbearing in their late 20s or early 30s, leaving more than 15 years of continued risk of unwanted pregnancy. Because of the risk of pill use at older ages and the lower reliability of alternative contraceptive methods, sterilization has become the most popular method of contraception among married individuals who have completed their families.

Slightly more than half of all sterilizations are performed on women. In addition to men being fearful of a vasectomy (which they sometimes equate with castration and the removal of their manhood), women may be more open to sterilization, despite its more invasive nature and longer recovery time than vasectomy. "I'm the one that ends up being pregnant and having the baby," said one woman. "So I want to make sure that I never get pregnant again."

Sterilization
Permanent surgical procedure that prevents reproduction

THINK ABOUT IT

Take a moment to answer the following questions. It may be difficult for younger individuals, and those who do not have children, to be sterilized. Do you think that people should be a certain age before physicians can legally perform sterilization procedures because they may change their minds, or do you feel this right belongs to any adult individual?

In addition, although some sterilizations for women have been reversed, a woman might consider sterilization only if she never wants to have a biological child. Eeckhaut and Sweeney (2018) noted that one-fourth of sterilized, reproductive-aged women in the United States express a desire to have their sterilization procedures reversed. The reason cited is a change in their context. Experiencing poststerilization union dissolution (e.g. they were no longer with a partner) or poststerilization union formation (e.g. they were with a new partner) were associated with elevated risk of regret.

12.2a Female Sterilization

Although a woman may be sterilized by removal of the ovaries (oophorectomy) or uterus (hysterectomy), these operations are not normally undertaken for the sole purpose of sterilization, because the ovaries produce important hormones (as well as eggs) and because both procedures carry the risks of major surgery.

The usual procedures of female sterilization are the salpingectomy and a variant of it, the laparoscopy. **Salpingectomy**, also known as *tubal ligation* or *tying the tubes*, is often performed under a general anesthetic while the woman is in the hospital (Figure 12-5). Many women elect to have this procedure performed just after they have delivered a baby. An incision is made in the lower abdomen, just above the pubic line, and the fallopian tubes are brought into view one at a time. A part of each tube is cut out; the ends are tied, clamped, or cauterized. The operation takes about 30 minutes.

A less expensive and quicker (about 15 minutes) form of salpingectomy is the **laparoscopy**, which is performed on an outpatient basis. Often using local anesthesia, the surgeon inserts a small, lighted viewing instrument (laparoscope) through the woman's abdominal wall just below the navel through which the uterus and the fallopian tubes can be seen. The surgeon then makes another small incision in the lower abdomen and inserts a special pair of forceps that carry electricity to cauterize the tubes. The laparoscope and the forceps are then withdrawn, the small wounds are closed with a single stitch, and small bandages are placed over the closed incisions. For this reason, laparoscopy is also known as "the Band-Aid® operation." The cost varies from $1,500 to $5,000 depending on what else (such as treating endometriosis) the physician does. As an alternative to reaching the fallopian tubes through an opening below the navel, the surgeon may make a small incision in the back of the vaginal barrel (vaginal tubal ligation).

12.2b Male Sterilization

The most common form of male sterilization is the **vasectomy** (Figure 12-6). There are two different ways for men to be sterilized, and both occur with local anesthetic in the physician's office. With incision methods, the health-care provider makes an incision on each side of the scrotum to reach each vas deferens—the tubes that carry sperm. In most procedures, each tube is blocked, and a small section of each tube is removed. Tubes may be tied off or blocked with surgical clips, or they may be closed

Salpingectomy
Sterilization procedure whereby the woman's fallopian tubes are cut out and the ends are tied, clamped, or cauterized so that eggs cannot pass down the fallopian tubes to be fertilized (also known as tubal ligation or tying the tubes)

Laparoscopy
Surgery using a laparoscope; sometimes used for tubal ligation

Vasectomy
Minor surgical procedure whereby the vas deferens are cut so as to prevent sperm from entering the penis

using an instrument with an electrical current. With the no-incision ("no-scalpel") method, the skin is not cut; rather, one tiny puncture is made to reach both tubes. The tubes are then tied off, cauterized, or blocked. The tiny puncture heals quickly. No stitches are needed, and no scarring takes place. The no-scalpel method reduces bleeding and decreases the possibility of infection, bruising, and other complications. Either procedure takes about 15–20 minutes, and the man can leave the physician's office within a short time.

Because sperm do not disappear from the ejaculate immediately after a vasectomy (some remain in the vas deferens below the severed portion), a couple should use another method of contraception until the man has had about 20 ejaculations. In about 1% of the cases, the vas deferens grows back, and the man becomes fertile again.

A vasectomy does not affect the man's desire for sex, ability to have an erection or an orgasm, amount of ejaculate (sperm make up only a minute portion of the seminal fluid), health, or chance of prostate cancer. Although in some instances a vasectomy may be reversed, men should get a vasectomy only if they do not want to have a biological child.

FIGURE **12-5** ‖ Female Sterilization: Tubal Sterilization

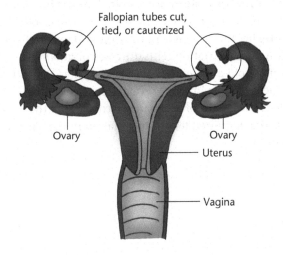

FIGURE **12-6** ‖ Male Sterilization: Vasectomy

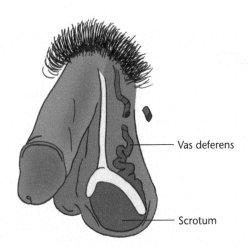

12.3 Abortion

Abortion
Deliberate termination of a pregnancy through chemical or surgical means

Induced abortion
The elective termination of a pregnancy through chemical or surgical means

Spontaneous abortion
The unintended termination of a pregnancy

Medical abortion
See pharmaceutical abortion

Pharmaceutical abortion
Intentional termination of pregnancy through the use of pharmaceutical drugs

Mifepristone
Synthetic steroid that effectively inhibits implantation of a fertilized egg by making the endometrium unsuitable for implantation, which, in effect, aborts the embryo; may be used in the first 10 weeks of pregnancy in the US (see also *RU-486*)

RU-486
Drug approved for use up to 10 weeks after the onset of the last menstrual period (also known as the abortion pill)

An **abortion** may be either an **induced abortion**, also known as an *elective abortion*, which is the deliberate termination of a pregnancy through chemical or surgical means, or a **spontaneous abortion** (miscarriage), which is the unintended termination of a pregnancy. While abortion is usually associated with relief, miscarriages often represent a significant loss that is associated with depression/anxiety.

12.3a Methods of Abortion

Prior to the availability of modern surgical techniques, induced abortion in the late 18th and early 19th centuries was performed by flushing the uterus with caustic substances (such as gunpowder, quinine, or oil of juniper) or by inserting sticks of silver nitrate into the cervix. In this section, we look at modern-day methods of abortion. The procedure used to perform an abortion depends largely on the stage of the pregnancy, as measured from the first day of the last menstrual period.

Pharmaceutical Abortion

Also called **medical abortion**, **pharmaceutical abortion** involves the intentional termination of pregnancy through the use of pharmaceutical drugs. In 1997, the drug **mifepristone** became available in the United States after being approved by the U.S. Food and Drug Administration. This drug was originally known by its French name, **RU-486**; it is now sold as Mifeprex® and is known as the abortion pill. Actual use of the drug to induce abortion involves several steps (see Figure 12-7). A health-care professional determines the length of pregnancy to make sure the woman is less than 10 weeks pregnant, as the permitted length of gestation in the United States for using Mifeprex is up to 10 weeks.

Almost one in three women will have had at least one abortion by menopause, and when you've got numbers like that, you can really see that it is an integral, normal, although much-stigmatized part of the lives of women and also of men. To criminalize abortion is to go back to where we were in the '50s, and what you had then was a tremendous amount of illegal abortion, which was often quite dangerous. I can't think why people would want to go back to that.

Katha Pollitt, American poet, quoted in (Roberts, 2019)

National DATA

According to the Guttmacher Institute (2019), in 2017, 18% of pregnancies (excluding miscarriages) ended in abortion. The 862,320 abortions performed represented a 7% decrease from the 926,190 performed in 2014. The 2017 abortion rate of 13.5 per 1,000 women, ages 15–44, was an 8% decrease from the 2014 rate of 14.6 per 1,000 and was the lowest rate observed in the US since the legalization of abortion in 1973. That year, the rate was 16.3 per 1,000.

Women most likely to get an abortion are in their 20s, are unmarried/not living with a partner, and/or already have a child. (Guttmacher Institute, 2019).

Women of all races and religions have abortions, with no one racial or religious group making up a majority of those having the procedure. The majority of people who had an abortion in 2014 identified as heterosexual (Jerman et al., 2016).

International **DATA**

Worldwide, 40% of the 213 million pregnancies that occur, about 85 million, are unintended (Guttmacher Institute, 2014a).

FIGURE **12-7** ‖ How Early Medical Abortion Works

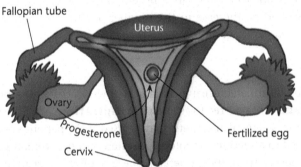

Progesterone is the hormone that supports changes in the uterine lining, allowing a fertilized egg to implant and develop in the uterus.

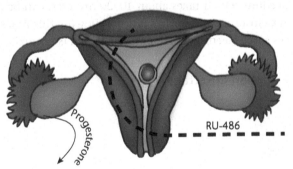

Mifepristone (RU-486) is an antiprogestin; when administered early in pregnancy, it prevents the uterus from supporting the fertilized egg.

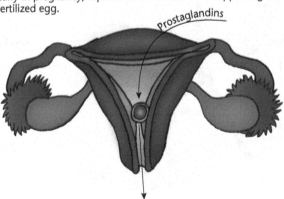

Two days later, prostaglandin is administered, which stimulates contractions of the uterus, expelling the products of conception.

Mifepristone is an antiprogestin that interferes with the uterine development that would support implantation of the fertilized egg. Two days after the mifepristone is administered, a prostaglandin (misoprostol) is administered, which causes stimulation of uterine contractions that help dislodge and expel the embryo. A heavy menstrual flow follows. The woman makes a final visit to the health-care professional to confirm that the abortion has been completed and to make sure the bleeding has stopped.

When women are offered a choice of surgical or medical abortion, most choose the medical method. The primary reasons for preferring medical abortions include greater privacy and autonomy (it can be done at home), less invasiveness, and greater naturalness. Another advantage of selecting a medical abortion is that the health-care professional can dispense such drugs in the privacy of an office, which means that women can avoid anti-abortion forces that target abortion clinics. A decade of experience with mifepristone in France, Great Britain, and Sweden has not shown that its availability has caused an increase in the number of abortions, though it has influenced their timing at earlier gestation.

Suction Curettage

Pregnancy may be terminated during the first 6–8 weeks through a procedure called **suction curettage**, also referred to as **vacuum aspiration**. After the administration of a local anesthetic (a general anesthetic may be used at the patient's request), a hollow plastic rod attached to a suction aspirator is inserted into the woman's uterus through the cervix. The device suctions the fetal tissue out of the uterus into a container. Following the suction procedure, the health-care professional may explore the uterine cavity with a small metal instrument (curette) to ensure that all the tissue has been removed. The procedure, which takes about 10–20 minutes, can be performed on an outpatient basis in a clinic or a physician's office. Following this procedure, the patient usually experiences some bleeding and cramping, which is normal (see Figure 12-8).

FIGURE **12-8** ‖ Suction Curettage

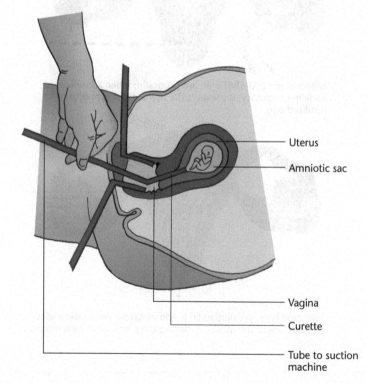

- Uterus
- Amniotic sac
- Vagina
- Curette
- Tube to suction machine

Suction curettage
Abortion procedure performed in the first 6–8 weeks of pregnancy, whereby a hollow plastic rod is inserted into the woman's uterus where the fetal tissue is evacuated

Vacuum aspiration
Synonym for suction curettage

Dilation and Suction

Dilation and suction (D & S), a method of abortion used during the first 12 weeks of pregnancy, is essentially the same as suction curettage, except that the cervix is dilated before the suction procedure. Cervical dilation may be achieved by inserting laminaria into the cervix the day before the abortion is performed. *Laminaria* are dried, sterile rods of compressed seaweed stems that increase in diameter after being inserted into the cervix to absorb moisture, thereby dilating the cervix. Cervical dilation may also be achieved by using a metal device designed to dilate the cervix just prior to the abortion. After suctioning the contents of the uterus, a physician uses a metal surgical instrument to remove any remaining fetal tissue and placenta from the uterine walls. This method is also known as **dilation and curettage** (D & C). A local or general anesthetic may be used.

Dilation and Evacuation

Dilation and evacuation (D & E), an abortion procedure used in the second trimester of pregnancy (13–24 weeks' gestation), involves dilating the cervix and dismembering the fetus inside the uterus so that the body parts can be more easily suctioned out. Extraction instruments called *ringed forceps* are also used to remove the fetal tissue. A local or general anesthetic may be used.

Intact Dilation and Extraction

An alternative to D & E is a procedure called **intact dilation and extraction** (D & X), which results in the whole fetus being aborted.

After dilating the cervix, a physician pulls the fetus down into the birth canal, feet first. Then, with the rest of the body delivered and the head still lodged against the cervix, the physician inserts an instrument to make an opening in the base of the skull, inserts a suction catheter into this hole, evacuates the contents, and removes the fetus. An advantage of this procedure, if the fetus is malformed, is that certain types of testing can be more easily performed on an intact fetus to assess the woman's chances for a normal pregnancy in the future.

Abortion opponents have labeled D & X abortions **"partial-birth" abortions** because the limbs and torso are typically delivered before the fetus has died. D & X abortions are typically performed because, at a late stage in the pregnancy, the fetus has been found to have a serious defect, the pregnancy jeopardizes the woman's health, or both. Dilation-and-extraction abortions, which are rare, are performed before the fetus's "age of viability," which is the age when a baby can survive outside of a uterus.

Induction Abortion

Induction abortion is the elective termination of a pregnancy by chemical or surgical means through induced labor and delivery of the fetus. Induction abortions are generally performed when a fatal or serious fetal defect is discovered at a late stage in the pregnancy or the woman's health is at stake or both. Some women whose fetuses have died spontaneously in utero also choose to have this procedure. Chemically, this procedure involves precipitating labor by injecting either saline or prostaglandins through the abdomen into the amniotic sac around the fetus. Prostaglandins may also be administered through vaginal suppositories. The injection or suppositories induce contractions that cause the cervix to dilate. An intravenous drip of oxytocin continues the labor contractions. The contractions are painful and can continue for several hours before the woman expels the fetus and placenta. Painkillers and local anesthesia are used to ease the woman's discomfort. This procedure is major surgery and must be performed in a hospital.

Dilation and suction
Abortion procedure during the first 12 weeks whereby the cervix is dilated before the suction procedure occurs

Dilation and curettage
Abortion procedure whereby a metal surgical instrument is used to remove any remaining fetal tissue and placenta from the uterine walls after suctioning the contents of the uterus

Dilation and evacuation
Abortion procedure during the second trimester (13–24 weeks' gestation), whereby the cervix is dilated and the fetal parts inside are dismembered so they can be suctioned out

Intact dilation and extraction
Abortion procedure involving breech delivery of fetus (except for the head) and partial evacuation of the brain, resulting in the vaginal delivery of a dead fetus

"Partial-birth" abortion
Nonmedical term used by abortion opponents to describe an abortion performed very late in pregnancy in which the terminated fetus is delivered (see *intact dilation and extraction*)

Induction abortion
Elective termination of a pregnancy through induced labor and delivery of the fetus; like other late-term abortions, generally performed when a fatal or serious fetal defect is discovered at a late stage in the pregnancy or the woman's health or life is at stake or both

12.3b Abortion Rights in the United States: Activism, Court Rulings, and Legislation

One of the most controversial political issues in US society is abortion legislation. After an overview of the historical background of the abortion rights movement, court rulings, and legislation, we will discuss the Supreme Court's landmark *Roe v. Wade* decision legalizing abortion and the recent surge of judicial and legislative action restricting abortion in the United States.

In the colonial United States, abortion was neither prohibited nor uncommon. During this time, the states were governed by English common law, which permitted abortion until *quickening*—the time when the woman could feel movement of the fetus (usually in the fourth or fifth month of pregnancy). Even if an abortion was performed after quickening, the woman was immune from prosecution.

Legal control of abortion by statute began in 1821. Because thousands of women had died taking medically prescribed poisons to induce abortions, Connecticut passed a law prohibiting the use of poisons to induce post-quickening abortions. This statute existed primarily to protect the lives of women. In 1828, New York enacted a law making abortion of a non-quickened fetus a misdemeanor crime and abortion of a quickened fetus second-degree manslaughter, unless the abortion was necessary to preserve the woman's life.

In the mid-19th century, the American Medical Association led the campaign to criminalize abortion. Their concerns were both economic and moral. Formally trained physicians competed economically with midwives, who assisted not only in births but also in abortions. Moral concerns in the medical community over abortion resulted in part from Christian-based religious concerns as well as advances in the scientific understanding of human development as a continuous process. These concerns led physicians to question the relevance of the distinction between quickened and non-quickened fetuses.

By 1900, abortion was illegal in all US jurisdictions. In most states, the sole legal reason an abortion could be performed was if continuation of the pregnancy threatened the life of the woman, though even with this medical proof, access was highly dependent on socioeconomic status and ethnicity, favoring women who had long-standing connections with sympathetic doctors. Women who sought abortions for personal, social, or economic reasons were forced to undergo more dangerous illegal abortions. In spite of the criminalization of abortion during this era, it is estimated that as many as one in three pregnancies was terminated by induced abortion (Rubin, 1987).

Roe v. Wade: A Landmark Decision

Reinforced by more than a decade of activism, the abortion rights movement reached a historic goal in 1973 when the U.S. Supreme Court ruled in the famous *Roe v. Wade* case that any restriction on abortions during the first trimester of pregnancy was unconstitutional. This ruling established that during the first 3 months of pregnancy, the decision to have an abortion would be between the pregnant woman and her physician. In the second trimester (the fourth through the sixth month of pregnancy), the state might regulate the abortion procedure (by requiring that the abortion take place in a hospital, for example) so as to protect the woman's health. During the last trimester, the state would have an interest in protecting the viable fetus, so the state might restrict or prohibit abortion.

In effect, the Supreme Court ruled that the fetus is a potential life and not a person until the third trimester. The *Roe v. Wade* decision was based on the right to privacy; government intrusion in the doctor-patient relationship and a woman's reproductive decisions was viewed as violating that right. The current abortion debate is a conflict between two fundamental values: the right of a potential life and the right of a woman to control her own body.

The right to abortion has had a positive impact on the health and well-being of US women and, up until recently, has gone largely unchallenged legally. The total number of abortions performed are at historic lows. In addition, because legal abortion is one of the safest medical procedures available, deaths are now extremely rare, plummeting to only 6 out of the more than 638,169 abortions performed in 2014 (Jatlaoui et al., 2018).

But with the increase in political interference in women's reproductive health care in 31 states, access to both legal abortion and contraceptive care has plummeted, with a concomitant rise in health risks and unwanted pregnancies. In Texas alone—per a 2016 study of the consequences of these politically motivated clinic closures (more than half the clinics in the state), restrictions, and defunding of women's health care by two thirds under the pretext of health concerns—nearly 200,000 women are now without reproductive health care. These closures have cut access not only to abortion services but also to contraceptives, as well as screenings for breast and cervical cancers, in addition to basic preventive care for hypertension and other major health problems, especially in rural, low-income areas. Women in cities are also impacted. A study done by researchers at the University of California, San Francisco, found that women living in 27 cities in the United States were living in "abortion deserts," meaning they had to travel more than 100 miles in order to obtain an abortion (Cartwright et al., 2018). And the problem is increasing. In state legislatures, anti-abortion legislators are cutting off funding to medical schools and hospitals that offer abortion education, resulting in nationwide repercussions: With fewer doctors being trained in the procedure, the remaining clinics throughout the country are increasingly under-staffed and overbooked

Anti-abortion domestic terrorism is also on the rise. In 2017, there was an 87% increase in the number of threats of harm and/or death threats that abortion providers received as compared to the prior year (National Abortion Federation, 2017). There was also a 103% increase in clinic blockades in that same time frame (https://prochoice.org/wp-content/uploads/2017-NAF-Violence-and-Disruption-Statistics.pdf). This means that women seeking their legal right to abortion can now face grave risks throughout the country.

Status of Abortion Legislation, September 2019

As of September 2019, 29 states in the US were considered hostile toward abortion rights, 14 states were considered supportive, and seven were considered in between (Guttmacher Institute, 2019). Examples of current restrictions in some states include (Guttmacher Institute, 2020a):

- Fetal heartbeat criteria: Georgia prohibits an abortion once a fetal heartbeat is present (about six weeks). Rape, incest, or mother's life exceptions. Alabama passed legislation to outlaw most abortions when there is a heartbeat (about six weeks) and criminalize the procedure for doctors. Only the life of the mother is a consideration in the abortion (rape and incest are not included).

- Physician requirements: Only a physician can perform an abortion; whereas before, skilled family nurse practitioners were legal providers.

- Hospital requirement: Abortion cannot be performed in a clinic—it must be performed in a hospital.
- Gestational limit: Abortion must be performed before fetal viability, unless the life of the mother is at stake.
- Late-term abortion: Prohibited in some states
- Public funds: Cannot be used to pay for an abortion.
- Private insurance: Is restricted from paying for abortion services in 11 states.
- Refusal to treat: Health-care providers and hospitals may refuse to perform an abortion.
- Waiting period: 27 states have mandatory waiting times. Often require 24–48 hours from the time of counseling to the procedure itself—in effect, the woman must make two trips to get an abortion, sometimes across state lines.
- State-mandated and misleading counseling: In 31 states, women seeking abortions are required to undergo state-based counseling designed to discourage them from obtaining the procedure, including myths that abortion causes breast cancer (American Cancer Society, 2014) and that aborted fetuses experience pain (Lee et al., 2005). A 2016 study revealed that one third of women seeking abortions in the United States are subjected to this mandatory misinformation (Malo, 2016).
- Parental involvement: One or both parents or legal guardians must agree to an abortion for a minor.

All in all, between 2011 and 2017, 401 abortion restrictions were enacted (Nash et al., 2017). Despite majority public support for access to both abortion and contraception, women's right to reproductive health care is far from secure in the 21st century.

12.3c Attitudes Toward Abortion

Few issues in human sexuality are as controversial as abortion. Attitudes toward abortion range from fierce opposition to abortion under all circumstances (including rape, compromised fetal health, and endangerment of a woman's life) to staunch support for legal and affordable access to abortion on request.

Anti-Choice Position

It is the right of every pregnant woman to give birth … and the right of every child to be born.

Birthright International

A dichotomy of attitudes toward abortion is reflected in two opposing groups of abortion activists. Individuals and groups who oppose a person's right to choose to have an abortion commonly refer to themselves as *pro-life*.

Of 2,958 undergraduate males surveyed, 20% disagreed that abortion is acceptable under certain conditions. Of 9,807 undergraduate females, 22% disagreed (Hall & Knox, 2019). Anti-abortion groups favor a complete ban on abortion. They essentially believe the following:

1. The unborn fetus has a right to life that should not be subject to a woman's decision.
2. Abortion is a violent and immoral solution to unintended pregnancy.

3. The life of an unborn fetus is sacred and should be protected, even in cases of rape or incest, and at the cost of individual difficulties or life-threatening health consequences for the pregnant woman.

Right to Choose Position

In the same survey of 2,958 undergraduate males, 66% along with 65% of 9,807 undergraduate females—agreed that "abortion is acceptable under certain conditions" (Hall & Knox, 2019).

Advocates for reproductive choice support the legal availability of abortion for all women. They essentially believe the following:

1. Freedom of choice and of bodily integrity are central values—as equal citizens under federal law, women must have the right to determine what happens to their own bodies.

2. Those who must personally bear the consequences of their moral choices have the right to make those choices.

3. Procreation choices must be free of governmental control because forced birth is contrary to human rights and democratic principles of full citizenship.

Some advocates for choice object to the label *pro-abortion* because some who are in favor of reproductive rights may still be personally opposed to abortion (hence the use of the term *pro-choice*). Others follow the "trust women" adage and advocate for abortion access without excuse or apology, stressing the basic right to bodily self-determination for both men and women.

> *I feel about Photoshop the way some people feel about abortion. It is appalling and a tragic reflection on the moral decay of our society ... unless I need it, in which case, everybody be cool.*
>
> Tina Fey, comedian

National DATA

In the US, 58% of adults say that abortion should be legal in all or most cases. (Pew Research Center, 2019a).

12.3d International Access

Around the world, abortion rights vary, with six countries—the Holy See (the Catholic Church's sovereign Vatican City State), Malta, Dominican Republic, El Salvador, Nicaragua, and Chile—banning the procedure altogether (see Figure 12-9). Another 13 countries have restrictions so onerous that abortion is essentially not available. Per a World Health Organization study, legality does not affect abortion rates, and studies connecting reduced maternal mortality to the legality of abortion have helped ease restrictions in some countries (Grimes et al., 2006). Until May 2018, the fetus in Ireland had an equal right to life as the woman carrying it. Repealing the 8th amendment of the Irish constitution in 2018 allowed women the right to get an abortion up to the 12th week of pregnancy—a blow to the Catholic Church.

12.3e Physical and Psychological Effects

Women who have experienced or are contemplating abortion may be concerned about its potential physical and psychological effects. Legal abortions, performed under safe conditions in such countries as the United States, are safer than childbirth. The earlier in the pregnancy the abortion is performed, the safer it is.

1. *Rates of mortality and complications:* The mortality rate of childbirth is 29.9 maternal deaths per 100,000 live births (Institute for Health Metrics and Evaluation, 2017). Mortality rates associated with legal abortion are 0.6 per 100,000 abortions. Women are nine times more likely to die from childbirth than from abortion (Raymond & Grimes, 2012).

   Post-abortion complications include the possibility of incomplete abortion, which occurs when the initial procedure misses the fetus and a repeat procedure must be done. Other possible complications include uterine infection; excessive bleeding; perforation or laceration of the uterus, bowel, or adjacent organs; and an adverse reaction to a medication or anesthetic. In legal abortion, complications are minimal. Interpretations on the data depend on whether prochoice or prolife is reporting.

2. *Long-term effects:* Suction curettage abortions, which make up most US abortions, and medical abortions (using medication) do not cause any risk to future childbearing. However, late-term abortions do increase the risk of subsequent miscarriages, premature deliveries, and babies with low birth-weight.

Of equal concern are the psychological effects of abortion. The American Psychological Association reviewed all outcome studies on the mental health effects of abortion and concluded the following:

> Based on our comprehensive review and evaluation of the empirical literature published in peer-reviewed journals since 1989, this Task Force on Mental Health and Abortion concludes that the most methodologically sound research indicates that among women who have a single, legal, first-trimester abortion of an unplanned pregnancy for nontherapeutic reasons, the relative risks of mental health problems are no greater than the risks among women who deliver an unplanned pregnancy (Major et al., 2008, p. 71).

Subsequent research has confirmed this position—abortion does not harm a woman's mental health (Steinberg & Rubin, 2014). In fact, the majority of women feel a sense of relief and happiness, per the Guttmacher Institute's research (Cohen, 2006).

What about the partner? Jones and colleagues (2011) examined data from 9,493 women who had obtained an abortion to find out the degree of their male partners' knowledge of the procedure. The overwhelming majority of women reported that the men with whom they got pregnant knew about the abortion, and most perceived these men to be supportive. Cohabiting men were particularly supportive. The researchers concluded that most women obtaining abortions are able to rely on male partners for social support.

PERSONAL DECISIONS 12-1

Deciding Whether to
Have an Abortion

Women who face the question of whether to have an abortion may benefit by considering the following guidelines:

- Consider all the alternatives available to you, realizing that no alternative may be all good or all bad. As you consider each option, think about both the short- and long-term consequences.
- Obtain objective information about each alternative course of action. Inform yourself about the medical, financial, and legal aspects of abortion, childbearing, parenting, and adoption.
- Talk with trusted family members, friends, or unbiased counselors. Talk with the man who participated in the pregnancy, if appropriate. If possible, talk with women who have had abortions, as well as women who have kept and reared their babies or placed them in adoptive homes. If you feel that someone is pressuring you in your decision-making, look for help elsewhere.
- Consider your own personal and moral commitments in life. Understand your own feelings, values, and beliefs concerning the fetus, and weigh those against the circumstances surrounding your pregnancy.

To what degree might women benefit from counseling? Brown (2013) interviewed 24 women between the ages of 16 and 20 who were waiting for, or had recently had, a surgical abortion to identify the process involved in making a decision regarding an abortion. All but one of the women had been offered counseling, but only two accepted. The women had decided that they wanted an abortion before accessing health services to request one. In making the decision, they had discussed their decision with someone close to them and did not feel the need to have further discussions with counselors.

Chapter Summary

Contraception

HORMONAL METHODS OF CONTRACEPTION currently available to women include the pill, NEXPLANON, Depo-Provera or Depo-subQ Provera 104, NuvaRing, and Ortho Evra. Barrier methods include the internal and external condom, spermicides, diaphragm and cervical cap. Intrauterine devices are an option of contraception that are either hormonal or nonhormonal. Natural family planning methods involve refraining from sexual intercourse during the 1–2 weeks each month when the woman is thought to be fertile. Withdrawal is another option, but it is not considered a reliable form of contraception.

Emergency contraception refers to various types of pills or the insertion of a postcoital IUD that are used when a woman has unprotected intercourse, when a contraceptive method fails (such as condom breakage or slippage), or when a woman is raped.

Sterilization

STERILIZATION is a surgical procedure that prevents fertilization, generally permanently, usually by blocking the passage of eggs or sperm through the fallopian tubes or vas deferens, respectively. The procedure for female sterilization is called salpingectomy or tubal ligation. Laparoscopy is a variation of tubal ligation. The most common form of male sterilization is vasectomy.

Abortion

AN ABORTION MAY BE EITHER induced, or spontaneous (miscarriage). Induced abortion methods will vary based on the stage of the pregnancy. Methods include suction curettage, dilation and suction, and dilation and evacuation. An abortion may also be induced by the use of the drug RU-486 (mifepristone, sold as Mifeprex and known as the abortion pill) if the woman is less than 10 weeks pregnant.

The United States is deeply divided over the issue of abortion. Abortion is accepted in all or most cases by a majority of the public. Although anti-abortion and abortion-rights groups dominate the public discourse on abortion, many people have mixed feelings.

Legal abortions, performed under safe conditions in such countries as the United States, are safer than childbirth. Research has indicated that abortion does not harm a woman's mental health.

Web Links

NARAL Pro-Choice America

http://www.naral.org/

Abortion Clinics Online

http://www.gynpages.com/

Bedsider: Birth Control Support Network

http://bedsider.org/

National Right to Life

http://www.nrlc.org/

Planned Parenthood

http://www.plannedparenthood.org/

Population Council

http://www.popcouncil.org

Key Terms

Abortion **324**

Cervical cap **317**

Coitus interruptus **319**

Condom use resistance **314**

Depo-Provera **311**

Diaphragm **317**

Dilation and curettage **327**

Dilation and evacuation **327**

Dilation and suction **327**

Emergency contraception **319**

Induced abortion **324**

Induction abortion **327**

Intact dilation and extraction **327**

Internal condom **314**

Intrauterine device **316**

Laparoscopy **322**

Medical abortion **324**

Mifepristone **324**

Mittelschmerz **318**

NEA-TDS (norethindrone acetate transdermal system) **312**

NEXPLANON **311**

NuvaRing **312**

"Partial-birth" abortion **327**

Periodic abstinence **317**

Pharmaceutical abortion **324**

Postcoital contraception **319**

RU-486 **324**

Salpingectomy **322**

Spermicide **315**

Spinnbarkeit **318**

Spontaneous abortion **324**

Stealthing **314**

Sterilization **321**

Suction curettage **326**

Today Sponge **316**

Vacuum aspiration **326**

Vasectomy **322**

CHAPTER 13

Pregnancy and Childbirth

There are two sides to being pregnant. There is the beautiful, wonderful blessing side. The second side—it sucks.

Tamar Braxton, American singer

Chapter Outline

13.1 Pregnancy 338
   13.1a Pregnancy Intention **338**
   13.1b Beginning of Pregnancy **338**
   Personal Decisions 13-1
      I Am an Egg Donor **339**
   13.1c Pregnancy Testing **340**
   13.1d Physical Changes
      During Pregnancy **340**
   13.1e Maternal Mortality **340**
   13.1f Prenatal Care and Exercise **342**
   13.1g Alcohol, Cigarette, and
      Drug Use **342**
   Social Policy 13-1
      Criminal Prosecution for
      Fetal Abuse? **344**
   13.1h Prenatal Testing **344**
   13.1i Miscarriage **346**
   13.1j Sex During Pregnancy **346**
13.2 Infertility 347
   13.2a Causes of Infertility **348**

Technology and Sexuality 13-1:
   Infertility, Birth Defects, and
   Information Sharing **349**
**13.3 Childbirth: Preparation
and Reality 349**
   13.3a Childbirth
      Preparation—Lamaze **349**
   13.3b Trends: Classes, Birth Centers, Home
      Birth, and VBAC **351**
   13.3c Pain Control in Labor
      and Delivery **351**
   13.3d First Stage of Labor **352**
   13.3e Second Stage of Labor **352**
   13.3f Third Stage of Labor **354**
   13.3g Cesarean Childbirth **354**
   13.3h Reactions to the Baby **355**
   13.3i Dangers of Childbirth for
      the Mother **355**

Web Links 356
Key Terms 357

Objectives

1. Identify the signs of pregnancy and the methods of testing for pregnancy
2. Review the physical and psychological changes that occur during pregnancy
3. Know what options are available for prenatal care and prenatal testing

4. Understand the effects of miscarriage
5. Review the Lamaze method of childbirth and the three stages of labor
6. Discuss the status of C-sections in terms of use and controversy

(Trevor Werb)

Truth — OR — Fiction?

T / F   1. The frequency of prepregnancy vaginal intercourse returns to the prepregnancy level after childbirth within 12 months and sexual satisfaction actually increases for first-time parents.

T / F   2. Couples are often secretive about the use of donor sperm and may not even tell close family members.

T / F   3. In the United States, maternal death due to childbirth and pregnancy-related causes has steadily decreased since the 1990s.

T / F   4. In spite of health risks, women are becoming more open to Caesarean childbirth.

T / F   5. Around 15% of couples are infertile.

Answers: 1. F   2. T   3. F   4. T   5. T

In her book *Counseling Couples Before, During, and After Pregnancy* (2018) Stephanie Buehler recounted her own pregnancy—"I felt awful." And, she noted that her husband was studying for the bar and "had about as much interest in being intimate with me as in his study guides" (Preface). Her experience removes the stereotypical "pregnancy glow" and replaces it with the reality of the personal and relationship impact of having a baby. Indeed, pregnancy and childbirth are events that change the life of the woman, her partner, and the couple forever. Physiologically, emotionally, socially, and economically, life will never be the same. In this chapter, we review the issues of pregnancy, infertility, childbirth, and reaction/adjustment to the birth of a baby.

Whether your pregnancy was meticulously planned, medically coaxed, or happened by surprise, one thing is certain—your life will never be the same.

Catherine Jones

Pregnancy is a joyous time of anticipation.

(Megan Smith)

13.1 Pregnancy

Pregnancy is a time of great change, not just for the mother, but also for others who will be active in the child's life. Pregnancy may be particularly challenging when it is unintended.

13.1a Pregnancy Intention

Deciding to have a child is an issue considered by many couples, regardless of sexual orientation. Gato et al. (2017) identified the various issues that impact the decision to have a child by lesbians and gay men. These factors include: sociodemographic (gender, age and cohort, and race/ethnicity), personal (internalization of anti-homosexual prejudice and openness about one's non-heterosexual orientation), relational (one's partner's parental motivation and social support), and contextual (work conditions; access to LGBT support networks; information and resources; and social, legal, and medical barriers). Adoption, use of a sperm donor and having a child with a previous partner are among the various avenues for lesbians and gay men. In the case of a biological child, there is a deliberate intention to get pregnant/become a parent.

Women who give birth resulting from an unintended pregnancy may be at higher risk of postpartum depression (Steinberg & Rubin, 2014). Their children are associated with higher negative outcomes later on in preschool, kindergarten, and beyond. The specific factors associated with negative outcomes include the mother not wanting the pregnancy, the father feeling that now is not the time for the pregnancy or not being present at all, and the parents being in conflict about wanting the baby.

The time prior to becoming pregnant is important. During this period, changes can be made physically, financially, and socially that can impact the health of both the baby and the parents. Some couples choose to have prenatal genetic testing before getting pregnant. While people of various populations are comfortable with prenatal genetic testing, Pivetti and Melotti (2013) found that less religious women tended to be more in favor of taking prenatal tests.

Umbilical cord
Flexible cord that connects the developing fetus and the placenta; contains two arteries and a vein that facilitate this exchange

Embryo
Developing organism from conception to the eighth week of pregnancy

Fetus
Developing organism from the eighth week of pregnancy forward

13.1b Beginning of Pregnancy

Immediately after the egg and sperm unite, typically in the fallopian tube, the egg begins to divide and is pushed by hairlike cilia down the tube into the uterus, where it attaches itself to the inner wall. The placenta forms in the endometrium of the woman's uterus and its blood vessels. The **umbilical cord** connects the developing fetus and the placenta. This flexible cord contains the two arteries and the vein that facilitate this exchange. Furnished with a rich supply of blood and nutrients, the developing organism is called an **embryo** for the first 8 weeks and a **fetus** thereafter (see Figure 13-1).

You never understand life until it grows inside of you.

Sandra Chami Kassis, Lebanese author

PERSONAL DECISIONS 13-1

I Am an Egg Donor*

I have a child I will never meet. My future children have a sibling they will never know, grow up with, or share memories with. But I comfort myself by knowing that I gave a precious life to a couple who spent almost a decade and tens of thousands of dollars to have a child. I also comfort myself by knowing that his or her parents are more than qualified to be the perfect parents and give him or her anything he/she needs.

I am an egg donor. Although I have been praised and commended for this wonderful deed, I could have never imagined me not doing it. I truly believe it is a calling.

I was 18 when I made the decision that I wanted to donate my eggs. After looking into the process and waiting to meet the age requirement, I applied and was accepted the next day. However, it was not until 6 months later that I received an email and a phone call saying that I had been chosen by a family. After completing a series of tests and psychological evaluations, I was on a plane to Los Angeles to have my first medical exam. Twenty-five pages of legal documents followed, including that the intended mother would have her name on the birth certificate, that the parents had the right to tell or not ever tell the child of its creation, and that I would have no rights to the child. After the documents were signed, I was sent the package of medications, needles for injections, and instructions I was to follow, which ended in me flying back out to Los Angeles, being sedated, and having my eggs retrieved.

Although the process was extensive, I feel joy that this couple will be able to celebrate Mother's/Father's Day, to wake up to a crying baby, and to enjoy the beautiful life of parenthood. This couple also gave me the chance to live comfortably through college and focus on my studies instead of worrying about working enough to pay rent.

*C. Ferron. Used by permission

FIGURE **13-1** ‖ The Developing Fetus

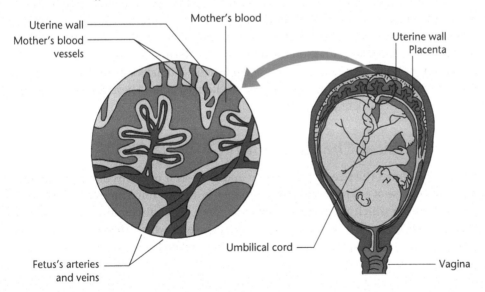

Detecting pregnancy as early as possible is important. Early detection not only enables the woman to begin prenatal precautions and medical care during the most vulnerable stage of fetal development, it also allows a woman with an unintended pregnancy time to consider whether she wants to have an abortion, which may then be performed early in pregnancy, when it is safest. Finally, early diagnosis may permit early detection of an **ectopic pregnancy**, in which the fetus develops outside the uterus, such as in the cervix, abdominal area, or ovary. Most ectopic pregnancies occur in the fallopian tube. The increase in tubal pregnancies in the past few years

Ectopic pregnancy
Condition in which a fertilized egg becomes implanted in a site other than the uterus

has been attributed to the rise in sexually transmitted infections, because infection-caused formation of scar tissue may interfere in the passage of the fertilized egg to the uterus.

An ectopic pregnancy is potentially dangerous because the tubal wall can be ruptured and cause severe bleeding, which can be lethal to the mother. Signs of such a pregnancy should be taken seriously. These signs include sudden intense pain in the lower abdomen, irregular bleeding, or dizziness that persists for more than a few seconds.

New treatments for ectopic pregnancy include microsurgery incisions that allow the physician to remove the embryo while leaving the reproductive system intact. In some cases, medication may be prescribed to destroy the pregnancy-related tissue.

13.1c Pregnancy Testing

Signs of pregnancy may include a missed period, morning sickness, enlarged and tender breasts, frequent urination, and excessive fatigue. However, pregnancy is best confirmed by laboratory tests and a physical examination.

Several laboratory tests for pregnancy have a high degree of accuracy. All of them depend on the presence of a hormone produced by the developing embryo, human chorionic gonadotropin (HCG), which appears in the pregnant woman's urine. One procedure, formally known as the *lutex agglutination slide test*, detects HCG in about 2.5 hours and can reveal within 14 days after the first missed menstrual period whether the woman is pregnant. All commercially available pregnancy tests use the lutex agglutination principle and are reasonably reliable in providing information about the existence of a pregnancy. The most common error in home pregnancy tests is that the woman takes the test too early in pregnancy and concludes that she is not pregnant when, in fact, she is (false negative).

HCG also appears in the bloodstream of the pregnant woman. A radioimmunoassay test, a laboratory examination of the blood, can determine whether a woman is pregnant within 8 days of conception. A new test, radioreceptor assay, also analyzes the blood and is 100% accurate on the first day after the first missed period. If the laboratory test indicates pregnancy, the physician usually conducts a pelvic examination to find out if the woman's uterus has enlarged or changed color. These changes take place around the sixth week of pregnancy.

13.1d Physical Changes During Pregnancy

Figure 13-2 shows the size of the embryo and fetus as it develops during pregnancy. The usual course of a typical 266-day pregnancy is divided into trimesters, or 3-month periods, during which the woman may experience some discomfort due to physical changes (see Table 13-1). Women vary in the degree to which they experience these changes. Some may experience few or none of the related symptoms, whereas others may experience many of them.

13.1e Maternal Mortality

Counter to a global trend of reduction, the maternal mortality rate in the United States—29.9 deaths per 100,000 births—is far higher than that of other developed countries, and it is rising. In 2017, the last year on record by the Institute for Health Metrics and Evaluation (2017), the US maternal mortality rate had risen by more than 50% since 1990 and was more than triple that found in Canada.

FIGURE **13-2** ‖ **Growth of the Embryo and Fetus from 2 to 15 Weeks After Conception**

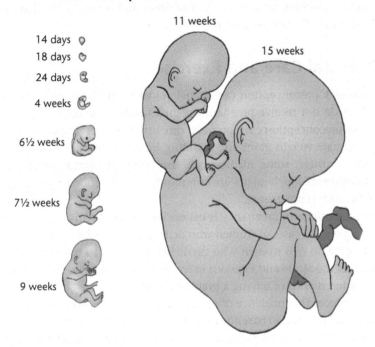

14 days
18 days
24 days
4 weeks
6½ weeks
7½ weeks
9 weeks
11 weeks
15 weeks

TABLE **13-1**	Side Effects of Pregnancy		
	First Trimester Weeks 0–14	Second Trimester Weeks 15–26	Third Trimester Weeks 27–40
Nausea	X		
Vomiting	X		
Frequent urination	X		X
Leg cramps	X		
Vaginal discharge	X	X	X
Fatigue	X	X	X
Constipation	X	X	X
Swelling		X	X
Varicose veins		X	X
Backache		X	X
Heartburn		X	
Shortness of breath		X	

Rather than pregnancy-related disease, childbirth, or associated trauma, the major causative factors for maternal mortality were chronic conditions and "lifestyle diseases" such as diabetes, cardiovascular problems, and obesity, as well as insufficient prenatal health care (Tavernise, 2016).

13.1f Prenatal Care and Exercise

Some women seek preconception care to help ensure a healthy pregnancy and baby, whereas others do not receive pregnancy-related health care until after they become pregnant. Like preconception care, prenatal care involves receiving adequate nutrition; achieving adequate weight gain; and avoiding harmful substances, such as alcohol, nicotine, illegal drugs, some medications, and toxic chemicals in the workplace. Vitamin and mineral supplements are commonly recommended, especially iron and folate (or folic acid) supplements.

In general, exercise in pregnancy is beneficial. Guendelman and colleagues (2013) compared data on 344 cases of women who delivered their babies preterm (at less than 37 weeks) to data on 698 women who carried their babies to full term. The research team found that moderate and vigorous exercise during the second trimester was associated with reduced odds of having a preterm delivery.

Exercise reduces the incidence of muscle cramps, fatigue, and shortness of breath. It also reduces the increase in baseline maternal heart rate that occurs normally in pregnancy. Women who undertake regular exercise have a lower incidence of third- and fourth-degree vaginal tears. In addition, children of exercising mothers have similar birth weights to children of sedentary mothers, and mental performance at age 5 is higher—the latter correlation may be due to the fact that active mothers may promote more interactive games/activities for their children than sedentary moms.

In the absence of specific obstetric or medical contraindications (such as anemia, hypertension, pain of any kind, fetal distress, heart palpitations, or vaginal or uterine bleeding), fit pregnant women can safely maintain the same level of fitness during pregnancy, although they may have to reduce the frequency with which they exercise and make some modifications. For example, certain yoga poses may need to be modified so that the woman is not lying flat on her back.

Amezcua-Prieto and colleagues (2013) collected data on 1,175 healthy pregnant women and found that just 27.5% and 19.4% of women fulfilled LTPA (leisure-time physical activity) recommendations prior to pregnancy and during pregnancy, respectively. The researchers found a decrease in LTPA throughout a woman's pregnancy, not only in frequency but also in duration and intensity.

13.1g Alcohol, Cigarette, and Drug Use

Fetal alcohol syndrome (FAS)
Possible negative consequences (intellectual disability, intrauterine growth restriction, facial malformation, low birth weight) for the fetus and infant of the mother who drinks alcohol during pregnancy

Pregnant women are strongly advised to eliminate their alcohol intake to avoid **fetal alcohol syndrome (FAS)**, the possible negative consequences for the fetus and infant of a mother who drinks alcohol. These consequences include increased risk of low birth weight (under 5 pounds), facial malformations, and intellectual disability. Avoiding alcohol intake during the early weeks of pregnancy (and before pregnancy, if no reliable method of birth control is being used) is particularly critical. Alcohol consumed in the later months may impede organ growth and cognitive ability. FAS is the leading cause of developmental disabilities in the United States.

In one study on alcohol consumption during pregnancy, half of 127 women reported that they had stopped drinking when they learned that they were pregnant. The researchers (Parackal et al., 2013) noted that women who were categorized as *risky drinkers* and those aged 16–24 years were more likely to drink or binge-drink in early pregnancy.

Smoking cigarettes during pregnancy is also associated with harm to the developing fetus. Negative consequences include lower-birth-weight babies, premature babies, and higher fetal or infant deaths. In one study of the smoking behavior of 10,890 women who had had one child and who were pregnant with a second, most did not smoke in either pregnancy. Of those who smoked during their first pregnancy, almost a third (30.9%) had quit by their second pregnancy. Factors associated with not smoking were lower stress, high education, and living with a partner who did not smoke (Hauge et al., 2013).

Paternal smoking may be equally hazardous. Tobacco smoke contains many mutagenic compounds that are easily absorbed into the blood and reach the testes. Paternal smoking is also associated with greater risk of perinatal mortality, lower birth weight, congenital malformation, and childhood cancers.

Concerned about the health of their babies, some pregnant women avoid not only alcohol and nicotine but also caffeine. In a review of the literature, Boylan and colleagues (2013) reaffirmed that caffeine during pregnancy increases the odds of fetal growth restriction.

Prescription drugs may also have negative consequences for the developing fetus. Medications for depression, such as selective serotonin reuptake inhibitors (SSRIs) and newer antidepressants used by pregnant women, have been associated with the birth of children small for their gestational age (Jensen et al., 2013).

Abuse of opiates, both illegal and prescription, is a major public health crisis in the United States and can be life-threatening for a pregnant woman and her fetus. Regular users of opiates who become pregnant need to seek medical care immediately to get a medically directed taper that reduces their dosage on a schedule; abrupt discontinuation can cause premature labor and fetal demise (ACOG, 2012, reaffirmed 2019).

National DATA

The most conservative annual estimate for attributing maternal binge-drinking to the number of preterm births (PTBs) is 8,701 and 5,627 low-birth-weight babies (below 5 lb., 8 oz.). The estimated rate of PTBs due to maternal binge-drinking was 1.57% among all PTBs to white women, 0.69% among black women, 3.31% among Hispanic women, and 2.35% among other races. Compared to other (preterm) age groups, women ages 40–44 had the highest adjusted binge-drinking rate and highest PTB rate due to maternal binge-drinking at 4.33% (Truong et al., 2013).

Even medications prescribed for pregnancy-related conditions can be risky. A commonly prescribed antinausea agent for morning sickness, ondansetron (marketed as Zofran®) has raised concerns about a possible association with fetal heart defects. Although research has produced inconsistent findings, the American College of Obstetricians and Gynecologists withdrew its support for the drug in 2015 and now recommends a combination of vitamin B6 and the antihistamine doxylamine, as well as ginger and adjustments in eating habits to focus on small, frequent, bland meals (ACOG, 2015, reaffirmed 2019).

With the Western world's increasing interest in its medicinal properties, marijuana (and, in the United States, Marinol®, its pharmaceutical counterpart) is now used as an alternative antiemetic option for severe nausea and vomiting due to chemotherapy and other factors and conditions. It has also been widely used in the developing world as a folk remedy for pregnancy-associated nausea and vomiting. A 2005 study revealed positive views of marijuana's effectiveness against morning sickness, per retroactive self-assessment (Westfall et al., 2006). However, further research is necessary and legal issues must be resolved before its use can be recommended.

Illegal drugs, such as methamphetamine and cocaine, should also be avoided. Methamphetamine has been linked with behavior problems in infants as late as 3–5 years of age who had been exposed to it in utero (LaGasse et al., 2012). Cocaine has been associated with preterm labor and delivery, lower-birth-weight babies, limb defects, lower IQ, and oversensitivity to stimulation. These "crack" or cocaine babies may enter the world disadvantaged, but because their mothers may have used various substances, it is difficult to isolate the specific effects of cocaine from malnutrition and lack of prenatal care. *Social Policy 13-1* introduces the question of whether women should be prosecuted for abusing substances that may harm their fetuses.

Pregnant women should also be careful of using herbal supplements, avoiding black cohosh in the third trimester, and should talk to their health-care provider about everything they are taking, including over-the-counter medications. A 2014 study found that infants of women who took acetaminophen (brand name Tylenol®) in pregnancy had a higher risk of attention-deficit/hyperactivity disorder and behavioral problems in childhood (Liew, 2014).

Social Policy 13-1

Criminal Prosecution for Fetal Abuse?

Should pregnant women who abuse alcohol, crack cocaine, and other drugs harmful to a fetus be prosecuted? Even though more than 100,000 infants have been exposed to such drugs while they were developing in utero, the courts have been reluctant to prosecute their mothers. Arguments against such prosecution are based on several issues: defining when the fetus becomes a person whose rights have been violated, the lack of warning to women that drug abuse during pregnancy may be a prosecutable offense, the vagueness of what exactly constitutes the crime, and the fact that fetal abuse is a lifestyle issue. Regarding the latter, many women who take drugs during their pregnancy live in poverty, which means they often lack prenatal care and have nutritional deficiencies. Indeed, prenatal care, drug treatment, and general health services are least accessible for poor and minority women. An additional problem is that sending pregnant women to jail or prison for drug abuse interferes with their ability to receive treatment during pregnancy.

13.1h Prenatal Testing

Prenatal care may also involve prenatal testing. Such tests range from screening measures routinely used in prenatal care to invasive diagnostic tests. The National Institutes of Health (NIH) now recommends routine prenatal genetic screening for cystic fibrosis, the most common inherited disease.

An **ultrasound scan** involves examining sound waves being intermittently beamed at the fetus, producing a detailed image on a video screen. This noninvasive test immediately provides pictures of the maternal and fetal outlines and inner organs.

Although its long-term effects are still being studied, ultrasound appears to be one of the safest procedures for the amount of information it provides. It allows the physician to determine the length of gestation (the age of the fetus) and assess the presence of structural abnormalities. High-resolution ultrasound has been shown to allow detection of risk of trisomy 21 (Down syndrome).

Other prenatal tests are used to identify fetuses with chromosomal and biochemical defects. These procedures are usually offered to women who have a child with a birth defect or some other risk factor (such as advanced maternal age, now defined at around age 35). Their purpose is to detect defects early enough so that if the test is positive, the woman can either be prepared for the birth of a child with health problems or terminate the pregnancy. Their availability has provided some women the confidence to initiate a pregnancy despite a familial history of serious genetic disease or prior birth of affected children.

Amniocentesis (performed after the 15th week of pregnancy) involves inserting a slender needle through the abdomen into the amniotic sac and taking about 1 ounce of fluid (see Figure 13-3). Fetal cells, which are present in this amniotic fluid, are sent to a laboratory, where they are cultured and then analyzed for defects.

FIGURE **13-3** ‖ Amniocentesis

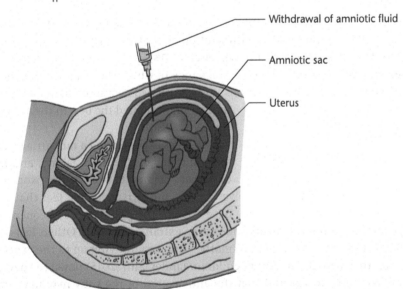

- Withdrawal of amniotic fluid
- Amniotic sac
- Uterus

Amniocentesis involves some risk. In rare cases (about 0.5% of the time, or 1 in 200 cases), the needle may damage the fetus, even though an ultrasound scan has been used to identify its position. Congenital orthopedic defects, such as clubfoot, and premature birth have been associated with amniocentesis. Also, even if no specific abnormality is detected (as is the case 97.5% of the time), this does not guarantee that the baby will be normal and healthy. Cleft palate, cleft lip, and most heart defects are not detected by amniocentesis.

Unfortunately, after the amniocentesis procedure at 16–17 weeks of gestation, an additional 3–4 weeks is required for cell tissue culture. By this time, the woman may be 20–22 weeks pregnant, the pregnancy is publicly visible, and she has probably felt fetal movement. Terminating a pregnancy at this juncture may be quite traumatic.

Ultrasound scan
Procedure whereby sound waves are used to project an image of the developing fetus on a video screen; used in prenatal testing

Amniocentesis
Prenatal test in which a needle is inserted (usually in the 16th or 17th week of pregnancy) into the pregnant woman's uterus to withdraw fluid, which is analyzed to see if the cells carry XX (female) or XY (male) chromosomes and to identify chromosomal defects

Chorionic villus sampling (CVS) may be performed at 10–12 weeks of gestation. Villi are the threadlike edges of the chorion, or membrane, surrounding the fetus. A small sample of the chorion can be obtained by passing a thin catheter, using ultrasound guidance, through the cervix and into the placenta. Sometimes, due to the placement of the placenta, the villi must be extracted through the abdomen, as in amniocentesis. The villi can then be analyzed directly or cultured and the chromosomes studied. CVS does not test for neural tube defects such as spina bifida; amniocentesis is used to detect these problems. A woman may choose CVS if she wants test results during the first 3 months of pregnancy. The risk of pregnancy interruption is slightly greater with CVS than amniocentesis (about 1.0%–1.5% risk of spontaneous abortion).

Deciding to undergo prenatal diagnosis can cause significant emotional strain to pregnant women, and waiting for results can cause depression and feelings of guilt and helplessness.

13.1i Miscarriage

A **miscarriage**, also known as spontaneous abortion, is the unintended loss of an embryo or fetus that occurs before the 20th week of pregnancy. Miscarriage is quite common, occurring in 10%–20% of all pregnancies, usually before the 12th week. It can also be associated with preterm birth, late prenatal care, history of childhood abuse, substance use, tobacco use, body mass index, race, and twin gestation (Goyal et al., 2015).

Women who experience a miscarriage often feel intense grief. Moore and Cote-Arsenault (2018) emphasized the difficult emotional journey of adjusting to a perinatal loss. Cote-Arsenault & Denney-Koelsch (2018) interviewed 16 mothers and their spouses who were confronted with a pregnancy in which there was a lethal fetal diagnosis. Couples in committed relationships who shared decision-making and provided mutual support fared the best in the aftermath of the baby's death.

> *A baby is something you carry inside you for nine months, in your arms for three years, and in your heart until the day you die.*
>
> Mary Mason, radio icon

Couples experiencing a miscarriage may also feel guilt, anger, a sense of failure, and jealousy of other pregnant women or women with children. They may blame themselves for the miscarriage. Some feel that they are being punished for something they have done in the past—such as frequent, casual, anonymous premarital sex; an abortion; or an extramarital affair. Others feel that they have failed, not only as a woman or mother, but also in living up to the expectations of their partner, parents, and other children. Lindemann (2015) noted the devastation that follows a miscarriage and that the anticipation of the baby may have included purchasing clothes for the infant but also starting a college fund—enormous investments, both emotional and financial, in the future of the unborn child.

13.1j Sex During Pregnancy

A sexual change for a couple in transition to parenthood is the gradual decline in vaginal intercourse that begins in the first trimester of pregnancy and continues throughout the pregnancy. Most couples resume vaginal intercourse after eight weeks but this behavior does not occur at pre-pregnancy frequencies till closer to 12 months (Jawed-Wessel & Sevick, 2017). While some studies have shown a loss of sexual interest during pregnancy, other studies have shown an increase in sexual activity. Buehler (2018) reviewed the literature and noted that some women report less responsiveness to clitoral contact. Rados and colleagues (2015) studied 105 men whose sexual partners

Chorionic villus sampling
Prenatal diagnostic test of cells from the chorion (membrane surrounding the fetus), performed at 10–12 weeks gestation to identify chromosomal abnormalities and some other diseases

Miscarriage
Unintended termination of a pregnancy

were in the third trimester who revealed that, while there was a decrease in sexual frequency, there was no corresponding decrease in sexual desire for two-thirds of the respondents. However, in general, participants perceived their sexual satisfaction to be high, with the more positive the relationship, the more positive the perception. Fear of hurting the fetus was the most common reason for not wanting to have sexual intercourse.

Sexual activity generally does not cause harm in pregnancy, although in advanced pregnancy, alternatives to intercourse can be more comfortable for the woman. Sexual functioning during the postpartum period may be influenced by pain disorders, hypoactive sexual desire, obstetric perineal damage, breastfeeding, postpartum mood changes, and the method used in delivery. Kelly and Jawed-Wessel (2019) found lower frequency of orgasm and intensity following vaginal versus Caesarean delivery.

Yildiz (2015) found that the couple's preconception sexual pattern is the best predictor of their sexual behavior during pregnancy and after the birth of the baby. Heidari et al. (2018) also found that pregnancy education alone provided to couples in which the woman was pregnant was effective in increasing the sexual satisfaction scores of participants over those in a control group.

There are conditions under which a pregnant woman should forgo intercourse and orgasmic activity. Women who are experiencing vaginal bleeding or abdominal pain, those whose amniotic membrane has ruptured, and those whose cervix has begun to efface or dilate after 24 weeks should abstain from sexual intercourse. Also, those with a history of premature delivery or a history of miscarriage should consult their physician or midwife about intercourse during pregnancy.

National DATA

Worldwide, 15% of couples are infertile (Fledderjohann & Barnes, 2018).

13.2 Infertility

Infertility is the inability to achieve a pregnancy after at least 1 year of regular sexual relations without birth control or the inability to carry a pregnancy to a live birth. Different types of infertility include the following:

1. *Primary infertility:* The woman has never conceived even though she wants to and has had regular sexual relations for the past 12 months.

2. *Secondary infertility:* The woman has previously conceived but is currently unable to do so even though she wants to and has had regular sexual relations for the past 12 months.

3. *Pregnancy wastage:* The woman has been able to conceive but has been unable to produce a live birth.

Shapiro (2012) emphasized the importance of conceiving in the 20s rather than delaying pregnancy until the 30s or 40s. The chance of conceiving per month in the 30s is 20%; in the 40s, it is 10%. MacDougall and colleagues (2013) interviewed women who delayed getting pregnant until age 40 or later—44% reported that they were "shocked" to learn that the ability to get pregnant declines so steeply as women move into their mid- to late 30s. Schmidt et al. (2012) also noted that delaying pregnancy

Infertility
Inability to achieve a pregnancy after at least 1 year of regular sexual relations without birth control, or the inability to carry a pregnancy to a live birth

until 35 and beyond is associated with higher risk of preterm births and stillbirths. A stillbirth is when a fetus dies in utero and is then delivered.

Considering these findings, women who want to bear children might plan their pregnancies before that period or, for delayed childbearing, consider freezing their eggs for future in vitro fertilization (IVF), if they are interested in that procedure, which carries risks and has a lower rate of success (4%–12%) than intercourse (Platt et al., 2014). Myers et al. (2017) interviewed young child-free women who had their eggs frozen not only to increase the chance of pregnancy in later life, but to help ensure that the eggs, which would be fertilized, would be healthier. The cost of freezing one's eggs is around $15,000 and a $500 annual fee to keep them frozen.

13.2a Causes of Infertility

Conception (also referred to as fertilization) refers to the fusion of the egg and sperm, whereas **pregnancy** is not considered to begin until 5–7 days later, when the fertilized egg is implanted (typically in the uterine wall). Hence, not all conceptions/fertilizations result in pregnancy. An estimated 30%–40% of conceptions are lost prior to or during implantation. Infertility problems can be attributed to the woman (40%), 40% to the man, and 20% to both of them. Some of the more common causes of infertility in men include low sperm production, poor semen motility, effects of STIs (such as chlamydia, gonorrhea, and syphilis), and interference with passage of sperm through the genital ducts due to an enlarged prostate. Additionally, there is some association between high body mass index in men and sperm that are problematic in impregnating a female (Sandlow, 2013).

Infertility in the woman is related to age, not having been pregnant before, blocked fallopian tubes, endocrine imbalance that prevents ovulation, dysfunctional ovaries, chemically hostile cervical mucus that may kill sperm, and effects of STIs (Van Geloven et al., 2013). Brandes and colleagues (2011) noted that unexplained infertility is one of the most common diagnoses in fertility care and is associated with a high probability of achieving a pregnancy.

Difficulty conceiving and carrying a fetus to term is a psychological challenge for both individuals and couples. Teskereci and Oncel (2013) reported data on 200 couples undergoing infertility treatment and found that the quality of life of the women in the study was lower than that of the men. Advanced age, low education level, unemployment status, lower income, and long duration of infertility were also associated with lower quality of life. Luk and Loke (2015) reviewed 20 articles on infertility that revealed a negative effect on the psychological well-being and sexual relationships of couples; evidence was inconclusive for the effect on marital relationships and quality of life. Kucur Suna and colleagues (2016) found that female sexual dysfunction was associated with infertility.

An at-home fertility kit, Fertell®, allows women to measure the level of their follicle-stimulating hormone on the third day of their menstrual cycles. An abnormally high level means that egg quality is low. The test takes 30 minutes and involves a urine stick. The same kit allows men to measure the concentration of motile sperm. Men provide a sample of sperm through masturbation, and the sperm swim through a solution similar to cervical mucus. This procedure takes about 80 minutes. Fertell has been approved by the Food and Drug Administration (FDA); no prescription is necessary, and the cost for the kit is about $100.

Conception
Fusion of the egg and sperm

Pregnancy
Fertilized egg implants (typically in the uterine wall) 5–7 days after conception

Technology and Sexuality 13-1: Infertility, Birth Defects, and Information Sharing

While women have been getting pregnant and giving birth for thousands of years without technology, the technological advances over the last several decades have certainly changed the process for many people. For couples who are coping with infertility, technology has provided many options. One solution is medication, which can help regulate ovulation. Some people will choose to combine fertility drugs with artificial insemination, where sperm are placed directly into a woman's uterus. Couples also have the option of using an assisted reproductive technique (ART), such as in vitro fertilization (IVF), a process in which an egg is fertilized by sperm in a lab and the resulting embryo is placed directly into the uterus. Donor sperm is sometimes used if the cause of the infertility is the partner's inadequate sperm. About a half a million women annually report having used donor sperm (alone or mixed with partner sperm). Donor sperm users are mostly white, urban, older, and college-educated with higher family incomes (Arocho et al. 2019). Frith et al. (2018) noted that couples often keep their use of donor sperm a secret. The first IVF baby in the United States was born in 1981.

Other methods of ART include gamete intra-fallopian transfer (GIFT), zygote intra-fallopian transfer (ZIFT), and intracytoplasmic sperm injection (ICSI). GIFT involves placing the sperm and egg into a woman's fallopian tubes with the goal of fertilization. ZIFT is similar, but involves implanting a zygote into the fallopian tube. ICSI involves a sperm being injected directly into an egg. If fertilization takes place, the embryo is then transferred into the uterus.

In an unprecedented use of ICSI to circumvent a mitochondrial DNA birth defect, on April 6, 2016, the world's first baby with three parents was born. The couple's first two children had died of a rare disease caused by defective genes carried in mitochondrial DNA. Through a controversial new technology—spindle nuclear transfer—the nucleus from the mother's egg was inserted into a denucleated donor egg. This egg, containing both the donor's mitochondrial DNA and the mother's nuclear DNA, was then fertilized by the father's sperm, and the resulting fetus was carried to term by the mother.

Infants conceived by previous mitochondrial transfers had fatal birth defects, so the process is not approved in the United States and was performed in Mexico. However, less than 1% of this baby's mitochondrial DNA carries the mutation, a percentage considered within the safe zone, and he has had no apparent health problems (Hamzelou, 2016).

Despite all of these options, IVF is not a widely used option for surmounting infertility and birth defects. These procedures are costly and do not always result in a live birth. ART is most successful for women under the age of 35, but even for this age group, only 31% of procedures result in a live birth (Centers for Disease Control and Prevention, 2019d).

Some infertile couples may want help when trying to conceive but cannot use fertility drugs or want something less invasive. For these individuals, there are apps that help identify when the woman is ovulating to increase the chance of getting pregnant during vaginal intercourse.

Apps and online communities can also help connect infertile individuals and carriers of genetic diseases with others who are going through a similar situation. This advantage has expanded access to an abundance of information now available during pregnancy. Easy access to information has also changed the relationship between the doctor or midwife and the parents-to-be. Today, parents are expected to "be a full participant in decision-making" not only during the pregnancy, but also through childbirth (Leggitt, 2013).

13.3 Childbirth: Preparation and Reality

13.3a Childbirth Preparation—Lamaze

At the beginning of the 20th century, around 95% of babies were born at home or in another nonmedical setting. Because there were few physicians and fewer hospitals, a midwife was usually summoned to the pregnant woman's home to assist the laboring mother-to-be with delivery. Home births gradually became less common due to the high infant mortality rate, the developing political strength of the medical profession, and the establishment of hospital facilities to handle difficult deliveries. Today, more than 98% of all births in the United States take place in a hospital.

Considerable controversy continues over whether physicians exercise too much control over the birthing process (referred to as the medicalization of childbirth). For example, in physician-controlled births, when the woman began to experience uterine contractions that were regular and intense, she was traditionally encouraged to check into the hospital, be prepped (the vaginal area was cleaned, the pubic hair shaved, and an enema was given), and complete labor in a special room near the delivery room. The husband or partner was usually not allowed to remain in the room during labor and delivery. The woman was confined to bed instead of being allowed to walk about during labor. The prescribed birthing position, the lithotomy position, had the woman lying on her back on the delivery table, legs in the air or in stirrups, and buttocks at the table's edge. In response to the feeling of being medically managed, expectant parents began to question physician-controlled births and emphasized that hospital childbirth procedures were too impersonal, autocratic, and rigid. They also felt that various childbirth interventions were used to accommodate physicians and hospital staff, not the mother. Higher Cesarean and episiotomy rates in physician-attended births compared to midwife-attended births also caused concern.

The natural childbirth movement, including the Lamaze method, provides an alternative to the medicalization of pregnancy and birth. Michaels (2014) noted that the Lamaze method, which began in Soviet Russia, was a response to the limited availability of pharmaceuticals to alleviate pain and led obstetricians to turn to psychological and breathing methods. The method received international attention when French obstetrician Fernand Lamaze visited the USSR in 1951. He returned to France and made modifications, which included classes beginning earlier in pregnancy, new educational materials, and the expectation that husbands become involved in preparation for the birth and birthing event.

The Lamaze method, also called *natural childbirth* or *prepared childbirth*, involves the woman and the partner (or other support person) taking 12 hours of instruction spread out over six to eight classes during the last trimester of pregnancy; the classes usually involve several other couples. The sessions aim to reduce the anxiety and pain of childbirth by viewing it as a natural process, by educating the couple about labor and delivery, and by giving them specific instructions to aid in the birth of their baby. Lamaze features several specific elements:

1. *Education about childbirth information:* Early sessions are about the anatomy and physiology of pregnancy and the stages of labor and delivery. The woman and partner or coach learn what is to happen at each stage of labor and delivery.

2. *Timed breathing exercises (respiration techniques):* Specific breathing exercises are recommended for each stage of labor to minimize the pain of the contractions. The purpose of the breathing exercises is to refocus the laboring woman's attention and keep the pressure of the diaphragm off the uterus. Lamaze breathing techniques also help maintain a balanced level of carbon dioxide and oxygen throughout labor and delivery. The couple practices the exercises between sessions so they will know when and how to use them when labor actually begins.

3. *Pain control exercises (conditioned relaxation):* The woman is taught to selectively tense and relax various muscle groups of the body (for example, the arm muscles). She then learns how to tense these muscle groups while relaxing the rest of the body, so that during labor the rest of the body can relax while the uterus is contracting involuntarily. In addition, the words of the coach serve as a conditioned stimulus for relaxation. The goal of such conditioned relaxation is to reduce pain.

4. *Visual focusing techniques:* The woman is encouraged to look at a specific spot on the wall as a diversion from attending to the physiological events of childbirth so as to minimize any feelings of pain.

5. *Social support via a coach:* A major advantage of the Lamaze method is the active involvement of a coach (often the husband or close partner) throughout the birthing. The coach prompts the woman to start and stop the various breathing exercises, gives psychological support throughout labor, lets her know what stage of the birthing process they are in, and responds to requests for such items as ice and blankets. The coach attends the classes with the woman, practices outside of class with her, and may photograph or record the birth.

13.3b Trends: Classes, Birth Centers, Home Birth, and VBAC

In the 1980s, hospitals regained their control over births, and the Lamaze method was used by fewer expectant couples. But recently, the natural approach is regaining popularity, with Lamaze-style, breathing-based childbirth classes commonly offered to expectant couples.

Birth centers, a less clinical alternative to the hospital setting, are also increasing in popularity. They provide professional medical care, including anesthesia and analgesia for women who request it, in a woman-centered setting, allowing women to move freely throughout the stages of labor as desired. Some even offer water features such as birthing tubs to ease pain and aid relaxation. Birth centers also welcome the presence of family members throughout the birth process.

Interest in home birth is also increasing. Between 2004 and 2009, home births in the United States increased by 29% (MacDorman et al., 2012). Of these home births, 62% involved midwives, who can also be attendants in hospital births. Home births occurred more frequently in mothers who were older than 35, who were married, and who had other children.

Vaginal birth after Cesarean (VBAC) was previously rare, with many physicians refusing to attempt the procedure due to concerns about possible uterine rupture and other potential problems. However, studies have revealed this risk to be less than 1% for laboring women who have had Cesareans, and the rate of VBACs has been steadily climbing over the past few years (Gregory et al., 2010).

13.3c Pain Control in Labor and Delivery

Many women—approximately 64% of women under a physician's care—seek pharmaceutical pain control in labor and delivery. The most commonly used treatments are epidural and spinal anesthesia or CSE (combined spinal/epidural).

The epidural block is the most widely used anesthesia for labor, with medication administered through a tube inserted in the lower back. The spinal block is a similar procedure, with medication injected into the spinal fluid.

The effects vary in duration, with the epidural offering prolonged pain relief, and the spinal block offering more immediate effects and a shorter duration, (approximately 1–2 hours). Both provide complete blocking of sensation throughout the pelvic and abdominal region, so that women feel nothing and must be instructed in pushing in the later stages of labor.

General anesthesia is also available but is administered mainly in emergencies due to increased health risks to both woman and fetus, as well as most women's desire to be conscious and "present" for the birth. Per the CDC, more than three out of five women who were attended by a doctor or osteopath had spinals or epidurals; that number fell to less than half for those women who were attended by midwives (Osterman & Martin, 2011).

13.3d First Stage of Labor

The beginning of labor signals the beginning of childbirth and the end of pregnancy. Labor occurs in three stages, and although there are great variations, it lasts an average of 13 hours for women having their first baby (who are referred to as **primigravida**) and about 8 hours if they have given birth before (**multigravida**). It is not known what causes the onset of labor, which is marked by uterine contractions of increasing intensity. But there are distinctions between the contractions of true labor and preparatory labor, also known as Braxton-Hicks contractions. Figure 13-4 depicts the birth process.

Labor begins with regular uterine contractions, at 15- to 20-minute intervals, that last from 10 to 30 seconds. The first stage of labor lasts for about 9 hours if it is the first baby and about 5 hours in subsequent deliveries. During this first stage, the woman often has cramps and backache. The membranes of the amniotic sac may rupture, spilling the amniotic fluid.

Throughout the first stage, the uterine contractions become stronger, (lasting for 30–45 seconds), and more frequent (every 3–5 minutes). These contractions result in effacement and dilation of the cervix. With **effacement**, the cervix flattens out and gets longer, and with **dilation**, the cervical opening through which the baby will pass gets larger. At the end of the first stage, the cervix is dilated 3.5–4 inches, and contractions occur every 1–2 minutes and last up to 1 minute.

During the first stage of labor, the baby is getting into position to be born. The fetal heart rate is monitored continually by stethoscope or ultrasound, and the woman's temperature and blood pressure are checked. She may experience leg cramps, nausea, or irritability during the first stage of labor.

13.3e Second Stage of Labor

Also known as the expulsive stage of labor, the second stage begins when the cervix is completely dilated and ends when the baby is born. It lasts about 50 minutes if it is the woman's first baby and 20 minutes for subsequent births. Uterine contractions may last 1.5 minutes and be 1–2 minutes apart. These contractions move the baby farther down into the vaginal birth canal. The woman may help this process through pushing movements. The head of the baby emerges first, followed by the shoulders and trunk. While most babies are born head first, some are born breech. In a **breech birth**, the baby's feet or buttocks come out of the vagina first. Breech deliveries are much more complicated.

To ease the birth, the health-care professional may perform an episiotomy, which involves cutting in one of two places on the *perineum*, the area between the vagina and the anus, to make a larger opening for the baby and to prevent uncontrolled tearing.

Cultural differences are a significant factor in episiotomy rates. In the last decade, though the procedure is less common than in the past, episiotomies are still performed in 50% of all births in the United States, in contrast to only 8% in the Netherlands and 14% in the United Kingdom. Although the procedure is purportedly performed to

Primigravida
Woman giving birth to her first baby

Multigravida
State of having given birth before

Effacement
During childbirth, the cervix flattening out and getting longer

Dilation
During childbirth, the increased size of the opening of the cervix through which the baby will pass

Breech birth
During childbirth, the baby's feet or buttocks come out of the vagina first

reduce tearing, researchers at the Royal College of Obstetricians and Gynaecologists found that reduced use of episiotomies was associated with decreased postpartum problems, including posterior perineal trauma and need for suturing, as well as healing complications. In addition, no difference in severe vaginal or perineal trauma, pain, urinary incontinence, or dyspareunia was seen (RCOG, 2015).

Immediately after the baby is born, the baby's nostrils are cleared of mucus using a small suction bulb. The umbilical cord is then clamped twice—about 1 and 2 inches from the infant's abdomen—and cut between the clamps. The baby is cleaned of placental matter and put in a temperature-controlled bassinet or held by the parents.

FIGURE **13-4** ‖ Stages of Labor

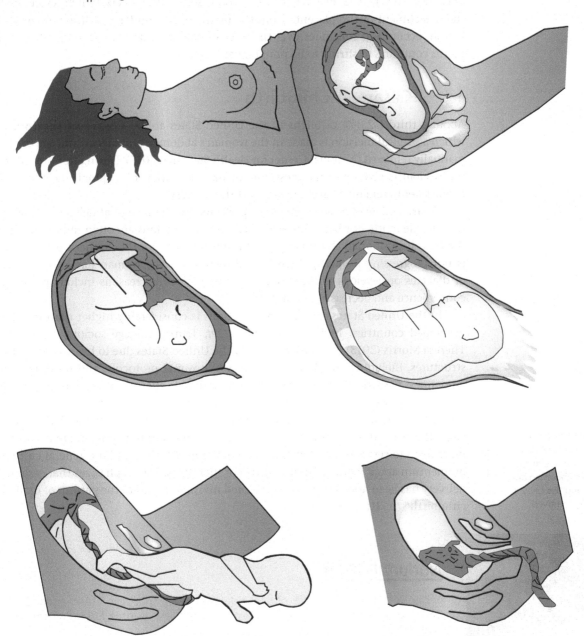

Drawn by–Rachel Jhala 2/11/16

13.3f Third Stage of Labor

After the baby is born, the *placenta*, or *afterbirth*, is delivered. Usually within 5 minutes after the birth of the baby, the placenta separates itself from the uterine wall and is expelled from the vagina. If it does not disengage easily and on its own, the birth attendant must manually remove it, taking care to ensure that no placental tissue is left in the woman's body to avoid postpartum infection. If an episiotomy was performed, the physician or midwife will repair it by stitching up the incision after the placenta is delivered.

The time from 1 to 4 hours after delivery is regarded by some physicians as a fourth stage of labor. During this time, the mother's uterus contracts, causing cramps, called *afterpains*, and shrinks. Bleeding of the blood vessels of the cervix, which results from the detachment of the placenta from the uterine wall, similar to a heavy menstrual period, occurs and continues over the next several days, decreasing gradually as the uterus continues to shrink to its nonpregnant state.

13.3g Cesarean Childbirth

About a third (32.3%) of births in the United States are by **Cesarean section,** in which a surgical incision is made in the woman's abdomen and uterus, and the baby is manually removed (National Center for Health Statistics, 2017). During this procedure, the woman is given general anesthesia or has the option of a spinal injection that enables her to remain awake and aware of the delivery.

Cesarean deliveries are most often performed when a vaginal delivery would be risky to the mother or baby. For example, Cesarean sections are often indicated when the fetus is positioned abnormally, the head is too large for the mother's pelvis, labor is not progressing properly, there is fetal distress, or the woman has an active STI or diabetes or develops toxemia during pregnancy. Other reasons include physician convenience and decreased use of forceps.

In the United States, the rate of C-sections is considerably higher than in other developed countries. In her book *Cut It Out,* Trinity College sociology professor Theresa Morris (2013) emphasized that in the United States due to health-care infra-structures, including standardized processes, hospital protocols, and minimal care guidelines, C-sections have escalated and are double the recommended percentage proposed by the World Health Organization. This is a concern because C-sections "are associated with a higher risk of injury and death to women and babies than vaginal birth" (Morris, 2013, p. 14). Jolly (2018) observed that women are becoming more open to cesarean childbirth in spite of the health risks and the general cultural momentum about women taking control of their lives. She emphasizes that cesarean delivery has been normalized and "rendered invisible as part of the pattern of modern childbirth" (p. 31).

Cesarean section
During childbirth, an incision is made in the woman's abdomen and uterus, and the baby is manually removed

National DATA

In the United States, the risk of death during and up to a year after pregnancy from pregnancy-related causes was 17 per 100,000 live births in 2013 (Zaharatos et al., 2018).

13.3h Reactions to the Baby

Most couples are thrilled at the birth of their baby; some are euphoric and cope well with the associated stresses. But for many, the reality of parenthood causes the new parents to become exhausted while coping with the reality of the infant, who requires continuous feeding and changing. A downturn in sexual satisfaction is a given among first time parents (Maas et al., 2018). However, mothers who blame their partners for the downturn report a larger drop in relationship satisfaction (Vannier et al., 2018).

While there is disagreement in regard to the definition and treatment of **postpartum depression**, about 11%–20% of new mothers experience a severe reaction beyond the usual baby blues, comprising sadness, hopelessness, lethargy, detachment or alienation from the baby, a sense of being overwhelmed, and even suicidal ideation. Only 15% of these women seek medical treatment (Stone, n.d.).

Postpartum depression usually occurs within a month of the baby's birth and is more common after a compli-cated delivery (Wickel, 2012) and when the partner is not

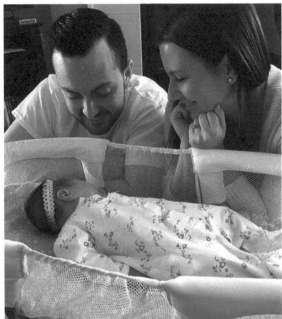
The focus of new parents turns from each other to their infant.

(Megan Smith)

supportive. Mothers who are perfectionistic are also more likely to report postpartum depression (Gelabert et al., 2012) in response to unrealistic cultural expectations of instant bonding and capability in infant care. Women who experience postpartum depression should seek counseling and treatment without shame as it is a common reaction among new mothers who feel unable to handle the pressures of parenting.

Treatment options include psychotherapy, antidepressants, bright light therapy, and alternative approaches, such as folic acid and omega-3 fatty acid supplements to help prevent depletion by the baby during pregnancy and breastfeeding. Lifestyle changes are also advised, such as increased exercise as tolerated, accepting assistance with baby care and other activities of daily living, establishing relationships with other new parents, strengthening ties with family and friends, and focusing on self-care (Stone, 2010). The clinical value of including partners in postpartum depression inter-ventions has limited research support (Alves et al., 2018).

While postpartum depression is well known, little attention has been given to **peripartum depression**—similar in symptoms to postpartum depression, these negative feelings may begin as early as 4 months into the pregnancy. Moncada & Natrajan-Tyagi (2018) interviewed 15 women who reported feeling anxious, depressed, and moody during the pregnancy. The *Diagnostic and Statistical Manual of Mental Disorders (DSM-5®)* was recently updated to include peripartum depression.

13.3i Dangers of Childbirth for the Mother

Citing data from the *Lancet* medical journal, Young (2018) noted that while the vast majority of mothers give birth without incident, 50,000 are severely injured and 700 die annually. Over half of these deaths could be prevented by following basic protocol—monitoring blood loss, high blood pressure, and fever.

Postpartum depression
Severe depression, anxiety, and alienation from infant experienced by 11%–20% of new mothers

Peripartum depression
Similar to postpartum depression but feelings begin as early as four months into pregnancy

Chapter Summary

Pregnancy

EARLY SIGNS OF PREGNANCY include lack of menstruation, nausea and vomiting (morning sickness), enlarged and tender breasts, frequent urination, and fatigue. Pregnancy is best confirmed by laboratory tests and a physical examination. Prenatal care helps ensure a healthy pregnancy and healthy baby. Miscarriages, or spontaneous abortions, are not uncommon in early pregnancy.

Infertility

INFERTILITY is the inability to achieve a pregnancy after at least 1 year of regular sexual relations without birth control, or the inability to carry a pregnancy to a live birth. Different types of infertility include primary, secondary, and pregnancy wastage. Infertility increases with age. The chance of conceiving per month in the 40s is 10% (preterm births and stillbirths are also higher with increased age).

Infertility causes attributed to the woman are 40%, 40% to the man, and 20% to both.

Childbirth: Preparation and Reality

IN THE UNITED STATES, while many babies are born in hospitals, there has been a growing trend to either do home births, or to use a birthing center. In preparation for the birth, some couples attend classes in Lamaze or other breath-focused techniques. The Lamaze method, also called natural childbirth or prepared childbirth, involves the woman and the partner (or other support person) taking six to eight classes during the last trimester of pregnancy, usually with several other couples. The goal of these sessions is to reduce the anxiety and pain of childbirth by viewing it as a natural process, by educating the couple about labor and delivery, and by giving them specific instructions to aid in the birth of their baby.

Most couples are thrilled, or even euphoric, at the birth of their baby, but for many, the reality of parenthood results in the new parents becoming exhausted. While there is disagreement in regard to the definition and treatment of postpartum depression, about 11%–20% of new mothers experience a severe reaction beyond baby blues. Postpartum depression usually occurs within a month of the baby's birth and is more likely after a complicated delivery and when the partner is not supportive.

Web Links

Planned Parenthood

http://www.plannedparenthood.org/

Population Council

http://www.popcouncil.org

Key Terms

Amniocentesis **345**

Breech birth **352**

Cesarean section **354**

Chorionic villus sampling **346**

Conception **348**

Dilation **352**

Ectopic pregnancy **339**

Effacement **352**

Embryo **338**

Fetal alcohol syndrome (FAS) **342**

Fetus **338**

Infertility **347**

Miscarriage **346**

Multigravida **352**

Peripartum depression **355**

Postpartum depression **355**

Pregnancy **348**

Primigravida **352**

Ultrasound scan **345**

Umbilical cord **338**

Intoxication, like sexual euphoria, is the privilege of the human animal. Sexual frenzy is our compensation for the tedious moments we must suffer in the passage of life. "Nothing in excess" professed the ancient Greeks. Why, if I spend half the month in healthy scholarship and pleasant sleep, shouldn't I be allowed the other half to howl at the moon and pillage the groins of Europe's great beauties?

Roman Payne, *The Wanderess*

Chapter Outline

14.1 **Definitions of Sexual Dysfunctions 360**
14.2 **Causes and Contributing Factors of Sexual Dysfunctions 362**
  14.2a Organic Factors **362**
  14.2b Sociocultural Factors **363**
  14.2c Psychological Factors **364**
  14.2d Relationship Factors **365**
  14.2e Cognitive Factors **365**
  14.2f Sexual Destiny? **366**
  Self-Assessment 14-1:
      Sexual Destiny Beliefs Measure **366**
14.3 **Interest/Arousal Dysfunctions 367**
  14.3a Female Sexual Interest/
      Arousal Disorder **367**
  Social Policy 14-1
      "Even the Score" Debate **371**
  14.3b Male Hypoactive Sexual
      Desire Disorder **372**
  14.3c Couple Discrepancy in Desire for
      Frequency of Sex **373**
14.4 **Other Male Sexual Dysfunctions 373**
  14.4a Premature Ejaculation **373**
  14.4b Erectile Disorder **375**

14.5 **Orgasm Dysfunctions 378**
  14.5a Female Orgasmic Disorder **378**
  14.5b Delayed Ejaculation **381**
14.6 **Genito-Pelvic Pain/
  Penetration Disorder 383**
  14.6a Vaginismus **384**
  14.6b Dyspareunia **384**
14.7 **Sex Therapy 386**
  14.7a Sex Therapist Requirements/Status
      of the Profession **386**
  14.7b Cognitive Behavioral
      Sex Therapy **386**
  Personal Decisions 14-1
      Finding a Sex Therapist **387**
  14.7c Masters and Johnson's Approach **387**
  14.7d Kaplan's Approach **388**
  14.7e PLISSIT Model Approach **389**
  14.7f LoPiccolo's Approach **389**
  14.7g Effectiveness of Sex Therapy **389**
  Technology and Sexuality 14-1:
      The Medicalization of
      Sexual Dysfunctions **390**

Web Links 392
Key Terms 393

Objectives

1. Identify the various elements that comprise the definition of sexual dysfunction
2. Understand the various causes and contributing factors to sexual dysfunctions
3. Review the various interest and arousal dysfunctions

4. Explain the two major male sexual dysfunctions
5. Discuss the two orgasm dysfunctions
6. Learn the two genito-pelvic pain and penetration disorders
7. Describe the various approaches used in sex therapy and their effectiveness

(Brenna Gilbert-Love)

Truth — OR — Fiction?

T / F 1. Sexual problems among college females are infrequent (less than 10 percent identify any sexual issues).

T / F 2. Too much alcohol was the top reason identified by women who reported infrequent orgasm during partnered sex.

T / F 3. Sex therapy has been amiss by providing services primarily to middle-class clients only.

T / F 4. Feeling desired is the top factor men identify as eliciting sexual desire just as being rejected is identified as inhibiting sexual desire.

T / F 5. Barry McCarthy popularized the concept of "good enough" sex.

Answers: 1. F   2. F   3. T   4. T   5. T

Psychiatrist Robert Sammons notes that among the couples he sees for sexual dysfunction, "the only thing that's important is that which is missing." His referent is sexual dysfunction, whether it be early ejaculation or lack of arousal/orgasm, the couple becomes obsessed with the sexual issue. Hinchliff et al. (2018) confirmed in a sample of 1,084 adults that sexual problems had a negative impact on the psychological well-being of the individual (e.g. frustration, depression, sadness) as well as on the individual's relationship. Hendrickx et al. (2019) noted personal and relationship distress in reference to sexual dysfunctions. Sexual problems are not infrequent. In one study of 271 female college students, three-fourths reported at least one sexual difficulty (Garneau-Fournier et al., 2014).

Personal REFLECTION

Take a moment to express your thoughts about the following questions. People vary in regard to their value of the importance of a good sexual relationship. For some, it is the prerequisite for a quality relationship; for others, it is irrelevant. On a 10-point scale, with 10 as the top, what value do you place on your sexual relationship with your partner? What number do you feel your partner would select? How discrepant can the numbers be before they impact the relationship?

Before we discuss sexual dysfunctions, let's examine the conditions under which partners report a satisfying sexual relationship. Factors associated with sexual competence in a relationship include the following (Grauvogl et al., 2015):

1. *Positive sexual attitudes:* The positive feelings about experiencing sexual behavior, as well as respect, expressed toward and received from the sexual partner

2. *Contraceptive use:* Using contraceptives to prevent sexually transmitted infections and unwanted pregnancy

3. *Communicating about sex:* Talking with your partner about promoting sexual hedonism and satisfaction for both yourself and your partner

4. *Refusing sex:* Being able to stop or disengage from undesirable sexual activities

5. *Sexual assertiveness:* The ability to stand up for your own rights and desires

6. *Addressing sexual problems:* Engaging your partner about how to resolve sexual dissatisfactions

> *He was now in that state of fire that she loved. She wanted to be burnt.*
>
> Anais Nin, American novelist

In one study of 100 married couples, about one-fourth of the husbands and one-third of the wives reported sexual problems (dealing with actual, desired, or intended sexual behaviors or displays of verbal and physical affection in the relationship). Average ages of the husbands and wives were 39 and 37, respectively, and they had been married an average of 12 years. Most had two or three children, with the range between one child and six (Papp et al., 2013). Notice that this study focused not on sexual dysfunctions but on general sexual issues in the relationship.

Barry McCarthy popularized the concept of "good enough" sex, whereby the focus was not on individual performance but a satisfying couple experience. Hence, couples can find what works for them rather than impose culturally scripted definitions of sexual satisfaction (Southern, 2019).

Sexual dysfunctions
A heterogeneous group of disorders that are typically characterized by a clinically significant disturbance in a person's ability to respond sexually or to experience sexual pleasure

14.1 Definitions of Sexual Dysfunctions

Sexual dysfunctions are a heterogeneous group of disorders that are typically characterized by a clinically significant disturbance in a person's ability to respond sexually or to experience sexual pleasure (American Psychiatric Association, 2013). An individual may have several sexual dysfunctions at once. The term *sexual dysfunction* is not appropriate if the sexual problem is caused by inadequate sexual stimulation.

As noted in Chapter 10, some individuals are asexual and are not aroused by, nor do they have an interest in, sexual behavior with a partner (Van Houdenhove et al., 2015). These people would not be labeled as having a sexual dysfunction, since asexuality is their identity and they do not regard their absence of interest in sex as negative.

One way to discuss sexual dysfunctions is in terms of the stages in which sexual problems occur across the sexual response cycle. However, doing so emphasizes the physical processes within the genitals—the **medicalization of sexual dysfunctions**—rather than a person's or couple's overall emotional relationship and sexual satisfaction. An example of the degree to which sexual dysfunctions have been medicalized is research by Leeners and colleagues (2013) that quantified satisfaction levels of female orgasm solely in reference to the pituitary hormone prolactin (PRL). More about this follows in the section on female orgasmic disorder.

Sexual problems have been medicalized in an attempt to identify medical sources for their causes and treatments. If a male loses his interest in sex or is not capable of getting and keeping an erection, the cause (we are reminded of regularly on television and in print ads) is low testosterone. A woman's libido drop is seen as an issue of hormones. What we're missing in this medical view, however, are the emotional and psychological factors that impact sexual feelings, interaction, and behavior.

Throughout the discussion of each sexual dysfunction, it is important to keep the cognitions and feelings of the individuals and their partners in mind. From this point of view, a couple may have various sexual issues yet still be happy with each other and their sexual relationship.

In this chapter, we review sexual dysfunctions as they are classified in the *Diagnostic and Statistical Manual of Mental Disorders*, 5th edition (commonly referred to as *DSM-5®*) (American Psychiatric Association, 2013). Although its title implies that mental disorders are distinct from physical disorders, there is much overlap between them. Note that the term *mental disorders* is used because an appropriate substitute has not been found. Although there are problems with this conceptualization, the *DSM-5* remains a widely used resource and is the standard diagnostic reference among health and mental health professionals in the United States.

According to the *DSM-5*, each sexual dysfunction identified may also be classified as being lifelong or acquired (American Psychiatric Association, 2013). A **lifelong dysfunction** (also referred to as a **primary dysfunction**) is one that a person has always experienced. For example, a person may have always lacked sexual desire. An **acquired dysfunction**, or **secondary dysfunction**, is one that a person is currently experiencing but has not always experienced. A person may also have a **situational dysfunction**, which occurs only with certain types of stimulation, situations, or partners, or a **generalized dysfunction**, which identifies sexual difficulties that are not limited to certain types of stimulation (APA, 2013). Basic causes may be organic, psychogenic, mixed, or unknown.

Medicalization of sexual dysfunctions
Emphasizes that sexual dysfunctions have a medical or biological basis rather than an emotional or relationship cause

Lifelong dysfunction
Sexual dysfunction that a person has always experienced; for example, a person may have always lacked sexual desire

Primary dysfunction
See lifelong dysfunction

Acquired dysfunction
Sexual dysfunction that a person is currently experiencing but has not always experienced

Secondary dysfunction
See acquired dysfunction

Situational dysfunction
Sexual dysfunction that occurs with one partner or in one situation only

Generalized dysfunction
Sexual dysfunction that occurs with all partners, in all contexts and settings

International DATA

Of 61,000 males in a National Health Insurance Database in Taiwan, 2% reported experiencing a sexual dysfunction (Chen et al., 2013). This low percentage is likely due to the cultural psychological repression of being open about one's sexuality.

How a sexual dysfunction is conceptualized and treated has changed across time. In addition, various treatments for a sexual dysfunction have regularly claimed to be revolutionary (Berry, 2013a). For example, over the years, erectile dysfunction has been seen as primarily psychological, then biopsychological. Today the focus is biochemical, with pharmacotherapy (as in Viagra, LEVITRA, and Cialis) as the treatment of choice. Caution is recommended in accepting any one conceptualization or treatment plan for a sexual dysfunction. Today, a broad approach encompassing biopsychosocial factors is preferred because any sexual dysfunction has both a biological basis and a psychological (anxiety) component, and it occurs in a social (interpersonal) context.

14.2 Causes and Contributing Factors of Sexual Dysfunctions

The numerous causes of sexual dysfunctions include organic, sociocultural, psychological, relationship, and cognitive factors.

14.2a Organic Factors

As noted in Chapter 11, the organic factors are important causes to consider for sexual dysfunctions. Shen (2019) analyzed national data on chronic disease burden, sexual frequency, and sexual dysfunction in partnered older adults and found that biological change concomitant with a disease and the negative impact on one's self-concept as a sexual partner resulted in a decrease in frequency and an increase in sexual dysfunction. In addition, a physical condition such as diabetes, arthritis, pituitary tumors, or vascular disease and its treatments may also interfere with physiological or anatomical mechanisms involved in sexual desire, arousal, or orgasm. As Burri (2013) further emphasized, "[U]nderstanding the genetic basis and therefore physiologic key mechanisms of sexual function and dysfunction has the potential for improved treatments (i.e., the development of new medication) and ultimately prevention." However, he noted the "scarcity of genetic epidemiologic research" as related to sexual dysfunction (p. 318).

Neurological conditions or diseases—such as stroke, multiple sclerosis (MS), Parkinson's disease (PD), epilepsy, and tumors—may alter the motor and sensory pathways and affect sexual performance. Weight is also related to sexual dysfunction. Researchers Erenel and Kilinc (2013) reported that 44% of 203 women who had applied to a diet center in a hospital said that being overweight affected their sex life. Metabolic syndrome, characterized by high blood pressure, blood sugar, and body fat, is also associated with sexual dysfunction in women (Otunctemur et al., 2015).

Although we discussed drugs and sexuality in Chapter 11, here we note that alcohol, marijuana, barbiturates, and amphetamines—as well as numerous medications used to treat various diseases and illnesses—affect sexuality and may cause or contribute to sexual dysfunction. For example, antipsychotic medications are associated with sexual dysfunctions. However, not all antipsychotic meds impact the body in the same way (Chiesa et al., 2013). If the goal is to reduce a patient's sexual dysfunction, either dose reduction or switching medication may be indicated. If you are currently taking a medication and have noticed a change in your sexual functioning, consult your health-care practitioner. It may be that either a dose reduction or medication change can help.

Age is also a factor in sexual dysfunction. As the body ages, so do the physical underpinnings of sexual functioning. For example, lubrication decreases in menopausal women, who report less frequent intimate contact and sexual intercourse (Lo & Kok, 2013). This is the most common sexual dysfunction in women. Penile erectile capacity in men also decreases with age.

Finally, sexual dysfunction often results from a combination of biological and psychosocial factors. For example, a woman may experience a lack of sexual desire because she is chronically fatigued (biological factor) from taking care of young children, a husband, aging parents, or a mother-in-law who lives in the house. Fuentealba-Torres et al. (2019) found women who breastfed reported a lower interest in sex. Compounding her fatigue is resentment (psychosocial factor) toward her husband for not sharing the childcare and housework and not helping to care for aging parents.

Cultural Diversity

Some religions, including Catholicism and Islam, teach that sex is only for procreation or that the only appropriate sexual relations are penile-vaginal and between husband and wife. Believers who depart from these cultural scripts may internalize negative feelings about sexuality (guilt), and these feelings may interfere with their ability to experience sexual desire, arousal, and orgasm.

14.2b Sociocultural Factors

In addition to physical and biological factors, sociocultural factors may cause or contribute to sexual dysfunction. These include restrictive upbringing and religious training. For example, in some families, parents may openly express negative attitudes toward sexuality by teaching their children that sex is dirty. Some parents punish children and adolescents for engaging in masturbation or other sexual exploration.

In many families, sex is never discussed with the children. Children who learn that sex is a taboo subject may come to regard sex as somehow wrong or shameful.

Another sociocultural factor that may contribute to sexual dysfunction is society's traditional gender role socialization. Women may be socialized to be sexually passive and to focus on pleasing their man, thus not giving emphasis to their own sexuality/pleasure; men may be taught to be sexually aggressive, entitled, and in control of sexual situations, thus missing the point of sexual sharing or experiencing a partner who guides the sexual experience. One of our female students noted, "I know a lot of women who love sex, but a lot of my friends engage in sex just to please their boyfriends. It is going to be a shock when their partner finds out otherwise." Women do indeed live in a different sociocultural world than men.

Still another sociocultural factor contributing to sexual dysfunction is society's emphasis on intercourse as the sexual act and on orgasm as the event necessary for satisfaction. Nongenital sexual expressions and sexual experiences that do not result in orgasm are given little recognition. The result is enormous pressure on couples to engage in *the act* and for orgasm to result.

I need sex for a clear complexion, but I'd rather do it for love.

Joan Crawford, actress of the 1950s

Finally, as the income of women continues to increase—so that more women earn more money than their husbands—what is the effect, if any, on the sexual relationship? Pierce and colleagues (2013) analyzed data on spouses in Denmark and found that men whose wives out-earn them are more likely to use erectile dysfunction medication than their male breadwinner counterparts, even when this inequality is small. In addition, breadwinner wives show increased insomnia and anxiety medication usage, with similar effects for men. The results emphasize that cultural factors and social norms play important roles in dictating how individuals respond sexually.

14.2c Psychological Factors

Positive sexual function is associated with the big five personality factors—extraversion, agreeableness, conscientiousness, emotional stability, and openness to experience (Velten et al., 2019). In contrast, negative psychological factors predict negative sexual function. Hence, numerous psychological factors are associated with sexual dysfunction.

1. *Child sexual abuse:* About a quarter of women worldwide report that they have been victims of child sexual abuse. Such an experience is associated with anxiety in sexual contexts, a depressed libido, difficulty in getting aroused, and anorgasmia. Victims of child sex abuse also tend to have negative self-concepts, abuse drugs, have early sexual debuts, and have numerous sexual partners.

2. *Anxiety:* Anxiety may be caused by thoughts and fears about sexual performance or the ability to please the partner. Other sources of anxiety may result from fear of intimacy, concern about the partner's commitment to the relationship, fear of rejection, and uncertainty about the partner's intentions or sexual expectations. One specific type of anxiety related to sexual dysfunction is **performance anxiety**, the excessive concern over adequate sexual performance. A person may become so anxious about having an orgasm or erection that the anxiety itself interferes with achieving both goals. Anxiety, in general, may also be problematic. In a survey of 3,800 respondents who had a regular heterosexual partner, 9% of the men and 12% of the women reported moderate psychological distress that was associated with low ratings of sexual and relationship satisfaction (Patrick et al., 2013).

3. *Fear:* Impairment in the desire, arousal, or orgasm phases of sexual response may result from fear of any of the following: unwanted pregnancy or sexually transmitted infections, intimacy or commitment, physical pain, displeasing a partner, or losing self-control during sexual arousal or orgasm. Fear of not measuring up may also be operative ("I'm too fat and fear I'm not a good lover").

4. *Guilt:* Guilt—which may be related to masturbation, choice of sexual partner, participation in forbidden or sinful sexual activity, or involvement in an extradyadic sexual relationship—may also interfere with sexual functioning.

5. *Depression and low self-esteem:* Sexual dysfunction may result from depression, which is known to suppress sexual drive. Related to depression is low self-esteem, which may cause an individual to feel unworthy of being loved or of experiencing sexual pleasure.

6. *Conflict concerning sexual orientation:* Because of the social stigma associated with being homosexual, some gay men and lesbians experience internal conflict about their sexual orientation. Some may deny their homosexuality and seek heterosexual relationships, only to find that sexual activity with other-sex individuals doesn't feel right for them and performance is difficult.

7. *Deployment adjustment:* Of 4,755 Iraq/Afghanistan veterans who sought treatment after returning from deployment, 5.5% reported having a sexual dysfunction (Hosain et al., 2013). The researchers noted the total number was likely undercoded for sexual dysfunction.

Performance anxiety
Excessive concern over adequate sexual performance, which may result in sexual dysfunction

8. *Stress:* Higher levels of stress are associated with lower levels of sexual interest, arousal, and satisfaction, particularly for women. This is the conclusion of a study of 228 women of reproductive age (Abedi et al., 2015).

Ecker et al. (2018) emphasized the value of sexual intimacy for recovery from severe mental illness. Hence, not only may psychological problems be associated with sexual dysfunction, recovery from psychological problems may be associated with sexual intimacy.

14.2d Relationship Factors

Sexual dysfunctions do not exist in isolation. Indeed, relationship satisfaction impacts sexual satisfaction. In a study of 351 individuals who had been involved in a relationship, those who regretted involvement in their relationship and agreed with the statement "I think I might have found a better relationship partner if I had kept looking instead of choosing to be with my current partner" were more likely to report less sexual satisfaction. This finding was truer of women than men (Cunningham et al., 2015). Rosen et al. (2017) confirmed the association between a positive relationship and sexual satisfaction.

Relationship, marriage, and sex therapists always focus on the relationship between the partners before addressing a specific sexual dysfunction such as lack of orgasm or erectile disorder (Nelson & Kenowitz, 2013). When a couple comes to therapy with a sexual problem, the therapist usually asks questions like, "Tell me about your relationship. How do you feel about each other? How much time do you spend together?"

In addition to the importance of relationship satisfaction, researchers Mark and Herbenick (2014) studied 176 women (mean age 35) in committed relationships and found that women who were increasingly attracted to their partners reported higher sexual satisfaction.

Working on the sexual problem is productive only if the couple has a good relationship. Anger, lack of trust, lack of intimacy, and/or lack of communication in a relationship contribute to sexual dysfunctions (lack of interest in sex, lack of orgasm, lack of satisfaction, unfulfilled expectations). Sexual dysfunctions may also contribute to relationship problems, and spouses who are not fulfilled sexually may be unhappy or angry and seek other sexual partners.

Not only is there a connection between relationship satisfaction and sexual satisfaction, but relationship satisfaction is also a good predictor of positive treatment outcome for women in sex therapy. In one study, women who reported high relationship satisfaction were the most likely to benefit from cognitive behavioral sex therapy (Stephenson et al., 2013).

The fact that sexual dysfunctions may have multiple causes (biological, psychogenic, interpersonal) raises questions about whether a physician, psychologist, marriage therapist, or sex therapist should be sought for treatment.

14.2e Cognitive Factors

Treatment of sexual dysfunction may include increasing one's awareness of what is happening to one's body. Other cognitive factors include identifying and deconstructing myths.

Consider the following examples: A woman in her 50s believes the myth that women her age should not be interested in sex. A man in his 50s believes the myth that men his age are unable to achieve an erection that is satisfactory for intercourse.

A heterosexual couple believes that the only appropriate way for the woman to have an orgasm is through sexual intercourse. A person believes that it is wrong to have sexual fantasies during lovemaking.

These are just a few examples of beliefs or myths (cognitions) that may interfere with sexual desire, arousal, or orgasm. Inadequate sex education can also contribute to belief in such myths and ignorance of sexual anatomy and physiology. For example, a woman who does not know where her clitoris is (or that it even exists) may have difficulty experiencing an orgasm.

14.2f Sexual Destiny?

Sexual destiny is the belief that couples "naturally" have a good sexual relationship, that it is not the result of working on their relationship and their sex life. The *Self-Assessment 14.1* provides a way for you to assess the degree to which you believe in sexual destiny.

Self-Assessment 14-1:
Sexual Destiny Beliefs Measure

Write the number to the left of each item which reflects your level of disagreement/ agreement:

1 (Strongly disagree), 2 (Disagree), 3 (Mildly disagree), 4 (Neutral), 5 (Mildly agree), 6 (Agree), 7 (Strongly agree)

1. __ Experiencing sexual problems is a sure sign that a couple is not sexually compatible.
2. __ Couples who experience sexual incompatibilities in their relationship will inevitably break up.
3. __ An unsatisfying sex life suggests that the relationship was never meant to be.
4. __ If a couple is truly in love, partners will naturally have high sexual chemistry.
5. __ Struggles in a sexual relationship are a sure sign that the relationship will fail.
6. __ A couple is either destined to have a satisfying sex life or they are not.
7. __ It is clear right from the start how satisfying a couple's sex life will be over the course of their relationship.
8. __ A passionate sex life is a sign that two partners are meant to be.
9. __ If sexual satisfaction declines over the course of a relationship, it suggests that a couple is not a good match.
10. __ If sexual partners are meant to be together, sex will be easy and wonderful.

Total score:

Scoring: Add the numbers you wrote before each item to obtain a total score. The higher your total score (77 is the highest possible score), the greater your belief in sexual destiny—that sexual satisfaction is a function of having a compatible partner (not "working" on your relationship). The lower your score (11 is the lowest possible score), the less you believe in sexual destiny (a good sexual relationship involves working on it). A score of 44 places you at the midpoint between not believing in sexual destiny and in believing in sexual destiny. Maxwell et al. (2017) found a small effect of sexual destiny beliefs on sexual satisfaction.

Source: Maxwell, J. A., Muise, A., MacDonald, G., Day, L. C., Rosen, N. O., Impett, E. A. (2017). How implicit theories of sexuality shape sexual and relationship well-being. *Journal of Personality & Social Psychology*, 112(2), 238–279. Copyright © 2017 American Psychological Association; reprint of table data permitted.

14.3 Interest/Arousal Dysfunctions

In this section we examine female sexual interest/arousal disorder and male hypoactive sexual desire disorder.

Is that a pistol in your pocket or are you just glad to see me?

Mae West, *actress of the 1930s*

14.3a Female Sexual Interest/Arousal Disorder

According to the *DSM-5*, diagnosis of **female sexual interest/arousal disorder** (previously known as *hypoactive sexual desire disorder*) involves the lack of, or significantly reduced, sexual interest/arousal as manifested by at least three of the following:

1. Absent/reduced interest in sexual activity
2. Absent or reduced sexual/erotic thoughts or fantasies
3. No initiation of sexual activity and unreceptive to partner's attempts to initiate
4. Absent or reduced sexual excitement during sexual activity in 75%–100% of the sexual encounters
5. Absent/reduced interest/arousal in response to sexual/erotic cues (such as sexting)
6. Absent/reduced genital and nongenital sensations during sexual activity

At least three of the above must have persisted for a minimum of 6 months. Gradations of the dysfunction would be mild, moderate, or severe. Therapists are careful to examine the relationship of the woman with her partner before determining the diagnosis of sexual interest/arousal disorder. For example, if the woman has a lower desire for sexual activity than her partner, this condition is not sufficient to label the woman as low interest/arousal disorder. The woman must be distressed by her lack of interest/arousal. If she has always viewed her lack of interest in sex as no problem, the label of *female sexual interest/arousal disorder* is not appropriate. The *DSM-5* presents no prevalent data for sexual interest/arousal disorder among females in the United States.

International DATA

Data from France reveal that, in the general female population, prevalence of female sexual interest/arousal disorder ranges from 24%–43% (Geonet et al., 2013).

There is professional disagreement about what constitutes female sexual arousal disorder (FSAD). While some authors have suggested that FSAD is more a subjective response rather than a genital response, others have suggested that desire and arousal disorders should be combined into one entity: *persistent genital arousal disorder (PGAD)*.

Regardless of the label, female sexual interest/arousal disorder means that the woman has no interest in sex and is not able to become or stay sexually aroused. Associated with the absence of interest/arousal is that the woman lacks genital lubrication and swelling. Like other sexual dysfunctions, female sexual arousal disorder may be lifelong, acquired, situational, or generalized. The diagnosis is not made if the woman is severely depressed, drug addicted, has a serious medical condition (such as diabetes), is in a physically abusive relationship, or has a partner who provides inadequate sexual stimulation. Hence, depression, substance abuse, and so on, would

Female sexual interest/arousal disorder
The persistent or recurrent inability to attain or maintain sufficient sexual excitement or a lack of genital lubrication/ swelling or other somatic responses

It was the wildness of it that got me going: the primal lust, the sheer needs of two people in heat, quickly finding ways to express their sacred hunger to each other in animal passion.

Fiona Thrust, *Naked and Sexual*

become the focus in therapy of the woman's problem, not the sexual side effect. It is not unusual for comorbidity to exist, meaning that the sexual interest/arousal problems occur at the same time as other factors, such as depression, thyroid problems, and so on.

Factors that may cause sexual interest/arousal difficulties include relationship dissatisfaction, restrictive upbringing, and exhaustion. Genetics may also be involved. "There appears to be a strong influence of genetic factors on vulnerability to sexual problems in women" (American Psychiatric Association, 2013, p. 435).

Female sexual interest/arousal dysfunction may also result from estrogen deficiency, the most common cause of which is menopause. Other biological factors that may be related to lack of sexual arousal in women include neurogenic disorders (such as multiple sclerosis) and some drugs (such as antihistamines and antihypertensives). Strong emotions—such as depression, fear, anger, and stress—may also interfere with sexual responsiveness.

Paterson et al. (2017) reported increased sexual interest/arousal on the part of 26 women who participated in an eight sessions of mindfulness-based cognitive group therapy for sexuality (MBCT-S). These gains occurred independent of treatment expectations, relationship duration, or low desire duration. Similarly, Velten et al. (2018) noted that "mindfulness-based interventions that encourage women to focus on physical arousal sensations in the here and now may be associated with women's improved sexual function by enhancing feelings of sexual arousal during sexual activity and by increasing concordance between subjective and genital sexual arousal." Palaniappan et al. (2018) also found that reading *A Tired Woman's Guide to Passionate Sex* was more effective in increasing a woman's sexual desire than taking a placebo pill identified as being helpful in increasing sexual desire. Treatment for women with low sexual interest who have difficulty experiencing sexual arousal usually includes an examination of the relationship with her partner. Not only is a loving, respectful context important for the woman's interest in sex, but the kind of stimulation required for arousal by her lover is also paramount. An insensitive, accusatory, selfish partner who does not nurture the love relationship with the partner and provide the time, type, and amount of stimulation their partner needs for arousal becomes the focus of therapeutic intervention. Indeed, research has confirmed that the sexual functioning of the woman's partner has an effect on the arousal, orgasm, and sexual satisfaction of the woman herself (Jiann et al., 2013).

While female sexual interest/arousal disorder may be present in all types of relationships, the concept of **lesbian bed death** has arisen in connection to long-term lesbian relationships. This term refers to a dramatic, sustained drop-off in sexual frequency that is believed to occur in some long-term lesbian couples (Iasenza, 2000). The belief is thought to have its origin in the fact that in lesbian couples, "[T]here is no man in the relationship to ensure initiation of sexual activity" (Iasenza, 2000, p. 59). Although some therapists have observed that lesbian women may not have been socialized to initiate sex, there is also evidence that, compared to heterosexual women, lesbian women may be more sexually aroused, comfortable using erotic or arousing language, and more likely to report a higher level of satisfaction with the quality of their sexual relationship. Indeed, lesbian bed death is a misconception. In addition, that part of the definition that suggests a drop-off in frequency of sex in long-term relationships is equally true of heterosexual relationships.

Lesbian bed death
Purported sustained drop-off in sexual frequency of lesbian couples in long-term relationships that is not backed up by scientific data

Cultural Diversity

Lower rates of sexual desire may be more common among East Asian women when compared with European women (American Psychiatric Association, 2013, p. 435). One explanation is that East Asian women are more likely taught to be passive and to serve their partners than to be focused on their own sexual needs (in contrast to the norm of individualism in Europe and the United States).

Treatment

Treatment for female sexual interest/arousal disorder depends on the underlying causes of the problem. Some of the ways in which lack of sexual desire may be treated include the following:

1. *Improve relationship satisfaction.* As noted earlier, "treating the relationship before treating the sexual problem" is standard therapy with any sexual dysfunction, including lack of interest in sex. A common prerequisite for being interested in sex with a partner, particularly from the viewpoint of a woman, is psychological intimacy—to be in love and to feel comfortable and secure with her partner. Couple's therapy that emphasizes a mutual loving relationship is the first stage of sex therapy.

2. *Change negative cognitions.* Researchers Geonet et al. (2013) emphasized the negative role cognitions play in scripting women out of a positive, pleasurable experience. These negative cognitions can be linked to their own self-image ("I am not beautiful enough"), their partner ("They disgust me"), or the marital relationship ("They are going to leave me," "They don't love me anymore"). Negative thoughts trigger emotions such as anxiety, shame, or guilt. Moreover, the cognitions will have a negative impact on sexual response. Indeed, the more negative thoughts are present, the less sexual arousal will be experienced. Consequently, during sexual intercourse, women with arousal issues tend to focus on negative thoughts rather than sexual excitements.

3. *Create the conditions for satisfying sex.* Women who report low interest in sex may not have a partner who created the stimulation, both physiological and psychological, who elicits her sexual feelings or desires. Identifying the conditions of satisfying sex for the woman becomes a goal.

4. *Practice sensate focus.* **Sensate focus** is an exercise whereby the partners focus on pleasuring each other in nongenital ways. Masters and Johnson (1966) developed sensate focus exercises to treat various sexual dysfunctions. Couples who are not experiencing sexual dysfunction but who want to enhance their sexual relationship may also use sensate focus.

   In practicing the sensate focus exercise, partners remove their clothing and take turns touching, feeling, caressing, and exploring each other in ways intended to provide sensual pleasure. In the first phase of sensate focus, genital touching is not allowed. The person being touched should indicate whether they find a particular touching behavior unpleasant and at which point the partner should stop or change the behavior.

Sensate focus
Treatment used in sex therapy developed by Masters and Johnson whereby the partners focus on pleasuring each other in nongenital ways

During the second phase of sensate focus, the person being touched is instructed to give positive as well as negative feedback (to indicate what is enjoyable as well as what is unpleasant). During the third phase, genital touching can be included, without the intention of producing orgasm. The goal of progressing through the three phases of sensate focus is to help the partners learn to give and receive pleasure by promoting trust and communication and reducing anxiety related to sexual performance.

5. *View/read erotic materials and invoke sexual fantasy.* Consistent with the principle of modeling, sexual desire can be encouraged by viewing and reading explicit material about people having explicit enjoyable sex or reading about a romantic sequence between two appealing people or invoking a fantasy that has been reliably erotic in the past.

6. *Replacing hormones.* After the social/relationship conditions for female sexual interest/arousal disorder (including low arousal and low orgasmic capacity) are assessed and treated, hormone assessment may be helpful. A physician may recommend androgen replacement therapy to increase desire, arousal, and satisfaction.

7. *Change medications or dosage (if possible) in cases in which medication interferes with sexual desire.* Selective serotonin reuptake inhibitors (SSRIs), such as Prozac® or Paxil®, which are used to treat depression, anxiety, or premenstrual dysphoric disorder, may interfere with interest, arousal, and performance. Careful monitoring of the effects of medication is indicated. It is important for people taking such medication to work closely with their health-care provider to plan dosage changes or medication discontinuation.

8. *Masturbate.* Masturbation may also be recommended on the premise that individuals may act themselves into a new way of thinking more quickly than they can think themselves into a new way of acting. Rather than trying to think themselves into sexual pleasure, they can masturbate (a vibrator may be helpful) to orgasm, which will provide an experiential basis for the development of positive thoughts and feelings about sex.

> *Among all types of sexual activity, masturbation is, however, the one in which the female most frequently reaches orgasm.*
>
> Alfred C. Kinsey, *Sexual Behavior in the Human Female*

9. *Rest and relax.* Other treatments for lack of sexual desire include rest and relaxation. This treatment is indicated when the culprit is chronic fatigue syndrome (CFS), the symptoms of which are overwhelming fatigue, low-grade fever, and sore throat, or simply ordinary fatigue from overwork. Women with young children sometimes report that they are exhausted and would rather sleep than have sex.

10. *Learn about alternate models of sexual response.* Some women have found it helpful to learn that not having spontaneous sexual desire can be normal. Sex therapists also note that desire is not a prerequisite for engaging in sexual behavior. Indeed, one may engage in sexual behavior out of feelings of emotional intimacy or to please the partner, although this should not be considered obligatory. The principle of acting one's self into a new way of feeling predicts that, once the person engages in sexual behavior with a loving and skilled sexual partner, the outcome may be sexual enjoyment.

Social Policy 14-1

"Even the Score" Debate

The existence of 26 medications for male sexual dysfunctions (premature ejaculation, impotence) has been met with an "Even the Score" campaign, which asks, "Where are the medications for women to enhance their sexuality?" The website http://www.eventhescore.org/ identifies the movement as a "Campaign for Women's Sexual Health Equity leading the fight for safe, FDA-approved treatment options for women's sexual dysfunction." Indeed, while lack of sexual interest, lack of arousal, and low orgasmic capacity are common sexual problems reported by women, only one medication has received FDA approval: Flibanserin, sold under the brand name of Addyi® and known as "Viagra for women," is taken daily at bedtime and works on brain chemicals rather than genital changes. The anticipated sales of Addyi did not occur.

In the summer of 2019, the FDA approved Vyleesi, generic name bremelanotide (designed to boost female desire and is being touted as "female Viagra"). While Vyleesi is also approved to treat hypoactice sexual desire disorder (HSDD), it differs from Addyi because it comes in the form of an injectable rather than a pill and is only to be used before sex rather than on a daily basis.

The counterargument to the minimal presence of FDA-approved drugs available to women is that most of the drugs that have been developed do not meet the research requirements to validate positive outcomes for the intended malady. Sponsored by Sprout Pharmaceuticals, flibanserin is a central nervous system serotonergic agent with effects on adrenaline and dopamine in the brain. The drug is supposed to have a positive impact on the woman's brain chemistry to make her body more responsive to sexual stimulation. The research on the effectiveness of the medication is tenuous, and social and economic pressure to approve the drug was enormous. Flibanserin must be taken daily, long-term, which raises concerns about side effects and long-term sequelae. All male drugs for sexual dysfunction, on the other hand, are taken as needed, which reduces toxicological effects.

There is also concern that the pharmaceutical industry is using the feminist movement as a front to get approval and sell a product. To be clear, flibanserin is designed to influence arousal. It is not a female Viagra, the latter being a male pill that effects only the physiological function—increasing blood flow to the penis. Viagra is said to work "below the waist," whereas flibanserin is designed to work "above the waist" on the biochemistry of the brain.

As noted in section (14.6), which discusses pain during intercourse, vaginally inserted estrogen cream, tablets, and slow-release rings are available and FDA approved to help with vaginal dryness and lubrication. While the potential for arousal may be increased as a function of reducing or removing pain, these products are not marketed specifically to increase a woman's desire for sex or arousal. Zestra® is an over-the-counter botanical oil. Research on its effectiveness has revealed an increase in arousal and orgasm (even among women taking antidepressants). However, many women report some burning or side effects, and many sex therapists report that a good lubricant is just as useful (Mintz, 2011).

Finally, there is an FDA-approved clitoral therapy device, Eros™, for treating difficulty or inability to orgasm. This device provides gentle suction to the clitoris. However, many sex therapists report that Eros is just an expensive vibrator; in fact, vibrators already on the market perform the same function (Mintz, 2015).

14.3b Male Hypoactive Sexual Desire Disorder

Male hypoactive sexual desire disorder is the male counterpart of female sexual interest/arousal disorder. It is the opposite of **hyperactive sexual desire disorder**. The following are the specific diagnostic criteria from the *DSM-5:*

1. Persistent or recurrent deficient (or absent) sexual/erotic thoughts or fantasies and desire for sexual activity is experienced. It is the clinician's call if the label applies, taking into account the age and context of the male patient.

2. The symptoms in the above criteria have persisted for a minimum of 6 months.

3. The symptoms cause significant distress. If the male is not concerned about having low sexual interest, the label does not apply.

4. The sexual dysfunction is not better explained by a nonsexual mental disorder, such as a severe relationship problem, substance abuse/medication, or another medical condition.

National DATA

Approximately 6% of younger men (ages 18–24) and 41% of older men (ages 66–74) report problems with sexual desire. However, persistent (6 months or more) lack of sexual interest in sex among men (ages 16–44) is rare—only 1.8% (American Psychiatric Association, 2013, p. 442).

Male hypoactive sexual desire disorder is sometimes associated with erectile dysfunction or premature ejaculation. The male feels embarrassed or ashamed, so he avoids sexual encounters and contexts, with concomitant loss of interest in sex. As with women, the dysfunction can be lifelong, acquired, generalized, or situational and is categorized as mild, moderate, or severe. Other terms sometimes used to refer to male hypoactive sexual desire disorder include *inhibited sexual desire, low sexual desire,* and *impaired sexual interest.*

Assessing whether a man has hypoactive sexual desire disorder is problematic. First, there are no clear criteria for determining abnormal levels of sexual desire. Two people can vary greatly in the degree to which they experience sexual interest or desire, and each may feel comfortable with their level. Hence, if the man's partner has a higher interest in sex, this fact does not mean that he should be labeled as having hypoactive sexual desire. Furthermore, sexual desire predictably decreases over time. The principle of **satiation** ensures that long-term lovers will not have sex with each other as frequently as when they were new to each other, since repeated exposure to anything reduces the stimulus value of that entity. It is important not to interpret normal declines in sexual interest and activity as a sexual dysfunction.

Causes and Contributing Factors

Causes and contributing factors of male hypoactive sexual desire disorder include satiation, relationship issues (poor communication/discrepancies in sexual interest), individual issues (poor body image, history of emotional/sexual abuse), cultural factors (religion), job stress/exhaustion, physical illness, depression, drugs, sexual dysfunctions of partner, and low hormone levels (testosterone, androgen). Murray et al. (2017) conducted 30 interviews with men (ages 30–65) about sexual desire and found that

Male hypoactive sexual desire disorder
Persistent or recurrent deficiency (or absence) of sexual fantasies, thoughts, and desire for (or receptivity to) sexual activity, which causes personal distress

Hyperactive sexual desire disorder
Very high (hyperactive) sexual interest, which influences persons to behave as though they are driven to sexual expression and the pursuit of sex, which may have negative effects on the health, relationships, or career of the individual

Satiation
Result of a stimulus losing its value with repeated exposure

"feeling desired" by one's partner was responsible for eliciting sexual desire in 73% of the respondents; feeling rejected was identified as the primary factor associated with inhibiting sexual desire.

Treatment

The course of treatment depends on the cause but, in general, follows the treatment for female sexual interest/arousal disorder: dealing with the relationship, job stress, physical well-being, depression, and so on. Focus might also be on other sexual dysfunctions, such as erectile dysfunction or premature ejaculation.

14.3c Couple Discrepancy in Desire for Frequency of Sex

For all the sexual problems that individuals experience, such as erectile dysfunction, rapid ejaculation, anorgasmia, pain during sex, couple problems such as a discrepancy in frequency of sex are more frequent. Kleimplatz et al. (2018) reported on the treatment of discrepancy in interest and frequency of sex for 14 couples who participated in 16 hours of group couples' therapy. The content of these sessions included addressing sexual myths, performance expectations, unlearning messages (e.g. always be aggressive or passive), improving relationship satisfaction, being attentive to the physical environment (e.g. safe, stress free), developing the capacities of being present/embodied in the moment, expressing sexual desires, cultivating trust, touch, and being playful. A comparison of pre- and post-test involvement revealed a significant positive change in the couples' satisfaction.

Specific options for resolving a discrepancy over frequency of sex include one or both partners reducing their expectations and satisfying these desires in another way (e.g. masturbation) or increasing one's participation with the partner. The latter may involve engaging in sex to comply with one's partner when the expense to one's self is minimal. "My partner needs sex more than I do," said one partner. "So I'm happy to take care of my partner even though I may not need anything for myself."

McCarthy and Oppliger (2019) reported on the treatment of discrepancy in sexual desire to include the use of the "good enough" perspective whereby "the demands of erection and intercourse as a pass-fail test for the man and orgasm during intercourse as the test for the woman" are substituted with each partner feeling as an intimate and erotic friend of the other. In some scenarios, one partner may simply hold the other as they masturbate to orgasm.

14.4 Other Male Sexual Dysfunctions

In addition to low interest in sex, male sexual dysfunctions include premature ejaculation and erectile disorder.

14.4a Premature Ejaculation

Premature ejaculation (PE) is regarded as the most common sexual dysfunction reported by men (McMahon et al., 2013). Also known as **rapid ejaculation**, PE is defined by various diagnostic criteria:

1. Persistent or recurrent pattern of ejaculation that occurs during partnered sexual activity within approximately 1 minute (some researchers indicate

---

Premature ejaculation
Ejaculation that always, or nearly always, occurs prior to or within about 1–2 minutes of vaginal penetration; the inability to delay ejaculation on all or nearly all vaginal penetrations; and the presence of negative personal consequences, such as distress, bother, frustration, and/or the avoidance of sexual intimacy

Rapid ejaculation
See *premature ejaculation*

2 minutes; Kaya et al., 2015) following vaginal penetration and before the individual wishes.

2. The symptom identified above must have been present for at least 6 months and experienced 75%–100% of the time.

3. The male is distressed about his early ejaculation.

4. The sexual dysfunction is not better explained by a nonsexual mental disorder or as a consequence of severe relationship distress or significant stressors and is not attributable to the effects of a substance/medication or other medical condition.

National DATA

More than 20%–30% of men, ages 18–70, report concern about how rapidly they ejaculate. When the definition of 1 minute is used, only 1%–3% of men would be diagnosed with the disorder (American Psychiatric Association, 2013, p. 442).

While there are differences in how PE is defined (Giami, 2013), the central themes of the definition are that ejaculation is quick, the man can't control it, he feels bad about it (with decreased self-esteem), and there are negative consequences for partner relationships. Premature ejaculation may be defined as "ejaculation before desired." Men who self-identified as being in one or both of these categories were more critical of themselves and their partners than men in the control group (Reed & Humpfer, 2014). As with other sexual dysfunctions, PE may be lifelong, acquired, generalized, or situational.

> *The only thing we don't have a god for is premature ejaculation ... but I hear that it's coming quickly.*
>
> Mel Brooks, comedian

Causes and Contributing Factors

Historically, attempts to explain the causes of PE have included both biological and psychological theories. Most of these explanations are not evidence-based and are speculative (McMahon et al., 2013). Biological causes suggest that some men are genetically wired to ejaculate quickly—they have a constitutionally hypersensitive sympathetic nervous system that predisposes them to it. Men with low testosterone levels, with prostate disease, and with hyperthyroidism also have higher incidences of PE (Maggi et al., 2013). Psychosocial factors associated with premature ejaculation include early learning experiences—such as the adolescent having to ejaculate quickly before being discovered—being anxious about having sex, and feeling as though he must hurry and ejaculate before losing his erection (McMahon et al., 2013).

The outcome of PE for men may be embarrassment and shame. For women, there is increased sexual dysfunction. In a comparison of women who were sexual partners of men with premature ejaculation, 78% were diagnosed with sexual dysfunction compared to 40% of women who were partnered with men not reporting PE (Kaya et al., 2015).

Treatment

Intervention is educational, interpersonal, and medical. The man should receive psychosexual education that includes an explanation of possible organic or psychological causes so as to relieve him of feeling responsible or ashamed. While involvement of the partner may be helpful, such involvement is not mandatory. Medical intervention is usually the first line of treatment for lifelong PE and may include drugs that are "usually effective in delaying ejaculation" (McMahon et al., 2013, p. 9). A specific recommendation used by many physicians is the drug paroxetine, which exerts the strongest ejaculation delay within 5–10 days of starting treatment, with the full therapeutic effect occurring in 2–3 weeks (p. 9). Dapoxetine has also been used with positive effect (Hoy & Scott, 2010). A person being prescribed these drugs should talk to their health-care provider about adverse side effects, including potential withdrawal.

Medical advances have made the use of more traditional techniques for PE (such as squeeze technique, pause technique) less viable. However, counseling focused on sex education and communication with the partner, expectations, and so on may still be a valuable adjunct to medical intervention. Some female partners may not be bothered by early, delayed, or no ejaculation. In heterosexual couples, when female pleasure/orgasm is the first priority (via oral sex, vibrator, digital simulation), when or if the male ejaculates becomes less of an issue. Men are typically more bothered by PE than their partners (Kempeneers et al., 2013).

14.4b Erectile Disorder

Erectile disorder is defined as having at least one of the three following symptoms that must be experienced in almost all, or 75%–100%, of sexual activity situations:

1. Marked difficulty in obtaining an erection during sexual activity
2. Marked difficulty in maintaining an erection until the completion of sexual activity
3. Marked decrease in erectile rigidity

In effect, the male cannot create or maintain a hard erection. In addition, the condition must have persisted for at least 6 months, cause significant distress to the male, cannot be better explained by a nonsexual mental disorder or in reference to severe relationship distress or other significant stressors, and is not attributable to the side effects of a substance/medication or other medical condition. Erectile problems are common in men diagnosed with depression or post-traumatic stress disorder (American Psychiatric Association, 2013). Occasional, isolated episodes of the inability to attain or maintain an erection are not considered dysfunctional; they are regarded as normal occurrences. Erectile dysfunction is most common in men after the age of 40.

Most cases of erectile dysfunction are caused by a chronic health problem (such as diabetes, hypertension, atherosclerosis, or kidney or liver failure) or physiological condition, including heavy smoking, alcohol or drug abuse, obesity, lack of exercise, blockage in the arteries, and various medications (for high blood pressure). Erectile dysfunction is also related to age—the older the man, the more likely he is to report difficulty creating and maintaining an erection.

What do you call it when a lizard can't get a boner?
eReptile dysfunction

Internet humor

Erectile disorder
Persistent or recurrent inability to attain, or to maintain until completion of sexual activity, an adequate erection

Psychiatric, emotional, and psychosocial problems may also interfere with erectile capacity. Examples include depression, fear (of unwanted pregnancy, intimacy, HIV, or other STIs), guilt, and relationship dissatisfaction. For example, the man who is having an extradyadic sexual relationship may feel guilty; this guilt may lead to difficulty in attaining or maintaining an erection in sexual interaction with the primary partner.

Anxiety may also inhibit the man's ability to create and maintain an erection. One source of anxiety is performance pressure, which may be self-imposed or imposed by a partner. In self-imposed performance anxiety, the man constantly checks (mentally or visually) to see that he is erect. Such self-monitoring, also referred to as **spectatoring**, creates anxiety because the man fears that he may not be erect.

Partner-imposed performance pressure involves the partner's communicating that the man must get and stay erect to be regarded as a good lover. Such pressure usually increases the man's anxiety, thus ensuring no erection. Whether self- or partner-imposed, the anxiety associated with performance pressure results in a vicious cycle—anxiety, erectile difficulty, embarrassment, followed by anxiety, erectile difficulty, and so on.

Performance anxiety may also be related to alcohol use. After consuming more than a few drinks, the man may initiate sex but may become anxious after failing to achieve an erection. Too much alcohol will interfere with erection. In Shakespeare's words, "Drink—it provokes the desire, but it takes away the performance" (*Macbeth*, Act II, scene iii). Although alcohol may be responsible for his initial failure, his erection difficulties may continue because of his anxiety or fear about not being able to get or keep an erection.

Men who expect to satisfy their partner with the use of only their penis are even more vulnerable to erectile failure. Men who are accustomed to satisfying their partner through cuddling, oral sex, the use of a vibrator, and/or digital stimulation feel they have various options for providing their partner with pleasure/orgasm. Hence, a flaccid penis is no cause for alarm—they just move to another option.

Treatment

In regard to the treatment of erectile dysfunction, successful oral therapies—namely, the phosphodiesterase type 5 inhibitors (PDE5-i; Viagra, Cialis, Levitra)—have been used. Viagra is typically the first option. For those men who aren't helped by Viagra or for those who are bothered by its side effects (headaches, flushed face, blue tint to vision), two similar drugs, tadalafil (Cialis) and vardenafil (Levitra), are available. Albersen and colleagues (2013) noted that the overall efficacy rates of these drugs for erectile dysfunction are 60%–70%. Interviews with 58 heterosexual men and 56 women, who dealt with erectile dysfunction, revealed a complex set of emotions about the problem and treatment. Erectile disorder depressed individual and relationship satisfaction and was not uniformly understood. In addition, the treatment was often feared as well as welcomed. Some women felt that the medication was only for old people, that it was not natural, and that their husbands would want sex all the time. Men were more relieved by treatment, as erections improved both their self-esteem and sexual satisfaction (McGraw et al., 2015).

Alternatives to the previously mentioned medications include penile injections, transurethral suppositories, rod implants, and the vacuum pump. In regard to injection therapy, CAVERJECT IMPULSE® or edex® (alprostadil) is injected directly into the side of the penis to produce an erection. The medication dilates the arteries of the penis and allows blood to flow in. An erection occurs from 5–15 minutes after the injection. The male gives himself the injection just before he wishes to engage in sexual activity. The erection lasts 30 minutes to an hour or up to orgasm.

Spectatoring
Self-monitoring your own sexual responses to the point that a sexual dysfunction may occur

THINK ABOUT IT

Take a moment to answer the following question. Because Viagra/Cialis/Levitra are assumed to be the fail-safe method for ensuring an erection, a man may panic if he discovers his erection is not forthcoming or is lost even though he has taken the "magic bullet." Sex therapists recommend that it is imperative that the man or couple prepare for such occasions because erections are not always predictable. What is needed is a cognitive strategy that accepts occasional erectile problems without undue stress/disappointment. To what degree do you feel men are able to adopt this cognitive perception?

Transurethral suppositories involve placing a medicated pellet about the size of a grain of rice 1 inch into the opening at the top of the penis. The only FDA-approved urethral suppository is MUSE® (Medicated Urethral System for Erection), which contains alprostadil. Within 5 to 10 minutes the medication is absorbed and an erection occurs. The erection may continue after ejaculation, and loss of erection usually occurs within an hour.

Penile implants are of two kinds, semirigid or those that inflate. They replace the spongy tissue (corpora cavernosa) inside the penis that fills with blood during erection. Surgery is required. Implants are used when medications such as Viagra are no longer effective or when the male has a medical condition that affects blood flow, such as diabetes.

The vacuum pump is considered an attractive second-line therapy. In select cases, such as post-prostatectomy penile rehabilitation, as well as in men who cannot use a PDE5-i, the vacuum device is considered first-line treatment (Brison et al., 2013). Indeed, the most effective treatment of erectile dysfunction encompasses both pharmacology (and alternatives) and psychotherapy in which cognitive aspects of poor sexual performance, including diminished self-esteem, lack of confidence, and perceived failures, are dealt with (Simopoulos & Trinidad, 2013).

For men who want to delay or avoid having problems with erectile dysfunction, the preventive behaviors are regular exercise, no smoking, moderate alcohol use, and maintaining appropriate weight (Glina et al., 2013).

Data from the United Kingdom reveals that prostate cancer is the third most frequent common cancer (Forbat et al., 2018). Since prostate cancer is associated with erectile dysfunction, there is interest in the most efficacious approach to treatment. But in a review of the literature on prostate cancer and male sexual dysfunction, the conclusion is that "while several preventive and treatment strategies for the preservation and recovery of sexual function are available, no specific recommendation or consensus guidelines exist regarding the optimal rehabilitation or treatment protocol" (Chung & Brock, 2013).

For men who have had a radical prostatectomy resulting in erectile dysfunction, the patient is taught to give himself an alprostadil injection in the penis—called IAI (intracavernous alprostadil injection). In a study of the sexual satisfaction of 152 women partnered with men who were being treated for erectile disorder with IAI, indexes of female sexual quality of life were low overall but were highly correlated with the partner's response level to IAI treatment. IAI-related pain, increased age, and poor urinary function of the male partner appeared to negatively impact their female partner's sex life (Yiou et al., 2013). Men who have cryotherapy for prostate cancer are able to avoid radical prostactectomy and the concomitant negative consequences.

Cultural Diversity

Cultures differ in the ways they treat sexual dysfunctions. In China, men with erectile dysfunction are sometimes regarded as "suffering from deficiency of Yang elements in the kidney." Their treatment is to drink a solution prepared with water and several chemicals designed to benefit kidney function. They may also be given acupuncture therapy (Shikai, 1990, p. 198).

14.5 Orgasm Dysfunctions

Orgasm dysfunctions include female orgasmic disorder and delayed ejaculation.

That's your orgasm talking. ... You're not really in love with me.

Laurie Elizabeth Flynn, novelist

14.5a Female Orgasmic Disorder

Female orgasmic disorder (FOD) is diagnosed under the following conditions (American Psychiatric Association, 2013):

1. A marked delay in, marked infrequency of, or absence of orgasm

2. Markedly reduced intensity of orgasmic features

3. Symptoms have persisted for a minimum of 6 months and cause distress.

4. The sexual dysfunction is not better explained by a nonsexual mental disorder, such as severe relationship distress (as in partner violence) or other significant stressors, and is not attributable to the effects of substance abuse/ medication or another medical condition.

National DATA

From 10% to 40% of US women report orgasmic problems depending on age, culture, duration, and severity of symptoms. Approximately 10% of women do not experience orgasm throughout their lifetime (American Psychiatric Association, 2013, p. 431).

Because women vary in their capacity to orgasm, a clinician making this diagnosis takes into consideration the woman's age (younger women are more likely to have orgasmic difficulties), previous sexual experiences, current relationship with the partner, and whether the sexual stimulation is adequate. Like other sexual dysfunctions, orgasmic disorder may be lifelong, acquired, situational, or generalized. Female orgasmic disorder may also occur in the presence of other sexual difficulties, such as lack of desire/arousal, no lubrication, and pain.

Cormier & O'Sullivan (2018) interviewed 53 heterosexual male and 53 female adolescents (ages 18–21); 71% of the women reported having difficulty having or reaching orgasm.

Female orgasmic disorder
A persistent or recurrent difficulty, delay in, or absence of experiencing orgasm following sufficient stimulation and arousal

International **DATA**

Reported prevalence figures for female orgasmic disorder range from 30% to 46% in Asia (Laan et al., 2013).

THINK ABOUT IT

Take a moment to answer the following question. A woman who does not achieve orgasm because of lack of sufficient stimulation is not considered to have a sexual dysfunction. To what degree do you feel a woman's partner views the woman's not having an orgasm as the partner not providing the necessary clitoral stimulation?

To what degree are reported sexual problems (including orgasmic dysfunction) related to sexual orientation? In a comparison of 390 lesbians with 1,009 heterosexual women, while there were no significant differences, heterosexual women reported lower rates of orgasm. Researchers Peixoto and Nobre (2015) noted that this discrepancy may be due to the fact that heterosexual women may not be getting the kind of clitoral stimulation that leads to orgasm.

Causes and Contributing Factors

Rowland et al. (2018) identified the reasons given by 452 women for their infrequent orgasm during partnered sex. The most commonly cited reasons were stress/anxiety, insufficient arousal, and lack of time during sex. Other factors less frequently cited were body image, pain, inadequate lubrication, and medical/medication issues. In regard to the latter issue, over half of women who take SSRI medications report delay or inhibition of orgasm (Laan et al., 2013).

Psychosocial and cultural factors associated with orgasmic dysfunctions are similar to those related to lack of sexual desire. Causes of orgasm difficulties in women include a restrictive upbringing and learning a passive female sexual role. Guilt, shame, disgust, fear of intimacy, fear of losing control, ambivalence about commitment, and spectatoring may also interfere with the ability to experience orgasm. Other women may not achieve orgasm because of their belief in the myth that women are not supposed to enjoy sex. Experiencing a traumatic event, such as being raped, may interfere with orgasmic capacity, as can being involved in a relationship with a partner who does not create a context of love, respect, and security.

For some women, lack of information can result in orgasmic difficulties; for example, some women do not know that clitoral stimulation is important for orgasm to occur. Finally, some women might not achieve orgasm with their partners because they are ashamed and insecure about telling their partners what they want in terms of sexual stimulation.

Treatment

See the following segment on "Helping Women to Achieve Orgasm."

Helping Women to Achieve Orgasm

Half of women (50%) ages 18–35 report that they cannot orgasm with a partner. While women struggling with this problem may think something is wrong with them, this large number reflects that something is wrong with our culture. The following provides essential information to overcome these cultural scripts and to become orgasmic.

1. *Clitoral knowledge and prioritization:* The vast majority of women need clitoral stimulation to reach orgasm. When women are asked their most reliable way to orgasm, almost all list clitoral stimulation, which can include oral sex, manual stimulation, or stimulation with a vibrator during sexual intercourse. Only 3%–10% of women reliably orgasm when vaginal penetration is the sole source of stimulation. Indeed, an over-focus on penile-vaginal intercourse is why the vast majority of women's orgasm problems occur in sexual encounters with men. Women are more likely to have an orgasm when masturbating or when having sex with a woman. This higher rate of orgasm is due to focusing on the clitoris (often with additional attention to the inner lips). When penetration is involved, we mistakenly assume both partners should orgasm this way. The solution is to value penetration and clitoral stimulation equally.

2. *Two mind-sets: Prioritization and mindfulness:* To hold penetration and clitoral stimulation equally, women need to believe that their pleasure is not secondary to their partners'. Prioritizing her own pleasure is a key mind-set for a woman's orgasm. In addition, a state of mindfulness is necessary for orgasm. Mindfulness is the ability to fully immerse oneself in the sensations of the moment. This is the opposite of the self-monitoring that many women engage in during sex ("Do I look fat?"; "Am I taking too long to orgasm?").

3. *Masturbation and communication:* What every woman needs to reach orgasm is unique, and what any one woman needs to orgasm can vary from one sexual encounter to another. This is why women need to first get to know their own bodies through masturbation and to develop communication skills to tell a partner what they need to orgasm. Take time to explore your body, especially your clitoris and inner lips. Try your fingers and a vibrator; lubrication is also recommended. Once you know how to bring yourself pleasure, learn how to be assertive—tell your partner how you need to be touched for orgasm. Don't be afraid to incorporate a vibrator into sex with a partner.

Sometimes more is needed than clitoral knowledge, the mind-set of women prioritizing their own pleasure, mindful immersion in the sensations of the moment, masturbation, and communication. If a woman has experienced sexual trauma, therapy is recommended. In addition, if lack of orgasm is a result of a negative body image or relationship problems, these will also need to be dealt with, often through therapy. However, for the vast majority of women, orgasm problems have cultural roots, particularly the false belief that penetration is the ideal way to reach orgasm and a concomitant lack of clitoral stimulation.

Source: Mintz, L. (2017). *Cliteracy.* New York, NY: Harper One.

Women who seek a therapist to become orgasmic discover that there is a typical protocol:

> A PLISSIT approach for treating orgasm disorder is recommended. This approach consists of Providing Permission, Limited Information, followed by Specific Suggestions if the problem is not resolved, followed by Intensive Therapy by clinicians/therapists specialized in providing sexological care. (Laan et al., 2013, p. 78)

We will detail the PLISSIT approach later in the chapter. For now, it is important to point out that intensive therapy, identified as part of the PLISSIT method, would not only include psychosocial aspects, such as the woman's learned attitudes about sex, but also her current relationship in terms of ensuring that it involves mutual love, respect, and security. Also, any previous sexual traumas, such as child sexual molestation or rape, should be dealt with.

National DATA

Herbenick et al. (2018) reported data on a national probability sample of women (1,055) ages 18–94. About 1 in 5 (18.4%) reported intercourse alone was sufficient for orgasm, over a third (36.6%) reported that clitoral stimulation was necessary for orgasm during intercourse, and another third (36%) said that orgasms "felt better" if their clitoris was stimulated during intercourse.

The most effective interventions for helping a woman become orgasmic include a combination of sexuality education, communication on general and sexual issues, attention to relationship and body image, and directed masturbation. Women may find valuable information from OMGyes at the organization's website, www.omgyes.com, particularly helpful in learning to experience sexual pleasure. Finally, a female therapist may be valuable in that she may serve as a model for the client in discussing her own masturbatory experience and recommending masturbatory sessions.

14.5b Delayed Ejaculation

For a diagnosis of **delayed ejaculation,** any of the following symptoms must be experienced with approximately 75%–100% of partnered sexual activity and without the partner desiring delay (American Psychiatric Association, 2013):

1. Marked delay in ejaculation

2. Marked infrequency or absence of ejaculation

3. Symptoms have persisted for a minimum of 6 months and cause distress.

4. The sexual dysfunction is not better explained by a nonsexual mental disorder, such as severe relationship distress or other significant stressors and is not attributable to the effects of substance abuse/medication or another medical condition.

    Like other sexual dysfunctions, delayed ejaculation may be lifelong, acquired, situational, or generalized. Delayed ejaculation is the least understood of the male sexual dysfunctions (Perelman, 2013).

Cormier & O'Sullivan (2018) interviewed 53 heterosexual male adolescents (ages 18–21); 38% of the men reported ejaculating too quickly.

Another term for delayed ejaculation is **inhibited male orgasm**. The clinician making the judgment about delayed ejaculation should take into account the man's age and whether the stimulation has been adequate in focus, intensity, and duration. The man's cultural background is also relevant. Traditional Chinese Taoist philosophy views avoiding ejaculation during intercourse in positive terms because this vital source of energy needs to be preserved (Tang et al., 1996).

Delayed ejaculation
Absence or delay of ejaculation

Inhibited male orgasm
Persistent or recurrent delay in or absence of orgasm following a normal sexual excitement phase

National DATA

Prevalence rates of delayed ejaculation in men are 1–4%. The percent is increasing due to greater use of pharmacotherapy, including 5-alpha reductase inhibitors (5αRIs) and SSRIs (Perelman, 2017).

Causes and Contributing Factors

Several medications may interfere with ejaculation, including some hormone-based medications, tranquilizers, barbiturates, antidepressants, and antihypertensives. Prozac and Paxil are particularly associated with delayed ejaculation. Injury or disease that impairs the neurological system may also interfere with orgasm in the male.

Psychosocial causes of delayed ejaculation include anxiety, fear, spectatoring, and negative attitudes toward sexuality. For example, traumatic experiences or embarrassing ones, such as being discovered by parents while masturbating, can lead to fear, anxiety, and punishment associated with impending orgasm. Thus, the sensation of impending orgasm can become conditioned to produce the response of fear and anxiety, which inhibits orgasm. Some men who are obsessed with trying to arouse and please their partners may become anxious and engage in spectatoring, which makes maintaining an erection more difficult. Fear of pregnancy and guilt may also interfere with a man's ability to achieve orgasm and ejaculate. Learning negative messages about genitals or sexual activities from one's parents or religious training may also lead to ejaculation difficulties.

Particular attention should also be given to psychological issues, including lack of confidence and poor body image. Either a sex therapist or physician should obtain a focused sexual history that includes, but is not limited to, perceived attractiveness of the man's partner, the use of fantasy during sex, anxiety about intercourse, and masturbatory patterns (Perelman, 2013).

Job/career difficulties or the presence of children in the household can also influence sexual performance. Men who have lost their jobs, are depressed about their economic future, or are anxious about children knocking on the door may find that their sexual focus is affected.

Just as with many women, some men are unable to orgasm because of a lack of sufficient stimulation. Some heterosexual men may have developed a pattern of masturbation that involves vigorous stimulation; they are then unable to obtain sufficient stimulation from the vagina during coitus.

Treatment

Treatment usually focuses on the psychosocial origins of delayed ejaculation and may consist of exploring the negative attitudes and cognitions that interfere with ejaculation and reeducating to change such negative attitudes. Treatment for delayed ejaculation may also involve changing medications and/or using sensate focus exercises. These exercises allow the couple to experience physical intimacy without putting pressure on the man to perform sexually. Eventually, the man's partner helps him ejaculate through oral or manual stimulation.

Research on treating delayed ejaculation has focused mainly on men in heterosexual relationships. After the couple is confident that the man can be brought to orgasm orally or manually, the partner stimulates him to a high level of sexual excitement and, at the moment of orgasm, inserts his penis into her vagina so that he ejaculates inside her. After several sessions, the woman gradually reduces the amount of time she orally or manually manipulates her partner and increases the amount of time she stimulates him with her vagina (Masters & Johnson, 1970). Alternatively, the goal in treating delayed ejaculation may be to enjoy sexual activities with a partner without the expectation that ejaculation must occur inside the vagina.

14.6 Genito-Pelvic Pain/ Penetration Disorder

Persistent genito-pelvic pain/penetration disorder (GPPD) is diagnosed as persistent or recurrent difficulties with one (or more) of the following (American Psychiatric Association, 2013):

1. Vaginal penetration during intercourse

2. Marked vulvovaginal or pelvic pain during vaginal intercourse or penetration attempts

3. Marked fear or anxiety about vulvovaginal or pelvic pain in anticipation of, during, or as a result of vaginal penetration

4. Marked tensing or tightening of the pelvic floor muscles during attempted vaginal penetration

5. The above symptoms have persisted for a minimum duration of approximately 6 months, and the individual is distressed about the symptoms.

6. The sexual dysfunction is not better explained by a nonsexual mental disorder or as a consequence of severe relationship distress, such as partner violence or other significant stressors, and is not attributable to the effects of substance abuse/medication or another medical condition.

Genito-pelvic pain/penetration disorder is characterized by difficulty having intercourse, genito-pelvic pain, fear of pain or vaginal penetration, and tension of the pelvic floor muscles. The diagnosis applies if there is distress in just one of the four areas. Like other sexual dysfunctions, genito-pelvic pain/penetration disorder may be lifelong, acquired, situational, or generalized. The disorder may also occur in the presence of other sexual difficulties, such as lack of desire/arousal, no lubrication, and pain. Both individuals with GPPD and their partners report low sexual satisfaction (Corsini-Munt et al., 2017). Glowacka et al. (2019) noted that a woman's self-worth is influenced by the degree to which she is able to function sexually in the absence of pain. Rosen & Bergeron (2019) suggested an interpersonal emotion regulation model whereby the partners work together to diffuse their negative emotions in reference to the GPPD.

The terms vaginismus and dyspareunia are also used to describe persistent genito-pelvic pain/penetration disorder. These two terms help sort out the two aspects of the disorder.

> **Persistent genito-pelvic pain/ penetration disorder**
> Involves recurrent difficulties accomplishing vaginal penetration during intercourse, pain during vaginal intercourse/ penetration attempts, and fear/anxiety surrounding such attempts

National DATA

Approximately 15% of women in North America report recurrent pain during intercourse (American Psychiatric Association, 2013, p. 438).

14.6a Vaginismus

Vaginismus is recurrent or persistent involuntary spasm of the musculature of the outer third of the vagina that makes vaginal penetration difficult. In a comparison of women with dyspareunia and vaginismus, those with the latter reported more sexual desire and less difficulty with lubrication compared to women with dyspareunia (Cherner & Reissing, 2013). Numerous sexual problems extending beyond vaginal penetration difficulties were confirmed, suggesting a need for broader treatment approaches not limited to the experience of vaginal penetration.

Causes and Contributing Factors

In women who experience dyspareunia (which may be caused by biological or psychosocial factors), vaginismus may be a protective response to prevent pain. In other words, if a woman anticipates coital pain, she may involuntarily constrict her vagina to prevent painful intercourse. A lack of sexual information and a deficit of knowledge of basic anatomy have been suggested as probable causes (American Psychiatric Association, 2013).

Vaginismus may also be related to psychosocial factors, such as a restrictive parental and religious upbringing, in which the woman learned to view intercourse as dirty and shameful. Other psychosocial factors include rape, incest, and childhood molestation.

Treatment

Treatment for vaginismus should begin with a gynecological examination to determine if an organic or physical problem is the cause. Treatment often involves teaching the woman to insert a dilator or objects of graduated size (such as her fingers) into her vagina while she is relaxed. After the woman is able to insert one finger into her vagina, she is instructed to introduce two fingers; this exercise is repeated until she feels relaxed enough to contain the penis. Both individual and partner involvement in the exercises has been used. Systematic desensitization, Kegel exercises, and therapy focusing on the woman's cognitions and perceptions about sex and sexuality with her particular partner may precede or accompany the insertion training.

14.6b Dyspareunia

Dyspareunia, a type of genital sexual pain (GSP), is pain during sexual intercourse. The pain may occur as soon as penile entry begins, during penile containment/movement, at ejaculation by the partner, or after intercourse; it may be experienced by either women or men. The symptoms range from mild discomfort to sharp pain. There is disagreement about whether dyspareunia should be regarded as a sexual dysfunction or as a localized GSP (Fugl-Meyer et al., 2013). Nevertheless, dyspareunia is one of the most commonly reported sexual dysfunctions in premenopausal women under the age of 40 (Pazmany et al., 2013). Also referred to as provoked vestibulodynia (PVD), it is the most frequent cause of unexplained genito-pelvic pain in premenopausal women (Rosen et al., 2017).

Causes and Contributing Factors

Dyspareunia in women may be caused by biological factors, many centering on inadequate lubrication. The most common cause of painful intercourse among postmenopausal women is lack of estrogen. Reduced estrogen levels can cause shrinkage of the vaginal mucosa, resulting in the narrowing of the vaginal opening (called *vaginal atrophy*), causing pain with penile insertion.

Vaginismus
Recurrent or persistent involuntary spasm of the musculature of the outer third of the vagina that interferes with vaginal penetration

Dyspareunia
The recurrent or persistent genital pain associated with intercourse or attempts at sexual intercourse

For postmenopausal dyspareunia, the most common solution is a vaginally inserted estrogen cream (a prescription is required) and a liberal use of a water-based (not glycerin-based) personal lubricant during foreplay and intercourse (Mintz, 2015). The Estriol (2 mg) vaginal suppository is a specific compound recommended by some physicians. Premarin® cream is the more readily available cream. Either is to be used with lubricants that are inserted prior to intercourse.

Dyspareunia may also be caused by vaginal or pelvic infections or inflammations or by allergic reactions to deodorants, douches, and contraceptive devices. Chronic discomfort or pain of the vulva, or **vulvodynia**, is a major cause of dyspareunia. Vulvodynia is diagnosed when a woman experiences burning, stinging, irritation, or knife-like pain of the vulva for more than 3 months, without obvious visible lesions. One subtype is *vulvar vestibulitis syndrome (VVS)*, in which a woman has painful areas on the vestibule (the area around the entrance to the vagina).

Dyspareunia may also be caused by a lack of lubrication, a rigid hymen, tender scarring following an episiotomy, or an improperly positioned uterus or ovary. Although there is no common etiology for dyspareunia, trauma is a common theme resulting from operations, vaginal delivery, and back injuries.

Psychological factors may also be involved in the etiology of dyspareunia. Pazmany and colleagues (2013) found that a more negative genital self-image was strongly and independently associated with an increased likelihood of reporting dyspareunia.

In men, inflammations of or lesions on the penis (often caused by herpes), Peyronie disease, and **urethritis** may cause pain. Because dyspareunia is often a symptom of a medical problem, a health-care provider should be consulted.

Dyspareunia may also be caused by psychosocial factors, including guilt, anxiety, or unresolved feelings about a previous trauma, such as rape or childhood molestation. Religious and parental prohibitions against sexual activity and relationship conflicts may also result in dyspareunia.

Treatment

Dyspareunia that is caused by biological factors may be treated by evaluating the medical condition that is causing the coital pain. Medical treatments for vulvodynia include the use of tricyclic antidepressants, though there have been no controlled studies of this treatment. Gabapentin, an anticonvulsant medication that is effective in reducing neuropathic pain, has been used successfully. Other treatments include acupuncture, biofeedback, pelvic-floor physiotherapy, lidocaine ointment, interferon, and surgical removal of vestibular tissue. Fortunately, many cases improve over time either with or without treatment. However, despite the distress caused by the puzzling problem, there have been few research treatment trials supporting any particular remedy. The National Vulvodynia Association (www.nva.org) has called for federal funding of vulvodynia research.

If medical or surgical procedures cannot resolve the pain, the person with dyspareunia may try different intercourse positions or other sexual activities that provide pleasure with no or minimal pain. When dyspareunia is caused by psychosocial factors, treatment may involve reeducation to replace negative attitudes toward sexual activity with positive ones. Individual therapy may help the person resolve feelings of guilt or anxiety associated with sexual activity. Couples therapy may be indicated to resolve relationship conflicts. Sensate focus exercises may help the individual relax and enjoy sexual contact. Ohnut is another alternative to reducing pain from vaginal penetration. Ohnut involves various rubber rings are placed over the penis to reduce the depth of penetration. Visit www.Ohnut.co for more information.

Vulvodynia
Burning, stinging, irritation, or knife-like pain of the vulva for more than 3 months without obvious visible lesions

Urethritis
Inflammation of the urethra

14.7 Sex Therapy

The sex was so good that even the neighbors had a cigarette.

Internet humor

Sex therapy is often delivered as part of another service, such as individual or relationship counseling. Most therapists function as physicians, marriage therapists, relationship counselors, or psychotherapists. Nevertheless, some specialize in sex therapy.

14.7a Sex Therapist Requirements/ Status of the Profession

The American Association of Sexuality Educators, Counselors and Therapists (AASECT), has established guidelines for a sex therapist certification. These requirements are outlined on the AASECT website (www.aasect.org) and include both academic (minimum of a master's degree from an accredited institution) and supervised clinical experience, a valid regulatory license from the state in which the therapist practices, and 90 clock hours of academic coursework on sexuality education. The training is prolonged and intensive.

As a profession, sex therapy is, and has been, in flux (Berry, 2013b). There is little agreement among sex therapists about how to treat various sexual problems. There have also been changes in treatment strategies across time. In the past, psychology and psychoanalysis dominated the treatment field. More recently, pharmacological treatment has become more prominent. In addition, there is a gender imbalance between professions. Most physicians working as sexologists are male, while most psychologists and psychoanalysts are female (Gogno et al., 2013). Female therapists also predominate among marriage and family therapists. These individuals also conduct sex therapy (Bernal et al., 2013). However, their training may be limited. Zamboni and Zaid (2017) surveyed 69 marriage and family therapy programs and found that most required only one course in human sexuality, and it was rare that anyone on the faculty had an expertise in sexuality. In addition, McCarthy and Ross (2018) also noted that sex therapy has been amiss by providing services primarily to middle-class individuals, that a broader demographic offering is warranted.

14.7b Cognitive Behavioral Sex Therapy

Cognitive therapy emphasizes that negative thoughts and attitudes about sex interfere with sexual interest, pleasure, and performance. **Cognitive behavioral sex therapy** is recognized as an effective treatment for sexual dysfunctions (Stephenson et al., 2013) and consists of identifying and stopping negative thoughts and replacing them with positive ones. For example, the individual who thinks that masturbation is sinful and selfish is asked to view it as a means of discovering the value of sexual self-pleasuring. Examples of beliefs women need to reevaluate are that "sex is meant to be a male activity and females should control urges and desires as it is a sin not to" (Nobre et al., 2003).

Negative cognitions may also interfere with personal, partner, and relationship functioning. "I'm too fat and not sexually desirable," "My partner is cheating on me," and "We should never have gotten married" are examples of negative thoughts that will affect sexual responsiveness. Addressing these cognitions and replacing them with different thoughts ("My partner loves me the way I am," "My partner is faithful to me," and "We are in our eighth year of a great relationship") become the goal of therapy.

Cognitive behavioral sex therapy
Treatment method emphasizing that negative thoughts and attitudes about sex interfere with sexual interest, pleasure, and performance

PERSONAL DECISIONS 14-1

Finding a Sex Therapist

"Let the client beware" applies to the person seeking sex therapy. The individual should be careful in choosing a sex therapist. A basic concern is training. With rare exceptions, there are no laws preventing persons from advertising that they are a sex therapist. In most communities, anyone can legally open an office and offer sex therapy. Academic degrees, therapy experience under supervision, and exposure to other aspects of formal training in human sexuality are not legally required to market one's self as a sex therapist in most US states. California and Florida are exceptions. To be licensed in California as a physician; psychologist; social worker; or marriage, family, or child counselor, a person must have had training in human sexuality. However, most physicians, psychologists, social workers, and marriage/family therapists in states other than California do not have adequate training in sexuality, and some may have had no training at all. Despite the fact that 30% of couples who see a marriage and family therapist have a clinically significant sexual problem (Peloquin et al., 2019), less than 1% of the research articles in journals for marriage and family therapists are focused on sex and sex therapy (Jones et al., 2019). Finally, sex therapists may be comfortable seeing only one partner of a dyad. But Gewirtz-Meydan & Finzi-Dottan (2018) emphasized the importance of both partners' perspectives in assessing/treating sexuality issues.

To help upgrade the skills of those providing sex therapy, AASECT offers a Certified Sex Therapist certificate to applicants who have a minimum of a master's degree in a clinical field (psychology, social work, nursing, marriage therapy), have conducted sex therapy under supervision for a minimum of 60 hours, and have attended a 2-day workshop on human sexuality (sponsored by AASECT) to sort out their own attitudes and values about human sexuality. AASECT guidelines indicate that the therapist should have a basic understanding of sexual and reproductive anatomy and physiology, sexual development (biological and psychological), interpersonal relationships, gender-related issues, marital and family dynamics, sociocultural factors in sexual values and behavior, medical issues affecting sexuality (including pregnancy, STIs, drugs, illness and disability, contraception, and fertility), sex research, sexual abuse, and personality theories. As a minimum, ask if your sex therapist is certified by AASECT. Help with sexual issues is also available online. Rosier and Tyler (2017) analyzed data on 40 couples who participated in an online sexual training program (Love Guru Program) and reported a decrease in apprehension in talking about sex, an increase in sexual knowledge/skill, and an increase in sexual and relationship satisfaction.

Aside from basic information about sexuality, there are various approaches to sex therapy.

Negative attitudes and cognitions about sex often result from sexual trauma, such as rape and incest. One way to change these negative attitudes and cognitions is for the therapist to teach traumatized patients to view themselves as survivors, rather than victims. In addition, the therapist can suggest that living well is the best revenge against the person who perpetrated the trauma.

Unrealistic expectations may also be operative in a couple who reports dissatisfaction with their sex life. Media messages suggest a very high bar, and the ubiquity and exploitation of sexuality in the commercial realm can help to create a sense of inadequacy.

14.7c Masters and Johnson's Approach

Masters and Johnson's approach to sex therapy was a key influence in the field of sex therapy. When the Masters and Johnson Institute in St. Louis began in the mid-1960s, couples went through an intensive 2-week sex therapy program. Treatment began with assessment procedures, including a physical examination and interviews with therapists who took medical and personal histories. On the third day, the therapists met with the couple to discuss their assessment of the nature, extent, and origin of the sexual problem; to recommend treatment procedures; and to answer any questions. All couples receiving treatment at the Masters and Johnson Institute were instructed to engage in sensate focus exercises.

The essential elements of the early Masters and Johnson (1970) approach to resolving sexual dysfunctions were as follows:

1. Both partners in a marital or coupled unit were expected to participate in sex therapy.

2. A male and a female sex therapist provided the treatment for heterosexual couples; in this way, each patient had a same-sex role model.

3. Sexual dysfunctions were conceptualized as having been learned. Hence, much of sex therapy was devoted to sex education and information.

4. Performance anxiety, fear of failure, and excessive need to please the partner were regarded as underlying causes of sexual problems and were addressed in therapy.

5. Communication between the partners was regarded as critical to a good sexual relationship. Hence, enhancing communication between the sexual partners became a goal.

6. The specific resolution of a sexual dysfunction involved behavioral change that was accomplished through the assignment of progressive tasks and behavioral prescriptions.

While having a male and female sex therapy team conducting each session is no longer practical and is too expensive, most of the other items of the Masters and Johnson approach are regarded as basic sex therapy.

Surrogates were also used for some of Masters and Johnson's patients. Also noted in the case study content of Chapter 2, section 2.6e (Zentner & Knox, 2013), surrogates provide real-time learning of new attitudes and behavior by clients. Some sex therapists today use certified sex surrogates in which the therapist works with the surrogate who meets with their clients (see links at end of chapter). Alternatively, some therapists use synthetic surrogates, also referred to as "companion dolls." Of course, there are advantages to using each type of surrogate.

14.7d Kaplan's Approach

The approach developed by Helen Kaplan (1974) of Cornell Medical Center does not have a rigid 2-week format, nor does it assume that therapy will continue indefinitely. The goal of this approach is to assist the partners in achieving their sexual goals in as short a time as possible. Sessions are usually held once or twice a week (with an occasional phone call during the week) while the partners continue to live at home. Although participation of both partners is seen as a crucial ingredient for successful sex therapy, Kaplan's approach does not require that sexual partners participate equally in the therapy program. For example, in the case of inhibited female orgasm, the therapist would spend most of the time working with the woman in individual sessions.

Kaplan also suggested that some individuals might not respond to behavioral interventions when the source of the sexual dysfunction was rooted in unconscious intrapsychic conflicts, deep-seated personality traits, or interpersonal dynamics. Thus, an important part of Kaplan's approach to sex therapy is insight therapy, through which the presumed deeper roots of sexual dysfunction are uncovered. There is considerable professional disagreement about the degree to which sexual problems are rooted in the unconscious.

14.7e PLISSIT Model Approach

Earlier in this chapter, we made reference to the PLISSIT model for treating sexual dysfunctions (Annon, 1976). The **PLISSIT model** outlines four treatment levels: permission, limited information, specific suggestions, and intensive therapy. The permission level of the PLISSIT model involves encouraging clients to discuss their sexual problems. The therapist may also assure clients that, in many cases, their thoughts, feelings, behaviors, and concerns are normal, common, and understandable. The second level of the PLISSIT model involves giving the client limited information, such as education about sexual response, sexual anatomy, or the effects of medications or alcohol on sexual functioning. This level of intervention also involves dispelling sexual myths. The third level of intervention involves specific suggestions such as teaching couples how to do sensate focus exercises or instructing women in masturbation techniques. The fourth level of treatment involves intensive therapy. This level of intervention focuses on anxiety, negative sexual learning events, and relationship conflicts.

14.7f LoPiccolo's Approach

Joseph LoPiccolo (1992) offered a three-part theory he dubbed "postmodern." Although his comments focused on erectile failure, the three theoretical elements he described are applicable to understanding other categories of sexual dysfunction as well:

1. *Systems theory:* LoPiccolo recommended that in assessing sexual dysfunction, the therapist should carefully examine the effect of the dysfunction on the relationship between the partners—for example, "[M]ight a husband feel more powerful and revert to a more authoritarian role with the wife if he became more 'potent' again? Might the wife find his sexual needs burdensome if the husband regained erectile function?" (LoPiccolo, 1992, p. 178).

2. *Integrated (physiological and psychological) planning:* Classifying people's dysfunctions as organic or psychogenic is often not useful and may be harmful. As noted, both organic and psychogenic factors are operating. LoPiccolo suggested that even when organic etiology is clearly established, a thorough psychological evaluation is also indicated.

3. *Sexual behavior patterns:* It is important to examine the specific sexual behaviors of the couple. What are the cues to sexual desire and arousal? Does the couple need to reconsider the methods, sites, or philosophies of stimulation?

14.7g Effectiveness of Sex Therapy

Providing data on the effectiveness of sex therapy is difficult for several reasons. First, the degree to which sex therapy is effective in resolving sexual problems depends on the problem: Some issues are easier to treat than others. In general, acquired problems are easier to treat than lifelong problems, and situational problems are easier to treat than generalized problems. Vaginismus and erectile dysfunction are likely to respond quickly to therapeutic intervention. Problems related to sexual desire may be the most difficult to treat. Second, the presence of restrictive religious beliefs, depression, or paraphilias makes achieving goals more difficult.

PLISSIT model
Method of sex therapy that involves four treatment levels: permission, limited information, specific suggestions, and intensive therapy

Sex therapy effectiveness rates may also vary because of the methodological problems in determining such rates. For example, who should decide whether treatment has failed or succeeded—the client or the therapist? What criteria should be used in determining success or failure? What if the client is successful in resolving sexual dysfunctions but is not successful in resolving related nonsexual issues, such as marital conflict, negative body image, and low self-esteem? What if the client is successful in resolving these related nonsexual issues but is still sexually dysfunctional? What criteria will be used to measure success and failure? Different answers to these questions will yield different results regarding reported success rates of sex therapy.

Technology and Sexuality 14-1: The Medicalization of Sexual Dysfunctions

In 2015, the Food and Drug Administration approved Addyi, a drug designed to help address issues of sexual desire for women. While some hailed it as a major advancement in helping to equalize the medical options available for women, others saw it as a continuation of the medicalization of sexuality.

Some researchers argue that the medicalization of sexual functioning is harmful for many reasons. First, taking a pill to fix lack of sexual interest implies that there is a normal level of sexual interest and that any deviation is a dysfunction and needs correction. For example, while some people may choose to be sexually active, others may choose to be abstinent. Of these options, is only one normal?

A second problem with an arbitrary definition of normal functioning is that there are some who may fit the clinical definition of having some type of dysfunction, yet be perfectly happy with their sexual lives. Imagine this scenario: A person discusses their sexual functioning with their physician. Due to the availability of medications and possible pressure to prescribe them by the pharmaceutical companies, the physician informs the patient that they have a dysfunction and that it can be treated with medication. This pronouncement results in a person who walked into the office feeling happy with their sex life walking out feeling bad about having a supposed dysfunction and being given a prescription for it. This prescription, which may or may not address a dysfunction that may or may not actually be present, could have a negative impact on other aspects of the person's sexual functioning or overall health.

One of the groups that has been vocal about the issue of the medicalization of sexuality is the New View Campaign (www.newviewcampaign.org), which has produced books, teaching manuals, and videos. Members of the campaign have testified numerous times at FDA hearings. While New View focuses specifically on female sexuality, the organization's primary message has been that the medicalization of sexuality has a negative impact on men, women, and couples.

Rather than a medical problem/pharmaceutical treatment perspective, an alternative view examines the ways society scripts perceptions of sexual functioning. In their document *The New View Manifesto: A New View of Women's Sexual Problems,* members of the New View Campaign identified four causes of sexual problems for females, the first of which is the sociocultural and political causes (The Working Group on a New View of Women's Sexual Problems, 2000). These factors include the lack of sexuality education on topics such as gender roles, aging, contraception, and STIs. The manifesto also identifies the impact of cultural beliefs about acceptable body shapes and sizes, as well as the anxiety and shame that people might feel when they do not meet these cultural norms. Other factors include relationship, psychological, and medical problems. A medication cannot possibly address all of these issues, which are often ignored during medical treatment.

The fact that many people are struggling with sexuality issues is a truth that cannot be ignored, but since any particular problem (such as female sexual desire) is complicated and multifaceted, attempts to address these issues need to be more holistic, rather than merely the prescription of a new pill.

Chapter Summary

Definitions of Sexual Dysfunctions

A SEXUAL DYSFUNCTION is a disorder that causes a significant disturbance in a person's ability to respond sexually or to experience sexual pleasure (American Psychiatric Association, 2013). Sexual dysfunctions may be lifelong, acquired, situational, or generalized.

Causes and Contributing Factors in Sexual Dysfunctions

THE NUMEROUS CAUSES of sexual dysfunctions include organic, sociocultural, psychological, relationship, and cognitive factors. Organic causes include physical illness, disease, or disability and use of some drugs.

Sociocultural factors (religious teachings that sex is dirty), psychological factors, (a history of child sexual abuse, fear, and guilt, relational factors (the couple do not love or respect each other), and cognitive (accepting the myth that sexual behavior ends with aging) can also cause sexual dysfunctions.

Interest/Arousal Dysfunctions

FEMALE SEXUAL INTEREST/AROUSAL DISORDER involves the woman not being able to become or stay sexually aroused, which implies that she lacks genital lubrication and swelling. Like other sexual dysfunctions, this disorder may be lifelong, acquired, situational, or generalized. Treatment involves taking a detailed sexual history to discover the etiology, often followed by the recommendation of masturbation.

Male hypoactive sexual desire disorder is a low interest in sex. The causes of hypoactive sexual desire may be organic, psychological, relational, or cognitive.

Other Male Sexual Dysfunctions

PREMATURE EJACULATION is regarded as the most common sexual dysfunction reported by men. It occurs when a man's ejaculation is quick, he can't control it, and he feels bad about it. There are several treatment options including medication, discussion of expectations, and communication with a partner.

Male erectile disorder, the inability to create and maintain an erection, may have a psychological or organic etiology. Medications such as Viagra are the first line of therapy for erectile disorder. Other treatments may include a vacuum pump or implants.

Orgasm Dysfunctions

FEMALE ORGASMIC DISORDER is defined as occurring when there is either a lack of orgasm, markedly diminished intensity of orgasmic sensations, or marked delay in orgasm. Biological, psychological, cultural, and relational factors contribute to the cause. Stress, anxiety, and insufficient arousal can all contribute to this disorder. The most effective interventions for helping a woman become orgasmic include a combination of sexuality education, communication on general and sexual issues, attention to relationship and body image, and directed masturbation.

Delayed ejaculation results in the man typically being unable to ejaculate, or a marked delay in ejaculation. Causes may be a combination of medication use, psychosocial, and psychological factors. Treatment will be based on specific causes and may involve using sensate focus.

Genito-Pelvic Pain/Penetration Disorder

GENITO-PELVIC PAIN/PENETRATION DISORDER is characterized by difficulty having intercourse, genito-pelvic pain, fear of pain or vaginal penetration, and tension of the pelvic floor muscles. The typical disorders are vaginismus (difficulty inserting an object into the vagina) and dyspareunia (pain during intercourse).

Sex Therapy

SEX THERAPY is and has been in flux. There is little agreement among sex therapists about how to treat a specific sexual problem. There have also been changes in treatment strategies over time. In the past, psychology and psychoanalysis dominated the treatment field. More recently, pharmacological treatment has become more prominent.

"Let the client beware" applies to the person seeking sex therapy. A Certified Sex Therapist certificate from the American Association of Sexuality Educators, Counselors, and Therapists is one credential to look for. Various modalities of sex therapy include cognitive behavioral sex therapy, the Masters and Johnson Approach, and the PLISSIT model approach. No matter what approach is used, providing data on the effectiveness of sex therapy is difficult.

Web Links

American Association of Sexuality Education, Counselors, and Therapists

http://www.aasect.org/

Surrogate Therapy

www.surrogatetherapy.org

Companion Dolls Used in Sex Therapy

www.syntheticsurrogates.com

Laurie Mintz PhD Blog on Sexual Issues: Stress and Sex

https://www.psychologytoday.com/blog/stress-and-sex

OMGyes

www.omgyes.com

Society for the Advancement of Sexual Health

http://www.sash.net

Society for Sex Therapy & Research

http://www.sstarnet.org/

Key Terms

Acquired dysfunction **361**

Cognitive behavioral
      sex therapy **386**

Delayed ejaculation **381**

Dyspareunia **384**

Erectile disorder **375**

Female orgasmic disorder **378**

Female sexual interest/
      arousal disorder **367**

Generalized dysfunction **361**

Hyperactive sexual
      desire disorder **372**

Inhibited male orgasm **381**

Lesbian bed death **368**

Lifelong dysfunction **361**

Male hypoactive sexual
      desire disorder **372**

Medicalization of
      sexual dysfunctions **361**

Performance anxiety **364**

Persistent genito-pelvic pain/
      penetration disorder **383**

PLISSIT model **389**

Premature ejaculation **373**

Primary dysfunction **361**

Rapid ejaculation **373**

Satiation **372**

Secondary dysfunction **361**

Sensate focus **369**

Sexual dysfunctions **360**

Situational dysfunction **361**

Spectatoring **376**

Urethritis **385**

Vaginismus **384**

Vulvodynia **385**

CHAPTER
15

Variant Sexual Behavior

There is a tendency to consider anything in human behavior that is unusual, not well known, or not well understood, as neurotic, psychopathic, immature, perverse, or the expression of some other sort of psychologic disturbance.

Alfred C. Kinsey

Chapter Outline

15.1 What Is Normal Sexual Behavior? 396
15.1a Criteria Used to Define Normal Sexual Behavior **396**
15.1b Historical Variations in Definitions of Normal Sexual Behavior **397**
15.1c Nudism **398**

15.2 Variant Sexual Behavior: Definitions and Overview 398
15.2a Legal Versus Illegal Paraphilias **400**
Personal Decisions 15-1
    Whose Business Is a Paraphilia? **401**

15.3 Types of Paraphilic Disorders 401
15.3a Voyeuristic Disorder **402**
15.3b Exhibitionistic Disorder **403**
15.3c Frotteuristic Disorder **404**
15.3d Sexual Masochism Disorder **405**
15.3e Sadism Disorder **407**
15.3f Pedophilic Disorder **408**
15.3g Fetishistic Disorder **410**
Self-Assessment 15-1:
    Salience of Fetishism Scale **410**
Technology and Sexuality 15-1:
    Finding Paraphilia Partners via the Internet **411**
15.3h Transvestic Disorder **412**
15.3i Other Paraphilias **412**

15.3j Pathologizing Kink **414**
15.3k "Sexual Addiction" **414**

15.4 The Origins of Paraphilias: Theoretical Perspectives 415
15.4a Psychoanalytic Theory **415**
Self-Assessment 15-2:
    Sexual Compulsivity Scale **416**
15.4b Feminist Theory **417**
15.4c Learning Theory **417**
15.4d Biological Theory **418**

15.5 Treatment of Paraphilias 418
15.5a Decreasing Deviant Sexual Arousal **419**
Social Policy 15-1
    Treating Paraphilic Sex Offenders with Hormones **419**
15.5b Aversive Conditioning **420**
15.5c Covert Sensitization **420**
15.5d Learning Social Skills **420**
Personal Decisions 15-2
    Can People Control Their Paraphilias? **421**
15.5e Changing Faulty Cognitions **421**
15.5f Resolving Sexual Dysfunctions **421**

Web Links 423
Key Terms 423

Objectives

1. Identify the criteria used to define normal sexual behavior
2. Understand the historical variations in defining normal sexual behavior
3. Review the personal decisions associated with paraphilia
4. Learn the differences between legal and illegal paraphilias
5. Identify the various types of paraphilias
6. Discuss the various theories that help explain the origins of paraphilias
7. Describe the various treatment options for paraphilias

(Chelsea Curry Edwards)

Truth ── OR ── Fiction?

T / F 1. The American Psychological Association and American Psychiatric Association recognize sex addiction.

T / F 2. Pedophiles typically focus on 1 of 4 age groups from infants to post-pubescent.

T / F 3. Compulsive Sexual Disorder is an alternative term being used for "sex addiction" to induce insurance companies to pay for treatment.

T / F 4. Women report voyeur behavior with equal frequency to men.

T / F 5. Both men and women report making out in public.

Answers: 1. F 2. T 3. T 4. F 5. T

Our sexualized culture reflects an increasing interest in more than what is considered "normal" or "vanilla" sex, and individuals are pushing cultural boundaries to explore new patterns of sexual expression. In this chapter, we look at sexual behavior viewed as atypical, or variant from the norm. We focus on paraphilias and controversies involved in the use of that term. We examine the terminology used for paraphilias identified in the *Diagnostic and Statistical Manual of Mental Disorders (DSM-5)* and how paraphilias are treated if they become a problem for the individual and/or society (American Psychiatric Association, 2013). We begin by addressing what is considered normal sexual behavior while emphasizing the importance of culture in defining what is normal.

15.1 What Is Normal Sexual Behavior?

Abnormal is so common, it's practically normal.
Cory Doctorow, journalist

One of the most frequent questions students in human sexuality classes ask is, "Am I normal?" Because sex is private and secretive, individuals are left to wonder if, indeed, their behavior is considered normal.

15.1a Criteria Used to Define Normal Sexual Behavior

Various criteria are used to define what is normal, including prevalence, moral correctness, naturalness, and adaptiveness/comfort.

Prevalence

We tend to assume that if most people engage in a sexual behavior, it is normal. For example, based on a national survey of US adult women ages 20–24, 80% reported having experienced vaginal intercourse in the past 12 months (Reece et al., 2012). Given this percentage, we tend to think of females in that age range having sexual intercourse as normal. These same women were asked if they had experienced anal sex in the last 12 months, and 23% reported in the affirmative (Reece et al., 2012). Individuals engage in sadistic sexual behavior even less frequently, so we tend to think that the lower the prevalence, the higher the abnormality or deviance.

Another way to conceptualize prevalence is via the *statistical model of normality*, better known as the *normal curve*. This statistical presentation of the prevalence of a phenomenon reveals the distribution in a large population. For example, in regard to the frequency of sexual intercourse of spouses, most will report their frequency as about once a week. However, there will be a few at both extremes, with some reporting sexual frequency at once a year, and some at three times a day.

Religion provides guidelines for the moral correctness of sexual behavior, most notably the Catholic Church approves only of procreative sex within marriage.

Moral Correctness

Sexual behaviors are also considered normal if they are viewed as morally correct. According to some religions, such as fundamentalist Christianity, penile-vaginal intercourse between husband and wife is the only morally correct form of sexual behavior. Other forms of sexual expression, including oral sex, masturbation, anal sex, sex between unmarried people, and sex between people of the same sex, are considered abnormal because they are viewed as immoral. One of the reasons some homosexuals seek the approval of the church despite its disapproval or rejection is that religion is such a powerful gatekeeper of definitions of sexual morality and normality.

What you do makes a difference, and you have to decide what kind of a difference you want to make.

Jane Goodall, British primatologist

THINK ABOUT IT

Take a moment to answer the following questions. Which of the four criteria used to define what is normal sexual behavior carries the most weight in your own personal view? What sexual behavior, if any, do you engage in or have you engaged in that might be labeled as abnormal or deviant?

Naturalness

Sexual behaviors also are viewed as natural or unnatural, largely depending on whether they result in procreation. Because masturbation, anal sex, and oral sex do not result in conception, they are sometimes viewed as unnatural—and, by implication, abnormal, perverted, or deviant. Sometimes people judge a behavior as natural if it occurs in the natural world (in the animal kingdom) or is biologically determined. People often ask whether homosexual behavior occurs in animals, implying that, if so, the behaviors of gays and lesbians are more natural and acceptable. Indeed, a variety of sexual behaviors occurs in the animal world, including same-sex behavior—but so do incest and assault. Although animal behavior is natural, it is also a questionable standard for humans.

Adaptiveness/Comfort

Sexual behaviors are more widely considered normal if they are adaptive, are comfortable, and have positive outcomes for the participants. Sexual behavior that causes physical or emotional harm or suffering or that interferes with personal or social functioning is considered abnormal. An example of sexual behavior considered abnormal is adults engaging in sexual acts with children, which is typically associated with negative outcomes for both adult and child.

Social Construction of Deviance

Michel Foucault, the influential mid-20th-century French historian and philosopher, emphasized that what is normal is socially defined and constructed: "What is accepted as normal and healthy sexuality is not determined by nature but changes with the values and norms of a particular society at a particular place and time" (De Block & Adriaens, 2013, p. 277).

15.1b Historical Variations in Definitions of Normal Sexual Behavior

Within the same culture, sexual behaviors may be labeled as normal at one historical time and abnormal at another. For example, although kissing in public is acceptable, normal behavior today (be aware of this PDA phenomenon on your campus), in the American colonial era, kissing in public was considered unacceptable and punishable by being "lodged in the stocks" in public. During that era, unmarried persons who were discovered to have engaged in intercourse were considered to have succumbed to the temptations of the flesh. After they were discovered, they had to make a public confession and were also subject to fines and a public lashing. Public kissing in Taiwan and in mainland China today is not illegal, but it is frowned upon—there is social disapproval for kissing one's beloved in public. The concept of voyeurism has also changed. Nudity is common in movies today, allowing viewers to become voyeurs.

15.1c Nudism

Nudism or naturism refers to the philosophy in which individuals practice/advocate nudity in private, in homes with other nudists or in public nudist contexts (e.g. nudist resorts). The goal of nudists is to enjoy being clothes-free and to enjoy the companionship of others who share this value. Nude beaches are common in Europe.

Wherever nudists gather, the norms emphasize nonsexual behavior. Staring and being sexually aggressive are not tolerated and the individual who does so is asked to leave. Some resorts include families where children of all ages are nude. Strict background checks on members and strict surveillance ensure the protection and safety of children. There are no laws that govern nudity of family members on private property.

> *I am strongly in favour of getting rid of every scrap of clothing ... I know the mischief done by making us ashamed of our bodies.*
>
> George Bernard Shaw, playwright

The American Association for Nude Recreation is the largest organization of nudists in North America. There are over 213,000 members throughout the United States, Canada, Mexico, and beyond. These members include those who go to small, private nudist venues (e.g. homes) as well as over 200 nudist resorts and affiliates.

A member of the first author's human sexuality class who identifies as a nudist visited a nude beach in Portugal and wrote the following:

> *When I think about the human body, I see it as beautiful—each and every shape. I believe we should be able to embrace our bodies. Nudity shouldn't be uncomfortable because without clothes we are who we are. Take off the Spanx, bras, and underwear and you are left nude in your own imperfect state. Maybe people don't like the idea of being nude because they feel so close to themselves. They are so used to masking what they are with clothes they forget who they are without them. Without clothes we are in our original primal state. Sometimes that can be perceived as sexual which is okay. But, we also need to be able to look at a body and think of it as art, think of it as pure and natural—flaw and all* (Bolden, 2018).

15.2 Variant Sexual Behavior: Definitions and Overview

What are determined to be acceptable sexual interests vary over time and across cultures. Scientific views of what is acceptable have changed drastically over time. Prior to 1850, the definition of sexual deviance was moral and theological. The Old Testament prohibited same-sex, masturbation, and anal-sexual behavior. With the replacement of "the clergy as authorities in the sexual domain," early psychiatrists conceptualized insanity as "diseases of the will and emotion." In his landmark work, *Psychopathia Sexualis*, Richard von Krafft-Ebing viewed sexual deviance as caused by "hereditary taintedness" in the family tree, which led to an imbalance of sexual instinct and inhibition. Hence, exhibitionists inherited a basic predisposition to behave in nonnormative ways that they felt powerless to control (De Block & Adriaens, 2013).

Freudian influence (sexuality was a fixation on early love objects and denial of a traumatizing sexual experience, such as with the Oedipal complex) overlapped with Germany's Magnus Hirschfeld, who founded the Institute for Sexual Science in Berlin. Hirschfeld, along with Havelock Ellis, viewed variant sexual behavior as neither pathological nor dangerous to society. Instead, they fostered the idea that there is a range of human sexual interests and behaviors, and these should not be

Nudism
Refers to the philosophy in which individuals practice/advocate nudity in private, in homes with other nudists, or in nudist resorts/beaches

considered pathological (including homosexuality and masturbation). The exception was when the behavior harmed someone else.

After a time, you may find that having is not so pleasing a thing, after all, as wanting.

Dr. Spock

In the *DSM-III*, use of the word *paraphilia* reaffirmed the idea that "unusual or bizarre imagery or acts necessary for sexual excitement" involved "sexual objects or situations that are not part of normative arousal-activity patterns and that in varying degrees may interfere with the capacity for reciprocal affectionate sexual activity." Hence, the downside of a paraphilia was that the individual might not be able to make a love connection.

Personal **REFLECTION**

Take a moment to express your thoughts about the following questions.
Sex-offending paraphilic behavior may go unnoticed for years. What paraphilic sexual behaviors have you encountered that escaped legal detection?

The term *paraphilia* is derived from the words *para*, meaning deviation, and *philia*, meaning attracted. Hence, the *paraphiliac* is attracted to a stimulus that is regarded by society as deviant. It is not unusual for a person to express more than one paraphilia.

The *DSM-5* defines **paraphilia** as being aroused by certain objects or situations that are not typical and that may interfere with the capacity for reciprocal, affectionate sexual activity with a partner. For example, a person who has a high-heel fetish may be unable to become aroused unless the partner wears high-heeled shoes. Although the partner may not mind wearing heels, feeling required to do so for the partner to become aroused may be problematic.

The essential elements of a paraphilia are recurrent, intense, sexually arousing fantasies, sexual urges, or behaviors, generally involving the following:

- Nonhuman objects (such as high-heel fetish)

- The actual suffering or humiliation of self or partner (not just simulated; as in sadism and masochism)

- Children or other nonconsenting persons (pedophilia, exhibitionism, voyeurism, frotteurism)

All three of these criteria need not necessarily be involved for the label of paraphilia to apply. For example, the pedophile focuses on human subjects (which leaves out the first criterion), and the cross-dresser focuses on clothing, not people (which leaves out the second and third criteria). What all paraphilias have in common is that the object being focused on becomes imbued with erotic value, and there is an intense yearning to experience that object. In some cases, the paraphilia is experienced as a compulsion that interferes with work and relationships. Using our example of the high-heel fetish, the person may spend hours and a great deal of money collecting high heels and require the partner to strut around in the shoes for show.

There is disagreement about whether paraphilias constitute a mental disorder. One position is that "nonnormative sexuality need not necessarily be a mental disorder" (De Block & Adriaens, 2013, p. 293). This conclusion is based on the observation that there is a difference between paraphilias (defined as atypical sexual behavior) and paraphilic disorders. The latter exists when a person's satisfaction of a paraphilia

Paraphilia
Overdependence on a culturally unacceptable or unusual stimulus for sexual arousal and satisfaction

THINK ABOUT IT

Take a moment to answer the following question. Some couples practice some sexually variant behaviors (sadism/masochism) with the goal of enhancing physical excitement. These behaviors may be a part of mature sexual expression when they are mutually agreed to and pleasurable for both parties. However, intervention may be needed if the behavior becomes compulsive and distressing to the individual or if it becomes coercive. To what degree do you think sexual behaviors that result in pain should be of concern to the law?

---

involves causing harm—or risk of harm—to self or others. Such an outcome of a paraphilia is not always the case, however, since any individual may have urges, fantasies, desires, or wishes without acting on them to harmful effect. Moran (2013) noted that "a paraphilia by itself does not automatically justify or require clinical intervention" and that "to warrant the diagnosis of paraphilic disorder the sexual behavior must cause distress, impairment in function or involve nonconsenting individuals."

Paraphilias vary in severity from disturbing fantasies (sometimes accompanied by masturbation) to sexual victimization, which may include murder (erotophonophilia, or lust murder, occurs when the partner is killed as a means of atoning for sex with the individual, as in a serial killer who murders sex workers after having sex with them). Although there are few classic profile characteristics (such as sexual orientation, ethnicity, socioeconomic background), paraphilias most often occur in men and are very rarely diagnosed in women. Among individuals seen clinically for the treatment of paraphilias, approximately half are married.

Some people with a paraphilia may become so preoccupied with the object that they feel out of control. They experience uncontrollable urges, feel unable to stop themselves from pursuing the activity, and increase the frequency and intensity of their involvement. In other cases, the person may feel in control of the paraphilic impulses and not driven to engage in the behavior.

The relationships of the person with a paraphilia may suffer if the partner becomes aware of it. For example, wives are sometimes shocked by the discovery of their husbands dressing in women's clothes. In some cases the spouse may be asked to participate in the paraphilia—for example, the partner is asked to be the recipient of the sexual sadist's paraphilia.

15.2a Legal Versus Illegal Paraphilias

The definitions of paraphilias presented in this chapter, which are based on the *DSM-5* developed by mental health professionals, do not necessarily meet legal or other nonmedical criteria for what constitutes mental disability. Paraphilias are legal or illegal depending on the degree to which the rights of others are affected. Formicophilia (arousal from ants or other insects crawling on the body) and klismaphilia (arousal from having enemas) do not infringe on the rights of others and are of little concern to the law. Voyeurism, exhibitionism, and pedophilia are examples of paraphilias that interfere with the rights of others and carry legal penalties. Voyeurism and exhibitionism are clinical terms—in the legal system, these criminal acts may be referred to as *secret peeping* and *indecent exposure*. They are usually regarded as misdemeanors and are punishable by a fine. Repeat offenses may involve mandatory outpatient treatment at a mental health facility. Pedophilic acts are punishable by imprisonment. Legal charges may range from taking indecent liberties with a minor to sodomy or rape. When people with paraphilias break the law, they are referred to as *sex offenders*. The majority of apprehended sex offenders are arrested for acts of exhibitionism, pedophilia, and voyeurism (American Psychiatric Association, 2013).

Laws regulating sexual behavior vary from state to state. Some states regard exhibitionism as a misdemeanor; others classify it as a felony. The penalty ranges from a fine to a prison term. If the exhibitionist is drunk or has a mental disability, police officers tend to regard this self-exposure differently from those who compulsively expose themselves and are repeatedly picked up for exhibitionism.

PERSONAL DECISIONS 15-1

Whose Business Is a Paraphilia?

Some paraphilias are illegal, and the person does not seek treatment unless forced to do so. An example is the pedophilic who agrees to treatment in exchange for a reduced prison term. Other paraphilias may be legal but harmful to the person with the paraphilia. Autoerotic asphyxiation involves the individual cutting off their air supply while masturbating. An example is a person who would "place pillows over his face, strangle himself with different cords, and lean over chairs to restrict his breathing during masturbation" (Faccini & Saide, 2012, p. 100). Sometimes the person restricts too much air and dies. Sometimes another person is involved, such as with asphyxiophilia (choking a partner during sex).

Some paraphilias, however, seem unusual but do not hurt anyone; examples include acrotomophilia (amputee partner) and autonepiophilia (wet diapers). Individuals with paraphilias that are not harmful to themselves or others might choose to disregard society's negative label of their behavior. Such a choice, in combination with a positive view of themselves, may have positive consequences for them, with no negative consequences for society. For example, crossdressing is a paraphilia that may be enjoyable for the individual and of limited consequence to the partner (assuming the partner's knowledge and acceptance).

15.3 **Types of Paraphilic Disorders**

In this section, we discuss the major types of paraphilias identified in the *DSM-5* (listed in Table 15-1) and briefly identify a variety of others (American Psychiatric Association, 2013). The emphasis in diagnosing a paraphilia is that it involves intense urges and fantasies, with action on the urges secondary and not necessarily needing to occur.

TABLE 15-1	Major Paraphilias by DSM-5
Paraphilia	Description
Voyeuristic disorder	Spying on others engaged in private (nude) behavior
Exhibitionistic disorder	Exposing one's genitals to strangers
Frotteuristic disorder	Touching or rubbing against an unsuspecting/nonconsenting person
Sexual masochism disorder	Becoming sexually aroused/enjoying being humiliated and/or hurt via being tied up, whipped, beaten, etc.
Sexual sadism disorder	Becoming sexually aroused/enjoying humiliating or causing physical pain in a partner
Pedophilic disorder	Being sexually aroused by children
Fetishistic disorder	Being sexually aroused by nonliving objects
Transvestic disorder	Being sexually aroused by cross-dressing

15.3a Voyeuristic Disorder

Voyeuristic disorder (also called **scopophilia**) is defined as recurrent and intense sexual arousal (over a period of at least 6 months) from observing an unsuspecting naked person. The individual is at least age 18 (American Psychiatric Association, 2013).

National DATA

Prevalence of voyeuristic disorder in the general population is unknown. Based on the voyeuristic sexual acts in nonclinical samples, the highest possible lifetime prevalence for voyeuristic disorder is approximately 12% in males and 4% in females (American Psychiatric Association, 2013, p. 688).

International DATA

In the province of Quebec, of 1,040 adults, 50% of males and 21% of females reported that they had engaged in at least one act of voyeurism (Joyal & Carpentier, 2017).

Voyeurs (sometimes referred to as *peeping Toms*) spend a lot of time planning to peep and will risk a great deal to do so. They regard climbing over fences, hiding in bushes, and shivering in the cold as worth the trouble. Peeping is the stimulus for sexual excitement, which most often results in ejaculation through masturbation either during the peeping or later. The target of the voyeur is usually a female stranger. Although some voyeurs are married, they may not derive excitement from watching their wives or any familiar woman undress. Persons who report they do not experience distress or shame for spying on others are regarded as having voyeuristic sexual interest but should not be diagnosed with voyeuristic disorder.

Voyeurism for men may be dysfunctional in that they may not learn how to relate to women as individuals but only as sexual body parts. Two researchers reviewed Gary Brooks's 1995 book *The Centerfold Syndrome: How Men Can Avoid Objectification and Achieve Intimacy with Women*. In it, Brooks emphasized that male socialization encourages voyeurism—looking at naked females (centerfolds in magazines and pornography on the internet)—which encourages objectification of the female, devoid of establishing emotionally intimate, sexually gratifying relationships with them (Elder et al., 2012). Brooks also noted men learning objectification of women from pornography, which is not "real sex" but performers paid to engage in specific sexual behaviors in a certain sequence, emitting certain sounds, and usually devoid of intimacy (though some "amateur porn" features real people involved in intimate relationships recording their sexual interaction). A man reported:

In pornography, typically, you don't see women expressing pain. So when she [his sexual partner] does say, "It hurts" or "Not anymore," you know, when there are things that in the "ideal world of sex" are not expressed, I think subconsciously, "Why can't it be like in porn, where everything's just perfect?" (Elder et al., 2012, p. 170)

Voyeuristic disorder
Paraphilia that involves recurrent, intense urges to look at unsuspecting people who are naked, undressing, or engaging in sexual behavior (also called *scopophilia*)

Scopophilia
See *voyeuristic disorder*

15.3b Exhibitionistic Disorder

Former New York Congressman Anthony Weiner gave visibility to the phenomenon of exhibitionism when he was discovered to have sent sexually explicit photos (sexting) of his penis to various women. After he resigned from office, it was revealed that he continued sexting (highlighting the compulsive nature of this fetish), and in September 2016, his sexts to an underage girl brought new approbation and prompted his wife to leave him. **Exhibitionistic disorder** is defined as recurrent and intense sexual arousal from the exposure of the genitals to an unsuspecting person as manifested in fantasies, urges, or behaviors (for a period of at least 6 months). The individual has acted on these urges with an unsuspecting person, or the sexual urges or fantasies cause significant distress (American Psychiatric Association, 2013).

National DATA

Prevalence of exhibitionistic disorder in the general population is unknown. Based on exhibitionistic sexual acts in nonclinical samples, the highest possible prevalence for exhibitionistic disorder in the male population is 2%–4%. The percentage for females is even more uncertain but believed to be much lower than in males (American Psychiatric Association, 2013, p. 690).

International DATA

In the province of Quebec, of 1,040 adults, 33% of males and 29% of females reported that they had engaged in at least one act of being an exhibitionist (Joyal & Carpentier, 2017).

Exhibitionists expose themselves to people they do not know for several reasons. Sexual excitement is a primary one. Hearing a victim yell and watching their horrified face is sexually stimulating for some individuals. Once sexually excited, the exhibitionist individual may masturbate to orgasm.

A male exhibitionist may expose himself to shock women. Exhibiting himself may be a way of directing anger and hostility toward women. Although the woman he exposes himself to likely has not injured him, other women may have belittled him (or he may have perceived it that way). Or perhaps he has recently been unable to have and maintain an erection, blames his lack of erection on women, and exposes himself as a way of getting back at them.

Some individuals expose themselves as a way of relieving stress. When the stress reaches a peak, individuals exhibit themselves, masturbate, and relieve the stress. Still others expose themselves with a sexually arousing fantasy in which the person observing them will become sexually aroused (American Psychiatric Association, 2013).

Some people have referred to exhibitionism, public masturbation, and voyeurism as victimless crimes; however, these behaviors can cause harm because victims may be distressed. An example is a student who was looking for a book in the library and pulled a book from a lower shelf, only to discover the penis of an exhibitionistic male who was exposing himself on the other side of the bookshelf. She was shocked, horrified, and distressed.

Exhibitionistic disorder
Paraphilia that involves an intense, recurrent (over a period of at least 6 months) sexual urge, often accompanied by sexually arousing fantasies, to expose one's genitals to a stranger

Ideally, if confronted by exhibitionism, try to make no response but quietly remove yourself from the situation and call the police. Law enforcement agencies may benefit from obtaining reports of minor offenses of exhibitionism and voyeurism, because a person who engages in one offense may engage again in the same offense or different types of offenses.

While it does not meet the criteria for a paraphilia, performing making out (PMO) refers to kissing, petting, and necking all of which are nonpenetrative. In an online questionnaire, 32% of 155 undergraduate females and 37% of undergraduate males reported having engaged in PMO (8% of the women and 2% of the men with same-sex partners). The motives for doing so included enhancing their image (e.g. making out with a very good-looking person), making someone jealous, demonstrating that they were in a relationship, being sexually arousing for men (as in the case of same-sex females putting on a show for heterosexual males), and just for fun and games. The latter involved drinking at a party and publically making out for adventure and excitement. Outcomes for men were to show off for their same-sex peers; the women were often slut-shamed since they were viewed as being public about their sexuality—the double standard (Esterline & Muehlenhard, 2017).

National DATA

It is estimated that 30% of adult males in the general population have engaged in frotteuristic behavior. About 10%–14% of adult males are seen in outpatient clinics for paraphilic disorders that meet the criteria for frotteuristic disorder (American Psychiatric Association, 2013, p. 693).

International DATA

In the province of Quebec, of 1,040 adults, 32% of males and 21% of females reported that they had engaged in at least one act of frotteurism (Joyal & Carpentier, 2017).

15.3c Frotteuristic Disorder

A crowded bar, concert, or subway is the ideal environment for the frotteur. According to the *DSM-5*, **frotteuristic disorder** is the recurrent and intense sexual arousal (for at least 6 months) from touching or rubbing against an unsuspecting person as manifested in fantasies, urges, or behaviors. The individual has acted on these urges with an unsuspecting person, or the sexual urges or fantasies cause significant distress (American Psychiatric Association, 2013).

Although the person may be distressed about the overwhelming urge to touch or rub against another, he also may act on those fantasies. The person usually chooses a crowded place for the activity. He presses against the sexually desired person while saying, "Excuse me," and then moves to another part of the crowd and presses against someone else. This behavior, known as *frottage*, usually goes unnoticed; however, the feelings aroused by pressing against another may be used in a masturbatory fantasy later.

Frotteuristic disorder
Paraphilia that involves recurring, intense, sexual urges (at least 6 months), accompanied by fantasies, of touching or rubbing—often with the genitals—against a nonconsenting person

International **DATA**

In the province of Quebec, of 1,040 adults, 14% of males and 24% of females reported that they had been in the role of a masochist (Joyal & Carpentier, 2017).

15.3d Sexual Masochism Disorder

BDSM is a generic term that refers to a spectrum of activities within bondage/discipline, dominance/submission, and sadism/masochism relationships. BDSM practitioners generally report higher education, are younger, and experience stigma due to the unfamiliarity of others with the practice. While 80% report having fantasized BDSM behavior, lower percentages (e.g. 10–35%) report being tied up, blindfolded, and/or spanked (Coppens et al., 2020). Martinez (2018) noted that BDSM roles are often gendered, with men tending to self-identify as dominant, master, top, or sadist (DMTS) (performing dominant roles) while women tend to self-identify as submissive, slave, bottom, or masochist (SSBM) (performing submissive roles). However, role fluidity sometimes occurs with the partners switching roles.

Sexual masochism disorder is diagnosed when there is recurrent and intense sexual arousal (over a period of at least 6 months) from the act of being humiliated, beaten, bound, or otherwise made to suffer as manifested in fantasies, urges, or behaviors. These fantasies, sexual urges, or behaviors cause significant distress (American Psychiatric Association, 2013, p. 694).

The masochist enjoys and is sexually aroused by physical pain and/or psychological humiliation. While the person may actually experience pain, the diagnosis only requires intense, recurrent urges and fantasies for at least 6 months. The person may have these fantasies while masturbating or while having sexual relations.

Age-play is a subset of BDSM whereby "littles" have a big daddy. Tiidenberg and Paasonen (2019) interviewed eight self-identified "little" informants, one of whom noted:

Being "collared" in the role of submissive is a turn-on for the masochist.

(Chelsea Curry Edwards)

He is always my Daddy. I am always baby, little, dolly, pet. … I just can't get myself to give over control very easily so it's not a space I go to with many people. He's been a safe place for my submission and because that's so rare, it's intoxicating. Topping often feels more service-y for me. I like it because I'm giving people what they want. I would be happy to switch with Daddy, if it was what he wanted. But Little submission is the money spot for me personally.

Her comments reveal great variation in being little, including switching. Sometimes being a little can be therapeutic—for both partners:

Personally, having a stable, loving, healthy relationship with my Daddy Dom is helping me to repair some pretty heavy childhood traumas. And interestingly, my Daddy, who doesn't have a positive relationship with his actual father, finds it therapeutic to know that these nurturing and loving qualities are inside of him, regardless of the fact that he didn't learn them by example. It has been powerfully healing for him too. (interview, 2017).

Sexual masochism disorder
Paraphilia characterized by recurrent, intense, sexual urges and sexually arousing fantasies of at least 6 months' duration, in which sexual arousal or gratification is obtained through enacting scripts that involve suffering and pain

Tiidenberg and Paasonen (2019) further assert that this type of age-play has been pathologized as paraphilic infantilism, an unfortunate, inaccurate depiction.

In the *Up Close 15-1* below a woman describes her involvement in dominance and submission.

My Entry/Enjoyment into the World of Dominance and Submission

The terms dominant and submissive never really meant much to me before I met Conrad. Sadomasochism was just this weird concept that conjured up images of gay men dressed in leather, spanking and beating each other: a caricature of abnormal sexual activities. I had no interest in that alternate lifestyle. I wasn't like that—I had normal sex. Unfortunately, this sex usually left me unsatisfied, but I didn't understand this dissatisfaction until I met Conrad my sophomore year of college. By introducing me to the world of domination and submission, he made me reconsider my previous notions of normality when it came to sex. What he showed me were not the stereotypes I had associated with this lifestyle, but rather a side of me I had never explored. What I had once thought was weird and abnormal had now become a part of my sexual identity—I became a submissive.

I met Conrad in one of my classes, and we quickly became friends. There was something about his demeanor, his ability to focus on me and listen to what I had to say, that attracted me. We shared common interests in literature, music, politics, film, etc. I admired his intelligence and his respect for me as a woman. I was not used to this respect—most boys treated me with a condescending attitude, as if my gender were a flaw. He was a soft-spoken Southern gentleman, and I was instantly attracted to him. If someone had told me that Conrad enjoyed dominating women with whips and paddles while they were tied to his bed, I would have laughed and said no way, not Conrad. He's not like that.

When we began having sex, nothing out of the ordinary happened. He didn't bring me into a dungeon and chain me to a wall; it was the same sex I had been having before: normal sex. But I did notice something different; I noticed a sexual connection between us. There was this sense of attentiveness that I had never experienced from a man before. Conrad seemed to be able to read my body: what it needed and what it wanted, and by doing this, I think he also witnessed the trust I quickly developed and invested in him.

Once this level of comfort was established, Conrad began to slowly introduce me to the world of domination and submission (D/S). His gradual introduction was perfect for me because I was hesitant at first. I trusted Conrad, but I didn't know how I would respond to the activities he had in mind. We began with spankings and bondage scenarios, which usually involved me being cuffed to the bed, spread-eagle. Shortly, we began using more toys rather than his hand: riding crops, paddles, whips, ball-gags, etc. After I had grown comfortable with this, Conrad applied power roles while we enacted sexual scenarios: he was the dominant, and I was the submissive, his slave. I had to say "please" and "thank you" after every sentence; I had to ask permission to orgasm. If at any point I was not enjoying myself, I used our safe word, "red," and Conrad stopped immediately to make sure I was all right.

The first time he placed a collar around my neck and told me to lick his boots, I realized this is what had been missing in my previous sexual activities. This loss of control, abandonment of power, was so erotic, so arousing, that it almost scared me. I was putting myself in a powerless position I never thought I would enjoy. All my life, I had been an outspoken leader, a feminist, an independent woman, someone who did not enjoy answering to authority. But here I was getting sexual pleasure out of being dominated, being treated like a slave, being beaten. It was difficult to balance my everyday sense of autonomy with this newfound loss of power, until I realized how to separate the two emotions. I am a different person in the bedroom; I don't need to bring my day into my night. At times I receive more respect from Conrad while he's dominating me than I do from people I encounter in my everyday life. For me, domination and submission is about love and respect.

People always ask me if we still have normal sex, or if we engage in a D/S relationship 24 hours a day. First, I ask them to define normal for me, and then I respond with no, we do not always engage in D/S when having sex. We have an even balance between vanilla sex (normal/ordinary sex) and D/S situations because we don't depend on D/S for sexual satisfaction; a dependency would diminish the eroticism for me. I don't need to be a submissive, but I enjoy being one for Conrad. The act of submission has allowed me to embrace my sexuality and has provided me with a kind of identity I never thought I could comfortably possess, until now.

International DATA

In the province of Quebec, of 1,040 adults, 7% of males and 4% of females reported that they had engaged in being a sadist at least once (Joyal & Carpentier, 2017).

15.3e Sadism Disorder

Sexual sadism disorder is diagnosed when there is recurrent and intense sexual arousal (for a period of at least 6 months) from the physical or psychological suffering of another person as manifested in fantasies, urges, or behaviors. The individual has acted on these sexual urges with a nonconsenting person, or the sexual urges or fantasies cause significant distress. Sexual sadism may also be defined as a paraphilia in which the infliction of pain or the humiliation of others is experienced as sexually gratifying. In an analysis of 1,020 adult male sexual offenders in an Austrian prison, the researchers found that sexual sadism occurred at the upper end of a continuum of sexual aggression/sexual violence rather than as a distinct separate sexual paraphilia (Mokros et al., 2014).

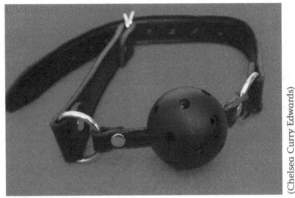

(Chelsea Curry Edwards)

Putting a ball and gag on the masochist may be part of the script for the sadist.

National DATA

Prevalence figures for sadism in the general population are unknown. Among civilly committed sex offenders in the United States, less than 10% have sexual sadism (American Psychiatric Association, 2013, p. 696).

The term *sadism* can be traced back to the French author, philosopher, and sado-masochist Marquis de Sade (1740–1814), who described the experiences of people who enjoyed hurting and dominating their sexual partners. The cries and suffering of the sexual partner were the source of sadistic sexual excitement. Such suffering may be by consenting masochistic partners or by those who are forced to participate. Sadistic acts or fantasies may involve several venues: dominance (forcing the victim to crawl), restraint or bondage (tying the victim to a chair), spanking, whipping, beating, burning, shocking (with electricity), cutting, strangling, mutilating, and/or killing.

There is a difference between sexual sadism disorder and being "kinky." Engaging in BDSM with a consensual partner is not a disorder. When the sadist and masochist get together, it is the sadist who enjoys inflicting the pain on the masochist. Such infliction of pain and social scripting ("Have you been a bad boy? Mommy must give you a good spanking" by the sadist and "Oh! Thank you, mistress. May I have some more, please, and harder?" by the masochist) normally occurs in the context of an explicit (and sometimes written) agreement between the parties as to the limits of what is acceptable (handcuffs, hot wax, whipping) and a safe word or action that alerts the sadist that the masochist wants to stop whatever is going on (and the sadist agrees to

Sexual sadism disorder
Paraphilia characterized by recurrent, intense sexual urges and sexually arousing fantasies, of at least 6 months' duration, involving acts that hurt or humiliate the sexual partner

stop when the masochist says this word or performs the specific action). Hence, sado-masochistic sexual behavior by partners who choose this pattern of sexual expression is consensual.

It may be difficult to understand how loving/intimate partners can hurt each other. Following is an example of a boyfriend revealing his feelings when his new girlfriend told him that she was a masochist (hence, she needed him to be her sadistic partner).

I never could figure out how hurting someone could come from love; now I realize it is one of the most intimate acts out there. To trust someone or be trusted that much is incredible; the amount of trust needed to know that those things can happen but it will never be abused, used outside of the right contexts, and will never cause problems takes the relationship to a level I never could have imagined. (Authors' files)

International **DATA**

In the province of Quebec, of 1,040 adults, 0.6% of males and 0.2% of females reported that they had had sex with a child at least once (Joyal & Carpentier, 2017).

15.3f Pedophilic Disorder

Pedophilic disorder is diagnosed when there is recurrent and intense (for a period of at least 6 months) sexually arousing fantasies, sexual urges, or behaviors involving sexual activity with a prepubescent child or children (generally age 13 or younger). The individual has acted on these sexual urges or the sexual urges or fantasies cause significant distress. The individual is at least age 16 and at least 5 years older than the child or children. Browne et al. (2018) noted that pedophiles are sexually aroused by their victims and plan/target to offend against their victims. The internet is sometimes used to find victims. De Santisteban and Gamez-Guadix (2018) found in a study of 2,732 minors (ages 12–15) that 16% of the females and 9% of the males reported sexual solicitation.

Pedophilic sexual interest may be deduced using psychophysiological measures (phallometric assessment of penile responses) and use of a Screening Scale (Helmus et al., 2015). Pedophilia may also be defined as having equal or greater sexual arousal to children than to adults (Tromovitch, 2014). Seto (2017) noted that pedophilia with its focus on prepubescent children is one of several chronophilias such as nepiophilia (infant/toddlers), pedophilia (prepubescent children), hebephilia (pubescent children), and ephebophilia (postpubescent, sexually maturing adolescents). He also suggested these chronophilia can be regarded as a sexual orientation in that the person is focused on/sexually attracted to these individuals.

Pedophiles can be categorized as four types. These types are based on 75 cases of sex offenders who used the internet to have sex with minors (Tener et al., 2015):

1. *Cynical* (35%): Without scruples, the cynic will often target a minor whom he knows.

2. *Expert* (32%): There may have been hundreds of victims he is working on or has had. He is relentless in doing whatever is necessary (such as lying) to accomplish the goal of sex with the minor.

Pedophilic disorder
Sexual arousal in reference to a child

3. *Affection-focused* (21%): He attempts to develop a mutual love relationship but the end game is sex.

4. *Sex-focused* (12%): The goal is immediate sex, with no concern for establishing a relationship with the victim.

Pedophiles are one of the most hated and feared social groups (even though they may not have committed any criminal act) (Jahnke et al., 2015). Not all individuals who have a sexual interest in children engage in aggressive sexual behavior directly; however, research strongly indicates that consumption of child pornography not only damages the children involved but also tends to encourage active behavior on the part of the viewer (Kim, 2004).

Given that 25% of women report being molested as children and estimates indicate that only 1 in 20 child sex abuse cases are reported, pedophilia is clearly a major human-rights problem. Per the Harvard Mental Health Letter (2010), researchers have found no effective treatment for pedophilia: "There is no cure, so the focus is on protecting children." Three key points are involved:

- Pedophilia is a sexual orientation and unlikely to change. Treatment aims to enable the pedophile to resist acting on these sexual urges.

- No intervention is likely to work on its own; outcomes may be better when the patient is motivated and treatment combines psychotherapy and medication.

- Parents should be aware that in most sexual abuse cases involving children, the perpetrator is someone the child knows.

Pedophiles are often in denial. Child sex offenders often distort reality to avoid their own culpability. For example, pedophiles may say that children often make up stories about adults having sex with them as a way of getting attention and deny they would ever sexually aggress against children (Nunes & Jung, 2013). Cranney (2018) noted the concept of "virtuous pedophiles" who explain/justify their sexual attraction to children as "God made me this way."

Cultural Factors

Mainstream cultural factors often send disturbing messages regarding sexuality and children. In the United States the sexualization of young girls is ubiquitous, from gendered clothing and toys to media and makeup. Nearly a third of clothing marketed for young girls and girl toddlers at 15 mainstream outlets in the United States featured sexualized characteristics (Goodin et al., 2011). Media also promotes sexualized appearance and behavior, with advertisements, movies, television shows, videos, music, and print material targeting even the youngest girls.

In 2007, an American Psychological Association (APA) task force review of research concluded that sexualization of girls is widespread in US culture. Per the report, this commercialization of sex has made "sexiness" a highly valued and imitated quality in girls as young as age 6. The abundance and influence of sexualized products, which is fostered by the adults who purchase them for their daughters, sisters, or nieces, has a wide range of consequences, including self-objectification, shame, anxiety, and dysfunction in girls from kindergarten through the teen years.

Adult reactions are a key component in both the sexualization of girls and its negative consequences. Researchers Graff and colleagues (2012) used images of a fifth-grade girl dressed in varying attire to analyze adult attitudes on girls' competence.

The reactions revealed that adults viewed the girl wearing sexualized clothing as "less competent, less intelligent, less moral, and less self-respecting." These results support the APA task force's findings that the combination of commercially driven sexualization and subsequent "slut-shaming" of girls who conformed to the advertised behaviors and appearances is connected to low self-esteem, depression, and eating disorders among elementary and middle school girls.

Though research on a direct connection to pedophilic crimes is still pending, a culture that views younger and younger girls with a sexual focus not only damages them, but also serves to normalize dangerous pedophilic attitudes and, perhaps, behavior.

15.3g Fetishistic Disorder

Fetishistic disorder is diagnosed when there is recurrent and intense sexual arousal (for at least 6 months) either from the use of nonliving objects or from a highly specific focus on nongenital body parts as manifested in fantasies, urges, or behaviors. The fantasies, sexual urges, or behaviors cause significant distress (American Psychiatric Association, 2013, p. 700). **Fetishism** is the generic term for various fetishes. A fetish may begin at the slight preference level and then it may progress in intensity to being a necessity and then to being a symbolic substitute for a sexual partner.

Autonepiophilia or paraphilic infantilism reflects individuals who refer to themselves as adult babies (AB), those who enjoy role-playing as infants, and diaper lovers (DL). As a group, they are referred to as adult baby/diaper lovers (ABDL). Zamboni (2018) studied members of an ABDL online community who reported that they usually told a new partner about their interest early in the relationship (80%); about 20% did not. Some of the respondents reported that their motive for wearing diapers was not sexual but as a means of relaxation (2019).

Fetishism
Paraphilia that involves a pattern, of at least 6 months' duration, of deriving sexual arousal or sexual gratification from actual or fantasized inanimate objects or nongenital body parts

---

Self-Assessment 15-1:
Salience of Fetishism Scale

This scale assesses the degree to which an individual has a foot fetish. The data were collected by researchers on a nonclinical sample; the researchers felt that the data they gathered voluntarily may have wider applicability to other fetishists besides their sample. You may be interested in reviewing the questions to determine the degree to which the fetish was central to the respondent's sex life.

1. Is foot play necessary for your sexual arousal?
2. Is foot fantasy necessary for your sexual arousal?
3. Is foot fantasy usually the main focus of your self-masturbation?
4. What was the frequency of masturbatory fantasies about feet during adolescence?
5. Are feet usually the main focus of your sexual activity with others?
6. How often do you self-masturbate without fantasizing about feet?
7. How often do you self-masturbate while fantasizing about feet?
8. Do you think you could stop fantasizing about feet if you wanted to?
9. Have you ever made a serious attempt to stop your interest in feet?
10. How often do you engage in sexual activity with another without foot play?
11. How often do you engage in sexual activity with another involving foot play?

Scoring and Interpretation

Since the variables used in the scales had different possible ranges, the researchers standardized the scores and made each variable range from 0 to 1. Then they summed the scores for each respondent. The results revealed that while there was a range of salience among the respondents, most clustered at the high end of the scale: 22% had the highest possible score on most of the variables. The salience of fetishism in the men's sex lives was not highly correlated to a measure of self-reported psychological problems. This showed that a man could report that fetishism was very important in his sex life but still have little in the way of psychological problems.

Source: "If the shoe fits. … Exploring male homosexual foot fetishism," by M. S. Weinberg, C. J. Williams, and C. Calhan, vol. 32, 17–27 (1995). Scale from page 25. Copyright 1995 Taylor & Francis Ltd, http://www.tandfonline.com. Reprinted by permission of the publisher.

Fetishes may be divided into two types: substance and form. A substance fetish means the substance itself is the fetish object. Leather is an example. Whatever forms the leather comes in—belt, shoe, clothes—it is imbued with an erotic connotation. A form fetish refers to a particular object, regardless of its makeup. For example, a person with a shoe fetish responds to shoes as an erotic stimulus, whether the shoes are made of plastic, leather, or cloth. The most common form of fetish objects are clothing items, including panties, stockings, lingerie, high-heeled shoes, and boots. Common substance fetishes include leather, satin, and latex. Fetishes may also include sounds (a particular song, the clicking of a train on the tracks) and scents (perfume, incense). *Self-Assessment 15-1: Salience of Fetishism Scale* is a way researchers assess the degree to which an individual has a foot fetish. However, almost any word can be substituted for foot (for example, leather or shoe) to assess the degree of an alternative fetish.

> *Now I can tell you something dirty. I like men who have a foot fetish. I absolutely think it's the most charming thing. It's just so romantic.*
>
> Elisabeth Rohm, German-American actress

Technology and Sexuality 15-1: Finding Paraphilia Partners via the Internet

The meeting of Christian and Ana in *Fifty Shades of Grey* was by chance. She interviewed him and they began to see each other. Later, he introduced her to his interest in BDSM. While she was open to his overtures, she did not bring a fetish for masochism to the relationship. Unlike their meetings, individuals with various paraphilias, fetishes, and proclivities can find each other more quickly via the internet.

For example, https://fetlife.com is a website connecting members who enjoy a range of paraphilias and fetishes. Not only can like-minded individuals meet/share stories about their fetish, but they can also alert each other to various events, conventions, parties, gear, and so on. A section on the FetLife® website features various groups. Examples of such groups include interracial kink, fire-play enthusiasts, men in corsets, group sex, cross-dressers, kinky seniors, naughty nurses, rope, foot worship, polyandry, spanking, public nudity, needles/cutting/blood play, voyeur, and coconut oil. Prior to the internet era, it was difficult to learn of others who shared a particular fetish.

There are also dating sites for those who are into a wide range of paraphilias. Sites like http://bdsm.com allow people who are interested in BDSM to connect with others. If a person's fetish involves high heels and/or feet, they might find https://heelsdating.com a helpful site.

Another website, Internet Paraphilias (http://knowyourmeme.com/memes/subcultures/internet-paraphilias), is more about information than connection. Examples of paraphilias discussed include inflation, transformation, and vore, among others. Individuals may learn about various fetishes and then seek someone who shares this interest on FetLife.

National **DATA**

Prevalence figures for cross-dressing in the general population are unknown. Fewer than 3% of males report having ever been sexually aroused by dressing in women's attire (American Psychiatric Association, 2013, p. 703).

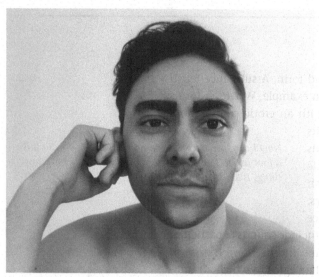

Cross-dressing typically involves a man presenting as a woman and does not involve distress. The photo is of a woman presenting as a man. She enjoys the experience. For her, cross-dressing is fun.

15.3h Transvestic Disorder

Transvestic disorder (also known as **transvestic fetishism**) is diagnosed when there is recurrent and intense sexual arousal (for at least 6 months) from cross-dressing as manifested by fantasies, sexual urges, or behaviors. The fantasies, urges, or behaviors cause significant distress. Cross-dressing typically involves a man dressing in women's clothes. Although women regularly cross-dress in terms of wearing pants and a bow tie, there is little to no cultural disapproval for doing so. However, men who cross-dress are subjects of considerable disapproval.

Most people who **cross-dress** are heterosexual men. At first, they may masturbate while dressed as the other gender. Over time, the sexual arousal motive for their cross-dressing diminishes and is replaced by the payoff of reducing anxiety, coping with depression, or creating a feeling of peace and calm.

Many men who cross-dress do not report motives of sexual excitement. When asked why he dressed up in women's clothes, one of the speakers for our human sexuality class said, "I feel more relaxed … like this is who I am. When I dress like a male, I feel anxious and 'not right.' Unless you are a cross-dresser, you won't understand." Another said, "I do it for the money. No makeup, no money." Performing in drag as a man carries both status and stigmatization in the LGBTQ community. Drag gender's multiple meanings are between gay and transgender politics (Levitt et al., 2018).

If the partner of the cross-dresser discovers the cross-dressing, they may ask him to stop. Some men resort to **purging**—throwing away their female attire in a desperate attempt to rid themselves of the urge to cross-dress. But the urge does not vanish with the clothes—new purchases are made, and the cross-dressing behavior resumes. Some wives adjust to the fetish of their husbands. "He's a good provider, family man, and faithful," said one wife. "Everyone comes with a catch, and I can put up with a dress as long as he only dresses up at home, not too often, and mostly when I am out of the house shopping" (authors' files).

15.3i Other Paraphilias

Although we have discussed the major paraphilias presented in the *DSM-5*, there are many others (American Psychiatric Association, 2013). While examples of other varieties are presented in Table 15-2, the list is not exhaustive. For example, autogynephilia is the paraphilic sexual arousal in a man by the thought or image of himself as a woman—cross-dressing is an example, but it may also include thoughts of breast-feeding or menstruating (Hsu et al., 2014).

Transvestic disorder
Paraphilia that involves recurrent, intense, sexual urges and sexually arousing fantasies, of at least 6 months' duration, that involve cross-dressing (such as a man dressing in a woman's clothes)

Transvestic fetishism
Sexual arousal by dressing in the gender of the other sex

Cross-dress
To dress in the clothes of the other gender, typically a man dresses in a woman's clothes

Purge
Act of throwing away or burning one's clothes as a desperate means of ending one's cross-dressing

THINK ABOUT IT

Take a moment to answer the following question. Individuals may wear nontraditional clothing for their gender for various reasons: They want to make a fashion statement or express their androgyny, cross-dressing makes them feel congruent with their self-identity, they want to entertain, or they want to experience sexual arousal. Would the reason a person is dressing the way they do impact how you view them?

Wignall and McCormack (2016) identified a form of kink—pup play, whereby one or both of the partners behaves like a dog. The pup moves around on all fours, nuzzles up to the "master," barks, and so on. An erotic sexual element may or may not be present.

Most of the activities identified in Table 15-2 are controversial and illegal in some jurisdictions, even when engaged in by consenting adults. However, learning about them can help explain part of the mystery and complexity of human sexual expression.

TABLE 15-2 | Other Paraphilias

Paraphilia	Description
Acrotomophilia	Deriving sexual arousal or gratification from engaging in sex with an amputee
Apotemnophilia	Becoming sexually aroused by the thought of becoming an amputee
Asphyxiophilia	Cutting off the air supply to enhance orgasm
Autonepiophilia	Regressive role-playing to an infant-like state
Avoniepiphilia	Deriving sexual arousal by wearing wet diapers
Coprophilia	Using feces for sexual arousal either by watching another defecate or by defecating on someone
Erotophonophilia	Committing lust murder in which the partner is killed as a means of atoning for sex with the individual
Fornicophilia	Becoming sexually aroused by ants, bugs, or other small, crawling creatures
Gerontophilia	Becoming sexually aroused by elderly individuals
Klismaphilia	Becoming sexually aroused by receiving an enema
Mysophilia	Deriving sexual excitement from filthy or soiled objects
Narratophilia	Listening to "dirty talk" as a means of becoming sexually aroused (phone sex companies depend on people with this paraphilia for their income)
Necrophilia	Deriving sexual arousal or gratification from sexual activity with a dead person (or a person acting the role of a corpse)
Olfactophilia	Becoming sexually aroused by certain scents
Partialism	Deriving sexual arousal or gratification from a specific nongenital body part (such as a foot)
Pictophilia	Becoming sexually aroused in reference to sexy photographs
Raptophilia	Becoming sexually aroused by surprise attack and violent assault
Scatalogia	Becoming sexually aroused by calling a stranger on the phone and either talking about sex or making sexual sounds (breathing heavily; also called telephonicophilia)
Somnophilia	Fondling a person (often a stranger) who is sleeping so as to become sexually aroused
Urophilia	Using urine for sexual arousal either by watching someone urinate or by urinating on someone
Zoophilia	Becoming aroused by sexual contact with animals (commonly known as bestiality)

Personal **REFLECTION**

Take a moment to express your thoughts about the following questions. Have you experienced a preference for a sexual stimulus that you feel borders on a compulsion? To what degree does such a proclivity affect you or your relationships? Are there any potential legal consequences for the transition of this preference into a compulsion?

15.3j Pathologizing Kink

While this chapter has referred to the *DSM-5* regarding various forms of sexual expression, it is important to emphasize that these definitions pathologize what others may consider normal. Haym et al. (2016) observed that the practice of communication, negotiation, and consent practiced by the BDSM/kink community could prove useful in sexual communication for the general population. Dr. Julie Fennell (personal communication, 2013) noted:

> In much the same way that gays and lesbians feel that their sexual desires were unfairly pathologized by the medical establishment prior to the removal of homosexuality as a mental disorder from the DSM, people who participate in BDSM ... feel that they have been unfairly pathologized for their sexual desires. People who engage in BDSM apply principles of consent to their practices—meaning that there are no victims or abusers, only "tops" and "bottoms." As explained by the National Coalition for Sexual Freedom, when BDSM is practiced correctly, only people who want to get hurt get hurt. People who have medical disorders associated with sadism and masochism are not engaging in consensual behaviors, and most people in the BDSM community view the diagnoses of "fetishism" and "transvestism" as obsolete and heteronormative, respectively.

15.3k "Sexual Addiction"

There is professional disagreement about the existence of sexual addiction since there are no diagnostic criteria. The *DSM-5* does not recognize the concept of "sex addiction or sexual addiction" (other terms include *out-of-control sexual behavior* (OCSB), *sexual compulsivity*, and hypersexuality). One reason for not using the term *addiction* in reference to sex is that there is no physiological withdrawal similar to that experienced with heroin. Moser (2013) questioned the validity of the term *sex* addiction:

> There are individuals who perceive their sexual behavior as "out of control" and there is no dispute that some of these individuals could benefit from psychiatric intervention. Nonetheless, the individual's perception of the problem may not be an accurate assessment or the "problem" may not be an actual problem. Appropriate clinical evaluation may demonstrate that their sexual behavior is a symptom or a result of another disorder (which should become the focus of treatment rather than their sexual behavior) or that the individual's behavior is within normal limits. (p. 48)

The American Association for Sexuality Educators, Counselors and Therapists (AASECT) Position Statement on Sex Addiction is that people may experience significant physical, psychological, spiritual and sexual health consequences related to their sexual urges, thoughts or behaviors. AASECT recommends that its members utilize models that do not unduly pathologize consensual sexual behaviors. AASECT 1) does not find sufficient empirical evidence to support the classification of sex addiction or porn addiction as a mental health disorder, and 2) does not find the sexual addiction training and treatment methods and educational pedagogies to be adequately informed by accurate human sexuality knowledge. Therefore, it is the position of AASECT that linking problems related to sexual urges, thoughts or behaviors to a porn/sexual addiction process cannot be advanced by AASECT as a standard of practice for sexuality education delivery, counseling or therapy. (American Association of Sexuality Educators, Counselors and Therapists, n.d.)

The International Statistical Classification of Diseases and Related Health Problems (ICD-11), published in 2018, uses the term Compulsive Sexual Behavior Disorder (Drescher, 2016). The implication of this change is pressure on insurance companies to pay for "treatment" for a malady professionals do not agree on. Hence, there is movement away from the term "addiction."

Depression (Christopher et al., 2014), substance abuse, STIs, unwanted pregnancy, and a feeling of having no meaning/purpose in life (existential anxiety) are all associated with hypersexuality (Giordano & Cecil, 2014). Giordano and Cecil's (2014) sample of 235 college students found that 11% were classified as hypersexual (men more than women). These behaviors may be the better target of therapy than sex addiction. Similarly, Braun-Harvey and Vigorito (2015) suggested that OCSB be treated as a sexual health issue not as an addiction.

While there may not be a clinical diagnosis of sex addiction, it does not mean that people are not facing issues related to their inability to control their own sexual behaviors. Just as the alcoholic craves alcohol, the sexually compulsive person feels compelled to seek sexual opportunities regardless of the consequences. In effect, the person behaves as though they are driven to sexual expression and will pursue sex, despite negative effects on their health (sexually transmitted infections), relationships (affair leading to divorce), or career (sex with coworkers/supervisors).

Self-Assessment 15-2 provides a way for you to assess the degree to which you are in control of your sexual urges and behaviors.

Up Close 15-2 reflects the presentation of a self-described sex addict to the first author's sexuality class. The speaker self-labeled his own behavior and noted that his addiction was one of several—gambling, alcoholism, and so on.

15.4 The Origins of Paraphilias: Theoretical Perspectives

Various theoretical perspectives offer explanations for why a particular individual develops paraphilias.

15.4a Psychoanalytic Theory

From a psychoanalytic perspective, paraphilias may be viewed as symptoms of unresolved subconscious conflicts. For example, an exhibitionistic man may frighten unsuspecting women by exposing himself to them as a way of rebelling against them. Such rebellion may stem from having a domineering mother or an unresolved Oedipal complex, which has left the person unable to engage in heterosexual intercourse. The urge to exhibit may be a subconscious, symbolic substitute that compensates for the inability to have sexual relations with women.

Self-Assessment 15-2: Sexual Compulsivity Scale

The purpose of this scale is to assess the degree to which you feel your sexual urges and behaviors are out of control.

Directions

After reading each sentence carefully, circle the number that best represents the degree to which you strongly disagree to strongly agree with the sentence. There are no right or wrong answers.

Please circle: 1 (Strongly disagree), 2 (Mildly disagree), 3 (Undecided), 4 (Mildly agree), 5 (Strongly agree)

1.	I feel that my sexual urges control me.	1 2 3 4 5
2.	I feel driven to do something sexual.	1 2 3 4 5
3.	I feel my sexual behavior is out of control.	1 2 3 4 5
4.	I feel powerless to curb my sexual urges.	1 2 3 4 5
5.	Others have told me I am too hypersexual.	1 2 3 4 5
6.	I have to keep secret how hypersexual I am.	1 2 3 4 5
7.	My hypersexuality could get me in trouble.	1 2 3 4 5
8.	It frightens me that I can't control my sex behavior.	1 2 3 4 5
9.	My hypersexuality has cost me some relationships.	1 2 3 4 5
10.	I have wondered if I am a sex addict.	1 2 3 4 5

Scoring

Add the numbers you circled. The lower your total score (10 is the lowest possible score), the more in control you are of your sexual urges and behavior. The higher your total score (50 is the highest possible score) the more you are controlled by your sexual urges and behavior. A score of 30 places you at the midpoint between the extremes.

Source: This scale was developed for this text. It is to be used for general assessment and is not designed to be a clinical diagnostic tool or as a research instrument.

"Hello, My Name Is KJ, and I'm a Sex Addict."

While I understand that there is disagreement about the validity of the term sexual addiction, I would like to assert that I am a sex addict and define the term as my inability to control my sexual behavior. While I am now in recovery (and have been for 7 years), I am constantly on alert to exercise control over my life by practicing recovery. Sex is only one of my addictions: I am also a gambler by compulsive stock trading, an alcoholic, and I am addicted to pornography. My life has been ruined by all of these, as I am now on my fifth marriage and have had very estranged relationships with my children.

Part of my recovery is to help others who feel helpless with control over their sexual behavior. I am a member of our local Sex Addicts Anonymous® organization, which uses the 12-step program of recovery, similar to recovering from alcoholism. I have authored a recovery workbook (*The Circle of Life: The Process of Sexual Recovery Workbook*) on sexual addiction, which is available in electronic format, as well as my own recovery story (*Dying to Live: Boulevard of Broken Dreams*) from Amazon.com®.

Source: A speaker in the first author's human sexuality class.

15.4b Feminist Theory

Paraphilias, such as pedophilia and sexual sadism, are, from a feminist perspective, expressions of aggression and status more than mere sexuality. The pedophile, sadist, and rapist express control and dominance through their paraphilic fantasies and behaviors.

Feminist theory explains why there are many more men with paraphilias than women with paraphilias: Our culture has perpetuated traditional gender roles that emphasize male dominance, entitlement, sexual aggression, and control. Men act out these fantasies and may become dependent on them for sexual arousal.

15.4c Learning Theory

Learning theorists emphasize that paraphilias are learned by means of both classical and operant conditioning. In 1966, Rachman demonstrated how a fetish could be learned through classical conditioning. Using an experimental design, Rachman paired women's boots with erotic slides of nude women. As a result, the participants began to experience erotic arousal at the sight of the boots alone.

Scarf, panty, and high-heeled shoe fetishes may be a result of classical conditioning. The person may have experienced sexual pleasure when in the presence of these objects, learned to associate these objects with the pleasure, and developed a preference for these objects during sex.

Operant conditioning may also account for the development of some paraphilias. For example, the exhibitionist may be reinforced by the startled response of a woman and seek conditions under which she will exhibit a startled response (exposing his penis). By exposing his penis, the exhibitionist causes her to yell, is reinforced, and wants to repeat the behavior with another new stranger. If the masochist has an orgasm while being tied up, the act of being bound is reinforced operantly.

Operant conditioning
Learning theory that behavior is learned in reference to its consequences; a behavior that is punished will decrease in frequency, while a behavior that is reinforced will increase in frequency

Similarly, paraphilias may result from negative reinforcement. *Negative reinforcement* is defined as the strengthening of a behavior associated with the removal of something aversive. A paraphilia may be learned because the associated behaviors remove feelings of anxiety, sadness, loneliness, and anger. Hence, when the exhibitionist exhibits to a victim, he feels a temporary reprieve from feelings of anxiety, which are replaced by feelings of excitement.

15.4d Biological Theory

The degree to which biological variables are responsible for the development of paraphilias is controversial. Just as one's sexual orientation may be based on biological predispositions, so may paraphilic tendencies. Some people may be biologically wired to respond erotically to atypical stimuli. Paraphilias are associated with having a mood disorder, major depression, bipolar disorder, anxiety disorder, impulse control disorder, or avoidant personality disorder. All of these may have their root in and be influenced by biological factors (Dunsieth et al., 2004). James Cantor's (2012) research on pedophiles revealed various physical differences from the general population including lower IQ.

15.5 Treatment of Paraphilias

The behavioral expression of some of the paraphilias we have discussed (such as exhibitionism and pedophilia) interferes with the rights of others. When people engaging in such behaviors come to the attention of the law, they are often required to enter a treatment program. Indeed, the U.S. Supreme Court has upheld the civil commitment of sexually violent predators for treatment as constitutional. In effect, these individuals may be legally kept in psychiatric hospitals or special facilities for the treatment of their sexual deviation prior to release. Whereas most people with paraphilias must be forced to address them, some individuals seek treatment voluntarily.

After the existence of the paraphilia has become socially visible, treatment of the sex offender begins with a thorough assessment. This assessment involves collecting information regarding the offense of record, as well as a sexual, social, and psychiatric history.

The therapist usually gathers the law enforcement report, victim statement, presentence investigation, and summaries of previous placements and treatment. Interviews with the client and relevant other people are conducted, and psychological testing may be done. The Multiphasic Sex Inventory obtains reports of deviant behaviors, as well as indications of sexual knowledge and cognitive distortions. Its scales measuring child molestation and rape are the most developed, although it does address other paraphilias. The polygraph is sometimes used to corroborate self-reports obtained in clinical interviews. Measurements of penile tumescence (changes in the volume and circumference of the penis) are also used to assess physiological arousal. The penile plethysmograph employs a sensor or transducer that measures and records changes in penis size in response to sexual stimuli (audiotapes or slides).

Models for treatment of paraphilias, particularly pedophilia, view sex as a biological drive that can be disturbed in both intensity and direction. After a thorough evaluation, treatment begins and is usually focused on decreasing deviant sexual arousal, increasing nondeviant sexual arousal, teaching social skills, changing faulty cognitions, resolving sexual dysfunctions, managing substance/alcohol abuse, or a combination of these tasks.

15.5a Decreasing Deviant Sexual Arousal

Effective treatment of a paraphilia involves decreasing the deviant sexual arousal response or the response to that which society regards as nonsexual stimuli. The therapeutic goal is for the person to no longer require the paraphilic target stimulus as a preferred or necessary condition of sexual arousal. Treatment that focuses on decreasing deviant sexual arousal may involve medications, aversive conditioning, and covert sensitization. Houtepen et al. (2016) noted that the use of adult pornography, masturbation, and sex with adults was helpful to pedophiles as a way of reducing arousal to minors. In regard to the use of medications to control paraphilias, there is considerable social debate. This controversy is discussed in *Social Policy 15-1.*

Social Policy 15-1

Treating Paraphilic Sex Offenders with Hormones

The use of hormones to quell the sexual lust of paraphiliac sex offenders involves a consideration of the rights of society to be protected from harm versus the rights of an offender to avoid being given medication that may have unwanted side effects. The rights of society have been established by the Supreme Court, which views the protection of children from pedophiles as paramount. California, Georgia, Montana, and Florida offer chemical castration as a condition of parole for repeat sex offenders.

Because sex is seen as a biological drive, hormones and neurotransmitters are used to mediate the intensity and direction of that drive. Anti-androgen drugs, such as Depo-Provera, may be used to lower the blood level of testosterone and seem to have a direct pharmacologic effect on brain pathways that mediate sexual behavior. These drugs may have the effect of removing the paraphilic preoccupation, while still allowing the person to act on his sexual interest in his partner without dysfunction. In other cases, Depo-Provera may result in a complete shutdown of eroticism. Although these treatments are controversial, these drugs may be used to treat pedophiles, exhibitionists, voyeurs, and rapists.

More recently, selective serotonin reuptake inhibitors (SSRIs), such as fluoxetine (brand name Prozac), have been used to treat paraphilias and to reduce an individual's sexually deviant fantasies, urges, masturbation, and sexual behavior. For severe cases, luteinizing hormone-releasing hormone agonists (LHRH agonists), which have the effect of pharmacological castration, may be used. One type of LHRH has been used to successfully reduce sexually aggressive behavior, as well as to reduce penile erection, ejaculation, masturbation, sexually deviant impulsiveness, and fantasies. These hormone and serotonin reuptake inhibitors, when combined with cognitive behavioral treatment, may provide some reduction in the urge to express paraphilic behaviors. However, there are also negative effects, such as loss of capacity to orgasm.

Turner and colleagues (2013) observed the effect of testosterone-lowering medications (TLMs) on sex offenders in Germany. Data were collected from the directors of 69 German forensic-psychiatric hospitals/outpatient clinics who oversaw the treatment of sex offenders (sex with children or sexual assault-rape). Almost all of the sex offenders were being treated psychotherapeutically, and 37% were receiving an additional pharmacological treatment. Of the sex offenders being treated with medication, 26%–75% showed improvements in such outcomes as reduction of frequency and intensity of sexual thoughts.

A rarely used alternative to chemical castration is surgical castration, whereby repeat child molesters may agree to the surgery in exchange for reduced jail time. The procedure results in reducing the man's interest in sex, sexual arousal, and activity in that it helps control sexually deviant compulsions.

15.5b Aversive Conditioning

Deviant sexual arousal may also be decreased through **aversive conditioning**. Such conditioning involves pairing an aversive or unpleasant stimulus with the paraphilic stimulus to decrease the deviant sexual arousal and reduce the probability of engaging in the paraphilic behavior. One example of an aversive stimulus is an unpleasant smell.

For the heterosexual male pedophile, during this type of aversion therapy, the patient listens to audio depictions of sexual activities with children and with adult women. After the taped narrative of sexual activity with the child is played, the therapist administers a noxious odor so that the patient associates this with the stimulus of the child. After removing the odor, the therapist changes the tape narrative to that of sexual activity with an adult woman. In this way, the patient associates relief from the noxious stimuli (and, consequently, a more pleasant feeling) with the stimulus of the adult woman.

Because it is believed that a fetish results from learning to associate a particular object with sexual pleasure, the stimulus object may be reconditioned by associating an unpleasant experience with it. For example, the person might be given emetic drugs to induce vomiting when in the presence of the fetish object. These procedures are still being researched.

15.5c Covert Sensitization

Covert sensitization involves using negative thoughts as a way of developing negative feelings associated with a deviant sexual stimulus. For example, a therapist may induce negative thoughts by saying the following to the patient:

> I want you to imagine going into the bedroom of your 7-year-old niece when her parents are in another part of the house. As you open the door, you see her asleep in her bed. But as you approach the bed, you begin to feel very nauseous and feel that you are going to throw up. You vomit and feel the particles in your mouth and the stench in your nostrils. You also think that if you act on your urges and are discovered, you will be shamed out of the family.

This scenario is designed to associate negative feelings and thoughts with acting on a sexual urge to touch a child so as to reduce the probability that the patient will engage in this behavior. Covert sensitization may be used to apply negative imagined consequences for offending and positive consequences for imagining alternatives to offending.

15.5d Learning Social Skills

People with paraphilias typically have low self-esteem, anxiety in social situations, and no skills in initiating and maintaining an intimate interpersonal relationship. Treatment of paraphilias often involves teaching the person how to initiate a conversation, empathize, listen, and keep a conversation going so that the person will be better able to develop a close emotional bond with an adult partner. Social skills training often takes place in a group therapy setting where group members may practice basic communication and interaction skills with each other.

Therapists seeing a client who lacks social skills can also devise an individual treatment plan to assist the client in learning these skills.

Aversive conditioning
Type of behavior therapy that involves pairing an aversive or unpleasant stimulus with a previously reinforcing stimulus; used in sex offender treatment to decrease deviant sexual arousal and reduce the probability of engaging in paraphilic behavior

Covert sensitization
Therapeutic technique that involves instructing the client to use negative thoughts as a way of developing negative feelings associated with a deviant sexual stimulus

PERSONAL DECISIONS 15-2

Can People Control Their Paraphilias?

Therapists disagree about the degree to which persons with paraphilias can control the behavioral expression of enacting them. Whereas some feel that those with pedophilia, exhibitionism, and voyeurism are uncontrollably and compulsively driven to express their paraphilia and will not be able to change their reaction to sexual cues, others suggest that these persons can exercise conscious control over their paraphilic behavior.

Pedophilia, exhibitionism, and voyeurism may be conceptualized as requiring a series of decisions leading to the expression of the paraphilic behavior. For example, a pedophile who fondles a young boy in the park on a summer afternoon is engaging in a behavior that was preceded by a number of decisions leading to that behavior. These decisions may have included taking off from work, looking at child pornography, drinking alcohol, going to the playground, buying candy, sitting on the bench where a young boy was also sitting, talking to the boy, offering the boy some candy, and so on. At any of these decision points, the pedophile may have chosen to engage in a behavior that was incompatible with child molestation. When taken alone, each decision along the way is relatively easier to make. The person might choose to stay at work, look at alternative magazines, and so forth.

Similarly, the exhibitionist who exposes himself in the library to a stranger may alternatively have chosen to masturbate at home, avoid alcohol, and go with a friend to a movie. Finally, the voyeur might choose to schedule time with others when he is particularly vulnerable to peeping, avoid walking on another person's property (where peeping often occurs), and select alternative behaviors, such as going to a movie during prime peeping time.

In addition to making deliberate decisions that are incompatible with the expression of paraphilic behaviors, the person who is concerned about his sexual interest may choose to seek therapy to address such issues as self-esteem, guilt, anxiety, sexual dysfunctions, and lack of social skills. By confronting these issues and ensuring that they do not contribute to unwanted behavior, the person is taking deliberate control of his sexual expression.

15.5e Changing Faulty Cognitions

Some paraphilic behaviors are continued on the basis of faulty cognitions. For example, the exhibitionist may think, "Women are really turned on by the sight of a naked penis and would enjoy someone exposing himself." The pedophile may believe that children profit from sexual experiences with adults as a form of sex education.

Correcting these cognitive distortions often occurs in the context of group therapy. Group members challenge each other's irrational beliefs and acknowledge their own. Irrational beliefs are replaced with new, realistic beliefs: Women are disgusted by exhibitionists, and children are harmed by adult sexual exploitation.

15.5f Resolving Sexual Dysfunctions

Some paraphilias continue because of sexual dysfunctions that prevent the individual with a paraphilia from engaging in sexual behavior with a partner. For example, the exhibitionist and voyeur may feel unable to engage in sex with a partner due to erectile disorder. They may also suffer rapid ejaculation or delayed ejaculation and want to avoid exposure of these dysfunctions in a relationship. Unless these sexual dysfunctions are treated, the individual with a paraphilia may continue to feel sexually inadequate and perceive no alternative for sexual gratification other than engaging in paraphilic behavior.

Chapter Summary

What Is Normal Sexual Behavior?

A SEXUAL BEHAVIOR may be defined as normal in regard to its prevalence (the higher the incidence, the more normal), moral correctness (religion supports penile-vaginal intercourse between spouses), naturalness (procreation), and adaptiveness/comfort (the more comfortable, the more normal). What is normal is socially defined and constructed.

Within the same culture, sexual behaviors may be labeled as normal in one historical time and abnormal in another. Kissing in public, prohibited during the colonial era, is now commonplace.

Variant Sexual Behavior: Definitions and Overview

A PARAPHILIA IS BEING AROUSED by a stimulus that society regards as deviant. There is disagreement about whether paraphilias constitute a mental disorder. Paraphilias most often occur in men and are rarely diagnosed in women. Paraphilias are legal or illegal depending on the degree to which the rights of others are affected. The majority of apprehended sex offenders are arrested for acts of exhibitionism, pedophilia, and voyeurism.

Types of Paraphilic Disorders

THE MAJOR PARAPHILIAS considered in this chapter are voyeurism, exhibitionism, frotteurism, sexual masochism, sexual sadism, pedophilia, fetishism, and transvestic fetishism. Professionals and the DSM-5 do not recognize the concept of sex addiction. Not being able to control sexual choices, such that they have consistent negative personal and interpersonal outcomes, is another way to conceptualize what others refer to as sexual addiction.

The Origins of Paraphilias: Theoretical Perspectives

THEORETICAL EXPLANATIONS FOR PARAPHILIAS include psychoanalytic (unconscious processes), feminist (control, power, aggression), learning (classical/operant paradigms), and biological (innate).

Treatment of Paraphilias

TREATMENT OF PARAPHILIAS involves decreasing deviant sexual arousal, aversive conditioning, covert sensitization, increasing nondeviant sexual arousal, developing interpersonal social skills, changing faulty cognitions, and resolving sexual dysfunctions.

Web Links

American Association for Nude Recreation

   https://www.aanr.com/about-aanr

@health

   http://athealth.com/topics/paraphilias-2/

FetLife

   www.fetlife.com

Sexaholics Anonymous®

   http://www.sa.org/

Sex Addicts Anonymous

   http://saa-recovery.org/

Internet Paraphilias

   http://knowyourmeme.com/memes/subcultures/internet-paraphilias

Key Terms

Aversive conditioning **420**

Covert sensitization **420**

Cross-dress **412**

Exhibitionistic disorder **403**

Fetishism **410**

Frotteuristic disorder **404**

Nudism **398**

Operant conditioning **417**

Paraphilia **399**

Pedophilic disorder **408**

Purge **412**

Scopophilia **402**

Sexual masochism disorder **405**

Sexual sadism disorder **407**

Transvestic disorder **412**

Transvestic fetishism **412**

Voyeuristic disorder **402**

CHAPTER 16

Sexually Transmitted Infections

Safe sex is an act of self love.

Miya Yamanouchi, *Embrace Your Sexual Self*

Chapter Outline

16.1 **Sexually Transmitted Infections: An Overview 426**
  16.1a Prevalence and Incidence of STIs in the United States 426
  16.1b Ignorance Promotes Infection 426
  16.1c Risk Factors for Sexually Transmitted Infections 427
  16.1d STI Testing 430
  Technology and Sexuality 16-1: Notification of Partners 431
  16.1e Consequences of Sexually Transmitted Infections 432
16.2 **Sexually Transmitted Infections: A Pandemic 434**
16.3 **Types of STIs 434**
  16.3a Ectoparasitic Infections 434
  16.3b Bacterial Infections 435
  16.3c Viral Infections 439
16.4 **HIV and AIDS 442**
  16.4a Definitions of HIV and AIDS 442
  16.4b Transmission 442
  16.4c Prevention and Control 445

16.5 **Protecting Yourself from STIs 445**
  16.5a Abstaining from Sex 446
  16.5b Reducing the Number of Sexual Partners and Mutual Monogamy 446
  16.5c Using Condoms Consistently and Effectively 446
  Self-Assessment 16-1: The UCLA Multidimensional Condom Attitudes Scale 448
  16.5d Preexposure Vaccination 449
  Social Policy 16-1 Condom Availability in High Schools 450
  16.5e Seeking STI Screening and Prompt Treatment 451
  Personal Decisions 16-1 Should You Be Screened for STIs? 451
  Social Policy 16-2 Legal Aspects of Disclosing an STI 452
16.6 **Accessing Sexual Health Services 453**

Web Links 455
Key Terms 455

Objectives

1. Identify current prevalence and incidence data on STIs in the United States and worldwide
2. Describe how technology can promote partners' communication about STIs
3. Describe the risks and consequences associated with STIs
4. Describe and compare the different types of STIs

5. Explain why STIs are regarded as a major individual and public health concern
6. Know how to actively protect yourself from acquiring and transmitting STIs
7. Review the various treatment options for STIs
8. Know the script for disclosing an STI

(Breanna Gilbert-Love)

Truth — OR — Fiction?

T / F   1. The more involved the couple, the lower the condom use.

T / F   2. The primary reason people do not get tested for STIs is cost.

T / F   3. PrEP is effective only about 10% of the time.

T / F   4. Men who perform oral sex are four times more likely to contract HPV, which can morph into cancer.

T / F   5. The percent of high school teens reporting first intercourse has dropped to 30%.

Answers: 1. T   2. F   3. F   4. T   5. T

I n this chapter, we present information about sexually transmitted infections (STIs). Although the term *sexually transmitted disease* (STD) is commonly used, we use the term *sexually transmitted infection* (STI) because not all STIs result in disease. A person with an STI may not have any disease symptoms, but they nevertheless may be contagious carriers of the infection. It is important for everyone who is sexually active to learn about STIs and how to prevent, treat, and manage them. STIs also present challenges for schools, communities, and states that are tasked with providing health education and/or health care to their members. After rates of three common STIs—syphilis, gonorrhea, and chlamydia—reached a record high in the United States in 2018, the executive director of the National Coalition of STD Directors called on national leaders to declare STDs a public health crisis (Howard, 2018).

16.1 Sexually Transmitted Infections: An Overview

Sexually transmitted infections (STIs) are caused by more than 30 different bacteria, viruses, and parasites and are spread predominantly by sexual contact (World Health Organization, 2016b). Some STIs can also be spread through nonsexual means such as transfusions or contact with infected blood or blood products. Many STIs can also be transmitted from mother to child during pregnancy and childbirth.

16.1a Prevalence and Incidence of STIs in the United States

Young people ages 15–24 account for half of all new STIs, although they represent just 25% of the sexually experienced population. In 2014, increases were seen in all three nationally reported STIs—chlamydia, gonorrhea, and syphilis—across all groups. The 1.7 million cases of chlamydia represent the highest number of annual cases of any condition ever reported to the CDC. Substantial increases were also seen among reported cases of gonorrhea (555,608) and syphilis (30,644). Many cases continue to go undiagnosed and unreported, and data on several additional STIs—such as human papillomavirus (HPV), herpes simplex virus, and trichomoniasis—are not routinely reported to the CDC. As a result, the annual surveillance report captures only a fraction of the true number of STIs in America. While young people and women are most severely affected by STIs, increasing rates among men (particularly gay and bisexual men) contributed to the overall increase in 2017 across all infections (Centers for Disease Control and Prevention, 2018g).

The most well publicized STI is HIV/AIDS. The CDC (2019k) estimates that about 1.1 million people in the United States were living with HIV at the end of 2016, the most recent year this information was available. Of those people, about 14% do not know they are infected.

Cultural Diversity

STIs have a profound impact on sexual and reproductive health worldwide. Each year, there are an estimated 376 million new infections with 1 of 4 STIs: chlamydia (127 million), gonorrhea (87 million), syphilis (6.3 million), and trichomoniasis (156 million). More than 500 million people are living with genital herpes simplex virus infection. And at any point in time, around 300 million women have an HPV infection, one of the most common STIs (World Health Organization, 2019c).

16.1b Ignorance Promotes Infection

Sexually transmitted infection

Infections transmitted primarily through sexual activity; a more recent, more specific term sometimes used to avoid the negative connotations sometimes associated with sexually transmitted disease (STD)

Despite the fact that much information has been learned about STIs, many people around the world remain largely ignorant of these infections. The vulnerability of young people to infection is compounded by their lack of knowledge. According to American College Health Association's (ACHA's) Fall 2018 National College Health Assessment (NCHA), 39.8% of students reported not receiving any information regarding STIs and STI prevention (American College Health Association, 2018). Individuals in developing countries are often unaware that STIs exist or that they are vulnerable to infection. Throughout the world, most young adults have not been tested for HIV and other STIs. Thus, many people are infected and do not even know it.

Many STIs are **asymptomatic** (do not produce symptoms or signs) or they yield symptoms so mild that they go unrecognized. As a result, people often assume they are uninfected and fail to seek medical care. People may be asymptomatic yet still be a carrier and pass on the infection to others. For example, about 5%–30% of women and 10% of men who are infected with chlamydia develop symptoms. They may not be aware of the infection until years later, when a significant health problem develops, such as infertility or ectopic pregnancy. It is estimated that untreated, chlamydia can cause 10%–15% of women to develop pelvic inflammatory disease (Centers for Disease Control and Prevention, 2016c).

Always use condom sense.

Taylor Puck, safe sex advocate

16.1c Risk Factors for Sexually Transmitted Infections

The risk of acquiring an STI depends on a variety of factors:

- *Exposure:* The rate of sexual contact between uninfected persons and infected individuals
- *Transmission:* The probability of an exposed person acquiring the infection
- *Duration:* The length of time an infected person is contagious and able to spread the disease
- *Level of arousal:* High levels of sexual arousal are associated with greater impulsivity/sexual risks (Cramer & Sparling, 2014).

The following biological, social, economic, and behavioral factors affect the spread of STIs.

Asymptomatic Nature of STIs

As mentioned above, asymptomatic infected persons often assume they are STI free, with the mind-set of "I would know if I had something." As a result, they fail to seek medical care and continue to put themselves and their partner(s) at an increased health risk. Often, a long interval, sometimes years, occurs between acquiring an STI and recognizing a clinically significant health problem.

Number of Sex Partners

The more sexual partners an individual has, the higher the risk of being exposed to an STI. According to the 2017 U.S. Youth Risk Behavior Surveillance System (YRBSS) report, which surveys high school students, of the 39.5% of students who had ever had sexual intercourse, 28.7% had had sexual intercourse during the 3 months before the survey (currently sexually active), and 9.7% had had sexual intercourse with four or more people during their life. Among currently sexually active students, only 53.8% had used a condom during their last sexual intercourse (Centers for Disease Control and Prevention, 2017a).

Age

Compared with older adults, sexually active adolescents ages 15–19 and young adults ages 20–24 are at higher risk of acquiring STIs for a combination of behavioral, biological, and cultural reasons. The CDC (2018b) estimates that 1 in 4 sexually active adolescent females has an STI, such as chlamydia or HPV. Higher rates may reflect multiple barriers to accessing quality STI prevention and management services, including inability to pay, lack of transportation, long waiting times, conflicts between clinic hours and work and school schedules, embarrassment attached to seeking STI services, method of specimen collection, and concerns about confidentiality.

Asymptomatic
Producing no symptoms or signs or, as with some STIs, yielding symptoms so mild that medical care is not sought

However, young people are not the only age group experiencing serious STI consequences. Many people aged 50 and older are sexually active, and have many of the same STI risk factors as younger people, including an unrealistic assumption of risk due to a lack of knowledge and how to prevent transmission, as well as multiple partners. Older people also face some unique issues, such as dating after a death or divorce, less use of barrier contraceptive methods due to no longer worrying about pregnancy, and being less likely to discuss their sexual habits or drug use with their doctors.

National DATA

Older adults account for 17% of new HIV diagnoses in the US and are more likely to be diagnosed with HIV later in the course of the disease compared to younger people. However, an estimated 83.7% of sexually active older adults never tested for HIV (Oraka et al., 2018).

Peers

Peers also influence STI exposure. Donenberg et al. (2018) noted that friends of young women are particularly influential in one's exposure to STIs because young women may engage in sexual activities in order to get approval from their friends.

Sex

The transmission of an STI (likelihood of acquiring the infection once exposed) is influenced by your sex. Women are biologically more susceptible than men to becoming infected if exposed to STIs. This is due to the larger mucosal surface area exposed to the virus in women, the greater amount of virus present in semen as compared with vaginal secretions, and the shortness and location of the female urethra (shorter distance for infectious organisms to travel). Table 16-1 reviews the different effects of STIs on women and men.

Although lesbians are not immune to HIV and other STIs, women who have sexual relations only with women (and whose partners do likewise) have a substantially lower risk of acquiring STIs than heterosexual women. The risk associated with the most common female-to-female sexual practices (oral sex and manual stimulation) is less than with heterosexual sexual intercourse. Hence, the main source of HIV infection among lesbians is related to injection drug use and sex with HIV-infected men.

Alcohol/Substance Use

Many studies document the association of substance abuse with STIs. At the community level, the introduction of new drugs can have a drastic influence on sexual behavior in high-risk sexual networks. Substance use increases the risk of STI transmission when it is associated with the exchange of sex for drugs, a greater number of anonymous sex partners, or decreases in the use of barrier protection (such as condoms) and in seeking medical care. At the individual level, substance use is associated with impaired judgment regarding sexual decisions.

TABLE 16-1	Ways STIs Affect Women Differently Than Men		
Description		Men	Women
1. Anatomy can place a unique risk for STIs.			X
2. Less likely to have symptoms of common STIs, such as chlamydia and gonorrhea.			X
3. More likely to confuse symptoms of an STI for something else.			X
4. May not see symptoms as easily.			X
5. STIs can lead to serious health complications and affect future reproductive plans.			X
6. Can pass STIs on to their babies.			X
7. Human papillomavirus is the most common STI and is the main cause of cervical cancer.			X

Source: Centers for Disease Control and Prevention. (n.d.). *Fact Sheet: How STDs Impact Women Differently from Men.*
Retrieved from: https://www.cdc.gov/nchhstp/newsroom/docs/factsheets/STDs-Women.pdf

Sexual Abuse

A history of sexual abuse increases the likelihood of a young woman beginning voluntary intercourse at an earlier age, an STI risk. Individuals who have been raped or sexually assaulted are also at risk for acquiring an STI because sexual coercion decreases the possibility of self-protection. Forced sexual activity is also more likely to result in vaginal or anal abrasions, thereby increasing susceptibility to HIV and other STIs. People who are physically abused (even if not through sexual violence) may engage in risky sexual behaviors out of fear and may be unable to negotiate use of condoms.

Racial and Ethnic Disparities

Surveillance data show higher rates of reported STIs among some racial or ethnic minority groups when compared with rates among whites. For example, African Americans

(Shutterstock)

Alcohol provides the context in which couples are more likely to have sex and more likely to have sex with more partners.

are most affected by HIV. In 2017, the most recent year this information was available, African Americans made up only 13% of the US population but had 43% of all new HIV infections. Hispanics/Latinos are also strongly affected, as they made up 17% of the US population but had 21% of all new HIV infections (Centers for Disease Control and Prevention, 2019j). In 2017, reported cases of chlamydia, gonorrhea, and syphilis in the United States were highest among African Americans, followed by American Indians/Alaska Natives, Native Hawaiians/other Pacific Islanders, and Hispanics (Centers for Disease Control and Prevention, 2018e).

Race and ethnicity in the United States are population characteristics that are correlated with other fundamental determinants of health status, such as high rates of poverty, income inequality, unemployment, and low educational attainment. People who struggle financially are often experiencing life circumstances that potentially increase their risk. Additionally, those who cannot afford basic necessities may have trouble accessing and affording quality sexual health services.

Sex Work

Many of the aforementioned risk factors converge in those who engage in sex work. Compounding their educational and economic disadvantages with unsafe sexual behaviors and the use of alcohol and other drugs, often in a context of coercion and violence, increases their risk for HIV/AIDS. Sex workers are also more likely to have histories of sexual partners at higher HIV risk (such as men who have sex with men, inject drugs, or are known to be HIV positive).

High-Risk Sexual Behavior

The term *high-risk group* implies that certain traits determine who will become infected with an STI; however, it is not the group that you belong to, but rather the behaviors that you practice that put you at risk for contracting an STI. Anyone who engages in risky sexual behavior is susceptible to acquiring STIs. These high-risk sexual patterns include having multiple partners, having sex with people who have multiple partners, males having unprotected sex with males, and alcohol/drug use.

Although worldwide, most cases of HIV and AIDS are found among the heterosexual population, in the United States, HIV rates are highest among men who have sex with men (MSM). In 2016, in the United States, gay and bisexual men accounted for 67% of the 40,324 new HIV diagnoses in the United States and 82% of males age 13 years and older (Centers for Disease Control and Prevention, 2018f). Their high-risk behaviors included unprotected anal intercourse, finding sex partners online, substance use, and failing to maintain prevention practices. High-risk behaviors among MSM may have increased due to optimism about the success of highly active antiretroviral therapy (HAART), the challenge of maintaining safer sex behaviors over time, and the younger MSM not having seen the toll of AIDS firsthand.

Sexuality, Stigma, and Secrecy

Perhaps the most important social factors contributing to the spread of STIs in the United States are the stigma associated with STIs and the general discomfort of discussing intimate aspects of life, especially those related to sex. These social factors separate the United States from industrialized countries with low rates of STIs (Healthy People 2020, 2019).

16.1d STI Testing

The CDC recommends regular STI testing for all sexually active individuals, especially young people. Many people do not get tested for STIs because they believe they are not infected. Many STIs are asymptomatic, or they have mild symptoms that can easily be overlooked. Thus, people may have an STI and not know it. Other individuals believe that if they aren't in a high-risk category, testing is not needed. Some individuals do not get tested because they fear the results may indicate they are infected. For this same reason, some individuals get tested but never follow up to get the results. Others fear being seen in a facility where STI testing occurs.

With many STIs, what you don't know can hurt you. The longer an STI goes undiagnosed and untreated, the more likely that it will produce serious health consequences, including infertility, cancer, and even death. The sooner an infected individual is tested and diagnosed, the sooner that individual can begin treatment for the disease and begin to change high-risk behaviors.

Early detection of HIV is especially important because it enables the infected individual to begin interventions that slow the growth of the virus and prevent opportunistic diseases. Early detection of other STIs can prevent or minimize the negative health effects they might otherwise produce. Because of the ulcerations caused by genital herpes, syphilis, and chancroid and the inflammation caused by gonorrhea, chlamydia, and trichomoniasis, these infections facilitate transmission of HIV. Therefore, rapid diagnosis and treatment of these STIs may help prevent sexual transmission of HIV.

STI testing is available at most local public health centers, STI clinics, family planning clinics, private health-care providers, hospitals, and university health centers. You can also get tested for STIs and HIV in the privacy of your home. Getting tested for STIs requires an investment of time, effort, and, potentially, money. It also requires you to overcome any embarrassment and fear associated with discussing your sexual behavior with health-care providers, having your genitals examined, and coping with the possibility of being told you have an STI.

However, the testing process itself can be quick and easy. Depending on the STI being tested, a health-care provider may take a blood sample, urine sample, or swab or do a physical exam (if symptoms are present or the patient is unsure). To prevent a false negative, an individual must not urinate within an hour before the appointment, and a swab (culture) must be done within 48 hours of onset of symptoms. Many people make the mistake of assuming that an annual medical checkup will include STI testing. The fact is that some providers might test for some infections, while others do not test for any STIs unless asked (American Sexual Health Association, 2019).

Technology and Sexuality 16-1: Notification of Partners

Preventing the spread of STIs can be accomplished in many ways: abstinence from intercourse (although other behaviors can carry risk for an STI), taking precautions, and being treated if you have an STI. Since an individual can have an STI without any symptoms, it is important for sexually active individuals to be tested regularly (not just during the month of April, which is STI Awareness Month).

Sometimes people find out through partner notification that they may have contracted an STI: someone who tests positive for an STI contacts a past and/or current partner(s) to tell them they have been exposed. Partner notification can be done by the person themselves or by health-care staff. People may be reluctant to tell a partner themselves because they fear a violent reaction or because they are ashamed. When health-care staff do partner notification, they will not divulge the name of the infected individual, which often helps mitigate any risk of unwanted contact or potential feelings of shame and embarrassment.

In the past, a person could do partner notification face-to-face, by phone, or by letter. As technology has advanced, there are more options available for partner notification, including text, email or social media. However, clinic survey data indicated that when respondents were faced with the hypothetical situation of being diagnosed with an STI, more than 90% would notify their partners in person; only 5% would use email or an online service (Rietmeijer et al., 2011).

Some challenges may arise when the infected individual does not know their past partners' phone numbers, email addresses, or even full names. In these situations, the internet may provide the means for contact. In 1999, there was a cluster of cases of syphilis among men who had met their partners online in a chat room. Given the anonymous nature of the chat room, traditional partner notification was not possible, so the local health department accessed the chat room and sent out a mass message about the syphilis cluster in the hopes of reaching some people who had been exposed. While technology can help provide alternative ways for conducting partner notification (whether by e-card, SMS, or email), the important issue is that notification should take place.

Personal **REFLECTION**

Take a moment to express your thoughts about the following questions. To what degree can you count on someone with an STI to reveal their infection? In one study, 83% of the respondents who had genital herpes reported that they told their last sex partner (Buhi & Myers, 2014). The primary reason for disclosure was a belief that the partner had a right to know. The most common reason for not disclosing was an expectation that the partner would react poorly/reject the informer if they knew.

16.1e Consequences of Sexually Transmitted Infections

In the United States, most teenagers and adults today are aware that HIV and AIDS can cause serious health consequences. However, HIV and other STIs can also cause psychological distress and place an economic burden on people and society.

Health Consequences

Untreated STIs can result in negative health consequences, particularly for women (e.g. infertility in women). Also, because women are less likely to produce symptoms, they are less likely to be diagnosed until severe problems develop (e.g. HPV causes almost all cervical cancer). Untreated STIs may cause infections of the cervix, uterus, and fallopian tubes, as well as life-threatening ectopic (tubal) pregnancy or **pelvic inflammatory disease** (PID). PID is a major health problem in women of reproductive age, often requiring hospitalization and surgery. It is associated with complications such as infertility, ectopic pregnancy, and chronic abdominal pain. Chlamydia and gonorrhea are common causes of PID in women.

STIs are also associated with health problems for pregnant women and infants. Various STIs may be transmitted to the fetus, newborn, or infant through the placenta (congenital infection), during passage through the birth canal (perinatal infection), or after birth through breastfeeding or close contact. Health consequences include spontaneous abortion, stillbirth, and premature delivery.

The health consequences of HIV and AIDS can often be life-threatening—AIDS causes more deaths than any other STI. Untreated syphilis can cause serious damage to the cardiovascular and nervous systems and may also cause blindness and death.

Economic Consequences

Pelvic inflammatory disease
Inflammation of the pelvic organs often requiring hospitalization and surgery, associated with complications, such as infertility, ectopic pregnancy, and chronic abdominal pain

The economic costs of STIs place a burden on individuals and their families and drain the tax dollars that support public health insurance (Medicaid) and public health-care facilities. The CDC conservatively estimates that the lifetime cost of treating the eight most common STIs contracted in just one year is $15.6 billion. Since viral STIs such as HIV are incurable and require lifelong treatment and care, they are by far the costliest. HPV is particularly costly due to the expense of treating HPV-related cancers. However, the annual cost of curable STIs is also significant at $742 million, especially considering that bacterial STIs have the potential to infect an individual more than once during their lifetime.

The HIV epidemic not only affects the health of individuals; it also impacts households, communities, and national development and economic growth. Many of the countries hardest hit by HIV also suffer from other infectious diseases, food insecurity, and other serious problems (The Henry J. Kaiser Family Foundation, 2015). Fortunately, in the United States, government and private programs can help pay for medications for eligible individuals. Some of these programs include the Ryan White AIDS Drug Assistance Program, Medicare Prescription Drug Coverage Plans, and Private Prescription Assistance Programs (Centers for Disease Control and Prevention, 2019b). By mid-2015, 15.8 million people living with HIV were receiving antiretroviral therapy (ART) globally. By the end of 2014, 40% of all people living with HIV were on ART (World Health Organization, 2016d).

Treatment is also expanding globally: Based on the World Health Organization's new "treat-all" recommendations to treat all people living with HIV, the number of people reportedly receiving ART has increased from 23 million to nearly 39 million people infected as of 2018. Expanding access to treatment is at the heart of a new set of targets for 2020, which aim to end the AIDS epidemic by 2030 (World Health Organization, 2019a).

Script for Disclosing an STI

I have something to say, and I want you to wait and hear all of the information before reacting. This is difficult for me to talk about, and I know this is going to sound and feel scary for you. The reason I want to talk to you about this is because I like you, care about you, and want to be honest with you. I have (insert STI). I have spoken to doctors, therapists, nurses (insert desired professionals) and feel confident in my abilities to keep it under control and keep you from contracting it. I feel very aware of when I am having a flare/outbreak and know how to stop it. (Insert detailed information about pertinent treatments and safe sex practices relevant to the specific STI.) I want us to be able to have a continued open dialog about concerns as they arise.

I know my telling you this can be unsettling. It unnerves me at times. I need for you to know that if this is too much for you and you need for us to stop seeing each other, I completely understand. I definitely want us to manage this together so that we can continue, but I want you to be completely free to say this is more than you bargained for. Additional thoughts about disclosing:

- The disclosing person might want to include sharing how they contracted the STI.
- The disclosing person might want to anticipate shock and initial fear from their partner until they hear the facts/learn more information from professionals or do their own internet research.
- The disclosing person should set aside a few hours to reveal having an STI. (The script may be short in writing, but it takes a long time to process the emotions and questions.)
- The disclosing person might want to include an escape clause to the disclosure script.

Source: Appreciation to colleagues Adrienne Alden and Samantha Scuderi, marriage/family/sex therapists, in Raleigh, North Carolina, for this script, which they use with their clients.

Psychological Consequences

Individuals who learn they are infected with an STI often experience psychological consequences similar to those experienced with other life crises. These reactions include shock, withdrawal from social interaction, anger (especially at the person who gave them the infection), fear, shame, and depression. Persons with STIs are also highly stigmatized, which impacts their seeking health-care and informing sexual partners of their STI (Dolan et al., 2014). Relationships may also be jeopardized. One of our students noted, "When my partner finds out she has herpes, she'll know it was me, and I'll be cooked. Everything will change." Telling your partner or a potential partner that you have an STI can be very stressful. Individuals infected with an STI often encounter rejection.

16.2 Sexually Transmitted Infections: A Pandemic

STIs represent a major individual and public health concern. An overview of US and global statistics on STIs reveals how widespread they are. The consequences of an STI on physical health, economic well-being, and psychological well-being convey the seriousness of the STI pandemic.

In the United States, more than 110 million individuals are infected with an STI (Centers for Disease Control and Prevention, 2013), and more than 1 million STIs are acquired every day worldwide. Recent studies estimate that there are approximately 2.3 million diagnosed cases of STIs in the US in 2018, which breaks the 2016 record by nearly 200,000 (Howard, 2018). Additionally, HIV continues to be a major global public health issue. By the end of 2017, approximately 36.9 million people were living with HIV (with 2 million people becoming newly infected), resulting in 1.2 million deaths from HIV-related causes globally (World Health Organization, 2019b).

If you slip between her thighs, be sure to condomize.

The Fresh Quotes

STIs and their consequences represent major public health problems, especially for developing countries, which lack resources for preventing and treating STIs. Africa has suffered the highest incidence of AIDS cases, and in sub-Saharan Africa, HIV/AIDS is the leading cause of death.

16.3 Types of STIs

STIs can be classified based on the type of microorganism that causes the infection and by the type of infection produced. Some STIs remain located at the site of infection, but others progress and affect body systems. Some are curable, and some are only treatable. The main agents responsible for STIs are parasites, bacteria, protozoa, and viruses.

16.3a Ectoparasitic Infections

An *ectoparasite* is a parasite that lives on or in the skin, but not within the body of the host. Pubic lice and scabies are common, sexually transmissible ectoparasites that are found throughout the world.

Pubic Lice

Pubic lice (*Pediculosis pubis*), also called *crab lice* or *crabs*, are parasitic insects. They attach themselves to the base of coarse pubic hair but may also be found on other

Pubic lice
Parasitic insects found in coarse body hair of humans, causing itching; also known as crabs

coarse hair of the body, such as hair on the legs, armpits, mustache, beard, eyebrows, or eyelashes. (Lice found on the head are head lice, not pubic lice.) They bite the skin to feed on blood; the bite causes severe itching. Crawling lice may be observed, although it is hard to see them because they move away quickly from light. Nits (lice eggs) may be visible. An infected person transmits pubic lice most often through sexual contact. Clothing, towels, and bedding may harbor the creatures, but infestation is rarely spread this way. Sitting on a toilet seat does not spread lice, as they are unable to hold onto smooth surfaces (Centers for Disease Control and Prevention, 2019k). A lice-killing lotion can be used to treat pubic lice and is available over-the-counter at a local drug store or pharmacy. These medications are safe and effective when used exactly according to the instructions. Prescription medications are also available but are restricted to patients who have failed treatment with or cannot tolerate other medications that pose less risk (Centers for Disease Control and Prevention, 2019k).

Scabies results from a microscopic mite, *Sarcoptes scabiei*, that penetrates the skin and lays eggs. The larvae of these eggs burrow tunnels under the skin and cause intense itching. They may cause skin rash, burrows, or pimple-like irritations between the fingers and in skin folds of the wrist, elbow, knee, penis, breast, or shoulder blades. Because the itching is intense, especially at night, scabies sufferers tend to scratch the affected area, which may result in sores on the body that may become infected. Scabies is spread by direct, prolonged skin-to-skin contact with an infested person (not a quick handshake or hug). In addition, it is easily spread to sexual partners and household members through clothing, towels, and bedding. Institutions such as nursing homes, extended-care facilities, and prisons are often sites of scabies outbreaks since it can spread rapidly under crowded conditions where skin-to-skin contact is frequent. Several prescription lotions are available to treat scabies, but no over-the-counter products have been proven to be effective. Household members and/or sexual partners should also be treated to prevent re-infestation. Machine-washing in hot water and drying on the hottest temperature of all bedding, clothing, and towels is advised (Centers for Disease Control and Prevention, 2010a; Workowski & Bolan, 2015).

16.3b Bacterial Infections

Gonorrhea

Also known as *the clap, the whites, morning drop, and the drip*, **gonorrhea** is caused by infection with the *Neisseria gonorrhea* bacterium, which infects the mucous membranes of the reproductive tract, including the cervix, uterus, and fallopian tubes in women and the urethra in women and men. It can also infect the mucous membranes of the mouth, throat, eyes, and rectum. The 555,608 reported cases of gonorrhea to the CDC in 2017 were an 18.6% increase from 2016 (Centers for Disease Control and Prevention, 2018d). Individuals most often contract gonorrhea through sexual contact with the penis, vagina, mouth, or anus of an infected partner. Gonococci cannot live long outside the human body. Even though these bacteria can be cultured from a toilet seat, there are no documented cases of gonorrhea being transmitted in any way other than intimate physical contact or perinatally, from mother to baby during childbirth. These bacteria thrive in warm, moist cavities, including the urinary tract, cervix, rectum, mouth, and throat.

Although many infected men are asymptomatic, when symptoms are present, they usually appear between 1 and 14 days after infection. Symptoms include dysuria (painful urination) or a white, yellow, or green urethral discharge. In cases where infection is complicated by epididymitis, men may also complain about testicular

Scabies
Infestation of the skin by microscopic mites that causes intense itching

Gonorrhea
Bacterial infection that is sexually transmitted; also known as the clap, the drip, the whites, and morning drop

As the most religious of 18 countries surveyed, the US also has the highest rates for teen pregnancies and for gonorrhea and syphilis.

Gwynne Dyer, Canadian journalist

or scrotal pain. Most women with gonorrhea have no symptoms; when they do, however, the symptoms are often so mild and nonspecific that they are mistaken for a bladder or vaginal infection. The initial symptoms include dysuria, increased vaginal discharge, or vaginal bleeding between periods. Symptoms of rectal infection can include anal itching, discharge, soreness, bleeding, and painful bowel movements. Pharyngeal infections may cause a sore throat but usually cause no symptoms (Centers for Disease Control and Prevention, 2019i).

Regardless of the presence or severity of symptoms, untreated gonorrhea can cause serious and permanent health problems. Often, a woman becomes aware of gonorrhea only after she feels extreme discomfort, which is usually a result of the untreated infection traveling up into her uterus and fallopian tubes, resulting in pelvic inflammatory disease (PID). PID can lead to internal abscesses, chronic pelvic pain, infertility, and ectopic pregnancy. The major complication for men is epididymitis, which may be signaled by severe scrotal pain. This could result in abdominal pain, infertility, and erectile problems. Untreated gonorrhea can eventually spread to the blood, causing disseminated gonococcal infection (DGI). DGI results in bone and joint disease and can be life-threatening. Untreated gonorrhea also increases a person's risk of acquiring or transmitting HIV (Centers for Disease Control and Prevention, 2019i).

The CDC now recommends dual therapy (using two drugs) for the treatment of gonorrhea. Although medication will cure the infection, it will not repair any permanent damage that has been done. Antimicrobial resistance in gonorrhea is of increasing concern, and successful treatment is becoming more difficult to achieve. If symptoms continue for more than a few days after receiving treatment, patients should return to a health-care provider to be reevaluated (Centers for Disease Control and Prevention, 2019i).

Syphilis

Syphilis is an STI caused by the bacterium *Treponema pallidum* that can cause long-term complications if not adequately treated. Trend data show that rates of syphilis are increasing at an alarming rate. The 30,644 cases of primary and secondary syphilis reported to the CDC in 2017 were a 10.5% increase from 2016. While rates have increased among both men and women, men account for more than 90% of all primary and secondary cases, with MSM accounting for 83% of male cases (Centers for Disease Control and Prevention, 2017c). Syphilis is transmitted from person to person by direct contact with a syphilitic sore, known as a *chancre*, during vaginal, anal, or oral sex. Additionally, infected pregnant women can transmit it to their unborn child.

Syphilis typically follows a progression of stages that can last for weeks, months, or even years. The average time between infection with syphilis and the start of the first symptom is 21 days, though this can range from 10 to 90 days. The appearance of a single chancre marks the primary stage, but there may be multiple sores. The chancre is usually firm, round, and painless. It appears at the location where syphilis entered the body (the vagina, penis, or anus), lasts 3–6 weeks, and heals regardless of whether the individual is treated. This is one of the tricky aspects of syphilis, because the chancre's disappearance leads infected people to believe they are cured. In reality, the disease is still present and doing great harm, even though there are no visible symptoms. Because the chancre is painless and often occurs internally in women, it is far more likely to remain undetected in women than in men. If untreated, the infection progresses to the secondary stage.

Syphilis
Sexually transmitted (or congenital) infection caused by a spirochete (*Treponema pallidum*); if untreated, it can progress to a systemic infection through three stages and be fatal

Skin rashes and/or mucous membrane lesions (sores in the vagina or anus) mark the secondary-stage symptoms. Rashes, which usually appear as rough, red, or reddish-brown spots both on the palms of the hands and bottoms of the feet, can appear when the primary chancre is healing or several weeks after the chancre has healed. However, rashes with a different appearance may occur on other parts of the body, sometimes resembling rashes caused by other diseases (mononucleosis, cancer, and psoriasis, for example). This is the reason syphilis has been called *the great pretender*. The rash could also be so faint that it goes unnoticed. Large, raised gray or white lesions, known as *condyloma lata*, may develop in warm, moist areas such as the mouth, underarm, or groin region. Additional symptoms may include fever, swollen lymph glands, sore throat, patchy hair loss, headaches, weight loss, muscle aches, and fatigue (Centers for Disease Control and Prevention, 2017c). Whatever the symptoms, they too will disappear without treatment, perhaps causing the person to again believe that nothing is wrong and enabling the infection to progress to the latent and possibly late stages of the disease.

During the latent (hidden) stage, the infected person will continue to have syphilis infection in their body even though there are no signs or symptoms. Latent syphilis can last for years. The late stages of syphilis can develop in about 15% of people who have not been treated and can appear 10–20 years after the infection was first acquired. In this stage, the disease may damage internal organs and cause difficulty coordinating muscle movements, paralysis, numbness, gradual blindness, dementia, and even death.

Syphilis is cured with a single intramuscular injection of an antibiotic in the primary, secondary, or early latent stage. Three doses at weekly intervals is the protocol recommended for individuals with late latent syphilis of unknown duration (Centers for Disease Control and Prevention, 2017c). Treatment will kill the infection and prevent further damage, but it cannot repair any damage that has been done.

Chlamydia

Chlamydia (clah-MID-ee-uh) is a commonly reported STI in the United States. It is caused by infection with the *Chlamydia trachomatis* bacterium. The 1,708,569 cases reported to CDC in 2017 were a 6.9% increase from 2016. Considering that a large number of cases are not reported because most people with chlamydia are asymptomatic and do not seek testing, the CDC indicates that diagnoses can increase, even as infection rates decrease (Centers for Disease Control and Prevention, 2018c).

Chlamydia is transmitted through sexual contact with the penis, vagina, mouth, or anus of an infected partner. The microorganisms are found most often in the urethra of men; the cervix, uterus, and fallopian tubes of women; and the rectum. Genital-to-eye transmission of the bacteria can also occur. If a person with a genital chlamydia infection rubs their eye (or touches the eye of a partner) after touching their infected genitals, the bacteria can be transferred to the eye. In addition, an infant can get chlamydia while passing through the cervix of its infected mother during delivery.

Chlamydia is known as a silent infection because most infected people are asymptomatic and lack abnormal physical examination findings. Given the relatively slow replication cycle of the bacteria, symptoms may not appear until several weeks after exposure in those people who develop symptoms. When men have symptoms, they usually have urethritis (inflammation of the urethra), with urethral discharge and painful urination. If left untreated, a minority of men develop epididymitis (inflammation of the epididymis) and have testicular pain and swelling.

In women, the bacteria initially infect the cervix, where the infection may cause cervicitis (discharge and bleeding) and sometimes urethritis. Untreated chlamydia can spread into the uterus and fallopian tubes and cause PID. Only 10%–15% of PID is symptomatic (Centers for Disease Control and Prevention, 2016e).

Chlamydia
Common sexually transmitted infection caused by the microorganism *Chlamydia trachomatis*, often asymptomatic, and therefore known as the *silent disease*

Chlamydia can be easily cured with antibiotics. Although medication will cure the infection, it will not repair any permanent damage done by the disease. If a person's symptoms continue for more than a few days after receiving treatment, they should return to a health-care provider to be reevaluated.

Nongonococcal Urethritis

Nongonococcal urethritis (NGU) is an infection of the urethra—the tube that carries urine from the bladder. Organisms that cause nongonococcal urethritis are transmitted through sexual contact and from mother to newborn. Several different sexually transmitted organisms cause NGU. The most common and most serious organism that causes NGU is chlamydia.

Because individuals with NGU are often asymptomatic, they unknowingly transmit infection to their partners. In men, symptoms of NGU include penile discharge, burning during urination, and burning or itching around the opening of the penis. Some men experience no symptoms or have symptoms so mild that they go unnoticed. In women, symptoms of NGU may include vaginal discharge, burning during urination, abdominal pain, bleeding between periods, and fever. Many infected women show no symptoms.

Once identified, NGU is treated with antibiotics. Even when symptoms are mild or nonexistent, untreated NGU can cause damage to the reproductive organs and lead to infertility; result in miscarriages; and cause eye, ear, and lung infections in newborns.

Vaginitis

Three types of **vaginitis**, or vaginal infection, are trichomoniasis, bacterial vaginosis (*Gardnerella*), and candidiasis. Most women get vaginitis at some time in their lives, and many do not develop it from sexual contact. It can be caused by anything that upsets the balance of vaginal microflora, including illness, antibiotics, or overgrowth of one organism. It may also be the result of bacteria from the rectum being transferred to the vagina, which can result from improper hygiene or anal intercourse and manipulation combined with vaginal intercourse. Vaginal infection may also result from foreign objects, such as tampons and diaphragms, being left in the vagina too long.

Although some infected women show no symptoms, trichomoniasis is usually characterized by a foul-smelling, thin, frothy discharge that may be green, yellow, gray, or white and causes an irritating rash in the vulva and painful intercourse if left untreated. Antibiotics, such as metronidazole (Flagyl®), are usually effective in treating trichomoniasis. When taking Flagyl, patients need to be aware of its nausea-inducing effect when combined with alcohol. Because the partner may harbor trichomoniasis organisms without symptoms, both the woman and her sexual partner should be treated.

Bacterial vaginosis, which is sometimes referred to as BV, may not cause symptoms or may result in a profuse discharge and a fishy odor. This organism is quite common. Estimates of prevalence of bacterial vaginosis range from 5% in college students up to 60% in STI clinics. It may also be treated with Flagyl, and partners should be treated.

The most common cause of vulvitis (irritation of the vulva) is **candidiasis**, also known as monilia or yeast infection. Candidiasis tends to occur in women during pregnancy, when they are on oral contraceptives, or when they have poor resistance to disease. Symptoms of candidiasis include vaginal irritation, itching, thick cottage cheese–like discharge, and pain during intercourse. Treatment involves inserting antifungal suppositories or creams into the vagina. Though commonly discussed with vaginitis, candida is caused by a fungus not bacteria. For this reason, antibiotics are not effective. This type of infection can spread to a partner, so it is important for both the identified patient and the sexual partner to be treated.

Nongonococcal urethritis
Infection of the urethra, the tube that carries urine from the bladder

Vaginitis
Infection of the vagina

Candidiasis
Vaginal yeast infection that tends to occur in women during pregnancy, when they are on oral contraceptives, or when they have poor resistance to infection

16.3c Viral Infections

Treatment for viral STIs is palliative (it may relieve symptoms or slow disease progression, but it does not cure the disease). The course of viral infections may include latent periods (times with no outward symptoms), but the symptoms may reappear.

Herpes

The term *herpes* refers to more than 50 related viruses (including the viruses that cause infectious mononucleosis, chickenpox, and shingles). One type of herpes virus is **herpes simplex virus type 2 (HSV-2)**, also known as **genital herpes**. Another type of herpes, known as **herpes simplex virus type 1 (HSV-1)**, is usually associated with cold sores around the mouth (oral-facial lesions). **Oral herpes** is very commonplace and is usually a benign infection. The World Health Organization estimates that two-thirds (67%) of the global population (more than 3.7 billion) under the age of 50 are infected with HSV-1. Although the two types of HSV have sites of preference, the estimates highlight that HSV-1 is also an important cause of genital herpes (World Health Organization, 2015). In the United States, 11.9% of persons aged 14–49 years have HSV-2 infection (Centers for Disease Control and Prevention, 2017b).

The herpes virus is spread by direct skin-to-skin contact, such as kissing or oral, vaginal, or anal sex, with an infected individual. Pregnant women can transmit the herpes virus to their newborn infants, most often during delivery. Fortunately, this type of transmission is rare in the United States. Herpes may also be spread from one part of the body to another by touching the infected area and then touching another area of the body. For example, touching a herpes infection can allow the virus to spread to a finger that has a cut or abrasion. This most often occurs during an initial outbreak. Although this type of transmission is not common, it is a good idea to avoid touching HSV lesions and avoid biting your nails if you have oral-facial herpes. Some people believe that herpes can be spread only when there are obvious signs or symptoms of the infection. However, it may be active without causing signs or symptoms. Herpes is often transmitted by people who are unaware that they are infected and by people who do not realize that their herpes infection is in its active phase. Wagoner (2018) followed 144 discordant couples over a median of 334 days and found that 14 of 144 partners were infected (9.7%). In 70% of the cases, the transmission occurred when the person was asymptomatic.

HSV-2 infection is more common among women than among men (15.9% versus 8.2% in people ages 14–49). Most infected persons are unaware of their infection, as an estimated 87.4% of people ages 14–49 infected with HSV-2 have never received a clinical diagnosis (Centers for Disease Control and Prevention, 2017b).

When a person is first infected with herpes, symptoms usually appear within 2 weeks after exposure. The initial symptoms of oral herpes infection often include small pimples or blisters (cold sores or fever blisters) on the mouth or face. Herpes may produce sores in the genital areas, and skin lesions may appear on the thighs or buttocks. These sores, resembling blisters or pimples, eventually crust over and scab. In the 2–4 weeks herpes sores need to heal, some people experience a second outbreak of lesions, and some will have flu-like symptoms, including fever, aches, and swollen glands. Primary infections may be treated with acyclovir.

After the symptoms of genital herpes subside (the sores dry up, scab over, and disappear, and the infected person feels well again), the virus settles in the nerve cells in the spinal column. HSV-2 causes repeated outbreaks in about one-third of those who are infected. Stress, menstruation, sunburn, fatigue, and the presence of other infections seem to be related. Recurrences of genital herpes due to HSV-1 are generally much less frequent than for HSV-2.

Herpes simplex virus type 2
See *genital herpes*

Genital herpes
Viral infection that may cause blistering, typically of the genitals, and may also infect the lips, mouth, and eyes

Herpes simplex virus type 1
Viral infection that may cause blistering, typically of the lips and mouth, and may also infect the genitals

Oral herpes
Sores of the lip and mouth, often caused by herpes simplex virus type I, but can also be caused by herpes simplex virus type II

There is no cure for herpes, but antiviral medications can prevent or shorten outbreaks during the time the person takes the medication. In addition, daily suppressive therapy (daily use of antiviral medication) can reduce the likelihood of transmission to partners. Several clinical trials have tested vaccines against genital herpes infection, but there is no commercially available vaccine that protects against it (Centers for Disease Control and Prevention, 2017b). Pregnant women with herpes outbreaks at the time of delivery can have Cesarean deliveries to prevent their newborns' exposure to the herpes virus.

Human Papillomavirus

The **human papillomaviruses (HPV)** are a group of more than 200 related viruses and are the most common STI. HPV is so common that nearly all sexually active people get it at some point in their lives. At any time there are approximately 79 million people in the United States with HPV. More than 40 HPV types can be easily spread through direct sexual contact, including oral, vaginal, and anal sex. It is also possible for HPV to be transmitted from an infected pregnant woman to her infant.

More than a dozen HPV types can cause warts in the skin around the vulva, cervix, penis, or anus (**genital warts**) or more subtle signs of infection in the genital tract. About 14 million people in the United States get HPV each year (Centers for Disease Control and Prevention, 2019a).

Many strains of HPV infection are asymptomatic. HPV can also remain inactive for months or years before any obvious signs of infection appear. This is why it is usually impossible to determine when or from whom HPV may have been contracted if the infected person has had multiple partners.

Some strains (primarily 6 and 11) cause small to large warts or bump-like growths that appear within 3–6 months after exposure. Warts may be pink or red and may appear in clusters or alone. In women, genital warts most commonly develop on the vulva, in the vagina, or on the cervix. They can also appear on or near the anus. In men, the warts appear most often on the penis but can also appear on the scrotum, around the anus, or within the rectum.

HPV may occur in oropharyngeal sites—the tongue, soft palate, tonsils, the throat behind the nasal cavity—and is four times more likely in men than women. HPV can morph into cancer and is usually only detected when the cancer is advanced. Although rare, HPV can produce warts around the mouth. Genital warts pose no health threat to the individual or partner and can be treated by several methods, depending on the number of warts and their location, the availability of equipment, the training of health-care providers, and the preferences of the patient. Treatment options for removing warts include cryotherapy (freezing), surgical removal, laser surgery, cauterization (burning), and topical application of chemicals such as podophyllin. In 90% of cases, the body's immune system clears HPV within 2 years; however, there is no way to determine which people who contract HPV will eventually develop health problems from it. However, people with a weakened immune system may be more susceptible (Centers for Disease Control and Prevention, 2019a).

High-risk types of HPV can cause cervical and other cancers, including cancer of the vulva, penis and anus. It often takes years, even decades, for these types to develop. More than 12,000 women in the United States get cervical cancer each year.

Consequently, vaccines play an important role in reducing the overall number of cases. Three HPV vaccines are currently available. The CDC (2016a) recommends that everyone ages 11 or 12 years old should get vaccinated. Catch-up vaccines are recommended for males through age 21 (26 for gay and bisexual men) and for females through age 26, if they did not get vaccinated when they were younger. (See Section 16.5d.)

Human papillomavirus
A group of more than 200 related viruses

Genital warts
See *human papillomavirus*

Hepatitis B

Hepatitis B (HBV) is an inflammatory disease of the liver caused by a virus. Other forms of hepatitis viruses include types A, C, D, and E. HBV is most often transmitted through vaginal, oral, or anal sexual contact with an infected individual. Infection may also occur from transfusions of contaminated blood or from sharing contaminated personal items, such as razors or needles (used for steroid injections, drug use, body piercing, or tattoos). Pregnant women may also transmit hepatitis B to their newborns. The rate of new HBV infections has declined from 8,036 in 2000, to 3,218 in 2016, likely attributable to the routine vaccination of children introduced in 1991 (Centers for Disease Control and Prevention, 2019f).

Most children under 5 years of age and newly infected immunosuppressed adults are asymptomatic, whereas 30%–50% of people 5 and older have initial signs and symptoms (Centers for Disease Control and Prevention, 2019f). The symptoms of acute HBV infection begin an average of 90 days (range: 60–150 days) after exposure and typically last for several weeks, though they can persist for up to 6 months. Symptoms can include fever, fatigue, loss of appetite, nausea, vomiting, abdominal pain, dark urine, clay-colored bowel movements, joint pain, and jaundice.

Persons with chronic HBV infection might be asymptomatic and have no evidence of liver disease, or they may have a spectrum of disease ranging from chronic hepatitis to cirrhosis or hepatocellular carcinoma (liver cancer). CDC reports that of those infected approximately 90% of infants and 25%–50% of children ages 1–5 will remain chronically infected with HBV. By contrast, approximately 95% of adults recover completely from HBV infection and do not become chronically infected (Centers for Disease Control and Prevention, 2019f). For acute infection, no medication is available. However, for chronic infection, several antiviral drugs are available; infected individuals require medical evaluation and regular monitoring.

The best way to prevent HBV is by getting vaccinated. The vaccination schedule most often used is three intramuscular injections, with the second and third doses administered 1 and 6 months after the first.

Emerging Infectious Disease: Zika Virus and Sexual Transmission

Zika virus is a vector-borne flavivirus primarily spread through the bite of an infected *Aedes aegypti* mosquito. Zika can also be transmitted through sexual contact, blood transfusion, and, rarely, from mother to child (Centers for Disease Control and Prevention, 2019g). Research by Oster and colleagues (2016) states that infection with Zika virus is asymptomatic in an estimated 80% of cases; when it does cause illness, symptoms are generally mild and self-limited. For this reason, many people may not realize they have been infected. The most common symptoms are similar to those of dengue and chikungunya and include headache, fever, rash, muscle and joint pain, or conjunctivitis (red eyes) lasting for several days to a week. According to the CDC, Zika virus remains in the blood of an infected person for about a week. Once infected, they are likely to be protected from future infections (Centers for Disease Control and Prevention, 2019g).

Sexual transmission of Zika virus is possible and is of particular concern for pregnant women, considering recent evidence that suggests a possible association between Zika virus and adverse fetal outcomes, such as congenital microcephaly, as well as a possible association with Guillain-Barré syndrome. However, as of June 2019 there have been reportedly zero cases of Zika being transmitted sexually in the United States (Centers for Disease Control and Prevention, 2019c). At this point, whether infected men who never develop symptoms can transmit Zika to their sex partners is unknown (Oster et al., 2016).

Hepatitis B
Inflammatory disease of the liver caused by a virus

Currently, there is no medication to treat persons infected with Zika virus and no vaccine to prevent it. People living in or traveling to areas of active Zika virus transmission should take steps to prevent mosquito bites. Steps include wearing long-sleeved shirts and long pants, using Environmental Protection Agency (EPA)–registered insect repellants, staying in air-conditioned places, installing mosquito nets and window and door screens, and treating clothing with permethrin or purchasing permethrin-treated items (Centers for Disease Control and Prevention, 2019g). All people living in or having traveled to an area of active Zika virus transmission who are concerned about sexual transmission of Zika virus should consider abstaining from sexual activity or should use condoms consistently and correctly during oral, vaginal, and anal sex.

Zika virus testing has been recommended to establish a diagnosis of infection in some groups, such as pregnant women who may have been exposed. Presently, testing for assessment of risk for sexual transmission is of uncertain value, because current understanding of the incidence and duration of shedding is that Zika can remain in semen for longer periods than in other body fluids, including vaginal fluids, urine, and blood (Centers for Disease Control and Prevention, 2019h). Testing of asymptomatic men for the purpose of assessing risk for sexual transmission is not recommended (Oster et al., 2016). As more cases are reported and studied, recommendations to prevent sexual transmission of Zika virus will be updated.

I tell you, it's funny because the only time I think about HIV is when I have to take my medicine twice a day.

Magic Johnson, basketball superstar

16.4 HIV and AIDS

Although HIV is caused by a virus, this separate section is warranted because of its serious global impact.

16.4a Definitions of HIV and AIDS

Human immunodeficiency virus (HIV) attacks the white blood cells (T-lymphocytes) in human blood and, if left untreated, can lead to **acquired immunodeficiency syndrome** (AIDS). AIDS is characterized by a breakdown of the body's immune system that makes individuals vulnerable to a variety of opportunistic diseases.

Before 1993, a diagnosis of AIDS was made only when an HIV-infected individual developed one of more than 20 serious illnesses—such as *Pneumocystis carinii* pneumonia, pulmonary tuberculosis, cervical cancer, or Kaposi sarcoma (a form of cancer)—as delineated by the CDC. Since 1993, the definition of AIDS has been expanded to include anyone with HIV whose immune system is severely impaired, as indicated by a T-cell (or CD4 cell) count of less than 200 cells per cubic millimeter of blood. T-cell counts in healthy people not infected with HIV range from 800–1,200 per cubic millimeter of blood.

16.4b Transmission

The human immunodeficiency virus can be transmitted in various ways, including:

- *Sexual contact:* HIV is found in several body fluids of infected individuals, including blood, semen, pre-seminal fluid (pre-cum), rectal fluids, and vaginal fluids. During sexual contact (anal, vaginal, or oral) with an infected individual, the virus may enter a person's bloodstream through broken skin or mucous membranes (wet, thin body tissue, as in the mouth, eyes, nose, vagina, rectum, and the opening of the penis). Worldwide, most new infections are transmitted heterosexually, although risk factors vary. In the

Human immunodeficiency virus

Virus that attacks the immune system and may lead to AIDS

Acquired immunodeficiency syndrome

Last stage of HIV infection in which the immune system of a person's body is so weakened that it becomes vulnerable to infection and disease (opportunistic infections)

United States, for example, gay and bisexual men are more severely affected by HIV than any other group. The incidence of new HIV infections in the United States continues to be greatest among MSM (Blackwell, 2018).

- *Intravenous drug use:* Drug users who are infected with HIV can transmit the virus to other drug users with whom they share needles, syringes, and other drug-related implements. This transmission method accounts for an increasing proportion of new HIV infections in Eastern Europe, South America, and Asia.

- *Blood transfusion:* HIV can be transmitted through HIV-infected blood or blood products. Currently, all blood donors are screened, and blood is not accepted from high-risk individuals. The US blood supply is considered among the world's safest supplies. Blood that is accepted from donors is tested for the presence of HIV. Testing began in 1985.

- *Mother-to-child transmission of HIV:* A pregnant woman infected with HIV can infect her unborn child in utero, during labor, and via breastfeeding. However, this risk is profoundly decreased if the mother receives anti-HIV treatment during pregnancy. Although HIV can be transmitted through breastfeeding, formula feeding reduces this risk. However, this solution can be problematic in developing countries in which there are problems obtaining adequate supplies of formula and clean water.

- *Organ or tissue transplants and donor semen:* Receiving transplant organs and tissues, as well as receiving semen for artificial insemination, could involve risk of contracting HIV if the donors have not been tested for it. Such testing is essential, and recipients should insist on knowing the HIV status of the organ, tissue, or semen donor.

- *Occupational transmission of HIV:* Certain occupational workers regularly come into contact with human blood and are therefore susceptible to occupational transmission of HIV. Health-care workers such as nurses and physicians, laboratory technicians, morgue technicians, rescue workers, dentists, police officers, prison guards, and other individuals who are likely to come into contact with bleeding individuals should use protection, such as latex gloves, before making physical contact with an injured or bleeding individual. Laypeople should also use latex gloves when coming into contact with another person's blood, and these gloves should be part of every first-aid kit.

HIV cannot be transmitted from casual contact (shaking hands, hugging, casual kissing) or from contact with objects in homes or in public settings (toilet seats, water fountains, doorknobs, dishes, drinking glasses, or food). Pets, animal bites, or insect bites do not transmit HIV. There has been no documented HIV transmission during sports participation.

The risk of getting HIV varies widely depending on the type of sexual activity. It also depends on several other factors, including condom use. If one person is HIV-positive, it can depend on whether the HIV-positive person is using ART and has suppressed a viral load and whether their HIV-negative partner is taking preexposure prophylaxis (PrEP) consistently and correctly.

Worldwide there has been a 47% decrease in new HIV infections since 1996, a 51% decrease in AIDS-related deaths since the peak in 2004, a 35% decrease in new HIV infections among children since 2010, and there were 21.7 million people accessing ART in 2017 (UNAIDS, 2019).

End the dread. Stop the spread.

Internet slogan

Symptoms

Although everyone infected with HIV is exposed to the same virus, there may be different symptoms at different stages. Some HIV-infected individuals display no symptoms at all for many years after exposure. Unless they are tested for HIV, many HIV-infected individuals don't know they are infected. When symptoms do appear, they may include rapid loss of weight, dry cough, recurrent fever or heavy night sweats, profound and unexplained fatigue, swollen lymph glands (in the armpits, groin, or neck), oral thrush (a white coating or spotting in the tongue, mouth, or throat), skin blotches (red, brown, pink, or purple), depression, memory problems, or other neurological dysfunctions.

If AIDS develops, severe immune system breakdown can lead to the onset of illnesses such as *Pneumocystis carinii* pneumonia, pulmonary tuberculosis, cervical cancer, and Kaposi sarcoma. A diagnosis of AIDS is made by a health-care professional based on specific criteria established by the Centers for Disease Control and Prevention.

No person should assume that if they have some of these symptoms they are infected with HIV, as other illnesses cause them as well. The only way to know if you are infected with HIV is to be specifically tested for it. The standard screening test for detecting HIV is the antibody screening test, which tests for the antibodies that your body makes against HIV. It is usually performed in a clinical setting on blood drawn from a vein. The newest tests can find HIV as soon as 3 weeks after exposure to the virus. Rapid tests and ones using oral fluid (not saliva) can also be performed; however, the rapid tests may give false-negative results, and the oral fluid tests take longer to provide results. Any test that is positive needs a follow-up test to confirm the results. Home-testing kits may be purchased at pharmacies and online. Similar to other forms of testing, a positive result is confirmed with a follow-up test. As an example, OraQuick® is an in-home HIV test that involves a mouth swab, with 99% accurate results available within 20–40 minutes.

Treatment

Presently, there is no cure for HIV or AIDS. However, the advent of the potent combination ART, which uses a cocktail of three or more antiretroviral drugs, has changed the course of the HIV epidemic. While these drugs do not cure HIV, they do slow the progression of the disease and increase survival rates in patients. A 2011 trial has confirmed that if an HIV-positive person adheres to an effective ART regimen, the risk of transmitting the virus to their uninfected sexual partner can be reduced by 96%. The World Health Organization's recommendation to initiate ART in all people living with HIV will contribute significantly to reducing HIV transmission (World Health Organization, 2019d).

There are currently four different classes of HIV drugs. Each class attacks the virus at different points in its life cycle, preventing it from replicating in the body. Patients are typically prescribed three drugs from two different classes of drugs that are designed to target HIV at different stages of replication and infection. This combination approach of physicians prescribing three drugs from two classes is referred to as *cocktail therapy;* the regimen is known as **highly active antiretroviral therapy** (HAART). This type of therapy can extend the life of an HIV-infected person by substantially restoring immune function. The downside of HAART therapy is that it may be so successful that

Highly active antiretroviral therapy
Combination of drugs an HIV-infected person takes to treat the virus; also known as *cocktail therapy*

HIV/AIDS may no longer be so feared as to induce safe-sex behavior. Indeed, research has shown that "successful treatment with antiretroviral therapies ... can prevent the onward transmission of HIV. As a result, health-care services are being challenged to find ways to roll out 'treatment as prevention' (TasP) as a public health measure" (Evans et al., 2015).

PrEP (Truvada®) is a prevention option for people who are at high risk of getting HIV. It is meant to be used consistently, as a pill taken every day by the person who is HIV negative and to be used with other prevention options, such as condoms. These medications can work to keep the virus from establishing a permanent infection. When taken consistently, PrEP has been shown to reduce the risk of HIV infection in people who are at high risk by up to 99%; it is much less effective if not taken consistently (Centers for Disease Control and Prevention, 2019e). Whitfield et al. (2019) found that use of PrEP was associated with sexual anxiety. On top of taking a daily pill, people who use PrEP must get regular checkups from their health-care provider every 3 months.

Treatment for HIV and AIDS also includes adopting lifestyle habits that promote well-being: a balanced diet, ample rest, regular exercise, and relaxation. It is also important for people with HIV/AIDS to avoid stressors on the immune system, such as tobacco, recreational drugs, and other STIs. Establishing a supportive network of family and friends is also essential in managing the stress of having HIV/AIDS.

16.4c Prevention and Control

It is no exaggeration to say that prevention of HIV promotes sexual health, saves lives, and averts devastating social and economic costs to people and countries. Currently, there is no vaccine to prevent HIV infection, so education is paramount. Herbst et al. (2018) confirmed positive outcomes from HIV prevention messages about self and partner benefits of ART and condom effectiveness on increased intentions for behavior change.

The risk of HIV transmission via semen is increased by concurrent infection with an STI. Ulcerations, lesions, or sores caused by many STIs provide a site for HIV to enter the bloodstream. Because STIs facilitate transmission of HIV, efforts to prevent, detect, and treat STIs may help reduce HIV transmission.

> *A woman is twice as likely as a man to get HIV infected from vaginal sex.*
>
> Lydia Hitchcock, health educator

Persons potentially exposed to HIV should use **post-exposure prophylaxis** (PEP). PEP is the use of antiretroviral drugs after a single high-risk event to stop HIV from making copies of itself and spreading through the body. PEP must be started as soon as possible to be effective—and always within 3 days of a possible exposure (Centers for Disease Control and Prevention, 2019b). PEP should be used only in emergency situations.

16.5 Protecting Yourself from STIs

According to the CDC (2016b), the most effective STI prevention strategies are as follows:

- Abstaining from sex
- Reducing the number of sexual partners and mutual monogamy

Post-exposure prophylaxis
The use of antiretroviral drugs after a single high-risk event to stop HIV from making copies of itself and spreading through the body

- Using condoms consistently and correctly
- Getting available vaccines
- Screening for STIs and treating promptly if infected

16.5a Abstaining from Sex

Abstinence from sexual intercourse, including oral sex, does provide protection from most STIs. However, certain diseases, such as herpes and HPV, can be transmitted from any sexual contact. A bigger problem with abstinence as an STI protection strategy is that it's just not a popular practice. Over half of US college students are sexually active, and 44.8% of college students in the annual National College Health Assessment reported that they have engaged in vaginal intercourse (American College Health Association, 2018).

Abstinent couples can achieve physical intimacy and pleasure by practicing **outercourse**—activities that do not involve exposing a partner to blood, semen, or vaginal secretions. Outercourse includes hugging, cuddling, masturbating, fantasizing, massaging, and rubbing body to body while clothed.

16.5b Reducing the Number of Sexual Partners and Mutual Monogamy

Individuals who engage in outercourse may reduce their risks of acquiring an STI by having sexual contact only with one partner who is not infected, who is also monogamous, and who does not inject drugs. A commitment to **mutual monogamy** is key to reducing STI risk. Mutual monogamy means that both partners agree to be sexually active only with each other.

Rather than rushing into sexual relationships, allow time to build trusting, caring, and honest relationships in which you can share your sexual histories. Also, carefully inspect your partner's genitals, as well as your own, before sexual contact. Although some STIs produce no visible signs, it is possible to see herpes blisters, chancres, genital warts, and rashes. If you notice anything unusual about your partner's genitals or your own, abstain from sexual contact and seek a medical examination. Also, be aware that even those who say they are in monogamous relationships can cheat. Vail-Smith and colleagues (2010) found that 27.2% of the males and 19.8% of the females out of 1,341 undergraduates reported having oral, vaginal, or anal sex outside of a relationship that their partner considered monogamous.

16.5c Using Condoms Consistently and Effectively

Of 2,223 undergraduate males, 43% reported that they used a condom the last time they had sexual intercourse, as did 42% of 7,176 undergraduate females (Hall & Knox, 2016). Milhausen et al. (2018) found that the more involved/committed a couple, the lower the condom use; similarly, casual hookup encounters are more likely to involve condom use. Older (50+) single individuals also have lower rates of condom use (Fileborn et al., 2018). Studies have shown that consistent and correct condom use reduces the overall risk of acquiring and transmitting HIV and other STIs. Laboratory studies have conclusively demonstrated that latex condoms provide an essentially impermeable barrier to STI pathogens (Centers for Disease Control and Prevention, n.d.). However, even when a condom is used, it does not offer a 100% guarantee against the transmission of STIs,

Outercourse
Sexual activities that do not involve exposing a partner to blood, semen, or vaginal secretions

Mutual monogamy
A relationship in which both partners agree to be sexually faithful to each other

for a variety of reasons. First, condoms are not always used consistently and correctly. The condom must be put on before penetration starts, to ensure effectiveness. Using a condom "most of the time" or "almost always" does not provide the same protection as using one every time a person engages in vaginal or anal intercourse or fellatio. Fehr et al. (2015) emphasized the importance of equal power in the relationship, which is associated with more consistent condom use.

Wright et al. (2012) reviewed the concept of condom assertiveness—the clear message that sex without a condom is unacceptable—and identified the characteristics of undergraduate women who are more likely to insist on condom use. These women have more faith in the effectiveness of condoms, believe more in their own condom communication skills, perceive that they are more susceptible to STIs, believe there are more relational benefits to being condom assertive, believe their peers are more condom assertive, and intend to be more condom assertive (Peasant et al., 2014). A problem with condom assertiveness is the false sense of security that insisting on a condom may involve. Stealthing is nonconsensual condom removal during sexual intercourse, which exposes victims to physical risks of pregnancy and disease (Brodsky, 2017).

Condom assertiveness is important not only for sexual and anal intercourse but also for oral sex. Not to use a condom or dental dam during oral sex or oral-anal contact is to increase the risk of contracting an STI. Indeed, individuals think "No way I am getting pregnant by having oral sex" only to discover HPV or another STI in their mouth or throat.

It is also important to use a condom correctly (see Table 16-2 on correct condom use). Even when a condom is used correctly, breakage and slippage may still occur.

Condoms do not protect against all STIs because some STI infections, such as HPV and herpes, can be located on the testicles and vulva, around the anus, and in other areas not protected by a condom. While not providing full protection, condom use may reduce the risk for HPV and HPV-associated diseases, such as genital warts and cervical cancer (Centers for Disease Control and Prevention, 2019a). In addition to external condoms (male condoms), internal condoms (female condoms) and dental dams may also be used to reduce the transmission of STIs.

TABLE 16-2	Correct Condom Use	
Do	**Don't**
<ul><li>use a condom every time you have sex.</li><li>put on a male condom or insert a female condom before having sex.</li><li>read the package and check the expiration date.</li><li>make sure there are no tears or defects.</li><li>store condoms in a cool, dry place.</li><li>use water-based or silicone-based lubricant to prevent breakage.</li></ul>	<ul><li>store condoms in your wallet because heat and friction can damage them.</li><li>use more than one condom at a time. This includes not using a male condom and a female condom together.</li><li>reuse a condom.</li></ul>

Source: Adapted from Centers for Disease Control and Prevention. (2016c, July). *Male Condom Use*. Retrieved from https://www.cdc.gov/condomeffectiveness/male-condom-use.html and Centers for Disease Control and Prevention. (2016d, November). *Female Condom Use*. Retrieved from https://www.cdc.gov/condomeffectiveness/Female-condom-use.html

One of the more controversial STI prevention strategies involves making condoms available to high school students. The *Social Policy 16-1* section looks at this controversy.

Self-Assessment 16-1:
The UCLA Multidimensional Condom Attitudes Scale

Directions

Indicate your level of agreement with each item by writing a number from 1 to 7 next to each item, based on the following answer key.

1 (Strongly disagree), 2 (Mostly disagree), 3 (Disagree a little), 4 (Neither agree nor disagree),

5 (Agree a little), 6 (Mostly agree), 7 (Strongly agree)

Reliability and Effectiveness

1. __ Condoms are an effective method of birth control.
2. __ Condoms are an effective method of preventing the spread of AIDS and other STIs.
3. __ I think condoms are an excellent means of contraception.
4.* __ Condoms are unreliable.
5.* __ Condoms do not offer reliable protection.

Pleasure

6. __ The use of condoms can make sex more stimulating.
7.* __ Condoms ruin the sex act.
8.* __ Condoms are uncomfortable for both partners.
9. __ Condoms are a lot of fun.
10.* __ Use of a condom is an interruption of foreplay.

Identity Stigma

11.* __ Men who suggest using a condom are really boring.
12.* __ If a couple is about to have sex and the man suggests using a condom, it is less likely that they will have sex.
13.* __ Women think men who use condoms are jerks.
14.* __ A woman who suggests using a condom does not trust her partner.

Embarrassment About Negotiation and Use

15.* __ When I suggest using a condom, I am almost always embarrassed.
16.* __ It is really hard to bring up the issue of using condoms with my partner.
17. __ It is easy to suggest to my partner that we use a condom.
18. __ I'm comfortable talking about condoms with my partner.
19.* __ I never know what to say when my partner and I need to talk about condoms or other protection.

Embarrassment About Purchase

20.* __ It is very embarrassing to buy condoms.
21.* __ When I need condoms, I often dread having to get them.
22. __ I don't think that buying condoms is awkward.
23.* __ It would be embarrassing to be seen buying condoms in a store.
24. __ I always feel really comfortable when I buy condoms.

Scoring

Reverse-score the items marked with an asterisk (*). To reverse-score, make the following changes in your answers: 1 = 7, 2 = 6, 3 = 5, 4 = 4 (no change), 5 = 3, 6 = 2, 7 = 1. After reversing the scores of the items indicated, compute a mean (average) score for each subsection. The higher the score, the more positive your attitudes toward condoms. You might pencil your mean scores in the spaces provided and compare them with those obtained in a study of 239 students ages 15–35 (mean age = 19) (Helweg-Larsen & Collins, 1994).

Subsection	Mean Score	
	Men	Women
1. Reliability and Effectiveness (measures attitudes toward the reliability and effectiveness of condoms)	5.4	5.3
2. Pleasure (measures the pleasure associated with condom use)	4.1	4.3
3. Identity Stigma (measures the stigma attached to being a condom user)	5.6	6.2
4. Embarrassment About Negotiation and Use (measures the embarrassment associated with the negotiation and use of condoms)	4.8	4.8
5. Embarrassment About Purchase (measures the embarrassment associated with the purchase of condoms)	4.3	3.5*
*P is less than 0.05.		

Discussion

After analyzing the scores of 239 students on the Multidimensional Condom Attitudes Scale, researchers found that overall, men were less embarrassed about purchasing condoms than women, whereas women were more positive about issues related to identity stigma (Helweg-Larsen & Collins, 1994).

Source: Helweg-Larsen, M., & Collins, B. E. (1994). The UCLA Multidimensional condom attitudes scale: Documenting the complex determinants of condom use in college students. *Health Psychology, 13*(3), 224–237. Copyright 1994 American Psychological Association; reprint of table data permitted.

16.5d Preexposure Vaccination

Preexposure vaccination is one of the most effective methods for preventing the transmission of HPV and HBV. HPV vaccination is recommended routinely for children ages 11 or 12 and can be administered beginning at age 9. Either bivalent, quadrivalent, or the 9-valent HPV vaccine is recommended for females, and quadrivalent vaccine or 9-valent vaccine is recommended for males. Vaccination is recommended through age 26 for all females and through age 21 for all males who did not receive any or all of the vaccine doses at a younger age. For persons with HIV infection and for MSM, HPV vaccination is recommended through age 26. HBV vaccination is recommended for all unvaccinated, uninfected persons being evaluated or treated for an STI. In addition, hepatitis A and HBV vaccines are recommended for MSM, injection-drug users, people with chronic liver disease, and people with HIV infections who have not yet been infected with the hepatitis virus (Centers for Disease Control and Prevention, 2019f, 2016a).

Social Policy 16-1

Condom Availability in High Schools

The 2017 CDC Youth Risk Behavior Surveillance System (YRBSS), a yearly national study, indicates that among US high school students:

- 39.5% had sexual intercourse.
- 3.4% had sexual intercourse for the first time before age 13.
- 9.7% had had sex with four or more people during their lifetime.
- 28.7% had had sexual intercourse during the previous three months.
- 11.3% of all female high school students had been raped ("physically forced to have sexual intercourse against their will"), including 12.1% and 11.3% of 11th and 12th grade girls, respectively; the statistic for boys is 3.5%.
- 53.8% did use a condom the last time they had sex.*
- 9.3% were ever tested for HIV infection.
- 18.8% drank alcohol or used drugs before last sexual intercourse.*
- 9.1% of female students who had dated in the last 12 months had been physically hurt on purpose by a person they were dating, and 10.7% had been forced to perform sexual acts against their will. Male statistics were 6.5% and 2.8%, respectively.

*Among students who were currently sexually active. (Centers for Disease Control and Prevention, 2018a)

Most US schools do not make condoms available to students. Indeed, most schools do not provide comprehensive sex education: 39 states and DC require that information on abstinence be provided, 19 states require instruction on the importance of engaging in sexual activity only within marriage, and only 17 states require that sex and HIV education programs be medically accurate. In addition, only nine states require that programs provide instruction that is not biased against any race, sex, or ethnicity (Guttmacher Institute, 2020).

Why aren't condoms made available to students in high schools? Despite evidence to the contrary, some parents are afraid that increased condom availability will encourage students to be more sexually active. Evangelical religious groups disapprove of making condoms available and feel that an unwanted pregnancy or STI is the natural punishment for engaging in this sinful behavior outside of marriage. In some states, there are legal restrictions against condom availability programs. Segments of the population, as well as powerful conservative groups such as the Family Research Council and Focus on the Family, strongly oppose school condom availability on the premise that giving young people condoms might seem to condone their sexual activities or encourage promiscuity.

16.5e Seeking STI Screening and Prompt Treatment

As mentioned previously, screening and prompt diagnoses and treatment of STIs are major prevention strategies. A *screening test*, or a test used for screening purposes, is one that is applied to someone with no symptoms or signs of the disease being assessed. If the person has either symptoms or signs of a particular STI, the test is not a screening test, but rather a *diagnostic test*. The CDC (2018d) recommends annual chlamydia screening for sexually active women ages 25 and under. Sexually active gay and bisexual men should be tested, at least annually, for HIV, syphilis, chlamydia, and gonorrhea. All residents of the United States should be screened at least once a year for HIV.

> *Treatment without prevention is unsustainable.*
> Bill Gates, billionaire philanthropist

Although symptoms may vary depending on the pathogen, the following are common to many STIs:

- Urethral discharge
- Genital ulcers
- Inguinal (groin) swelling
- Scrotal swelling
- Vaginal discharge
- Lower abdominal pain

It must be remembered that some STIs are asymptomatic and are, consequently, less likely to be diagnosed and potentially more likely to lead to long-term consequences. *Personal Decisions 16-1* explores whether you should be screened for STIs.

PERSONAL DECISIONS 16-1

Should You Be Screened for STIs?

The CDC offers the following guidelines for STI screening. Based on these guidelines, do you think you should be screened?

- At least one HIV test for all adults and adolescents ages 15–65
- Annual chlamydia screening for all sexually active women younger than 25 years, as well as older women with risk factors such as new or multiple sex partners or a sex partner who has an STI
- Annual gonorrhea screening for all sexually active women younger than 25 years, as well as older women with risk factors, such as new or multiple sex partners or a sex partner with an STI
- Syphilis, HIV, chlamydia, and hepatitis B screening for all pregnant women, and gonorrhea screening for at-risk pregnant women starting early in pregnancy, with repeat testing as needed, to protect the health of mothers and their infants
- Screening at least once a year for syphilis, chlamydia, and gonorrhea for all sexually active gay, bisexual, and other MSM (MSM who have multiple or anonymous partners should be screened more frequently for STIs at 3- to 6-month intervals.)
- HIV testing at least once a year for anyone who has unsafe sex or shares injection drug equipment (Sexually active gay and bisexual men may benefit from more frequent testing, such as every 3–6 months.)

Source: Centers for Disease Control and Prevention. (2015, June). 2015 Sexually Transmitted Diseases Treatment Guidelines. Screening Recommendations Referenced in Treatment Guidelines and Original Recommendation Sources. Retrieved from: https://www.cdc.gov/std/tg2015/screening-recommendations.htm

Social Policy 16-2

Legal Aspects of Disclosing an STI

Research has confirmed that individuals with STIs (including HIV) do not always disclose their infection to their sexual partners (Sullivan et al., 2013a). Individuals often struggle over whether, or how, to tell a partner about their sexual health condition or history. If a person in a committed relationship becomes infected with an STI, that individual—or their partner—may have had sex with someone outside the relationship. Thus, disclosure of an STI may also mean confessing your own infidelity or confronting your partner about their infidelity. Of course, it is possible the infection may have occurred prior to the current relationship but was undetected.

For partners in abusive relationships, telling their partner that they have an STI often involves fear that their partner will react violently. Individuals who are infected with an STI and who are beginning a new relationship face a different set of concerns. Will their new partner view them negatively? Will they want to continue the relationship or end the relationship abruptly?

The following is an example of what an individual who had herpes disclosed, and the reaction:

> I told five partners in an up-front manner on the first date. Trying to make it a little funny, I said, "I guess I should tell you something. ... Before you fall madly in love with me and we run away and get married, ... I have herpes." In every case, five out of five, the first date was the last!

Although telling a partner about having an STI may be difficult and embarrassing, avoiding disclosure or lying about having an STI represents a serious ethical violation. Even if condoms are used ("I won't tell; I'll just use a condom"), they do not provide 100% protection; and the partner has a right to have the information of the presence of an STI so that they can make a decision about taking a risk.

While the responsibility to inform a partner of an STI—before having sex with that partner—is a moral one, there are also legal reasons for disclosing a sexual health condition to a partner. If you have an STI and you do not tell your partner, you may be liable for damages if you transmit the disease to your partner. In more than half the states, transmission of a communicable disease, including many STIs, is considered a crime.

Some states and cities have **partner notification laws** that require health-care providers to advise all persons with serious STIs about the importance of informing their sex or needle-sharing partner (or partners). Partner notification laws may also require health-care providers to either notify any partners of the infected person's names or forward the information about the partners to the Department of Health, where public health officers will notify the partner (or partners) that they have been exposed to an STI and schedule an STI testing appointment. The privacy of the infected individual is protected by not revealing their name to the partner being notified of potential infection. In cases in which the infected person refuses to identify partners, standard partner notification laws require doctors to undertake notification without cooperation if they know who the partner or spouse is. Although there is some public support for partner notification laws, the American Civil Liberties Union is against such laws. The organization fears that such mandatory reporting laws will discourage people from being tested for HIV. See *Technology and Sexuality 16-1: Notification of Partners* for more information on this topic.

One of the underlying causes for the spread of STIs among college-age students is the fear that telling a potential partner will result not only in personal rejection but also with the whole university knowing about it. To express appreciation for the honesty of the disclosure, to show compassion, and to guarantee confidentiality would be a welcome response to the disclosing party. One student disclosed to a partner that she had an STI. She said of his response, "He held me, told me he knew it was hard for me to tell him, and that we would get through this. He was wonderful and we are still together."

Partner notification laws
Set of laws that require health-care providers to advise all persons with serious sexually transmitted infections about the importance of informing their sex or needle-sharing partner or partners

16.6 **Accessing Sexual Health Services**

Public clinics, agencies, health centers, and private health-care providers provide sexual health services including screening, diagnostic testing, and STI treatment. Denison et al. (2017) identified the reasons individuals do not get tested for STIs. These reasons included individual (underestimate the risk, view STIs as not serious), structural (cost), and social (fear of being stigmatized). Access is also a barrier to sexual health services. To improve accessibility, more STI prevention and control programs need to be delivered through alternative approaches, such as school health programs, peer teen outreach, and mobile clinics. Stigma is also operative, so norms need to change so that buying condoms, getting the HPV vaccine, and getting STI tested are normative and socially approved. Recent attacks on funding for reproductive health clinics make it even more difficult for people in the affected states to access no-to-low-cost STI testing.

In addition to access to sexual health services, efforts to prevent and control STIs involve modifying high-risk behaviors, delivering public and private sexual health care, reducing the sharing of potentially infected needles, using computer technology, providing educational interventions, and initiating community development. Gariepy et al. (2018) noted the successful use of video games to improve condom and contraception self-efficacy, risk perceptions, and high-risk sexual knowledge. Exposure to eight sessions of POWER (Providing Opportunities for Women's Empowerment, Risk-Reduction, and Relationships) for 521 incarcerated women prior to their release was associated with greater condom use outside a monogamous relationship 3 and 6 months after release from prison (Fogel et al., 2015). Such training programs might also be made available outside the prison system. STI intervention programs might also include an emphasis on alcohol control/moderation, particularly since alcohol use is associated with high-risk sexual behavior (not using a condom, or having sex with high-risk partners) (Hutton et al., 2015). Additionally, since illicit drug use is associated with high-risk sexual behavior, such as drug use (including drugs being injected), it might also become a focus for treatment (Thamotharan et al., 2015). Increasing the sales tax on alcohol may also decrease STI rates. Staras and colleagues (2015) confirmed that an increase in the alcohol tax in the state of Maryland was associated with a decrease by 24% in the reported rate of gonorrhea the following year.

Chapter Summary

Sexually Transmitted Infections: An Overview

SEXUALLY TRANSMITTED INFECTIONS (STIs) are infections spread primarily through person-to-person sexual contact. There are more than 30 different sexually transmissible bacteria, viruses, and parasites. Young people ages 15–24 account for half of all new STIs. People at greatest risk for an STI have had many sexual partners or have sex with those who have had many sexual partners, are adolescents and/or young adults, are female, use drugs, have been sexually abused, and are of minority status. The CDC recommends regular STI testing for all sexually active individuals, especially young people.

Sexually Transmitted Infections: A Pandemic

STIs represent a major individual and public health concern. STI rates in the United States have been increasing. STIs and their consequences represent major public health problems, worldwide.

Types of STIs

THE MAIN AGENTS RESPONSIBLE FOR STIs are bacteria, protozoa, parasites, and viruses. Some STIs are curable, and some are only treatable. Many STIs are asymptomatic, so regular screening is key to diagnosis and treatment. Treatment for viral STIs is palliative: It may relieve symptoms or slow down the disease progression, but it does not cure the disease.

HIV and AIDS

HIV is TRANSMITTED through sexual contact, intravenous drug use, blood transfusion, mother-to-child transmission of HIV, organ or tissue transplants, donor semen, and occupational transmission of HIV. Treatment for HIV and AIDS includes taking drugs and adopting lifestyle habits that promote well-being, such as eating a balanced diet and getting ample rest, regular exercise, and relaxation.

Protecting Yourself from STIs

THE MOST EFFECTIVE STI prevention strategies include abstaining from sex, reducing the number of sexual partners and mutual monogamy, and using condoms consistently and correctly. It is also important to get available vaccines and to be screened for STIs and treated promptly if infected.

Accessing Sexual Health Services

SEXUAL HEALTH SERVICES—including screening, diagnostic testing, and STI treatment—are provided by public clinics, health centers, and private health-care providers.

Web Links

The Foundation for AIDS Research

http://www.amfar.org

American Sexual Health Association

http://www.ashasexualhealth.org/

Centers for Disease Control and Prevention (CDC)

http://www.cdc.gov/STD/

Joint United Nations Programme on HIV/AIDS

http://www.unaids.org

Medline Plus on STDs

http://www.nlm.nih.gov/medlineplus/sexuallytransmitteddiseases.html

myLAB Box: Online STI Testing Firm

http://www.mylabbox.com/

World Health Organization—Sexualy and Reproductive Health

http://who.int/reproductivehealth/topics/rtis/en/

Key Terms

Acquired immunodeficiency syndrome **442**

Asymptomatic **427**

Candidiasis **438**

Chlamydia **437**

Genital herpes **439**

Genital warts **440**

Gonorrhea **435**

Hepatitis B **441**

Herpes simplex virus type 1 **439**

Herpes simplex virus type 2 **439**

Highly active antiretroviral therapy **444**

Human immunodeficiency virus **442**

Human papillomavirus **440**

Mutual monogamy **446**

Nongonococcal urethritis **438**

Oral herpes **439**

Outercourse **446**

Partner notification laws **452**

Pelvic inflammatory disease **432**

Post-exposure prophylaxis **445**

Pubic lice **434**

Scabies **435**

Sexually transmitted infection **426**

Syphilis **436**

Vaginitis **438**

I speak up to contribute to the end of the conspiracy of silence.

Lupita Nyongo, in reference to her sexual harassment by Harvey Weinstein

Chapter Outline

17.1 Sexual Coercion: Rape and Sexual Assault 458
17.1a Definitions of Rape 459
Self-Assessment 17-1:
 Revised Sexual
 Coercion Inventory 460
Personal Experience 17-1
 "And the Lights Went Out" 462
17.1b Prevalence and Contexts
 of Rape 462
17.1c Characteristics of Men Who
 Rape Women 463
17.1d Men as Victims of Rape 466
17.2 Theories of Rape 467
17.2a Evolutionary and Biological
 Theories of Rape 467
17.2b Psychopathological Theory
 of Rape 468
Technology and Sexuality 17-1:
 Resources for Safety, Information,
 and Support 468
17.2c Feminist Theory of Rape 469
17.2d Social Learning Theory of Rape 469
Self-Assessment 17-2:
 Rape Supportive Attitude Scale 470
17.2e Rape Culture 471
17.2f Sexual Assault and Harassment in
 the Military 472
**17.3 Consequences of Rape and Treatment
for Rape Survivors 473**
17.3a Reporting a Rape and Title IX 473
17.3b Consequences of Rape 474
17.3c Treatment for Rape Survivors 475
17.4 Prevention of Rape 475
17.4a Teaching Women to Avoid Rape 476
17.4b Teaching Men Not to Rape 476
17.4c Campaigns to Address Rape 477
Social Policy 17-1
 The #MeToo Movement—Have We
 Gone Too Far? 478

17.5 Child Sexual Abuse 479
17.5a Intrafamilial Child
 Sexual Abuse 480
Personal Experience 17-2
 "Child Sex Abuse by My Father" 481
17.5b Extrafamilial Child
 Sexual Abuse 483
17.5c Stages of Grooming 483
17.5d Recovered Memories of Abuse 483
**17.6 Consequences and Treatment of Child
Sexual Abuse 484**
17.6a Impact of Child Sexual Abuse 484
17.6b Treatment of Sexually Abused
 Children and Adults Sexually Abused
 as Children 485
**17.7 Prevention of Child
Sexual Abuse 485**
Social Policy 17-2
 Megan's Law 486
**17.8 Treatment of Rape and Child Sexual
Abuse Perpetrators 486**
17.9 Sexual Harassment 487
17.9a Definition and Incidence of
 Sexual Harassment 488
17.9b Theories of Sexual Harassment 489
17.9c Profile of Sexually Harassed Victims
 and Perpetrators 490
Social Policy 17-3
 Sexual Harassment Policy in
 the Workplace 490
17.9d Consequences of
 Sexual Harassment 491
17.9e Responses to Sexual Harassment 491
Personal Decisions 17-1
 Confronting Someone Who Sexually
 Harasses You 492

Web Links 495
Key Terms 496

(Trevor Werb)

Objectives

1. Know the definitions and prevalence of rape and sexual assault
2. Explain the various theories of rape
3. Review the consequences of rape and the treatment for rape survivors
4. Describe the various strategies for the prevention of rape
5. Discuss intrafamilial and extrafamilial child sexual abuse
6. Know the consequences, treatment, and prevention of child sexual abuse
7. Review the definition, theories, and consequences of sexual harassment

Truth OR Fiction?

T / F   1. Increasingly, faculty members are required to report sexual assault even if the student does not want this.

T / F   2. Pressure from a man is the primary reason women report texting a sex photo.

T / F   3. Sex offenders have two to three times the testosterone levels of non-sex offenders.

T / F   4. The current criteria for determining guilt in a sexual assault on campus is "preponderance of evidence."

T / F   5. Tolerance of rampant sexism must be eliminated if sexual harassment in the military is to be curbed.

Answers: 1. T   2. T   3. F   4. F   5. T

Harvey Weinstein (Hollywood mogul) was accused by over 80 women to have sexually harassed and/or assaulted them. He was subsequently indicted by a grand jury for charges including first degree rape and sentenced to 23 years in prison. His victims had kept silent out of fear—he could decimate their careers. After the story initially broke, social media was flooded with hundreds of thousands of women from 85 countries in response to the Twitter hashtag #MeToo (Gill & Orgad, 2018). A cascade of celebrities and executives became exposed as perpetrators of sexual assault and harassment, some with negative consequences to their careers (e.g. Netflix removed Kevin Spacey from *House of Cards*, Charlie Rose was fired from PBS, as was Matt Lauer from *The Today Show*). Indeed, 94% of 834 Hollywood women reported "sexual misconduct" as part of their professional journey (Puente & Kelly, 2018). Also in 2018, Bill Cosby was found guilty of rape and sexual assault of three women (60 had come forward charging that he had drugged and raped them) and sentenced to prison. In a final example, 150 women confronted Larry Nassar (former USA Gymnastics and University of Michigan physician) at his sentencing hearing. He pleaded guilty to sexual misconduct and was sentenced to 175 years in prison. These examples, plus the televised questioning of Supreme Court nominee Brett Kavanaugh, who was accused of sexual assault, emphasize that sexual harassment/coercion is a frequent phenomenon in our society. Pellegrini (2018) noted that while women have experienced sexual harassment for decades, the context of Donald Trump's, election which exposed "his record of misogynist statements and assaultive behavior, may have fueled #MeToo."

The Hunting Ground, a documentary on rape crimes on US college and university campuses, exposes the devastation in the lives of victims from not only the assault itself, but also from the widespread institutional cover-ups that follow. The title comes from the fact that males on campus can hunt for and rape their prey with relative impunity; while 20% of female university students have reported being sexually assaulted, as with most rape statistics, the actual number is estimated to be far higher. One in five college students is sexually assaulted (Muehlenhard et al., 2017). Although we tend to think of sexual involvement as a series of voluntary, gentle, and intimate encounters, the data reveal that an alarming percentage of people are forced to have sex against their will by both intimates and strangers. In this chapter we discuss the various forms of sexual coercion, the victims, and the perpetrators. At the outset, we emphasize that forced sex occurs in dating, cohabiting, and marriage contexts in all types of relationships, regardless of the genders and orientations of those involved. Unwanted sexual contact, including sexual coercion, is the most frequent sexual assault complaint among college women (Fedina et al., 2018).

> *I believed he was going to rape me.*
> Dr. Christine Blasey Ford of Supreme Court nominee Brett Kavanaugh

17.1 Sexual Coercion: Rape and Sexual Assault

While showing sexual interest in a partner and attempting to be physically intimate have positive personal and relationship outcomes such as increased satisfaction, improved communication, and less conflict (Leavitt & Willoughby, 2015), **sexual coercion**, which involves using force (actual or threatened) to engage a person in sexual acts against that person's will, has predictable negative outcomes. While legal definitions vary from state to state, there are four types of sexual coercion, including verbal coercion until the person gives in, someone doing something sexual to a partner without asking for consent, someone doing something sexual to the person while that person is intoxicated

Sexual coercion
Use of force (actual or threatened) to engage a person in sexual acts against that person's will

or asleep, or using or threatening to use physical force (Mustapha & Muehlenhard, 2014). French et al. (2017) emphasized that sexual coercion can be both a result of manipulation (e.g. saying "I love you" and promising marriage) as well as using alcohol/drugs and physical force (see Self-Assessment 17-1). But even formal consent may overlook the fact that the partner may not be fully capacitated. The following statement is from a man who "technically, would only have sex with a woman who gave consent" … but

> *Like, I'm not gonna go to a party and the woman's just laying there drunk and I'm just gonna pull up her skirt and take out a latex and go at it. I mean, I'll wake her up, and I'll tell her lies like, "You look amazing," even though she's got throw up on her face. But I'm not gonna start right away. (Strang & Peterson, 2017, p. 980)*

Apps have surfaced to handle the awkward area of agreement in regard to sex. Consent Amour, LegalFling, and YesMeansYes are examples. Another is The Consent App where an individual asserts that they are of legal age, understand the laws of legal consent, and declare that the agreement is made of one's own free will. After signing, the person gives it to the partner who also signs and the couple take a selfie, which goes in the "vault" of the company. The drawback is that the individual may change their mind (Blag, 2018).

Although sexual coercion has existed for centuries, only in the past couple of decades have individuals, social scientists, medical and mental health professionals, and politicians been confronted with the pervasiveness of sexually coercive acts. Examples of what television and print media have revealed about sex abuse include the sex abuse scandal of the Catholic Church and sexual harassment in the military.

Research by Perkins et al. (2020) revealed that 75% of their respondents (mostly female) revealed that they had vetted a potential or current romantic partner. While individuals might vet potential partners, some apps do not. Many of the free dating apps (including Tinder, OkCupid, Hinge and Plenty of Fish) do not screen whether users are registered sex offenders. Janine Dunphy (one of 10 million who used these sites) met someone on Plenty of Fish who turned out to be a registered sex offender (he raped her the night they met). These apps are owned by Match Group, operator of the fee-based site Match.com, which does screen for sex offender registries (Battiste, 2019). Sexual coercion may also take place in the context of an abusive relationship, which is referred to as *co-victimization* (Katz & Rich, 2015). Emotional, physical, and sexual aggression are more likely to occur in committed relationships (69%), but may also occur in casual sexual relationships (31%–36%), such as friends with benefits, booty calls, and hook-up relationships (Klipfel et al., 2014). A study of individuals who persisted in obtaining sex after an initial refusal noted that verbal pressure, existing intoxication, and promoting intoxication were the primary tactics to get a partner to relent (Smeaton et al., 2014).

17.1a Definitions of Rape

One of the difficulties in studying rape and sexual assault is that these terms are variously defined in legal codes and research literature. Criminal law distinguishes between forcible rape and statutory rape. **Forcible rape** includes three elements: penetration of the vagina, mouth, or anus; force or threat of force; and no consent of the victim. **Statutory rape** involves sexual intercourse without use of force with a person below the legal age of consent. The age of consent for sex varies by state in the United States, from age 14 for the male in Iowa to age 18 for the female in 14 states. In most states, the legal age for sex between men and women is 17. **Marital rape**, now recognized in all states, is forcible rape by a spouse. In no state is a person legally entitled to force their spouse to have sex.

Forcible rape
Sexual force involving three elements: vaginal, oral, or anal penetration; the use of force or threat of force; and nonconsent of the victim

Statutory rape
Sexual intercourse without the use of force with a person below the legal age of consent in the United States; the age of legal consent varies by state

Marital rape
Forcible rape by one's spouse; now illegal in all states

Self-Assessment 17-1:
Revised Sexual Coercion Inventory*

Instructions

Sometimes in a relationship, one partner wants to become more sexually involved than the other does. For the following list, indicate whether you have ever been pressured by a peer to engage in sexual behaviors (meaning vaginal, oral, or anal intercourse) even though you did not want to participate. For this questionnaire, only refer to sexual experiences with a nonrelative peer (such as a boyfriend/girlfriend, friend, acquaintance, stranger, etc. but do not include potential sexual experiences with a family member) since you were 12 years old.

If the type of incident happened to you, indicate if it resulted in kissing and/or fondling, attempted sexual intercourse, or completed sexual intercourse. If you have had more than one experience with an incident that resulted in the same level of severity (such as two different people have threatened to stop seeing you if you didn't have sex and they *both* resulted in completed sexual intercourse) please provide the information for the *last* event that occurred.

*It is important that you answer all questions honestly to the best of your ability. All information you provide will remain confidential.

		Has this ever happened to you?	If this happened to you, indicate the most severe sexual behavior this resulted in.		
			Kissing and/or fondling	Attempted sexual intercourse	Completed sexual intercourse
1	A sexual partner has threatened to stop seeing me.	Yes No	1	2	3
2	A sexual partner has given me alcohol without my knowledge and then took advantage of me sexually.	Yes No	1	2	3
3	A sexual partner has threatened to tell lies about me.	Yes No	1	2	3
4	A sexual partner has threatened to tell private things about me.	Yes No	1	2	3
5	A sexual partner has encouraged me to drink and then took advantage of me sexually.	Yes No	1	2	3
6	A sexual partner has said things to make me feel guilty (e.g., "It's your duty.")	Yes No	1	2	3
7	A sexual partner has begged me and would not stop until I agreed.	Yes No	1	2	3
8	A sexual partner has given me drugs without my knowledge and then took advantage of me sexually.	Yes No	1	2	3
9	A sexual partner has encouraged me to use drugs and then took advantage of me sexually.	Yes No	1	2	3
10	A sexual partner would not let me leave although I wanted to go.	Yes No	1	2	3
11	A sexual partner has tried to interest me by touching me sexually but I was not interested.	Yes No	1	2	3
12	A sexual partner has made false promises (e.g., "We'll get married").	Yes No	1	2	3
13	A sexual partner has said things that later proved to be untrue (e.g., "I love you").	Yes No	1	2	3

		Has this ever happened to you?	If this happened to you, indicate the most severe sexual behavior this resulted in.		
			Kissing and/or fondling	Attempted sexual intercourse	Completed sexual intercourse
14	A sexual partner has physically held me down.	Yes No	1	2	3
15	A sexual has partner threatened to use or did use a weapon.	Yes No	1	2	3
16	A sexual partner has threatened to use physical force (e.g., slapping, hitting).	Yes No	1	2	3
17	A sexual partner has used physical force.	Yes No	1	2	3

Scoring Instructions

For unweighted score (to assess victimization rates):

Item = 1 if participant indicated "Yes, this happened to me"

Item = 0 if participant indicated "No, this did not happen to me"

Items are summed.

Scores range from 0 to 17 with higher scores reflecting higher rates of victimization.

For weighted scores (to assess victimization based on severity):

If participant indicated "Yes" to an item, score ranges from 1 to 3 based on response.

If participant indicated "No" to an item, score = 0.

Items are summed.

Scores range from 0 to 51 with higher scores reflecting higher levels of severity of victimization.

Subscales based on French et al., 2017:

- Manipulation = Items 4, 6, 7, 11, 12, 13

  Scores range from 0 to 6 with higher scores reflecting higher rates of manipulation.

  Weighted subscales range from 0 to 18 for manipulation.

- Substance use and aggression = Items 2, 3, 8, 10, 14, 16, 17

  Scores range from 0 to 7 with higher scores reflecting higher rates of substance use/aggression.

  Weighted subscales range from 0 to 21 for substance abuse/ and aggression.

Source: "Exploratory Factor Analysis and Psychometric Properties of the Sexual Coercion Inventory," by Bryana French, Han Na Suh, and Brooke Arterberry, (2016). *The Journal of Sex Research, 54*(8), 1–9. Copyright 2016 Taylor & Francis Ltd., http://www.tandfonline.com. Reprinted by permission of the publisher and Bryana H. French, Graduate School of Professional Psychology, University of St. Thomas. Bryana.french@stthomas.edu.

Because legal definitions of rape are varied and restrictive, the term *forced sex* is more descriptive. In this section, we use the terms **forced sex** and **rape** interchangeably to refer to acts of sex (or attempted sex) in which one party is nonconsenting, regardless of the age and sex of the offender and victim and regardless of whether the act meets the criteria for what legally constitutes rape. Pressure to engage in sex is another way of describing forced sex, though it is subtler and the partner may relent (thus the murkiness of deciding whether to call the act *rape*).

A team of researchers examined the reasons sexually active women cited for giving in to pressure to have sex. One reason was "wanting to please." Reflecting on this theme, one respondent said, "I believe that, if they aren't requiring something you're specifically uncomfortable with, you should have sex with your long-term partner to help ensure their happiness." A second theme was "giving up" in the sense of being tired of resisting. A final and related theme was "wanting the pressure to end."

Forced sex

Acts of sex (or attempted sex) in which one party is nonconsenting, regardless of the age and sex of the offender and victim and whether or not the act meets criteria for what legally constitutes rape (also called rape)

Rape

See forced sex

In effect, there was the perception that the partner was not going to stop the pressure, so the individual engaged in the sexual behavior because she was pressured to get it over with (Budge et al., 2015). Gender roles are strongly involved in pressure and "giving in," with women acquiescing to sexual pressure to please the partner, promote intimacy, and avoid an argument (Conroy et al., 2014).

Personal Experience 17-1 reveals the horror of an undergraduate female who was raped when she visited a friend for consolation after breaking up with a boyfriend.

PERSONAL EXPERIENCE 17-1

"And the Lights Went Out"

I was in my first semester of my freshmen year. It was on a regular Thursday night in the dorm. A girl down the hall from me had her boyfriend and some of his guys over that night and we were all hanging out. We all were drinking and ended up getting way more drunk than any of us thought. Some people went downtown but me and another girl and the guys' friends stayed back. I stayed back because I was too drunk. I remember just hanging out and drinking more but then the girl that was in the room with me left. So it was just me and the guys in there now. The next thing I knew is that one of the guys turned the lights off while the other started feeling me up. I remember specifically saying "stop." I only said it once because one of the guys started choking me and threatening me if I didn't stop talking. I remember being thrown on the bed and basically being tag teamed. When it was over I remember being so dizzy and confused and scared as to what just happened. The lights ended up being turned on and I was the only one in the room. I went to the bathroom and threw up because I was so nauseous and anxious about what had happened.

(Amberlynn Bishop)

Then I remember just going to bed and falling asleep. The next morning, I had remembered what happened, went to the bathroom and saw the marks on my neck and wrists. I started crying, my hall advisor heard me, came in and convinced me to call the cops and get a rape kit at the student health center. I ended up not pressing charges because I couldn't remember the names or faces of the guys. The girl that knew their names wouldn't tell me so as to protect them because they had athletic scholarships.

Girls need to know the extent some guys will take to have a good night at college and how they will hang out with you and laugh with you but then hurt you and abandon you. My life was changed that night. But through therapy and an amazing boyfriend (who is loving, supportive and patient), I feel happy and safe.

17.1b Prevalence and Contexts of Rape

The fact that there are many definitions of rape can obscure data accuracy. When men are asked if they have "ever coerced someone to have intercourse by holding them down," they are more likely to admit having engaged in the behavior than if asked, "Have you ever raped somebody?"—they are more likely to deny when the label *rape* is used (Koss, 1998).

National DATA

More than 1 in 3 women in the US has been a victim of rape, stalking, or domestic violence (Aizer et al., 2018).

Regardless of the official numbers, it is estimated that 75%–95% of women raped are not reported (Fisher & Pina, 2013). While the estimates indicate that 1 in 10 rapes involve a male victim, underreporting is also an issue when men are the victims (Planty et al., 2013, rev. 2016). In the 2015 US transgender survey, 47% of trans people reported having been sexually assaulted (James et al., 2016).

Rape by an acquaintance (80% of reported rapes) can be seen as a sequence of events—flirting, alcohol, physical intimacy in the form of kissing, isolation from the person's support network, and movement to an isolated place such as an apartment. Alcohol and drugs are a major contextual factor in rape (McCauley et al., 2013). In their study of 353 college women, Messman-Moore and colleagues (2013) categorized 15.6% of the rapes as "alcohol-involved rape." Heavy episodic drinking was particularly associated with being raped. Also important, Schnittker (2019) found that depression played as significant a role as alcohol abuse disorder in its association with being vulnerable to being the victim of sexual coercion. Hence the person who is very depressed may drink a great deal and increase their vulnerability to rape.

There is also the complex interaction of alcohol, beliefs about alcohol, and gender norms, including male entitlement, sex scripts, and rape myths, that normalize male dominance and violence against women (Crowley, 2014). Adolescents vulnerable to being sexually victimized by a partner include those with a risky lifestyle (getting drunk, having sex) and having deviant friends. Those with strict mothers and conservative sexual attitudes predicted a lower likelihood of subsequent assault (East & Hokoda, 2015).

"Why are you afraid of women?" I asked a group of men. "We're afraid they'll laugh at us," replied the men. "Why are you afraid of men?" I asked a group of women. "We're afraid they'll kill us," replied the women.

Margaret Atwood, Canadian poet/novelist

17.1c Characteristics of Men Who Rape Women

Most rapists are men who believe in **rape myths**. Also referred to as **rape-supportive beliefs**, rape myths are attitudes and beliefs that are false but are widely and persistently held. They serve to deny and/or justify male sexual aggression against women. Such rape myths include that women have a secret desire to be controlled/raped, that when a woman says "no" she really means "yes," that only strangers commit rape, and that women who dress provocatively are really asking for sex. Moser and Ballard (2017) surveyed 549 undergraduates and found that males and those in Greek life were more likely to support rape myths.

Rape myths
False but widely held attitudes and beliefs that serve to justify male sexual aggression against women (also called *rape-supportive beliefs*)

Rape-supportive beliefs
See *rape myths*

Think About It

THINK ABOUT IT

One unintended consequence of the cultural revelations of "#metoo" is to overgeneralize and assume that most men are libidinous lechers who target their partners, threaten them, sexually assault them, and engage in harmful, pathological behavior. Most men are respectful of women and do not engage in these behaviors. How can we as a society address some of these changes post #metoo?

THINK ABOUT IT

Take a moment to answer the following question. Because men with whom the women were acquainted or romantically involved perpetrate most rapes of adult women, rape is one of the most underreported violent crimes in the United States. What social changes do you feel can be made to increase the reporting of rape?

The acceptance of rape myths is associated with psychopathic qualities in both incarcerated and non-incarcerated individuals. In a sample of 308 college males, those who believed that females were responsible for their own rapes (they dress provocatively, they drink too much) also had the traits of being callous and manipulative. In addition, those who thought "rape is trivial" also reported being both impulsive and antisocial (Mouilso & Calhoun, 2013).

In addition to believing in rape myths, men who rape may share several other characteristics. They ignore personal space (hands all over you), abuse alcohol or other drugs (reduced judgment), sexualize conversations, are dominant/aggressive, have rigid gender roles, use threats in displays of anger, have a quick temper, are sadistic/narcissistic, and are impersonal/aloof emotionally. Men who rape may also be sexually aroused by a misperception that their partner is interested (Bouffard & Miller, 2014). Men who rape may be an acquaintance, boyfriend, husband, or stranger. The rape may be perpetrated by one individual or by a group. An example of the latter is a woman who said she awakened upstairs in a fraternity house to discover that eight of the fraternity brothers had already had sex with her. While fraternities have been prominent in the news about gang rape allegations and are thought to be contexts for socializing men to be sexually aggressive (Boyle, 2015), data comparing sexual assault and fraternity status revealed no significant differences (Jozkowski & Canan, 2014).

College women may also buy into rape myths. In a sample of first- and fourth-year college women (Deming et al., 2013), the respondents were ambivalent about the definition of when rape has occurred when there are other contributing factors: alcohol consumption (Should the woman not have had so much to drink? Should she have been more in control?), varying degrees of consent (The woman consented to the man coming back to her apartment or to being unclothed), and the woman knowing the perpetrator (boyfriend versus just a hookup).

Acquaintance as Rapist

Most rapists know the person they rape. One form of **acquaintance rape** is sometimes referred to as **date rape**. Date rape refers to nonconsensual sex between people who are dating, on a date (the concept includes individuals who are sexually active and who previously dated), or hooking up. Thirty-nine percent of 10,004 undergraduate females and 21% of 3,035 undergraduate males reported that they had been pressured to have sex by a person they were dating (Hall & Knox, 2019).

Acquaintance rapes most often occur in the context of alcohol or drugs. Indeed, alcohol is the primary drug men use to reduce the inhibitions or to alter the judgment of their target female. The word *target* is used deliberately. Some men spend time with or drink with women for the express purpose of getting them drunk and having sex with them.

Two illegal drugs that have been associated with date rape cases are Rohypnol® and gamma hydroxybutyrate (GHB). **Rohypnol** (also known as *dulcitas*, the "forget-me drug") causes profound and prolonged sedation and short-term memory loss. It has 10 times the potency of Valium by weight and lasts for about 8 hours. **GHB** is also

Acquaintance rape
Nonconsensual sex between people who are dating or on a date (also called *date rape*)

Date rape
See *acquaintance rape*

Rohypnol
Drug used in date rape scenarios that causes profound and prolonged sedation, a feeling of well-being, and short-term memory loss; also known as *dulcitas,* the "forget me drug"

GHB (gamma hydroxybutyrate)
Also known as "liquid ecstasy" because, like X, it inspires a tendency to be touchy-feely and relaxed; however, it is more powerful, can cause deep sedation, and can be fatal

known as "liquid Ecstasy" because, like X, it inspires a tendency to be touchy-feely and relaxed. However, it is far more powerful than Ecstasy and can be fatal. GHB acts faster than Rohypnol to induce confusion, intense sleepiness, unconsciousness, and memory loss. Although most symptoms last 3–6 hours, the drowsiness may last for 3 days. Police in Los Angeles County routinely test date rape victims for both Rohypnol and GHB.

Although both of these drugs may be used to incapacitate a woman, alcohol is more typically used. It is legal, available, and normative—the woman sees her friends drinking, so its use is not questioned.

Cultural Diversity

An unconscionable and tragic example of force is gender communal terrorism in the form of gang rape. This strategy was used during the Bosnian War (1992–1995) and the Second Congo War (1998–2003), as part of a large-scale campaign to wipe out ethnic groups (the Second Congo War has been considered the worst in the history of humankind) (Matusitz, 2017). Such gang rape reflects various symbolic themes: (1) identicide (or ethnic cleansing), (2) punishment, (3) conquering territory, (4) proof of manhood, (5) wounded femininity, (6) wounded community, (7) rejection from family, and (8) abjection. The latter means that the raped are viewed as disgusting by family members so their sense of self and family are destroyed—they are no longer wanted (Matusitz, 2017).

Boko Haram kidnapped 276 girls at Government Secondary School Chibok, Borno State, Nigeria, in 2014 in an act of sexual and gender-based violence against women. Boko Haram terrorists conducted mass rapes of women, impregnated them, and then kidnapped the offspring. About 200 of the captured schoolchildren remain missing (Oriola 2017). The abuse continues—in 2018 one hundred teenage girls were seized by Boko Haram in the town of Dapchi in Nigeria's north-eastern Yobo tribe.

Husband as Rapist

Marital rape may occur as part of a larger pattern of verbal and emotional abuse. Historically, husbands could not be prosecuted for rape because the wife was the husband's property and taking her sexually was his right. Today, every state in the United States recognizes marital rape as a crime. Most wives are reluctant to press charges, but those who do are usually successful in seeing their husbands convicted. One reason for such a high conviction rate is that such rapes are often particularly brutal.

Stranger as Rapist

Rape by a stranger is known as **predatory rape** or **classic rape** and may involve a weapon (a gun or knife). Historically the courts haven't taken rapes by strangers more seriously, and prosecuted rapists who do not know their victims are more often convicted. Although the 2015 case involving Brock Turner would indicate that while convictions may occur, the sentencing may be lenient. Of 10,004 undergraduate females, 21% reported that they have been pressured to have sex by a stranger (Hall & Knox, 2019).

Gang Rape

Some rape involves multiple perpetrators who are either strangers or acquaintances. Gang rape by strangers involves a group of men targeting a woman they do not know and raping her. One example is a woman who was jogging in the park where three male friends were hanging out and decided to rape her. Gang rape by acquaintances involves a group of men the woman knows. Or she may be at a fraternity party, know several of the brothers, and be gang-raped one night while she is drunk.

Predatory rape
Rape by a stranger which may involve a weapon (also called *classic rape*)

Classic rape
See *predatory rape*

Gang rape is also common in war, where men enter a context in which there are females whom they can control or rape, and they do so in a group. Men may be responsible for war rape not only as individuals but also as "collective bystanders, facilitators and beneficiaries" (Paul, 2013).

Several social-psychological factors can help explain why group members who individually would not commit rape would do so in a group context. First, the group context allows members to diffuse responsibility for the gang rape by blaming others in the group ("They were just all having sex with her, so I went along."). Second, in a group setting, modeling of aggression occurs. Not only does watching while group members rape a woman convey to other group members that this behavior is considered appropriate and fun, it also demonstrates techniques of how to force someone to have sex.

Gang rape of male victims may be part of hazing and initiation rituals in some groups, like sports teams (Jeckell et al., 2018). While sexual assault as part of hazing is not new, there has recently been an increase in the media coverage due in part to incidents involving high school students in Maryland and Texas.

17.1d Men as Victims of Rape

While male rape is often thought of as a gay issue with men raping men, male rape is actually either men or women raping men (Javaid, 2018). Male rape is underreported since men are restrained by culture from making visible their abuse due to myths such as real men can't be raped, rape is a homosexual issue, and rape by a woman is not serious. In addition, masculine sexual scripts do not account for unwanted sex, which makes processing of these experiences difficult. Nevertheless, men are traumatized by the experience and have limited healing venues. O'Brien et al. (2016) studied rape in the military and confirmed that half of military sexual assault survivors are men.

In an analysis of 209 cases of stranger rape involving male offenders and male victims, three themes of offender-victim interaction were observed:

1. *Hostility:* This is characterized by demeaning, threatening, and hurting the victim, such as forceful anal penetration by the hand or object.

2. *Involvement intimacy:* The male perpetrator attempted to create a pseudo-intimate relationship by revealing personal information and asking for the same. Almost half (49%) of the male-to-male offenses were classified as involving intimacy.

3. *Involvement exploitative:* The offender had a weapon (gun or knife) and required the victim to perform sexual acts on the offender. In most cases (92%), the request was verbal, and the individual was urged to comply (Lundrigan & Mueller-Johnson, 2013).

In another study, researchers Griffith and Kimball (2014) analyzed data on 590 undergraduate males, 17% of whom reported an unwanted sexual experience—sexual assault, child sexual molestation, or silent reluctance (did not feel comfortable saying no). Of 12,293 rapes in the United Kingdom, 852 were recorded as rapes of men (Fisher & Pina, 2013). In the United Kingdom, research on rape of men by women is problematic since rape is defined in reference to penetration by a penis. Hence, no legal definition exists for a female who rapes a male. Even though women report sexual assault/abuse of males, the legal definition of rape remains gender biased in the United Kingdom. The absence of a legal definition for a female raping a male in the United Kingdom has important legal outcomes. Since a woman can be charged with sexual assault, not rape, the penalty for assault is much lower (maximum of 10 years in prison) than the penalty for rape (life imprisonment).

US law allows for rape to be the penetration of any orifice; a penis is not required. Thus, a woman could be considered a rapist if she used a penis-shaped vibrator and penetrated a male anally or aroused him and inserted his penis into her vagina.

Just as there are female rape myths, there are male rape myths. These myths include that men are stronger than women and can't be raped and that men who are raped by women lose their masculinity. Acceptance of the male rape myths results in considerable underreporting since people may believe that "males can't really be raped." Men also often fear that they will be held responsible for whatever happened.

While underreported, men are also the victim of rape by both women and men.

(Shutterstock)

Regardless of definitions or frequencies, some of the negative consequences for a man who is sexually assaulted or raped by a woman are the same as those for a woman who was raped by a man. There can be long-term psychological (depression, substance abuse), relationship (insecurity, instability), and physical (insomnia, anxiety) problems. Sexual dysfunction is particularly problematic after a heterosexual assault against a male by a female because it can affect current and future relationships with women (Turchik & Hassija, 2014). One fear is that if the male is sexual with a woman, she will begin another assault.

The consequences of rape vary considerably depending on gender. For example, female victims must contend with the possibility of pregnancy; gender-based differences in size and physical strength often lead to physical injury for women; and women and men face different degrees of secondary victimization. While male rape myths can lead to male victims not being taken seriously, the double standard means that female victims face "slut shaming" by authorities and rejection by friends and family. In some cultures, women rape survivors and even those who have been accused of any sexual activity are at risk of being murdered in "honor killings" (see *Cultural Diversity: Honor Killing* later in this chapter).

Sexual assaults on lesbians, gay men, and bisexuals also occur at rates similar to or higher than their heterosexual counterparts. These assaults are less often reported, in part because the victim may fear the consequences of being outed.

17.2 Theories of Rape

Various theories have been suggested in an attempt to explain why rape occurs. Because the vast majority of rapes are perpetrated by men who rape women, this discussion focuses only on those relevant theories and does not explore the reasons for women raping men, rapes that involve same-gender victims and rapists, or those that target trans people.

17.2a Evolutionary and Biological Theories of Rape

Evolutionary and biological theories explain rape on the basis of anatomy, biologically based drives, and natural selection for reproductive success. In addition to men's greater physical strength, some biological theories of rape emphasize that it results from a strong biological sex drive in men. The high level of androgens and other sex hormones to which the male brain is exposed explains, in part, this strong sex drive. Evolutionary/biological theories of rape have been criticized on the basis that societies differ in their rape rates, suggesting that such rates are due to social, not biological, influences and that being genetically programmed to rape is nonsense.

17.2b Psychopathological Theory of Rape

According to the psychopathological theory of rape, rapists are viewed as having a mental disorder. Most people in the general population agree with this theory and think of rapists as being crazy. According to this theory, these individuals do not have the proper social controls to inhibit their sexual impulses.

The psychopathological theory of rape may be criticized on the basis that the subject populations used for studies on rapists have been made up of incarcerated rapists. Also, not all rapists display the same symptomology or show marked deviation on standard psychological tests. Finally, the theory does not adequately explain why rape is so widespread.

Technology and Sexuality 17-1: Resources for Safety, Information, and Support

Some individuals think of the internet and technology as dangerous (stories of online predators luring children to their death, nude photos being posted by a revengeful ex-partner, and a private email account being hacked), but technology can also be used as a means to help victims of abuse, rape, and sexual assault stay safe, be informed, and seek help via online support groups.

Several apps are available to help people remain safe. One app, Circle of 6, allows you to select six people to be in your circle. Once you open the app, with a push of a button, you can send a request that someone pick you up; that message will be sent to your circle of six and will include your current location. You can also send out a request for someone to call you to interrupt whatever might be happening if you feel you are in a situation that may become unsafe or is simply uncomfortable. There are also quick links to hotlines and emergency numbers on the Circle of 6 app. Another award-winning app is OnWatch, which is free for Android and iPhone users. The app connects to different emergency contacts—campus police, 911, and has a timer feature for a walk home—after the timer expires, it asks you to check in, and if you don't, it sends out alerts with your GPS location. Another app, bSafe, has an SOS system that can be activated by touch or by your voice saying a key phrase, and can livestream and record during whatever emergency you're in. bSafe also has a timer alarm and siren-like alarm.

Some colleges and universities have developed their own apps that allow students to communicate directly with their campus police department.

While apps like these can be helpful during an emergency, technology also provides support for people who are in an unhealthy relationship or who are looking for support after an abusive event has occurred.

The Rape, Abuse, and Incest National Network (RAINN), in addition to providing information, offers a link to the National Sexual Assault Online Hotline. This online chat gives people who are struggling with an abusive relationship or the repercussions of rape an opportunity to text online in real time with a volunteer. The site also lists information for visitors on how to clear a computer cache, user history, and cookies after the conversation to prevent an abusive partner from finding out that they are reaching out for help. SafetiPin is a mobile app that provides information on safety, including the lack of safety in public places. Used in five countries, the app provides a safety score based on lighting, security, openness, visibility, walking paths, and so on. Individuals use the app to determine if it is safe to go to a particular part of town (Viswanath & Ashish, 2015).

In addition to finding immediate help for sexual abuse, involvement in an online support group may offer the first step toward healing. These online support groups can not only provide emotional support but also be a source of information (Yeager, 2012). Hence, technology can serve many functions: It can help people feel safe, provide information about unhealthy/abusive relationships, and provide access to assistance and support.

17.2c Feminist Theory of Rape

The feminist theory of rape emphasizes the unequal distribution of power between men and women in society. Proponents of this theory believe that because men dominate women in the personal, political, economic, and cultural sphere, rape is an extension of the dominance, power, and control men exert over women. Hence, rape is viewed as an act of power and dominance that employs sex as a method, not simply an act of sex.

Support for the view that rape is essentially a male behavior associated with social inequality between the sexes is provided by a culture-based analysis. Data indicate that the prevalence of rape in different societies varies according to the degree of inequality between women and men. In one study of 95 societies (Sanday, 1981), rape was either absent or rare in almost half (47%) of the cases. In these cultures (the Ashanti of West Africa, for example), women tend to have equal status with men. "In 'rape-free' societies, women are treated with considerable respect, and prestige is attached to female reproductive and productive roles" (Sanday, 1981, p. 16).

Feminist scholarship and activism have ... led to a paradigmatic shift away from the notion of women as temptress of innocent men and toward the insistence on male responsibility for his actions in the perpetration of violence against women.

Patricia Rozee and Mary Koss, research professors

17.2d Social Learning Theory of Rape

The social learning theory of rape views it as "behavior that males learn through the acquisition of social attitudes favorable to rape, and through the imitation of depictions of sexuality interlinked with aggression" (Ellis, 1989, p. 16). Men learn aggressive behavior toward women, including rape behavior, through the following four interrelated processes (also see *Self-Assessment 17-2*):

- *The sex-violence linkage effect:* This process refers to the association of sexuality and violence. For example, many slasher and horror films, television shows, the most popular pornography, and music videos depict sex and violence together, thus causing the viewer to form a link or association between sex and violence.

- *The modeling effect:* This process involves imitating rape scenes and other acts of violence toward women that are seen in real life and in the mass media. Some data also reveal that childhood maltreatment is associated with being sexually coercive as an adult (Forsman et al., 2015).

- *The desensitization effect:* This process involves becoming desensitized to the pain, fear, and humiliation of sexual aggression through repeated exposure to sexual aggression. Since it is common to see men sexually aggressing against women in mass media, men slowly adapt to believing that such sexually aggressive behavior is normative.

- *The rape myth effect:* In this process, men learn to view women as "really wanting it" and to deny that their force constitutes rape (Ellis, 1989).

If you want to be safe, walk in the middle of the street. I'm not joking. In the States, someone is killed in a car accident on average every 12.5 minutes, while someone is raped on average every 2.5 minutes.

Emilie Autumn, American author, *The Asylum for Wayward Victorian Girls*

Self-Assessment 17-2: Rape Supportive Attitude Scale

Directions

Indicate whether you strongly disagree (1), disagree (2), are undecided or have no opinion (3), agree (4), or strongly agree (5). The scale takes about 10 minutes to complete.

1. __ Being roughed up is sexually stimulating to many women.

2. __ A man has some justification in forcing a female to have sex with him when she led him to believe she would go to bed with him.

3. __ The degree of a woman's resistance should be the major factor in determining if a rape has occurred.

4. __ The reason most rapists commit rape is for sex.

5. __ If a girl engages in necking or petting and she lets things get out of hand, it is her fault if her partner forces sex on her.

6. __ Many women falsely report that they have been raped because they are pregnant and want to protect their reputation.

7. __ A man has some justification in forcing a woman to have sex with him if she allowed herself to be picked up.

8. __ Sometimes the only way a man can get a cold woman turned on is to use force.

9. __ A charge of rape 2 days after the act has occurred is probably not rape.

10. __ A raped woman is a less desirable woman.

11. __ A man is somewhat justified in forcing a woman to have sex with him if he has had sex with her in the past.

12. __ In order to protect the male, it should be difficult to prove that a rape has occurred.

13. __ Many times a woman will pretend she doesn't want to have intercourse because she doesn't want to seem loose, but she's really hoping the man will force her.

14. __ A woman who is stuck-up and thinks she is too good to talk to guys deserves to be taught a lesson.

15. __ One reason that women falsely report rape is that they frequently have a need to call attention to themselves.

16. __ In a majority of rapes the victim is promiscuous or had a bad reputation.

17. __ Many women have an unconscious wish to be raped and may then unconsciously set up a situation in which they are likely to be attacked.

18. __ Rape is the expression of an uncontrollable desire for sex.

19. __ A man is somewhat justified in forcing a woman to have sex with him if they have dated for a long time.

20. __ Rape of a woman by a man she knows can be defined as a "woman who changed her mind afterward."

Scoring and Interpretation

All of the items are scored in the same direction. To determine your score for the scale, add the responses (coded 1–5) to the 20 items (possible range 20–100). The higher the score, the more rape supportive or victim-callous attitudes are supported. This scale measures seven beliefs that have been found to promote rape and also interfere with the recovery of rape survivors:

> (a) women enjoy sexual violence, (b) women are responsible for rape prevention, (c) sex rather than power is the primary motivation for rape, (d) rape happens only to certain kinds of women, (e) a woman is less desirable after she has been raped, (f) women falsely report many rape claims, and (g) rape is justified in some situations. (Lottes, 1998, p. 504).

The Rape Supportive Attitude Scale was administered to college students, mostly single and in the 19- to 22-year-old age range, at schools in the northeastern United States (Lottes, 1991). Men scored significantly higher on the scale than women.

The Rape Supportive Attitude Scale was one measure used in a university study in the United Kingdom that investigated sexually aggressive attitudes and behaviors among 298 male students who participated in contact sports and noncontact sports, as well as nonathletes (Smith & Stewart, 2003). This study's findings were consistent with prior research that men who held rape-supportive beliefs and were hostile to women were more likely than other men to have committed rape. However, the study did not find that being an athlete was correlated with being sexually aggressive toward women; rather, the characteristics of being very win-oriented and strongly desiring to dominate one's opponent were found to be correlated with those who committed rape.

Reliability and Validity

The Cronbach alpha value for both samples of students was 0.91, showing high internal reliability (Lottes, 1991). A single dominant factor emerged from a principal components analysis of the data, which accounted for 37% of the variance. Men's scores on the Rape Supportive Attitude Scale were correlated with scores on the Hypermasculinity Inventory. For men and women, scores on the Rape Supportive Attitude Scale were significantly correlated with measures of non-egalitarian gender role beliefs, traditional attitudes toward female sexuality, adversarial sexual beliefs, arousal to sexual violence, and non-acceptance of homosexuality.

Source: From Lottes, I. L. (2009). Rape Supportive Attitudes Scale. In C. M. Davis, W. L. Yarber, R. Bauserman, G. Schreer, & S. L. Davis (Eds.), *Handbook of sexuality-related measures* (p. 516). Copyright Taylor & Francis, LTD. Republished with permission of Taylor & Francis, LTD; permission conveyed through Copyright Clearance Center, Inc.

17.2e Rape Culture

As in the Koss study cited earlier, in which men admitted to raping women when questions used euphemistic terminology instead of the word rape, Edwards et al.'s (2014) study of college males revealed similar findings. In the study, more than 1 in 3 college men admitted "intentions to force women to have sexual intercourse," while denying that this act constitutes rape. These studies reveal a disturbing and pervasive social dynamic identified as rape culture.

Rape culture establishes and normalizes male entitlement to women's bodies as products to be consumed ("getting a piece") and holds women responsible as the cause of their victimization ("she asked for it," "she shouldn't have had that second drink," etc.). In US society, rape culture is sustained by the advertising industry, in which women and girls are portrayed primarily as objects for display and sexual use by men.

As the underlying framework of rape culture, violence against women is not only a societal norm; it is also viewed as sexually exciting in itself. The connection between sex and violence is woven throughout the social fabric of Western culture, evident in the prevalence of rape itself—with nearly a quarter of women reporting it and up to 95% of rapes going unreported (Horvath & Brown, 2010). In addition, the sex-and-violence conflation is apparent in the nearly universal rates of street and workplace harassment of women, high rates of intimate partner violence, high risk of physical abuse faced by sex workers, and the extreme violence against and degradation of women in what is now mainstream, widely consumed pornography.

These misogynistic attitudes and behaviors are ubiquitous throughout the world, created and sustained in patriarchal societies with rigid gender roles in which women have diminished status.

I'm critical of your client sticking his hand under my skirt and grabbing my ass.

Taylor Swift, pop star, responding to a question about whether she was critical of her bodyguard in her testimony against Colorado DJ David Mueller, whom she said groped her bare backside at a meet-and-greet in 2013. Mueller was found guilty of assault and battery and paid a symbolic $1 to Swift.

Rape culture
The widespread social framework in highly gendered patriarchal cultures characterized by male entitlement and objectification of women, in which violence is normalized and viewed as sexually exciting and women are blamed for being victimized

17.2f Sexual Assault and Harassment in the Military

In 2018, there were 20,500 reports of unwanted sexual contact by military personnel, a 38% increase from 2016 (Vanden Brook, 2019b).

Most assaults in the military are not reported because the victims fear they will lose their jobs, not be taken seriously, or be derogated. Even when a complaint is filed, the "good ol' boy" system has ensured that most victims are ignored or denigrated. Indeed, 62% of those service members who filed a claim experienced retaliation, including administrative punishments such as being forced to leave the service, as well as social harassment or ostracizing (Department of Defense, 2015). The 2012 documentary *The Invisible War* details sexual assault in the military, featuring interviews with women who were raped and felt that their complaints were ignored and their careers ruined.

> *It is essentially the woman who is on trial, and the trial can be worse than the rape.*
>
> Colonel Elspeth Ritchie, retired U.S. Army psychiatrist

Congressional hearings on sexual harassment and rape in the military continue to be held on Capitol Hill, but actual changes are minimal. Per the Rand Corporation's 2014 Military Workplace study, 22% of women on active military duty reported sexual harassment, with 85% of it perpetrated by a fellow member of the military; 52% of those women experienced professional or social retaliation for reporting.

Clearly, the military remains an environment where men dominate, may prey on women, and use the system to escape punishment and enact secondary victimization. An undergraduate in the first author's class who visited an Army base to "party" reflected on her experience of being raped:

> *The military base on which the rape occurred was not helpful. They did not tell me the process of what to do, and of course I had no idea; I had never been to a courtroom before. One day I got a phone call stating that I had a court date. I was not given a lawyer, just somebody that would represent the state. With my anxiety worse than ever before, I found myself crying on the stand trying to tell the judge everything that happened on that night of "the incident." I ended up losing the case, mostly because the guy who put me in this situation said that he thought it was consensual. That was all he had to say to make me lose the court case. I probably heard from the military base one time after that to see how I was doing, but it was just a routine call; they really didn't care.* (name withheld by request)

Harris et al. (2018) emphasized that sexual harassment/assault continues in the U.S. military due to the tolerance of sexism and that reduction must address/remove this ideology. Indeed, the Pentagon delayed the release of new research figures on sexual assault out of fear that the data would harm recruiting. The new data showed a 10% increase in reports (to almost 7,000) of sexual assaults at over 200 military installations from 2016 to 2017 (Vanden Brook, 2018). Data on military academies showed a 50% increase from 2017 to 2018 (Vanden Brook, 2019a): 16% of women and 2% of men reported having been sexually assaulted.

International DATA

About 11% of rapes in England are reported to the police (Lundrigan & Mueller-Johnson, 2013).

17.3 Consequences of Rape and Treatment for Rape Survivors

17.3a Reporting a Rape and Title IX

Academic institutions have been slow to take sexual assault complaints seriously. Based on a survey of 440 four-year institutions of higher education, many universities and colleges show a lack of knowledge of the scope of the sexual assault problem, a failure to encourage reporting, a lack of adequate sexual assault training, a lack of adequate services for survivors, and a lack of trained and coordinated law enforcement; they also reported that sexual assault often goes uninvestigated (McCaskill, 2014). In a random sample of the student body of a large Southern university, exactly half of the female respondents believed that complaints are taken seriously, while a third believed that sexual assault perpetrators get away with it (O'Neill et al., 2015a).

In what has become an international scandal, many cities in the United States have delayed prosecution for rape or abandoned it altogether, with thousands of rape kits containing evidence collected from women who were raped languishing unprocessed in labs due to deprioritization by the criminal justice system (Reilly, 2015).

Title IX of the Educational Amendment of 1972 is designed to prevent sex-based discrimination in any institution, program, or activity receiving federal funding. The law empowers students to combat campus violence/rape, requiring federally funded colleges and universities to take every complaint of violence, rape, or sexual assault seriously by filing a federal complaint or a civil lawsuit. Schools that do not comply are fined $150,000 per violation and up to 1% of their operating budget for failure to investigate reports of sexual assault on campus. However, Betsy De Vos, education secretary under the Trump administration, relaxed the aggressiveness with which campuses are to pursue sexual assault cases and changed the standard of guilt from "preponderance of the evidence" to the "clear and convincing" standard. The former means that it's more likely than not that sexual harassment or violence occurred while the latter requires campus investigators to determine the accusations are highly probable or reasonably certain. The result is greater power to the perpetrator with fewer women victims coming forward.

Some university faculty members are mandated to report a sexual assault to the Title IX coordinator, even if the student does not want the assault reported (Ward & Chang, 2015). Those faculty who are mandated to report are regarded as responsible employees—they are the supervisor of a university employee or are responsible for supervising clinical education experiences, practicums, and/or internships. Even the typical faculty member conducting a class who hears a student talking about having been raped may be required to report the event. However, to remove ambiguity and prevent a student's rape from being reported if the student does not want this, the faculty member may alert the students, "If you make me aware of a rape or sexual assault, I may need to report this, even without your permission."

Unfortunately, individuals who seek help from legal and medical personnel often experience **secondary victimization**, in which they are blamed for the rape ("You didn't lead him on, did you?" "You weren't dressed provocatively, were you?" "How much did you have to drink?").

When a person discloses a rape, it is often to a close friend. In a survey of 2,000 female college students, 40% reported that a friend had told them about a rape, but the police were usually not contacted. Reasons for not reporting to the police

Secondary victimization
The process of organizations or individuals blaming the person who reports a rape

No person in the United States shall, on the basis of sex, be excluded from participation in, be denied the benefits of, or be subjected to discrimination under any education program or activity receiving Federal financial assistance.

Title IX

include not wanting others to know, not acknowledging the rape due to victim blaming by others and self (for being drunk or "leading him on"), and fear of secondary victimization by friends or family as well as law enforcement (Cohn et al., 2013).

17.3b Consequences of Rape

Reactions to being raped are variable. Canan and Jozkowski (2019) revealed the aftermath of 933 women's sexual assault experiences, including their self-reflections (e.g., self-absolution versus self-blame), reactions of perpetrators (e.g., apologized versus acted like nothing had happened), reactions of parents (e.g., "said I was lying"), and personal outcome (e.g., "got pregnant and gave up baby for adoption"). In most cases, an individual who has been raped has been traumatized. Initial reactions to rape include an acute period of disorganization, helplessness, vulnerability, anger, guilt, dread, fear, anxiety, and shame (Budge et al., 2015). The person may also blame themselves for the incident. The most devastating aspect of rape is not only the genital contact but also the sense of cognitive and emotional violation. The person who felt that their environment was safe and predictable, that other people were trustworthy, and that they were competent and autonomous may become someone who is fearful of their surroundings, suspicious of other people, and unsure of their ability to control their life.

DiMauro et al. (2018) reported outcomes on sexual assault of 225 females to include significantly lower sexual satisfaction, greater post-traumatic stress disorder (PTSD)/ depressive symptoms, and higher suicidal ideation. Pandey et al. (2018) noted that military women who experienced sexual trauma were also more likely to report PTSD as well as weight gain. Sexual victimization has also been associated with increased alcohol use to cope with the sexual distress rather than to enhance the sexual experience (Bird et al., 2019). However, a qualitative study on 45 survivors of sexual assault revealed that while some lost interest in sex and became celibate, others increased their number of sexual partners ("What did it matter once I had been raped" or "I was looking for love") (O'Callaghan et al. 2019).

Victims often display **rape trauma syndrome**, or the acute and long-term reorganization process that occurs as a result of forcible rape or attempted rape (Burgess & Holstrom, 1974). The acute phase involves fear, anxiety, crying, and restlessness. Long-term reorganization may involve moving to another community and changing phone numbers. Nightmares, sexual dysfunctions, and phobias associated with the rape may also occur. Examples of the latter include fear of being alone, of being in the dark, or of touching someone's penis.

Other descriptions for rape aftereffects are acute stress disorder and **post-traumatic stress disorder** (PTSD), both of which include a particular set of reactions to traumatic events such as military combat, natural disasters, or other events that invoke terror, helplessness, and fear of loss of life. Another aftereffect of rape is the abuse of alcohol, which may be used to cope with the psychological and emotional consequences of victimization. Alcohol use is also associated with repeat victimization—the person gets drunk and is vulnerable to being raped again (Yeater et al., 2015).

In addition to the psychological and interpersonal consequences, rape victims also face the physical consequence of STI and HIV infection. A review of 21 studies on coerced/forced sexual initiation and sexual intimate partner violence (sexual IPV) revealed a significant contribution to a woman's risk for STI and HIV infection.

Rape trauma syndrome
Acute and long-term reorganization process that occurs as a result of forcible or attempted rape

Post-traumatic stress disorder
Mental health diagnostic category that characterizes a particular set of symptoms following traumatic events (including military combat, natural disasters, or other events that invoke terror, helplessness, and fear of loss of life); experienced by many rape victims

Cultural Diversity

Honor Killing

The ultimate example of secondary victimization occurs when a woman is murdered via an **honor killing**. Unmarried women in countries such as Pakistan, India, Morocco, Jordan, Egypt, and Lebanon who have intercourse before or outside of marriage (even if through rape) are viewed as bringing shame on their parents and siblings and may be killed; this action is referred to as an honor crime or honor killing. Over 1,000 annually are killed in Pakistan alone (5,000 worldwide). The legal consequence is typically minimal to nonexistent. For example, a brother may kill his sister if she has intercourse with a man she is not married to and spend no more than a month or two in jail as the penalty (his parents forgive the killing so prosecution is limited). New laws are being passed to address this, such as in Pakistan, which carries a minimum penalty of 25 years in jail for an honor killing. But a loophole is that the death must be officially ruled as an honor crime to warrant this sentence.

17.3c Treatment for Rape Survivors

Crisis counseling may last from a few days to several months after the assault. The primary goals of crisis counseling include establishing a therapeutic relationship, encouraging emotional expression, and providing information about reporting rape to the police. The therapist may also promote adjustment of immediate role responsibilities, which may take the form of encouraging the person to take time off from work or eliciting the support of others to provide a period for processing the rape experience.

Exposure techniques may involve survivors retelling the traumatic event or writing a narrative to be used in treatment to reduce rape-related fears. Jaycee Dugard (kidnapped at age 11, raped for 18 years) wrote *A Stolen Life* (2011) as part of her therapy.

17.4 Prevention of Rape

In the face of the pervasive social influence of violent masculinity and an advertising industry sexualizing women and girls for profit, ending rape culture is a major cultural challenge. First, identification is essential. Instead of asking, "What was she wearing?" we need to ask, "How could 1 in 3 college men be would-be rapists?" Myers (2019) found that policies used by fraternities to curb sexual assaults at parties are beginning and included sober brothers responsible for identifying/monitoring "sketchy" male attendees. Sororities reported having rules about everyone leaving the party together, a ban on entering a private room/leaving common areas, and designating sober members for each party.

Comprehensive rape prevention includes addressing issues in all people, regardless of gender. While women's awareness and actions for self-protection must be enhanced until we can put an end to rape culture, above all else, the culture of masculinity as defined by the capacity for violence must be identified, with men taking the responsibility for redefining it. Elementary schools should include education in self-respect and speaking out. They should also teach respect for women and nonviolence for boys. In the home, fathers and mothers can make an effort to model and teach egalitarian and respectful interactions for their children. In higher education, colleges can expand Title IX programs and actively investigate and prosecute cases of sexual harassment, sexual assault, and rape. In the workplace, mandatory workshops in nonsexist behavior

Honor killing
Killing of a woman in certain cultures who is raped or who has intercourse before or outside of marriage, which brings great shame to her parents/family; the killing absolves the family of the shame

and identifying sexual harassment can help make the workplace more secure for everyone. Programs on sexual assault might also be provided. However, Moser and Ballard (2017) found that attendance at sexual assault educational programs was unrelated to lower beliefs in rape myths.

17.4a Teaching Women to Avoid Rape

Women must acknowledge that rape is a real possibility, particularly acquaintance rape, and that until we live in a world that isn't dominated by rape culture, they must monitor their alcohol/drug consumption to keep their wits about them. They must also identify the signs of an impending rape. The male who sexualizes the conversation, who encourages the woman to drink, who is all hands, who seeks to isolate her from her friends, and who does not take no for an answer—all should be identified as dangerous, and the woman should extricate herself or escape from such a person as quickly as possible. Exercising sexual agency—making a decision and being assertive early in the chain of events—is important (Bay-Cheng, 2019). Sell et al. (2018) identified various protective behavioral strategies that may reduce rape when used in combination. These include deciding to limit one's use of alcohol ahead of time, letting others know one's whereabouts, and avoiding mixing alcohol types. Others include going to and returning from a party with trusted friends, staying with your friends at the party (not leaving alone), watching your drink being made, and never leaving it unattended (Monroe, 2019).

17.4b Teaching Men Not to Rape

Men must take full responsibility for sexual violence and abuse (Salazar & Ohman, 2015). Teaching men not to rape involves alerting them that US society provides the context for them to be socialized to dominate women and to believe in rape myths such as "no means yes." Correction of the tendency to believe in rape myths must begin early (Reyes & Foshee, 2013). Rejecting sexual myths and respecting the dignity and privacy of women must be followed by not sexualizing conversations, not getting her drunk, and not isolating her for sex. Men must also remember that a woman being in an altered state (alcohol/drugs) and passive does not imply consent to have sex. Having sex with a woman who is cognitively altered is against the law in some states.

Bystander behavior (intervening when a woman is observed getting drunk and her date is moving her toward sex) may reduce the number of rapes. In a random university sample, 80% of both men and women reported that it is their responsibility to intervene if they witness an assault and/or questionable behavior. Both males and females believe they would be more likely to intervene if they knew the victim and, somewhat less so, the aggressor (O'Neill et al., 2015a). In a study of 126 female and 83 male college students, 38% of the women and 27% of the men reported observing a sexually coercive situation (usually a man coercing a woman). The most common reason for hesitating was fear of the coercer (Kutchko & Muehlenhard, 2015).

Bystander programs to teach individuals to intervene when they see sexual coercion are particularly effective when led by peer educators rather than by professionals (Hines & Palm Reed, 2015). Focus must be on attacking rape culture myths, because bystanders are less likely to act when they believe the victims have done something that makes them culpable in the act being perpetrated against them (O'Neill et al., 2015b).

But depending on bystander support is not enough to dismantle rape culture. Early education can also play a vital role in teaching respect for girls as independent beings with their own values and rights. The commercial sexualization of young girls and the culture of toxic masculinity for boys must move beyond the unhealthy polarization of these limited gender roles toward a more egalitarian mindset, and men must re-evaluate their own sense of privilege and entitlement to women's bodies.

Stronger legislation, education, and adequate funding can help the criminal justice system to become a vital defense against, rather than a bulwark of, rape culture. Workplace equality laws, along with education on and protection against rape and sexual harassment, must not only be instituted but also actively enforced. In addition, political figures and celebrities can call out the commercial conflation of sex and violence in mainstream media and pornography as a toxic influence on and enforcement of rape culture. At the 2016 Academy Awards ceremony, former Vice President Joe Biden made a plea to "change the culture" and "take the pledge" to intervene as indicated and necessary. Other prominent figures, from Michelle and Barack Obama to singers Beyoncé and John Legend and actors Ryan Gosling and Will Smith, are taking the lead in speaking out for a safer, healthier culture based on gender equality and respect for women. Online resources against rape culture, including many men's groups, are also increasingly available.

At the college level, Spencer et al. (2015) emphasized the importance of changing the entire cultural college community context/norms to reduce sexual assaults. Finally, men must ensure that their sexual partners are not just passively going along with sex, but are adamant that they want sex to happen. California passed a law in 2014 that requires "an affirmative, unambiguous and conscious decision" by each party to engage in sexual activity. "Yes means yes" has been the law of the land in Canada since 1992 and should be enforced in the United States as well.

17.4c Campaigns to Address Rape

The culture has exploded with media attention to the rape of women, especially on campus. Playwright Eve Ensler wrote and produced *The Vagina Monologues*, a play performed on campuses and in theaters across the country, leading to an HBO® presentation that launched V-Day (Violence Against Women Day), a global nonprofit movement that offers presentations and raises money for groups working to end violence against women. And as noted earlier, the documentary *The Hunting Ground* has heightened awareness of college campuses as a context for rape by exposing the reality of the danger women experience on campus.

Take Back the Night has the goal of ending sexual violence in all forms. The organization is international (30 countries) and involves marches, rallies, and vigils (often on university campuses) intended as a protest and direct action against rape. Presentations usually follow a march and a gathering at night with candles/lights to "take back the night."

RAINN (Rape, Abuse, and Incest National Network) operates the National Sexual Assault Hotline (1-800-656-HOPE) in conjunction with 1,100 rape crisis centers across the nation. In addition, RAINN operates the National Sexual Assault Online Hotline, which provides online help.

Male Athletes Against Violence, Men Can Stop Rape, Men Stopping Violence, and White Ribbon Campaign are all designed to increase the awareness of men to take more responsibility for reducing the level of violence against women and ending rape culture. These groups offer programs that can help men advocate for a culture of greater safety and equity for women and girls, as well as a healthier sexuality for both men and women. More resources for men, some focusing on athletes, fathers, and students, can be found at http://menstoppingviolence.org

Social Policy 17-1

The #MeToo Movement—Have We Gone Too Far?

The #MeToo Movement took off in 2017 when the actress Alyssa Milano wrote on Twitter that "women who have been sexually harassed or assaulted" write "Me too" in the wake of American film producer Harvey Weinstein's exposure. Soon, women and men came forward in America and 85 other countries (Gill & Orgad, 2018). While awareness of harassment, assaults, and exploitation is imperative, has the movement gone too far (Knox & Hilliard, 2019)?

Culture of Fear

Reaction to the #MeToo Movement has been the development of a culture of fear whereby male mentors fear that women will charge them with sexual harassment/assault and ruin their careers (Soklaridis et al., 2018). The fear surrounding the #MeToo Movement is data based. Bennhold (2019) noted that over 200 prominent men have lost their jobs and most have been replaced by women. "Basically, the #MeToo Movement has become a risk-management issue for men," said Laura Liswood, secretary general of the Council of Women World Leaders, an organization for former and current female political leaders.

The costs are real. Not only will few women find mentors to guide them (to high status powerful positions themselves), the mentors will miss the opportunity to learn from the mentees—about work/life balance, diversity, and the issues that women are sensitive to (Agarwal, 2019). In addition, mentors will miss the opportunity to nurture bright, insightful women who will make enormous contributions to their profession and society.

Unintended Consequences in Corporations

Sandberg and Pritchard (2019) revealed research on corporate America such that 60% of managers who are men report that they are uncomfortable participating in common job-related activities with women, such as mentoring, working alone together, or socializing together. In 2018, that number was 46%. Senior men are more hesitant to work with junior women than junior men across a range of activities. For example, in regard to one-on-one meetings, senior men are 12 times more hesitant to meet with a woman than a man. Business travel: nine times more likely to hesitate. Work dinners: six times more likely. Mentoring a woman: 16% of male managers in the US say they are hesitant to do so.

Unintended Consequences in Medicine

In addition to corporate America, the #MeToo Movement has had an impact on the training of medical students. With females being half of all incoming medical students, the need for mentors for females is outstripping demand. Daar et al. (2019) noted that only 10% of full professor surgeons are women, yet 30% of resident surgeons are female. The numbers belie the possibility that there are enough women to serve as mentors for other women. Male mentors must get in and stay in the game:

> Male surgeons must consciously pursue intentional mentorship relationships, which by definition encompass 2 major functions: (1) career-related support through "sponsorship, exposure and visibility, coaching, and protection," and (2) psychosocial support, which enhances the mentee's "competence, identity, and effectiveness," in the professional setting.

Changes Needed

The #MeToo Movement should be acknowledged as having value, but a warning should sound that it can have unintended negative consequences if allowed to go unquestioned in terms of unwarranted stigmatization, which is occurring and being perpetuated. In the context of this perspective, five changes are suggested:

1) Institutional change. Corporations must value all talent and set norms that mentoring is valuable. This includes being specific about men mentoring women. Sheryl Sandberg of Facebook stated, "Let's make sure we're not telling men not to be alone with women" (McGregor, 2019).

2) Individual/mentor change. Mentors must reject the cultural stigmatization and focus on the goal—nurturing talent, which includes women. This involves not being driven by fear but by what is right—to be a guide to whomever is interested in learning the details of one's profession. When men are asked why they are withdrawing from mentoring or socializing with a woman, 36% say they were nervous about how it would look. Men should stop being nervous and focus on their role of mentoring.

3) Change contexts. If one-on-one interaction is uncomfortable, change to group meetings. If being alone in one's office is disconcerting, open the door or go to a coffee shop.

4) Use informal information. Salem (2019) noted that some companies provide informal networks to women about who the creepy mentors are so women can avoid them.

5) Listen to and acknowledge the legitimate claims of women who have been harassed/assaulted/exploited by men in power positions.

17.5 Child Sexual Abuse

Child sexual abuse may be both physical and emotional. Physical sexual abuse includes sexual intercourse or penetration, genital or anal fondling or touching, oral sex, kissing, and/or forced performing of fellatio and cunnilingus of a minor by an adult or to an adult. Emotional sexual abuse of a child can include behaviors such as forcing a minor to watch sexual acts, encouraging the child to undress in front of others, and/or making lewd comments about a minor. In either case, the child experiences a breakdown of trust, destruction of boundaries, and a sense of violation.

Researchers have noted that 1 in 4 women in the general population report having been sexually abused as a child. When women in therapy are considered, the number rises to 7 in 10 females reporting childhood sexual encounters (Blumer et al., 2013). Child sexual abuse can be limited to one incident, or it can last for years. Comedian Margaret Cho revealed that she was molested by a family friend for more than 7 years, beginning when she was 5 (Couch, 2015).

We showed no care for the little ones; we abandoned them.

Pope Francis

National & International DATA

The global prevalence of child sexual abuse is 26% (Jeong & Cha, 2019). In a study of 1,928 Canadian children ages 4–14 years, 22% of the females and 8% of the males reported having been sexually abused (MacMillan et al., 2013). There are 800,000 registered sex offenders, and 2,350 therapists in the United States who provide court-mandated treatment (Dockterman, 2018).

Factors associated with child sexual abuse include poverty, growing up in an urban area, parental adversity, and child physical abuse. Siblings of sexually abused children are also at increased risk for sexual abuse themselves (MacMillan et al., 2013). Victims of child sex abuse may be any gender, and any orientation. In a study of 183 gay and bisexual men, 51% reported child sexual abuse (Hequembourg et al., 2015).

17.5a Intrafamilial Child Sexual Abuse

Perpetrators of child sexual abuse are often categorized based on whether they are members of the child's family (intrafamilial child sex abuse) or external to the family (extrafamilial child sex abuse).

Also known as incestuous child abuse, **intrafamilial child sexual abuse** refers to exploitative sexual contact or attempted or forced sex that occurs between relatives when the victim is under the age of 18. In this instance, relatives include biologically related individuals, stepparents, and stepsiblings, who make up about 34% of all perpetrators (RAINN, n.d.). Child sexual abuse occurs in any family regardless of income, race, ethnicity, religion, education, occupation, political affiliation, and social class.

Before I worked in sex crimes, I would see kids getting off the school bus and imagine those kids running into the house being greeted by a hug and anxious to talk about their day. After sex crimes, I worried that every single one of those kids dreaded going in that house because they knew they were going to be molested by someone in their house before mom got home from work.

Prosecutor in Sex Crimes Unit

Fathers as Perpetrators

Father-daughter incest is the type of incest that has received the most attention in society. Such incest is a blatant abuse of power and authority. Compared to women who had not experienced child sexual abuse, adult women who experienced father-daughter incest were more likely to endorse feeling like damaged goods, to think that they had suffered psychological injury, and to have undergone psychological treatment for child sexual abuse (Stroebel et al., 2013).

Factors contributing to father-daughter incest include extreme paternal dominance (the daughter learns to be obedient to her father), maternal disability (the mother ceases to function as an emotional and sexual partner for the husband), and imposition of the mothering role on the oldest daughter (she becomes responsible for housework and child care). An added consequence of the oldest daughter taking over the role of the mother is her belief that she is responsible for keeping the family together. This implies not only doing what the father wants but also keeping it a secret because she or her father will be expelled from the family for disclosure.

Although some fathers may force themselves on their daughters, incest may begin with affectionate cuddling between father and daughter. The father's motives may be sexual; his daughter's are typically nonsexual. Indeed, the daughter is generally unaware of any sexual connotations of her behavior; her motive is to feel acceptance and love from her father.

Intrafamilial child sexual abuse
Exploitative sexual contact or attempted or forced sex that occurs between related individuals when the victim is under the age 18 (also known as *incestuous child abuse*)

PERSONAL EXPERIENCE 17-2

"Child Sex Abuse by My Father"

(Mary Evelyn Thomas)

I was brought up by my biological dad. I didn't even know I had a mother till I was 8. Everyone thought he was the perfect dad. But behind closed doors I was physically, emotionally, psychologically, verbally, and most of all, sexually abused from age 6 to 13. It started when I was really young with him having me sleep in his bed while he would kiss me, hold me, touch me and had me do things that little girls should not be doing, especially with their father.

Why didn't I say or do something? Lots of reasons:

- I was scared, he was very aggressive and mean, especially when drunk or under the influence of drugs
- I was young and didn't really understand
- He was the only parent I had
- I thought that it was normal until I got a lot older
- I didn't want to be the reason my little sister lost the only parent we had
- I thought that no one would believe me
- I didn't want to push him towards my little sister
- I didn't want anyone to look at me a certain way and feel bad for me

When I was about 14 I couldn't take it any more. I finally made the decision and left with my younger sister to a family that had been kind to me. My mother and the police soon got involved and I told the police what my father had done. He is now in prison.

The negative effects of his sexual abuse on me have been:

- Lots of physical/emotional/psychological instability. Trust issues. Lots of bad dreams
- My dad was not there and won't be there for me and various life events—i.e. proms, graduations, first day of college, to walk me down the aisle, grandkids etc.
- Not being able to say "no" to things I should say no to
- Not being able to build relationships easily; not being able to really love someone
- I missed having a normal childhood
- When my mom died, I had no support from my dad since he was in prison
- Promises and apologies don't mean anything to me because time and time again he would promise me one thing, or apologize for his wrong doings but then turn around and do it over and over
- Really hard for me to explain to a guy I am dating where my dad is and why

The "positives" of my horrific experience are:

- I have learned to forgive, not hold grudges, and to move on
- I have grown up fast and am very independent
- A burden was lifted off me when I finally told the police what I had experienced and I was removed from the situation

I also want others who are or who have been sexually abused as a child to consider deciding to:

- Notify the police
- Talk with a counselor who is trained in how to help rape victims. Counseling can help you learn how to cope with the emotional and physical impacts of the assault. You can find a counselor by contacting a local rape crisis center, a hotline, a counseling service, or RAINN. RAINN is a national victim assistance organization, at 1-800-656-HOPE. RAINN will connect you to a rape crisis center in your area.

Brothers as Perpetrators

Sibling sexual abuse, primarily perpetuated by bothers against their sisters, is more common than parental sexual abuse (Yates, 2018). When compared with controls (those who had experienced no incest), the female victims of brother-sister incest were more likely to endorse feeling like damaged goods, to endorse thinking that they had suffered psychological injury, and to have undergone psychological treatment for child sexual abuse. However, the victims of father-daughter incest were worse off than the victims of brother-sister incest, with consequences including depression, substance abuse, and sexual dysfunction for the former (Stroebel et al., 2013).

Cultural Diversity

Although brother-sister incest taboos are nearly universal across cultures, there are exceptions. Siblings in royal families in ancient Egypt, Hawaii, and the Incas of Peru were permitted to have sex to keep power invested in a small group.

Whether sex between children and adults is considered acceptable varies across societies and historical periods. Bullough (1990) observed that "what appears obvious from a historical overview is that adult/child and adult/adolescent sexual behavior has had different meanings at different historical times" (p. 70). For example, during the 18th and 19th centuries in England, a child of 12 could consent to sexual behavior with a middle-aged adult. Even children under 12 "could be seduced with near impunity in privacy" (p. 74).

Women as Perpetrators

Women also sexually abuse children (McLeod, 2015). Data from the National Child Abuse and Neglect Data System revealed that 20% of 66,765 substantiated child sex abuse cases involved a female perpetrator, though questions about the study's methodology have been raised. Other sources, including the U.S. Department of Justice, estimate the number being about 4% female; the National Center for the Victims of Crime's National Sex Offender Public Website (NSOPW) stated that perpetrators are "overwhelmingly male."

Characteristics of female perpetrators suggest that they are typically drug abusers, intellectually/physically challenged, or mentally ill, with a mean age of 33.4. They are generally the biological or the adoptive parent. The target of the female sex offender is typically a 10-year-old female (Bolen, 2001, p. 193). Some women offend in a group context—they talk their boyfriends into participating or vice versa, or they participate in luring in the child victim (Wijkman et al., 2015). Williams and Bierie (2015) compared female and male sex offenders and found that women more often offended when accompanied by a male accomplice and were more likely to offend against a victim of the same sex. The partner with whom they co-offend is often also a sex offender (Gillespie et al., 2015).

Female sex offenders are also more likely to have a history of being sexually abused as a child, being emotionally neglected as a child, and being reared by parents with problems of their own who were ill equipped to protect them as children (Levenson et al., 2015). Women may also be co-offenders of abuse by failing to protect the child. Indeed, some treatment models for incest require that mothers apologize to their child for not protecting them.

17.5b Extrafamilial Child Sexual Abuse

Another pattern of child sexual abuse is extrafamilial child sexual abuse, non-family members who know the child, such as family friends, babysitters, child-care providers, and neighbors. Strangers make up only 10% of extrafamilial child sexual abusers (National Center for Victims of Crime, n.d.). Technically, **extrafamilial child sexual abuse** is defined as attempted or completed forced sex with a child, before the child reaches the age of 14, by a person who is unrelated to the child by blood or marriage. The nature of the sexual behavior may range from touching breasts and genitals to rape. The sex abuse scandal of the Catholic Church is the most recognized example of extrafamilial child sex abuse, involving over 3,000 priests and an estimated payout cresting $3 billion. The latest unconscionable child sex abuses have been detailed by a Pennsylvania grand jury report of over 300 priests violating over 1,000 children in 54 of 67 counties with pervasive and consistent institutional cover-ups. Due to the statute of limitations on sex abuse crimes, only two have been prosecuted criminally (Courthouse News Service, 2018). Less visible are children with learning disabilities who are also at risk (Franklin & Smeaton, 2018).

17.5c Stages of Grooming

Winters and Jeglic (2017) identified the stages of grooming child sex predators use on their victims. The first stage is selection of the victim, which may be because the child is viewed as pretty, wears particular clothes, or is small. Gaining access is the second stage whereby the predator infiltrates the social world of the child with the goal of isolating the child both physically and emotionally. Becoming a teacher, camp counselor, or bus driver are roles that provide access to children. Trust development is the third phase whereby the parents or teachers are befriended so that the child feels "safe." The final stage is increasing physical contact in the form of hugging, wrestling, or tickling, which establish that touching is normative. Later, the predator will escalate the contact to include sexual contact.

17.5d Recovered Memories of Abuse

In any discussion on child sexual abuse, it is important to comment on the issue of *recovered memories of abuse* (also known as *delayed, recovered,* and *discontinuous memory*). A number of factors may be involved to account for the fact that traumatic memories may be forgotten. They include failure to encode (no memory was created at the time of the event), repression (active prevention of retrieval of memory), and long-term depression (cellular changes that suppress transmission of data from some cells to others) (Roth & Friedman, 1998).

Along with discussions of how memory is affected, there is debate among professionals, as well as the general public, as to whether some sexual molestation charges are the product of a therapist's suggestion or the client's imagination. One can indeed imagine events that never happened, thus creating a false memory. Laboratory research on memory has shown that children can be persuaded to remember a traumatic event that did not actually happen to them, such as being separated from a parent on a shopping trip (Loftus, 1993).

Extrafamilial child sexual abuse
Attempted or completed forced sex, before a child reaches the age of 14, by a person who is unrelated to the child by blood or marriage

In an effort to provide a balanced report on the scientific knowledge base of the reality of repressed memories of childhood trauma, the International Society for Traumatic Stress Studies summarized the research on traumatic memory and its implications for clinical and forensic practice (Roth & Friedman, 1998). They reviewed a number of research studies showing that a significant proportion (20%–60%) of adult women and men with documented cases of child sexual abuse did not seem to recall the abuse when they were interviewed as young adults. The younger the person at the time of the trauma, the more likely they were to have forgotten and to report recovered memories.

Cognitive psychologists and neurobiologists studying human memory processes explain that memory does not perfectly represent an event (like a photograph). Instead, the memory processes prioritize information based on what is thought to be the most important when the event occurred. Memory storage has been compared to a spider web in which specific memories are represented by the pattern of connections among fibers in the entire network. Memory is not a process of locating intact bits of information but rather involves partially recreating a pattern of associated threads of information across an entire network. (Roth & Friedman, 1998, p. 11)

In addition, there may be differences in how traumatic and nontraumatic memories are encoded, consolidated, and retrieved. Ferguson and Malouff (2016) suggested that around 5% of accusations of sexual assault to the police are false.

17.6 Consequences and Treatment of Child Sexual Abuse

In this section, we look at the impact of—and the treatment alternatives for—child sexual abuse.

> *When the clergy sex scandal broke in 2002, some staunch Catholics defended the church, calling the outpouring of abuse stories anti-Catholic.*
>
> Sharon Otterman and Elizabeth Povoledo, *The New York Times*

17.6a Impact of Child Sexual Abuse

Child sexual abuse is associated with numerous negative outcomes: depression, anxiety, PTSD, alcohol/substance abuse, sexual dysfunction, distrust in relationships, difficulties with intimacy, lower self-esteem, and eating disorders (Blumer et al., 2013). These negative outcomes have an impact on the mental health of adolescents and adults of all orientations (Conley & Wright, 2014).

In addition, a team of researchers studied the histories of 60 individuals who had experienced physical/sexual abuse and observed a lower capacity to invest in relationships in an emotionally and mutually engaging manner. This deficit contributed to higher levels of PTSD symptomatology. The individuals also tended to view the world as threatening and painful in regard to interactions with others (Bedi et al., 2013). Sexual health outcomes over time were reported by Fava et al. (2018) who found that children who were sexually abused can be described as resilient and end up having fulfilling lives.

Suicide is also related to child sexual abuse, particularly for males. An analysis of data on 487 men (ages 19–84) who were sexually abused during childhood revealed that five variables—duration of the sexual abuse, use of force during the sexual abuse, high conformity to masculine norms, level of depressive symptoms, and suicidal ideation—increased the odds of a suicide attempt in the past 12 months (Easton et al., 2013).

17.6b Treatment of Sexually Abused Children and Adults Sexually Abused as Children

Incest is viewed as a family problem in terms of assessment and intervention. In the example of stepfather/stepdaughter, counseling begins immediately; the individuals are first seen alone and then as a family. Depending on the case, the perpetrator is incarcerated or denied access/proximity under restraining orders to create a safe space for the victim. The focus of the counseling is to open channels of communication among the family members and to develop or reestablish trust between the parents. Another aspect of the program involves a confrontation between the perpetrator and the victim, in which the perpetrator apologizes and takes full responsibility for the sexual abuse. The ideal outcome of therapy is for the abuser to take complete responsibility for the sex abuse, for the mother (if the perpetrator is the father or stepfather; if not, both parents) to take responsibility for not having been more vigilant, and for the child to feel completely absolved of any guilt for having participated in the sex abuse. Of course, the abuser may be the biological father, aunt, uncle, brother, and so forth.

Researchers emphasize that in working with children who were sexually abused as children, the focus should be on "empowering the survivor to take control over their own life, ... which involves challenging the survivor to redefine many aspects of themselves and their external relationships" (Blumer et al., 2013). For example, the woman who was molested as a child will be encouraged to redefine her sense of guilt, shame, and self-blame. A beginning is to stop using the term *victim,* "which implies a power differential where the client is vulnerable, helpless, and hopeless," and begin to use the term *survivor,* which "inspires hope and helps the client take back the power stolen from them as a child" (Blumer et al., 2013).

Trauma-focused cognitive behavior therapy is the treatment of choice for victims of child sex abuse. This modality emphasizes removing the avoidance the person has had to think or talk about the abuse, facing it as an event in life that was *not* their fault, and using the experience to develop strength, power, and control of their life.

Jeong and Cha (2019) reviewed the qualitative studies on healing from CSA (child sexual abuse) and found several themes—dissociating oneself from the memories of CSA, disclosure as the start of healing, involvement in safe relationships, sharing experiences/connecting with CSA survivors, and accepting CSA as part of one's life history and stepping forward. In effect the CSA survivor recognized their experiences as real but determined they would not be defined by them and move on.

> *You can recognize survivors of abuse by their courage. When silence is so very inviting, they step forward and share their truth so others know they are not alone.*
>
> Jeanne McElvaney, author, *Healing Insights*

Some individuals who have experienced child sexual abuse prefer to avoid mainstream therapy and seek self-help groups. Rham and colleagues (2013) studied 87 women who had been sexually abused and who participated in self-help groups. Results revealed that these women were in poor mental health and more than half were at risk for developing PTSD.

17.7 Prevention of Child Sexual Abuse

Helping to ensure that children live in safe neighborhoods where it is known if neighbors are former convicted child molesters is important for preventing child sexual abuse and is the basis of Megan's Law (see *Social Policy 17-2*).

Social Policy 17-2

Megan's Law

In 1994, Jesse Timmendequas lured 7-year-old Megan Kanka into his house in New Jersey on the pretext of seeing a puppy. He then raped and strangled her and left her body in a nearby park. Timmendequas had two prior convictions for sexually assaulting girls, and Megan's mother, Maureen Kanka, argued that she would have kept her daughter away from her neighbor if she had known about his past sex offenses. She campaigned for a law, known as **Megan's Law**, requiring that communities be notified of a neighbor's previous sex convictions. Every state has enacted similar laws, and President Bill Clinton signed a federal version in 1996.

Megan's Law
Federal law that requires that convicted sex offenders register with local police when they move into a community

While most child sex offenders are members of the child's immediate or extended family, the law requires that convicted sexual offenders register with local police in the communities in which they live. It also requires the police to go out and notify residents and certain institutions (such as schools) that a dangerous sex offender has moved into the area. It is this provision of the law that has been challenged by critics who argue that convicted child molesters who have been in prison have paid for their crime and that to stigmatize them in communities as sex offenders may further alienate them from mainstream society and increase their vulnerability for repeat offenses.

17.8 Treatment of Rape and Child Sexual Abuse Perpetrators

The U.S. Justice Department reported that convicted sex offenders are much more likely to recommit sex offenses than any other type of felon. Sex offenders rarely seek treatment on their own volition prior to any involvement with legal authorities. Most sex offenders in treatment are required to be there by legal authorities, and many therapists in outpatient programs refuse to take voluntary clients. The timing of therapy is important. Unless therapy occurs when the offender is facing a court sentencing or as a condition of probation, the perpetrator usually denies the existence of a problem and has little motivation for treatment. Experienced clinicians typically request a court order before beginning treatment or recommending a period of inpatient treatment.

Therapeutic alternatives used in the treatment of sex offenders include the use of testosterone-lowering medications (TLMs) in conjunction with psychotherapy. However, the lack of controlled clinical trials requires caution in interpreting the results. Wong and Gravel (2018) summarized the research of 20 electronic databases regarding the testosterone differences between sex offenders and non-sex offenders—there were none.

THINK ABOUT IT

Take a moment to answer the following questions. Assume that you have a young child. A convicted child molester has been released from prison and now lives in your neighborhood. What do you feel your rights are as a parent in terms of knowing about the presence of this person? What about this person's right to privacy? (Of course, while we have been discussing the child molester next door, the person most likely to sexually abuse the child lives in the family of the child.)

Other treatments used for sex offenders include group therapy, learning relaxation techniques and stress management, communication skills training, impulse control, increasing arousal to appropriate stimuli, and dealing with the offender's own past sexual or physical abuse. Some treatment programs involve after-care treatment designed to assist the client when he is released from treatment. After-care treatment may include assisting the client in gaining further education or in securing employment. While not a treatment, Spruin et al. (2018) noted that polygraph testing during supervision of sexual offenders may be helpful in aiding offender compliance with supervision agreements.

Unfortunately, researchers conducting a study for the Harvard Medical School concluded that, despite the many modalities described above, there is no effective treatment for pedophilia. Therefore, the focus is on protecting children. With 25% of women reporting molestation as children and estimates that only 1 in 20 child sex abuse cases are reported, all in a culture that normalizes sexualization of young girls and male entitlement to women's and girls' bodies, the prognosis for improvement is grim (Harvard Mental Health Letter, 2010).

17.9 Sexual Harassment

Taylor Swift brought nationwide attention in 2017 to the issue of sexual harassment with her legal vindication in the jury trial over ex-Denver radio DJ David Mueller, who groped her in 2013. During late 2017, there was a nationwide revelation of women who were sexually harassed by celebrities and bosses with a #metoo hashtag (later to be #keeptellingpeople). Like rape or child sexual abuse, **sexual harassment** may be another form of sexual coercion. However, while sexual harassment typically refers to "sexual" harassment, Herbenick et al. (2019) noted that it is much more:

> *sexual harassment is more often gender-based, or "nonsexual." This includes derogating someone on the basis of their gender/sex or violations of their gender/sex norms, as with sexual minorities, nonsexual heterosexual men, or sexually agentic women, etc., and gender-based insults, jokes, and discrimination. Sexual harassment may be physical or verbal, in-person or electronic, isolated or repeated, or occur in groups or one-on-one. In our experience, sexual harassment can also be reflected in colleagues seeing/treating women or feminine people (especially young ones) at conferences as only one of two things: potential sexual partners or irrelevant. (p. 997)*

Sexual harassment
Unwelcome sexual advances, gestures, comments, demands, and other verbal or physical conduct of a sexual nature; unreasonably interferes with work or school performance and creates an intimidating, hostile, or offensive work, educational, or domestic environment

Legally, sexual harassment is a form of sex discrimination that violates Title VII of the Civil Rights Act of 1964 and has been defined as sexual terrorism.

17.9a Definition and Incidence of Sexual Harassment

According to the Equal Employment Opportunity Commission (EEOC), sexual harassment in the workplace is defined as unwelcome sexual advances, requests for sexual favors, and other verbal or physical conduct of a sexual nature that unreasonably interferes with an individual's work performance or creates an intimidating, hostile, or offensive work environment (Equal Employment Opportunity Commission, 2009). A similar definition applies to sexual harassment in educational institutions.

Although definitions vary across studies, there is agreement on two elements: Sexual harassment occurs when sexual behavior is (a) inappropriate for the context and (b) unwanted by a participant or observer. Sexual harassment may involve harassing anyone, although harassers are generally men who target women.

Two other types of sexual harassment have also been identified. **Hostile-environment sexual harassment** refers to deliberate or repeated unwanted sexual comments or behaviors that affect performance at work or school. **Quid pro quo sexual harassment** (*quid pro quo* means "this for that") sets up workplace consequences contingent upon sexual favors, such as requiring sexual favors to obtain a raise or promotion or to prevent being fired or demoted. Some common sexual harassment behaviors include unwanted touching, asking sexual questions, asking to be alone with the person, making sexual comments about dress or appearance, and sexual graffiti such as placing notes or material with sexual content on a target's desk. The victim does not have to be the person harassed; it could be anyone affected by the offensive conduct. For example, someone else in the office may not be the target of direct sexual harassment, but observing this behavior may make them uncomfortable.

Sexual harassment may also occur via sending erotic images that intimidate or upset the target person. The impact of this is often not discussed but can have a significant impact on the victim: Per Henry (2015, p. 104), "Current legal and policy approaches fail to adequately capture the social and psychological harm that results from the use of sexual imagery to harass, coerce or blackmail women."

In one context of sexual harassment, hotel cleaning staff members are targeted. In a study of 46 female room attendants in five-star hotels, 41% reported that they had been sexually harassed—for example, the guest would ask them to sit and talk, have dinner later, or get them a sex worker. Some guests made direct sexual advances. The context is one in which the woman is in a low-status power position compared to the guest. Whether she refuses or complies, she can lose her job. If she is too solicitous, she loses her integrity and risks assault. For these reasons, hotel cleaning staff workers can experience considerable stress in their job (Kensboc et al., 2015).

The form of harassment that women experience most commonly is street harassment: "Hey, baby," obscenities, whistles and sexual gestures, following, threats, and so on (Logan, 2015). More than 81% of women and 43% of men in the United States report being harassed and/or assaulted, with 68% of women and 23% of men reporting that the harassment took place in public—on a street or in a store or restaurant (Stop Street Harassment, 2019).

Sexual harassment of women is pervasive online, as well. The GamerGate incident revealed the misogyny prevalent in the gaming community, which has traditionally been a predominantly male group. In 2014, this insular "boys' club" environment fostered an onslaught of abuse targeting feminist commentator Anita Sarkeesian. She published a video series critiquing sexist tropes in the depictions of female characters in videogames and defending a woman game developer who had been harassed online. Sarkeesian herself was then targeted, receiving hundreds of obscene tweets, threats, and other online hate messages that escalated to viable death threats with photographs

Hostile-environment sexual harassment
Environment whereby deliberate or repeated unwanted sexual comments or behaviors affect one's performance at work or school

Quid pro quo sexual harassment
Type of sexual harassment whereby the individual is provided benefits (promotions, salary raises) in exchange for sexual favors

of an arsenal of automatic weapons. She had to cancel a presentation at a Utah college due to death threats from a gamer who was outraged that she had spoken out about the online gaming community's sexism (Dockterman, 2014).

Other women authors, columnists, and scientists, including Australian author and blogger Clementine Ford and senior research fellow Dr. Emma Jane of the University of New South Wales, also commonly receive hundreds of obscene messages and threats of rape and murder for daring to express their views online (McNally, 2015).

Online, sexual harassment is widespread, not just for commentators but for all women. They must regularly navigate verbal and visual misogyny, not to mention unsolicited "dick pix," on their social media feeds and email. In her poem "Reclaim the Internet," poet Agnes Török and the Dangerous Women's Project challenge and inspire resistance to online sexual harassment.

While ostensibly consensual and thus not defined as sexual harassment per se, voluntary sexual relationships between a supervisor and a subordinate are problematic and exist in a gray zone, as exemplified by President Bill Clinton's self-admitted "inappropriate" relationship with a young female intern in 1995–1996. Considering the disparity in their ages and the status differential between a president and an intern, an abuse of power was clearly in effect.

The most common form of male-on-male harassment targets men who are thought to be homosexual, with a Human Rights Campaign survey finding that GBQT men are as much as 47% more likely to experience sexual violence than men who are heterosexual (Human Rights Campaign, 2020).

17.9b Theories of Sexual Harassment

Five theories have been advanced to explain sexual harassment (Sbraga & O'Donohue, 2000). Some of them are the same theories used to explain other types of sexual coercion. While anyone can harass anyone, regardless of gender, here we discuss the more usual phenomenon of men harassing women.

- The *natural/biological model* implies that sexual harassment is a natural consequence of men's sex drive. The sociobiological model fits here with the assumption that men engage in sexual harassment to increase their probability of gaining sexual access to more women.

- The *sociocultural model* considers the social and political context of male dominance in the society. Male and female workers often act on gender roles and stereotypes at work. Luo (2013) emphasized that sexual harassment is patriarchal oppression of women.

- The *organizational model* considers the power hierarchies, norms, and situations within an organization that may be conducive to sexual harassment. For example, women may be subject to gender-specific demands related to personal appearance, requirements for travel, or working behind closed doors that men do not face.

- The *gender-role spillover model* hypothesizes that workers bring gender-biased behavior expectancies into the workplace, even if these beliefs are not appropriate for work. When the sex-role stereotypes are discrepant from the work demands, conflicts arise. Therefore, women in work roles that do not involve nurturing or being an object of sexual attention are more likely to be harassed.

- The *four-factor model*, offered by O'Hare and O'Donohue (1998), offers a more comprehensive model. It states that for sexual harassment to occur, four factors must be present: (a) motivation to harass, (b) overcoming internal inhibitions that might suppress harassment, (c) overcoming external inhibitions, and (d) overcoming victim resistance. This model takes into consideration the complexity of a combination of factors such as human predispositions, social values and norms, organizational policy, and sex-role beliefs.

(Chelsea Curry Edwards)

Sexual harassment takes place in a context of unequal power where the male often is inappropriately sexually aggressive.

17.9c Profile of Sexually Harassed Victims and Perpetrators

The person most likely to be sexually harassed is the adult woman who is financially insecure. Aside from street harassment, among the professions that reflect the context of men in high-status roles working with women in low-status roles are medicine, military service, office work, and nursing. Indeed, workplace sexual harassment is often directed toward young, unmarried women in traditionally all-male organizations. Sexual harassment of men does occur, but it is less common and less reported because men have greater power in society. Marcum et al. (2017) studied cyberstalkers who logged into the social media sites of former romantic partners to create a negative presence. These individuals were found to have low self-control and deviant peer associations. Due to increased visibility of sexual harassment suits in our society via the exposure of Harvey Weinstein and other celebrities/politicians, awareness of policies to react to such harassment have become more visible. These policies are the topic of *Social Policy 17-3*.

Social Policy 17-3

Sexual Harassment Policy in the Workplace

The Equal Employment Opportunity Commission (EEOC) of the federal government, major companies, and academic institutions have developed sexual harassment policies. Formally, these policies mandate that public organizations, companies, and schools must go on record as being against sexual harassment, discourage employees from engaging in sexually harassing behavior, and provide a mechanism through which harassment victims can inform management. The policies' informal goals are to provide the organization with guidelines for reacting to allegations of harassment and to protect the organization from being taken to court and being forced to pay punitive damages. Organizations and schools also offer educational programs about sexual harassment by developing and distributing brochures and conducting training workshops. Increasingly, policies emphasize the rights of the harassed and the responsibility of the organization to prevent harassment and provide mechanisms for dealing with it when it occurs. In spite of the public policies, 295 million dollars in penalties have been paid in public penalties to settle harassment claims in the last seven years (Bomey & Della Cava, 2017).

Persons who file sexual harassment suits may encounter empathy for their experiences, or they may discover that the full weight of the organization is being used against them. Both the institution and the alleged harasser may be willing and have the resources to launch a full-scale attack on the professional, personal, and sexual life of the complainant—but even large corporations can lose. A sexual harassment lawsuit against Red Lobster® resulted in a $160,000 payment by Red Lobster Restaurants to three workers in Baltimore, Maryland, who were subjected by a chef "to severe and pervasive sexual harassment, including pressing his groin against them, grabbing and groping them" (Equal Employment Opportunity Commission, 2015).

17.9d Consequences of Sexual Harassment

Sexual harassment, like rape, can be devastating for its victims. Direct experiences with harassment can lead to a shattering of victims' core assumptions about the world and themselves, which, in turn, can result in considerable psychological distress. Victims complain of depression, anxiety, anger, fear, guilt, helplessness, sexual dysfunction, isolation from family/friends, and substance abuse. A former student recalled how her boss was giving favors to several of the female workers in the office and paying their rent bills, letting them come in late/leave early, and so on. When she was asked to "have a drink" (translated to "become sexual") and she refused, she reported that her boss "turned her life into a living hell" by complaining about her work, dumping unreasonable amounts of work on her, refusing to let her leave early, and so forth.

17.9e Responses to Sexual Harassment

Victims' most frequent response to sexual harassment is to ignore it. Almost half (46%) of Americans believe that it remains a major problem that women who complain about sexual harassment are not believed (Graf, 2018). Unfortunately, ignoring harassment does not make it go away. Many victims try to avoid the harasser by dropping a class, changing a position, or quitting a job. These indirect strategies are not very effective and do nothing to deter the harasser from violating others. That a new era of openness about sexual harassment had begun was evidenced by *Time* magazine awarding in 2017 its person of the year award to several women who had come forward to reveal their having been sexually harassed. With the Time's Up Movement barreling forward, these revelations are likely to continue, and with threatened exposure to perpetrators, hopefully a decrease in such behavior.

THINK ABOUT IT

Take a moment to consider the following. Addie Zinone is a former *Today Show* staff person who reported that 17 years ago she had a brief consensual sexual relationship with Matt Lauer (former co-anchor of *Today Show*), which she described on the *Today Show* in 2017 as an "abuse of power" (Kelly, 2017). The cultural response to such an accusation is typically to fault Lauer on the "abuse of power" charge. Alternatively, is there any responsibility on the part of women who use their youth/beauty/sexuality (the source of their power) to advance their careers via consensual sex? Sir Ian McKellen says that women tell directors they will sleep with them to win roles. The result of consensual sex for Ms. Zinone was to remain on her career path; for Matt Lauer, who also consented to the sexual relationship, the result was further career demise. The Women's Movement emphasizes equality. The term consensual implies agreement. Are youth/beauty/sexuality as enticements for consensual sex with a man irrelevant when the man is charged with using status in his career to entice a woman for consensual sex?

PERSONAL DECISIONS 17-1

Confronting Someone Who Sexually Harasses You

Aside from ignoring or avoiding a sexual harasser, a victim has at least three choices: verbal, written, or institutional/legal action. The verbal choice consists of telling the harasser what behavior they are engaging in that creates discomfort and then asking the person to stop. Some harassers might respond with denial, such as, "What are you talking about? I was just joking." Others might apologize and stop the behavior. Still others can respond with violence, sometimes lethal; so, if possible, have a witness and carry personal security.

If direct communication is not successful in terminating the harassment in an academic or organizational setting, a written statement of the concerns is the next level of intervention. Such a letter should detail the sexual harassment behaviors (with dates of occurrence) and include a description of the consequences (personal distress, depression, sleep-lessness). The letter should end with a statement of what the victim would like to happen in the future. For example, "I ask that our future interaction be formal and professional."

The letter should be sent immediately after it becomes clear that the offender did not take the verbal requests for change seriously. If the desired behavior is not forthcoming, the letter can be used as evidence of an attempt to alert the offender of the sexual harassment problem. Use of this evidence may be internal (inside the organization) or external (a formal complaint filed with the Equal Employment Opportunity Commission). Information for filing a complaint with the EEOC can be found at https://www.eeoc.gov/

Unfortunately, people who take the direct approach to confront the harasser are at greater risk for experiencing adverse and even dangerous reactions than those who attempt to solve the problem indirectly. Although the direct approach is assertive, harassment victims who speak up often encounter reprisals, counter allegations, forced time off from work, slander, and, in extreme cases, even assault or death. "My boss had a team of lawyers waiting on any female who did not play along," recalled a former student.

Chapter Summary

Sexual Coercion: Rape and Sexual Assault

SEXUAL COERCION INVOLVES using force (actual or threatened) to engage a person in sexual acts against that person's will. One of the difficulties in studying rape and sexual assault is that these terms are variously defined in legal codes and research literature. These different definitions make it difficult to obtain data on the prevalence of rape.

Theories of Rape

THEORIES OF RAPE include evolutionary/biological theory (men are predisposed to rape women to plant their seed and reproduce), psychopathological theory (rapists have a mental disorder), feminist theory (rape is due to unequal status between men and women in society), and social learning theory (men are socialized that it is okay to rape women).

Consequences of Rape and Treatment for Rape Survivors

RAPE IS A TRAUMATIC EXPERIENCE, and the effects of successful treatment develop slowly. Initial reactions to rape include an acute period of disorganization, helplessness, vulnerability, anger, guilt, dread, anxiety, and shame. The victims may also blame themselves for the incident. In some cases, the most devastating aspect of rape may not be the genital contact itself, but rather the aftermath and feelings of cognitive and emotional violation. Even when reported, many rapes are not prosecuted. Post-traumatic stress disorder may follow if the assault invoked terror, helplessness, or fear of loss of life or if the report was not followed by conviction. The rape survivor may also display rape trauma syndrome, which includes symptoms such as fear, crying, and nightmares. Treatment for rape survivors includes crisis counseling, which may last from a few days to several months after the assault. Some may require long-term therapy.

Prevention of Rape

ENDING RAPE CULTURE is a major cultural challenge. Comprehensive rape prevention includes addressing issues in both women and men. While women's awareness and actions for self-protection must be enhanced until we can put an end to rape culture, above all else, the culture of masculinity as defined by the capacity for violence must be identified, with men taking the responsibility for redefining it.

Bystander behavior (intervening when a woman is observed getting drunk and her date is moving her toward sex) may help reduce the number of rapes. An important focus must be attacking rape culture myths, since bystanders are less likely to act when they believe the victim has done something that makes her culpable in the act being perpetrated against her (i.e., she was dressed provocatively and getting drunk).

Many organizations and resources for men seeking to end sexual violence are active online, including RAINN, Men Against Violence, and sites specific to fathers, athletes, and other groups.

Child Sexual Abuse

CHILD SEXUAL ABUSE may be both physical and emotional. Physical child sexual abuse includes sexual intercourse or penetration, genital or anal fondling or touching, oral sex, kissing, and/or forced performing of fellatio and cunnilingus of a minor by an adult or to an adult. Emotional sexual abuse of a child can include behaviors such as forcing a minor to watch sexual acts, encouraging the child to undress in front of others, and/or making lewd comments about a minor. In either case of child sexual abuse, the child experiences a breakdown of trust, destruction of boundaries, and a sense of violation. Perpetrators of child sexual abuse are often categorized based on whether they are members of the child's family (intrafamilial child sex abuse) or external to the family (extrafamilial child sex abuse).

Consequences and Treatment of Child Sexual Abuse

CHILD SEXUAL ABUSE is associated with numerous negative outcomes: depression, anxiety, PTSD, alcohol/substance abuse, sexual dysfunction, distrust in relationships, difficulties with intimacy, lower self-esteem, and eating disorders. Researchers emphasize that in working with children who were sexually abused, the focus should be on empowering the survivors, which includes seeing themselves as survivors instead of victims. Traumatic-focused cognitive behavior therapy is the treatment of choice for victims of child sex abuse. However, some individuals prefer to avoid mainstream therapy and seek self-help groups.

Prevention of Child Sexual Abuse

HELPING TO ENSURE THAT CHILDREN live in safe neighborhoods where it is known if neighbors are former convicted child molesters is important for preventing child sexual abuse. The goal of Megan's Law was to alert parents of a neighbor who had been convicted of being a child molester.

Treatment of Rape and Child Sexual Abuse Perpetrators

SEX OFFENDERS rarely seek treatment on their own prior to any involvement with legal authorities. The timing of therapy is important. Unless therapy occurs when the offender is facing a court sentencing or as a condition of probation, the perpetrator usually denies the existence of a problem and has little motivation for treatment. Therapeutic interventions include techniques to reduce deviant arousal and to increase arousal to appropriate stimuli. Other treatments include group therapy, learning relaxation techniques/stress management, communication skills training, impulse control, and dealing with the offender's own past sexual or physical abuse.

Sexual Harassment

SEXUAL HARASSMENT is defined as unwelcome sexual advances, requests for sexual favors, threats, and other verbal or physical conduct of a sexual nature on the street or when submission to or rejection of this conduct explicitly or implicitly affects an individual's employment. The vast majority of women report having been sexually harassed, although victims of harassment can be of any gender, and any orientation. Direct experiences with sexual harassment can lead to a shattering of victims' core assumptions about the world and themselves, which, in turn, can result in considerable psychological distress.

Web Links

Stop It Now: Campaign to Prevent Child Abuse

http://www.stopitnow.com/

Equal Employment Opportunity Commission:
Red Lobster Sexual Harassment Lawsuit

http://www.eeoc.gov/eeoc/newsroom/release/4-29-15a.cfm

Know Your Title IX

http://knowyourix.org/

National Sexual Assault Telephone Hotline

800.656.HOPE (4673)

Rape, Abuse, and Incest National Network (RAINN)

http://www.rainn.org

National Sex Offender Public Website

http://www.nsopw.gov/

SAFE: Sexual Assault Facts & Education

http://rivervision.com/safe/index.html

Stop Rape Now

http://www.stoprapenow.org

Hollaback!

http://www.ihollaback.org

Men Stopping Violence

http://menstoppingviolence.org

Men Can Stop Rape

http://www.mencanstoprape.org/Resources/us-mens-anti-violence-organizations.html

Reclaim the Internet: Agnes Török and the Dangerous Women's Project.

https://www.youtube.com/watch?v=XeoLRDqsMXs

Key Terms

Acquaintance rape **464**

Classic rape **465**

Date rape **464**

Extrafamilial child
sexual abuse **483**

Forced sex **461**

Forcible rape **459**

GHB (gamma
hydroxybutyrate) **464**

Honor killing **475**

Hostile-environment
sexual harassment **488**

Intrafamilial child
sexual abuse **480**

Marital rape **459**

Megan's Law **486**

Post-traumatic stress disorder **474**

Predatory rape **465**

Quid pro quo
sexual harassment **488**

Rape **461**

Rape culture **471**

Rape myths **463**

Rape-supportive beliefs **463**

Rape trauma syndrome **474**

Rohypnol **464**

Secondary victimization **473**

Sexual coercion **458**

Sexual harassment **487**

Statutory rape **459**

CHAPTER
18
Commercialization of Sex

Software is like sex: it's better when it's free.

Linus Torvalds, software engineer

Chapter Outline

18.1 Sex in Advertising 500

18.2 Sexuality Online 500

18.2a Benefits of Sexuality Online 500

Social Policy 18-1
Government Control of Online
Sexual Content 501

18.2b Disadvantages of
Sexuality Online 504

18.3 Sex and the Law 506

18.4 Sex-Related Businesses 507

18.4a Phone Sex 507

18.4b Camming 507

18.4c Strip Clubs 507

Personal Decisions 18-1
"Camming from
My Apartment" 508

Personal Decisions 18-2
What It's Like to Be a
Stripper—Two Stories 509

18.4d Erotic Massage Parlors 510

18.4e Community Attitudes toward
Adult Businesses 510

18.5 Pornography 511

18.5a Defining Pornography
and Erotica 511

Technology and Sexuality 18-1:
Online Porn, Commercial vs.
Amateur, and "Pornification" 512

Self-Assessment 18-1:
The Problematic Pornography
Consumption Scale (PPCS) 513

18.5b Pornography and the Law 514

18.5c Effects of Pornography on Individuals
and Relationships 515

Personal Experience 18-1
Porn in My Marriage 517

18.6 Sex Work 517

18.6a Definition of Prostitution as
Sex Work 517

18.6b Types of Sex Workers 518

18.6c Becoming a Sex Worker 521

18.6d Life as a Sex Worker 523

18.6e Impact of Sex Work on Personal
Intimate Relationships 523

Personal Decisions 18-3
Sex Workers Speak Out 524

18.6f Clients of Sex Workers 524

18.6g Prostitution and the Law 526

18.6h Sex Workers and STIs/HIV 526

Social Policy 18-2
Should Sex Work
Be Decriminalized? 527

18.6i Sex Trafficking 528

Web Links 532
Key Terms 533

Objectives

1. Explain the impact of sex in advertising
2. Understand the various expressions of sexuality on the internet, including the benefits
3. Discuss sex and the law
4. Describe the four types of sexuality businesses
5. Review the data on the effects of exposure to pornography
6. Know the different types of prostitution and the demographics of "Johns"
7. Learn about sex trafficking
8. Discuss sex trafficking

Truth — OR — Fiction?

T / F   1. Higher pornography use and feeling "out of control" are associated with lower relationship and sexual satisfaction.

T / F   2. Sugar babies emphasize the emotional aspects of their relationships to avoid the stigma associated with sex work.

T / F   3. Technology can help people maintain long-distance relationships.

T / F   4. The primary reason sex workers want to exit the business is that it interferes with their family and romantic relationships.

T / F   5. FOSTA/SESTA has led to sex workers having to take on violent clients.

Answers: 1. T   2. T   3. T   4. T   5. F

The Girlfriend Experience was a Showtime television series that focused on how the principal character purported to offer genuine emotion for her clients. Doing so allowed her clients the illusion that they were not a "John" or a "trick" but someone the escort cared about. This mirage was presented against the backdrop of her leaving one client and going to another, often juggling several "relationships" at the same time.

In this chapter we review the supply side of sexual offerings that are commercially available (pornography, erotic massage, stripping, and prostitution) and the consequences for the providers and consumers.

The advertising slogan "Get your hands on a Toyota" is not about a car.

Anonymous

18.1 Sex in Advertising

Burger King® featured the photo of the BK Super Seven Incher sandwich in one of its advertisements with the open mouth of a woman inches away; the caption read, "It will blow your mind away." Other slogans for commercial products that use sexual inference include "Just do it" (Nike®), "Reach out and touch someone" (AT&T®), and "The best a man can get" (Gillette®). Another example is a television commercial that shows an affectionate couple dressed in skimpy attire. As the announcer intones, "Be ready for the moment," the word *Levitra* (the quick-start Viagra) appears.

Advertisers use sex to get the attention of the viewer and then punch in the product. In this chapter, we examine sex itself as the product and discuss the various ways in which it is offered, sold, and consumed.

18.2 Sexuality Online

Internet sex searches range from seeking educational sexual material (www.siecus.org/) to sex therapists; shopping for, purchasing, or selling sexuality-related items (books, DVDs, sex toys) for entertainment or masturbation use offline; finding strip clubs/massage parlors; engaging in mutual erotic dialogue; and having **cybersex**. The internet is also used by people of all orientations to find sex partners and serves as a virtual storehouse of sex, open 24 hours a day, with millions of users online seeking and finding kindred spirits with similar sexual interests. In earlier chapters, we noted the controversial use of the term "addiction." Here we use it as loss of control. In regard to "cybersex addiction," Giordano and Cashwell (2017) found that 10% of 339 US undergraduates scored in the clinical range for cybersex addiction, with males more likely to score in the clinical range than females.

Online sexual content is extensive, with pornography and webcams with which some people strip and dance for their long-distance viewers. Other webcam strippers generate income by doing as the customer requests (strip, masturbate). Countries vary in the degree of control they levy on the sexual content of the internet (see *Social Policy 18-1*).

Cybersex
Engaging in self-stimulation while online, including looking at images or videos, engaging in sexual chat, exchanging explicit sexual emails, and sharing mutual sexual fantasies while masturbating

18.2a Benefits of Sexuality Online

Sex online has both positive and negative consequences and poses many ethical dilemmas. The following are some advantages regarding sexuality on the internet.

Cultural Diversity

While the US government recommends an unrestricted internet, other countries are very restrictive of online policies for all citizens. The Chinese government has customized internet blocking strategies for what it considers to be inappropriate websites. In Singapore, the government requires internet service providers to block access to certain websites that contain pornography or that inflame political, religious, or racial sensitivities. China's largest service provider blocks at least 100 sites, including Playboy™ (Feng & Guo, 2013).

Social Policy 18-1

Government Control of Online Sexual Content

Should the government censor sexual content online? This question is the focus of an ongoing public debate that concerns protecting children from sexually explicit content. One side of the issue is reflected in the Communications Decency Act, passed by the U.S. Congress in 1996, which prohibited sending indecent messages over the internet to people under age 18. The Supreme Court rejected the law in 1997, however, citing that the law was too broadly worded and violated free-speech rights in that it restricted too much material that adults might want to access. A similar ruling in 2002 has hampered government crackdowns on pornography, including virtual child pornography. In support of not limiting sexual content on the internet, the American Civil Liberties Union emphasized that governmental restrictions threaten material protected by the First Amendment, including sexually explicit poetry and material educating disabled persons on how to experience sexual pleasure.

Congress passed another law (Child Online Protection Act, or COPA) in 1998, which made it a crime to knowingly make available to people under age 17 any web materials that, based on "contemporary community standards," were designed to pander to prurient interests. The law required commercial operators to verify that a user was an adult through credit card information and adult access codes. Businesses that broke the law would be subject to a $50,000 fine and 6 months in jail. An inadvertent effect of the act has been to require public libraries to install internet filters to block access to objectionable sites. These filters are not configured with sufficient sophistication and sometimes prevent people from doing research on important topics, such as breast cancer. A U.S. appeals court and a panel of federal judges have struck down this law on the basis that it violates free speech guaranteed by the First Amendment.

Other than child pornography, there are virtually no restrictions on sexual content on the internet in the United States. There is consensus that adults should have access to pornography but that such material should be restricted from children (Diamond, 2009). However, technology security company BitDefender's internal statistics indicate that 10% of online porn consumers are under 10 years of age. Although porn websites are designed for adults, there is no confirmation required; thus, anyone who clicks the "I'm 18" dialog box is allowed full access to unlimited porn. Some of this material is racist, is misogynistic, and if not literally pedophilic, focuses on teens. In fact, in 2015, "teen" was the highest-ranking category viewed on Pornhub in 19 Western, Midwest, and Northeastern states. BitDefender's senior e-threat analyst Bogdan Botezatu recommends that parents install parental control tools that block access to websites they deem inappropriate for their children (Curtis, 2016).

In the United States, parents—not the government—are expected to be responsible for regulating children's use of the internet. Software products, such as Net Nanny®, Qustodio®, Mobicip®, and uKnowKids® Premier, are marketed to help parents control what their children view online. These software programs allow parents to block unapproved websites and categories (such as pornography), as well as transmission of personal data (such as address and telephone numbers). They also scan pages for sexual material before they are viewed and track internet usage. NQ Family Guardian™ provides a smartphone for children that has a web filter (parents can block inappropriate websites), an app filter (which ensures child-friendly apps), a contacts filter (parents can choose what numbers to block), monitors (allows parents to know where their children are as well as their texts, photos, and browsing history), and scheduling (allows parents to set up times their children can use the phone, including blocking its use for school and bedtime). *PC Magazine* lists the year's top 10 parental control software programs at http://bvtlab.com/E9hZP (Rubenking, 2016).

Parents can also go online with their children both to monitor what their children are viewing and to teach them values about what they believe is right and wrong online. Some parents believe that children must learn how to safely surf the internet. One parent reported that the internet is like a busy street—just as you must teach your children how to safely cross in traffic, you must teach them how to avoid giving information to strangers online.

In a study of sex-related internet use by Doornwaard et al. (2017), while adolescents acknowledged potential negative influences (e.g., pornography creating unrealistic expectations) they felt that they had the skills to make judgments to navigate the online sexual landscape in a responsible way.

One of the challenges facing our society is where adults learn about pornography. Sex education in schools in the United States often doesn't discuss the existence of pornography, let alone provide instruction on how to understand the messages that one learns from pornography. For adults, unless they're enrolled in a college course that discusses these issues, there is no formal education on this topic.

Sex Information and Education

The internet is a source of sex education. Smith (2013) conducted 51 interviews with young adults who revealed their online use, which was motivated by curiosity about sex, sexually explicit material, sex with romantic partners/in groups, or individual sexual pleasure. Many participants described incorporating ideas learned online into their sexual experiences.

Go Ask Alice! is an online question-and-answer health information resource sponsored by Columbia University (http://www.goaskalice.columbia.edu/). "Alice" (not a real person but a team of professionals) includes a section on sex and reproductive health, relationships, drugs, and other topics. No question is taboo. Scarleteen, a comprehensive site (http://www.scarleteen.com/) providing "sex ed for the real world" is staffed with sex-ed professionals and teen volunteers who offer information, emergency advice, and community support. Other sex education sites are, https://www.plannedparenthood.org/teens (a sexuality teen site sponsored by Planned Parenthood), and http://www.iwannaknow.org/teens/index.html (a teen sexual health and STI information site sponsored by the American Social Health Association).

https://goaskalice.columbia.edu/category/sexual-reproductive-health

Go Ask Alice! is a website dedicated to answering sexual questions.

Anonymous STI Testing

For persons who wish to avoid going to a clinic for STI testing, the internet provides a quick anonymous alternative. Google "STI online testing," for various kits capable of testing for various STIs, have the kit sent to your home, collect a urine/blood sample (depending on what STIs you want to assess), send back the specimen, and go online to check the results.

THINK ABOUT IT

Take a moment to answer the following questions. Internet infidelity is an issue about which some partners disagree. Does developing an online emotional relationship involving the exchange of sexual fantasies constitute being unfaithful to a partner? Does such interaction degrade the value of faithfulness an individual has toward a partner and relationship? What amount of time emailing others is appropriate?

Find a Partner

Using the internet to find a partner is losing its stigma. It's less common for members of a couple to lie about how they met; they simply say, "We met on Match" and laugh. A person can log on to one of the hundreds of dating services (such as Match.com®, eHarmony®, Tinder). There are specialty sites for people based on their interests, their religion, or their age, like OurTime, which is designed for people who are 50 and older.

> *It's right there in the name. It's not "Great Cupid" or even "Good Cupid." It's "OK Cupid."*
>
> Helen Hong, comedienne

For people who meet online, their relationship can develop differently than face-to-face relationships. Due to the speed of communication through texting and emailing, partners can develop an emotional bond quickly. If people want to continue their relationship offline, they should be aware that there might be an adjustment period as they begin to spend time together outside of their phones and tablets. If the goal is to move the relationship offline, we recommend meeting the person soon after there is established mutual interest, since the person presented on texting and email may be very different from the actual person.

Find a Sex Partner

While people use the internet to find lifetime partners, they also use the internet to find hook-up partners. Some of the profiles on Match.com reveal the person's sexual motives: "Looking for someone to be physically intimate without strings attached." Hooking up is becoming normative. In a survey of 483 first-year female college students, 40% reported hooking up during the first year. Tinder and Grindr are known as hookup apps and are ways of meeting a hookup partner.

Maintain a Long-Distance Relationship

Technology can help partners bridge the distance and maintain long-distance relationships. Couples separated due to career, education, family responsibilities, or military deployment can connect with each other daily. Such frequent contact helps nurture the relationship and reduces the negative effect of being separated.

Experience Cybersex

Individuals with similar sexual interests and fetishes may exchange photos and play out their sexual fantasies online. Cybersex may occur with one's partner, a known non-partner, or a stranger. Courtice and Shaughnessy (2018) studied cybersex among sexual minority women and noted that more women engage in cybersex with a primary partner compared to men, and that more men than women report cybersex outside a committed-partner context and engage in it more frequently. Cybersex is also safe sex in that there is no risk of pregnancy or someone contracting an STI.

Connect Disenfranchised or Marginalized Individuals

People who have unique demographic features or backgrounds may find others who share their background. People who have been raped; who have STIs (herpes, HPV, HIV); or who are paraplegic/disabled, a cross-dresser, or asexual may find others on the internet who share these experiences and communicate with them. Doing so reduces the feeling of isolation and increases feeling *normal* because others share the same phenomenon.

Try Out a New Identity

The internet provides a way to gain information about a set of practices or an identity concept and to try out a new identity online. A person who experiences feelings of being attracted to same-sex individuals may interact with others online to experience how such interaction feels without the attendant anxiety of doing so in person.

Buy Sex Products Online

People who are shy or embarrassed about buying sex toys, books, or pornography in a store can purchase these items online. Internet access also allows them to buy products that may not be available locally. This is especially important for those with physical limitations who are looking for products that might not be stocked at their local store.

18.2b Disadvantages of Sexuality Online

Sexual uses of the internet may also involve negative consequences.

Cybersex Crime

Examples of cybersex crimes include obscene emails, unsolicited porn, spam, and the posting of false personal ads advertising the victim's availability for sex. These behaviors are also an example of online sexual harassment.

Deception in Finding a Partner

Finding a partner on the internet also involves deception, with potential partners presenting inaccurate information about their marital status, weight, height, income, bad habits (e.g., alcoholism), and so on. Adults who are connecting with other adults might set up a time to meet at a public place to provide a reality check on who is behind the computer screen. The term "catfishing" has become a phrase in popular culture that refers to creating a false persona online in order to lure a partner.

Online "Sex Addiction"

Related to the controversy on the existence of sex addiction, there is debate as to whether online sex addiction exists because there are no clinical diagnostic criteria. A review of the literature on online sex addiction can be summarized as follows:

> The advent of the [i]nternet has added another medium in which people can engage in sexual behavior. This ranges from the passive consumption of online pornography to the interactive exchange of sexual content in cybersex chat rooms. It is believed that access, affordability, and anonymity are critical factors that make the [i]nternet viable for the acquisition, development, and maintenance of online sexuality. For some, sexual behaviors online are used as a complement to their offline sexuality, whereas for others, they serve as a substitute, potentially resulting in [i]nternet sex addiction, which can

be conceptualized as the intersection between [i]nternet addiction and sex addiction. Based on the five qualitative and nine quantitative studies, ... it was concluded that engaging in sexual behaviors on the [i]nternet can go awry and result in [i]nternet sex addiction, as it can lead to a wide variety of negative consequences for the individuals affected. (Griffiths, 2012, p. 111)

Among these consequences is an example of a man who lost his job (since he spent 12 hours a day on the internet looking at porn) and almost lost his marriage. His wife had not known about his online porn consumption.

One of the potential negative consequences of online sex addiction for individuals is that their partners may feel betrayed and replaced. Because social, emotional, and sexual connections can be made quickly on the computer, people sometimes abandon face-to-face relationships for virtual ones. Indeed, they may become so socially isolated with their computer relationships that they neglect the development of their live inter-personal skills and relationships. One woman complained, "He's always in there on the computer and would rather be in chat rooms than in the room talking with me" (authors' files). However, self-acknowledged sex addiction related to online pornography is rare. In an Australian national study of 9,963 men and 10,133 women ages 16–69, 4% of the men and 1% of the women self-reported that they were "addicted" (Rissel et al., 2017). The Problematic Pornography Consumption Scale (PPSC) in *Self-Assessment 18-1* provides a way to measure the degree to which pornography is regarded as a problem by the individual (Bothe et al., 2018).

Treatment for online/pornography addiction includes becoming involved in a group (Sex Addicts Anonymous), being assigned a sponsor, and installing strong anti-porn software on your computer. The urge to view pornography must be managed daily just like other addictions such as the urge to drink or gamble. Learning how to develop a relationship that includes a sexual component rather than a sex-focused relationship also becomes an emphasis of treatment.

Pedophiles Online

The internet is used by pedophiles to lure victims into forced sex. Wolak and Finkelhor (2013) analyzed national data on 2,653 arrests for internet-related sex crimes against minors. The charges included statutory rape (nonforcible illegal sexual activity with underage youth) or noncontact offenses, such as child pornography production.

Through the internet, dissemination of child pornography has become pervasive because pedophiles can connect with each other and share pictures in relative anonymity. Youth can be used in pornography without contact between the child and the perpetrator because images of a child can be digitally transformed into pornography and distributed without the victim's knowledge. Pornographic images can be a source of repeated, long-term victimization that can last for years.

Although the internet has become one of the most valuable information and educational tools of our society, it can be lethal if children are not properly supervised in its use. Pedophiles posing as friends may enter chat rooms with unsuspecting prepubescents, interact with them as though they are peers, arrange to meet them at the mall or other public place, and abduct them. Awareness of the presence of pedophiles on the internet has become a concern for parents who want their children to become computer literate. Pedophiles have no shortage of sites.

Websites such as GetNetWise® (www.getnetwise.org/) address safe internet use by children. *Personal Decisions 18-1* presents a recommended agreement between parents and children. Parental supervision of a child's or adolescent's smartphone is equally important; as noted earlier in this chapter, software is available to monitor all activity.

18.3 Sex and the Law

US society has an ongoing debate on the issue of private rights versus social morality. For example, should consenting adults be permitted to engage in any sexual behaviors they choose, or should the law define morally acceptable parameters?

In his classic 1859 "On Liberty," British philosopher and freethinker John Stuart Mill (1859; new edition 1985) emphasized the rights of the individual by arguing that the only purpose of government should be to protect its citizens from harm by others. He also advocated that:

> The liberty of the individual must be thus far limited; he must not make himself a nuisance to other people. But if he refrains from molesting others in what concerns them, and merely acts according to his own inclination and judgment in things which concern himself, ... he should be allowed, without molestation, to carry his opinions into practice at his own cost. (pp. 119–120)

In contrast, the 1986 Meese Commission Report on pornography reflected a version of legislating morality. The commission took the position that the protection of society's moral environment was a legitimate purpose of government and recommended more restrictive laws on pornography. The George W. Bush administration launched a new "war on pornography."

One of the ways that society has achieved compromise and balance between the radically opposing views of private versus public morality has been to view certain sexual behaviors on a continuum of offensiveness and to assign relative penalties for engaging in them. For example, child sexual abuse and rape are regarded as severely offensive and are subject to strong social sanctions. However, frottage may go unrecognized in criminal statistics because such behavior is likely to be prosecuted under a more generalized category, such as assault.

The following are five categories of sexual acts, according to criminal classification:

- *Category I:* Criminal acts that require enforcement to protect society (Rape and child molestation are examples.)

- *Category II:* Sexual acts with potential victimization (Exhibitionism and voyeurism are examples. Although these behaviors may not be regarded as morally severe, they may create harm to the victims, who deserve protection.)

- *Category III:* Sexual acts midway between those considered morally reprehensible and those creating victims (Sex work and adultery are examples. Both are said to reflect immorality, and both have the potential to produce victims—the sex workers, or the spouse or children of the adulterer.)

- *Category IV:* Sex acts between consenting adults (In some states, for example, oral sex is still against the law.)

- *Category V:* Behaviors that do not involve sexual contact but are either criminalized or considered to be sex crimes (Abortion in countries where it is illegal and the sale and distribution of child pornography are examples.)

18.4 Sex-Related Businesses

18.4a Phone Sex

Phone sex (sometimes referred to as *guided masturbation*) is a telephone conversation between a caller and a sex worker (also referred to as a phone actress, fantasy artist, or adult phone entertainer) who verbally arouses, stimulates, and moves the caller toward orgasm in exchange for money. Phone sex advertisements (usually provocative photos with toll-free numbers) are in men's magazines, on websites, and on late-night cable TV. The individual calls the 800 or 900 number, tells the sex worker the kind of sex fantasy or dirty talk desired, and masturbates to the words of the sex worker. Phone sex is not prostitution because there is no live, face-to-face, body-to-body exchange of sexual service for money. Popular in the 1980s and 1990s, phone sex has largely been replaced by webcam sex in which a person connects online with someone and directs them to do specific things (discussed in the next section).

I wanna be the reason you tilt your phone away from others when you read my message.

Pinterest

A number of businesses exist to sell sex. Their products include sexual fantasy (phone sex), nudity (stripping), and orgasm (erotic massage parlors).

18.4b Camming

Camming allows the customer to feel like they have a direct connection with the performer. The customers can talk about their fantasies and what they want the performer to do. Many websites offer camming.

18.4c Strip Clubs

Modern strip clubs (euphemistically called *adult entertainment*) owe their heritage to the art of striptease, which flourished in the 1940s and 1950s. Upscale strip clubs are referred to as gentlemen's clubs, in which the women wear evening gowns and then strip rather than just walk about in a bikini. Mount (2018) reemphasized the fact that strip clubs are businesses, a fact customers forget or are oblivious to:

> People just don't understand the other side of the curtain when it comes to these bars. They go in, they see a certain thing, "oh, look at that hot chick!" And everyone's havin' fun and drinkin,' this and that. They don't realize what goes on, you know ... behind the curtain, in the dressing rooms, it's such an act, everything is a show. It's just not ... what people think it is.

Phone sex
Telephone conversation between a caller and a sex worker who verbally arouses, stimulates, and moves the caller toward orgasm in exchange for money

Camming
The use of a webcam to facilitate the customer seeing, directing, and interacting with a performer

PERSONAL DECISIONS 18-1

"Camming from My Apartment"

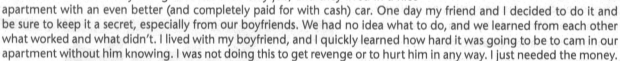

As a college sophomore, I found myself always running low on money and trying to find ways to make lots of cash fast. My friend knew somebody who cammed and made a lot of money doing it. It was their only job, and they lived in a nice apartment with an even better (and completely paid for with cash) car. One day my friend and I decided to do it and be sure to keep it a secret, especially from our boyfriends. We had no idea what to do, and we learned from each other what worked and what didn't. I lived with my boyfriend, and I quickly learned how hard it was going to be to cam in our apartment without him knowing. I was not doing this to get revenge or to hurt him in any way. I just needed the money.

To start off as a cam model is not easy; you have to sit there while revealing your body to get people interested in you, possibly for hours on end without getting any tips, which later are exchanged for paychecks. Once you create a fan base of people who enjoy watching you, that's when the money starts coming in, and you find people wanting to know if you have an Amazon Wish List so they could buy things for you too. Tips and gifts are mostly all in exchange for a show.

The shows of a cam model vary model by model. Some don't show anything but their boobs, while others do anal with their male partners. I was in the middle; I would do a strip show, and if that wasn't enough for the client, I would masturbate for them. Most of the time I would not orgasm, but I would fake it. The goal is to make the person paying for your show to orgasm; that's why they come to the website to view cam models in the first place.

Shortly after I started camming, I was found by a very reputable agent. He was very impressed by my show confidence and looks and wanted to know if I would go into business with him. He would do all my promoting and scheduling, and I would just have to show up and do my show. I was very excited, especially after learning that he would only take 10% of the profits I make. So I decided to go through with it. Unfortunately, the day after I signed the contract to work with the agent, my boyfriend found out about me doing camming. Obviously very upset, he demanded I choose him or being a cam model. At this time, I was making over $1,000 a month, and I was only camming about an hour or two every other day and having to do it very secretly. Since I have been dating him for over 2 years and am fully in love with him, I chose him over the money. I ended the contract with the agent and promised my boyfriend that I would never do it again.

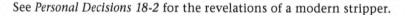

See *Personal Decisions 18-2* for the revelations of a modern stripper.

Although some strip clubs feature male strippers for gay men and female strippers for women, the overwhelming majority exist for the heterosexual man, and that is the focus of this section. Due to internet pornography/webcams, men have access to whatever they want to watch, so the pressure on strippers is to do less tease and just take off their clothes. Laws about how much clothing a dancer is required to leave on differ from county to county.

Table dance
Type of dance in which a person dances or disrobes on the customer's table or in front of the seated customer

Lap dance
Type of dance that involves varying amounts of physical contact and can result in sexual release on the part of the customer (also known as friction dance or straddle dance)

The dancer knows the script, so she strips quickly, picks up the money, and returns to her dressing room or to the floor to solicit a private **table dance**, in which she dances or disrobes on the customer's table or in front of the seated customer. Although the dancer may put her hands on the shoulders of the customer, typically he is not to touch her; and there must be a 1-foot distance between the dancer and the customer. Some strip clubs offer a **lap dance**, also known as friction dance or straddle dance, which allows for varying amounts of physical contact and can result in sexual release on the part of the customer. Still other strip clubs offer manual manipulation, oral sex, and sexual intercourse. Déjà Vu® operates 100 adult-oriented retail stores and theaters in 16 states and has private rooms with small, cushioned sofas. No hand jobs, oral sex, or sexual intercourse are allowed.

Cultural
Diversity

Iceland is the first country in the world to ban strip clubs for feminist rather than religious reasons. Kolbrún Halldórsdóttir, the politician who first proposed the ban, said of the law, "It is not acceptable that women or people in general are a product to be sold." Prostitution is also illegal for johns and pimps, but not for prostitutes. In addition, pornography is against the law, though a thriving illegal market persists, http://bvtlab.com/637u9.

PERSONAL DECISIONS 18-2

What It's Like to Be a Stripper— Two Stories

While some people refer to what I do as stripping, to me, I am a dancer. I have always loved to dance. I was a cheerleader in high school and on the dance team—I have always been a dancing performer, and I love it.

I got into dancing on a lark. One night my girlfriends and I were out and decided to go to amateur night at a local club. Three of us got up and danced. I found that I liked it, did not mind taking my clothes off, and when the music stopped, I was hooked.

I've been dancing for 5 months, and I'm on the 2-year plan. I'll make enough money to take care of getting me through dental hygiene school. The lowest I have made in a night was $10; the highest, $700.

Both my parents know I dance, and they are okay with it. My mom came to the club and was impressed that it was upscale. Both parents asked that I not tell their parents (my grandparents), since they would not understand.

I don't have a boyfriend. I'm happy without one for now. Guys can't handle their lady being a dancer, so I am going to avoid the drama. I have close relationships with my family and girlfriends.

I have been offered money for sex three times in 5 months. The highest offer was a guy who offered me $5,000 to do him and his wife. I am not for sale, so it was easy to say no.

I think the hardest part of my job is that some people look down on me. I work hard for my money, am not promiscuous, am good to people, so I'm sorry they don't understand.

***

Stripping for me has been about getting money to pay for my heroin. Were it not for my addiction, I would not consider stripping. But I needed the money and I needed a lot of it, fast. I had no shame being a stripper and meeting customers after work for more money (in exchange for more sex). I was a stripper for two years and spiraled downward with my drug abuse till I was fired. A lot of the girls where I worked were on drugs. I went to a Sober Living Home (rehab center) in California and have been clean for two years.

Whereas some strip clubs pay the dancers an hourly fee and let them keep their tips, others charge the dancers stage fees ($50) for dancing privileges and a $200 commission for each 6-hour shift. In effect, the stripper may feel pressure to offer more explicit sex to generate money from customers. Strippers must present two social images. One is at work, where the woman must project a sexy, profitable image to keep the dollars flowing from clients. Outside of work, the woman must present a different image to avoid being stigmatized as a stripper (Morrow, 2012).

I understood and agreed that from a feminist perspective working in a strip club was extremely problematic, but I was saving money to travel and making more in one night than most of my friends made in a week. Plus, it was interesting.

Periel Aschenbrand, *On My Knees: A Memoir*

Most research on stripping has been on female strippers. Scull (2019) interviewed 22 male strippers and revealed their joy in using the context to have sex with women (some in the parking lot) with an enhancement to their own self-concept. Scull's research revealed the double standard—that women are devalued and stigmatized for stripping but males benefit (by sexual access) rather than being punished from presenting their sexual selves in public.

18.4d Erotic Massage Parlors

Erotic massage parlors are places that provide sexual services (manual manipulation, oral sex, and sometimes sexual intercourse) in exchange for money. Homeowners who live near these massage parlors often consider them undesirable and object to their presence. Not only is there a moral concern; they may also depress property values. Many erotic massage parlor workers are trafficked women. Erotic massage is to be differentiated from **therapeutic massage**, which requires academic training at one of the more than 400 accredited programs, a supervised internship, and a license. The more than 45,000 therapeutic massage therapists often struggle for professional status and credibility because of a common association of massage with eroticism and sex work. The professional associations of therapeutic massage specify that sex is not only "never appropriate in massage—it's illegal."

Get 'em in, get 'em up, get 'em off, and get 'em out.

Motto of sex worker in erotic massage parlor

Professional organizations of persons offering therapeutic massage are ABMP (Associated Bodywork & Massage Professionals®) and AMTA (American Massage Therapy Association). The National Certification Board for Therapeutic Massage & Bodywork® (NCBTMB) is the only national certifying group of massage therapists in the United States. This organization provides the test that professional massage therapists take in the United States, even if their states don't offer licensure, in an effort to demonstrate their knowledge.

Erotic massage parlors make little pretense of providing anything other than sexual release. "Want a happy ending?" is a typical question erotic massage parlor workers may ask their customers.

18.4e Community Attitudes toward Adult Businesses

Residents of a community usually do not want adult businesses near where they live. Communities attempt to control adult business by restricting where they can locate. Strip clubs are often subjected to an ordinance that prohibits exotic entertainment businesses from opening within 2,000 feet of a school, religious building, public park, hotel, or home. Although most people do not want to live near an adult business, the belief that an increased crime rate is associated with such places may be unfounded. Linz and colleagues (2004) studied the effect of 20 topless nightclubs on the surrounding areas (500- and 1,000-foot radii) in terms of reported crime and then matched these with similar sites with no adult businesses. They found lower numbers of reported crimes in the areas surrounding adult businesses.

Erotic massage parlors
Places that provide sexual services (manual manipulation, oral sex, and sometimes sexual intercourse) in exchange for money

Therapeutic massage
Nonerotic massage by a person who has received academic training at one of the more than 400 accredited programs, completed a supervised internship, and has a therapeutic massage license

18.5 Pornography

18.5a Defining Pornography and Erotica

The term **pornography**—derived from the words *porne* ("prostitute") and *graphein* ("to write")—originally meant "stories of prostitutes." Shim et al. (2015) provided a content analysis of pornographic online magazines and identified four themes: dominance/submission (who controls sexual acts), reciprocity (mutual satisfaction), exploitation (one uses the other—buys a prostitute, drugs the woman), or autoerotic (masturbation scene). In comparing the content aimed at women or men, the researchers found that websites aimed at men included more autoerotic (33%) and dominant themes (16%) than did those aimed at women (7.6% and 11.4%, respectively). Websites aimed at women contained more reciprocal themes (53.2%) than did those aimed at men (4%). Sites aimed at men were also more likely to depict themes of sexual inequality than those aimed at women.

Not all sexually explicit material is pornographic. There is debate over what is pornography and what is **erotica**. Although the perception of what is pornographic or what is erotic is subjective to a degree, erotica can be artistic or literary in nature, generally depicting consensual sex. Although some sex researchers have found neutral to positive effects from exposure to sexually explicit material (Rosser et al., 1995), concerns about the extreme porn that is widespread online are growing.

Pornography tells lies about women. But pornography tells the truth about men.

John Stoltenberg, radical feminist activist

There are different types of pornography. **Degrading pornography** is sexually explicit material that degrades, debases, and dehumanizes people—generally, women. **Violent pornography** is sexually explicit material that endorses the utility and normativeness of sexual violence, again usually directed by men toward women. Pornography has become more brazen and extreme in recent years. The acronym CURBFHP refers to the type of pornography that has been the target of federal prosecution: children, urination, rape, bestiality, fisting, homicide, and pain (Kirk & Boyer 2002). Unfortunately, this "gonzo" porn that focuses on degradation and violence against women is increasingly popular, and some researchers consider it a public health issue (Bridges et al., 2010). Davis et al. (2018) surveyed 517 young (15–29) heterosexual Australians in regard to what they perceived to be the content of pornography. Men's pleasure (83%) was seen by the highest proportion of the respondents with 70% reporting the man being dominant. It is unclear if degradation and violence were included in the categories of men's pleasure and being dominant that were identified.

Pornography is also categorized as *softcore* and *hardcore*. Soft pornography refers to romance novels, photos of women in revealing swimsuits, and sex scenes in major Hollywood movies, while hardcore pornography refers to graphic scenes of sexual encounters, three-way sex scenes, and so on. Hardcore is more often thought of when the term *pornography* is used (Willoughby et al., 2014a). Canadian law restricts what pornography may be made or shown in Canada. Scenes of rape, force, degradation, and so on are prohibited (Covell, 2016), whereas the United States is less restrictive. Feminist porn has also entered the marketplace focusing on faces, relationships, consent, mutuality, respect, different ages, body types, and ethnicities (Ryan, 2017). Ericka Lust is a Swedish filmmaker who emphasizes these qualities in her videos.

Pornography
Sexually explicit pictures, writing, or other images, usually pairing sex with power and violence

Erotica
Sexually explicit material that is neither a degrading nor violent portrayal of consensual sexual activity

Degrading pornography
Sexually explicit material that degrades, debases, and dehumanizes people, typically women

Violent pornography
Sexually explicit visual images of sexual violence, usually directed by men toward women

National DATA

Pornography Consumption

Based on an internet sample of 1,392 adults in the US, ages 18–73, 92% of men and 60% of women reported having viewed pornography in the last month. Men reported primarily watching videos while women reported reading written pornography more often. The primary function of pornography was to enhance masturbation (Solano, et al. 2020). Reports of viewing pornography are usually lower than actual viewing due to social desirability bias (Rasmussen et al., 2018). With that caveat in mind, Frutos and Merrill (2017) analyzed data on 11,372 adults who reported viewing an explicit sexual movie in the past year. Findings included significantly greater exposure in men than women (35% vs. 16%); blacks than whites (33% vs. 22%); and never married (41% vs. 18% married, 31% separated, and 24% divorced). It also decreased with older age, higher education, and more children in the household. When does pornography exposure begin? Over a thousand (1,408) men and women reported their age at first exposure: 11% ages 7–11, 38% ages 12–15, 20% ages 16–17, and 31% ages 18–30 (Young-Petersen et al., 2016).

Technology and Sexuality 18-1: Online Porn, Commercial vs. Amateur, and "Pornification"

Whether it was the automobile, Polaroid® camera, or VHS™, technological advances have had an impact on sexual behavior. Cars gave people mobility, whether it was to visit sex workers or brothels or to elude the watchful eyes of parents as they explored each other's bodies. The Polaroid instant camera provided the option of taking nude photos and sharing them. The VHS video recorder and player gave people the ability to watch pornography at home.

Like other new forms of technology, the internet has had a major impact on our sexuality. It has allowed us to find information on a variety of sexuality topics, to meet new people with whom to have sexual experiences, and to connect with others in search of a long-term partner.

The internet has also made a variety of pornography more accessible—interracial, gay/lesbian, fetish, you name it. Webcams provide a way for long-distance couples to talk/interact in the nude, but they also allow amateurs to get into the porn business. One of our students noted that all she had to do was close her bedroom door, turn on her webcam, and start charging money for men to see her naked. In addition to webcamming, some individuals and couples record their own sexual behavior and post the video on sites like Pornhub® and Xtube™.

Some people claim that amateur porn has expanded the type of bodies regarded as sexy. While this may be true, the portrayal of normal body types as sexual is not limited to amateur porn. "Sex-positive" porn produced commercially also features a variety of body shapes, as well as more variety in terms of the actors' gender fluidity and race (Center for Sexual Pleasure & Health, n.d.).

Commercial porn has regulations and protocols that are lacking in amateur porn. In commercial porn, actors and actresses agree ahead of filming about what will be taking place with whom, although these standards may be ignored. Commercial porn is subject to regulations about the use of condoms to protect against STIs and the need for HIV testing to protect the participants.

While some couples record themselves having sex and try to market it, there has been an increase in the amount of amateur porn that doesn't involve off-screen couples; rather, they use actors and actresses doing amateur work. Like professional porn actors, these individuals may feel pressure to engage in behaviors that make them uncomfortable (Andelloux, 2013).

Both commercial and amateur porn can be problematic in content and effects, with unlimited free online access to all ages due to insufficient screening technology. Today's mainstream online porn is far more extreme than it was even a decade ago: brutal images may now be mainstream. In terms of commercial production and consumption, "sex-positive" porn gets a miniscule market share (Bindel, 2010).

For adolescent girls, the risks of porn-based sexualization are intensified with social media. Near-obligatory soft-porn selfies can garner "Likes" and boost social status, but they also expose girls to criticism and "slut-shaming." Nancy Jo Sales's 2016 book *American Girls: Social Media and the Secret Lives of Teenagers,* a study of girls ages 3–19 in 10 states, reveals a "pornified" subculture of misogynistic double standards and male entitlement, characterized by self-objectification and anxiety for girls, with boys demanding painful and degrading porn-style sexual behaviors and blackmailing girls for nude photos that they then share with friends (Sales, 2016). Along with the commercial sexualization of young girls, porn culture has permeated the mainstream in ways that objectify and damage girls and women.

Self-Assessment 18-1:
The Problematic Pornography Consumption Scale (PPCS)

Think back to the past six months and indicate on the following 7-point scale how often or to what extent the statements apply to you. There is no right or wrong answer. Write down the number that indicates the answer that most applies to you.

1 (Never), 2 (Rarely), 3 (Occasionally), 4 (Sometimes), 5 (Often), 6 (Very Often), 7 (All the Time)

1. __ I felt that porn is an important part of my life.
2. __ I used porn to restore the tranquility of my feelings.
3. __ I felt porn caused problems in my sexual life.
4. __ I felt that I had to watch more and more porn for satisfaction.
5. __ I unsuccessfully tried to reduce the amount of porn I watch.
6. __ I became stressed when something prevented me from watching porn.
7. __ I thought about how good it would be to watch porn.
8. __ Watching porn got rid of my negative feelings.
9. __ Watching porn prevented me from bringing out the best in me.
10. __ I felt that I needed more and more porn in order to satisfy my needs.
11. __ When I vowed not to watch porn anymore, I could only do it for a short time.
12. __ I became agitated when I was unable to watch porn.
13. __ I continually planned when to watch porn.
14. __ I released my tension by watching porn.
15. __ I neglected other leisure activities as a result of watching porn.
16. __ I gradually watched more "extreme" porn, because the porn I watched before was less satisfying.
17. __ I resisted watching porn for only a little while before I relapsed.
18. __ I missed porn greatly when I didn't watch it for a while.

Scoring:

For the total score, add all the scores of the items. A score of 76 or higher indicates possible problematic pornography use.

Source: "The Development of the Problematic Pornography Consumption Scale (PPCS)," by Bothe, B., Toth-Kiraly, I., Zsila, A., Griffiths, M. D., Demetrovicsis, Z., & Orosz, G., *The Journal of Sex Research, 55*(3), 395-406. Copyright 2018 Taylor & Francis Ltd, http://www.tandfonline.com. Reprinted by permission of the publisher and Dr. B. Bothe (bothe.beata@ppk.elte.hu)

Obscenity has been legally defined by meeting three criteria. First, the dominant theme of the material must appeal to a prurient interest in sex. Such interest implies that the material is sexually arousing in a lewd way. Second, the material must be patently offensive to the community. In general, a community can dictate what its standards are regarding the sale, display, and distribution of sexual materials. Third, the sexual material must have no redeeming social value. If the material can be viewed as entertaining or educational (if it helps with the sexual communication of couples, for example), a case can be made for its social value.

18.5b Pornography and the Law

The Supreme Court has made a number of decisions regarding obscenity and child pornography. In 1973, the Court decided in *Miller v. California* that a work is obscene if, taken as a whole, it appeals to the prurient interest; portrays sexual conduct in a patently offensive way, as measured by community standards; and lacks serious social value (literary, artistic, etc.). Shortly thereafter, in *New York v. Ferber*, the Court decided that the "states have a compelling interest in protecting children; that child pornography is inextricably intertwined with child exploitation and abuse and that child pornography has very little social, scientific, political, literary or artistic value" (Ferraro & Casey, 2005, p. 16). In effect, the Court distinguished child pornography from obscenity—material need not be obscene to be illegal child pornography. Furthermore, in *Osborne v. Ohio*, the Court found that the mere possession of child pornography was illegal.

Child pornography is defined as an image that depicts a clearly prepubescent human being in a sexually explicit manner. It is also referred to as **kiddie porn** and **chicken porn**. Seto et al. (2015) found that 4% of 1,978 Swedish men ages 17–20 reported ever having viewed child pornography. Having viewed violent sexual pornography and having a sexual interest in children predicted child pornography viewing behavior. A strong cultural value views the use of children in sex films as immoral and abusive. These children do not have the option of free choice and are manipulated or forced into participation. Pornography involving children may result in devastating consequences to child participants.

The Communications Decency Act of 1996 (which made it a crime—punishable by a $250,000 fine or up to 2 years in prison—for anyone to make "indecent" material available to children on the internet) was designed to protect children from pornography. Although the Act was found to be constitutionally too broad, subsequent federal initiatives have included the 1998 Child Online Protection Act, which mandates that commercial pornographers require potential users of adult pornographic websites to acknowledge that they are over age 18. However, as previously noted, no verification process is required, so these limitations are largely ineffective. The 2000 Children's Internet Protection Act denies federal funds to libraries unless they have installed software preventing minors from accessing harmful material (Federal Communications Commission, 2019).

Possession of child porn carries a 5-year prison sentence. Greater involvement may involve stronger penalties. For example, Thomas Reedy, owner of Landslide Operation, was convicted on federal charges related to possessing and distributing child pornography and received 1,335 years in prison (Johnson, 2001). However, Jared Fogle, former spokesman for Subway®, received only 15 years for distributing and receiving child porn and for traveling to engage in illicit sexual conduct with a child.

Obscenity
Label for sexual material that meets three criteria: (a) The dominant theme of the material must appeal to a prurient interest in sex; (b) the material must be patently offensive to the community; and (c) the sexual material must have no redeeming social value

Child pornography
Image that depicts a clearly prepubescent human being in a sexually explicit manner (also called kiddie porn and chicken porn)

Kiddie porn
See *child pornography*

Chicken porn
See *child pornography*

The law is being questioned in regard to sexting among minors. In North Carolina, a 17-year-old was arrested and is facing charges for sexually exploiting a minor for sending naked photos of himself to his girlfriend. Because of his age, he is being charged with sexually exploiting himself (a minor), and yet he is being charged as an adult. Henshaw et al. (2017) focused on online child pornography offenders (CPOs) as compared to those who have sexual contact with children. In general, CPOs have been found to be relatively high functioning and generally pro-social individuals with less extensive and diverse offending histories than contact offenders. CPOs also display high levels of sexual preoccupation that surpass those of contact offenders. The courts are still trying to figure out how to protect children without censoring the content available to adults (Mauro, 1997). The U.S. Customs Service is the country's front line of defense to combat the illegal importation and proliferation of child pornography.

18.5c Effects of Pornography on Individuals and Relationships

The effects of pornography have been studied extensively. Dawson et al. (2020) reviewed the outcomes of watching pornography including low "addiction" reports (4% for men; 1% for women), low frequency reports of any negative personal or relationship

Experiences with pornography are complex and nuanced, often paradoxical, varying among and within individuals.

Sarah Ashton, sex researcher

outcomes, and frequent positive reports including reduction of boredom/stress and orgasm intensity and learning new ideas. Emmers-Sommer (2018) noted that the primary reason for using pornography identified by 143 online participants (ages 18–48) was as a solitary aid for masturbation that results in a positive physical outcome. Positive attitudes toward premarital sex (Wright, 2015) and being narcissistic are also associated with pornography use (Kasper et al., 2014). Daspe et al. (2018) noted that pornography use is higher and the person was more likely to feel a "lack of control" when relationship and sexual satisfaction in the relationship was lowest.

To what degree does pornography use impact one's relationship happiness? The answer is in reference to masturbation. According to Perry (2020), watching pornography only has a negative impact on one's relationship happiness if doing so is accompanied by solo masturbation. Willoughby and Leonhardt (2020) also found that watching pornography as a couple was associated with higher sexual satisfaction for both partners. So what is the effect of pornography use on relationships? The answer may depend on whether the partners watch together, separately or alone. Kohut et al. (2018) identified pornography use as shared (both partners watch pornography together), concordant (both partners watch pornography independently/alone), or discordant (one watches, the other does not). Partners who shared pornography reported more open sexual communication/relationship closeness whereas partners who had discordant use reported both lower sexual communication and relationship closeness.

McKeown et al. (2018) noted the benefits of consumption of online pornography for women to include helping them to fulfill their sexual needs, embrace and explore their sexual selves, connect with sexual partners, and normalize their sexual desires. Wright et al. (2017) conducted an analysis of 50 studies, including more than 50,000 participants from 10 countries and found that, in regard to pornography consumption and intrapersonal satisfaction (satisfaction with oneself or one's body), there were no effects for either men or women. Perry and Schleifer (2018) found that beginning pornography use during marriage was associated with subsequent divorce. However, it is possible that there was a reverse causation such that a spouse may be unhappy and begin viewing pornography, and it is the unhappiness—not the pornography—that may be associated with divorce. In regard to pornography use and sexual satisfaction of adolescents, Milas et al. (2020) revealed that pornography viewing by adolescents did not significantly impact their reported sexual satisfaction. Another study of high school students viewing pornography revealed that adolescent females who do so are more likely to report greater likelihood of having sex and having a higher number of sexual partners (Huntington et al., 2019).

Previously, the U.S. Commission on Obscenity and Pornography found no evidence that explicit sexual material played a significant role in causing individual or social harm. Rather, such material seemed to be sought for entertainment and educational purposes and seemed to enhance sexual communication. Further, the commission recommended that all federal, state, and local legislation prohibiting the sale, exhibition, and distribution of sexual material to adults be repealed. This study was published in 1967—the U.S. Senate and President Richard Nixon rejected the committee's recommendations.

In the summer of 1986, the U.S. Surgeon General's Workshop on Pornography and Public Health was convened in Arlington, Virginia, with 19 specialists in the area of pornography. Conclusions about the workshop's presentations and discussions (Koop, 1987) follow:

1. Prolonged exposure to pornography results in people believing that less common sexual practices are more common than they are.

2. Pornography depicting sexual aggression as pleasurable to the victim increases the acceptance of the use of coercion in sexual relations.

3. Acceptance of aggression may increase the chance of engaging in sexual aggression.

4. Children who participate in the production of pornography experience adverse and enduring effects.

Revenge porn, sometimes known as when one posts nude photos of a former partner on the internet and social media to get back at the partner, can have catastrophic consequences when employers and parents view these photos. A more accurate term is nonconsensual pornography, which is the distribution of sexually graphic images of individuals without their consent. Cyber Civil Rights Initiative is an organization to help victims. Hall & Hearn (2019) noted that men are most likely to engage in revenge porn against their ex partners and legitimize their doing so because the "victim"—their partner—was unfaithful, took their children, etc. Hence, revenge porn by men may be another form of violence against women and "blaming the victim."

In regard to increasing the positive impact of pornography, Dawson et al. (2020) emphasized the need for porn literacy in sex education programs—the focus should be on reducing the shame of watching pornography and increasing critical skills in regard to body image comparisons/dissatisfactions, the importance of consent, and the unrealistic standards of sex promoted in pornography.

Revenge porn
When one posts nude photos of a former partner on the internet to get back at a partner

The format of America's cultural conversation about pornography is primarily negative; no one will stand up for pornography and those who do are perceived as immoral, anti-family, anti-child, and anti-woman.

Marty Klein, *America's War on Sex*

Personal Experience 18-1

Porn in My Marriage*

While my spouse and I have been married for over a year, we have been together for six years. My husband has always watched porn. In the beginning, I was angry and jealous—why would he watch porn when he had me? Was I not pretty enough or sexy enough or what?

He would also ask me to do things he saw during his porn watching. This further angered me since I felt he wanted me to be like those porn stars.

It is now several years later and we have worked all of this out. I no longer feel upset with his porn watching. I know he loves me and he no longer pressures me to do what his porn princesses do. Rather, we now watch porn together as an elixir, which gets us going. And, I have begun to enjoy porn watching myself—both alone and together. In fact, as bad as I once thought porn was, I now feel it is a positive for our relationship.

*Name withheld by request

18.6 Sex Work

Robert Kraft (age 77), owner of the New England Patriots, gave renewed visibility to the issue of sex work when he was charged with two counts of solicitation or prostitution in 2019. When people hear the term *sex for sale*, they think of prostitution. Prostitutes (also called call girls, escorts, courtesans, harlots, hookers, hustlers, sluts, streetwalkers, strumpets, tramps, and sex workers) are the focus of this section.

18.6a Definition of Prostitution as Sex Work

Prostitution is defined as providing sexual behavior through the use of a person's body (typically manual stimulation, oral sex, sexual intercourse, anal sex) in exchange for money, drugs, or other goods. Prostitution is one type of **sex work** in which people earn their living by providing sexual services. A team of researchers (Benoit et al., 2017a) interviewed 218 sex workers about why they entered the business. Three reasons emerged: critical life events such as being abused/neglected, which led to a feeling of no self-worth; the need for money (e.g., literally to buy food and pay rent); and attraction to the role (e.g., "I like money and sex, so why not combine?"). One sex worker (new to the business) said that she was astonished that for 15 minutes she earned $250. Wilson and Flicker (2018) revealed the motivations of young black women in Canada for trading sex for money. These included the need for access to resources and the contexts ranged from being a sugar baby to a prostitute in a brothel-like den.

Other types of sex work include posing/acting for pornographic photographs/DVDs, being a phone sex actor, stripping, lap dancing, providing erotic massages, and being a professional dominant. Although sex workers are typically thought of as adult women, men are also sex workers (gigolos), as are children.

Red-light districts are known as the places where sex workers work. In America the term *red light* has its origin "from the days when railroad men left their red signal lanterns outside the brothels while paying a visit to a lady of the evening—so they could be found in an emergency" (MacKell, 2004, p. 1).

Prostitution
Act of providing sexual behavior (typically manual stimulation, oral sex, sexual intercourse, anal sex) through the use of one's body in exchange for money, drugs, or other goods

Sex work
Way in which one earns a living by providing sexual services, such as acting in a pornographic video, being a stripper, or being a phone sex worker

Until they come, the nightly scum, with drunken eyes aflame; Your sweethearts, sons, ye scornful ones—'tis I who know their shame. The gods, ye see, are brutes to me—and so I play the game.

Robert W. Service, Yukon poet, *The Harpy*

18.6b Types of Sex Workers

There is a status hierarchy among sex workers in terms of working conditions, clients, and income.

Streetwalker

Sex workers who are referred to as *streetwalkers* get this name because they approach individuals waiting at a street corner, walk alongside them/propositioning them, or negotiate with a potential customer in a car who stops at the street corner. The sex act takes place in a rented room, street alley, or the customer's car. Streetwalkers are the least respected and lowest level of sex workers.

Streetwalkers live in a context of violence, both physical and sexual. Oselin and Blasyak (2013) interviewed 17 streetwalkers who revealed the horror and danger of working on the streets.

> *I thought I was going to die in the life … that I would die using or be killed by a trick because I didn't see any way out no matter how much I wanted it to end. I wasn't expecting my life to be too much longer out there because things were getting worse on the streets day by day. I've seen about five girls I knew who were working the streets along with me end up dead in garbage cans. One girl that used to live with me they found her rolled up in a carpet in back of this restaurant in the area we used to prostitute together. When I found out about her death [she shakes her head] … I knew her … I knew her children and her husband.*

Apartment Sex Worker

In some European cities, such as Amsterdam, sex workers may legally rent one-room apartments and solicit customers from behind windows. Patrons walk by and are enticed to come inside. The sex worker identifies what the customer wants, negotiates the price, and the service begins.

Erotic Massage Parlor Worker

Although therapeutic massage is a legitimate service provided by educated, trained, and licensed masseuses, some massage parlors are fronts for prostitution, offering hand jobs, oral sex, and intercourse. These type of sex workers are discussed earlier in the chapter.

Cultural Diversity

Prostitution has been legal in Switzerland since the 1940s. More recently (2012), Zurich taxpayers set aside 2 million to build "Strichplatz" areas, also known as "sex boxes," where clients drive in, park their cars, and negotiate sex with one of 24 sex workers on duty. For those who want more space, small wooden structures with plank beds are available. The result of these government-sponsored cubicles, which amount to parking one's car in a mini garage cubicle for 20 minutes, is a reduction in violence against sex workers and a reduction in human trafficking. The clients pay for access to the structures, the sex workers pay taxes on their earnings, and everyone is safe—a win-win (Bachmann, 2018). In rural India, family sanctioned prostitution has been a long tradition for the lower caste Bedia community. Since prostitution is the primary family income, girls are trained and groomed to become sex workers to provide for their families (Della, et al., 2019).

House Sex Worker

Some sex workers work out of an established house or **brothel** (also known as a *whorehouse, cathouse,* or *bordello*). In the past, a **madam,** who took care of the business and the girls, ran a brothel.

Some modern brothels are run more like other service-based businesses, although many are fronts for trafficked women forced to prostitute themselves against their will. The Moonlite Bunny Ranch™ in Las Vegas, Nevada, is a legal brothel that houses around 15 sex workers. Men come in, select from a lineup, have a drink, go to the woman's room, negotiate a price, and pay the money to the woman, who then leaves the room and takes it to the manager. The service, called a "party," begins on her return. When the time is up, if the customer wants another party (more time, two women, etc.), the negotiation starts over. The sex worker pays the owner a percentage of what the customer pays. The house sex worker is relatively safe from violence because a video camera may be in every room, and a bouncer is on the premises. The workers generally have regular STI/HIV checks and require their customers to use condoms. Prices at brothels may range from $500 to $10,000, depending on what the customer wants in terms of time (20 minutes to all-night hours), activities, and number of participants. Durant & Couch (2019) interviewed men in Dandenong, Victoria, Australia, about their experience with brothel sex workers. The former were described as "When you go into a brothel, it's like going to Macca's (a McDonald's Restaurant). You just get handed this booklet thing that has all their services and other stuff in it and you choose what you want [from it] …"

Call Girl

The **call girl** is a sex worker who is called on the phone and asked to come to the customer's room to provide a sexual service. Call girls can be trafficked sex slaves, or may come from the top hierarchy of sex workers, as personified by Heidi Fleiss (known as the Hollywood Madam) and Sydney Biddle Barrows (known as the Mayflower Madam). Both Fleiss and Barrows began as high-priced call girls who—because of their youth, intelligence, and social skills—were able to command considerable fees. Later, these women attracted other women with similar credentials and became madams of large-scale call-girl rings. Both Fleiss and Barrows were eventually caught and prosecuted.

Escort is another term for call girl; this term implies a wider range of behavior, such as being a social companion for an evening that typically ends in sexual interaction. Burghart (2018) revealed the ways in which escorts marketed themselves to clients over the internet in reference to factors including romance, safety/discretion, body, level of sophistication/social class, submissiveness, one-off encounter (client who seeks sexual experience over sexual intimacy), and relationship (the "girlfriend" or "boyfriend" experience). An example of an advertisement for the latter, one advertisement read: *"I would be happy to arrange an evening tailored especially to your taste. Or available for overnights or long weekends away."*

The escort may entertain their patron in their own residence, the patron's, or a hotel room. Although some escort services offer nonsexual services, most are fronts for prostitution. Some escorts evade the illegality of prostitution by referring to their service as a *sensuality coach.* Still another variation is the heterosexual escort in developing countries who offers romance and sex for wealthy women. Jacobs (2014) noted a thriving business in Kenya, where the locals provide romance and sex in exchange for gifts, food, adventure, and cash. While it is men who most often buy sex from women, Berg et al. (2020) reviewed the research on women who pay men for sex. While rare, such women (often more mature, financially independent women) take global vacations (often to Caribbean islands) to secure the sexual and romantic (companionship)

Brothel
Place, typically a house or rented space, where prostitutes service their customers

Madam
Woman who runs a house of prostitution

Call girl
Sex worker who is called on the phone and asked to come to the customer's room to provide sexual service

Escort
Another term for call girl that implies a wider range of behavior, such as being a social companion for an evening that typically ends in sexual intimacy

services of an idolized, hypersexual black male. Male escorts sell themselves as a "date" and view themselves as "desirable entrepreneurs" and "besness" men to avoid the stigma. In reality, they are young, uneducated, low-income drug users/sellers. In this transactional sex, the woman is in charge and gets the sex and the illusion of romance in exchange for money.

Finally, while escort services are thought of as mainly those offered by women, Schrimshaw et al. (2017) noted the use of gay male escorts who use gay hookup apps and sites to find customers. Tewksbury and Lapsey (2018) conducted a content analysis of 627 online narratives of male escorts. Findings revealed that sexual services and sexual skills are only one aspect of what male escorts provide. Sometimes more important, were issues of intimacy, social interactions, and personality. While the "girlfriend" experience of female sex workers has been emphasized as a value to clients, little visibility has been given to the emotional aspect of male escort services.

Sugar Baby

A **sugar baby** is a person who exchanges friendship and sometimes sex for mentoring and money from an older, wealthy man, called a **sugar daddy**. Sugar babies are typically young, attractive, articulate females who want to find a source to pay for school rather than a minimum-wage job or who lack money to pay off enormous student loan debt.

An anonymous source wrote of 160 students at Tulane University in Louisiana in search of "Sugar Daddies" or "Sugar Mommies" on the website www.seeking.com. Over a third of the site's 900,000 members are college students. The founder, Brandon Wade, states that the site is not about prostitution; rather, it is a place where women can find wealthy boyfriends (Nola Defender, 2011). There is debate in the legal profession about whether sugar-daddy sites promote prostitution. One attorney has recommended they be investigated (Motyl, 2013). Nayar (2017) analyzed blog content to discover the nuances of the relationship between sugar babies and sugar daddies/sugar mamas and noted that while the economic exchange was important, aspects of the relationship were emotional, intimate, chemistry laden, etc. These later labels were invoked to legitimize the arrangement as separate from sex work.

One of the students in our sexuality class noted that she was a sugar baby who received $4,000 a month from her sugar daddy to cover her expenses. In exchange, she would meet him at conferences he flew her to and act as his girlfriend for the weekend. She reported that her sugar daddy was married and had four children. The downside was that he fell in love with her and wanted to marry her. She broke off the arrangement, reminding him that theirs was a business deal.

Male Sex Worker

Although the term *prostitute* is most often used in reference to women, male sex workers (also referred to as *escorts, hustlers,* or *rent boys*) are not uncommon. Male sex workers may service men (escorts), women (gigolos), or both (taxi boys).

Sugar baby
Woman who exchanges friendship and sex for mentoring and money from an older, wealthy man

Sugar daddy
Wealthy man who provides mentoring and money to a younger female in exchange for friendship and sex

While the internet is thought mainly as being used in reference to female escorts, Kumar (2017) provided a global overview of male escort websites via a content analysis of 499 websites. Most were independent and not affiliated with escort agencies; the majority also catered to male escorts soliciting male clients. The sites are becoming more visible and are globally dispersed with Asian, European, and South American countries as major market hubs.

Cultural Diversity

Organizational Structure of Sex Workers

In addition to these various types of sex workers, another way of categorizing sex workers is whether they work for themselves, work for a pimp, or are forced into prostitution—that is, they are bought and sold as sex slaves either domestically or taken from other countries. Some call girls are independent workers who set up their own clients on their cell phones. Others work for escort agencies or trafficking agents that have a central office, where prospective clients call and identify what they want (blue-eyed blonde, providing bondage and discipline, etc.). The call is then routed to the woman who has the characteristics or meets the requests of the caller.

Other sex workers (more often streetwalkers) have a pimp who controls them and takes a percentage of their earnings. They are not free to leave the business but are free to walk about when they are not turning tricks. Many sex workers are actually enslaved girls and women who have been bought and sold, often as children, by owners who put them in brothels, massage parlors, or on the streets to service men daily. These girls and women are not free to leave, are beaten into submission, and live horrible lives. Some illegal immigrants are, in effect, sex slaves forced into prostitution to pay for their travel and expenses—which are never paid off. We will discuss sex trafficking further in this chapter.

18.6c Becoming a Sex Worker

Studies on recruitment into prostitution have focused on the characteristics associated with women who work as sex workers. Early first sexual experiences, childhood physical/sexual abuse, estrangement from parents, and low economic status are background characteristics of most sex workers. Some parents sell their children into prostitution as a means of providing income for the family (generally in India and other developing countries), and many women around the world and domestically are tricked or forced into trafficked sex slavery.

A common theme of recruitment into sex work is the need for money. Hampton & Lieggi (2020) emphasized that homeless, runaway, and transgender youth are at high risk for commercial sexual exploitation in the United States. Girls quickly learn that selling sex is one of the fastest ways to earn a lot of cash (and the alternative of working at a minimum-wage job cannot pay the bills). An exotic dancer in one of the authors' classes noted that she can make up to $1,500 a week, and this money is not taxed. One-fourth of adjunct college professors are on public assistance. They are known as the "fast food workers of the academic world." Some turn to sex work (Gee, 2017).

Some women report peer influence and stumbling into the connection between sex and money. Another student in the authors' classes noted the following:

> It was amateur night at the local titty bar. I went with my friends to see another of our friends who was dancing. We got liquored up and dared each other to get on stage and do a dance. I got a lot of tips and loved the attention. It wasn't long before I was a regular. Then the strip bar closed, but the owner wanted five of us to work for him at a new club. The men there were older and had more money. I got used to the money and was hooked. It wasn't long before I was turning tricks. (Authors' files)

Others are seduced into the role of sex work by a *loverboy* or *pimp*. While prostitution is often called the oldest profession, pimping is considered the second oldest profession. Researchers Van San and Bovenkerk (2013) interviewed 13 loverboys (then in prison) about their experiences of seducing young women into the role of prostitute. The respondents claimed that the women initiated the idea and implied or said they would perform sex work if the boyfriend (loverboy) would not break up with them.

Hence, the loverboys presented the prostitution as motivated by the girl and that their role was only as protectors—they denied violent force (which was a lie, according to police reports).

The loverboys pointed out that they knew how to spot a vulnerable girl. She was "on the stupid side" and could be easily manipulated:

> *Listen, these are mostly problem girls. They have problems with their parents or they have debts; a long-term relationship has recently ended, or they just broke up with their boyfriend. They're at an all-time low, and then a loverboy comes along. Someone with a lot of money, who takes her out to all the right places, pays for everything, spoils her or what have you. Eventually, there comes a time when the girl who gets everything from her man is expected to do something for him in return, but they often don't know how. Sooner or later these girls are simply going to be manipulated.*
> (Van San & Bovenkerk, 2013)

The set of steps include the pimp making the girl fall in love with him by spending money on her and making promises ("We'll open a club together"), isolating the girl from her friends and family so that the loverboy is the only person in her life, and telling her he was broke or needed money so the girl turned tricks for him. Some of the loverboys gave the girls drugs to get them addicted, so that they would do sex work for drugs. Progression through the various steps takes months or years and often includes the loverboy spinning up several women at once so that he eventually gets them competing against each other for his favor. Women may also be lured into prostitution by scams whereby men pose as wanting a mail order bride (Yakushko & Rajan, 2017).

International DATA

Statistics on Women who are Sex Workers

The vast majority of prostituted women have experienced severe early trauma and face a range of life-threatening risks. In her 2006 review of international studies, clinical and research psychologist Melissa Farley compiled these global statistics:

- 65%–95% of prostituted women were sexually assaulted as children.
- 70%–95% were physically assaulted in prostitution.
- 60%–80% were raped in prostitution.
- 75% have been homeless at some point in their lives.
- 85%–95% of those in prostitution want to escape it but have no other options for survival.
- 68% of 854 people in strip clubs, massage, and street prostitution in nine countries met criteria for post-traumatic stress disorder.
- 95% experience sexual harassment that would be legally actionable in another job.
- 80%–90% of those in prostitution experience verbal abuse and social contempt that adversely affect them.

Source: Farley, M. (2006, October 1). Prostitution, trafficking, and cultural amnesia: What we must not know in order to keep the business of sexual exploitation running smoothly. *Yale Journal of Law and Feminism*. Retrieved from http://digitalcommons.law.yale.edu/cgi/viewcontent.cgi?article=1243&context=yjlf

18.6d Life as a Sex Worker

Most women who work as sex workers in the United States are poor, have limited education, and have little opportunity of acquiring the job skills to increase their job prospects. Many are trafficked—some from other countries—as sex slaves in childhood or adolescence. In addition to financial concerns, some women choose sex work as an occupation because it provides them with more freedom, flexible work hours, and the ability to manage their dual responsibilities of being a nurturer (mother) and provider (Sinha, 2015). Blithe and Wolfe (2017) emphasized how sex workers in Nevada's legal brothel industry become trapped in the sex worker role (e.g., literally on lockdown in some brothels), are stigmatized, living an illusion of "work now, live later." Some sex workers are drug addicts. Regardless of the motivation, most are vulnerable to HIV infection and vulnerable to being beaten up or murdered.

Male sex workers experience similar stigma that negatively affects "their social supports and ability to develop and maintain noncommercial romantic relationships" (Jiao & Bungay, 2019). One male sex worker noted the impact on friendships:

> *If you're trying to go out to have some fun with some friends, and then this stranger comes up to you and he is offering you money and telling you all these things he wants to do ... your friends hear all of it, and then they're gone because they don't want to be friends anymore. (p. 245)*

Not all sex workers are destitute, regard their profession as particularly dangerous, or want to exit. Some, especially call girls at the top of the prostitution hierarchy who work in a relatively safe environment with regular clients and run a lucrative business, feel that they are unfairly harassed for earning a living the way they choose. They argue that they are abused by the courts and the police who harass them. These women note that sex workers are more often women than men and are more often arrested than the men they serve.

18.6e Impact of Sex Work on Personal Intimate Relationships

In a study of 44 couples in which one partner was involved in sex work (Syvertsen et al., 2013), respondents emphasized the emotional toll of the sex work on them as individuals and on their relationship. According to the researchers, "Couples employed multiple strategies to cope with sex work, including psychologically disconnecting from their situation, telling 'little lies,' avoiding the topic, and, to a lesser extent, superficially discussing their risks" (p. 1). Hence, the partners circumnavigated the fact that one partner was a sex worker by withholding information or minimizing the information that was available. The researchers added, "While such strategies served to protect both partners' emotional health by upholding illusions of fidelity and avoiding potential conflict, nondisclosure of risk behaviors may exacerbate the potential for HIV/STI acquisition" (Syvertsen et al., 2013, p. 1). This is important given that a study by Guida et al. (2019) found that sex workers reported less likelihood of using condoms with boyfriends/husbands. Drucker and Nieri (2018) interviewed 27 sex workers who discussed their intentions to exit the business. Reasons for wanting to exit sex work included that it interfered with outside interests and relationships, the desire to reconnect with family members, and wanting to improve current romantic relationships.

Our discussion of sex workers has focused on female sex workers. In a study comparing the behavior of male escorts with their male clients to their sexual behavior with noncommercial male partners, the sexual encounters with noncommercial partners were much more likely to include kissing, anal receptive sex, and sex without condoms (Rodriguez-Diaz et al., 2014). Jiao & Bungay (2019) interviewed Canadian gay male escorts, one of whom reported how sex work impacted his interest in sex:

> but when you do something for work, you lose interest in it (sex and relationships) outside of work. And sex is a big thing in a lot of people's lives, but you have absolutely no interest. ... It is like something got turned off and it can't be turned back on. (p. 645)

PERSONAL DECISIONS 18-3

Sex Workers Speak Out

India: It was typical for me to have 10–12 buyers every night. They were usually abusive, treating me as if they owned my body. I have a deep scar on my neck from a knife blade, which I got trying to save a young girl in my house from being gang raped. It almost killed me. When people tell me that women choose this life, I can't help but laugh. Do they know how many women like me have tried to escape, but have been beaten black and blue when they are caught? To the men who buy us, we are like meat. To everybody else in society, we simply do not exist.[1]

US: Prostitution is serial rape of our bodies. ... To this day, I have physical problems, and my emotional problems will fill a book. When I was in it, getting out seemed impossible because my sense of self-worth was nonexistent. I have no solution as long as men pay to do this terrible thing to us; the damage to us is massive. Maybe there is really no escape from this rape prison called prostitution.[2]

UK: The punters [buyers of sex] are the problem. Prostitution, apart from professional boxing, is the only job where people fully expect you to accept serious physical violence every day without complaint. That's not the sex workers' fault—it's the fault of the messed-up punters. Solving the problem of violence against sex workers goes much deeper than just creating "tolerance zones" where women (and men) can be legally ignored day in and day out.[2]

US: I had started having sex at 10 years old; I knew how to please men, even if it killed me. But at night when I came home and I showered, I scrubbed and lathered to try and get the streets off me. I hated being touched by tricks. Each time I did a call, I felt as if I was being raped again ... My best friend was raped in the room next to me, and I never heard a sound. The trick muffled her cries and walked out like nothing was wrong.[3]

US: For a great part of 1992, I lived in a beautiful apartment. I drove my expensive car. I bought lovely clothes and traveled extensively out of the country. I felt invincible. And I was miserable to the core. I hated myself because I hated my life. All the things I came to possess meant nothing. I could not face myself in the mirror. Working in prostitution lost my soul.[4]

Sources:

[1] Ayesha. (2016, August 22). India. *Equality Now.* Retrieved from http://www.equalitynow.org/campaigns/trafficking-survivor-stories/ayesha

[2] BBC News. (2006, December 19) Prostitutes speak of their ordeals. Retrieved from http://news.bbc.co.uk/2/hi/in_depth/6183491.stm

[3] Nekome. (2010, February 24). How prostitution chose me. *Prostitution Research & Education.* Retrieved from http://prostitutionresearch.com/pre_blog/2010/02/24/un_commission_on_the_status_of/

[4] Boyer, D., Chapman, L., & Marshall, B. (1993). *Survival sex in King County: Helping women out.* King County Women's Advisory Board, Seattle, WA: Northwest Resource Associates.

If only sex work were not criminal, sex workers could do so much more for themselves and each other.

Melissa Grant, *Playing the Whore*

18.6f Clients of Sex Workers

Clients of sex workers are both single and married and of all social classes, ethnicity, and age (Serughetti, 2013). Five types of males who seek sex workers include (Sanders, 2008):

- *Explorers:* Men focused on the desire for sexual experimentation, curiosity, and fantasy.

- *Yo-yoers:* Men in their 30s who had stopped seeing sex workers when in a relationship but then start again when the relationship with their primary partner becomes unsatisfactory.

- *Compulsives:* Men who seek/have sex with sex workers as a compulsive behavior/fetish.

- *Bookends:* Men who have initial sexual experiences with sex workers and go back to buying sex in later life as the ultimate chance to satisfy their sexual desires.

- *Permanent purchasers:* Men who seek paid sex sporadically throughout their lifetime.

According to a sex worker who ran a call service in Los Angeles, "a large percentage of clients were a cross-section of lawyers, city administrators, law enforcement officers, and businessmen." She noted, "It is ironic that the people who use the services and benefit from prostitution are the same people that beat the drum against prostitution." (BBC News, 2006).

An analysis of data on 1,342 heterosexual men arrested for soliciting streetwalkers revealed the behavior that sex workers were most likely to engage in with clients was fellatio or vaginal intercourse. Fellatio was more likely to occur regardless of the customer's age or marital status (Sabbah, 2013).

In another study, Grov and colleagues (2014) reported data from an online survey of 495 male clients who paid for sex with male escorts. Most clients were white/Caucasian (87.7%), HIV negative (89.5%), employed full time (71.1%), single (58.6%), with a mean age of 54. Three quarters of clients were gay identified, 18% bisexual, and 4% heterosexual. Oral sex was common (80% gave, 69% received), 30% reported anal insertive sex, and 34% reported anal receptive sex. In total, few (12%) reported unprotected anal sex. Satisfaction with encounters was high.

Kong (2016) observed that men who buy sex from women:

negotiate four major risks at the normative "edge" of social behavior while enjoying the thrill of commercial sex: the consumption risk of overindulgence, the emotional risk of mixing love and sex, the moral risk of being discovered and the legal risk of being caught. (p. 105)

Men who buy sex from women vary in their perceptions of the experience. General attitudes are revealed by statements such as "Being with a prostitute is like having a cup of coffee. When you're done, you throw it out" and "[I'm] renting an organ for 10 minutes." Dominance and hostility play a primary role for many buyers: "She gives up the right to say no" and "I think about getting even [during sex with prostitutes]." Another man explains his expectations to the women whose services he buys: "I paid for this. You have no rights. You're with me now" (Farley et al., 2011).

Milrod and Monto (2015) provided data on 60- to 84-year-old heterosexual males and found that the older the man, the more frequent his behavior with sex workers. While fellatio was the most frequent service provided, many clients sought the girl-friend experience, which includes making the client feel important and pretending to genuinely care about his woes without sharing their own burdens. Mai (2017) also noted the "boyfriend experience" provided by Tunisian professional boyfriends for tourists. These arrangements not only involved providing regular sex for the females on vacation but sometimes escalated to include marriage and moving to Europe, all of which was to get money for their parents and partners back home. For potential clients who want to investigate hiring a sex worker, Horswill and Weitzer (2018) noted how The Erotic Review website not only provides information about sex workers but socializes the novice in regard to the use of sex services.

Males as tourists (e.g., Egypt) may also seek sex with young children. Although officially sex with children is prohibited, Soliman et al. (2018) reported that some young children in Egypt are encouraged/allowed by their parents to "marry" tourists to circumvent laws preventing the tourists having sex with children.

Prior and Peled (2019) noted four themes which permeated being a sex tourist: the financial experience, in which the men saw themselves as enriching the lives of the sex workers by lavishing money on them for their services; the cultural/exotic experience, in which the sex workers were viewed as hypersexual/lustful by nature; the girlfriend experience; and the masculinity boosting experience, in which they hire the youngest, most beautiful girl. Most of the men reported having unsatisfactory sex lives, viewed sex as a natural/biological drive, viewed seeking sex as what men do, and as a connection for intimacy.

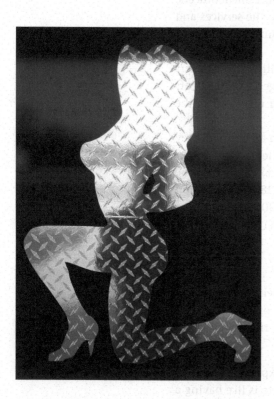

18.6g Prostitution and the Law

While sex workers are often stigmatized and blamed for their choice to be involved in sex work, Shdaimah and Wiechelt (2013) emphasized that they occupy a unique position of being both victim and criminal. They are victims in that sex workers, particularly streetwalkers, "suffer from a variety of problems including past and current trauma and abuse, substance abuse, mental and physical health disorders, and housing instability" (p. 23). The researchers interviewed and conducted focus groups with 17 women currently or formerly engaged in prostitution, which revealed that both survival needs and coercion were factors in their becoming involved in prostitution. In response, the State's Attorney's Office of the City of Baltimore began an initiative to create an alternative for people who are charged with prostitution, which is a crime in Maryland. Rather than treat the sex workers as criminals, they were viewed as individuals who are victims of economics, structure, and socialization and who could benefit from compassion and help toward an alternative job. *Social Policy 18-2* addresses the controversy of whether sex work should be decriminalized.

18.6h Sex Workers and STIs/HIV

Sex workers are at high risk for infecting (and being infected by) their clients with STIs, including HIV. Such a related risk occurs worldwide. The consequences of HIV among sex workers are devastating. Not only can they infect clients, but their children may be born with HIV. As the sex worker becomes progressively weaker, her children may be forced into prostitution themselves to survive. When the mother dies, the child may be left alone in the streets or grow up in an orphanage.

Social Policy 18-2

Should Sex Work Be Decriminalized?

Sex work is a controversial topic, with some individuals viewing it as a form of sexual abuse and exploitation, and others considering it a legitimate way of earning a living, in which adults have the right to engage.

Proponents of the prostitution-as-abuse perspective argue that the concept of consent is problematic and unrealistic, considering the vast inequity in gender, race, and economics targeting women. The dangers of prostitution are high: an increased risk of murder, rape, beatings, robbery, psychological abuse, emotional pain, and vulnerability to diseases—particularly HIV. Most prostituted women have a long history of sexual abuse and poverty. (See *Personal Decisions 18-3*.)

Others contend that although sex workers are physically, morally, and economically exploited, they have a right to be sex workers. Both camps believe that sex workers should be legally protected.

COYOTE (an acronym for Call Off Your Old Tired Ethics) is a sex worker advocacy group that was formed in San Francisco in 1973 by ex-sex worker Margo St. James. COYOTE promotes the creation of a sex workers' union to change their public image and to fight the moral and legal discrimination to which they are subjected. The organization supports programs to assist sex workers in their choice to change their occupation, works to prevent scapegoating and abuse, and aims to educate sex workers and their clients to use safe sex practices. COYOTE's affiliates identify three main claims: (1) Not all prostitution is forced but often is voluntarily chosen, (2) prostitution is a type of service work and should be destigmatized, and (3) not allowing a woman to work as a sex worker (under conditions of her choice) is a violation of her civil rights. A goal of COYOTE is decriminalization of sex work and the elimination of unjust treatment by police and health-care workers (Grant, 2014).

However, some human rights activists and lawyers who stand against discrimination and abuse of sex workers note that the service-work model of sex work is a simplistic view of a complex situation. International human rights lawyer Dianne Post, who advocates for trafficked women, states that prostitution "brands all women as something that can be bought and sold; and therefore ... less than full humans" (Post, 2013).

The United Nations Special Report on Trafficking pointed out in a 2006 report that the concept of consent is far from viable for many women. "Power and vulnerability in this context must be understood to include power disparities based on gender, race, ethnicity, and poverty. ... [T]he road to prostitution and life within 'the life' is rarely one marked by empowerment or adequate options" (Huda, 2006). Even among women who are not trafficked, poverty and ethnic and gender inequity can serve as limitations that make prostitution the only means of survival—a path that is far from voluntary.

Sex researchers, enforcement officials, politicians, and sex workers continue to debate the issue of whether prostitution should be legalized or decriminalized in the United States. Among the arguments for the legalization of prostitution, it would permit the taxation of the billions of currently untaxed dollars spent on prostitution, help control and regulate the criminal activity associated with prostitution, help prevent teenage prostitution, and help protect sex workers against abuse by pimps and clients by enabling sex workers to report abuse without fear of being arrested.

Furthermore, if prostitution were legal, public health regulations could require sex workers to use condoms and have regular gynecological exams to ensure they are not infected with an STI and to treat any diseases they may acquire. Just as restaurants must pass a health inspection and display a rating certificate, sex workers could be required to obtain a similar certificate of health. For example, in some districts of rural Nevada, prostitution has been legalized, and sex workers there are checked regularly by a physician for STIs.

The human rights organization Amnesty International has recommended complete global decriminalization for both buyers and sellers of sex. The rationale is that by decriminalizing sex work, sex workers may seek protection from abuse and avail themselves of medical and social services. Fritsch et al. (2016) also noted how the decriminalization of sex work can aid in the erotic lives of disabled people.

In Australia, approximately 20,000 sex workers spend an average of 2.5 years in the industry. In Victoria, Australia, sex work is legal in licensed brothels, while street-based sex work and sex work in unlicensed brothels remain illegal. Begum and colleagues (2013) interviewed 14 women in three focus groups who currently or recently were sex workers in a legal brothel and over age 18. The women reported that while legalization has brought increased safety (condom use, less violence), still the stigma remains. They also commented that being a legal sex worker is both economically rewarding and entrapping (women stay in the profession since they can't earn high incomes outside of prostitution). In addition, while the women felt empowered (they were earning good incomes), they also felt demeaned by the male clients. One woman said:

But I think my worst experience ... is ... men ... just disrespecting you—they can pound you because they've paid that money, they can do what they want. They can put their fingers inside, they can do those extra things ...

Surprisingly, some sex workers oppose legalizing their trade. In Nevada, where prostitution is legalized, some sex workers resent the legal conditions of their employment. They are not allowed to discriminate against certain customers by refusing to service them. They also feel that the law interferes with their private lives. Sex workers can go to town only during certain hours and cannot appear in the company of a client in a restaurant. This stigmatization of the profession, including fingerprinting and registration, also makes it difficult for sex workers to leave the profession and enter another.

As with other uses of technology, sex workers turned to the internet as a way to market themselves. While many posted advertisements on craigslist.com, others turned to websites like backpage.com. In 2018, the website backpage.com was shut down by federal agencies.

Providing services through these websites allowed many sex workers to move away from working under pimps, and allowed them to control their own sex worker businesses. Research by Cunningham et al. (2019) found that as a result of moving off the street to craigslist.com, there may have been a 10%–17% decrease in homicides of female sex workers. One reason for this decrease was that sex workers were no longer forced to walk the streets to attract clients but used the website to avoid clients they felt might be dangerous.

In 2018, FOSTA (Fight Online Sex Trafficking Act) and SESTA (Stop Enabling Sex Traffickers Act) bills were signed into law, which virtually eliminated the internet as a mechanism to secure clients. As many sex workers feared, these laws made their work unsafe. In a survey that was conducted soon after the bills went into effect, 60% of sex workers reported "that they had to take on potentially violent clients to make ends meet" (Peterson et al., 2019, p. 190).

https://polarisproject.org/human-trafficking

18.6i Sex Trafficking

Sex trafficking
Using force and deception to transfer persons into situations of extreme exploitation; related to prostitution

According to the Victims of Trafficking and Violence Protection Act of 2000, **sex trafficking** is the "recruitment, harboring, transportation, provision, or obtaining of a person for the purpose of a commercial sex act." The Act criminalizes the forced or deceptive movement of people into exploitative conditions of labor and provides services to victims. The law makes a symbolic distinction (although it holds no legal meaning) between sex and nonsex trafficking (i.e., movement into forced prostitution and movement into other forced labor sectors), thereby marking sex trafficking as a special category (Peters, 2013).

National DATA

The United States is one of the largest trafficking destination countries, where approximately 50,000 women and children are trafficked into the country each year. The average age for recruitment is between 11 and 14 (Hom & Woods, 2013).

Earlier, in 1910, the Mann Act, also known as the White Slave Traffic Act, was enacted to prohibit transporting women across state lines for the purpose of prostitution. The Act, which was strengthened in 1986, "prohibits coercion or enticement and transportation of minors (under 18) for prostitution or criminal sexual activity" (Stetson, 2004, p. 255).

The commercial sexual exploitation of women and girls through forced prostitution and sex trafficking is a major human rights and public health issue in the United States (Hom & Woods, 2013). Survivors face complex physical and mental health problems from the trauma and violence they experience. Several aspects of their background include:

1. *Pimp enculturation:* Perkins (2019) identified the characteristics of girls vulnerable to being trafficked as having backgrounds of homelessness, past violence, and foster care. Other life events leading up to the induction into sex trafficking often include a difficult home life with early abuse, rape by parent/stepparent, running away from home, and being vulnerable to a pimp. Sex workers are kept in the sex trade (13–15 customers a day) by being told by the pimp that he is the only one who cares about them and will take care of them, and that they have no place to go; threats to the family are also commonly made. Some are sold by their parents to traffickers as a way of providing income for the family. The women are also controlled by violent means—beatings, starvation, coercive drug use, and rape. One service provider reported knowing women who had suffered "ruptured spleens, broken bones that never healed, stabbings, and gunshot wounds, ... sexually transmitted infections, pregnancy, HIV, and complications from abortions" (Hom & Woods, 2013).

2. *Aftermath:* The effects of trafficking and sexual exploitation include physical damage, STIs, post-traumatic stress disorder, dissociation, anxiety, sleep disorders/nightmares, low self-esteem, and depression. These women often are unable to return to their families upon rescue or escape because of the shame and social rejection associated with being a prostitute or having been trafficked.

3. *Healing the wounds:* Talking with an outreach person who establishes trust and encourages the victims to consider an alternative life can offer the possibility of escape. The prostitutes are given trafficking hotline numbers and told that there are people, other than their pimp or trafficker, who really care about them. The recovery path is slow and holistic, encompassing the psychological and physical needs of trafficked women. Their immediate needs are also intensive—safe shelter, food, and acquiring identification, as well as future requirements essential to starting a new life, including education and skills training for an alternative job.

By 2018, every state had enacted anti-trafficking legislation. Most focus on the sex trafficking of children and the development of rehab services for them. Most states also no longer treat victims of sex trafficking as criminals to be prosecuted and put in jail, but as victims who are exploited. Hence, victims of sex trafficking are put into treatment systems that include safety from their pimps, education to learn alternative skills for becoming independent, and help in healing from prior abuse. However, in many states, programs are underfunded, making access a challenge. Steiner et al. (2018) studied trafficked survivors and noted the theme of empowerment for survivors. In addition, the governmental context needed to be engaged in promoting the recognition of human trafficking.

> *The only way to stop this trafficking is for prostitution to be legalized. Legalization will open it up to regulation, and regulation means safety.*
>
> Jeannette Angell, call girl

Chapter Summary

THIS CHAPTER REVIEWS the supply side of sexual offerings commercially available and the consequences for the providers and consumers.

Sex in Advertising

SEX IN ADVERTISING is common. The advertiser uses sex to get the attention of the viewer and punches in the product.

Sexuality Online

SEX ONLINE HAS both positive and negative consequences and poses many ethical dilemmas. Advantages of sexuality on the internet is that people can search for information, find a partner, maintain a long-distance relationship, connect disenfranchised or marginalized individuals, and buy sex products. Disadvantages of sexuality on the internet include online sexual harassment, and people misrepresenting themselves to potential partners.

The internet features erotic photos and webcams in which some people strip/dance for their long-distance partners. Other webcam strippers generate income from a nude show. Benefits of online sexuality include learning sex information, anonymous STI testing, finding a mate or sex partner, experiencing sexual fantasies/cybersex, connecting with disenfranchised/marginal groups, and enabling individuals to try out a new identity. Disadvantages include the spread of STIs/HIV, cybersex crime, deception, and supporting internet addiction.

Sex and the Law

THE UNITED STATES HAS AN ONGOING DEBATE on the issue of private rights versus social morality: Should consenting adults be permitted to engage in any sexual behaviors they choose, or should the law define morally acceptable parameters? One of the ways that society has achieved compromise and balance between the radically opposing views of private versus public morality has been to view certain sexual behaviors on a continuum of offensiveness and to assign relative penalties for engaging in them.

Sex-Related Businesses

PHONE SEX, STRIP CLUBS, EROTIC MASSAGE PARLORS, AND CAMMING are examples of businesses that sell sex.

Pornography

LITERALLY TRANSLATED, PORNOGRAPHY MEANS "stories of prostitutes." Something is deemed obscene if it appeals to a prurient interest in sex, is offensive to the community, and has no redeeming social value. Pornography has become more brazen and extreme in recent years. The acronym CURBFHP—children, urination, rape, bestiality, fisting, homicide, and pain—reflects the type of contemporary pornography that is becoming the target of federal prosecution.

Although many adults consume porn without negative effects, prolonged exposure to pornography results in people believing that less common sexual practices are more common than they are.

Sex Work

BEING INVOLVED IN PROSTITUTION IS NEGOTIATING the exchange of sexual behavior (typically manual stimulation, oral sex, sexual intercourse, and anal sex) for money, drugs, or other goods. It is a type of sex work in which people earn their living by providing sexual services.

Sex trafficking is the "recruitment, harboring, transportation, provision, or obtaining of a person for the purpose of a commercial sex act." The consequences are devastating for those who are sex-trafficked. These survivors face complex mental health problems from the trauma and violence they are exposed to.

Web Links

ECPAT: Every Child Protected Against Trafficking

> http://www.ecpat.org.uk

COYOTE (Call Off Your Old Tired Ethics)

> http://coyoteri.org/wp/

Cyber Civil Rights Initiative

> https://www.cybercivilrights.org/

CyberPatrol/Net Nanny

> http://www.cyberpatrol.com/

Cybersitter

> http://www.cybersitter.com/

Fight the New Drug

> http://www.fightthenewdrug.com

National Center for Missing and Exploited Children

> http://www.missingkids.com

Regulation of Pornography and Child Pornography on the Internet

> http://www2.warwick.ac.uk/fac/soc/law/elj/jilt/1997_1/akdeniz1/

Your Brain on Porn

> http://www.yourbrainonporn.com

Exotic Dancers Alliance

> http://www.bayswan.org/eda-sf/

Rapeis.org

> http://www.rapeis.org

Key Terms

Brothel **519**

Call girl **519**

Camming **507**

Chicken porn **514**

Child pornography **514**

Cybersex **500**

Degrading pornography **511**

Erotica **511**

Erotic massage parlors **510**

Escort **519**

Kiddie porn **514**

Lap dance **508**

Madam **519**

Obscenity **514**

Phone sex **507**

Pornography **511**

Prostitution **517**

Revenge porn **516**

Sex trafficking **528**

Sex work **517**

Sugar baby **520**

Sugar daddy **520**

Table dance **508**

Therapeutic massage **510**

Violent pornography **511**

Glossary

A

Abortion

Deliberate termination of a pregnancy through chemical or surgical means

Absolutism

A belief system based on the unconditional power and authority of religion, law, or tradition

Abstinence

State of refraining from having sexual intercourse

Acquaintance rape

Nonconsensual sex between people who are dating or on a date (also called *date rape*)

Acquired dysfunction

Sexual dysfunction that a person is currently experiencing but has not always experienced

Acquired immunodeficiency syndrome

Last stage of HIV infection in which the immune system of a person's body is so weakened that it becomes vulnerable to infection and disease (opportunistic infections)

Adolescence

Developmental period in which a youth moves from childhood to adulthood

Agender

Individuals who do not identify as having a gender identity

Agnosia

Loss of auditory, sensory, or visual comprehension

Ally development model

Combating homophobia by exposing children in K–12 grades to the nature of prejudice and discrimination toward LGBTQIA individuals

Alzheimer's disease

Progressive and degenerative brain disease progressing from mild memory loss, through significant cognitive impairment, to very serious confusion and the loss of ability to manage activities of daily living, such as dressing, eating, and bathing

Ambivalence

Conflicting feelings that coexist, producing uncertainty or indecisiveness about a person, object, idea, or course of action

Amenorrhea

Absence of menstruation for 3 or more months during which a woman is not pregnant, is menopausal, or is breastfeeding

Amniocentesis

Prenatal test in which a needle is inserted (usually in the 16th or 17th week of pregnancy) into the pregnant woman's uterus to withdraw fluid, which is analyzed to see if the cells carry XX (female) or XY (male) chromosomes and to identify chromosomal defects

Analingus

Licking and/or insertion of the tongue into the partner's anus (also known as *rimming*)

Androgyny

Having traits stereotypically associated with both masculinity and femininity

Aphasia

Impaired communicative ability

Aphrodisiac

Any food, drink, drug, scent, or device that arouses and increases sexual desire

Apraxia

Inability to perform coordinated movements

Areola

Darkened ring around the nipple that keeps the nipples lubricated by secretions of oil during breastfeeding

Asceticism

Belief that rising above carnal lust and the pursuit of sensual pleasure into a life of self-discipline and self-denial is desirable

Asexual

Refers to people who do not experience sexual attraction/arousal to a partner; however, they may form emotional attachments, masturbate, and experience sexual pleasure

Asexuality

Absence of sexual attraction to anyone

Asymptomatic

Producing no symptoms or signs or, as with some STIs, yielding symptoms so mild that medical care is not sought

Atypical anatomical development

Refers to congenital variations in the reproductive system, sometimes resulting in ambiguous genitalia

Autoerotic asphyxiation

Cutting off one's air supply to enhance one's orgasm but misjudging the extent of doing so such that accidental death occurs

Aversive conditioning

Type of behavior therapy that involves pairing an aversive or unpleasant stimulus with a previously reinforcing stimulus; used in sex offender treatment to decrease deviant sexual arousal and reduce the probability of engaging in paraphilic behavior

B

Bartholin glands

Glands located at the base of the minor lips of the female genitalia that secrete a small amount of mucus to the inner surfaces of the labia minora

Benign prostatic hyperplasia

Normal enlargement of the man's prostate as he ages that may eventually require treatment

Biosexology

Study of the biological aspects of sexuality

Biosocial framework

Theoretical framework that emphasizes the interaction of one's biological/genetic inheritance with one's social environment to explain and predict human behavior

Biphobia

Fearful, negative, discriminatory reactions toward bisexuals

Bisexuality

Emotional and sexual attraction to members of both sexes

Blended orgasm

Orgasm whereby the woman experiences both vulval contractions and deep uterine enjoyment

Brainstorming

Problem-solving strategy of suggesting as many alternatives as possible without evaluating them

Breast-conserving therapy

Removal of the cancerous lump rather than the whole breast (also called lumpectomy)

Breech birth

During childbirth, the baby's feet or buttocks come out of the vagina first

Brothel

Place, typically a house or rented space, where prostitutes service their customers

C

Call girl

Sex worker who is called on the phone and asked to come to the customer's room to provide sexual service

Camming

The use of a webcam to facilitate the customer seeing, directing, and interacting with a performer

Candidiasis

Vaginal yeast infection that tends to occur in women during pregnancy, when they are on oral contraceptives, or when they have poor resistance to infection

Case study

Research method that involves conducting an in-depth, detailed analysis of an individual, group, relationship, or event

Catfishing

The process of luring someone into believing that a fake person they meet online is actually real

Celibacy

Condition of refraining from sexual intercourse, especially by reason of religious vows; also used to refer to being unmarried

Cerebral palsy

Condition, often caused by brain damage that occurs before or during birth or in infancy, resulting in muscular impairment and sometimes speech and learning disabilities

Cervical cap

Thimble-shaped contraceptive device made of rubber or polyethylene that fits tightly over the cervix and is held in place by suction

Cervix

Narrower portion of the uterus that projects into the vagina

Cesarean section

During childbirth, an incision is made in the woman's abdomen and uterus, and the baby is manually removed

Chastity

State of not having had sexual intercourse; also implies moral purity or virtuousness in both thought and conduct

Chicken porn

See *child pornography*

Childhood

Developmental time frame that extends from ages 2–12 and involves physical, cognitive, social, and sexual development

Child pornography

Image that depicts a clearly prepubescent human being in a sexually explicit manner (also called kiddie porn and chicken porn)

Chlamydia

Common sexually transmitted infection caused by the microorganism *Chlamydia trachomatis*, often asymptomatic, and therefore known as the *silent disease*

Chorionic villus sampling

Prenatal diagnostic test of cells from the chorion (membrane surrounding the fetus), performed at 10–12 weeks gestation to identify chromosomal abnormalities and some other diseases

Chromosomes

Threadlike structures of DNA within the cell nucleus that carry genes and transmit hereditary information

Chronic obstructive pulmonary disease

Collective term for diseases that affect the flow of air into the body, such as asthma, bronchitis, and emphysema (Individuals with COPD often experience fatigue due to decreased oxygen intake and the effort involved in breathing.)

Circumcision

Surgical procedure in which the foreskin of the penis is pulled forward and cut off (also known as *male genital mutilation*)

Cisgender

Individuals who feel that their identity matches their biological sex

Classical conditioning

Behavior modification technique whereby an unconditioned stimulus and a neutral stimulus are linked to elicit a desired response

Classic rape

See *predatory rape*

Climacteric

Term often used synonymously with menopause; refers to changes that both men and women experience at midlife

Clitoris

Sensory organ located at the top of the labia minora of the female genitalia

Closed-ended question

Type of question that yields little information and can be answered in one word

Cognitive/affective theory

As related to sexuality, a theory that emphasizes the role of thought processes and emotions in sexual behavior

Cognitive behavioral sex therapy

Treatment method emphasizing that negative thoughts and attitudes about sex interfere with sexual interest, pleasure, and performance

Cognitive-developmental theory

Theory that views gender role acquisition as based on both biology and social learning

Cohabitation

Also known as living together, cohabitation is when two unrelated adults involved in a relationship sleep in the same residence at least 4 nights a week for 3 months.

Coitus

See *sexual intercourse*

Coitus interruptus

Practice whereby the man withdraws the penis from the vagina before he ejaculates (also known as *withdrawal*)

Coming out

(Shortened form of "coming out of the closet") Process of defining yourself as gay in sexual orientation and disclosing your self-identification to others

Communication

Exchange of messages between two or more people

Compersion

The opposite of jealousy, whereby a person feels positive about a lover's emotional and sexual enjoyment with another

Complementary needs theory

Individuals tend to select a mate whose needs are opposite or complementary to their own needs

Comprehensive sex education programs

Programs that discuss abstinence as well as the use of contraception

Conception

Fusion of the egg and sperm

Condom use resistance

Successful attempt to engage in unprotected sexual intercourse with a partner who wants to use a condom

Conflict theory

Sociological theory that views society as consisting of different parts competing for power and resources

Conversion therapy

Therapy designed to change a person's sexual orientation, usually gay to heterosexual

Coolidge effect

The effect of novelty and variety on sexual arousal—for example, when a novel partner is available, a sexually satiated male regains capacity for arousal

Corona

Raised rim on the glans of the penis that is especially sensitive to touch

Correlation

Statistical index that represents the degree of relationship between two variables

Cougar

Older woman who pursues younger sexual partners

Covert sensitization

Therapeutic technique that involves instructing the client to use negative thoughts as a way of developing negative feelings associated with a deviant sexual stimulus

Cowper glands

Pea-sized structures attached to the urethra in the penis that secrete droplets of clear, sticky fluid prior to ejaculation (also known as *bulbourethral glands*)

Critical sexuality studies

Generic term for current core content of sexuality theory and research that is multifaceted and multidisciplinary (crossing several social science and humanities disciplines)

Cross-dress

To dress in the clothes of the other gender, typically a man dresses in a woman's clothes

Cryptorchidism

Undescended testes

Cunnilingus

Stimulation of the clitoris, labia, and vaginal opening of the woman by her partner's tongue and lips

Curvilinear correlation

Relationship that exists when two variables vary in both the same and opposite directions

Cybersex

Engaging in self-stimulation while online, including looking at images or videos, engaging in sexual chat, exchanging explicit sexual emails, and sharing mutual sexual fantasies while masturbating

Cystitis

Bladder inflammation and infection

D

Date rape

See *acquaintance rape*

Deductive research

Sequence of research starting with a specific theory, generating a specific expectation or hypothesis based on that theory, and then gathering data that will either support or refute the theory

Defense of Marriage Act

Legislative act that denied federal recognition of same-sex marriage and allowed states to ignore same-sex marriages licensed elsewhere

Degrading pornography

Sexually explicit material that degrades, debases, and dehumanizes people, typically women

Delayed ejaculation

Absence or delay of ejaculation

Dementia

Brain disorder involving multiple cognitive deficits, including memory impairment and at least one of the following: aphasia; agnosia; apraxia; or loss of ability to think abstractly and to plan, initiate, sequence, monitor, and stop complex behavior

Dental dam

Thin piece of latex that covers the vulva during cunnilingus or the anus during analingus

Dependent variable

Variable that is measured to assess what, if any, effect the independent variable has on it

Depo-Provera

A synthetic compound, similar to progesterone, injected into the woman's arm or buttock that protects her against pregnancy for 3 months by preventing ovulation

Descriptive research

Qualitative or quantitative research that describes sexual processes, behaviors, and attitudes, as well as the people who experience them

Diabetes mellitus

Chronic disease in which the pancreas fails to produce sufficient insulin, which is necessary for metabolizing carbohydrates and fats

Diaphragm

Shallow rubber dome attached to a flexible, circular steel spring, 2–4 inches in diameter, that can be inserted vaginally to cover the cervix and prevent sperm from entering the uterus

Dichotomous model

(Also referred to as the *either-or model of sexuality*) Way of conceptualizing sexual orientation that prevails not only in views on sexual orientation but also in cultural understandings of biological sex (male versus female) and gender (masculine versus feminine)

Digisexuality

The use of radical new sexual technologies (e.g. teledildonics, virtual sex, sex robots)

Dilation

During childbirth, the increased size of the opening of the cervix through which the baby will pass

Dilation and curettage

Abortion procedure whereby a metal surgical instrument is used to remove any remaining fetal tissue and placenta from the uterine walls after suctioning the contents of the uterus

Dilation and evacuation

Abortion procedure during the second trimester (13–24 weeks' gestation), whereby the cervix is dilated and the fetal parts inside are dismembered so they can be suctioned out

Dilation and suction

Abortion procedure during the first 12 weeks whereby the cervix is dilated before the suction procedure occurs

Disability

Health condition that involves functional deficits in performing activities of daily living

Discrimination

Behavior that involves treating categories of individuals unequally

Disorders of sex development

An umbrella term that includes many different conditions that occur when "a less-common path of sex development is taken"

Double mastectomy

Removal of both breasts

Down low

Behavior of keeping sexual activity private; term used to describe men who have sex with men but do not label themselves as gay or bisexual

Dysmenorrhea

Painful menstruation

Dyspareunia

The recurrent or persistent genital pain associated with intercourse or attempts at sexual intercourse

E

Eclectic view

View that recognizes the contribution of multiple perspectives to the understanding of sexuality

Ecstasy

Drug with both stimulant and psychedelic effects that can result in increased energy; enhanced sense of pleasure and self-confidence; and feelings of peacefulness, acceptance, and closeness with others; also known as MDMA, X, Molly, or E (use is also associated with dangerous risks, such as heart failure)

Ectopic pregnancy

Condition in which a fertilized egg becomes implanted in a site other than the uterus

Effacement

During childbirth, the cervix flattening out and getting longer

Ego

Freud's term for that part of the individual's psyche that deals with objective reality

Ejaculatory inevitability

The feeling a male has when he becomes aware that he is going to ejaculate and cannot stop the process

Embryo

Developing organism from conception to the eighth week of pregnancy

Emergency contraception

Contraceptive administered within 72 hours following unprotected intercourse; referred to as the morning-after pill

Emission

First phase of a male orgasm in which semen pools in the urethral bulb and ejaculatory pressure builds

Empirical evidence

Data that can be observed, measured, and quantified

Endogamy

The cultural expectation to select a marriage partner with one's own social group

Endometriosis

Growth of endometrial tissue outside the uterus, in the fallopian tubes or abdominal cavity, which may cause pain

Epididymis

Part of the spermatic duct system connecting the testicles with the vas deferens

Erectile disorder

Persistent or recurrent inability to attain, or to maintain until completion of sexual activity, an adequate erection

Erotica

Sexually explicit material that is neither a degrading nor violent portrayal of consensual sexual activity

Erotic massage parlors

Places that provide sexual services (manual manipulation, oral sex, and sometimes sexual intercourse) in exchange for money

Erotophilia

Propensity to have very positive views of and emotional responses to sexuality

Erotophobia

Propensity to have very negative views of and emotional responses to sexuality

Escort

Another term for call girl that implies a wider range of behavior, such as being a social companion for an evening that typically ends in sexual intimacy

Evolutionary theory

Theory that explains human sexual behavior and sexual anatomy on the basis of human evolution (See also *sociobiological theory*)

Exchange theory

In mate selection, refers to selecting a partner who offers the greatest rewards at the lowest cost

Excitement phase

Phase of sexual response cycle whereby increasing arousal is manifested by increases in heart rate, blood pressure, respiration, overall muscle tension, and vasocongestion, or increased blood flow to the genital region

Exhibitionistic disorder

Paraphilia that involves an intense, recurrent (over a period of at least 6 months) sexual urge, often accompanied by sexually arousing fantasies, to expose one's genitals to a stranger

Exogamy

The cultural expectation to marry outside your own family group

Experimental research

Research methodology that involves manipulating the independent variable to determine how it affects the dependent variable

Expulsion

Second phase of a male orgasm in which semen is expelled by vigorous contractions of the muscles surrounding the root of the penis, pelvic region, and genital ducts

External locus of control

The perspective that successes and failures are determined by fate, chance, or some powerful external source

Extradyadic affair

Betrayal (sexual, emotional, cybersexual) by an individual in an "exclusive" relationship

Extrafamilial child sexual abuse

Attempted or completed forced sex, before a child reaches the age of 14, by a person who is unrelated to the child by blood or marriage

Extramarital affair

Sexual involvement between a spouse and someone other than the person they are married to

F

Fallopian tubes

Oviducts, or tubes, that extend about 4 inches laterally from either side of the uterus to the ovaries; they transport the ovum from an ovary to the uterus

Family balancing

Act of selecting the sex of a child before it is conceived, ostensibly for a "balanced" one boy/one girl family; involves separating sperm carrying the X and Y chromosomes

Family of origin

Family into which an individual is born

Family of procreation

Family you begin by finding a mate and having and rearing children

Fellatio

Oral stimulation of a man's genitals

Female genital cutting

Cutting or amputating some or all of the female external genitalia: the prepuce (or hood) of the clitoris and shaft of the clitoris, the labia minora, and the labia majora (also called female genital alteration)

Female orgasmic disorder

A persistent or recurrent difficulty, delay in, or absence of experiencing orgasm following sufficient stimulation and arousal

Female sexual interest/arousal disorder

The persistent or recurrent inability to attain or maintain sufficient sexual excitement or a lack of genital lubrication/swelling or other somatic responses

Feminist theory

Perspectives that analyze discrepancies in equality between men and women and how these imbalances affect sexuality, research studies in sexuality, and sexual health-care delivery

Fetal alcohol syndrome (FAS)

Possible negative consequences (intellectual disability, intrauterine growth restriction, facial malformation, low birth weight) for the fetus and infant of the mother who drinks alcohol during pregnancy

Fetishism

Paraphilia that involves a pattern, of at least 6 months' duration, of deriving sexual arousal or sexual gratification from actual or fantasized inanimate objects or nongenital body parts

Fetus

Developing organism from the eighth week of pregnancy forward

Field research

Method of data collection that involves observing and studying social behaviors in settings in which they occur naturally

Fisting

Insertion of several fingers or an entire closed fist and forearm (typically lubricated with a nonpetroleum-based lubricant) into a partner's rectum and sometimes the lower colon; term also used to describe insertion of hand into vagina

Focus group

Interviews conducted in a small group and typically focused on one subject

Follicle-stimulating hormone

Hormone responsible for the release of an egg from the ovary

Forced sex

Acts of sex (or attempted sex) in which one party is nonconsenting, regardless of the age and sex of the offender and victim and whether or not the act meets criteria for what legally constitutes rape (also called rape)

Forcible rape

Sexual force involving three elements: vaginal, oral, or anal penetration; the use of force or threat of force; and nonconsent of the victim

Frenulum

Thin strip of skin on the underside of the head of the penis that connects the glans with the shaft

Friends with benefits

Friends who get together regularly for sex but who do not have a romantic relationship

Frotteuristic disorder

Paraphilia that involves recurring, intense, sexual urges (at least 6 months), accompanied by fantasies, of touching or rubbing—often with the genitals— against a nonconsenting person

Fundus

Broad, rounded part of the uterus

G

Gender

Social and psychological characteristics associated with being female or male

Gender binary

An either/or concept of gender as feminine or masculine, used by previous generations

Gender fluid

Individuals who change conceptions of how they feel and how they view themselves

Gender identity

Psychological state of viewing yourself as a girl or a boy, and later as a woman or man, or in the case of genderqueer individuals, as a blend of the two

Gender postmodernism

Abandonment of the notion of gender as natural and recognition that gender is socially constructed; dissolution of male and female categories as currently conceptualized in Western capitalist society

Genderqueer

Individuals who consider themselves a blend of both feminine and masculine

Gender role ideology

Socially prescribed role relationships between women and men in any given society

Gender roles

Social norms that dictate culturally appropriate female and male behavior

Gender role transcendence

Abandonment of gender schema, or becoming gender aschematic, so that personality traits, social and occupational roles, and other aspects of life are independent from gender categories

Generalized dysfunction

Sexual dysfunction that occurs with all partners, in all contexts and settings

Genital herpes

Viral infection that may cause blistering, typically of the genitals, and may also infect the lips, mouth, and eyes

Genital warts

See *human papillomavirus*

GHB (gamma hydroxybutyrate)

Also known as "liquid ecstasy" because, like X, it inspires a tendency to be touchy-feely and relaxed; however, it is more powerful, can cause deep sedation, and can be fatal

Glans

Small, rounded body of tissue on the head of the penis that can swell and harden

Gonorrhea

Bacterial infection that is sexually transmitted; also known as the clap, the drip, the whites, and morning drop

G-spot

Alleged highly sensitive area on the front wall of the vagina, 1–2 inches into the vaginal canal (also called the Gräfenberg spot)

H

Hate crimes

Bringing harm to an individual because they are viewed as belonging to a group you don't approve of

Hedonism

Sexual value that reflects a philosophy that the pursuit of pleasure and the avoidance of pain are the ultimate values and motivation for sexual behavior

Hepatitis B

Inflammatory disease of the liver caused by a virus

Herpes simplex virus type 1

Viral infection that may cause blistering, typically of the lips and mouth, and may also infect the genitals

Herpes simplex virus type 2

See *genital herpes*

Heterosexism

Belief, stated or implied, that heterosexuality is superior (morally, socially, emotionally, and behaviorally) to homosexuality

Heterosexuality

Sexual orientation in which the predominance of emotional and sexual attraction is to people of the other sex

Highly active antiretroviral therapy

Combination of drugs an HIV-infected person takes to treat the virus; also known as *cocktail therapy*

Homogamy theory

Individuals tend to be attracted to and involved with persons similar to themselves in age, race, religion, and so on

Homonegativity

Term that refers to antigay responses, including negative feelings (fear, disgust, anger), thoughts, and behavior

Homophobia

Negative emotional responses toward, and aversion to, gay individuals

Homosexuality

Sexual orientation in which the predominance of emotional and sexual attraction is to people of the same sex

Honor killing

The killing of an unmarried female who has had sex (which is thought to bring dishonor to her parents) by the parents or another family member in order to restore the family's honor (The practice occurs in Middle Eastern countries such as Jordan.)

Hooking up

Meeting someone and becoming sexually involved that same evening with no commitment or expectation beyond the encounter

Hormones

Chemical messengers that travel from cell to cell via the bloodstream

Hostile-environment sexual harassment

Environment whereby deliberate or repeated unwanted sexual comments or behaviors affect one's performance at work or school

Human immunodeficiency virus

Virus that attacks the immune system and may lead to AIDS

Human papillomavirus

A group of more than 200 related viruses

Hymen

Thin mucous membrane that may partially cover the vaginal opening

Hyperactive sexual desire disorder

Very high (hyperactive) sexual interest, which influences persons to behave as though they are driven to sexual expression and the pursuit of sex, which may have negative effects on the health, relationships, or career of the individual

Hyperventilation

Abnormally heavy breathing, resulting in loss of carbon dioxide from the blood, sometimes resulting in lowered blood pressure and fainting

Hypothesis

A tentative and testable proposal or an educated guess about the outcome of a research study

Hysterectomy

Surgical removal of the uterus

I

Id

Freud's term that refers to instinctive biological drives, such as the need for sex, food, and water

Independent variable

Variable that is presumed to cause or influence the dependent variable

Induced abortion

The elective termination of a pregnancy through chemical or surgical means

Induction abortion

Elective termination of a pregnancy through induced labor and delivery of the fetus; like other late-term abortions, generally performed when a fatal or serious fetal defect is discovered at a late stage in the pregnancy or the woman's health or life is at stake or both

Inductive research

Sequence of research that begins with specific empirical data, which are then used to formulate a theory to explain the data

Infancy

First year of life following birth

Infertility

Inability to achieve a pregnancy after at least 1 year of regular sexual relations without birth control, or the inability to carry a pregnancy to a live birth

Informed consent

In the context of participants in a research project, voluntary agreement to participate based on the provision of full information as to the project's risks and dangers

Inhibited male orgasm

Persistent or recurrent delay in or absence of orgasm following a normal sexual excitement phase

Intact dilation and extraction

Abortion procedure involving breech delivery of fetus (except for the head) and partial evacuation of the brain, resulting in the vaginal delivery of a dead fetus

Intellectual disability

Condition that involves subaverage intellectual functioning and deficits in adaptive behavior (also referred to as *mental retardation*)

Internal condom

Lubricated, polyurethane condom that is about 6.5 inches long and has flexible rings at both ends—one inserted vaginally, which covers the cervix, and one external, which partially covers the labia

Internal locus of control

The belief that successes and failures in life are attributable to one's own abilities and efforts

Intersexed

Individuals who have characteristics of both sexes

Interstitial cells

Cells that are housed in the testes and produce testosterone (They are also known as Leydig cells)

Interview survey research

Type of research in which trained interviewers ask respondents a series of questions and either take written notes or record the respondents' answers, over the telephone, online, or face-to-face

Intrafamilial child sexual abuse

Exploitative sexual contact or attempted or forced sex that occurs between related individuals when the victim is under the age 18 (also known as *incestuous child abuse*)

Intrauterine device

Object inserted into the uterus by a physician to prevent the fertilized egg from implanting on the uterine wall

Introitus

Vaginal opening

Involuntary abstinence

Condition of not having sexual relations due to environmental factors, such as not having a partner or being confined to an institution that does not encourage sexual expression

"I" statements

Statements that focus on the feelings and thoughts of the communicator without making a judgment on what the other person says or does

J

Jealousy

Emotional reaction to a perceived or real threat to a valued love relationship

K

Kegel exercise

Voluntary contraction of the PC muscle, as though stopping the flow of urine after beginning to urinate, that may be performed several times at several sessions per day

Kiddie porn

See *child pornography*

Klinefelter syndrome

Condition that occurs in males and results from the presence of an extra X sex chromosome (XXY), resulting in aberrant testicular development, infertility, low interest in sex (low libido), and, in some cases, mental disability

L

Labia majora ("major lips")

Two elongated folds of fatty tissue that extend from the mons veneris to the perineum

Labia minora ("little lips")

Two smaller elongated folds of fatty tissue that enfold the urethral and vaginal openings

Laparoscopy

Surgery using a laparoscope; sometimes used for tubal ligation

Lap dance

Type of dance that involves varying amounts of physical contact and can result in sexual release on the part of the customer (also known as friction dance or straddle dance)

Lesbian bed death

Purported sustained drop-off in sexual frequency of lesbian couples in long-term relationships that is not backed up by scientific data

LGBTQIA

Lesbian, gay, bisexual, transgender, questioning/queer, intersex, asexual, or ally

Libido

The sex drive

Lifelong dysfunction

Sexual dysfunction that a person has always experienced; for example, a person may have always lacked sexual desire

Locus of control

An individual's beliefs about the source or cause (internal or external) of his or her successes and failures

Looking-glass self

Idea that the image people have of themselves is a reflection of what other people tell them they are

M

Madam

Woman who runs a house of prostitution

Male "G-spot"

The prostate gland, which can be stimulated by a partner who inserts an index finger, up to the second knuckle (facing the partner) into the anus, and bends the finger in a "come hither" motion

Male hypoactive sexual desire disorder

Persistent or recurrent deficiency (or absence) of sexual fantasies, thoughts, and desire for (or receptivity to) sexual activity, which causes personal distress

Mammogram

Low-dose X-ray technique used by radiologists to detect small tumors inside the breast

Marital rape

Forcible rape by one's spouse; now illegal in all states

Mastectomy

Surgical removal of one breast

Masturbation

Natural, common, and nonharmful means of sexual self-pleasuring that is engaged in by individuals of all ages, sexual orientations, and levels of functioning (also called autoerotic behavior)

Meatus

Opening to the urethra at the tip of the penis

Medical abortion

See *pharmaceutical abortion*

Medicalization of sexual dysfunctions

Emphasizes that sexual dysfunctions have a medical or biological basis rather than an emotional or relationship cause

Medical model (view of intellectual disability)

Views the intellectually disabled individual as coping with a personal tragedy—which implies adjusting to limited functioning; views their sexual needs as nonexistent (also called the biological model)

Megan's Law

Federal law that requires that convicted sex offenders register with local police when they move into a community

Menarche

First menstruation

Menopause

Permanent cessation of menstruation that occurs in middle age

Menorrhagia

Excessive or prolonged menstruation

Menstrual extraction

Self-help manual suction technique to control the menstrual cycle or provide very early termination of pregnancy

Menstrual suppression

Use of hormones or drugs to inhibit menstruation

Menstrual synchrony

Increased tendency for women living in close proximity to have their menstrual cycles occur at relatively the same time

Menstruation or menses

Sloughing off of blood, mucus, and lining of the uterus

Mental disorders

Mental states characterized by mild to severe disturbances in thinking, mood, or behavior associated with distress or impaired functioning (sometimes called mental illness)

Middle age

Commonly thought to occur between the ages of 40 and 60

Mifepristone

Synthetic steroid that effectively inhibits implantation of a fertilized egg by making the endometrium unsuitable for implantation, which, in effect, aborts the embryo; may be used in the first 10 weeks of pregnancy in the US (see also *RU-486*)

Miscarriage

Unintended termination of a pregnancy

Mittelschmerz

Ovulatory pain

Mons veneris

Soft cushion of fatty tissue that lies over the pubic symphysis (joint between the left and right pubic bones)

Multidimensional model

Way of conceptualizing sexual orientation that suggests that a person's orientation consists of various independent components—including emotions, lifestyle, self-identification, sexual attraction, fantasy, and behavior—and that these components may change over time

Multigravida

State of having given birth before

Multiple sclerosis

Progressive disease that attacks the central nervous system

Mutual monogamy

A relationship in which both partners agree to be sexually faithful to each other

Myotonia

Muscle contractions

N

Natural selection

Theory that individuals who have genetic traits that are adaptive for survival are more likely to survive and pass on their genetic traits to their offspring

NEA-TDS (norethindrone acetate transdermal system)

A contraceptive patch worn continuously for 7 days and then replaced with a new patch (rotating sites on the abdomen, buttocks, or hips)

Negative correlation

Relationship between two variables that change in opposite directions

NEXPLANON

A single, flexible, plastic-rod subdermal implant the size of a matchstick that releases a progestin hormone called etonogestrel and provides up to 3 years of protection against pregnancy

Nomophobia

Dependence on virtual reality environments to the point that one has a social phobia

Nongonococcal urethritis

Infection of the urethra, the tube that carries urine from the bladder

Nonparticipant observation

Type of research in which investigators observe the phenomenon being studied but do not actively participate in the group or the activity

Nonverbal messages

Type of communication in which facial expressions, gestures, bodily contact, and tone of voice predominate

Nudism

Refers to the philosophy in which individuals practice/advocate nudity in private, in homes with other nudists, or in nudist resorts/beaches

NuvaRing

Soft, flexible, and transparent ring, approximately 2 inches in diameter, that is worn inside the vagina and provides month-long pregnancy protection

O

Obscenity

Label for sexual material that meets three criteria: (a) The dominant theme of the material must appeal to a prurient interest in sex; (b) the material must be patently offensive to the community; and (c) the sexual material must have no redeeming social value

Obsessive relational intrusion

Stranger or acquaintance repeatedly invades the physical or symbolic space of another with the goal of having an intimate relationship

Occupational sex segregation

Tendency for women and men to pursue different occupations

Oligomenorrhea

Irregular monthly periods

Oophorectomy

Surgical removal of the ovaries

Open-ended question

Broad question designed to elicit a great deal of information

Open relationship

Each partner agrees that the other can have sexual (and sometimes emotional) relationships with someone outside the couple relationship

Operant conditioning

Learning theory that behavior is learned in reference to its consequences; a behavior that is punished will decrease in frequency, while a behavior that is reinforced will increase in frequency

Operant learning theory

Explanation of human behavior that emphasizes that the consequences of a behavior influence whether that behavior will occur in the future

Operational definition

Working definition; how a variable is defined in a particular study

Operationalize

Define how a variable will be measured

Oral herpes

Sores of the lip and mouth, often caused by herpes simplex virus type I, but can also be caused by herpes simplex virus type II

Orchiectomy

Surgical removal of the testicles

Orgasm

Climax of sexual excitement, experienced as a release of tension involving intense pleasure

Orgasmic headache

A sudden and severe headache that occurs at the time of orgasm or shortly afterward

Orgasmic meditation

Holistic practice whereby one individual strokes the clitoris of the partner in a way that is designed to increase the emotional connection between the partners, not to create an orgasm

Os

Opening of the cervix (opening to the uterus)

Ostomy surgery

Surgery whereby a portion of the large or small intestine or urinary system is rerouted and brought to the skin surface of the abdomen, where the contents are collected in a bag (Cancers of the colon, rectum, bladder, cervix, or ovaries are typical causes of ostomy surgery.)

Outercourse

Sexual activities that do not involve exposing a partner to blood, semen, or vaginal secretions

Ovaries

Female gonads, attached by ligaments on both sides of the uterus, that have the following two functions: producing ova and producing the female hormones—estrogen and progesterone

P

Pansexuality

The state in which someone is attracted to people, regardless of their gender identity

Pap test

Procedure in which surface cells are scraped from the vaginal walls and cervix, transferred to a slide, and examined under a microscope to detect the presence of cancer cells

Paraphilia

Overdependence on a culturally unacceptable or unusual stimulus for sexual arousal and satisfaction

Paraplegia

Paralysis of the lower half of the body

Parental investment

Any investment by a parent that increases the offspring's chance of surviving and thus increases reproductive success

"Partial-birth" abortion

Nonmedical term used by abortion opponents to describe an abortion performed very late in pregnancy in which the terminated fetus is delivered (see *intact dilation and extraction*)

Participant observation

Type of observation in which the researcher participates in the phenomenon being studied to obtain an insider's perspective of the people and/or behavior being observed

Partner notification laws

Set of laws that require health-care providers to advise all persons with serious sexually transmitted infections about the importance of informing their sex or needle-sharing partner or partners

Patriarchy

The global system in which females are subordinate to or the property of a male, usually their husbands and/or fathers

Pedophilic disorder

Sexual arousal in reference to a child

Pelvic inflammatory disease

Inflammation of the pelvic organs often requiring hospitalization and surgery, associated with complications, such as infertility, ectopic pregnancy, and chronic abdominal pain

Penectomy

Surgical removal of part or all of the penis

Penile strain gauge

Flexible band that fits around the base of the penis and expands as the penis enlarges, measuring circumference—a way of measuring male arousal via penis size

Penis

Primary male external sex organ that, in the unaroused state, is soft and hangs between the legs

Performance anxiety

Excessive concern over adequate sexual performance, which may result in sexual dysfunction

Perineum

Area of skin between the opening of the vagina and the anus

Periodic abstinence

Refraining from sexual intercourse during the 1 to 2 weeks each month when the woman is thought to be fertile; (also known as *rhythm method, fertility awareness,* and *natural family planning*)

Peripartum depression

Similar to postpartum depression but feelings begin as early as four months into pregnancy

Persistent genito-pelvic pain/penetration disorder

Involves recurrent difficulties accomplishing vaginal penetration during intercourse, pain during vaginal intercourse/penetration attempts, and fear/anxiety surrounding such attempts

Peyronie's disease

A curved or deformed penis that is a result of accumulated scar tissue

Pharmaceutical abortion

Intentional termination of pregnancy through the use of pharmaceutical drugs

Pheromones

Chemicals that activate the behavior of same-species organisms

Phone sex

Telephone conversation between a caller and a sex worker who verbally arouses, stimulates, and moves the caller toward orgasm in exchange for money

Physiological theory

Theory that describes and explains how physiological processes affect and are affected by sexual behavior

Plateau phase

Second phase of Masters and Johnson's model of the sexual response cycle, which involves the continuation of sexual arousal, including myotonia (muscle contractions), hyperventilation (heavy breathing), tachycardia (heart rate increase), and blood pressure elevation

PLISSIT model

Method of sex therapy that involves four treatment levels: permission, limited information, specific suggestions, and intensive therapy

Polyamory

Involvement of more than two individuals in a pair-bonded relationship (some of the individuals may be married to each other) who have an emotional, sexual, and sometimes parenting relationship

Polyfidelity

Partners in the group remain faithful (sexually exclusive) to everyone else in the group

Pornography

Sexually explicit pictures, writing, or other images, usually pairing sex with power and violence

Positive correlation

Relationship between two variables that exists when both variables change in the same direction

Postcoital contraception

See *emergency contraception*

Post-exposure prophylaxis

The use of antiretroviral drugs after a single high-risk event to stop HIV from making copies of itself and spreading through the body

Postpartum depression

Severe depression, anxiety, and alienation from infant experienced by 11%–20% of new mothers

Post-traumatic stress disorder

Mental health diagnostic category that characterizes a particular set of symptoms following traumatic events (including military combat, natural disasters, or other events that invoke terror, helplessness, and fear of loss of life); experienced by many rape victims

Preconception sex selection

Selection of the sex of a child before it is conceived (See also *family balancing*)

Predatory rape

Rape by a stranger which may involve a weapon (also called *classic rape*)

Pre-ejaculatory fluid

Fluid released from the Cowper glands during sexual arousal

Pregnancy

Fertilized egg implants (typically in the uterine wall) 5–7 days after conception

Premature ejaculation

Ejaculation that always, or nearly always, occurs prior to or within about 1–2 minutes of vaginal penetration; the inability to delay ejaculation on all or nearly all vaginal penetrations; and the presence of negative personal consequences, such as distress, bother, frustration, and/or the avoidance of sexual intimacy

Premenstrual dysphoric disorder

A proposed diagnostic category indicating a more severe form of PMS that interferes with work, social activities, and the relationships of a woman

Premenstrual syndrome

Physical and psychological symptoms caused by hormonal changes from the time of ovulation to the beginning of, and sometimes during, menstruation

Prenatal sex selection

Selection of whether to continue the pregnancy based on the sex of the fetus

Primacy/recency effect

Tendency of individuals to remember best what occurs first and last in a sequence

Primary dysfunction

See *lifelong dysfunction*

Primary sex characteristics

Characteristics that differentiate women and men, such as external genitalia (vulva and penis), gonads (ovaries and testes), sex chromosomes (XX and XY), and hormones (estrogen, progesterone, and testosterone)

Primigravida

Woman giving birth to her first baby

Principle of least interest

The person with the least interest controls the relationship

Prostate gland

Chestnut-sized structure in the male, located below the bladder and in front of the rectum, that produces much of the seminal fluid

Prostitution

Act of providing sexual behavior (typically manual stimulation, oral sex, sexual intercourse, anal sex) through the use of one's body in exchange for money, drugs, or other goods

Psychoanalytic theory

Sigmund Freud's theory that emphasizes the role of unconscious processes in life

Psychosexology

Area of sexology focused on how psychological processes influence and are influenced by sexual development and behavior

Puberty

Developmental stage in which a youth achieves reproductive capacity

Pubic lice

Parasitic insects found in coarse body hair of humans, causing itching; also known as crabs

Pubococcygeus

Muscle surrounding the opening to the vagina that can influence sexual functioning; if it is too tense, vaginal entry may be difficult or impossible

Punishment

Consequence that decreases or terminates a behavior

Purge

Act of throwing away or burning one's clothes as a desperate means of ending one's cross-dressing

Q

Quadriplegia

Paralysis from the neck down

Queer

A blanket term that many gender nonconforming individuals prefer

Quid pro quo sexual harassment

Type of sexual harassment whereby the individual is provided benefits (promotions, salary raises) in exchange for sexual favors

R

Radical prostatectomy

Surgical removal of the prostate

Rape

See *forced sex*

Rape culture

The widespread social framework in highly gendered patriarchal cultures characterized by male entitlement and objectification of women, in which violence is normalized and viewed as sexually exciting and women are blamed for being victimized

Rape myths

False but widely held attitudes and beliefs that serve to justify male sexual aggression against women (also called *rape-supportive beliefs*)

Rape-supportive beliefs

See *rape myths*

Rape trauma syndrome

Acute and long-term reorganization process that occurs as a result of forcible or attempted rape

Rapid ejaculation

See *premature ejaculation*

Reflective listening

Communication technique in which one person restates the meaning of what their partner has said in a conversation

Reinforcement

Consequence that maintains or increases a behavior

Relativism

Sexual value that emphasizes that sexual decisions should be made in the context of a particular situation

Representative sample

Sample the researcher studies that is representative of the population from which it is taken

Resolution phase

Final phase of Masters and Johnson's model of the sexual response cycle that describes the body's return to its pre-excitement condition

Retrograde ejaculation

Ejaculation during which a man experiences an orgasm where the ejaculate does not come out of the penis, but is emptied, instead, into the bladder

Revenge porn

When one posts nude photos of a former partner on the internet to get back at a partner

Rohypnol

Drug used in date rape scenarios that causes profound and prolonged sedation, a feeling of well-being, and short-term memory loss; also known as *dulcitas*, the "forget me drug"

RU-486

Drug approved for use up to 10 weeks after the onset of the last menstrual period (also known as the abortion pill)

S

Salpingectomy

Sterilization procedure whereby the woman's fallopian tubes are cut out and the ends are tied, clamped, or cauterized so that eggs cannot pass down the fallopian tubes to be fertilized (also known as tubal ligation or tying the tubes)

Sample

Portion of the population that the researcher studies to attempt to make inferences about the whole population

Satiation

A stimulus loses its value with repeated exposure

Satiation

Result of a stimulus losing its value with repeated exposure

Scabies

Infestation of the skin by microscopic mites that causes intense itching

Schizophrenia

Mental disorder characterized by social withdrawal and disturbances in thought, motor behavior, and interpersonal functioning

Scopophilia

See *voyeuristic disorder*

Scrotum

The sac located below the penis that contains the testicles

Secondary dysfunction

See *acquired dysfunction*

Secondary sex characteristics

Characteristics that differentiate males and females that are not linked to reproduction (facial hair in men, breasts in women)

Secondary victimization

The process of organizations or individuals blaming the person who reports a rape

Self-fulfilling prophecy

Behaving in such a way to make expectations come true; for example, caustically accusing a partner of infidelity may lead that partner to be unfaithful

Semenarche

A boy's first seminal ejaculation

Semen-conservation doctrine

From early Ayurvedic teachings in India, the belief that general good health in both sexes depends on conserving the life-giving power of vital fluids (semen and vaginal fluids)

Seminal vesicles

Two small glands about 2 inches in length, located behind the bladder in the male, that secrete fluids that mix with sperm to become semen

Seminiferous tubules

Part of the spermatic duct system, located within the testicles

Sensate focus

Treatment used in sex therapy developed by Masters and Johnson whereby the partners focus on pleasuring each other in nongenital ways

Sex

The biological distinction between female and male, usually categorized on the basis of the reproductive organs and genetic makeup

Sexism

Prejudice and discrimination, typically against women, on the basis of sex

Sexology

Unique discipline that identifies important questions related to sexuality issues and finds and integrates answers from biology, psychology, and sociology based on scientific methods of investigation

Sex party

The gathering of 6 or more people where full nudity is allowed and people openly engage in sexual and/or kinky activities

Sex roles

Roles filled by women or men that are defined by biological constraints and can be enacted by members of one biological sex only, such as wet nurse or sperm donor

Sex trafficking

Using force and deception to transfer persons into situations of extreme exploitation; related to prostitution

Sexual anatomy

Term referring to internal and external genitals, also called sex organs

Sexual coercion

Use of force (actual or threatened) to engage a person in sexual acts against that person's will

Sexual competence

Refers to four criteria—use of contraception, autonomy of decision, equally willing, and the "right time" as to when a person is ready for first intercourse

Sexual compliance

The concept whereby an individual willingly agrees to participate in sexual behavior without having the desire to do so

Sexual debut

First sexual intercourse

Sexual double standard

One standard for women and another for men regarding sexual behavior (In the United States, for example, it is normative for men to have more sexual partners than women do.)

Sexual dysfunctions

A heterogeneous group of disorders that are typically characterized by a clinically significant disturbance in a person's ability to respond sexually or to experience sexual pleasure

Sexual fantasies

Cognitions, thoughts, and/or images that are sexual in nature

Sexual fluidity

Capacity for variation in erotic responses depending on the situation

Sexual growth

The term for sexual satisfaction that results from work and effort with one's partner for a good sex life

Sexual guilt

Feeling that results from violating your sexual values

Sexual harassment

Unwelcome sexual advances, gestures, comments, demands, and other verbal or physical conduct of a sexual nature; unreasonably interferes with work or school performance and creates an intimidating, hostile, or offensive work, educational, or domestic environment

Sexual intercourse

Sexual union of a man's penis and a woman's vagina (also known as coitus)

Sexually transmitted infection

Infections transmitted primarily through sexual activity; a more recent, more specific term sometimes used to avoid the negative connotations sometimes associated with sexually transmitted disease (STD)

Sexual masochism disorder

Paraphilia characterized by recurrent, intense, sexual urges and sexually arousing fantasies of at least 6 months' duration, in which sexual arousal or gratification is obtained through enacting scripts that involve suffering and pain

Sexual orientation

Classification of individuals as heterosexual, bisexual, or homosexual based on their emotional, cognitive, and sexual attractions, as well as their self-identity and lifestyle

Sexual physiology

Vascular, hormonal, and central nervous system processes involved in genital functioning

Sexual sadism disorder

Paraphilia characterized by recurrent, intense sexual urges and sexually arousing fantasies, of at least 6 months' duration, involving acts that hurt or humiliate the sexual partner

Sexual self-concept

The way you think and feel about your body, self-evaluation of your interest in sex, and evaluation of yourself as a sexual partner

Sexual self-efficacy

The way you think and feel about your own competence to function sexually or to be a good sexual partner

Sexual touching

The broad category of activities that are usually undertaken with the goal of increasing your own and/or your partner's sexual arousal and pleasure

Sexual values

Moral guidelines for making sexual decisions

Sex work

Way in which one earns a living by providing sexual services, such as acting in a pornographic video, being a stripper, or being a phone sex worker

Situational dysfunction

Sexual dysfunction that occurs with one partner or in one situation only

Social learning theory

Framework that emphasizes the process of learning through observation and imitation

Social learning theory

Theory that emphasizes the role of reward and punishment in acquisition of gender role behavior

Social model (view of intellectual disability)

Views the intellectually disabled individual as the product of specific social definitions that involve oppression and discrimination

Social scripts

Shared interpretations that have three functions: define situations, name actors, and plot behaviors

Sociobiological theory

Framework that explains human sexual behavior and sexual anatomy as functional for human evolution (See also *evolutionary theory*)

Sociobiology

Framework in which social behavior is viewed as having a biological basis in terms of being functional in human evolution

Sociosexology

Aspect of sexology that is concerned with the way social and cultural forces influence and are influenced by sexual attitudes, beliefs, and behaviors

Spectatoring

Self-monitoring your own sexual responses to the point that a sexual dysfunction may occur

Spermicide

Chemical that kills sperm. It can be placed in a condom and/or deep in the vagina to prevent sperm from entering the cervix

Spinnbarkeit

The slippery, elastic, raw egg white consistency of the cervical mucus that becomes evident at the time of ovulation and signals that it is likely a woman has ovulated

Spontaneous abortion

The unintended termination of a pregnancy

Spurious correlation

Pattern that exists when two variables appear to be related but only because they are both related to a third variable

Stalking

An extreme form of obsessive relational intrusion that may involve behaviors like home invasion or threats of physical harm

Statutory rape

Sexual intercourse without the use of force with a person below the legal age of consent in the United States; the age of legal consent varies by state

Stealthing

Nonconsensual removal during sexual intercourse of a condom which exposes the victim to pregnancy and disease

Sterilization

Permanent surgical procedure that prevents reproduction

Stoma

Protruding portion of the large or small intestine (bowel) or urinary system that is rerouted and brought to the skin surface of the abdomen during ostomy surgery (also called ostomy)

Structural-functional theory

Framework that views society as a system of interrelated parts that influence each other and work together to achieve social stability

Substance abuse

The overuse or overdependence on drugs or chemicals that results in a failure to fulfill obligations at work, school, or home, the effects of which include danger (such as driving while impaired), recurrent substance-related legal problems, and continued substance use despite its negative effect on social or interpersonal relationships (also called substance dependence)

Suction curettage

Abortion procedure performed in the first 6–8 weeks of pregnancy, whereby a hollow plastic rod is inserted into the woman's uterus where the fetal tissue is evacuated

Sugar baby

Woman who exchanges friendship and sex for mentoring and money from an older, wealthy man

Sugar daddy

Wealthy man who provides mentoring and money to a younger female in exchange for friendship and sex

Superego

Freud's term for the conscience, which functions by guiding the individual to do what is morally right and good

Surgical menopause

Sudden decrease in estrogen resulting from removal of the ovaries that can lead to decreased desire, vaginal dryness, and dyspareunia

Survey research

Research that involves eliciting information from respondents using questions

Swingers

Spouses who agree that they will have sexual encounters with other couples

Symbolic interaction theory

Sociological theory that focuses on how meanings, labels, and definitions learned through interaction affect one's attitudes, self-concept, and behavior

Syphilis

Sexually transmitted (or congenital) infection caused by a spirochete (*Treponema pallidum*); if untreated, it can progress to a systemic infection through three stages and be fatal

Systems theory

Theoretical framework that emphasizes the interpersonal and relationship aspects of sexuality

T

Table dance

Type of dance in which a person dances or disrobes on the customer's table or in front of the seated customer

Tachycardia

Increased heart rate

Testes

Male glands that develop from the same embryonic tissue as the female gonads (the ovaries) and produce spermatozoa and male hormones (They are also called *testicles*)

Theory

Set of ideas designed to answer a question or explain a particular phenomenon

Therapeutic massage

Nonerotic massage by a person who has received academic training at one of the more than 400 accredited programs, completed a supervised internship, and has a therapeutic massage license

Today Sponge

Disk-shaped polyurethane device containing the spermicide nonoxynol-9 that protects for repeated acts of intercourse over 24 hours without the need for supplying additional spermicide

Touch-and-ask rule

Sexual technique whereby each touch and caress is accompanied by the question, "How does that feel?" and is followed by feedback from the partner

Transgender

Term that refers to individuals of one biological sex (female or male) who identify with the other and express behavior that "is different from cultural expectations based on the sex they were assigned at birth"

Transsexual

An older term for a person who has had hormonal or surgical intervention to change their body to align with their gender identity

Transvestic disorder

Paraphilia that involves recurrent, intense, sexual urges and sexually arousing fantasies, of at least 6 months' duration, that involve cross-dressing (such as a man dressing in a woman's clothes)

Transvestic fetishism

Sexual arousal by dressing in the gender of the other sex

Traumatic brain injury

Closed head injury that results from an exterior force and creates a temporary or enduring impairment in brain functioning

Turner syndrome

Condition that occurs in females resulting from the absence of an X chromosome (XO)

U

Ultrasound scan
Procedure whereby sound waves are used to project an image of the developing fetus on a video screen; used in prenatal testing

Umbilical cord
Flexible cord that connects the developing fetus and the placenta; contains two arteries and a vein that facilitate this exchange

Unidimensional continuum model
Identification of sexual orientation on a scale from 0 (exclusively heterosexual) to 6 (exclusively gay), suggesting that most people are not on the extremes but somewhere in between

Urethra
Short tube that connects the bladder with the urethral opening

Urethritis
Inflammation of the urethra

Uterine orgasm
In contrast to clitoral orgasm, an orgasm caused by deep intravaginal stimulation and involving contractions in the uterus as well as the vagina

Uterus
Also called the womb, the hollow, muscular organ in which a fertilized egg may implant and develop

V

Vacuum aspiration
Synonym for suction curettage

Vagina
Muscular tube 3–5 inches long that extends from the vulva to the cervix of the uterus

Vaginismus
Recurrent or persistent involuntary spasm of the musculature of the outer third of the vagina that interferes with vaginal penetration

Vaginitis
Infection of the vagina

Variable
Any measurable event or characteristic that varies or is subject to change

Vas deferens
Tube from the ejaculatory ducts to the testes that transports sperm

Vasectomy
Minor surgical procedure whereby the vas deferens are cut so as to prevent sperm from entering the penis

Vasocongestion
Increased blood flow to the genital region

Vees
Three-person relationships in which one member is sexually connected to each of the two others

Verbal messages
Words individuals say to each other

Vestibule
Smooth tissue surrounding a woman's urethral opening

Violent pornography
Sexually explicit visual images of sexual violence, usually directed by men toward women

Virginity
State of not having experienced sexual intercourse

Voluntary abstinence
State of forgoing sexual intercourse for a period of time by choice

Voyeuristic disorder
Paraphilia that involves recurrent, intense urges to look at unsuspecting people who are naked, undressing, or engaging in sexual behavior (also called *scopophilia*)

Vulva
External female genitalia

Vulval orgasm
An orgasm that results primarily from manual stimulation of the clitoris and is characterized by contractions of the outer third of the vagina (also called *clitoral orgasm*)

Vulvodynia
Burning, stinging, irritation, or knife-like pain of the vulva for more than 3 months without obvious visible lesions

W

Win-win solution

Outcome of an interpersonal conflict whereby both people feel satisfied with the agreement or resolution

Y

Yang

In Chinese thought, the male force that is viewed as active

Yin

In Chinese thought, the female force that is seen as passive

"You" statements

In communication theory, those statements that blame or criticize the listener and often result in increasing negative feelings and behavior in the relationship

References

Abbasi, I. S., & Alghamdi, N. G. (2018). The pursuit of romantic alternatives online: Social media friends as potential alternatives. *Journal of Sex & Marital Therapy, 44*(1), 16–28.

Abedi, P., Afrazeh, M., Javadifar, N., & Saki, A. (2015). The relation between stress and sexual function and satisfaction in reproductive-age women in Iran: A cross-sectional study. *Journal of Sex & Marital Therapy, 41*(4), 384–390.

Abma, J. C., & Martinez, G. M. (2017, June 22). *Sexual activity and contraceptive use among teenagers in the United States, 2011–2015. National Health Statistics Report, Number 104*, Centers for Disease Control and Prevention. Retrieved from https://www.cdc.gov/nchs/data/nhsr/nhsr104.pdf

Acuña, M. J., Martin, J. C., Graciani, M., Cruces, A., & Gotor, F. (2010). A comparative study of the sexual function of institutionalized patients with schizophrenia. *Journal of Sexual Medicine, 7*(10), 3414–3423.

Adamson, K. (2014, March). Polyamory. Lecture presented to Sociology 3325, Sociology of Human Sexuality, East Carolina University, Greenville, NC.

Adeagbo, O. A. (2018). Are same-sex relationships anti-family?: Investigating relationship stability among interracial gay partners in South Africa. *Journal of Gender Studies, 27*(2), 165–176.

Adkins, T., England, P., Risman, J., & Ford, J. (2015). Student bodies: Does the sex ratio matter for hooking up and having sex at college? *Social Currents, 2*(2), 144–162.

Adler, A., & Ben-Ari, A. (2018). "How we stay together without going crazy:" Reconstruction of reality among women of mixed-orientation relationships. *Journal of Homosexuality, 65*(5), 640–658.

Adolfsen, A., Iedema, J., & Keuzenkamp, S. (2010). Multiple dimensions of attitudes about homosexuality: Development of a multifaceted scale measuring attitudes toward homosexuality. *Journal of Homosexuality, 57*(10), 1237–1257.

Agarwal, P. (2019, February 18). *In the era of #Metoo are men scared of mentoring women?* Forbes, Retrieved from https://www.forbes.com/sites/pragyaagarwaleurope/2019/02/18/in-the-era-of-metoo-are-men-scared-of-mentoring-women/#6a3420707d0d

Aguilar, J. (2013). Situational sexual behaviors: The ideological work of moving toward polyamory in communal living groups. *Journal of Contemporary Ethnography, 42*(1), 104–129.

Aizer, A., Stroud, L., & Buka, S. (2018, October 25). *Intimate-partner domestic violence in the US: Costs, consequences, causes and possible solutions.* National Science Foundation. Retrieved from https://www.nsf.gov/discoveries/disc_summ.jsp?cntn_id=297021&WT.mc_id=USNSF_1

Albersen, M., Linsen, L., Tinel, H., Sandner, P., & Van Renterghem, K. (2013). Synergistic effects of BAY 60-4552 and Vardenafil on relaxation of corpus cavernosum tissue of patients with erectile dysfunction and clinical phosphodiesterase type 5 inhibitor failure. *Journal of Sexual Medicine, 10*(5), 1268–1277.

Allan, P. (2018, June). *How to protect yourself from online dating scams*. Lifehacker. Retrieved from https://lifehacker.com/how-to-protect-yourself-from-online-dating-scams-1827106759

Allen, P. L. (2000). *The wages of sin: Sex and disease, past and present*. Chicago, IL: University of Chicago Press.

Allison, R. & Risman, B. J. (2017). Marriage delay, time to play? Marital horizons and hooking up in college. *Sociological Inquiry, 87*(3), 472–500.

Alonzo, D. J., & Buttitta, D. J. (2019). Is "coming out" still relevant? Social implications for LGB-membered families. *Journal of Family Theory & Review, 11*(3), 354–366. doi: https://doi.org/10.1111/jftr.12333

Alves, S., Martins, A., Fonseca, A., Canavarro, M. C., & Pereira, M. (2018). Preventing and treating women's postpartum depression: A qualitative systematic review on partner-inclusive interventions. *Journal of Child & Family Studies, 27*(1), 1–25.

Alzheimer's Association. (2019). *Alzheimer's disease facts and figures*. Retrieved from https://www.alz.org/alzheimers-dementia/facts-figures

American Academy of Pediatrics. (2012). Circumcision policy statement: Task force on circumcision. *Pediatrics, 130*(3), 585–586.

American Association of Sexuality Educators, Counselors and Therapists. (n.d.). *AASECT Position on Sex Addiction*. Retrieved from https://www.aasect.org/position-sex-addiction

American Cancer Society. (2014, June 19). *Abortion and breast cancer risk*. Retrieved from http://www.cancer.org/cancer/breastcancer/moreinformation/is-abortion-linked-to-breast-cancer

American Cancer Society. (2019a). *How common is breast cancer?* Retrieved from http://www.cancer.org/cancer/breastcancer/detailedguide/breast-cancer-key-statistics

American Cancer Society. (2019b, August 1). *About Prostate Cancer*. Retrieved from https://www.cancer.org/content/dam/CRC/PDF/Public/8793.00.pdf

American Cancer Society. (2019c, January 8). *Key Statistics for Testicular Cancer*. Retrieved from https://www.cancer.org/cancer/testicular-cancer/about/key-statistics.html

American College Health Association. (2018, December). *Frequency Report on STD/I Information in College*. National College Health Assessment: Fall 2018 Reference Group Data Report. Retrieved from: https://www.acha.org/documents/ncha/NCHA-II_Fall_2018_Reference_Group_Data_Report.pdf

American College of Obstetricians and Gynecologists. (2007, September). *Committee opinion: Vaginal "rejuvenation" and cosmetic vaginal procedures*. Retrieved from http://www.acog.org/Resources-And-Publications/Committee-Opinions/Committee-on-Gynecologic-Practice/Vaginal-Rejuvenation-and-Cosmetic-Vaginal-Procedures

American College of Obstetricians and Gynecologists. (2012, May; reaffirmed 2019). *Committee opinion: Opioid abuse, dependence, and addiction in pregnancy*. Retrieved from https://www.acog.org/Clinical-Guidance-and-Publications/Committee-Opinions/Committee-on-Obstetric-Practice/Opioid-Use-and-Opioid-Use-Disorder-in-Pregnancy?IsMobileSet=false

American College of Obstetricians and Gynecologists. (2015, December). *Committee opinion: Physical activity and exercise during pregnancy and the postpartum period*. Retrieved from http://www.acog.org/Resources-And-Publications/Committee-Opinions/Committee-on-Obstetric-Practice/Physical-Activity-and-Exercise-During-Pregnancy-and-the-Postpartum-Period

American Psychiatric Association. (2013). *Diagnostic and statistical manual of mental disorders* (5th ed.). Arlington, VA: Author.

American Psychological Association. (2010). *Ethical principles of psychologists and code of conduct*. Retrieved from http://www.apa.org/ethics/code/

American Sexual Health Association. (2019). *Get Tested*. Retrieved from: http://www.ashasexualhealth.org/stdsstis/get-tested/

American Society for Plastic Surgeons (2018). *2017 Plastic Surgery Statistics*. Retrieved from https://www.plasticsurgery.org/documents/News/Statistics/2017/plastic-surgery-statistics-report-2017.pdf

Amezcua-Prieto, C., Olmedo-Requeno, R., Jimenez-Mejias, E., Hurtado-Sanchez, F., Mozas-Moreno, J., Lardelli-Claret, P., & Jimemez-Moleon, J. J. (2013). Changes in leisure time physical activity during pregnancy compared to the prior year. *Maternal and Child Health Journal, 17*(4), 632–638.

Andelloux, M. (2013, July 28). *Where can I find ethical pornography?* [Video file]. Retrieved from https://www.youtube.com/watch?v=TSluPg1H6Hc

Anderson, H. & Daniels, M. (2017, April). *Film dialogue from 2,000 screenplays, broken down by gender and age.* The Pudding. Retrieved from https://pudding.cool/2017/03/film-dialogue/

Anderson, L. (2013, September 12). *Abortion education under pressure in U.S. medical schools.* Thomson Reuters Foundation. Retrieved from http://news.trust.org//item/20130912080731-3jnub/

Andersson, G., & Titov, N. (2014). Advantages and limitations of Internet-based interventions for common mental disorders. *World Psychiatry, 13*(1), 4–11.

Andrews, T., & Knaak, S. (2013). Medicalized mothering: Experiences in breastfeeding in Canada and Norway. *The Sociological Review, 61*(1), 88–110.

Angel, L., Wiesler, J., Pettijohn, T., Terranova, A., Hooper, C., & Phillips, C. (2016, November). *A comparison of the effects of human sexuality courses on students' attitudes, behavior, and knowledge at three colleges.* Poster presented at annual meeting of the Society for the Scientific Study of Sexuality, Phoenix, AZ.

Annon, J. (1976). The PLISSIT model: A proposed conceptual scheme for behavioral treatment of sex problems. *Journal of Sex Education and Therapy, 2*(1), 1–15.

Arakawa, D. R., Flanders, C. E., & Heck, R. (2013). Positive psychology: What impact has it had on sex research publication trends? *Sexuality & Culture, 17*(2), 305–320.

ARC. (2015, April 28). *Intellectual disability.* Retrieved from http://www.thearc.org/learn-about/intellectual-disability

Arocho, R., Lozano, E. B., & Halpern, C. T. (2019). Estimates of donated sperm use in the United States: National Survey of Family Growth 1995–2017. *Fertility and Sterility, 112*(4), 718–723.

Ashton, S., McDonald, K., & Kirkman, M. (2018) Women's experiences of pornography: A systematic review of research using qualitative methods. *Journal of Sex Research, 55*(3), 334–347.

Aubrey, J. S., Behm-Morawitz, E., & Kim, K. (2014). Understanding the effects of MTV's *16 and Pregnant* on adolescent girls' beliefs, attitudes, and behavioral intentions toward teen pregnancy. *Journal of Health Communication, 19*(10), 1145–1160.

Aubrey, J. S., & Smith, S. E. (2013). Development and validation of the endorsement of the hookup culture index. *Journal of Sex Research, 50*(5), 435–448.

AVEN. (2001). *The Asexuality Visibility and Education Network.* Retrieved from http://www.asexuality.org/home/

Averett, S. H., Corman, H., & Reichman, N. E. (2013). Effects of overweight on risky sexual behavior of adolescent girls. *Economic Inquiry, 51*(1), 605–619.

Ayesha. (2016, August 22). *Ayesha - India.* Equality now. Retrieved from http://www.equalitynow.org/campaigns/trafficking-survivor-stories/ayesha

Babin, E. A. (2013). An examination of predictors of nonverbal and verbal communication of pleasure during sex and sexual satisfaction. *Journal of Social and Personal Relationships, 30*(3), 270–292.

Bacchus, N. S. (2017). Shifting sexual boundaries: Ethnicity and premarital sex in the lives of South Asian American women. *Sexuality & Culture, 21*(3), 776–794.

Bachmann, H. (2018, August 24). Sex in the city: Zurich's prostitution "sex boxes" deemed success in Switzerland. *USA Today,* p. A1. Retrieved from https://www.usatoday.com/story/news/world/2018/08/24/sex-boxes-make-legal-prostitution-safe-zurich-switzerland-europe/1083444002/

Bahouq, H., Fadoua, A., Hanan, R., Ihsane, H., & Najia, H. (2013). Profile of sexuality in Moroccan chronic low back pain patients. *BMC Musculoskeletal Disorders, 14*(63), 1472.

Bailey, B. (2014, November 14). "Tennessee Williams," by John Lahr. *New York Times.* Retrieved from http://www.nytimes.com/2014/11/16/books/review/tennessee-williams-by-john-lahr.html?_r=0

Bal, D. M., Yilmaz, S. D., & Beji, N. K. (2013). Sexual health in patients with gynecological cancer: A qualitative study. *Sexuality and Disability, 31*(1), 83–92.

Baldas, T. (2017, April 25). Genital mutilation victims break their silence: "This is Demonic." *USA Today.* p. 1A.

Balderrama-Durbin, C., Stanton, K., Snyder, D. K., Cigrang, J. A., Talcott, G.W., Smith Slep, A. M., ... Cassidy, D. G. (2017). The risk for marital infidelity across a year long deployment. *Journal of Family Psychology, 32*(5), 629–634.

Ballester-Arnal, R., Calvo, J. C., Gil-Llario, M. D., Gil-Julia, B., & Castro Calvo, J. (2017). Cybersex addiction: A study on Spanish college students. *Journal of Sex & Marital Therapy, 43*(6), 567–585.

Balzarini, R., Holmes, B., McDonald, J., & Kohut, T. (2016, November). *Studying polyamory using traditional measures: Insights into potential pitfalls.* Session at the annual meeting of the Society for the Scientific Study of Sexuality, Phoenix, AZ.

Bandini, E., Fisher, A. D., Castellini, G., Lo Sauro, C., Lelli, Z. L., Meriggiola, M. C., ... Ricca, V. (2013). Gender identity and disorder and eating disorders: Similarities and differences in terms of body uneasiness. *Journal of Sexual Medicine, 10*(4), 1012–1023.

Barber, L. L., & Cooper, M. L. (2014). Rebound sex: Sexual motives and behaviors following a relationship breakup. *Archives of Sexual Behavior, 43*(2), 251–265.

Barnett, M. D., Martin, K. J., & Melugin, P. R. (2018). Making and breaking abstinence pledges: Moral foundations and the Purity movement. *Sexuality & Culture, 22*(1), 288–298.

Barrett, E. S., Tran, V., Thurston, S., Jasienska, G., Furberg, A. S., Ellison, P. T., & Thune, I. (2013). Marriage and motherhood are associated with lower testosterone concentrations in women. *Hormones and Behavior, 63*(1), 72–79.

Barriger, M., & Velez-Blasini, C. J. (2013). Descriptive and injunctive social norm overestimation in hooking up and their role as predictors of hook-up activity in a college student sample. *Journal of Sex Research, 50*(1), 84–94.

Bartz, D., & Greenberg, J. (2008). Sterilization in the United States. *Obstetrics & Gynecology, 1*(1), 23–32. Retrieved from http://www.ncbi.nlm.nih.gov/pmc/articles/PMC2492586/

Basson, R. (2001a). Are the complexities of women's sexual function reflected in the new consensus definitions of dysfunction? *Journal of Sex & Marital Therapy, 27*(2), 105–112.

Basson, R. (2001b). Human sex-response cycles. *Journal of Sex & Marital Therapy, 27*(1), 33–43.

Battiste, N. (2019, December 3). Report finds many free dating apps don't screen for sex offenders. *CBS Evening News with Norah O'Donnell.*

Batuman, E. (2018, April 30). A theory of relativity: Japan's rent-a-family industry. *The New Yorker,* 50–61.

Bay-Cheng, L. (2019). Agency is everywhere, but agency is not enough: A conceptual analysis of young women's sexual agency. *The Journal of Sex Research, 56*(4–5), 462–474.

Bay-Cheng, L. Y., Maguin, E., & Bruns, A. E. (2018). Who wears the pants: The implications of gender and power for youth heterosexual relationships. *Journal of Sex Research, 55*(1), 7–20.

Bay-Cheng, L. Y. (2017) Seeing how far I've come: The impact of the Digital Sexual Life History Calendar on young adult research participants. *Journal of Sex Research, 54*(3), 284–295.

BBC News. (2006, December 19). *Prostitutes speak of their ordeals.* Retrieved from http://news.bbc.co.uk/2/hi/in_depth/6183491.stm

Beale, K., Maynard, E., & Bigler, M. (2016, November). *The intersection of religion and sex: Sex guild resiliency among Baptists, Catholics, and Latter-day Saints.* Paper presented at the annual meeting of the Society for the Scientific Study of Sexuality, Phoenix, AZ.

Bearak, J. M. (2014). Casual contraception in casual sex: Life-cycle change in undergraduates' sexual behavior in hookups. *Social Forces, 93*(2), 483–513.

Becasen, J. S., Ford, J., & Hogben, M. (2015). Sexual health interventions: A meta-analysis. *Journal of Sex Research, 52*(4), 433–443.

Bedi, R., Muller, R. T., & Thornback, K. (2013). Object relations and psychopathology among adult survivors of childhood abuse. *Psychological Trauma: Theory, Research, Practice, and Policy, 5*(3), 233–240.

Bedor, E. (2016). It's not you, it's your (old) vagina: Osphena's articulation of sexual dysfunction. *Sexuality & Culture, 20*(1), 38–55.

Begley, S. (2009, September 2). Why parents may cause gender differences in kids. *Newsweek.* Retrieved from http://www.newsweek.com/why-parents-may-cause-gender-differences-kids-79501

Begum, S., Hocking, J. S., Groves, J., Fairley, C. K., & Keogh, L. A. (2013). Sex workers talk about sex work: Six contradictory characteristics of legalized sex work in Melbourne, Australia. *Culture, Health & Sexuality, 15*(1), 85–100.

Bell, S. N., & McClelland, S. I. (2018). When, if, and how: Young women contend with orgasmic absence. *Journal of Sex Research, 55*(6), 679–91.

Bell, S., & Reissing, E. D. (2017). Sexual well-being in older women: The relevance of sexual excitation and sexual inhibition. *The Journal of Sex Research, 54*(9), 1153–1165.

Belous, C. K., & Bauman, M. L. (2017). What's in a name? Exploring pansexuality online. *Journal of Bisexuality, 17*(1), 58–72.

Bennett, M. (2019, November). *"This feels so good.!": A qualitative examination of communication during sexual activity.* Poster presented at the Society for the Scientific Study of Sex annual meeting, Denver, CO.

Bennhold, K. (2019, January 27). Another Side of #MeToo: Male Managers Fearful of Mentoring Women. *New York Times.* Retrieved from https://www.nytimes.com/2019/01/27/world/europe/metoo-backlash-gender-equality-davos-men.html

Benoit, C., Quellet, N., Jansson, M., Magnus, S., & Smith, M. (2017a). Would you think of doing sex for money? Structure and agency in deciding to sell sex in Canada. *Work, Employment & Society, 31*(5), 731–747.

Benoit, C., Saelaert, M., Hannes, K., & Bilsen, J. (2017b). The sexual adjustment process of cancer patients and their partners: A qualitative evidence synthesis. *Archives of Sexual Behavior, 46*(7), 2059–2083.

Berdychevsky, L. (2017). Toward the tailoring of sexual health education messages for young women: A focus on tourist experiences. *The Journal of Sex Research, 54*(9), 1171–1187.

Berenguer, C., Rebolo, C., & Costa, R. M. (2019). Interoceptive awareness, alexithymia, and sexual function. *Journal of Sex & Marital Therapy, 45*(8), 729–738.

Bergdall, A. R., Kraft, J. M., Andes, K., Carter, M., Hatfield-Timajchy, K., & Hock-Long, L. (2012). Love and hooking up in the new millennium: Communication technology and relationships among urban African American and Puerto Rican young adults. *Journal of Sex Research, 49*(6), 570–582.

Berg, R. C., Molin, S. B., & Nanavati, J. (2020). Women who trade sexual services from men: A systematic mapping service. *Journal of Sex Research, 57*(1), 104–118.

Bermant, G. (1976). *Sexual behavior: Hard times with the Coolidge effect.* In M. H. Siegel & H. P. Zeigler (Eds.), Psychological research: The inside story (pp. 76–103). New York, NY: Harper and Row.

Bernal, A. T., D'aniello, C., & Vasquez, W. F. (2013). Gender distribution in COAMFTE-accredited programs. *Journal of Feminist Family Therapy: An International Forum, 25*(2), 93–111.

Berry, M. D. (2013a). Historical revolutions in sex therapy: A critical examination of men's sexual dysfunctions and their treatment. *Journal of Sex & Marital Therapy, 39*(1), 21–39.

Berry, M. D. (2013b). The history and evolution of sex therapy and its relationship to psychoanalysis. *International Journal of Applied Psychoanalytic Studies, 10*(1), 53–74.

Bersamin, M. M., Zamboanga, B. L., Schwartz, S. J., Donnellan, M. B., Hudson, M., Weisskirch, R. S., ... Caraway, S. J. (2014). Risky business: Is there an association between casual sex and mental health among emerging adults? *Journal of Sex Research, 51*(1), 43–51.

Bettina, S., Wander, K., Hernlund, Y., & Moreau, A. (2013). Legislating change? Responses to criminalizing female genital cutting in Senegal. *Law & Society, 47*(4), 803–835.

Bindel, J. (2010, July 2). *The truth about the porn industry.* The Guardian. Retrieved from https://www.theguardian.com/lifeandstyle/2010/jul/02/gail-dines-pornography

Bird, E. R., Stappenbeck, C. A., Neilson, E. C., Gulati, N. K., George, W. H., Cooper, M. L., & Davis, K. C. (2019). Sexual victimization and sex-related drinking motives: How protective is emotion regulation. *The Journal of Sex Research, 56*(2), 156–165.

Bishop, C. J. (2015). Emotional reactions of heterosexual men to gay imagery. *Journal of Homosexuality, 62*(1), 51–66.

Blackstrom, L., Armstrong, E. A., & Puentes, J. (2012). Women's negotiation of cunnilingus in college hookups and relationships. *Journal of Sex Research, 49*(1), 1–12.

Blackwell, C. W. W. (2018). Reducing risk: Counseling men infected with HIV who have sex with men on safer sex practices with serocondordant partners. *Social Work in Public Health, 33*(5), 271–279.

Blackwell, C. W., & Dziegielewski, S. F. (2012). Using the Internet to meet sexual partners: Research and practice implications. *Journal of Social Service Research, 38*(1), 46–55.

Blag, E. C. (2018, September 27). Can you give sexual consent using an App? *USA Today*, p. B1.

Bland, A. M & McQueen, K. S. (2018). The distribution of Chapman's Love Languages in couples: An exploratory cluster analysis. *Couple and Family Psychology: Research and Practice, 7*(2), 103–126. doi: http://dx.doi.org/10.1037/cfp0000102

Blaszcznski, A., & Morandini, J. (2014, November). *Essentialist beliefs, internalized homonegativity and psychological wellbeing in gay men.* Poster session presented at the annual meeting of the Society for the Scientific Study of Sexuality, Omaha, NE.

Bleakley, A., Ellithorpe, M. E., Hennessy, M., Khurana, A., Jamieson, P., & Weitz, I. (2017). Alcohol, sex, and screens: Modeling media influence on adolescent alcohol and sex co-occurrence. *The Journal of Sex Research, 54*(8), 1026–1037.

Blithe, S. J., & Wolfe, A. W. (2017). Work-life management in legal prostitution: Stigma and lockdown in Nevada's brothels. *Human Relations, 70*(6), 725–750.

Blodgett, J., Chandler, K. D., & Tominey, S. (2019, November). *Gender matters: Parents' reflections on their gender socialization practices with adolescents.* Poster presented at the National Council on Family Relations annual meeting, Fort Worth, TX.

Brodsky, A. (2017). 'Rape-Adjacent': Imagining legal responses to nonconsensual condom removal. *Columbia Journal of Gender and Law, 32*(2). Retrieved from https://ssrn.com/abstract=2954726

Blumer, M., & Bergdall, M. (2014, November). *E-visibility management of LGB identities.* Poster session presented at the annual meeting of the Society for the Scientific Study of Sexuality, Omaha, NE.

Blumer, M., Haym, C., Iantaffi, A., & Prouty, A. (2015, November). *Managing monogamism: Clinical practice with consensually open non-monogamous relationship and family systems.* Workshop presented at the annual meeting of the Society for the Scientific Study of Sexuality, Albuquerque, NM.

Blumer, M. L., Papaj, A. K., & Erolin, K. S. (2013). Feminist family therapy for treating female survivors of childhood sexual abuse. *Journal of Feminist Family Therapy: An International Forum, 25*(1), 65–79.

Blunt-Vinti, H., Jozkowski, K. N., & Hunt, M. (2019). Show or tell? Does verbal and/or nonverbal sexual communication matter for sexual satisfaction. *Journal of Sex & Marital Therapy, 45*(3), 206–217.

Bockting, W. O., Miner, M. H., Swinburne Romine, R. E., Hamilton, A., & Coleman, E. (2013). Stigma, mental health, and resilience in an online sample of U.S. transgender population. *American Journal of Public Health, 103*(5), 943–951.

Boislard, M., Dussault, F., Boisvert, I., Belley, M., Blais, M., Beaulieu-Prevost, D., … Otis, J. (2016, November). *Coital virginity in emerging adulthood: Findings from two French-Canadian studies.* Session 42 at the annual meeting of the Society for the Scientific Study of Sexuality, Phoenix, AZ.

Bolden, S. (2018). *Presentation on nudism.* Sociology of Human Sexuality course, Spring semester. East Carolina University, NC.

Bolen, R. M. (2001). *Child sexual abuse: Its scope and our failure.* New York, NY: Kluwer Academic/Plenum.

Bomey, N., & Della Cava, M. (2017, December 1). Harassment long tolerated in the world of big business. *USA Today,* p. A1.

Bonet, M. L., Marchand, M., Kaminski, A., Fohran, A., Betoko, A., Charles, M. A., & Blondel, B. (2013). Breastfeeding duration, social and occupational characteristics of mothers in the French "EDEN mother-child" cohort. *Maternal and Child Health Journal, 17*(4), 714–722.

Boonstra, H. D. (2014, September 3). What is behind the decline in teen pregnancy rates? *Guttmacher Policy Review, 17*(3). Retrieved from https://www.guttmacher.org/about/gpr/2014/09/what-behind-declines-teen-pregnancy-rates

Bothe, B., Toth-Kiraly, I., Zsila, A., Griffiths, M. D., Demetrovices, Z., & Orosz, G. (2018). The Development of the Problematic Pornography Consumption Scale (PPCS). *Journal of Sex Research, 55*(3), 395–406.

Bouffard, J., & Miller, H. (2014). The role of sexual arousal and overperception of sexual intent within the decision to engage in sexual coercion. *Journal of Interpersonal Violence, 29*(11), 1967–1986.

Bowleg, L., del Rio-Gonzalez, A. M., Holt, S. L., Perez, C., Massie, J. S., Mandell, J. E. & Boone, C. A. (2017) Intersectional epistemologies of ignorance: How behavioral and social science research shapes what we know, think we know, and don't know about U. S. black men's sexualities. *The Journal of Sex Research, 54*(4–5), 577–603.

Boyer, D., Chapman, L., & Marshall, B. (1993). *Survival sex in King County: Helping women out.* King County Women's Advisory Board, Seattle, WA: Northwest Resource Associates.

Boylan, S. M., Greenwood, D. C., Alwan, N., Cooke, M. S., Dolby, V. A., Hay, W. M., … Cade, J. E. (2013). Does nausea and vomiting of pregnancy play a role in the association found between maternal caffeine intake and fetal growth restriction? *Maternal and Child Health Journal, 17*(4), 601–608.

Boyle, K. M. (2015). Social psychological processes that facilitate sexual assault with the fraternity party subculture. *Sociology Compass, 9*(5), 386–399.

Bragg, B., Chang, I. J., & Knox, D. (2018). *Some traditions die as slow as molasses: Are male children still preferred?* Poster presented at the National Council on Family Relations annual meeting, San Diego, CA.

Braksmajer, A. (2017). "That's kind of one of our jobs": Sexual activity as a form of care work among women with sexual difficulties. *Archives of Sexual Behavior, 46*(7), 2085–2095.

Brandes, M., Hamilton, C., van der Steen, J., de Bruin, J., Bots, R., Nelen, W., & Kremer, J. (2011). Unexplained infertility: Overall ongoing pregnancy rate and mode of conception. *Human Reproduction, 26*(2), 360–368.

Branfman, J., Stiritz, S., & Anderson, E. (2018). Relaxing the straight male anus: Decreasing homohysteria around anal eroticism. *Sexualities, 21* (1–2, 109–127.

Braun-Harvey, D., & Vigorito, M. (2015, November). *Treating out of control sexual behavior: A sexual health approach.* Workshop presented at the annual meeting of the Society for the Scientific Study of Sexuality, Albuquerque, NM.

BreastCancer.org. (2019, March 19). *Going flat: Choosing no reconstruction.* Retrieved from http://www.breastcancer.org/treatment/surgery/reconstruction/no-reconstruction

Breedlove, S. M. (2017). Prenatal influences on human sexual orientation: Expectations versus data. *Archives of Sexual Behavior, 46*(6), 1583–1592.

Breuer, R., Pericak, S., Watson, E., Milhausen, R., & Maitland, S. (2014, November). *Examining the relationships between recreational physical activity, body image, and sexual functioning and sexual satisfaction in heterosexual women.* Poster session presented at the annual meeting of the Society for the Scientific Study of Sexuality, Omaha, NE.

Bridges, A. J., Wosnitzer, R., Scharrer, E., Chyng, S., & Liberman, R. (2010). Aggression and sexual behavior in best-selling pornography videos: A content analysis update. *Violence Against Women, 16*(10), 1065–1085.

Bridle, E., & Humphreys, T. (2019, November). *Together when we're apart: The role of sexting in long distance relationships.* Poster presented at the Society for the Scientific Study of Sex annual meeting, Denver, CO.

Brison, D., Seftel, A., & Sadeghi-Nejad, H. (2013). The resurgence of the vacuum erection device (VED) for treatment of erectile dysfunction. *Journal of Sexual Medicine, 10*(4), 1124–1135.

Brizendine, L. (2006). *The female brain.* New York, NY: Broadway Books.

Brodsky, A. (2017). 'Rape-Adjacent': Imagining legal responses to nonconsensual condom removal. *Columbia Journal of Gender and Law, 32*(2). Retrieved from https://ssrn.com/abstract=2954726

Brooks, G. R. (1995). *The centerfold syndrome: How men can overcome objectification and achieve intimacy with women.* San Francisco, CA: Jossey-Bass.

Brooks-Gunn, J., & Ruble, D. N. (1980). The menstrual attitude questionnaire. *Psychosomatic Medicine, 42*(5), 503–512.

Brown, S. (2013). Is counseling necessary? Making the decision to have an abortion. A qualitative interview study. *The European Journal of Contraception & Reproductive Health Care, 18*(1), 44–48.

Brown, Z., & Tiggemann, M. (2016). Attractive celebrity and peer images on Instagram: Effect on women's mood and body image. *Body Image, 19,* 37-43.

Browne, K. D., Hines, M., & Tully, R. J. (2018). The differences between sex offenders who victimize older women and sex offenders who offend against women. *Aging & Mental Health, 22*(1), 11–18.

Brumbaugh-Johnson, S. M., & Hull, K. E. (2019). Coming out as transgender: Navigating the social implications of a transgender identity. *Journal of Homosexuality, 66*(8), 1148–1177.

Buck, A. E., Lange, K. M., Sackett, K., & Edlund, J. E. (2019). Reactions to homosexual, transgender, and heterosexual public displays of affection. *Journal of Positive Sexuality, 5*(2), 34–47.

Budge, S. L., Keller, B. L., & Sherry, A. R. (2015). Sexual minority women's experiences of sexual pressure: A qualitative investigation of recipients' and initiators' reports. *Archives of Sexual Behavior, 44*(4), 813–824.

Buehler, S. (2018). *Counseling couples before, during, and after pregnancy: Sexuality and intimacy issues.* New York: Springer Publishing Co.

Buhi, E., & Myers, J. (2014, November). *Genital herpes disclosure: Reasons people do and do not tell sex partners.* Presented at the annual meeting of the Society for the Scientific Study of Sexuality, Omaha, NE.

Bullough, V. L. (1990). History in adult human sexual behavior with children and adolescents in Western societies. In J. R. Frierman (Ed.), *Pedophilia: Biosocial dimensions* (pp. 69–90). New York, NY: Springer-Verlag.

Bullough, V. L. (2003). Masturbation: An historical overview. In W. O. Bockting & E. Coleman (Eds.), *Masturbation as a means of achieving sexual health* (pp. 17–33). New York, NY: Haworth.

Bunt, S., & and Hazelwood. Z. J. (2017). Walking the walk, talking the talk: Love languages, self-regulation, and relationship satisfaction. *Personal Relationships, 24*(2) 280–290.

Burgess, A. W., & Holstrom, L. L. (1974). Rape trauma syndrome. *American Journal of Psychiatry, 131*(9), 981–986. Retrieved from http://ajp.psychiatryonline.org/doi/abs/10.1176/ajp.131.9.981

Burghart, K. O. (2018). What's on sale? A discourse analysis of four distinctive online escort advertisement websites. *Sexuality & Culture, 22*(1), 316–335.

Burke Winkleman, S., Vail-Smith, K., Brinkley, J., & Knox, D. (2014). Sexting on the college campus. *Electronic Journal of Human Sexuality, 17.* Retrieved from http://www.ejhs.org/volume17/Sexting.html

Burri, A. (2013). Bringing sex research into the 21st century: Genetic and epigenetic approaches on female sexual function. *Journal of Sex Research, 50*(3–4), 318–328.

Burris, C. T., & Munteanu, A. R. (2015). Greater arousal in response to expansive female pubic hair is linked to more positive reactions to female sterility among heterosexual men. *Canadian Journal of Human Sexuality, 24*(1), 63–68.

Busby, D. M., & Yoshida, K. (2015). Challenges with online research for couples and families: Evaluating nonrespondents and the differential impact of incentives. *Journal of Child and Family Studies, 24*(2), 505–513.

Business Wire. (2018). *Global online sex toys market 2018–2022.* Retrieved on October 26, 2018 from https://www.businesswire.com/news/home/20180822005299/en/Global-Online-Sex-Toys-Market-2018-2022-Adult

Buss, D. M. (1989). Sex differences in human mate preferences: Evolutionary hypotheses tested in 37 cultures. *Behavioral and Brain Sciences, 12*(1), 1–13.

Butler, M. H., Meloy, K. C., & Call, M. L. (2015). Dismantling powerlessness in addiction: Empowering recovery through rehabilitating behavioral learning. *Sexual Addiction & Compulsivity: Journal of Treatment & Prevention, 22*(1), 26–58.

Butler, S. M., Procopio, M., Ragan, K., Funke, B., & Black, D. R. (2014). Assessment of university condom distribution programs: Results of a national study. *Electronic Journal of Human Sexuality, 17.* Retrieved from http://www.ejhs.org/volume17/distribution.html

Buunk, A. P., Goor, J., & Solano, A. C. (2010). Intrasexual competition at work: Sex differences in the jealousy-evoking effect of rival characteristics in work settings. *Journal of Social and Personal Relationships, 27*(5), 671–684.

Buxton, A. P. (2000). Writing our own script: How bisexual men and their heterosexual wives maintained their marriages after disclosure. *Journal of Bisexuality, 1*(2–3), 155–189.

Cambridge, P., Beadle-Brown, J., Milne, A., Mansell, J., & Whelton, B. (2011). Patterns of risk in adult protection referrals for sexual abuse and people with intellectual disability. *Journal of Applied Research In Intellectual Disabilities, 24*(2), 118–132.

Campa, M. I., Leff, S. Z., & Tufts, M. (2018). Reaching high-need youth populations with evidence-based sexual health education in California. *American Journal of Public Health, 108*(S1), S32-S37.

Canan, S., & Jozkowski, K. (2017). Sexual health education topics in schools: Inclusion and timing preferences of a sample of southern U.S. college students. *Sexuality Research & Social Policy, 14*(2), 143–156.

Canan, S. N., & Jozkowski, K. N. (2019, November). *Aftermath: 933 Women's qualitative accounts of what happened after their sexual assault.* Poster presented as Society for the Scientific Study of Sex annual meeting, Denver, CO.

Cantor, J. M. (2012). Brain research and pedophilia: What it says and what it means. *Sex Offender Law Report, 13*(6), 81–85.

Cantor, J. M., Blanchard, R., Paterson, A. D., & Bogaert, A. F. (2002). How many gay men owe their sexual orientation to fraternal birth order? *Archives of Sexual Behavior, 31*(1), 63–71.

Carey, A. R., & Trap, P. (2013, May 30). Frequent users of social network sites/services. *USA Today*, p. A1.

Carlson, D. L., Miller, A. J., Sassler, S., & Hanson, S. (2016a). The gendered division of housework and couples' sexual relationships: A reexamination. *Journal of Marriage and Family, 78*(4), 975–995.

Carlson, D. L., Hanson, S., & Fitzroy, A. (2016b). The division of child care, sexual intimacy, and relationship quality in couples. *Gender & Society, 30*(3), 442–466.

Caron, S. (2013). *The sex lives of college students: Two decades of attitudes and behaviors.* Orono, ME: Maine College Press.

Caron, S. L., & Hinman, S. P. (2013). "I took his V-card": An exploratory analysis of college student stories involving male virginity loss. *Sexuality & Culture, 17*(4), 525–539.

Carpenter, L. M. (2011). Like a virgin ... again?: Secondary virginity as an ongoing gendered social construction. *Sexuality & Culture, 14*(2), 115–140.

Carter, J., Stabile, C., Guinn, A., & Sonoda, Y. (2013). The physical consequences of gynecologic cancer surgery and their impact on sexual, emotional, and quality of life issues. *Journal of Sexual Medicine, 10*(S1), 21–34.

Cartwright, A. F., Karunaratne, M., Barr-Walker, J., Johns, N. E., & Upadhyay, U. D. (2018). Identifying national availability of abortion care and distance from major US cities: Systematic online search. *Journal of Medical Internet Research, 20*(5), e186.

Carvalheira, A., Godinho, L., & Costa, P. (2017). The impact of body dissatisfaction on distressing sexual difficulties among men and women: the mediator role of cognitive distraction. *Journal of Sex Research, 54*(3), 331–340.

Cashman, E. G., & Walters, A. S, (2018, June 14). *I made my Facebook page name benefits so when you add me it says, "You're Friends with Benefits": Young adults' attitudes about FWB relationships.* Poster presented at the American Association of Sexuality Educators, Counselors and Therapists annual meeting, Denver, CO.

Cassell, C. (2015, November). *"It just happened:" The paradox of magical thinking, risky sex, and unwanted pregnancy in this age of contraception.* Presented at the annual meeting of the Society for the Scientific Study of Sexuality, Albuquerque, NM.

Caughlin, J. P., & Basinger, E. D. (2015). Completely open and honest communication: Is that really what we want? *Family Focus, FF64*. Minneapolis, Minnesota: National Council on Family Relations.

Cavazos-Rehg, P. A., Krauss, M. J., Spitznagel, E. L., Schootman, M., Cottler, L. B., & Bierut, L. (2013). Characteristics of sexually active teenage girls who would be pleased with becoming pregnant. *Maternal & Child Health Journal, 17*(3), 470–476.

Center for Sexual Pleasure & Health. (n.d.). *Sex-positive and feminist-friendly porn*. Retrieved from http://www.thecsph.org/the-csph-resources /web-resources/sex-positive-basics/pleasure/sex-positive-and-feminist-friendly-porn/

Centers for Disease Control and Prevention. (2010, November 2). *Parasites—scabies*. Retrieved from http://www.cdc.gov/parasites/scabies/

Centers for Disease Control and Prevention. (n.d.). Condoms and STDs: Fact sheet for public health personnel. Retrieved from https://www.cdc.gov /condomeffectiveness/docs/condoms_and_stds.pdf

Centers for Disease Control and Prevention. (2013, February). *Incidence, prevalence, and cost of sexually transmitted infections in the United States*. Retrieved from http://www.cdc.gov/std/stats/sti-estimates-fact-sheet-feb-2013.pdf

Centers for Disease Control and Prevention. (2015, June). *2015 Sexually Transmitted Diseases Treatment Guidelines. Screening Recommendations Referenced in Treatment Guidelines and Original Recommendation Sources*. Retrieved from: https://www.cdc.gov/std/tg2015/screening-recommendations.htm.

Centers for Disease Control and Prevention. (2016a, December). *Vaccines and Preventable Diseases. HPV Vaccine Recommendations*. Retrieved from: https://www.cdc.gov/vaccines/vpd/hpv/hcp/recommendations.html

Centers for Disease Control and Prevention. (2016b, January 21). *How you can prevent sexually transmitted diseases*. Retrieved from http://www.cdc.gov /std/prevention/default.htm

Centers for Disease Control and Prevention. (2016c, July). *Male Condom Use*. Retrieved from https://www.cdc.gov/condomeffectiveness /male-condom-use.html

Centers for Disease Control and Prevention. (2016d, November). *Female Condom Use*. Retrieved from https://www.cdc.gov/condomeffectiveness /Female-condom-use.html

Centers for Disease Control and Prevention. (2016e, October). *Chlamydia*. Detailed Fact Sheet. Retrieved from: https://www.cdc.gov/std/chlamydia /stdfact-chlamydia-detailed.htm

Centers for Disease Control and Prevention-a. (2017a). *Youth Risk Behavior Survey Data Summary & Trends Report 2007 – 2017*. Retrieved from https://www.cdc.gov/healthyyouth/data/yrbs/pdf/trendsreport.pdf

Centers for Disease Control and Prevention. (2017b, January). *Genital Herpes Fact Sheet (Detailed)*. Retrieved from: https://www.cdc.gov/std/herpes /stdfact-herpes-detailed.htm

Centers for Disease Control and Prevention. (2017c, January). *Sexually Transmitted Diseases (STDs). Syphilis Fact Sheet (Detailed)*. Retrieved from: https://www.cdc.gov/std/syphilis/stdfact-syphilis-detailed.htm

Centers for Disease Control and Prevention. (n.d.). *Fact Sheet: How STDs Impact Women Differently from Men*. Retrieved from: https://www.cdc.gov /nchhstp/newsroom/docs/factsheets/STDs-Women.pdf

Centers for Disease Control and Prevention. (2018a, June 15). *Youth Risk Behavior Surveillance System (YRBSS)—United States, 2017*. Retrieved from https://www.cdc.gov/healthyyouth/data/yrbs/pdf/2017/ss6708.pdf

Centers for Disease Control and Prevention. (2018b, July). *Sexually Transmitted Disease Surveillance 2017: Adolescents and Young Adults*. Retrieved from: https://www.cdc.gov/std/stats17/adolescents.htm

Centers for Disease Control and Prevention. (2018c, July). *Sexually Transmitted Diseases Surveillance 2017: Chlamydia*. Retrieved from: https://www.cdc.gov/std/stats17/chlamydia.htm

Centers for Disease Control and Prevention. (2018d, July). *Sexually Transmitted Diseases and Surveillance 2017: Gonorrhea*. Retrieved from: https://www.cdc.gov/std/stats17/gonorrhea.htm

Centers for Disease Control and Prevention. (2018e, July). *Sexually Transmitted Disease and Surveillance 2017: Racial and Ethnic Minorities*. Retrieved from: https://www.cdc.gov/std/stats17/minorities.htm

Centers for Disease Control and Prevention. (2018f, September). *HIV/AIDS: HIV and Gay and Bisexual Men*. Retrieved from: https://www.cdc.gov /hiv/group/msm/index.html

Centers for Disease Control and Prevention. (2018g, September). *Reported STDs in the United States, 2017: High Burden of STDs Threatens Millions of Americans*. Retrieved from: https://www.cdc.gov/nchhstp/newsroom/docs/factsheets/std-trends-508.pdf

Centers for Disease Control and Prevention. (2019a, August). *Genital HPV - Fact Sheet*. Retrieved from: https://www.cdc.gov/std/hpv/stdfact-hpv.htm

Centers for Disease Control and Prevention. (2019b, December 3). *Living with HIV*. Retrieved from http://www.cdc.gov/actagainstaids/campaigns /hivtreatmentworks/stayincare/costoftreatment.html

Centers for Disease Control and Prevention. (2019c, December). *Zika Virus. 2019 Case Counts (Provisional Data)*. Retrieved from: https://www.cdc.gov /zika/reporting/2019-case-counts.html

Centers for Disease Control and Prevention. (2019d, January 16). *Infertility FAQs*. Retrieved from http://www.cdc.gov/reproductivehealth /infertility/#14

Centers for Disease Control and Prevention. (2019e, May). *PrEP (pre-exposure prophylaxis)*. Retrieved from: https://www.cdc.gov/hiv/risk/prep /index.html

Centers for Disease Control and Prevention. (2019f, May). *Viral Hepatitis. Q&As for Health Professionals: Overview and Statistics*. Retrieved from: https://www.cdc.gov/hepatitis/hbv/hbvfaq.htm#overview

Centers for Disease Control and Prevention. (2019g, May). *Zika Basics. Zika Basics and How to Protect Yourself*. Retrieved from: https://www.cdc.gov /zika/pdfs/fs-zika-basics.pdf

Centers for Disease Control and Prevention. (2019h, May). *Zika virus: Prevention and transmission*. Retrieved from http://www.cdc.gov/zika /prevention/index.html

Centers for Disease Control and Prevention. (2019i, November). *Gonorrhea Fact Sheet (Detailed)*. Retrieved from: https://www.cdc.gov/std /gonorrhea/stdfact-gonorrhea-detailed.htm

Centers for Disease Control and Prevention. (2019j, November). *HIV/AIDS: Basic Statistics*. Retrieved from: https://www.cdc.gov/hiv/basics /statistics.html

Centers for Disease Control and Prevention. (2019k, September). *Pubic "crab" lice: Treatment*. Retrieved from http://www.cdc.gov/parasites/lice /pubic/treatment.html

Center for Positive Sexuality. (2019). *About Us*. Retrieved from http://positivesexuality.org/about-us/

Center for Reproductive Rights. (2019, April 26). *The World's Abortion Laws*. Retrieved from https://reproductiverights.org/sites/default /files/documents/World-Abortion-Map.pdf

Cerebralpalsy.org. (2018). *About cerebral palsy*. Retrieved from https://www.cerebralpalsy.org/about-cerebral-palsy

Chadwick, S. B., & Van Anders, S. M. (2017). Do women's orgasms function as a masculinity achievement for men? *The Journal of Sex Research, 54*(9), 1128–1140.

Chalker, R., & Downer, C. (1998). *A woman's book of choices: Abortion, menstrual extraction, RU-486.* New York, NY: Seven Stories Press.

Chang, I. J., & Ward, R. (2017, November 17). *Disney Princess going to college: Using Disney Princess films as catalyst for discussion.* Poster presented at the annual meeting of National Council on Family Relations, Orlando, FL.

Chang, J., Ward, R., Padgett, D., & Smith, M. F. (2012, November). *Do feminists hook up more? Examining pro-feminism attitude in the context of hooking up.* Paper presented at the National Council on Family Relations, Phoenix, AZ.

Chapman, G. (2010). *The five love languages: The secret to love that lasts.* Chicago: Northfield Publishing.

Chen, Y. J., Chen, C. C., Lin, M. W., Chen, T. J., Li, C. Y., Hwang, C. Y., ... Liu, H. N. (2013). Increased risk of sexual dysfunction in male patients with psoriasis: A nationwide population-based follow up study. *Journal of Sexual Medicine, 10*(5), 1212–1218.

Cherner, R. A., & Reissing, E. D. (2013). A psychological investigation of sexual arousal in women with lifelong vaginismus. *Journal of Sexual Medicine, 10*(5), 1291–1303.

Chevallier, D., Haertig, A., Faix, A., & Droupy, S. (2013). Cosmetic surgery of the male genitalia. *Progrès en Urologie: Journal de l'Association Française d'Urologie et de la Société Française d'Urologie, 23*(9), 685–695.

Chi, X., Bongardt, D., & Hawke, S. T. (2015). Intrapersonal and interpersonal sexual behaviors of Chinese university students: Gender differences in prevalence and correlates. *Journal of Sex Research, 52*(5), 532–542.

Chiesa, A., Leucci, V., Serretti, A., & De Ronchi, D. (2013). Antipsychotics and sexual dysfunction: Epidemiology, mechanisms and management. *Clinical Neuropsychiatry, 10*(1), 31–36.

Cho, S. B., Ming, C., & Claridge, A. M. (2018). Cohabiting parents' marriage plans and marriage realization. *Journal of Social & Personal Relationships, 35*(2), 137–158.

Chonody, J. M. (2013). Measuring sexual prejudice against gay men and lesbian women: Development of the Sexual Prejudice Scale (SPS). *Journal of Homosexuality, 60*(6), 895–926.

Christensen, M. C., Wright, R., & Dunn, J. (2017). 'It's awkward stuff': conversations about sexuality with young children. *Child & Family, 22*(2), 711–720.

Christopher, S., Garos, S., & Reid, R. (2014, November). *Exploring typologies in men assessed with hypersexual disorder.* Poster session presented at the annual meeting of the Society for the Scientific Study of Sexuality, Omaha, NE.

Chung, E., & Brock, G. (2013). Sexual rehabilitation and cancer survivorship: A state of art review of current literature and management strategies in male sexual dysfunction among prostate cancer survivors. *Journal of Sexual Medicine, 10*(1), 102–11.

Cimpian, J. R., Timmer, J. D., Birkett, M. A., Marro, R. L., Turner, B. C., & Phillips II, G. L. (2018). Bias from potentially mischievous responders on large-scale estimates of lesbian, gay, bisexual, or questioning (LGBQ)-Heterosexual youth health disparities. *American Journal of Public Health, 108*(s4), s258–s265.

Cinthio, H. (2015). "You go home and tell that to my dad!" Conflicting claims and understandings on hymen and virginity. *Sexuality & Culture: An Interdisciplinary Quarterly, 19*(1), 172–189.

Clarke, V., & Smith, M. (2015). "Not hiding, not shouting, just me": Gay men negotiate their visual identities. *Journal of Homosexuality, 62*(1), 4–32.

Coakley, T. M., Randolf, S. D., Shears, J., & Collins, P. (2017a). Values that fathers communicate to sons about sex, sexuality, relationships and marriage. *Social Work in Public Health, 32*(5), 355–368.

Coakley, T. M., Randolf, S., Shears, J., Beamon, E. R., Collins, P., & Sides, T. (2017b). Parent-youth communication to reduce at-risk sexual behavior: A systematic literature review. *Journal of Human Behavior in the Social Environment, 27*(6), 609–624.

Coffman, H., & Jozkowski, K. (2015, November). *A study of the relationship among sexual debut, sexual attitudes, and self-esteem.* Presented at the annual meeting of the Society for the Scientific Study of Sexuality, Albuquerque, NM.

Cohen, J. N., & Byers, E. S. (2014). Beyond lesbian bed death: Enhancing our understanding of the sexuality of sexual-minority women in relationships. *Journal of Sex Research, 51*(8), 893–903.

Cohen, M. T. (2016a). An exploratory study of individuals in non-traditional, alternative relationships: How 'open' are we? *Sexuality & Culture, 20*(2), 295–315.

Cohen, M. T. (2016b). It's not you, it's me ... no, actually it's you: Perceptions of what makes a first date successful or not. *Sexuality & Culture, 20*(1), 173–191.

Cohen, S. A. (2006, August 1). Abortion and mental health: Myths and realities. *Guttmacher Policy Review, 9*(3). Retrieved from https://www.guttmacher.org/about/gpr/2006/08/abortion-and-mental-health-myths-and-realities

Cohn, A. M., Zinzow, H. M., Resnick, H. S., & Kilpatrick, D. G. (2013). Correlates of reasons for not reporting rape to the police: Results from a national telephone probability sample of women with forcible or drug or alcohol facilitated/incapacitated rape. *Journal of Interpersonal Violence, 28*(3), 455–473.

Colapinto, J. (2000). *As nature made him: The boy who was raised as a girl.* New York, NY: Harper Collins.

Coleman, E., & Allen, M. P. (2014, November). *Gender variance: A cross cultural comparison.* Presented at the annual meeting of the Society for the Scientific Study of Sexuality, Omaha, NE.

Collazo, E., Barnhart, K., & Herbenick, D. (2014, November). *"Love. Fun. The baby was asleep." Reasons for sex across the lifespan.* Poster session presented at the annual meeting of the Society for the Scientific Study of Sexuality, Omaha, NE.

Collins, M. E. (1991). Body figure perceptions and preferences among preadolescent children. *International Journal of Eating Disorders, 10*(2), 199–208.

Conley, C., & Wright, E. (2014, November). *Impact of adverse childhood experiences and sexual identity distress on adult lesbian, gay, and bisexual (LGB) mental health.* Presented at the annual meeting of the Society for the Scientific Study of Sexuality, Omaha, NE.

Conley, T. D., Piemonte, J. L., Gusakova, S., & Rubin, J. D. (2018). Sexual satisfaction among individuals in monogamous and consensually non-monogamous relationships. *Journal of Social and Personal Relationships, 35*(4), 509–532.

Connell, K. M., Coates, R., & Wood, F. M. (2015). Burn injuries lead to behavioral changes that impact engagement in sexual and social activities in females. *Sexuality and Disability, 33*(1), 75–91.

Conroy, N., Krishnakumar, A., & Leone, J. (2014, November). *The hidden role of social coercion in sexual acquiescence.* Paper presented at the annual meeting of the National Council on Family Relations, Baltimore, MD.

Consortium on the Management of Disorders of Sex Development. (2006). *Handbook for parents.* Retrieved from http://www.accordalliance.org /dsdguidelines/parents.pdf

Cooley, C. H. (1964). *Human nature and the social order.* New York, NY: Schocken.

Cooper, A., & Gordon, B. (2015). Young New Zealand women's sexual decision making in casual sex situations: A qualitative study. *The Canadian Journal of Human Sexuality, 24*(1), 69–76.

Cooper, M. L. (1994). Motivations for alcohol use among adolescents: Development and validation of a four-factor model. *Psychological Assessment, 6*(2), 117–128.

Coppens, V., Brink, S. T., Huys, W., Fransen, E., & Morrens, M. (2020). A survey on BDSM-related activities: BDSM experience correlates with age of first exposure, interest profile, and role identity. *Journal of Sex Research, 57*(1), 129–136.

Corbett, S. L., & Morgan, K. D. (1983). The process of lesbian identification. *Free Inquiry in Creative Sociology, 11*(1), 81–83.

Cormier, L. A., & O'Sullivan, L. F. (2018). Anti-climactic: Investigating how late adolescents perceive and deal with orgasm difficulty in the context of their intimate relationships. *Canadian Journal of Human Sexuality, 27*(2), 111–122.

Corsini-Munt, S., Bergeron, S., Rosen, N. O., Beaulieu, N., & Steben, M. (2017). A dyadic perspective on childhood mistreatment for women with provoked vestibulodynia and their partners: Associations with pain and sexual and psychosocial functioning. *Journal of Sex Research, 54*(3), 308–318.

Costa, R. M., Miller, G. F., & Brody, S. (2012). Women who prefer longer penises are more likely to have vaginal orgasms (but not clitoral orgasms): Implications for an evolutionary theory of vaginal orgasm. *Journal of Sexual Medicine, 9*(12), 3079–3088.

Costello, M., Rukus, J. & Hawdon, J. (2019). We don't like your type around here: Regional and residential differences in exposure to online hate material targeting sexuality. *Deviant Behavior, 40*(3), 385–401.

Cote-Arsenault, D. & Denney-Koelsch, E. (2018). "Love is a choice": Couple responses to continuing pregnancy with a lethal fetal diagnosis. *Illness, Crisis & Loss, 26*(1), 5–22.

Couch, A. (2015, October 14). Margaret Cho opens up about her experience with rape, abuse: "Sharing the suffering alleviates the burden." *People*. Retrieved from http://www.people.com/article/margaret-cho-talks-abuse-bullying-rape

Courthouse News Service. (2018, July 16). *40th Statewide Report Investigating Grand Jury, Report 1, Interim—Redacted*. Retrieved from https://www.courthousenews.com/wp-content/uploads/2018/08/pa-abuse-report.pdf

Courtice, E. L. & Shaughnessy, K. (2018). The partner context of sexual minority women's and men's cybersex experiences: Implications for traditional sexual script. *Sex Roles, 78*(3–4), 722–285.

Covell, T. (2016, March). To know ourselves: Possible meanings in Canadian pornography. *Sexuality & Culture, 20*(1), 124–139.

Cramer, K., & Sparling, S. (2014, November). *Sexual arousal's impact on elements of sexual decision making: How sexual arousal affects condom adherence.* Paper presented at the annual meeting of the Society for the Scientific Study of Sexuality, Omaha, NE.

Cranney, S. (2017). Sex life satisfaction in Sub-Saharan Africa: A descriptive and exploratory analysis. *Archives of Sexual Behavior, 46*(7), 1961–1972.

Cranney, S. (2018, April 27). Why did God make me this way? Religious coping and framing in the virtuous pedophile community. *Society for the Scientific Study of Religion*, Online. doi: https://doi.org/10.1111/jssr.12480

Crowley, A. D. (2014). "Let's get drunk and have sex": The complex relationship of alcohol, gender, and sexual victimization. *Journal of Interpersonal Violence, 29*(7), 1258–1278.

Culp-Ressler, T. (2015, January 8). *This doctor moved her clinic to the middle of the ocean to help women get safe abortions.* Retrieved from https://thinkprogress.org/this-doctor-moved-her-clinic-to-the-middle-of-the-ocean-to-help-women-get-safe-abortions-8219378afaf0/

Cunningham, K., German, N. M., & Mattson, R. E. (2015). Regretful liaisons: Exploring the role of partner regret in the association between sexual and relationship satisfaction. *Journal of Sex & Marital Therapy, 41*(3), 325–338.

Cunningham, S., DeAngelo, G., & Tripp, J. (2019, February). *Craigslist's reduced violence against women.* Retrieved from http://scunning.com/craigslist110.pdf.

Curtis, S. (2016, September 19). One in 10 visitors to porn sites are under 10 years old, report claims. *Mirror*. Retrieved from http://www.mirror.co.uk/tech/one-10-visitors-porn-sites-8868796

Cutler, W. B., Friedmann, E. F., & McCoy, N. L. (1998). Pheromonal influences on sociosexual behavior in men. *Archives of Sexual Behavior, 27*(1), 1–13.

D'Amico, E., & Julien, D. (2012). Disclosure of sexual orientation and gay, lesbian, and bisexual youths' adjustment: Associations with past and current parental acceptance and rejection. *Journal of GLBT Family Studies, 8*(3), 215–242.

Daar, D. A., Abdou, S. A., Wilson, S. C., Hazen, A., & Saadeh, P. B. (2019). A call to action for male surgeons in the wake of the #MeToo Movement: Mentor Female Students. *Annals of Surgery, 20*(20), 1–3.

da Silva Lara, L. A., dos Santos Lima, M. L., Romao, G. S., Ferriani, R. A., & de Albuquerque Salles Navarro, P. A. (2016). Factors related to coital frequency of women in their thirties. *Journal of Sex & Marital Therapy, 42*(5), 403–412.

Daspe, M. E., Vaillancourt-Morel, M. P., Lussier, Y., Sabourin, S., & Ferron, A. (2018). When pornography use feels out of control: The moderation effect of relationship and sexual satisfaction. *Journal of Sex & Marital Therapy, 44*(4), 343–353.

Davies, E., Mangongi, N. P., & Carter, C. L. (2013). Is timing everything? A meeting report of the Society for Women's Health Research roundtable on menopausal hormone therapy. *Journal of Women's Health, 22*(4), 303–311.

Davis, A. C., Carrotte, E. R., Hellard, M. E., & Lim, M. S. C. (2018). What behaviors do young heterosexual Australians see in pornography? *Journal of Sex Research, 55*(3), 310–319.

Davis, G., & Wakefield, C. (2017). The intersex kids are all right? Diagnosis disclosure and the experiences of intersex youth. *Sociological Studies of Children & Youth, 23*, 43–65.

Davis, K. N., & Olmstead, S. B. (2017, March). *Reasons for having sex among emerging adults: A developmental perspective.* Poster presented at the annual meeting of Southeastern Council on Family Relations, Charlotte, NC.

Dawson, K., Gabhainn, S. N., & MacNeela, P. (2020) Toward a model of porn literacy: Core concepts, rationales, and approaches. *Journal of Sex Research, 57*(1), 1–15.

De Block, A., & Adriaens, P. (2013). Pathologizing sexual deviance: A history. *Journal of Sex Research, 50*(3–4), 276–298.

De Groot, K. (2017). Psychiatrist, gay rights trailblazer honored in Philadelphia. *The Washington Times*, Oct 1. Retrieved from https://m.washingtontimes.com/news/2017/oct/1/psychiatrist-gay-rights-trailblazer-honored-in-phi

DeHaan, S., Kuper, L. E., Magee, J. C., Bigelow, L., & Mustanski, B. S. (2013). The interplay between online and offline explorations of identity, relationships, and sex: A mixed-methods study with LGBT youth. *Journal of Sex Research, 50*(5), 421–434.

DeHart, D. D., & Birkimer, J. C. (1997). Trying to practice safer sex: Development of the sexual risks scale. *Journal of Sex Research, 34*(1), 11–25.

De Jong, D. C., Adams, K. N., & Reiss, H. T. (2018). Predicting women's emotional responses to hooking up. Do motives matter? *Journal of Social and Personal Relationships, 35*(4): 532–556.

Della, R. L., Erwin, S., Peter, J., Roselius, K., & Thrasher, A. (2019, November 19–23). *Family-sanctioned sex trafficking: studying risk and male partner relationship dynamics among the Bedia of India.* Paper presented at the annual conference of national Council of Family Relations, Fort Worth, TX.

Deming, M. E., Covan, E. K., Swan, S. C., & Billings, D. L. (2013). Exploring rape myths, gendered norms, group processing, and the social context of rape among college women: A qualitative analysis. *Violence Against Women, 19*(4), 465–485.

Denison, H. J., Bromihead, C., Grainger, R. Dennison, E. M., & Jutel, A. (2017). Barriers to sexually transmitted infection testing in New Zealand: A qualitative study. *Australian & New Zealand Journal of Public Health, 41*(4), 432–437.

Dennis, A. (2018). The strange survival and apparent resurgence of sociobiology. *History of the Human Sciences, 31*(1), 19–35.

Department of Defense. (2015, May 18). *Embattled: Retaliation against sexual assault survivors in the U.S. military.* Retrieved from https://www.hrw.org/report/2015/05/18/embattled/retaliation-against-sexual-assault-survivors-us-military

DePaulo, B. M., Ansfield, M. E., Kirkendol, S. E., & Boden, J. M. (2004). Serious lies. *Basic & Applied Social Psychology, 26*(2–3), 147–167.

DePaulo, B. M., Kiekendol, S. E., Kashy, D. A., Wyer, M. M., & Epstein, J. A. (1996). Lying in everyday life. *Journal of Personality and Social Psychology, 70*(5), 979–997.

Derlega, V. J., Metts, S., Petronio, S., & Marulis, S. T. (1993). *Self-disclosure.* Newbury Park, CA: Sage.

De Santis, J. P., Provencio-Vasquez, E., Mata, H. J., & Mancera, B. (2017). A comparison of sexual relationships among Hispanic men by sexual orientation: Implications for HIV/STI prevention. *Sexuality & Culture, 21*(3), 692–702.

De Santisteban, P., & Gamez-Guadix, M. (2018). Prevalence and risk factors among minors for online sexual solicitations and interactions with adults. *Journal of Sex Research, 55*(7), 939–950.

de Vries, A. L., McGuire, J. K., Steensma, T. D., Wagenaar, E. C., Doreleijers, T. A., & Cohen-Kettenis, P. T. (2014, September 2). Young adult psychological outcome after puberty suppression and gender reassignment. *Pediatrics.* Retrieved from http://pediatrics.aappublications.org/content/early/2014/09/02/peds.2013-2958

Diamond, M. (1995). Biological aspects of sexual orientation and identity. In L. Diamont & R. D. McAnulty (Eds.), *The psychology of sexual orientation, behavior, and identity: A handbook* (pp. 45–80). Westport, CT: Greenwood Press.

Diamond, M. (2009). Pornography, public acceptance and sex related crimes: A review. *International Journal of Law and Psychiatry, 32*(5), 304–314.

Diamond, M., & Sigmundson, H. K. (1997). Sex reassignment at birth. Long-term review and clinical implications. *Archives of Pediatrics & Adolescent Medicine, 151*(3), 298–304.

DiMauro, J., Renshaw, K. D., & Blais, R. K. (2018). Sexual vs. non-sexual trauma, sexual satisfaction and function, and mental health in female veterans. *Journal of Trauma & Dissociation, 19*(4), 403–416.

Dines, G. (2006). The white man's burden: Gonzo pornography and the construction of black masculinity. *Yale Journal of Law & Feminism, 18*(1), 283–297.

Diokno, A. C., Brown, M. B., & Herzog, A. R. (1990). Sexual functioning in the elderly. *Archives of Internal Medicine, 150*(1), 197–200.

Diop, M. K. & Stewart, P. (2014, November). *The role of men in the perpetuation and eradication of female genital mutilation.* Paper presented at the annual meeting of the National Council on Family Relations, Baltimore, MD.

DiPlacidio, J. (1998). Minority stress among lesbians, gay men, and bisexuals. In G. M. Herek (Ed.), *Stigma and sexual orientation: Understanding prejudice against lesbians, gay men, and bisexuals* (pp. 138–159). Davis, CA: Sage Publications.

Dobson, K., Campbell, L., & Stanton, C. E.. (2018). Are you coming on to me? Bias and accuracy in couples' perceptions of sexual advances. *Journal of Social and Personal Relationships, 35*(4), 460–484.

Dockterman, E. (2018, May 21). Can bad men change: What it's like inside sex offender therapy. *Time.* Retrieved from https://time.com/5272337/sex-offenders-therapy-treatment/

Dockterman, E. (2014, October 16). What is #GamerGate and why are women being threatened about video games? *Time.* Retrieved from https://time.com/3510381/gamergate-faq/

Dolan, K. (2019, January). *Gender fluidity and gender identity.* Presentation at Sociology of Human Sexuality, East Carolina University, Greenville, NC..

Dolan, A., Fowler, E., Moors, A., Matsick, J., Ziegler, A., & Conley, T. (2014, November). *Unwarranted stigma surrounding sexual behaviors.* Poster session presented at the annual meeting of the Society for the Scientific Study of Sexuality, Omaha, NE.

Donatello, R. A., De Rosa, C. J., Moulton, B. D., Viola, R., Rohrbach, A., & Afifi, A. A. (2017). Patterns of sexual experience among urban Latino and African American ninth grade students. *The Journal of Sex Research, 54*(4–5), 619–630.

Donenberg, G., Emerson, E., Mackesy-Amiti, M. E., Fletcher, F. (2018). Sexual risk among African-American girls seeking psychiatric care: A social-personal framework. *Journal of Consulting and Clinical Psychology, 86*(1), 24–38.

Donovan, M. K. (2017). The looming threat to sex education: A resurgence of Federal funding for abstinence-only programs? *Guttmacher Policy Review, 20,* 44-47. Online at https://www.guttmacher.org/sites/default/files/article_files/gpr2004417.pdf

Donnelly, J. (1997). Sexual satisfaction for a woman with severe cerebral palsy. *Sexuality and Disability, 15*(1), 16–17.

Doornwaard, S. M., Boer, F. D., Vanwesenbeeck, I., Van Nijnatten, C. H. C. J., Ter Bogt, T. F. M., & Van Den Eijnden, R. J. J. M. (2017). Dutch adolescents' motives, perceptions, and reflections toward sex-related Internet use: Results of a web-based focus-group study. *The Journal of Sex Research, 54*(8), 1038–1050.

Döring, N., Daneback, K., Shaughnessy, K, Grov, C., & Byers, E. S. (2017). Online sexual activity experiences among college students: A four-country comparison. *Archives of Sexual Behavior, 46*(6), 1641–1652.

Döring, N., & Pöschl, S. (2018). Sex toys, sex dolls, sex robots: Our under-researched bed-fellows. *Sexologies: European Journal of Sexology and Sexual Health, 27*(3), e51–e55.

Dosch, A., Ghisletta, P., & Van der Linden, M. (2016). Body image in dyadic and solitary sexual desire: The role of encoding style and distracting thoughts. *The Journal of Sex Research, 53*(9), 1193-1206.

Dossett, J. (2014, November). *How important is sex? The development and validation of the sexual importance scale.* Presented at the annual meeting of the Society for the Scientific Study of Sexuality, Omaha, NE.

Dourado, M., Finamore, C., Barroso, M. F., Santos, R., & Laks, J. (2010). Sexual satisfaction in dementia: Perspectives of patients and spouses. *Sexuality and Disability, 28*(3), 195–203.

Doyle, C., Swain, W. A., Ewald, H. A., Cook, C. L., & Ewald, P. W. (2015). Sexually transmitted pathogens, depression, and other manifestations associated with premenstrual syndrome. *Human Nature, 26*(3), 277–291.

Drescher, J. (2016, August 15). Gender diagnoses and ICD-11. *Psychiatric News.* Published online. Retrieved from http://psychnews.psychiatryonline.org/doi/full/10.1176/appi.pn.2016.8a15

Driemeyer, W. , Janssen, E., Wiltfang, J., & Elmerstig, E. (2017) Masturbation experiences of Swedish senior high school students: Gender differences and similarities. *The Journal of Sex Research, 54*(4–5), 633–641.

Drouin, M., Vogel, K. N., Surbey, A., & Stills, J. R. (2013). Let's talk about sexting, baby: Computer-mediated sexual behaviors among young adults. *Computer in Human Behavior, 29*(5), A25–A30.

Drouin, M., Hernandez, E., & Wehle, S. M. (2018). "Tell me lies, tell me sweet little lies:" Sexting deception among adults. *Sexuality & Culture, 22*(3), 865–880.

Drucker, J., & Nieri, T. (2018). Female online sex workers' perceptions of exit from sex work. *Deviant Behavior, 39*(1), 1–19.

Dube, S., Lavoie, F., Blais, M., & Hebert, M. (2017). Consequences of casual sex relationships and experiences on adolescents' psychological well-being: A prospective study. *The Journal of Sex Research, 54*(8), 1006–2017.

Ducharme, J. K., & Kollar, M. M. (2012). Does the "marriage benefit" extend to same-sex union? Evidence from a sample of married lesbian couples in Massachusetts. *Journal of Homosexuality, 59*(4), 580–591.

Dufur, M. J., Hoffmann, J. P., & Erickson, L. D. (2018). Single parenthood and adolescent sexual outcomes. *Journal of Child & Family Studies, 27*(3), 802–815.

Duncan, B. L., & Rock, J. W. (1993, January 1). The power of the unpredictable: How one person can initiate change in a troubled relationship. *Psychology Today*. Retrieved from https://www.psychologytoday.com/articles/199301/the-power-the-unpredictable

Duncan, D., Prestage, G., & Grierson, J. (2015). Trust, commitment, love and sex: HIV, monogamy, and gay men. *Journal of Sex & Marital Therapy, 41*(4), 345–360.

Dunsieth, N. W., Nelson, E. B., Brusman-Lovins, L. A., Holcomb, J. L., Beckman, D., Welge, J. A., ... McElroy, S. L. (2004). Psychiatric and legal features of 113 men convicted of sexual offenses. *Journal of Clinical Psychiatry, 65*(3), 293–300.

DuPree, M. G., Mustanski, B. S., Bocklandt, S., Nievergelt, C., & Hamer, D. H. (2004). A candidate gene study of CYP19 (Aromatase) and male sexual orientation. *Behavior Genetics, 34*(3), 243–250.

Durant, B., & Couch, J. (2019). "It's just more, you know, natural:" The perceptions of men who buy sex in an emerging street sex market. *Sexualities, 22*(3), 310–324.

East, P., & Hokoda, A. (2015). Risk and protective factors for sexual and dating violence victimization: A longitudinal, prospective study of Latino and African American adolescents. *Journal of Youth and Adolescence, 44*(6), 1288–1300.

Easterling, B. D., Knox, D., & Brackett, A. (2012). Secrets in romantic relationships: Does sexual orientation matter? *Journal of GLBT Family Studies, 8*(2), 196–208.

Easton, S. D., Renner, L. M., & O'Leary, P. (2013). Suicide attempts among men with histories of child sex abuse: Examining abuse severity, mental health, and masculine norms. *Child Abuse and Neglect, 37*(6), 380–387.

Eaton, N. R., Thompson, Jr., R. G., Hu, M. C., Goldstein, R. B., Saha, T. D., & Hasin, D. S. (2015). Regularly drinking alcohol before sexual activity in a nationally representative sample: Prevalence, sociodemographics, and associations with psychiatric and substance use disorders. *American Journal of Public Health, 105*(7), 1387–1393.

Ecker, J., Cherner, R., Rae, J., & Czechowski, K. (2018). Sexual intimacy, mental illness, and homelessness. *American Journal of Community Psychology, 61*(1–2), 131–140.

Edelman, A. (2018, April). *Plan C: Ensuring that your plan B works*. Conference on Contraceptive Technology, Washington, DC.

Edwards, S. R., Bradshaw, K. A., & Hinsz V. B. (2014). Denying rape but endorsing forceful intercourse: Exploring differences among responders. *Violence and Gender, 1*(4), 188–193.

Eeckhaut, M. C. W., & Sweeney, M. M. (2018). Understanding sterilization regret in the United States: The role of relationship context. *Journal of Marriage & Family, 80*(5), 1259–1270.

Efrati, Y. (2019). God, I can't stop thinking about sex! The rebound effect in unsuccessful suppression of sexual thoughts among religious adults. *The Journal of Sex Research, 56*(2), 146–155.

Eiseman, P., & Peterson, Z. (2014, November). *Definitions of "cheating" in an undergraduate sample: Comparisons and correlates*. Presented at the annual meeting of the Society for the Scientific Study of Sexuality, Omaha, NE.

Elder, W. B., Brooks, G. R., & Morrow, S. L. (2012). Sexual self-schemas of heterosexual men. *Psychology of Men and Masculinity, 13*(2), 166–179.

Elias, V. L., Fullerton, A. S., & Simpson, J. M. (2015). Long-term changes in attitudes toward premarital sex in the United States: Reexamining the role of cohort replacement. *Journal of Sex Research, 52*(2), 129–139. doi: http://dx.doi.org/10.1080/00224499.2013.798610

Eliason, M. (2000). Bi-negativity: The stigma facing bisexual men. *Journal of Bisexuality, 1*(2–3), 137–154.

Ellis, L. (1989). *Theories of rape: Inquiries into the causes of sexual aggression*. New York, NY: Hemisphere.

Ellis, L. (1996). Theories of homosexuality. In R. C. Savin-Williams & K. M. Cohen (Eds.), *The lives of lesbians, gays, and bisexuals: Children to adults* (pp. 11–34). Fort Worth, TX: Harcourt Brace.

Ellis, L., & Ames, M. A. (1987). Neurohormonal functioning and sexual orientation: A theory of homosexuality-heterosexuality. *Psychological Bulletin, 101*(2), 233–258.

Ellis, L. D., & Walters, A. S. (2018, June). *Like a virgin: The porous definitions of virginity and virginity loss among lesbians and gay men*. Poster presented at the annual meeting of the American Association of Sexuality Educators, Counselors and Therapists, Denver, CO.

Emmers-Sommer, T. M. (2018). Reasons for pornography consumption: Associations with gender, psychological and physical sexual satisfaction, and attitudinal impacts. *Sexuality & Culture, 22*(1), 48–62.

Emmers-Sommer, T. M., Allen, M., Schoenbauer, K. V., & Burrell, N. (2018). Implications of sex guilt: A meta-analysis. *Marriage & Family Review, 54*(5), 417–437.

Epstein, S. & Mamo, L. (2017). The proliferation of sexual health: Diverse social problems and the legitimation of sexuality. *Social Science & Medicine, 188*, 176–190.Equal Employment Opportunity Commission. (2009, December 14). Facts about sexual harassment. Retrieved from http://www.eeoc.gov/eeoc/publications/fs-sex.cfm

Equal Employment Opportunity Commission. (2015, April 29). *Red Lobster restaurants will pay $160,000 to settle EEOC sexual harassment lawsuit* [Press release]. Retrieved from http://www.eeoc.gov/eeoc/newsroom/release/4-29-15a.cfm

Erbil, N. (2013). The relationships between sexual function, body image and body mass index among women. *Sexuality and Disability, 31*(1), 63–70.

Erenel, A. S., & Kilinc, F. N. (2013). Does obesity increase sexual dysfunction in women? *Sexuality and Disability, 31*(1), 53–62.

Erichsen, K., & Dignam, P. (2016, April). *From hookup to husband: Courtship attitudes among college students*. Paper presented at the annual meeting of the Southern Sociological Society, Atlanta, GA.

Erichsen, K., & Knox, D. (2015, March). *Transitioning casual involvement to committed relationship*. Paper presented at the annual meeting of the Southern Sociological Society, New Orleans, LA.

Esterline, K. M., & Muehlenhard, C. L. (2017). Wanting to be seen: Young people's experiences of performative making out. *The Journal of Sex Research, 54*(8), 1051–1063.

Estill, A., Mock, S. E., Schryer, E., & Eibach, R. P. (2018). The effects of subjective age and aging attitudes on mid- to late-life sexuality. *Journal of Sex Research, 55*(2), 146–151.

Evans, C., Bennett, J., Croston, M., Brito-Ault, N., & Bruton, J. (2015). "In reality, it is complex and difficult": UK nurses on "treatment as prevention" within HIV care. *AIDS Care, 27*(6), 753–7.

Faccini, L., & Saide, M. A. (2012). "Can you breathe?" Autoerotic asphyxiation and asphyxiophilia in a person with an intellectual disability and sex offending. *Sexuality and Disability, 30*(1), 97–101.

Fahs, B. (2016). Methodological mishaps and slippery subjects: Stories of first sex, oral sex, and sexual trauma in qualitative sex research. *Qualitative Psychology, 3*(2), 209–225.

Farivar, C. (2018). *Cybersex toy industry heats up as infamous "teledildonics" patent climaxes.* Retrieved on October 28, 2018 from https://arstechnica.com/tech-policy/2018/08/cybersex-toy-industry-heats-up-as-infamous-teledildonics-patent-climaxes/

Farvid, P., & Braun, V. (2017). Unpacking the "pleasures" and "pains" of heterosexual casual sex: Beyond singular understandings. *The Journal of Sex Research, 54*(1), 73–90.

Fass, P. S., & Mason, M. A. (1995). *Childhood in America.* New York, NY: NYU Press.

Farris, C., Treat, T. A., Viken, R. J., & McFall, R. M. (2008). Sexual coercion and the misperception of sexual intent. *Clinical Psychology Review, 28*(1), 48–66. doi: 10.1016/j.cpr.2007.03.002

Farley, M. (2006, October 1). Prostitution, trafficking, and cultural amnesia: What we must not know in order to keep the business of sexual exploitation running smoothly. *Yale Journal of Law and Feminism.* Retrieved from http://digitalcommons.law.yale.edu/cgi/viewcontent.cgi?article=1243&context=yjlf

Farley, M., Schuckman, E., Golding, J. M., Houser, K., Jarrett, L., Qualliotine, P., & Decker, M. (2011, July). *Comparing sex buyers with men who don't buy sex: "You can have a good time with the servitude" vs. "You're supporting a system of degradation."* Paper presented at the annual conference of the Psychologists for Social Responsibility, Boston, MA.

Farr, R. H., Salomon, I., Brown-Iannuzzi, J. L., & Brown, C. S. (2019). Elementary school-age children's attitudes toward children in same-sex parent families. *Journal of GLBT Family Studies, 15*(2), 127–150.

Faustino, M. J., (2018). Rebooting an old script by new means: Teledildonics—The technological return to the 'Coital imperative'. *Sexuality & Culture, 22*(1), 243–257. doi: https://doi.org/10.1007/s12119-017-9463-5

Fausto-Sterling, A. (2019). Gender/sex, sexual orientation, and identity are in the body: How did they get there? *The Journal of Sex Research, 56*(4–5), 529–555.

Fava, N. M., Bay-Cheng, L. Y., Nochajski, T. H., Bowker, J. C., & Hayes, T. (2018). A resilience framework: Sexual health trajectories of youth with maltreatment histories. *Journal of Trauma & Dissociation, 19*(4), 444–460.

Favez, N., Tissot, H., Gisletta, P., Golay, P., & Cairo Notari, S. (2016). Validation of the French version of the Experiences in Close Relationships—Revised (ECR-R) adult romantic attachment questionnaire. *Swiss Journal of Psychology, 75*(3), 113–121.

Federal Communications Commission. (2019, December 30). Children's Internet Protection Act. Retrieved from https://www.fcc.gov/consumers/guides/childrens-internet-protection-act

Fedewa, A. L., Black, W. W., & Soyeon, A. (2015). Children and adolescents with same-gender parents: A meta-analytic approach in assessing outcomes. *Journal of GLBT Family Studies, 11*(1), 1–34.

Fedina, L., Holmes, J. L., Backes, B. L. (2018). Campus sexual assault: A systemic review of prevalence from 2000 to 2015. *Trauma, Violence & Abuse, 19*(1), 76–93.

Fehr, S. K., Vidourek, R. A., & King, K. A. (2015). Intra- and inter-personal barriers to condom use among college students: A review of the literature. *Sexuality & Culture, 19*(1), 103–121.

Feng, G. C., & Guo, S. Z. (2013). Tracing the route of China's Internet censorship: An empirical study. *Telematics and Informatics, 30*(4), 335–345.

Ferguson, C. E., & Malouff, J. M. (2016). Assessing police classifications of sexual assault reports: A meta-analysis of false reporting rates. *Archives of Sexual Behavior, 45*(5), 1185–1193.

Ferraro, M. M., & Casey, E. (2005). *Investigating child exploitation and pornography.* Boston, MA: Elsevier Academic Press.

Ferreira, J. M., Collins, M., Palmqvist, H., Pasquino, N., Bahamondes, L., & Brotto, L. A. (2019). Analysis of 16 years of calls and emails to the Options for Sexual Health "Sex Sense" information and referral service. *The Canadian Journal of Human Sexuality, 28*(1), 38–45.

Ferris, S. (2015, September 13). *GOP: Defund Planned Parenthood even if it didn't break the law.* The Hill. Retrieved from http://thehill.com/policy/healthcare/253452-gop-defund-planned-parenthood-even-if-it-didnt-break-the-law

Fetterolf, J. C., & Sanchez, D. T. (2015). The costs and benefits of perceived sexual agency for men and women. *Archives of Sexual Behavior. 44*(4), 961–970.

Fielder, R. L., Carey, K. B., & Carey, M. P. (2013). Are hookups replacing romantic relationships? A longitudinal study of first-year female college students. *Journal of Adolescent Health, 52*(5), 657–659.

Fileborn, B., Brown, G., Lyons, A., Hinchliff, S., Heywood, W., Minichiello, V., ... Crameri, P. (2018). Safer sex in later life: Qualitative interviews with older Australians on their understandings and practices of safer sex. *Journal of Sex Research, 55*(2), 164–177.

Fileborn, B., Hinchliff, S., Lyons, A., Heywood, W., Minichiello, V., Brown, G., ... Cameri, P. (2017). The importance of sex and the meaning of sex and sexual pleasure for men aged 60 and older who engage in heterosexual relationships: Findings from a qualitative interview study. *Archives of Sexual Behavior, 46*(7), 2097–2110.

Finer, L. B., & Philbin, J. M. (2013). Sexual initiation, contraceptive use, and pregnancy among young adolescents. *Pediatrics, 131*(5), 886–891.

Fiorini, M. (2019, November). *Dimisexuality and its clinical considerations.* Poster presented at the Society for the Scientific Study of Sex annual meeting, Denver, CO.

Fishburn, E., Fu, T., Dodge, B., & Herbenick, D. (2016, November). *The impact of alcohol and drug use on desire for sex among a probability sample of U. S. college students.* Poster presented at the annual meeting of the Society for the Scientific Study of Sexuality, Phoenix, AZ.

Fisher, A. D., Bandini, E., Rastrelli, G., Corana, G., Monami, M., Mannucci, E., & Maggi, M. (2012a). Sexual and cardiovascular correlates of male unfaithfulness. *Journal of Sexual Medicine, 9*(6), 1508–1518.

Fisher, N. L., & Pina, A. (2013). An overview of the literature on female perpetrated adult male sexual victimization. *Aggression and Violent Behavior, 18*(1), 54–61.

Fitzgerald, C., & Withers, P. (2013). "I don't know what a proper woman means": What women with intellectual disabilities think about sex, sexuality and themselves. *British Journal of Learning Disabilities, 41*(1), 5–12.

Flanders, C. E., Anderson, R. E., Tarasoff, L. A., & Robinson, M. (2019a). Bisexual stigma, sexual violence, and sexual health among bisexual and other plurisexual women: A cross-sectional survey study. *The Journal of Sex Research, 56*(9), 1115–1127.

Flanders, C. E., Legge, M. M., Plante, I., Goldberg, A. E., & Ross, L. E. (2019b). Gender socialization practices among bisexual and other nonmonosexual mothers: A longitudinal qualitative examination. *Journal of GLBT Family Studies, 15*(2), 105–126.

Flanders, C. E, Tarasoff, L. A., Legge, M. M., Robinson, M., & Gos, G. (2017). Positive experiences of young bisexual and other nonmonosexual people: A qualitative inquiry. *Journal of Homosexuality, 64*(8), 1014–1032.

Fledderjohann, J., & Barnes, L. W. (2018). Reimagining infertility: A critical examination of fertility norms, geopolitics and survey bias. Health Policy & Planning, 33(1), 34–40.

Fletcher, G., Dowsett, G. W., Duncan, D., Slavin, S., & Corboz, J. (2013). Advancing sexuality studies: A short course on sexuality theory and research methodologies. *Sex Education, 13*(3), 319–335.

Flores, A. R., Herman, J. L., Gates, G. J., Brown, T. N. T. (2016, June). *How Many Adults Identify as Transgender in the United States?* The Williams Institute. Retrieved from http://williamsinstitute.law.ucla.edu/wp-content/uploads/How-Many-Adults-Identify-as-Transgender-in-the -United-States.pdf.

Florres, D., & Barroso, J. (2017). 21st century parent-child sex communication in the United States: A process review. *The Journal of Sex Research, 54*(4–5), 532–548.

Flotynska, J., Uruska, A., Michalska, A., Araszkiewicz, A., & Zozulinska-Ziolkiewicz, D. (2019). Sexual dysfunction is a more common problem in young women with type 1 diabetes than in healthy. *Journal of Marital & Sex Therapy, 45*(7), 643–651. doi: https://doi-org.jproxy.lib.ecu.edu /10.1080/0092623X.2019.1610121

Flynn, E. (2019, September). Who's behind the screen? *The Sun.* Retrieved from https://www.thesun.co.uk/fabulous/1754916/catfishing-meaning -identity-steal-online-dating-law/

Fogel, C. I., Crandell, J. L., Neevel, A. M., Parker, S. D., Carry, M., White, B. L. & Gelaude, D. J. (2015). Efficacy of an adapted HIV and sexually transmitted infection prevention intervention for incarcerated women: A randomized controlled trial. *American Journal of Public Health, 105*(4), 802–809.

Fogel, J., & Kovalenko, L. (2013). Reality television shows focusing on sexual relationships are associated with college students engaging in one-night stands. *Journal of Cognitive & Behavioral Psychotherapies, 13*(2), 321–331.

Forbat, L., Robertson, J., & Mcnamee, P. (2018). Couple therapy following prostate cancer surgery: a manual to guide treatment. *Journal of Family Therapy, 40*(s1), s86–s110.

Forbes, M. K. , Baillie, A. J., Eaton, N. R., & Krueger, R. F. (2017a). A place for sexual dysfunction in the empirical taxonomy of psychopathology. *The Journal of Sexual Behavior, 54*(4–5), 465–485.

Forbes, M. K., Eaton, N. R., & Kruger, R. F. (2017b). Sexual quality of life and aging: A prospective study of a nationally representative study. *Journal of Sex Research. 54*(2), 137-148.

Forsman, M., Johansson, A., Santtila, P., Sandnabba, K., & Langstrom, N. (2015). Sexually coercive behavior following childhood maltreatment. *Archives of Sexual Behavior, 44*(1), 149–156.

Fortenberry, J. D. (2019). Trust, sexual trust, and sexual health: An interrogative review. *The Journal of Sex Research, 56*(4–5), 425–439.

Fox, K., Knox, D., Hall, S.S., & Kuck, D. (2019, April). *Religiosity: Impact on love, relationships, and sexual values/behavior.* Poster presented at annual meeting of the Southern Sociological Society, Atlanta, GA.

Fox, K., & Kuck, D. (2018, April). *Self-identified religiosity and its impact on multiple sex partners, attitudes toward extra-marital sex, sex education in schools.* Poster presented at the annual meeting of the Southern Sociological Society, New Orleans, LA.

Franco, O. H., Chowdhury, R., Troup, J., Voortman, T., Kunutsor, S., Kavousi, M., … Muka, T. (2016). Use of plant-based therapies and menopausal symptoms: A systematic review and meta-analysis. *Journal of the American Medical Association, 315*(23), 2554–2563.

Frank, S. E. (2018). Intersex and intimacy: Presenting concerns about dating and intimate relationships. *Sexuality & Culture, 22*(1), 127–147.

Franklin, A., & Smeaton, E. (2018). Listening to young people with learning disabilities who have experienced, or are at risk of, child sexual exploitation in the UK. *Children & Society, 32*(2), 98–109.

Freeman, C., Bernadette, C., & Hay-Smith, E. J. C. (2017). Couple's experiences of relationship maintenance and intimacy in acute spinal cord injury rehabilitation: An interpretative phenomenological analysis. *Sexuality and Disability, 35*(4), 433–444.

French, B. H., Suh, H. N., & Arterberry, B. (2017). Exploratory factor analysis and psychometric properties of the Sexual Coercion Inventory. *The Journal of Sex Research, 54*(8), 962–970.

Freysteinsdóttir, F. J., Skulason, S., Halligan, C., & Knox, D. (2014). U.S. and Icelandic college student attitudes toward relationships/sexuality. *College Student Journal, 48*(3), 355–361.

Frith, L., Blyth, E., Crawshaw, M., & Van den Aaker, O. (2018). Secrets and disclosure in donor conception. *Sociology of Health & Illness, 40*(1), 188–203.

Fritsch, K., Heynen, R., Ross, A. M., & van der Meulen. (2016). Disability and sex work: Developing affinities through decriminalization. *Disability & Society, 31*(1), 184–199.

Frost, K., Franzoi, S., Oswald, D. & Shields, S. (2018). Revising the Body Esteem Scale with a U.S. college student sample: Evaluation, validation and uses for the BES-R. *Sex Roles, 78*(1/2), 1–17.

Frutos, A., & Merrill, R. (2017). Explicit sexual movie viewing in the United States according to selected marriage and lifestyle, work and financial, religious and political factors. *Sexuality & Culture, 21*(4), 1062–1082.

Frye-Cox, N. E., & Hesse, C. R. (2013). Alexithymia and marital quality: The mediating roles of loneliness and intimate communication. *Journal of Family Psychology, 27*(2), 203–211.

Fuentealba-Torres, M., Cartagena-Ramos, D., Lara, L. A. S., Alves, J. D., Ramos, A. C. V., Campoy, L. T., … Arcêncio, R. A. (2019). Determinants of female sexual function in breastfeeding women. *Journal of Sex & Marital Therapy, 45*(6), 538–549.

Fugl-Meyer, K. S., Bohm-Starke, N., Damsted Petersen, C., Fugl-Meyer, A., Parish, S., & Giraldi, A. (2013). Standard operating procedures for female sexual pain. *Journal of Sexual Medicine, 10*(1), 83–93.

Fulle, A., Chang, J., & Knox, D. (2016, April). *Sexual hedonism: A comparison of undergraduate women and men.* Poster session presented at the annual meeting of the Southern Sociological Society, Atlanta, GA.

Fulle, A., Knox, D., & Chang, J. (2015, March). *Female sexual hedonism: Navigating stigma.* Poster session presented at the annual meeting of the Southern Sociological Society, New Orleans, LA.

Gagnon, J. H. (1977). *Human sexualities.* Glenview, IL: Scott Foresman.

Gagnon, J. H., & Simon, W. (1973). *Sexual conduct: The social sources of human sexuality.* Chicago, IL: Aldine.

Gaither, T. W., Allen, I. E., Osterberg, E. C., Alwal, A., Harris, C. R., & Breyer, B. N. (2017). Characterization of genital dissatisfaction in a national sample of U.S. men. *Archives of Sexual Behavior, 46*(7), 2123–2130.

Galinsky, A. M. (2012). Sexual touching and difficulties with sexual arousal and orgasm among U.S. older adults. *Archives of Sexual Behavior, 41*(4), 875–890.

Galperin, A., Haselton, M. G., Frederick, D. A., Poore, J., Hippel, W. V., Buss, D. M., & Gonzaga, D. C. (2013). Sexual regret: Evidence for evolved sex differences. *Archives of Sexual Behavior, 42*(7), 1145–1161.

Gao, J., Zhang, X., Su, P., Liu, J., Xia, L., Yang, J., … Liang, C. (2013). Prevalence and factors associated with the complaint of premature ejaculation and the four premature ejaculation syndromes: A large observational study in China. *Journal of Sexual Medicine, 10*(7), 1874–1881.

Gariepy, A. M., Hieftje, K, Pendergrass, T., Miller, E., Dziura, J. D., & Fiellin, L. E. (2018). Development and feasibility testing of a videogame intervention to reduce high-risk sexual behavior in Black and Hispanic adolescents. *Games for Health Journal, 7*(6). Published online November 30. doi: https://doi.org/10.1089/g4h.2017.0142

Garneau-Fournier, J., Dubois, R., McBain, S., & Turchik, J. A. (2014, August). *Predictors of sexual dysfunction in female college students*. Poster session presented at the annual meeting of the American Psychological Association, Washington, DC.

Gartrell, N., Bos, H., & Koh, A. (2018, July 19). National longitudinal lesbian family study—Mental health of adult offspring. *New England Journal of Medicine, 379*(3), 297–299.

Gato, J., Santos, S., & Fontaine, A. (2017). To have or not to have children? That is the question. Factors influencing decisions among lesbians and gay men. *Sexuality Research & Social Policy: Journal of NSRC, 14*(3), 310–323.

Gatzeva, M., & Paik, A. (2011). Emotional and physical satisfaction in noncohabitating, cohabitating and marital relationships: The importance of jealous conflict. *Journal of Sex Research, 48*(1), 29–42.

Gee, A. (2017). *Facing poverty, academics turn to sex work and sleeping in cars*. The Guardian, September. Retrieved from https://www.theguardian.com/us-news/2017/sep/28/adjunct-professors-homeless-sex-work-academia-poverty?CMP=Share_iOSApp_Other

Geher, G., & Wedberg, N. (2019). *Positive evolutionary psychology: Darwin's guide to living a richer life*. Oxford, England: Oxford University Press.

Gelabert, E., Subirà, S., García-Esteve, L., Navarro, P., Plaza, A., Cuyàs, E., ... Martin-Santos, R. (2012). Perfectionism dimensions in major postpartum depression. *Journal of Affective Disorders, 136*(1–2), 17–25.

Geonet, M., De Sutter, P., & Zech, E. (2013). Cognitive factors in female hypoactive sexual desire disorder. *Sexologies: European Journal of Sexology and Sexual Health, 22*(1), 9–15.

George, W. H. (2019). Alcohol and sexual health behavior: "What we know and how we know it." *The Journal of Sex Research, 56*(4-5), 409–424.

Gerdts, C., Fuentes, L., Grossman, D., White, K., Keefe-Oates, B., Baum, S. E., ... Potter, J. E. (2016, February 14). Impact of clinic closures on women obtaining abortion services after implementation of a restrictive law in Texas. *American Journal of Public Health, 106*(5), 857–864.

Gesselman, A. N., Webster, G. D., & Garcia, J. R. (2017). Has virginity lost its virtue? Relationship stigma associated with being a sexually inexperienced adult. *The Journal of Sex Research, 54*(2), 202–213.

Gewirtz-Meydan, A., & Finzi-Dottan, R. (2018). Sexual satisfaction among couples: The role of attachment orientation and sexual motives. *Journal of Sex Research, 55*(2), 178–190.

Ghajarzadeh, M., Tanha, F. D., Akrami, M., Mohseni, M., Askari, F., & Farsi, L. (2014). Do Iranian women with endometriosis suffer from sexual dysfunction? *Sexuality and Disability, 32*(2), 189–195.

Ghanem, H., Glina, S., Assalian, P., & Buvat, J. (2013). Position paper: Management of men complaining of a small penis size despite an actually normal size. *Journal of Sexual Medicine, 10*(1), 294–303.

Giami, A. (2013). Social epidemiology of premature ejaculation. *Sexologies, 22,* 27–32.

Gibbs, N. (2012, August). Your life is fully mobile: We walk, talk and sleep with our phones. But are we more—or less—connected?. *Time, 180*(9). Retrieved from http://techland.time.com/2012/08/16/your-life-is-fully-mobile/

Gill, R., & Orgad, S. (2018). The shifting terrain of sex and power: From the 'sexualization of culture' to #MeToo. *Sexualities, 21*(8), 1313–1324.

Gill, T. (2014, November). *Transforming queer culture: There's an app for that*. Presented at the annual meeting of the Society for the Scientific Study of Sexuality, Omaha, NE.

Gillespie, S. M., Williams, R., Elliott, I. A., Eldridge, H. J., Ashfield, S., & Beech, A. R. (2015). Characteristics of females who sexually offend: A comparison of solo and co-offenders. *Sexual Abuse: A Journal of Research & Treatment, 27*(3), 284–301.

Giordano, A. L., & Cashwell, C. S. (2017). Cybersex addiction among college students: A prevalence study. *Sexual Addiction & Compulsivity, 24*(1-2), 47–57.

Giordano, A. L., & Cecil, A. L. (2014). Religious coping, spirituality, and hypersexual behavior among college students. *Sexual Addiction & Compulsivity, 21*(3), 225–239.

Gkyamerah, A. O., Collier, K. L., Reddy, V., & Sandfort, T. G. M. (2019). Sexuality disclosure among black family South African MSM and responses by family. *The Journal of Sex Research, 56*(9), 1203–1218.

Glina, S., Sharlip, I. D., & Hellstrom, W. J. (2013). Modifying risk factors to prevent and treat erectile dysfunction. *Journal of Sexual Medicine, 10*(1), 115–119.

Glowacka, M., Bergeron, S., Delisle, I., & Rosen, N. O. (2019). Sexual distress mediates the associations between sexual contingent self-worth and well-being in women with genitopelvic pain: A dyadic daily experiences study. *The Journal of Sex Research, 56*(3), 314–326.

Gogno, M., Jones, D., & Ibarlucia, I. (2013). The challenges of sexology in Argentina. *International Journal of Sexual Health, 25*(1), 13–26.

Gold, R. B., & Hasstedt, K. (2016). Lessons from Texas: Widespread consequences of assaults on abortion access. *American Journal of Public Health, 106*(6), 970–971.

Goldfarb, E., Lieberman, L., Santos, P., & Kwiatkowski, S. (2018). Silence and censure: A qualitative analysis of young adults' reflections on communication with parents prior to first sex. *Journal of Family Issues, 39*(1), 28–54.

Goldfarb, E., Lieberman, L., & Santos, P. (2016, November*). Listening to the voices of GBQ young men about navigating first sex: Implications for families, schools, and public health*. Session 42 at the annual meeting of the Society for the Scientific Study of Sexuality, Phoenix, AZ.

Gontero, P., Di Marco, M., Giubilei, G., Bartoletti, R., Pappagallo, G., Tizzani, A., & Mondaini, N. (2009). A pilot phase-II prospective study to test the 'efficacy' and tolerability of a penile-extender device in the treatment of "short penis." *BJU International, 103*(6), 793–797.

Gonzalez-Rivas, S., Kern, S., & Peterson, Z. (2016, November).*Women's sexual initiation in other-sex and same-sex relationships*. Paper presented at the annual meeting of the Society for the Scientific Study of Sexuality, Phoenix, AZ.

Gonzalez-Rivas, S. & Peterson, Z. (2014, November). *Sexual satisfaction in infertile couples: A comparison of sex for conception and sex not for conception*. Paper presented at the annual meeting of the Society for the Scientific Study of Sexuality, Omaha, NE.

Goodin, S. M., Van Denburg, A., Murnen, S. K., & Smolak, L. (2011). "Putting on" sexiness: A content analysis of the presence of sexualizing characteristics in girls' clothing. *Sex Roles, 65*(1), 1–12.

Goodman, D. L. (2017). Development and validation of the pretending orgasm reasons measure. *Archives of Sexual Behavior, 46*(7), 1973–1991.

Gottman, J. (1994). *Why marriages succeed or fail ... and how you can make yours last*. New York, NY: Simon & Schuster.

Gottman, J. M., Coan, J., Carrere, S., & Swanson, C. (1998). Predicting marital happiness and stability from newlywed interactions. *Journal of Marriage and the Family, 60*(1), 5–22.

Gowen, L. K., & Winges-Yanez, N. (2014). Lesbian, gay, bisexual, transgender, queer and questioning youths' perspectives of inclusive school-based sexuality education. *Journal of Sex Research, 51*(7), 788–800.

Goyal, N. K., Hall, E. S., Greenberg, J. M., & Kelly, E. A. (2015). Risk prediction for adverse pregnancy outcomes in a Medicaid population. *Journal of Women's Health, 24*(8), 681–688.

Graf, N. (2018). *Sexual harassment at work in the era of #MeToo*. Pew Research Center. Retrieved from http://www.pewsocialtrends.org/2018/04/04/sexual-harassment-at-work-in-the-era-of-metoo/?utm_source=Pew+Research+Center&utm_campaign=63c18076fb-SDT_2018_04_04&utm_medium=email&utm_term=0_3e953b9b70-63c18076fb-399483133

Graff, K., Murnen, S. K., & Smolak, L. (2012). Too sexualized to be taken seriously? Perceptions of a girl in childlike vs. sexualizing clothing. *Sex Roles, 66*(11), 764–775.

Graham, S. (1848). *Lecture to young men on chastity, intended also for the serious consideration of parents and guardians* (10th ed.). Boston, MA: C. H. Price.

Grant, M. G. (2014). *Playing the whore*: The work of sex work. New York: Verso.

Granville, L., & Pregler, J. (2018). Women's sexual health and aging. *Journal of the American Geriatrics Society, 66*(3), 595–601.

Grauvogl, A., Peters, M. L., Evers, S. M. A., & van Lankveld, J. J. (2015). A new instrument to measure sexual competence and interaction competence in youth: Psychometric properties in female adolescents. *Journal of Sex & Marital Therapy, 41*(5), 544–556.

Greaves, L. M., Sibley, C. G., Fraser, G., & Barlow, F. K. (2019). Comparing pansexual- and bisexual-identified participants on demographics, psychological well-being, and political ideology in a New Zealand national sample. *The Journal of Sex Research, 56*(9), 1083–1090.

Greeff, A. P., & De Bruyne, T. (2000). Conflict management style and marital satisfaction. *Journal of Sex and Marital Satisfaction, 26*(4), 321–334.

Green, E. (2014, November). *Does education effectively reduce anti-transgender prejudice? Findings from a national study*. Paper presented at the annual meeting of the Society for the Scientific Study of Sexuality, Omaha, NE.

Green, R. J., Bettinger, M., & Zacks, F. (1996). Are lesbian couples fused and gay male couples disengaged? In J. Laird & R. J. Green (Eds.), *Lesbians and gays in couples and families* (pp. 185–230). San Francisco, CA: Jossey Bass.

Gregory, K. D., Fridman, M., & Korst, L. (2010, March). *Trends and patterns of vaginal birth after cesarean availability in the United States*. Paper presented at the NIH Consensus Development Conference on Vaginal Birth After Cesarean: New Insights, Bethesda, MD.

Griffith, S., & Kimball, C. (2014, August). *Men's stories of unwanted sexual and pornography exposure experiences: A qualitative analysis*. Poster session presented at the annual meeting of the American Psychological Association, Washington, DC.

Griffiths, M. D. (2012). Internet sex addiction: A review of empirical research. *Addiction Research & Theory, 20*(2), 111–124.

Grimes, D. A., Benson, J., Singh, S., Romero, M., Ganatra, B., Okonofua, F. E., & Shah, I. H. (2006). Unsafe abortion: The preventable pandemic. *The Lancet Sexual and Reproductive Health Series, 4*. Retrieved from http://www.who.int/reproductivehealth/publications/general/lancet_4.pdf

Grose, R. (2014, November). *Applying empowerment theory: A paradigm for understanding women's sexual pleasure*. Paper presented at the annual meeting of the Society for the Scientific Study of Sexuality, Omaha, NE.

Grossman, J. M., Richer, A. M., Charmaraman, L., Ceder, I., & Erkut, S. (2018). Youth perspectives on sexuality communication with parents and extended family. Family Relations, *67*(3), 368–380.

Grov, C., Wells, B. E., & Parsons, J. T. (2013). Self-reported penis size and experiences with condoms among gay and bisexual men. *Archives of Sexual Behavior, 42*(2), 313–322.

Grov, C., Wolff, M., Smith, M. D., Koken, J., & Parsons, J. T. (2014). Male clients of male escorts: Satisfaction, sexual behavior, and demographic characteristics. *Journal of Sex Research, 51*(7), 827–837.

Grubbs, J. B., & Perry, S. L. (2019). Moral incongruence and pornography use: A critical review and integration. *The Journal of Sex Research,56*(1), 29–37.

Guendelman, S., Pearl, M., Kosa, J. L., Graham, S., Abrams, B., & Kharrazi, M. (2013). Association between preterm delivery and pre-pregnancy body mass (BMI), exercise and sleep during pregnancy among working women in Southern California. *Maternal and Child Health Journal, 17*(4), 723–731.

Guida, J., Liangyuan, H., & Liu, H. (2019). Sexual behavior with noncommercial partners: A concurrent partnership study among middle-aged female sex workers in China. *The Journal of Sex Research, 56*(4–5), 670–680.

Guler, T., Yavuz, U., Ozkum, D., & Demirdamar, R. (2013). Effects of perimenstrual complaints on sexuality and disability and coping strategies of university students. *Sexuality and Disability, 31*(1), 93–101.

Gunderson, C., Hill, C., Haag, A., & Merkler, M. (2014, November). *Romantic and sexual interest in relation to implicit and explicit sexual motives*. Poster session presented at the annual meeting of the Society for the Scientific Study of Sexuality, Omaha, NE.

Guo, Y. (2019). Sexual double standards in White and Asian Americans: Ethnicity, gender, and acculturation. *Sexuality & Culture, 23*(1), 57–95.

Gupta, K. (2017). "And now I'm just different, but there's nothing actually wrong with me": Asexual marginalization and resistance. *Journal of Homosexuality, 64*(8), 991-1013.

Guttmacher Institute. (2014a, September 17). *New study finds that 40% of pregnancies worldwide are unintended*. Retrieved from http://www.guttmacher.org/media/nr/2014/09/17/sfp-sedgh-up.html

Guttmacher Institute. (2019, September). *Fact sheet: Induced abortion in the United States*. https://www.guttmacher.org/fact-sheet /induced-abortion-united-states

Guttmacher Institute. (2020a, January 1). *An Overview of Abortion Laws*. Retrieved from https://www.guttmacher.org/state-policy/explore /overview-abortion-laws

Guttmacher Institute. (2020b, January 1). *State laws and policies: Sex and HIV education*. Retrieved from https://www.guttmacher.org/state-policy /explore/sex-and-hiv-education

Haapsamo, H., Kuusikko-Gauffin, S., Ebeling, H., Larinen, K., Penninkilampi-Kerola, V., Soini, H., & Moilanen, I. (2013). Communication development and characteristics of influencing factors: A follow-up study from 8 to 36 months. *Early Child Development and Care, 183*(2), 321–334.

Haas, A. L., Barthel, J. M., & Taylor, S. (2017). Sex and drugs and starting school: Differences in precollege alcohol-related sexual risk taking by gender and recent blackout activity. *The Journal of Sex Research, 54*(6), 741–751.

Hafner, J. (2019, March 29-31). The "pill" for men: So close, yet so far. *USA Today*, p. A1.

Hahn, H. A., You, D. S., Sferra, M., Hubbard, M., Thamotharan, S., & Fields, S. A. (2018). Is it too soon to meet? Examining differences in Geosocial Networking App use and sexual risk behavior of emerging adults. *Sexuality & Culture, 22*(1), 1–21.

Hakim, C. (2015). The male sexual deficit: A social fact of the 21st century. *International Sociology, 30*(3), 314–335.

Hall, M. (2015). "When there's no underbrush the tree looks taller": A discourse analysis of men's online groin shaving talk. *Sexualities, 18*(8), 997–1017.

Hall, M., & Hearn, J. (2019). Revenge pornography and manhood acts: a discourse analysis of perpetrators' accounts. *Journal of Gender Studies, 28*(2), 158–170.

Hall, K. S., Moreau, C., & Trussell, J. (2012). Young women's perceived health and lifetime sexual experience: Results from the National Survey of Family Growth. *Journal of Sexual Medicine, 9*(5), 1382–1391.

Hall, S. & Knox, D. (2019) *College student attitudes and behaviors survey of 13,070 undergraduates*. Unpublished data collected for this text. Department of Family, Consumer, and Technology Education Teachers College, Ball State University and Department of Sociology, East Carolina University, Greenville, NC.

Hall, S., & Knox, D. (2016). *Relationship and sexual behaviors of a sample of 9,948 university students.* Unpublished raw data, Ball State University, Muncie, IN, and East Carolina University, Greenville, NC.

Halligan, C., Knox, D., & Brinkley, J. (2015, March)."*Once you go black, you never go back?": Stereotypes and realities.* Poster session presented at the annual meeting of the Southern Sociological Society, New Orleans, LA.

Hammack, P. L, Frost, D. M., & Hughes, S. D. (2019). Queer intimacies: A new paradigm for the study of relationship diversity. *The Journal of Sex Research, 56*(1–4), 556–592.

Hampton, M. D., & Lieggi, M. (2020). Commercial sexual exploitation of youth in the United States: A qualitative systematic review. *Trauma, Violence & Abuse, 21*(1), 57–70.

Hamzelou, J. (2016, September 27). Exclusive: World's first baby born with new "3 parent" technique. *New Scientist.* Retrieved from https://www.newscientist.com/article/2107219-exclusive-worlds-first-baby-born-with-new-3-parent-technique/?cmpid=SOC%7CNSNS%7C2016-Echobox&utm_campaign=Echobox&utm_medium=Social&utm_source=Twitter#link_time=1474985189

Hankes, K. (2016, January 5). How the extremist right hijacked Star Wars, Taylor Swift and the Mizzou student protests to promote racism. *Southern Poverty Law Center.* Retrieved from https://www.splcenter.org/hatewatch/2016/01/05/how-extremist-right-hijacked-%E2%80%98star-wars%E2%80%99-taylor-swift-and-mizzou-student-protests-promote

Hannaford, P. C., & Iverson, L. (2013). Mortality among oral contraceptive users: An evolving story. *The European Journal of Contraception & Reproductive Health Care, 18*(1), 1–4.

Hargie, O., Mitchell, D. H., & Somerville, I. J. A. (2017). 'People have a knack of making you feel excluded if they catch on to your difference': Transgender experiences of exclusion in sport. *International Review for the Sociology of Sport, 52*(2), 223–239.

Harknett, K. & Cranney, S. (2017). Majority rules: Gender composition and sexual norms and behavior in high schools. *Population Research & Policy Review, 36*(4), 469–500.

Harris, A. L., & Vitzthum, V. J. (2013). Darwin's legacy: An evolutionary view of women's reproductive and sexual functioning. Journal of Sex Research, 50(3–4), 207–246.

Harris Poll on behalf of GLAAD, Frank Pompa (2018). *Accelerating Acceptance 2018.* Retrieved from https://www.glaad.org/files/aa/Accelerating%20Acceptance%202018.pdf

Harris, R., J., McDonald, D. P., & Sparks, C. S. (2018). Sexual harassment in the military. *Armed Forces & Society, 44*(1), 25–43.

Harvard Health Letter. (2013, January). Considering testosterone therapy? *Harvard Health Publications, 38*(5). Retrieved from http://www.health.harvard.edu/mens-health/considering-testosterone-therapy

Harvard Mental Health Letter. (2010, July). Pessimism about pedophilia: There is no cure, so the focus is on protecting children. *Harvard Health Publications.* Retrieved from http://www.health.harvard.edu/newsletter_article/pessimism-about-pedophilia

Haselton, M. G. (2003). The sexual overperception bias: Evidence of a systematic bias in men from a survey of naturally occurring events. *Journal of Research in Personality, 37*(1), 34–47. doi: 10.1016/S0092-6566(02)00529-9

Hauge, L. J., Aaro, L. E., Torgersen, L., & Vollrath, M. E. (2013). Smoking during consecutive pregnancies among primiparous women in the population-based Norwegian mother and child cohort study. *Nicotine & Tobacco Research, 15*(2), 428–434.

Haupert, M. L., Moors, A. C., Gesselman, A. N., & Garcia, J. R. (2017). Estimates and correlates of engagement in consensually non-monogamous relationships. *Current Sexual Health Reports, 9*(3), 155–165.

Haym, C., Mack, J., & Hechter, S. (2016, November). *Thinkin' kinkin': A modern look at current kink research in psychotherapy.* Annual meeting of the Society for the Scientific Study of Sexuality, Phoenix, AZ.

Haywood, C. (2018). 'Leaving masculinity at the car door': Dogging, de-subjectification and the pursuit of pleasure. *Sexualities, 21*(4), 587–604.

Hazan, C., Merrill, S., Laurita, A. C., Surenkok, G., Fletcher, K., & Zayas, V. (2014, November). *Fooled around and fell in love: Sexual behavior as a marker of adult attachment.* Poster session presented at the annual meeting of the Society for the Scientific Study of Sexuality, Omaha, NE.

Healthy People 2020. (2019, December). *Sexually transmitted diseases.* Retrieved from http://www.healthypeople.gov/2020/topics-objectives/topic/sexually-transmitted-diseases

Heidari, M., Amin Shokravi, F., Zayeri, F., Azin, S. A., & Merghati-Khoei, E. (2018). Sexual life during pregnancy: Effect of an educational intervention on the sexuality of Iranian couples: A quasiexperimental study. *Journal of Sex & Marital Therapy, 44*(1), 45–55.

Hellman, J. (2017, June 6), Abstinence education advocate named to HHS post, *The Hill.* Retrieved from https://thehill.com/policy/healthcare/336620-abstinence-education-advocate-named-to-hhs-post

Helmus, L., Ó Ciardha, C., & Seto, M. C. (2015). The Screening Scale for Pedophilic Interests (SSPI): Construct, predictive, and incremental validity. *Law and Human Behavior, 39*(1), 35–43.

Helweg-Larsen, M., & Collins, B. E. (1994). The UCLA multidimensional condom attitudes scale: Documenting the complex determinants of condom use in college students. *Health Psychology, 13*(3), 224–237.

Hendrick, S. S., & Hendrick, C. (1992). *Romantic love.* Newbury Park, CA: Sage.

Hendrickx, L., Gijs, L., & Enzlin, P. (2019). Who's distressed by sexual difficulties? Exploring associations between personal, perceived partner and relational distress and sexual difficulties in heterosexual men and women. *The Journal of Se Research, 56*(3), 300–313.

Henry, N. (2015). Beyond the "sext": Technology-facilitated sexual violence and harassment against adult women. *Australian & New Zealand Journal of Criminology, 48*(1), 104–118.

Henshaw, M., Ogloff, J. R. P., & Clough, J. A. (2017). Looking beyond the screen; A critical review of the literature on the online child pornography offender. *Sexual Abuse: A Journal of Research & Treatment, 29*(5), 416–445.

Hequembourg, A. L., & Dearing, R. L. (2013). Exploring shame, guilt, and risky substance use among sexual minority men and women. *Journal of Homosexuality, 60*(4), 615–638.

Hequembourg, A. L., Parks, K. A., Collins, R. L., & Hughes, T. L. (2015). Sexual assault risks among gay and bisexual men. *Journal of Sex Research, 52*(3), 282–295.

Herbenick, D. (2012). *Sex made easy: Your awkward questions answered—for better, smarter, amazing sex.* Philadelphia, PA: Running Press Book Publishers.

Herbenick, D., Fu, T., Arter, J., Sanders, S. A., & Dodge, B. (2018). Women's experiences with genital touching, sexual pleasure, and orgasm: Results from a U.S. probability sample of women ages 18 to 94. *Journal of Sex & Marital Therapy, 4*(2), 201–212.

Herbenick, D., Hensel, D., Smith, N. K., Schick, V., Reece, M., Sanders, S. A., & Fortenberry, J. D. (2013). Pubic hair removal and sexual behavior: Findings from a prospective daily diary study of sexually active women in the United States. *Journal of Sexual Medicine, 10*(3), 678–685.

Herbenick, D., Reece, M., Schick, V., Sanders, S. A., Dodge, B., & Fortenberry, D. (2010). Sexual behavior in the United States: Results from a national probability sample of men and women ages 14–94. *Journal of Sexual Medicine, 7*(5), 255–265.

Herbenick, D., Van Anders, S. M., Brotto, L. A., Chivers, M. L., Jawed-Wessel, S., & Galarza, J. (2019). Sexual harassment in the field of sexuality research. *Archives of Sexual Behavior, 48*(4), 997–1006.

Herbst, J. H., Mansergh, G., Pitts, N., Denson, D., Mimiaga, M., & Holman, J. (2018). Effects of brief messages about antiretroviral therapy and condom use benefits among Black and Latino MSM in three U.S. cities. *Journal of Homosexuality, 65*(2), 154–166.

Hernandez, B. F., Peskin, M. F., Markham, C. M. Burr, J., Roberts, T., & Emery, S. T. (2018). The context of sexual decisions and intrapersonal factors related to sexual initiation among female military-dependent youth. *Journal of Sex Research, 55*(1), 73–83.

Hernandez-Kane, K. M., & Mahoney, A. (2018). Sex through a sacred lens: Longitudinal effects of sanctification of marital sexuality. *Journal of Family Psychology, 32*(4), 425–434.

Heron, K. E., & Smyth, J. M. (2013). Body image discrepancy and negative affect in women's everyday lives: An ecological momentary assessment evaluation of self-discrepancy theory. *Journal of Social and Clinical Psychology, 32*(3), 276–295.

Heywood, W., Lyons, A., Fileborn, B., Hinchliff, S., Minichiello, V., Malta, S., Barrett, C. & Dow, B. (2018) Sexual satisfaction among older Australian heterosexual men and women: Findings from the Sex, Age & Me Study. *Journal of Sex & Marital Therapy, 44*(3), 295–307.

Hille, J. (2014, November). *Asexuals and masturbation: Pleasure beyond sexuality.* Poster session presented at the annual meeting of the Society for the Scientific Study of Sexuality, Omaha, NE.

Hilliard, T. E., Edwards, A. L., Hall, S. S., & Knox, D. (2019a, November). *Who is the sexiest of them all? Racial differences in body language of female undergraduates.* Poster presented at the National Council on Family Relations annual meeting, Fort Worth, TX.

Hilliard, T., Knox, D. & Brenner, R. (2019b, March).*"This is how I like it": Association of feminist attitudes with sexual satisfaction.* Paper presented at the annual meeting of Eastern Sociological Society.

Hilliard, T., Knox, D., & Hall, S. (2019c, November). *Sexual value changes after a romantic breakup.* Poster presented at Society for the Scientific Study of Sex annual meeting, Denver, CO.

Hilliard, T., Knox, D., Stoner, M., & Aamlid, C. (2018, April). *What Parents Don't Know: International students' romantic relationships in the United States.* Paper presented at annual meeting of the Southern Sociological Society, New Orleans, LA.

Hinchliff, S., Tetley, J., Lee, D., & Nazroo, J. (2018). Older adults' experiences of sexual difficulties: Qualitative findings from the English longitudinal study on ageing. *Journal of Sex Research, 55*(2), 152–163.

Hines, D. A., & Palm Reed, K. M. (2015). An experimental evaluation of peer versus professional educators of a bystander program for the prevention of sexual and dating violence among college Students. *Journal of Aggression, Maltreatment & Trauma, 24*(3), 279–298.

Hines, T. M. (2001). The G-spot: A modern gynecologic myth. *American Journal of Obstetrics & Gynecology, 185*(2), 359–362.

Hintistan, S., & Cilingir, D. (2013). Sexual dysfunction in Turkish men and women with type 2 diabetes mellitus. *Sexuality and Disability, 31*(1), 31–41.

Ho, P. S. Y., Jackson, S., Cao S., & Kwok, C. (2018) Sex with Chinese characteristics: Sexuality research in/on 21st-century China. *Journal of Sex Research, 55*(4–5), 486–521.

Holland, L., Matthews, T. L., & Schott, M. R. (2012). "That's So Gay!" Exploring college students' attitudes toward the LGBT population. *Journal of Homosexuality, 60*(4), 575–595.

Holway, G. V., Umberson, D., & Donnelly, R. (2018). Health and health behavior concordance between spouses in same-sex and different-sex marriages. *Social Currents, 5*(4), 319–327.

Hom, K. A., & Woods, S. J. (2013). Trauma and its aftermath for commercially sexually exploited women as told by front-line providers. *Issues in Mental Health Nursing, 34*(2), 75–81.

Hope, D., & Meidlinger, P. (2014, November). *Measurement and implications of disclosure and concealment in lesbian, gay, and bisexual individuals.* Paper presented at the annual meeting of the Society for the Scientific Study of Sexuality, Omaha, NE.

Horowitz, A. D., & Bedford, E. (2017). Graded structure in sexual definitions: Categorizations of having "had sex" and virginity loss among homosexual and heterosexual men and women. *Archives of Sexual Behavior, 46*(6), 1653–1665.

Horswill, A., & Weitzer, R. (2018). Becoming a client: The socialization of novice buyers of sexual services. *Deviant Behavior, 39*(2), 148–158.

Horvath, M., & Brown, J. (2010). Between a rock and a hard place. *The British Psychological Society, 23,* 556–559.

Hosain, G. M., Latini, D. M., Kauth, M., Goltz, H. H., & Helmer, D. A. (2013). Sexual dysfunction among male veterans returning from Iraq and Afghanistan: Prevalence and correlates. *Journal of Sexual Medicine, 10*(2), 516–523.

Hoskins, R., Blair, K., and Jenson, K. (2016, November). *Dignity versus diagnosis: Sexual orientation and gender identity differences in reports of one's greatest concern about receiving a sexual health exam.* Poster presented at the annual meeting of the Society for the Scientific Study of Sexuality, Phoenix, AZ.

Houtepen, J. A., Sijtsema, J. J., & Bogaerts, S. (2016). Being sexually attracted to minors: Sexual development, coping with forbidden feelings, and relieving sexual arousal in self-identified pedophiles. *Journal of Sex & Marital Therapy, 42*(1), 48–69.

Howard, J. (2018, August 28). Rates of three STDs in US reach record high, CDC says. CNN. Retrieved from https://www.cnn.com/2018/08/28/health/std-rates-united-states-2018-bn/index.html

Hoy, A. (2018). Invisibility, illegibility and stigma: The citizenship experiences of divorced days and lesbians. *Journal of Divorce & Remarriage, 59*(2), 69–91.

Hoy, S. M., & Scott, L. J. (2010). Dapoxetine: In premature ejaculation. *Drugs, 70*(11), 1433–1443.

Hsu, K. J., Rosenthal, A. M., & Bailey, J. M. (2015). The psychometric structure of items assessing autogynephilia. *Archives of Sexual Behavior, 44*(5), 1301–1312.

Huang (2018). Cherry picking: Virginity loss definitions among gay and straight cisgender men. *Journal of Homosexuality, 65*(6), 727–740.

Huda, S. (2006, February 20). *Integration of the human rights of women and a gender perspective.* UN Commission on Human Rights, sixty-second session. Retrieved from http://www.refworld.org/docid/48abd53dd.html

Hudson, A., Kaminsky, G., Black, S. W., Owen, J., & Fincham, F. (2018, June 14). *Short-term sex and long-term effects: A longitudinal investigation of hook ups and holistic well-being among college students.* Poster presented at the American Association of Sexuality Educators, Counselors and Therapists annual meeting, Denver, CO.

Hughes, L. (2018). Alternative rites of passage: Faith, rights, and performance in FGM/C abandonment campaigns in Kenya. *African Studies, 77*(2), 274–292.

Human Rights Campaign. (n.d.). *Sexual orientation and gender identity definitions.* Retrieved from http://www.hrc.org/resources/sexual-orientation-and-gender-identity-terminology-and-definitions

Human Rights Campaign. (2014, June). *A resource guide to coming out for African Americans.* Retrieved from http://www.hrc.org/resources/resource-guide-to-coming-out-for-african-americans

Human Rights Campaign. (2016). *The lies and dangers of efforts to change sexual orientation or gender identity.* Retrieved from http://www.hrc.org/resources/the-lies-and-dangers-of-reparative-therapy

Human Rights Campaign. (2020). Sexual Assault and the LGBTQ Community. Retrieved from https://www.hrc.org/resources/sexual-assault-and-the-lgbt-community

Hummel, S. B., Van Lankyeld, J. J., Oldenburg, H. S., Hahn, D. E, Kieffer, J. M., & Gerritsma, M. A. (2018). Internet-based cognitive behavioral therapy realizes long-term improvement in the sexual functioning and body image of breast cancer survivors. *Journal of Sex & Marital Therapy*, *44*(5), 485–496. doi: doi.org/10.1080/0092623X.2017.1408047

Humphreys, L. (1975). *Tearoom trade: Impersonal sex in public places* (Enlarged edition with a retrospect on ethical issues). New York, NY: Aldine.

Humphreys, T. P. (2013). Cognitive frameworks of virginity and first intercourse. *Journal of Sex Research*, *50*(7), 664–675.

Humphries-Waa, H. (2014). The use of hormone therapy in the male-to-female transgender population: Issues for consideration in Thailand. *International Journal of Sexual Health*, *26*(1), 41–51.

Hunt, M., & Jozkowski, K. (2014, November). *"There is nothing to work towards if they are getting it already": Emerging themes in college students' sexual decision-making regarding hooking up.* Paper presented at the annual meeting of the Society for the Scientific Study of Sexuality, Omaha, NE.

Huntington, C., Atkins, D., & Rhoades, G. (2019, November). *Pornography viewing and sexual attitudes and behavior: Differential associations by gender.* Poster presented at the Society for the Scientific Study of Sex annual meeting, Denver, CO.

Hutton, H. E., McCaul, M. E., Norris, J., Valliant, J. D., Abrefa-Gyan, T., & Chander, G. (2015). Sex-related alcohol expectancies among African American women attending an urban STI clinic. *Journal of Sex Research*, *52*(5), 580–589.

Iasenza, S. (2000). Lesbian sexuality post-stonewall to post-modernism: Putting the "lesbian bed death" concept to bed. *Journal of Sex Education and Therapy*, *25*(1), 59–69.

Ingraham, C. (2015). Americans truly are exceptional—at least when it comes to circumcision. *The Washington Post*. Retrieved from https://www.washingtonpost.com/news/wonk/wp/2015/05/26/americans-truly-are-exceptional-at-least-when-it-comes-to-circumcision/

Ingraham, C. (2019). The share of Americans not having sex has reached a record high. *The Washington Post*. Retrieved from https://www.washingtonpost.com/business/2019/03/29/share-americans-not-having-sex-has-reached-record-high/?utm_term=.2115aeb8950d

Institute for Health Metrics and Evaluation. (2017). *SDG Index, United States, 2017*. Retrieved from https://vizhub.healthdata.org/sdg/

International Lesbian, Gay, Bisexual, Trans and Intersex Association. (2016, June). *Sexual orientation laws in the world: Overview*. Retrieved from http://ilga.org/downloads/03_ILGA_WorldMap_ENGLISH_Overview_May2016.pdf

Introcaso, C. E., Xu, F., Kilmarx, P. H., Zaidi, A., & Markowitz, L. E. (2013). Prevalence of circumcision among men and boys aged 14 to 59 years in the United States, National Health and Nutrition Examination Surveys 2005–2010. *Sexually transmitted diseases*, *40*(7), 521–525.

Irvine, J. M. (2015). The other sex work: Stigma in sexuality research. *Social Currents*, *2*(2), 116–125.

Ivanski, C. & Kohut, T. (2017). Exploring definitions of sex positivity through thematic analysis. *The Canadian Journal of Human Sexuality*, *26*(3), 216–225. doi: 10.3138/cjhs.2017-0017

Iveniuk, J., & Waite, L. J. (2018). The psychosocial sources of sexual interest in older couples. *Journal of Social & Personal Relationships*, *35*(4), 615–631.

Iwamoto, D., Grivel, M., Kaya, A., & Clinton, L. (2014, August). *"Real men" and casual sex: Conformity to masculine norms, disinhibition, and number of sexual partners.* Poster session presented at the annual meeting of the American Psychological Association, Washington, DC.

Jäckle, S., & Wenzelburger, G. (2015). Religion, religiosity and the attitudes towards homosexuality: A multilevel analysis of 79 countries. *Journal of Homosexuality*, *62*(2), 207–241.

Jackman, M. (2014). Understanding the cheating heart: What determines infidelity intentions? *Sexuality & Culture: An Interdisciplinary Quarterly*, *19*(1), 72–84. Retrieved from http://link.springer.com/article/10.1007/s12119-014-9248-z

Jacobs, H. (2014, October 21). *Wealthy older women are hiring men in Kenya to romance them*. Business Insider. Retrieved from http://www.businessinsider.com/wealthy-older-women-are-hiring-men-in-kenya-to-romance-them-2014-10?op=1#ixzz3ZFj2LHtz

Jahnke, S., Imhoff, R., & Hoyer J. (2015). Stigmatization of people with pedophilia: Two comparative surveys. *Archives of Sexual Behavior*, *44*(1), 21–34.

Jaishankar, K. (2009). Sexting: A new form of victimless crime? *International Journal of Cyber Criminology*, *3*(1), 21–25.

James, S. E., Herman, J. L., Rankin, S., Keisling, M., Mottet, L., & Anafi, M. (2016). *The Report of the 2015 US Transgender Survey: Executive Summary*. National Center for Transgender Equality. Retrieved from https://www.transequality.org/sites/default/files/docs/USTS-Full-Report-FINAL.PDF

James, R. (2014, November). *Examining the relationship of sexual shame, sexual orientation, and substance misuse in a sample of women in treatment: A mixed-methods approach.* Presented at the annual meeting of the Society for the Scientific Study of Sexuality, Omaha, NE.

James-Kangal, N., Weitbrecht, E. M., Francis, T. E., & Whitton, S. W. (2018). Hooking up and emerging adults' relationship attitudes and expectations. *Sexuality & Culture*, *22*(3), 706–723.

Jardin, C., Garey, L., & Zvolensky, M. J. (2017). Measuring sexual motives: A test of the psychometric properties of the sexual motivations scale. *The Journal of Sex Research*, *54*(9), 1209–1219.

Jasper, M. (2015, March). *Covert sexism on the radio waves*. Poster session presented at the annual meeting of the Southern Sociological Society, New Orleans, LA.

Jatlaoui, T.C., Boutot, M.E., Mandel, M.G., Whiteman, M.K., Ti, A., Petersen, E., Pazol, K. (2018). Abortion Surveillance — United States, 2015. Surveillance Summaries, 67(13):1–45. doi: http://dx.doi.org/10.15585/mmwr.ss6713a1

Javaid, A. (2018). Theorising vulnerability and male sexual victimization. *Australian & New Zealand Journal of Criminology*, *51*(3), 454–470.

Jawed-Wessel, S., & Sevick, E. (2017). The impact of pregnancy and childbirth on sexual behaviors: A systematic review. *The Journal of Sex Research*, *54*(4–5), 411–423.

Jayson, S. (2011, March 30). More college "hookups," but more virgins, too. *USA Today*. Retrieved from http://usatoday30.usatoday.com/news/health/wellness/dating/story/2011/03/More-hookups-on-campuses-but-more-virgins-too/45556388/1

Jayson, S. (2012, October 17). Living together not just for the young, new data show. *USA Today*. Retrieved from http://www.usatoday.com/story/news/nation/2012/10/17/older-couples-cohabitation/1630681/

Jayson, S. (2013, February 5). What singles want: Survey looks at attraction, turnoffs. *USA Today*. Retrieved from https://www.usatoday.com/story/news/nation/2013/02/04/singles-dating-attraction-facebook/1878265/

Jeanfreau, M. M., & Mong, M. (2019). Barriers to marital infidelity. *Marriage and Family Review*, *55*(1), 23–37, doi: 10.1080/01494929.2018.1518821

Jeckell, A. S., Copenhaver, E. A., & Diamond, A. B. (2018). The spectrum of hazing and peer sexual abuse in sports: a current perspective. *Sports health*, *10*(6), 558–564.

Jeltsen, M. (2016, March 30). 3 women are killed every day by their partners. Here are 59 ideas on how to stop the violence. *The Huffington Post*. Retrieved from http://www.huffingtonpost.com/entry/how-to-stop-domestic-violence-murder_us_56eeb745e4b09bf44a9d85f6

Jenkins, I. (2014). Bias and male circumcision. *Mayo Clinic Proceedings*, *89*(11), 1588.

Jensen, H. M., Gron, R., Lidegaard, O., Pedersen, L. H., Andersen, P. K., & Kessing, L. V. (2013). The effects of maternal depression and use of antidepressants during pregnancy on risk of a child small for gestational age. *Psychopharmacology*, *228*(2), 199–205.

Jeong, S., & Cha, C. (2019). Healing from childhood sexual abuse: A meta-synthesis of qualitative studies. *Journal of Child Sexual Abuse*, *28*(4), 383–399.

Jerman, J., Jones, R. K., & Onda, T. (2016). *Characteristics of U.S. abortion patients in 2014 and changes since 2008.* Guttmacher Institute, New York. Retrieved from https://www.guttmacher.org/report/characteristics-us-abortion-patients-2014.

Jesser, C. J. (1978). Male responses to direct verbal sexual initiatives of females. *The Journal of Sex Research, 14*(2), 118–128.

Jiann, B. P., Su, C. C., & Tsai, J. Y. (2013). Is female sexual function related to the male partner's erectile function? *Journal of Sexual Medicine, 10*(2), 420–429.

Jiao, S. & Bungay, V. (2019). Intersections of stigma, mental health, and sex work: How Canadian men engaged in sex work navigate and resist stigma to protect their mental health. *The Journal of Sex Research, 56*(4–5), 641–649.

Jing., S., Lay, A., Weis, L., & Furnham, A. (2018). Attitudes toward, and use of, vibrators in China. *Journal of Sex & Marital Therapy, 14*(1), 102–109.

Joel, D., Berman, Z., Tavor, I., Wexler, N., Gaber, O., Stein, Y., ... Assaf, Y. (2015). Sex beyond the genitalia: The human brain mosaic. *Proceedings of the National Academy of Sciences of the United States of America (PNAS), 112*(50), 15468–15473.

Johnson, K. (2001, August 9). 100 arrested in net child porn ring: Children as young as 4 were abused. *USA Today*, 1A.

Johnston, L., McLellan, T., & McKinlay, A. (2014). (Perceived) size really does matter: Male dissatisfaction with penis size. *Psychology of Men & Masculinity, 15*(2), 225–228.

Jolly, N. (2018). Cutting through the discussion on caesarean delivery: birth practices as social practices. *Health Sociology Review, 27*(1), 31–44.

Jones, A., Johnson, N. C., Wenglein, S., & Elshershaby, S. T. (2019). The state of sex research in MFT and family studies literature: A seventeen-year content analysis. *Journal of Marital & Family Therapy, 45*(2), 275–295.

Jones, J. H. (1993). *Bad blood: The Tuskegee syphilis experiment* (Rev. ed.). New York, NY: The Free Press.

Jones, R. K., Moore, A. M., & Frohwirth, L. F. (2011). Perceptions of male knowledge and support among U.S. women obtaining abortions. *Women's Health Issues, 21*(2), 117–123.

Jones, R. L., Almack, K., & Scicluna, R. (2018). Older bisexual people: Implications for social work from the "Looking Both Ways" study. *Journal of Gerontological Social Work, 61*(3), 334–347.

Jordan-Young, R., & Rumiati, R. I. (2012). Hardwired for sexism? Approaches to sex/gender in neuroscience. *Neuroethics, 5*(3), 305–315.

Joshi, P., Overton, M., & Cole, K. (2016). Association of Sexual Orientation and Bullying among High School Students. *Public Health Research, 6*(6), 157–160.

Jovanovic, J., & Williams, J.C. (2018). Gender, sexual agency and friends with benefits. *Sexuality & Culture, 22*(2), 555–576.

Joyal, C. C., & Carpentier, J. (2017). The prevalence of paraphilic interests and behaviors in the general population: A provincial survey. *The Journal Sex Research, 54*(2), 161–171.

Jozkowski, K., & Canan, S. (2014, November). *Sexual assault in Greek fraternity and sorority life: An analysis of rape myth acceptance and token resistance in Greek and non-Greek college students.* Poster session presented at the annual meeting of the Society for the Scientific Study of Sexuality. Omaha, NE.

Jozkowski, K., Canan, S., Rhoads, K. & Hunt, M. (2016, November). *Understanding the action in "Lights, camera, action": Examining sexual behaviors and sexual consent portrayals in mainstream films.* Session at the annual meeting of the Society for the Scientific Study of Sexuality, Phoenix, AZ.

Kaestle, K, E. (2019). Sexual orientation trajectories based on sexual attractions, partners, and identity: A longitudinal investigation from adolescent through youth adulthood using a U.S. representative sample. *Journal of Sex Research, 56*(7), 811–826.

Kahn, N. F., & Halpern, C. T. (2018). The relationship between cognitive ability and experiences of vaginal, oral, and anal sex in the United States. *Journal of Sex Research, 55*(1), 99–105.

Kaiser, A., Reid, D., & Boschen, K. A. (2012). Experiences of parents with spinal cord injury. *Sexuality and Disability, 30*(2), 123–137.

Kalfoglou, A., Kammersell, M., Philpott, S., & Dahl, E. (2013). Ethical arguments for and against sperm sorting for non-medical sex selection: A review. *Reproductive BioMedicine Online, 26*(3), 231–239.

Kane, M. D. (2013). Finding "safe" campuses: Predicting the presence of LGBT student groups at North Carolina colleges and universities. *Journal of Homosexuality, 60*(6), 828–852.

Kann, L., McManus, T., Harris, W., Shanklin, S., Flint, K., Queen, B., ... Ethier, K. (2018, June 15). *Youth Risk Behavior Surveillance — United States, 2017/Surveillance Summaries,* Centers for Disease Control and Prevention. Retrieved from https://www.cdc.gov/mmwr/volumes/67/ss/ss6708a1.htm#conclusion

Kaplan, H. (1979). *Disorders of sexual desire.* New York, NY: Brunner/Mazel.

Kaplan, H. S. (1974). The classification of the female sexual dysfunctions. *Journal of Sex and Marital Therapy, 1*(2), 124–138.

Karioris, F. G., & Allan, J. A. (2019). When two become one: sexuality studies and critical studies of men and masculinities. *Journal of Gender Studies, 28*(3), 247–256.

Karraker, A., & DeLamater, J. (2013). Past-year inactivity among older married persons and their partners. *Journal of Marriage and Family, 75*(1), 142–163.

Kasper, T. E., Short, M. B., & Milam, A. C. (2015). Narcissism and Internet pornography use. *Journal of Sex & Marital Therapy, 41*(5), 481–486.

Kattari, S. K. (2014). Sexual experiences of adults with physical disabilities: Negotiating with sexual partners. *Sexuality and Disability, 32*(4), 499–513.

Kattari, S. K., O'Connor, A. A., & Kattari, L. (2018). Development and validation of the Transgender Inclusive Behavior Scale (TIBS) *Journal of Homosexuality, 65*(2), 181–196.

Katz, J., & Rich, H. (2015). Partner covictimization and post-breakup stalking, pursuit, and violence: A retrospective study of college women. *Journal of Family Violence, 30*(2), 189–199.

Kaya, C., Gunes, M., Gokce, A. M., & Kalkan, S. (2015). Is sexual function in female partners of men with premature ejaculation compromised? *Journal of Sex & Marital Therapy, 41*(4), 379–383.

Kearney, M. S., & Levine, P. B. (2014, January). Media influences on social outcomes: The impact of MTV's *16 and Pregnant* on teen childbearing. *American Economic Review, American Economic Association, 105*(12), 3597–3632.

Kedde, H., van de Wiel, H. B., Weijmar Schultz, W. C., & Wijsen, C. (2013). Sexual dysfunction in young women with breast cancer. *Supportive Care in Cancer, 21*(1), 271–280.

Kelemen, A., Cagle, J., & Groninger, H. (2016). Screening for intimacy concerns in a palliative care population: Findings from a pilot study. *Journal of Palliative Medicine, 19*(10), 1102–1105.

Kelly, C. R., & Hoerl, K. E. (2015). Shaved or saved? Disciplining women's bodies. *Women's Studies in Communication, 38*, 141–145. Retrieved from http://digitalcommons.butler.edu/ccom_papers/87/

Kelly, A., & Jawed-Wessel. S. (2019, November). *Quantitative analysis of sexual function of mothers up to 1 year post-partum.* Brief communication at the Society for the Scientific Study of Sex annual meeting, Denver, CO.

Kelly, M. (2017, December 18). *Today Show staffer: Consensual relationship with Matt Lauer was abuse of power.* Retrieved from https://www.today.com/video/ex-today-staffer-consensual-relationship-with-matt-lauer-was-abuse-of-power-1118847555843

Kemerer, B., Quinn-Nilas, C., & Milhausen, R. (2019, November). *The impact of health on sexual functioning and sexual satisfaction at midlife: Insights from a National Sample of married midlife Canadians*. Brief communication at the Society for the Scientific Study of Sex annual meeting, Denver, CO.

Kempeneers, P., Andrianne, R., Bauwens, S., Georis, I., Pairous, J. F., & Blairy, S. (2013). Functional and psychological characteristics of Belgian men with premature ejaculation and their partners. *Archives of Sexual Behavior, 42*(1), 51–66.

Kendler, K. S., Thomton, L. M., Gilman, S. E., & Kessler, R. C. (2000). Sexual orientation in a U.S. national sample of twin and nontwin sibling pairs. *The American Journal of Psychiatry, 157*(11), 1843–1846.

Kennedy, H. R., Dalla, R. L., & Dreesman, S. (2018). "We are two of the lucky ones": Experiences with marriage and wellbeing for same sex couples. *Journal of Homosexuality, 65*(9), 1207–1231.

Kensboc, S., Bailey, J., Jennings, G., & Patiar, A. (2015). Sexual harassment of women as room attendants within 5-star hotels. *Gender, Work & Organization, 22*(1), 36–50.

Kerr, D. L., Santurri, L., & Peters, P. (2013). A comparison of lesbian, bisexual, and heterosexual college undergraduate women on selected mental health issues. *Journals of American College Health, 61*(4), 185–194.

Kerr, Z. Y., Pollack, L. M., Woods, W. J., Blair, J., & Binson, D. (2015). Use of multiple sex venues and prevalence of HIV risk behavior: Identifying high-risk men who have sex with men. *Archives of Sexual Behavior, 44*(2), 443–451.

Kettrey, H. H. (2018). "Bad girls" say no and "good girls" say yes: Sexual subjectivity and participation in undesired sex during heterosexual college hookups. *Sexuality & Culture, 22*(3), 685–705.

Kijak, R. (2013). The sexuality of adults with intellectual disability in Poland. *Sexuality and Disability, 31*(2), 109–123.

Kilimnik, C., & Humphreys, T. (2014, November 9). *The role of erotophobia-erotophilia on sexual consent perspectives*. Paper presented at the annual meeting of the Society for the Scientific Study of Sexuality, Omaha, NE.

Killoren, S. E., Campione-Barr, N. M., Jones, S. K., & Giron, S. E. (2019). Adolescent girls' disclosure about dating and sexuality. *Journal of Family Issues, 40*(7), 887–910.

Kim, J., Muise, A., & Impett, E. A. (2018). The relationship implications of rejecting a partner for sex kindly versus having sex reluctantly. *Journal of Social and Personal Relationships, 35*(4), 485–508.

Kim, C. (2004, November 3). From fantasy to reality: The link between viewing child pornography and molesting children. *Child Sexual Exploitation Update, 1*(3). Retrieved from https://web.archive.org/web/20080111204617/http://www.ndaa.org/publications/newsletters/child_sexual_exploitation_update_volume_1_number_3_2004.html

Kimberly, C., & Hans, J. D. (2015). From fantasy to reality: A grounded theory of experiences in the swinging lifestyle. *Archives of Sexual Behavior, 46*(3),789–799. Retrieved from http://link.springer.com/article/10.1007/s10508-015-0621-2

Kimberly, C., Williams, A., & Creel, S. (2018). Women's introduction to alternative sexual behaviors through erotica and its association with sexual and relationship satisfaction. *Sex Roles, 78*(1–2), 119–129.

Kimbrough, A. M., Guadagno, R. E., Muscanell, N. L., & Dill, J. (2013). Gender differences in mediated communication: Women connect more than men do. *Computers in Human Behavior, 29*(3), 896–900.

Kimmons, J., & Moore, T. (2014, November). *Widows of a certain age: Reluctance to formation of new intimate relationships*. Paper presented at the annual meeting of the Society for the Scientific Study of Sexuality, Omaha, NE.

King, A. L. S., Valenca, A. M., Silva, A. C. O., Baczynski, T., Carvalho, M. R., & Nardi, A. E. (2013). Nomophobia: Dependency on virtual environments or social phobia? *Computers in Human Behavior, 29*(1), 140–144.

King, B. M., Duncan, L. M., Clinkenbeard, K. M., Rutland, M. B., & Ryan, K. M. (2019a). Social desirability and young men's self-reports of penis size. *Journal of Sex & Marital Therapy, 45*(5) 452–455. doi: 10.1080/0092623X.2018.1533905

King, B. M., Scott, A. E., Van Doorn, E. M., Abele, E. E., & McDevitt, M. E. (2019b). Reasons students at a US university do or do not enroll in a human sexuality course. *Sex Education*. doi: 10.1080/14681811.2019.1606793

Kinsey, A. C., Pomeroy, W. B., & Martin, C. E. (1948). *Sexual behavior in the human male*. Philadelphia, PA: Saunders.

Kinsey, A. C., Pomeroy, W. B., Martin, C. E., & Gebhard, P. H. (1953). *Sexual behavior in the human female*. Philadelphia, PA: Saunders.

Kirby, B. J., & Michaelson, C. (2015). Comparative morality judgments about lesbians and gay men teaching and adopting children. *Journal of Homosexuality, 62*(1), 33–50.

Kirk, K. M., Bailey, J. M., Dunne, M. P., & Martin, N. G. (2000). Measurement models for sexual orientation in a community twin sample. *Behavior Genetics, 30*(4), 345–356.

Kirk, M., & Boyer, P. J. (2002). *American porn (a PBS Frontline home video)*. Boston, MA: WGBH Educational Foundation.

Kirkman, L., Fox, C., & Dickson-Swift, V. (2016). A case for sexual health policy that includes midlife and older adult sexuality and sexual health. *The International Journal of Aging and Society, 6*(2), 17–27.

Kirsch, A. C., & Murnen, S. K. (2015). "Hot" girls and "cool dudes": Examining the prevalence of the heterosexual script in American children's television media. *Psychology of Popular Media Culture, 4*(1), 18–30.

Kleimplatz, P. J. , Paradis, N., Charest, M., Lawless, S., Neufeld, M., Neufeld, R., … Rosen, L. (2018, January). From sexual desire discrepancies to desirable sex: Creating the optimal connection. *The Journal of Sex & Marital Therapy, 44*(5), 438–449. doi: doi.org/10.1080/0092623X.2017.1405309

Klein, A., & Golub, S. A. (2016). Family rejection as a predictor of suicide attempts and substance misuse among transgender and gender nonconforming adults. *LGBT Health, 3*(3), 193–199. doi: doi.org/10.1089/lgbt.2015.0111

Klein, K., Holtby, A., Cook, K., & Travers, R. (2015). Complicating the coming out narrative: Becoming oneself in a heterosexist and cissexist world. *Journal of Homosexuality, 62*(3), 297–326.

Klein, V., Becker, I., & Štulhofer, A. (2018). Parenting, communication about sexuality, and the development of adolescent women's sexual agency: A longitudinal assessment. *Journal of Youth & Adolescence, 47*(7), 1486–1498.

Klettke, B., Hallford, D. J., Clancy, E., Mellor, D., & Toumbourou. (2019). Sexting and psychological distress: The role of unwanted and coerced sexts. *Cyberpsychology, Behavior, and Social Networking, 22*(4), 237–242. doi: doi.org/10.1089/cyber.2018.0291

Klipfel, K. M., Claxton, S. E., & van Dulmen, M. H. (2014). Interpersonal aggression victimization within casual sexual relationships and experiences. *Journal of Interpersonal Violence, 29*(3), 557–569.

Knox, D. & Hilliard, T. (2019, November). *The #MeToo Movement: Have we gone too far?* Roundtable at the Society for the Scientific Study of Sex annual meeting, Denver, CO.

Knox, D., Schacht, C., & Turner, J. (1993). Sexual lies among university students. *College Student Journal, 27*(2), 269–272.

Knox, D., Huff, S., & Chang, I. J. (2017). Sex dolls - Creepy or healthy?: Attitudes of undergraduates. *Journal of Positive Sexuality, 3*(2) 32–37.

Kohlberg, L. (1966). A cognitive-developmental analysis of children's sex-role concepts and attitudes. In E. E. Maccoby (Ed.), *The development of sex differences* (pp. 82–172). Stanford, CA: Stanford University Press.

Kohlberg, L. (1969). State and sequence: The cognitive-developmental approach to socialization. In D. A. Goslin (Ed.), *Handbook of socialization theory and research* (pp. 347–480). Chicago, IL: Rand McNally.

Kohlberg, L. (1976). Moral stages and moralization: The cognitive-developmental approach. In T. Lickona (Ed.), *Moral development and behavior* (pp. 31–53). New York, NY: Holt, Rinehart, & Winston.

Kohut, T., Balzarini, R. N., & Fisher, W. A. (2018). Pornography's associations with open sexual communication and relationship closeness as a function of dyadic patterns of pornography use within heterosexual relationships. *Journal of Social & Personal Relationships, 35*(4), 655–676.

Komarnicky, T., Shakoon-Sparling, S., Milhausen, R. R., & Breuer, R. (2019). Genital self-image: Associations with other domains of body image and sexual response. *Journal of Sex & Marital Therapy, 45*(6), 524–537. doi: doi.org/10.1080/0092623X.2019.1586018

Kong, T. S. (2016). Buying sex as edgework: Hong Kong male clients in commercial sex. *British Journal of Criminology, 56*(1), 105–122.

Kongsved, S. M., Basnov, M., Holm-Christensen, K., & Hjollund, N. H. (2007). Response rate and completeness of questionnaires: A randomized study of internet versus paper-and-pencil versions. *Journal of Medical Internet Research, 9*(3), e25.

Kontula, O. (2014, November). *What boys really desire to know about sex.* Poster session presented at the annual meeting of the Society for the Scientific Study of Sexuality, Omaha, NE.

Koop, C. E. (1987). Report of the Surgeon General's Workshop on Pornography and Public Health. *American Psychologist, 42*(10), 944–945.

Koss, M. P. (1998). Hidden rape: Sexual aggression and victimization in a national sample in higher education. In A. M. Burgess (Ed.), *Rape and sexual assault* (Vol. II, pp. 3–25). New York, NY: Garland Press.

Kozin, A. (2016). Flirtation: Deconstructed. *Sexuality & Culture, 20*(2), 358–372.

Krajewski, S. (2019). Killer whales and killer women: Exploring menopause as a 'Satellite taboo' that orbits madness and old age. *Sexuality & Culture, 23*(2), 605–620.

Kucur Suna, K., Ilay, G., Aysenur, A., Kerem Han, G., Eda Ulku, U., Pasa, U., & Fatima, C. (2016). Effects of infertility etiology and depression on female sexual function. *Journal of Sex & Marital Therapy, 42*(1), 27–35.

Kuhle, B. X., Melzer, D. K., Cooper, C. A., Merkle, A. J., Pepe, A., Ribanovic, … Wettstein, T. L. (2015). The "birds and the bees" differ for boys and girls: Sex differences in the nature of sex talks. *Evolutionary Behavioral Sciences, 9*(2), 107–115.

Kumar, N., Minichiello, V., Scott, J., & Harrington, T. (2017). A global overview of male escort websites. *Journal of Homosexuality, 64*(12), 1731–1744.

Kuortti, M., & Lindfors, P. (2014). Girls' stories about their first sexual intercourse: Readiness, affection and experience-seeking in the process of growing into womanhood. *Sexuality & Culture, 18*(3), 505–526.

Kuper, L. E., Nussbaum, R., & Mustanski, B. (2012). Exploring the diversity of gender and sexual orientation identities in an online sample of transgender individuals. *Journal of Sex Research, 49*(2–3), 244–254.

Kurdek, L. A. (1994). Conflict resolution styles in gay, lesbian, heterosexual nonparent, and heterosexual parent couples. *Journal of Marriage and the Family, 56*(3), 705–722.

Kurdek, L. A. (2008). Change in relationship quality for partners from lesbian, gay male, and heterosexual couples. *Journal of Family Psychology, 22*(5), 701–711.

Kutchko, V., & Muehlenhard, C. (2015, November). *Bystander experiences with sexual coercion: Real-life experiences.* Presented at the annual meeting of the Society Scientific Study of Sexuality, Albuquerque, NM.

Kwak, T. I., Oh, M., Kim, J. J., & Moon du, G. (2011). The effects of penile girth enhancement using injectable hyaluronic acid gel, a filler. *Journal of Sexual Medicine, 8*(12), 3407–3413.

Kwon, K. A., Han, S., Jeon, H. J., & Bingham, G. E. (2013). Mothers' and fathers' parenting challenges, strategies, and resources in toddlerhood. *Early Child Development and Care, 183*(3–4), 415–429.

Laan, E., Rellini, A. H., & Barnes, T. (2013). Standard operating procedures for female orgasmic disorder: Consensus of the International Society for Sexual Medicine. *Journal of Sexual Medicine, 10*(1), 74–82.

LaGasse, L. L., Derauf, C., Smith, L. M., Newman, E., Shah, R., Neal, C., … Lester, B. M. (2012, March). Prenatal methamphetamine exposure and childhood behavior problems at 3 and 5 years of age. *Pediatrics.* Retrieved from http://pediatrics.aappublications.org/content/early/2012/03/14/peds.2011-2209

Lammers, J., & Maner, J. (2016). Power and attraction to the counternormative aspects of infidelity. *Journal of Sex Research, 53*(1), 54–63.

Langevin, R., & Lang, R. A. (1987). The courtship disorders. In G. D. Wilson (Ed.), *Variant sexuality: Research and theory* (pp. 202–228). Baltimore, MD: Johns Hopkins University Press.

Langlais, M. R., & Schwanz, S. J. (2018). Centrality of religiosity of relationships for affectionate and sexual behaviors among emerging adults. *Sexuality & Culture, 22*(2), 405–421.

Laumann, E. O., Levinson, W., O'Muircheartaigh, C. A., & Waite, L. J. (2007). A study of sexuality and health among older adults in the United States. *The New England Journal of Medicine, 357*, 762–774.

Laura, G. T. (2018, January 29). *Barriers to breastfeeding: Why U.S. breastfeeding rates are so low.* WeHaveKids. Retrieved from https://wehavekids.com/parenting/Barriers-to-Breastfeeding-Why-US-Breastfeeding-Rates-Are-So-Low.

Laverty, E., Bouchard, L. & Wentland, J. (2016, November). *Friends having sex: What benefits do you expect?* Poster presented at the annual meeting of the Society for the Scientific Study of Sexuality, Phoenix, AZ.

Lazo, G., & Cole, S. (2014, November). *Religiousness and sexual beliefs about gender roles.* Poster session presented at the annual meeting of the Society for the Scientific Study of Sexuality, Omaha, NE.

Leavitt, C. E., & Willoughby, B. J. (2015). Associations between attempts at physical intimacy and relational outcomes among cohabiting and married couples. *Journal of Social & Personal Relationships, 32*(2), 241–262.

Leavitt, C., Leonhardt, N. D., & Busby, D. M. (2019). Different ways to get there: Evidence of a variable female sexual response cycle. *Journal of Sexual Response, 56*(7), 899–912.

Lee, J. W., Ha, Y. S., Park, S. C., Seo, Y. I., & Lee, H. S. (2013). Orgasmic headache treated with nimodipine. *Journal of Sexual Medicine, 10*(7), 1893–1896.

Lee, M., & Crofts, T. (2015). Gender, pressure, coercion and pleasure: Untangling motivations for sexting between young people. *British Journal of Criminology, 55*(3), 454–473.

Lee, S. J., Ralston, H. J., Drey, E. A., Partridge, J. C., & Rosen, M. A. (2005). Fetal pain: A systematic multidisciplinary review of the evidence. *The Journal of the American Medical Association, 294*(8), 947–954.

Leickly, E., Nelson, K., & Simoni, J. (2017). Sexually explicit online media, body satisfaction, and partner expectations among men who have sex with men: A qualitative study. *Sexuality Research & Social Policy: Journal of NSRC, 14*(3), 270–274.

Leeming, D., Williamson, I., Lyttle, S., & Johnson, S. (2013). Socially sensitive lactation: Exploring the social context of breastfeeding. *Psychology and Health, 28*(4), 450–468.

Leeners, B., Kruger, T. H., Brody, S., Schmidlin, S., Naegli, E., & Egli, M. (2013). The quality of sexual experience in women correlates with post-orgasmic prolactin surges: Results from an experimental prototype study. *Journal of Sexual Medicine, 10*(5), 1313–1319.

Lefkowitz, E. S., Vasilenko, S. A., & Leavit, C. E. (2016). Oral vs. vaginal sex experiences and consequences among first-year college students. *Archives of Sexual Behavior, 45*(2), 329–337.

Lefkowitz, E., Wesche, R., & Vasilenko, S. (2014, November). *Sexual behavior patterns in romantic and nonromantic partnerships*. Poster session presented at the annual meeting of the Society for the Scientific Study of Sexuality, Omaha, NE.

Leggitt, K. (2013, July 2). How has childbirth changed in this century? Retrieved from http://www.takingcharge.csh.umn.edu/explore-healing-practices/holistic-pregnancy-childbirth/how-has-childbirth-changed-century

Lehmiller, J., Vrangalova, Z., Mark, K., & Maas, M. (2014, November). *Keeping the science in sex: Disseminating sex research to broad audiences*. Continuing education session presented at the annual meeting of the Society for the Scientific Study of Sexuality, Omaha, NE.

Leonhardt, N., Willoughby, B., Busby, D., Yorgason, J., & Holmes, E. (2017). *Power of the female orgasm: A nationally representative dyadic study of newlywed orgasm experience*. Poster presented at annual meeting National Council on Family Relations, Orlando, Florida.

Lermann, J., Haberle, L., Merk, S., Henglein, K., Beckmann, M., Mueller, A., & Mehlhorn, G. (2013). Comparison of prevalence of hypoactive sexual desire disorder (HSDD) in women after five different hysterectomy procedures. *European Journal of Obstetrics & Gynecology and Reproductive Biology, 167*(2), 210–213.

Levenson, J. S., Willis, G. M., & Prescott, D. S. (2015). Adverse childhood experiences in the lives of female sex offenders. *Sexual Abuse: A Journal of Research and Treatment, 27*(3), 258–283.

Lever, J. (1994, August 23). The 1994 Advocate survey of sexuality and relationships: The men. *The Advocate: The National Gay and Lesbian Newsmagazine, 661–662*, 16–24.

Levin, D. (2016, November). *Learning from adults: Exploring the role of teachers in school-based sex education*. Session 46 at the annual meeting of the Society for the Scientific Study of Sexuality, Phoenix, AZ.

Levine, D., & Kantor, L. (2016, November). *Serving LGBTQ youth through digital support*. Session 53 at the annual meeting of the Society for the Scientific Study of Sexuality, Phoenix, AZ.

Levitt, H. M., Surace, F. I., Wheeler, E. E., Maki, E., Alcántara, D., Cadet, M., ... Ngai, C. (2018). Drag gender: Experiences of gender for gay and queer men who perform drag. *Sex Roles, 78*(5–6), 367–384.

Levitt, H. M., & Ippolito, M. R. (2014). Being transgender: The experience of transgender identity development. *Journal of Homosexuality, 61*(12), 1727–1758.

Levitt, M. J., Silver, M., & Franco, N. (1996). Troublesome relationships: A part of human experience. *Journal of Social and Personal Relationships, 13*(4), 523–536.

Lew-Starowicz, M., & Rola, R. (2013). Prevalence of sexual dysfunctions among women with multiple sclerosis. *Sexuality and Disability, 31*(2), 141–153.

Liao, L. M., Taghinejadi, N., & Creighton, S. M. (2012, November 12). An analysis of the content and clinical implications of online advertisements for female genital cosmetic surgery. *BMJ Open, 2*(6). Retrieved from http://bmjopen.bmj.com/content/2/6/e001908.abstract

Lien, I. L. (2017). The perspectives of Gambian men on the sexuality of cut and uncut women. *Sexualities, 20*(5–6), 521–534.

Liew, Z., Ritz, B., Rebordosa, C., Lee, P. C., & Olson, J. (2014). Acetaminophen use during pregnancy, behavioral problems, and hyperkinetic disorders. *JAMA Pediatrics, 168*(4), 313–320.

LifeWay Student Ministry. (2014). *True love waits*. Retrieved from http://www.lifeway.com/n/Product-Family/True-Love-Waits

Lindemann, H. (2015). Miscarriage and the stories we live by. *Journal of Social Philosophy, 46*(1), 80–90.

Ling, J., Mahoney, J., McGuire, P., & Freeze C. (2018, April 24) *The 'incel' community and the dark side of the internet*. Retrieved from https://www.theglobeandmail.com/canada/article-the-incel-community-and-the-dark-side-of-the-internet/

Linton, K. F., & Rueda, H. A. (2015). Dating and sexuality among minority adolescents with disabilities: An application of sociocultural theory. *Journal of Human Behavior in the Social Environment, 25*(2), 77–89.

Linz, D., Paul, B., Land, K. C., Williams, J. R., & Ezell, M. E. (2004). An examination of the assumption that adult businesses are associated with crime in surrounding areas: A secondary effects study in Charlotte, North Carolina. *Law & Society Review, 38*(1), 69–104.

Liong, M., & Cheng, G. H. L. (2019). Objectifying or liberating? Investigation of the effects of sexting on body image. *The Journal of Sex Research, 56*(3), 337–344.

Lippman, J. R., & Campbell, S. W. (2014). Damned if you do, damned if you don't ... if you're a girl: Relational and normative contexts of adolescent sexting in the United States. *Journal of Children and Media, 8*(4), 371–386.

Lo, S. S., & Kok, W. M. (2013). Sexuality of Chinese women around menopause. *Maturitas, 74*(2), 190–195.

Loftus, E. F. (1993). The reality of repressed memories. *American Psychologist, 48*(5), 518–537.

Logan, L. S. (2015). Street harassment: Current and promising avenues for researchers and activists. *Sociology Compass, 9*(3), 196–211.

Loiacano, D. K. (1993). Gay identity among Black Americans: Racism, homophobia, and the need for validation. In L. D. Garnets & D. C. Kimmel (Eds.), *Psychological perspectives on lesbian and gay male experiences* (pp. 364–375). New York, NY: Columbia University Press.

Lomash, E., & Galupo, M. P. (2016, November). *LGBTQ experiences with microaggressions in religious and spiritual communities*. Poster presented at the annual meeting of the Society for the Scientific Study of Sexuality, Phoenix, AZ.

Lomas, T. (2018). The flavours of love: A cross-cultural lexical analysis. *Journal for the Theory of Social Behavior, 48*(1), 134–152.

Londo, S., & Thompson, A. (2016, November). *Till death do us part?: The examination of monogamy expectations and agreements within romantic relationships*. Poster presented at the annual meeting of the Society for the Scientific Study of Sexuality, Phoenix, AZ.

Longest, K. C., & Uecker, J. E. (2018). Moral communities and sex: The religious influence on young adult sexual behavior and regret. *Sociological Perspectives, 61*(3), 361–382.

LoPiccolo, J. (1992). Postmodern sex therapy for erectile failure. In R. C. Rosen & S. R. Leiblum (Eds.), *Erectile disorders: Assessment and treatment* (pp. 171–197). New York, NY: Guilford Press.

Lorimer, K., DeAmics, L., Dalrymple, J., Frankis, J., Jackson, L., Lorgelly, P., McMillan, L., and Ross, J. (2019). A rapid review of sexual wellbeing definitions and measures: Should we now include sexual wellbeing freedom? *Journal of Sex Research, 56*(7), 843–853.

Loshek, E., & Terrell, H. K. (2015). The development of the Sexual Assertiveness Questionnaire (SAQ): A comprehensive measure of sexual assertiveness for women. *Journal of Sex Research, 52*(9), 1017–1027.

Lottes, I. L. (1991). Belief systems: Sexuality and rape. *Journal of Psychology & Human Sexuality, 4*(1), 37–59.

Lottes, I. L. (2009). Rape Supportive Attitudes Scale. In C. M. Davis, W. L. Yarber, R. Bauserman, G. Schreer, & S. L. Davis (Eds.), *Handbook of sexuality-related measures* (p. 516). Copyright Taylor & Francis, LTD. Republished with permission of Taylor & Francis, LTD; permission conveyed through Copyright Clearance Center, Inc.

Luk, B. H., & Loke, A. Y. (2015). The impact of infertility on the psychological well-being, marital relationships, and quality of life of couples: A systematic review. *Journal of Sex and Marital Therapy, 41*(6), 610–625.

Lulu, R. A., & Alkaff, S. N. H. (2018). Of lust and love: A cross-cultural study of sex and relationship advice in women's magazines. *Sexuality & Culture, 22*(2), 479–496.

Lund, E. M., & Johnson, B. A. (2015). Asexuality and disability: Strange but compatible bedfellows. *Sexuality and Disability, 33*(1), 123–132.

Lundrigan, S., & Mueller-Johnson, K. (2013). Male stranger rape: A behavioral model of victim-offender interaction. *Criminal Justice and Behavior, 40*(7), 763–783.

Luo, T. Y. (2013). After sexual harassment: Secondary harm from women coping with sexual harassment incident. *Chinese Journal of Guidance and Counseling, 33,* 155–191.

Lyne, K. (2014, November). *Resiliency in same-sex couples.* Poster session presented at the annual meeting of the Society for the Scientific Study of Sexuality, Omaha, NE.

Lyyerzapf, H., Visse, M., De Beer, A., & Amba, T. A. (2018). Gay-friendly elderly care: creating space for sexual diversity in residential care by challenging the hetero norm. *Ageing & Society, 38*(2), 352–377.

Ma, P., Brewer-Asling, M., & Magnus, J. H. (2013). A case study on the economic impact of optimal breastfeeding. *Maternal and Child Health Journal, 17*(1), 9–13.

Maas, M. K., & Lefkowitz, E. S. (2015). Sexual esteem in emerging adulthood: Associations with sexual behavior, contraception use, and romantic relationships. *Journal of Sex Research, 52*(7), 795–806.

Maas, M. K., McDaniel, B. T., Feinberg, M. E., & Jones, D. E. (2018). Division of labor and multiple domains of sexual satisfaction among first-time parents. *Journal of Family Issues, 39*(1), 104–127.

Macapagal, K., Greene, G. J., Rivera, Z., & Mustanski, B. (2015). "The best is always yet to come": Relationship stages and processes among young LGBT couples. *Journal of Family Psychology, 29*(3), 309–320.

MacDorman, M. F., Mathews, T. J., & Declercq, E. (2012, January 26). Home births in the United States, 1990–2009. *National Center for Health Statistics Data Brief No. 84.* Retrieved from http://www.cdc.gov/nchs/products/databriefs/db84.htm

MacDougall, K., Beyene, Y., & Nachtigall, R. D. (2013). Age shock: Misperceptions of the impact of age on fertility before and after IVF in women who conceived after age 40. *Human Reproduction, 28*(2), 350–356.

MacKell, J. (2004). *Brothels, bordellos, & bad girls: Prostitution in Colorado, 1860–1930.* Albuquerque, NM: University of New Mexico Press.

MacMillan, H. L., Tanaka, M., Duku, E., Vaillancourt, T., & Boyle, M. H. (2013). Child physical and sexual abuse in community sample of young adults: Results from the Ontario Child Health Study. *Child Abuse & Neglect, 37*(1), 14–21.

Madden, M., Lenhart, A., Duggan, M., Cortesi, S., & Gasser, U. (2013, March 13). *Teens and technology 2013: Main findings.* Retrieved from http://www.pewinternet.org/2013/03/13/main-findings-5/

Maggi, M., Buvat, J., Corona, G., Guay, A., & Torres, L. O. (2013). Hormonal causes of male sexual dysfunctions and their management (hyperprolactinemia, thyroid disorders, GH disorders, and DHEA). *Journal of Sexual Medicine, 10*(3), 661–677.

Mai, N. (2017). Mobile orientations: An autoethnography of Tunisian professional boyfriends. *Sexualities, 20*(4), 482–496.

Maier, T. (2009). *Masters of sex: The life and times of William Masters and Virginia Johnson.* New, York, NY: Perseus.

Maines, R. P. (2001). *The technology of orgasm: "Hysteria," the vibrator, and women's sexual satisfaction.* Baltimore, MD: Johns Hopkins University Press.

Major, B., Appelbaum, M., Beckman, L., Dutton, M. A., Russo, N. F., & West, C. (2008). *Report of the APA task force on mental health and abortion.* Washington, DC: American Psychological Association.

Majumdar, C. (2018). Attitudes toward premarital sex in India: Traditionalism and cultural change. *Sexuality & Culture, 22*(2), 614–631.

Mallory, A. B., Stanton, A. M., & Handy, A. B. (2019). Couples' sexual communication and dimensions of sexual function: A meta-analysis. *Journal of Sex Research, 56*(7), 882–898.

Malo, S. (2016, February 29). Study: One-third of U.S. women seeking abortions get misleading information. *Thomson Reuters Foundation.* Retrieved from http://news.trust.org/item/20160229223700-slhm2/?source=dpagehead

Manago, A. M., Ward, L. M., Lemm, K. M., Reed, L., & Seabrook, R. (2015). Facebook involvement, objectified body consciousness, body shame, and sexual assertiveness in college women and men. *Sex Roles, 72*(1), 1–14.

Manning, J. (2015a). Communicating sexual identities: A typology of coming out. *Sexuality & Culture: An Interdisciplinary Quarterly, 19*(1), 122–138.

Manning, J. (2015b). Positive and negative communicative behaviors in coming-out conversations. *Journal of Homosexuality, 62*(1), 67–97.

Mar, A. (2017). Love in the time of robots: Are we ready for intimacy with robots? *Wired.* Retrieved from https://www.wired.com/2017/10/hiroshiishiguro-when-robots-act-just-like-humans/

March, E., & Wagstaff, D. L. (2017). Sending nudes: Sex, self-rated mate value, and trait Machiavellianism predict sending unsolicited explicit images. *Frontiers in Psychology, 8*(2210). doi: 10.3389/fpsyg.2017.02210

Marcum, C., Higgins, G., & Nicholson, J. (2017). I'm watching you: Cyberstalking behaviors of university students in romantic relationships. *American Journal of Criminal Justice, 42*(2), 373–388.

Marelich, W. D., & Lundquist, J. (2008). Motivations for sexual intimacy: Development of a needs-based sexual intimacy scale. *International Journal of Sexual Health, 20*(3), 177–186.

Marelich, W. D., Shelton, E., & Grandfield, E. (2013). Correlates and factor replication of the need for sexual intimacy scale (NSIS). *Electronic Journal of Human Sexuality, 16*(6). Retrieved from http://www.ejhs.org/volume16/NSIS.html

Marini, I., Wang, X., Etzbach, C. A., & Del Castillo, A. (2013). Ethnic, gender, and contact differences in intimacy attitudes toward wheelchair users. *Rehabilitation Counseling Bulletin, 56*(3), 135–145.

Mark, K. P., & Herbenick, D. (2014). The influence of attraction to partner on heterosexual women's sexual and relationship satisfaction in long-term relationships. *Archives of Sexual Behavior, 43*(3), 563–570.

Markman, H., Stanley, S., & Blumberg, S. L. (1994). *Fighting for your marriage: Positive steps for preventing divorce and preserving a lasting love.* San Francisco, CA: Jossey-Bass.

Martin, C. L., Kornienko, O., Schaefer, D. R., Hanish, L. D., Fabes, R. A., & Goble, P. (2013). The role of sex of peers and gender-typed activities in young children's peer affiliative networks: A longitudinal analysis of selection and influence. *Child Development, 84*(3), 921–937.

Martinez, K. (2018). BDSM role fluidity: A mixed-methods approach to investigating switches within dominant/submissive binaries. *Journal of Homosexuality, 65*(10), 1299–1324.

Martino, L. L., Youngpaioj, S., & Vermund, S. H. (2004). Vaginal douching: Personal practices and public policies. *Journal of Women's Health, 13*(9), 1048–1065.

Masci, D., Brown, A., & Kiley, J. (2017, June 26). 5 facts about same-sex marriage. *Pew Research Center.* Retrieved from http://www.pewresearch.org/fact-tank/2017/06/26/same-sex-marriage/

Masters, N. T., Casey, E., Wells, E. A., & Morrison, D. M. (2013). Sexual scripts among young active men and women: Continuity and change. *Journal of Sex Research, 50*(5), 409–420.

Masters, W. H., & Johnson, V. E. (1966). *Human sexual response.* Boston, MA: Little Brown.

Masters, W. H., & Johnson, V. E. (1970). *Human sexual inadequacy.* Boston, MA: Little Brown.

Masters, W. H., & Johnson, V. E. (1976). *The pleasure bond.* New York, NY: Random House.

Masters, W. H., & Johnson, V. E. (1979). *Homosexuality in perspective.* Boston, MA: Little Brown.

Match.com. (2017). *2016 Singles in America Study.* Retrieved from www.singlesinAmerica.com

Match.com (2016) *Annual survey on Singles in America (2016).* Retrieved from www.singlesinamerica.com

Matthews, J., & Cramer, E. P. (2008). Using technology to enhance qualitative research with hidden populations. *The Qualitative Report, 13*(2), 301–315. Retrieved from http://www.nova.edu/ssss/QR/QR13-2/matthews.pdf

Matusitz, J. (2017). Gender communal terrorism or war rape: Ten symbolic reasons. *Sexuality & Culture, 21*(3), 830–844.

Mauro, T. (1997, March 18). Taming the internet court's task to protect kids but not censor. *USA Today,* p. 1A.

Maxwell, J. A., Muise, A., MacDonald, G., Day, L. C., Rosen, N. O., Impett, E. A. (2017). How implicit theories of sexuality shape sexual and relationship well-being. *Journal of Personality & Social Psychology, 112*(2), 238–279.

Mayo Clinic Staff. (2019, September 5). *Depo-Provera (contraception injection): About.* Retrieved from https:// https://www.mayoclinic.org /tests-procedures/depo-provera/about/pac-20392204

Mayo Clinic Staff. (2017, June 22). *Penis-enlargement products: Do they work?* Retrieved from http://www.mayoclinic.org/healthy-lifestyle /sexual-health/in-depth/penis/art-20045363

Mays, V. M. (2012). Research challenges and bioethics responsibilities in the aftermath of the presidential apology to the survivors of the U.S. Public Health Services Syphilis Study at Tuskegee. *Ethics and Behavior, 22*(6), 419–430.

McArthur, N., & Twist, M. (2016, November). *The rise of digisexuality: Therapeutic challenges and possibilities.* Paper presented at annual meeting of the Society for the Scientific Study of Sexuality, Phoenix, AZ.

McBride, K. R., Sanders, S. A., Hill, B. J., & Reinisch, J. M. (2017). Heterosexual women's and men's labeling of anal behaviors as having "had sex." *The Journal of Sex Research, 54*(9), 1166–70.

McCarthy, B., & McCarthy, E. (1984). *Sexual awareness: Enhancing sexual pleasure.* New York, NY: Carroll & Graf.

McCarthy, B., & Wald Ross, L. (2018). Expanding the types of clients receiving sex therapy and sexual health services. *Journal of Sex & Marital Therapy, 44*(1), 96–101.

McCarthy, B., & Oppliger, T. R. (2019). Treatment of desire discrepancy: One clinician's approach. *Journal of Sex & Marital Therapy, 45*(7), 585–593.

McCaskill, C. (2014, July 9). Sexual violence on campus: How too many institutions of higher education are failing to protect students. *Association of Title Administrators.* Retrieved from https://cdn.atixa.org/website-media/atixa.org/wp-content/uploads/2014/07/12194119 /Summary-of-Sexual-Violence-on-Campus-McCaskill.pdf

McCauley, J. L., Kilpatrick, D. G., Walsh, K., & Resnick, H. S. (2013). Substance use among women receiving post-rape medical care, associated post-assault concerns and current substance abuse: Results from a national telephone household probability sample. *Addictive Behaviors, 38*(4), 1952–1957.

McChesney, K. Y. (2015). Successful approaches to ending female genital cutting. *Journal of Sociology & Social Welfare, 42*(1), 3–24.

McClelland, S., & Holland, K. J. (2016). Toward better measurement: The role of survey marginalia in critical sexuality research. *Qualitative Psychology, 3*(2), 166–185. doi: http://dx.doi.org/10.1037/qup0000056

McClintock, M. K. (1971). Menstrual synchrony and suppression. *Nature, 229,* 244–245.

McCoy, K., & Snider, M. (2017, November 8). Valeant sells off its "female Viagra" after losing money. *USA Today.* p. 4B.

McGraw, S. A., Rosen, R. C., Althof, S. E., Dunn, M., Cameron, A., & Wong, D. (2015). Perceptions of erectile dysfunction and phosphodiesterase type 5 inhibitor therapy in a qualitative study of men and women in affected relationships. *Journal of Sex & Marital Relationships, 41*(2), 203–220.

McGregor, J. (2019). #MeToo backlash: More male managers avoid mentoring women or meeting alone with them. *The Washington Post.* May 17.

McKeown, J. K. L., Parry, D. C., & Penny Light, T. (2018). "My iPhone changed my life": How digital technologies can enable women's consumption of online sexually explicit materials. *Sexuality & Culture, 22*(2), 340–354.

McKinney, E. Louise. (2018). Two's company, three's a crowd: disabled people, their carers and their partners. *Disability & Society, 33*(2), 272–284.

McLaren, S., Gibbs, P. M., & Watts, E. (2013). The interrelations between age, sense of belonging, and depressive symptoms among Australian gay men and lesbians. *Journal of Homosexuality, 60*(1), 1–15.

McLaughlin, A. (2015, February 5). 3 myths about female sexuality—and why people keep believing them. *The Huffington Post.* Retrieved from http://www.huffingtonpost.com/august-mclaughlin/female-sexual-arousal-myths-and-why-they-keep-coming_b_5993620.html

McLelland, M. (2017) "Not in front of the parents!" Young people, sexual literacies and intimate citizenship in the internet age. *Sexualities, 20*(1–2), 234–254.

McLeod, D. A. (2015). Female offenders in child sexual abuse cases: A national picture. *Journal of Child Sexual Abuse, 24*(1), 97–114.

McMahon, C. G., Jannini, E., Waldinger, M., & Rowland, D. (2013). Standard operating procedures in the disorders of orgasm and ejaculation. *Journal of Sexual Medicine, 10*(1), 204–229.

McNally, G. (2015, July 30). All feminists should be gang-raped: Inside the disturbing world of online misogyny. *The Daily Telegraph.* Retrieved from http://www.dailytelegraph.com.au/news/nsw/why-do-men-threaten-women-with-rape-to-shut-them-up-on-the-web/news-story /0abd8403e59747a51717f54b81a21b46

McNeil, J., Rehman, U. S., & Fallis, E. (2018). The influence of attachment styles on sexual communication behavior. *Journal of Sex Research, 55*(2), 191–201.

Mead, M. (1928). *Coming of age in Samoa: A psychological study of primitive youth for Western civilization.* New York, NY: William Morrow & Company.

Meese, G. (2013). Successful bonding is important. *Deutsches Arzteblatt International, 110*(1–2), 13.

Meltzer, A. L., & McNulty, J. K. (2014). "Tell me I'm sexy … and otherwise valuable": Body valuation and relationship satisfaction. *Personal Relationships, 21*(1), 68–87.

Mena, J. A., & Vaccaro, A. (2013). Tell me you love me no matter what: Relationships and self-esteem among GLBQ young adults. *Journal of GLBT Family Studies, 9*(1), 3–23.

Merrill, J., & Knox, D. (2010). *When I fall in love again: A new study on finding and keeping the love of your life.* Santa Barbara, CA: Praeger.

Merta, C. (2010, June 10). *Kinsey institute fights for funding for sexuality research.* Retrieved from http://www.idsnews.com/article/2010/06 /kinsey-institute-fights-for-funding-for-sexuality-research

Messman-Moore, T. L., Ward, R. M., & DeNardi, K. A. (2013). The impact of sexual enhancement alcohol expectancies and risky behavior on alcohol-involved rape among college women. *Violence Against Women, 19*(4), 449–464.

Michael, R. T., Gagnon, J. H., Laumann, E. O., & Kolata, G. (1994). *Sex in America: A definitive survey.* Boston, MA: Little, Brown.

Michaels, P. A. (2014). *Lamaze: An international history.* Oxford, UK: Oxford University Press.

Michel, K, & Mark, K, (2019). *"I've never seen an uncircumcised one": A qualitative analysis of American women's circumcision status preferences.* Brief communication at annual meeting of Society for the Scientific Study of Sex, Denver, CO.

Mikolajczak, M., & Pietrzak, J. (2014). Ambivalent sexism and religion: Connected through values. *Sex Roles, 70*(9), 387–399.

Milas, G., Wright, P., and Stulhofer, A. (2020). Longitudinal assessment of the association between pornography use and sexual satisfaction in adolescence. *Journal of Sex Research, 57*(1), 16–28.

Milhausen, R., & Murray, S. (2014, November). *Maintaining sexual desire in long-term relationships: Themes from four qualitative studies of women and men.* Paper presented at the annual meeting of the Society for the Scientific Study of Sexuality, Omaha, NE.

Milhausen, R. R., McKay, A., Graham, C. A., Sanders, S. A., Crosby, R. A., Yarber, W. L., & Wood, J. (2018). Do associations between pleasure ratings and condom use during penile-vaginal intercourse vary by relationship type? A study of Canadian university students. *Journal of Sex Research, 55*(1), 21–30.

Mill, J. S. (1859/1985). *On liberty.* New York, NY: Penguin.

Miller, C. C. (2015, October 30). Boys and girls, constrained by toys and costumes. *New York Times.* Retrieved from http://www.nytimes.com/2015/10/31/upshot/boys-and-girls-constrained-by-toys-and-costumes.html?_r=2

Miller, S. (2018, April 18). Record number of states banning conversion therapy. *USA Today*, p. 3a.

Milrod, C., & Monto, M. (2015, November). Gray foxes, hobbyists and the girlfriend experience: Elderly male clients of heterosexual prostitution. Presented at the annual meeting of the Society for the Scientific Study of Sexuality, Albuquerque, NM.

Mintz, L. (2011, July 31). The menopausal symptom women don't tell friends about [Blog post]. Retrieved from https://www.psychologytoday.com/blog/stress-and-sex/201107/the-menopausal-symptom-women-don-t-tell-friends-about

Mintz, L. (2017). *Cliteracy.* New York, NY: Harper One.

Mitchell, K. R., Mercer, C. H., Prah, P., Clifton, S., Tanton, C., Welllings, K., & Copas, A. (2019). Why do men report more opposite-sex sexual partners than women? Analysis of the gender discrepancy in a British national probability survey. *The Journal of Sex Research, 56*(1), 1–8.

Mitchell, H., & Hunnicutt, G. (2019). Challenging accepted scripts of sexual "Normality": Asexual narratives of non-normative identity and experience. *Sexuality & Culture, 23*(2), 507–524.

Mitchison, D., Hay, P., Griffiths, S., Murray, S. B., Bentley, C., Gratwick-Sarll, K., ... & Mond, J. (2017). Disentangling body image: The relative associations of overvaluation, dissatisfaction, and preoccupation with psychological distress and eating disorder behaviors in male and female adolescents. *International Journal of Eating Disorders, 50*(2), 118-126.

Mizrahi, M., Kanat-Maymon, Y., & Birnbaum, G. E. (2018). You haven't been on my mind lately: Partner responsiveness mediates the link between attachment insecurity and sexual fantasies. *Journal of Social and Personal Relationships, 35*(4), 440–459.

Moilanen, K. L., & Manuel, M. L. (2018). Mechanisms linking self-regulation and sexual behaviors in never-married young adults. *Journal of Sex Research, 55*(1), 120–133.

Mokros, A., Schilling, F., Weiss, K., Nitschke, J., & Eher. R. (2014). Sadism in sexual offenders: Evidence for dimensionality. *Psychological Assessment, 26*(1), 137–147.

Molinares, C., Kolobova, I., & Knox, D. (2017, March). Anal sexual practices among undergraduate students. *Journal of Positive Sexuality, 3*(1), 21–36.

Moller, N. P., & Vossler, A. (2015). Defining infidelity in research and couple counseling: A qualitative study. *Journal of Sex & Marital Therapy, 41*(5), 487–497.

Moncada, J., & Natrajan-Tyagi, R. (2019, November 8). *Recollections of peripartum depression: A lived experience storytelling of peripartum depression among Latina women.* Poster presented at the National Council on Family Relations, San Diego, CA.

Money, J. (1986). *Lovemaps: Clinical concepts of sexual/erotic health and pathology, paraphilia, and gender transportation in childhood, adolescence, and maturity.* New York, NY: Irvington.

Money, J. (1987). Sin, sickness or status? Homosexual gender identity and psychoneuroendocrinology. *American Psychologist, 42*(4), 384–399.

Money, J. (1988). *Gay, straight, and in-between.* New York, NY: Oxford University Press.

Mongeau, P. A., Knight, K., Williams, J., Eden, J., & Shaw, C. (2013). Identifying and explicating variation among friends with benefits relationships. *Journal of Sex Research, 50*(1), 37–47.

Monro, S. (2000). Theorizing transgender diversity: Towards a social model of health. *Sexual and Relationship Therapy, 15*(1), 33–42.

Monroe, D. (2019, February 6). *kNOw MORE: A journey of rape prevention.* Presentation, Human Sexuality class, East Carolina University, Greenville, NC.

Montemurro, B. (2014a). *Deserving desire: Women's stories of sexual evolution.* New Brunswick, NJ: Rutgers University Press.

Montemurro, B. (2014b). Getting married, breaking up and making up for lost time: Relationship transitions as turning points in women's sexuality. *Journal of Contemporary Ethnography, 43*(1), 63–93.

Montemurro, B., Bartasavich, J., & Wintermute, L. (2015). Let's (not) talk about sex: The gender of sexual discourse. *Sexuality & Culture, 19*(1), 139–156.

Montemurro, B., & Siefken, J. M. (2014). Cougars on the prowl? Perceptions of older women's sexuality. *Journal of Aging Studies, 28*, 35–43.

Montemurro, B., & Chewning, L. (2018). Unscripted: Exploring representations of older unpartnered women's sexuality. *Journal of Women & Aging, 30*(2),127–144.

Montes, K. S., Blanco, L., & LaBrie, J. W. (2017). The relationship between perceived hookup attitudes and negative hookup consequences: Do perceived attitudes of close friends matter? *The Journal of Sex Research, 54*(9), 1128–1140.

Montgomery, M. J., & Sorell, G. T. (1997). Differences in love attitudes across family life stages. *Family Relations, 46*(1), 55–61.

Monto, M. A., & Carey, A. G. (2014). A new standard of sexual behavior? Are claims associated with the "hookup culture" supported by general social survey data? *Journal of Sex Research, 51*(6), 605–615.

Moon, D. (2014). Beyond the dichotomy: Six religious views of homosexuality. *Journal of Homosexuality, 61*(9), 1215–1241.

Moore, S. E., & Cote-Arsenault, D. (2018). Navigating an uncertain journey of pregnancy after perinatal loss. *Illness, Crisis & Loss, 26*(1) 58–74.

Moore, T. J., & Sailor, J. L. (2018). A phenomenological study of romantic love for women in late life. *Journal of Women & Aging, 30*(2), 2011–126.

Moors, A. C. (2017). Has the American public's interest in formation related to relationships beyond "the couple" increased over time? *Journal of Sex Research, 54*(6), 677–684.

Moors, A., Conley, T., Valentine, B., Harman, J., Selterman, D., & Rubin, J. (2014, November). *Departures from monogamy: A focus on more than one love*. Symposium presented at the annual meeting of the Society for the Scientific Study of Sexuality, Omaha, NE.

Morales, E., Gauthier, V., Edwards, G., Courtois, F., Lamontagne, A., & Guérette, A. (2018). Co-designing sex toys for adults with motor disabilities. *Sexuality & Disability, 36*(1), 47–68.

Moran, M. (2013, May 3). DSM to distinguish paraphilias from paraphilic disorders. *Psychiatric News*. Retrieved from http://psychnews. psychiatryonline.org/doi/10.1176/appi.pn.2013.5a19

Morell, V. (1998). A new look at monogamy. *Science, 282*(5390), 882.

Moreno, J. A., Arango-Lasprilla, J. C., Gan, C., & McKerral, M. (2013). Sexuality after traumatic brain injury: A critical review. *NeuroRehabilitation, 32*(1), 69–85.

Morgentaler, A. (2009, January 19). Penis size: The measure of a man? *Psychology Today*. Retrieved from https://www.psychologytoday.com/blog/men-sex-and-testosterone/200901/penis-size-the-measure-man

Morotti, E., Battaglia, B., Paradisi, R., Persico, N., Zampieri, M., Venturoli, S., & Battaglia, C. (2013). Body mass index, Stunkard Figure Rating Scale, and sexuality in young Italian women: A pilot study. *Journal of Sexual Medicine, 10*(4), 1034–1043.

Morris, H., Chang, I. J., & Knox, D. (2016). Three's a Crowd or Bonus? College students' threesome experiences. *Journal of Positive Sexuality, 2*, 62–76.

Morris, T. (2013). Cut it out: The C-section epidemic in America. New York, NY: New York University Press.

Morrison, D. M., Masters, N. T., Wells, E. A., Casey, E., Beadnell, E., & Hoppe, M. J. (2015). "He enjoys giving her pleasure": Diversity and complexity in young men's sexual scripts. *Archives of Sexual Behavior, 44*(3), 655–668.

Morrissey Stahl, K. A., Gale, J., Lewis, D. C., & Kleiber, D. (2018). Sex after divorce: Older adult women's reflections. *Journal of Gerontological Social Work, 61*(6), 659–674.

Morrow, L. C. (2012). Cyclical role-playing and stigma: Exploring the challenges of stereotype performance among exotic dancers. *Deviant Behavior, 33*(5), 357–374.

Moser, A. & Ballard, S. (2017, April 5). Rape myth acceptance among ECU students. Poster presented at Research and Creative Week at ECU, April 5. East Carolina University, Greenville, NC.

Moser, A. (2019). The influence of cannabis on sexual functioning and satisfaction. (Thesis). Department of Human Development and Family Science, East Carolina University, NC.

Moser, C. (1992). Lust, lack of desire, and paraphilias: Some thoughts and possible connections. *Journal of Sex and Marital Therapy, 18*(1), 65–69.

Moser, C. (2013). Hypersexual disorder: Searching for clarity. *Sexual Addiction & Compulsivity: Journal of Treatment & Prevention, 20*,(1–2), 48–58.

Moss-Racusin, C. A., & Johnson, E. R. (2016). Backlash against male elementary educators. *Journal of Applied Social Psychology, 46*(7), 379–393.

Motyl, J. (2013). Trading sex for college tuition: How sugar daddy "dating" sites may be sugar coating prostitution. *Penn State Law Review, 117*(3). Retrieved from http://www.pennstatelawreview.org/117/3/Motyl%20final.pdf

Mouilso, E. R., & Calhoun, K. S. (2013). The role of rape myth acceptance and psychopathy in sexual assault perpetration. *Journal of Aggression, Maltreatment & Trauma, 22*(2), 159–174.

Mount, L. (2018). "Behind the curtain": Strip clubs and the management of competition for tips. *Journal of Contemporary Ethnography, 47*(1), 60–87.

Muccigrosso, L. (1991). Sexual abuse prevention strategies and programs for persons with developmental disabilities. *Sexuality and Disability, 9*(3), 261–271.

Muehlenhard, C. L., Peterson, S. D., Humphreys, T. P., & Jozkowski. (2017). Evaluating the one-in-five statistic: Women's risk of sexual assault while in College. *The Journal of Sex Research, 54*(4–5), 549–576.

Muise, A., Maxwell, J. A,. & Impett, E. A. (2018). What theories and methods from relationship research can contribute to sex research. *Journal of Sex Research, 55*(4–5), 540–562.

Muise, A., Boudreau, G. K., & Rosen, N. O. (2017a). Seeking a connection versus avoiding disappointment: An experimental manipulation of approach and avoidance sexual goals and the implications of desire and satisfaction. *Journal of Sex Research, 54*(3), 296–307.

Muise, A., Kim, J. J., Impett, E. A., & Rosen, A. (2017b).Understanding when a partner is not in the mood: Sexual communal strength in couples transitioning to parenthood. *Archives of Sexual Behavior, 46*(7), 1993–2006.

Muise, A., Schimmack, U. S., & Impett, E. A. (2016). Sexual frequency predicts greater well-being, but more is not always better. *Social Psychological & Personality Service, 7*(4), 295–302.

Mullinax, M., Dennis, S., Dennis, B., Higgins, B., Higgins, J., Fortenberry, J. D., & Reece, M. How condom discontinuation occurs: Interviews with emerging adult women. *The Journal of Sex Research, 54*(4–5), 642–650.

Murphy, M. (2016). Hiding in plain sight: The production of heteronormativity in medical education. *Journal of Contemporary Ethnography, 45*(3). 256–289.

Murray, K., Willis, M., & Jozkowski, K. (2019, November). *Consent and contraceptives: An investigation of dyadic processes within sexual relationships*. Brief communication at the Society for the Scientific Study of Sex annual meeting, Denver, CO.

Murry, S. H., Milhausen, R. R., Graham, C. A., & Kuczynski, L. (2017). A qualitative exploration of factors that affect sexual desire among men aged 30 to 65 in long-term relationships. *Journal of Sex Research, 54*(3), 319–330.

Mustanski, B., Greene, G. J., Ryan, D., & Whitton, S. W. (2015). Feasibility, acceptability, and initial efficacy of an online sexual health promotion program for LGBT youth: The queer sex ed intervention. *Journal of Sex Research, 52*(2), 220–230.

Mustapha, A., & Muehlenhard, C. (2014, November). *Women's and men's reactions to being sexually coerced: A quantitative and qualitative analysis*. Poster session presented at the annual meeting of the Society for the Scientific Study of Sexuality, Omaha, NE.

Myers, K. (2017). "If I'm going to do it, I'm going to do it right": Intensive mothering ideologies among childless women who elect egg freezing, *Gender & Society, 31*(6), 777–803.

Myers, J. L. (2019, November). *Alcohol risk reduction as sexual assault risk reduction*. Poster presented at the Society for the Scientific Study of Sex annual meeting, Denver, CO.

Nakić Radoš, S. N., Soljаćić Vraneš, H., & Šunjić, M. (2015). Sexuality during pregnancy: What is important for sexual satisfaction in expectant fathers? *Journal of Sex & Marital Therapy, 41*(3), 282–293.

Nakku, M. E. (2019, February). *Effects of female genital mutilation on the lives of women and girls in the district of Amudati, Uganda*. Poster presented at American Association of Behavioral and Social Sciences annual meeting, Las Vegas, NV.

Napper, L. E., Kenney, S. R., & LaBrie, J. W. (2015). The longitudinal relationships among injunctive norms and hooking up attitudes and behaviors in college students. *Journal of Sex Research, 52*(5), 499–506.

Nash, E., Gold, R.B., Mohammed, L., Ansari-Thomas, Z., Cappello, O. (2018, January 2). Policy Trends in the State, 2017. Guttmacher Institute. Retrieved from https://www.guttmacher.org/article/2018/01/policy-trends-states-2017

National Abortion Federation. (2017). 2017 Violence and Disruption Statistics. Retrieved from https://prochoice.org/wp-content/uploads/2017-NAF-Violence-and-Disruption-Statistics.pdf

National Center for Health Statistics. (2017, August 30). *2003 revisions of the U.S. standard certificates of live birth and death and the fetal death report.* Retrieved from http://www.cdc.gov/nchs/nvss/vital_certificate_revisions.htm

National Center for Injury Prevention and Control, Division of Violence and Prevention, Centers for Disease Control and Prevention. (2019, March 12). *Preventing Sexual Violence.* Retrieved from https://www.cdc.gov/violenceprevention/sexualviolence/fastfact.html

National Center for Victims of Crime. (n.d.). *Statistics on perpetrators of child sexual abuse.* Retrieved from https://victimsofcrime.org/media/reporting-on-child-sexual-abuse/statistics-on-perpetrators-of-csa

National Coalition of Anti-Violence Programs. (2016). Lesbian, gay, bisexual, transgender, queer, and HIV-affected hate violence in 2016. New York, NY: Emily Waters.

National Coalition of Anti-Violence Programs. (2014). *A report from the National Coalition of Anti-Violence programs: Lesbian, gay, bisexual, transgender, queer, and HIV-affected hate violence in 2013.* New York, NY: Author.

National Eating Disorders Association. (n.d.). *Get the facts on eating disorders.* Retrieved from https://www.nationaleatingdisorders.org/get-facts-eating-disorders

National Institute of Justice. (2012, April 20). *Intimate partner stalking.* Retrieved from http://www.nij.gov/topics/crime/intimate-partner-violence/stalking/pages/welcome.aspx

National Multiple Sclerosis Society. (2019). *MS prevalence.* Retrieved from https://www.nationalmssociety.org/About-the-Society/MS-Prevalence

National Survey of Family Growth. (2015). *Number of lifetime sexual partners.* Retrieved from https://www.cdc.gov/nchs/nsfg/key_statistics/n.htm#numberlifetime

Nayar, K. I. (2017). Sweetening the deal: dating for compensation in the digital age. *Journal of Gender Studies, 26*(3), 335–346.

Nekome. (2010, February 24). How prostitution chose me. *Prostitution Research & Education.* Retrieved from http://prostitutionresearch.com/pre_blog/2010/02/24/un_commission_on_the_status_of/

Nelms, B. J., Knox, D., & Easterling, B. (2012). The relationship talk: Assessing partner commitment. *College Student Journal, 46*(1), 178–182.

Nelson, C. J., & Kenowitz, J. (2013). Communication and intimacy-enhancing interventions for men diagnosed with prostate cancer and their partners. *Journal of Sexual Medicine, 10*(1), 127–132.

Nelson, C. J., & Mulhall, J. P. (2013). Psychological impact of Peyronie's disease: A review. *Journal of Sexual Medicine, 10*(3), 653–660.

Nesi, J., Widman, L., Chokas-Bradley, S., & Pristein, M. J. (2017). Technology-based communication and the development of interpersonal competencies within adolescent romantic relationships: A preliminary investigation. *Journal of Research on Adolescence, 27*(2), 471–477.

Netting, N. S. & Reynolds, M. K. (2018). Thirty years of sexual behavior at a Canadian university: Romantic relationships, hooking up, and sexual choices. *Canadian Journal of Human Sexuality, 27*(1), 55–68.

Neuman, H. B., Park, J., Fuzesi, S., & Temple, L. K. (2012). Rectal cancer patients' quality of life with a temporary stoma: Shifting perspectives. *Diseases of the Colon and Rectum, 55*(11), 1117–1124.

Nguyen, H., Shiu, C. S., & Hardesty, M. (2016). Extramarital sex among Vietnamese married men: Results of a survey in urban and rural areas of Northern and Southern Vietnam. *Journal of Sex Research, 53*(9), 1065–1081.

Nicoletti, A. (2007). Female genital cutting. *Journal of Pediatric & Adolescent Gynecology, 20*(4), 261–262.

Niehuis, O., Buellesbach, J., Gibson, J. D., Pothmann, D., Hanner, C., Mutti, N. S., ... Schmitt, T. (2013). Behavioural and genetic analysis of Nasonia shed light on the evolution of sex pheromones. *Nature, 494*(7437), 345–348.

Nikkelen, S. W. C., & Kreukels, B. (2018). Sexual experiences in transgender people: The role of desire for gender-confirming interventions, psychological well-being and body satisfaction. *Journal of Sex & Marital Therapy, 44*(4), 370–381.

Nobre, P. J., Gouveia, J. P., & Gomes, F. A. (2003). Sexual dysfunctional beliefs questionnaire: An instrument to assess sexual dysfunctional beliefs as vulnerability factors to sexual problems. *Sexual & Relationship Therapy, 18*(2), 171–204. doi:10.1080/1468199031000061281

Nola Defender. (2011, September 21). *Tulane students seek sugar daddies.* Retrieved from http://www.noladefender.com/content/tulane-students-seek-sugar-daddies

Norona, J. C., Olmstead, S. B., & Welsh, D. P. (2018). Betrayals in emerging adulthood: A developmental perspective of infidelity. *Journal of Sex Research, 55*(1), 84–98.

North, F., Ward, W. J., Varkey, P., & Tulledge-Scheitel, S. M. (2012). Should you search the Internet for information about your acute symptom? *Telemedicine and e-Health, 18*(3), 213–218.

Norton, A. M., & Baptist, J. (2012, November). *Couple boundaries for social networking: Impact of trust and satisfaction.* Paper presented at the annual meeting of the National Council on Family Relations, Phoenix, AZ.

Notarius, C., & Markman, H. (1994). *We can work it out. Making sense of marital conflict.* New York, NY: Putnam.

NPR. (2002, July 25). *Remembering Tuskegee.* Retrieved from https://www.npr.org/templates/story/story.php?storyId=1147234

Nunes, K. L., & Jung, S. (2013). Are cognitive distortions associated with denial and minimization among sex offenders? *Sex Abuse: Journal of Research and Treatment, 25*(2), 166–188.

O'Brien, C., Keith, J., & Shoemaker, L. (2016). Don't tell: Military culture and male rape. *Psychological Services, 12*(4), 357–365.

O'Callaghan, E., Shepp, V., Ullman, S. E., & Kirkner, A. (2019) Navigating sex and sexuality after sexual assault: A qualitative study of survivors and informal support providers. *Journal of Sex Research, 56*(8), 1045–1057.

O'Donnell, N. (correspondent). (2018). The Theranos Deception: How a company with a blood-testing machine that could never perform as touted went from billion-dollar baby to complete bust. In K. Textor & H. Rosenberg, *60 Minutes.* New York, NY: CBS News. Retrieved from https://www.cbsnews.com/news/the-theranos-elizabeth-holmes-deception/

Oeffinger, K. C., Fontham, E. T., Etzioni, R., Herzig, A., Michaelson, J. S., Shih, Y. C., ... Wender, R. (2015). Breast cancer screening for women at average risk: 2015 guideline update from the American Cancer Society. *The Journal of the American Medical Association, 314*(15), 1599–1614.

Ogden, G. (2013). *Expanding the practice of sex therapy.* New York, NY: Routledge.

O'Hare, E. A., & O'Donohue, W. (1998). Sexual harassment: Identifying risk factors. *Archives of Sexual Behavior, 27*(6), 561–580.

O'Neill, J. L., Van Willigen, M., & Hatch, A. (2015a, March). *Sexual assault campus climate survey: Rape culture, safety, and perception of university response.* Paper presented at the annual meeting of the Southern Sociological Society, New Orleans, LA.

O'Neill, J., Van Willigen, M., Knox, D., & Hatch, A. (2015b, October). *Increasing bystander intervention via rape culture myth victim responsibility.* Paper presented at the annual meeting of the Georgia Sociological Society, Jekyll Island, GA.

Onwu, C. N. (2019). Understanding female genital cutting in the United Kingdom within immigrant communities. *Columbia Social Work Review, 13*(1). Retrieved from https://journals.library.columbia.edu/index.php/cswr/article/view/1865

Onyulo, T. (2018, January 21) Teen girls decry painful illegal "circumcision." *USA Today,* p. 3A.

Oraka, E., Mason, S. & Xia, M. (2018). Too old to test? Prevalence and correlates of HIV testing among sexually active older adults. *Journal of Gerontological Social Work, 61*(1), 460–470.

Oriola, T. B. (2017). "Unwilling Cocoons": Boko Haram's war against women. *Studies in Conflict & Terrorism, 40*(2), 99–121.

Orozco-Lapray, D. Kim, S. Y. Cance, J. (2016, November). *Saliency of sexuality in early parenting: Parenting couples discuss their child's sexuality development.* Session at the annual meeting of the Society for the Scientific Study of Sexuality, Phoenix, AZ.

Osborn, J. L. (2012). When TV and marriage meet: A social exchange analysis of the impact of television viewing on marital satisfaction and commitment. *Mass Communication and Society, 15*(5), 739–757.

Oselin, S. S., & Blasyak, A. (2013). Contending with violence: Female prostitutes' strategic responses on the streets. *Deviant Behavior, 34*(4), 274–290.

Oster, A. M., Russell, K. K, Stryker, J. E., Friedman, A., Kachur, R. E., Petersen, E. E. ... Brooks, J. T. (2016). Update: Interim guidance for prevention of sexual transmission of Zika virus—United States, 2016. *Morbidity and Mortality Weekly Report (MMWR), 65*(12), 323–325.

Osterman, M. J., & Martin, J. A. (2011, April 6). Epidural and spinal anesthesia use during labor: 27-state reporting area, 2008. *National Vital Statistics Reports, 59*(5). Retrieved from https://www.cdc.gov/nchs/data/nvsr/nvsr59/nvsr59_05.pdf

Oswald, F., Lopes, A., Skoda, K., Hesse, C. L., & Pedersen, C. L. (2019, July 18). I'll Show You Mine so You'll Show Me Yours: Motivations and Personality Variables in Photographic Exhibitionism. *The Journal of Sex Research*, 1–13.

Oswalt, S. B., & Wyatt, T. J. (2011). Sexual orientation and differences in mental health, stress, and academic performance in a national sample of U.S. college students. *Journal of Homosexuality, 58*(9), 1255–1280.

Otunctemur, A., Dursun, M., Ozbek, E., Sahin, S., Besiroglu, H., Koklu, I., ... Bozkurt, M. (2015). Effect of metabolic syndrome on sexual function in pre- and postmenopausal women. *Journal of Sex & Marital Therapy, 41*(4), 440–449.

Oyefara, J. K. (2015). Female genital mutilation (FGM) and sexual functioning of married women in Oworonshoki community, Lagos State, Nigeria. *African Population Studies, 29*(1), 1527–1541.

Pahlajani, G., Raina, R., Jones, S., Ali, M., & Zippe, C. (2012). Vacuum erection devices revisited: Its emerging role in the treatment of erectile dysfunction and early penile rehabilitation following prostate cancer therapy. *Journal of Sexual Medicine, 9*(4), 1182–1189.

Palaniappan, M., Heatherly, R., Mintz, L. B., Connelly, K., Wimberley, T., Balzer, A., ... Vogel Anderson, K. (2018). Skills vs. pills: Comparative effectiveness for low sexual desire in women. *Journal of Sex & Marital Therapy, 44*(1), 1–15.

Palmer, M. J., Clarke, L., Ploubidis, G. B., Mercer, C. H., Gibson, L. J., Johnson, A. M., ... Wellings, K. (2017). Is "sexual competence" at first heterosexual intercourse associated with subsequent sexual health status? *The Journal of Sex Research, 54*(1), 91–104.

Pandey, N., Ashfaq, S. N., Dauterive, E. W., MacCarthy, A. A., Copeland, L. A. (2018). Military sexual trauma and obesity among women veterans. *Journal of Women's Health, 27*(3), 305–310.

Papp, L. M., Goeke-Morey, M. C., & Cummings, E. M. (2013). Let's talk about sex: A diary investigation of couples' intimacy conflicts in the home. *Couple and Family Psychology: Research and Practice, 2*(1), 60–72.

Parackal, S. M., Parackal, M. K., & Harraway, J. A. (2013). Prevalence and correlates of drinking in early pregnancy among women who stopped drinking on pregnancy recognition. *Maternal and Child Health Journal, 17*(3), 520–529.

Parchomiuk, M. (2013). Model of intellectual disability and the relationship of attitudes towards the sexuality of persons with an intellectual disability. *Sexuality and Disability, 31*(2), 125–139.

Pariera, K. L., & Brody, E. (2018). "Talk more about it": Emerging adults' attitudes about how and when parents should talk about sex. *Research & Social Policy: Journal of NSRC, 15*(2), 219–229.

Parker, M. G., & Yau, M. K. (2012). Sexuality, identity and women with spinal cord injury. *Sexuality and Disability, 30*(1), 15–27.

Parks, A., & Moore, D. (2016, November). *The scientific study of pansexuality.* Presented at the annual meeting of the Society for the Scientific Study of Sexuality, Phoenix, AZ.

Paterson, L. Q. P., Handy, A. B., & Brotto, L. A. (2017). A pilot study of eight-session mindfulness-based cognitive therapy adapted for women's sexual interest/arousal disorder. *Journal of Sex Research, 54*(7), 850–861.

Patrick, K., Heywood, W., Smith, A. M., Simpson, J. M., Shelley, J. M., Richters, J., & Pitts, M. K. (2013). A population-based study investigating the association between sexual and relationship satisfaction and psychological distress among heterosexuals. *Journal of Sex and Marital Therapy, 39*(1), 56–70.

Patterson, C. L., Nobel, C. M., & Walters, A. S. (2018). *"Fantasies: New and lovely images follow me everywhere I go": Women's fantasies and sexual behavior.* Poster presented at the American Association of Sexuality Educators, Counselors and Therapists annual meeting, Denver, CO.

Paul, K. (2013). Refusing to be a man? Men's responsibility for war rape and the problem of social structures in feminists and gender theory. *Men and Masculinities, 16*(1), 93–114.

Pazmany, E., Bergeron, S., Van Oudenhove, L., Verhaeghe, J., & Enzlin, P. (2013). Body image and genital self-image in pre-menopausal women with dyspareunia. *Archives of Sexual Behavior, 42*(6), 999–1010.

Pearson, J. (2018). High school context, heterosexual scripts, and young women's sexual development. *Journal of Youth & Adolescence, 47*(7), 1469–1485.

Peasant, C., Parra, G. R., and Okwumabua, T. M. (2014). Condom negotiation: Findings and future directions. *The Journal of Sex Research, 52*(4), 470–483.

Pedrelli, P., Bentley, K., Vitali, M., Clain, A. J., Nyer, M., Fava, M., & Farabaugh, A. H. (2013). Compulsive use of alcohol among college students. *Psychiatry Research, 205*(1–2), 95–102.

Peixoto, M. M., & Nobre, P. (2015). Prevalence of sexual problems and associated distress among lesbian and heterosexual women. *Journal of Sex & Marital Therapy, 41*(4), 427–439.

Pellegrini, A. (2018). #MeToo: Before and after. *Studies in Gender & Sexuality, 19*(4), 262–264.

Peloquin, K., Byers, E. S., Callaci, M., & Tremblay, N. (2019). Sexual portrait of couples seeking relationship therapy. *Journal of Marital & Family Therapy, 45*(1), 120–133.

Perales, F. & Baxter, J. (2018). Sexual identity and relationship quality in Australia and the United Kingdom. *Family Relations, 67*(1), 55–69.

Perel, E. (2017). The state of affairs: Rethinking infidelity. New York: Harper.

Perelman, M. A. (2017, January). Delayed ejaculation in couple and family therapy. *Encyclopedia of Couple and Family Therapy*, pp. 1–6. doi: 10.1007/978-3-319-15877-8_456-1

Perelman, M. A. (2013). Delayed ejaculation. *Journal of Sexual Medicine, 10*(4), 1189–1190.

Perkins, E. (2019, February 25). *An examination of vulnerability in domestic minor sex trafficking using attachment theory.* Poster presented at the American Association for Behavioral and Social Sciences annual meeting, Las Vegas, NV.

Perkins, E. B., Dyer, C., Hilliard, T., & Knox, D. (2020, February). *"Let's hang out. ... After I vet you": Vetting in romantic relationships.* Presented at the American Association of Behavioral and Social Sciences Conference, Las Vegas, NV.

Perry, S. L. (2020). Is the link between pornography use and relational happiness really more about masturbation? *Journal of Sex Research, 57*(1), 64–76.

Perry, S. L., & Schleifer, C. (2018). Till porn do us part? A longitudinal examination of pornography use and divorce. *Journal of Sex Research, 55*(3), 284–296.

Persson, T. J., Drury, K. M., Gluch, E., & Wiviott, G. (2016). Sex education groups in a psychiatric day hospital: Clinical observations. *Journal of Sex & Marital Therapy, 42*(1), 18–26.

Persson, T. J., & Pfaus, J. G. (2015). Bisexuality and mental health: Future research directions. *Journal of Bisexuality, 15*(1), 82–98.

Peta, C., Mckenzie, J., Kathard, H., & Africa, A. (2017). We are not asexual beings: Disabled women in Zimbabwe talk about their active sexuality. *Sexuality Research & Social Policy: Journal of NSRC, 14*(4), 410–424.

Peters, A. W. (2013). "Things that involve sex are just different." U.S. anti-trafficking law and policy on the books in their minds and in action. *Anthropological Quarterly, 86*(1), 221–255.

Peterson, M., Robinson, B., & Shih, E. (2019). The new virtual crackdown on sex workers' rights: Perspectives from the United States. *Anti-Trafficking Review, 12,* 189–193.

Peterson, Z., Humphreys, T., Jozkowski, K., & Kern, S. (2016, November). *Young women's preparation for first intercourse: Implications for wantedness, satisfaction, and regret.* Session 42 at the annual meeting of the Society for the Scientific Study of Sexuality, Phoenix, AZ.

Pew Research Center. (2019a, August 29). *Public opinion on abortion.* Retrieved from https://www.pewforum.org/fact-sheet/public-opinion-on-abortion/

Pew Research Center (2019b, June 12). *Internet/Broadband Fact Sheet.* Retrieved from http://www.pewinternet.org/fact-sheet/internet-broadband

Pew Research Center. (2019c, June 12). *Mobile Fact Sheet: Who owns cellphones and smartphones?* Retrieved from http://www.pewinternet.org/fact-sheet/mobile/

Pew Research Center. (2019d, October 28). *Same-sex marriage around the world.* Retrieved from https://www.pewforum.org/fact-sheet/gay-marriage-around-the-world/

Pfeifer, L. R., Miller, R. B., Li, T. S., & Hsiao, Y. L. (2013). Perceived marital problems in Taiwan. *Contemporary Family Therapy: An International Journal, 35*(1), 91–104.

Pham, J. M. (2017) Beyond hookup culture: Current trends in the study of college student sex and where to next. *Sociology Compass. 11*(8), 11.

Pierce, L., Dahl, M. S., & Nielsen, J. (2013). In sickness and in wealth: Psychological and sexual costs of income comparison in marriage. *Personality and Social Psychology Bulletin, 39*(3), 359–374.

Pilver, C. E., Libby, D. J., & Hoff, R. A. (2013). Premenstrual dysphoric disorder as a correlate of suicidal ideation, plans, and attempts among a nationally representative sample. *Social Psychiatry and Psychiatric Epidemiology, 48*(3), 437–446.

Pinon, Jr., R. (2002). *Biology of human reproduction.* Sausalito, CA: University Science Books.

Pinto, N., Bhola, P., & Chandra, P. S. (2019). "End-of-life care is more than wound care": Health-care providers' perceptions of psychological and interpersonal needs of patients with terminal cancer. *Indian Journal of Palliative Care, 25*(3), 428.

Pivetti, M., & Melotti, G. (2013). Prenatal genetic testing: An investigation of determining factors affecting the decision-making process. *Journal of Genetic Counseling, 22*(1), 76–89.

Planty, M., Langton, L., Krebs, C., Berzofsky, M., & Smiley-McDonald, H. (2013, rev. 2016, May 31). *Female victims of sexual violence, 1994-2010. Special Report. (No. NCJ 240655).* Office of Justice Programs, Bureau of Justice Statistics. U.S. Department of Justice. Washington, DC. Retrieved from https://www.bjs.gov/content/pub/pdf/fvsv9410.pdf

Platt, L. F., Wolf, J. K., & Scheitle, C. P. (2018). Patterns of mental health care utilization among sexual orientation minority groups. *Journal of Homosexuality, 65*(2), 135–153.

Platt, L. F., & Bolland, K. S. (2017). Trans* partner relationships: A qualitative exploration. *Journal of GLBT Family Studies, 13*(2), 163–185.

Platt, I., Chen, C., & Mazzucco, A. E. (2014). Delayed childbearing: Should women freeze their eggs? *National Center for Health Research.* Retrieved from http://www.center4research.org/delayed-childbearing-women-freeze-eggs/

Pollitt, A. M., Robinson, B. A., & Umberson, D. (2018). Gender conformity, perceptions of shared power, and marital quality in same and different sex marriages. *Gender & Society, 32*(1), 109–131.

Pomeranz, J. L. (2018). Challenging and preventing policies that prohibit local civil rights protections for lesbians, gay, bisexual, transgender and queer people. *American Journal of Public Health, 108*(1), 67–72.

Pornhub. (2016, February 6). United States top searches. *Pornhub insights.* Retrieved from http://www.pornhub.com/insights/united-states-top-searches

Post, D. (2013, December 6). Prostitution cannot be squared with human rights or the equality of women. *Cato Unbound: A Journal of Debate.* Retrieved from https://www.cato-unbound.org/2013/12/06/dianne-post/prostitution-cannot-be-squared-human-rights-or-equality-women

Potarca, G., Mills, M., & Neberich, W. (2015). Relationship preferences among gay and lesbian online daters: Individual and contextual influences. *Journal of Marriage and Family, 77*(2), 523–541.

Power to Decide. (2019). *National data.* Retrieved from https://thenationalcampaign.org/data/landing

Prior, A., & Peled, E. (2019). Paying for sex while traveling as tourists: The experiences of Israeli men. *Journal of Sex Research, 56*(4–5), 659–669.

ProQuest. (2019). *ProQuest Statistical abstract of the United States 2019.* Retrieved from https://www.proquest.com/products-services/statabstract.html

Pruthi, S. (2019, May 8). *Mammogram guidelines: What are they?* Retrieved from http://www.mayoclinic.org/tests-procedures/mammogram/expert-answers/mammogram-guidelines/faq-20057759

Puckett, J. A., Horne, S. G., Surace, F., Carter, A., Noffsinger-Frazier, N., Shulman, J., ... & Mosher, C. (2017). Predictors of sexual minority youth's reported suicide attempts and mental health. *Journal of Homosexuality, 64*(6), 697–715.

Puckett, J., Cleary, P., Rossman, K., Mustanski, B., & Newcomb, M. (2018). Barriers to gender-affirming care for transgender and gender nonconforming individuals. *Sexuality Research & Social Policy: Journal of NSRC, 15*(15), 48–59.

Puente, M. & Kelly, C. (2018, February 22) Hollywood's 'me too' woes ... 94%. *USA Today International Edition,* p. A1.

Quidley-Rodriguez, N., & De Santis, J. P. (2019). A concept analysis of bear identity. *Journal of Homosexuality, 66*(1), 60–76.

Quinlon, M. (2000). *Swearing on one's testicles.* Retrieved from http://www.worldwidewords.org/qa/qa-swe1.htm

Quinn, C., Happell, B., & Browne, G. (2012). Opportunity lost? Psychiatric medications and problems with sexual function: a role for nurses in mental health. *Journal of Clinical Nursing, 21*(3–4), 415–423.

Quinn, C., Happell, B., & Welch, A. (2013). Talking about sex as part of our role: Making and sustaining practice change. *International Journal of Mental Health Nursing, 22*(3), 231–240.

Quinn-Nilas, C., and Kennett D. J. (2018). Reasons why undergraduate women comply with unwanted, non-coercive sexual advances: A serial indirect effect model integrating sexual script theory and sexual self-control perspectives. *Journal of Social Psychology, 158*(5), 603–615.

Quinn, H., Flood, S., Mendelowitz, E., Marrie, R. A., & Foley, F. (2015). Predictors of fear of sexual rejection in individuals with multiple sclerosis. *Sexuality and Disability*, *33*(1), 53–61.

Quinn, K., Dickson-Gomez, J., & Pacella, M. (2019). "Running trains" and "sexing-in": The functions of sex within adolescent gangs. *Youth & Society*, *51*(2), 151–169.

Radosh, A., & Simkin, L. (2017, November). *What is sexual bereavement? Why do we need to know more about it?* Presented at the annual meeting of Society for Scientific Study of Sex, Atlanta, GA.

RAINN. (n.d.) Perpetrators of Sexual Violence: Statistics. Retrieved from https://www.rainn.org/statistics/perpetrators-sexual-violence

Rako, S., & Friebely, J. (2004). The pheromonal influences on sociosexual behavior in postmenopausal women. *Journal of Sex Research*, *41*(4), 372–380.

Ram, L., & Devillers, L. (2016, November). *The modern gay relationship: Results from 2016 National Survey and contemporary literature review*. Paper presented at the annual meeting of the Society for the Scientific Study of Sexuality, Phoenix, AZ.

Ramirez, M., & Kim, J. (2018). Traversing gender, sexual orientation, and race-ethnicity. *Journal of Gay & Lesbian Social Services*, *30*(2), 192–208.

Ramo, D. E., & Prochaska, J. J. (2012). Broad reach and targeted recruitment using Facebook for an online survey of young adult substance use. *Journal of Medical Internet Research*, *14*(1), e28.

Rappleyea, D. L., Taylor, A. C., & Fang, X. (2014). Gender differences and communication technology use among emerging adults in the initiation of dating relationships. *Marriage & Family Review*, *50*(3), 269–284.

Rasmussen, K. R., Grubbs, J. B., Pargament, K. I., & Exline, J. J. (2018). Social desirability bias in pornography-related self-reports: The role of religion. *Journal of Sex Research*, *55*(3), 381–394.

Ravanipour, M., Gharibi, T., & Gharibi, T. (2013). Elderly women's views about sexual desire during old age: A qualitative study. *Sexuality and Disability*, *31*(2), 179–188. doi:10.1007/s11195-013-9295-7

Raymond, E. G., & Grimes, D. A. (2012). The comparative safety of legal induced abortion and childbirth in the United States. *Obstetrics and Gynecology*, *119*(2 Pt 1), 215–219.

Rayne, K. (2015). *Breaking the hush factor: Ten rules for talking with teenagers about sex*. Austin, TX: Impetus Books.

Reece, M., Herbenick, D., Fortenberry, J. D., Dodge, B., Sanders, S. A., & Schick, V. (2012). [Graph of sexual behavior by age group, October 1, 2010]. *National Survey of Sexual Health and Behavior*. Retrieved from http://www.nationalsexstudy.indiana.edu

Reed, H., & Humpfer, J. (2014, November). *Attributional tendencies in men with ejaculatory issues*. Presented at the annual meeting of the Society for the Scientific Study of Sexuality, Omaha, NE.

Regnerus, M., Price, J., & Gordon, D. (2017). Masturbation and partnered sex: Substitutes or complements? *Archives of Sexual Behavior*, *46*(7), 2111–2121.

Reilly, S. (2015, July 30). Tens of thousands of rape kits go untested across USA. *USA Today*. Retrieved from http://www.usatoday.com/story/news/2015/07/16/untested-rape-kits-evidence-across-usa/29902199/

Retznik, L., Wienholz, Seidel, Pantenburg, B., Conrad, I., Michel, M., & Riedel-Heller, S. G. (2017). Relationship status: Single? Young adults with visual, hearing, or physical disability and their experiences with partnership and sexuality. *Sexuality and Disability*, *35*(4), 415–432.

Reverby, S. M. (2012). Reflections on apologies and the studies in Tuskegee and Guatemala. *Ethics and Behavior*, *22*(6), 493–495.

Reyes, H. L., & Foshee, V. A. (2013). Sexual dating aggression across grades 8 through 12: Timing and predictors of onset. *Journal of Youth and Adolescence*, *42*(4), 581–595.

Rham, G., Renck, B., & Ringsberg, K. C. (2013). Psychological distress among women who were sexually abused as children. *International Journal of Social Welfare*, *22*(3), 269–278.

Ricketts, M., Maloney, C., Marcum, C., & Higgins, G. (2015). The effect of Internet related problems on the sexting behaviors of juveniles. *American Journal of Criminal Justice*, *40*(2), 270–284.

Rickman, E. (2018, April). *Celebrity culture, romance, and young adults*. Poster presented at the Southern Sociological Society Annual Meeting, New Orleans, LA.

Riddle, K., & De Simone, J. J. (2013). A Snooki effect? An exploration of the surveillance subgenre of reality TV and viewers' beliefs about the "real" real world. *Psychology of Popular Media Culture*, *2*(4), 237–250.

Rietmeijer, C. A., Westergaard, B., Mickiewicz, T. A., Richardson, D., Ling, S., Sapp, T., … McFarlane, M. (2011). Evaluation of an online partner notification program. *Sexually Transmitted Diseases*, *38*(5), 359–364.

Rinehart, J. K., Nason, E. E., Yeater, E. A., & Miller, G. F. (2017). Do some students need special protection from research on sex and trauma? New evidence for young adult resilience in "sensitive topics" research. *Journal of Sex Research*, *54*(3), 273–283.

Ringrose, J., & Lawrence, E. (2018). Remixing misandry, manspreading, and dick pics: Networked feminist humour on Tumblr. *Feminist Media Studies*, *18*(4), 686–704. doi: 10.1080/14680777.2018.1450351

Rissel, C., Richters, J., de Visser, R. O., McKee, A., Yeung, A., & Caruana, T. (2017). A profile of pornography users in Australia: Findings from the second Australian study of health and relationships. *The Journal of Sex Research*, *54*(2), 227–240.

Ritter, L., Morris, H., & Knox, D. (2018, June). Who's getting the best sex?: A comparison by sexual orientation. *Sexuality and Culture*, *23*(4), 1466–1489. doi:10.1007/s12119-018-9538-y. Retrieved from https://link.springer.com/article/10.1007/s12119-018-9538-y

Roberts, Michael. (2016, September 22). Six Myths About Abortion From Katha Pollitt, *Westword*. Retrieved from https://www.westword.com/news/six-myths-about-abortion-from-katha-pollitt-8332578

Robinson, B., & Connor, J. (2014, November). *Sexuality, behavior, HIV prevention, and female genital cutting: Perspectives from Somali women living in the U.S.* Presented at the annual meeting of the Society for the Scientific Study of Sexuality, Omaha, NE.

Robinson, M. (2013). Polyamory and monogamy as strategic identities. *Journal of Bisexuality*, *13*(1), 21–38.

Rodoo, P., & Hellberg, D. (2013). Girls who masturbate in early infancy: Diagnostics, natural course and long-term follow-up. *Acta Paediatrica*, *102*(7), 762–766.

Rodrigues, D., Lopes, D., & Smith C. V. (2017). Caught in a "bad romance"? Reconsidering the negative association between sociosexuality and relationship functioning. *The Journal of Sex Research*, *54*(9), 1118–1127.

Rodriguez-Diaz, C., Grov, C., Jovet-Toledo, G., & Parsons, J. (2014, November). *Comparing male escorts' sexual behavior with their last male client versus non-commercial male partner*. Presented at the annual meeting of the Society for the Scientific Study of Sexuality, Omaha, NE.

Rodriguez, E. M., Etengoff, C., & Vaughan, M. D. (2019). A quantitative examination of identity integration in gay, lesbian, and bisexual people. *Journal of Homosexuality*, *66*(1), 77–99.

Roen, K. (2019). Intersex or diverse sex development: Critical review of psychosocial health care research and indications for practice. *The Journal of Sex Research*, *56*(4–5), 511–528.

Rosa's Law. (2010, October 5). Public law 111-256. 111th Congress. Retrieved from https://www.gpo.gov/fdsys/pkg/PLAW-111publ256/pdf/PLAW-111publ256.pdf

Rosen, N. O., Dewitte, M., Merwin, K., & Bergeron, S. (2017). Interpersonal goals and well-being in couples coping with genitor-pelvic pain. *Archives of Sexual Behavior, 46*(7), 2007–2019.

Rosen, N. O., & Bergeron, S. (2019) Genito-pelvic pain through a dyadic lens: Moving toward an interpersonal emotion regulation model of women's sexual dysfunction. *The Journal of Sex Research, 56*(4–5), 440–461.

Rosier, J. G., & Tyler, J. M. (2017). Finding the Love Guru in you: Examining the effectiveness of a sexual communication training program for married couples. *Marriage & Family Review, 53*(1), 65–87.

Ross, L. E., Salway, T., Tarasoff, L. A., MacKay, J. M., Hawkins, B. W., & Fehr, C. P. (2018). Prevalence of depression and anxiety among bisexual people compared to gay, lesbian, and heterosexual individuals: A systematic review and meta-analysis. *Journal of Sex Research, 55*(4–5), 435–456.

Rosser, B. R., Dwyer, M., Coleman, E., Miner, M., Metz, M., Robinson, B. E., & Bockting, W. O. (1995). Using sexually explicit material in adult sex education: An eighteen-year comparative analysis. *Journal of Sex Education and Therapy, 21*(2), 117–128.

Rossi, E., Poulin, F., & Boislard, M. A. (2017). Trajectories of annual number of sexual partners from adolescence to emerging adulthood: Individual and family predictors. *Journal of Youth & Adolescence, 46*(5), 995–1008.

Rossi, N. E. (2010). "Coming out" stories of gay and lesbian young adults. *Journal of Homosexuality, 57*(9), 1174–1191.

Roth, S., & Friedman, M. J. (1998). Childhood trauma remembered: A report on the current scientific knowledge base and its applications. *Journal of Child Sexual Abuse, 7*(1), 83–109.

Rothman, E. F., Sullivan, M., Keyes, S., & Boehmer, U. (2012). Parents' supportive reactions to sexual orientation disclosure associated with better health: Results from a population-based survey of LGB adults in Massachusetts. *Journal of Homosexuality, 59*(2), 186–200.

Rowland, D. L., Cempel, L. M., & Tempel, A. R. (2018). Women's attributions regarding why they have difficulty reaching orgasm. *Journal of Sex & Marital Therapy, 44*(5), 475–484. doi: doi.org/10.1080/0092623X.2017.1408046

Rowland, D. L., Adamski, B. A., Neal, C. J. Myers, A. L., & Burnett, A. L. (2015). Self-efficacy as a relevant construct in understanding sexual response and dysfunction. *Journal of Sex & Marital Therapy, 41*(1), 60–71.

Royal College of Obstetricians & Gynaecologists. (2015, June). The management of third- and fourth-degree perineal tears. *Green-top Guidelines No. 29.* Retrieved from https://www.rcog.org.uk/globalassets/documents/guidelines/gtg-29.pdf

Rubel, A. N., & Bogaert, A. F. (2015). Consensual nonmonogamy: Psychological well-being and relationship quality correlates. *Journal of Sex Research, 52*(9), 961–982.

Rubenking, N. J. (2019, June 27). The best parental control software for 2020. *PC Magazine.* Retrieved from http://www.pcmag.com/article2/0,2817,2346997,00.asp

Rubin, E. (1987). *Abortion, politics, and the courts: Roe v. Wade and its aftermath* (2nd ed.). Westport, CT: Greenwood Press.

Rullo, J. E., Lorenz, T., Ziegelmann, M. J., Meihofer, L., Herbenick, D., & Faubion, S. S. (2018). Genital vibration for sexual function and enhancement: a review of evidence. *Sexual & Relationship Therapy, 33*(3), 263–274.

Runfola, C. D., Von Holle, A., Trace, S. E., Brownley, K. A., Hofmeier, S. M., Gagne, D. A., & Bulik, C. M. (2013). Body dissatisfaction in women across the lifespan: Results of the UNC-SELF and Gender and Body Image (GABI) studies. *European Eating Disorders Review, 21*(1), 52–59.

Russell, S. T., Ryan, C., Toomey, R. B., Diaz, R. M., & Sanchez, J. (2011). Lesbian, gay, bisexual and transgender adolescent school victimization: Implications for young adult health and adjustment. *Journal of School Health, 81*(5), 223–230.

Russell, V. M., Baker, L. R., & Mcnulty, J. K. (2013). Attachment insecurity and infidelity in marriage: Do studies of dating relationships really inform us about marriage? *Journal of Family Psychology, 27*(2), 241–251.

Rutagumirwa, S. K., & Bailey, A. (2018). "The heart has desires but the body refuses": Sexual scripts, older men's perceptions of sexuality, and implications for their mental and sexual health. *Sex Roles, 78*(9–10), 653–668.

Ryan, P. (2017, June 7). Can porn be feminist? These directors say 'yes'. *USA Today,* p. 2D.

Sabbah, K. (2013). *Sex and the married John: Profiling male sexual behaviors with street prostitutes.* Presented at the 18th annual symposium at California State University Northridge, Northridge, CA.

Sahay, R. D., Haynes, E. N., Rao, M. B., & Pirko, I. (2012). Assessment of sexual satisfaction in relation to potential sexual problems in women with multiple sclerosis: A pilot study. *Sexuality and Disability, 30*(2), 227–236.

Sakaluk, J. K., & Fisher, A. N. (2019). Measurement memo I: Updated practices in psychological measurement for sexual scientists. *Canadian Journal of Human Sexuality, 28*(2), 84–92. doi: 10.3138/cjhs.2019-0018

Salazar, M., & Ohman, A. (2015). Negotiating masculinity, violence, and responsibility: A situational analysis of young Nicaraguan men's discourses on intimate partner and sexual violence. *Journal of Aggression, Maltreatment & Trauma, 24*(2), 131–149.

Salem, S. (2019, January 29). What happens when men are too afraid to mentor women? Ripple effect of #MeToo that women did not ask for: fewer champions. *New York Times.*

Sales, N. J. (2016). *American girls: Social media and the secret life of teenagers.* New York, NY: Knopf Doubleday.

Sanday, P. R. (1981). The socio-cultural context of rape: A cross-cultural study. *Journal of Social Issues, 37*(4), 5–27.

Sanday, P. R. (1995). Pulling train. In P. S. Rothenberg (Ed.), *Race, class, and gender in the United States* (3rd ed., pp. 396–402). New York, NY: St. Martin's Press.

Sandberg, S., & Pritchard, M. (2019, May 17). The number of men who are uncomfortable mentoring women is growing. *Fortune Magazine.* Retrieved from http://fortune.com/2019/05/17/sheryl-sandberg-lean-in-me-too/

Sandberg-Thoma, S. E., & Kamp Dush, C. M. (2014). Casual sexual relationships and mental health in adolescence and emerging adulthood. *Journal of Sex Research, 51*(2), 121–130.

Sanders, T. L. (2008). *Paying for pleasure: Men who buy sex.* Cullompton, Devon, UK: Willan.

Sandlow, J. I. (2013). Size does matter: Higher body mass index may mean lower pregnancy rates for microscopic testicular sperm extraction. *Fertility and Sterility, 99*(2), 347.

Sanjakdar, F. (2018). Can difference make a difference? A critical theory discussion of religion in sexuality education. *Discourse: Studies in the Cultural Politics of Education, 39*(3), 393–407.

Santelli, J. S., Kantor, L. M., Grilo, S. A., Speizer, I. S., Lindberg, L. D., Heitel, J. ... Ott, M.A. (2017). Abstinence-only-until-marriage: An updated review of U.S. policies and programs and their impact. *Journal of Adolescent Health, 61*(3), 273–280.

Santelli, J. S., Lindberg, L. D., Grilo, S. A., Kantor, L. M. (2019). Ideology or evidence? Examining the population-level impact of US government funding to prevent pregnancy. *American Journal of Public Health, 109*(3), 356–357. doi: 10.2105/AJPH.2018.304940.

Sarrel, P. M., Njike, V. Y., Vinante, V., & Katz, D. L. (2013). The mortality toll of estrogen avoidance: An analysis of excess deaths among hysterectomized women aged 50 to 59 years. *American Journal of Public Health, 103*(9), 1583–1588.

Sassler, S., & Miller, A. J. (2014). "We're very careful ...": The fertility desires and contraceptive behaviors of cohabiting couples. *Family Relations, 63*(4), 538–553.

Satinsky, S., & Jozkowski, K. N. (2015). Female sexual subjectivity and verbal consent to receiving oral sex. *Journal of Sex & Marital Therapy, 41*(4), 413–426.

Sato, A., Aramaki, E., Shimamoto, Y., Tanaka, S., & Kawakami, K. (2015). Blog posting after lung cancer notification: Content analysis of blogs written by patients or their families. *Journal of Medical Internet Research, 1*(1), e5.

Savin-Williams, R. C. (2018). An exploratory study of exclusively heterosexual, primarily heterosexual, and mostly heterosexual young men. *Sexualities, 21*(1–2), 16–29.

Sawyer, A. N., Smith, E. R., & Benotsch, E. G. (2018). Dating application use and sexual risk behavior among young adults. *Sexuality Research & Social Policy, 15*(2), 183–191.

Sbraga, T. P., & O'Donohue, W. (2000). Sexual harassment. *Annual Review of Sex Research, 11*(1), 258–285.

Schaafsma, D., Kok, G., Stoffelen, J. M., & Curfs, L. M. (2015). Identifying effective methods for teaching sex education to individuals with intellectual disabilities: A systematic review. *Journal of Sex Research, 52*(4), 412–432.

Schade, L. C., Sandberg, J., Bean, R., Busby, D., & Coyne, S. (2013). Using technology to connect in romantic relationships: Effects on attachment, relationship, satisfaction, and stability in emerging adults. *Journal of Couple & Relationship Therapy, 12*(4), 314–338.

Scheim, A. I., & Bauer, G. R. (2015). Sex and gender diversity among transgender persons in Ontario, Canada: Results from a respondent-driven sampling survey. *Journal of Sex Research, 52*(1), 1–14.

Scheim, A. I., & Bauer, G. R. (2019). Sexual inactivity among transfeminine persons: A Canadian respondent-driven sampling survey. *The Journal of Sex Research, 56*(2), 264–273.

Scheitle, C. P., & Wolf, J. K. (2017). The religious origins and destinations of individuals identifying as a sexual minority. *Sexuality & Culture, 21*(3), 719–740.

Scherrer, K. S., Kazyak, E., & Schmitz, R. (2015). Getting "bi" in the family: Bisexual people's disclosure experiences. *Journal of Marriage and Family, 77*(3), 680–696.

Schmidt, L., Sobotka, T., Bentzen, G., Andersen, A. N., & ESHRE Reproduction and Society Task Force. (2012). Demographic and medical consequences of the postponement of parenthood. *Human Reproduction Update, 18*(1), 29–43.

Schmitz, R. M., & Tyler, K. A. (2018). LGBTQ+ young adults on the street and on campus: Identity as a product of social context. *Journal of Homosexuality, 65*(2), 197–223.

Schneider, S., & Courey, M. (2016, June 17). Transgender voice and communication – vocal health and considerations, University of California, San Francisco, Transgender Care. Retrieved from https://transcare.ucsf.edu/guidelines/vocal-health

Schnittker, J. (2019). Sexual violence and major depression among women: Evidence from reciprocal relationships. *Social Currents, 6*(6), 575–589.

Schoentjes, E., Deboutte, D., & Friedrich, W. (1999). Child sexual behavior inventory: A Dutch-speaking normative sample. *Pediatrics, 104*(4–1), 885–893.

Schrimshaw, E. W., Downing, M. J., Cohn, D. J., & Siegel, K. (2014). Conceptions of privacy and the non-disclosure of same-sex behaviour by behaviourally-bisexual men in heterosexual relationships. Culture, *Health & Sexuality, 16*(4), 351–365.

Schrimshaw, E. W., Siegel, K., & Meunier, E. (2017). Venues where male sex workers meet partners: The emergence of gay hookup apps and web sites. *American Journal of Public Health, 107*(12), 1866–1867.

Schulz, E. E, Cary, K. M., Maas, M K., & McCauley, H. L. (2019, November). *Sex toys to close orgasm gap: Differences in orgasm methods between relationship status and gender among college students*. Poster presented at the annual meeting of the Society for Scientific Study of Sexuality, Denver, CO.

Scoats, R., Joseph, L. J., & Anderson, E. (2018). 'I don't mind watching him cum': Heterosexual men, threesomes, and the erosion of the one-time rule of homosexuality. *Sexualities, 21*(1–2), 30–48.

Scroggs, B., Madrigal, R., & Faflick, N. (2019). Adolescent sexual guilt and the development of self-esteem during the transition to adulthood: The moderating effect of race. *Sexuality & Culture, 23*(2), 641–656.

Scuka, R. R. (2015). A clinician's guide to helping couples heal from the trauma of infidelity. *Journal of Couple & Relationship Therapy, 14*(2), 141–168.

Scull, M. T. (2019, November). *Male strippers and the toll of exotic dance*. Poster presented at the Society for the Scientific Study of Sex annual meeting, Denver, CO.

Seavey, C. A., Katz, P. A., & Zalk, S. R. (1975). Baby X: The effect of gender labels on adult responses to infants. *Sex Roles, 1*(2), 103–109.

Seeman, M. V. (2013). Clinical interventions for women with schizophrenia: Pregnancy. *Acta Psychiatrica Scandinavica, 127*(1), 12–22.

Seguin, L., Blais, M, Goyer, M. F., Rodrique, C., Magontier, C., Adam, B. D., & Lavoie, F. (2017). Examining relationship quality across three types of relationship agreements. *Sexualities, 20*(1–2), 86–104.

Seguin, L. J., Milhausen, R. R., & Kukkonen, T. (2015). The development and validation of the motives for feigning orgasms scale. *Canadian Journal of Human Sexuality, 24*(1), 31–48.

Sell, N. M., Turrisi, R., Scaglione, N. M., Cleavland, M. J., & Mallett, K. A. (2018). Alcohol consumption and use of sexual assault and drinking protective behavioral strategies. *Psychology of Women Quarterly, 42*(1), 1–22.

Sells, T. G. C., & Ganong, L. (2017). Emerging adults' expectations and preferences for gender role arrangements in long-term heterosexual relationships. *Sex Roles, 76*(3–4), 125–137.

Selterman, D., Garcia, J. R., & Tsapelas, I. (2019). Motivations for extradyadic infidelity revisited. *The Journal of Sex Research, 56*(3), 273–286.

Selvaggi, G., & Bellringer, J. (2011). Gender reassignment surgery: An overview. *Nature Reviews Urology, 8*, 274–282.

Semigran, H. L., Linder, J. A., Gidengil, C., & Mehrotra, A. (2015). Evaluation of symptom checkers for self diagnosis and triage: Audit study. *British Medical Journal, 351*. Retrieved from http://www.bmj.com/content/351/bmj.h3480

Serughetti, G. (2013). Prostitution and clients' responsibility. *Men and Masculinities, 16*(1), 35–48.

Seto, M. C. (2017) The puzzle of male chronophilias. *Archives of Sexual Behavior, 46*(1), 3–22.

Seto, M. C., Hermann, C. A., Kjellgren, C., Priebe, G., Svedin, C. G., & Langstroom, N. (2015). Viewing child pornography: Prevalence and correlates in a representative community same of young Swedish men. *Archives of Sexual Behavior, 44*(1), 67–79.

Setzer, K. (2015, April 16). *Open dialogue: ECU experts discuss marriage rights*. East Carolina University News Services. Retrieved from http://www.ecu.edu/cs-admin/news/marriagepanel.cfm

Sevecke, J. R., Rhymer, K. N., Almazan, E. P., & Jacob, S. (2015). Effects of interaction experiences and undergraduate coursework on attitudes toward gay and lesbian issues. *Journal of Homosexuality, 62*(6), 821–840.

Sewell, K. K., McGarrity, L. A., & Strassberg, D. S. (2017). Sexual behavior, definitions of sex, and the role of self-partner context among lesbian, gay, and bisexual adults. *Journal of Sex Research, 54*(7), 825–831.

Shapiro, C. H. (2012, November). *Decade of change: New interdisciplinary needs of people with infertility*. Paper presented at the annual meeting of the National Council on Family Relations, Phoenix, AZ.

Sharma, A., Garofalo, R., Hidalgo, M. A., Hoehnle, S., Mimiaga, M. J., Brown, E. ... Stephenson, R. (2019). Do male couples agree on their sexual agreements? An analysis of dyadic data. *Archives of Sexual Behavior, 48*(4), 1203–1216.

Sharp, M., & Dohme, B. V. (2016, March). *FDA-approved patient labeling: Nexplanon®.* Retrieved from http://www.merck.com/product/usa/pi_circulars/n/nexplanon/nexplanon_ppi.pdf

Shaw, L. K., Sherman, K. A., Fitness, J., & Breast Cancer Network Australia. (2016). Women's experiences of dating after breast cancer. *Journal of Psychosocial Oncology, 34*(4), 318–335.

Shdaimah, C. S., & Wiechelt, S. A. (2013). Crime and compassion: Women in prostitution at the intersection of criminality and victimization. *International Review of Victimology, 19*(1), 23–35.

Shear, M. D. (2015, April 8). Obama calls for end to "conversion therapies" for gay and transgender youth. *New York Times.* Retrieved from http://www.nytimes.com/2015/04/09/us/politics/obama-to-call-for-end-to-conversion-therapies-for-gay-and-transgender-youth.html

Sheff, E. (2014). *The polyamorists next door: Inside multiple-partner relationships and families.* Lanham, MD: Rowman & Littlefield.

Shen, S. (2019). Chronic disease burden, sexual frequency, and sexual dysfunction in partnered older adults. *Journal of Sex & Marital Therapy, 45*(8), 706–720.

Shikai, X. (1990). Treatment of impotence in traditional Chinese medicine. *Journal of Sex Education and Therapy, 16*(3), 198–200.

Shim, J. W., Kwon, M., & Cheng, H. I. (2015). Analysis of representation of sexuality on women's and men's pornographic websites. *Social Behavior and Personality, 43*(1), 53–62.

Shin, K. H., Yang, J. A., & Edwards, C. (2010). Gender role identity among Korean and American college students: Links to gender and academic achievement. *Social Behavior and Personality: An International Journal, 38*(2), 267–272.

Shrout, M. R., & Weigel, D. J. (2018) Infidelity's aftermath: Appraisals, mental health, and health-compromising behaviors following a partner's infidelity. *Journal of Social and Personal Relationships, 35*(8), 1067–1091.

Shin, S. H., Hong, H. G., & Jeon, S. M. (2012). Personality and alcohol use: The role of impulsivity. *Addictive Behaviors, 37*(1), 102–107.

SIECUS (Sexuality Information and Education Council of the U.S.). (2018a, August). Position statement. Retrieved from http://siecus.org/index.cfm?fuseaction=Page.ViewPage&pageId=494 https://siecus.org/wp-content/uploads/2018/07/Position-Statements-2018-2.pdf

SIECUS (Sexuality Information and Education Council of the U.S.). (2018b). State laws and policies across the United States. Retrieved from https://siecus.org/wp-content/uploads/2018/07/SIECUS-SP-FY17-State-Law-and-Policy-Chart.pdf

SIECUS (Sexuality Information and Education Council of the U.S.). (2015, March 23). *Position statement on homosexuality.* Retrieved http://www.dianedew.com/siecus.htm

Silva, T. (2017). Bud-sex: Constructing normative masculinity among rural straight men that have sex with men. *Gender & Society, 31*(1), 51–73.

Silva, T. J., & Bridges Whaley, R. (2018). Bud-sex, dude-sex, and heteroflexible men: The relationship between straight identification and social attitudes in a nationally representative sample of men with same-sex attractions or sexual practices. *Sociological Perspectives, 61*(3), 426–443.

Silver, K. E., Goodenow, S., Martella, A., Rossey, A., Davidson, K., Anderson, R. A., & Delanhanty, D. (2018). *A qualitative analysis of college men's perceptions of sex.* Annual meet of Society for the Scientific Study of Sex. Montreal, Canada, Nov 9.

Simbar, M., Nazarpour, S., Mirzababaiee, M., EmamHadi, M. A., Tehrani, F. R., & Maid, H. A. (2018). Quality of life and body image of individuals with gender dysphoria. *Journal of Sex & Marital Therapy, 44*(6), 523–532. doi.org/10.1080/0092623X.2017.1419392

Simister, J. G. (2010). Domestic violence and female genital mutilation in Kenya: Effects of ethnicity and education. *Journal of Family Violence, 25*(3), 247–257.

Simon, J., Caramelli, K., Thomas, H., & Reape, K. (2013). Efficacy and safety of a weekly progestin-only transdermal system for prevention of pregnancy. *Contraception, 88*(2), 316.

Símonardóttir, S., & Gíslason, I. V. (2018). When breast is not best: Opposing dominant discourses on breastfeeding. *Sociological Review, 66*(3) 665–681.

Simopoulos, E. F., & Trinidad, A. C. (2013). Male erectile dysfunction: Integrating psychopharmacology and psychotherapy. *General Hospital Psychiatry, 35*(1), 33–38.

Simpson, P., Wilson, C. B., Brown, L. J. E., Dickinson, T., & Horne, M. (2018). 'We've had our sex life way back': older care home residents, sexuality and intimacy. *Ageing & Society, 38*(7), 1478–1501.

Singer, I. (1973). *The goals of human sexuality.* New York, NY: Norton.

Sinha, S. (2015). Reasons for women's entry into sex work: A case study of Kolkata, India. *Sexuality & Culture, 19*(1), 216–235.

Sizemore, K. M., & Olmstead, S. B. (2017). Willingness to engage in consensual nonmonogamy among emerging adults: A structural equation analysis of sexual identity, casual sex attitudes, and gender. *The Journal of Sex Research, 54*(9), 1106–1117.

Smeaton, G., Anderson, P., Fagen, J., & Bohn, R. (2014, November). *Gender majority status and tactics used to gain sex from a reluctant partner.* Poster session presented at the annual meeting of the Society for the Scientific Study of Sexuality, Omaha, NE.

Smith, D., & Stewart, S. (2003). Sexual aggression and sports participation. *Journal of Sport Behavior, 26*(4), 384–394.

Smith, M. (2013). Youth viewing sexually explicit material online: Addressing the elephant on the screen. *Sexuality Research and Social Policy, 10*(1), 62–75.

Snapp, S., Lento, R., Ryu, E., & Rosen, K. S. (2014). Why do they hook up? Attachment style and motives of college students. *Personal Relationships, 21*(3), 468–481.

Sneha, S. (2018) An autoethnography about recovering awareness following brain injury: Is my truth valid? *Qualitative Inquiry, 24*(1), 56–69.

Snipes, D. J., & Benotsch, E. G. (2013). High-risk cocktails and high-risk sex: Examining the relation between alcohol mixed with energy drink consumption, sexual behavior, and drug use in college students. *Addictive Behaviors, 38*(1), 1418–1423.

Soh, D. (2019). Guest on HBO's *Bill Mahr Live.* June 21.

Soklaridis, S., Zahn, C., Kuper, A., Gillis, D., Taylor, V. H., & Whitehead, C. (2018). Men's fear of mentoring in the #MeToo Era — What's at stake for academic medicine? *The New England Journal of Medicine, 379*(23), 2270–2274.

Solano, I., Eaton, N. R., & O'Leary, K. D. (2020). Pornography consumption, modality and function in a large Internet sample. *Journal of Sex Research, 57*(1), 92–103.

Soliman, H. H., Alsharqawi, N. I., & Younis, M. A. (2018). Is tourism marriage of young girls in Egypt a form of child sexual abuse? A family exploitation perspective. *Journal of Child Sexual Abuse, 27*(2), 122–140.

Sommers, M., & Abboud, S. (2014, November). *Understanding virginity from the perspectives of Arab-American women: A phenomenological approach.* Presented at the annual meeting of the Society for the Scientific Study of Sexuality, Omaha, NE.

Southern, S. (2019). Good enough sex: An interview with Barry McCarty. *Family Journal, 27*(1), 5–10.

Spencer, C., Mallory, A., Smith, S., & Tripodi, J. (2015, November). *Reducing sexual violence on college campuses.* Poster session presented at the annual meeting of the National Council on Family Relations, Vancouver, BC.

Sprecher, S., Barbee, A., & Schwartz, P. (1995). "Was it good for you, too?": Gender differences in first sexual intercourse experiences. *Journal of Sex Research, 32*(1), 3–15.

Sprecher, S., & Treger, S. (2015). Virgin college students' reasons for and reactions to their abstinence from sex: Results from a 23-year study at a Midwestern U.S. university. *Journal of Sex Research, 52*(8), 936–948.

Spruin, E., Wood, J. L., Gannon, T. A., & Tyler, N. (2018). Sexual of offender's experiences of polygraph testing: a thematic study in three probation trusts. *Journal of Sexual Aggression, 24*(1), 12–24.

Stanton, R., Milstein, S., Knox, D., & Hall, S. (2018, June). *Sexual values: Variations by sexual identity and relationship status.* Poster presented at the American Association of Sexuality Educators, Counselors and Therapists annual meeting, Denver, CO.

Stappenbeck, C. A., Gulati, N. K., & Davis, K. C. (2019). A prospective examination of men's condom use resistance: Event-level associations with sexual aggression, alcohol consumption and trait anger. *Journal of Sex Research, 56*(8), 947–956.

Staras, S. A., Livingston, M. D., & Wagenaar, A. C. (2015). Maryland alcohol sales tax and sexually transmitted infections: A natural experiment. *American Journal of Preventive Medicine, 50*(3), e73-e80.

Stein, J. B., Mongeau, P., Posteher, K., & Veluscek, A. (2019). Netflix and chill? Exploring and refining differing motivations in friends with benefits relationships. *The Canadian Journal of Human Sexuality, 28*(3), 317–327.

Steinberg, J. R., & Rubin, L. R. (2014). Psychological aspects of contraception, unintended pregnancy, and abortion. *Policy Insights from the Behavioral and Brain Sciences, 1*(1), 239–247.

Steiner, J., Kynn, J., Stylianou, A. M., & Postmus, J. L. (2018). Providing services to trafficking survivors: Understanding practices across the globe. *Journal of Evidence-informed Social Work, 15*(2), 150–168.

Steinke, E. E., Jaarsma, T., Barnason, S. A., Bryne, M., Doherty, S., Dougherty, C. M., … Moser, D. K. (2013, October 29). Sexual counseling for individuals with cardiovascular disease and their partners: A consensus document from the American Heart Association and the ESC Council on Cardiovascular Nursing and Allied Professions (CCNAP). *Circulation, 28*(18). Retrieved from http://circ.ahajournals.org/content/128/18/2075.full

Stephenson, K. R., & Meston, C. M. (2015). The conditional importance of sex: Exploring the association between sexual well-being and life satisfaction. *Journal of Sex & Marital Therapy, 41*(1), 25–38.

Stephenson, K. R., Rellini, A. H., & Meston, C. M. (2013). Relationship satisfaction as a predictor of treatment response during cognitive behavioral sex therapy. *Archives of Sexual Behavior, 42*(1), 143–152.

Stepler, R. (2017). Number of U.S. adults cohabiting with a partner continues to rise, especially among those 50 and older. *Pew Research Center.* Retrieved from http://www.pewresearch.org/fact-tank/2017/04/06/number-of-u-s-adults-cohabiting-with-a-partner-continues-to-rise-especially -among-those-50-and-older/

Stern,, L. (2018, April 6). *Clinical tools to facilitate contraception satisfaction and continuation.* Presented at the Conference on Contraceptive Technology, Washington, DC.

Sternberg, R. J. (1986). A triangular theory of love. *Psychological Review, 93*(2), 119–135.

Stetson, D. M. (2004). The invisible issue: Trafficking of women and girls in the United States. In J. Outshoorn (Ed.), *The politics of prostitution: Women's movements, democratic states and the globalization of sex commerce* (pp. 245–264). New York, NY: Cambridge University Press.

Stewart-Williams, S., Butler, C. A., & Thomas, A. G. (2017). Sexual history and present attractiveness: People want a mate with a bit of a past, but not too much. *The Journal of Sex Research, 54*(9), 1097–1105.

Stone, K. (n.d.). The Symptoms of Postpartum Depression & Anxiety (in Plain Mama English). *Postpartum Progress.* Retrieved from https://postpartumprogress.com/the-symptoms-of-postpartum-depression-anxiety-in-plain-mama-english

Stone, K. (2010, April 20). The best alternative treatment options for postpartum depression. *Postpartum Progress.* Retrieved from http://www.postpartumprogress.com/the-best-complementary-alternative-medicine-treatment-options-postpartum-depression

Stop Street Harassment. (2019). *Measuring #MeToo: A National Study on Sexual Harassment and Assault.* Retrieved from http://www.stopstreetharassment.org/wp-content/uploads/2012/08/Street-Harassment-Factsheet-2019-Study.pdf

Strang, E. & Peterson, Z. D. (2017). Unintentional misreporting on self-report measures of sexually aggressive behavior: An interview study. *The Journal of Sex Research, 54*(8), 971–983.

Stroebel, S. S., O'Keefe, S. L., Beard, K. W., Kuo, S. Y., Swindell, S., & Stroupe, W. (2013). Brother-sister incest: Data from anonymous computer assisted self-interviews. *Journal of Child Sexual Abuse, 22*(3), 255–276.

Strommen, E. F. (1989). "You're a what?" Family member reactions to the disclosure of homosexuality. *Journal of Homosexuality, 18*(1–2), 37–58.

Struckman-Johnson, C., Nalan, K., & Allemang, H. (2014, November). *Sexting and Snapchat behaviors among college students.* Presented at the annual meeting of the Society for the Scientific Study of Sexuality, Omaha, NE.

Struckman-Johnson, C., Nalan-Sheffield, K., Gaster, S., & Struckman-Johnson. D. (2017). Sexual behavior in parked cars reported by Midwestern college men and women. *The Journal of Sex Research, 54*(8), 1064–1076.

Stuhlsatz, G., & Lohman, B. (2014, November). *Hooking up behaviors and romantic relationship desires among young adults.* Poster session presented at the annual meeting of the Society for the Scientific Study of Sexuality, Omaha, NE.

Sue, V. M., & Ritter, L. A. (2012). *Conducting online surveys* (2nd ed.). Los Angeles, CA: Sage.

Sullivan, A. K., Savage, E. J., Lowndes, C. M., Paul, G., Murphy, G., Carne, S., … Gill, O. N. (2013a). Non-disclosure of HIV status in U.K. sexual health clinics—a pilot study to identify non-disclosure within a national unlinked anonymous seroprevalence survey. *Sexually Transmitted Infections, 89*(2), 120–121.

Sullivan, J. F., Stember, D. S., Deveci, S., Akin-Olugbade, Y., & Mulhall, J. P. (2013b). Ejaculation profiles of men following radiation therapy for prostate cancer. *Journal of Sexual Medicine, 10*(5), 1410–1416.

Suschinsky, K. D., & Chivers, M. L. (2018). The relationship between sexual concordance and orgasm consistency in women. *Journal of Sex Research, 55*(6), 704–718.

Sutton, K. S., Stratton, N., Pytyck, J., Kolla, N. J., & Cantor, J. M. (2015). Patient characteristics by type of hypersexuality referral: A quantitative chart review of 115 consecutive male cases. *Journal of Sex & Marital Therapy, 41*(6), 563–580.

Syme, M. L., Klonoff, E. A., Macera, C. A., & Brodine, S. K. (2013). Predicting sexual decline and dissatisfaction among older adults: The role of partnered and individual physical and mental health factors. *Journals of Gerontology Series B: Psychological Sciences and Social Sciences, 68*(3), 323–332.

Syvertsen, J. L., Robertson, A. M., Rolon, M. L., Palinkas, L. A., Martinez, G., Rangel, M. G., & Strathdee, S. A. (2013). "Eyes that don't see, heart that doesn't feel": Coping with sex work in intimate relationships and its implications for HIV/STI prevention. *Social Science and Medicine, 87*, 1–8.

Taff, K, D., & Limke-McLean, A. (2019, November). *All the ways you love me: Links between love languages and relationship outcomes.* Poster presented at the Society for the Scientific Study of Sex annual meeting, Denver, CO.

Tamilin, E. R., Quinlan, M. M., & Bates, B. R. (2017). Assessing womanhood: Jenna Talackova and the marking of a beauty queen. *Sexuality & Culture, 21*(3), 703–718.

Tang, C. S., Siu, B. N., Lai, F. D., & Chung, T. K. (1996). Heterosexual Chinese women's sexual adjustment after gynecologic cancer. *Journal of Sex Research, 33*(3), 189–195.

Tannahill, E. (1982). *Sex in history.* New York, NY: Scarborough.

Tannen, D. (1990). *You just don't understand: Women and men in conversation.* London, UK: Virago.

Tavernise, S. (2016, September 21). Maternal mortality rate in U.S. rises, defying global trend, study finds. *The New York Times.* Retrieved from http://www.nytimes.com/2016/09/22/health/maternal-mortality.html?_r=1

Taylor, J. (2018). Out of the darkness and into the shadows: The evolution of contemporary bisexuality. *The Canadian Journal of Human Sexuality, 27*(2), 103–109.

Taylor, B. M. (1995). Gender-power relations and safer sex negation. *Journal of Advanced Nursing, 22*(4), 687–693.

Taylor, D, McCarthy, M., & Sikore, A. (2015, November). *Increased risk of depression and suicidality in adolescents who report same sex attraction in later life: Findings from a nationally representative longitudinal study.* Presented at the annual meeting of the Society for the Scientific Study of Sexuality, Albuquerque, NM.

Tener, D., Wolak, J., & Finkelhor, D. (2015). A typology of offenders who use online communications to commit sex crimes against minors. *Journal of Aggression, Maltreatment & Trauma, 24*(3), 319–337.

Teskereci, G., & Oncel, S. (2013). Effect of lifestyle on quality of life of couples receiving infertility treatment. *Journal of Sex & Marital Therapy, 39*(6), 476–492.

Teter, J. (2014, November). *They do it, too! The evaluation and clinical application of sexuality and clients with autism.* Continuing education session presented at the annual meeting of the Society for the Scientific Study of Sexuality, Omaha, NE.

Tewksbury, R., & Lapsey, D. (2018). It's more than just a big dick: Desires, experiences, and how male escorts satisfy their customers. *Deviant Behavior, 39*(1), 126–135.

Thamotharan, S., Grabowski, K., Stefano, E., & Sherecce, F. (2015). An examination of sexual risk behaviors in adolescent substance users. *International Journal of Sexual Health, 27*(2), 106–124.

The Henry J. Kaiser Family Foundation. (2015, November). *The global HIV/AIDS epidemic.* Retrieved from http://files.kff.org/attachment/fact-sheet-the-global-hivaids-epidemic

The Working Group on a New View of Women's Sexual Problems. (2000). *The new view manifesto: A new view of women's sexual problems.* Retrieved from http://www.newviewcampaign.org/manifesto.asp

Thibodeau, M. E., Lavoie, F., Hebert, M., & Blais, M. (2017). Pathways linking childhood maltreatment and adolescent sexual risk behaviors: The role of attachment anxiety. *The Journal of Sex Research, 54*(8), 994–1005.

Thompson, H. (2015, January 9). Female ejaculation comes in two forms. *New Scientist.* Retrieved from http://www.newscientist.com/article/dn26772-female-ejaculation-comes-in-two-forms-scientistsfind.html#.VLIFeSfCK4

Thomsen, D., & Chang, I. J. (2000, November). *Predictors of satisfaction with first intercourse: A new perspective for sexuality education.* Poster session presented at the annual conference for the National Council on Family Relations, Minneapolis, MN.

Tiidenberg, K., & Paasonen, S. (2019). Littles: Affects and aesthetics in sexual age-play. *Sexuality & Culture, 23*(2), 375–393.

Timmermans, E., & Courtois, C. (2018). From swiping to casual sex and/or committed relationships: Exploring the experiences of Tinder users. *Information Society, 34*(2), 59–70.

Tissot, S. A. (1758/1766). *Onania, or a treatise upon the disorders produced by masturbation* (A. Hume, Trans.). London, UK: J. Pridden (original work published 1758).

Tolentino, J. (2018, May 15). The rage of the incels. *The New Yorker.* Retrieved from https://www.newyorker.com/culture/cultural-comment/the-rage-of-the-incels.

Topco. (n.d.). *About Topco.* Retrieved from http://www.topcosales.com/pages/about-topco

Towne, A. (2019). Clitoral stimulation during penile-vaginal intercourse: A phenomenological study exploring sexual experiences in support of female orgasm. *The Canadian Journal of Human Sexuality, 28*(1), 68–80.

Traeen, B., Samuelsen, S. O., & Roen, K. (2016). Sexual debut ages in heterosexual, lesbian, gay, and bisexual young adults in Norway. *Sexuality & Culture, 20*(3), 699–716.

The Trevor Project. (n.d.). *About The Trevor Project: Programs and services.* Retrieved from http://www.thetrevorproject.org

Tromovitch, P. (2014, November). *The prevalence of pedophilia among normal men.* Poster presented at the annual meeting of the Society for the Scientific Study of Sexuality, Omaha, NE.

Truong, K. D., Reifsnider, O. S., Mayorga, M. E., & Spitler, H. (2013). Estimated number of preterm births and low birth weight children born in the United States due to maternal binge drinking. *Maternal and Child Health Journal, 17*(4), 677–688.

Tsatali, M., & Tsolaki, M. (2014). Sexual function in normal elders, MCI and patients with mild dementia. *Sexuality and Disability, 32*(2), 205–219.

Turchik, J., & Hassija, C. (2014). Female sexual victimization among college students: Assault severity, health risk behaviors, and sexual functioning. *Journal of Interpersonal Violence, 29*(13), 2439–2457.

Turetsky, B., Steil, J., Turetsky, K., Levine J., Perry, M., & Levine, C. (2014, August). *Cross-cultural conceptions of intimacy, marriage and close relationships.* Poster presented at the annual meeting of the American Psychological Association, Washington, DC.

Turner, D., Basdekis-Jozsa, R., & Briken, P. (2013). Prescription of testosterone-lowering medications for sex offender treatment in German forensic-psychiatric institutions. *Journal of Sexual Medicine, 10*(2), 570–578.

Tyiska, C. G. (1998, January 24). *Working with victims of crime with disabilities* [Bulletin]. Office for Victims of Crime. Retrieved from https://www.ncjrs.gov/ovc_archives/factsheets/disable.htm

Udry, J. R. (1998). Doing sex research on adolescents. In G. G. Brannigan, E. R. Allgeier, & A. R. Allgeier, *The sex scientists* (pp. 49–60). New York, NY: Longman.

Umberson, D., Thomeer, M. B., & Lodge, A. C. (2015). Intimacy and emotion work in lesbian, gay, and heterosexual relationships. *Journal of Marriage and Family, 77*(2), 542–556.

UNAIDS. (2019). *Global HIV & AIDS Statistics—2018 Fact Sheet.* Retrieved from: https://www.unaids.org/en/resources/fact-sheet

Unitarian Universalist Association. (2016, July 26). *Our whole lives: Lifespan sexuality education.* Retrieved from http://www.uua.org/re/owl

U.S. Government Accountability Office. (2016, June 30). *Female genital mutilation/cutting: Existing federal efforts to increase awareness should be improved.* Retrieved from http://www.gao.gov/products/%20GAO-16-645

Usigan, Y. (2011, September 30). Teen sexting driven by peer pressure, says study. *CBS News.* Retrieved from http://www.cbsnews.com/news/teen-sexting-driven-by-peer-pressure-says-study/

Ussher, J. M., & Perz, J. (2013). PMS as a gendered illness linked to the construction and relational experience of hetero-femininity. *Sex Roles, 68*(1), 132–150.

Vaillancourt, K. T., & Few-Demo, A. L. (2014). The relational dynamics of swinging relationships: An exploratory study. *The Family Journal, 22*(3), 311–320.

Vail-Smith, K., Whetstone, L., & Knox, D. (2010). The illusion of safety in "monogamous" undergraduate relationships. *American Journal of Health Behavior, 34*(1), 12–20.

van Bergen, D. D., Bos, H. M., van Lisdonk, J., Keuzenkamp, S., & Sandfort, T. G. (2013). Victimization and suicidality among Dutch lesbian, gay, and bisexual youths. *American Journal of Public Health, 103*(1), 70–72.

van de Grift, T. C., Elaut, E., Cerwenka, Cohen-Kettenis, P. T., & Kreukels, B. (2018). Surgical satisfaction, quality of life, and their association after gender-affirming surgery: A follow-up study. *Journal of Sex & Marital Therapy, 44*(2), 138–148.

Van den Brink, F., Vollmann, M., Smeets, M. A. M., Hessen, D. J., & Woertman, L. (2018). Relationship between body image, sexual satisfaction, and relationship quality in romantic couples. *Journal of Family Psychology, 32*(4), 466–474.

Vanden Brook, T. (2018, September 10) Pentagon hangs on to sexual assault study. *USA Today*, p. 3A.

Vanden Brook, T. (2019a, January 31) Sexual assault, harassment spikes at military academies, strategies fail to stem crisis. *USA Today*. p. A1.

Vanden Brook, T. (2019b, May 2). Shanahan calls for reforms as military sexual assaults rise by 38%; highest for young women. *USA Today*. p. A1.

Van Geloven, N., Van der Veen, F., Bossuyt, P. M., Hompes, P. G., Zwinderman, A. H., & Mol, B. W. (2013). Can we distinguish between infertility and subfertility when predicting natural conception in couples with an unfulfilled child wish? *Human Reproduction, 28*(3), 658–665.

Van Houdenhove, E., Gijs, L, T'Sjoen, G., & Enzlin, P. (2015). Stories about asexuality: A qualitative study on asexual women. *Journal of Sex & Marital Therapy, 41*(3), 262–281.

van Lankveld, J., & Mevissen, F. E. (2015). Bibliotherapy and internet-based programmes for sexual problems. In K. Wylie (Ed.), *ABC of sexual health*, (3rd ed.). (pp. 118–120). Awest Sussex, UK: John Wiley & Sons.

Van Ouytsel, J., Van Gool, E., Wolrave, M., Ponnet, K., and Peeters, E. (2017). Sexting: adolescents' perceptions of the applications for, motivations for, and consequences of sexting. *Journal of Youth Studies, 20*(4), 446–470.

Van San, M., & Bovenkerk, F. (2013). Secret seducers: True tales of pimps in the red light district of Amsterdam. *Crime Law and Social Change, 60*(1), 67–80.

Van Willigen, M. (2015, April). *Continuing debates around federal, state and individual rights: The case of marriage in the United States*. Panel discussion at East Carolina University, Greenville, NC.

Vannier, S. A., Adare, K. E., & Rosen, N. O. (2018). Is it me or you? First time mothers' attributions for postpartum sexual concerns are associated with sexual and relationship satisfaction in the transition to parenthood. *Journal of Social and Personal Relationships, 35*(4), 577–599.

Vanman, E. (2018, July). We asked catfish why they trick people online—it's not about money. *The Conversation*. Retrieved from https://phys.org/news/2018-07-catfish-people-onlineit-money.html

Varjas, K., Meyers, J., Kiperman, S., & Howard, A. (2013). Technology hurts? Lesbian, gay and bisexual youth perspectives of technology and cyberbullying. *Journal of School Violence, 12*(1), 27–44.

Vault Careers. (2019, February 14). *Attention Cubicle Cupids: The 2019 Office Romance Survey Results Are In!*. Retrieved from https://www.vault.com/blogs/workplace-issues/2019-vault-office-romance-survey-results

Vazsonyi, A. I., & Jenkins, D. D. (2010). Religiosity, self-control, and virginity status in college students from the "Bible belt": A research note. *Journal for the Scientific Study of Religion, 49*(3), 561–568.

Veale, D., Miles, S., Bramley, S., Muir, G., & Hodsoll, J. (2015). Am I normal? A systematic review and construction of nomograms for flaccid and erect penis length and circumference in up to 15,521 men. *BJU International, 115*(6), 978–986.

Velotti, P., Balzarotti, S. Tagliabue, T., English, G., Zavattini, C., & Gross, J. J. (2016). Emotional suppression in early marriage: Actor, partner, and similarity effects on marital quality. *Journal of Social and Personal Relationships, 33*(3), 277–302.

Velten, J., Margraf, J., Chivers, M. L., & Brotto, L. A. (2018). Effects of a mindfulness task on women's sexual response. *Journal of Sex Research, 55*(6), 747–757.

Vickers, R. (2010, March 22). *Sexuality of the elderly*. Presented during Sociology of Human Sexuality, East Carolina University, Greenville, NC.

Villar, F. Serrat, R., Celdran, M., Faba, J., & Martinez, T. (2019). Disclosing a LGB sexual identity: When living in an elderly long-term care facility: Common and best practices. *Journal of Homosexuality, 66*(7), 970–988.

Vissing, Y. (2018). Sexual debut education: Cultivating a health approach to young people's sexual experiences. *Sociological Studies of Children & Youth, 23*(23), 177–200.

Viswanath, K., & Basu, A. (2015). SafetiPin: An innovative mobile app to collect data on women's safety in Indian circles. *Gender & Development, 23*(1), 45–60.

Vitis, L., & Gilmour, F. (2017). Dick pics on blast: A woman's resistance to online sexual harassment using humour, art and Instagram. *Crime, Media, Culture, 13*(3), 335–355. doi: 10.1177/1741659016652445

Vogels, E. (2016, November). Porn, peers, and performing oral sex: The mediating role of peer norms on porn's influence regarding oral sex. Session 57 at the annual meeting of the Society for the Scientific Study of Sexuality, Phoenix, AZ.

Vogels, E., & Stewart, H. (2018, November). *Sexy messages or sexual harassment: Experiences of individuals who have received "dick pics."* Poster presented at the annual meeting of the Society for the Scientific Study of Sexuality, Montreal, Canada.

von der Osten-Sacken, T., & Uwer, T. (2007). Is female genital mutilation an Islamic problem? *Middle East Quarterly, Winter*, 29–36. Retrieved from http://www.meforum.org/1629/is-female-genital-mutilation-an-islamic-problem

Von Krafft-Ebing, R. F. (1965). *Psychopathia sexualis*. New York, NY: Arcade.

Vrangalova, Z. (2015). Hooking up and psychological well-being in college students: Short-term prospective links across different hookup definitions. *Journal of Sex Research, 52*(5), 485–498.

Wada, M., Hurd Clark, L., & Mortenson, W. B. (2019). 'I am busy independent woman who has sense of humor, caring about others': older adults' self-representations in online dating profiles. *Ageing & Society, 39*(5), 951–976.

Wagoner, Van. N. (2018, April 6). *Genital herpes: The sore and more*. Presented at the Conference on Contraceptive Technology, Washington, DC.

Wahlig, J. L. (2015). Losing the child they thought they had: Therapeutic suggestions for an ambiguous loss perspective with parents of a transgender child. *Journal of GLBT Family Studies, 11*(4), 305–326.

Waling, A., & Pym, T. (2017). 'C'mon, no one wants a dick pic': Exploring the cultural framings of the 'dick pic' in contemporary online publics. *Journal of Gender Studies, 28*(1), 70–85. doi: 10.1080/09589236.2017.1394821

Walker, J. J., Golub, S. A., Bimbi, D. S., & Parsons, J. T. (2012). Butch bottom—femme top? An exploration of lesbian stereotypes. *Journal of Lesbian Studies, 16*(1), 90–107.

Waller, W., & Hill, R. (1951). *The family: A dynamic interpretation*. New York, NY: Holt, Rinehart and Winston.

Wallien, M. S., & Cohen-Kettenis, P. T. (2008). Psychosexual outcome of gender-dysphoric children. *Journal of the American Academy of Child and Adolescent Psychiatry, 47*(12), 1413–1423.

Walters, A. S., & Burger, B. D. (2013). "I love you, and I cheated": Investigating disclosures of infidelity to primary romantic partners. *Sexuality & Culture, 17*(1), 20–49.

Wang, H. L. (2014, February 15). Walking down the widening isle of interracial marriages. *NPR*. Retrieved from http://www.npr.org/sections /codeswitch/2014/02/13/276516736/walking-down-the-widening-aisle-of-interracial-marriages

Wang, R. H., Jian, S. Y., & Yang, Y. M. (2011). Psychometric testing of the Chinese version of the Contraceptive Behavior Scale: A preliminary study. *Journal of Clinical Nursing, 22*(7–8), 1066–1072.

Wang, Y., Griffith, J., & Grande, G. (2018). The influence of gender identities on body image and breast health among sexual minority women in Taiwan: Implications for healthcare practices. *Sex Roles, 78*(3–4), 242–254.

Ward, K. M., Atkinson, J. P., Smith, C. A., & Windsor, R. (2013). A friendships and dating program for adults with intellectual and developmental disabilities: A formative evaluation. *Intellectual and Developmental Disabilities, 51*(1), 22–32.

Ward, L. M., Seabrook, R. C., Grower, P., Giaccardi, S., & Lippman, J. R. (2018). Sexual object or sexual subject? Media use, self-actualization, and sexual agency among undergraduate women. *Psychology of Women Quarterly, 42*(1), 29–43.

Ward, R., & Chang, I. J. (2015, November). *An exploration of the implementation of Title IX in regard to sexual violence on college campuses.* Roundtable discussion presented at the annual meeting of the National Council on Family Relations, Vancouver, BC.

Watson, E., & Pericak, S. (2014, November). *A snapshot of marginalized sexualities: Understanding reports of sexual satisfaction and sexual functioning in individuals who identify as pansexual.* Poster session presented at the annual meeting of the Society for the Scientific Study of Sexuality, Omaha, NE.

WebMD. (2019, October). *Drugs Linked to Erectile Dysfunction.* Rev. by N. Q. Bandukwala, Retrieved from https://www.webmd.com/erectile-dysfunction/guide/drugs-linked-erectile-dysfunction

Weill, K. (2017, April 24). North Carolina's Duggar-approved sex ed: The anti-gay, pro-life Focus on the Family may soon be crafting conservative sex ed curricula for North Carolina's public schools. *The Daily Beast.* Retrieved from http://www.thedailybeast.com/articles/2015/09/17/north -carolina-s-duggar-approved-sex-ed.html

Weinberg, M. S., Williams, C. J., & Calhan, C. (1995). "If the shoe fits …": Exploring male homosexual foot fetishism. *Journal of Sex Research, 32*(1), 17–27.

Weise, E., & Strauss, G. (2013, June 26). Across nation, gays celebrate court rulings. *USA Today*. Retrieved from http://www.usatoday.com/story /news/2013/06/26/supreme-court-rulings-applauded-by-gays/2459279/

Weiser, D. A., & Weigel, D. J. (2017). Exploring intergenerational patterns of infidelity. *Personal Relationships, 24*(4): 933–952.

Weisskirch, R., Drouin, S. M., & Delevi, R. (2017). Relational anxiety and sexting. *The Journal of Sex Research, 54*(6), 685–693.

Wells, B., Vrangalova, Z., Brill, A., Bird, E., & Lock. L. (2016, November). *Characteristics of sex parties and sex party attendees in the United States: Results of a national survey.* Session 37 at the annual meeting of the Society for the Scientific Study of Sexuality, Phoenix, AZ.

Wertheim, E., Paxton, S., & Blaney, S. (2009). Body image in girls. In L. Smolak & J. K. Thompson (Eds.), *Body image, eating disorders, and obesity in youth: Assessment, prevention, and treatment* (2nd ed., pp. 47–76). Washington, DC: American Psychological Association.

Wesche, R., Walsh, J. L., Shepardson, R. L., Carey, K. B., & Carey, M. P. (2019). The association between sexual behavior and affect: Moderating factors in young women. *Journal of Sex Research, 56*(8), 1058–1069.

Westfall, R. E., Janssen, P. A., Lucas, P., & Capler, R. (2006). Survey of medicinal cannabis use among childbearing women: Patterns of its use in pregnancy and retroactive self-assessment of its efficacy against "morning sickness." *Complementary Therapies in Clinical Practice, 12*(1), 27–33.

Whatley, M. (2006). *Attitudes toward infidelity scale* [Survey]. Published data from Valdosta State University, Valdosta, GA. Retrieved from https://www.scribd.com/doc/152231639/Attitudes-Toward-Infidelity-Scale

Whipple, B., & Komisaruk, B. R. (1999). Beyond the G spot: Recent research on female sexuality. *Psychiatric Annals, 29*(1), 34–37.

White, F. A., Verrellli, S., Maunder, R. D., & Kervinen, A. (2019). Using electronic contact to reduce homonegative attitudes, emotions, and behavioral intentions among heterosexual women and men: A contemporary extensions of the contact hypothesis. *The Journal of Sex Research, 56*(9), 1179–2019.

Whitfield, T. H. F., Jones, S. S., Wachman, M., Parsons, J. T., & Rendina, H. J. (2019). The Impact of Pre-Exposure Prophylaxis (PrEP) Use on Sexual Anxiety, Satisfaction, and Esteem Among Gay and Bisexual Men. *The Journal of Sex Research, 56*(9), 1128–1135.

Whithead, A. L. (2018). Homosexuality, religion and the family: The effects of religion on American's appraisals of the parenting abilities of same-sex couples. *Journal of Homosexuality, 65*(1), 42–65.

Whitton, S. W., Weitbrecht, E. M., Kuryluk, A. D., & Bruner, M. R. (2013). Committed dating relationships and mental health among college students. *Journal of American College Health, 61*(3), 176–183.

Wickel, K. (2012, November). *Partner support and postpartum depression: A review of the literature.* Poster session presented at the annual meeting of the National Council on Family Relations, Phoenix, AZ.

Widman, L., Golin, C. E., Kamke, K., Burnette, J. L., & Prinstein, M. (2018). Sexual assertiveness skills and sexual decision-making in adolescent girls: Randomized controlled trial of an online program. *American Journal of Public Health, 108*(1), 96–102. doi: 10.2105/AJPH.2017.304106

Wiederman, M. W. (1999). Volunteer bias in sexuality research using college student participants. *Journal of Sex Research, 36*(1), 59–66.

Wignall, L., & McCormack, M. (2015, December 14). An exploratory study of a new kink activity: "Pup play." *Archives of Sexual Behavior, 46*(3), 801–11. Retrieved from http://link.springer.com/article/10.1007/s10508-015-0636-8

Wijkman, M., Weerman, F., Bijleveld, C., & Hendriks, J. (2015). Group sexual offending by juvenile females. *Sexual Abuse: A Journal of Research & Treatment, 27*(3), 335–356.

Wiley, D., & Wilson, K. (2014, November). *Examining differences between perceived sexual partner reactions to condom use among adolescents.* Poster session presented at the annual meeting of the Society for the Scientific Study of Sexuality, Omaha, NE.

Wilkenfeld, B., & Ballan, M. (2011). Educators' attitudes and beliefs towards the sexuality of individuals with developmental disabilities. *Sexuality and Disability, 29*(4), 351–361.

Wilkinson, V. J., Theodore, K., & Raczka, R. (2015). "As normal as possible": Sexual identity development in people with intellectual disabilities transitioning to adulthood. *Sexuality and Disability, 33*(1), 93–105.

Williams, R. H., Irby, C. A., & Warner, R. S. (2018). "Dare to be different": How religious groups frame and enact appropriate sexuality and gender norms among young adults. *Sociological Studies of Children & Youth, 23*, pp. 1–22.

Williams, K. M., DeFazio, K., & Goins, R. M. (2014). Transitions: Negotiating sexual decision making in the life of students attending a Christian university. *Sexuality & Culture, 18*(3), 547–559.

Williams, K. S., & Bierie, D. M. (2015). An incident-based comparison of female and male sexual offenders. *Sexual Abuse: A Journal of Research and Treatment, 27*(3), 235–257.

Williams, L., & Russell, S. (2013). Shared social and emotional activities within adolescent romantic and non-romantic sexual relationships. *Archives of Sexual Behavior, 42*(4), 649–658.

Williams, L. R., Wray-Lake, L., Loken, E., & Maggs, J. L. (2012). The effects of adolescent heavy drinking on the timing and stability of cohabitation and marriage. *Families in Society, 93*(3), 181–188.

Willoughby, B. J., & Carroll, J. S. (2012). Correlates of attitudes toward cohabitation: Looking at the associations with demographics, relational attitudes, and dating behavior. *Journal of Family Issues, 33*(11), 1450–1476.

Willoughby, B. J., Carroll, J., & Busby, D. (2014a, November). *What is porn? Exploring variations in the self-definition of pornography.* Presented at the annual meeting of the Society for the Scientific Study of Sexuality, Omaha, NE.

Willoughby, B. J., Carroll, J. S., Nelson, L. J., & Padilla-Walker, L. (2014b). Associations between relational sexual behaviour, pornography use, and pornography acceptance among U.S. college students. *Culture, Health & Sexuality, 16*(9), 1052–1069.

Willoughby, B. J., & Leonhardt, N. B. (2020). Behind closed doors: Individual and joint pornography use among romantic couples. *Journal of Sex Research, 57*(1), 77–91.

Willoughby, B. J., Young-Petersen, B., & Leonhardt, N. D. (2018). Exploring trajectories of pornography use through adolescence and emerging adulthood. *The Journal of Sex Research, 55*(3), 297–309.

Wilson, C. L., & Flicker, S. (2018). Let's talk about sex for money: An exploration of economically motivated relationships among young black women in Canada. *Sociological Studies of Children & Youth, 23*, 97–119.

Wilson, K., Kortes-Miller, K., & Stinchcombe, A. (2018). Staying out of the closet: LGBT older adults' hopes and fears in considering end of life. *Canadian Journal on Aging, 37* (1), 22–31.

Winters, G. M., & Jeglic, E. L. (2017). Stages of sexual grooming: Recognizing potentially predatory behaviors of child molesters. *Deviant Behavior, 38*(6), 724–733.

Witcomb, G. L., Bouman, W. P., Brewin, N., Richards, C., Fernandez-Aranda, F., & Arcelus, J. (2015). Body image dissatisfaction and eating-related psychopathology in trans individuals: A matched control study. *European Eating Disorders Review, 23*(4), 287–293.

Wittmann, D., Northouse, L., Crossley, H., Miller, D., Dunn, R., Nidetz, J., … Montie, J. E. (2015). A pilot study of potential pre-operative barriers to couples' sexual recovery after radical prostatectomy for prostate cancer. *Journal of Sex & Marital Therapy, 41*(2), 155–168.

Wlodarski, R., & Dunbar, R. I. (2013). Examining the possible functions of kissing in romantic relationships. *Archives of Sexual Behavior, 42*(8), 1415–1423.

Woerner, J., & Abbey, A. (2017). Positive feelings after casual sex: The role of gender and traditional gender-role beliefs. *The Journal of Sex Research, 54*(6), 717–727.

Wolak, J., & Finkelhor, D. (2013). Are crimes by online predators different from crimes by sex offenders who know youth in-person? *Journal of Adolescent Health, 53*(6), 736–741.

Wolfe, L. (2016a, November). *Herpes: Folklore, fear and realities.* Session 39 at the annual meeting of the Society for the Scientific Study of Sexuality, Phoenix, AZ.

Wolfe, L. (2016b, November). *The culture of cybersex and Internet chat.* Poster presented at the annual meeting of the Society for the Scientific Study of Sexuality, Phoenix, AZ.

Wolff, M., Wells, B., Ventura-DiPersia, C., Renson, A., & Gro, C. (2017). Measuring sexual orientation: A review and critique of U. S. data collection efforts and implications for health policy. *The Journal of Sexual Research, 54*(4–5), 507–531.

Wolfinger, N. (2018). Does sexual history affect marital happiness? *Institute for Family Studies.* October 22, 2018. Retrieved from https://ifstudies.org/blog/does-sexual-history-affect-marital-happiness

Wollstonecraft, M. (1792). *A vindication of the rights of women: With strictures on political and moral subjects.* Boston, MA: Peter Edes.

Women's Health Initiative. (2008, March 4). *WHI follow-up study confirms health risks of long-term combination hormone therapy outweigh benefits for postmenopausal women.* Retrieved from https://www.nih.gov/news-events/news-releases/whi-follow-study-confirms-health-risks-long-term-combination-hormone-therapy-outweigh-benefits-postmenopausal-women

Women's Health Initiative (WHI). (2010, February 15). *WHI study data confirm short-term heart disease risks of combination hormone therapy for postmenopausal women.* Retrieved from https://www.nih.gov/news-events/news-releases/whi-study-data-confirm-short-term-heart-disease-risks-combination-hormone-therapy-postmenopausal-women

Women's Health Research Institute. (n.d.). *Stages of menopause: Before, during & after.* Retrieved from http://menopause.northwestern.edu/content/stages-menopause

Women's Health Specialists of California. (n.d.). *What is menstrual extraction?* Retrieved from http://www.womenshealthspecialists.org/self-help/menstrual-extraction/

Wong, J. S., & Gravel, J. (2018). Do sex offenders have higher levels of testosterone? Results from a meta-analysis. *Sexual Abuse: A Journal of Sex Research & Treatment, 30*(2), 147–168.

Wong, W. I., & Hines. M. (2015). Effects of gender color-coding on toddler's gender-typical toy play. *Archives of Sexual Behavior, 44*(5), 1233–1242.

Wood, J., Crann, S., Cunningham, S., Money, D., & D'Doherty, K. (2017). A cross-sectional survey of sex toy use, characteristics of sex toy use hygiene behaviors, and vulvovaginal health outcomes. *The Canadian Journal of Human Sexuality, 26*(3), doi: 10.3138/cjhs.2017-0016

Wood, J., Desmarais, S., Burleigh, T., & Milhausen, R. (2018). Reasons for sex and relational outcomes in consensually nonmonogamous and monogamous relationships. *Journal of Social & Personal Relationships, 35*(4), 632–654.

Workowski, K., & Bolan, G. (2015). Centers for Disease Control and Prevention: Sexually transmitted disease treatment guidelines, 2015. *Morbidity and Mortality Weekly Report, 64*(RR3), 1–137.

World Association for Sexual Health. (2019, October). *Declaration on Sexual Pleasure.* Presented at Mexico City World Congress of Sexual Health, Mexico City, MX. Retrieved from https://worldsexualhealth.net/declaration-on-sexual-pleasure/

World Health Organization Department of Reproductive Health and Research (WHO/RHR) and Johns Hopkins Bloomberg School of Public Health/ Center for Communication Programs (CCP). (2018 update). Knowledge for Health Project. *Family Planning: A Global Handbook for Providers.* (Baltimore and Geneva: CCP and WHO). Retrieved from http://fphandbook.org/sites/default/files/global-handbook-2018-full-web.pdf

World Health Organization. (2015, October 28). *Globally, an estimated two-thirds of the population under 50 are infected with herpes simplex virus type 1.* Retrieved from http://www.who.int/mediacentre/news/releases/2015/herpes/en/

World Health Organization. (2019a, August 2). *Global Health Observatory Data Repository. Antiretroviral Therapy Coverage Data and Estimates by WHO Region.* Retrieved from: http://apps.who.int/gho/data/view.main.23300REGION?lang=en

World Health Organization. (2019b, August 2). *Global Health Observatory Data Repository. Number of People (All Ages) Living with HIV Estimates by WHO Region.* Retrieved from: http://apps.who.int/gho/data/view.main.22100WHO?lang=en

World Health Organization. (2019c, June 14). *Sexually transmitted infections (STIs).* Fact Sheet. Retrieved from: https://www.who.int/news-room/fact-sheets/detail/sexually-transmitted-infections-(stis)

World Health Organization. (2019d, November 15). *HIV/AIDS. Key Facts.* Retrieved from: https://www.who.int/news-room/fact-sheets/detail/hiv-aids

Wright, P. J., Tokunaga, R. S., Kraus, A., & Klann, E. (2017). Pornography consumption and satisfaction: A meta-analysis. *Human Communication Research, 43*(3), 315–343. doi:10.1111/hcre.12108

Wright, P. J. (2013). U.S. males and pornography, 1973–2010: Consumption, predictors, correlates. *Journal of Sex Research, 50*(1), 60–71.

Wright, P. J. (2015). Americans' attitudes toward premarital sex and pornography consumption: A national panel analysis. *Archives of Sexual Behavior, 44*(1), 89–97.

Wright, P. J., Randall, A. K., & Hayes, J. G. (2012). Predicting the condom assertiveness of collegiate females in the United States from the expanded health belief model. *International Journal of Sexual Health, 24*(2), 137–153.

Wright, R. G., Leblanc, A. J., & Badgett, L. (2013). Same-sex legal marriage and psychological well-being. Findings from the California health interview survey. *American Journal of Public Health, 103*(2), 339–346.

Wu, S., & Ward, J. (2018) The mediation of gay men's lives: A review of gay dating app studies. *Sociology Compass, 12*(2), 1–10.

Xishan, H., Xiso-Lu, Z., Juan, Z., Lin, Z., & Shiomi, K. (2012). Relationships among androgyny, self-esteem, and trait coping style of Chinese university students. *Social Behavior & Personality: An International Journal, 40*(6), 1005–1014.

Yacan, L., & Erol, O. (2019). Evaluation of sexual function among women with or without diabetes. *Sexuality and Disability, 37*(1), 77–90.

Yakushko. O., & Rajan, I. (2017). Global love for sale: Divergence and convergence of human trafficking with "mail order brides" and international arranged marriage phenomena. *Women & Therapy, 40*(1–2), 190–206.

Yaman, S., & Ayaz, S. (2016). Psychological problems experienced by women with gynecological cancer and how they cope with it: A phenomenological study in Turkey. *Health and Social Work, 41*(3), 173–181.

Yates, P. (2018). "Siblings as Better Together": Social worker decision making in cases involving sibling sexual behavior. *British Journal of Social Work, 48*(1), 176–194.

Yazedjian, A., Toews, M. L., & Daniel, K. (2014, November). *College males' and females' perceptions of and experiences with hooking up.* Poster session presented at the annual meeting of the National Council on Family Relations, Baltimore, MD.

Yeager, J. (2012). A content analysis of an online support group for survivors of sexual violence. *E-Health Communities and Online Self-Help Groups, 85–105.* Retrieved from http://www.igi-global.com/chapter/content-analysis-online-support-group/59978

Yeater, E., Montanaro, E., & Bryan, A. (2015). Predictors of sexual coercion and alcohol use among female juvenile offenders. *Journal of Youth & Adolescence, 44*(1), 114–126.

Yelland, E., & Hosier, A. (2017). Public attitudes toward sexual expression in long-term care: Does context matter? *Journal of Applied Gerontology, 36*(8), 1016–1031.

Yildiz, H. (2015). The relation between prepregnancy sexuality and sexual function during pregnancy and the postpartum period: A prospective study. *Journal of Sex & Marital Therapy, 41*(1), 49–59.

Yiou, R., Ebrahiminia, V., Mouracade, P., Lingombet, O., & Abbou, C. (2013). Sexual quality of life in women partnered with men using intracavernous alprostadil injections after radical prostatectomy. *Journal of Sexual Medicine, 10*(5), 1355–1362.

Yockery, R. A., King, K. A., Vidourek, R., Burbage, M., & Merianos, A. (2019). The depiction of sexuality among university students on Snapchat. *Sexuality & Culture, 23*(1),132–141.

Youn, G. (2018). Attitudinal changes toward homosexuality during the past two decades (1994-2014) in Korea. *Journal of Homosexuality, 65*(1), 100–116.

Young, A. (2018, June 27). Hospitals know how to protect mothers: They just aren't doing it. *USA Today*, p. 1A.

Young-Petersen, B., & Willoughby, B. (2016, November) *Early exposure to pornography: Individual and relational outcomes.* Presented at the annual meeting of the Society for the Scientific Study of Sexuality, Phoenix, AZ.

Youssouf, S. (2013). Female genital mutilations: A testimony. *The European Journal of Contraception & Reproductive Health Care, 18*(1), 5–9.

Zaharatos, J., St. Pierre, A., Cornell, A., Pasalic, E., & Goodman, D. (2018). Building U.S. capacity to review and prevent maternal deaths. *Journal of Women's Health, 27*(1), 1–5.

Zamboni, B. D. (2018) Partner knowledge and involvement in adult baby/diaper lover behavior. *Journal of Sex & Marital Therapy, 44*(2), 159–171.

Zamboni, B. D., & Zaid, S. J. (2017). Human sexuality education in marriage and family therapy graduate programs. *Journal of Marital & Family Therapy, 43*(4), 605–616.

Zammitt, K. A., Pepperell, J., & Coe, M. (2015). Implementing an ally development model to promote safer schools for LGB youth: A trans-disciplinary approach. *Journal of Homosexuality, 62*(6), 687–700.

Zapien, N. (2017) Participation bias and social desirability effects in research on extramarital affairs: Considerations of meaning and implications for sexual behavior research. *Archives of Sexual Behavior, 46*(60), 1565–1571.

Zentner, M., & Knox, D. (2013). Surrogates in relationship therapy: A case study in learning how to talk, touch, and kiss. *Psychology Journal, 10*(2), 63–68.

Zeigler, B. S., & Muscarella, F. (2019, November). *Sex and sexual orientation differences in emotional expression.* Poster presented at the Society for the Scientific Study of Sex annual meeting, Denver, CO.

Zhang, X. (2010). Charging children with child pornography: Using the legal system to handle the problem of "sexting." *Computer Law & Security Review, 26*(3), 251–259.

Ziv, I., Lubin, B. H., & Asher, S. (2018). "I swear I will never betray you": Factors reported by spouses as helping them resist extra marital sex in relation to gender, marriage, length, and religiosity. *Journal of Sex Research, 55*(2), 236–251.

Zivony, A., & Saguy, T. (2018). Stereotype deduction about bisexual women. *Journal of Sex Research, 55*(4–5), 666–678.

Zsok, F., Haucke, M., DeWit, C. Y., & Barelds, D. P. H. (2017). What kind of love is love at first sight? An empirical investigation. *Personal Relationships, 24*(4), 869–885.

Zwier, S. (2014). "What motivates her": Motivations for considering labial reduction surgery as recounted on women's online communities and surgeons' websites. *Sexual Medicine, 2*(1), 16–23.

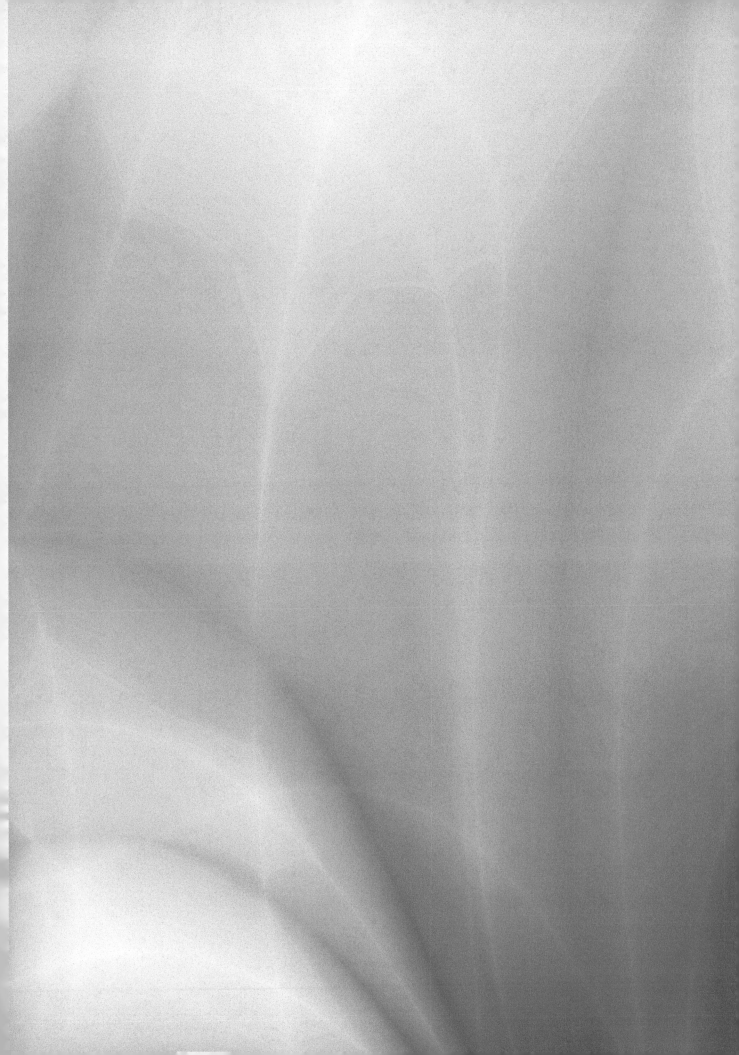

Author Index

A

Abbasi, I. S. 20
Abedi, P. 365
Abma, J. C. 222
Acuña, M. J. 292
Adamson, K. 149
Adeagbo, O. A. 49, 261
Adkins, T. 144
Adler, A. 260
Adolfsen, A. 266
Agarwal, P. 478
Aguilar, J. 148
Aizer, A. 463
Albersen, M. 376
Allan, P. 179
Allen, P. L. 195, 196, 197
Allison, R. 143
Alonzo, D. J. 259
Alves, S. 355
Amezcua-Prieto, C. 342
Andelloux, M. 512
Anderson, H. 126
Andersson, G. 46
Andrews, T. 69
Angel, L. 21
Annon, J. 389
Arakawa, D. R. 30
Arocho, R. 349
Ashton, S. 52
Aubrey, J. S. 143, 226
Averett, S. H. 221
Ayesha 524

B

Babin, E. A. 170
Bacchus, N. S. 20
Bachmann, H. 518
Bahouq, H. 293
Bailey, B. 197
Bal, D. M. 282
Baldas, T. 66
Balderrama-Durbin, C. 232
Balzarini, R. 146
Bandini, E. 111
Barber, L. L. 231
Barnett, M. D. 8
Barrett, E. S. 230
Barriger, M. 143
Bartz, D. 321
Basson, R. 83, 84
Battiste, N. 459
Batuman, E. 231
Bay-Cheng, L. 476
Bay-Cheng, L. Y. 49, 115
Beale, K. 156
Bearak, J. M. 308
Becasen, J. S. 13
Bedi, R. 484

Bedor, E. 243
Begley, S. 123
Begum, S. 527
Belous, C. K. 257
Bennett, M. 169
Bennhold, K. 478
Benoit, C. 282, 517
Berdychevsky, L. 9
Bergdall, A. R. 173
Berg, R. C. 519
Bermant, G. 235
Bernal, A. T. 386
Berry, M. D. 362, 386
Bersamin, M. M. 9, 211
Bettina, S. 68
Bindel, J. 512
Bird, E. R. 474
Bishop, C. J. 269
Blackstrom, L. 144
Blackwell, C. W. 261
Blackwell, C. W. W. 443
Blag, E. C. 459
Bland, A. M. 139
Blaszcznski, A. 255
Bleakley, A. 19, 24
Blithe, S. J. 523
Blodgett, J. 124
Blumer, M. 146, 256
Blumer, M. L. 479, 484, 485
Blunt-Vinti, H. 166
Bockting, W. O. 111
Boislard, M. 207
Bolden, S. 398
Bolen, R. M. 482
Bomey, N. 490
Bonet, M. L. 69
Boonstra, H. D. 224
Bothe, B. 505, 513
Bouffard, J. 464
Bowleg, L. 44
Boyer, D. 524
Boylan, S. M. 343
Boyle, K. M. 464
Bragg, B. 117
Braksmajer, A. 165, 232
Brandes, M. 348
Branfman, J. 205
Braun-Harvey, D. 415
Breedlove, S. M. 254, 255
Breuer, R. 7, 210
Bridges, A. J. 511
Bridle, E. 175
Brison, D. 377
Brizendine, L. 121
Brodsky, A. 314, 447
Brooks-Gunn, J. 78, 79
Brown, S. 333
Brown, Z. 19
Browne, K. D. 408
Brumbaugh-Johnson, S. M. 256
Buck, A. E. 266
Budge, S. L. 462, 474

Buehler, S. 337, 346
Buhi, E. 432
Bullough, V. L. 197, 482
Bunt, S. 139
Burgess, A. W. 474
Burghart, K. O. 519
Burke Winkleman, S. 177
Burri, A. 362
Burris, C. T. 64
Busby, D. M. 45
Buss, D. M. 122
Butler, S. M. 23
Buunk, A. P. 155
Buxton, A. P. 260

C

Cambridge, P. 292
Campa, M. I. 14
Canan, S. 23
Canan, S. N. 474
Cantor, J. M. 254, 418
Carey, A. R. 184
Carlson, D. L. 107
Caron, S. 64
Caron, S. L. 192
Carpenter, L. M. 192
Carter, J. 295
Cartwright, A. F. 329
Carvalheira, A. 6
Cashman, E. G. 145
Cassell, C. 308
Caughlin, J. P. 180
Cavazos-Rehg, P. A. 224
Chadwick, S. B. 82
Chalker, R. 76
Chang, J. 143, 144
Chapman, G. 139
Chen, Y. J. 361
Cherner, R. A. 384
Chevallier, D. 94
Chi, X. 202
Chiesa, A. 362
Cho, S. B. 227
Chonody, J. M. 268, 269
Christensen, M. C. 218
Christopher, S. 415
Chung, E. 377
Cimpian, J. R. 45
Cinthio, H. 66
Clarke, V. 256
Coakley, T. M. 19, 20, 223
Coffman, H. 11
Cohen, J. N. 262
Cohen, M. T. 151, 166
Cohen, S. A. 332
Cohn, A. M. 474
Colapinto, J. 109
Coleman, E. 130
Collazo, E. 136, 216
Collins, M. E. 221

Conley, C. 484
Conley, T. D. 151
Connell, K. M. 293
Conroy, N. 462
Cooley, C. H. 176
Cooper, A. 16
Cooper, M. L. 300
Coppens, V. 405
Corbett, S. L. 262
Cormier, L. A. 378, 381
Corsini-Munt, S. 383
Costa, R. M. 92
Costello, M. 266
Cote-Arsenault, D. 346
Couch, A. 479
Courtice, E. L. 503
Covell, T. 511
Cramer, K. 427
Cranney, S. 227, 409
Crowley, A. D. 463
Cunningham, K. 365
Cunningham, S. 528
Curtis, S. 501
Cutler, W. B. 86

D

Daar, D. A. 478
D'Amico, E. 258
da Silva Lara, L. A. 206
Daspe, M. E. 515
Davies, E. 240
Davis, A. C. 511
Davis, G. 120
Davis, K. N. 225
Dawson, K. 515, 516
De Block, A. 397, 398, 399
De Groot, K. 271
DeHaan, S. 259
DeHart, D. D. 229
De Jong, D. C. 144
Della, R. L. 518
Deming, M. E. 464
Denison, H. J. 453
Dennis, A. 33
DePaulo, B. M. 179
Derlega, V. J. 184
De Santis, J. P. 261
De Santisteban, P. 408
De Vries, A. L. 114
Diamond, M. 110, 255, 501
DiMauro, J. 474
Diokno, A. C. 86
Diop, M. K. 68
DiPlacidio, J. 257
Dobson, K. 165
Dockterman, E. 479, 489
Dolan, A. 434
Dolan, K. 110
Donatello, R. A. 222
Donenberg, G. 428
Donnelly, J. 286
Donovan, M. K. 51
Doornwaard, S. M. 501
Döring, N. 21, 201
Dosch, A. 6

Dossett, J. 5
Dourado, M. 288
Doyle, C. 80
Drescher, J. 415
Driemeyer, W. 200
Drouin, M. 175, 177
Drucker, J. 523
Dube, S. 146
Ducharme, J. K. 272
Dufur, M. J. 220
Duncan, B. L. 173
Duncan, D. 261
Dunsieth, N. W. 418
DuPree, M. G. 254
Durant, B. 519

E

East, P. 463
Easterling, B. D. 178
Easton, S. D. 484
Eaton, N. R. 298
Ecker, J. 365
Edwards, S. R. 471
Eeckhaut, M. C. W. 322
Efrati, Y. 22
Eiseman, P. 178
Elder, W. B. 402
Elias, V. L. 8
Eliason, M. 274
Ellis, L. 255, 469
Ellis, L. D. 12
Emmers-Sommer, T. M. 156, 515
Epstein, S. 14
Erbil, N. 127
Erenel, A. S. 362
Erichsen, K. 31, 42, 144
Esterline, K. M. 404
Estill, A. 239
Evans, C. 445

F

Faccini, L. 401
Fahs, B. 45
Farivar, C. 201
Farley, M. 522, 525
Farris, C. 175
Farr, R. H. 266
Farvid, P. 10, 13
Faustino, M. J. 201
Fausto-Sterling, A. 254
Fava, N. M. 484
Favez, N. 155
Fedewa, A. L. 273
Fedina, L. 458
Fehr, S. K. 447
Feng, G. C. 500
Ferguson, C. E. 484
Ferraro, M. M. 514
Ferreira, J. M. 12
Fetterolf, J. C. 11
Fielder, R. L. 144
Fileborn, B. 239, 242, 446
Finer, L. B. 222

Fiorini, M. 253
Fishburn, E. 24
Fisher, A. D. 236
Fisher, N. L. 463, 466
Fitzgerald, C. 290
Flanders, C. E. 124, 253, 257, 273
Fledderjohann, J. 347
Fletcher, G. 48
Flores, A. R. 111, 218
Flotynska, J. 286
Flynn, E. 179
Fogel, C. I. 453
Fogel, J. 226
Forbat, L. 377
Forbes, M. K. 243
Forsman, M. 469
Fortenberry, J. D. 165
Fox, K. 21
Franco, O. H. 240
Frank, S. E. 120
Franklin, A. 483
Freeman, C. 284
French, B. H. 459, 461
Freysteinsdóttir, F. J. 139
Frith, L. 349
Fritsch, K. 527
Frost, K. 6, 7
Frutos, A. 512
Frye-Cox, N. E. 184
Fuentealba-Torres, M. 363
Fugl-Meyer, K. S. 384
Fulle, A. 11, 38, 126, 128, 156

G

Gagnon, J. H. 38
Gaither, T. W. 93
Galinsky, A. M. 102, 203
Galperin, A. 7
Gao, J. 102
Gariepy, A. M. 453
Garneau-Fournier, J. 359
Gartrell, N. 273
Gato, J. 338
Gatzeva, M. 155
Gee, A. 521
Geher, G. 201
Gelabert, E. 355
Geonet, M. 367, 369
George, W. H. 24
Gesselman, A. N. 191
Gewirtz-Meydan, A. 387
Ghajarzadeh, M. 293
Ghanem, H. 94
Giami, A. 374
Gibbs, N. 173
Gill, R. 458, 478
Gill, T. 253
Gillespie, S. M. 482
Giordano, A. L. 415, 415
Gkyamerah, A. O. 258
Glina, S. 377
Glowacka, M. 383
Gogno, M. 386
Goldfarb, E. 222, 223
Gontero, P. 94

Gonzalez-Rivas, S. 115
Goodin, S. M. 409
Goodman, D. L. 82
Gottman, J. 168
Gottman, J. M. 168
Gowen, L. K. 23
Goyal, N. K. 346
Graf, N. 491
Graff, K. 409
Graham, S. 197
Grant, M. G. 527
Granville, L. 239
Grauvogl, A. 360
Greaves, L. M. 251
Greeff, A. P. 183
Green, E. 23
Green, R. J. 262
Gregory, K. D. 351
Griffith, S. 466
Griffiths, M. D. 505
Grimes, D. A. 331
Grose, R. 11
Grossman, J. M. 20
Grov, C. 92, 525
Grubbs, J. B. 21
Guendelman, S. 342
Guida, J. 523
Guler, T. 79
Gunderson, C. 207
Guo, G. 10
Gupta, K. 250

H

Haapsamo, H. 184
Haas, A. L. 24
Hafner, J. 321
Hahn, H. A. 13
Hakim, C. 128
Hall, K. S. 209
Hall, M. 92, 516
Hall, S. 8, 9, 128, 142, 145, 150, 155,
    157, 178, 190, 203, 204, 210, 230,
    249, 298, 320, 330, 331, 446, 464, 465
Halligan, C. 209
Hammack, P. L. 250
Hampton, M. D. 521
Hamzelou, J. 349
Hankes, K. 153
Hannaford, P. C. 311
Hargie, O. 111
Harknett, K. 18
Harris, A. L. 76, 80, 85
Harris, R. J. 472
Haselton, M. G. 175
Hauge, L. J. 343
Haupert, M. L. 152
Haym, C. 414
Haywood, C. 261
Hazan, C. 144
Heidari, M. 347
Hellman, J. 23
Helmus, L. 408
Helweg-Larsen, M. 449
Hendrick, S. S. 140
Hendrickx, L. 359

Henry, N. 488
Henshaw, M. 515
Hequembourg, A. L. 273, 480
Herbenick, D. 64, 73, 239, 381, 487
Herbst, J. H. 445
Hernandez, B. F. 207
Hernandez-Kane, K. M. 22
Heron, K. E. 127
Heywood, W. 8, 243
Hille, J. 250
Hilliard, T. 11, 20, 158, 170
Hilliard, T. E. 125
Hinchliff, S. 359
Hines, D. A. 476
Hines, T. M. 73
Hintistan, S. 286
Ho, P. S. Y. 30
Holland, L. 269
Holway, G. V. 265
Hom, K. A. 529
Hope, D. 257
Horowitz, A. D. 11
Horswill, A. 526
Horvath, M. 471
Hosain, G. M. 364
Hoskins, R. 259
Houtepen, J. A. 419
Howard, J. 425, 434
Hoy, A. 272
Hoy, S. M. 375
Hsu, K. J. 412
Huang 12
Huda, S. 527
Hudson, A. 143
Hughes, L. 68
Humphreys, L. 47
Humphreys, T. P. 192
Humphries-Waa, H. 114
Hunt, M. 142
Huntington, C. 516
Hutton, H. E. 453

I

Iasenza, S. 368
Ingraham, C. 96, 224
Introcaso, C. E. 95
Irvine, J. M. 29
Ivanski, C. 4
Iveniuk, J. 242
Iwamoto, D. 112

J

Jäckle, S. 269
Jackman, M. 232
Jacobs, H. 519
Jahnke, S. 409
James, R. 262
James, S. E. 463
James-Kangal, N. 144
Jardin, C. 11
Jasper, M. 126
Jatlaoui, T. C. 329
Javaid, A. 466

Jawed-Wessel, S. 346
Jayson, S. 144, 210, 227
Jeanfreau, M. M. 237
Jeckell, A. S. 466
Jenkins, I. 95
Jensen, H. M. 343
Jeong, S. 479, 485
Jerman, J. 324
Jesser, C. J. 167
Jiann, B. P. 368
Jiao, S. 523, 524
Jing, S. 200
Joel, D. 121
Johnson, K. 514
Johnston, L. 7, 92, 93
Jolly, N. 354
Jones, A. 387
Jones, J. H. 46
Jones, R. K. 332
Jones, R. L. 263
Jordan-Young, R. 121
Joshi, P. 258
Jovanovic, J. 145
Joyal, C. C. 402, 403, 404,
    405, 407, 408
Jozkowski, K. 19, 464

K

Kaestle, K. E. 253
Kahn, N. F. 289
Kaiser, A. 284
Kalfoglou, A. 117
Kane, M. D. 269
Kann, L. 222
Kaplan, H. 84
Kaplan, H. S. 388
Karioris, F. G. 128
Karraker, A. 243
Kasper, T. E. 515
Kattari, S. K. 111, 113, 282
Katz, J. 459
Kaya, C. 374
Kearney, M. S. 226
Kedde, H. 296
Kelly, A. 347
Kelly, C. R. 64
Kelly, M. 491
Kemerer, B. 242
Kempeneers, P. 375
Kendler, K. S. 254
Kennedy, H. R. 272
Kensboc, S. 488
Kerr, D. L. 273
Kerr, Z. Y. 265
Kettrey, H. H. 127
Kijak, R. 289
Kilimnik, C. 190
Killoren, S. E. 221
Kim, C. 409
Kim, J. 170
Kimberly, C. 146, 151
Kimbrough, A. M. 184
Kimmons, J. 231
King, A. L. S. 174
King, B. M. 3, 92

Kinsey, A. C. 21, 197, 202, 251, 252
Kirby, B. J. 273
Kirk, K. M. 254
Kirk, M. 511
Kirkman, L. 231
Kirsch, A. C. 126
Kleimplatz, P. J. 84, 373
Klein, A. 111, 112
Klein, K. 256
Klein, V. 20
Klettke, B. 175
Klipfel, K. M. 459
Knox, D. 20, 138, 179, 201, 478
Kohlberg, L. 123, 124
Kohut, T. 515
Komarnicky, T. 6
Kong, T. S. 525
Kongsved, S. M. 46
Kontula, O. 221
Koop, C. E. 516
Koss, M. P. 462
Kozin, A. 166
Krajewski, S. 242
Kucur Suna, K. 348
Kuhle, B. X. 124
Kumar, N. 520
Kuortti, M. 222
Kurdek, L. A. 260, 261
Kutchko, V. 476
Kwak, T. I. 94
Kwon, K. A. 124

L

Laan, E. 379, 380
LaGasse, L. L. 344
Lammers, J. 232
Langlais, M. R. 21
Laura, G. T. 69
Laverty, E. 145
Lazo, G. 126
Leavitt, C. 83
Leavitt, C. E. 458
Lee, J. W. 102
Lee, M. 175, 177
Lee, S. J. 330
Leeming, D. 69
Leeners, B. 361
Lefkowitz, E. 136
Lefkowitz, E. S. 210
Leggitt, K. 349
Lehmiller, J. 30
Leickly, E. 261
Leonhardt, N. 82
Lermann, J. 295
Levenson, J. S. 482
Lever, J. 255
Levin, D. 23
Levine, D. 259
Levitt, H. M. 256, 412
Levitt, M. J. 181
Lew-Starowicz, M. 282
Liao, L. M. 64
Lien, I. L. 67, 68
Liew, Z. 344
Lindemann, H. 346

Ling, J. 193
Linton, K. F. 282
Linz, D. 510
Liong, M. 175
Lippman, J. R. 175
Lo, S. S. 363
Loftus, E. F. 483
Logan, L. S. 488
Loiacano, D. K. 258
Lomas, T. 136
Lomash, E. 269
Londo, S. 165
Longest, K. C. 21
LoPiccolo, J. 389
Lorimer, K. 14
Loshek, E. 115, 127
Lottes, I. L. 470, 471
Luk, B. H. 348
Lulu, R. A. 19
Lund, E. M. 282
Lundrigan, S. 466, 472
Luo, T. Y. 489
Lyne, K. 261
Lyyerzapf, H. 273

M

Ma, P. 69
Maas, M. K. 128, 355
Macapagal, K. 260
MacDorman, M. F. 351
MacDougall, K. 347
MacKell, J. 517
MacMillan, H. L. 479, 480
Madden, M. 46
Maggi, M. 374
Mai, N. 525
Maier, T. 43
Maines, R. P. 200
Major, B. 332
Majumdar, C. 18
Mallory, A. B. 164
Malo, S. 330
Manago, A. M. 19
Manning, J. 257
Mar, A. 150
March, E. 175
Marcum, C. 490
Marelich, W. D. 37
Marini, I. 283
Mark, K. P. 365
Markman, H. 181
Martin, C. L. 125
Martinez, K. 405
Martino, L. L. 64
Masci, D. 272
Masters, N. T. 38
Masters, W. H. 43, 81, 82,
   83, 141, 369, 382, 388
Matthews, J. 46
Matusitz, J. 465
Mauro, T. 515
Maxwell, J. A. 17, 366
Mays, V. M. 47
McArthur, N. 20
McCarthy, B. 373, 386

McCaskill, C. 473
McCauley, J. L. 463
McChesney, K. Y. 68
McClelland, S. 45
McClintock, M. K. 75
McGraw, S. A. 376
McGregor, J. 479
McKeown, J. K. L. 515
McKinney, E. 283
McLaren, S. 258
McLaughlin, A. 126
McLelland, M. 220
McLeod, D. A. 482
McMahon, C. G. 373, 374, 375
McNally, G. 489
McNeil, J. 168
Mead, M. 18
Meese, G. 69
Meltzer, A. L. 7
Mena, J. A. 258
Merrill, J. 210
Merta, C. 51
Messman-Moore, T. L. 463
Michael, R. T. 127, 227, 230
Michaels, P. A. 350
Michel, K. 95
Mikolajczak, M. 126
Milas, G. 516
Milhausen, R. 243
Milhausen, R. R. 206, 446
Mill, J. S. 506
Miller, C. C. 111
Miller, S. 256
Milrod, C. 525
Mintz, L. 198, 371, 380, 385
Mitchell, H. 250
Mitchell, K. R. 127
Mitchison, D. 222
Mizrahi, M. 201
Moilanen, K. L. 24
Mokros, A. 407
Molinares, C. 205
Moller, N. P. 232
Moncada, J. 355
Money, J. 255
Mongeau, P. A. 145, 146
Monro, S. 130
Monroe, D. 476
Montemurro, B. 38, 49,
   165, 225, 231, 239
Montes, K. S. 19
Montgomery, M. J. 140
Monto, M. A. 144
Moon, D. 269
Moore, S. E. 346
Moore, T. J. 241
Moors, A. C. 146
Morales, E. 201
Moran, M. 400
Morell, V. 236
Moreno, J. A. 289
Morgentaler, A. 93
Morotti, E. 7
Morris, H. 150, 211
Morris, T. 354
Morrison, D. M. 38
Morrissey Stahl, K. A. 231

Morrow, L. C. 509
Moser, A. 299, 463, 476
Moser, C. 271, 414
Moss-Racusin, C. A. 114
Motyl, J. 520
Mouilso, E. R. 464
Mount, L. 507
Muccigrosso, L. 292
Muehlenhard, C. L. 458
Muise, A. 55, 165, 202, 207, 232
Mullinax, M. 308
Murphy, M. 276
Murray, K. 164, 372
Mustanski, B. 23
Mustapha, A. 459
Myers, J. L. 475
Myers, K. 348

N

Nakku, M. E. 66
Napper, L. E. 19
Nash, E. 330
Nayar, K. I. 520
Nekome 524
Nelms, B. J. 115
Nelson, C. J. 95, 365
Nesi, J. 174
Netting, N. S. 9
Neuman, H. B. 297
Nguyen, H. 233
Nicoletti, A. 67
Niehuis, O. 86
Nikkelen, S. W. 264
Nobre, P. J. 6, 386
Norona, J. C. 235
North, F. 287
Norton, A. M. 174
Notarius, C. 168
Nunes, K. L. 409

O

O'Brien, C. 466
O'Callaghan, E. 49, 474
O'Donnell, N. 44
Oeffinger, K. C. 71
O'Hare, E. A. 490
O'Neill, J. 476
O'Neill, J. L. 473, 476
Onwu, C. N. 67
Onyulo, T. 68
Oraka, E. 428
Oriola, T. B. 465
Orozco-Lapray, D. 217
Osborn, J. L. 226
Oselin, S. S. 518
Oster, A. M. 441, 442
Osterman, M. J. 352
Oswald, F. 175
Oswalt, S. B. 275
Otunctemur, A. 362
Oyefara, J. K. 67

P

Pahlajani, G. 94
Palaniappan, M. 368
Palmer, M. J. 223
Pandey, N. 474
Papp, L. M. 360
Parackal, S. M. 343
Parchomiuk, M. 290, 291
Pariera, K. L. 218
Parker, M. G. 284
Parks, A. 250
Paterson, L. Q. P. 368
Patrick, K. 364
Patterson, C. L. 201
Paul, K. 466
Pazmany, E. 384, 385
Pearson, J. 21
Peasant, C. 447
Pedrelli, P. 298
Peixoto, M. M. 379
Pellegrini, A. 458
Peloquin, K. 387
Perales, F. 261, 262
Perel, E. 237
Perelman, M. A. 381, 382
Perkins, E. 529
Perkins, E. B. 459
Perry, S. L. 515
Persson, T. J. 262, 293
Peta, C. 284
Peters, A. W. 528
Peterson, M. 528
Peterson, Z. 222
Pfeifer, L. R. 184
Pham, J. M. 44
Pierce, L. 363
Pilver, C. E. 80
Pinon Jr., R. 98
Pinto, N. 194
Pivetti, M. 338
Platt, I. 348
Platt, L. F. 263, 265, 273
Pollitt, A. M. 115
Pomeranz, J. L. 276
Post, D. 527
Potarca, G. 262, 272
Prior, A. 526
Pruthi, S. 71
Puckett, J. 269
Puckett, J. A. 258
Puente, M. 458

Q

Quidley-Rodriguez, N. 250
Quinn, C. 293
Quinn, H. 285, 292
Quinn, K. 19
Quinn-Nilas, C. 232

R

Radosh, A. 231
Rako, S. 86
Ram, L. 261
Ramirez, M. 259
Ramo, D. E. 46
Rappleyea, D. L. 140
Rasmussen, K. R. 512
Ravanipour, M. 22
Raymond, E. G. 332
Rayne, K. 223
Reece, M. 12, 127, 204, 205, 209, 396
Reed, H. 374
Regnerus, M. 195
Reilly, S. 473
Retznik, L. 282
Reverby, S. M. 47
Reyes, H. L. 476
Rham, G. 485
Ricketts, M. 177
Rickman, E. 18
Riddle, K. 226
Rietmeijer, C. A. 431
Rinehart, J. K. 45
Ringrose, J. 175
Rissel, C. 505
Ritter, L. 266
Robinson, B. 68
Robinson, M. 148
Rodoo, P. 194
Rodrigues, D. 152
Rodriguez-Diaz, C. 524
Rodriguez, E. M. 269
Roen, K. 120
Rosen, N. O. 365, 383, 384
Rosier, J. G. 387
Ross, L. E. 274
Rosser, B. R. 511
Rossi, E. 222
Rossi, N. E. 258
Roth, S. 483, 484
Rothman, E. F. 258
Rowland, D. L. 6, 379
Rubel, A. N. 148
Rubenking, N. J. 501
Rubin, E. 328
Rullo, J. E. 201
Runfola, C. D. 127
Russell, S. T. 258
Russell, V. M. 232
Rutagumirwa, S. K. 242
Ryan, P. 511

S

Sabbah, K. 525
Sahay, R. D. 285
Sakaluk, J. K. 54
Salazar, M. 476
Salem, S. 479
Sales, N. J. 513
Sanday, P. R. 275, 469
Sandberg, S. 478
Sandberg-Thoma, S. E. 9
Sanders, T. L. 524

Sandlow, J. I. 348
Sanjakdar, F. 22
Santelli, J. S. 23
Sarrel, P. M. 240
Sassler, S. 308
Satinsky, S. 170
Sato, A. 46
Savin-Williams, R. C. 252
Sawyer, A. N. 13
Sbraga, T. P. 489
Schaafsma, D. 290
Schade, L. C. 140
Scheim, A. I. 111
Scheitle, C. P. 270
Scherrer, K. S. 257
Schmidt, L. 347
Schmitz, R. M. 256
Schneider, S. 114
Schnittker, J. 463
Schoentjes, E. 216, 217
Schrimshaw, E. W. 256, 520
Schulz, E. E. 87
Scoats, R. 211
Scroggs, B. 218
Scuka, R. R. 237
Scull, M. T. 510
Seavey, C. A. 123
Seeman, M. V. 292
Seguin, L. 151
Seguin, L. J. 82
Sell, N. M. 476
Sells, T. G. C. 115
Selterman, D. 235, 236
Selvaggi, G. 114
Semigran, H. L. 287
Serughetti, G. 524
Seto, M. C. 408, 514
Setzer, K. 272
Sevecke, J. R. 276
Sewell, K. K. 11
Shapiro, C. H. 347
Sharma, A. 165
Sharp, M. 311
Shaw, L. K. 295
Shdaimah, C. S. 526
Shear, M. D. 256
Sheff, E. 148
Shen, S. 362
Shikai, X. 378
Shim, J. W. 511
Shin, K. H. 129
Shin, S. H. 298
Shrout, M. R. 237
Silva, T. J. 252
Simbar, M. 112
Simister, J. G. 67, 68
Simon, J. 312
Símonardóttir, S. 69
Simopoulos, E. F. 377
Simpson, P. 244
Singer, I. 82
Sinha, S. 523
Sizemore, K. M. 235
Smarr, J. 219
Smeaton, G. 459
Smith, D. 471
Smith, M. 502

Snapp, S. 19
Sneha, S. 289
Snipes, D. J. 298
Soh, D. 224
Soklaridis, S. 478
Solano, I. 512
Soliman, H. H. 526
Sommers, M. 65
Southern, S. 360
Spencer, C. 477
Sprecher, S. 127, 190
Spruin, E. 487
Stappenbeck, C. A. 314
Staras, S. A. 453
Stein, J. B. 145
Steinberg, J. R. 332, 338
Steiner, J. 530
Steinke, E. E. 297
Stephenson, K. R. 6, 13, 365, 386
Stepler, R. 227
Stern, L. 309
Sternberg, R. J. 138, 159
Stetson, D. M. 529
Stewart-Williams, S. 11, 190
Stone, K. 355
Strang, E. 459
Stroebel, S. S. 480, 482
Strommen, E. F. 260
Struckman-Johnson, C. 18, 177
Stuhlsatz, G. 144
Sue, V. M. 46
Sullivan, A. K. 452
Sullivan, J. F. 99
Suschinsky, K. D. 198
Sutton, K. S. 190
Syme, M. L. 243, 294
Syvertsen, J. L. 523

T

Taff, K. D. 139
Tamilin, E. R. 112
Tang, C. S. 381
Tannahill, E. 196
Tannen, D. 184
Tavernise, S. 342
Taylor, B. M. 308
Taylor, D. 273
Taylor, J. 250
Tener, D. 408
Teskereci, G. 348
Teter, J. 290
Tewksbury, R. 520
Thamotharan, S. 453
Thibodeau, M. E. 19
Thompson, H. 82
Thomsen, D. 142
Tiidenberg, K. 405, 406
Timmermans, E. 144
Tissot, S. A. 196
Tolentino, J. 193
Towne, A. 65
Traeen, B. 194
Tromovitch, P. 408
Truong, K. D. 343
Tsatali, M. 288

Turchik, J. 467
Turetsky, B. 139
Turner, D. 419
Tyiska, C. G. 292

U

Udry, J. R. 50
Umberson, D. 262
Usigan, Y. 175
Ussher, J. M. 80

V

Vaillancourt, K. T. 146
Vail-Smith, K. 446
van Bergen, D. D. 258, 275
van de Grift, T. C. 112
Van den Brink, F. 6
Vanden Brook, T. 472
Van Geloven, N. 348
Van Houdenhove, E. 250, 361
van Lankveld, J. 287
Vanman, E. 179
Vannier, S. A. 232, 355
Van Ouytsel, J. 175
Van San, M. 521, 522
Van Willigen, M. 273
Varjas, K. 259
Vazsonyi, A. I. 190
Velotti, P. 184
Velten, J. 364, 368
Vickers, R. 242
Villar, F. 256
Vissing, Y. 222
Viswanath, K. 468
Vitis, L. 175
Vogels, E. 175, 204
von der Osten-Sacken, T. 67
Vrangalova, Z. 143, 144

W

Wada, M. 243
Wagoner, Van. N. 439
Wahlig, J. L. 112
Waling, A. 174, 175
Walker, J. J. 262
Waller, W. 154
Wallien, M. S. 114
Walters, A. S. 179
Wang, H. L. 153
Wang, R. H. 309
Ward, K. M. 292
Ward, L. M. 18
Ward, R. 473
Watson, E. 263
Weill, K. 218
Weinberg, M. S. 411
Weise, E. 272
Weiser, D. A. 19
Weisskirch, R. 175
Wells, B. 147
Wertheim, E. 221

Wesche, R. 144
Westfall, R. E. 344
Whatley, M. 234
Whipple, B. 83
White, F. A. 267
Whitfield, T. H. F. 445
Whithead, A. L. 273
Whitton, S. W. 13, 127
Wickel, K. 355
Widman, L. 14
Wiederman, M. W. 48
Wignall, L. 413
Wijkman, M. 482
Wiley, D. 308
Wilkenfeld, B. 290
Wilkinson, V. J. 290
Williams, K. M. 8
Williams, K. S. 482
Williams, L. 127
Williams, L. R. 298
Williams, R. H. 22
Willoughby, B. J. 48, 227, 511, 515
Wilson, C. L. 517
Wilson, K. 256
Winters, G. M. 483
Witcomb, G. L. 7
Wittmann, D. 296
Wlodarski, R. 202
Woerner, J. 128
Wolak, J. 505
Wolfe, L. 19, 21
Wolff, M. 251
Wolfinger, N. 9
Wong, J. S. 486
Wong, W. I. 130
Wood, J. 151, 200
Workowski, K. 435
Wright, P. J. 447, 515
Wright, R. G. 272
Wu, S. 13

X

Xishan, H. 129

Y

Yacan, L. 286
Yakushko, O. 522
Yaman, S. 297
Yates, P. 482
Yazedjian, A. 38, 143
Yeager, J. 468
Yeater, E. 474
Yelland, E. 244
Yildiz, H. 347
Yiou, R. 377
Yockery, R. A. 18
Youn, G. 251
Young, A. 355
Young-Petersen, B. 512
Youssouf, S. 67

Z

Zaharatos, J. 354
Zamboni, B. D. 29, 178, 386, 410
Zammitt, K. A. 276
Zapien, N. 45, 232
Zeigler, B. S. 136, 253
Zentner, M. 52, 388
Zhang, X. 177
Ziv, I. 237
Zivony, A. 257
Zsok, F. 139
Zwier, S. 64

Subject Index

A

abortion
  attitudes toward 330–331
  decision-making 333
  defined 324
  effects 332
  international access 331
  legislation 328–330
  methods 324–327
absolutism 8
abstinence
  celibacy 192
  defined 193
  and disability 282
  in family planning 317
  involuntary 193–194, 244
  and male focus 64
  and parental communication 19
  and positive sexuality 4
  and sex education 23, 51
  and sexually transmitted infection
    (STI) prevention 431, 446
  voluntary 193
acquaintance rape 464–465
acquired dysfunction 361
acquired immunodeficiency
    syndrome (AIDS) 442–445
adolescence 220–221
advertising 500
affair
  attitudes self-assessment 234
  avoiding 237
  cultural influences 233
  motivations 235–237
  overview 232
  recovery from 237, 238
  social media impacts 20
  types 233, 238
agender 110
agnosia 288
alcohol use
  among sexual minorities 257, 258
  campus 298
  consequence of abuse 474, 484
  and dementia 288
  factor in rape 463, 464–465
  factor in sexual dysfunction
    299, 362, 376
  and hooking up 143
  impact on sexual decisions 24, 211
  long-term effects 299
  and pregnancy 342–344
  self-assessment 300
  and sexuality 299, 301
  and sexually transmitted
    infections (STIs) 428
ally development model 276
Alzheimer's disease 288
ambivalence 15
amenorrhea 79

amniocentesis 117, 345
anal intercourse 205–206
analingus 205
androgyny 129
aphasia 288
aphrodisiac 86
apps 13
apraxia 288
areola 70
asceticism 192
asexual 250
asexuality 194
asymptomatic 427
atypical anatomical development 120
autoerotic asphyxiation 198
aversive conditioning 420

B

Bartholin glands 63
benign prostatic hyperplasia (BPH) 99
biosexology 32
biosocial framework 33
biphobia 274
bisexuality 250
blended orgasms 82
brainstorming 183
breast-conserving therapy (BCT) 295
breast self-examination 71
breastfeeding 69
breech birth 352
brothel 519

C

call girl 519–520
camming 507, 508
candidiasis 438
case study 52
casual sex 10
catfishing 179
celibacy 192. See also abstinence
cerebral palsy (CP) 286
cervical cap 317
cervix 74
Cesarean section 354
chastity 192
chicken porn. See child pornography
childbirth
  Cesarean section 354
  depression 355
  Lamaze method 349–351
  maternal mortality 355
  pain control 351–352
  stages 352–354
  trends 351
childhood 216–217
child pornography
  effects 516

child pornography (cont.)
  legislation 501, 514–515
  online 505
  and pedophilic disorder 409
  and sexting 177
child sexual abuse
  effects 484–485
  extrafamilial 483
  grooming 483
  intrafamilial 480–482
  overview 479–480
  perpetrator treatment 486–487
  prevention 485–486
  recovered memories 483–484
chlamydia 437–438
Chorionic villus sampling (CVS) 346
chromosomes 116, 118
chronic obstructive pulmonary
    disease (COPD) 294
circumcision 95
cisgender 110
classic rape 465
classical conditioning 34–35
climacteric 240
clitoris 63–65
closed-ended question 170–171
cognitive/affective theories 35
cognitive behavioral sex
    therapy 386–387
cognitive-developmental
    theory 123–124
cohabitation 227
coitus 206
coitus interruptus 319
coming out 256–260, 264
communication
  defined 164
  gender differences in 165, 184
  honesty vs. dishonesty 177–181
  importance 164, 165
  message congruency 166
  principles 168–173
  and technology 173–175
  theory 176–177
  timing 165
compersion 148–149
complementary needs theory 154
comprehensive sex education
    programs 23
conception 348
condom use resistance 314
condoms
  and alcohol use 24
  and anal intercourse 205
  attitude self-assessment 448–449
  and communication importance 165
  contraceptive comparison 320
  effective use 446–447, 453
  and fellatio 204
  high school availability 450
  and hooking up 143
  internal 110, 314–315, 321

condoms (cont.)
  and open relationships 150
  overview 313–315
  and pre-ejaculatory fluid 100
  sex work use 512, 519, 523, 524
  sexual risk self-assessment 228–229
  and sexually transmitted infections
    (STIs) 310, 442, 452
  and spermicides 315
conflict 181–183
conflict theory 39
contraception. *See also* condoms
  barrier methods 312–317
  behavior self-assessment 309
  emergency 319
  hormonal methods 309–312
  method comparisons 320
  natural methods 317–319
  overview 308
  postcoital 319
  sterilization 75, 321–323
  withdrawal method 319
conversion therapy 255–256
Coolidge effect 235
corona 93
correlation 52–53
cougar 239
covert sensitization 420
Cowper glands 100
crabs. *See* pubic lice
critical sexuality studies 30
cross-dress 412
cryptorchidism 98
cunnilingus 204
curvilinear correlation 53
cybersex
  benefits 500, 502–504
  camming 507, 508
  defined 500
  disadvantages 504–505
  government regulation 500–501
cystitis 66, 206

D

date rape 464
deductive research 31
degrading pornography 511
delayed ejaculation 381–382
dementia 288
dental dam 204
dependent variable 42
Depo-Provera 311
descriptive research 52
determinism 25
diabetes mellitus 286
diaphragm 317
dichotomous model 251
digisexuality 20–21
dilation 352
dilation and curettage (D & C) 327
dilation and evacuation (D & E) 327
dilation and suction (D & S) 327
disability 281–283
discrimination 273–274, 276
disorders of sex development (DSD) 116

diverse sex development (dsd).
  See atypical anatomical
  development
double mastectomy 295
double standard. *See* sexual
  double-standard
down low 236
dysmenorrhea 79
dyspareunia 384–386

E

eclectic view 40–42
ecstasy 299
ectopic pregnancy 74, 339–340
effacement 352
ego 34
ejaculatory inevitability 101
embryo 338
emergency contraception 319
emission 101
empirical evidence 31
endogamy 153
endometriosis 79, 293–294
epididymis 98
erectile disorder 375–377
erectile dysfunction 301
erotic massage parlors 510, 518
erotica 511
erotophilia 190, 191
erotophobia 190, 191
escort 519–520
evolutionary theory 33, 41
exchange theory 154
excitement phase 81
exhibitionistic disorder 403–404
exogamy 153
experimental research 48
expulsion 101
external locus of control 24
extradyadic affair 233
extrafamilial child sexual abuse 483
extramarital affair 233

F

fallopian tubes 74–75
family balancing 117
family of origin 135
family of procreation 135
fellatio 203–204
female genital cutting (FGC) 66–68
female orgasmic disorder
  (FOD) 378–381
female sexual interest/arousal
  disorder 367–371
feminist theory 39–40, 41
fetal alcohol syndrome (FAS) 342
fetishism 410–411, 412
fetus 338
field research 50
fisting 205
focus group 49
follicle-stimulating hormone (FSH) 75
forced sex 461

forcible rape 459
free will 25
frenulum 93
friends with benefits 145–146
frotteuristic disorder 404
fundus 74

G

G-spot 73, 99
gender
  brain characteristics 121–122
  communication differences 165, 184
  defined 108
  emotional expression
    differences 136, 253
  overview 108–110
  and puberty 120–121, 221–222
  rape consequence differences 467
  relationship differences 145
  roles. *See* gender roles
  and sexual harassment 487, 489
gender binary 108
gender fluid 110
gender identity 110–111
gender postmodernism 130
gender role ideology 115–116
gender role transcendence 129
gender roles
  changes in 129–130
  cultural effects on 107–108
  defined 112
  and homonegativity 270, 275
  and hooking up 38
  overview 112–116
  and paraphilias 405, 417
  and rape culture 471, 477
  and relationships 263
  and sexual dysfunction 363
  and sexual harassment 489
  socialization agents 124–126
  socialization effects on
    sexuality 126–128
  theories 122–124
genderqueer 110
generalized dysfunction 361
genital herpes 439
genital warts 440
GHB 464
glans 93
gonorrhea 435–436
guilt 156

H

hate crimes 274
hedonism 9–11
hepatitis B (HBV) 441
herpes simplex virus type 1 (HSV-1) 439
herpes simplex virus type 2 (HSV-2) 439
heterosexism 266–268
heterosexuality 250
highly active antiretroviral
  therapy (HAART) 444
homogamy theory 153

homonegativity 269–273
homophobia 269, 274–275
homosexuality 250
honor killing 65, 475
hooking up 31, 143–145
hormones
   and contraception 309–
      312, 316, 318, 321
   defined 85
   female 75
   fetal 118–119
   and gender differences 122
   and gender transitioning 114
   male 96, 99
   and menopause 239–241
   menstrual cycle 75–76, 79–80
   pubertal 120–121, 221
   and rape theories 467
   and sex offender treatment 419
   and sexual dysfunction 361, 370, 372
   and sexual orientation 255
   and sexual response 85
   and spousal intercourse 230
hostile-environment sexual
      harassment 488
Human immunodeficiency
      virus (HIV) 442–445
human papillomaviruses (HPV) 440
hymen 65
hyperactive sexual desire disorder 372
hyperventilation 81
hypothesis 42
hysterectomy 295

I

"I" statements 172
id 34
independent variable 42
induced abortion 324
induction abortion 327
inductive research 31
infancy 216
infertility 339, 347–349
infidelity. *See* affair
informed consent 46
inhibited male orgasm 381
intact dilation and extraction
      (D & X) 327
intellectual disability (ID) 289–292
internal condom 314–315
internal locus of control 24
interstitial cells 96
interview survey research 49
intrafamilial child sexual
      abuse 480–482
intrauterine device (IUD) 316
introitus 65
involuntary abstinence 193

J

jealousy 155–156

K

Kegel exercises 73
kiddie porn. *See* child pornography
kissing 202
Klinefelter syndrome 118

L

labia majora 63
labia minora 63
lap dance 508
laparoscopy 322
lesbian bed death 368
LGBTQIA 250
libido 34
lice. *See* pubic lice
lifelong dysfunction 361
locus of control 24
looking-glass self 176
love
   attitudes self-assessment 137–138
   continuum 136–138
   cultural differences in 139
   elements of 138–139
   languages 139
   partner selection 153–154
   polyamory 146–150
   relationship challenges 155–158
   styles 140–143
   workplace 147–148

M

madam 519
male "G-spot" 99
male hypoactive sexual desire
      disorder 372–373
mammogram 71
marital rape 459
masochism. *See* sexual
      masochism disorder
massage 510, 518
mastectomy 295
Masters and Johnson
   research overview 43
   sex therapy 369–370, 387–388
   sexual response model
      81–83, 100–103
masturbation
   cons 199
   defined 194
   negative attitudes toward 195–198
   overview 194–195
   pros 198
   vibrators 200–201
#MeToo Movement 458, 478–479
meatus 93
medical abortion 324
medical model of intellectual
      disability 290
medicalization of sexual
      dysfunctions 361
Megan's Law 486

menarche 75
menopause 239–241, 295
menorrhagia 79
menstrual extraction 76
menstrual suppression 76
menstrual synchrony 75
menstruation (menses)
   attitudes toward 77–79
   definition 75
   overview 75
   phases 76
   problems 79–80
   suppression 76
mental disorders 292–293
middle age 238–241
mifepristone 324–326
miscarriage 324, 346
Mittelschmerz 318
mons veneris 62
multidimensional model 253
multigravida 352
multiple sclerosis (MS) 285
mutual monogamy 446
myotonia 81

N

natural selection 33
NEA-TDS (norethindrone acetate
      transdermal system) 312
negative correlation 53
NEXPLANON 311
nomophobia 174
nongonococcal urethritis (NGU) 438
nonparticipant observation 50
nonverbal messages 166
nudism 398
nudity 220
NuvaRing 312

O

obscenity 514
obsessive relational intrusion
      (ORI) 156–157
occupational sex segregation 114
oligomenorrhea 79
oophorectomy 295
open-ended question 170–171
open relationships 150–151
operant conditioning 417–418
operant learning theory 35, 41
operational definition 44
operationalize 44
oral herpes 439
orchiectomy 296
orgasm 82, 101–102
orgasm dysfunctions 378–382
orgasmic headache 102
orgasmic meditation (OM) 203
os 74
ostomy surgery 296
ovaries 75

P

pansexuality 250
Pap test 74
paraphilia
   defined 399–400
   legal vs. illegal 400–401
   overview 399–400
   theories 415–418
   treatment 418–421
   types 401, 413
paraplegia 284
parental investment 122
"partial-birth" abortions 327
participant observation 50
partner notification laws 452
partner selection 153–154
patriarchy 39
pedophilia 505
pedophilic disorder 408–410
pelvic inflammatory disease (PID) 432
penectomy 296
penile strain gauge 100
penis 92–95
performance anxiety 364
perineum 63
periodic abstinence 317
peripartum depression 355
persistent genito-pelvic pain/
    penetration disorder
    (GPPD) 383–385
Peyronie's Disease (PD) 95
pharmaceutical abortion 324–326
pheromones 86–87
phone sex 507
physiological theory 33, 41
plateau phase 81–82
PLISSIT model 380, 389
polyamory 146–150
polyfidelity 149
pornography
   and body image 64, 93
   child. (*see* child pornography)
   commercial vs. amateur 512
   consumption 512–513
   and cosmetic surgery 64
   defined 511
   effects on individuals 48, 52, 516
   effects on relationships 52, 515–517
   effects on young people 20
   and pedophilic disorder 419
   and rape 469, 471, 477
   self-assessment 513
   and technology 501, 512–513
   theories 41
   types 511, 516
   and voyeuristic disorder 402
positive correlation 52
positive sexuality 4
post-exposure prophylaxis (PEP) 445
post-traumatic stress disorder
    (PTSD) 474
postcoital contraception 319
postpartum depression 355
pre-ejaculatory fluid 100
preconception sex selection 117
predatory rape 465

pregnancy
   defined 348
   early 338–340
   ectopic 74, 339–340
   intention 338
   maternal mortality 340
   prenatal care 342, 344–346
   prevention. (*see* contraception)
   sex during 346–347
   substance use effects 342–344
   teen 224, 225
   testing for 340
premature ejaculation (PE) 373–375
premenstrual dysphoric
    disorder (PMDD) 80
premenstrual syndrome (PMS) 79
primacy/recency effect 168
primary dysfunction 361
primary sex characteristics 108
primigravida 352
principle of least interest 154
prostate cancer 100
prostate gland 99
prostitution 517, 521–522,
    526. *See also* sex work
psychoanalytic theory 33–34
psychosexology 32
puberty 221
pubic hair 64
pubic lice 434–435
pubococcygeus 73
punishment 35
purging 412

Q

quadriplegia 284
queer 250
quid pro quo sexual harassment 488

R

radical prostatectomy 296
rape. *See also* sexual assault
   attitude self-assessment 470–471
   definitions 459–462
   effects of 190, 474–475
   and emergency contraception
    225, 319
   and homophobia 275
   male victims 466–467
   #MeToo Movement 478
   military 472
   perpetrator characteristics 463–466
   perpetrator treatment 486–487
   prevalence 462–463
   prevention 475–477
   resources 468
   and sex trafficking 529
   and sexually transmitted
    infections (STIs) 429
   in sex work 522, 524, 527
   survivor treatment 475
   theories 34, 467–469
   and Title IX 473–474

rape culture 471
rape myths 463
rape-supportive beliefs 463
rape trauma syndrome 474
rapid ejaculation 373
reflective listening 171
reinforcement 35
relationships. *See also* love
   bisexual 262–263
   challenges in 155–158
   communication in.
    (*see* communication)
   gay male 261
   and gender role 115, 116, 126–128
   and hooking up 31, 144
   lesbian 262
   mixed-orientation 260
   non-monogamous 146–147, 148–152
   pansexual 263
   pornography effects on 515–517
   and sexual dysfunction 365
   and technology 140
   trans partner 263–265
relativism 8–9
religion 21–22
representative sample 48
research, sex
   caveats 44–46
   data analysis 52–55
   early 40–42
   ethics 46–47
   funding 51
   Masters and Johnson 43
   methods 48–52
   overview 30–32
   process 42–44
resolution phase 83
retrograde ejaculation 102
revenge porn 516
risk self-assessment 228–229
rohypnol 464
RU-486 324–326

S

sadism. *See* sexual sadism disorder
salpingectomy 322–323
sample 48
satiation 230, 372
scabies 435
schizophrenia 292
scopophilia 402
scrotum 96
secondary dysfunction 361
secondary sex characteristics 69
secondary victimization 473
self-concept. *See* sexual self-concept
self-efficacy. *See* sexual self-efficacy
self-fulfilling prophecy 168
semen-conservation doctrine 196
semenarche 221
seminal vesicles 99
seminiferous tubules 98
sensate focus 369
sex, biological 108, 116–120

sex education
    influence on sexual decisions 21
    and intellectual disability (ID) 290
    internet 502
    and mental illness 293
    parental 218, 225
    and porn literacy 501, 516
    and positive sexuality 4
    and religion 22
    school 23, 218–220, 450, 501
    sex app 13
    and sexual dysfunction 366, 375
    and sexually transmitted infection
        (STI) prevention 445
sex party 147
sex positivity 4
sex roles 114
sex therapy 386–390
sex trafficking
    in brothels 519
    and call girls 519
    defined 528
    in erotic massage parlors 510
    overview 528–530
    and sex work decriminalization 527
    and sex work entry 521, 523
    and sex work organization 521
sex work
    clientele 524–526
    defined 517
    entry into 521–523
    and the law 526, 527–528
    life in 522–524
    relationship impacts 523–524
    trafficking. (see sex trafficking)
    types 507–510, 518–521
sexism 126
sexology 32
sexting 174–175, 177, 403, 515
sexual abuse. See child sexual abuse
sexual addiction 414–415, 416–417
sexual anatomy 61
sexual assault 39, 275, 292,
        293. See also rape
sexual behavior. See sexual decisions
sexual coercion 458–459, 460–461.
        See also rape; sexual assault
sexual competence 223
sexual compliance 232
sexual debut 218, 222–223
sexual decisions
    cultural influences 18, 21
    and education 21, 23
    making 16–18
    media influences 18–19
    nature of 14–15
    in new relationships 209–211
    psychological factors 24–25
    relational influences 19–20
    and religion 21–22
    sexual compliance 232
    sexual risk self-assessment 228–229
    and substance use 24
    and technology 20–21
sexual destiny 366
sexual double standard 10

sexual dysfunctions
    cognitive factors 365–366
    definitions 360–362
    erectile disorder 375–377
    female sexual interest/arousal
        disorder 367–371
    male hypoactive sexual desire
        disorder 372–373
    medicalization of 390
    organic factors 362–363
    orgasm dysfunctions 378–382
    persistent genito-pelvic pain/
        penetration disorder
        (GPPD) 383–385
    premature ejaculation (PE) 373–375
    psychological factors 364–365
    relationship factors 365
    sociocultural factors 363
    therapy 386–390
sexual fantasies 201–202
sexual fluidity 253
sexual growth 16–17
sexual guilt 156. See
        also sexual decisions
sexual harassment
    confronting 492
    consequences 491
    defined 487–488
    incidence 488–489
    #MeToo Movement 478–479
    responses 491
    in sex work 522
    theories 489–490
    victim characteristics 490
    workplace policies 490–491
sexual intercourse
    defined 206
    diagram 206
    in new relationships 209–211
    positions 207–209
    statistics 206–207, 209
sexual masochism disorder 405–406
sexual orientation
    defined 250
    discrimination 273–274
    and health 265
    models 251–253
    prevalence 253
    and relationships. (see relationships)
    theories 254–255
sexual physiology 61
sexual response
    and aphrodisiacs 86–87
    female 81–84
    gender differences 103
    hormone role 85–89
    male 100–102
    and pheromones 86
sexual risk self-assessment 228–229
sexual sadism disorder 407–408
sexual self-concept 6–7
sexual self-efficacy 6
sexual technologies 13, 20–21.
        See also cybersex
sexual touching 203
sexual values 7–11

sexuality theories
    biological 33
    observations 41
    psychological 33–37
    sexual orientation 254–255
    sociological 37–40
sexualization
    in advertising 500
    in the media 18–19
    and pedophilia 409–410
    and pornography 513
    and rape 477
sexually transmitted infection
        (STI) prevention
    abstinence 446
    accessing health services 453
    condom use 446–449, 450
    partner reduction 446
    screening 451
    vaccination 449
sexually transmitted infections (STIs)
    acquired immunodeficiency
        syndrome (AIDS) 442–445
    candidiasis 438
    chlamydia 437–438
    defined 426
    disclosing 433, 452
    effects 432–434
    gonorrhea 435–436
    hepatitis B (HBV) 441
    herpes 439–442
    human immunodeficiency
        virus (HIV) 442–445
    human papillomaviruses (HPV) 440
    nongonococcal urethritis (NGU) 438
    prevalence 426–427
    prevention. (see sexually transmitted
        infection (STI) prevention)
    pubic lice 434–435
    risk factors 427–430
    scabies 435
    and sex work 526
    syphilis 436–437
    testing 430–431, 502
    vaginitis 438
    Zika virus 441–442
situational dysfunction 361
social learning theory 35, 123
social model of intellectual
        disability 290
social scripts 38, 41
sociobiological theory 33
sociobiology 122–123
sociosexology 32
spectatoring 376
spermicide 315–316
Spinnbarkeit 318
spontaneous abortion 324, 346
spurious correlation 53
stalking 157
statutory rape 459
stealthing 314
sterilization 75, 321–323
stoma 296
strip clubs 507–510
structural-functional theory 38–39, 41
substance abuse 298–301

suction curettage 326
sugar baby 520
sugar daddy 520
superego 34
surgical menopause 295
survey research 48–50
swingers 146, 150–151
symbolic interaction theory 38
syphilis 436–437
systems theory 40, 41

T

table dance 508
tachycardia 81
teen pregnancy 224, 225
testes 96–98
theory 32
therapeutic massage 510
Today Sponge 316
touch-and-ask rule 170
trafficking. *See* sex trafficking
transgender 111–112, 113, 114
transsexual 111
transvestic disorder 412
transvestic fetishism 412
traumatic brain injury (TBI) 289
tubal ligation 322–323
Turner syndrome 118

U

ultrasound scan 345
umbilical cord 338
unidimensional continuum
　　model 251–252
urethra 66
urethritis 385
uterine orgasms 82
uterus 74

V

vacuum aspiration 326
vagina 72–73
vaginismus 384
vaginitis 438
values. *See* sexual values
variable 42
vas deferens 99
vasectomy 322–323
vasocongestion 81
vees 150
verbal messages 166
vestibule 65
violent pornography 511
virginity 190–193
voluntary abstinence 193
voyeuristic disorder 402
vulva 62
vulval orgasms 82
vulvitis 438
vulvodynia 385

W

win-win solution 182

Y

yang 196
yin 196
"you" statements 172

Z

Zika virus 441–442